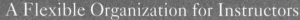

A Flexible Organization for Instructors

Text "Looking Ahead"
Learning Objectives
form the framework for organizing your lectures, selecting support materials, and customizing tests for your students.

Test Bank Questions
are grouped by learning objective, so that you can thoroughly test all objectives — or emphasize the ones you feel are most important. Correlation tables at the beginning of each chapter make it easy to prepare tests that cover the objectives at the level of difficulty appropriate for your students.

MicroExam 4.0

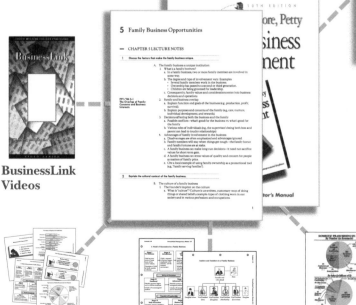

BusinessLink
Videos

Transparencies

Transparency Masters

PowerPoint

All Lecture Support Materials
come together under their appropriate objectives in the *Instructor's Manual Lecture Notes*, for thorough coverage of all objectives. Annotations tell you the appropriate times to integrate transparencies, transparency masters, PowerPoint slides, and BusinessLink videos into your lectures.

Small Business Management

An Entrepreneurial Emphasis

Justin G. Longenecker
Baylor University

Carlos W. Moore
Baylor University

J. William Petty
Baylor University

SOUTH-WESTERN College Publishing

An International Thomson Publishing Company

Editor-in-Chief: Valerie A. Ashton
Acquisitions Editor: Randy G. Haubner
Developmental Editors: Cinci Stowell, Ann Sass
Production Editor: Judith O'Neill
Production: Lifland et al., Bookmakers
Cover and Internal Design: Michael H. Stratton
Photo Editor: Jennifer Mayhall
Photo Research: Images Resources
Cover Photograph: Joyce Photography
Manufacturing Coordinator: Sue Disselkamp
Marketing Manager: Stephen E. Momper

Photo credits on pages 699–700 constitute a continuation of the copyright page.

3 4 5 6 7 KI 2 1 0 9 8 7 6

Printed in the United States of America

Library of Congress Cataloging-in-Publication Data

Longenecker, Justin Gooderl, 1917–
    Small business management: an entrepreneurial emphasis/ Justin G. Longenecker, Carlos W. Moore, J. William Petty. — 10th ed.
        p.   cm.
    Includes bibliographical references and index.
    ISBN 0-538-85077-9
    1. Small business—Management.   I. Moore, Carlos W.   II. Petty, J. William, 1942- .   III. Title.
    HD62.7.L66   1997
    658.02'2—dc20   96-6330
                                                                              CIP

I(T)P
International Thomson Publishing

South-Western College Publishing is an ITP Company. The ITP trademark is used under license.

To the memory of

Dr. H. N. Broom,
1911–1994,

whose vision, along with that of coauthor Justin G. Longenecker,
helped launch the first edition in 1961

TO THE STUDENT

As authors of *Small Business Management: An Entrepreneurial Emphasis,* we must measure our success by the effectiveness of our presentation to you. Although you may not be involved in selecting this textbook, we still consider you our customer and wish to be sensitive to your needs in learning the material presented. For this reason, we have made every effort to make it understandable and relevant. We have also tried to consider your viewpoint in each chapter we have written.

We extend our best wishes to you for a challenging and successful course.

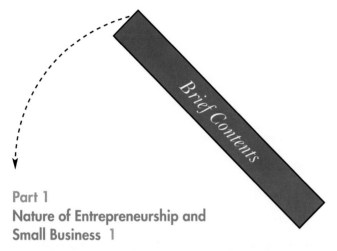

Brief Contents

Part 1
Nature of Entrepreneurship and Small Business 1

1 Entrepreneurs: The Energizers of Small Business 2

2 Small Business: Vital Component of the Economy 22

Part 2
Seeking Entrepreneurial Opportunities 41

3 Startup and Buyout Opportunities 42

4 Franchising Opportunities 66

5 Family Business Opportunities 91

Part 3
Developing the New Venture Business Plan 113

6 The Role of a Business Plan for a New Venture 114

7 Creating a Competitive Advantage 137

8 Analyzing the Market and Formulating the Marketing Plan 159

9 Selecting the Management Team and Form of Organization 182

10 Choosing the Location and Physical Facilities 206

11 Accounting Statements and Financial Requirements 228

12 Finding Sources of Financing 254

Part 4
Small Business Marketing 281

13 Consumer Behavior and Product Strategy 282

14 Pricing and Credit Strategies 305

15 Promotion: Personal Selling, Advertising, and Sales Promotion 329

16 Distribution Channels and Global Markets 349

Part 5
Managing Small Business Operations 371

17 Professional Management in the Growing Firm 372

18 Managing Human Resources 396

19 Quality Management and the Operations Process 415

20 Purchasing and Managing Inventory 436

21 Computer-Based Technology for Small Businesses 454

Part 6
Financial Management in the Entrepreneurial Firm 475

22 Evaluating Financial Performance 476

23 Working-Capital Management and Capital Budgeting 498

24 Risk and Insurance Management 534

Part 7
Social and Legal Environment 553

25 Social and Ethical Issues 554

26 Working Within the Law 571

Cases 593

Appendixes 665

Endnotes 691

Photo Credits 699

Glossary 701

Index 717

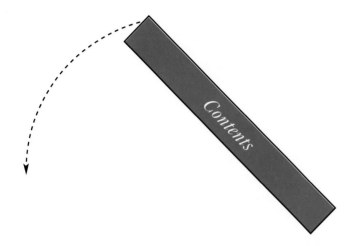

Walk Through xi

Preface xxv

About the Authors xxxi

Part 1
Nature of Entrepreneurship and Small Business 1

1   Entrepreneurs: The Energizers of Small Business 2

Opportunities for Entrepreneurial "Energizers" 3   Rewards and Drawbacks of
Entrepreneurship 6   Characteristics of Entrepreneurs 9   Readiness for
Entrepreneurship 12   Diversity in Entrepreneurship 15

2   Small Business: Vital Component of the Economy 22

Definition of Small Business 23   Small Business as Producer of Goods and Services 24
Special Contributions of Small Business 29   The Small Business Failure Record 34
Causes of Business Failure 36

Part 2
Seeking Entrepreneurial Opportunities 41

3   Startup and Buyout Opportunities 42

The Startup: Creating a New Business 43   Buying an Existing Business 50   Increasing the
Chances of a Successful Startup: Lessons from High-Growth Firms 61

4   Franchising Opportunities 66

Understanding the Franchise Option 67   Advantages and Disadvantages of
Franchising 69   Evaluating Franchise Opportunities 78   Selling a Franchise 83
Understanding the Franchisor/Franchisee Relationship 83

5   Family Business Opportunities 91

The Family Business: A Unique Institution 92   The Culture of a Family Business 96
Family Roles and Relationships 98   Special Features of Family Firm Management 102
The Process of Leadership Succession 105   Transfer of Ownership 108

Part 3
Developing the New Venture Business Plan 113

6   The Role of a Business Plan for a New Venture 114

What Is a Business Plan? 115   The Need for a Business Plan 116   How Much Business
Plan Is Needed? 120   Preparing a Business Plan 122   Where to Go for More
Information 128   The Business Plan 136

7   Creating a Competitive Advantage 137

Competitive Advantage 138   Market Segmentation Strategies 142
Niche Marketing 147   Customer Service Management 150   The
Business Plan 158

**8   Analyzing the Market and Formulating the
Marketing Plan 159**

Small Business Marketing 160   Marketing Research for the New
Venture 162   Estimating Market Potential 170   Components of
the Formal Marketing Plan 175   The Business Plan 181

**9   Selecting the Management Team and Form of
Organization 182**

The Management Team 183   Legal Forms of Organization
185   The Board of Directors 195   Federal Income Taxes and
the Form of Organization 199   The Business Plan 205

10   Choosing the Location and Physical Facilities 206

The Location Decision 207   Site Selection 211   Home-Based
Businesses 217   The Building and Its Layout 219   Equipment and Tools 223   The
Business Plan 227

11   Accounting Statements and Financial Requirements 228

Accounting Statements: Tools for Determining Financial Needs 229   Assessing
Profitability 240   A Firm's Financial Requirements 243   The Business Plan 253

12   Finding Sources of Financing 254

Debt or Equity Financing? 255   Sources of Financing 259   Individuals as Sources of
Funds 262   Business Suppliers and Asset-Based Lenders as Sources of Funds 265

Commercial Banks as Sources of Funds 267   Government-Sponsored Agencies as
Sources of Funds 273   Other Sources of Funds 274   Keeping the Right Perspective 276
The Business Plan 280

Part 4
Small Business Marketing 281

13   Consumer Behavior and Product Strategy 282

Understanding the Customer 283   Product Management 291
Product Strategy Alternatives for Small Businesses 295   Building
the Total Product Offering 299

14   Pricing and Credit Strategies 305

Setting a Price 306   Using Break-Even Analysis for Pricing 310
Selecting a Pricing Strategy 313   Offering Credit 316
Managing the Credit Process 320

**15   Promotion: Personal Selling, Advertising, and
Sales Promotion 329**

Promotion and the Communication Process 330   Determining
Promotional Expenditures 331   Personal Selling Techniques
for Small Firms 334   Advertising Considerations for Small
Firms 339   Sales Promotion Options for Small Firms 343

16   Distribution Channels and Global Markets 349

The Role of Distribution Activities in Marketing 350   Structuring a Distribution System 353
Global Marketing Challenges 355   Initial Preparations for Global Marketing 358
Sources of Trade and Financing Assistance 364

Part 5
Managing Small Business Operations 371

17   Professional Management in the Growing Firm 372

Distinctive Features of Small Firm Management 373   The Nature of Managerial
Work 376   Time Management 385   Outside Management Assistance 387

18   Managing Human Resources 396

Recruiting Personnel 397   Evaluating Prospects and Selecting Employees 401   Training
and Development 404   Compensation and Incentives for Small Business Employees 407
Special Issues in Human Resources Management 409

19   Quality Management and the Operations Process 415

Total Quality Management 416   The Operations Process 425   Improving Productivity 430

20   Purchasing and Managing Inventory 436

Purchasing Processes and Policies 437   Relationships with Suppliers 443   Objectives of
Inventory Management 445   Controlling Inventory Costs 446

21   **Computer-Based Technology for Small Businesses 454**

Overview of Available Technology 455   Computer Systems: Hardware
and Software 458   Communication Among Computers 463   Office and
Production Technology 465   Purchasing and Managing Technology 468
Trends in Computer-Based Technology 471

Part 6
Financial Management in the Entrepreneurial Firm 475

22   **Evaluating Financial Performance 476**

Accounting Activities in Small Firms 477   Assessing a Firm's
Financial Performance 482

23   **Working-Capital Management and Capital
     Budgeting 498**

The Working-Capital Cycle 499   Managing Cash Flow 505
Managing Accounts Receivable 510   Managing Inventory 511
Managing Accounts Payable 513   Capital Budgeting 514

**Appendix 23A: Time Value of Money: Finding the Present Value of a
Dollar 524**

**Appendix 23B: Discounted Cash-Flow Techniques: Computing a Project's
Net Present Value and Internal Rate of Return 527**

24   **Risk and Insurance Management 534**

Defining and Classifying Risk 535   Risk Management 542   Insurance for the Small
Business 544

Part 7
Social and Legal Environment 553

25   **Social and Ethical Issues 554**

Social Responsibilities and Small Business 555   The Special Challenges of
Environmentalism and Consumerism 558   The Small Business Context for Ethical
Decisions 559   Putting Ethical Precepts into Practice 563

26   **Working Within the Law 571**

Government Regulation and Small Business Opportunity 572   Government Regulation
and Protection of the Marketplace 576   Business Agreements and the Law 586   The
Challenge of Taxation 588

Case 1   **King's Beauty Supply 593**

Case 2   **Construction Equipment Dealership 595**

Case 3   **Stitch Craft 597**

Case 4   Operating a Kiosk Franchise 600

Case 5   The Brown Family Business 603

Case 6   Robinson Associates, Inc. 605

Case 7   The Fantastic Catalogue Company 610

Case 8   ScrubaDub Auto Wash 614

Case 9   VMG Products 618

Case 10   Logan Beach 619

Case 11   WJP Partners 622

Case 12   Walker Machine Works 624

Case 13   Silver Lining 627

Case 14   The Jordan Construction Account 629

Case 15   Litter Ridder 631

Case 16   NovaSoft Systems Inc. 634

Case 17   Central Engineering 636

Case 18   Gibson Mortuary 639

Case 19   Douglas Electrical Supply, Inc. 642

Case 20   Mather's Heating and Air Conditioning 644

Case 21   Franklin Motors 646

Case 22   The Style Shop 648

Case 23   Barton Sales and Service 653

Case 24   Fox Manufacturing 657

Case 25   The Martin Company 660

Case 26   Diaper Dan 662

Appendix A Sample Business Plan 665

Appendix B Present Value of $1 683

Appendix C Present Value of an Annuity of $1 for *n* Periods 687

Endnotes 691

Photo Credits 699

Glossary 701

Index 717

Special Features

Before You Open The Door To The 10th Edition of Small Business Management: An Entrepreneurial Emphasis, take a walk through the special features of the text, detailed on the next few pages. The topic of small business holds special interest for us, and we are excited to share what we know with you. Whether you already have plans to start your own business and are looking for hands-on, practical guidance, or you are simply interested in the possibility but aren't sure if it would be right for you, this text has what you need. As you'll see on the next few pages, we offer a variety of rich and interesting features to help you develop practical skills for managing a small business as well as an awareness and appreciation for the challenges involved. **COME ON IN!**

Beginning with the "Looking Ahead" learning objectives that open each chapter, the text is organized as an integrated learning system. To keep the central ideas before you, the opening objectives are repeated in key places: at the beginning of the section where the objective is fulfilled and within the "Looking Back" summary where the key points of each objective are recapped.

To help you organize your study, we have structured the Student Learning Guide around these same learning objectives. An icon beginning each section of the Guide identifies the corresponding learning objective. First, we recap each key section in the chapter, grouped by learning objectives. Next, a "Quick Identification and Explanation" section reviews important terms in the chapter. Next come True-False, Multiple-Choice, Fill-In, and Essay Questions —all organized according to the learning objectives they test.

6 The Role of a Business Plan for a New Venture

— LEARNING OBJECTIVES

1 Answer the question "What is a business plan?"

- A business plan identifies the nature and context of the business opportunity, and it presents the approach to be taken by the entrepreneur to capture the opportunity.

2 Explain the need for a business plan from the perspective of the entrepreneur and the investor.

- A business plan clearly states goals and strategies for internal purposes, and it is used as a selling document to outsiders.
- A business plan must be designed to communicate effectively and quickly to prospective investors, who need to know how the business will help achieve the investor's personal goal—to maximize the potential return on investment through the cash flows that will be received from the investment, while minimizing personal risk exposure.
- Most investors are more market-oriented than product-oriented.

3 Describe what determines how much planning an entrepreneur and a management team are likely to do.

- The allocation of two scarce resources, time and money, affects how much planning will be done.
- [...] t affect the extent of planning include (a) management style and ability, [...] references, (c) the complexity of the business, (d) the competitive environment, [...] uncertainty in the environment.

[...] ns to follow in writing a business plan, [...] mponents of a business plan.

[...] will be more effective if you follow these suggestions: (a) provide a table of [...] ach section for easy reference; (b) use a loose-leaf binder to package the plan and [...] ns; (c) use charts, graphs, diagrams, tabular summaries, and other visual aids to [...] d provide an effective presentation that is easy to follow; (d) maintain [...] the plan; and (e) ask carefully chosen third parties to give their assessment of the [...]

[...] of a business plan are (a) a cover page, (b) an executive summary, (c) a general [...] on, (d) products and/or services plan, (e) a marketing plan, (f) a management [...] ng plan, (h) a financial plan, and (i) an appendix.

5 Identify sources available for assistance in preparing a business plan.

- Professionals such as attorneys, accountants, and other entrepreneurs can provide useful suggestions and assistance in the preparation of a business plan.
- A large number of business plan computer software packages and books are available.

— QUICK IDENTIFICATION AND EXPLANATION

1 Answer the question "What is a business plan?"

1. **business plan:** a document containing the basic idea underlying a business and related considerations for starting up

4 List practical suggestions to follow in writing a business plan, and outline the key components of a business plan.

2. **executive summary:** a section of the business plan, written to convey a clear and concise picture of the proposed venture
3. **products and/or services plan:** a section of the business plan describing the product and/or service to be provided and explaining its merits
4. **marketing plan:** a section of the business plan describing the user benefits of the product or service and the type of market that exists
5. **management plan:** a section of the business plan describing the key players in a new firm and their experience and qualifications
6. **operating plan:** a section of the business plan describing the new firm's facilities, labor, raw materials, and processing requirements
7. **financial plan:** a section of the business plan providing an account of the new firm's financial needs and sources of financing and a projection of its revenues, costs, and profits
8. **pro forma financial statements:** reports that provide projections of a firm's financial conditions

[...]ESTIONS

[...] T, if it is true, or with an F, if it is false.
[...] an is primarily a selling document.

[...]ness plan from the perspective of
[...]nvestor.

[...] an provides a clear statement of goals and strategies.
[...] an is not seen by customers, suppliers, or investors.
[...] ne starting a business faces the task of raising financial resources.
[...] an is a legal document for raising needed capital.
[...] is a legal document for warning potential investors about the possible risks
[...]ment.
[...] l of most investors is to maximize the return on the investment.
[...] an should be lengthy and detailed.

Chapter 6   The Role of a Business Plan for a New Venture   51

4 List practical suggestions to follow in writing a business plan, and outline the key components of a business plan.

8. The _____ is usually at the beginning of the business plan and summarizes the total plan.
   a. executive summary
   b. products and/or services plan
   c. marketing plan
   d. management plan

9. Prospective investors and lenders attach a high priority to the
   a. operating plan.
   b. marketing plan.
   c. products and/or services plan.
   d. appendix.

5 Identify sources available for assistance in preparing a business plan.

10. A _____ allows an entrepreneur to experiment with various scenarios and quickly ascertain their effect on the firm's balance sheet, operating profits, and cash flows.
    a. word-processing package
    b. computer spreadsheet
    c. business calculator
    d. business plan

— FILL-IN-THE-BLANK QUESTIONS

Write the correct word in the blank provided.

1 Answer the question "What is a business plan?"

1. A _____ is a written document containing the basic idea underlying a business and related considerations for starting up.
2. Planning should be a continuing process in the _____ of any business.

2 Explain the need for a business plan from the perspective of the entrepreneur and the investor.

3. There are two reasons for writing a business plan: to clearly state goals and strategies for internal purposes and to create a _____ document to be shared with outsiders.
4. A business plan can be used to enhance the firm's _____ with prospective customers and suppliers.
5. Most entrepreneurs need to raise _____ resources to supplement personal savings.
6. A _____ contains all the information needed to satisfy security laws related to warning potential investors about possible risks of an investment.
7. The basic goal of an investor is to maximize _____ on investment.
8. A business plan should seldom exceed _____ pages in length.

This tightly integrated learning system is designed to help you study efficiently. After reading the chapter, review the summary and key definitions. Then work through the Student Learning Guide questions. If you find from these review activities that you need further study on a particular objective, you can easily locate all applicable material by simply looking for the appropriate numbered learning objective in the text and Learning Guide.

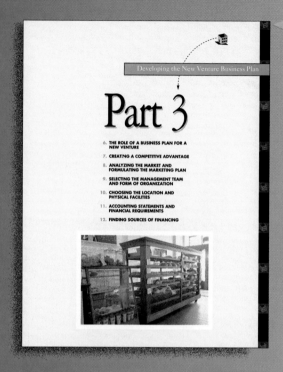

Part 3: Developing the New Venture Business Plan, Step-by-Step.
In this edition, we've given the business plan the emphasis it deserves. Each chapter in Part 3 presents a major part of the business plan.

Laying the Foundation.
Designed around a series of questions, these chapter-end exercises lead you through the building of your own business plan, guiding you to reflect upon critical issues that will impact your small business.

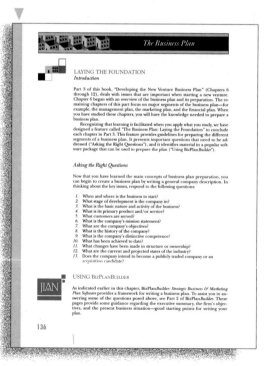

BizPlan*Builder* and *BizPlanBuilder* Express.
Now you can prepare your business plan using the software that real entrepreneurs use: *BizPlanBuilder* or the abridged *BizPlanBuilder Express* designed especially for students. This commercially successful software is available to you at a reduced price from **South-Western College Publishing**. At the end of every chapter in Part 3, we send you to the appropriate sections in *BizPlanBuilder* for preparing the portion of your plan discussed in the chapter.

Appendix A: A Sample Business Plan.

This appendix shows you a real business plan. Use this example to see how the pieces come together. Refer to it as you build your own plan—either as a class project, or later, when you are ready to go into business!

SiBōn
Beverage Corporation
P.O. Box 1927
202 Simmons Way
Jasper, Texas 75951-1927
1-800-755-0000

Ph. 409-383-0000   Fax: 409-383-0000

EXECUTIVE SUMMARY

The "New Age" beverage market is the result of a spectacular boom in demand for drinks that have nutritional value, are made from environmentally safe ingredients, and use water that comes from deep, clear, clean springs free of chemicals and pollutants. SiBōn Beverage Corporation ("SiBōn") will produce and market a full line of sparkling fruit drinks, flavored waters, and sports drinks of the highest quality and purity. These drinks have taste appeal similar to that of soft drinks, while using the most healthful fruit juices, natural sugars, and the purest spring water—the hallmark of the New Age drink market.

New Age beverages are relatively new in the $28 billion soft drink market, growing in sales from $117 million (wholesale) in 1985 to over $1 billion in 1993. The industry has grown tenfold in sales in less than two years, and demand has simply outpaced supply. The product is distinguished by rich natural fruit concentrates, spring waters, and all natural ingredients. A New Age drink is defined as a beverage that is perceived by consumers as (1) healthy, allowing consumers to feel good about themselves, and (2) a natural product, free of artificial ingredients, preservatives, and flavors.

SiBōn projects gross sales and earnings as follows:

	1994	1995	1996
Gross sales	$1,446,731	$5,082,302	$8,095,825
Pre-tax income	($ 169,719)	$ 307,146	$1,261,782

SiBōn proposes to finance its building and land, located in the Jasper Industrial Park, with an acceptable Jasper Bank, using a financial guarantee from the Jasper Economic Development Corporation (JEDC). The following business plan details SiBōn's projected operations to support JEDC's guarantee.

3
DEVELOPING A SIMPLE BUSINESS PLAN: CLASSROOM LEARNING EXERCISES

This chapter demonstrates the process of writing a business plan. To some extent, the process has been simplified. We will provide an overview of a business plan but will avoid extensive elaboration of the subject matter. Our intention is to focus attention on the framework of the plan and the necessary information for putting it together.

As you later formulate personal plans for real ventures, you will need to amplify or modify this document as required by the characteristics of the specific venture. In most cases, for example, you should project cash flow on a monthly basis. In the sample plan, cash flow is presented only by years. The additional material presented in Chapter 4 will help you decide how to expand your "real-world" plan and will also make you aware of additional resources for developing those plans.

AN EXAMPLE OF A SIMPLIFIED PLAN

In this section of the chapter, we present a scenario for a potential small business and a simple business plan developed on the basis of that scenario. In a subsequent section of this chapter, other assignment scenarios are described as a basis for you to gain "hands-on" experience in developing a plan. By examining the completed plan for the first scenario, you should learn how to develop a plan for the assignment scenario(s). A set of worksheets is provided to assist you in this assignment.

The sample plan that follows will give you clues concerning what you need to cover when you develop your plan, but it will not provide all of the details. Since the business described in your plan will differ from the venture contemplated in this sample plan, you will need to develop sales estimates, cost figures, marketing approaches, and so on that are appropriate for that venture.

The Sample Plan Scenario
(Report-Plus)

Valerie Wright is a sophomore English major attending Southern University, a small liberal arts college in southern Florida. She is the current president of the college journalism club which is where she first met her dorm roommate, Cheri Perez. Cheri is a junior computer science major. Valerie and Cheri have become good friends and have been discussing the possibility of a new business venture. Both entrepreneurs were born and raised in rural areas and feel a need to supplement the meager financial support currently provided by their parents.

After months of brainstorming, they have agreed to start a venture called "Report-Plus" which would serve the needs of students and local businesses by typing and binding reports and term papers. Both young entrepreneurs recently attended a seminar entitled "How to Start a New Business." From this experience, they realize the need for a basic business plan document to help them better visualize their business venture and also to assist in obtaining some additional financial resources.

17

Preparing the Business Plan: Resources for the Classroom.

This brief supplement walks you through the preparation of a simple business plan with a practical, nuts-and-bolts approach. Later, this guide serves as a quick reference as you prepare the comprehensive plan for your own small business.

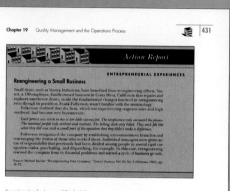
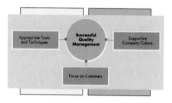

A Special Emphasis on the Internet

The Internet as a Selling Tool.
Surfing the Net. Everybody's doing it. That's why you, as a potential small business manager, need to know how to take advantage of the Internet to reach this growing potential market for your products. We'll help you do this.

"Exploring the Web" Experiential Exercises.
The Internet is more than a sales tool. It offers a wealth of resources from all over the world to help you manage your business. **"Exploring the Web" Experiential Exercises** take you "surfing" to see the kinds of information out there for small businesses. You will browse Web sites of real small businesses. You will even investigate the site for your text!

Internet Action Reports.
Throughout the book special **"Action Reports"** devoted to Internet topics will show you some creative ways that small companies are taking advantage of this powerful communication tool. Maybe you can think of some new ways.

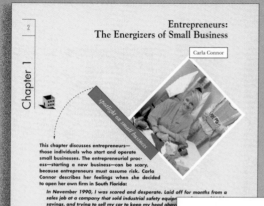

Throughout the text, we integrate real-world experiences. Each chapter opens with a **"Spotlight,"** profiling a small business that exemplifies topics to come in the chapter. **"Action Reports"** throughout each chapter use real experiences to illustrate how today's small firms cope with issues related to ethics, technology, quality, entrepreneurship, and global trends. Taken from sources such as *Inc., Forbes, Entrepreneur, The Wall Street Journal,* and *Nation's Business,* these reports offer current examples from the world of small business.

Spotlight on
Small Business

Action Report:
Technological Applications

▼

▲
Action Report:
Entrepreneurial
Experiences

Action Report:
Quality Goals ▶

Action Report:
Ethical Issues ▶

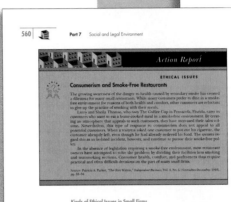

Action Report:
Global Opportunities
▼

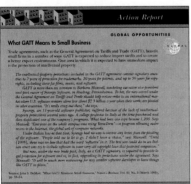

◀ **Icons.**
These same topics also appear within the
chapter narrative. Icons identical to those on
the Action Reports mark quality, ethics,
global, and technological discussions for you.

To be a successful small business manager, you need practice. Without it, you have a book that whets your appetite but doesn't bring you any closer to the table. In addition to offering practical information ready to put to use, each chapter concludes with realistic application exercises and references that send you to the chapter-specific cases at the end of the text.

You Make the Call.

These scenarios put you in the place of a small business person and ask what you would do in the same situation.

Experiential Exercises.

Designed to connect "book learning" to the real world, these exercises often send you into your community to gather information and ideas from small business managers. They also encourage you to consider your own experiences in the context of chapter concepts.

Case References ▶

Small Business Management

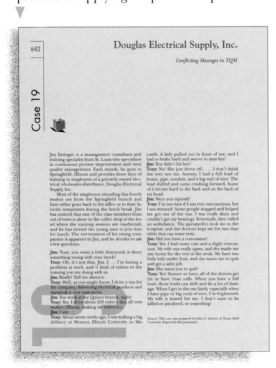

NovaSoft Systems Inc.
Not So Innocent Abroad

Case 16
634

With the homes they'd pledged for seed capital on the line and the seed money running thin, Sureyya "Ray" Ciliv and Robin Hillyard, engineer-founders of a software startup outside Boston, planned to test a business basic: Sales generate cash. However, another business basic—a stock-market crash—intervened. NovaSoft Systems Inc. was down to its last $250 when the panic of 1987 hit, reducing its chances of attracting risk capital to nil.

CEO Ciliv and chief technical officer Hillyard didn't dare begin marketing in the United States without resources. So they decided to begin marketing overseas without resources. As novice owners of a nearly broke company, they nonetheless had an asset no one abroad did—the latest technology in computer-based engineering document management systems. They would prove their product could sell and then ride that momentum back to the United States.

"When you market in the United States," Ciliv notes, "you have to advertise and do PR and attend large trade shows—all of which costs money. Then you have to build a sales organization, but salespeople don't become 100 percent productive for maybe nine months, and that's also a cost. The usual routine is to make an investment, then wait for a return. But if you don't have the cash to make that investment, obviously, you don't have a choice." Accordingly, he invested what remained in NovaSoft's treasury in a ticket to Europe.

The strategy called for establishing distributorship agreements with, Ciliv says, "solid, well-

staffed companies that already had sales forces and support organizations in place and were dealing with the kind of companies that would be our target customers." Ciliv began in Rome. "Italians would be open-minded and spontaneous," the Turkish-born Ciliv had theorized.

His instincts were right. In July 1988, hardly two months after NovaSoft had begun operations, he closed a deal with Italcad, a large Italian distributor of computer-aided design and computer-aided manufacturing equipment. It wasn't a hard sell, Ciliv says. The company even gave him a quick $100,000 up front. "It was supplying other products and could anticipate the appeal of ours within its customer base. Any kind of agreement—even a royalty advance—represented little risk to it; essentially, it had already done the market research." Within weeks, Italcad had placed NovaSoft's systems with Fiat.

Buoyed by that debut, Ciliv convinced Hewlett Packard that running his software would show off the manufacturer's hardware to good advantage. While Ciliv was presenting a NovaSoft program at a Hewlett-Packard booth at a large trade exhibition in Germany, some executives from the international conglomerate Siemens, based in Munich, happened by. The company arranged to send a representative to NovaSoft's U.S. facilities to evaluate the technology. "That," Ciliv recalls, "was unnerving. We

Source: Robert A. Mamis, "Not So Innocent Abroad," *Inc.*, Vol. 15, No. 9 (September 1993), pp. 110–111. Reprinted with permission, *Inc.* magazine (September 1993). Copyright 1993 by Goldhirsh Group, Inc. 38 Commercial Wharf, Boston, MA 02110.

Cases.

The 26 short cases located at the end of the text are designed for specific chapters. End-of-chapter references briefly describe the main case for that chapter and offer alternative selections as well. Based on actual experiences of small business managers, these cases give you practice in applying chapter concepts.

Douglas Electrical Supply, Inc.
Conflicting Messages in TQM

Case 19
642

Jim Essinger is a management consultant and training specialist from St. Louis who specializes in continuous process improvement and total quality management. Each month, he goes to Springfield, Illinois and provides three days of training to employees of a privately owned electrical wholesaler-distributor, Douglas Electrical Supply, Inc.

Most of the employees attending this fourth session are from the Springfield branch and have either gone back to the office or to their favorite restaurants during the lunch break. Jim has noticed that one of the class members from out of town is alone in the coffee shop of the hotel where the training sessions are conducted, and he has invited the young man to join him for lunch. The nervousness of his young companion is apparent to Jim, and he decides to ask a few questions.

Jim: Tony, you seem a little distracted; is there something wrong with your lunch?
Tony: Oh, it's not that, Jim. I . . . . I'm having a problem at work, and it kind of relates to the training you are doing with us.
Jim: Really? Tell me about it.
Tony: Well, as you might know, I drive a van for the company, delivering electrical products and materials to our customers.
Jim: You work at the Quincy branch, right?
Tony: Yes. I drive about 250 miles a day, all over western Illinois, making my deliveries.
Jim: I see.
Tony: About seven weeks ago, I was making a big delivery at Western Illinois University in Ma-

comb. A lady pulled out in front of me, and I had to brake hard and swerve to miss her!
Jim: You didn't hit her?
Tony: No! She just drove off . . . . I don't think she ever saw me. Anyway, I had a full load of boxes, pipe, conduit, and a big reel of wire. The load shifted and came crashing forward. Some of it hit me hard in the back and on the back of my head.
Jim: Were you injured?
Tony: I'm not sure if I was ever unconscious, but I was stunned. Some people stopped and helped me get out of the van. I was really dizzy and couldn't get my bearings. Eventually, they called an ambulance. The paramedics took me to the hospital, and the doctors kept me for two days while they ran some tests.
Jim: Did you have a concussion?
Tony: Yes, I had some cuts and a slight concussion. My wife was really upset, and she made me stay home for the rest of the week. We have two little kids under four, and she wants me to quit and get a safer job.
Jim: She wants you to quit?
Tony: Yes! Sooner or later, all of the drivers get hit or have close calls. When you have a full load, those loads can shift and do a lot of damage. When I get in the van lately, especially when I have pipe or big reels of wire, I'm frightened. My wife is scared for me. I don't want to be killed or paralyzed, you know.

Source: This case was prepared by John E. Schien of Texas A&M University. Reprinted with permission.

Welcome! Thank you for selecting our text for your students. We are excited about the new edition and its related teaching tools. As you well know, many students at some point in their lives will own or work for a small business. Therefore, this field of study is relevant to more individuals each year, making our role as educators both challenging and productive. *Our goal is to provide a teaching package that will help you help your students.*

For more than three decades, *Small Business Management: An Entrepreneurial Emphasis* has been the most widely used text in its field. In the tradition of earlier editions, we have prepared a tenth edition that incorporates current theory and practice related to starting and managing small firms. Our diverse academic backgrounds in business management, marketing, and finance have enabled us to provide well-balanced coverage of small business issues. In preparing this book, we kept three primary goals in mind. First, we sought to offer a complete treatment of each topic. Second, we gave readability a high priority by continuing to write in the same clear and concise style that students have appreciated over the last nine editions. Finally, we included numerous real-world examples to help students understand how to apply the concepts.

Ultimately, however, it is your evaluation that is important to us. We want to know what you think. Please contact any of us as questions or needs arise. (Our telephone numbers, fax numbers, and E-mail addresses are provided at the end of this preface.) We view ourselves as partners with you in this venture, and we wish to be sensitive to your wishes and desires whenever possible.

Innovations for You and Your Students

As we prepared the tenth edition, we tried to include the latest teaching tools to help you plan your course and the most current concepts and real-world examples to help you keep your course up to date. A description of some of these new features follows.

- **Integrated Learning System.** In this edition, we structured the text and supplements around the learning objectives, to create an integrated learning system. The numbered objectives in each Looking Ahead section also appear in the margins throughout the chapter. In the Looking Back section at the end of the

New!

chapter, material that fulfills each objective is identified. These same objectives introduce related exercises in the *Student Learning Guide*. If students find that they are having trouble with a certain concept, they can easily locate all related materials in the text and the *Student Learning Guide* simply by looking for the appropriate objective.

For you, the instructor, the integrated learning system makes lecture and test preparation easier. The lecture notes in the *Instructor's Manual* are grouped by learning objective and identify the appropriate acetates, masters, and *PowerPoint* slides to display as you cover each objective. Questions in the *Test Bank* are grouped by objective as well. A correlation table at the beginning of each *Test Bank* chapter helps you to select questions that cover all objectives or to emphasize those objectives you believe are most important.

New!

- **Emphasis on Building a Business Plan.** The ability to create a business plan is a critical skill for potential small business managers. In this edition, we devote all seven chapters in Part 3 to business plan topics. At the end of each of these chapters, a Laying the Foundation section helps students identify what they are trying to achieve with their own business plans. We include a complete sample business plan in Appendix A as an example.

In the real world, small business owners/managers often use software specifically designed for business plan writing. To bring this realism into the classroom, we have partnered with Jian to offer its commercially successful Biz-Plan*Builder* software to your students at a reduced price. Ask your South-Western/ITP sales representative about bundling this popular software with the textbook. A special Using BizPlan*Builder* section at the end of each chapter in Part 3 sends students to the appropriate place in BizPlan*Builder* to prepare the portion of the plan discussed in that chapter. For more about BizPlan-*Builder*, see the Jian home page on the Internet:

http://www.jianusa.com

If you want your students to use software but time is limited, try BizPlan-*Builder, Express.* This abridged version of BizPlan*Builder* was designed specifically for student use.

If you prefer not to use business plan software, consider using the print supplement *Preparing the Business Plan: Resources for the Classroom.* This booklet was designed as a simplified practical guide to business plans. Ask your South-Western/ITP sales representative about this supplement.

New!

- **Exploring the 🌐.** The Internet offers a whole world of helpful resources, as well as marketing opportunities, for small businesses. To help students become familiar with what's out there, we have included Internet activities among the end-of-chapter experiential exercises. These activities, called Exploring the Web, send students to specific locations on the World Wide Web, such as the home pages for the Small Business Administration and Dun & Bradstreet. Specific questions require students to search and evaluate the small business—related information found there.

In addition, this text has its own home page at

HOME PAGE
Longenecker
http://www.thomson.com/swcp
/mm/longenecker.html

http://www.thomson.com/swcp/mm/longenecker.html

Experiential Exercise 5 in Chapter 1 prompts students to explore its contents.

Action Reports in several chapters introduce students to small businesses with home pages on the Web. Through these Action Reports, even students without Internet access can become acquainted with how small companies are taking advantage of this unique communication medium.

- **Topical Boxed Features.** This edition, for the first time, includes boxed Action Reports featuring topical themes of special interest to today's small business managers. Each theme is identified by its own icon:

| Global | Quality | Technology | Ethics | Internet Technology |

For example, an Action Report in Chapter 16, identified by a global icon, explains how GATT affects small business.

Additional Action Reports and Spotlight on Small Business features focus on the experiences of particular entrepreneurs. For example, the Action Report in Chapter 7 describes entrepreneur Carol Weinstock's strategy of targeting ethnic markets with appropriate greeting card designs. In Chapter 19, an Action Report looks at a small firm that states its customer orientation forcefully: "Kill yourself for your customers."

- **Theme Topics Integrated Throughout the Text.** Discussion of technology, ethics, quality, and global opportunities is not limited to special boxed features—it is integrated throughout the text. Since these topics are of special interest to students today, we have highlighted them with marginal icons identical to those used in the Action Reports.

Popular Features Retained and Improved

In this edition, we have retained and improved many of the features that have made this text so popular among students and instructors.

- Chapter-opening Spotlights and Action Reports feature small firms applying the concepts developed in the chapter. The majority of these are new to this edition.
- Definitions of key terms appear in the margins and in the Glossary. A list of each chapter's new terms and concepts appears at the end of the chapter, with page references.
- Looking Ahead learning objectives and a Looking Back summary appear in each chapter, to keep students focused on the most important points. To simplify review, we organized the summaries as bulleted key points in this edition.
- Discussion questions, experiential exercises including Exploring the Web activities, and an increased number of real-world decision-making situations in You Make the Call at the end of each chapter offer students practice in applying chapter concepts.
- A total of 26 short cases illustrating realistic business situations appear at the end of the text. In this edition, we have added references at the end of each chapter to direct you to the cases appropriate for that chapter. These cases afford students an opportunity to enhance their understanding of chapter concepts.

New!

New!

Revision Highlights in the Tenth Edition

A major goal of our revision effort was to include topics that are a part of *today's* exciting world of small business management. As we incorporated this material, we also improved the arrangement of chapter material. Here is a quick summary of the results, in addition to those already mentioned:

- The discussion of accounting statements has been moved forward to Chapter 11, to provide an early foundation for the introduction of initial financial requirements.
- Finding sources of financing, a major challenge in starting a business, is now the focus of an entire chapter—Chapter 12.
- Chapter 21, which covers computer-based technology for the small firm, incorporates a discussion of the Internet.
- The discussion of global marketing in Chapter 16 has been updated to reflect the ever-growing importance of offshore markets.
- Quality management has been made the primary focus of Chapter 19, and the chapter has been restructured to highlight that theme.
- Current topics of importance to small business have been added or updated within the narrative. These topics include

    Re-engineering
    Customer focus of quality management
    Internet/E-mail
    Cash flow management
    Family business succession
    Valuing the firm
    Benchmarking
    Networking
    Outsourcing
    Work teams

The Complete Teaching Package

All package components with *Small Business Management: An Entrepreneurial Emphasis*, Tenth Edition, have been designed to fit a variety of teaching styles and classroom situations. You have the opportunity to choose the resources that best suit your teaching style and student needs. The following supplements are available.

- *Student Learning Guide.* This supplement presents key points of each text chapter, brief definitions, and a variety of self-testing material, including true/false, multiple-choice, fill-in-the-blank, and essay questions. It serves as an excellent tool for students to pursue their own self-study of the text material.
- *Instructor's Manual.* The *Instructor's Manual* has been completely redesigned to make it more usable. It contains lecture notes, sources of audio/video and other instructional materials, answers to discussion questions, comments on You Make the Call situations, and teaching notes for cases. Transparency masters are also provided for each chapter.
- *Instructor's Manual on Disk.* To help you customize your lectures, the *Instructor's Manual* is available on disk in ASCII. You can quickly and easily adapt our lecture materials to include your own notes, examples, and ways of presenting the materials in class.
- *Acetates.* Acetates for each chapter are provided free to adopters. Notes in the *Instructor's Manual* lecture outlines suggest when to use the acetates and pro-

vide discussion prompts for each one. If you want handouts, you can use the Transparency Masters in the *Instructor's Manual* as photocopy masters for all non-text transparencies.

- *PowerPoint.* The complete transparency package is now available on *PowerPoint.* Computer-driven projection makes it easy to use these colorful images to add excitement to your lectures. All you need is Windows to run the *PowerPoint* viewer and an LCD panel for classroom display.

- *Videos.* Since this text is used by INTELECOM as part of the telecourse *Something Ventured,* you can receive, at no cost, videos from this program. Also available upon request are custom-produced videos that are part of South-Western's new *BusinessLink* video series. These videos show real small businesses dealing with such issues as whether to expand ("Kropf: A Study in Planning"), improving quality ("Wainwright: A Study in Quality), and startup decisions ("Second-Chance Co.: Entrepreneurship").

- *Test Bank.* A comprehensive *Test Bank* includes true/false, multiple-choice, and discussion questions. A correlation table at the beginning of each chapter in the *Test Bank* helps you prepare tests with the coverage and type of questions appropriate for your students.

- *Computerized Test Bank.* The complete *Test Bank* is available on easy-to-use *MicroExam 4.0* disks. You can create exams by selecting, modifying, or adding questions within *MicroExam.* The software will run on MS-DOS computers with a minimum of 640K memory, a 3½" disk drive, and a hard drive.

- *Preparing the Business Plan: Resources for the Classroom.* This short booklet includes background articles, detailed exercises, instructions for preparing business plans, and sample business plans.

Special Thanks and Acknowledgments

There are numerous individuals to whom we owe a debt of gratitude for their assistance in making this project a reality. In particular, we thank our friends at South-Western College Publishing. We are indebted to Acquisitions Editor Randy Haubner, Developmental Editors Cinci Stowell and Ann Sass, Production Editor Judy O'Neill, and Copyeditor Jeanne Yost. They are all true professionals!

We especially appreciate the support of Mr. and Mrs. Edwin W. Streetman, our former Dean, Richard C. Scott, and our present Dean, Terry Maness. We also thank Doris Kelly for her excellent word-processing skills. Once again, we appreciate the understanding and support of our wives, Frances and Donna, during this process.

For their helpful revision suggestions during our preparation of the tenth edition, we are especially grateful to the following individuals:

David Anstett
The College of St. Scholastica

Aline Arnold
Eastern Illinois University

Barry Ashmen
Bucks County Community College

Ronald Cook
Rider University

Michael Graves
Portland Community College

Cecil Green
Riverside Community College

Max Harbert
West Virginia State College

Neil Hilkert
Delaware Valley College

Carl Kovelowski
Mercer County College

John Lea
Arizona State University

Charles Matthews
University of Cincinnati

John Maurer
Wayne State University

Timothy Mescon
Kennesaw State College

William Motz, Jr.
Lansing Community College

Douglas Naffziger
Ball State University

Joan Nichols
Emporia State University

Joseph Platts
Miami-Dade Community College

Elaine Powell
Sinclair Community College

Nicholas Sarantakes
Austin Community College

Winston Stahlecker
West Texas A&M University

James Swenson
Moorhead State University

Bernard Weinrich
St. Louis Community College

Jonnie Williams
Grand Rapids Community College

As a final word, we express our sincere thanks to the many instructors who use our text in both academic and professional settings. We thank you for letting us serve you.

Justin G. Longenecker
Tel.: (817) 755-1111, ext. 4258
Fax: (817) 755-1093

Carlos W. Moore
Tel.: (817) 755-1111, ext. 6176
Fax: (817) 755-1068
E-mail: Carlos_Moore@Baylor.edu

J. William Petty
Tel.: (817) 755-1111, ext. 2260
Fax: (817) 755-1092
E-mail: Bill_Petty@Baylor.edu

ABOUT THE AUTHORS

JUSTIN G. LONGENECKER
Baylor University

Justin G. Longenecker's authorship of *Small Business Management: An Entrepreneurial Emphasis* began with the first edition of this book and continues with an active, extensive involvement in the preparation of the present edition. He has authored a number of books and numerous articles in such journals as *Journal of Small Business Management, Academy of Management Review, Business Horizons,* and *Journal of Business Ethics.* Active in a number of professional organizations, he has served as president of the International Council for Small Business.

Dr. Longenecker attended Central College, a two-year college in McPherson, Kansas. He earned his bachelor's degree in Political Science from Seattle Pacific University, his M.B.A. from Ohio State University, and his Ph.D. from the University of Washington.

CARLOS W. MOORE
Baylor University

Carlos W. Moore is the Edwin W. Streetman Professor of Marketing at Baylor University, where he has been an instructor for more than 20 years. He has been honored as a Distinguished Professor by the Hankamer School of Business, where he teaches both graduate and undergraduate courses. Dr. Moore has authored articles in such journals as *Journal of Small Business Management, Journal of Business Ethics, Organizational Dynamics, Accounting Horizons,* and *Journal of Accountancy.* His authorship of this textbook began with its sixth edition.

Dr. Moore received an Associate Arts degree from Navarro Junior College in Corsicana, Texas, where he was later named Ex-Student of the Year. He earned a B.B.A. degree from The University of Texas at Austin, an M.B.A. from Baylor University, and a Ph.D. from Texas A&M University.

Besides his academic experience, Dr. Moore has business experience as co-owner of a small ranch and as a partner in a small business consulting firm.

J. WILLIAM PETTY
Baylor University

J. William Petty is Professor of Finance and the W. W. Caruth Chairholder in Entrepreneurship at Baylor University. One of his primary responsibilities is teaching entrepreneurial finance, at both the undergraduate and the graduate level. He has also taught "Financing the Small Firm" at the University of Texas at Austin. He is a co-author of a leading corporate finance textbook and a co-author of *Financial Management of the Small Firm.* He is also a contributor to the *Portable MBA on Entrepreneurship.* He was the 1995 president of the Academy of Small Business Finance. Dr. Petty has published research in numerous academic and practitioner journals, including *Financial Management, Accounting Review, Journal of Financial and Quantitative Analysis, Journal of Managerial Finance,* and the *Journal of Small Business Finance.* He has served as a consultant to several small and middle-market companies. He is the editor of the *Journal of Small Business Finance.*

Dr. Petty received his undergraduate degree in marketing from Abilene Christian University, and both his M.B.A. and his Ph.D. in finance and accounting from The University of Texas at Austin. He is a C.P.A. in the state of Texas.

Part 1

1. **ENTREPRENEURS: THE ENERGIZERS OF SMALL BUSINESS**

2. **SMALL BUSINESS: VITAL COMPONENT OF THE ECONOMY**

Chapter 1

Entrepreneurs:
The Energizers of Small Business

Carla Connor

spotlight on small business

This chapter discusses entrepreneurs—those individuals who start and operate small businesses. The entrepreneurial process—starting a new business—can be scary, because entrepreneurs must assume risk. Carla Connor describes her feelings when she decided to open her own firm in South Florida:

In November 1990, I was scared and desperate. Laid off for months from a sales job at a company that sold industrial safety equipment, down to $100 in savings, and trying to sell my car to keep my head above water, the only thing I was sure of was that I no longer wanted to work for someone else. On the other hand, I was afraid to fail and wasn't entirely comfortable with the idea of being in business on my own.

Drawing on her corporate experience and using her home as a base, Connor started C&B Industrial Safety, Inc. to sell industrial safety equipment.

Although C&B was named for my two whippet dogs—Candy and Buva—I'm sure people thought it stood for "Carla & Somebody." They had no idea or concern that I was a one-person company, that the back supports I sold were stored behind my couch, that I stored safety glasses in my linen closet, and that my dining room table doubled as the shipping department.

Despite such humble beginnings, C&B Industrial Safety has succeeded, with four employees and more than $700,000 in 1993 sales revenue. Connor's startup illustrates the entrepreneurial process in the 1990s.

Source: Carla Connor, "Entrepreneur's Notebook: Personal Growth, Professional Success," *Nation's Business*, Vol. 82, No. 2 (February 1994), p. 6. Reprinted by permission. Copyright 1994, U.S. Chamber of Commerce.

Have you ever thought about your own prospects for entrepreneurship? For example, what kinds of opportunities exist? How attractive are the rewards? Must entrepreneurs possess special characteristics in order to succeed? Is there a right time to launch a business? What kinds of entrepreneurs are there, and what kinds of businesses do they operate? By discussing such questions, this chapter will present an introduction to the formation and management of small firms.

Entrepreneurs are energizers who take risks, provide jobs, introduce innovations, and spark economic growth. Although some writers restrict the term **entrepreneur** to founders of business firms, we use a broader definition that includes all active owner-managers and encompasses second-generation members of family-owned firms and owner-managers who buy out the founders of existing firms. However, the definition excludes salaried managers of large corporations, even those who are described as entrepreneurial because of their flair for innovation and their willingness to assume risk.

Looking Ahead

After studying this chapter, you should be able to:

1 Discuss the availability of entrepreneurial opportunities and give examples of highly successful businesses started by entrepreneurs.

2 Identify three rewards and three drawbacks of entrepreneurial careers.

3 Identify personal characteristics often found in entrepreneurs.

4 Discuss factors that indicate a readiness for entrepreneurship.

5 Describe the various types of entrepreneurs, entrepreneurial leadership, and entrepreneurial firms.

entrepreneur
a person who starts and/or operates a business

OPPORTUNITIES FOR ENTREPRENEURIAL "ENERGIZERS"

Prospective entrepreneurs are constantly searching for opportunities, that is, for markets and situations in which they can operate a business successfully. In this section, we first point out a kind of entrepreneurial mind-set or orientation that is most appropriate for today's opportunities. Then, to communicate the reality and excitement of entrepreneurial opportunities, we describe three entrepreneurs who have experienced outstanding success. These entrepreneurs faced the same competitive business world, with its threats and opportunities, that you face as a prospective entrepreneur.

1 Discuss the availability of entrepreneurial opportunities and give examples of highly successful businesses started by entrepreneurs.

Do It Better—Beat the Competition

Business opportunities exist for those who can produce products or services desired by customers. If a business can make its product or service especially attractive, it will find its prospects brightened considerably. The opportunities today, however, are greatest for firms that add to their attractive products and services an emphasis on superior quality and unquestionable integrity. Customers like to do business with companies that do good work and that show honesty in their relationships.

As we approach the year 2000, customers are placing heavy emphasis on quality and service. Because of this, the future is bright for entrepreneurs who stress quality. In many cases, entrepreneurs can become successful simply by doing the task better than their competitors—that is, providing levels of service and quality that exceed those of others. One route to successful entrepreneurship, therefore, is the achievement of superior performance and quality in meeting customers' needs. The Blue Chip Enterprises program for small firms—sponsored jointly by Con-

QUALITY

necticut Mutual Life Insurance Company, the U.S. Chamber of Commerce, and *Nation's Business*—illustrates this point: Its four national award winners in 1993 were companies having a strong emphasis on quality.[1]

The future is also bright for firms that add to quality and service a solid reputation for honesty and dependability. Customers respond to evidence of integrity because they are aware of ethical issues. Experience has taught them that advertising claims are sometimes unbelievable, that the fine print in contracts is sometimes detrimental to their best interests, and that businesses sometimes fail to stand behind their work. If a small business is consistently ethical in its relationships, it can earn the loyalty of a skeptical public. For example, a small diesel-engine service business performed a major overhaul on an engine for a large construction company. Such an overhaul is extremely expensive, often costing from $15,000 to $20,000. Soon after the initial overhaul, the engine malfunctioned again. At considerable expense to itself, the small business performed additional repair work at no additional charge. The customer was so impressed with this firm's unquestionable dependability that it often sends equipment 200 miles or more, past other repair centers, to the firm that demonstrated trustworthiness in a very practical way. A major customer was won through quality work and integrity in customer relationships.

The doors to entrepreneurial opportunity are wide open, as is evident in the business successes occurring all around you. The following examples will help you visualize the great variety of opportunities that await you.

CRACKER BARREL (LEBANON, TENNESSEE) The construction of interstate highways ruined the financial stability of many gasoline stations, motels, and other small businesses located on local roads. At the same time, the change created business opportunities along the new routes. In the small town of Lebanon, Tennessee, ex-Marine Dan Evins saw this opportunity and responded by building a gasoline station (combined with a restaurant and gift shop) just off the interstate highway.[2]

With a nostalgic atmosphere, down-home food, and affordable prices, Dan Evins, founder of the Cracker Barrel Old Country Store, attracts interstate travelers in droves.

(Evins had gained some experience in this area by working for an oil company owned by his family, which operated some rural gasoline stations.)

In 1969, Evins borrowed $40,000 to build his first facility in Lebanon; he called it the Cracker Barrel Old Country Store. The restaurant featured down-home food—biscuits, grits, country ham, and the like—at prices families could afford. The atmosphere was that of an old-fashioned country store.

The new firm prospered and earned a profit in its very first month. Evins sold off poorly located gas stations for the family-owned oil company and concentrated on the new type of business. By 1978, he had opened 15 Cracker Barrels, and by 1995, the number had reached 230. In fiscal year 1995, Cracker Barrel Old Country Store, Inc. earned $66 million on sales of $783 million.

Evins is a classic entrepreneur who responded to change in the highway system and capitalized on the opportunities presented by that change. By selling off the small gas stations, he faced up to the changing environment, refusing to drift downward with the declining market. By successfully meeting the needs of those traveling over interstate highways, Evins was able to achieve large financial rewards.

COLDWATER CREEK (SANDPOINT, IDAHO)   The beautiful lake and snow-capped mountains near the Canadian border in Idaho lured Dennis and Ann Pence into entrepreneurship.[3] They had tired of the rat race of their business careers in New Jersey, where Dennis served as national marketing manager for a major corporation and Ann worked as a freelance advertising copywriter. In 1983, the Pences packed up a U-Haul and headed west to Sandpoint, Idaho.

> *Why Sandpoint? The little town happens to be smack in one of the most beautiful wildernesses in the nation. Situated on the shores of Lake Pend Oreille, a 43-mile-long pristine body of deep blue water, Sandpoint is flanked by two snow-capped mountain ranges. Ospreys and eagles fly overhead; grizzly bears and caribou are occasionally sighted in the nearby mountains. And since the town is just west of the Continental Divide, its climate is not so frigid as it is in neighboring Montana.*[4]

Employment opportunities are limited in northern Idaho, so the Pences decided to start a mail-order business, which they named Coldwater Creek. Since both were experienced in marketing, this business idea built on their personal strengths. The Pences searched for nature-related gifts, largely from regional artisans. Some examples from their catalog are belt buckles and earrings in Native American designs, craft items, and tee shirts and sweat shirts with pictures of wild animals on them.

Like most successful entrepreneurs, the Pences carefully planned their startup and kept their focus on potential customers:

> *Ann Pence never lost sight of her customer. Even the catalog's size—9 ⅛ inches square—was carefully calculated. "This is the easiest size to hold on your stomach in bed, reading," says Ann. "That's the only time most of our customers have to read catalogs."*[5]

Started in 1984, the business grew to $18 million in revenue in only eight years. With 80 employees, Coldwater Creek has become one of the largest employers in the entire county and has contributed significantly to the population growth of Sandpoint.

In this case, the new business provided a number of entrepreneurial rewards. The obvious financial gains rewarded the owners for risks they assumed when they left their established careers and moved west. In addition, they realized the benefits of a beautiful location, freedom from restraints of corporate careers, and a lifestyle that was attractive to them.

PROCTOR AND GARDNER ADVERTISING (CHICAGO, ILLINOIS)   After earning an English degree at a small Alabama college, Barbara Gardner Proctor found a job as an advertising copywriter in Chicago.[6] As she gained experience, she also developed an appreciation for quality in advertising. A concept being developed by the agency for a TV commercial struck her as tasteless and offensive, and this difference of opinion with management led to her being fired. Following her dismissal, Proctor applied to the Small Business Administration for a loan of $80,000 and promptly opened her own agency in 1970.

Proctor and Gardner Advertising is still a relatively small advertising agency, but it is well established (having almost $11 million in billings in 1994) and respected.

It specializes in advertising, public relations, and event management and counts Kraft Foods and American Family Insurance among its clients. Chicago's Jewel Food Stores chain credits the agency with helping make its generic foods campaign a success in 1978.

As an entrepreneur in the area of business services, Barbara Gardner Proctor succeeded by selecting a strategic niche in which she could compete effectively. The knowledge and skills she developed as a salaried employee also contributed to the success of the agency.

Unlimited Entrepreneurial Opportunities

In a private enterprise system, any individual is free to enter business for himself or herself. We have described four different kinds of persons who took that step—an unemployed woman in Florida, an ex-Marine in Tennessee, an executive couple in Idaho, and an advertising copywriter in Illinois. In contrast to many others who have tried and failed, these individuals achieved outstanding success.

At any time, such potentially profitable opportunities exist in the environment. But these opportunities must be recognized and grasped by individuals with abilities and desire strong enough to assure success. Of course, there are thousands of variations and alternatives for independent business careers. In fact, you may achieve great success in some business endeavor far different from those described here. And the varied types of entrepreneurship present a number of potential rewards. We turn now to a consideration of these benefits.

2 **Identify three rewards and three drawbacks of entrepreneurial careers.**

REWARDS AND DRAWBACKS OF ENTREPRENEURSHIP

Individuals are *pulled* toward entrepreneurship by a number of powerful incentives, or rewards (see Figure 1-1). These rewards may be grouped, for the sake of simplicity, into three basic categories: profit, independence, and a satisfying life-style.

Profit

The financial return of any business must compensate its owner for investing his or her personal time (a salary equivalent) and personal savings (an interest and/or

Figure 1-1

Entrepreneurial Incentives

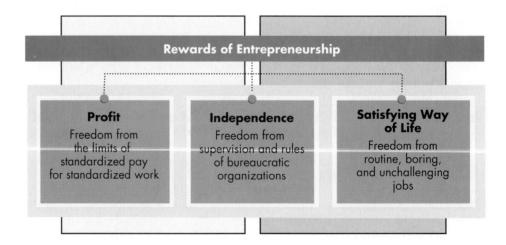

dividend equivalent) before any true profits are realized. Entrepreneurs expect a return that will not only compensate them for the time and money they invest but also reward them well for the risks and initiative they take in operating their own businesses.

Not surprisingly, the profit incentive is a more powerful motivator for some entrepreneurs than for others. For example, Bob Minchak, founder of *J.B. Dollar Stretcher* magazine, published in northeastern Ohio, explains his motivation in simple terms: "The formula is for me to get all the money." Referring to his wife and himself as the sole stockholders, he adds: "Our mission is to maximize our own personal gain." Minchak's life-style confirms his profit orientation: "I have all the toys—a yacht, a pool, fountains, maids."[7]

Bob Minchak is an example of an entrepreneur who possesses a strong interest in financial rewards. However, there are also those for whom profit is primarily a way of "keeping score." Such entrepreneurs may spend their profit on themselves or give it away, but most are not satisfied unless they make what they consider to be a reasonable profit. Indeed, some profit is necessary for survival because a firm that continues to lose money eventually becomes insolvent.

Independence

Freedom to operate independently is another reward of entrepreneurship. Its importance as a motivational factor is evidenced by a 1991 survey of small business owners.[8] Thirty-eight percent of those who had left jobs at other companies said their main reason for leaving was that they wanted to be their own boss. Like these entrepreneurs, many of us have a strong desire to make our own decisions, take risks, and reap the rewards. Being one's own boss seems an attractive ideal.

Some entrepreneurs use their independence to provide flexibility in their personal lives and work habits. A rather extreme example of this type is John Nicholson, owner of New York's popular Cafe Nicholson, who sets the schedule of cafe operation to fit his personal preferences.

> For seven years, Mr. Nicholson has closed his restaurant when the city's climate isn't to his liking. "I hate the winters in New York, and the summers are horrible," explains the 75-year-old restaurateur. "So I go away." He also closes the tiny 10-table restaurant on several days when other restaurateurs do a brisk business—such as Thanksgiving.[9]

Nicholson doesn't notify patrons of future closings, knowing that they don't expect the cafe to be open all the time. One magazine called the restaurant, which is still a profitable business, "The Cafe That's Never Open."

Obviously, most entrepreneurs don't carry their quest for flexibility to such lengths. But entrepreneurs in general appreciate the independence inherent in entrepreneurial careers. They can do things their own way, reap their own profits, and set their own schedules.

Of course, independence does not guarantee an easy life. Most entrepreneurs work very hard for long hours. But they do have the satisfaction of making their own decisions within the constraints imposed by economic and other environmental factors.

A Satisfying Way of Life

Entrepreneurs frequently speak of the personal satisfaction they experience in their own businesses; some even refer to business as "fun." Part of their enjoyment may derive from their independence, but some of it apparently comes from the

The desire to operate independently is a powerful motivator for most entrepreneurs. These new restaurant owners expect the rewards of profit, independence, and personal satisfaction in providing customers with freshly made soups, entrees, and baked goods.

particular nature of the business, the entrepreneur's role in the business, and the entrepreneur's opportunities to be of service.

In 1981, Larry Mahar took early retirement from a major advertising agency and with his wife, Hazel, embarked on a new business venture for the fun of it. They began to create and sell a product somewhat similar to greeting cards. However, their product is printed on parchment and is suitable for framing. They coined the name "Frameables" and the slogan "When a mere card is not enough." Their personal satisfaction in operating the business is expressed in these words:

> *A lot of entrepreneurs want their business to be big. We have resisted bigness. We're more interested in enjoying what we do—just as long as we are making a nice living. We travel three days a week to meet with our customers; we know every one by name. We take our time, enjoy the scenery, and relax sometimes at quaint restaurants along the way.*[10]

A different type of satisfaction is enjoyed by Bruce Wilson, an entrepreneur with a passion for preservation of the environment.[11] His company, Healthy Planet Products, in Petaluma, California produces cause-related greeting cards. Operating at the $3.5 million sales level, the firm produces cards for the Humane Society of the United States, the Sierra Club, and others. Wilson's satisfaction with his role is evident in his statement: "We're helping fulfill the dream of a healthy planet."

Drawbacks of Entrepreneurship

Although the rewards of entrepreneurship are enticing, there are also drawbacks and costs associated with business ownership. Starting and operating one's own business typically demands hard work, long hours, and much emotional energy. Many entrepreneurs describe their careers as exciting but very demanding.

The frustrations of reaching a satisfactory profit level, for example, may be very wearing on the entrepreneur. Frank DeLuca, who runs a training and consulting firm called Resource Development Group, has spoken of the stress involved in getting enough business on a consistent basis: "I had to devote so much energy to selling my service that I didn't have enough time for the creative aspects of my work."[12]

The possibility of business failure is a constant threat to entrepreneurs. No one guarantees success or agrees to bail out a failing owner. As we discuss later in this chapter, entrepreneurs must assume a variety of risks related to failure. No one likes to be a loser, but that is always a possibility for the person who starts a business.

In deciding on an entrepreneurial career, therefore, you should look at both positive and negative aspects. The drawbacks noted here call for a degree of commitment and some sacrifice on your part if you expect to reap the rewards.

CHARACTERISTICS OF ENTREPRENEURS

3 Identify personal characteristics often found in entrepreneurs.

A common stereotype of the entrepreneur emphasizes such characteristics as a high need for achievement, a willingness to take moderate risks, and strong self-confidence. As we look at specific entrepreneurs, you will meet individuals who, for the most part, fit this image. However, we must sound two notes of caution. First, proof of the importance of these characteristics is still lacking.[13] Second, there are exceptions to every rule, and individuals who do not fit the mold may still be successful entrepreneurs.

Need for Achievement

Psychologists recognize that people differ in the degree of their **need for achievement.** Individuals with a low need for achievement seem to be contented with their present status. On the other hand, individuals with a high need for achievement like to compete with some standard of excellence and prefer to be personally responsible for their own assigned tasks.

need for achievement
a desire to succeed, where success is measured against a personal standard of excellence

A leader in the study of achievement motivation is David C. McClelland, a Harvard psychologist.[14] He discovered a positive correlation between the need for achievement and entrepreneurial activity. According to McClelland, those who become entrepreneurs have, on average, a higher need for achievement than do members of the general population. While research continues to find that entrepreneurs are high achievers, the same characteristic has also been found in successful corporate executives.[15]

This drive for achievement is apparent in the ambitious individuals who start new firms and then guide them in their growth. In some individuals, such entrepreneurial drive is evident at a very early age. For example, a child may take a paper route, subcontract it to a younger brother or sister, and then try another venture. Also, a college student may take over or start a student-related venture that he or she can operate while pursuing an academic program.

Willingness to Take Risks

The risks entrepreneurs take in starting and/or operating their own businesses are varied. By investing their own money, they assume financial risk. If they leave secure jobs, they risk their careers. The stress and time required in starting and running a business may also place their families at risk. And entrepreneurs who identify closely with particular business ventures assume psychic risk as they face the possibility of failure.

David C. McClelland discovered in his studies that individuals with a high need

for achievement also have moderate risk-taking propensities.[16] This means that they prefer risky situations in which they can exert some control over the outcome, in contrast to gambling situations in which the outcome depends on pure chance. This preference for moderate risk reflects another entrepreneurial characteristic, self-confidence (to be discussed below).

The extent to which entrepreneurs actually have a distinctive risk-taking propensity is still debated, however. Some studies have found them to be similar to professional managers, while other studies have found them to have a greater willingness to assume risk.[17] This debate should not be allowed to obscure the fact that entrepreneurs must be willing to assume risks. They typically place a great deal on the line when they choose to enter business for themselves.

Self-Confidence

Individuals who possess self-confidence feel they can meet the challenges that confront them. They have a sense of mastery over the types of problems they might encounter. Studies show that most successful entrepreneurs are self-reliant individuals who see the problems in launching a new venture but believe in their own ability to overcome these problems.

internal locus of control
believing that one's success depends upon one's own efforts

external locus of control
believing that one's life is controlled more by luck or fate than by one's own efforts

Some studies of entrepreneurs have measured the extent to which they are confident of their own abilities. According to J. B. Rotter, a psychologist, those entrepreneurs who believe that their success depends on their own efforts have an **internal locus of control.** In contrast, those who feel that their lives are controlled to a greater extent by luck or chance or fate have an **external locus of control.**[18] Research has indicated that entrepreneurs have a higher internal locus of control than is true of the population in general, although they may not differ significantly from other managers on this characteristic.

A Need to Seek Refuge

Although most people go into business to obtain the rewards of entrepreneurship, some become entrepreneurs to escape from something (see Figure 1-2). Professor

Action Report

GLOBAL OPPORTUNITIES

Foreign Refugees to Global Entrepreneurs

GLOBAL

Immigrants who start new businesses are so-called foreign refugees who seek a better life through their entrepreneurial endeavors. In Miami, two such refugees discovered a great money-making opportunity that is global in scope.

> Three years ago, in a flash of inspiration, Roberto Rodriguez pulled his 1986 Audi into an auto body shop and stuck neon lights all over it.
> Today, Rodriguez, 32, and his brother, Efrain, 40, Peruvian immigrants who have run a neon and electrical signage business in Miami since 1985, have a lucrative sideline of selling brightly colored neon lighting kits for cars and other vehicles.
> Last year, Motion Neon, Inc. raked in close to $2 million in sales of something that nobody really needs but that lots of people all over the world apparently are clamoring to buy: pink, blue, yellow, red, green, aqua, peach, and purple neon accessories that light up the underbodies of vehicles and encircle car stereo speakers and license plates.

Neon auto accessories may prove to be only a fad, but the Rodriguez brothers are exploiting the current opportunity and attempting to develop a longer-term demand. In addition to selling the products in the United States, they sell to 1,500 dealers in 25 countries from South Africa and Australia to Mexico, France, and Japan. Export sales account for 55 percent of the company's revenues.

Source: Rosalind Resnick, "Hot Lights on Wheels," *Nation's Business*, Vol. 82, No. 6 (June 1994), pp. 14–16. Reprinted by permission. Copyright 1994, U.S. Chamber of Commerce.

Russell M. Knight of the University of Western Ontario has identified some environmental factors that "push" people to found new firms and has labeled entrepreneurs affected by such factors **refugees.**[19]

In thinking about these refugees, you should recognize that many entrepreneurs are motivated as much or more by entrepreneurial rewards than by an escapist mind-set. Indeed, often a mixture of positive and negative considerations is operating. Nevertheless, this characterization of some entrepreneurs as refugees clarifies certain important considerations involved in much entrepreneurial activity.

THE FOREIGN REFUGEE   Many individuals escape the political, religious, or economic constraints of their homeland by crossing national boundaries. Frequently, such **foreign refugees** face discrimination or handicaps in seeking salaried employment in the new country. As a result, many of them go into business for themselves.

THE CORPORATE REFUGEE   Individuals who flee the bureaucratic environment of big (or even medium-size) business by going into business for themselves are identified by Knight as **corporate refugees.** Employees of large corporations often find the corporate atmosphere or decisions or the relocations required by their jobs to be undesirable. Entrepreneurship provides an attractive alternative for many such individuals.

For example, after 13 years in an executive capacity with the H.J. Heinz Company, Jim Kilmer lost enthusiasm for corporate life.[20] After holding a variety of responsible and satisfying positions, he began to experience a sense of frustration.

refugee
a person who becomes an entrepreneur to escape an undesirable situation

foreign refugee
a person who leaves his or her native country and becomes an entrepreneur in the new country

corporate refugee
a person who leaves big business to go into business for himself or herself

When a new boss took over, Kilmer found his own power to make decisions slipping away. Things that needed quick attention were held up for weeks or even longer. As a result, Kilmer became a corporate refugee as he launched a new business marketing a little-known, low-calorie vegetable called spaghetti squash. His new firm purchases raw squash and peels, chops, and packages it for supermarket customers.

OTHER REFUGEES   Additional types of refugees identified by Knight are the following:

- The *parental (paternal) refugee,* who leaves a family business to show the parent that "I can do it alone"
- The *feminist refugee,* who experiences discrimination and elects to start a firm in which she can operate independently without the interference of male co-workers
- The *housewife refugee,* who starts her own business after her children are grown or at some other point when she can free herself from household responsibilities
- The *society refugee,* who senses some alienation from the prevailing culture and expresses it through entrepreneurial activity such as a soil conservation business or an energy-saving business
- The *educational refugee,* who tires of academia and decides to go into business

READINESS FOR ENTREPRENEURSHIP

 Discuss factors that indicate a readiness for entrepreneurship.

Many people think about getting into business for themselves if and when the right opportunity comes along. When the opportunity does come along, they must consider the combination of age, education, and experience they need to be successful. There are, in fact, four kinds of entrepreneurial opportunities, or routes to entrepreneurship, and each requires proper preparation.

Four Routes to Entrepreneurship

As we noted earlier, the term *entrepreneur* is sometimes restricted to those who build entirely new businesses. Accordingly, the only real entrepreneurial career opportunity is thought to be starting a new firm. If we broaden the concept to include various independent business options, it becomes apparent that launching an entirely new business is only one of four alternatives. The spectrum of opportunities comprises the following:

1. Start a new business
2. Buy an existing business
3. Open a franchised business
4. Enter a family business

By following any one of these four paths, an individual can become an independent business owner. Chapters 3, 4, and 5 discuss these options in greater detail.

Age and Entrepreneurial Opportunity

Education and experience are key elements in the success of most entrepreneurs. Although the requirements for these elements vary with the nature and demands

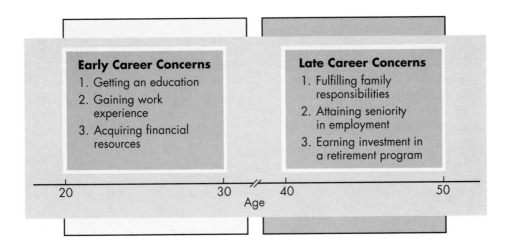

Figure 1-3

Age Concerns in Starting a Business

of a particular business, some type of know-how is needed. In addition, prospective entrepreneurs must build their financial resources in order to make initial investments. Time is required, therefore, to gain education, experience, and financial resources.

Even though there are no hard-and-fast rules concerning the right age for starting a business, some age deterrents do exist. As Figure 1-3 shows, young people are discouraged from entering entrepreneurial careers by inadequacies in their preparation and resources. On the other hand, older people develop family, financial, and job commitments that make entrepreneurship seem too risky; they may have acquired interests in retirement programs or achieved promotions to positions of greater responsibility and higher salaries.

The ideal time for entrepreneurship, then, appears to lie somewhere between these two periods, from the late 20s to the early 40s, when there is a balance between preparatory experiences on the one hand and family obligations on the other. Obviously, there are exceptions to this generalization. Some teenagers start their own firms. And older persons, even 50 or 60 years of age, walk away from successful careers in big business when they become excited by the prospects of entrepreneurship.

Precipitating Events

Many potential entrepreneurs never take the fateful step of launching their own business ventures. Some who actually make the move are stimulated by a **precipitating event** such as job termination, job dissatisfaction, or an unexpected opportunity.

Loss of a job, for example, caused Mary Anne Jackson to start her own business in Deerfield, Illinois.[21] Jackson was director of business and operations planning for Swift-Eckrich, a division of Beatrice Foods, until a leveraged buyout put her back in the job market in 1986. Well educated, with a bachelor's degree in accounting and a master's degree in business administration, she soon received attractive job offers. However, she decided instead to strike out on her own by producing nutritious meals in vacuum-sealed plastic pouches for children 2 to 10 years old.

Losing a job is only one of many types of experiences that may serve as a catalyst to taking the plunge as an entrepreneur. Some individuals become so disenchanted with formal academic programs that they simply walk away from the classroom and start new lives as entrepreneurs. Others become exasperated with rebuffs or perceived injustices at the hands of superiors in large organizations and

precipitating event
event, such as losing a job, that moves an individual to become an entrepreneur

Action Report

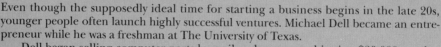

ENTREPRENEURIAL EXPERIENCES

College-Age Entrepreneurship

Even though the supposedly ideal time for starting a business begins in the late 20s, younger people often launch highly successful ventures. Michael Dell became an entrepreneur while he was a freshman at The University of Texas.

Dell began selling computer parts by mail and was soon shipping $80,000 worth a month! The prospects were so attractive that he dropped out of school to devote full time to the business. In 1985, his company, Dell Computer Corporation, started selling IBM PC clones created with off-the-shelf parts and priced at less than $1,000. For the year ending January 31, 1995, sales of the company exceeded $3 billion.

Youth was no barrier to Dell's success. He is a real entrepreneur, an energizer, who started with nothing and created a small business that quickly grew into a very big one. Are Dell's entrepreneurial skills sufficient to make Dell Computer Corporation—now the fourth-largest personal computer maker in the United States—a powerful competitor in the big business world of IBM, Apple, and Compaq? We can only wait and see.

Source: The story above has been widely reported in the business press.

leave in disgust to start their own businesses. In a more positive vein, other entrepreneurs unexpectedly stumble across business opportunities.

Many prospective entrepreneurs, of course, plan for and seek out independent business opportunities. No precipitating event is directly involved in their decision to become entrepreneurs. It is difficult to say what proportion of new entrepreneurs make their move because of some particular event. However, many who launch new firms or otherwise go into business for themselves are helped along by precipitating events.

Preparation for Entrepreneurial Careers

As we have suggested, proper preparation for entrepreneurship requires some mixture of education and experience. How much or what kind of each is necessary is extremely difficult to specify. Different types of ventures call for different kinds of preparation. The background and skills needed to start a company to produce computer software are obviously different from those needed to open an automobile repair shop. There are also striking differences in the backgrounds of those who succeed in the same industry. For these reasons, we must be cautious in discussing entrepreneurial qualifications, realizing that there are exceptions to every rule.

Some fascinating entrepreneurial success stories feature individuals who dropped out of school to start their ventures. This should not lead one to conclude, however, that education is generally unimportant. As shown in Figure 1-4, the formal education of new business owners is superior to that of the general adult population. This suggests that entrepreneurial success is not furthered by a substandard education.

In recent years, colleges and universities have greatly expanded their offerings in entrepreneurship and small business. Thousands of students across the country are now taking how-to-start-your-own-business courses. The usefulness of such

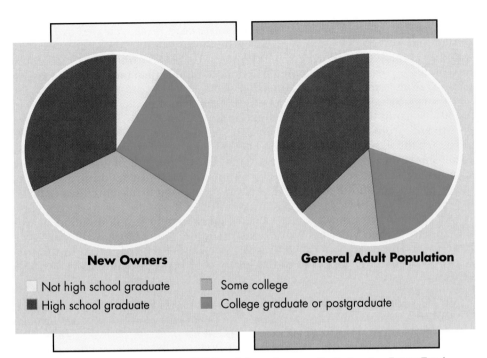

Source: Data developed and provided by the NFIB Foundation and sponsored by the American Express Travel
Related Services Company, Inc.

courses is widely debated, with some critics holding that entrepreneurs are born
and not made or that early childhood influences are more important than education. Those who offer entrepreneurship courses believe that such instruction can
contribute positively to the success of new business owners, even though it will not
be perfectly correlated with their success.

Even though it is not possible to delineate educational and experiential requirements for entrepreneurial success with great precision, we urge prospective
entrepreneurs to maximize their preparation within the limits of their time and resources. At best, however, such preparation can never completely prepare one for
the world of business ownership. Warren Buffett, the well-known investor, has expressed it this way: "Could you really explain to a fish what it's like to walk on land?
One day on land is worth a thousand years of talking about it, and one day running
a business has exactly the same kind of value."[22] In other words, get as much relevant education and experience as you can, but realize that you will still need a lot
of on-the-job entrepreneurial training.

DIVERSITY IN ENTREPRENEURSHIP

The field of small business encompasses a great variety of entrepreneurs and entrepreneurial ventures. This section identifies the various types of people and firms
that exist within the spectrum of entrepreneurship.

Women as Entrepreneurs

The number of female entrepreneurs has risen dramatically during the last two
decades. Between 1979 and 1990, the number of women-owned businesses increased at a rate of 8.4 percent, nearly double the 4.5 percent rate of growth in

5 Describe the various
types of entrepre-
neurs, entrepreneurial
leadership, and entre-
preneurial firms.

men-owned businesses.[23] A study by economist David Birch, released in 1992, reported that women owned 28 percent of the businesses in the United States and that they employed 10 percent of the country's workers.[24] Although women's business ownership has been expanding much more rapidly than men's, women are expanding from a smaller base of ownership.

Women are not only starting more businesses than they did previously, but they are also starting them in nontraditional industries and with ambitious plans for growth and profit. Not too many years ago, female entrepreneurs confined themselves, for the most part, to operating beauty shops, small clothing stores, or other establishments catering especially to women. Even though most women's business startups are still in services, women's ownership of construction firms rose by nearly 60 percent and their ownership of manufacturing firms more than doubled between 1982 and 1987.[25]

An example of a woman who became an entrepreneur in a nontraditional area is Claudette Weber. She runs Brero Construction in Santa Clara, California—the largest woman-owned general contracting firm in the United States. In the construction business, she has found that many people do not automatically take a woman seriously.

> *In 1984, while bidding on a small job to expand a church, Weber was accompanied by a vice president and a construction supervisor—both of them men—at a meeting with church elders. The church officials didn't even look her in the eye, she recalls. Then, when it came time to ink the deal, Weber suddenly pulled out a pen and signed the paper, leaving her new clients speechless. "They were astonished that a woman owned a construction business," Weber says.[26]*

Female entrepreneurs obviously face problems common to all entrepreneurs. However, they must also contend with difficulties associated with their newness in entrepreneurial roles. Lack of access to credit has been a problem frequently cited by women who enter business. This is a troublesome area for most small business owners, but many women feel they carry an added burden of discrimination. Loan officers point out that female applicants often lack a track record in financial management and argue that this creates problems in loan approval. Women entrepreneurs have also found that some male loan officers still have stereotypical ideas of what women can accomplish.

Another barrier for some women is the limited opportunity they find for business relationships with others in similar positions. It takes time and effort for them

Women's business ownership has increased significantly over the last 20 years. Claudette Weber operates the largest woman-owned general contracting company in the United States, Brero Construction.

to gain full acceptance and to develop informal relationships with others in local, mostly male, business and professional groups. Women are attacking this problem by increasing their participation in predominantly male organizations and also by forming networks of their own—the female equivalent of the "old boy network."

Founders and Other Entrepreneurs

Although the categories tend to overlap, entrepreneurial leadership may be classified into three types: founders, general managers, and franchisees.

FOUNDERS   Generally considered to be the "pure" entrepreneurs, **founders** may be inventors who initiate businesses on the basis of new or improved products or services. They may also be artisans who develop skills and then start their own firms. Or they may be enterprising individuals, often with marketing backgrounds, who draw on the ideas of others in starting new firms. Whether acting as an individual or as part of a group, these people bring firms into existence by surveying the market, raising funds, and arranging for the necessary facilities. After the firm is launched, the founding entrepreneur may preside over the subsequent growth of the business or sell out and move on to other ventures.

founder
an entrepreneur who brings a new firm into existence

GENERAL MANAGERS   As a new firm becomes well established, the founder often becomes less innovative and more administrative. Thus, we recognize another class of entrepreneurs called **general managers.** General managers preside over the operation of successful ongoing business firms. They manage the week-to-week and month-to-month production, marketing, and financial functions of small firms. The distinction between founders and general managers is often hazy. In some cases, small firms grow rapidly, and their orientation is more akin to the founding than to the management process. Nevertheless, it is helpful to distinguish those entrepreneurs who found or substantially change firms (the "movers and shakers") from those who direct the continuing operations of established firms.

general manager
an entrepreneur who functions as an administrator of a business

FRANCHISEES   A third category of entrepreneurs comprises franchisees. **Franchisees** differ from general managers in the degree of their independence. Because of the constraints and guidance provided by contractual relationships with franchising organizations, franchisees function as limited entrepreneurs. Chapter 4 presents more information about franchisees.

franchisee
an entrepreneur whose power is limited by a contractual relationship with a franchising organization

High-Growth and Low-Growth Firms

Small business ventures differ greatly in their potential for growth and profits. Some create millionaires, while others produce less spectacular results. To account for these differences, we distinguish firms as being in the following categories: marginal firms, attractive small companies, and high-potential ventures. In writing about small businesses, one can easily fall into the trap of considering only one end of the spectrum. Some authors treat only the tiny, marginal firms whose owners barely survive; others focus entirely on high-growth, high-technology firms. A balanced view must recognize the entire range of ventures with the varied problems and rewards presented by each point on the spectrum.

MARGINAL FIRMS   Some dry cleaners, beauty shops, service stations, appliance repair shops, and other small firms that provide very modest returns to their owners

marginal firm
any small firm that provides minimal profits to its owner(s)

are **marginal firms.** We do not call them marginal because they are in danger of bankruptcy, however. Although it is true that some marginal firms are on thin ice financially, their distinguishing feature is their limited ability to generate significant profits. Entrepreneurs who devote personal effort to such ventures receive a profit return that does little more than compensate them for their time. Part-time businesses typically fall into the category of marginal firms.

attractive small firm
any small firm that provides substantial profits to its owner(s)

ATTRACTIVE SMALL COMPANIES   In contrast to marginal firms, **attractive small firms** offer substantial rewards to their owners. Entrepreneurial income from these ventures may easily range from $100,000 to $300,000 or more annually. They represent the strong segment of small business—the good firms that can provide rewarding careers.

high-potential venture (gazelle)
a small firm that has great prospects for growth

HIGH-POTENTIAL VENTURES   A few businesses have such great prospects for growth that they may be called **high-potential ventures,** or **gazelles.** Frequently, these are also high-technology ventures. At the time of such a firm's founding, the owners often anticipate rapid growth, a possible merger, or going public within a few years. Some striking examples in this category are Microsoft, Wal-Mart, McDonald's, and Toys "R" Us. In addition to such widely recognized successes, thousands of less well-known ventures are constantly being launched and experiencing rapid growth. Entrepreneurial ventures of this type appeal to many engineers, professional managers, and venture capitalists who see the potential rewards and exciting prospects.

Artisan Entrepreneurs and Opportunistic Entrepreneurs

Perhaps because of their varied backgrounds, entrepreneurs display great variation in their styles of doing business. They analyze problems and approach decision making in drastically different ways. Norman R. Smith has suggested two basic entrepreneurial patterns: artisan, or craftsman, entrepreneurs and opportunistic entrepreneurs.[27]

artisan entrepreneur
a person who starts a business with primarily technical skills and little business knowledge

THE ARTISAN ENTREPRENEUR   According to Smith, the education of the **artisan entrepreneur** is limited to technical training. Such entrepreneurs have technical job experience, but they typically lack good communication skills. Their approach to business decision making is characterized by the following features:

- They are paternalistic (meaning that they direct their businesses much as they might direct their own families).
- They are reluctant to delegate authority.
- They use few (one or two) capital sources to create their firms.
- They define marketing strategy in terms of the traditional components of price, quality, and company reputation.
- Their sales efforts are primarily personal.
- Their time orientation is short, with little planning for future growth or change.

A mechanic who starts an independent garage and a beautician who operates a beauty shop are examples of artisan entrepreneurs.

opportunistic entrepreneur
a person who starts a business with both sophisticated managerial skills and technical knowledge

entrepreneurial team
two or more people who work together as entrepreneurs

THE OPPORTUNISTIC ENTREPRENEUR   Smith's definition of an **opportunistic entrepreneur** is one who has supplemented his or her technical education by studying such nontechnical subjects as economics, law, or English. Opportunistic entrepreneurs avoid paternalism, delegate authority as necessary for growth, employ various marketing strategies and types of sales efforts, obtain original capitalization from more than two sources, and plan for future growth. An example of an opportunistic entrepreneur is a small building contractor and developer who uses a relatively sophisticated approach to management; because of the complexity of the industry, successful contractors use careful record keeping and budgeting, precise bidding, and systematic market research.

In Smith's model of entrepreneurial styles, we see two extremes. At one end, we find an artisan in an entrepreneurial position. At the other end, we find a well-educated and experienced manager. The former "flies by the seat of the pants," and the latter uses systematic management procedures and something resembling a scientific management approach. In practice, of course, the distribution of entrepreneurial styles is less polarized than suggested by Smith's model, with entrepreneurs scattered along a continuum of managerial sophistication. This book is intended to help you move toward the opportunistic end and away from the artisan end of the continuum.

Entrepreneurial Teams

So far, we have assumed that entrepreneurs are individuals. And, of course, this is usually the case. However, the entrepreneurial team is becoming increasingly common, particularly in ventures of substantial size. An **entrepreneurial team** is formed when two or more individuals come together to function in the capacity of entrepreneurs.

Each year, *Inc.* magazine compiles a list of the 500 fastest-growing, pri-

1 Discuss the availability of entrepreneurial opportunities, and give examples of highly successful businesses started by entrepreneurs.

- Entrepreneurs who provide quality and integrity can still find opportunities, even in a highly competitive marketplace.
- Cracker Barrel, Coldwater Creek, and Proctor and Gardner Advertising are examples of highly successful businesses started by entrepreneurs.
- Unlimited entrepreneurial opportunities exist for those who recognize them.

2 Identify three rewards and three drawbacks of entrepreneurial careers.

- Entrepreneurial rewards include profit, independence, and a satisfying way of life.
- Drawbacks to entrepreneurship include hard work, personal stress, and danger of failure.

3 Identify personal characteristics often found in entrepreneurs.

- Individuals who become entrepreneurs often have a high need for achievement, a willingness to take moderate risks, and a high degree of self-confidence.
- Many entrepreneurs have entered entrepreneurial careers as refugees from corporate life or other restrictive environments.

4 Discuss factors that indicate a readiness for entrepreneurship.

- Routes to entrepreneurship include starting a new business, buying an existing business, opening a franchise, and entering a family business.
- The period between the late 20s and early 40s is the time when a person's education, work experience, and financial resources are most likely to enable him or her to become an entrepreneur.
- Entry into entrepreneurial careers is often triggered by a precipitating event, such as losing a job.
- Successful entrepreneurship requires a combination of education and experience appropriate for the particular type of endeavor.

5 Describe the various types of entrepreneurs, entrepreneurial leadership, and entrepreneurial firms.

- The number of women becoming entrepreneurs is growing rapidly, and they are entering many nontraditional fields.
- Entrepreneurs may be categorized as founders of firms, general managers, or franchisees.
- Entrepreneurial firms may be classified as marginal firms, attractive small companies, or high-potential ventures (gazelles).
- In their management styles, entrepreneurs may be characterized as artisan entrepreneurs or opportunistic entrepreneurs.
- Entrepreneurial teams consist of two or more individuals who come together to function as entrepreneurs.

New Terms and Concepts

entrepreneur *3*	precipitating event *13*	artisan entrepreneur *18*
need for achievement *9*	founder *17*	opportunistic entrepreneur *18*
internal locus of control *10*	general manager *17*	entrepreneurial team *18*
external locus of control *10*	franchisee *17*	
	marginal firm *18*	
refugee *11*	attractive small firm *18*	
foreign refugee *11*		
corporate refugee *11*	high-potential venture (gazelle) *18*	

You Make the Call

Situation 1 Following is a statement in which a business owner attempts to explain and justify his preference for slow growth in his business:

I limit my growth pace and make every effort to service my present customers in the manner they deserve. I have some peer pressure to do otherwise by following the advice of experts—that is, to take on partners and debt to facilitate rapid growth in sales and market share. When tempted by such thoughts, I think about what I might gain. Perhaps I could make more money, but I would also expect a lot more problems. Also, I think it might interfere somewhat with my family relationships, which are very important to me.

Question 1 Should this venture be regarded as entrepreneurial? Is the owner a true entrepreneur?
Question 2 Do you agree with the philosophy expressed here? Is the owner really doing what is best for his family?
Question 3 What kinds of problems is this owner avoiding?

Situation 2 When Amy Clark was growing up, her father owned several service stations where she pumped gas and developed some knowledge of station operation. When she graduated from high school, Amy entered business college and trained to be a secretary. She married soon after school, and her husband entered the service station business. Recently, Amy decided that she would like to operate a station of her own. A station with three service bays and facilities for minor auto repair is available if she can persuade the oil company—the same one that franchises her husband's station—that she is qualified to have a franchise. Clark has expressed her philosophy as follows: "I'm a person who likes to get things done. I like to keep excelling and to do bigger and better things than I've ever done before. I guess that's why I'd like to have a station of my own."

Question 1 Evaluate Amy Clark's qualifications for the proposed venture. Should the oil company accept her as a dealer?
Question 2 As a female entrepreneur, what problems should she anticipate in relationships with customers, employees, the franchising oil company, and her family?

Continue on next page

vately held companies in the United States. In its 1992 survey, *Inc.* found that 58 percent of the chief executives of companies in this group began with at least one partner.[28] Even though very small firms are underrepresented in this survey, it does suggest that founding teams are not unusual.

By forming a team, founders can secure a broader range of managerial talents than is otherwise possible. For example, a person with manufacturing experience can team up with a person who has marketing experience. The need for such diversified experience is particularly acute in new high-technology businesses.

DISCUSSION QUESTIONS

1. What is meant by the term *entrepreneur*?
2. The outstanding success stories at the beginning of the chapter are exceptions to the rule. What, then, is their significance in illustrating entrepreneurial opportunity? Are these stories misleading?
3. Concerning the entrepreneur you know best, what was the most significant reason for his or her following an independent business career?
4. The rewards of profit, independence, and a satisfying way of life attract individuals to entrepreneurial careers. What problems might be anticipated if an entrepreneur were to become obsessed with one of these rewards, that is, feel an excessive desire for profit or independence or a particular life-style?
5. Explain the internal locus of control and its significance for entrepreneurship.
6. Identify a foreign refugee entrepreneur and explain the circumstances surrounding his or her entry into entrepreneurship.

7. Why is the period from the late 20s to the early 40s considered to be the best time of life for becoming an entrepreneur?
8. What is a precipitating event? Give some examples.
9. Distinguish between an artisan entrepreneur and an opportunistic entrepreneur.
10. What is the advantage of using an entrepreneurial team?

EXPERIENTIAL EXERCISES

1. Analyze your own education and experience as qualifications for entrepreneurship. Identify your greatest strengths and weaknesses.
2. Explain your own interest in each type of entrepreneurial reward—profit, independence, satisfying way of life, or other. Point out which of these is most significant for you personally and tell why.
3. Interview someone who has started a business, being sure to ask for information regarding that entrepreneur's background and age at the time the business was started. In the report of your interview, indicate whether the entrepreneur was in any sense a refugee and show how the timing of her or his startup relates to the ideal time for startup explained in this chapter.
4. Interview a female entrepreneur about what problems, if any, she has encountered because she is a woman.

Exploring the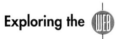

5. Using a personal computer, find the home page for this book, *Small Business Management: An Entrepreneurial Emphasis,* by accessing the World Wide Web. Then prepare a one-page report summarizing the content of this home page. The Web address is

http://www.thomson.com/swcp/mm/longenecker.html

 CASE 1
King's Beauty Supply (p. 593)

This case describes the entrepreneurial struggles and eventual success of a native South Korean in the United States.

Alternative Case for Chapter 1: Case 2, "Construction Equipment Dealership," p. 595

Situation 3 An idealistic artisan is contemplating starting his own business. He loves woodworking and wants to produce handcrafted tables, cabinets, and other furniture items. Previously, he, with three partners, had successfully produced elegant rosewood and walnut conference tables for some large business firms in his city. This prospective entrepreneur expresses a personal philosophy that some consider more idealistic than businesslike. He believes that employees who enjoy producing something will turn out high-quality products and have a sense of self-esteem as well as pride in their work. He hopes to be successful by creating an atmosphere that permits employees to experience that sense of professional joy. He even intends, after an allowance for a substantial personal salary for himself, to share profits with the employees.

Question 1 What appear to be the prospective rewards of entrepreneurship for this individual? How are they likely to affect the firm's chances for success?

Question 2 In view of this prospective entrepreneur's obvious woodworking skills, is he likely to succeed? Would you be willing to invest in his new business? What additional information would you seek?

Small Business:
Vital Component of the Economy

Chapter 2

Linda and
Lawrence Link

spotlight on small business

Steins, population zero, is a tiny fly-speck on the map of western New Mexico. It boasts no corporate offices, but it is home to an imaginative entrepreneurial venture that was conceived in the minds of Lawrence and Linda Link. In the late 1980s, the Links bought Steins, an abandoned ghost town, for $50,000. There were no large corporations bidding against them because big business is not good in finding isolated opportunities of this nature. The Links, however, saw a deserted railroad village (once a stagecoach stop) that could be restored to preserve a part of the history of the Old West. It would not be Disneyland, but it could offer a glimpse of pioneer life to tourists traveling I-10.

Most of the dozen or so small adobe, stone, and wood buildings were in disrepair. The Links have been restoring the property to its original condition. Even in its partially restored form, the village attracts several hundred visitors a day. Steins is a ghost town with a bright future because two entrepreneurs risked their savings to bring it back to life. This is a small business with no big business competition. Although large and small firms exist side by side, millions of small firms such as this one serve specialized markets that are totally unsuited to large corporations.

Looking Ahead

After studying this chapter, you should be able to:

1 Define small business and identify criteria that may be used to measure the size of business firms.

2 Compare the relative importance of small business in the eight major industries and explain the trend in small business activity.

3 Identify five special contributions of small business to society.

4 Discuss the rate of small business failure and the costs associated with such failure.

5 Describe the causes of business failure.

start here

It is easy to overestimate the importance of big business because of its high visibility. Small businesses seem dwarfed by such corporate giants as General Motors (693,000 employees), Citicorp ($163 billion in deposits), Wal-Mart (2,855 stores), and Exxon ($5 billion of annual profits). Yet small firms, even though less conspicuous, are a vital component of the economy. In this chapter, we examine not only the extent of small business activity but also the unique contributions of small businesses that help preserve the nation's economic well-being. But first, we will look at the criteria used to define small business.

DEFINITION OF SMALL BUSINESS

1 Define small business and identify criteria that may be used to measure the size of business firms.

Establishing a size as the standard to define small business is necessarily arbitrary, because people adopt particular standards for particular purposes. Legislators, for example, may exclude small firms from certain regulations if they have fewer than 10 or 15 employees. Moreover, a business may be described as "small" when compared to larger firms, but "large" when compared to smaller ones. Most people, for example, would classify independently owned gasoline stations, neighborhood restaurants, and locally owned retail stores as small businesses. Similarly, most would agree that the major automobile manufacturers are big businesses. Firms of in-between sizes, however, are characterized as large or small on the basis of individual viewpoints.

Size Criteria

Even the criteria used to measure the size of businesses vary. Some **size criteria** are applicable to all industrial areas, while others are relevant only to certain types of business. Examples of criteria used to measure size are

size criteria
criteria by which the size of a business is measured

- Number of employees
- Volume of sales
- Value of assets
- Insurance in force (for insurance companies)
- Volume of deposits (for banks)

Although the first criterion listed above—number of employees—is the one most widely used, the best criterion in any given case depends on the user's purpose.

SBA STANDARDS The Small Business Administration (SBA) establishes size standards that determine eligibility for SBA loans and for special consideration in bid-

Table 2-1

*Examples of SBA Size
Standards for Classifying
a Business as Small*

Type of Business	Maximum Sales ($) or Number of Employees
Advertising agencies	$3.5 million
Copper ore mining	500 employees
Employment agencies	$3.5 million
Furniture stores	$3.5 million
General contractors (Single-family houses)	$17.0 million
Hardware wholesaling	100 employees
Insurance agents, brokers, and service	$3.5 million
Meat-packing plants	500 employees
Metal can manufacturing	1,000 employees
Mobile home dealers	$6.5 million
Radio and television repair shops	$3.5 million
Radio broadcasting	$3.5 million

Source: "Standard Industrial Classification Codes and Size Standards," *Code of Federal Regulations,* Title 13, Section 121.601, 1994.

SBA standards
the standards set by
the Small Business
Administration (SBA)
that specify size limits
for small firms

ding on government contracts. Some **SBA standards** are stated in terms of number of employees and others in terms of sales volume. As you can see in Table 2-1, these standards vary by industry, with 500 employees and $3.5 million in sales being typical limits.

CRITERIA USED IN THIS BOOK   In this book, we use the following general criteria for defining a small business:

1. Financing of the business is supplied by one individual or a small group. Only in a rare case would the business have more than 15 owners.
2. Except for its marketing function, the firm's operations are geographically localized.
3. Compared to the biggest firms in the industry, the business is small.
4. The number of employees in the business is usually fewer than 100.

Obviously, some small firms fail to meet *all* of the above standards. For example, a small executive search firm—a firm that helps corporate clients recruit managers from other organizations—may operate in many sections of the country and thereby fail to meet the second criterion. Nevertheless, the discussion of management concepts in this book is aimed primarily at the type of firm that fits the general pattern outlined by these criteria.

**Compare the relative
importance of small
business in the eight
2 major industries and
explain the trend
in small business
activity.**

SMALL BUSINESS AS PRODUCER OF GOODS AND SERVICES

In this section, our purpose is to describe the contribution made by small business as part of the total economic system. This entails a look at small business in the major industries and its relative importance as compared to big business.

Small Business in the Major Industries

Small firms operate in all industries, but their nature and importance differ widely from industry to industry. Consideration of their economic contribution, therefore, requires identifying the major industries (as classified by the U.S. Department

Table 2-2

The Eight Major Industries

Industry	Examples of Small Firms
Wholesale trade	Wholesale drug companies Petroleum bulk stations
Construction	General building contractors Electrical contractors
Retail trade	Hardware stores Restaurants
Services	Travel agencies Beauty shops
Finance, insurance, and real estate	Local insurance agencies Real estate brokerage firms
Mining	Sand and gravel companies Coal mines
Transportation, communication, and utilities	Taxicab companies Local radio stations
Manufacturing	Bakeries Machine shops

of Commerce) and noting the types of small firms that function in these industries. The eight **major industries** and two examples of the types of small firms in each are listed in Table 2-2.

major industries
the eight largest groups of businesses as specified by the U.S. Department of Commerce

Number of Small Businesses

Widely divergent statements about the number of U.S. businesses appear in print. The numbers range from 5 million to more than 20 million firms! Much of the confusion arises from different definitions of what constitutes a business.

The larger numbers are typically based on Internal Revenue Service data. In 1992, for example, an estimated 21.3 million business tax returns were filed.[1] Does this mean that 21.3 million businesses exist? The answer depends on how "business" is defined. Many tax returns report hobbies and part-time activities as businesses even though these show little revenue and often no profit. A homemaker, for example, may give piano lessons to two or three neighborhood children and file a business tax return to report the income.

Table 2-3 shows, for the major industries, the number of firms having one or more paid employees. The total of 5,073,795 is a conservative estimate, excluding

Table 2-3

Number of Small Firms by Major Industry

Industry	Number
Services	1,921,767
Retail trade	1,109,703
Construction	597,272
Finance, insurance, and real estate	419,963
Wholesale trade	374,283
Manufacturing	327,036
Transportation, communication, and utilities	180,900
Mining	24,309
U.S. total	5,073,795

Source: *The State of Small Business: A Report of the President 1993* (Washington: U.S. Government Printing Office, 1993), pp. 48–51.

as it does most of the hobby, part-time, and other very small one-person operations. More than 98 percent of these 5,073,795 firms have fewer than 100 employees. This percentage tells us that a huge number of small firms operate in the United States—about 5 million according to this conservative estimate and many more if very small business activities were included.

Emphasizing the large number of small business units may distort your impression of the overall importance of small business. There is a great difference between the small business proportion of all business units and the small business proportion of all business activity. The output of one large corporation may easily exceed the combined output of thousands of small firms. The fact that more than 98 percent of all businesses are small, therefore, does not mean that 98 percent of all products and services are produced by small business. In the section at the bottom of this page, we compare the overall role of small businesses with that of big businesses as producers of goods and services.

The Global Reach of Small Business

The growing participation of small firms in international trade has caused a modification of the traditional image of small businesses as strictly domestic. Even though small firms are typically situated in one locality, many of them export or import products across national boundaries. As the volume of international business has grown, therefore, small businesses have become increasingly involved in the global market.

As just one example, Auburn Farms, Inc., a small Sacramento, California snack foods company, has started importing products from South Africa.[2] Auburn Farms, whose annual sales volume is $15 million, has become the exclusive U.S. importer of Beacon Sweets & Chocolates of South Africa, a candy maker that exports to 23 other countries. The strategy is meant to broaden Auburn Farms's product line of fat-free snack foods and help make the company a more general supplier of specialty foods.

Most small firms, of course, are not directly involved in international business. Nevertheless, the number of small firms functioning as importers and exporters is growing, along with the overall volume of international business. Thus, small business is very much a part of the global economy. Its role in international business is discussed more fully in Chapter 16.

In the service industry, small businesses, such as beauty salons, are more important than large businesses. Service firms with fewer than 100 workers employ 42.3 percent of U.S. workers, and those with fewer than 500 workers employ 59.6 percent of U.S. workers.

Relative Economic Importance of Small Business

The fact that numerous small firms exist in each major industry does not reveal much about their relative importance. Small firms may be merely on the fringe of some industries. Or they may be so numerous and productive that their collective output exceeds that of large firms. The question then is this: What percentage of the economy's total output of goods and services comes from small business?

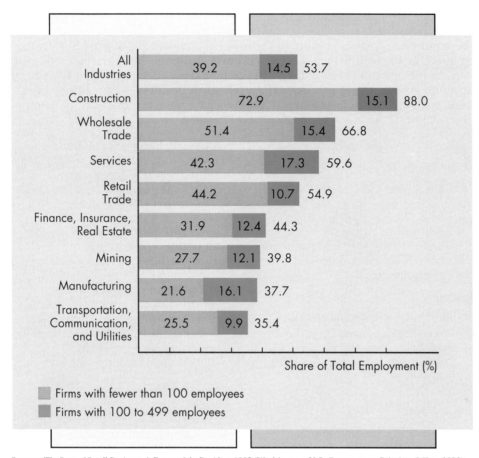

Figure 2-1

Percentage of Employees in Small Firms

Source: *The State of Small Business: A Report of the President 1993* (Washington: U.S. Government Printing Office, 1993), pp. 48–51.

One simple way to measure this percentage is to compare the number of employees who work in small firms with the number of employees who work in large firms. We can do this for each industry and for the economy as a whole. Figure 2-1 presents such a comparison.

As you can see, the small business share of total U.S. employment is 39.2 percent based on the 100-employee criterion; an additional 14.5 percent is added for firms with 100 to 499 employees, making a total of 53.7 percent based on the 500-employee criterion. Individual industries differ, naturally, from this overall average. In the construction industry, where small business is strongest, 88 percent of all employees work in firms with fewer than 500 employees. Assuming that all workers are equally productive, we can infer that 88 percent of that industry's output comes from small business.

In four of the industries portrayed in Figure 2-1—construction, wholesale trade, services, and retail trade—small business appears to be relatively more important than big business. In the other four industries, large business is dominant. Big business is strongest in the transportation, communication, and utilities category, representing 64.6 percent of all employment.

As previously noted, for industry as a whole, firms with fewer than 500 employees account for 53.7 percent of the nation's employment and, presumably, the same percentage of the nation's output. It is apparent that much—roughly 50 percent—of U.S. business may be classified as small.

The Trend in Small Business Activity

For a number of decades prior to the mid-1970s, the share of total business accounted for by small firms had slowly eroded. Although small business still produced a major share of the nation's gross national product, it was gradually giving up some ground to big business. However, small business is evidently staging a comeback. Even popular business periodicals have observed the phenomenon, as indicated by the following report from *The Economist*:

> *Despite ever-larger and noisier mergers, the biggest change coming over the world of business is that firms are getting smaller. The trend of a century is being reversed. Until the mid-1970s the size of firms everywhere grew; the numbers of self-employed fell. ... No longer. Now it is the big firms that are shrinking and small ones that are on the rise. The trend is unmistakable—and businessmen and policymakers will ignore it at their peril.*[3]

The quest of large corporations for efficiency through downsizing no doubt contributed to the apparent resurgence of small business. Many corporations shed peripheral divisions and activities during the 1980s as they sought to increase efficiency by building on the strength of their core competencies.

On balance, small business has maintained a position of overall strength during recent decades. Bennett Harrison, professor of political economy at Carnegie Mellon University, argues that large corporations are still the dominant force in economic life but agrees that the share of all jobs accounted for by small companies with fewer than 100 employees has hardly changed since the 1960s.[4]

Reasons for the continuing strength of small firms may include such factors as the following:

- New technologies, such as numerically controlled machine tools, may permit more efficient production on a smaller scale.
- Greater flexibility is required as a result of increased global competition, a requirement that favors small firms.
- Small firms may be more flexible in employing the increasing numbers of working mothers in the labor force.
- Consumers appear to prefer personalized products over mass-produced goods, and this opens a door of opportunity for smaller business.[5]
- The earlier advantage of large firms in working with the international banking system has been reduced.

Small business just held its own for several decades. Now, however, with such new technologies as personal computers, faxes, and modems allowing firms to produce more efficiently on a smaller scale, small and home-based businesses are on the rise.

The vigor of small business is evident in the entrepreneurial boom in the United States. From 1950 to 1975, the number of new incorporations—a proxy for new business formation—simply kept pace with the growth of the economy. After 1975, however, the entrepreneurial pace picked up. In 1991, despite the recession, 630,000 companies incorporated—twice the rate of incorporations in 1975.[6] The spirit of entrepreneurship is obviously far from dead, and its effect has been to strengthen small business as a continuing, important part of the U.S. economy.

SPECIAL CONTRIBUTIONS OF SMALL BUSINESS

3 Identify five special contributions of small business to society.

As part of the business community, small firms unquestionably contribute to the nation's economic welfare. As we noted earlier, they produce roughly 50 percent of total U.S. goods and services. Thus, their general economic contribution is similar to that of big business. Small firms, however, possess some qualities that make them more than miniature versions of big business corporations. They make exceptional contributions as they provide new jobs, introduce innovations, stimulate competition, aid big business, and produce goods and services efficiently.

Providing New Jobs

Small businesses provide many of the new job opportunities needed by a growing population. There is evidence, indeed, that small firms create the lion's share of new jobs, sometimes adding jobs while large corporations are downsizing and laying off employees. Between 1980 and 1986, for example, firms with fewer than 20 employees accounted for more of total job growth than did firms of 500 or more employees.[7]

The powerful role of small business in generating new jobs was discovered by David L. Birch in his research during the 1980s.[8] Later studies have supplied support for Birch's findings. Acs and Audretsch, for example, found that 1.3 million new jobs in manufacturing were created by small firms between 1976 and 1986, while the number of manufacturing jobs in large firms decreased by 100,000.[9] Although some scholars still question this virtue of small business, our conclusion at this point is that small firms provide a large, disproportionate share of new jobs.[10]

This does not mean, of course, that all or even most small firms are adding new jobs. Numerous small businesses show no growth whatever. Birch concludes that 10 to 15 percent of all small enterprises create most of the growth.[11]

Small firms that add jobs soon become medium or large firms. As medium and large corporations, they often continue to add jobs. The small business sector, therefore, contributes to new job growth in two ways—first by the formation of new ventures and subsequently by the further expansion of these businesses.

Introducing Innovation

New products that originate in the research laboratories of big business make a valuable contribution to people's standard of living. Some people question, however, the relative importance of big business in achieving truly significant innovations. The record shows that many scientific breakthroughs have originated with independent inventors and small organizations. Here are some twentieth-century examples of new products created by small firms:

- Photocopiers
- Insulin
- Vacuum tube
- Penicillin
- Cotton picker
- Zipper
- Automatic transmission
- Jet engine
- Helicopter
- Power steering
- Color film
- Ballpoint pen

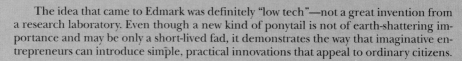

Action Report

ENTREPRENEURIAL EXPERIENCES

TopsyTail: A Case of Nontechnical Innovation

Tomima Edmark can remember the exact moment when the Idea Worth Millions came to her. It was August 20, 1989.

Walking with her mother into a movie theater in Seattle, the Dallas entrepreneur, then 32, got a glimpse of a woman's beautifully styled hair done in a French twist.

"I'll never forget it," Edmark says. "I said to my mother, 'I wonder if you can turn a pony-tail inside out?'"

The idea that came to Edmark was definitely "low tech"—not a great invention from a research laboratory. Even though a new kind of ponytail is not of earth-shattering importance and may be only a short-lived fad, it demonstrates the way that imaginative entrepreneurs can introduce simple, practical innovations that appeal to ordinary citizens.

After the movie, Edmark went to her mother's home and played with her own long blond ponytail, trying to flip it inside out.

First she tried using a toothbrush with a rubber band attached to one end. Then she tried a pencil with a paper clip attached to the eraser.

Circular knitting needles finally did the trick. She cut the plastic string that holds the needles together, then relooped one string, forming a circle at the top of one needle.

She stuck the end of the needle into her hair between her head and the elastic band, pushed her ponytail through the loop and pulled it down. Voila! A topsy-turvy ponytail. A TopsyTail.

After two large hair-product companies rejected the idea, Edmark started selling the product directly. In three months, she sold 3.6 million TopsyTails at $15 each! In 1993, retail sales reached approximately $80 million. The product is sold not only in the United States but also in Canada, Europe, Mexico, Japan, and South America.

Source: Glenna Whitley, "Turning a Hairdo into Gold," reprinted with permission from the December, 1993 issue of *Texas Monthly.*

Jeffrey A. Timmons suggests, on the basis of several studies by the U.S. Department of Commerce, that 50 percent of all innovations and 95 percent of all radical innovations since World War II have come from new and smaller firms. As examples, Timmons mentions the microcomputer, the pacemaker, overnight express packages, the quick oil change, fast food, and oral contraceptives.[12]

Research departments of big businesses tend to emphasize the improvement of existing products. Some ideas may be sidetracked because they are not related to existing products or because of their unusual nature. Unfortunately, preoccupation with an existing product can sometimes obscure the value of a *new* idea. The jet engine, for example, had difficulty winning the attention of those who were accustomed to internal combustion engines.

Studies of innovation have shown the greater effectiveness of small firms in research and development. Figure 2-2, based on a study by Edwards and Gordon, shows that small firms are superior innovators in both increasing-employment and decreasing-employment industries. More recent research continues to provide sup-

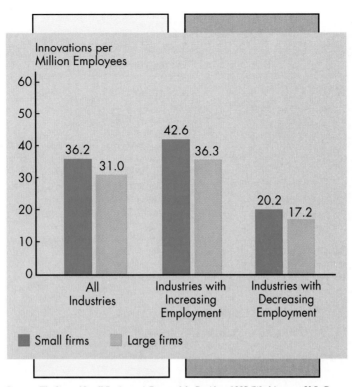

Source: *The State of Small Business: A Report of the President 1985* (Washington: U.S. Government Printing Office, 1985), p. 128; Keith L. Edwards and Theodore J. Gordon, "Characterization of Innovations Introduced on the U.S. Market in 1982" (Glastonbury, CT: Prepared for the U.S. Small Business Administration, Office of Advocacy, under Award No. SBA-6050-OA-82, March 1984), p. 46.

port for the important small business role in innovation. A recent summary reads as follows:

> *We can say with assurance that the role of small companies has become more, not less, important. From steel to computers, small companies continue to lead. In the all-important biotechnology industry small companies have a virtual monopoly on innovations.*[13]

Stimulating Economic Competition

Many economists, beginning with Adam Smith, have expounded the values inherent in **economic competition.** In a competitive business situation, individuals are driven by self-interest to act in a socially desirable manner. Competition acts as the regulator that transforms their self-interest into service.

When producers consist of only a few big firms, however, the customer is at their mercy. They may set high prices, withhold technological developments, exclude new competitors, or otherwise abuse their position of power. If competition is to have a cutting edge, there is need for small firms.

The fall of communist governments in Eastern Europe and the breakup of the Soviet Union made possible a start toward a competitive economic system in that area of the world. Communism's economic system, lacking a free market and business competition, was a dismal failure. Scrapping the system of state-owned enterprise opened the way for independent business firms, many of them small, to compete and thereby to increase productivity and raise the standard of living.

economic competition
a situation in which businesses vie for sales

Action Report

GLOBAL OPPORTUNITIES

Competing Effectively in the Global Market

Many small firms compete successfully with big corporations and even international companies. This is good for consumers and the economy as a whole, as well as for the small firms that manage to outhustle their giant competitors.

JoLene Company, a small children's apparel manufacturer in Provo, Utah, experienced this kind of competition in 1985. Its sales dropped by 25 percent because of competition from imports. The sales drop, in turn, made it difficult to obtain financing, which delayed production and shipments to customers.

Led by its president, Donald W. Geis, JoLene regained sales and eventually expanded its sales volume by following these steps:

1. Adding to its one-person sales staff by creating an independent sales force in 15 U.S. cities
2. Hiring a consultant to improve scheduling and timeliness of shipments
3. Obtaining $1.2 million from a private source to finance growth
4. Reorganizing its design department under the direction of Melodee Chin, a designer who understood how to combine trend-setting designs with cost-effective production

Source: Sharon Nelton, "Beating Back the Competition," *Nation's Business*, Vol. 82, No. 9 (September 1994), pp. 18–25. Excerpted by permission. Copyright 1994, U.S. Chamber of Commerce.

Not every competitive effort of small firms is successful, but big business may be kept on its toes by small business. For example, a small jelly manufacturer, Sorrell Ridge of Port Reading, New Jersey, challenged giant Smucker's, whose commercials say, "With a name like Smucker's, it has to be good."[14] Tiny Sorrell Ridge introduced a line of no-sugar, all-natural fruit spreads and twitted its larger rival in its commercials: "With a name like Smucker's, is it really so good? Sorrell Ridge—with 100% fruit, it has to be better." Smucker's soon introduced an all-fruit line of its own. Small companies like Sorrell Ridge keep larger companies like Smucker's on their toes.

However, there is no guarantee of competition in numbers alone. Many small firms may be no match for one large firm or for several firms that dominate an industry. Nevertheless, the existence of many healthy small businesses in an industry may be viewed as a bulwark of the U.S. capitalistic system.

Aiding Big Business

The fact that some functions are more expertly performed by small business enables small firms to contribute to the success of larger ones. If small businesses were suddenly removed from the contemporary scene, big businesses would find themselves saddled with a myriad of activities that they could perform only inefficiently. Three functions that small business can often perform more efficiently than big business are the distribution function, the supply function, and the service function.

DISTRIBUTION FUNCTION Few large manufacturers find it desirable to own wholesale and retail outlets. Small businesses carry out the **distribution function** for such products as toiletries, books, lawnmowers, musical instruments, gasoline, food items, personal computers, office supplies, clothing, kitchen appliances, automobiles, tires, auto parts, furniture, and industrial supplies. Wholesale and retail establishments, many of them small, perform a valuable economic service by linking customers and the producers of these products.

Small businesses are usually more efficient than large manufacturers in many types of distribution. Distribution of grocery store produce is one example of a function small firms can perform to aid larger ones.

SUPPLY FUNCTION In performing the **supply function,** small businesses act as suppliers and subcontractors for large firms. Large firms recognize the growing importance of their suppliers by using terms such as *partnership* and *strategic alliance* to describe the ideal working relationship. Japanese manufacturers have pioneered in developing strong relationships by working closely with trusted, long-term suppliers. To some extent, U.S. manufacturers are implementing this same approach, granting long-term contracts to suppliers in return for a specified level of quality, lower prices, and cost-saving ideas.

distribution function
a small business activity that links producers and customers

supply function
an activity in which small businesses function as suppliers and subcontractors for larger firms

SERVICE FUNCTION In addition to supplying services directly to large corporations, small firms perform the **service function** for customers of big business. For example, they service automobiles, repair appliances, and clean carpets produced by large manufacturers.

service function
an activity in which small businesses provide repair and other services that aid larger firms

Producing Goods and Services Efficiently

Consideration of the contributions of small business must include a concern with an underlying question of small business efficiency. Common sense tells you that the most efficient size of a business varies with the industry. You can easily recognize, for example, that big business is better in manufacturing automobiles and that small business is better in repairing them.

The continued existence of small business in a competitive economic system is in itself evidence of efficient small business operation. If small firms were hopelessly inefficient and made no useful contribution, they would be forced out of business quickly by stronger competitors.

Although research has identified some cost advantages for small firms over big businesses, the economic evidence related to firm size and productivity is limited. Some of the reasons for the relative economic strength of small business are summarized in the following:

New contributions to the theory of business organization and operation suggest that small firms are less encumbered by the complex, multi-echelon decision-making structures that inhibit the flexibility and productivity of many large firms. Because the owners of small

Action Report

TECHNOLOGICAL APPLICATIONS

TECHNOLOGY

Efficient Operation by a Small Manufacturer

Small firms sometimes distinguish themselves by superior performance in highly competitive industries. One example is Fadal Engineering Company, a family-owned manufacturer of metalworking machines, whose performance has won the grudging admiration of large rivals in both the United States and Japan.

> *Compared with the machine tools catering to big manufacturers, Fadal's machine had fewer parts and simpler electronic controls. Also, Fadal offers preprogrammed functions and routines designed for smaller shops making anything from dental braces to guitar necks.*
>
> *With Fadal, buyers get the Volkswagen Beetle of the industry. The machines are functional and durable, yet Fadal charges $74,500 for its main model, at least $15,000 less than the typical lowest-price competing machine that does the same job. What's more, Fadal, with few exceptions, uses American-made, off-the-shelf parts, so repairs are generally a routine matter.*

Source: "Fadal's Attractions," October 22, 1990 issue of *Business Week*. Used by special permission. © 1990.

firms are often also their managers, small firms are less likely to be affected adversely by the separation of owners' interests from managerial control. Empirical evidence of small firm survival and productivity suggests that, where firm size is concerned, bigger is not necessarily better.[15]

Additional economic research will undoubtedly shed more light on the most effective combination of small and large businesses. In the meantime, we believe that small business contributes in a substantial way to the economic welfare of our society.

---

4 Discuss the rate of small business failure and the costs associated with such failure.

THE SMALL BUSINESS FAILURE RECORD

A balanced view of small business in the economy requires us to also consider its darker side—that is, the record of business failure. Although we wish to avoid pessimism, we must deal realistically with this matter.

Small Business Failure Rate

Business failure is not the only reason that firms cease operation. In some cases, for example, owners shut down their businesses without loss to anyone. In other cases, businesses are sold to new owners, and the original firms no longer exist. Some terminations, however, result in losses to creditors, and these are clearly recognized as business failures.

The existence of various kinds of discontinuances and lack of accurate data as to why particular firms cease operation make it difficult to measure the **failure rate**

failure rate
the proportion of businesses that close with a loss to creditors

accurately. This leads to some confusion concerning the life expectancy of small firms. You may have heard pronouncements such as "Four out of five firms fail within the first five years." This startling statement has the ring of truth, but it is totally false. Prospects for small business survival are much, much better.

Business failure data compiled by **Dun & Bradstreet,** a company that operates a credit-rating service, have been used over the years to track the fortunes of business in general and small business in particular.[16] Discontinuances are classified as failures only if there is a financial loss to creditors. From year to year, there is some fluctuation in the Dun & Bradstreet failure rate. In general, the rate of failure is lower during periods of prosperity and higher during economic recessions. Overall, however, the rate has been quite low. In 1993, for example, 96 firms failed out of each 10,000 (firms of all sizes) in Dun & Bradstreet's records. This means that fewer than 1 percent failed. This figure indicates that chances for success are excellent! In light of such data, you might be encouraged to consider business ownership because of its bright prospects, rather than shun it because of fear of failure.

Some of the reasons for the popular perception of an inflated failure rate among small businesses are as follows:

- A business may cease operation because its profits are unsatisfactory, not because it is losing money. To an outsider, this may seem to be a failure.
- A business may close one office or store to consolidate operations—another apparent failure.
- A business may relocate, and the empty building may signal failure to those on the outside.
- A business may change ownership, making it seem that the original business has failed.

Recent research by Bruce A. Kirchoff, professor of entrepreneurship at New Jersey Institute of Technology, supports the more optimistic view of prospects for small business survival. His summary of findings regarding failure or survival over an eight-year period follows:

> *The research reported here suggests that something in excess of 50 percent of small business owners survive in their small business ownership experience for eight or more years. And, under the worst set of assumptions, no more than 18 percent terminate with losses to creditors.*[17]

The fact that 82 percent of business owners can make it through eight years without failing to the extent that creditors lose money is indeed encouraging.

It is desirable, of course, that we learn from the experiences of those who fail. However, apprehension of failure should not be permitted to stifle an inclination toward an independent business career. While prospective entrepreneurs should understand that failure is possible, they should also recognize that the odds are far from overwhelming.

The Costs of Business Failure

The costs of business failure involve more than financial costs to the business owner and creditors. Costs also include those of a psychological, social, and economic nature. We consider all these types of costs next.

LOSS OF ENTREPRENEUR'S AND CREDITORS' CAPITAL   The owner of a business that fails suffers a loss of invested capital, either in whole or in part. In some cases, this

Dun & Bradstreet
a company that researches and publishes business credit information

financial setback means the loss of a person's lifetime savings! The entrepreneur's loss of capital, however, is augmented by the losses of business creditors. Thus, the total capital loss is greater than the sum of the entrepreneurial losses in any one year.

INJURIOUS PSYCHOLOGICAL EFFECTS   Individuals who fail in business suffer a blow to their self-esteem. The businesses they started with enthusiasm and high expectations of success have gone under. Older entrepreneurs, in many cases, lack the vitality to recover from the blow. Unsuccessful entrepreneurs may relapse into employee status for the balance of their lives.

Failure need not be totally devastating to entrepreneurs, however. They may recover from the failure and try again. Albert Shapero offered these encouraging comments: "Many heroes of business failed at least once. Henry Ford failed twice. Maybe trying and failing is a better business education than going to a business school that has little concern with small business and entrepreneurship."[18] The key, therefore, is the response of the person who fails and that person's ability to learn from failure.

SOCIAL AND ECONOMIC LOSSES   The failure of a firm may mean the elimination of goods and services that the public needs and wants. Moreover, the number of jobs available in the community is reduced. The resulting unemployment of the entrepreneur and the firm's employees causes the community to suffer from the loss of a business payroll. Finally, the failed business was a taxpayer that contributed to the tax support of schools, police and fire protection, and other governmental services.

CAUSES OF BUSINESS FAILURE

5 Describe the causes of business failure.

Specifying the reasons that businesses fail is notoriously difficult. The factors involved in a failure form a complex web, and a great deal of subjective judgment is necessary in trying to pinpoint the most basic reasons for a firm's going under. Inadequate sales, for example, may be offered as the explanation for the demise of a firm. The inadequate sales, however, might have resulted from economic conditions beyond the control of the manager or from pricing or advertising decisions that represented management mistakes.

Table 2-4 shows what Dun & Bradstreet considers to be the causes of business failure in 1993. As you can see, finance causes were the most numerous. The largest segment of these finance causes is identified by Dun & Bradstreet as "heavy operat-

Table 2-4

Causes of Business Failure

Cause	Percentage of Failures
Finance	47.3
Economic factors	37.1
Disaster	6.3
Neglect	3.9
Fraud	3.8
Strategy	1.0
Experience	0.6

Source: *Business Failure Record* (New York: Dun & Bradstreet, Inc., 1993), p. 19.

ing expenses." Control of operating expenses is a responsibility of management, and a problem with operating expenses usually reflects managerial weakness. Under economic factors, Dun & Bradstreet lists such causes as high interest rates, inadequate sales, and inventory difficulties. Some of these may likewise result from management errors.

A study of British business failure, published in 1992, reported the perceptions of owners as to why their businesses failed.[19] Overwhelmingly, the owners identified problems in operational management as the major reasons for their failure. These problems included undercapitalization, poor management of debt, inaccurate costing and estimating, poor management accounting, poor supervision of staff, and so on. Obviously many of these can be viewed as management deficiencies.

Although there are numerous possible explanations of small business failure, we believe the most basic reason is weakness in management. As will be evident in the discussion of management processes in Chapter 17, hundreds of thousands of small firms limp along and occasionally even prosper with little that can be recognized as good management. Their management decisions lack careful analysis, and their financial records are fragmentary at best. To the extent that this is true, the incidence of failure could be reduced further by upgrading the expertise of small business management.

DISCUSSION QUESTIONS

1. In view of the numerous definitions of small business, how can you decide which definition is correct?

1 Define small business and identify criteria that may be used to measure the size of business firms.

- Small business definitions are necessarily arbitrary and differ according to purpose.
- SBA standards are based on annual sales volume (typically $3.5 million) or number of employees (typically 500).
- This book emphasizes firms with one or a few investors, situated in one locality, small compared to others in same industry, and having fewer than 100 employees.

2 Compare the relative importance of small business in the eight major industries and explain the trend in small business activity.

- There are approximately 5 million firms having one or more employees, over 98 percent of which are small.
- In four of the eight major industries—construction, wholesale trade, services, and retail trade—small business is relatively more important than big business.
- Small business accounts for about 50 percent of all business activity.
- Over the past several decades, small business has maintained its share of total employment.

3 Identify five special contributions of small business to society.

- Small business provides a disproportionate share of new jobs needed for a growing labor force.
- Small firms introduce many innovations and make scientific breakthroughs involving products such as photocopiers and pacemakers.
- Small firms keep large corporations and others on their toes by providing vigorous competition.
- Small businesses aid big businesses by acting as suppliers, distributors, and service providers.
- Small firms produce goods and services more efficiently than do larger firms in many areas of business.

4 Discuss the rate of small business failure and the costs associated with such failure.

- The rate of failure calculated by Dun & Bradstreet is much lower than commonly believed—less than 1 percent annually.
- One major study found that more than one-half of all startup firms survived at least eight years.
- Costs of business failure include loss of capital, possible injurious psychological effects, and economic losses to the community.

5 Describe the causes of business failure.

- Dun & Bradstreet cites finance and economic factors as the most common causes of failure.
- Although there are many possible explanations of failure, the most basic reason is weakness in management.

New Terms and Concepts

size criteria *23*	distribution	Dun & Bradstreet *35*
SBA standards *24*	function *33*	
major industries *25*	supply function *33*	
economic	service function *33*	
competition *31*	failure rate *34*	

You Make the Call

Situation 1   In the 1980s, a major food company began a push to increase its share of the nation's pickle market. To build market share, it used TV advertising and aggressive pricing. The price of its 46-ounce jar of pickles quickly dropped in one area from $1.89 to $0.79—a price some believed was less than the cost of production. This meant strong price competition for a family-owned business that had long dominated the pickle market in that area. This family firm, whose primary product is pickles, must now decide how to compete with a powerful national corporation whose annual sales volume amounts to billions of dollars.

Question 1   How should the family business react to the price competition?
Question 2   What advertising changes might be needed?
Question 3   How can a family business survive in such a setting?

Situation 2   The entrepreneurial failure of Ron A. Berger is described in the following account:

> In 1979 Berger was hot. His four-year-old brainchild, *Photo Factory*, was pulling in $40 million a year. He had 57 stores in eight states, and he was rolling.
> Then, suddenly, he was broke.
> His business had been leveraged with a $1-million line of credit. Interest rates skyrocketed, and the bank called in his loan. Because Berger had personally guaranteed the loan, he was forced to declare personal bankruptcy. Overnight, Berger plummeted from a net worth of about $5 million to zip. Job searches and depression followed. "I couldn't come to grips with it," Berger says today. "I felt like a total failure. I questioned my own worth and every business decision I'd ever made."

Source: "Building on Failure," *Nation's Business*, Vol. 75, No. 4, p. 50. Reprinted by permission, *Nation's Business*, April 1987. Copyright 1987, U.S. Chamber of Commerce.

Question 1   What was the cause of Berger's failure? Explain your answer.
Question 2   What should he learn from this failure, and how should he deal with his negative feelings?

Continue on next page

2. Of the businesses with which you are acquainted, which is the largest that you consider to be in the small business category? Does it conform to the size standards used in this book?

3. What generalizations can you make about the relative importance of large and small business in the United States?

4. In which sectors of the economy is small business most important? What accounts for its strength in these areas?

5. What special contribution is made by small business in providing jobs?

6. How can you explain the unique contributions of small business to product innovation?

7. What changes would be necessary for Ford Motor Company to continue operation if all firms with fewer than 500 employees were eliminated? Would the new arrangement be more or less efficient than the present one? Why?

8. What is the difference between saying "most firms fail within five years" and "most firms that fail do so within five years"? Which statement is more nearly correct? Based on the statistics on business failure, would you describe the prospects for new startups as bright or bleak?

9. List and describe the nonfinancial costs of business failure.

10. Explain the significance of the quality of management as a cause of failure.

EXPERIENTIAL EXERCISES

1. Visit a local firm and prepare a report describing the number of owners, geographical scope of operation, relative size in the industry, number of employees, and sales volume (if the firm will provide sales data). In your report, discuss the size of the firm (whether large or small) in terms of standards outlined in this chapter and the industry of which it is a part.

2. Interview a small business owner-manager concerning the type of big business competition faced by his or her firm and that owner-manager's "secrets of success" in competing with big business. Report on the insights offered by this entrepreneur.

3. Select a recent issue of *Inc.* and report on the types of new products or services being developed by small firms.

4. Select a section of 20 businesses listed in the Yellow Pages of the telephone directory. Label each of these businesses as large or small on the basis of the limited information provided, and give your rationale or assumptions for your classification of each. Then call five of these firms and ask whether the firm is a large or small business. Ask the individual you're speaking with to explain why he or she sees the business as small or large—for example, because of sales volume, number of employees, or other factors. Compare the responses to your own classification.

Situation 3 Dover Sporting Goods Store occupies an unimpressive retail location in a small city in northern Illinois. Started in 1935, it is now operated by Duane Dover—a third-generation member of the founding family. He works long hours trying to earn a reasonable profit in the old downtown area.

Dover's immediate concern is an announcement that Wal-Mart is considering opening a store at the southern edge of town. As Dover reacted to this announcement, he was overwhelmed by a sense of injustice. Why should a family business that had served the community honestly and well for 60 years be attacked by a large corporation that would take big profits out of the community and give very little in return? Surely, he reasoned, the law or the constitution must give some kind of protection against big business predators of this kind. Dover also wondered whether small stores such as his had ever been successful in competing against business giants such as Wal-Mart.

Question 1 Is Dover's feeling of unfairness justified? Is his business entitled to some type of protection against moves of this type?

Question 2 How should Dover plan to compete against Wal-Mart if and when this becomes necessary?

 CASE 2

Construction Equipment Dealership (p. 595)

This case presents the dilemma of a student who must choose between running the family business and accepting a big business career opportunity.

Alternative Cases for Chapter 2: Case 13, "Silver Lining," p. 627
Case 18, "Gibson Mortuary," p. 639

Seeking Entrepreneurial Opportunities

Part 2

3. **STARTUP AND BUYOUT OPPORTUNITIES**

4. **FRANCHISING OPPORTUNITIES**

5. **FAMILY BUSINESS OPPORTUNITIES**

Chapter 3

Startup and Buyout Opportunities

Harold Finch

spotlight on small business

Sometimes business ideas arrive like a bolt from the blue. Others are pursued more matter of factly by prospective entrepreneurs. Harold Finch, CEO of CottageCare in Overland Park, Kansas, has done it both ways. His first startup was Padgett-Thompson, a management-training company. Finch recalls, "When I asked how to do it, I was told, 'Just do it.' And I made every mistake in the book." After some nerve-racking months, the venture took off, and annual sales eventually reached $30 million. They then sold the company, which gave Finch the money and the time to research his next venture.

Finch spent six months at the library studying economic trends and identified three he thought were key to the success of his next business: the rise of service, franchising, and the working woman. So he began to consider fast food, child care, and housecleaning. That's when his next business partner approached him. Tom Schrader had started a housecleaning company 17 years earlier but had underestimated the capital requirements and had to sell the company to cover debts. He and Harold Finch got together in the right place at the right time, and Cottage-Care was born for the purpose of providing professional housecleaning.

Finch goes to a hotel room at least once a month, with nothing but a pad and pencil, to think up ways to do his work more effectively. But he recognizes the practical limits of research: "At some point, you have to stop reading, stop talking, stop studying, and do it."

Source: Leslie Brokaw, "How to Start an *Inc. 500* Company," *Inc. 500* (Special Issue), 1994, pp. 54–57.

start here

Creating a business from scratch—a **startup**—is the route that usually comes to mind when discussing entrepreneurship. There is no question that startups represent a significant opportunity for many entrepreneurs. However, an even greater number of individuals realize their entrepreneurial dreams through other alternatives—by purchasing an existing firm (a **buyout**), by franchising, or by entering a family business. Figure 3-1 depicts the four different types of small business ownership opportunities: startups, buyouts, franchises, and family businesses. This chapter examines the startup and buyout options for entering small business. Chapters 4 and 5 will explore franchising and family businesses.

Looking Ahead

After studying this chapter, you should be able to:

1 Give three reasons for starting a *new* business rather than buying an existing firm or acquiring a franchise.

2 Distinguish the different types and sources of startup ideas.

3 Identify five factors that determine whether an idea is a good investment opportunity.

4 List some reasons for buying an existing business.

5 Summarize four basic approaches for determining a fair value for a business.

6 Describe the characteristics of highly successful startup companies.

THE STARTUP: CREATING A NEW BUSINESS

There are several reasons for starting a business from scratch, rather than pursuing other alternatives, such as franchising. Such reasons include the following:

* To begin a new type of business based on a recently invented or newly developed product or service
* To take advantage of an ideal location, equipment, products or services, employees, suppliers, and bankers
* To avoid undesirable precedents, policies, procedures, and legal commitments of existing firms

Assuming that one of these reasons—or others—exists, several basic questions need to be addressed:

* What are the different types of startup ideas you might consider?
* What are some sources for new ideas?

> 1 Give three reasons for starting a *new* business rather than buying an existing firm or acquiring a franchise.

startup
creating a new business from scratch

buyout
purchasing an existing business

Figure 3-1

Alternative Routes to Small Business Ownership

Startup

Franchising

Small Business Ownership

Buyout

Family Business

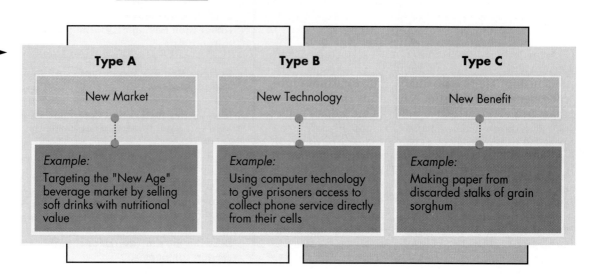

Figure 3-2   *Types of Ideas That Develop into Startups*

- How can you identify a genuine opportunity that promises attractive financial rewards?
- How should you refine your idea?
- What might you do to increase your chances that the startup business will be successful?

Let's look at each of these questions.

2 Distinguish the different types and sources of startup ideas.

Kinds of Startup Ideas

Figure 3-2 portrays the three basic categories of new venture ideas: new markets, new technologies, and new benefits.

Many startups are developed from **Type A ideas**—those that concern providing customers with a product or service that does not exist in their market but already exists somewhere else. The SiBôn Beverage Corporation, founded in 1993 by Robert J. Hall and other entrepreneurs, is an example of such a startup. The business is located close to natural water springs in eastern Texas and is intended to compete in the "New Age" beverage market, a niche market of the soft drink industry which features soft drinks with nutritional value. The market grew from $117 million in 1985 to over $1 billion by 1993—an annual compound growth rate of 31 percent. (See Appendix A for SiBôn's Business Plan.)

Some startups are based on **Type B ideas**—those that involve a technically new process. DeWayne Eidson, for example, developed the computer technology needed to provide cost-efficient phone service for inmates in county prisons. In the late 1980s, many states guaranteed prisoners access to a phone. In most prisons, the guards had to dial each call and hold the phone while the inmate talked. This legal right thus became an increasing cost factor in operating a prison. Using Eidson's phone system, however, the prisoners could make collect calls directly from their cells, and the prison received a percentage of the revenue from the collect calls.

Type C ideas probably account for the largest number of all startups. They represent concepts for performing old functions in new and improved ways. In fact, most new ventures, especially in the service industry, are founded on "me, too" strategies, differentiating themselves through superior service or cheaper cost. For

Type A ideas
startup ideas to provide customers with an existing product not available in their market

Type B ideas
startup ideas to provide customers with a new product

Type C ideas
startup ideas to provide customers with an improved product

example, Pat Odell, a professor at Baylor University, has developed a way to make paper—not exactly a new product. Instead of using trees as the raw product for the paper, Odell makes paper from the stalks of grain sorghum (known as maize in some parts of the country). After farmers raise and harvest grain sorghum, they are left with the stalks of the plant, which they must dispose of, usually by burning. Odell has applied existing technology to make paper from these unwanted grain sorghum stalks. Besides saving trees, he can produce comparable paper at a cheaper cost. As of 1995 Odell was trying to raise the capital to implement his idea.

Sources of Startup Ideas

Since startups begin with ideas, let's consider some sources for new ideas. Several studies have sought to discover where new ideas for small business startups originate. Figure 3-3 gives the results of a study by the National Federation of Independent Business Foundation, which found that "prior work experience" accounts for 45 percent of the new ideas. "Personal interest/hobby" represents 16 percent of the total, and a "chance happening" accounts for 11 percent. Another study found that 73 percent of the ideas underlying the 1994 *Inc. 500* firms came from an in-depth understanding of the industry and the market.[1] Clearly, these studies emphasize the importance of knowledge of the product or service the new firm is to develop and sell.

Keep these thoughts about the sources of ideas in mind as we consider in more detail the circumstances that tend to create new ideas. Although numerous possibilities exist—a new idea can come from virtually anywhere—we will focus on four sources: personal experience, hobbies, accidental discovery, and deliberate search.

PERSONAL EXPERIENCE   The primary basis for startup ideas is personal experience, either at work or at home. The knowledge gleaned from a present or recent job often allows a person to see possibilities for modifying an existing product, improving a service, or duplicating a business concept in a different location. Natalie

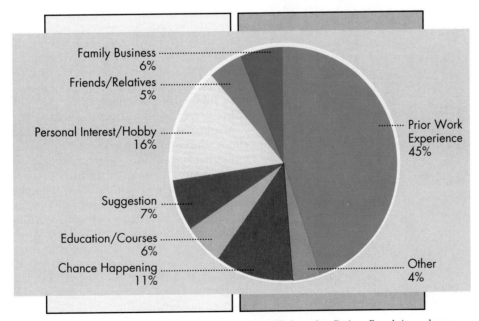

Figure 3-3

Sources of Startup Ideas

Family Business
6%

Friends/Relatives
5%

Personal Interest/Hobby
16%

Suggestion
7%

Education/Courses
6%

Chance Happening
11%

Prior Work Experience
45%

Other
4%

Source: Data developed and provided by the National Federation of Independent Business Foundation and sponsored by the American Express Travel Related Services Company, Inc.

Stiles, the founder and president of OCS Consulting Services, started the firm based on personal experience in her work. After graduation, Stiles went to work for Litton Industries as that company's first female programmer. She then moved to Xerox, and eventually to General Electric's Consulting Services division, G-Con. At G-Con, she reached a point where she no longer felt challenged in her work. In her words, "There was no room at the top for mavericks. You were supposed to do what you were told and make your numbers." So Stiles began her own company, relying heavily on what she had learned in her former job. Five years later, with 40 employees, her firm had $2.4 million in sales, and GE was one of her largest clients.[2]

HOBBIES   Sometimes hobbies grow beyond their status as hobbies to become businesses. For instance, a student who loves snow skiing might start a ski equipment rental business as a way to make income from an activity that she enjoys. Another example is Vickie Henry, who converted her shopping ability into a thriving business. Her firm, Feedback Plus, dispatches professional shoppers posing as amateurs to visit stores, try out merchandise, and make purchases—all to assess how employees treat customers. To help meet the demand for the shopping service, she has a database of 8,800 people who act as "mystery shoppers." In the first few years, the firm's revenues have been growing at 50 percent per year.[3]

ACCIDENTAL DISCOVERY   Another source of new startup ideas—accidental discovery—involves something called **serendipity,** or the seeming ability to make desirable discoveries by accident. Any person may stumble across a useful idea in the ordinary course of day-to-day living. DeWayne Eidson's idea of developing specialized phone technology for county prisons, described earlier, came with little forethought after he had designed a phone system for university dormitories. When a friend who owned a prison complained about the expense of providing phone service for the inmates, Eidson quickly converted his system to fit the prison's needs. The result was a successful business meeting an unanticipated need.

serendipity
the faculty for making
desirable discoveries
by accident

Personal experience is an excellent source of startup ideas. Hobbies are the basis for a variety of successful businesses, including a shopping service that sends out mystery shoppers to evaluate how well a company's employees treat customers.

DELIBERATE SEARCH   A startup idea also may emerge from a prospective entrepreneur's deliberate search—a purposeful exploration to find a new idea. Such a deliberate search may be useful because it stimulates a readiness of mind. Prospective entrepreneurs who are thinking seriously about new business ideas will be more receptive to new ideas from any source.

Magazines and other periodicals are excellent sources of startup ideas. One way of generating startup ideas is by reading about the creativity of other entrepreneurs. For example, most issues of *Inc.* feature many kinds of business opportunities in the section called "The American Dream." Visiting the library and looking through the Yellow Pages of the telephone directories of other cities for your type of business can be productive. Also, traveling to other cities to visit with entrepreneurs in the same line of business is extremely helpful.

Action Report

ENTREPRENEURIAL EXPERIENCES

Starting a Business Without Personal Experience

Over a quarter-century, Marvin Saul built Junior's delicatessen into a successful restaurant in Los Angeles. But, he says, he experienced an embarrassing and expensive failure when trying to branch out by starting a fancy catering business: "I was the comic who wanted to play Hamlet."

A group of entrepreneurs had convinced him that he could make money as a caterer, by serving squab, French pastries, and the like for home and office parties. "It was going to be a real white-glove operation," says Saul, who made his fortune selling lox and bagels.

Saul put up the money and hired the people with the idea to help run the operation. Unfortunately, they knew little about running a business. They persuaded him to lease fancy offices and a big commissary. "I am still paying off the lease," he says.

While the business was piling up overhead, nobody was signing up customers. The venture undercharged the few customers it did attract. After about a year and a half in the red, Saul pulled the plug. He estimates that he lost several hundred thousand dollars. Saul made the mistake of going into a business he didn't know and then turning it over to people who weren't up to the job.

Source: John R. Emshwiller, "Pass the Bagel; Hold the Squab," *The Wall Street Journal*, October 16, 1992, p. R4.

Entrepreneurs can evaluate their own capabilities and then look at the new products or services they may be capable of producing, or they can first look for needs in the marketplace and then relate these needs to their own capabilities. The latter approach has apparently produced more successful startups, especially in the field of consumer goods and services.

Bill Waugh, the founder of the restaurant chain Taco Bueno, helped develop the concept of Mexican fast-food restaurants in the 1960s after extensive research into the fast-food industry in general and Mexican food in particular. After completing the research, he wanted to acquire a franchise from El Chico, a national chain of Mexican restaurants, but he was turned down as a prospective franchisee. He decided that the research he had done had given him enough understanding to start his own Mexican restaurant. Eighty-four restaurants later, he sold his firm to Unigate, Ltd., a firm from London, for $34 million. Then, in the late 1980s, Waugh began the research process again, looking for his next venture. This time, he developed a concept for a new fast-food restaurant selling hamburgers, which he named Burger Street. By 1994, and as a result of his research, he had successfully opened and was operating 25 restaurants.

A truly creative person can find useful ideas in many different ways. The sources of new venture ideas discussed here are suggestive, not exhaustive. We encourage you to seek and reflect on new venture ideas in whatever circumstances you find yourself.

Identify five factors that determine whether an idea is a good investment opportunity.

3

Identifying and Evaluating Investment Opportunities

Experience shows that a good idea is not necessarily a good investment opportunity. In fact, most people tend to become infatuated with an idea and underestimate the difficulty involved in developing market receptivity to the idea. To qualify as a good investment opportunity, a product must meet a real need with respect to functionality, quality, durability, and price. The opportunity ultimately depends on convincing consumers (the market) of the benefits of the product or service. According to Amar Bhide, a professor at Harvard Business School, "Startups with products that do not serve clear and important needs cannot expect to be 'discovered' by enough customers to make a difference."[4] Thus, the market ultimately determines whether an idea has potential as an investment opportunity.

There are many other criteria for judging whether a new business idea is a good investment opportunity. Some of the fundamental requirements are as follows:

1. There must be a clearly defined market need for the product, and the timing must be right. Opportunities arise in what some call "real time." Even if the product or service concept is good, poor timing can prevent it from being a viable investment opportunity. Success demands that the window of opportunity be open and that it remain open long enough for an entrepreneur to exploit the opportunity.

2. The proposed business must be able to achieve a durable or sustainable competitive advantage. Failure to understand the nature and importance of having a competitive advantage has resulted in the failure of many small startups. This widespread problem is addressed further in Chapter 7.

3. The economics of the venture need to be rewarding, and even forgiving, allowing for significant profit and growth potential. That is, the profit margin (profit as a percentage of sales) and return on investment (profit as a percentage of the size of the investment) must be high enough to allow for errors and mistakes and still yield significant economic benefits.

4. There must be a good fit between the entrepreneur and the opportunity. In other words, the opportunity must be captured and developed by someone who has the appropriate skills and experience and who has access to the critical resources necessary for the venture's growth.

5. There must be no fatal flaw in the venture—that is, no circumstance or development that could in and of itself make the business a loser. An example of such a flaw is described in the following story:

> By the late 1980s, Arthur Benson had sweated for more than two decades to build his Sure Air Ltd. into a national provider of maintenance work for retail stores. An acquaintance suggested that they try selling franchises for the sale and repair of satellite dishes.
>
> Mr. Benson says that he, the acquaintance, and a third partner spent months and "lots of money" on the project—calling people in the industry, printing "gorgeous" brochures, and delineating franchise territories all across the United States.
>
> The group sold exactly one franchise. Benson says he realizes now that he badly miscalculated demand—not of homeowners for satellite dishes, but of entrepreneurs for his franchising idea.
>
> The problem, he says, is that he tried to sell franchises to the same people whom he deals with in his main business—providers of air-conditioning, electrical and plumbing services to retailers. The new venture would have required them to switch their emphasis from service to sales. At the same time, they also would have had to sell an unfamiliar product, satellite dishes, to an unfamiliar market, residential households. "It was too much of a leap for them," he says. "My plan sounded so good, but it was so far afield."[5]

The five evaluation criteria just described are elaborated on somewhat in Table 3-1. The point being made in this section may be stated as follows: Beware of being

Table 3-1

Evaluation Criteria for a Startup

Criterion	Attractiveness	
	Favorable	**Unfavorable**
Marketing Factors		
Need for the product	Well identified	Unfocused
Customers	Reachable; receptive	Unreachable; strong product loyalty for competitor
Value created by product or service for the customer	Significant	Not significant
Life of product	Use extends beyond time for customer to recover investment plus profit	To be used for a time less than that required for customer to recover investment
Market structure	Emerging industry; not highly competitive	Highly concentrated competition; mature or declining industry
Market size	$100 million sales or more	Unknown, less than $10 million sales, or multibillion-dollar sales
Market growth rate	Growing by at least 30% annually	Contracting, or growth less than 10% annually
Competitive Advantage		
Cost structure	Low-cost producer	No production cost advantage
Degree of control over:		
Price	Moderate to strong	Nonexistent
Costs	Moderate to strong	Nonexistent
Channels of supply	Moderate to strong	Nonexistent
Barriers to entry:		
Proprietary information or regulatory protection	Have or can develop	Not possible
Response/lead-time advantage	Resilient and responsive	Nonexistent
Legal, contractual advantage	Proprietary or exclusive	Nonexistent
Contacts and networks	Well-developed	Limited
Economics		
Return on investment	25% or more; durable	Less than 15%; fragile
Investment requirements	Small to moderate amount; easily financed	Large amount; financed with difficulty
Time to break-even profits or to reach positive cash flows	Under 2 years	More than 3 years
Management Capability	Proven experience, with diverse skills among the management team	Solo entrepeneur with no related experience
Fatal Flaw	None	One or more

Source: Adapted from Jeffry A. Timmons, *New Venture Creation* (Homewood, IL: Irwin, 1994), pp. 93, 94.

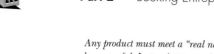

Any product must meet a "real need" among customers to be successful. Just as important is the fit between entrepreneur and opportunity. Only a devoted gardener or flower arranger would want to tackle the startup of a dried flower shop.

deluded into thinking that an idea is a "natural" and cannot miss. The market can be a harsh disciplinarian for those who have not done their homework. However, for those who succeed in identifying a meaningful opportunity, the rewards can be sizable.

Refining a Startup Idea

A startup idea often requires an extended period of time for refinement and testing. This is particularly true for original inventions that require developmental work to make them operational. Almost any idea for a new business deserves careful study and typically requires modification as opening day for the new business approaches.

The need to refine an idea is the basis for the MIT Enterprise Forum at the Massachusetts Institute of Technology. Here, aspiring entrepreneurs present their business plans to a panel of individuals familiar with company startups. The panel generally consists of a venture capitalist, a private investor, a banker, an accountant, and an attorney, among others. These individuals read the business plan and serve at a public forum where the entrepreneur makes an oral presentation of the plan to an audience of interested individuals. The panel members then, one by one, offer their suggestions for strengthening the venture proposed. Finally, the audience has an opportunity to ask questions and make suggestions. The Enterprise Forum has now spread to most major cities across the United States and has been a vehicle for thousands of entrepreneurs seeking someone with expertise to review their plans. Whether through the Enterprise Forum or another group, an entrepreneur should seize the opportunity to have others evaluate the idea being put forth—better sooner than later.

The process of preparing a business plan, which will be discussed in Chapter 6, helps the individual to think through an idea and consider all aspects of a proposed business. Outside experts can be asked to review the business plan, and their questions and suggestions can help improve it.

We now shift our attention from creating a totally new business to buying an existing firm as a way to ownership of a small company.

---

4 | List some reasons for buying an existing business.

BUYING AN EXISTING BUSINESS

Would-be entrepreneurs can choose to buy an established business as an alternative to starting from scratch, buying a franchise, or joining a family business. This decision should be made only after careful consideration of the advantages and disadvantages.

ENTREPRENEURIAL EXPERIENCES

A Startup That Was a Good Investment Opportunity

While attending Harvard Business School in the mid-1970s, James McCurry and Gary Kusin often talked about starting a business together but were short on ideas. After graduation, the two went their separate ways—McCurry into consulting and Kusin into retailing.

Then, in 1982, McCurry had a brainstorm. While consulting with a video game maker out of Bain & Co.'s San Francisco office, McCurry was surprised that so few stores were selling computer software. McCurry ran the idea by Kusin, who was then head of merchandising for Federated Department Stores' Sanger-Harris division in Dallas. Kusin saw parallels with the business in which he was engaged. As he puts it: "The specialty stores were killing department stores. This was our real chance."

At the end of 1982, the two left their jobs. They almost failed to survive their first few months as entrepreneurs. However, in February 1983, they received a call from Ross Perot, who knew Kusin's family from Texarkana. Recalls McCurry: "He kept asking us, 'You've left your jobs? You haven't found any money? And you're still at this thing?'" Perot, who clearly admired the pair's persistence, offered to guarantee a $3 million line of credit to the fledgling firm in exchange for a third of the company. He also gave some practical advice to the two upstarts. Originally, they were planning to open 20 stores the first month. Instead, Perot recommended they open one store and run it themselves, morning, noon, and night. Steep themselves in business. Learn what the customers were like and what they wanted.

In May 1983, McCurry and Kusin opened a small software store in a north Dallas mall. They called it Babbage's after Charles Babbage, the nineteenth-century British mathematician generally credited with inventing the first computing machine. Says Kusin: "Everybody thought we were crazy."

They took turns opening and closing the store. In its first full year, the company lost $560,000 on $3 million in sales. Financing its growth through a series of private placements, the 23-store company broke even in fiscal 1987 on sales of $10 million. Today, Babbage's is one of the biggest consumer software retailers in the country, with 246 stores in 37 states. In its 1992 fiscal year, the company earned a record $5.6 million on $168 million in sales.

Source: Claire Poole, "Learn to Walk Before You Try to Run," *Forbes*, Vol. 150, No. 14 (December 21, 1992), pp. 96–98.

Reasons for Buying an Existing Business

The reasons for buying an existing business can be condensed into three general categories:

1. To reduce some of the uncertainties and unknowns that must be faced when starting a business from the ground up
2. To acquire a business with ongoing operations and already established relationships
3. To obtain an ongoing business at a bargain price—a price below what it would cost to start a new business

Let's examine each of these reasons in more detail.

REDUCTION OF UNCERTAINTIES   A successful business has already demonstrated its ability to attract customers, control costs, and make a profit. Although future operations may be different, the firm's past record shows what it can do under actual market conditions. For example, the satisfactory location of a going concern eliminates one major uncertainty. Although traffic counts are useful in assessing the value of a potential location, the acid test comes when a business opens its doors at that location. This test has already been met in the case of an existing firm. The results are available in the form of sales and profit data. Noncompetition agreements are needed, however, to discourage the seller from starting a new company that will compete directly with the one being sold.

ACQUISITION OF ONGOING OPERATIONS AND RELATIONSHIPS   The buyer of an existing business typically acquires its personnel, inventories, physical facilities, established banking connections, and ongoing relationships with trade suppliers. Extensive time and effort would be required to build these elements from scratch. Of course, buying an established firm is an advantage only under certain conditions. For example, a firm's skilled, experienced employees constitute a valuable asset only if they will continue to work for the new owner. The physical facilities must not be obsolete, and the firm's relationships with banks and suppliers must be healthy. Also, new agreements will probably have to be negotiated with current vendors and leaseholders—a fact that could impact negatively on the decision to buy an existing business.

A BARGAIN PRICE   An existing business may become available at what seems to be a low price. If the seller is more eager to sell the business than the buyer is to buy it, the firm may be available at a discounted price. However, whether it is actually a good buy must be determined by the prospective new owner. The price may appear low, but several factors could make a "bargain price" anything but a bargain. For example, the business may be losing money, the location may be deteriorating, or the seller may intend to reopen another business as a competitor. On the other hand, the business may indeed be a bargain and turn out to be a wise investment.

Finding a Business to Buy

Frequently, in the course of day-to-day living and working, a would-be buyer comes across an opportunity to buy an existing business. For example, a sales representative for a manufacturer or a wholesaler may be offered an opportunity to buy a customer's retail business. In other cases, the prospective buyer may need to search for a business to buy.

Sources of leads about business firms available for purchase include suppliers, distributors, trade associations, and even bankers. Realtors—particularly those who specialize in the sale of business firms and business properties—can also provide leads. In addition, there are specialized brokers, called **matchmakers,** who handle all the arrangements for closing a buyout. At least 2,000 matchmakers handle the mergers and acquisitions of small and mid-sized companies in the United States.

matchmakers specialized brokers who bring together buyers and sellers of businesses

Investigating and Evaluating the Existing Business

Regardless of the source of leads, each business opportunity requires a background investigation and careful evaluation. As a preliminary step, the buyer needs to acquire information about the business. Some of this information can be obtained through personal observation or discussion with the seller. Talking with other informed parties, such as suppliers, bankers, and customers of the business, is also important.

RELYING ON PROFESSIONALS   Although some of the background investigation requires personal checking, the buyer can also seek the help of outside experts. The two most valuable sources of such assistance are accountants and lawyers. The time and money spent on professional help in investigating a business can pay big dividends—now and in the future. However, the prospective buyer should never relinquish the final decision to the experts. Too often, advisors have a personal interest in whether the acquisition is made. For one thing, their fees may be greater if the business is acquired.

Although advisors are usually valuable in these situations—especially when the buyer is inexperienced—the final consequences of purchasing a business, good and bad, are borne by the buyer. As a result, it is a mistake to assume that professional help is unbiased and infallible. Seek advice and counsel, but the final decision is too important to entrust to someone else. Also, it is wise to seek out others who have acquired a business, to learn from their experience. Their perspective will be different from that of a consultant, and it will bring some balance to the counsel received.

KNOWING WHY THE BUSINESS IS FOR SALE   The seller's *real* reasons for selling a going concern may or may not be the *stated* ones. When a company is for sale, always question why the owner is trying to get rid of it. There is a real possibility that the company is not doing well or that there are latent problems that will affect its future performance. The buyer must be wary, therefore, of taking the seller's explanations at face value. Here are some of the most common reasons that owners offer their businesses for sale:

- Old age or illness
- Desire to relocate in a different section of the country
- Decision to accept a position with another company
- Unprofitability of the business
- Discontinuance of an exclusive sales franchise
- Maturation of the industry and lack of growth potential

As a matter of caution, the prospective buyer cannot be certain that the seller-owner will be honest in presenting all the facts about the business, especially concerning financial matters. Too frequently, the seller may have "cooked the books" or have been taking unreported cash out of the business. The only way to avoid an unpleasant surprise later is for the buyer to do his or her best to determine whether the seller is an ethical person.

When purchasing a business, the buyer may be wise to buy the assets only, rather than the business as a whole. When a business is purchased as a total entity, the buyer takes control of the assets but also assumes any outstanding debt, including any hidden or unknown liabilities. Even if the financial records are audited, these debts may not surface, and the new owners will be liable. If the buyer instead purchases only the assets, the seller is responsible for settling any outstanding debts previously incurred. Also, an indemnification clause in the sales contract regarding any unreported debt may protect the buyer.

EXAMINING THE FINANCIAL DATA   There are two basic stages in evaluating the financial health of a firm: (1) a review of the financial statements and tax returns for the past five years (or for as many years as are available), and (2) an appraisal, or valuation, of the firm. The first stage helps determine whether the buyer and seller are in the same ballpark. In the second stage, the parties begin refining the terms, including the price to be paid for the firm.

To start, the buyer should determine the history of the business and the direction in which it is moving. To this end, the buyer examines financial data pertaining to the company's operation. If financial statements are available for the past five years, the buyer can get some idea of trends for the business. As an ethical matter, the prospective buyer is obligated to show the financial statements to others only on a need-to-know basis. To do otherwise is a violation of trust and confidentiality.

The buyer should recognize that financial statements may be misleading and may require normalizing to yield a realistic picture of the business. For example, business owners sometimes understate business income in an effort to minimize taxable income. On the other hand, expenses such as for employee training or advertising may be reduced to abnormally low levels, in an effort to make the income look good in the hopes of selling the business.

Other items that may need adjustment include personal expenses and wage or salary payments. For example, costs related to personal use of business vehicles frequently appear as a business expense. In some situations, family members receive excessive compensation or none at all. "I don't touch 80 percent of the businesses. . . . Even when you have the books and records, it's a fiction . . . the owners hide the perks," cautions Stanley Salmore, a Beverly Hills business broker.[6] All items must be examined carefully to be sure that they relate to the business and are realistic.

Figure 3-4 shows an income statement that has been adjusted by a prospective buyer. Note carefully the buyer's reasons for the adjustments that have been made. Naturally, many other adjustments can be made as well.

The buyer should also scrutinize the seller's balance sheet to see whether asset book values are realistic. Property often appreciates in value after it is recorded on the books. In contrast, physical facilities, inventory, or receivables may decline in value, so their actual worth is less than their inflated accounting book value. Adjustments to recognize these changes in value are generally not made in the accountant's records but should be considered by the prospective buyer. However, making adjustments to the financial statements serves only as the beginning point for valuing the firm.

5 Summarize four basic approaches for determining a fair value for a business.

asset-based valuation approach determination of the value of a business by estimating the value of its assets

modified book value approach determination of the value of a business by adjusting book value to reflect differences between the historical cost and the current value of the assets

Valuation of the Business

In deciding whether to buy a company, the buyer must arrive at a fair value for the firm. Valuing a company is not easy or exact, even in the best of circumstances. While buyers might prefer audited financial statements, some companies are still run out of a shoe box. For such companies, the buyer will have to examine federal tax returns and state sales tax statements. It may also be helpful to scrutinize invoices and receipts—with both customers and suppliers—as well as the bank statements.

Although numerous techniques of valuing a company are used, they are typically derivations of four basic approaches: (1) asset-based valuation, (2) market-based valuation, (3) earnings-based valuation, and (4) cash flow–based valuation.

ASSET-BASED VALUATION   The **asset-based valuation approach** assumes that the value of a firm can be determined by estimating the value of its underlying assets. Three variations of this approach involve estimating (1) a modified book value for the assets, (2) the replacement value of the assets, and (3) the assets' liquidation value. The **modified book value approach** uses the firm's book value, as shown in the balance sheet, and adjusts this value to reflect any obvious differences between the historical cost of an asset and its current value. For instance, marketable securi-

Income Statement as Adjusted by Prospective Buyer | Figure 3-4 |

Original Income Statement			Required Adjustments	Adjusted Income Statement	
Estimated sales	$172,000			$172,000	
Cost of goods sold	84,240			84,240	
Gross profit		$87,760			$87,760
Operating expenses:					
Rent	$20,000		Rental agreement will expire in six months; rent is expected to increase 20%.	$24,000	
Salaries	19,860			19,860	
Telephone	990			990	
Advertising	11,285			11,285	
Utilities	2,580			2,580	
Insurance	1,200		Property is under-insured; adequate coverage will double present cost.	2,400	
Professional services	1,200			1,200	
Credit card expense	1,860		Amount of credit card expense is unreasonably large; approximately $1,400 of this amount should be classified as personal expense.	460	
Miscellaneous	1,250	60,225		1,250	$64,025
Net income		$27,535			$23,735

ties held by the firm may have a market value totally different from their historical book value. The same may be true for real estate. The second asset-based approach, the **replacement value approach,** attempts to determine what it would cost to replace each of the firm's assets. The third method, the **liquidation value approach,** estimates the amount of money that would be received if the firm ended its operations and liquidated the individual assets.

The asset-based valuation approaches are not especially effective in helping a prospective buyer decide what to pay for a firm. Historical costs shown on the balance sheet may bear little relationship to the current value of the assets. The book value of an asset was never intended to measure present value. Although making adjustments for this misapplication may be better than not recognizing the inherent weakness, it builds an estimate of value on a weak foundation. Also, all three asset-based techniques fail to recognize the firm as a going concern. On the other hand, they do estimate the value that could be realized if the business were liquidated, which is good information to have.

replacement value approach
determination of the value of a business based on the cost necessary to replace the firm's assets

liquidation value approach
determination of the value of a business based on the money available if the firm were to liquidate its assets

An estimate of a firm's value is sometimes based on the sale prices of comparable firms. An entrepreneur must also carefully examine a firm's business records when attempting to determine its value.

MARKET-BASED VALUATION The **market-based valuation approach** relies on financial markets in estimating a firm's value. This method looks at the actual market prices of firms that are similar to the one being valued and have been recently sold, or that are traded publicly on a stock exchange. For instance, as a prospective buyer, you might find recently sold companies having growth prospects and levels of risk comparable to the firm you wish to value. For each of these companies, you could calculate the price-to-earnings ratio, measured as follows:

$$\text{Price-to-earnings ratio} = \frac{\text{Market price}}{\text{After-tax earnings}}$$

market-based valuation approach determination of the value of a business based on the sale prices of comparable firms

You then apply this ratio to estimate the prospective company's value as if it had the same price-to-earnings ratio as the similar firms that were recently sold.

The market-based valuation approach is not as easy as it might appear, because it is often difficult to find even one company that provides a good comparison in every way. It is not enough simply to find a firm in the same industry, although that might provide a rough approximation. Instead, the ideal company is in the same or a similar type of business and has a similar growth rate, financial structure, asset turnover ratio (sales/total assets), and profit margin (profits/sales). However, there is considerable published information about company purchases. For instance, Mergerstat Review publishes the price for all company sales announced in the public media. Also, many large accounting firms have departments that can sometimes provide information about the selling prices of comparable companies.

As an example, assume that you are considering the purchase of the Aberdeen Company, which has after-tax earnings (net income) of $80,000. You are interested in determining a fair price for the company and have located three comparable firms that recently sold, on average, for six times their earnings after taxes. That is,

$$\text{Price-to-earnings ratio} = \frac{\text{Market price}}{\text{After-tax earnings}} = 6$$

Using this information, you estimate the market value of Aberdeen's equity as follows:

$$\frac{\text{Aberdeen's market value}}{\text{Aberdeen's after-tax earnings}} = 6$$

or

$$\text{Aberdeen's market value} = 6\left(\frac{\text{Aberdeen's}}{\text{after-tax earnings}}\right)$$

Given Aberdeen's after-tax earnings of $80,000, you estimate its equity market value (the owner's value) to be $480,000:

$$\text{Aberdeen's market value} = 6(\$80,000)$$
$$= \$480,000$$

Thus, it could be reasonably argued that the market value of Aberdeen Company's equity ownership, a price you might be willing to pay for the firm, is about $480,000.

EARNINGS-BASED VALUATION We now provide a different perspective, in which the value of a firm is not determined by historical or replacement costs or by market comparables, but by future returns from the investment. That is, the estimated value of the firm is based on its ability to produce future income or profits—thus, the name **earnings-based valuation approach.**

Different procedures are used in valuing a company based on its earnings, but the underlying concept is generally the same: (1) determine normalized earnings, and (2) divide this amount by a capitalization rate. That is,

$$\text{Firm's value} = \frac{\text{Normalized earnings}}{\text{Capitalization rate}}$$

Normalized earnings are earnings that have been adjusted for any unusual items, such as a one-time loss in the sale of real estate or as the consequence of a fire. Also, the buyer should be certain that all relevant expenses are included, such as a fair salary for the owner's time. The appropriate **capitalization rate** is based on the riskiness of the earnings and the expected growth rate of these earnings in the future. The relationships are as follows:

1. The more (less) *risky* the business, the higher (lower) the *capitalization rate* to be used, and, as a consequence, the lower (higher) the firm's value.
2. The higher (lower) the *projected growth rate* in future earnings, the lower (higher) the *capitalization rate* to be used and, therefore, the higher (lower) the firm's value.

These relationships are presented graphically in Figure 3-5.

In practice, the capitalization rate is determined largely by rules of thumb; that is, it is based on conventional wisdom and the experience of the person perform-

earnings-based valuation approach
determination of the value of a business based on its potential future earnings

normalized earnings
earnings that have been adjusted for unusual items, such as fire damage

capitalization rate
a figure, determined by the riskiness of current earnings and the expected growth rate of future earnings, that is used to assess the earnings-based value of a business

Figure 3-5

Determinants of a Firm's Capitalization Rate

Risk			
	High	High Capitalization Rate	Low Firm Value
	Low	Low Capitalization Rate	High Firm Value

Projected Growth			
	High	Low Capitalization Rate	High Firm Value
	Low	High Capitalization Rate	Low Firm Value

ing the valuation. For example some appraisers assign capitalization rates for different types of firms as follows:

Small, well-established businesses, vulnerable to recession	15 percent
Small companies requiring average executive ability but operating in a highly competitive environment	25 percent
Firms that depend on the special, often unusual, skill of one individual or small group of managers	50 percent

Assume that the normalized earnings for a company are $130,000 (before deducting anything for the owner's salary) and that fair compensation for the owner's time would be $50,000. Using the earnings-based valuation technique, the appraiser would capitalize the $80,000 in earnings that remains after the owner's salary is deducted ($130,000 – $50,000). If the appraiser uses a 25 percent capitalization rate, the firm would be valued at $320,000, calculated as follows:

$$\text{Firm's value} = \frac{\text{Normalized earnings}}{\text{Capitalization rate}}$$

$$= \frac{\$80,000}{0.25}$$

$$= \$320,000$$

cash flow–based valuation approach determination of the value of a business by a comparison of the expected and required rates of return on the investment

CASH FLOW–BASED VALUATION   Although not popular, a **cash flow–based valuation approach**—valuing a company based on the amount and timing of its future cash flows—makes a lot of sense. The earnings-based valuation approach, while used more often in practice, presents a conceptual problem. It considers earnings, rather than cash flows, as the item to be valued. From an investor's or owner's perspective, the value of a firm should be based on future cash flows, not reported earnings—especially not a single year of earnings. Valuation is just too complex a process to be captured by a single earnings figure. For one thing, there are simply too many ways to influence a firm's earnings favorably (even when using generally accepted accounting principles) while having no effect on future cash flows, or, even worse, reducing cash flows.

Buying a business is in one sense similar to investing in a savings account in a bank. With a savings account, you are interested in the cash (capital) you have to put in the account and the future cash flows you will receive in the form of interest. Similarly, when you buy a company, you should be interested in future cash flows received relative to capital invested. In a cash flow–based valuation, a comparison is made between the expected rate of return on investment (the interest rate promised by the bank) and the required rate of return to determine whether the investment (savings account) is satisfactory.

Two steps are involved in measuring the present value of a company's future cash flows:

1. Estimate the future cash flows that can be expected by the investor.
2. Decide on the investor's required rate of return.

The first step—projecting cash flows—is no simple matter and is beyond the scope of this book. However, anyone serious about valuing a company would be well advised to develop an understanding of the technique or to seek assistance from someone who can help in this regard.

The second step involves selecting a discount rate to be used in bringing the firm's future cash flows back to their present value.[7] This rate is not the same as the capitalization rate used for earnings. The capitalization rate is used to convert a single point estimate of the current or normalized earnings into value. A required rate of return is used as a discount rate that is applicable to a stream of projected future cash flows. The required rate of return is, therefore, the opportunity cost of the funds: An investor must think, "If I do not make this investment (buy this company), what is the best rate of return that I could earn on another investment having a similar level of risk?" The answer to this question provides the appropriate discount rate to be used in valuing future cash flows.

The required rate of return also equals the existing risk-free rate in the capital markets, such as the rate earned on short-term U.S. government securities, plus a return premium for assuming risk (**risk premium**). In other words,

risk premium

Required rate of return = Risk-free rate of return + Risk premium

For example, assume the current rate on U.S. Treasury Bills, a short-term government security, is 7 percent. If, for a given investment, such as buying a company, the risk premium is 15 percent, then the required rate of return should be 22 percent (7 percent + 15 percent).

How the risk premium is estimated is clearly an important ingredient in determining the required rate of return. Although there are no hard-and-fast rules that can be used in determining the required rate of return, the smaller companies listed on the New York Stock Exchange have provided investors an average risk premium of 9 percent. So if the rate of return on a government security is 6 percent, an investor should expect at least a 15 percent rate of return on her or his investment (6 percent risk-free rate + 9 percent risk premium)—and even more if the firm being valued is riskier.

In fact, for most very small firms, the rate should be significantly more than 15 percent. Suggested risk premiums to be required above and beyond the risk-free rate are presented in Table 3-2. As you look at the different categories, you will see that categories 4 and 5 apply to small companies. (Small firms also frequently fall in category 3.) Thus, the risk premium—the rate above the risk-free rate—should,

risk premium the difference between the required rate of return on a given investment and the risk-free rate of return

Table 3-2

Suggested Risk Premium Categories

Category	Description	Risk Premium
1	Established businesses with a strong trade position that are well financed, have depth in management, have stable past earnings, and whose future is highly predictable.	6–10%
2	Established businesses in a more competitive industry that are well financed, have depth in management, have stable past earnings, and whose future is fairly predictable.	11–15%
3	Businesses in a highly competitive industry that require little capital to enter, have no management depth, and have a high element of risk, although past record may be good.	16–20%
4	Small businesses that depend on the special skill of one or two people or large established businesses that are highly cyclical in nature. In both cases, future earnings may be expected to deviate widely from projections.	21–25%
5	Small "one-person" businesses of a personal services nature, where the transferability of the income stream is in question.	26–30%

Source: James H. Schilt, "Selection of Capitalization Rates—Revisited," *Business Valuation Review,* American Society of Appraisers, P. O. Box 17265, Washington, DC 20041 (June 1991), p. 51.

according to one experienced appraiser, be at least 16 percent, and possibly as much as 30 percent, depending on the riskiness of the firm being valued. Given the required rate of return for valuing a company, an appraiser can then use the rate to calculate the present value of the firm's future cash flows.

Nonquantitative Factors to Consider in Valuing a Business

In addition to the above quantitative methods of valuation, there are a number of other factors to consider in evaluating an existing business. Although only indirectly related to a company's future cash flows and financial position, they should be mentioned. Some of these factors are

- *Competition.* The prospective buyer should look into the extent, intensity, and location of competing businesses. In particular, the buyer should check to see whether the business in question is gaining or losing in its race with competitors.
- *Market.* The adequacy of the market to maintain all competing business units, including the one to be purchased, should be determined. This entails market research, study of census data, and personal, on-the-spot observation at each competitor's place of business.
- *Future community development.* Examples of community development planned for the future that could have an indirect impact on a business include changes in zoning ordinances already enacted but not yet in effect and change from two-way traffic flow to one-way traffic flow.
- *Legal commitments.* These commitments may include contingent liabilities, unsettled lawsuits, delinquent tax payments, missed payrolls, overdue rent or installment payments, and mortgages of record against any of the real property acquired.
- *Union contracts.* The prospective buyer should determine what type of labor agreement, if any, is in force, as well as the quality of the firm's employee relations.
- *Buildings.* The quality of the buildings housing the business, particularly any fire hazards involved, should be checked. In addition, the buyer should determine whether there are restrictions on access to the building.
- *Product prices.* The prospective owner should compare the prices of the seller's products with manufacturers' or wholesalers' catalogs and prices of competing products in the locality. This is necessary to ensure full and fair pricing of goods whose sales are reported on the seller's financial statements.

Negotiating and Closing the Deal

The purchase price of the business is determined by negotiation between buyer and seller. Although the calculated value may not be the price eventually paid for the business, it gives the buyer an estimated value to use in negotiating price. Typically, the buyer tries to purchase the firm for something less than the full estimated value. Of course, the seller tries to get more than that value.

An important part of this negotiation is the terms of purchase. In many cases, the buyer is unable to pay the full price in cash and must seek extended terms. The seller may also be concerned about taxes on the profit from the sale. Terms may become more attractive to the buyer and the seller as the amount of the down payment is reduced and/or the length of the repayment period is extended.

Like a purchase of real estate, the purchase of a business is closed at a specific time. The closing may be handled by a title company or an attorney. Preferably, the closing occurs under the direction of an independent third party. If the seller's attorney is suggested as the closing agent, the buyer should exercise caution. A buyer should never go through a closing without an experienced attorney who represents only the buyer.

A number of important documents are completed during the closing. These include a bill of sale, certifications as to taxing and other governmental regulations, and agreements pertaining to future payments and related guarantees to the seller. Also, the buyer should be certain to apply for new federal and state tax identification numbers. Otherwise, the buyer may be responsible for past obligations associated with the old numbers.

INCREASING THE CHANCES OF A SUCCESSFUL STARTUP: LESSONS FROM HIGH-GROWTH FIRMS

6 Describe the characteristics of highly successful startup companies.

Anyone who has a dream of owning and operating a small business should do everything possible to enhance the chances of success. Observing successful role models is one way to increase the likelihood of realizing the dream.

A key determinant of success is a firm's growth in sales, provided, of course, that the profits and cash flows generated from the sales are adequate. Higher sales enable a firm to cover fixed costs by achieving economies of scale. Although a significant increase in sales can cause financial problems, sales growth is necessary to get beyond mere survival. Growing firms can fail, but the chance for creating economic value—a key barometer of success—and for creating jobs within a community where the business is located is greatly enhanced through growth.

The right beginning is important to a new company's eventual success. Leslie Brokaw has identified several characteristics that are common to high-growth firms.[8] His views are based on a study of *Inc. 500* companies, firms identified by *Inc.* magazine as the fastest-growing businesses in the United States during the prior five years. Brokaw says:

Companies that grow begin differently from the ones that don't in a handful of starkly identifiable ways. The distinguishing traits of a successful startup have to do with the kind of experience and knowledge its founders possess. They have to do with a startup's ability to seek and nurture alliances, whether for financing or product development. And they have to do with the market ambitions a company adopts right at the outset.

Brokaw continues by describing the observable features of these high-growth firms, which include the following:

1. The venture is most often a team effort. The vast majority of high-growth firms are started by a group that brings diversity and balance to the business.
2. The founders bring meaningful experience to the business. They are not learning the business as they begin the operations.
3. The founders of high-growth firms often have started other businesses in the past. In 50 percent of the 1992 *Inc. 500* firms, the president had started at least one business before starting the most recent venture. However, many of these early startups resulted in failure—only 27 percent of the earlier companies were still in existence.
4. Most frequently, high-growth companies are in service or manufacturing industries. Almost half of the *Inc. 500* firms are classified as high tech, with 25 percent being manufacturers, compared to 56 percent in services. Only 7 percent are in retailing.

1 **Give three reasons for starting a new business rather than buying an existing firm or acquiring a franchise.**

- A new business can feature a recently invented or newly developed product or service.
- A new business can take advantage of an ideal location, equipment, products or services, employees, suppliers, and bankers.
- A new business avoids undesirable precedents, policies, procedures, and legal commitments of existing firms.

2 **Distinguish the different types and sources of startup ideas.**

- The different types of startup ideas include existing concepts redirected to new markets, technologically derived ideas, and ideas to perform existing functions in a new and improved manner.
- Ideas for new startups come from a variety of sources, including personal experiences, hobbies, accidental discovery, and deliberate search.

3 **Identify five factors that determine whether an idea is a good investment opportunity.**

- The timing must be good.
- The firm must have the ability to achieve a durable or sustainable competitive advantage.
- There must be significant profit and growth potential.
- There should be a good fit between the entrepreneur and the opportunity.
- No fatal flaws can exist.

4 **List some reasons for buying an existing business.**

- Buying an existing company can reduce uncertainties.
- In acquiring an existing firm, the entrepreneur can take advantage of the company's ongoing operations and established relationships.
- It may be a bargain.

5 **Summarize four basic approaches for determining a fair value for a business.**

- A firm's value is based on the assets it owns (asset-based valuation).
- A firm's value is based on the market price of similar companies (market-based valuation).
- A firm's value is based on the amount of earnings the business produces (earnings-based valuation).
- A firm's value is based on the present value of the firm's future cash flows (cash flow–based valuation).

6 **Describe the characteristics of highly successful startup companies.**

- Most high-growth companies began through a team effort.
- The founders have related experience.
- The founders have often started other businesses.
- High-growth companies are frequently found in service or manufacturing industries.
- High-growth firms are better financed—but not by much.
- The founders of high-growth companies share ownership in the business.
- High-growth firms do not limit themselves to local markets.

5. High-growth firms are better financed—but not by much. High-growth companies begin with more money, but only slightly more.

6. The founders of high-growth companies share ownership in the business. In high-growth firms, the founders do not keep all the equity; they frequently own less than half of it. They think it is better to own a part of something large than all of something small.

7. High-growth firms do not limit themselves to local markets. The majority of the *Inc. 500* companies receive more than half of their sales from outside their local region. Over one-third of these businesses have sales from overseas customers.

Brokaw concludes with some predictions about the trends of highly successful startups:

> We'll find that larger percentages of successful startups will have formed alliances with major companies in their early years. More will be exporting ever greater portions of their output to customers overseas. Today's startups, we'll discover, will have continued to modify the ways they're set up, whom they become dependent on, and how far-reaching they try to be, all in response to the increasing globalization—and increasing complexity—of the marketplace.

The preceding viewpoint presumes that the goal is to grow—and grow fast. As was suggested earlier, however, growth has its good side and its bad side. Many firms have encountered severe, if not fatal, consequences from growing too fast. Jim Hindman, the founder of Jiffy Lube, lost sight of that fact and took the firm during its early years beyond its capacity to finance the growth. The result was chaos and such severe financial distress that Hindman is no longer part of the firm he conceived and built. Also, some entrepreneurs prefer not to grow too large or too quickly. They prefer to remain small or at least to control the level of growth at what for them is a manageable rate when everything is considered, including priorities for their personal lives. Finally, a startup should avoid increasing sales when the profits associated with the sales are not sufficient to provide an attractive return on the capital invested —an issue we will discuss more completely in Chapters 6 and 23. However, even with the preceding caveats in mind, an entrepreneur cannot ignore the importance of achieving an adequate level of sales. In this regard, we emphasize learning from those who do it well—the kinds of firms that have been described by Brokaw.

DISCUSSION QUESTIONS

1. Why would an entrepreneur prefer to launch an entirely new venture rather than buy an existing firm?

2. Suggest a product or a service not currently available that might lead to a new small business. How safe would it be to launch a new business depending solely on that one new product or service? Why?

3. Use the categories in Figure 3-2 to classify a mobile car service that changes oil and filters in parking lots. Can you think of a similar but different business that might fit the other two categories? Explain.

4. Suppose that a business available for purchase has shown an average net profit of $40,000 for the past five years. During these years, the amount of profit fluc-

New Terms and Concepts

startup *43*
buyout *43*
Type A ideas *44*
Type B ideas *44*
Type C ideas *44*
serendipity *46*
matchmakers *52*
asset-based valuation approach *54*
modified book value approach *54*

replacement value approach *55*
liquidation value approach *55*
market-based valuation approach *56*
earnings-based valuation approach *57*
normalized earnings *57*

capitalization rate *57*
cash flow–based valuation approach *58*
risk premium *59*

You Make the Call

Situation 1 After selling his small computer business, James Stroder set out on an 18-month sailboat trip with his wife and young children. He had founded the business several years earlier, and it had become a million-dollar enterprise. Now, he was looking for a new venture.

While giving his two sons reading lessons on board the sailboat (they each had slight reading disabilities), Stroder had an inspiration for a new company. He wondered why a computer could not be programmed to drill special education students who needed repetition to recognize and pronounce new words correctly.

Source: Based on an article in *The Wall Street Journal.* (Names are fictitious.)

Question 1 How would you classify Stroder's startup idea?
Question 2 What was the source of Stroder's new idea?
Question 3 Do you think Stroder might develop his idea with a startup or a buyout? Why?

Situation 2 Four years after starting their business, Bill and Janet Brown began to have thoughts of selling out. Their business, Bucket-to-Go, had been extremely successful, as indicated by an average 50 percent increase in revenue in each of its years in existence. Bucket-to-Go began when Bill turned his hobby of making wooden buckets into a full-time business. The buckets were marketed nationwide in gift shops and garden centers.

Sam Kline learned of the buyout opportunity after contacting a business broker. Kline wanted to retire from corporate life and thought this business would be an excellent opportunity.

Question 1 Which valuation technique do you think Kline should use to value the business? Why?
Question 2 What accounting information should Kline consider? What adjustments might be required?
Question 3 What qualitative information should Kline evaluate?

Continue on next page

Situation 3   Stuart Mize had worked with his father in a successful building materials business. The family had sold the company, and Mize received a portion of the sales price. After several months, Mize began thinking about starting or buying a company. One of his hobbies was backpacking; he had hiked the highest peaks in 30 of the 50 states. In his search for a new business, Mize heard of a company that made small trailers for motorcycles. These trailers were fairly popular with retirees who were cyclists and with individuals who liked to travel on motorcycles in order to go into the backwoods where a car could not go.

After several meetings, Mize and the current owner of the firm negotiated a selling price and the deal was consummated. Immediately after the purchase, Mize moved the business from its present location to his own town, several hundred miles away.

Question 1   Why should Mize buy the company instead of starting his own firm?

Question 2   What are the pros and cons for Mize's buying of this particular business?

Question 3   Do you think Mize made a mistake in moving the business to his hometown?

tuated between $20,000 and $60,000. The business is in a highly competitive industry, and its purchase requires only a small capital outlay. Thus, the barriers to entry are low. State your assumptions, and then calculate the value that you might use in negotiating the purchase price.

5. Contrast the market-based valuation approach with the earnings-based approach. Which is easier to apply? Which is more appropriate?

6. Using the earnings-capitalization technique, value the following companies:

   a. The normalized net income is $50,000. The business requires average executive ability and a comparatively small capital investment. Established goodwill, however, is of distinct importance.

   b. The normalized net income is $80,000. The firm is a small industrial business in a highly competitive industry and requires a relatively small capital outlay. Anyone with a little capital may enter the industry.

   c. The normalized net income is $30,000. The business depends on the special skills of a small group of managers. The business is highly competitive, and the failure rate in the industry is relatively high.

   d. The normalized net income is $60,000. The firm is a personal service business. Little, if any, capital is required. The earnings of the enterprise reflect the owner's skill; the owner is not likely to be able to create an organization that will successfully carry on.

7. Describe the relationship between a firm's capitalization rate and (1) the riskiness of the firm, and (2) the firm's prospects for growth.

8. Differentiate between a capitalization rate and a required rate of return.

9. What is the present risk-free rate, as reported in *The Wall Street Journal*? Select a small company, and estimate what you believe to be an appropriate risk premium and total required rate of return if you were to buy the company.

10. If your goal is to start a business with high-growth potential, how should you structure the company?

EXPERIENTIAL EXERCISES

1. Look through some small business periodicals in your school's library for profiles of five or six new startups. Report to the class, describing the sources of the ideas.

2. Consult the Yellow Pages of your local telephone directory to locate the name of a business broker. Interview the broker and report to the class on how she or he values businesses.

3.   Select a startup you are familiar with and then write a description of your experiential and educational background. Evaluate the extent to which you are qualified to operate that startup.

4.   Consult your local newspaper's new business listings and then contact one of the firms to arrange a personal interview. Report to the class on how the idea for the new business originated. Classify the type of idea, according to Figure 3-2.

Exploring the

5.   Do a word search on the Web for "startup business." Report on five of the references you found in your search.

CASE 3
Stitch Craft (p. 597)

This case describes an opportunity to take over a small business.

Alternative Cases for Chapter 3: Case 1, "King's Beauty Supply," p. 593
Case 4, "Operating a Kiosk Franchise," p. 600
Case 12, "Walker Machine Works," p. 624
Case 26, "Diaper Dan," p. 662

Franchising Opportunities

Chapter 4

Cruise
Holidays
International

spotlight on small business

Successful ventures are not always rooted in spectacular and innovative products or services. Often an entrepreneur simply recognizes an empty market niche and provides an ordinary product or service to receptive customers through appropriate marketing strategies.

Such is the case with Cruise Holidays International, a franchisor headquartered in San Diego, California. In 1984, Cruise Holidays was launched as the first cruise-only travel agency. Most insiders and travel agents laughed at the idea of a specialized, cruise-only agency. But the founder believed that the market niche was large enough to support the venture. Cruise Holidays built its reputation on identifying and fulfilling each individual customer's needs. Because Cruise Holidays concentrates solely on cruises, it is more focused and is able to customize each cruise package.

Mike London became president of Cruise Holidays in 1992. His vision for franchising growth is reflected in this statement: "We're welcoming people who wish to combine their spirit of independence with the huge competitive advantage of international franchise affiliation . . . who share our belief that profits are driven by exemplary customer service and knowledgeable, personalized cruise travel counseling. . . ." Apparently, specialization and attention to people have been a winning combination for this number one cruise-only agency.

Source: Informational materials provided by Cruise Holidays International.

start here

Chapter 3 examined the alternatives of creating an entirely new venture or buying an existing business—startups and buyouts. This chapter examines a third alternative—beginning a business by franchising. This is a viable alternative since the growth pattern for franchised businesses historically has been steady.

One of the first franchise arrangements was a nineteenth-century distribution relationship between Singer Sewing Machine Company and its dealers. Post–World War II franchise growth was based on the expansion of the franchising principle into such businesses as motels, variety shops, drugstores, and employment agencies. Then came the boom in the 1960s and 1970s, which featured franchising of fast-food outlets. Franchising growth has continued into the 1990s with a major emphasis on global franchising. Canada has provided the biggest market for U.S. franchisors, although Europe and Japan have also been extremely receptive. Even China and Russia have allowed some franchising from abroad, such as McDonald's.

G L O B A L

It is expected that franchising will continue to help thousands of entrepreneurs realize their business ownership dreams each year. First, let's examine the language and structure of the franchising system.

UNDERSTANDING THE FRANCHISE OPTION

1 Describe the basic concept of franchising and some of the important approaches.

The phrase *business opportunity* is used so much in promoting franchising that it seems to relate to franchising in a special way. However, franchising is just one type of business opportunity. It involves a formalized arrangement and a set of relationships that govern the way a business is operated. Franchise companies usually provide members of the system (franchisees) with names, logos, products, operating procedures, and more.

From the perspective of an entrepreneur, franchising may reduce the overall risk of starting and operating a business. The franchise arrangement allows new

The recent proliferation of fast-food franchises overseas vividly illustrates the success of franchising. This Moscow McDonald's has an employee turnover rate of only 3 percent; these young workers earn more than their parents do.

franchising
a marketing system revolving around a two-party legal agreement, whereby the franchisee conducts business according to terms specified by the franchisor

franchisee
an entrepreneur whose power is limited by a contractual relationship with a franchising organization

franchisor
the party in a franchise contract who specifies the methods to be followed by and the terms to be met by the other party

business operators to benefit from the accumulated business experience of all members of the franchise system. It is estimated that one of every twelve businesses is a franchise.[1]

The Language of Franchising

The term *franchising* is defined in many ways. In this book, we use a broad definition to encompass the term's wide diversity. **Franchising** is a marketing system revolving around a two-party legal agreement whereby one party (the **franchisee**) is granted the privilege to conduct business as an individual owner but is required to operate according to methods and terms specified by the other party (the **franchisor**). The legal agreement is known as the **franchise contract,** and the privilege it conveys is called the **franchise.**

The potential value of any franchising arrangement is defined by the rights contained in the franchise contract. The extent and importance of these rights are quite varied. For example, a potential franchisee may desire the right to use a widely recognized product or name. The term commonly used to describe this relationship between franchisor (supplier) and franchisee (buyer) is **product and trade name franchising.** Gasoline service stations, automobile dealerships, and soft drink bottlers are typical examples. Currently, product and trade name franchising accounts for about 30 percent of all franchise businesses but almost 70 percent of all franchise sales.[2]

Alternatively, the potential franchisee may want an entire marketing system and an ongoing process of assistance and guidance. This type of relationship is referred to as **business format franchising.** Fast-food outlets, hotels and motels, and business services are examples of this type of franchising. The volume of sales and the number of franchise units owned through business format franchising have increased steadily since the early 1970s.

Piggyback franchising refers to the operation of a retail franchise within the physical facilities of a host store. Examples of piggyback franchising include a cookie franchise doing business inside an Arby's fast-food outlet or a car-phone franchise within an automobile dealership. This form of franchising benefits both parties. The host store is able to add a new product line, and the franchisee obtains a location near prospective customers.

A **master licensee** is a firm or individual having a continuing contractual relationship with a franchisor to sell its franchises. This independent company or businessperson is a type of sales agent. Master licensees are responsible for finding new franchisees within a specified territory. Sometimes they will even provide support services such as training and warehousing, which are traditionally provided by the franchisor. Another franchising strategy gaining widespread usage is **multiple-unit ownership,** a situation that occurs when one franchisee owns more than one unit. Some of these franchisees are called **area developers,** individuals or firms that obtain the legal right to open several outlets in a given area. For example, Richard Jenkins's company, Boddie-Noell Enterprises of Rocky Mountain, North Carolina, is a large area developer that operates 350 Hardee's restaurants.[3]

The Structure of the Franchising Industry

Three types, or levels, of franchising systems offer various relationships for entrepreneurs. Figure 4-1 depicts each of these systems and provides examples. In **System A franchising,** the producer/creator (the franchisor) grants a franchise to a wholesaler (the franchisee). This system is often used in the soft drink industry. Dr Pepper and Coca-Cola are examples of System A franchisors.

franchise contract
the legal agreement between franchisor and franchisee

franchise
the privileges in a franchise contract

product and trade name franchising
a franchise relationship granting the right to use a widely recognized product or name

business format franchising
an agreement whereby the franchisee obtains an entire marketing system and ongoing guidance from the franchisor

piggyback franchising
the operation of a retail franchise within the physical facilities of a host store

master licensee
firm or individual acting as a sales agent with the responsibility for finding new franchisees within a specified territory

multiple-unit ownership
a situation in which a franchisee owns more than one franchise from the same company

area developers
individuals or firms that obtain the legal right to open several franchised outlets in a given area

System A franchising
a franchising system in which a producer grants a franchise to a wholesaler

Alternative Franchising Systems   ⬚ *Figure 4-1* ⬚

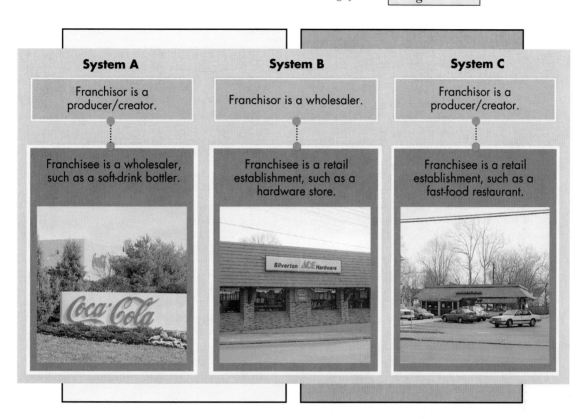

System A

Franchisor is a producer/creator.

Franchisee is a wholesaler, such as a soft-drink bottler.

System B

Franchisor is a wholesaler.

Franchisee is a retail establishment, such as a hardware store.

System C

Franchisor is a producer/creator.

Franchisee is a retail establishment, such as a fast-food restaurant.

In the second type, designated as **System B franchising,** the wholesaler is the franchisor. This system prevails among supermarkets and general merchandising stores. Ben Franklin and Ace Hardware are examples of System B franchisors.

The third type, **System C franchising,** is the most widely used. In this system, the producer/creator is the franchisor, and the retailer is the franchisee. Automobile dealerships and gasoline service stations are prototypes of this system. In recent years, it has also been used successfully by many fast-food outlets and printing services. Notable examples of System C franchisors are Burger King and Kwik-Kopy.

Most of the sales in franchising are derived from the traditional franchising areas (see Table 4-1). For example, approximately 50 percent of franchise sales in 1990 came from auto and truck franchisees. Interestingly, this sector represented only 5 percent of the total number of franchise establishments in that year. Nonretail trade continued to grow as a percent of total franchise sales over the period of 1970 to 1990—from 10 percent to over 15 percent.

The larger franchisors are the dominant force in the franchising industry. Franchisors with more than 500 units accounted for only 6 percent of the estimated 3,000 franchisors in 1990, but they accounted for almost two-thirds of all franchise sales.[4]

System B franchising
a franchising system in which a wholesaler is the franchisor

System C franchising
the most widely used franchising system in which a producer is the franchisor and a retailer is the franchisee

ADVANTAGES AND DISADVANTAGES OF FRANCHISING

2 Identify the major advantages and disadvantages of franchising.

"Look before you leap" is an old adage that should be heeded by potential franchisees. Entrepreneurial enthusiasm should not cloud your eyes to the realities,

Table 4-1

Percentage of Franchised Establishments and Franchising Sales by Industry, 1970, 1980, and 1990

	Franchised Establishments			Franchising Sales		
	1970	**1980**	**1990**	**1970**	**1980**	**1990**
Retail Trade	**83.5%**	**71.1%**	**63.5%**	**89.8%**	**87.2%**	**85.1%**
Auto and truck dealers	9.4	6.7	5.2	49.1	42.8	50.6
Gasoline stations	56.0	35.8	21.0	24.5	28.1	16.1
Restaurants	8.2	13.6	19.2	3.8	8.7	10.7
Convenience stores	2.2	3.5	3.3	1.4	2.3	2.0
Nonfood retailers	7.7	8.0	10.2	11.0	3.1	4.0
Food retailers	—	3.5	4.8	—	2.2	1.7
Other Sectors	**14.6**	**28.9**	**36.5**	**10.2**	**12.8**	**14.9**
Business services	2.7	9.2	12.6	0.6	2.0	2.7
Total	**100.0**	**100.0**	**100.0**	**100.0**	**100.0**	**100.0**

Source: U.S. Small Business Administration, *The State of Small Business: A Report of the President, 1993* (U.S. Government Printing Office, Washington, DC, 1993), p. 114.

both good and bad, of franchising. Therefore, we will first look at the advantages of buying a franchise and then examine the limitations. The choice of franchising over alternative methods of starting your own business is ultimately based on weighing all the pluses and minuses of franchising. Figure 4-2 illustrates the major factors in this evaluation. Franchising will not be the ideal choice for all prospective entrepreneurs, because the various factors carry different weights for different individuals, depending on their personal goals and circumstances. However, many people find a franchise to be the best choice.[5] Study these advantages and disadvantages carefully, and remember them when you are evaluating the franchising option.

Advantages of Franchising

Buying a franchise can be attractive for a variety of reasons. The greatest overall advantage by far is its probability of success! Business failure data are difficult to find and evaluate. Nevertheless, the success rate for franchises seems much higher than that for nonfranchised businesses. One U.S. government publication indi-

Figure 4-2

Major Pluses and Minuses in the Franchising Calculation

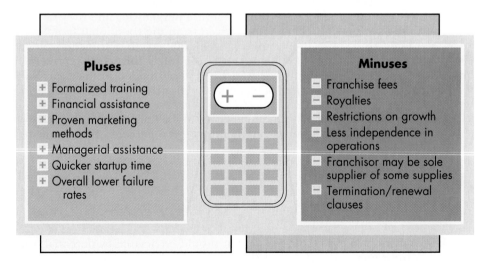

Pluses

+ Formalized training
+ Financial assistance
+ Proven marketing methods
+ Managerial assistance
+ Quicker startup time
+ Overall lower failure rates

Minuses

− Franchise fees
− Royalties
− Restrictions on growth
− Less independence in operations
− Franchisor may be sole supplier of some supplies
− Termination/renewal clauses

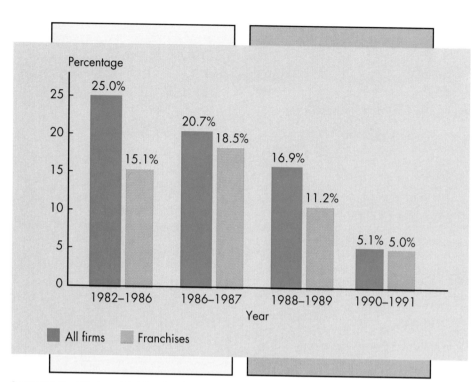

Source: U.S. Small Business Administration, *The State of Small Business: A Report of the President, 1993* (U.S. Government Printing Office, Washington, DC, 1993), p. 127.

Figure 4-3

Failure Rates of Eating Places Holding SBA Loans for Selected Time Periods Between 1982 and 1991

cates that franchise companies report annual turnover of fewer than 5 percent of their franchisees.[6] Figure 4-3 presents failure information for one industry segment over a period of 10 years, based solely on SBA loan data. Note that the failure rate for franchised eating places is lower than the rate for all firms in this area.

Also, a 1991 study by Arthur Andersen, the accounting firm, found that nearly 97 percent of franchisee-owned units opened five years previously were still in operation.[7] There appears to be little question that the failure rate for independent small businesses in general is much higher than that for franchised businesses.

One explanation for the lower failure rate of franchises is that most franchisors are highly selective when granting a franchise. Many potential franchisees who qualify financially are rejected. "You have to be discriminating," says Edward Kushell, president of The Franchise Consulting Group in Century City, California. Many of the large franchisors get 10 applicants for every one they accept.[8]

There are three additional, and more specific, reasons why a franchise opportunity is appealing. A franchise is typically attractive because it offers (1) training, (2) financial assistance, and (3) operating benefits. Naturally, all franchises are not equally strong in all these aspects. But these advantages motivate people to consider the franchise arrangement.

TRAINING   The training received from the franchisor is important because of the managerial weakness typical of many small entrepreneurs. To the extent that it can help alleviate this weakness, the training program offered by the franchisor constitutes a major benefit. Training by the franchisor often begins with an initial period of a few days or a few weeks at a central training school or at another established location. For example, the Holiday Inn franchise chain operates the hotel industry's largest training center, Holiday Inn University, which was built in 1972 at a cost

Action Report

QUALITY GOALS

QUALITY

Kwik-Kopy Campus

One of the major reasons for buying a Kwik-Kopy franchise is good, quality training. Kwik-Kopy's training covers the technical aspects of running a printing business as well as the standard topics of accounting, computers, and leadership. However, Kwik-Kopy's training facility is unique. Located at picturesque Northwest Forest, a few miles from Houston, Texas, the Kwik-Kopy campus of 131 acres looks like an amusement park with a full-size replica of the Texas Alamo. The founder of the company, Bud Hadfield, likes to do things differently. Trainees also like to have fun.

But franchise trainees quickly realize that the three-week training program is hard. Classes usually start at 7:00 A.M. and conclude at 6:00 P.M., Mondays through Fridays, and they continue for a half-day on Saturdays. It is not much time to train the franchisees, but it is not mission impossible.

The training program must be working. Today Kwik-Kopy has approximately 1,000 franchises spread among 39 states in the United States and 13 other countries.

Source: Excerpted from Kwik-Kopy materials.

of $5 million. Initial training programs cover not only the operating procedures to be used by the business, but also broader topics such as record keeping, inventory control, insurance, and human relations.

Another very famous franchisor, McDonald's, describes its franchisee training effort as follows:

This year Hamburger University (HU) celebrates 30 years of training in the fine points of Quality, Service and Cleanliness. More than 40,000 owner/operators, managers and employees have graduated with degrees in hamburgerology since 1961, when the first sessions were held in the basement of a restaurant in Des Plaines, Illinois. Today HU is located at McDonald's Office Campus in Oak Brook, Illinois. It is an international management training center with more than 30 classrooms and labs, and a staff of more than 30 professors. Since courses are accredited by the American Council on Education, students who have satisfied the operations training requirements of the McDonald's System can receive up to 32 hours of college credit. In addition, HU's in England, Germany and Japan support international growth.[9]

The Mister Donut franchise requires an initial training course of four weeks, including such topics as doughnut making, accounting and controls, advertising and merchandising, scheduling of labor and production, purchasing, and so on. Naturally, the nature of the product and the type of business affect the amount and type of training required for the franchisee. In most cases, training constitutes an important advantage of the franchising system and permits individuals who have had little training and education to start and succeed in businesses of their own.

Initial training is ordinarily supplemented with subsequent training and guidance. This may involve refresher courses and/or visits by a traveling company representative to the franchisee's location from time to time. The franchisee may also receive manuals and other printed materials that provide guidance for the business. However, in particular cases, it may be difficult to distinguish between guidance and control. The franchisor normally places considerable emphasis on observing strict controls. Still, much of the continued training goes far beyond the application of controls. Although some franchising systems have developed excellent training programs, this is by no means universal. Some unscrupulous promoters falsely promise satisfactory training.

Figure 4-4 displays selected listings from a U.S. Department of Commerce publication entitled *Franchise Opportunities Handbook*. This handbook contains a comprehensive listing of franchisors with a brief statement about their nature and requirements. Note the entry describing the training provided to franchisees.

FINANCIAL ASSISTANCE   The costs of starting an independent business are often high, and the typical entrepreneur's sources of capital quite limited. The entrepreneur's standing as a prospective borrower is weakest at this time. By teaming up with a franchising organization, the aspiring franchisee may enhance the likelihood of obtaining financial assistance.

If the franchising organization considers the applicant to be a suitable prospect with a high probability of success, it frequently extends a helping hand financially. For example, the franchisee is seldom required to pay the complete cost of establishing the business. In addition, the beginning franchisee is normally given a payment schedule that can be met through successful operation. Also, the franchisor may permit delay in payments for products or supplies obtained from the parent organization, thus increasing the franchisee's working capital.

Association with a well-established franchisor may also improve a new franchisee's credit standing with a bank. The reputation of the franchising organization and the managerial and financial controls that it provides serve to recommend the new franchisee to a banker. Also, the franchisor will frequently cosign a note with a local bank, thus guaranteeing the franchisee's loan.

OPERATING BENEFITS   Most franchised products and services are widely known and accepted. For example, consumers will readily buy McDonald's hamburgers or Baskin-Robbins ice cream, because they know the reputation of these products. Travelers may recognize a restaurant or a motel because of its name, type of roof, or some other feature such as the "Golden Arches" of McDonald's. Travelers may turn into a Denny's Restaurant or a Holiday Inn because of their previous experiences and the knowledge that they can depend on the food and service that these outlets provide. Thus, franchising offers both a proven line of business and product or service identification.

The entrepreneur who enters a franchising agreement acquires the right to use the franchisor's nationally advertised trademark or brand name. This serves to identify the local enterprise with the widely recognized product or service. Of course, the value of product identification differs with the type of product or service and the extent to which it has received widespread promotion. In any case, the franchisor maintains the value of its name by continued advertising and promotion.

Popular franchises in the 1990s include stores that sell secondhand merchandise. Once Upon A Child is a growing chain of stores that sells secondhand children's goods.

Figure 4-4 *Information Profile of Selected Franchisors*

COOKIE BOUQUET / COOKIES BY DESIGN
6757 Arapaho Rd., # 761
Dallas, TX 75248
Telephone: (800) 945-2665;
(214) 239-7474
Fax: (214) 239-1144
**Mr. David Patterson, Vice President
of Franchise Development**
Number of Franchised Units: 72
Number of Company-Owned Units: 1
Number of Total Operating Units: 73

In Business Since: 1983
Franchising Since: 1987

Description of Operation: Unique retail opportunity! Gift bakery, specializing in hand-decorated cookie arrangements and gourmet cookies created for special events, holidays, centerpieces, etc. Clientele include both individual and corporate customers. A wonderful, delicious alternative to flowers or balloons.

Equity Capital Needed: $43,500–$98,000

Franchise Fee: $18,500

Royalty Fee: 6%

Financial Assistance: None

Managerial Assistance: Cookie Bouquet produces complete training, operations, design, decorating, and employee manuals. Stores receive periodic visits from corporation representatives. The corporation publishes a monthly newsletter and holiday bulletins and also holds an annual convention.

Training Provided: An extensive 2-week "Cookie College" at the corporate headquarters in Dallas, TX will show new franchise owners a working store, where they can have hands-on training in every aspect of the business.

Information Submitted: November 1993

MCDONALD'S CORPORATION
One McDonald's Plaza, Kroc Dr.
Oak Brook, IL 60521
Telephone: (708) 575-6196
Fax: (708) 575-5645
Franchising Department
Number of Franchised Units: 10,229
Number of Company-Owned Units: 3,768
Number of Total Operating Units: 13,997

In Business Since: 1955
Franchising Since: 1955

Description of Operation: McDonald's is the world's leading food-service retailer in the global consumer market place, with nearly 14,000 restaurants in 70 countries. 85% of McDonald's restaurant businesses in the United States are locally owned and operated by independent entrepreneurs.

Equity Capital Needed: Minimum of $75,000 in non-borrowed personal resources to consider an individual for a franchise

Franchise Fee: $22,500, plus $15,000 noninterest-bearing franchise security deposit paid to McDonalds

Royalty Fee: A monthly service fee of 3.5% of sales, plus the greater of monthly base rent or % rent of sales

Financial Assistance: McDonald's does not provide financing or loan guarantees.

Managerial Assistance: Operations, training, maintenance, accounting, and equipment manuals are provided. McDonald's makes available promotional advertising material, plus field operations support.

Training Provided: Prospective franchisees are required to participate in a training and evaluation program, which may, on a part-time basis, take 2 years or longer to complete.

Information Submitted: April 1994

QUALITY

In addition to offering a proven line of business and readily identifiable products or services, franchisors have developed and tested their methods of marketing and management. The operating manuals and procedures supplied to franchises enable them to operate more efficiently from the start. This is one reason why franchisors insist on the observance of quality methods of operation and performance. If some franchises were allowed to operate at substandard levels, they could easily destroy customers' confidence in the entire system.

CRUISE HOLIDAYS INTERNATIONAL
9665 Chesapeake Dr., # 401
San Diego, CA 92123
Telephone: (800) 866-7245;
              (619) 279-4780
Fax: (619) 279-4788
Franchise Development Department
Number of Franchised Units: 160
Number of Company-Owned Units:0
Number of Total Operating Units: 160

In Business Since: 1984
Franchising Since: 1984

Description of Operation: Cruise Holidays International is the oldest and largest chain of cruise-only agencies in the world, specializing in the sale of cruise vacations to the general public. Cruising has become the fastest-growing and most profitable segment of the travel industry. Cruise Holidays offers comprehensive training, national advertising, and no inventory. Cruise Holidays represents all the major cruise lines.

Equity Capital Needed:
$84,000–$130,000

Franchise Fee: $29,500

Royalty Fee: 1% or $525.50

Financial Assistance: Financial assistance to veterans who qualify under the VetFran program. Franchisor will finance up to 50% of the franchise fee through a small interest note.

Managerial Assistance: We provide 2 weeks of comprehensive training in marketing, advertising, sales, customer service, product knowledge, business operations, and accounting. A free cruise is included as part of the training. On-site visits and assistance. Group and convention sales and advanced training available.

Training Provided: Same as above.

Information Submitted: March 1994

KWIK-COPY PRINTING
One Kwik-Kopy Ln.
Cypress, TX 77429
Telephone: (800) 942-9526;
              (713) 373-9142
Fax: (800) 542-8539
**Ms. LaDonna Meadows Allen,
Vice President**
Number of Franchised Units: 516
Number of Company-Owned Units: 0
Number of Total Operating Units: 516

In Business Since: 1967
Franchising Since: 1967

Description of Operation: Centers offer fine printing, quality copied materials, design, typesetting, and other services, primarily to the business community.

Equity Capital Needed:
$138,500–$146,000, plus $45,000 working capital

Franchise Fee: $25,000

Royalty Fee: Maximum of 8%

Financial Assistance: Financing is available to qualified applicants for balance.

Managerial Assistance: Our support system is unequaled in the industry.

Training Provided: We provide 5 weeks of hands-on classroom and field training. Training continues with an annual conference and trade show. Custom software, public relations, and direct mail programs.

Information Submitted: March 1994

Source: U.S. Department of Commerce, *Franchise Opportunities Handbook* (Washington, DC: U.S. Government Printing Office, October 1994).

The existence of proven products and methods, however, does not guarantee that a franchised business will succeed. For example, what the franchisor's marketing research techniques show to be a satisfactory location may turn out to be inferior. Or the franchisee may lack ambition or perseverance. However, the fact that a franchisor has a record of successful operation proves that the system can work and has worked elsewhere.

Figure 4-5   *A Low Franchise Fee Is Not Everything*

Limitations of Franchising

Franchising is like a coin—it has two sides. We have examined the positive side of franchising, but we must also look at the negative side. In particular, three shortcomings permeate the franchise form of business. These are (1) the cost of a franchise, (2) the restrictions on growth that can accompany a franchise contract, and (3) the loss of entrepreneurial independence.

COST OF A FRANCHISE   The total franchise cost has several components, *all* of which need to be examined. The cost of a franchise begins with the franchise fee. Generally speaking, higher fees are charged by well-known franchisors (see Figure 4-5).

Other costs include royalty payments, promotion costs, inventory and supply costs, and building and equipment costs. When these expenditures are considered along with the franchise fee, the total investment may be surprisingly large. For example, a McDonald's franchise may require over $500,000 in initial costs! Other franchises require only a few thousand dollars. In addition to initial costs, it is often recommended that funds be available for at least six months to cover pre-opening expenses, training expenses, personal expenses, and emergencies. A reputable franchisor should always provide a detailed estimate of investment cost. Figure 4-6 provides an example of how these items are presented in promotional materials offered by the franchisor of Cookies by Design.

If entrepreneurs could earn the same income independently, they would save the franchise fee and some of these other costs. However, an objection to paying the fee is not valid if the franchisor provides the benefits previously described. In that case, franchisees are paying for the advantages of their relationship with the franchisor, and this may prove to be a very good investment.

RESTRICTIONS ON GROWTH   A basic way to achieve business growth is to expand existing sales territory. However, many franchise contracts restrict the franchisee to a defined sales territory, thereby eliminating this means of growth. Usually, the franchisor agrees not to grant another franchisee the right to operate within the same territory. The potential franchisee, therefore, should weigh territorial limitation against the advantages cited earlier.

Estimated Franchise Cost for a Cookies By Design Shoppe | Figure 4-6 |

CATEGORIES OF EXPENSES	COSTS	
Initial Franchise Fee	$ 10,000 -	25,000
Opening Inventory	3,500 -	4,500
Major Equipment	10,000 -	25,000
Leasehold Improvements	10,000 -	20,000
Furniture & Fixtures	1,000 -	3,000
Signs	2,000 -	5,000
First Month's Rent	2,000 -	3,000
Security Deposit / Insurance Deposits	1,500 -	5,000
Training	1,000 -	1,500
Working Capital	5,000 -	15,000
Licenses & Permits	+ 100 -	500
	$ 46,100 -	107,500

These figures are estimates only. Costs will differ according to a variety of variables that include the following: geographical area, the size and location of your shoppe, inflation, cost of labor and materials, and the terms of your lease.

Explanation of Expenses:

Initial Franchise Fee

Two types of franchises are available: (a) Individual Store Franchise Agreement - this agreement grants rights to open one shoppe in a specific location, which is generally defined by multiple U.S. Postal Zip Codes.

(b) Area Development Agreement - this agreement grants the rights to develop multiple shoppes within a defined territory according to an agreed-upon development schedule. The defined area is most often a large metropolitan area.

Opening Inventory

Various supplies are included in this category such as ingredients, plaster, baskets, and other materials needed in production for the first month of business.

Major Equipment

This category includes major bakery equipment and computer software and hardware, as well as any installation costs.

Leasehold Improvements

These consist of store construction costs, which include such things as plumbing, painting, electrical work, cabinetry work, contractor's fee, etc.

Furniture & Fixtures

This category includes tables, chairs, shelving and other miscellaneous furniture items, as well as any associated installation costs.

Signs

Storefront and illuminated signs are included in this category, along with installation costs.

First Month's Rent

This category includes the monthly rent and common area maintenance charges for the first month of operation.

Security Deposit / Insurance Deposits

Utility deposits and rent security deposits are included in this category. Insurance down payments are also included.

Training (per person)

This category includes amounts for transportation and room and board for each person while attending Cookie College.

Working Capital

This consists of salary, occupancy costs, and other expenses that will be incurred during approximately the first three months of operation.

Licenses and Permits

This category includes the cost for the various business licenses and permits that may be required depending on your location.

LOSS OF INDEPENDENCE   Frequently, individuals leave salaried employment for entrepreneurship because they dislike working under the direct supervision and control of others. By entering into a franchise relationship, such individuals may simply find that a different pattern of close control over personal endeavors has taken over. The franchisee does surrender a considerable amount of independence in signing a franchise agreement. This situation is described by Aris Mardirossian, president of 6-Twelve Convenient Mart, Inc., of Rockville, Maryland: "If you can't follow somebody else, don't buy a franchise, because your life will be miserable and the franchisor's life will be miserable."[10]

Even though the franchisor's influence on business operations may be helpful in ensuring success, the level of control exerted may be unpleasant to an entrepreneur who cherishes independence. In addition, some franchise contracts go to extremes by covering unimportant details or specifying practices that are more helpful to others in the chain than to the local operation. Thus, as an operator of a franchised business, the entrepreneur occupies the position of a semi-independent businessperson.

<table>
<tr><td>

3 Discuss the process for evaluating a franchise.

</td></tr>
</table>

EVALUATING FRANCHISE OPPORTUNITIES

After deciding to buy a franchise, the prospective franchisee still has much to do before the opportunity is a reality. He or she must first locate the right franchise and then investigate it completely. As we discuss the process, we will incorporate examples based on Cruise Holidays, the franchise company introduced in this chapter's opening.

Locating a Potential Franchise

With the growth of franchising over the years, the task of initially locating an appropriate franchise has become quite easy. Personal observation frequently sparks interest, or awareness may begin with exposure to an advertisement in a newspaper or magazine. These advertisements generally have headlines that appeal to the financial and personal rewards sought by the entrepreneur. *The Wall Street Journal, Entrepreneur, Nation's Business,* and *Inc.* are examples of publications that include advertisements of franchisors. For example, an advertisement for Cruise Holidays, which appeared in *Entrepreneur* magazine, is shown in Figure 4-7.

<table>
<tr><td>

Figure 4-7

Cruise Holidays Advertisement

</td><td>

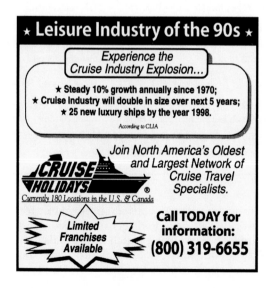

</td></tr>
</table>

Global Franchising Opportunities

There is a great opportunity for small business firms in the United States to franchise in other countries. Traditionally, U.S. franchisors have done most of their international franchising in Canada, because of Canada's proximity and language similarity. However, this is changing. A combination of events—the structuring of the European Economic Community, the collapse of the Soviet Union, the passage of the North American Free Trade Agreement, to mention only a few—have turned the eyes of U.S. franchisors to other foreign markets. A recent study by a major accounting firm indicates that half of the U.S. franchisors currently focused on domestic operations have plans to expand to international markets.

Recently, the U.S. Department of Commerce pegged 10 countries—Argentina, Brazil, China, India, Indonesia, Mexico, Poland, South Africa, South Korea, and Turkey—as prime franchising locations. "These markets comprise about half the world's population, and their gross national products are growing more rapidly than those of a number of developed countries," says Fred Elliott, a franchising specialist with the Commerce Department.[11]

Although the appeal of foreign markets is substantial, the task of franchising there is not easy. One franchisor's manager of international development expressed the challenge this way:

> *In order to successfully franchise overseas, the franchisor must have a sound and successful home base that is sufficiently profitable. The financial position of the franchisor must be secure and [the franchisor] must have resources which are surplus to—or can be exclusively diverted from—[its] domestic requirements. [The franchisor] must also have the personnel available to devote solely to international operations, and above all . . . must be patient. On the whole, the development of international markets will always take longer and make greater demands on the resources of the franchisor than first anticipated.*[12]

Investigating the Franchise

The nature of the commitment required in franchising justifies careful investigation. A franchised business typically involves a substantial financial investment, usually many thousands of dollars. Furthermore, the business relationship is one that may be expected to continue over a period of years.

The evaluation process is a two-way effort. The franchisor wishes to investigate the franchisee, and the franchisee obviously wishes to evaluate the franchisor and the type of opportunity offered. Time is required for this kind of analysis. You should be skeptical of a franchisor who pressures franchisees to sign at once, without allowing for proper investigation.

What should be the prospective entrepreneur's first step in evaluating a franchising opportunity? What sources of information are available? Do governmental agencies provide information on franchising? These and other questions should be considered. Basically, three sources of information should be tapped: (1) the franchisors themselves; (2) existing and previous franchisees; and (3) several independent, third-party sources.

THE FRANCHISOR AS A SOURCE OF INFORMATION   The franchisor being evaluated should be the primary source of information about a franchise. Obviously, information provided by a franchisor must be viewed in light of its purpose—to promote a franchise. However, there is no quicker source of information.

There are several ways to obtain information from a franchisor. One way is to correspond directly with the franchisor. Another method is to contact the franchisor indirectly by responding on reader service cards, provided by most business magazines. In Figure 4-7, note the toll-free telephone number at the bottom of the advertisement for Cruise Holidays. We called the number and, within a few days, received an attractive brochure describing Cruise Holidays and a cover letter from their marketing representative. These are items typically received as an initial response. The brochure included the Decision Making Checklist (shown in Figure 4-8), which can assist the prospective franchisee with his or her evaluation process.

Financial data are sometimes provided in the information packet sent initially by the franchisor. However, it is important for potential franchisees to remember that many of the financial figures are only estimates. Profit claims are becoming

Figure 4-8

Decision Making Checklist Provided by Franchisor

CRUISE HOLIDAYS ®

Franchise Development Department
9665 Chesapeake Dr., Suite 401
P.O. Box 23559
San Diego, CA 92193
(800) 866-7245

Decision Making Checklist
Confidential Pre-Interview Form

The Decision Making Checklist is designed to provide you with a step-by-step guide to the items you need to understand, complete, or schedule in order to make an informed business decision about the Cruise Holidays franchise opportunity. Refer to this Checklist often as you review this opportunity to make sure your information and understanding are complete.

Analysis of Opportunity (approximately 1 to 3 months from initial inquiry)   Anticipated Opening Date ____/____/____

Initial Inquiry: _____

- ❏ 1. I have received and reviewed the Franchise Promotional Package.
- ❏ 2. I have returned the completed Request for Consideration.

Initial Interview with Marketing Representative: _____

- ❏ 3. My Request for Consideration has been approved.
- ❏ 4. I have completed the initial interview with a Franchise Manager or Director.
- ❏ 5. I understand the mission statement of Cruise Holidays International, Inc.
- ❏ 6. I understand the industry and the market niche for the Cruise Holidays concept.
- ❏ 7. I understand the Cruise Holidays International Inc. support system.
- ❏ 8. I understand franchising and I am committed to work within the Cruise Holidays franchise system.
- ❏ 9. I have obtained information regarding site selection.
- ❏ 10. I have received the Prospectus (UFOC) and have signed and returned the Acknowledgment of Receipt form.
- ❏ 11. I have received the Franchise Agreement.

Second Interview with Marketing Representative: _____

- ❏ 12. I have spoken to cruise line executives regarding Cruise Holidays.
- ❏ 13. I have spoken with existing franchisees and made my own financial projections.
- ❏ 14. I have conducted store visitations, if possible.
- ❏ 15. I have received answers to all disclosure documents and franchise agreement questions.
- ❏ 16. I have received satisfactory answers to all questions regarding the Cruise Holidays opportunity.

Concluding Interview: _____

- ❏ 17. I have had a concluding interview with the Franchise Manager or Director.
- ❏ 18. I have visited the Cruise Holidays corporate office.
- ❏ 19. I have signed a Franchise Agreement and other paperwork and paid the Initial Franchise Fee.
- ❏ 20. I have had my location approved by Corporate.
- ❏ 21. I have scheduled training for all attendees.

Other Activities: _____

- ❏ _____ Target completion date ____/____/____
- ❏ _____ Target completion date ____/____/____

more common, partly because tough economic times make it difficult to sell a franchise without giving potential franchisees some idea of what they can earn.[13] Reputable franchisors are careful not to misrepresent what a franchisee can expect to attain in terms of sales, gross income, or profits. The importance of earnings to a prospective franchisee makes the subject of earnings claims a particularly sensitive one. "Historically, the misuse of earnings claims–type information has been a rampant form of misconduct in the sale of franchises and has thus been a priority of all government agencies regulating franchising," says Andrew C. Selden, a franchising lawyer. "What you're seeing in [recent FTC] enforcement actions is a crackdown on a subtler form of earnings claims abuse—the manipulation of data in the offering circular."[14]

After an entrepreneur has expressed further interest in a franchise by completing the application form and the franchisor has tentatively qualified the potential franchisee, a meeting is usually arranged to discuss the disclosure document. A disclosure document is a detailed statement of such information as the franchisor's finances, experience, size, and involvement in litigation. The document must inform potential franchisees of any restrictions, costs, and provisions for renewal or cancellation of the franchise. Important considerations related to this document are examined more fully in a later section.

EXISTING AND PREVIOUS FRANCHISEES AS SOURCES OF INFORMATION   There may be no better source of franchise facts than existing franchisees. Sometimes, the location of a franchise may preclude a visit to the business site. However, a simple telephone call can provide you with the viewpoint of someone in the position you are considering. If possible, also talk with franchisees who have left the business. They can offer valuable input about their decisions.

INDEPENDENT, THIRD-PARTY SOURCES OF INFORMATION   State and federal governments are valuable sources of franchising information. Since most states require registration of franchises, a prospective franchisee should not overlook state offices as a source of assistance. The federal government publishes the *Franchise Opportunities Handbook,* which is a useful directory of hundreds of franchisors. Also, a comprehensive listing of over 5,000 franchisees can be found in the *Franchise Opportunities Guide,* which is published by the International Franchise Association (IFA). The information in Figure 4-9 is taken from this publication; note the entry for Cruise Holidays. The IFA, which refers to itself as "The Voice of Franchising," is a nonprofit trade association whose membership comprises more than 600 franchisors, accounting for nearly 300,000 establishments. In October 1993, the IFA opened its membership to franchisees, and as of October 1995, over 34,000 franchisees had become members. The IFA sponsors legal and government affairs symposiums, franchise management workshops, franchisor/franchisee relations seminars, and trade shows. The IFA is highly selective, and not all companies applying for membership are accepted.

Business publications are also an excellent source of data on specific franchisors, and several include regular features on franchising. *Entrepreneur, Inc., Nation's Business, Success,* and *The Wall Street Journal,* to name a few, can be found in most libraries.

Continuing with our hypothetical evaluation of the Cruise Holidays franchise, we researched several business publications and, in the process, located two informative articles on Cruise Holidays—one in *Entrepreneur* and the other in *The Wall Street Journal.* Frequently, material provided in these kinds of articles is not available from the franchisor or from governmental offices. Articles in business publications often give an extensive profile of franchise problems and strategy changes. The third-party coverage adds credibility to the information in these articles.

Figure 4-9

Sample Entries in the Franchise Opportunities Guide

Supplemental Listings (Non-Members)

Air Brook Limousine
(201) 843-6100
P.O. Box 123
Rochelle Park, NJ 07662
Dynamic Air Freight, Inc.
(800) 736-0011
P.O. Box 167848
Irving, TX 75016
Franklin Traffic Service, Inc.
(716) 731-3131
P.O. Box 100
Ransomville, NY 14131
InTransit, Inc.
(800) 547-2053
P.O. Box 1147
Medford, OR 97501

TRAVEL AGENCIES
IFA MEMBERS

CARLSON TRAVEL NETWORK
(612) 449-2278
P.O. Box 59159, Minneapolis, MN 55459-8207
full member

TYPE OF BUSINESS: Travel Agencies

HISTORY: Over 1,100 franchised units; in business since 1888, franchising since 1984.

CASH INVESTMENT: Conversion franchise. No start ups. Financial assistance not available.

QUALIFICATIONS: Established travel agencies, leaders in local markets $1.5 million plus in volume.

CONTACT: Terry Robertson, Executive Vice President and General Manager of the Associate Division

CRUISE HOLIDAYS INTERNATIONAL, INC.
(800) 866-7245
(619) 279-4788 FAX
9665 Chesapeake Drive, Suite 401, P.O. Box 23559, San Diego, CA 92193
full member

TYPE OF BUSINESS: World's oldest and largest cruise-only travel center franchise.

HISTORY: 175 franchised units; in business since 1984, franchised since 1984.

CASH INVESTMENT: $29,500 franchise fee plus start-up costs and working capital. $100,000 plus, total investment.

QUALIFICATIONS: People who are aggressive and have marketing, sales, and business management ability.

CONTACT: Terry Mammen, CEO

FRANCHISING INTERNATIONALLY: Canada (will consider other countries).

THE THOMAS COOK GROUP
(44) 71-4084169
45 Berkeley Street, London, England W1A 1EB
associate member

TYPE OF BUSINESS: Travel Agency

CONTACT: J. J. Doran, Travel Development-International

TRAVEL AGENTS INTERNATIONAL
(813) 894-1537
(800) 678-8241
111 Second Ave. N.E., 15th Floor, Box 31005, St. Petersburg, FL 33731-8905
full member

TYPE OF BUSINESS: Retail travel agencies.

HISTORY: 393 franchised units, 1 company-owned; in business 13 years.

CASH INVESTMENT: $30,000 and operating capital. Includes furniture, equipment, indoor signs, training, advertising program, ongoing advertising, accounting and sales assistance. Qualified support staff. Assistance in site location and hiring of qualified personnel.

QUALIFICATIONS: Aggressive, outgoing individual with a record of personal accomplishment and a strong desire for success in his/her own business.

CONTACT: Lori Langenhahn, Franchise Coordinator

FRANCHISING INTERNATIONALLY: Canada

TRAVEL NETWORK, LTD.
(201) 567-8500
(800) 669-9000
560 Sylvan Avenue, Englewood Cliffs, NJ 07632
full member

TYPE OF BUSINESS: Full service computerized travel agency franchise chain.

HISTORY: 267 franchised units; 1 company-owned unit; in business since 1982; franchising since 1982.

CASH INVESTMENT: $45,000 start up cash; $85,000 total investment required. In cooperation with SBA-approved company we provide 80% financing of total investment.

QUALIFICATIONS: No travel experience needed; good business background and education.

CONTACT: Michael Y. Brent, President, CEO

FRANCHISING INTERNATIONALLY: Worldwide

Another useful source of franchise information is *The Franchise Annual,* which is published by Franchise News, Inc., an independent business publisher. This publication lists business format franchisors. The 1995 edition contains over 5,000 listings, including over 1,500 Canadian and overseas listings.

In recent years, franchise consultants have appeared in the marketplace to assist individuals seeking franchise opportunities. Some consulting firms present seminars on choosing the right franchise; one such firm is Franchise Seminars, Inc.

of Minneapolis, Minnesota. Of course, the prospective franchisee needs to be careful to select a reputable consultant. Since franchise consultants are not necessarily attorneys, an experienced franchise attorney should evaluate all legal documents.

SELLING A FRANCHISE

4 Explain the benefits derived from becoming a franchisor.

Franchising contains opportunities for both the buyer and the seller. We have already presented the franchising story from the viewpoint of buying a franchise. Now let's briefly consider the franchising option from the perspective of a potential franchisor.

Why would a businessperson wish to become a franchisor? At least three general benefits can be identified:

1. *Reduction of capital requirements.* Franchising allows you to expand without diluting your capital. The firm involved in franchising, in effect, through fee and royalty arrangements, borrows capital from the franchisee for channel development and thus has lower capital requirements than does a wholly owned chain.
2. *Increase in management motivation.* Franchisees, as independent businesspeople, are probably more highly motivated than salaried employees because of profit incentives and their vested interest in the business. Since franchising is decentralized, the franchisor is less susceptible to labor-organizing efforts than are centralized organizations.
3. *Speed of expansion.* Franchising lets a business enter many more markets much more quickly than it could using only its own resources.

There are also distinct drawbacks associated with franchising from the franchisor's perspective. At least three drawbacks can be isolated:

1. *Reduction in control.* A franchisor's right of control is greatly reduced in the franchising form of business because the franchisees are not employees. This is a major concern for most franchisors.
2. *Sharing of profits.* Only part of the profits from the franchise operation belongs to the franchisor.
3. *Increase in operating support.* There is generally more expense associated with nurturing the ongoing franchise relationships—providing accounting and legal services—than there is with centralized organization.

Among the older and highly successful large franchisors, such as McDonald's, are many small businesses that are finding success as franchisors. For example, David Martin, president of Steak-Out, made the transition from an independent businessperson to a franchisor. The steak and burger home-delivery franchise is based in Huntsville, Alabama. In 1987, Martin and his wife, Rhonda, who is operations manager, decided to franchise. The Martins closely followed the advice of their franchising consultant, and the company has grown to 17 locations.[15]

UNDERSTANDING THE FRANCHISOR/FRANCHISEE RELATIONSHIP

5 Describe the critical franchisor/franchisee relationship.

The basic features of the relationship between the franchisor and the franchisee are embodied in the franchise contract. The contract is typically a complex docu-

Action Report

ENTREPRENEURIAL EXPERIENCES

The Shoe May Not Fit

In 1986, Shelagh Watson chose to pursue expansion of her shoe store business through franchising. She had started Magnifete in downtown Cincinnati, Ohio only a year earlier. Her store specializes in hard-to-find women's oversized shoes. After $367,000 in gross sales in 1986, sales reached $600,000 in 1987. In light of this success, Watson opened two more company stores and began to market franchises through national trade shows.

Now, six years later and after $250,000 in expenses, Watson has closed the franchise company. She says her entry into franchising was premature. "Our franchisee profile was not working. . . . The people who were interested wanted to be absentee owners, or couldn't get the financing, or thought they would turn a 15 percent profit in the first year," says Watson. Watson was also concerned with the potential for franchise litigation over the life of a franchise contract: "I'd rather say that this [franchise program] was a nice research project for a quarter of a million dollars than be in a lawsuit for a million or more because we hadn't supported [the franchisee] properly."

After pulling out of franchising, Watson introduced a catalog of oversized shoes, and sales have increased by 30 percent.

Source: Meg Whittemore, "Is There a Franchise in Your Future?" *Nation's Business*, Vol. 80, No. 6 (June 1992), p. 63. Reprinted by permission. Copyright 1992, U.S. Chamber of Commerce.

ment, often running to many pages. Because of its extreme importance as the legal basis for the franchised business, no franchise contract should ever be signed by the franchisee without legal counsel. As a matter of fact, reputable franchisors insist that the franchisee have legal counsel before signing the agreement. An attorney may anticipate trouble spots and note objectionable features of the franchise contract.

In addition to consulting an attorney, a prospective franchisee should use as many other sources of help as practical. In particular, she or he should discuss the franchise proposal with a banker, going over it in as much detail as possible. The prospective franchisee should also obtain the services of a professional accounting firm in examining the franchisor's statements of projected sales, operating expenses, and net income. An accountant can give valuable help in evaluating the quality of these estimates and in discovering projections that may be unlikely to occur.

One of the most important features of the contract is the provision relating to termination and transfer of the franchise. Some franchisors have been accused of devising agreements that permit arbitrary cancellation. Of course, it is reasonable for the franchisor to have legal protection in the event that a franchisee fails to obtain a satisfactory level of operation or to maintain satisfactory quality standards. However, the prospective franchisee should be wary of contract provisions that contain overly strict cancellation policies. Similarly, the rights of the franchisee to sell the business to a third party should be clearly stipulated. A franchisor who can restrict the sale of the business to a third party could potentially assume ownership of the business at an unreasonably low price. The right of the franchisee to renew the contract after the business has been built up to a successful operating level should also be clearly stated in the contract.

The Uniform Franchise Offering Circular

The offer and sale of a franchise are regulated by both state and federal laws. At the federal level, the minimum disclosure standards are specified by Rule 436 of the Federal Trade Commission. Additionally, 15 states have their own regulations. A document, called the **Uniform Franchise Offering Circular (UFOC),** has been the accepted format for satisfying the franchise disclosure requirements of the Federal Trade Commission. It is intended to provide basic information about the franchise offering and the franchisor. A revised version of the UFOC was written by the North American Securities Administrators Association (NASAA). The new version promises to be more readable and less intimidating. Figure 4-10 provides a listing of some of the items covered in the new UFOC.

The UFOC is somewhat technical, and some prospective entrepreneurs mistakenly fail to read it or to get professional assistance. All disclosure statements must carry a statement on the front page advising the reader to study the document and show it to an accountant or lawyer.

Uniform Franchise Offering Circular (UFOC)
a document accepted by the Federal Trade Commission as satisfying its franchise disclosure requirements

Franchising Frauds

Every industry has its share of shady operations, and franchising is no exception. Unscrupulous fast-buck artists offer a wide variety of fraudulent schemes to attract unsuspecting investors. The franchisor in such cases is merely interested in obtaining the capital investment of the franchisee and not in a nurturing relationship. One source has suggested the following ten warning signs of a franchise scam:

1. *The Rented Rolls Royce Syndrome.* The overdressed, jewelry-laden sales representative is designed to impress you with an appearance of success. These people reek of money—and you hope, quite naturally, that it will rub off on you. *Motto:* "Don't you want to be like me?" *Antidote:* Check the financial statements in the offering document; they must be audited.

1. The franchisor, its predecessors and affiliates	14. Patents, copyrights, and proprietary information
2. Business experience	15. Obligation to participate in the actual operation of the franchise
3. Litigation	16. Restrictions on what the franchisee may sell
4. Bankruptcy	
5. Initial franchise fee	17. Renewal, termination, transfer, and dispute resolution
6. Other fees	
7. Initial investment	18. Public figures
8. Restrictions on sources of products and services	19. Earnings claims
	20. List of outlets
9. Franchisee's obligations	21. Financial statements
10. Financing	22. Contracts
11. Franchisor's obligations	23. Receipt
12. Territory	
13. Trademarks	

Figure 4-10

Items Covered in the New UFOC

Source: Excerpted from NASAA material dated April 25, 1993, p. 5.

Action Report

ETHICAL ISSUES

A New Code of Ethics

In 1994, the International Franchise Association revised its 1992 code of conduct for its members. Its "Code of Principles and Standards of Conduct" prescribes principles and standards "well beyond what would generally be considered to be ethical principles," according to Lewis G. Rudnick, counsel to the IFA. The 1992 code was rooted in the recognition by the IFA that the media, government officials, and the public did not understand the ethics that most U.S. franchising firms believe in. The code is considered to be a living document; therefore, the 1994 revisions are simply intended to make franchising more effective.

The four major principles set forth in the new code are that franchisors are to

1. Conduct business professionally, truthfully, accurately, fairly, and responsibly.
2. Use ethical business practices in dealing with franchisees, consumers, and government.
3. Comply with applicable law.
4. Offer equal opportunities to minorities, women, and disabled persons.

The new code also contains standards of conduct relating to 10 elements of the franchise relationship: (1) franchise sales and disclosure, (2) good faith dealing, (3) franchise advisory councils and franchisee associations, (4) termination of franchise agreements, (5) expiration of franchise agreements, (6) transfer of franchise, (7) system expansion, (8) supply sources, (9) disputes, and (10) discrimination.

Source: Lewis G. Rudnick, "IFA Conduct Code Revised," *Franchising World*, July-August, 1994, p. 6.

2. *The Hustle.* The giveaway sales pitch is "Territories are going fast. . . . Act now or you'll be shut out" or "I'm leaving town on Monday afternoon, so make your decision now." They make you feel like a worthless, indecisive dreamer if you do not take immediate action. *Motto:* "Wimps need not apply." *Antidote:* Take your time, and recognize The Hustle for the crude closing technique that it is.

3. *The Cash-Only Transaction.* An obvious clue that the company is running its program on the fly is that it wants cash so that there's no way to trace it and so that you can't stop payment if things crash and burn. *Motto:* "In God we trust; all others pay cash." *Antidote:* Insist on a check—made out to the company, not to an individual. Better yet, walk away.

4. *The Boast.* "Our dealers are pulling in six figures. We're not interested in small thinkers. If you think big, you can join the ranks of the really big money earners in our system. The sky's the limit." This statement was in answer to your straightforward question about the names of purchasers in your area. *Motto:* "We never met an exaggeration we didn't like." *Antidote:* Write your own business plan, and make it realistic. Don't try to be a big thinker—just a smart one.

5. *The Big-Money Claim.* Most state authorities point to exaggerated profit claims as the biggest problem in business opportunity and franchise sales. "Earn

$10,000 a month in your spare time" sounds great, doesn't it? If it is a franchise, any statement about earnings (regarding others in the system or your potential earnings) must appear in the Uniform Franchise Offering Circular (Item 19). *Motto:* "We can sling the zeros with the best of 'em." *Antidote:* Read the UFOC, and find five franchise owners who have attained the earnings claimed.

6. *The Couch Potato's Dream.* "Make money in your spare time. . . . This business can be operated on the phone while you're on the beach. . . . Two hours a week earns $10,000 a month." Understand this and understand it now: The only easy money in a deal like this one will be made by the seller. *Motto:* "Why not be lazy *and* rich?" *Antidote:* Get off the couch, and roll up your sleeves for some honest and rewarding work.

7. *Location, Location, Location.* Buyers are frequently disappointed by promises of services from third-party location hunters, such as "We'll place these pistachio dispensers in prime locations in your town." Turns out all the best locations are taken, and the bar owners will not insure the machines against damage by their inebriated patrons. Next thing you know, your dining room table is loaded with pistachio dispensers—and your kids don't even like pistachios. *Motto:* "I've got 10 sweet locations that are going to make you rich." *Antidote:* Get in the car, and check for available locations.

8. *The Disclosure Dance.* "Disclosure? Well, we're, uh, exempt from disclosure because we're, uh, not a public corporation. Yeah, that's it." No business format franchisor, with very rare exceptions, is exempt from delivering a disclosure document at your first serious sales meeting or at least 10 business days before the sale takes place. *Motto:* "Trust me, kid." *Antidote:* Disclosure: Don't let your money leave your pocket without it.

9. *The Registration Ruse.* You try to check out the franchisor with state authorities, and they respond, "Who?" Franchisors are required to register in 15 states; in Florida, Nebraska, and Texas, franchisors may file for exemption. *Motto:* "Registration? We don't need no stinking registration!" *Antidote:* If you are in a franchise registration state and the company is not registered, find out why. (Some companies are legitimately exempt.)

10. *The Thinly Capitalized Franchisor.* This franchisor dances lightly around the issue of its available capital. *Motto:* "Don't you worry about all that bean-counter hocus-pocus. We don't." *Antidote:* Take the UFOC to your accountant and learn what resources the franchisor has to back up its contractual obligations. If its capitalization is too thin or it has a negative net worth, it's not necessarily a scam, but the investment is riskier.[16]

The possibility of such fraudulent schemes requires alertness on the part of prospective franchisees. Only careful investigation of the company and the product can distinguish between fraudulent operators and legitimate franchising opportunities. Sometimes, even careful investigation is not enough. Consider the following situation:

Rose Gregg found out first-hand. The 35-year-old single mother from Cincinnati invested all of her modest savings two years ago with American Legal Distributors, an Atlanta concern that billed itself as a provider of prepaid legal services. She saw the business—marketing the company's services in local shopping malls—as work that would let her spend more time with her son, who has cerebral palsy.

"They had the biggest booth at the show, surrounded by legitimate franchises I recognized," she says. "I spent a week in a training seminar. I talked to other people who said they'd been successful. They even sent a bouquet of flowers after I invested."

Looking Back

1 **Describe the basic concept of franchising and some of the important approaches.**

- Franchising is a formalized arrangement that describes a certain way of operating a small business.
- The potential value of any franchising arrangement is determined by the rights contained in the franchise contract.
- Product trade franchising and business format franchising are the two types of franchising.
- Piggyback franchising, master licensees, multiple-unit ownership, and area developers are special approaches to franchising.
- Three levels of franchising systems—A, B, and C—offer various relationships between franchisor and franchisee.

2 **Identify the major advantages and disadvantages of franchising.**

- The overall attraction of franchising is its potential for a high rate of success.
- A franchise may be favored over other alternatives because it offers training, financial assistance, and operating benefits.
- The major limitations of franchising are its cost, restrictions on growth, and loss of entrepreneurial independence.

3 **Discuss the process for evaluating a franchise.**

- The substantial investment required by most franchises justifies careful investigation by a potential franchisee.
- The most logical source of the greatest amount of information about a franchise is the franchisor.
- Existing and previous franchisees are good sources of information for evaluating a franchise.
- Independent third parties, such as the government and the IFA, are valuable sources of franchise information.

4 **Explain the benefits derived from becoming a franchisor.**

- The major benefits of becoming a franchisor are reduced capital requirements, increased management motivation, and speed of expansion.
- The major drawbacks to franchising are reduction in control, sharing of profits, and increasing operating support.

5 **Describe the critical franchisor/franchisee relationship.**

- A franchise contract is a complex document and should be given to an attorney for evaluation.
- An important feature of the franchise contract is the provision relating to termination and transfer.
- A revised Uniform Franchise Offering Circular has been approved by the FTC.
- A revised code of ethics has been approved by the International Franchising Association.
- Prospective franchisees should be alert to possible franchising frauds.

That was all she got. Ms. Gregg was one of 375 people bilked out of more than $4 million by American Legal, with individual losses ranging from Ms. Gregg's $5,500 nest egg to more than $25,000, according to court documents. The scam's organizer, Harold H. Pasley, was sentenced last month to 15 years in prison, while four "singers," people who were paid to pose as successful franchisees, also received stiff sentences. James C. Strayhorn, Mr. Pasley's attorney, says his client disputes the charges and intends to pursue an appeal of his sentence.[17]

In conclusion, we need to point out that franchising has enabled many individuals to enter business who otherwise would never have escaped the necessity of salaried employment. Thus, franchising has contributed to the development of many successful small businesses.

DISCUSSION QUESTIONS

1. What makes franchising different from other forms of business? Be specific.
2. What is the difference between product and trade name franchising and business format franchising? Which one accounts for the majority of franchising activity?
3. Explain the three types of franchising systems. Which is most widely used?
4. Discuss the advantages and disadvantages of franchising from the viewpoints of the potential franchisee and the potential franchisor.
5. Should franchise information provided by a franchisor be discounted? Why or why not?

6. Do you believe the government-required disclosure document is useful for franchise evaluation? Defend your position.

7. Evaluate loss of control as a disadvantage of franchising from the franchisor's perspective.

8. What types of restrictions on franchisee independence might be included in a typical franchise contract?

9. What problems might arise when consulting previous franchisees in the process of evaluating a franchise?

10. What types of franchise information could you expect to obtain from business periodicals that you could not secure from the franchisor?

EXPERIENTIAL EXERCISES

1. Interview a local owner-manager of a widely recognized retail franchise such as McDonald's. Ask the person to explain the process of how he or she obtained the franchise and the advantages of franchising over starting a business from scratch.

2. Find a franchise advertisement in a recent issue of a business magazine. Research the franchise and report back to class with your findings.

3. Consider the potential for a hypothetical new fast-food restaurant to be located next to your campus. (Be as specific about the assumed location as you can.) Divide into two groups. Ask one group to favor a franchised operation and the other to support a nonfranchised business. Plan a debate on the merits of each operation for the next class meeting.

New Terms and Concepts

franchising *67*
franchisee *67*
franchisor *67*
franchise contract *68*
franchise *68*
product and trade name franchising *68*

business format franchising *68*
piggyback franchising *68*
master licensee *68*
multiple-unit ownership *68*
area developers *68*

System A franchising *68*
System B franchising *69*
System C franchising *69*
Uniform Franchise Offering Circular (UFOC) *85*

You Make the Call

Situation 1 While still a student in college in 1992, Adrian Johnson began his first business venture. He took his idea for a laundromat to a local bank and brought back a $90,000 loan. After finding a suitable site close to his campus, he signed a 10-year lease and opened for business. Over the first three days, the business averaged over 1,000 customers per day.

The attraction of Adrian's laundromat was its unique atmosphere. The business was carpeted, with oak paneling and brass fittings. There was a snack bar and a big-screen television for patrons to enjoy while waiting for their laundry. Within a week of opening day, Adrian had an offer to sell his business at twice his investment. He rejected the offer because he was considering the possibility of franchising his business concept.

Question 1 What major considerations should Adrian evaluate before he decides to franchise?
Question 2 Would piggyback franchising have potential for this type of business?
Question 3 If Adrian does indeed franchise his business, what types of training and support systems would you recommend he provide to franchisees?

Situation 2 Hard times in the agricultural commodities market led broker Bill Landers to leave his independent business and look for new opportunities. This time around, Bill was committed to going into business with his wife, Gwen, and their teenage son and daughter. His goal was to keep the family close and reduce the stress in their lives. In his previous job as a broker, Bill would leave home early and return late, with little time for his wife or children.

Before leaving his job, Bill looked at several franchise opportunities. One opportunity he and Gwen were seriously considering was a custom framing franchise that had been in existence for over 10 years and had almost 100 stores nationwide. However, the Landers were concerned about their lack of experience in this area and also about how long it would take to get the business going.

Continue on next page

Question 1 How important should their lack of prior experience be to Bill and Gwen's decision?

Question 2 What other characteristics of the franchise should they investigate? What sources for this information would you recommend?

Question 3 Can they reasonably expect to have a different life-style while owning a franchise? Explain.

Situation 3 When Donna Smith wanted to expand her three-year-old maternity clothing business in 1984, she approached an attorney for advice. She could not expand her Portland, Oregon firm, Pro Creations Maternity Leasewear, without spending a lot of money. Without hesitation, the attorney told the 54-year-old entrepreneur, "Franchise!" Confident in her attorney's advice, she set out to franchise her business.

Question 1 Do you think Smith's decision was made too quickly? If so, what should she have done before making a decision?

Question 2 What do you see as other expansion alternatives?

4. Research articles that discuss current fraudulent franchisors and report on your findings.

Exploring the

5. Locate the Franchise Conxions site on the World Wide Web:

http://www.franchise-conxions.com

Write a one-page summary describing three different franchisors you find listed at the site. For each franchisor be sure to include the head office location, current franchise locations, and the required investment level.

 CASE 4
Operating a Kiosk Franchise (p. 600)

This case describes an entrepreneur's venture into franchising.

Alternative Case for Chapter 4: Case 6, "Robinson Associates, Inc.," p. 605

Family Business Opportunities

Chapter 5

Seven Sisters

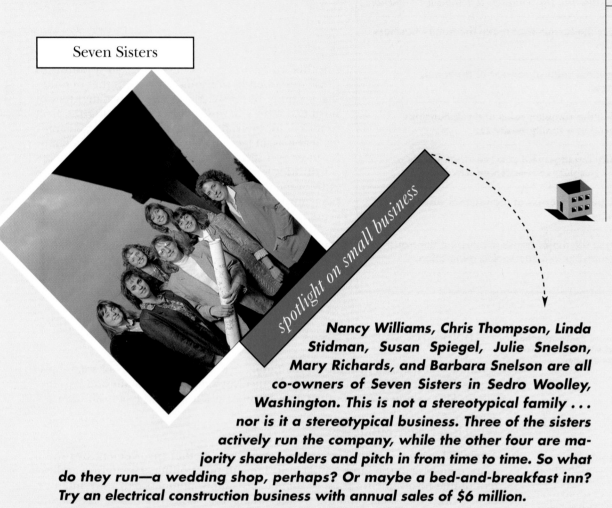

spotlight on small business

Nancy Williams, Chris Thompson, Linda Stidman, Susan Spiegel, Julie Snelson, Mary Richards, and Barbara Snelson are all co-owners of Seven Sisters in Sedro Woolley, Washington. This is not a stereotypical family . . . nor is it a stereotypical business. Three of the sisters actively run the company, while the other four are majority shareholders and pitch in from time to time. So what do they run—a wedding shop, perhaps? Or maybe a bed-and-breakfast inn? Try an electrical construction business with annual sales of $6 million.

With seven sisters involved, this firm is very much a *family* business. In a sense, the firm is also a second-generation business. Some of the sisters had worked with their father, Bill Snelson, who owned a mechanical contracting company. Nancy Williams, president of Seven Sisters, had worked her way up to a division manager position. She and her six sisters then purchased the electrical engineering division from their father.

This company is one of many different types of family business operations. The three sisters who run the firm each have different jobs and never meddle in another sister's territory. They also make a special effort to separate work time and family time.

Source: Erika Kotite, "Sister Act," *Entrepreneur,* Vol. 21, No. 9 (September 1993), p. 172. Reprinted with permission from Entrepreneur Magazine.

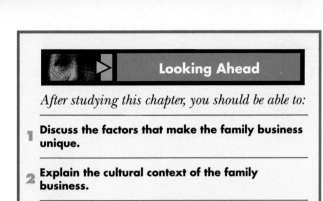

Looking Ahead

After studying this chapter, you should be able to:

1 Discuss the factors that make the family business unique.

2 Explain the cultural context of the family business.

3 Outline the complex roles and relationships involved in a family business.

4 Identify management practices that enable a family business to function effectively.

5 Describe the process of managerial succession in a family firm.

6 Analyze the major issues involved in the transfer of ownership to a succeeding generation.

start here

Another route to entrepreneurship, in addition to those described in previous chapters, is that of entering a family business. Many sons and daughters of business owners have the option of joining the firm founded by their parents or grandparents. Family leaders may, in fact, strive for continuation of a family business over several generations, thereby creating opportunities for children or other relatives to pursue entrepreneurship in that business. Young family members must then decide, often during their college years, whether to prepare for a career in the family business. This decision should be based on an understanding of the dynamics of such a business. This chapter, therefore, examines the distinctive features that characterize the family business as one type of entrepreneurial alternative.

THE FAMILY BUSINESS: A UNIQUE INSTITUTION

1 Discuss the factors that make the family business unique.

A number of features distinguish the family firm from other types of small businesses. Its decision making, for example, involves a mixture of family and business values. This section examines the family business as a unique type of institution.

What Is a Family Business?

family business
a company in which family members are directly involved in the ownership and/or functioning

A **family business** is characterized by ownership or other involvement by two or more members of the same family in its life and functioning. The nature and extent of that involvement varies. In some firms, family members may work full-time or part-time. In a small restaurant, for example, one spouse may serve as host and manager, the other may keep the books, and the children may work in the kitchen or as servers.

A business is also distinguished as a family business when it passes from one generation to another. For example, Thompson's Plumbing Supply is now headed by Bill Thompson, Jr., son of the founder, who is deceased. Bill Thompson III has started to work on the sales floor, after serving in the stockroom during his high school years. He is the heir apparent, who will someday replace his father. People in the community recognize Thompson's Plumbing Supply as a family business.

Most family businesses, including those we are concerned with in this book, are small. However, family considerations may continue to be important even when such businesses become large corporations. Companies such as Wal-Mart Stores, Levi Strauss and Company, Ford Motor Company, and Marriott Corporation are still recognized, to some extent, as family businesses.

Family and Business Overlap

Any family business is composed of both a family and a business. Although these are separate institutions—each with its own members, goals, and values—they overlap in the family firm (see Figure 5-1).

Action Report

GLOBAL OPPORTUNITIES

Family Business with a Global Reach

Although most family businesses are small, some expand across national borders to reach a global market. One example is McCain Foods Limited in Florenceville, New Brunswick, Canada. This family business was started by two brothers in 1957 in a remote province of Canada. At first, they exported Canadian potatoes to Europe.

> *Today McCain has 50 production facilities in nine countries, including Japan, New Zealand, and Australia. It churns out frozen french fries, dinners, vegetables, desserts, pizzas, and juices. Estimates are that Europe generates as much as 45 percent of sales; Canada and the United States generate perhaps 25 percent and 20 percent, respectively.*

This firm, still wholly owned and managed by the McCain family, is now known as the world's "French Fry King." It attained this position by being a tough competitor. However, the firm's attitude toward competitors, described by a former executive as "What's mine is mine, what's yours is mine," has apparently also created conflicts in decisions regarding family succession. Things have reportedly turned "nasty," with both brothers jockeying to have their own children assume management control.

Source: Toddi Gutner, "What's Yours Is Mine," *Forbes*, Vol. 152, No. 3 (August 2, 1993), pp. 68–69; and Toddi Gutner Block, "Food Fight!" *Forbes*, Vol. 155, No. 6 (March 13, 1995), p. 14.

Families and businesses exist for fundamentally different reasons. The family's primary function relates to the care and nurture of family members, while the business is concerned with the production or distribution of goods and/or services. The family's goals are the fullest possible development of each member, regardless of limitations in ability, and the provision of equal opportunities and rewards for each member. The business's goals are profitability and survival. These goals may be either in harmony or in conflict, but it is obvious that they are not identical. In the short run, what's best for the family may or may not be what's best for the business.

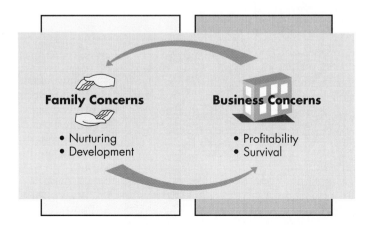

Family Concerns
- Nurturing
- Development

Business Concerns
- Profitability
- Survival

Figure 5-1

The Overlap of Family Concerns and Business Interests

In many cases, one decision may serve both sets of overlapping interests. However, the differing interests can also create tension and sometimes lead to conflict. Relationships among family members in a business are more sensitive than they are among unrelated employees. For example, a manager may become angry at an employee who consistently arrives late, but disciplining the employee is much more problematic if he or she is also a family member.

Decisions Affecting Both Business and Family

The overlap of family concerns and business interests in the family firm complicates the management process. Many decisions impact both business and family. Consider, for example, a performance review session between a parent-boss and a child-subordinate. Even with nonfamily employees, performance reviews can be potential minefields. The existence of a family relationship adds emotional overtones that vastly complicate the review process.

Which comes first, the family or the business? In theory, at least, most people opt for the family. Few business owners would knowingly allow the business to destroy their family. In practice, however, the resolution of such tensions becomes difficult. For example, a parent, motivated by a sense of family responsibility, may become so absorbed in the business that he or she spends insufficient time with the children.

If the business is to survive, its interests cannot be unduly compromised to satisfy family wishes. To grow, family firms must recognize the need for professional management and the fact that family concerns must sometimes be secondary. An example is found in the experience of Pierre DuPont, a member of the founding family of E. I. duPont de Nemours:

> *As far as Pierre was concerned, the large firm did not have the obligation to provide the family with jobs; instead, it should ensure them of large dividends. Of course, when the firm expanded, there would be increased employment opportunities for younger relatives.*[1]

Family members may be more willing than other employees to defer their own rewards for the sake of the firm. Siblings Hamish, Cynthia, and Arjester Reed, owners of Branches Medical Inc. of Lauderhill, Florida, exemplify the benefits of strong family ties in a business.

The health and survival of a family business require a proper balancing of business and family interests. Otherwise, results will be unsatisfactory to both.

Advantages of Family Involvement in the Business

Problems associated with family businesses can easily blind young people to the advantages that can be derived from participation of family members in the business. The many positive values associated with family involvement should be recognized and used in the family firm.

A primary benefit comes from the strength of family relationships. Members of the family are drawn to the

---

Action Report

ENTREPRENEURIAL EXPERIENCES

Business Benefits from Family Relationships

One benefit a business can derive from family relationships is the willingness of family members to sacrifice during times of crisis. Computerware, Inc., a computer retailer run by four brothers, their parents, and one outsider, drew on that kind of strength during down cycles:

> *Budget tightening, says president and eldest brother John Kovalcik, Jr., was easier to impose on family members. First went perks like afternoons of golf. Next were the company credit cards, so that managers had to fill out T&E forms for reimbursement of expenses. Salaries were frozen for everyone in the company, and the seven owners took 10 percent pay cuts.*
>
> *"It was just done, and it was accepted," says Kovalcik. "Our family said, 'OK, we'll pitch in.' And this was a good amount of our income; what we earn right now isn't even within industry standards."*

Source: Leslie Brokaw, "Why Family Businesses Are Best," *Inc.*, Vol. 14, No. 3 (March 1992), p. 74. Reprinted with permission, *Inc.* magazine, March 1992. Copyright 1992 by Goldhirsh Group, Inc., 38 Commercial Wharf, Boston, MA 02110.

---

business because of family ties, and they tend to stick with the business through thick and thin. A downturn in business fortunes might cause nonfamily managers to seek greener pastures elsewhere. A son or daughter, however, is reluctant to leave. The family name, the family welfare, and, possibly, the family fortune are at stake. In addition, a person's reputation as a family member may hinge on whether he or she can continue the business that Mom or Grandfather built.

Family members may also sacrifice income to keep a business going. Rather than draw large salaries or high dividends, they permit such resources to remain in the business for current needs. Many families have gone without a new car or new furniture long enough to let the new business get started or to get through a period of financial stress.

Some family businesses use the family theme in advertising to distinguish themselves from their competitors. Such advertising campaigns attempt to convey the fact that family-owned firms have a strong commitment to the business, high ethical standards, and a personal commitment to serving their customers and the local community.

Other features of the family firm can also contribute to superior business performance. Peter Davis, director of the Wharton Applied Research Center at the Wharton School in Philadelphia, provides as examples the three following features:[2]

1. *Preserving the humanity of the workplace.* A family business can easily demonstrate higher levels of concern and caring for individuals than are found in the typical corporation.
2. *Focusing on the long run.* A family business can take the long-run view more easily than can corporate managers who are being judged on year-to-year results.
3. *Emphasizing quality.* Family businesses have long maintained a tradition of providing quality and value to the consumer.

2 Explain the cultural context of the family business.

organizational culture
patterns of behaviors and beliefs that characterize a particular firm

THE CULTURE OF A FAMILY BUSINESS

Family firms, like other business organizations, develop certain ways of doing things and certain priorities that are unique to each particular firm. These special patterns of behaviors and beliefs are often described as **organizational culture.** As new employees and family members enter the business, they tend to pick up these special viewpoints and ways of operating.

The Founder's Imprint on the Culture

The distinctive values that motivate and guide an entrepreneur in the founding of a firm may help to create a competitive advantage for the new firm. For example, the founder may cater to customer needs in a special way and make customer service a guiding principle for the firm. The new firm may go far beyond normal industry practices in making sure customers are satisfied, even if it means working overtime or making a delivery on Saturday. Those who work in the business quickly learn that customers must always be handled with very special care.

In a family business, the founder's core values may become part of both the business culture and the family code—"the things we believe as a family." John Robben, the second-generation CEO of RobToy, Inc., describes the legacy of his father, who founded the firm:

> *But he left us much more than his confidence, and his willingness to take a chance. My father never lied; nor did he ever cheat anyone or take a dollar he didn't honestly earn. He passed these values on, first to me and then, through me, to his grandchildren. It's funny how that worked. He never talked about these things, he just did them.*[3]

The last sentence above tells us something about the way cultural values are transmitted. Family members and others in the firm learn what's important and absorb the traditions of the firm simply by functioning as part of the organization.

Cultural Patterns in the Firm

The culture of a particular firm includes numerous distinctive beliefs and behaviors. By examining those beliefs and behaviors closely, we can discern various cultural patterns that help us understand the way in which the firm functions.

cultural configuration
the total culture of a family firm, made up of the firm's business, family, and governance patterns

W. Gibb Dyer, Jr., a professor at Brigham Young University, has identified a set of cultural patterns that apply to three facets of family firms: the actual business, the family, and the governance (board of directors) of the business.[4] As illustrated in Figure 5-2, the business pattern, the family pattern, and the governance pattern combine to form an overall **cultural configuration** that constitutes a family firm's total culture.

An example of a business pattern is a firm's system of beliefs and behaviors concerning the importance of quality. Members of an organization tend to adopt a common viewpoint concerning the extent to which effort, or even sacrifice, should be devoted to product and service quality. When leaders of a firm consistently demonstrate a commitment to quality, they encourage others to appreciate the same values. By decisions and practices that place a high priority on quality, therefore, leaders in a family business can build a business pattern that exhibits a strong commitment to producing high-quality goods and services.

In the early stages of a family business, according to Dyer, a common cultural configuration includes a paternalistic business culture, a patriarchal family culture,

QUALITY

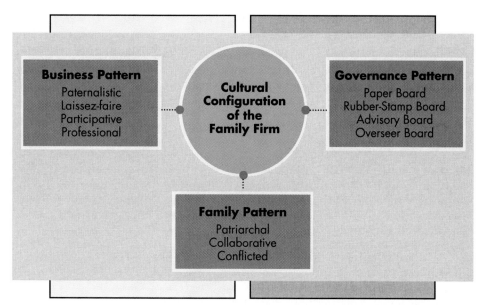

Figure 5-2

Cultural Configuration of a Family Firm

Source: W. Gibb Dyer, Jr., *Cultural Change in Family Firms* (San Francisco: Jossey-Bass, 1986), p. 22. Reprinted with permission.

and a rubber-stamp board of directors. This simply means that family relationships are more important than professional skills, that the founder is the undisputed head of the clan, and that the board automatically supports the founder's decisions.

Cultural Patterns and Leadership Succession

The process of passing the leadership from one generation to another is complicated by, and interwoven with, changes in the family business culture. To appreciate this point, think about the paternalistic-patriarchal configuration mentioned above—which is quite common in the early days of a family business. Changing conditions may render that cultural configuration ineffective. As a family business grows, it requires a greater measure of professional expertise. Thus, the firm may be pressured to break from the paternalistic mold that gives first priority to family authority and less attention to professional abilities. Likewise, the aging of the founder and the maturation of the founder's children tend to weaken the patriarchal family culture with its one dominant source of authority—a parent who "always knows best."

Succession may occur, therefore, against the backdrop of a changing organizational culture. In fact, leadership change itself may play a role in introducing or bringing about changes in the culture and making a break with traditional methods of operation. To some extent, the successor may act as a change agent. For example, a son or daughter with a business degree may eliminate the dated managerial practices of an earlier generation and substitute a more professional approach.

Growth of the business and changes in leadership over time will thus make some cultural change necessary. However, certain values are timeless and should never be changed—the commitment to honesty, for example. While some traditions may embody inefficient business practices and require change, others may be basic to the competitive strength and integrity of the firm.

3 Outline the complex roles and relationships involved in a family business.

FAMILY ROLES AND RELATIONSHIPS

As we noted earlier, a family business represents the overlapping of two institutions—a family and a business. This fact makes the family firm incredibly difficult to manage. This section examines a few of the many possible family roles and relationships that contribute to this managerial complexity.

Mom or Dad, the Founder

A common figure in family businesses is the man or woman who founded the firm and plans to pass it on to a son or a daughter. In most cases, the business and the family grow simultaneously. Some founders achieve a delicate balance between their business and family responsibilities. Others must exert great diligence to squeeze out time for weekends and vacations with the children.

Entrepreneurs who have children typically think in terms of passing the business on to the next generation. Parental concerns involved in this process include the following:

- Does my son or daughter possess the temperament and ability necessary for business leadership?
- How can I, the founder, motivate my son or daughter to take an interest in the business?
- What type of education and experience will be most helpful in preparing my son or daughter for leadership?
- What timetable should I follow in employing and promoting my son or daughter?
- How can I avoid favoritism in managing and developing my son or daughter?
- How can I prevent the business relationship from damaging or destroying the parent-child relationship?

Of all the relationships in a family business, the parent-child relationship has been the most troublesome. The problem has been recognized informally for generations. In more recent years, counseling has developed, seminars have been created, and books have been written about such relationships. In spite of this extensive attention, however, the parent-child relationship continues to perplex numerous families involved in family businesses.

Couples in Business

Some family businesses are owned and managed by husband-wife teams. Their roles may vary depending on their backgrounds and expertise. In some cases, the husband serves as general manager and the wife runs the office. In other cases, the wife functions as operations manager and the husband keeps the books. Whatever the arrangement, both parties are an integral part of the business.

A potential advantage of the husband-wife team is the opportunity it affords a couple to share more of their lives. For some couples, however, the potential benefits become eclipsed by problems related to the business. Differences of opinion about business matters may carry over into family life. And the energies of both parties may be so dissipated by their work in a struggling company that little zest remains for a strong family life.

Adele Bihn and Murray P. Heinrich of San Jose, California have experienced both the joys and strains of working together as business partners.[5] After 12 years

Action Report

ETHICAL ISSUES

Business Versus Family: A Clash of Values

While some couples grow strong by working together, others break up because of the strain involved in running a business. Mary and Phil Baechler experienced the latter. They started a business in Yakima, Washington in 1984 to produce a jogger's stroller that Phil had invented so that he could continue to jog following the birth of their son Travis.

The family grew with the birth of two more children, and the business prospered. Both Mary and Phil worked so hard in the business that they found it difficult to take time for themselves and their marriage. They also differed in the priority they assigned to the business. Mary felt that she had a bigger dose of ambition for the business than Phil did and believed that Phil viewed it more as a means to an end. As Mary expressed it, "I was always making choices that he couldn't understand, and I couldn't figure out why he wouldn't go that extra mile." In spite of their mutual affection and respect, the business was pulling them apart.

Rather poignantly, Mary described her feelings the day before the court dissolved the marriage:

In the morning, I'll be divorced. Every time I imagine standing up in the courtroom, answering the judge, I blubber shamelessly. And I know that if Phil goes there with me, we'll both be crying, and the judge will wonder why the heck we are doing this. Then, in my imagination, Phil will hold me while I cry on his shoulder. Pals to the end.

Source: Mary Baechler, "Death of a Marriage," *Inc.*, Vol. 16, No. 4 (April 1994), pp. 74–78. Reprinted with permission, *Inc.* magazine, April 1994. Copyright 1994 by Goldhirsch Group, Inc., 38 Commercial Wharf, Boston, MA 02110.

of marriage and collaboration in their business, Data Marketing, Inc., they are described as "still blissfully happy." Adele, mother of their four children, owns 50 percent of the company and serves as president. Murray owns the other 50 percent and heads up product research. To maintain their happiness, they must deal with strains imposed by the business. They have worked together to resolve these pressures by using a variety of methods, including semiannual visits with a marriage counselor, annual away-from-work business strategy sessions, Saturday morning breakfast dates without the children, and annual separate vacations. Their experience shows that entrepreneurial couples can maintain good marriages, but it also shows that such couples must devote special effort to both business and family concerns.

Sons and Daughters

Should sons and daughters be groomed for the family business, or should they pursue careers of their own choosing? In the entrepreneurial family, a natural tendency is to think in terms of a family business career and to push a child, either openly or subtly, in that direction (see Figure 5-3). Little thought, indeed, may be given to the basic issues involved, which include the child's talent, aptitude, and temperament. The child may be a chip off the old block but may also be an individual with different bents and aspirations. He or she may prefer music or medi-

Figure 5-3 *Following the Founder's Footsteps*

Source: WINTHROP reprinted by permission of NEA, Inc.

cine to the world of business and may fit the business mold very poorly. It is also possible that the abilities of the son or daughter may simply be insufficient for a leadership role. (Of course, a child's talents may be underestimated by parents simply because there has been little opportunity for development.)

Another issue is personal freedom. We live in a society that values the right of the individual to choose his or her own career and way of life. If this value is embraced by a son or daughter, that child must be granted the freedom to select a career of his or her own choosing.

A son or daughter may feel a need to go outside the family business, for a time at least, to prove that "I can make it on my own." To build self-esteem, he or she may wish to operate independently of the family. Entering the family business immediately after graduation may seem stifling—"continuing to feel like a little kid with Dad telling me what to do."

If the family business is profitable, it does provide opportunities. A son or daughter may be well advised to give serious consideration to accepting such a challenge. If the business relationship is to be satisfactory, however, family pressure must be minimized. Both parties must recognize the choice as a business decision as well as a family decision—and as a decision that may conceivably be reversed.

Sibling Cooperation, Sibling Rivalry

In families with a number of children, two or more may become involved in the family firm. This depends, of course, on the interests of the individual children. In some cases, parents feel fortunate if even one child elects to stay with the family firm. Nevertheless, it is not unusual for several siblings to take positions in a family business. Even those who do not work in the business may be more than casual observers on the sidelines because of their stake as heirs or partial owners.

At best, siblings work as a smoothly functioning team, each contributing services according to his or her respective abilities. Just as some families experience excellent cooperation and unity in their family relationships, so family businesses can benefit from effective collaboration among brothers and sisters.

However, just as there are sometimes squabbles within a family, there can also be sibling rivalry within a family business. Business issues tend to generate competition, and this affects family, as well as nonfamily, members. Two siblings, for example, may disagree about business policy or about their respective roles in the business. Sibling rivalry has been identified as a problem in the operation of Johnson Products Company, a Chicago hair-products manufacturer and one of the largest black-owned companies in the United States.[6] Joan M. Johnson clashed with her older brother, Eric G. Johnson, who served as president, over her role in the business. The conflict led to Eric's resignation in 1992 and the subsequent elevation of Joan to a newly created office of the president. (Their father and company founder, George E. Johnson, had resigned as chairperson and given up his stake in the company as part of a divorce settlement in 1989. Their mother, Joan B. Johnson, owns 61 percent of the company and serves as chairperson.)

In-Laws In and Out of the Business

As sons and daughters marry, the daughters-in-law and sons-in-law become significant actors in the family business drama. Some in-laws become directly involved in the drama by accepting positions in the family firm. If a son or daughter is also employed in the firm, rivalry and conflict may develop. How do the rewards for performance and progress of an in-law compare with the rewards for performance and progress of a son or daughter?

For a time, effective collaboration may be achieved by assigning family members to different branches or roles within the company. Eventually, competition for top leadership will force decisions that distinguish among children and in-laws employed in the business. Being fair and retaining family loyalty become more difficult as the number of family employees increases.

Sons, daughters, sons-in-law, and daughters-in-law who are on the sidelines are also participants with an important stake in the business. For example, they are often married to someone on the family payroll. Whatever the relationship, the view from the sideline has both a family and a business dimension. A decision by a parent affecting a family member is seen from the sideline as a family *and* a business decision. Giving the nod to a daughter or a son-in-law, for example, is more than merely promoting another employee in a business.

The Entrepreneur's Spouse

One of the most critical roles in the family business drama is that of the entrepreneur's spouse. Traditionally, this has been the entrepreneur's wife and the mother of his children. However, more women are becoming entrepreneurs, and many husbands have now assumed the role of entrepreneur's spouse.

A spouse plays a supporting role to the entrepreneur's career; as parent, she or he helps prepare their children for possible careers in the family business. This creates a need for communication between spouse and entrepreneur and a need for the spouse to be a good listener. The spouse needs to hear what's going on in the business; otherwise, she or he feels detached and must compete for attention. The spouse can offer understanding and act as a sounding board only if there is communication on matters of obvious importance to them both individually and as a family.

It is easy for the spouse to function as worrier for the family business. This is particularly true if there is insufficient communication about business matters. One spouse said:

> *I've told my husband that I have an active imagination—very active. If he doesn't tell me what's going on in the business, well, then I'm going to imagine what's going on and blow it all out of proportion. When things are looking dark, I'd rather know the worst than know nothing.*[7]

The spouse may also serve as mediator in business relationships between the entrepreneur and the children. One wife's comments to her husband, John, and son Terry illustrate the nature of this function:

- "John, don't you think that Terry may have worked long enough as a stockperson in the warehouse?"
- "Terry, your father is going to be very disappointed if you don't come back to the business after your graduation."
- "John, do you really think it is fair to move Stanley into that new office? After all, Terry is older and has been working a year longer."
- "Terry, what did you say to your father today that upset him?"

Ideally, the entrepreneur and spouse form a team committed to the success of both the family and the family business. They share in the processes that affect the fortunes of each. Such teamwork does not occur automatically; it requires a collaborative effort by both parties to the marriage.

SPECIAL FEATURES OF FAMILY FIRM MANAGEMENT

4   Identify management practices that enable a family business to function effectively.

The complexity of relationships in family firms creates a demand for enlightened management. To a considerable extent, this just means good professional management. However, certain special techniques are useful in dealing effectively with the complications inherent in the family firm.

The Need for Good Management

Good management is necessary for the success of any business, and the family firm is no exception. Significant deviations for family reasons from what we might call

After Sam Ash died without a will, wife Rose divided control of Sam Ash Music Corporation among six heirs. There's a lot of talent in the business, but lack of a single chief makes the firm slow to adapt.

good management practices, therefore, only serve to weaken the firm. Such a course of action runs counter to the interests of both the firm and the family. For the benefit of both, we suggest three management concepts that are particularly relevant to the family firm:

1. *A family firm must be able to rely on the competence of its professional and managerial personnel.* It cannot afford to accept and support family members who are incompetent or who lack the potential for development.
2. *Favoritism in personnel decisions must be avoided.* If possible, the evaluation of family members should involve the judgment of nonfamily members—those in supervisory positions, outside members of the board of directors, or managers of other companies in which family members have worked.
3. *Plans for succession, steps in professional development, and intentions regarding changes in ownership should be developed and discussed openly.* Founders who recognize the need for managing the process of succession can work out plans carefully rather than drift toward it haphazardly. Lack of knowledge regarding the plans and intentions of key participants creates uncertainty and possible suspicion. The planning process can begin as the founder or the presiding family member shares his or her dream for the firm and family participation in it.

The family firm is a business—a competitive business. The observance of these and other fundamental precepts of management will help the business thrive and permit the family to function as a family. Disregard of such considerations will pose a threat to the business and impose strains on family relationships.

Nonfamily Employees in a Family Firm

Even those employees who are not family members are affected by family considerations. In some cases, their opportunities for promotion are lessened by the presence of family members who seem to have the inside track. What parent is going to promote an outsider over a competent daughter or son who is being groomed for future leadership? The potential for advancement of nonfamily members, therefore, may be limited, and they may experience a sense of unfairness and frustration.

One young business executive, for example, worked for a family business that operated a chain of restaurants. When hired, he had negotiated a contract that gave him a specified percentage of the business based on performance. Under this arrangement, he was doing extremely well financially—that is, until the owner called on him to say, "I am here to buy you out." When the young man asked why, the owner replied, "Son, you are doing too well, and your last name is not the same as mine!"

The extent of limitations on nonfamily employees will depend on the number of family members active in the business and the number of managerial or professional positions in the business to which nonfamily employees might aspire. It will also depend on the extent to which the owner demands competence in management and maintains an atmosphere of fairness in supervision. To avoid future problems, the owner should make clear, when hiring nonfamily employees, the extent of opportunities available and identify the positions, if any, that are reserved for family members.

Those outside the family may also be caught in the crossfire between family members who are competing with each other. Family feuds make it difficult for outsiders to maintain strict neutrality. If a nonfamily employee is perceived as siding with one of those involved in the feud, he or she will lose the support of other family members. Hard-working employees often feel that they deserve hazard pay for working in a firm plagued by an unusual amount of family conflict.

Family Retreats

family retreat
a gathering of family members, usually at a remote location, to discuss family business matters

Some families hold retreats in order to review family business concerns. A **family retreat** is a gathering of family members, usually at a remote location, to discuss family business matters. An attempt is made to create an informal atmosphere. Nancy Upton, founder of the Institute for Family Business at Baylor University, has conducted many family retreats. She has described the general purpose and format of such retreats as follows:

> *The purpose of the retreat is to provide a forum for introspection, problem solving and policy making. For some participants this will be their first opportunity to talk about their concerns in a nonconfrontational atmosphere. It is also a time to celebrate the family and enhance its inner strength.*
>
> *A retreat usually lasts two days and is held far enough away so you won't be disturbed or tempted to go to the office. Every member of the family, including in-laws, should be invited.*[8]

The prospect of sitting down together to discuss family business matters sometimes seems threatening. As a result, some families avoid extensive communication, fearing that it will stir up trouble. They assume that decision making that occurs quietly or secretly will preserve harmony. Unfortunately, such an approach often conceals serious differences that become increasingly troublesome. Family retreats are designed to open lines of communication and to bring about understanding and agreement on family business issues.

Initiating such discussions is difficult, so family leaders often invite an outside expert or facilitator to lead early sessions. The facilitator can help develop an agenda and establish ground rules for discussion. By moderating early sessions, the facilitator can help to develop a positive tone that emphasizes family achievements and encourages rational consideration of sensitive issues. Families that hold such meetings often speak of the joy of sharing family values and stories of past family experiences. In this way, the meetings can strengthen the family as well as the business.

Family Councils

family council
an organized group of family members who gather periodically to discuss family-related business issues

A family retreat could pave the way for creation of a family council. A **family council** functions as the organizational and strategic planning arm of a family; in it, family members meet to discuss values, policies, and direction for the future. The council provides a forum for the ongoing process of listening to the ideas of all members and discovering what they believe in and want from the business. A family council formalizes the participation of the family in the business to a greater extent than does the family retreat. It can also be the focal point for the future planning of the individuals, the family, the business, and how each relates to the other.

A council should be recognized as a formal organization that holds regular meetings, keeps minutes, and makes suggestions to the firm's board of directors. Experts recommend that it should be open to all interested family members and spouses of all generations. The first several meetings are often used to generate an acceptable mission statement as well as a family creed.

Family businesses that have these councils find them useful for developing family harmony. Meetings are often fun and informative and may include speakers who discuss items of interest. Time is often set aside for sharing achievements, milestones, and family history. The younger generation is encouraged to participate because much of the process is designed to increase their understanding of family traditions and business interests and to prepare some of them for working effectively in the business.

As with family retreats, an outside facilitator may be useful in getting a council organized and helping in initial meetings. Subsequently, the organization and leadership of meetings can rotate among family members.

THE PROCESS OF LEADERSHIP SUCCESSION

5 Describe the process of managerial succession in a family firm.

The task of preparing family members for careers and, ultimately, leadership within the business is difficult and sometimes frustrating. Professional and managerial requirements tend to become intertwined with family feelings and interests. This section looks at the development and transfer process and some of the difficulties associated with it.

Available Family Talent

A stream can rise no higher than its source, and the family firm can be no more brilliant than its leader. The business is dependent, therefore, on the quality of leadership talent provided by the family. If the available talent is deficient, the owner must bring in outside leadership or supplement family talent to avoid a decline under the leadership of second- or third-generation family members.

The question of competency is both a critical issue and a delicate issue. With experience, individuals can improve their abilities; younger people should not be judged too harshly too early. Furthermore, potential successors may be held back by the reluctance of a parent-owner to delegate realistically to them.

Perhaps the most appropriate philosophy is to recognize the right of family members to prove themselves. A period of testing may occur either in the family business or, preferably, in another organization. As children show themselves to be capable, they earn the right to increased leadership responsibility. If potential successors are found, through a process of fair assessment, to have inadequate leadership abilities, preservation of the family business and the welfare of family members demand that they be passed over for promotion. The appointment of competent outsiders to these jobs, if necessary, increases the value of the firm for all family members who have an ownership interest in it.

Stages in the Process of Succession

Sons or daughters do not typically assume leadership of a family firm at a particular moment in time. Instead, a long, drawn-out process of preparation and transition is customary—a process that extends over years and often decades. Figure 5-4 portrays this process as a series of **stages in succession.**[9]

stages in succession phases in the process of transferring leadership from parent to child in a family business

PRE-BUSINESS STAGE   In Stage I, a potential successor becomes acquainted with the business as a part of growing up. The young child accompanies a parent to the office, store, or warehouse or plays with equipment related to the business. There

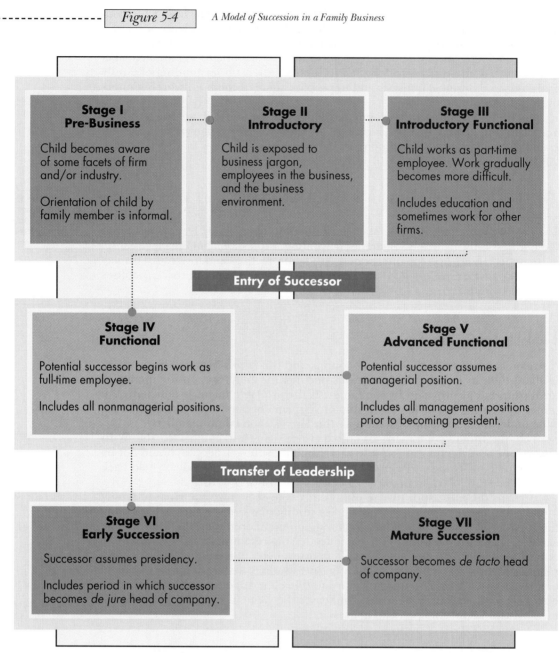

Figure 5-4   *A Model of Succession in a Family Business*

Stage I
Pre-Business

Child becomes aware of some facets of firm and/or industry.

Orientation of child by family member is informal.

Stage II
Introductory

Child is exposed to business jargon, employees in the business, and the business environment.

Stage III
Introductory Functional

Child works as part-time employee. Work gradually becomes more difficult.

Includes education and sometimes work for other firms.

Entry of Successor

Stage IV
Functional

Potential successor begins work as full-time employee.

Includes all nonmanagerial positions.

Stage V
Advanced Functional

Potential successor assumes managerial position.

Includes all management positions prior to becoming president.

Transfer of Leadership

Stage VI
Early Succession

Successor assumes presidency.

Includes period in which successor becomes *de jure* head of company.

Stage VII
Mature Succession

Successor becomes *de facto* head of company.

Source: Adapted from Justin G. Longenecker and John E. Schoen, "Management Succession in the Family Business," *Journal of Small Business Management*, Vol. 16 (July 1978), pp. 1–6.

is no formal planning for the child's preparation for entering the business in this early period. This first stage forms a foundation for the more deliberate stages of the process that occur in later years.

INTRODUCTORY STAGE   Stage II also includes experiences that occur before the successor is old enough to begin part-time work in the family business. It differs from Stage I in that family members deliberately introduce the child to certain people associated directly or indirectly with the firm and to other aspects of the business. In an industrial equipment dealership, for example, a parent might explain the difference between a front loader and a backhoe or introduce the child to the firm's banker.

INTRODUCTORY FUNCTIONAL STAGE   In Stage III, the son or daughter begins to function as a part-time employee, often during vacation or after school. At this stage, the son or daughter develops an acquaintance with some of the key individuals employed in the firm. Often, such work begins in the warehouse, office, or production department and may involve assignments in various functional areas as time goes on. The introductory functional stage includes the child's formal education as well as experience gained in other organizations.

FUNCTIONAL STAGE   Stage IV begins when the potential successor enters full-time employment, typically following the completion of his or her formal education. Prior to moving into a management position, the son or daughter may work as an accountant, a salesperson, or an inventory clerk, possibly gaining experience in a number of such positions.

ADVANCED FUNCTIONAL STAGE   As the potential successor assumes supervisory duties, he or she enters the advanced functional stage, or Stage V. The management positions at this stage involve directing the work of others but not managing the entire firm.

EARLY SUCCESSION STAGE   In Stage VI, the son or daughter is named president or general manager of the business. As *de jure* head of the business, he or she presumably exercises overall direction, but a parent is still in the background. The leadership role does not transfer as easily or absolutely as the leadership title does. The successor has not necessarily mastered the complexities of the role, and the predecessor may be reluctant to give up all decision making.

MATURE SUCCESSION STAGE   Stage VII is reached when the transition process is complete. The successor is leader in fact as well as in name. In some cases, this does not occur until the predecessor dies. Perhaps optimistically, we will assume that Stage VII begins two years after the successor assumes the leadership title.

Reluctant Parents and Ambitious Children

Let's assume the business founder is a father who is preparing his son or daughter to take over the family firm. The founder's attachment to the business must not be underestimated. Not only is he tied to the firm financially—it is probably his primary, if not his only, major investment—but he is also tied to it emotionally. The business is his "baby," and he is understandably reluctant to entrust its future to one who is immature and unproven. (Unfortunately, parents often have a way of seeing their children as immature long after their years of adolescence.)

The child may be ambitious, possibly well educated, and insightful regarding the business. His or her tendency to push ahead—to try something new—often conflicts with the father's caution. As a result, the child may see the father as excessively conservative, stubborn, and unwilling to change.

A recent study examined 18 family-owned businesses in which daughters worked as managers with their fathers. Interviews with family members produced this picture of the daughters' positions:

> *In 90 percent of the cases, the daughters reported having to contend with carryover, conflict, and ambiguity in their business roles in the firm and as daughters. While the major-*

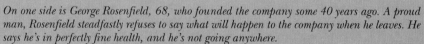

Action Report

ENTREPRENEURIAL EXPERIENCES

Reluctant Father and Ambitious Daughter

Children often feel they are ready to take control before their parents are ready to acknowledge it. This is true of Tasco Corporation, a Miami-based distributor of optical products such as telescopes and rifle scopes. The intensity of the father's and daughter's feelings is evident in this account:

> On one side is George Rosenfield, 68, who founded the company some 40 years ago. A proud man, Rosenfield steadfastly refuses to say what will happen to the company when he leaves. He says he's in perfectly fine health, and he's not going anywhere.
>
> In the other corner is Rosenfield's daughter, Sheryl Rosenfield. Headstrong, 39 years old and eager to take charge of the company, Sheryl has worked at Tasco for her entire 17-year business career and currently carries the title of executive vice president. At the very least, she would like to become a partner with her dad. She figures she's entitled.
>
> Dad disagrees. "I'm still in charge, and she doesn't seem to understand it," says he. "You can't run a business where two people are in charge." Retorts Sheryl: "Dad's ideal daughter is one who would be there for him but one who wouldn't want the throne. That's not me."

Source: Dyan Machan, "'It Would Be Stupid to Quit Now,'" *Forbes*, Vol. 145, No. 7 (April 2, 1990), pp. 178–180.

ity of the women interviewed had previously worked in other organizations, and had developed their identities as businesswomen, they discovered that when they joined the family business they were torn between their roles as daughter and their business roles. They found their relationships with the boss transformed, since the boss was not only the boss, but the father as well. These daughters reported that they often found themselves reduced to the role of "daddy's little girl" (and, in a few cases, "mommy's little girl"), in spite of their best intentions.[10]

At the root of many such difficulties is a lack of a clear understanding between parent and child. They work together without a map showing where they are going. Children in the business, and also their spouses, may have expectations about progress that, in terms of the founder's thinking, are totally unrealistic. The successor tends to sense such problems much more acutely than does his or her parent. But much of the problem could be avoided if a full discussion about the development process took place.

transfer of ownership
the final step in conveyance of power from parent to child, that of distributing ownership of the family business

Analyze the major issues involved in the transfer of ownership to a succeeding generation.

6

TRANSFER OF OWNERSHIP

A final and often complex step in the succession process in the family firm is the **transfer of ownership.** Questions of inheritance affect not only the leadership successor but also other family members having no involvement in the business. In distributing their estate, parents-owners typically wish to treat all their children fairly, both those involved in the business and those on the outside.

One of the most difficult decisions is determining the future ownership of the business. If there are several children, for example, should they all receive equal shares? On the surface, this seems to be the fairest approach. However, such an arrangement may play havoc with the future functioning of the business. Suppose that each of five children receives a 20 percent ownership share even though only one of them is active in the business. The child active in the business—the leadership successor—becomes a minority stockholder completely at the mercy of relatives on the outside.

Ideally, the founder has been able to arrange his or her personal holdings to create wealth outside the business as well as within it. In this way, he or she may bequeath comparable shares to all heirs while allowing business control to remain with the child or children active in the business.

Tax considerations are relevant, of course, and they tend to favor gradual transfer of ownership to all heirs. As noted above, however, transfer of equal ownership shares to all heirs may be inconsistent with future efficient operation of the business. Tax laws should not be allowed to blind one to possible adverse effects on management.

One creative ownership transfer plan was worked out by a warehouse distributor in the tire industry.[11] The distributor's son and probable successor was active in the business. The distributor's daughter was married to a college professor at a small southern university. Believing the business to be their most valuable asset, the owner and his wife were concerned that both the daughter and the son receive a fair share. Initially, the parents decided to give the business real estate to their daughter and the business itself to their son, who would then pay rent to his sister. After discussing the matter with both children, however, they developed a better plan whereby both the business property and the business would go to the son.

1 Discuss the factors that make the family business unique.

- Family members have a special involvement in a family business.
- Business interests (production and profitability) overlap family interests (care and nurturing) in a family business.
- The advantages of a family business include a strong commitment of family members and focus on people, quality, and long-term goals.

2 Explain the cultural context of the family business.

- Special patterns of belief and behavior constitute the family business culture.
- The founder often leaves a deep imprint on the culture of a family firm.
- The cultural configuration includes business patterns, family patterns, and governance (or board-of-directors) patterns.
- Changes in culture often occur as leadership passes from one generation to the next.

3 Outline the complex roles and relationships involved in a family business.

- A primary relationship is that between founder and son or daughter.
- Some couples in business together find their relationship with each other strengthened, while others find it weakened.
- Sons, daughters, in-laws, and other relatives may experience collaboration or conflict with other relatives.
- The role of the founder's spouse is especially important, as he or she often serves as a mediator in family disputes.

4 Identify management practices that enable a family business to function effectively.

- Good management practices are very important in a family business.
- Family members should be treated fairly and consistently in accordance with their ability and performance.
- Motivation of nonfamily employees can be enhanced by open communication and fairness.
- Family retreats bring all family members together to discuss business and family matters.
- Family councils provide a formal framework for the family's ongoing discussion of family and business issues.

5 Describe the process of managerial succession in a family firm.

- Succession is a long-term process starting early in the successor's life.
- The seven stages in the succession process include such periods as pre-business, part-time work, and full-time managerial work.
- Tension often exists between the founder and the potential successor as the latter gains experience.

6 Analyze the major issues involved in the transfer of ownership to a succeeding generation.

- Transfer of ownership involves issues of fairness, taxes, and managerial control.
- Planning and discussion of transfer plans are sometimes difficult but usually desirable.

New Terms and Concepts

family business *92*	family retreat *104*	transfer of
organizational culture *96*	family council *104*	ownership *108*
cultural configuration *96*	stages in succession *105*	

You Make the Call

Situation 1

The three Dorsett brothers are barely speaking to each other. "Phone for you" is about all they have to say.

It hasn't always been like this. For more than 30 years, Tom, Harry, and Bob Dorsett have run the successful manufacturing business founded by their father. For most of that time, they have gotten along rather well. They've had their differences and arguments, but important decisions were thrashed out until a consensus was reached.

Each brother has two children in the business. Tom's oldest son manages the plant, Harry's oldest daughter keeps the books, and Bob's oldest son is a rising outside salesman. The younger children are learning the ropes in lower-level positions.

The problem? Compensation. Each brother feels that his own children are underpaid and that some of his nieces and nephews are overpaid. After violent arguments, the Dorsett brothers just quit talking while each continued to smolder.

The six younger-generation cousins are still on speaking terms, however. Despite the differences that exist among them, they manage to get along with one another. They range in age from 41 down to 25.

The business is in a slump but not yet in danger. Because the brothers aren't talking, important business decisions are being postponed.

The family is stuck. What can be done?

Source: "Anger Over Money Silences Brothers," *Nation's Business*, Vol. 78, No. 10 (October 1990), p. 62. Reprinted by permission, *Nation's Business*, October 1990. Copyright 1990, U.S. Chamber of Commerce.

Question 1 Why do you think the cousins get along better than their fathers?

Question 2 How might this conflict over compensation be resolved?

Situation 2
Harrison Stevens, second-generation president of a family-owned heating and air conditioning business, was concerned about his 19-year-old son, Barry, who worked as a full-time employee in the firm. Although Barry had made it through high school, he had not distinguished himself as a student or shown interest in further education. He was somewhat indifferent in his attitude toward his work, although he did reasonably, or at least minimally, satisfactory work. His father saw Barry as immature and more interested in riding motorcycles than in building a business.

Stevens wanted to provide his son with an opportunity for personal development. This could begin, as he saw it, by learning to work hard. If he

Continue on next page

The daughter would receive all non-business assets plus an instrument of debt from her brother, intended to balance the monetary values. This plan was not only fair but also workable in terms of the operation and management of the firm.

Planning and discussing the transfer of ownership is not easy, but such action is recommended. Over a period of time, the owner must reflect seriously on family talents and interests as they relate to the future of the firm. The plan for transfer of ownership can then be firmed up and modified as necessary when it is discussed with the children or other potential heirs.

DISCUSSION QUESTIONS

1. A computer software company began operation with a three-member management team whose skills were focused in the areas of engineering, finance, and general business. Is this a family business? What might cause it to be classified as a family business or to become a family business?

2. Suppose that you, as founder of a business, have a vacant sales manager position. You realize that sales may suffer somewhat if you promote your son from sales representative to sales manager. However, you would like to see your son make some progress and earn a higher salary to support his wife and young daughter. How would you go about making this decision? Would you promote your son?

3. What benefits result from family involvement in a business?

4. Why does a first-generation family business tend to have a paternalistic business pattern and a patriarchal family pattern?

5. As a recent graduate in business administration, you are headed back to the family business. As a

result of your education, you have become aware of some outdated business practices in the family firm. In spite of them, the business is showing a good return on investment. Should you rock the boat? How should you proceed in correcting what you see as obsolete traditions?

6. Describe a founder-son or founder-daughter relationship in a family business with which you are familiar. What strengths or weaknesses do you see in that relationship?

7. Should a son or daughter feel an obligation to carry on a family business? What is the source of such a feeling?

8. Assume that you are an ambitious, nonfamily manager in a family firm and that one of your peers is the son or daughter of the founder. What, if anything, would keep you interested in pursuing your career with this company?

9. Identify and describe the stages outlined in the model of succession shown in Figure 5-4.

10. Should estate tax laws or other factors be given greater weight than family concerns in decisions about transferring ownership of a family business from one generation to another? Why?

liked the work and showed promise, Barry might eventually be groomed to take over the business. His father also held a faint hope that hard work might eventually inspire him to get a college education.

In trying to achieve these goals, Stevens sensed two problems. First, Barry obviously lacked proper motivation. The second problem related to his supervision. Supervisors seemed reluctant to be exacting in their demands on Barry. Possibly because they feared antagonizing the boss by being too hard on his son, they allowed Barry to get by with marginal performance.

Question 1 In view of Barry's shortcomings, should Harrison Stevens seriously consider him as a potential successor?

Question 2 How can Barry be motivated? Can Harrison Stevens do anything more to improve the situation, or does the responsibility lie with Barry?

Question 3 How can the quality of Barry's supervision be improved so that his work experience will be more productive?

Situation 3 Two brothers share management responsibilities in a company that produces neckties. Petty bickering between them following the death of their father has taken their focus off the quality of the product being produced for customers. Although neckties are becoming bolder fashion statements, this firm continues to turn out dull and uninspired patterns, primarily because of the brothers' involvement in the family squabble and their consequent neglect of the business. Two major customers have reduced their orders for neckties. It is evident that the market for this firm's products is cooling. The product-quality problem has emerged as a serious issue.

Question 1 Is this firm's quality problem caused by family conflict or by some other underlying factor?

Question 2 If you were one of the brothers, what steps would you take to solve the problem?

EXPERIENTIAL EXERCISES

1. Interview a college student who has grown up in a family business about the way he or she may have been trained or educated, both formally and informally, for entry into the business. Prepare a brief report, relating your findings to the stages in succession shown in Figure 5-4.

2. Interview another college student who has grown up in a family business about parental attitudes toward his or her possible entry into the business. Submit a one-page report describing the extent of pressure on the student to enter the family business and the direct or indirect ways in which expectations have been communicated.

3. Identify a family business and prepare a brief report on its history, including its founding, family involvement, and any leadership changes that have occurred.

4. Read and report on a biography or history book pertaining to a family in business or a family business.

Exploring the

5. With the keyboard search capability of the Internet, browse information appearing under the caption "family business." Prepare a one-page report identifying the kinds of data available, and include references to at least two academic programs having home pages on the Web.

CASE 5
The Brown Family Business (p. 603)

This case presents the philosophy, criteria, and procedures adopted by one family to regulate work opportunities for family members in the family business.

Alternative Cases for Chapter 5:   Case 2, "Construction Equipment Dealership," p. 595
Case 17, "Central Engineering," p. 636
Case 18, "Gibson Mortuary," p. 639
Case 25, "The Martin Company," p. 660

Part 3

6. **THE ROLE OF A BUSINESS PLAN FOR A NEW VENTURE**

7. **CREATING A COMPETITIVE ADVANTAGE**

8. **ANALYZING THE MARKET AND FORMULATING THE MARKETING PLAN**

9. **SELECTING THE MANAGEMENT TEAM AND FORM OF ORGANIZATION**

10. **CHOOSING THE LOCATION AND PHYSICAL FACILITIES**

11. **ACCOUNTING STATEMENTS AND FINANCIAL REQUIREMENTS**

12. **FINDING SOURCES OF FINANCING**

The Role of a Business Plan for a New Venture

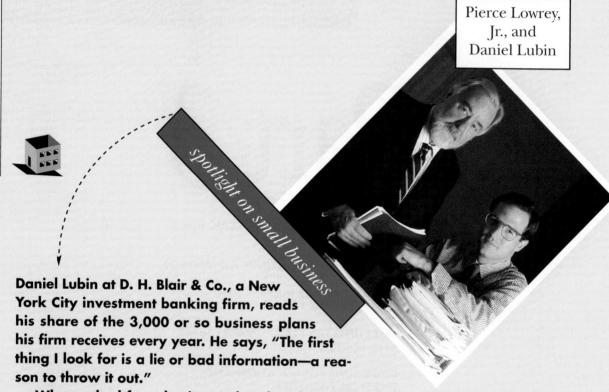

Chapter 6

Pierce Lowrey, Jr., and Daniel Lubin

spotlight on small business

Daniel Lubin at D. H. Blair & Co., a New York City investment banking firm, reads his share of the 3,000 or so business plans his firm receives every year. He says, "The first thing I look for is a lie or bad information—a reason to throw it out."

When asked for a business plan that demonstrates the qualities of a good plan, he offered Pierce Lowrey, Jr.'s plan for Imtech. The first quality of the plan mentioned by Lubin was brevity. "Make it easy to read. Venture capitalists don't have a lot of time," he says. "Also, remember that for money-raising purposes, a plan isn't supposed to showcase how much you know—it's meant to get the venture capitalist salivating." Lowrey's plan ultimately raised $4.5 million in a Blair-backed stock issue, in exchange for 28 percent of Imtech's stock.

Source: Adapted with permission, Ellyn E. Spragins, "Venture Capital Express," *Inc.*, Vol. 12, No. 11 (November 1990), p. 159.

Think back to the last term paper you wrote. Do you recall the frustration of not knowing what to write about and the difficulty you had in just getting started? The all too frequent result is procrastination. Many times, students only begin the writing process when they are faced with an impending deadline.

In some ways, preparing a business plan is similar to writing a term paper. It is agonizing to begin and difficult to know what to say, especially when you lack experience and are at a loss as to what needs to be included. Even when you know the questions, you may have difficulty finding good answers. But just as you learn from writing a term paper, you increase your understanding of what you want to accomplish in a new business by carefully preparing a business plan.

As we begin this chapter, we give several reasons for writing a business plan. None, however, is as important as its use as a selling document—selling your ideas and even yourself to others. If you have felt pride on completing a term paper, you will feel exhilaration from writing an effective business plan. The business plan—its preparation, content, and organization—will serve as the thread that weaves a common purpose through Chapters 6–12.

> ## Looking Ahead
>
> *After studying this chapter, you should be able to:*
>
> **1** Answer the question "What is a business plan?"
>
> **2** Explain the need for a business plan from the perspective of the entrepreneur and the investor.
>
> **3** Describe what determines how much planning an entrepreneur and a management team are likely to do.
>
> **4** List practical suggestions to follow in writing a business plan, and outline the key components of a business plan.
>
> **5** Identify available sources of assistance in preparing a business plan.

WHAT IS A BUSINESS PLAN?

1 Answer the question "What is a business plan?"

business plan
a document containing the basic idea underlying a business and related considerations for starting up

For the entrepreneur starting a new venture, a **business plan** is a written document that accomplishes two basic objectives. First, it identifies the nature and the context of the business opportunity—why does such an opportunity exist? Second, the business plan presents the approach the entrepreneur plans to take to exploit the opportunity.

A business plan explains the key variables for success or failure. It can help you anticipate the different situations that may occur—to think about what can go right and what can go wrong. But, as we noted earlier, a business plan is, first and foremost, a selling document. It is the tool that extols the merits of an investment opportunity. In another sense, it is the game plan—it crystallizes the dreams and hopes that provide your motivation. The business plan should lay out your basic idea, describe where you are now, point out where you want to go, and outline how you propose to get there.

The business plan is the entrepreneur's blueprint for creating the new venture; in this sense, it might be called the *first creation*. Without first mentally visualizing the desired end result, the entrepreneur probably will not see it become a physical reality, or the *second creation*. For anything that is built—a house or a business—there is always a need for a written plan. This blueprint is, in essence, a bridge between the mental and the physical, between an idea and reality. The role of the business plan is to provide a clear visualization of what the entrepreneur intends to do.

A business plan, as presented here, is a proposal for launching a new business. The venture itself is the outgrowth of the business plan. As part of the plan, an entrepreneur projects the marketing, operational, and financial aspects of a proposed business for the first three to five years. In some cases, a business plan may address a major expansion of a firm that has already started operation. For example, an entrepreneur may open a small local business and then recognize the possibility of opening additional branches or extending the businesses's success in other ways. A business plan may also be a response to some change in the external environment (government, demographics, industry, and so on) that may lead to new opportunities.

More mature businesses may prepare strategic and operational plans that contain many of the features described in this chapter. In fact, planning should be a continuous process in the management of any business. That is, you should think of a business plan as an ongoing process, and not as an end product. This last point deserves repeating: *Writing a business plan is primarily an ongoing process and only secondarily a product or outcome.*

2 Explain the need for a business plan from the perspective of the entrepreneur and the investor.

THE NEED FOR A BUSINESS PLAN

Most entrepreneurs are results-oriented, and for good reason. A "can do" attitude is essential when starting a new business. Otherwise, the danger of paralysis by inaction or, equally bad, paralysis by analysis can become overwhelming. Getting the business operational should be a high priority. However, using the need for action as an excuse to neglect planning is also a big mistake.

Reasons for Preparing a Business Plan

There are two reasons for writing a business plan: (1) to create a selling document to be shared with outsiders, and (2) to provide a clearly articulated statement of goals and strategies for internal purposes. Figure 6-1 provides an overview of those who might have an interest in a business plan. One group of users shown in the figure consists of outsiders who are critical to the firm's success; the remaining group consists of the internal users of the business plan. Let's consider the internal users first.

Figure 6-1

Users of Business Plans

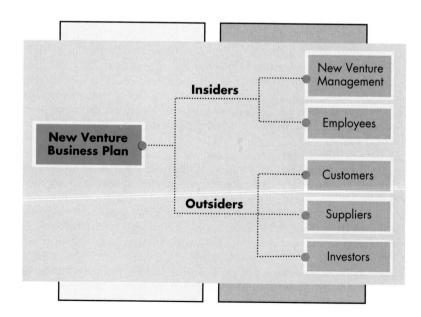

Using the Business Plan Internally

Any activity that is initiated without adequate preparation tends to be haphazard. This is particularly true of such a complex process as initiating a new business. Although planning is a mental process, it must go beyond the realm of thought. Thinking about a proposed new business must become more rigorous as rough ideas are crystallized and quantified. A written plan is essential to ensure systematic coverage of all the important features of a new business. It becomes a model of what the entrepreneur wants to happen by identifying the variables that can affect the success or failure of the business. Modeling, or planning, helps the entrepreneur focus on the important issues and activities.

Preparing a formal written plan thereby imposes needed discipline on the entrepreneur and the team of managers. In order to prepare a written statement about marketing strategy, for example, the team must perform some sort of market research. Likewise, a study of financing requirements requires a review of projected receipts and expenditures month by month. Otherwise, even a good opportunity can fail because of negative cash flows. In short, business plan preparation forces an entrepreneur to exercise the discipline that good managers must possess.

A business plan should also be effective in selling ideas to others, even to those within the company. In this way, the business plan provides a structure for communicating the entrepreneur's mission to employees of the firm, both current and prospective.

The Business Plan and Outsiders

The business plan can be an effective selling tool to use with customers, suppliers, and investors. It can enhance the firm's credibility with prospective suppliers and customers. Suppliers, for example, extend trade credit, which is often an important part of a new firm's financial plan. A well-prepared business plan may be helpful in gaining a supplier's trust and securing favorable credit terms. Occasionally, a business plan can also improve sales prospects—for example, by convincing a potential customer that the new firm is likely to be around to service a product or to continue as a procurement source.

Almost anyone starting a business faces the task of raising financial resources to supplement personal savings. Unless an entrepreneur has a rich relative who will supply funds, he or she must appeal to bankers, individual investors, or venture capitalists. The business plan serves as the entrepreneur's calling card when approaching these sources of financing.

A business plan can be effective in convincing outsiders of the firm's value. It is particularly useful when an entrepreneur is seeking financial resources; bank officers will require a business plan before approving any type of a loan.

Both lenders and investors can use the business plan to better understand the business, the type of product or service it offers, the nature of the market, and the qualifications of the entrepreneur or entrepreneurial team. A venture capital firm or other sophisticated investors would not consider investing in a new business before reviewing a properly prepared business plan. The plan can also be helpful in establishing a good relationship with a commercial bank, a relationship that is important for a new firm. The significance of the business plan in dealing with outsiders is aptly expressed by Mark Stevens:

> *If you are inclined to view the business plan as just another piece of useless paperwork, it's time for an attitude change. When you are starting out, investors will justifiably want to know a lot about you and your qualifications for running a business and will want to see a step-by-step plan for how you intend to make it a success. If you are already running a business and plan to expand or diversify, investors and lenders will want to know a good deal about the company's current status, where it is headed and how you intend to get it there. You must provide them with a plan that makes all of this clear.*[1]

The business plan is not, however, a legal document for actually raising the needed capital. When it comes time to solicit investors for money, a *prospectus*, or offering memorandum, is used. This document contains all the information needed to satisfy the federal and state security laws for warning potential investors about the possible risks of the investment. As a consequence, the prospectus alone is not an effective marketing document with which to sell a concept. You must first use the business plan to create interest in your startup, followed by a formal offering memorandum to those investors who seem genuinely interested.

Understanding the Investor's Perspective

If you intend to use the business plan to raise capital, you must understand the investor's basic perspective. You have to see the world as the investor sees it; that is, you must think as the investor thinks. For most entrepreneurs, this is more easily said than done. The entrepreneur generally perceives a new venture very differently than the investor does. The entrepreneur will characteristically focus on the positive potential of the startup—what will happen if everything goes right. The prospective investor, on the other hand, plays the role of the skeptic, thinking more about what could go wrong. An entrepreneur's failure not only to understand but also to appreciate this difference in perspectives greatly increases the chance of rejection by an investor.

At the most basic level, a prospective investor has a single goal: to maximize potential return on the investment through the cash flows that will be received, while minimizing personal risk exposure. Even venture capitalists, who are thought to be great risk takers, want to minimize their risk. Like any informed investor, they will look for ways to shift risk to the entrepreneur.

Given the fundamental differences between the investor and the entrepreneur, the important question becomes "How do I write a business plan that will capture a prospective investor's interest?" There is no easy answer, but two things are certain: (1) Investors have a short attention span, and (2) certain features appeal to investors, while others are distinctly unappealing.

THE INVESTOR'S SHORT ATTENTION SPAN In the 1980s, Kenneth Blanchard and Spencer Johnson wrote a popular book about being a one-minute manager—a manager who practices principles that can be applied quickly but produce large results.[2] Investors in startup and early-stage companies are, in a sense, one-minute investors. Because they receive many business plans, they cannot read them in any detailed fashion. Tim Smith, an officer of the Capital Southwest Corporation, a Dallas-based venture capital firm, observed that "we receive some 300 or more plans per year but invest only in three or four firms in any given year. Thus, we simply do not have the luxury to analyze each opportunity thoroughly."

The speed with which business plans are reviewed requires that they be designed to communicate effectively and quickly to prospective investors. They must not sacrifice thoroughness, however, or substitute a few snappy phrases for basic factual information. After all, someone will eventually read the plan carefully. To get that careful reading, however, the plan must first gain the interest of the reader(s), and it must be formulated with that purpose in mind. While many factors may stimulate an investor's interest, some basic elements of a business plan that tend to attract or repel prospective investors deserve consideration.

BUSINESS PLAN FEATURES THAT ATTRACT OR REPEL INVESTORS   Based on their experience with the MIT Enterprise Forum, Stanley R. Rich and David E. Gumpert have identified the type of business plan that wins funding. (The MIT Enterprise Forum sponsors sessions in which prospective entrepreneurs present business plans to panels of venture capitalists, bankers, marketing specialists, and other experts.) Figure 6-2 lists some of the features of successful business plans that are important from an investor's perspective. For instance, to be effective, the plan cannot be extremely long or encyclopedic in detail; it should seldom exceed 40 pages in length. Investors generally have a tendency to look at brief reports and to avoid those that take too long to read. Also, the general appearance of the report

Figure 6-2

Features of Business Plans That Succeed

- It must be arranged appropriately, with an executive summary, a table of contents, and chapters in the right order.
- It must be the right length and have the right appearance—not too long and not too short, not too fancy and not too plain.
- It must give a sense of what the founders and the company expect to accomplish three to seven years into the future.
- It must explain in quantitative and qualitative terms the benefit to the user of the company's products or services.
- It must present hard evidence of the marketability of the products or services.
- It must justify financially the means chosen to sell the products or services.
- It must explain and justify the level of product development that has been achieved and describe in appropriate detail the manufacturing process and associated costs.
- It must portray the partners as a team of experienced managers with complementary business skills.
- It must suggest as high an overall "rating" as possible of the venture's product development and team sophistication.
- It must contain believable financial projections, with the key data explained and documented.
- It must show how investors can cash out in three to seven years, with appropriate capital appreciation.
- It must be presented to the most potentially receptive financers possible to avoid wasting precious time as company funds dwindle.
- It must be easily and concisely explainable in a well-orchestrated oral presentation.

Source: "Plans That Succeed," pp. 126–127 from *Business Plans That Win $$$: Lessons from the MIT Enterprise Forum* by Stanley R. Rich and David E. Gumpert. Reprinted by permission of Sterling Lord Literistic, Inc. Copyright © 1985 by Stanley R. Rich and David E. Gumpert.

should be attractive, and it should be well organized, with numbered pages and a table of contents.

Investors are more *market-oriented* than *product-oriented*. We are not suggesting that they are not interested in new product development. The essence of the entrepreneurial process relates to identifying new products, but only if they meet an identifiable customer need. Investors realize that most inventions, even those that are patented, never earn a dime for the inventors. Thus, it is essential for the entrepreneur to appreciate this market orientation and, more importantly, to join investors in their concern about market prospects.

Some other factors presumably interest investors:

- Evidence of customer acceptance of the venture's product or service
- An appreciation of investors' needs, through recognition of their particular financial-return goals
- Evidence of focus, through concentration on only a limited number of products and/or services
- Proprietary position, as represented by patents, copyrights, and trademarks[3]

Prospective investors may also be unimpressed by a business plan. Some of the features that create unfavorable reactions are the following:

- Infatuation with the product or service rather than familiarity with and awareness of marketplace needs
- Financial projections at odds with accepted industry norms
- Growth projections out of touch with reality
- Custom or applications engineering, which make substantial growth difficult[4]

HOW MUCH BUSINESS PLAN IS NEEDED?

3 Describe what determines how much planning an entrepreneur and a management team are likely to do.

Entrepreneurs' levels of commitment to the writing of a business plan vary greatly. However, expert advice in its preparation provides direction as well as another's perspective on key issues.

We have given the impression to this point that writing a business plan is a matter of either/or—either you do it, or you don't. We have done so in an effort to make a compelling case for writing a plan, to persuade you that a plan is important both as a guide for future action and as a selling document.

In reality, preparing a business plan is a matter of degree. That is, even if you are convinced that a business plan is necessary, the question remains as to the level of effort to be given to the plan. A plan can be written on the back of an envelope at one extreme, or it can be a comprehensive plan filled with intricate detail at the other extreme—or you can target a plan somewhere in between. The point is, you must choose from somewhere along a continuum.

In making a decision regarding the extent of planning, an entrepreneur must deal with tradeoffs. Preparing a business plan requires both time and money, two resources that are usually in limited supply. Other considerations come into play as well:

Action Report

ENTREPRENEURIAL EXPERIENCE

Planning Can Make the Difference

For Harlan Accola, 1986 was one horrendous year. His aerial-photography business, Skypix, hit a wall and nearly vanished from sight. And he had only himself to blame.

Skypix had started as a hobby. After high school, Accola began selling his aerial shots of farms and homes to help pay for his pilot's license, his flying time, and his photography habit. His brother Conrad, also a pilot, joined in to make a few bucks.

In 1980, when their sideline unexpectedly evolved into a business and made money, the brothers had visions of sales booming to $3 million, and then $10 million. "We thought that's the way it happens," Harlan says. "You hit a niche and an opportunity, and it's magic."

A bookkeeper and later a certified public accounting firm furnished financial statements that Harlan didn't understand. "I didn't know anything about business," he admits. "And worse, I didn't think it was important. I thought a financial statement was just something you had to give the bank to keep your loan okay. So I took it, looked at the bottom line, and tossed it into a desk drawer." The brothers' earliest "business plan" was simple: Always have enough cash to pay next week's bills.

For a time, the Accolas' seat-of-the-pants style held the business together. By 1986, however, their world was coming unglued. Harlan Accola blames his age—he was 19 when he started Skypix—and the hubris born of early success. "I thought if I made enough sales, everything else would take care of itself. But I confused profits with cash flow."

"We grew too fast," he confesses, "and it was simply from lack of planning. We must have looked like a real comedy team to our suppliers." Since those madcap days, Accola has turned religious about planning. American Images is now a $4.7 million business with 54 employees and 22 independent sales reps. The company's seven single-engine Cessnas operate in 31 states from its base in Marshfield, Wisconsin.

Source: Reprinted with permission, Jay Finegan, "Everything According to Plan," *Inc.*, Vol. 17, No. 3 (March 1995), pp. 78–85.

- *Management style and ability.* The extent of planning depends, in part, on the ability of the entrepreneur to grasp multiple and interrelated dimensions of the business, to keep all that is necessary in his or her head, and to be able to retrieve it in an orderly fashion. Further, whether to plan depends on the lead entrepreneur's management style. These are practical matters that affect the *actual* amount of planning, but they may not lead to the *ideal* amount of planning.
- *Preferences of the management team.* The amount of planning by a firm also depends on the management team's personal preferences. Some management teams want to participate in the planning process, and others do not. These preferences, it should be noted, could lead to insufficient planning.
- *Complexity of the business.* The complexity of a business will affect how much planning is appropriate.
- *Competitive environment.* If the firm will be operating in a highly competitive environment, where it must be kept lean and tightly disciplined to survive, more planning will be needed.

- *Level of uncertainty.* Some ventures face a volatile, rapidly changing environment and must be prepared for contingencies. In such cases, a greater amount of planning is needed. However, in reality, entrepreneurs are frequently more inclined to plan when there is less uncertainty because they can better anticipate future events—which is the opposite of what they should be thinking.[5]

So the issue goes beyond the question, "Do I plan?" The decision includes the question of *how much* to plan, and this, in turn, involves difficult tradeoffs. Let's now consider the actual preparation of the business plan.

List practical suggestions to follow in writing a business plan, and outline the key components of a business plan.

4

PREPARING A BUSINESS PLAN

Two issues are of primary concern when preparing a business plan: (1) the basic format and effectiveness of the written presentation, and (2) the content of the plan.

Formatting and Writing a Business Plan

The quality of a completed business plan depends on the quality of the underlying business concept. A defective new venture idea cannot be rescued by good writing. A good concept may be destroyed, however, by writing that fails to communicate.

A business plan must be clearly written in order to give credibility to the ideas being presented. Factual support must be supplied for any claims or promises being made. When making a promise to provide superior service or explaining the attractiveness of the market, for example, the entrepreneur must provide strong supporting evidence. In short, the plan must be believable.

Skills in written communication are necessary to present the business concept in an accurate, comprehensible, and enthusiastic way. Although this book cannot cover general writing principles, it may be useful to include some practical suggestions specifically related to the business plan. The following hints are given by the public accounting firm Arthur Andersen and Company in its booklet *An Entrepreneur's Guide to Developing a Business Plan*:

- Provide a table of contents and tab each section for easy reference.
- Use a typewritten 8½ x 11 format and photocopy the plan to minimize costs. Use a loose-leaf binder to package the plan and to facilitate future revisions.
- To add interest and improve comprehension—especially by prospective investors who lack the day-to-day familiarity that your management team has— use charts, graphs, diagrams, tabular summaries, maps, and other visual aids.
- You almost certainly will want prospective investors, as well as your management team, to treat your plan confidentially, so indicate on the cover and again on the title page of the plan that all information is proprietary and confidential. Number each copy of the plan and account for each outstanding copy by filing the recipient's memorandum of receipt.
- Given the particularly sensitive nature of startup operations based on advanced technology, it is entirely possible that many entrepreneurs will be reluctant to divulge certain information—details of a technological design, for example, or the highly sensitive specifics of marketing strategy—even to a prospective investor. In that situation, you still can put together a highly effective document to support your funding proposal by developing an in-depth plan for internal purposes, and using appropriate extracts from it in a plan designed for outside use.

- As you complete major sections of the plan, ask carefully chosen third parties—entrepreneurs who have themselves raised capital successfully, accountants, lawyers and others—to give their perspectives on the quality, clarity, reasonableness, and thoroughness of the plan. After you pull the entire plan together, ask these independent reviewers for final comments before you reproduce and distribute the plan.[6]

Content of a Business Plan

The business plan for each new venture is unique, and that uniqueness must be recognized. However, a prospective entrepreneur needs a guide to follow in preparing a business plan. While no single standard format is in general use, there is considerable similarity in basic content among many business plans.

Figure 6-3 summarizes the major segments common to most business plans, providing a bird's-eye view of the content of the end product. Chapters 7 through 12 will look at the respective segments of the business plan in more detail. However, now we will briefly introduce each of the sections.

COVER PAGE The cover page, or title page, is the first page of the business plan and should contain the following information:

- Company name, address, and phone number
- Logo, if available
- Names, titles, addresses, and phone numbers of the owners and key executives
- Date on which the plan is issued
- Number of the copy (to help keep track of how many copies are outstanding)
- Name of the preparer

EXECUTIVE SUMMARY The **executive summary** is crucial for getting the attention of the one-minute investor. It must, therefore, convey a clear and concise picture of the proposed venture and, at the same time, create a sense of excitement regarding its prospects. This means that it must be written and, if necessary, rewritten to achieve clarity and interest. Even though the executive summary comes at the beginning of the business plan, it provides an overview of the whole plan and should be written last. A sample executive summary for the business plan of an all-natural baby and children's food company is shown in Figure 6-4. This particular example is provided by Ernst & Young, a Big Six accounting firm, and may be slightly too long. Conciseness is definitely a virtue for the executive summary. In addition, it would be helpful if a mission statement for the firm were included in this summary.

> **executive summary**
> a section of the business plan, written to convey a clear and concise picture of the proposed venture

GENERAL COMPANY DESCRIPTION The main body of the business plan begins with a brief description of the company. If the firm is already in existence, its history is included. This section informs the reader as to the type of business being proposed, the firm's objectives, where the firm is located, and whether it is serving a local or international market. In many cases, legal issues—especially the form of organization—are addressed in this section of the plan. In writing this section, the entrepreneur must answer certain questions:

- What is the basic nature and activity of the business?
- When and where was this business started?
- What achievements have been made to date?
- What changes have been made in structure or ownership?
- What is the company's stage of development—seed stage, full product line?
- What is the company's mission statement and objectives?
- What is its primary product or service?

- What customers are served?
- What is the company's distinctive competence?
- What is the industry and its current and projected state?
- What is the company's form of organization—sole proprietorship, partnership, or corporation? (The legal issues are discussed more completely in Chapter 9.)
- Does the company intend to become a publicly traded company or an acquisition candidate?

Figure 6-3

Abbreviated Business Plan Outline

Cover Page: Name of venture and owners, date prepared, and contact person.

Executive Summary: A one- to three-page overview of the total business plan. Written after the other sections are completed, it highlights their significant points and, ideally, creates enough excitement to motivate the reader to continue.

General Company Description: Explains the type of company and gives its history if it already exists. Tells whether it is a manufacturing, retail, service, or other type of business. Also describes the proposed form of organization—sole proprietorship, partnership, or corporation. This section should be organized as follows: name and location; company objectives; nature and primary product or service of the business; current status (startup, buyout, or expansion) and history (if applicable); and legal form of organization.

Products and/or Services Plan: Describes the product and/or service and points out any unique features. Explains why people will buy the product or service. This section should be organized as follows: description of products and/or services; features of product/service providing a competitive advantage; legal protection—patents, copyrights, trademarks; and dangers of technical or style obsolescence.

Marketing Plan: Shows who the firm's customers will be and what type of competition it will face. Outlines the marketing strategy and specifies what will give the firm a competitive edge. This section should be organized as follows: analysis of target market and profile of target customer; methods to identify and attract customers; selling approach, type of sales force, and distribution channels; types of sales promotion and advertising; and credit and pricing policies.

Management Plan: Identifies the key players—the active investors, management team, and directors. Cites the experience and competence they possess. This section should be organized as follows: description of management team; outside investors and/or directors and their qualifications; outside resource people and their qualifications; and plans for recruiting and training employees.

Operating Plan: Explains the type of manufacturing or operating system to be used. Describes the facilities, labor, raw materials, and processing requirements. This section should be organized as follows: operating or manufacturing methods; description of operating facilities (location, space, and equipment); quality-control methods; procedures to control inventory and operations; and sources of supply and purchasing procedures.

Financial Plan: Specifies financial needs and contemplated sources of financing. Presents projections of revenues, costs, and profits. This section should be organized as follows: historical financial statements for last three to five years or as available; pro forma financial statements for three to five years, including income statements, balance sheets, cash flow statements, and cash budgets, monthly for first year and quarterly for second year; break-even analysis of profits and cash flows; and planned sources of financing.

Appendix: Provides supplementary materials to the plan. This section should be organized as follows: management team biographies; other important supporting data; and ethics code.

PRODUCTS AND/OR SERVICES PLAN   As revealed by its title, the **products and/or services plan** discusses the products and/or services to be offered to the firm's customers. If a new or unique physical product is to be offered and a working model or prototype is available, a photograph of it should be included. Investors will naturally show the greatest interest in products that have been developed, tested, and found to be functional. Any innovative features should be identified and patent protection, if any, explained. In many instances, of course, the product or service may be similar to that offered by competitors—electrical contracting, for example. However, any special features should be clearly identified. Chapters 13 and 16 discuss this topic more fully.

products and/or services plan
a section of the business plan describing the product and/or service to be provided and explaining its merits

MARKETING PLAN   As we stated earlier, prospective investors and lenders attach a high priority to market considerations. A product may be well engineered but unwanted by customers. The **marketing plan,** therefore, must identify user benefits and the type of market that exists. Depending on the type of product or service being offered, the marketing plan may be able not only to identify but also to quantify the user's financial benefit—for example, by showing how quickly a user can recover the cost of the product or service through savings in operating costs. Of course, benefits may also take the form of savings in time or improvements in attractiveness, safety, health, and so on.

marketing plan
a section of the business plan describing the user benefits of the product or service and the type of market that exists

The business plan should document the existence of customer interest by showing that a market exists and that customers are ready to buy the product or service. The market analysis must be detailed enough for a reasonable estimate of demand to be achieved. Estimates of demand must be analytically sound and based on more than assumptions if they are to be accepted as credible by prospective investors.

The marketing plan must also examine the competition and present elements of the proposed marketing strategy—for example, by specifying the type of sales force and methods of promotion and advertising that will be used. Chapter 8 presents fuller coverage of the marketing plan.

MANAGEMENT PLAN   Prospective investors look for well-managed companies. Of all the factors that may be considered, the management team is paramount—it is even more important than the product or service. Unfortunately, the ability to conceive an idea for a new venture is no guarantee of managerial ability. The **management plan,** therefore, must detail the proposed firm's organizational arrangement and the backgrounds of those who will fill its key positions.

management plan
a section of the business plan describing the key players in a new firm and their experience and qualifications

Ideally, investors desire a well-balanced management team, one that includes financial and marketing expertise as well as production experience and innovative talent. Managerial experience in related enterprises and in other startup situations is particularly valuable in the eyes of prospective investors. The factors involved in preparing the management plan are discussed in detail in Chapter 9.

OPERATING PLAN   The **operating plan** offers information on how the product will be produced or the service provided. The importance of the operating plan varies from venture to venture. This plan touches on such items as location and facilities—how much space the business will need and what type of equipment it will require. The operating plan should explain the proposed approach to assuring quality, controlling inventory, and using subcontracting or obtaining raw materials. These aspects are treated at greater length in Chapter 10.

operating plan
a section of the business plan describing the new firm's facilities, labor, raw materials, and processing requirements

Figure 6-4

An Example of an Executive Summary

Executive Summary for Good Foods, Incorporated

This business plan has been developed to present Good Foods, Incorporated (referred to as GFI or The Company) to prospective investors and to assist in raising the $700,000 of equity capital needed to begin the sale of its initial products and finish development of its complete product line.

The Company

GFI is a startup business with three principals presently involved in its development. The main contact is Judith Appel of Nature's Best, Inc., 24 Woodland Road, Great Neck, New York (516-555-5321).

During the past three years, GFI's principals have researched and developed a line of unique children's food products based on the holistic health concept—if the whole body is supplied with proper nutrition, it will, in many cases, remain healthy and free of disease.

Holism is the theory that living organisms should be viewed and treated as whole beings and not merely as the sum of different parts. The holistic concept, which *Health Food Consumer* determined is widely accepted among adult consumers of health foods, is new to the child-care field.

Hence, GFI plans to take advantage of the opportunities for market development and penetration that its principals are confident exist. GFI also believes that the existing baby-food industry pays only cursory attention to providing high-quality, nutritious products, and that the limited number of truly healthy and nutritious baby foods creates a market void that GFI can successfully fill.

Based on the detailed financial projections prepared by The Company's management, it is estimated that $700,000 of equity investment is required to begin The Company's operations successfully. The funds received will be used to finance initial marketing activities, complete development of The Company's product line, and provide working capital during the first two years of operation.

Market Potential

GFI's market research shows that the United States is entering a "mini-baby boom" that will increase the potential market base for The Company's products. This increase, combined with an expected future 25 percent annual growth rate of the $2.4 billion health food industry, as estimated by *Health Foods Business* in 1985, will increase the demand for GFI's products. Additionally, health food products are more frequently being sold in supermarkets, which is increasing product visibility and should help to increase popularity.

The Company will approach the marketplace primarily through health food stores and natural food centers in major supermarket chain stores, initially in the Northeast and California. Acceptance of the GFI concept in these areas will enable The Company to expand to a national market.

---

financial plan
a section of the business plan providing an account of the new firm's financial needs and sources of financing and a projection of its revenues, costs, and profits

pro forma statements
reports that provide projections of a firm's financial condition

FINANCIAL PLAN   Financial analysis constitutes another crucial piece of the business plan. The **financial plan** presents **pro forma statements,** or projections of the company's financial statements over the next five years (or longer). These forecasts include balance sheets, income statements, and cash flow statements on an annual basis for the five years and cash budgets on a monthly basis for the first year, a quarterly basis for the second and third years, and annually for the fourth and fifth years. It is vital that the financial projections be supported by well-substantiated assumptions and explanations of how the figures have been determined.

The specific target markets GFI will approach through these outlets are:

- Parents who are concerned about their health and their children's health and who thus demand higher and more nutritionally balanced foods and products

- Operators of child-care centers who provide meals to children

Major Milestones

Approximately two-thirds of GFI's product line is ready to market. The remaining one-third is expected to be ready within one year.

Distinctive Competence

GFI is uniquely positioned to take advantage of this market opportunity due to the managerial and field expertise of its founders, and its products' distinct benefits.

Judith Appel, George Knapp, M.D., and Samuel Knapp, M.D., all possess several years of experience in the child-care industry. Ms. Appel is a nutritionist and has served as director for the Children's Hospital for Special Services in White Plains, New York. In addition, she has nine years of business experience, first as marketing director for Healthy Harvest Foods in Yonkers, New York, then as owner/president of Nature's Best, Inc. Both Drs. Knapp have worked extensively with children, in hospital-based and private practices.

Together, the principals have spent the last three years developing, refining, testing, and selling GFI's products through Nature's Best, Inc., the retail outlet in Great Neck, a Long Island suburb of New York City.

GFI's product line will satisfy the market demand for a natural, nutritious children's food. The maximum amount of nutrients will be retained in the food, providing children with more nutritional benefit than most products presently on the market. The menu items chosen will reflect the tastes most preferred by children. A broad product line will provide for diverse meal plans.

Financial Summary

Based on detailed financial projections prepared by GFI, if The Company receives the required $700,000 in funding, it will operate profitably by year 3. The following is a summary of projected financial information (dollars in thousands).

	Year 1	Year 2	Year 3	Year 4	Year 5
Sales	$1,216	$1,520	$2,653	$4,021	$5,661
Gross margin	50%	50%	50%	50%	50%
Net income after tax	$(380)	$(304)	$15	$404	$633
Net income after tax/ sales	—	—	0.6%	10.0%	11.2%
Return/equity	0.0%	0.0%	10.8%	73.9%	53.6%
Return/assets	0.0%	0.0%	2.6%	44.5%	36.2%

Source: Eric Siegel, Loren Schultz, Brian Ford, and Jay Bornstein, *The Ernst & Young Business Plan Guide*, pp. 47–50. Copyright © 1993, John Wiley & Sons. Reprinted by permission of John Wiley & Sons, Inc.

While all the financial statements are important, cash flow statements deserve special attention, because a business may be profitable but fail to produce positive cash flows. A cash flow statement identifies the sources of cash—how much will be raised from investors and how much will be generated from operations. It also shows how much money will be devoted to such investments as inventories and equipment. The cash flow statement should clearly indicate how much cash is

Although an operating plan may need to be more detailed for a manufacturing firm than for a service business, the information it provides is essential to every firm's physical operations. The entrepreneur must consider the details of production, as well as the firm's space and equipment requirements.

needed from prospective investors and the intended purpose for the money. Investors also want to be told how and when they may expect to cash out of the investment. Most investors want to invest in a privately held company for only a limited period. Experience tells them that the eventual return on their investment will be largely dependent on their ability to cash out of the investment. Therefore, the plan should outline what mechanism will be available for exiting the company. The preparation of pro forma statements and the process of raising the needed capital are discussed more fully in Chapters 11 and 12.

APPENDIX   The appendix should contain various supplementary supporting materials and attachments to expand the reader's understanding of the plan. These include items that are referenced in the text of the business plan, such as résumés of the key investors and managers; photographs of products, facilities, and buildings; professional references; marketing research studies; pertinent published research; signed contracts of sale; and other such materials.

WHERE TO GO FOR MORE INFORMATION

5 Identify available sources of assistance in preparing a business plan.

We have just presented an overview of the business plan. More extensive descriptions are provided in books on the subject, and computer software is available to guide you step by step through the preparation of a business plan. (A listing of some books and computer software packages is provided at the end of this chapter, on pp. 134–135. Several word-processing packages are described in Chapter 21.) While such resources can be invaluable, caution is advised if you are tempted to rely on an existing business plan and adapt it to your own use. For instance, changing the numbers and some of the verbiage of another business's plan is simply not effective.

Computer-Aided Business Planning

A computer facilitates preparation of a business plan. Its word-processing capabilities, for example, can speed up the writing of narrative sections of the report, such as the description of the product and the review of key management personnel. By using word-processing software, the entrepreneur can begin with an original version of the narrative, go through a series of drafts as corrections and refinements are made, and print out the final plan as it is to be presented to investors or others.

Action Report

ENTREPRENEURIAL EXPERIENCES

Using Business Plan Consultants

A decade ago, even questionable business ventures could often find seed money. Now, banks, venture capitalists, and private investment groups require business plans from entrepreneurs who seek funds. No wonder business plan consulting is a fast-growing service industry.

"So many small businesses need this service," says Marcia Layton, founder of Layton & Co., a business plan consulting firm in Rochester, New York. "[Research has found that] a business plan makes an enterprise much more likely to succeed."

An AT&T Small Business Study published last year reported that of businesses with less than $20 million in sales during 1992, fewer than 42 percent use formal business plans to guide their daily operations. Among businesses with sales of less than $500,000, which make up 68 percent of the total, only one-third have carried out even the most basic planning efforts. Those who do, however, are likely to be rewarded: More than half (59 percent) of the small businesses that exhibited growth over the past two years said they used formal business plans.

"A lot of people just can't get started [on a plan]," says Layton. She encourages clients to buy books on the subject because it helps them think through how they're going to start their business. "I can do some counseling and advise them on marketing [and operating] strategies," she says, "but I cannot make the decisions for them."

Linda T. Elkins, owner of Business Plan Writing in Mechanicsville, Maryland, describes her technique: "I either get clients to write a draft on their own, which is ideal, or guide them through a series of questions. I show them the things that need to go into a business plan. I say, 'Tell me about your market. Describe your customers. How many are there? How do you know? Let's go get the data. Who are your competitors? Let's get their sales literature.' I prompt them for the information, then I put it together to see if it makes a logical whole. We go back and edit it and make more decisions; then we sit down and do the financials."

Source: Reprinted with permission from Ken Ohlson, "A Higher Plan," *Entrepreneur*, Vol. 22, No. 8 (August 1994), pp. 172–175.

The computer is an even more helpful tool for preparing the financial statements needed in the plan. Since the various parts of a financial plan are interwoven in many ways, a change in one item—sales volume, interest rates, or cost of goods sold, for example—will cause a ripple effect through the entire plan. A long, tedious set of calculations are required if the entrepreneur wishes to check out various assumptions. By using a computer spreadsheet, she or he can accomplish this task electronically. A computer spreadsheet enables an entrepreneur to experiment with best-case and worst-case scenarios and quickly ascertain their effect on the firm's balance sheet, operating profits, and cash flows.

Finally, as we mentioned above, there are many business plan software packages. Their basic objective is to help you think through the important issues in beginning a new company and to organize your thoughts into an effective presentation. They are not capable, however, of producing a *unique* plan, and thus may limit the entrepreneur's creativity and flexibility.

1 Answer the question "What is a business plan?"

- A business plan identifies the nature and context of the business opportunity and answers the question "Why is there an opportunity?"
- A business plan describes the approach the entrepreneur will take to exploit the opportunity.

2 Explain the need for a business plan from the perspective of the entrepreneur and the investor.

- The business plan provides a clearly articulated statement of the firm's goals and strategies.
- The business plan helps identify the important variables that will determine the success or failure of the firm.
- The business plan is used as a selling document to outsiders.
- An investor plays the role of a skeptic, thinking more about what could go wrong than what will go right.
- An investor needs to know how the business will help achieve the investor's personal goal—to maximize the potential return on investment through the cash flows that will be received from the investment, while minimizing personal risk exposure.
- An investor needs to know how he or she will cash out of the investment.

3 Describe what determines how much planning an entrepreneur and a management team are likely to do.

- The allocation of two scarce resources, time and money, affects how much planning will be done.
- Other factors that affect the extent of planning include (1) management style and ability, (2) management preferences, (3) the complexity of the business, (4) the competitive environment, and (5) the level of uncertainty in the environment.

4 List practical suggestions to follow in writing a business plan, and outline the key components of a business plan.

- A business plan will be more effective if you follow these suggestions: (1) provide a table of contents and tab each section for easy reference; (2) use a loose-leaf binder to package the plan and to facilitate revisions; (3) use charts, graphs, diagrams, tabular summaries, and other visual aids to create interest and provide an effective presentation that is easy to follow; (4) maintain confidentiality of the plan; and (5) ask carefully chosen third parties to give their assessment of the quality of the plan.
- Key components of a business plan are (1) a cover page, (2) an executive summary, (3) a general company description, (4) a products and/or services plan, (5) a marketing plan, (6) a management plan, (7) an operating plan, (8) a financial plan, and (9) an appendix.

5 Identify sources available for assistance in preparing a business plan.

- A variety of books and software packages are available to assist in the preparation of a business plan.
- Professionals who have expertise, such as attorneys, accountants, and other entrepreneurs, can provide useful suggestions and assistance in the preparation of a business plan.

One of the business plan software packages described in the list at the end of this chapter is BizPlan*Builder*. We have chosen BizPlan, which can be purchased as a supplement to this text, to use in a feature of this book called "The Business Plan: Laying the Foundation." At the conclusion of each chapter in this section of the book (Chapters 6 through 12), we present questions to be answered in the process of writing a business plan. We then identify the part of BizPlan that will help you work through the given set of questions.

Locating Assistance in Preparing a Business Plan

The founder of a company is most notably a doer. Such a person often lacks the breadth of experience and know-how, and possibly the inclination, needed for planning. Consequently, he or she must supplement personal knowledge and skills by obtaining the assistance of outsiders or by adding individuals with planning skills to the management team.

Securing help in plan preparation does not relieve the entrepreneur of direct involvement. He or she must be the primary planner. The entrepreneur's basic ideas are necessary to produce a plan that is realistic and believable. Furthermore, the plan eventually will have to be interpreted and defended to outsiders. An entrepreneur can be effective in such a presentation only by having complete familiarity with the plan.

However, after the founder has the basic ideas clarified, other individuals may be able to render assistance in preparing the business plan. Calling on outside help to finish and polish the plan is appropriate and wise. The use of business plan consultants is described in the Action Plan on p. 129. Other outside sources of assistance are listed below:

- Attorneys can make sure that the company has the necessary patent protection, review contracts, consult on liability and environmental concerns, and advise on the best form of organization.
- Marketing specialists can perform market analysis and evaluate market acceptance of a new product.
- Engineering and production experts can perform product development, determine technical feasibility of products, and assist in plant layout and production planning.
- Accounting firms can guide in developing the written plan, assist in making financial projections, and advise in establishing a system of financial control.
- Incubator organizations offer space for fledgling companies and advise on structuring new businesses. (Incubators are discussed at greater length in Chapters 10 and 17.)
- Small business development corporations (SBDCs) and regional and local economic development offices can offer general assistance.

Now that you are more aware of the importance and fundamentals of the business plan, we will look more closely at each of its components in the chapters that follow.

DISCUSSION QUESTIONS

1. What benefits are associated with the preparation of a written business plan for a new venture? Who uses such a plan?
2. Why do entrepreneurs tend to neglect initial planning? Why would you personally be tempted to neglect it?
3. In what way could a business plan be helpful in recruiting key management personnel?
4. Recall the statement that an investor in new ventures is a

New Terms and Concepts

business plan *115*	marketing plan *125*	pro forma statements *126*
executive summary *123*	management plan *125*	
products and/or services plan *125*	operating plan *125*	
	financial plan *126*	

You Make the Call

Situation 1   New ventures are occasionally more successful than their initial business plans projected. One such company is Compaq Computer Corporation. Ben Rosen and L. J. Sevin invested in this company even though they had reservations about its projected sales volume. They were astonished by the excellent returns.

In 1982, Rosen and Sevin invested in a company then called Gateway Technology, Inc. Gateway's plan stated that the company would make a portable computer compatible with IBM's personal computer and would sell 20,000 machines for $35 million in its first year—"Which we didn't believe for a moment," says Rosen. The sales projection for the second year was even more outrageous: $198 million. "Can you imagine seeing a business plan like this for a company going head-on against IBM, and projecting $198 million?" he asks. He and Sevin told the fledgling company to scale down its projections.

Gateway later changed its name to Compaq Computer Corporation. In its first year, the company sold an estimated 50,000 machines, more than twice the plan's forecast, for $111 million. In the second year, Compaq's sales were $329 million.

Source: Adapted with permission from *Inc.* magazine, Vol. 9, No. 2 (February 1987). Copyright © 1987 by Goldhirsh Group, Inc., 38 Commercial Wharf, Boston, MA 02110.

Question 1   In view of the major underestimation of Compaq's projected sales, what benefits, if any, may have been realized through initial planning?
Question 2   What implications for the preparation of a business plan are evident in the investors' skepticism concerning sales projections?
Question 3   In view of the circumstances in this case, do you think that entrepreneurs or investors are likely to be more accurate and realistic in making projections for business plans? Why?

Situation 2   A young journalist contemplates launching a new magazine that will feature wildlife, plant life, and the scenic beauty of nature throughout the world. The prospective entrepreneur intends each issue to contain several feature articles—for example, on the dangers and benefits of forest fires, features of Rocky Mountain National Park, wildflowers found at high altitudes, and the danger of acid rain. The magazine will make extensive use of color photographs, and its articles will be technically accurate and interestingly written. Unlike *National Geographic*, the proposed publication will avoid articles dealing with the general culture and confine itself to topics closely related to nature itself. Suppose you are a venture capitalist examining a business plan prepared by this journalist.

Continue on next page

Question 1 What are the most urgent questions you would want the marketing plan to answer?

Question 2 What details would you look for in the management plan?

Question 3 Do you think this entrepreneur would need to raise closer to $1 million or $10 million in startup capital? Why?

Question 4 At first glance, are you inclined to accept or reject the proposal? Why?

Situation 3 In 1993, Ed Jones and John Rose decided to start a new business to manufacture noncarbonated soft drinks. They believed that their location in eastern Texas, close to high-quality water, gave them a competitive edge. Although Jones and Rose had never worked together, Jones had 17 years of experience in the soft drink industry. Rose had recently sold his own firm and had funds to help finance the venture; however, the partners needed to raise additional money from outside investors. Both men were excited about the opportunity and spent almost 18 months developing their business plan. The first paragraph of their executive summary reflected their excitement:

> The "New Age" beverage market is result of a spectacular boom in demand for drinks that have nutritional value from environmentally safe ingredients and waters that come from deep, clear springs free of chemicals and pollutants. Argon Beverage Corporation will produce and market a full line of sparkling fruit drinks, flavored waters, and sports drinks that are of the highest quality and purity. These drinks have the same or similar delicious taste appeal as that of soft drinks while using the most healthful fruit juices, natural sugars, and the purest spring water, the hallmark of the "New Age" drink market.

With the help of a well-developed plan, the two men were successful in raising the necessary capital to begin their business. They leased facilities and got underway. However, after almost two years, the plan's goals were not being met. There were cost overruns, and profits were not nearly up to expectations.

Question 1 What problems might have contributed to the firm's poor performance?

Question 2 Although several problems were encountered in implementing the business plan, the primary reason for low profits was embezzlement. Jones was diverting company resources for personal use, even taking some of the construction material purchased by the company and using it to build his own house.

a. What could Rose have done to avoid this situation?

b. What are his options after the fact?

---

one-minute investor. Would an intelligent investor really make a decision based on such a hasty review of a business plan?

5. Investors are said to be more market-oriented than product-oriented. What does this mean? What is the logic behind this orientation?

6. Why shouldn't a longer business plan be better than a shorter one, since it could include more data and supporting analysis?

7. What advantages are realized by using a computer in preparing narrative sections of a business plan? In preparing the financial plan?

8. How might you quantify user benefit for a new type of production tool?

9. The founders of Apple Computer, Inc. eventually left or were forced out of the company's management. What implications does this have for the management plan of a new business?

10. If the income statement of a financial plan shows that the business will be profitable, why is there a need for a cash flow statement?

EXPERIENTIAL EXERCISES

1. Assume that you wish to start a business to produce and sell a device to hold down a tablecloth on a picnic table so that the wind will not blow it off. Prepare a one-page outline of the marketing plan for this product. Be as specific and comprehensive as possible.

2. A former chef wishes to start a business to supply temporary kitchen help (chefs, sauce cooks, bakers, meat cutters, and so on) to restaurants that are in need of staff during busy periods. Prepare a one-page report explaining which section or sections of the business plan are most crucial in this case and why.

3. Suppose that you wish to start a tutoring service for college students in elementary accounting courses. List the benefits you would realize from preparing a written business plan.

4. Interview a person who has started a business within the past five years. Prepare a report describing the extent to which the entrepreneur engaged in preliminary planning and his or her views about the value of business plans.

Exploring the

5. Locate the home page for BizPlan*Builder* and report what information is available on this home page. The address for BizPlan*Builder* is

http://www.jianusa.com/

CASE 6
Robinson Associates, Inc. (p. 605)

This case presents a business plan for a proposed management consulting firm.

Alternative Cases for Chapter 6:   Case 11, "WJP Partners," p. 622
Case 12, "Walker Machine Works," p. 624

BOOKS AND COMPUTER SOFTWARE ON PREPARING BUSINESS PLANS

Books

The following supplement to this book discusses the preparation of business plans more completely and includes sample plans:

Longenecker, Justin G., Carlos W. Moore, and J. William Petty, *Preparing the Business Plan* (Cincinnati, OH: South-Western, 1995).

Other helpful references include the following:

Abrams, Rhonda M., *The Successful Business Plan: Secrets and Strategies*, 2nd ed. (Grants Pass, OR: Oasis Press, 1993).
Bangs, David H., Jr., *The Business Planning Guide: Creating a Plan for Success in Your Own Business*, 6th ed. (Dover, NH: Upstart Publishing, 1992).
Business Plan for Small Service Firms (U.S. Small Business Administration, Washington, DC, 1990).
The Business Plan: A Touche Ross Guide to Writing an Effective Business Plan (Los Angeles: Touche Ross, 1991).
An Entrepreneur's Guide to Developing a Business Plan (Chicago: Arthur Andersen and Company, 1990).
Gumpert, David E., *How to Really Create a Successful Business Plan* (Boulder, CO: *Inc.* Business, 1990).
Lasher, William, *The Perfect Business Plan Made Simple* (Garden City, NY: Doubleday, 1994).
Luther, William M., *The Start-up Business Plan* (Englewood Cliffs, NJ: Prentice Hall, 1991).
McKeever, Mike, *How to Write a Business Plan*, 4th ed. (Berkeley, CA: Nolo Press, 1992).
Pinson, Linda, and Jerry Jinnett, *Anatomy of a Business Plan*, 2nd ed. (Chicago: Enterprise/Dearborn, 1993).
Pinson, Linda, and Jerry Jinnett, *Business Plan for the Small Construction Firm* (U.S. Small Business Administration, Washington, DC, 1990).
Pinson, Linda, and Jerry Jinnett, *Business Planning for the Small Retailer* (U.S. Small Business Administration, Washington, DC, 1990).
Rich, Stanley R., and David E. Gumpert, *Business Plans That Win $$$: Lessons from the MIT Enterprise Forum* (New York: HarperCollins, 1987).
Schilt, W. Keith, *The Entrepreneur's Guide to Preparing a Winning Business Plan and Raising Venture Capital* (Englewood Cliffs, NJ: Prentice Hall, 1990).
Siegel, Eric, Loren Schultz, Brian Ford, and Jay Bornstein, *The Ernst & Young Business Plan Guide* (New York: John Wiley & Sons, 1993).

Software

The following four software packages illustrate the types of computerized assistance that are available for preparing business plans:

1. ***Inc. Business Plan,*** developed by *Inc.* magazine. The *Inc.* package provides a first-time user with the tools needed to prepare a business plan with relative ease. This may or may not be in the best interest of the preparer; a quality plan requires careful thought.

To start the program, the user is taken through a series of instructions set up to show how the program works and how to access different parts of it. The instructions are brief and to the point. Once the user is in the program, getting started with actual data is quite simple. Each step is explained in terms of the information needed.

The plan is organized along conventional lines. It is very detailed and includes references to such items as insurance and worker's compensation.

2. ***How to Write a Business Plan,*** developed by the American Institute of Small Business. This package is designed to help the user build a business plan by using already written text that offers five or six different options in each section. In this way, the text demonstrates the basic points contained in a business plan.

The software is designed for use with WordPerfect and Lotus 1-2-3, but it will also run with Word for Windows and Excel. However, some of the calculations in the financial part of the plan must be done outside the spreadsheet.

The organizational plan of the software includes such areas as the executive summary, general company description, a description of the firm's products and/or services, industry conditions, a marketing plan, a production plan, and a financial plan.

3. ***Business DISC Entrepreneur's Kit,*** developed by Maryland Institute Technologies. This software primarily targets the small business startup. Its main purpose is to assist a new company in developing a very simple but efficient business plan in the area of operations.

The Kit consists of two separate programs: the Business DISC and the Data/Companion, which can be used together or separately. However, using the programs together provides a wider range of possible modifications to the plan. The software can be considered an expert system because of the built-in questions that the user must answer when going through the development process.

The Business DISC consists of four main modules: a business profile, personal income statement, cash flow projections, and letter of intent. In each module, the user must make a series of decisions. Depending on the business area chosen, the program generates appropriate questions to assist the user. All the information is saved on a data/companion diskette, which can be used separately with Lotus 1-2-3 once the model plan has been designed. Also, with an additional utility program called FisCal, a sensitivity analysis can be performed to show the effect of changes in certain key variables in the model.

4. **BizPlan*Builder: Strategic Business & Marketing Plan Software,*** developed by South-Western Publishing. This software has word-processing and spreadsheet capabilities that take the user through the preparation of a business plan. The different sections of the presentation begin with opening comments that explain what should be covered in a given section. Sentences and paragraphs (as much as possible) are already started; the user completes them as appropriate. To prompt the user, X's appear where information needs to be provided. Explanations, suggestions, and/or instructions are presented near each blank area.

The word-processing files are provided in Microsoft Word, WordPerfect, and, as a last resort, ASCII (American Standard Code for Information Interchange). Most DOS- or Windows-based word processors can read one or more of these file formats. The spreadsheet files are provided in Lotus 1-2-3 (Versions 1-A and 2.01).

LAYING THE FOUNDATION
Introduction

Part 3 of this book, "Developing the New Venture Business Plan" (Chapters 6 through 12), deals with issues that are important when starting a new venture. Chapter 6 began with an overview of the business plan and its preparation. The remaining chapters of this part focus on major segments of the business plan—for example, the management plan, the marketing plan, and the financial plan. When you have studied these chapters, you will have the knowledge needed to prepare a business plan.

Recognizing that learning is facilitated when you apply what you study, we have designed a feature called "The Business Plan: Laying the Foundation" to conclude each chapter in Part 3. This feature provides guidelines for preparing the different segments of a business plan. It presents important questions that need to be addressed ("Asking the Right Questions"), and it identifies material in a popular software package that can be used to prepare the plan ("Using BizPlan*Builder*").

Asking the Right Questions

Now that you have learned the main concepts of business plan preparation, you can begin to create a business plan by writing a general company description. In thinking about the key issues, respond to the following questions:

1. When and where is the business to start?
2. What stage of development is the company in?
3. What is the basic nature and activity of the business?
4. What is its primary product and/or service?
5. What customers are served?
6. What is the company's mission statement?
7. What are the company's objectives?
8. What is the history of the company?
9. What is the company's distinctive competence?
10. What has been achieved to date?
11. What changes have been made in structure or ownership?
12. What are the current and projected states of the industry?
13. Does the company intend to become a publicly traded company or an acquisition candidate?

USING BizPlanBuilder

As indicated earlier in this chapter, BizPlan*Builder: Strategic Business & Marketing Plan Software* provides a framework for writing a business plan. To assist you in answering some of the questions posed above, see Part 2 of BizPlan*Builder*. These pages provide some guidance regarding the executive summary, the firm's objectives, and the present business situation—good starting points for writing your plan.

Creating a Competitive Advantage

Louis Brown, Jr.

spotlight on small business

An entrepreneur who begins a new venture increases the odds for success by seeking a market niche not targeted by big businesses. This is precisely the strategy followed by Louis Brown, Jr., of Beltsville, Maryland when he started his business. Raised on a dairy farm, Brown earned an engineering degree from Johns Hopkins University in 1966. In 1970, after working for Armco Steel and Hewlett-Packard, he and two engineering friends started a computer-design company.

Along the way, [Brown] also did some consulting work for a company that made electronic cash registers. He decided to start making smart cash registers, too. But rather than take on NCR Corp. or IBM, Brown decided to specialize in registers for restaurants. He named his new company Micros Systems, Inc.

The register he developed enables managers to compare sales data, track each item on a menu, and cross-check information against a system's inventory records. In fiscal year 1994, Micros Systems's profits were about $12 million, and it was ranked 100th on *Forbes*'s 1995 list of the 200 Best Small Companies in the United States.

By following a niche strategy, Micros Systems gained an immediate competitive advantage. After a decade of hard work, Micros Systems has approximately a 12 percent share of the fragmented market for restaurant computer systems. "I firmly believe," Brown says, "that the driving force behind me was the good Lord looking out for me. If I'd been born a generation earlier, I'd have been a farmer."

Source: Kate Bohner Lewis, "Thou Better Not Steal," *Forbes*, Vol. 154, No. 11 (November 7, 1994), pp. 216–217. Reprinted By Permission of FORBES Magazine © Forbes Inc., 1994.

Looking Ahead

After studying this chapter, you should be able to:

1 Identify the forces that determine the nature and degree of competition within an industry.

2 Identify and compare strategy options for building competitive advantage.

3 Define the different types of market segmentation strategies.

4 Explain the concept of niche marketing and its importance to small business.

5 Discuss the importance of customer service to the successful operation of a small business.

start here

A competitive advantage may just happen, or it may result from careful thought about the mission of a firm. Unfortunately, many entrepreneurs are unaccustomed to the kind of systematic investigation required to develop a real competitive advantage and then to describe their strategy in a business plan. They typically have difficulty finding an appropriate starting point.

Nevertheless, after examining opportunities, risks, and resources, the successful entrepreneur *must* decide on a competitive advantage and develop a basic strategy. Ideally, these strategic plans are then committed to writing in the business plan to ensure completion of the strategy-determination process and to provide a basis for subsequent planning.

These brief introductory comments regarding a firm's competitive advantage indicate the complexity of the task. Therefore, it is not surprising that creation of a meaningful strategy requires a conscious commitment by the entrepreneur to devote considerable time and energy to the process. This chapter describes key building blocks for the development of a small firm's overall competitive advantage strategy: the central concept of competitive advantage and the related activities of market segmentation, niche marketing, and customer service management. We will discuss the translation of overall strategy into detailed action in later chapters.

COMPETITIVE ADVANTAGE

> **1** Identify the forces that determine the nature and degree of competition within an industry.

competitive advantage
a benefit that exists when a firm has a product or service that is seen by its target market as better than that of a competitor

A **competitive advantage** exists when a firm has a product or service that is perceived by its target market customers as better than that of its competitors. Unfortunately, entrepreneurs are often confronted with two myths surrounding the creation of a competitive advantage. One is that most good business opportunities are already gone. The other is that small firms cannot compete well with big companies. Both of these ideas are erroneous! Nevertheless, existing companies, large and small, do not typically welcome competitors. As one well-respected author, Karl H. Vesper, puts it:

> *Established companies do their best to maintain proprietary shields . . . to ward off prospective as well as existing competitors. Consequently, the entrepreneur who would create a new competitor to attack them needs some sort of "entry wedge," or strategic competitive advantage for breaking into the established pattern of commercial activity.*[1]

Before choosing such an entry wedge, the entrepreneur needs to understand the basic nature of the competition he or she faces in the marketplace. Only then can a competitive advantage be developed properly.

The Basic Nature of Competition

The following strategies of three entrepreneurs show the simplicity of many successful competitive advantages:

- Dale Dunning and his two partners started Wall Street Custom Clothiers in 1986, with suits selling for $700 to $2,000. Dunning targets upscale consumers by traveling to their offices, instead of waiting for customers in a retail shop.[2]
- Ron Sanculi spent two years developing the perfect salsa recipe before packaging it in an ordinary mason jar with a generic label and seeking shelf space along with many other brands. Since 1991, Sanculi has sold nearly 500,000 bottles of Mad Butcher's Salsa.[3]
- Allen Conway, Sr., is the founder of Discount Labels, a company launched in 1980 to meet the needs of customers who require small quantities of printed labels quickly—a market of little interest to established companies. Because of its ability to fill orders within 24 hours, the company is the nation's largest short-run manufacturer of custom labels.[4]

These entrepreneurs compete successfully within their respective industries. Each understands the nature of competition and follows a simple but sound strategy. But what are the basic factors in a competitive market?

A number of factors determine the level of competition within an industry. Several typologies have been developed to categorize these competitive forces. For example, Michael Porter, in his book *Competitive Advantage*, identifies five factors that determine the nature and degree of competition in an industry:

1. Bargaining power of buyers
2. Threat of substitutes
3. Bargaining power of suppliers
4. Rivalry among existing competitors
5. Threat of new competitors

Figure 7-1 depicts these five factors as weights, offsetting the attractiveness of a target market.

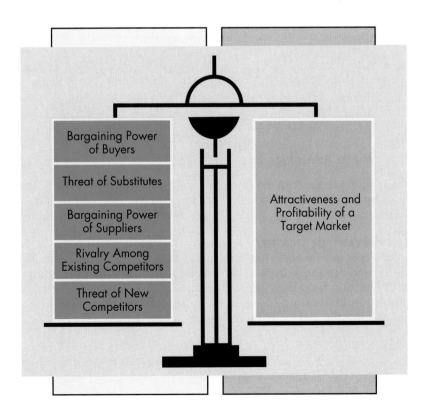

Figure 7-1

Major Factors Offsetting Market Attractiveness

To a large degree, these five market forces collectively determine the ability of a firm, whether large or small, to be successful. Obviously, all industries are not alike; therefore, each force has varying impact from one situation to the next. Porter identifies numerous elements of industry structure that influence these five factors. Detailed explanation of them is, however, beyond the scope of this discussion. Briefly stated, these factors influence the creation of a competitive advantage as follows:

> *Buyer power influences the prices that firms can charge, for example, as does the threat of substitution. The power of buyers can also influence cost and investment, because powerful buyers demand costly service. The bargaining power of suppliers determines the cost of raw materials and other inputs. The intensity of rivalry influences prices as well as the costs of competing in areas such as plant, product development, advertising, and sales force. The threat of entry places a limit on prices and shapes the investment required to deter entrants.*[5]

The more completely entrepreneurs understand the underlying forces of competitive pressure, the better they will be able to assess market opportunities or threats facing their venture. Obviously, which forces dominate industry competition depend on the particular circumstances. Therefore, the challenge to the entrepreneur is to recognize and understand these forces so that the venture is positioned best to cope with the industry environment.

Porter has identified several fatal flaws that plague entrepreneurs' strategic thinking regarding their competitive situation. Three of these flaws are

1. *Possessing no true competitive advantage.* Imitation of rivals is both hard and risky and reflects a lack of any competitive advantage.
2. *Pursuing a competitive advantage that is not sustainable.* The entrepreneur must make sure that the competitive advantage cannot be quickly imitated.
3. *Misreading industry attractiveness.* The most attractive industry may not be the fastest-growing or the most glamorous.[6]

This chapter focuses on concepts that assist entrepreneurs in overcoming these flaws. If entrepreneurs create a true competitive advantage, maintain that advantage, and correctly understand industry potential, they will greatly enhance their likelihood of success.

2 Identify and compare strategy options for building competitive advantage.

Competitive Advantage Strategies

Many strategies can build a firm's competitive advantage in the marketplace. However, two broad-based options are used most frequently. One option involves creating a cost advantage; the other involves creating a marketing advantage.

COST-ADVANTAGE STRATEGY   The cost-advantage strategy requires a firm to be the lowest-cost producer within the market. The sources of this advantage are quite varied and can range from low-cost labor to efficiency in operations. For example, Max Duncan, founder of Integrity Industries in Kingsville, Texas, created a cost advantage by locating his new chemical blending operation in a vacant facility whose owner he persuaded to sign on as a partner.

> [Then] *he found an experienced sales manager willing to take another third of the company in lieu of a year's salary. Duncan bought used equipment for "pennies on the dollar"; he ordered free samples from chemical companies for his initial raw materials. . . .*

Duncan quickly found customers. The reason was simple: His costs were so low that he could charge 10 percent to 20 percent less than the competition. . . . "We're able to make healthy profit margins and keep prices low by maintaining extreme efficiency in operation," he explains.[7]

Integrity Industries continues to grow but has not abandoned its key cost advantage.

Another example of the use of a cost advantage is found in the strategy of Hull Industries, Inc., a Twinsburg, Ohio startup. Entrepreneur Edwin Hull, Jr., plans to take on the market leader—Winner International Corporation, maker of the Club—with an automobile antitheft device called Lockjaw.

Lockjaw offers retailers two enticements. Its one-size-fits-all design cuts their inventory expenses. (The Club comes in 14 models with suggested retail prices ranging from $29.95 to $99.95, depending on the size, color, and quality of the lock.) And Lockjaw's wholesale cost is about $5 less than that of the Club's comparable model, improving stores' profit margins. (Lockjaw's suggested retail price is $39.95.)[8]

MARKETING-ADVANTAGE STRATEGY   The second broad-based option for building a competitive advantage is creation of a marketing advantage, which requires efforts that differentiate the firm's product or service in some way other than cost. A firm that can create and sustain such a differentiation will be a successful performer in the marketplace. The uniqueness of the product or service can be real or simply consumer perception. A wide variety of operational and marketing tactics—ranging from promotion to product design—lead to product and/or service differentiation.

Inventor Henry Artis entered the home composting market by creating a competitive marketing advantage through product design. Traditional composters have been designed as fixed rectangular bins. Such a stationary design requires periodic stirring to introduce oxygen into the leaves, grass clippings, and discarded food. Other designs use elevated tubes that are rotated with a hand-operated crank. Artis's idea, called TumbleBug, features a giant hollow plastic ball that can be rolled across the yard to achieve the necessary agitation to create compost. Selling

Inventor Henry Artis created a competitive marketing advantage for the Tumblebug, a home composter, through his product design. A gardener can achieve the agitation necessary to make compost by rolling this large hollow plastic ball across the yard.

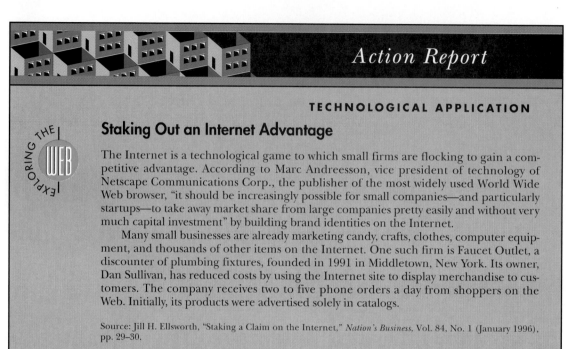

Action Report

TECHNOLOGICAL APPLICATION

Staking Out an Internet Advantage

The Internet is a technological game to which small firms are flocking to gain a competitive advantage. According to Marc Andreesson, vice president of technology of Netscape Communications Corp., the publisher of the most widely used World Wide Web browser, "it should be increasingly possible for small companies—and particularly startups—to take away market share from large companies pretty easily and without very much capital investment" by building brand identities on the Internet.

Many small businesses are already marketing candy, crafts, clothes, computer equipment, and thousands of other items on the Internet. One such firm is Faucet Outlet, a discounter of plumbing fixtures, founded in 1991 in Middletown, New York. Its owner, Dan Sullivan, has reduced costs by using the Internet site to display merchandise to customers. The company receives two to five phone orders a day from shoppers on the Web. Initially, its products were advertised solely in catalogs.

Source: Jill H. Ellsworth, "Staking a Claim on the Internet," *Nation's Business*, Vol. 84, No. 1 (January 1996), pp. 29–30.

at a relatively expensive $169, Artis's product provides "better looks, no odors, higher temperatures, and faster composting."[9] This venture relies on product differentiation rather than cost for its competitive advantage.

MARKET SEGMENTATION STRATEGIES

The previously discussed competitive advantages—cost and marketing—apply to a marketplace that is relatively homogeneous or uniform in nature. They can also be used to focus on a limited market within an industry. Michael Porter refers to this type of competitive strategy as a focus strategy. In other words, cost and marketing advantages can be achieved within narrow market segments as well as in the overall market.

market segmentation
division of a market into several smaller groups with similar needs

Within marketing circles, this focus strategy is generally called **market segmentation**. Formally defined, it is the process of dividing the total market for a product or service into groups with similar needs such that each group is likely to respond favorably to a specific marketing strategy. A small business may view its market in either general or focus terms. The personal computer industry is a good example of real-world market segmentation. Originally, computer manufacturers aimed at the corporate market and practiced very little market segmentation. But, as corporate demand declined, the personal computer industry focused on market segments such as small businesses, home offices, and educational institutions.

The Need for Market Segmentation

If a business had control of the only known water supply in the world, its sales volume would be huge. This business would not be concerned about differences in personal preferences concerning taste, appearance, or temperature. It would con-

Action Report

QUALITY GOALS

Quality Segmentation by the Bottle

Discerning consumers are making his company's market segmentation strategy successful, according to Greg Steltenpohl, founder and chairman of Odwalla, Inc., which produces all-natural fresh fruit and vegetable juices:

> *"People today are looking for higher quality in every area of their lives, and that includes what they drink," Steltenpohl says. "They're more discerning about the content, taste, and consistency of juice, and that is what is driving our success."*

Odwalla, Inc. began operation in 1980 in Santa Cruz, California and has recently shifted production to a 65,000-square-foot plant in Dinuba, California. The company produces about 20 different juices that have no artificial ingredients or preservatives and are not pasteurized. Therefore, they retain enzymes and vitamins, which translates into better aroma and subtle sensations of freshness.

Named for a character in a song-poem called "Illistrum," Odwalla is successful because it produces a quality product and delivers it quickly to its target market. The company recently went public, and Steltenpohl believes it can hit sales near $100 million in about five years.

Source: Steven B. Kaufman, "Freshness by the Bottle," *Nation's Business*, Vol. 82, No. 2 (February 1994), p. 14. Reprinted by permission. Copyright 1994, U.S. Chamber of Commerce.

sider its customers to be *one* market. As long as the water product was wet, it would satisfy everyone. However, if someone else discovered a second water supply, the view of the market would change. The first business might discover that sales were drying up and turn to a modified strategy. It would need to segment the market to reflect differences in consumer preferences as it attempted to be competitive.

In the real world, a number of preferences for drinks exist, creating a heterogeneous market. The different preferences may take a number of forms: Some may relate to the way consumers react to the taste or to the container; others may relate to the price of the drink or to the availability of "specials." Preferences might also be uncovered with respect to different distribution strategies or to certain promotional tones and techniques. In other words, many markets are actually composed of several submarkets.

Types of Market Segmentation Strategies

There are several types of market segmentation strategies. The three types we discuss in this section are the unsegmented approach, the multisegmentation approach, and the single-segmentation approach. These strategies can be best illustrated by using an example—a hypothetical small firm called the Community Writing Company.

THE UNSEGMENTED STRATEGY   When a business defines the total market as its target, it is following an **unsegmented strategy** (also known as mass marketing). This

unsegmented strategy
defining the total market as a target market

strategy can sometimes be successful, but it assumes that all customers desire the same general benefit from the product or service. This may hold true for water but certainly does not for shoes, which satisfy numerous needs through many styles, prices, colors, and sizes. Using an unsegmented strategy, a firm develops a single marketing mix—one combination of product, price, promotion, and distribution. Its competitive advantage must be derived from either a cost or a marketing advantage. The unsegmented strategy of the Community Writing Company is shown in Figure 7-2. The Community Writing Company's product is a lead pencil that is sold at the one price of $0.79 and is promoted through a single medium and distribution plan. Note how the marketing mix is aimed at all potential users of a writing instrument.

multisegmentation strategy
recognizing different preferences of individual market segments and developing a unique marketing mix for each

THE MULTISEGMENTATION STRATEGY With a view of the market that recognizes individual segments with different preferences, a firm is in a better position to tailor marketing mixes to various segments. For example, a firm may think that two or more market segments can be profitable. If it then develops a unique marketing mix for each segment, it is following a **multisegmentation strategy.**

Let's assume that the Community Writing Company has recognized three separate market segments: students, professors, and executives. Following the multisegmentation approach, the company develops a competitive advantage with three

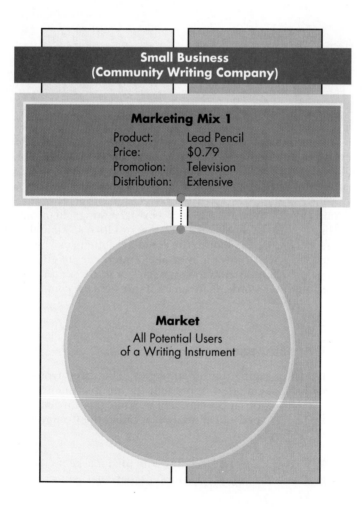

Figure 7-2

An Unsegmented Market Strategy

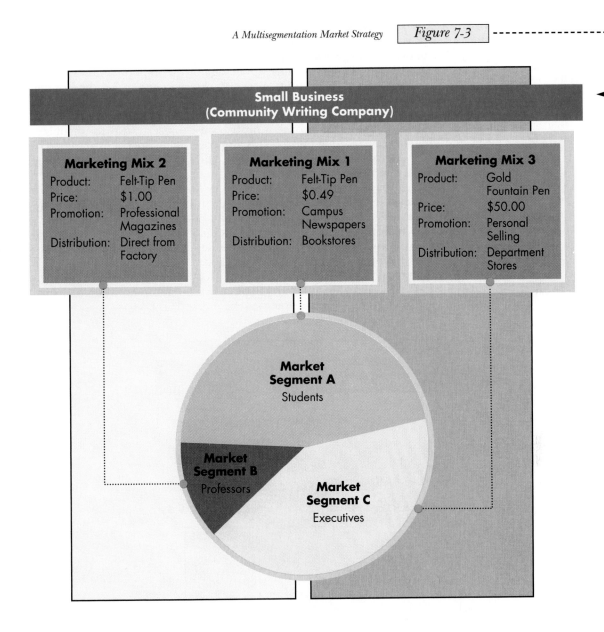

A Multisegmentation Market Strategy | Figure 7-3 |

Small Business (Community Writing Company)

Marketing Mix 2
Product: Felt-Tip Pen
Price: $1.00
Promotion: Professional Magazines
Distribution: Direct from Factory

Marketing Mix 1
Product: Felt-Tip Pen
Price: $0.49
Promotion: Campus Newspapers
Distribution: Bookstores

Marketing Mix 3
Product: Gold Fountain Pen
Price: $50.00
Promotion: Personal Selling
Distribution: Department Stores

Market Segment A
Students

Market Segment B
Professors

Market Segment C
Executives

marketing mixes, based on differences in pricing, promotion, distribution, or the product itself, as shown in Figure 7-3. Mix #1 consists of selling felt-tip pens to students through bookstores at the lower-than-normal price of $0.49 and supporting this effort with a promotional campaign in campus newspapers. With Mix #2, the company markets the same pen to universities for use by professors. Professional magazines are the promotional medium used in this mix, distribution is direct from the factory, and the product price is $1.00. Finally, with Mix #3, which is aimed at corporate executives, the product is a gold fountain pen that is sold only in exclusive department stores, promoted by personal selling, and priced at $50.00. Note the distinct differences in these three marketing mixes. Small businesses, however, tend to resist the use of the multisegmentation strategy because of the risk of spreading resources too thinly among several marketing efforts.

single-segmentation strategy
recognizing the existence of several distinct market segments, but pursuing only the most profitable segment

THE SINGLE-SEGMENTATION STRATEGY   When a firm recognizes that several distinct market segments exist but chooses to concentrate on reaching only one segment, it is following a **single-segmentation strategy.** The segment selected is the one that seems to be the most profitable. Once again, a competitive advantage is achieved through a cost or marketing strategy. As shown in Figure 7-4, the Community Writing Company selects the student market segment in deciding to pursue a single-segmentation approach.

The single-segmentation approach is probably the wisest strategy for small businesses during initial marketing efforts. This approach allows such a firm to specialize and make better use of its limited resources. Then, when a reputation has been built, it is easier to enter new markets.

A single-segmentation strategy was followed by Elias and Gaynell Hendricks in 1988, when they started Wee Care Academy, Inc. in Birmingham, Alabama. They wanted to fill a void in the market by providing a preschool where "kids of all races could enjoy a challenging, fun curriculum that incorporates African and African American viewpoints." They used the single-segmentation strategy to build a successful business, with 1994 revenues over $2 million.[10]

A variation of the single-segmentation approach has become known in recent years as a niche strategy. Because of its popularity and potential value to a small firm's success, we devote a later section to niche marketing.

Figure 7-4

A Single-Segmentation Market Strategy

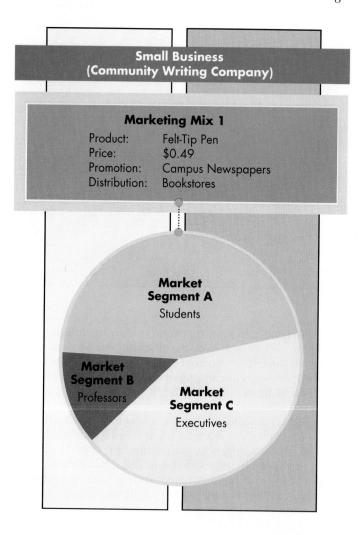

Segmentation Variables

A firm's target market could be defined simply as "anyone who is alive" in that market. However, this is too broad to be useful even for a firm that follows an unsegmented approach. A **market** is a group of customers or potential customers who have purchasing power and unsatisfied needs. In any type of market analysis, some degree of segmentation must be made. Note in Figure 7-2 (on page 144), which presents an unsegmented market strategy, that the market does not include everyone in the universe—just those who might use writing instruments.

In order to divide the total market into appropriate segments, an entrepreneur must consider segmentation variables. Basically, **segmentation variables** are labels that identify the particular dimensions that are thought to distinguish one form of market behavior from another. Two broad sets of segmentation variables that represent major dimensions of a market are benefit variables and demographic variables.

BENEFIT VARIABLES   The definition of a market highlights the unsatisfied needs of customers. **Benefit variables** are related to customer needs in that they are used to identify segments of a market according to the benefits sought by customers. For example, the toothpaste market has several benefit segments. The principal benefit to parents may be cavity prevention for their young children, while the principal benefit to a teenager might be fresh breath. In both cases, toothpaste is the product, but it has two different market segments.

DEMOGRAPHIC VARIABLES   Benefit variables alone are insufficient for market analysis. It is impossible to implement forecasting and marketing strategy without defining the market further. Therefore, small businesses commonly use demographics as part of market segmentation. Typical demographics are age, marital status, sex, occupation, and income. Recall the definition of a market—customers with purchasing power and unsatisfied needs. Thus, **demographic variables** refer to certain characteristics that describe customers and their purchasing power.

NICHE MARKETING

Niche marketing is a special type of segmented market strategy in which entrepreneurs try to isolate themselves from market forces, such as competitors, by focusing on a specific target market segment. The strategy can be implemented through any element of the market mix—price, product design, service, packaging, and so on. A niche market strategy is particularly attractive to a small firm that is building a competitive advantage while trying to escape direct competition with industry giants.

Niche marketing can be effective in both domestic and international markets. Noted author John Naisbitt foresees a huge global economy with smaller and smaller market niches. He believes success in those niches "has to do with swiftness to market and innovation, which small companies can do so well."[11]

Selecting a Market Niche

Many new ventures fail because of poor market positioning or lack of a perceived advantage by customers in their target market. To minimize this chance of failure, an entrepreneur should consider the benefits of exploiting gaps in a market rather

market
a group of customers or potential customers who have purchasing power and unsatisfied needs

segmentation variables
the parameters used to distinguish one form of market demand from another

benefit variables
variables that distinguish market segments according to the benefits sought by customers

demographic variables
specific characteristics that describe customers and their purchasing power

4 Explain the concept of niche marketing and its importance to small business.

niche marketing
choosing market segments not adequately served by competitors

than going head-to-head with competition. Niche marketing can be implemented by using any of the following strategies:

- Restricted focus on a single market segment
- Emphasis on a single product or service
- Limitation to a single geographical region
- Concentration on superiority of the product or service

The following examples of firms pursuing one or more of these strategies demonstrate the successful efforts of creative entrepreneurs:

> *City Family, published quarterly by Arthur Schiff, is targeted at poor people while other publishers chase upscale demographics. Mr. Schiff says that, in two years, the magazine's circulation has climbed to 200,000 from 10,000. . . . Library Journal magazine named City Family one of the 10 best new magazines of 1993, the first full year of [its] publication.*[12]

> *Tom Frye opened an insurance claims–adjusting business . . . based in Belmont, California, four years ago [1990]. Frye saw the need for an independent regional company that would be small enough to know you but large enough to serve you. He took advantage of technology in a way that his competitors did not. "Every one of our staff in the field has a fax machine, has a voice-mail pager, has a car phone."*[13]

> *Atlantic Publication Group, Inc. (APG) spent four years offering broad-based, general-interest magazines . . . before Marvin Jenkins, the president, began developing products for particular niches in 1989. Now, this small company in Charleston, South Carolina, produces 28 publications for all kinds of organizations [for example, Pro Basketball, The Lehigh Valley, International Perspective.] Every APG product is developed in response to a particular need. "First, we identify readers and what they are looking for," Jenkins says. "A business must differentiate itself in ways that are important to the customer. . . . Niche marketing is really refinement of product. . . . The trick is to be open-minded. Look at what you're doing—honestly—and whether it is working. Small companies have the flexibility to change direction."*[14]

strategic decision
a decision regarding the direction a firm will take in relating to its customers and competitors

By selecting a particular niche, an entrepreneur decides on the basic direction of the firm. Such a choice affects the very nature of the business and is thus referred to as a **strategic decision**. A firm's overall strategy is formulated, therefore, as its leader decides how the firm will relate to its environment—particularly to the customers and competitors in that environment. One small business analyst expresses a word of caution about selecting a niche market:

By focusing on specific market segments, entrepreneurs protect their businesses from competitors. The chef-owner of this restaurant targets customers who enjoy indulging in freshly made pastries and confections.

ENTREPRENEURIAL EXPERIENCES

Greetings to a Market Niche

Targeting neglected niche markets is an intelligent and profitable competitive advantage strategy. The greeting card industry, for example, is not one broad market but rather the sum of many segmented markets—some with little or no competition.

According to the Greeting Card Association, the overall $5.9 billion market in 1994 was shared by roughly 1,500 companies. Opportunities for small firms exist where established card publishers have left gaps. Carol Weinstock's greeting card company addresses one of these gaps. Her company, EthnoGraphics, of Santa Barbara, California, targets ethnic markets with appropriate greeting card designs. When she first researched the greeting card industry, she saw a real void. Although ethnic groups represent 20 percent of the country's population, these groups weren't being served by the greeting card industry.

EthnoGraphic's current product line includes almost 800 different cards. All card designs are created by artists who belong to the ethnic group targeted.

Source: Gayle Sato Stodder, "The Greeting of America," *Entrepreneur,* Vol. 22, No. 9 (September 1994), pp. 210–211. Reprinted with permission of Entrepreneur Magazine, September 1994.

Ventures that seek to capture a market niche, not transform or create an industry, don't need extraordinary ideas. Some ingenuity is necessary to design a product that will draw customers away from mainstream offerings and overcome the cost penalty of serving a small market. But features that are too novel can be a hindrance; a niche market will rarely justify the investment required to educate customers and distributors about the benefits of a radically new product.[15]

Selection of a very specialized market is, of course, not the only possible strategy for a small firm. Nevertheless, finding a niche that can be exploited is a popular strategy. It allows a small firm to operate in the gap that exists between larger competitors. If a small firm chooses to go head-to-head in competition with other businesses, particularly large corporations, it must be prepared to distinguish itself in some way—for example, by attention to detail, highly personal service, or speed of service—in order to make itself a viable competitor.

Maintaining Niche Potential

Those firms that adopt a niche strategy tread a narrow line between maintaining a protected market and attracting competition. Entrepreneurs must be prepared to encounter competition if their ventures prove profitable. In his book *Competitive Advantage,* Michael Porter cautions that a segmented market can erode under any of four conditions:

1. The focus strategy is imitated.
2. The target segment becomes structurally unattractive because of erosion of the structure, or because demand simply disappears.

3. The target segment's differences from other segments narrow.
4. New firms subsegment the industry.[16]

Minnetonka, a small firm widely recognized as the first to introduce liquid hand soap, provides an example of how a focus strategy can be imitated. The huge success of its brand, Softsoap, quickly attracted several of the industry giants, including Procter & Gamble. Minnetonka's competitive advantage was soon washed away. Some analysts believe the company focused too much on the advantages of liquid soap in general and not enough on the particular benefits of Softsoap.

Sometimes it is difficult to anticipate the exact source of competition. For example, before Bob Lindberg started his upscale apparel shop in Tustin, California, he felt that he had adequately researched the market, including potential competition. "The only other upscale retailer, as far as I know, [had] no plans to expand here," said Lindberg, whose research showed him customers weren't worried about price—they wanted quality-brand merchandise and good service. Lindberg opened A.J. & Co. Big and Tall in October 1993, and a steady flow of customers began to patronize his business. Shortly thereafter, Lindberg realized his competition was more than just other upscale retailers. Several catalog retailers were offering similar merchandise, and Lindberg had failed to anticipate the impact on his sales. "Catalogs offer convenience retailers find hard to match—especially for men who have experienced a lot of shopping frustration in the past. Almost everyone who comes into my store has purchased something from a catalog," he says.[17] A.J. & Co. Big and Tall offers competitive pricing and maintains its competitive advantage by providing a wide selection, accurate sizing, and—most important—personalized service. This strategy enables the firm to compete effectively, even against catalog retailers.

Another example of maintaining a market niche can be seen in the efforts of Sheri Poe. Poe had tried almost every brand of athletic shoes during years of working out, only to suffer severe lower back and knee pain. She concluded that existing women's athletic shoes were only sized-down versions of men's shoes. Poe believed that an entrepreneur could carve out a niche that the larger companies had overlooked. Her company, Rykä, developed a fitness shoe built specifically for women, a patented design for better shock absorption and durability, and introduced the shoe at a trade show in 1988. Poe says, "As a new manufacturer in a big industry, we had a realistic fear that established companies would target us and market us right out of business." The strategy Rykä used to combat the threat was one that did not challenge the established shoe companies on all fronts but only in a narrow niche. Rykä started with shoe designs for several applications—running, tennis, and so on. However, Poe cut back to aerobic shoes not only because she didn't have the budget to build several different markets at once, but because she recognized the key to success is to target a strong niche and stay focused. In 1993, sales at Rykä reached $14 million. The Rykä business venture is an example of how niche marketing can work for a small firm, allowing it to step into the land of giants.[18]

Clearly, niche marketing does not guarantee a sustainable competitive advantage. But small firms can extend their prosperity by developing competitive clout.

CUSTOMER SERVICE MANAGEMENT

5 Discuss the importance of customer service to the successful operation of a small business.

In the previous sections, we described possible tactics for creating a competitive advantage. We also provided several real-world examples. Now we give special attention to perhaps the most important tactic for creating and maintaining a com-

Customer service is generally thought to be an area in which small firms have a competitive advantage. Danny Wegman, president of Wegmans Food Markets, heads a chain noted for its dedication to customer satisfaction.

petitive advantage—customer service. Three basic beliefs serve as the foundation for our approach to customer service:

1. Customer satisfaction is not a means to achieve a certain goal; rather, it *is* the goal.
2. Customer service can provide a competitive edge.
3. Small firms are potentially in a much better position to achieve customer satisfaction than are big businesses.

These beliefs, particularly the last one, suggest that *all* small business managers should implement customer service management. A small business that ignores customer service is jeopardizing its chances for success.

Customer Satisfaction—The Key Ingredient

Customer service can provide a competitive edge for small firms regardless of the nature of the business. A **customer satisfaction strategy** is a marketing plan that has customer satisfaction as its goal. Such a strategy applies to consumer products and services as well as industrial products. Customer service should be the rule rather than the exception.

The use of outstanding customer service to earn a competitive advantage is certainly not new. Longtime retailer Stanley Marcus, of Dallas-based Neiman-Marcus, is famous for his commitment to customer service. What is relatively new to small firms is the recognition that top-notch customer service is smart business.

A recent survey by *Communication Briefings* revealed that, in general, customers do not feel they get what they deserve. Responses to the question "How would you rate the quality of customer service you receive from most organizations you do business with?" are summarized as follows:

Excellent:	6 percent
Good:	45 percent
Fair:	43 percent
Poor:	5 percent

customer satisfaction strategy
a marketing plan that emphasizes customer service

Here are some other findings of the study:

- Over one-third of the respondents said the biggest customer service mistake was failing to make customers feel important.
- Almost one-fourth of the respondents indicated that clerks are rude to customers and management dismisses customer complaints.
- Nearly one-half of the respondents said that in the past year they had ceased doing business with three or more businesses because of poor customer service.[19]

What is the special significance of these statistics for small businesses? The answer is that small firms are *potentially* in a much better position to achieve customer satisfaction than are big businesses. Why? Ask yourself if the problems identified by the survey are more solvable within firms having fewer employees. For example, with fewer employees, a small firm can vest authority for dealing with complaints in each employee. On the other hand, a large business will usually charge a single individual or department with that responsibility.

Consider the following two firms' success with customer service tactics. Sewell Village Cadillac, a car dealer in Dallas, Texas, is famous for its customer service. Its owner, Carl Sewell, began the service journey in 1967 when Sewell Village was in third place among the three Dallas Cadillac dealers. Sewell "realized that most people didn't like doing business with car dealers. . . . They looked forward to seeing us about as much as they did going to the dentist," he says. Therefore, he simply began asking customers what they didn't like about car dealers. Three points of major dissatisfaction were identified—service hours, being without a car during service, and repair done incorrectly. By responding to these concerns, Sewell Village Cadillac increased its customer satisfaction rating.[20]

Another firm reaping the benefits of providing superior customer satisfaction is the Phelps Country Bank, headquartered in Rolla, Missouri. This little bank has prospered at the expense of its big competitors because of its chief executive Emma Lou Brent, who has developed a different kind of banking environment. The following are among the customer service strategies implemented by the bank's 55 employees:

- *The lobby opens five minutes before 9:00 A.M. and closes five minutes after 3:00 P.M.—there are no disgruntled customers peering in and looking angrily at their watches.*
- *[A customer] is upset because he lost track of his checkbook balance and now doesn't want to pay the overdraft charge? A rep . . . might refund the amount if she thinks it was an honest mistake. Or she might propose splitting it with him.*
- *Employees do not keep customers waiting while they finish paperwork.*
- *The bank's newspaper ads carry lending officers' home phone numbers, as do the officers' business cards. Customers are encouraged to call nights or weekends on urgent matters.*[21]

High levels of customer service do not come cheaply. There are definite costs associated with offering superior service before, during, and after a sale. However, many customers are willing to pay for good service. These costs can be reflected in a product's or service's price, or they can sometimes be scheduled separately, based on the amount of service requested. For example, David and Linda West, owners of San Luis Sourdough Co. in San Luis Obispo, California, price according to how much service their clients (supermarkets and specialty food stores) require. "If a supermarket is happy to have the bread dropped off at the back door, the wholesale price is $0.97. If the store wants to be able to return day-old bread for full

Action Report

ENTREPRENEURIAL EXPERIENCES

Try My Service On for Size

A marketing strategy emphasizing good customer service should provide the entrepreneur with a distinct advantage. An excellent example is the quality service policy of small business owner Gail Sundling. Sundling operates Delmar Bootery in Albany, New York, where she is a 1992 state designee in the Blue Chip Enterprise program. (The program is jointly sponsored by Connecticut Mutual Life Insurance Co., the U.S. Chamber of Commerce, and *Nation's Business* magazine.) "I give my people on the floor every bit of my authority" to keep the customers happy, she says. Sundling estimates the cost of retaining a customer to be one-fifth of what it takes to gain a new one.

Several customer service techniques have worked well for her store. For example, anyone who buys a pair of shoes at her bootery gets free shoe shines for the life of the shoes. Sundling has learned that this policy not only creates goodwill but results in customers purchasing a lot of extras when they come in for a free shine.

Source: Bradford McKee, "If the Shoe Fits, They'll Be Back," *Nation's Business*, Vol. 80, No. 7 (July 1992), p. 8. Reprinted by permission. Copyright 1992, U.S. Chamber of Commerce.

credit, the cost is $1.02 a loaf." The Wests figure the price covers the cost of the service.[22]

Because there is a great deal of current interest in applying the principles of total quality management to controlling customer service and creating a competitive advantage, we will briefly examine this topic in the next section.

Customer Service and Total Quality Management

Total quality management (TQM) is an umbrella term encompassing intensive quality control programs that have become popular in U.S. businesses in the past several years.[23] TQM is rooted in the superior quality of Japanese products in the 1970s. Large U.S. manufacturers responded to the Japanese challenge with similar quality control programs.

Increasingly, small manufacturing firms are feeling the need to implement TQM, partly as a result of pressure from the big companies they supply. Other small firms are interested in TQM because they recognize the potential for creating a better competitive advantage. TQM principles, therefore, extend beyond manufacturing to firms offering final consumer products and services. We will briefly examine the elements of a TQM program as they relate to offering final consumer products and services. (The use of TQM in operations management is analyzed in Chapter 19.)

Quality improvement starts with the culture of the organization. Consider the remarks of Jim Zawacki, owner and president of Grand Rapids Spring & Wire Products in Grand Rapids, Michigan—a small firm with 160 employees. Zawacki believes

total quality management (TQM)
an all-encompassing management approach to providing high-quality products and services

QUALITY

that "getting people to understand why we're in business" and building "trust, relationships, integrity, and communication" are the keys to developing the appropriate organizational culture for TQM. His firm is seeing results.[24]

Entrepreneurs should place top priority on creating and controlling quality customer service. One recent study indicates that small firms are keenly aware of the importance of customer service when they compete with big business. As Figure 7-5 shows, approximately 70 percent of the small firms surveyed mentioned "customer service" as a successful competitive tactic. Also note that "quality of employees" was mentioned quite frequently. Obviously, employees are critical ingredients in a quality customer service program.

Making customer satisfaction the number one priority is not necessarily as natural as it might seem. Business has used the phrase "The customer is always right" for decades, but have U.S. businesses achieved a high level of customer satisfaction? Here are some results of a survey for which one-half of the respondents were companies with 500 or fewer employees:

- Only 57 percent of the businesses rate "meeting customer needs" as their number one priority.
- In 62 percent of the companies, not everyone is aware of what customers do with the company's product or service.
- Fewer than half of new products and services are developed or improved based on customer suggestions and complaints, despite an MIT study showing that the best innovations come from customers.
- Only 59 percent of the firms contact lost customers; 7 percent do nothing

Figure 7-5

Areas in Which Small Companies Believe They Have an Advantage over Big Competitors

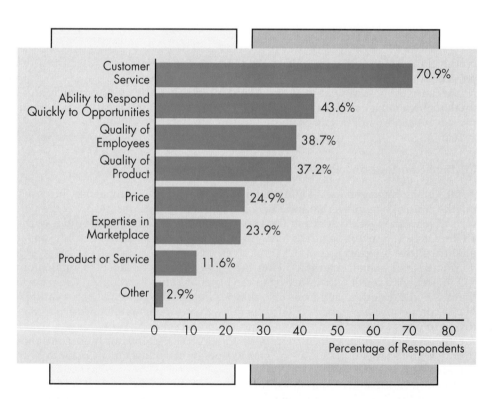

Source: Reprinted with permission, *Inc.* magazine (July 1990). Copyright 1990 by Goldhirsh Group, Inc., 38 Commercial Wharf, Boston, MA 02110.

when they lose a customer.

- In some companies (17 percent), not even salespeople talk to customers. It gets worse for senior management (22 percent don't talk to them), marketing (29 percent), and R&D (67 percent).
- Only 60 percent report that they base their competitive strategy primarily on "attention to customer needs." (And they say that only 29 percent of their competitors emphasize this.)
- Thirty-three percent say that their marketing strategy aims to produce business from new, as opposed to repeat, customers.[25]

It seems fair to say that there is room to improve customer satisfaction.

Evaluating Customer Service

The most common way that problems with customer service are recognized is through customer complaints. Every firm strives to eliminate customer complaints. When they occur, however, they should be analyzed carefully to discover possible weaknesses in customer service.

A customer complaint form can be an effective tool for handling customer complaints. For example, Electronic Controls Co., based in Boise, Idaho, had its customer service team develop a way to tabulate complaints and deal with them systematically. A secretary enters each complaint into a database, which is used to generate a monthly report that summarizes the complaints. "Once we know what the most common complaints are, we can identify what's causing them," says Ed Zimmer, who is in charge of sales and marketing.[26]

Managers can also learn about customer service problems through personal observations and undercover techniques. A manager can evaluate service by talking directly to customers or by playing that role anonymously—for example, by a telephone call to one's own business. Some restaurants and motels invite feedback on customer service by providing comment cards to customers. Whatever method is used, evaluating customer service is essential to any business.

1 Identify the forces that determine the nature and degree of competition within an industry.

- The major forces that determine the level of competition are (1) the threat of new competitors, (2) the threat of substitutes, (3) the bargaining power of buyers, (4) the bargaining power of suppliers, and (5) the rivalry among existing competitors.

2 Identify and compare strategy options for building competitive advantage.

- A firm's competitive advantage can be based on a cost or marketing advantage.
- A cost advantage requires the firm to become the lowest-cost producer.
- Product differentiation is frequently used as a means to gain a marketing advantage.

3 Define the different types of market segmentation strategies.

- Market segmentation, sometimes called a focus strategy, is the process of dividing the total market for a product or service into groups, each of which is likely to respond favorably to a specific marketing strategy.
- The three types of market segmentation strategy are (1) the unsegmented approach, (2) the multisegmentation approach, and (3) the single-segmentation approach.

4 Explain the concept of niche marketing and its importance to small business.

- Selecting a niche market is a special segmentation strategy that small firms can use successfully.
- The choice of a niche strategy encompasses the following activities: (1) strict concentration on a single market segment, (2) concentration on a single product, (3) reliance on close customer contact, (4) restriction to a single geographical region, and (5) emphasis on substantive product superiority.

5 Discuss the importance of customer service to the successful operation of a small business.

- It is important that small firms use outstanding service to gain a competitive advantage.
- Small firms are potentially in a much better position than are large firms to implement a customer satisfaction strategy.
- Total Quality Management is a term describing programs devoted to creating and controlling quality products and customer service.
- A customer complaint form is an effective tool for handling customer complaints.

New Terms and Concepts

competitive
advantage *138*

market
segmentation *142*

unsegmented
strategy *143*

multisegmentation
strategy *144*

single-segmentation
strategy *146*

market *147*

segmentation
variables *147*

benefit
variables *147*

demographic
variables *147*

niche marketing *147*

strategic
decision *148*

customer satisfaction
strategy *151*

total quality
management
(TQM) *153*

You Make the Call

Situation 1   Tom Jones is a retired factory worker who invented a rectangular case with wheels on one end and a retractable handle on the other. The suitcase can hold about four days' worth of clothes and be pulled easily down narrow airplane aisles. Jones exhibited his new product at the luggage industry's 1995 annual trade show. The bag, named Roll'o Bag, created little excitement among buyers. They complained that the suitcase stood on its side, which looked unnatural.

Question 1   What particular market niche, if any, do you think Jones can successfully reach with this product? Why?
Question 2   Do you think he will face an immediate challenge from competitors? If so, how should he react?
Question 3   What type of quality concerns should he have regarding the product?

Situation 2   Amy Wright is the owner of Fit Wright Shoes, a manufacturer of footwear located in Alice, Texas. Her company has pledged that all customers will have a lifetime replacement guarantee on all footwear bought from the company. This guarantee applies to the entire shoe, even though parts of the product are made by another company.

Question 1   Do you think a lifetime guarantee is too generous for this kind of product? Why or why not?
Question 2   What impact will this policy have on quality standards in the company? Be specific.
Question 3   What alternative customer service policies would you suggest?

Situation 3   Shopping cart theft is no small problem: Each cart costs about $100, and the Food Marketing Institute estimates that lost carts total around one million yearly. Carson Anderson believes that there may be a demand for a firm that recovers stolen carts. He plans to target southern California, where over 100,000 carts were stolen in 1994. Anderson estimates his startup capital will be represented by an old truck and a tank of gas.

Question 1   Do you believe there is adequate demand for his service? Why or why not?
Question 2   If he is successful, what sources of competition should he expect?

DISCUSSION QUESTIONS

1. Think of one experience as a buyer of a product or service in which you were extremely displeased. What was the primary reason for your dissatisfaction?
2. What are the two basic strategy options for creating a competitive advantage, as discussed in the chapter?
3. What advantages, if any, does a small firm have in creating a competitive advantage?
4. What are the five forces that dictate competition in any industry? How do they relate to the level of competition?
5. Explain the difference—if any—between a multisegmentation strategy and a single-segmentation strategy. Which one may be more appealing to a small firm? Why?
6. What types of variables are used for market segmentation? Would a small firm use the same variables as a large business? Why or why not?
7. Explain what is meant by the term *niche marketing*.
8. Discuss the role of quality customer service in the creation of a competitive advantage.
9. Think of a recent customer service policy you encountered as a consumer. What made the service you received a special event?
10. What is meant by the term *total quality management*?

EXPERIENTIAL EXERCISES

1. Examine a recent issue of a business publication and report on the type of target market strategy you believe this magazine uses.
2. Visit a local small retailer and ask the manager to describe the firm's customer service policies.

3. Select a new product that is familiar to most of the class. Working in small groups, write a brief but specific description of the best target market for that product. Have a member of each group read the market profile to the class.
4. Interview several friends regarding their satisfaction or dissatisfaction with a shopping experience in a small retail firm. Summarize their stories and report to the class.

 CASE 7
The Fantastic Catalogue Co. (p. 610)

This case describes the experiences of a female entrepreneur as she attempts to gain a competitive advantage in the mail-order market.

Alternative Cases for Chapter 7: Case 8, "ScrubaDub Auto Wash," p. 614
Case 10, "Logan Beach," p. 619

LAYING THE FOUNDATION
Asking the Right Questions

As part of laying the foundation to preparing your own business plan, respond to the following questions regarding your market and customer satisfaction strategies.

Market Strategy Questions

1. What is the nature of your competitive advantage?
2. What is the nature of the cost advantage, if any, of your idea?
3. What is the nature of the marketing advantage, if any, of your idea?
4. Which type of market segmentation strategy do you plan to follow?
5. What market segments exist?
6. What is your target market?
7. What is the profile of your target market customer?
8. What share of the market do you expect to get?
9. Who are your strongest competitors?
10. Are competing businesses growing or declining?
11. What is the future outlook of your competitors?

Customer Satisfaction Questions

1. How will customers benefit by using your product and/or service?
2. What is your customer satisfaction goal?
3. What customer service tactics do you plan to include in your customer satisfaction strategy?
4. What quality control techniques do you plan to include in your customer service program?

USING BizPlanBuilder

If you are using BizPlan*Builder*, refer to Part 3 for information about customers and markets that should be reflected in the business plan. Then turn to Part 2 for instructions on using the BizPlan software to create this section of the plan.

Analyzing the Market and Formulating the Marketing Plan

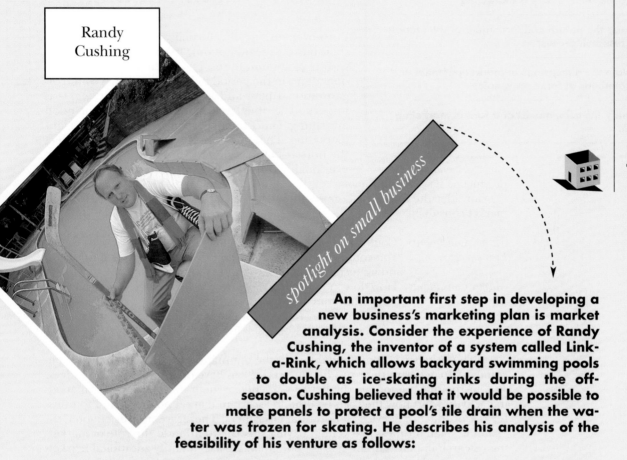

Randy
Cushing

spotlight on small business

An important first step in developing a new business's marketing plan is market analysis. Consider the experience of Randy Cushing, the inventor of a system called Link-a-Rink, which allows backyard swimming pools to double as ice-skating rinks during the off-season. Cushing believed that it would be possible to make panels to protect a pool's tile drain when the water was frozen for skating. He describes his analysis of the feasibility of his venture as follows:

1. *First, I needed to determine if my idea was unique. I asked pool dealers about the existence of such a system. (All advised against skating in a pool.) Then I checked with exhibitors at a pool trade show. No one suggested that such a product existed.*
2. *Next, I paid the National Spa and Pool Institute for data on pool ownership in the United States and Canada. I also studied the average daily temperatures of 290 cities over the past 30 years.*
3. *I then hired as a consultant a former professor . . . [who] was an expert on polymers and plastics and I asked him to determine the most suitable material for the protective panels.*

After being granted a U.S. patent, Cushing searched for and found a manufacturer. Armed with a prototype and marketing research, he raised $500,000 and began selling conversion kits.

Source: Randy Cushing, "The Iceman Cometh to a Pool near You," *Nation's Business*, Vol. 81, No. 11 (November 1993), p. 6 . Quoted by permission. Copyright 1993, U.S. Chamber of Commerce.

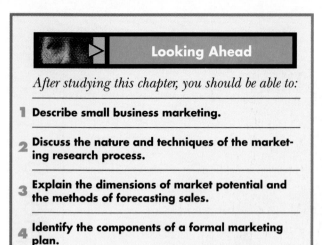

After studying this chapter, you should be able to:

1 Describe small business marketing.

2 Discuss the nature and techniques of the marketing research process.

3 Explain the dimensions of market potential and the methods of forecasting sales.

4 Identify the components of a formal marketing plan.

start here

Entrepreneurs need a formal marketing strategy in their business plan, not only to convince potential investors to commit funds, but also to guide marketing operations in the period following startup. A sound organizational plan and a good financial strategy—as important as they are—cannot substitute for good marketing. Unfortunately, many entrepreneurs slight marketing. They concentrate on the cart and neglect the horse—emphasizing the product or service while overlooking the marketing activities that will pull the product or service into the market.

Consider the following conversation between a first-time entrepreneur and a market consultant:

Market Consultant: "Could I see your marketing plan?"
Entrepreneur: "You could if I had one, but I don't. We have a great product, and we just know people will want to buy it."
Market Consultant: "How do you know that these people will be so eager to buy? Is this what your consumer research indicates?"
Entrepreneur: "I don't have any research but all our friends told us it was a fantastic idea that would sell like hotcakes."

Such optimism is commendable, but the temptation for entrepreneurs to become infatuated with their product or service can have devastating consequences. At some point—the sooner, the better—an entrepreneur must understand marketing activities and how they can be used to ascertain market potential and to transfer the product or service to potential customers. Therefore, in this chapter, we examine small business marketing, paying special attention to the role of marketing research in determining market potential. We also identify additional marketing activities that can help transform the entrepreneur's idea into reality and become part of the formal marketing section of the business plan.[1] More detailed discussions of marketing strategy are found in Chapters 13–16.

SMALL BUSINESS MARKETING

1 Describe small business marketing.

Marketing was once viewed simply as the performance of business activities that affect the flow of goods and services from producer to consumer or user. Note that this definition implies that distribution is the essence of marketing. Other definitions portray marketing as little more than selling. Unfortunately, some entrepreneurs still choose to view marketing in this simplistic manner. In reality, marketing consists of numerous activities, many of which occur even before a product is produced and ready for distribution and sale.

In order to portray the true scope of small business marketing, we use a more comprehensive definition. **Small business marketing** consists of those business activities that relate directly to (1) identifying a target market, (2) determining target market potential, and (3) preparing, communicating, and delivering a bundle of satisfaction to the target market.

small business marketing
identifying target markets, assessing their potential, and delivering satisfaction

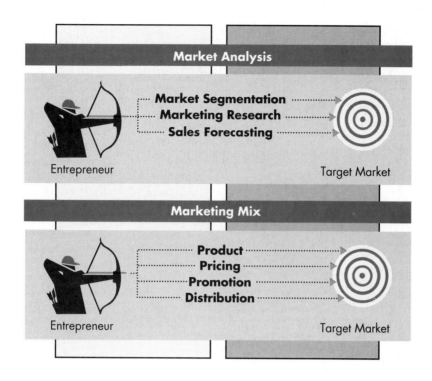

Figure 8-1

Small Business Marketing Activities

This task-oriented definition encompasses marketing activities essential to every small business. A condensed representation of the more essential activities is presented in Figure 8-1. The arrows represent the marketing activities emphasized in this chapter. Market segmentation, marketing research, and sales forecasting are integral parts of what is commonly called **market analysis**. Product, pricing, promotion, and distribution activities combine to form the firm's **marketing mix**.

market analysis
evaluation process that encompasses market segmentation, marketing research, and sales forecasting

marketing mix
product, pricing, promotion, and distribution activities

Adopting a Consumer Orientation

An individual's personal philosophy about life will influence the tactics she or he uses to achieve a personal goal. For example, a person who believes that others should be treated with the same respect that she or he would like to receive will probably not cheat or defraud another person. Similarly, a football coach who believes in "three yards and a cloud of dust" will use the running attack rather than passing as a major offensive weapon. Likewise, an entrepreneur's marketing philosophy shapes a firm's marketing activities.

Historically, three distinct marketing philosophies have been evident among firms. These are commonly referred to as the production-oriented, sales-oriented, and consumer-oriented philosophies. For a firm subscribing to a production-oriented philosophy, the product is the most important part of the business. The firm concentrates on producing the product in the most efficient manner, even if this means slighting promotion, distribution, and other marketing activities. A business operating with a sales-oriented philosophy de-emphasizes production efficiencies and customer preferences in favor of making sales. Finally, a firm may hold a consumer-oriented philosophy, which says that everything, including production and sales, originates with consumer needs. The priority is the customer; all marketing efforts begin and end with the consumer.

A business that subscribes to a consumer-oriented philosophy places customer satisfaction above all other concerns. This tailor's reputation depends on his ability to fashion clothing to meet his customer's individual needs.

Beginning in the late nineteenth century, U.S. businesses have gradually shifted their marketing emphasis from production to sales and, more recently, to the consumer. Is this same evolution necessary within a new small business? It need not be. Indeed, it *should* not be. A small business can *begin* with a consumer orientation. Is this philosophy more consistent with success? The answer is yes. No matter what the type of business, nothing is better than a consumer orientation.

The production- and sales-oriented philosophies may each occasionally permit success. However, the consumer orientation is preferable because it not only recognizes production efficiency goals and professional selling but also adds concern for customer satisfaction. In effect, a firm that adopts a consumer orientation is incorporating the best of each philosophy. Remember, customer satisfaction is not a means to achieving a certain goal; rather, it *is* the goal!

Factors That Influence a Marketing Philosophy

Why have some small firms failed to adopt a consumer orientation? The answer lies in three key factors. First, the state of competition always affects a firm's orientation. If there is little or no competition and if demand exceeds supply, a firm is likely to emphasize production efficiency. This is usually a short-run situation, however, and one that can lead to disaster.

Second, small business managers show a wide range of interests and abilities. For example, some small business managers are strongest in production and weakest in sales. Naturally, production considerations receive their primary attention.

Third, some managers are simply shortsighted. A sales-oriented philosophy, for example, is a shortsighted approach to marketing. Emphasis on moving merchandise can often create customer dissatisfaction, if high-pressure selling is used with little regard for customers' needs. On the other hand, a consumer orientation contributes to long-term survival by emphasizing customer satisfaction.

2 Discuss the nature and techniques of the marketing research process.

MARKETING RESEARCH FOR THE NEW VENTURE

Entrepreneurs can make marketing decisions based on intuition alone, or they can supplement their judgment with sound market information. It is often a good idea to put entrepreneurial enthusiasm on hold until marketing research facts are collected and evaluated. A survey of 173 small to medium-size companies in the United States demonstrated that these firms use a variety of marketing research sources for new products and services. As shown in Figure 8-2, current customers, networking (contact with other key people), gut instinct, and the polling of potential customers are the top four sources of market information.

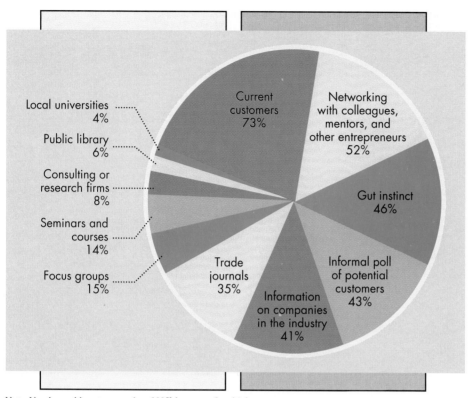

Note: Numbers add up to more than 100% because of multiple responses.

Source: A survey of 173 CEOs, 57% with sales of $10 million or less, by *Inc.* and The Executive Committee, San Diego, 1992. *Inc.*, Vol. 14, No. 6 (June 1992), p. 108. Reprinted with permission, *Inc.* magazine, June 1992. Copyright 1992 by Goldhirsh Group, Inc., 38 Commercial Wharf, Boston, MA 02110.

Figure 8-2

Top Sources of Market Research for New Products

As important as marketing research can be, it should never be used to suppress entrepreneurship and a hands-on feel for the market. It should be viewed as a supplement—not a replacement—for intuitive judgment and a sense of "cautious experimentation in launching new products and services."[2]

Nature of Marketing Research

Marketing research may be defined as the gathering, processing, reporting, and interpreting of market information. A small business typically conducts less marketing research than a big business, partly because of a lack of understanding of the basic research process. Our discussion of marketing research will emphasize the more widely used practical techniques that small business firms can use as they analyze their market and make other operating decisions.

Cost is another reason why small firms tend to neglect research. A manager should compare the cost of research with the expected benefits. Although such analysis is difficult, it will often show that marketing research can be conducted within resource limits. For example, Biosite Diagnostics, Inc., a six-year-old biotechnology startup in San Diego, California, commissioned two market surveys at a cost of $150,000. Biosite hired a research firm first to survey physicians and laboratory technicians and then to conduct focus groups of about 100 potential users of its drug-testing device. The company used the research information to help redefine

marketing research gathering, processing, reporting, and interpreting market information

Action Report

ENTREPRENEURIAL EXPERIENCES

Surveying Customers

Of the many potential sources of market information, one of the most important is customers. Surveying customers and potential customers is a smart strategy.

Christopher Fish, owner of Northwest Industrial Coatings (NIC) in White City, Oregon, can attest to that. He conducted a simple customer survey four years ago and learned about customer dissatisfaction:

But while Fish's questionnaire showed that his customers were satisfied with the quality of NIC's work, they were finding it hard to place orders [by telephone]. "We were surprised that the phone lines were so tied up. On our end things seemed to be rolling along smoothly with four lines," says Fish.

In response to this information, NIC installed new telephone and fax lines. Fish has continued to conduct customer surveys to assist in developing NIC's marketing plan.

Source: Kim T. Gordon, "Tuning In to Your Customers," *Independent Business*, Vol. 4, No. 1 (January-February 1993), p. 24.

---

its potential market and reshape its business strategy. Biosite also used this relatively costly research to approach investors. "That may have turned off investors who like to invest in grander schemes, but it greatly helped our ability to be a real operating company," says Kim Blickenstaff, Biosite's co-founder.[3] In this case, the benefits justified the investment in marketing research.

Although an entrepreneur can frequently conduct useful marketing research without the assistance of an expert, the cost of hiring such an expert can be considered a bargain, especially if the results of a study greatly increase revenues or cut costs. Marketing researchers are trained, experienced professionals, not unlike attorneys or architects. Accordingly, the first-time research buyer may be startled by prices for research services. For example, focus groups run about $3,000 to $10,000 each, and a telephone survey could range anywhere from $5,000 to $25,000 or more, depending on the number of interviews and the length of the questionnaire.

Because costs of this size represent a substantial investment for most small businesses, owners should ask themselves the following questions before contacting a research firm:

- *Is the research really necessary?* In some cases, maybe a "best guess" would prove just as effective as a well-designed research project. In other cases, however, research may be absolutely necessary. For example, many lending institutions require a feasibility study of a proposed business idea, using marketing research, before they make any loan.
- *Is the research worth doing?* Will the outcome of the research result in a benefit exceeding the cost of the research itself? Spending $20,000 on a research project to realize an increase in company revenues of $1,000 a year simply doesn't make sense.
- *Can I do the research myself?* This is probably the hardest question to answer. You must be able to determine the complexity of the research problem and the risk

involved if the research was not done. To strike an analogy, several companies offer do-it-yourself legal guides that allow the small business owner to create contracts, incorporate, and so forth. If you feel comfortable with this type of approach, fine; if not, see an attorney. The same holds true for marketing research.[4]

Steps in the Marketing Research Process

An understanding of good research methodology helps a manager evaluate the validity of research done by others and better direct his or her own efforts. Typical steps in the marketing research procedure include identifying informational needs, searching for secondary data, collecting primary data, and interpreting the data gathered.

IDENTIFY THE INFORMATIONAL NEED   The first step in marketing research is to identify and define the informational need. Although this may seem too obvious to mention, the fact is that entrepreneurs sometimes conduct surveys without pinpointing the specific information that is relevant to their venture. For example, an entrepreneur contemplating a location for a restaurant may conduct a survey to ascertain customer menu preferences and reasons for eating out when, in fact, the more relevant informational needs are whether residents of the area ever eat out and how far they are willing to drive to eat in a restaurant.

In another situation, an entrepreneur may specifically define his or her informational need correctly. With a precise definition, the survey that is conducted can concentrate on the specific need. Figure 8-3 displays a survey questionnaire developed by an entrepreneur to ascertain customer satisfaction. This businessperson determined his informational need to be "what are customers' attitudes concerning the car wash I have purchased."

SEARCH FOR SECONDARY DATA   Information that has already been compiled is known as **secondary data.** Generally speaking, secondary data is less expensive to gather than new data. Therefore, a small business should exhaust all available sources of secondary data before going further into the research process. Marketing decisions can often be made on the basis of secondary data. "It's a myth that only the big guys have the wherewithal to do market research," says Mary Beth Campau, assistant vice-president for reference services at Dun & Bradstreet Information Services. "There is a wealth of timely information from a variety of sources available in public and university libraries throughout the United States. Just ask the librarians, and they'll be happy to point you in the right direction."[5]

secondary data
market information that has been previously compiled by others

Secondary data may be internal or external. *Internal* secondary data consists of information that exists within the firm. *External* secondary data abounds in numerous periodicals, trade association publications, private information services, and government publications. A helpful source of external data for the small business is the Small Business Administration (SBA). This agency publishes extensive bibliographies relating to many decision areas, including market analysis. The SBA also provides a nationwide electronic bulletin board called SBA On-Line, which has these features:

- Internet E-mail that allows users to communicate and network with other online service users worldwide
- The new Reach Strategic Venture Partner program, which provides growth opportunities for small exporters through international trade leads, such as a list of foreign companies interested in forming joint ventures with U.S. businesses

TECHNOLOGY

Figure 8-3

*Small Business Survey
Questionnaire*

PLEASE—WE NEED YOUR HELP!

You're The Boss. All of us here at Genie Car Wash have just one purpose . . .
TO PLEASE YOU!

Date _____   Time _____ of Visit

How are we doing?

1. Personnel—courteous and helpful?   **Yes**   **No**
   Service writer ....   ☐   ☐
   Vacuum attendants ....   ☐   ☐
   Cashier ....   ☐   ☐
   Final finish & inspection ....   ☐   ☐
   Management ....   ☐   ☐

2. Do you feel the time it took to wash your car was . . .
   Right amount of time ....   ☐
   Too much time ....   ☐
   Not enough time ....   ☐

3. How do you judge the appearance of the personnel? **Excel** **Good** **Avg** **Poor**
                                                          ☐   ☐   ☐   ☐

4. Please rate the quality of workmanship on the interior
   of your car.
   Inside vacuum ....   ☐   ☐   ☐   ☐
   Dashboard ....   ☐   ☐   ☐   ☐
   Doorjambs ....   ☐   ☐   ☐   ☐
   Ash trays ....   ☐   ☐   ☐   ☐
   Windows ....   ☐   ☐   ☐   ☐
   Console ....   ☐   ☐   ☐   ☐

5. Please rate the quality of workmanship on the exterior
   of your car.
   Tires and wheels ....   ☐   ☐   ☐   ☐
   Bumpers and chrome ....   ☐   ☐   ☐   ☐
   Body of car ....   ☐   ☐   ☐   ☐
   Grill ....   ☐   ☐   ☐   ☐

6. Please rate the overall appearance of our facility.
   Outside building & grounds ....   ☐   ☐   ☐   ☐
   Inside building ....   ☐   ☐   ☐   ☐
   Rest rooms ....   ☐   ☐   ☐   ☐

7. Please rate your overall impression of the experience
   you had while at Genie Car Wash. ....   ☐   ☐   ☐   ☐

*It is important that we clean your car to your satisfaction. Additional comments will be
appreciated.*

_____

_____

_____

OPTIONAL Your Name _____

Address _____

City _____ State _____ Zip _____

Thank you!

- Information on government contracting opportunities and a collateral purchases database that contains information on equipment, land, or business property sales
- Access to the SBA's extensive network of local resources and small business management experts, including the newest feature, Ask SCORE, which allows users to communicate directly with the Service Corps of Retired Executives (SCORE) counselors by leaving a message in the Ask SCORE mailbox (all inquiries are confidential and are answered within 48 hours)
- Access to more than 60 other government agencies' electronic bulletin boards and listings for contacting other groups, including the U.S. Senate and House of Representatives, the IRS, the U.S. Patent and Trademark Office, chambers of commerce, and other agencies
- Downloadable application forms such as the Procurement Automated Source System application for companies seeking to do business with the federal government and the SBA's new LowDoc loan form, a one-page loan application designed to simplify the loan process for qualified applicants
- Communication via E-mail, enabling entrepreneurs in fields such as advertising, aviation, computer services, education, mail order, and more to discuss business issues with others who share their interests.[6]

Another well-known source of secondary data is Dun & Bradstreet, which provides many kinds of useful information.

A wealth of D&B information is also available at libraries. A parachute maker in New Jersey who was planning to export his product abroad was pleasantly shocked to discover a D&B book called the Exporters' Encyclopedia that gave him the nuts and bolts of exporting. Available in well-stocked libraries' business sections, the Encyclopedia gave him a crash course in exporting basics, from government regulations to documentation requirements.

Start-up and established businesses alike can take advantage of D&B reference sources, including State Sales Guides, D&B's Regional Business Directories, D&B's family of CD-ROM products and many others.

A good place to start is with D&B's State Sales Guides. These 51 volumes, which cover all the states plus the District of Columbia, let entrepreneurs quickly check a company's estimated financial condition and overall credit appraisal by looking at its D&B rating. The guides also provide the telephone number, the Standard Industrial Classification code, and the year the business was started.

To help identify new prospects, qualify sales leads and assess market potential, more detailed information can be found in one of D&B's Regional Business Directories. Besides basic information (telephone number, address and company description), the directories also tell you when the company was started, sales volume, number of employees, parent company (if any) and, if it's a public company, on which exchange it's traded.

If you're planning to develop a targeted marketing campaign, [you might consult] D&B's Million Dollar Disc family, which includes three CD-ROM disks. The first lists the 200,000 businesses in the United States that do more than $25 million in sales annually, employ 250 or more people, or have a net worth of $500,000 or more. The second disk lists 150,000 middle-market companies, and the third covers 200,000 public administration and service businesses, including nonmanufacturing enterprises such as government agencies, police and fire departments, doctors, lawyers and other consultants. This CD-ROM series also includes biographical information on company owners or officers, giving you insight into their background and business experience.

For a wide view of your potential marketplace there's D&B's Census of American Business, a directory that lists business characteristics in each state, providing statistics on industries and the number of workers by region of the country. If you're considering opening a gas station, restaurant or pizza chain, for example, the directory can tell you how many people are employed in a region, thus pinpointing potential markets for your products or potential labor sources.

For more specialized targets, there's D&B's Directory of Service Companies, which lists 50,000 service companies in the United States, and D&B's Health Care Directory, a hefty tome listing health-care suppliers and providers (hospitals, nursing homes, hospices, pharmaceutical companies, distributors, insurers and more).[7]

The list of secondary data sources goes on and on. Entrepreneurs should always consult local libraries for assistance in identifying these sources.

Unfortunately, several problems accompany the use of secondary data. One problem is that such data may be outdated and, therefore, less useful. Another problem is that the units of measure in the secondary data may not fit a current problem. For example, a firm's market might consist of individuals with incomes between $20,000 and $25,000, while the secondary data show the number of individuals with incomes between $15,000 and $50,000. Finally, the question of credibility is always present. Some sources of secondary data are less trustworthy than others. Mere publication of data does not in itself make the data valid and reliable.

COLLECT PRIMARY DATA   If the secondary data are insufficient, a search for new information, or **primary data,** is the next step. Several techniques can be used in accumulating primary data. These techniques are often classified as observational methods and questioning methods. Observational methods avoid contact with respondents, while questioning methods involve some degree of contact with respondents.

primary data
market information that is gathered by the entrepreneur through various methods

Observational Methods   Observation is probably the oldest form of research in existence. Indeed, learning by observing is quite common. Thus, it is hardly surprising that observation can provide useful information for small businesses. An excellent example of observational research has been conducted by Jack Kahl, president and CEO of Manco, Inc., which markets a line of tapes, weather stripping, and mailing supplies. Since 1977, Kahl has transformed Manco into a major retail supplier by observing the strategy of such big firms as Wal-Mart. "You've got to keep your eyes on the giants all the time," Kahl says. "All I know is that if I study excellent companies, I come up with excellent ideas."[8]

Observational methods can be very economical. Furthermore, they avoid the potential bias that can result from a respondent's contact with an interviewer during questioning. Observation—as in counting customers going in a store, for example—can be conducted by a person or by mechanical devices, such as hidden video cameras. Mechanical observation devices are rapidly coming down in cost, bringing them within the budget of many small businesses.

Questioning Methods   Both surveys and experimentation are questioning methods that involve contact with respondents. Surveys can be conducted by mail, telephone, or personal interviews. Mail surveys are often used when respondents are widely dispersed; however, they usually yield low response rates. Telephone surveys and personal interview surveys achieve higher response rates. However, personal interview surveys are more expensive than either mail or telephone surveys. Moreover, individuals are often reluctant to grant personal interviews because they feel that a sales pitch is forthcoming.

A questionnaire is the basic instrument for guiding the researcher and the respondent when surveys are being taken. The questionnaire should be developed carefully and pretested before it is used in the market. Several major considerations should be kept in mind when designing and testing a questionnaire:

Action Report

TECHNOLOGICAL APPLICATIONS

TECHNOLOGY

Surveys Pay Dividends

Small businesses sometimes avoid customer surveying because they are afraid that direct contact will annoy customers and thereby have a negative impact on goodwill for the firm. Computer technology applied to surveying is helping lessen this concern.

One example is an electronic desktop device called the "Point of View" survey box. This device is about the size of a laptop computer and has two rows of large keyboard numbers. When a respondent presses a start button, the display asks questions and the response is entered via the keyboard.

Small firms exhibiting at trade shows have used the device successfully, according to Bill Lipscomb, a marketing consultant from Georgetown, Texas. With this technology, Lipscomb says, "We're able to ask questions, get tabulated answers, graphs, and reports quickly." This device provides feedback from people viewing a firm's display booth with minimal effort on their part.

Source: Eric J. Adams, "Boost Your Booth Power with the Latest Tech Wizardy," *Independent Business*, Vol. 5, No. 1 (January-February, 1994), pp. 40–42.

- Ask questions that relate to the decision under consideration. An "interesting" question may not be relevant. Assume an answer to each question, and then ask yourself how you would use that information. This provides a good test of relevance.
- Select a form of question that is appropriate for the subject and the conditions of the survey. Open-ended and multiple-choice questions are two popular forms.
- Carefully consider the order of the questions. The wrong sequence can cause biases in answers to later questions.
- Ask the more sensitive questions near the end of the questionnaire. Age and income, for example, are usually sensitive subjects.
- Carefully select the words of each question. They should be as simple, clear, and objective as possible.
- Pre-test the questionnaire by administering it to a small sample of respondents representative of the group to be surveyed.

Refer to the questionnaire shown in Figure 8-3 on page 166 which was developed by a car wash owner. This survey instrument illustrates how the above considerations can be incorporated into a questionnaire. Note the use of both multiple-choice and open-ended questions. Responses to the open-ended request were particularly useful for this firm.

INTERPRET THE DATA   After the necessary data have been accumulated, they should be transformed into usable information. Large quantities of data are only facts without a purpose. They must be organized and molded into meaningful information. Numerous methods of summarizing and simplifying information for users include tables, charts, and other graphic methods. Descriptive statistics such as the mean, mode, and median are most helpful during this step in the research procedure. Inexpensive personal computer software is now available to perform statistical calculations and generate report-quality graphics. Some of these programs are identified in Chapter 21.

It should be re-emphasized that formal marketing research is not always necessary when launching a new venture. Bill Madway, founder and president of Madway Business Research, Inc. in Malvern, Pennsylvania, says, "Sometimes, you cannot answer a question with research . . . you just have to test it. Then the question is whether you can afford to test something that might not work. If there's very little risk involved or you can test it on a very small scale, you might decide to jump in. But the bigger the risk, the more valuable advance information becomes."[9]

ESTIMATING MARKET POTENTIAL

3 Explain the dimensions of market potential and the methods of forecasting sales.

A small business can be successful only if an adequate market exists for its product or service. The sales forecast is the typical indicator of adequacy. A sales estimate is particularly important prior to starting a business. Without it, the entrepreneur enters the marketplace much like a high diver who leaves the board without checking the depth of the water. Many types of information from numerous sources are required for determining market potential. In this section, we examine the ingredients of a market and the forecasting process.

Ingredients of a Market

The term *market* means different things to different people. Sometimes, it refers to a location where buying and selling take place, as in "They went to the market." On other occasions, the term is used to describe selling efforts, as when business managers say, "We must market this product aggressively." Still another meaning is the one we emphasize in this chapter: A **market** is a group of customers or potential customers who have purchasing power and unsatisfied needs. Note carefully the three ingredients in this definition of a market.

market
a group of customers or potential customers who have purchasing power and unsatisfied needs

First, a market must have buying units, or *customers*. These units may be individuals or business entities. For example, consumer products are sold to individuals, and industrial products are sold to business users. Thus, a market is more than a geographic area. It must contain potential customers.

Second, customers in a market must have *purchasing power*. Assessing the level of purchasing power in a potential market is very important. Customers who have unsatisfied needs but who lack money and/or credit are poor markets because they have nothing to offer in exchange for a product or service. In such a situation, no transactions can occur.

Third, a market must contain buying units with *unsatisfied needs*. Consumers, for instance, will not buy unless they are motivated to do so. Motivation can occur only when an individual recognizes unsatisfied needs. It would be difficult, for example, to sell luxury urban apartments to desert nomads! (Chapter 13 investigates consumer behavior characteristics more fully.)

In light of our definition of a market, therefore, determining market potential is the process of locating and investigating buying units that have purchasing power and needs that can be satisfied with the product or service that is being offered.

The Sales Forecast

sales forecast
a prediction of how much will be purchased within a market during a defined time period

Formally defined, a **sales forecast** estimates how much of a product or service will be purchased within a given market for a defined time period. The estimate can be stated in terms of dollars and/or units.

Note that a sales forecast revolves around a specific target market; therefore, the market should be defined as precisely as possible. The market description forms the forecasting boundary. For example, consider the sales forecast for a manual shaving device. If the market for this product is described simply as "men," the sales forecast will probably be extremely large. A more precise definition, such as "men between the ages of 15 and 25 who are dissatisfied with electric shavers," will result in a smaller but more useful forecast.

Also note that the sales forecast implies a defined time period. One sales forecast may cover a year or less, while another may extend over several years. Both short-term and long-term forecasts are needed in a well-constructed business plan.

A sales forecast for wool might be used to determine how many sheep should be sheared within a given time period or to provide an estimate of the dollar amount that can be expected in return for the sheep's wool.

The sales forecast is a critical component of the business plan for assessing the feasibility of a new venture. If the market is insufficient, the business is destined for failure. The sales forecast is also useful in other areas of business planning. Production schedules, inventory policies, and personnel decisions—to name a few—all start with the sales forecast. Obviously, forecasts can never be perfect. Furthermore, the entrepreneur should remember that a forecast can be wrong in either of two directions—underestimating potential sales or overestimating potential sales.

Limitations to Forecasting

For a number of practical reasons, forecasting is used less frequently by small firms than by large firms. First, forecasting circumstances in a new business are unique. Entrepreneurial inexperience coupled with a new idea present the most difficult forecasting situation, as illustrated in Figure 8-4. An ongoing business that needs only an updated forecast for its existing product is in the most favorable forecasting position.

Second, a small business manager may be unfamiliar with methods of quantitative analysis. This is not to say that all forecasting must be quantitatively oriented. Qualitative forecasting is helpful and may be sufficient. However, quantitative methods have proven their value in forecasting over and over again.

Third, the typical small business entrepreneur lacks familiarity with the forecasting process and/or personnel with such skills. To overcome these deficiencies, some small firms attempt to keep in touch with industry trends through contacts with appropriate trade associations. Because it has professional staff members, a trade association is frequently better qualified to engage in business forecasting. Most libraries have a copy of *National Trade and Professional Associations of the United States*, which lists these groups. Entrepreneurs can also provide themselves with current information about business trends by regularly reading trade publications and economic newsletters such as the *Kiplinger Washington Letter, Business Week*, and *The Wall Street Journal*. Government publications, such as *Survey of Current Business*, the *Federal Reserve Bulletin*, and *Monthly Labor Review*, are also of interest in a general

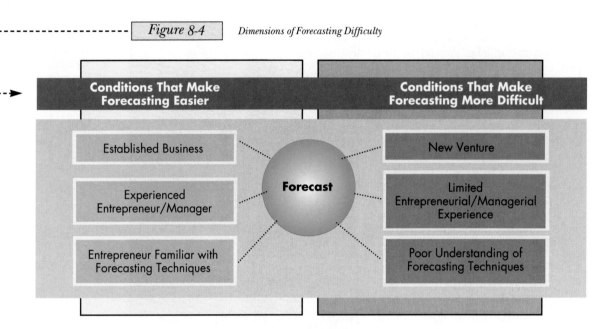

Figure 8-4 Dimensions of Forecasting Difficulty

way. Subscribing to professional forecasting services is a way to obtain forecasts of general business conditions or specific forecasts for given industries.

Despite the limitations, a small business entrepreneur should not slight the forecasting task. Instead, he or she should remember how important the sales outlook is to the business plan when obtaining financing. The statement "We can sell as many as we can produce" does not satisfy the information requirements of potential investors.

The Forecasting Process

Estimating market demand with a sales forecast is a multistep process. Typically, the sales forecast is a composite of several individual forecasts, so the process of sales forecasting involves merging these individual forecasts properly.

The forecasting process can be characterized by two important dimensions: (1) the point at which the process is started, and (2) the nature of the predicting variable. The starting point is usually designated by the term *breakdown process* or *buildup process*. The nature of the predicting variable is denoted by either direct forecasting or indirect forecasting.

breakdown process a forecasting method that begins with a macro-level variable and works down to the sales forecast

THE STARTING POINT A **breakdown process,** sometimes called a chain-ratio method, begins with a variable that has a very large scope and systematically works down to the sales forecast. This method is frequently used for consumer products forecasting. The initial variable might be a population figure encompassing the targeted market. By the use of percentages, the appropriate link is built to generate the sales forecast. For example, consider the market segment identified in Chapter 7 (page 144) by the hypothetical company, the Community Writing Company. Let's now assume that the targeted market is older students (25 years of age or over) seeking convenience and erasability in their writing instrument. Assume further that the initial geographic target is the state of Idaho. Table 8-1 outlines the breakdown process. Obviously, the more links in the forecasting chain, the greater the potential for error.

Table 8-1

Sales Forecasting with the Breakdown Method

Linking Variable	Source	Estimating Value	Market Potential*
1. Idaho state population	U.S. census of population		1,000,000
2. State population in target age category	*Sales & Marketing Management Survey of Buying Power*	12%	120,000
3. Target age enrolled in colleges and universities	Idaho Department of Education	30%	36,000
4. Target age college students preferring convenience over price	Student survey in a marketing research class	50%	18,000
5. Convenience-oriented students likely to purchase new felt-tip pen within next month	Personal telephone interview by entrepreneur	75%	13,500
6. People who say they are likely to purchase who actually buy	Article in *Journal of Consumer Research*	35%	4,725
7. Average number of pens bought per year	Personal experience of entrepreneur	4 units	18,900
SALES FORECAST FOR IDAHO		18,900 units	

*Figures in this column, for variables 2–7, are derived by multiplying the percentage or number in the estimating value column times the amount on the previous line of the market potential column.

Kenneth Seiff, founder of Pivot Corporation, used the breakdown method to estimate the market for his company's golf-related sportswear. The 25 million U.S. golfers, as estimated by the National Golf Foundation, served as his starting point—with particular emphasis on the large segment in the 20- to 29-year-old range. His research suggested that about half of these golfers play less than seven times a year. Furthermore, he estimated that many of these occasional golfers never saw the inside of a country club but would nevertheless purchase a golf shirt or sweater from a store. He concluded that there is a market niche of adequate size for golf-related sportswear. Pivot's sportswear is now in such upscale stores as Nordstrom and Bloomingdale's.[10]

In contrast to the breakdown process, the **buildup process** calls for identifying all potential buyers in a market's submarkets and then adding up the estimated demand. For example, a local dry-cleaning firm forecasting demand for cleaning high school letter jackets might first estimate its market share as 20 percent within each school. Then, by determining the number of high school students obtaining a letter jacket in each area school—maybe from the school yearbook—a total could be forecasted.

The buildup method is especially helpful for industrial goods forecasting. Data from the census of manufacturers by the U.S. Department of Commerce is often used to estimate potential. The information can be broken down according to the Standard Industrial Classification (SIC) code—a classification system that presents information according to the type of industry. This classification system identifies potential industrial customers by SIC code, allowing the forecaster to obtain information on the number of establishments and their geographic location, number of employees, and annual sales. By summing this information for several relevant SIC codes, a sales potential can be constructed.

buildup process
a forecasting method that identifies all potential buyers in submarkets and adds up the estimated demand

Action Report

ENTREPRENEURIAL EXPERIENCES

Learning to Forecast

Sales forecasting is vital to a complete business plan, and it continues to be an important guide for ongoing marketing activities. An important characteristic of successful forecasting for any small firm is employee participation. For example, employees contribute to the forecasting process developed by Alan Burkhard, CEO of The Placers, Inc., a temporary-personnel and job search firm based in Wilmington, Delaware. At The Placers, the forecasting process runs from October to December each year, and every employee is involved. Burkhard implemented the current forecasting process after several early years of "guesstimating" that never worked out. The five essential phases of his forecasting system are summarized as follows:

1. *The preplanning session.* An initial all-day meeting with the senior management team to set the overall tone and context that will guide the process is held in mid-October. Issues such as current market trends and competitive developments are discussed.
2. *The leadership session.* The executive vice-president of operations meets next with the company's "leadership" team—the 12 employees who supervise offices or departments. This group generates actual numbers for sales and expenditures reflecting the overall "picture" of the market set by senior management.
3. *The research process.* During November, all employees, guided by a worksheet, project how many temporaries will be placed at each location, corresponding billing rates, and operating expenses. To obtain good numbers, salespeople are encouraged to telephone major clients.
4. *Collation of results.* Department heads collect each employee's projections and enter the numbers into the company computer. Burkhard and his management team analyze this data and suggest changes where appropriate.
5. *The final forecast.* By December, the final forecast is compiled and then circulated to each employee by the first of the next year.

On a weekly basis, all salespeople are sent budget updates comparing forecasted sales with actual results. "We tell people we expect them to stay on target. And, if they're not meeting their forecasted numbers, they've got to figure out why not, how they can adjust their performance, and whether variances represent problems for the business," says Burkhard.

Source: Jill Andresky Fraser, "On Target," *Inc.*, Vol. 13, No. 4 (April 1991), pp. 113–114. Reprinted with permission, *Inc.* magazine, April 1991, Copyright 1991 by Goldhirsh Group, Inc., 38 Commercial Wharf, Boston, MA 02110.

direct forecasting
a forecasting method that uses sales as the predicting variable

indirect forecasting
a forecasting method that uses variables related to sales to project the sales forecast

THE PREDICTING VARIABLE In **direct forecasting,** sales is the forecasted variable. This is the simplest form of forecasting. Many times, however, sales cannot be predicted directly and other variables must be used. **Indirect forecasting** takes place when these surrogate variables are used to project the sales forecast. For example, a firm may lack information about industry sales of baby cribs but may have data on births. The figures for births can help forecast industry sales for baby cribs because of the strong correlation between the two variables.

COMPONENTS OF THE FORMAL MARKETING PLAN

4 Identify the components of a formal marketing plan.

After market analysis is completed, the entrepreneur is ready to write the formal marketing plan. Each business venture is different, and, therefore, each marketing plan will be unique. An entrepreneur should not feel that he or she must develop a cloned version of a plan created by someone else. The marketing plan should include sections on market analysis, the competition, and marketing strategy. In this section, we describe these major elements of the formal marketing plan. A more detailed discussion of marketing activities and strategies for both new and ongoing small businesses is provided in Chapters 13–16.

Market Analysis

In the market analysis section of the marketing plan, the entrepreneur should describe the customers in the targeted market. This description of potential customers is commonly called a **customer profile.** Information compiled with marketing research—both secondary and primary data—can be used to construct this profile. A detailed discussion of the major customer benefits provided by the new product or service should be included. Obviously, these benefits must be reasonable and consistent with statements in the "Products and Services" section of the business plan.

customer profile
a description of potential customers

Advances in computer software allow small business owners to evaluate potential markets much more quickly and to include professional market profiles in the business plan. Consider the following description of one such software program:

> One of the newest software products for uncovering niche markets is ArcView II, from Environmental Systems Research Institute Inc. (ESRI) in Redlands, California. Designed for the computer novice, it uses Geographic Information Systems (GIS), which guided soldiers and missiles to targets in the Persian Gulf War, and has been used to analyze crime patterns; now, you can use it to identify new markets.
>
> "The GIS links graphic [map] information to [database] information to reveal more than either set of data would provide alone," says ESRI spokesperson Mike Michelsen, Jr. "By moving a mouse and typing a command, you can call up a color-coded map displaying the desired information."
>
> For example, suppose you're a restaurant supplier considering selling your products in a new territory. ArcView offers a computerized map showing the location of your current and potential customers, highlighted with sales figures, competitors, and even the best way to service these locations. ArcView is available in many libraries, or can be purchased for about $495. Specific information costs around $195, depending on the type of information and how detailed it is.[11]

TECHNOLOGY

If an entrepreneur envisions several target markets, each segment must have its corresponding customer profile. Likewise, several target markets may necessitate an equal number of different marketing strategies.

Another major element of market analysis is the actual sales forecast. It is usually desirable to include more than one sales forecast. The three sales scenarios of "most likely," "pessimistic," and "optimistic" provide investors and the entrepreneur with different forecasts on which to base their evaluation.

As we pointed out earlier in this chapter, forecasting sales for a new venture is extremely difficult. Assumptions will be necessary but should be minimized. The forecasting method should be described and supported by empirical data wherever feasible.

Action Report

ENTREPRENEURIAL EXPERIENCES

A Prisoner to Competition

The reality of competition is sometimes found in strange places—even behind bars. Several small companies, producing products ranging from draperies to audio cables, are facing a marketing disadvantage resulting from government contracts being given Federal Prison Industries, Inc., which is a government corporation operating under the name Unicor.

The traditional prison-shop activity of stamping out license plates has evolved into a "professional-looking catalog listing 150 products in 46 industries." Small firms contend the prison industry is encroaching unfairly on their potential markets. Richard Secter, Unicor's chief executive, says a recent market study found Unicor's impact on the private sector to be "insignificant."

However, Stephen Heller, who operates Hiltronics, a family business in Stony Point, New York, contends prison-made products are forcing the shutdown of his company. Hiltronics makes one product—audio cables used in airplanes and helicopters. Its military orders have dropped to one from two dozen four years ago.

Also, Thomas W. Raftery, Inc., a drapery manufacturer in Hartford, Connecticut, saw its government sales slide last year after Unicor began bidding on government drapery orders. "We became pretty dependent on the federal market, [and] they simply took the customers away from us," says Gary Rigolletti, Raftery's president.

Small business is lobbying for a change, according to Leslie Aubin, a representative of the National Federation of Independent Business. "It's fine for prisoners to have factories. . . . We're just asking for a level playing field," she says.

Source: Eugene Carlson, "Some Small Companies Find Competition Is in Prisons," *The Wall Street Journal*, December 9, 1991, p. B2. Reprinted by permission of *The Wall Street Journal*, © 1991 Dow Jones & Company, Inc. All Rights Reserved Worldwide.

The Competition

Frequently, entrepreneurs ignore the reality of competition for their new ventures. They apparently believe that the marketplace contains no close substitutes or that their success will not attract other entrepreneurs! This is simply not reality.

Existing competitors should be studied carefully. They should be profiled, and the names of key management personnel should be listed. A brief discussion of competitors' overall strengths and weaknesses should be a part of this section of the plan. Also, a list of related products currently being marketed or tested by competitors should be noted. An assessment should be made of the likelihood that each of these firms will enter the entrepreneur's target market. For example, consider the competitive situation of Worthington Foods, Inc. of Worthington, Ohio:

> *Worthington is a pioneer in fat-free foods but its growth has attracted competition. From 1987 to 1991, Worthington's sales doubled, to $70 million, but profit margins have been squeezed below that of other specialty food companies such as McCormick and J. M. Smucker. In part, this is because the competitors are huge companies with marketing muscle.*[12]

Marketing Strategy

A well-prepared market analysis and a discussion of the competition are important to the formal marketing plan. But the information covering marketing strategy is the most detailed and, in many respects, subject to the closest scrutiny from potential investors. Such strategy plots the course of marketing actions that will give life to the entrepreneur's vision.

Four areas of marketing strategy should be addressed: (1) marketing decisions that will transform the basic product or service idea into a total product or service, (2) promotional decisions that will communicate the necessary information to target markets, (3) decisions regarding the distribution of a product to customers, and (4) pricing decisions that will set an acceptable exchange value on the total product or service. Recall that these four areas of marketing strategy are referred to collectively as a firm's marketing mix.

Obviously, the nature of a new venture has a direct bearing on the emphasis given to each of these areas. For example, a service business will not have the same distribution problems as a product business, and the promotional challenges facing a new retail store will be quite different from those faced by a new manufacturer. Despite these differences, we can offer a generalized format for presenting marketing strategy in a business plan.

THE TOTAL PRODUCT OR SERVICE   Within this section of the marketing plan, the entrepreneur includes the product or service name and why it was selected. Any legal protection that has been obtained should be described. It is very important to explain the logic behind the name selection. An entrepreneur's family name, if used for certain products or services, may make a positive contribution to sales. In other situations, a descriptive name that suggests a benefit of the product may be more desirable. Regardless of the logic behind the name, the selection should be defended.

Other components of the total product, such as the package, should be presented via drawings. Sometimes, it may be desirable to use professional packaging consultants to develop these drawings. Customer service plans such as warranties and repair policies also need to be discussed. These elements of the marketing strategy should be tied directly to customer satisfaction. (Consumer behavior and product or service strategy are discussed in more depth in Chapter 13.)

PROMOTIONAL PLAN   The promotional plan should describe the entrepreneur's approach to creating customer awareness of the product or service and motivating customers to buy. The entrepreneur has many promotional options. Personal selling and advertising are two of the most popular alternatives.

Advertising agencies can be helpful to a small business that is trying to develop a promotional plan. An advertising executive provides a professional perspective on messages the firm might want to send to customers and on the media with which to communicate them.

1 Describe small business marketing.

- Small business marketing consists of numerous activities including market analysis and determining the marketing mix.
- Three distinct marketing philosophies are production-, sales-, and consumer-oriented.
- A small business should adopt a consumer orientation.

2 Discuss the nature and techniques of the marketing research process.

- Marketing research is the gathering, processing, reporting, and interpreting of marketing information.
- The cost of marketing research should be evaluated against its benefits.
- The steps of marketing research include identifying the problem, searching for secondary and primary data, and interpreting the data.

3 Explain the dimensions of market potential and the methods of forecasting sales.

- A market is a group of customers or potential customers who have purchasing power and unsatisfied needs.
- A sales forecast is an estimation of how much of a product or service will be purchased within a market during a defined time period.
- The forecasting process begins with either a breakdown or a buildup process and uses either direct or indirect methods.

4 Identify the components of a formal marketing plan.

- The marketing plan should include sections on market analysis, the competition, and marketing strategy.
- The market analysis should include a customer profile.
- Four areas of marketing strategy should be addressed: the total product or service, promotion, distribution, and pricing.

If personal selling is appropriate, the plan should outline how many salespeople will be employed and how they will be compensated. Plans for training the sales force should be mentioned. If advertising is to be used, a list of the specific media should be included and the advertising themes should be described. Often, it is advisable to seek the services of a small advertising agency. In this case, the name and credentials of the agency should be provided. A brief mention of successful campaigns supervised by the agency can add to the value of this section of the marketing plan. (Personal selling and advertising are discussed more extensively in Chapter 15.)

DISTRIBUTION PLAN Quite often, new ventures will use established intermediaries to structure their channels of distribution. This distribution strategy expedites the process and reduces the necessary investment. How those intermediaries will be convinced to carry the new product should be explained in the distribution plan. If the new business intends to license its product or service, this strategy should also be covered in this section.

Some new retail ventures require fixed locations; others require mobile stores. The layouts and configurations of these retail outlets should be explained.

When a new business begins by exporting, the distribution plan must discuss the relevant laws and regulations governing that activity. Knowledge of exchange rates and distribution options must be reflected in the material included in this section. (Exporting and other distribution concepts are explained in detail in Chapter 16.)

PRICING PLAN At the very minimum, the price of a product or service must cover the costs of bringing it to customers. Therefore, the pricing plan must include a schedule of both production and marketing costs. Break-even computations should be included for alternative prices. Naturally, the analysis in this section should be consistent with the forecasting methods used in preparing the market analysis section. However, setting a price based exclusively on break-even analysis ignores other aspects of pricing. If the entrepreneur has truly found a unique niche, she or he may be able to charge a premium price—at least for initial operating periods.

The closest competitor should be studied to learn what that firm is charging. The new product or service will most likely have to be priced within a reasonable range of that price. (Chapter 14 examines break-even analysis and pricing strategy in more depth.)

DISCUSSION QUESTIONS

1. Can you think of one purchase with which you were completely satisfied? If so, explain the circumstances surrounding that experience. If not, what made a good purchase less than completely satisfactory?
2. How do the three marketing philosophies differ? Select a product and discuss the marketing tactics that could be used to implement each philosophy.
3. Do you believe that small businesses can achieve a higher level of customer satisfaction than big businesses? Why or why not?
4. What are the steps in the marketing research process?
5. What research methods could you use to estimate the number of male students with cars at your school?
6. Identify and briefly explain the three components of the definition of a market presented in this chapter.
7. Explain the concept of a market niche, using as an example the marketing of a new electronic poison-alert device, which emits a warning beep whenever a cabinet or drawer containing harmful materials is opened.
8. Why is it so important to understand the target market? What difference would it make if an entrepreneur simply ignored the characteristics of the market's customers?
9. Explain why forecasting is used more successfully by large firms than by small ones.
10. Briefly describe each of the components of a formal marketing plan.

New Terms and Concepts

small business marketing *160*

market analysis *161*

marketing mix *161*

marketing research *163*

secondary data *165*

primary data *168*

market *170*

sales forecast *170*

breakdown process *172*

buildup process *173*

direct forecasting *174*

indirect forecasting *174*

customer profile *175*

You Make the Call

Situation 1 James Mitchell was born and raised in the cattle country of southern Oklahoma, where he continued to ranch for almost 20 years until falling beef prices in the mid-1970s drove him out of business. After a brief stint in the restaurant business, Mitchell, now 64, wants to try a new venture in car-care service.

His business will be an automobile inspection service. There is currently no other business of this type in the city of 150,000 residents where he lives, and he has leased a good location adjacent to a major traffic artery. Mitchell does not plan to do mechanical work, other than minor jobs such as fuse and headlight replacements that are necessary to get a car up to inspection standards. Since the state mandates that automobiles pass an inspection yearly, he feels market demand will be stable.

Question 1 Write a brief description of what you see as Mitchell's strategic marketing position. Do you think his venture is likely to succeed? Why or why not?

Question 2 What methods of marketing research can Mitchell use to gather helpful marketing information?

Question 3 What name might be appropriate for Mitchell's business? What forms of promotion should be in his marketing plan?

Question 4 What type of pricing strategy would you suggest Mitchell adopt? Why?

Situation 2 Carson Smith is an employee of a small family-owned manufacturing plant located in his hometown, Malone, Mississippi. One day, while waiting to see someone at a competitor's business, he noticed a memo tacked to a bulletin board and read it. The memo described a forthcoming promotional campaign and details of a new pricing strategy. Upon leaving the plant, Carson returned to his office and informed management of the details of the memo.

Question 1 Is this a legitimate form of marketing research? Why or why not?

Question 2 Do you consider Carson's behavior spying?

Question 3 What would you have done in Carson's situation?

Continue on next page

Situation 3 Mary Wilson is a 31-year-old wife and mother who wants to start her own company. She has no previous business experience but has an idea to market an animal-grooming service, using an approach similar to that used for pizza delivery: When a customer calls, she will arrive in a van in less than 30 minutes and provide the grooming service. Many of her friends think the idea is unusual, and they usually smile and remark, "Oh, really?" However, Wilson is not discouraged; she is setting out to purchase the van and necessary grooming equipment.

Question 1 What target market or markets can you identify for Wilson? How could she forecast sales for her service in each market?

Question 2 What advantage does her business have compared to existing grooming businesses?

Question 3 What business name and what promotional strategy would you suggest to Wilson?

EXPERIENTIAL EXERCISES

1. Interview a local small business manager about what he or she believes is (are) the competitive advantage(s) offered by the business.
2. Assume you are planning to market a new facial tissue. Write a detailed customer profile, and explain how you would develop the sales forecast for this product.
3. Interview a local small business owner to determine the type of marketing research, if any, he or she has used.
4. Visit a local small retailer and observe the marketing efforts—salesperson style, store atmosphere, and warranty policies, for example. Report to the class and make recommendations for improving these efforts to increase customer satisfaction.

 CASE 8
ScrubaDub Auto Wash (p. 614)

This case examines the financial rewards being reaped by a company that realized the importance of a marketing plan.

Alternative Cases for Chapter 8: Case 7, "The Fantastic Catalogue Company," p. 610
Case 26, "Diaper Dan," p. 662

LAYING THE FOUNDATION
Asking the Right Questions

As part of laying the foundation for your own business plan, respond to the following questions regarding marketing research, forecasting, and the marketing plan.

Marketing Research Questions
1. What types of research should be conducted to collect the information you need?
2. How much will this research cost?
3. What sources of secondary data will be useful to your informational needs?
4. What sources of relevant data are available in your local library?
5. What sources of outside professional assistance have you considered using to help with marketing research?

Forecasting Questions
1. How do you plan to forecast sales for your product or service?
2. What sources of forecasting assistance have you consulted?
3. What forecasting techniques are most appropriate to your needs?
4. What is the sales forecast for your product or service?

Marketing Plan Questions
1. What is your customer profile?
2. How will you identify prospective customers?
3. What geographical area will you serve?
4. What are the distinguishing characteristics of your product or service?
5. What steps have already been taken to develop your product or service?
6. What do you plan to name your product or service?
7. Will there be a warranty?
8. How will you set the price for your product or service?
9. What channels of distribution will you use?
10. Will you export to other countries?
11. What type of selling effort will you use?
12. What special selling skills will be required?
13. What types of advertising and sales promotion will you use?

USING BizPlanBuilder

If you are using BizPlan*Builder*, refer to Part 2 for information about products and services, market analysis, and marketing strategy that should be reflected in the business plan.

Chapter 9

Selecting the Management Team and Form of Organization

Jerry Fiddler
and
David Wilmer

spotlight on small business

Partnerships are fraught with risk for many aspiring partners. The following story tells of two partners who made good on their venture.

A talented software programmer in his own right, Jerry Fiddler didn't need a scientist for a partner. But when his landlord evicted him and his embryonic enterprise from a garage in 1983, Fiddler seized the moment to do some traveling. He paid an engineer friend, David Wilmer, to mind what was left of the store. On Fiddler's return, Wilmer announced that at the current salary, he no longer cared to work for Fiddler. Work with me then, Fiddler offered, and the two shook hands on a 50-50 share of, essentially, nothing. "There was no capital," Fiddler relates. "If we needed equipment, one or the other would spring for it."

When they officially incorporated Wind River Systems, it was capitalized not in dollars but in the paraphernalia each owned. The union blossomed, and soon the partners had to decide who would take engineering and who would be responsible for operations. A personality-grading test revealed Wilmer's insistence on detail and susceptibility to anxiety; it also revealed the laid-back Fiddler's diametric inclinations. "I hadn't thought of us as fragmented before," says Fiddler, "but it must be good to be opposite in those ways, since we've never had a fight." So Fiddler took the position of CEO; Wilmer became vice-president of engineering. On the day their company went public . . . its market value was $79 million.

Source: "Two Who Made Good," *Inc.*, Vol. 16, No. 6 (June 1994), pp. 40, 42.

Looking Ahead

After studying this chapter, you should be able to:

1 Describe the characteristics and value of a strong management team.

2 Identify the common legal forms of organization used by small businesses and describe the characteristics of each.

3 Identify factors to consider in making a choice among the different legal forms of organization.

4 Describe the effective use of boards of directors and advisory councils.

5 Explain how different forms of businesses are taxed by the federal government.

6 Describe the special features and restrictions of a Subchapter S corporation.

A business plan takes on life as the entrepreneur assembles the management team and decides on the form of organization. As a first step, the entrepreneur must find the people who will help in operating the business. In addition, the entrepreneur must select the most appropriate legal form of organization to use. We look at both of these issues in this chapter.

THE MANAGEMENT TEAM

Unless a firm is extremely small, the founder will not be the only individual in a leadership role. The concept of a management team, therefore, is relevant. In general, the **management team,** as we envision it here, includes both managers and other professionals or key persons who help give a new company its general direction.

Value of a Strong Management Team

1 Describe the characteristics and value of a strong management team.

management team managers and other key persons who give a company its general direction

The quality of the management team is generally recognized as vital to a firm's effective operation. As we noted in Chapter 2, poor management is a significant contributor to business failure. Strong management can make the best of any business idea and provide the resources to make it work. Of course, even a highly competent management team cannot rescue a firm that is based on a weak business concept or that lacks adequate resources.

A management team brings greater strength to many ventures than does an individual entrepreneur. For one thing, a team can provide a diversity of talent to meet various staffing needs. This is particularly true for high-tech startups, but it may be true for any venture. Also, a team can provide greater assurance of continuity since the departure of one member of a team would be less devastating than the departure of a sole entrepreneur.

The importance of strong management to startups is evident in the attitudes of prospective investors. From an investor's perspective, the single most important factor in the decision to invest or not is the quality of a new venture's management.

Building a Complementary Management Team

The management team includes individuals with supervisory responsibilities—for example, a financial manager who supervises a small office staff—and all others who play key roles in the business even though they are not supervisors. A new firm, for example, might begin with only one individual conducting its marketing effort. Because of the importance of the marketing function, that person would be a key member of the management team.

The type of competence needed in a management team depends on the type of business and the nature of its operations. For example, a software development firm and a restaurant call for different types of business experience. Whatever the business, a small firm needs managers with an appropriate combination of educa-

Action Report

ENTREPRENEURIAL EXPERIENCES

Building a Management Team

A complete management team is not always in place when a business plan is formulated or when a new business begins operation. Sometimes, entrepreneurs fail to recognize the need for a management team until the business begins to struggle. This was the situation with Engineering Data Systems and its founders, Scott Taylor and John Biver, of Dubuque, Iowa.

After writing some basic software for their personal drafting tasks, they quit their jobs in 1984 and, with a $7,500 PC, began a software development company. Over the next several years, their business merely survived. Then the two entrepreneurs were introduced to Rodney Blum. "We recognized right away that this guy could help us," says Biver. Blum was a part-time consultant who had previous marketing experience with a medical claims data-processing company.

Within six months, Blum joined the management team, receiving part ownership. Subsequently, Engineering Data Systems grew to 145 employees. Blum's marketing expertise took the company to second place among competitors in the niche market for land surveying and civil engineering software.

How do the original entrepreneurs feel toward the new team member? Taylor says, "I feel more in control today than I did five years ago."

Source: Damon Darlin, "Right Here in Little Dubuque," *Forbes*, Vol. 151, No. 7 (March 29, 1993), pp. 86–88. Reprinted By Permission of *FORBES* Magazine © Forbes Inc., 1993.

tional background and experience. In evaluating the qualifications of those who will fill key positions, the entrepreneur needs to know whether an applicant is experienced in a related type of business, whether the experience has included any managerial responsibilities, and whether the individual has ever functioned as an entrepreneur.

Not all members of a management team need competence in all areas. The key is balance. Is one member competent in finance? Does another have an adequate marketing background? Is there someone who can supervise employees effectively?

Even when entrepreneurs recognize the need for team members with varying expertise, they frequently seek to duplicate their own personalities and management styles. While personal compatibility and cooperation of team members are necessary for effective collaboration, a healthy situation exists when each team member is unique. Dr. Stephen R. Covey, a management consultant, puts it this way:

> *In my opinion, the No. 1 mistake that most entrepreneurs make is that they never know how to develop a complementary team. They're always kind of cloning themselves, that is, trying to turn their employees into duplicates of themselves. . . . You have to empower other people and build on their strengths to make your own weaknesses irrelevant.*[1]

Planning the company's leadership, then, should produce a team that is able to give competent direction to the new firm. The management team should be balanced in terms of covering the various functional areas and offering the right combination of education and experience. It may comprise both insiders and outside specialists.

In addition to selecting members of the management team, the entrepreneur must design an organizational structure. Relationships among the various positions need to be understood. Although such relationships need not be worked out in great detail, planning should be sufficient to permit an orderly functioning of the enterprise and to avoid a jumble of responsibilities that invites conflict.

The management plan should be drafted in a way that provides for business growth. Unfilled positions should be specified, and job descriptions should spell out the duties and qualifications for such positions. Methods for selecting key employees should also be explained. For a partnership, the partners need to look ahead to the possible breakup of the partnership. The ownership share, if any, needs to be thought out carefully. Similarly, compensation arrangements, including bonus systems or other incentive plans for key organization members, warrant scrutiny and planning.

Outside Professional Support

The managerial and professional talent of the management team for a new venture can be supplemented by drawing on outside assistance. This may take various forms. For example, a small firm may shore up weak areas by carefully developing working relationships with external professionals, such as a commercial bank, a law firm, and a certified public accounting firm. Also, the Small Business Administration (SBA) provides managerial assistance, which will be explained more completely in Chapter 12. To some extent, reliance on such outside advisors can compensate for the absence of sufficient internal staffing.

An active board of directors can also provide counsel and guidance to the management team. Directors may be appointed on the basis of their business or technical expertise, or because of their financial investment in the company. (The selection of and compensation for directors are discussed later in this chapter.)

Nonmanagerial Personnel

In many cases, the entrepreneur or the members of the management team are the only employees when a business begins operations. However, additional personnel will be required as the business grows. The selection and training of such employees are treated in Chapter 18.

LEGAL FORMS OF ORGANIZATION

Human resources—the people involved in the business—require a formal organizational structure in which to operate. We now turn our attention to the various legal forms of organization available to small businesses. Several options are appropriate only for very specialized applications. A new form, the limited liability company, is now recognized in some states. However, as Figure 9-1 shows, the forms currently in wide use by small business are the sole proprietorship, the partnership, and the corporation. Two basic types of partnership exist—the general partnership and the limited partnership. The two types of corporation are the regular, or C, corporation and the Subchapter S corporation.

The sole proprietorship is the most popular form of organization among small businesses. This popularity is evident across all industries. Nevertheless, many small businesses operate as partnerships or as corporations, which suggests that there are circumstances that favor those forms. About 70 percent of the firms in the United States are sole proprietorships, 20 percent are corporations, and 10 percent are partnerships.[2]

> **2** Identify the common legal forms of organization used by small businesses and describe the characteristics of each.

Figure 9-1

*Forms of Legal
Organization for
Small Businesses*

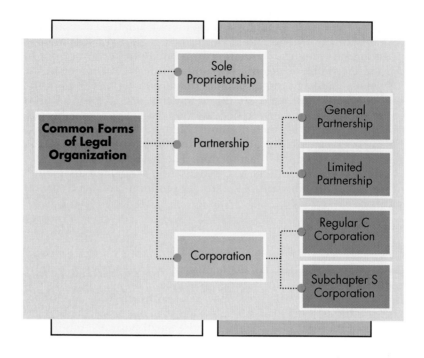

The Sole Proprietorship Option

sole proprietorship
a business owned and
operated by one
person

A **sole proprietorship** is a business owned and operated by one person. An individual proprietor has title to all business assets, subject to the claims of creditors. He or she receives all of the business's profits but must also assume all losses, bear all risks, and pay all debts. A sole proprietorship is the simplest and cheapest way to start operation and is frequently the most appropriate form for a new business.

In a sole proprietorship, an owner is free from interference by partners, shareholders, directors, and officers. However, it lacks some of the advantages of other legal forms. For example, there are no limits on the owner's personal liability; that is, the owner of the business has **unlimited liability.** This means that the owner's personal assets can be taken by creditors if the business fails. In addition, sole proprietors are not employees and cannot receive the tax-free advantage of the fringe

unlimited liability
owner's liability that
extends beyond the
assets of the business

*The sole proprietorship is
the most popular form of
small business organiza-
tion in the United States.
As a sole proprietor, this
copy shop owner receives
all of the business's profits
but is also responsible for
its losses and debts.*

benefits customarily provided by corporations, such as insurance and hospitalization plans.

The death of the owner terminates the legal existence of a business that is organized as a sole proprietorship. The possibility of the owner's death may cloud relationships between a business and its creditors and employees. It is important that the owner have a will because the assets of the business minus its liabilities belong to the heirs. In a will, an owner can give an executor the power to run the business for the heirs until they can take it over or it can be sold.

Another contingency that must be provided for is the possible incapacity of the sole proprietor. If she or he were badly hurt in an accident and unconscious for an extended period, the business could be ruined. The sole proprietor can guard against this by giving a competent person a legal power of attorney to carry on in such circumstances.

In some cases, the sole proprietorship option is virtually ruled out by the circumstances. For example, if the nature of a business involves a high exposure to legal risks, as in the case of a manufacturer of a potentially hazardous, chemical-based product, a legal form that provides greater protection against personal liability will be required.

The Partnership Option

A **partnership** is a voluntary association of two or more persons to carry on, as co-owners, a business for profit. Because of its voluntary nature, a partnership can be set up quickly without many of the legal procedures involved in creating a corporation. A partnership pools the managerial talents and capital of those joining together as business partners. However, partners do share unlimited liability.

partnership
a voluntary association of two or more persons to carry on, as co-owners, a business for profit

QUALIFICATIONS OF PARTNERS   Any person capable of contracting may legally become a business partner. Individuals may become partners without contributing capital or sharing in the assets at the time of dissolution. Such persons are partners only in regard to management and profits. The formation of a partnership, however, requires serious consideration of aspects other than legal issues. A strong partnership requires partners who are honest, healthy, capable, and compatible.

Operating a business as a partnership has its benefits, but it is also fraught with problems. When *Inc.* magazine surveyed individuals about their opinions regarding the partnership form of ownership, almost 60 percent of the respondents considered a partnership to be a "bad way to run a business."[3] The respondents were also asked to identify what they believed to be good and bad qualities associated with the partnership form. Their responses are given in Table 9-1. Interestingly, few of the perceived pros or cons are directly associated with financial matters. For instance, only 6 percent of the respondents thought that the dilution of equity was a good reason not to have a partner. Instead, those disliking partnerships focused more on the deterioration of relationships. Many spoke of a partner's dishonesty at worst and differing priorities at best. However, some of the respondents who considered a partnership a bad way to run a business did note some redeeming quali-

Source: "The *Inc.* FaxPoll: Are Partners Bad for Business?" *Inc.*, Vol. 14, No. 2 (February 1992), p. 24. Reprinted with permission, *Inc.* magazine (February 1992). Copyright 1992 by Goldhirsh Group, Inc., 38 Commercial Wharf, Boston, MA 02110.

Table 9-1

An Opinion Survey About the Pros and Cons of Partnerships

Question	Perceived Pros and Cons	Percentage Responding
Why is a partnership good?	Spreads the workload	55
	Spreads the emotional burden	41
	Buys executive talent not otherwise affordable	40
	Spreads the financial burden	33
	Makes company office less lonely	26
Why is a partnership bad?	Personal conflicts outweigh the benefits	60
	Partners never live up to one another's expectations	59
	Companies function better with one clear leader	53
	Dilutes equity too much	6
	You can't call your own shots	6

Personal compatibility is an important consideration when forming a business partnership. Partners share the workload and the financial responsibilities of their business, as well as its profits.

ties. Similarly, the advocates of a partnership noted some inherently bad qualities. Thus, the issue is not black and white. The important point of these findings is that a partnership should be formed only if it is clearly the best option when *all* matters are considered.

The following questions should be asked before choosing a business partner. The objective of these questions is to clarify expectations before a partnership agreement is finalized.

- *What's our business concept?* This is a big, broad topic, and sometimes it helps to ask a third party to listen in, just to see if the partners are on each other's wavelength. First, the partners need to decide who will make the widgets and who will sell them. Then they need to talk about growth. Are they building the company to sell it, or are they after long-term growth? It's also important to discuss exactly how the business will be run. Do they want participative management, or will employees simply hunker down at machines and churn out parts? "If one guy is a fist pounder with a 'do-it-as-I-say' mentality, and the other believes that people ought to feel good about their jobs, that probably represents an irreconcilable difference," says Sam Lane, a consultant who works with partners.
- *How are we going to structure ownership?* It sounds great for two people to scratch out 50-50 on a cocktail napkin and leave it at that. But, in practice, splitting the company down the middle can paralyze the business. If neither is willing to settle for 49 percent, then the partners should build some arbitration into the partnership agreement.
- *Why do we need each other?* "I thought it would be much less scary with two of us," says Arthur Eisenberg, explaining his rationale for teaming up with his partner. That may be so, but bringing on a partner means sharing responsibility and authority. "If you are taking on a partner because you are afraid of going it alone, find some other way to handle the anxiety," advises Mardy Grothe, a psychologist.
- *How do our life-styles differ?* The fact that one partner is single and the other has a family, for example, can affect more than just the time each puts in. It may mean that one partner needs to pull more money out of the business. Or it may affect a partner's willingness to take risks with the company. "All of this stuff needs to get talked out," says Peter Wylie, a psychologist. "The implications are profound."[4]

As already suggested, the failure to clarify expectations is a frequent deterrent to building an effective working relationship.

RIGHTS AND DUTIES OF PARTNERS   Partners' rights and duties should be stated explicitly and in writing in **articles of partnership.** These articles should be drawn up before the firm is operating and, at the very least, should cover the following items:

articles of partnership
a document that states explicitly the rights and duties of partners

1. Date of formation of the partnership
2. Names and addresses of all partners
3. Statement of fact of partnership
4. Statement of business purpose(s)
5. Duration of the business

During startup, partners are likely to fill various roles, including mover and interior designer. For the long term, however, articles of partnership should be drawn up to clarify business partners' rights and duties.

6. Name and location of the business
7. Amount invested by each partner
8. Sharing ratio for profits and losses
9. Partners' rights, if any, regarding withdrawal of funds for personal use
10. Provision for accounting records and their accessibility to partners
11. Specific duties of each partner
12. Provision for dissolution and sharing of the net assets
13. Restraint on partners' assumption of special obligations, such as endorsing a note of another
14. Provision for protection of surviving partners, decedent's estate, and so forth in the event of a partner's death

Unless specified otherwise in the articles, a partner is generally recognized as having certain implicit rights. For example, partners share profits or losses equally if they have not agreed on a different ratio.

In a partnership, each partner has **agency power,** which means that a partner can bind all members of the firm. Good faith, together with reasonable care in the exercise of managerial duties, is required of all partners in a business. Since the partnership relationship is fiduciary in character, a partner cannot compete in business and remain a partner. Nor can a partner use business information solely for personal gain.

agency power
the ability of any partner to legally bind in good faith the other partners

TERMINATION OF A PARTNERSHIP   Death, incapacity, or withdrawal of any one of the partners ends a partnership and necessitates liquidation or reorganization of the business. While liquidation often results in substantial losses to all partners, it may be legally necessary, because a partnership is a close personal relationship of the parties that cannot be maintained against the desire of any one of them.

This disadvantage may be partially overcome at the time a partnership is formed by stipulating in the articles that surviving partners can continue the business after buying the decedent's interest. This can be facilitated by having each partner carry life insurance that names the other partners as beneficiaries.

limited partnership
a partnership with at least one general partner and one or more limited partners

THE LIMITED PARTNERSHIP   A small business sometimes finds it desirable to use a special form of partnership called the **limited partnership.** This form consists of at least one general partner and one or more limited partners. The **general partner**

general partner
the partner with unlimited personal liability in a limited partnership

limited partner
a partner who is not active in the management of a limited partnership and who has limited personal liability

remains personally liable for the debts of the business. **Limited partners** have limited personal liability as long as they do not take an active role in the management of the partnership. In other words, limited partners risk only the capital they invest in the business. An individual with substantial personal assets can, therefore, invest money in a limited partnership without exposing his or her total estate to liability claims that might arise through activities of the business. If a limited partner becomes active in management, the limited liability is lost.

To form a limited partnership, partners must file a certificate of limited partnership with the proper state office. State law governs this form of organization.

The Corporation Option

corporation
a business organization that exists as a legal entity

legal entity
a business organization that is recognized by the law as having a separate legal existence

In 1819, Chief Justice John Marshall of the United States Supreme Court defined a **corporation** as "an artificial being, invisible, intangible, and existing only in contemplation of the law." With these words, the Supreme Court recognized the corporation as a **legal entity,** meaning that a corporation can sue and be sued, hold and sell property, and engage in business operations that are stipulated in the corporate charter. For tax purposes, there are two types of corporations—C corporation and Subchapter S corporation—which are discussed in more detail later in this chapter.

The corporation is chartered under state laws. The length of its life is independent of its owners' (stockholders') lives. The corporation, and not its owners, is liable for debts contracted by the business. The directors and officers serve as agents to bind the corporation.

corporate charter
the document that establishes a corporation's existence

THE CORPORATE CHARTER To form a corporation, one or more persons must apply to the secretary of state for permission to incorporate. After preliminary steps, including payment of an incorporation fee, have been completed, the written application (which should be prepared by an attorney) is approved by the secretary of state and becomes the corporation's charter. In some states, documents showing that the corporation exists are called *articles of incorporation* or *certificates of incorporation.* A **corporate charter** typically provides the following information:

1. Name of the company
2. Formal statement of the company's formation
3. Purposes and powers—that is, type of business
4. Location of principal office in the state of incorporation
5. Duration (perpetual existence, 50-year life and renewable charter, or other)
6. Classes and preferences of classes of stock
7. Number and par (or stated) value of shares of each class of stock authorized
8. Voting privileges for each class of stock
9. Names and addresses of incorporators and first year's directors
10. Names and addresses of and amounts subscribed by each subscriber to capital stock
11. Statement of limited liability of stockholders (if required specifically by state law)
12. Statement of alterations of directors' powers, if any, from the general corporation law of the state

A corporation's charter should be brief, in accord with state law, and broad in the statement of the firm's powers. Details should be left to the bylaws.

RIGHTS AND STATUS OF STOCKHOLDERS   Ownership in a corporation is evidenced by **stock certificates,** each of which stipulates the number of shares owned by a stockholder. An ownership interest does not confer a legal right to act for the firm or to share in its management. It does provide the stockholder with the right to receive dividends in proportion to stockholdings—but only when the dividends are properly declared by the firm. Ownership of stock typically carries a **pre-emptive right,** or the right to buy new shares, in proportion to the number of shares already owned, before new stock is offered for public sale.

The legal status of stockholders is fundamental, of course, but it may be overemphasized. In many small corporations, the owners typically serve both as directors and as managing officers. The person who owns most or all of the stock can control a business as effectively as if it were a sole proprietorship. Thus, the corporate form works well for individual- and family-owned businesses, where maintaining control of the firm is important.

Major stockholders must be concerned about their working relationships, as well as their legal relationships, with other owners who are active in the business. Cooperation among all owners and managers of a new corporation is necessary for its success. Specifying legal technicalities is important, but it is an inadequate basis for successful collaboration. Owners and the members of their management team need to clarify their expectations of each others' roles as best they can. Failure to have clear expectations about working relationships can result in one or more persons feeling that others serving as managers or co-owners are not honoring their word. In reality, the problem may result from not taking the time and effort to clarify and reconcile everyone's expectations. In short, unrealistic or unfulfilled expectations can wreak havoc within a business, in spite of the best intentions—and in spite of the best legal contracts.

LIMITED LIABILITY OF STOCKHOLDERS   To owners, their limited liability is one of the advantages of the corporate form of organization. Their financial liability is limited to the amount of money they have invested in the business. Creditors cannot require them to sell personal assets to pay off the corporation's debts. However, small corporations are often in somewhat shaky financial condition during their early years of operation. As a result, a bank that makes a loan to a small company may insist that the stockholders assume personal liability for the company's debts by signing the promissory notes not only as representatives of the firm but personally as well. Then, if the corporation is unable to repay the loan, the banker can look to the owners' personal assets to recover the amount of the loan. In this way, the corporate advantage of limited liability is lost.

Why would owners agree to personally guarantee a company's debt? Simply put, they may have no choice if they want the money. Most bankers are not willing to loan money to an entrepreneur who is not prepared to put his or her own personal assets at risk. If the entrepreneur is not confident enough about the business to risk his or her own funds, the banker will not put the bank's funds at risk.

The courts may also override the concept of limited liability for shareholders and hold them personally liable in certain unusual cases—for example, if personal and corporate funds have been mixed together or if the corporation was formed to try to evade an existing obligation.

DEATH OR WITHDRAWAL OF STOCKHOLDERS   Unlike ownership in a partnership, ownership in a corporation is readily transferable. Exchange of shares of stock is all that is required to convey an ownership interest to a different individual.

Stock of large corporations is exchanged constantly without noticeable effect on the operations of the business. For a small firm, however, a change of owners,

stock certificate
a document specifying the number of shares owned by a stockholder

pre-emptive right
the right of stockholders to buy new shares of stock before they are offered to the public

Action Report

ENTREPRENEURIAL EXPERIENCES

Minority Stockholder Beware!

Wayne Ragan was a successful GMC truck dealer in Lubbock, Texas, but he sold the business in 1987. He later served as a consultant to several firms, both in and out of the truck and automobile industry. Then, in 1989, a banker approached Ragan about helping to find new owners for a car dealership. The bank had extended credit to a dealership that had later encountered financial difficulties. In an effort to protect its loan position, the bank wanted to bring in new owners.

Ragan called on Richard Harris, who had the financial means to buy the dealership and a possible interest in such an investment. Ragan and Harris then contacted Mike Tarhill to see if he would have an interest in investing in the dealership and serving as its operating manager. A deal was struck. Harris and Tarhill were each to have 47 percent of the company's stock, and Ragan was to receive the remaining 6 percent for helping to put the deal together and for continuing to act as an adviser to the business.

At the outset, everything worked well, and the firm appeared to be on its way back to profitability. However, Harris and Tarhill soon began having problems working together. It finally reached a point where they could not agree on much of anything. Ragan became the mediator, trying to work out a plan both men could accept. After several months, Ragan became convinced that the two men could no longer work together. He recommended that one of them buy the other's stock. However, Tarhill could not raise the necessary funds, and he was unwilling to sell to Harris.

Ragan again tried to resolve the problems between the two men, but with no success. At this point, Ragan met with Tarhill and urged him to let Harris purchase his interest in the business. When Tarhill again refused, Ragan told him, "Mike, you have not been successful at getting the financing to buy Harris's stock, so you need to let Harris buy you out. If you won't, then at the stockholders' meeting this month, I will make a motion that you be dismissed as the operating manager and that your salary be terminated at the appropriate time. Though I own only 6 percent of the company, we both know that Harris will vote with me."

Ragan did make the motion at the next stockholders' meeting, and Tarhill was removed as the manager of the dealership. Fortunately, Ragan and Tarhill remained friends. However, this example demonstrates a fact of corporate life. Minority stockholders in a small firm often do not have any say in business decisions, even at times when they would most like to influence those decisions.

though legally just as straightforward, can involve numerous complications. For example, finding a buyer for the stock of a small firm may prove difficult. Also, a minority stockholder in a small firm is vulnerable. If two of three equal shareholders in a small business sold their stock to an outsider, the remaining shareholder would then be at the mercy of that outsider. The minority stockholder might be removed from any managerial post he or she happened to hold or be legally ousted from the board of directors and no longer have any voice in the management of the business.

The death of a majority stockholder can also have unfortunate repercussions in a small firm. An heir, the executor, or a purchaser of the stock might well insist on direct control, with possible adverse effects for the other stockholders. To prevent problems of this nature from arising, legal arrangements should be made at the time of incorporation to provide for management continuity by surviving stockholders, as well as for fair treatment of a stockholder's heirs. As in the case of the partnership, mutual insurance may be carried to ensure ability to buy out a deceased stockholder's interest. This arrangement would require an option for the corporation or surviving stockholders to (1) purchase the decedent's stock before it is offered to outsiders, and (2) specify the method for determining the stock's price per share. A similar arrangement might be made to protect remaining stockholders in case one of the owners wished to retire from the business at any time.

Choosing an Organizational Form

It should be apparent by now that it is not easy to choose the best form of organization. A number of criteria must be considered, and some tradeoffs are necessary. Table 9-2 provides an overview of the more important criteria. The bottom row of the table suggests the preferred form of business organization, given the particular list of factors shown.

The factors listed in Table 9-2 summarize the main considerations in selecting a form of ownership:

- *Organizational costs.* Initial organizational costs increase as the formality of the organization increases. That is, a sole proprietorship is typically less expensive to form than a partnership, and a partnership is usually less expensive to create than a corporation. However, this consideration is of minimum importance in the long term.
- *Limited versus unlimited liability.* A sole proprietorship and a general partnership have the inherent disadvantage of unlimited liability. For these organizations, there is no distinction between business assets and the owners' personal assets. Creditors lending money to the business can require the owners to sell personal assets if the firm is financially unable to repay its loans. In contrast, both the limited partnership and the corporation limit the owners' liability to their investment in the company. However, if a corporation is small, its owners are often required to guarantee a loan personally.
- *Continuity.* A sole proprietorship is immediately dissolved on the owner's death. Likewise, a general partnership is terminated on the death or withdrawal of a partner, unless stated otherwise in the partnership agreement. A corporation, on the other hand, offers the greatest degree of continuity. The status of an investor does not affect the corporation's existence.
- *Transferability of ownership.* The ability to transfer ownership between persons is intrinsically neither good nor bad. Its desirability depends largely on the owners' preferences. In certain businesses, owners may want the option of evaluating any prospective new investors. In other circumstances, unrestricted transferability may be preferred.
- *Management control.* A sole proprietor has absolute control of the firm. Control within a general partnership is normally based on the majority vote. An increase in the number of partners reduces each partner's voice in management. A separation of ownership from control exists in a limited partnership. A general partner controls the firm's operations, but limited partners generally have most of the ownership. Within a corporation, control has two dimensions: (1) the formal control vested in the stockholders who own the majority of the voting common shares, and (2) the functional control exercised by the corporate officers in conducting daily operations. For a small corporation, these two forms of control usually rest in the same individuals.
- *Raising new equity capital.* A corporation has a distinct advantage when raising new equity capital, due to the ease of transferring ownership through the sale

Identify factors to consider in making a choice among the different legal forms of organization.

Table 9-2

*Comparison of Legal
Forms of Organization*

Form of Organization	Initial Organizational Requirements and Costs	Liability of Owners	Continuity of Business
Sole proprietorship	Minimum requirements; generally no registration or filing fee.	Unlimited liability	Dissolved upon proprietor's death
General partnership	Minimum requirements; generally no registration or filing fee; written partnership agreement not legally required but is strongly suggested.	Unlimited liability	Unless partnership agreement specifies differently, dissolved upon withdrawal or death of partner
Limited partnership	Moderate requirements; written certificate must be filed; must comply with state law.	General partners: unlimited liability. Limited partners: liability limited to investment in company.	General partners: same as general partnership. Limited partners: withdrawal or death does not affect continuity of business.
Corporation	Most expensive and greatest requirements; filing fees; compliance with state regulations for corporations.	Liability limited to investment in company.	Continuity of business unaffected by shareholder withdrawal or death
Form of organization preferred	Proprietorship or general partnership	Limited partnership or corporation	Corporation

of common shares and the flexibility in distributing the shares. In contrast, the unlimited liability of a sole proprietorship and a general partnership discourages new investors. Between these extremes, the limited partnership provides limited liability for the limited partners, thereby tending to attract wealthy investors. However, the impracticality of having a large number of partners and the difficulty often encountered in selling an interest in a partnership make the limited partnership less attractive than the corporation for raising large amounts of new equity capital.

- *Income taxes.* Income taxes frequently have a major effect on an owner's selection of a form of organization. The sole proprietorship, partnership, and S corporation are not taxed directly; their owners report business profits on their personal income tax returns. Earnings from these types of company are taxable to the owner, regardless of whether the profits have been paid out to the owner. On the other hand, a C corporation reports and pays taxes as a separate and distinct entity. The corporation's income is taxed again if and when it is distributed to shareholders in the form of dividends.

An especially important factor in choosing the legal form of organization is its relationship to income taxes. In the last section of this chapter, we will look more closely at federal taxes as they relate to choosing a form of organization.

Transferability of Ownership	Management Control	Attractiveness for Raising Capital	Income Taxes
May transfer ownership in company name and assets	Absolute management freedom	Limited to proprietor's personal capital	Income from the business is taxed as personal income to the proprietor
Requires the consent of all partners	Majority vote of partners required for control	Limited to partners' ability and desire to contribute capital	Income from the business is taxed as personal income to the partners
General partners: same as general partnership. Limited partners: may sell interest in the company.	General partners: same as general partnership. Limited partners: not permitted any involvement in management	General partners: same as general partnership. Limited partners: limited liability provides a stronger inducement for raising capital.	General partners: same as general partnership. Limited partners: same as general partnership.
Easily transferred by transferring shares of stock	Shareholders have final control, but usually board of directors controls company policies.	Usually the most attractive form for raising capital	The C corporation is taxed on its income and the stockholder is taxed if and when dividends are received. The S corporation is taxed as a partnership.
Depends on the circumstances	Depends on the circumstances	Corporation	Depends on the circumstances

THE BOARD OF DIRECTORS

A common stockholder may ordinarily cast one vote per share in stockholders' meetings. Thus, the stockholder indirectly participates in management by helping elect the directors. The **board of directors** is the governing body for corporate activity. It elects the firm's officers, who manage the enterprise with the help of management specialists. The directors also set or approve management policies, consider reports on operating results from the officers, and declare dividends (if any).

All too often, the majority stockholder (the entrepreneur) in a small corporation appoints a board of directors only to fulfill a legal requirement. Such owners make little or no use of directors in managing their companies. In fact, the entrepreneur may actively resent efforts of managerial assistance from these directors. When appointing a board of directors, such an entrepreneur tends to select personal friends, relatives, or businesspersons who are too busy to analyze the firm's circumstances and are not inclined to argue. In board meetings, the entrepreneur and other directors may simply engage in long-winded, innocuous discussions of broad general policies, leaving no time for serious, constructive questions. Some entrepreneurs, however, have found an active board to be both practical and beneficial.

4 Describe the effective use of boards of directors and advisory councils.

board of directors the governing body of a corporation, elected by the stockholders

A strong board of directors lends credibility to a small firm. In addition to formally reviewing major policy decisions, board members can provide valuable advice informally.

Use of Outside Directors by Small Companies

A survey of the fastest-growing U.S. companies shows that most of them make only limited use of outside directors. As illustrated in Figure 9-2, 43 percent of the companies do not have anyone outside the company serving on the board, and over half of them have fewer than 20 percent of board members coming from outside the company.

Objectivity is the most valuable contribution of outside directors. Outside directors may also serve a small firm by scrutinizing and questioning its ethical standards. Operating executives, without outside directors to question them, may rationalize unethical or illegal behavior as being in the best interest of the company.

Contribution of Directors

A properly assembled board of directors can bring supplementary knowledge and broad experience to corporate management. The board should meet regularly to provide maximum assistance to the chief executive. In such board meetings, ideas should be debated, strategies determined, and the pros and cons of policies explored. In this way, the chief executive is assisted by the experience of all the board members. Their combined knowledge makes possible more intelligent decisions on major issues.

Utilizing the experience of a board of directors does not mean that the chief executive of a small corporation is abdicating active control of its operations. Instead, it simply means that she or he is consulting with, and seeking the advice of, the board's members in order to draw on a larger pool of business knowledge. Better decisions are typically made when there is group involvement, and not just a single individual working in isolation.

An active board of directors serves management in several important ways: by reviewing major policy decisions, by advising on external business conditions and on proper reaction to the business cycle, and by providing informal advice from

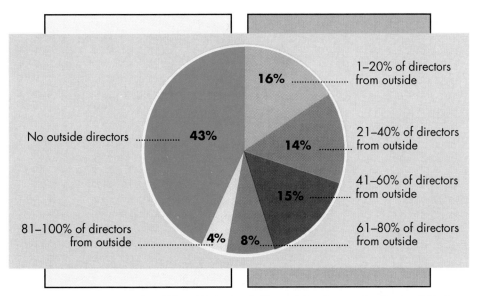

Figure 9-2

Percentage of Outside Directors for High-Growth U.S. Companies

Source: *Inc.*, Vol. 12, No. 10 (October 1990), p. 151. Reprinted with permission, *Inc.* magazine (October 1990). Copyright © 1990 by Goldhirsh Group, Inc., 38 Commercial Wharf, Boston, MA 02110.

time to time on specific problems that arise. With a strong board, the small firm gains greater credibility with the public, as well as with the business and financial community.

Selection of Directors

Many sources are available to an owner attempting to assemble a cooperative and experienced group of directors. The firm's attorney, banker, accountant, other business executives, and local management consultants might all be considered as potential directors. However, such individuals lack the independence needed for critical review of an entrepreneur's plans. Also, the owner is already paying for their expertise. For this reason, the owner needs to consider the value of an outside board—one with members whose income does not depend on the corporation.

Although the following excerpt refers specifically to a family business, it expresses the importance to any firm of selecting a truly independent group of board members:

> *Probably the strongest argument for adding outsiders to the family business board is to make qualified and objective confidants available to the chief executive. Too many family business directors seek to tell the CEO what he wants to hear. That is understandable if the directors are other family members, employees, or outsiders who depend on the family for income.*[5]

The nature and needs of a business will help determine the qualifications needed in its director. For example, a firm that faces a marketing problem may benefit greatly from the counsel of a board member with a marketing background. Business prominence in the community is not essential, although it may help give the company credibility and enable it to attract other well-qualified directors.

After deciding on the qualifications to look for, a business owner must seek suit-

Action Report

ENTREPRENEURIAL EXPERIENCES

Outside Directors Are an Asset Inside Small Companies

For many small companies, outside directors, if they exist at all, are compliant and content to rubber-stamp the ideas of their friend, the board chairman. But, for some companies, the perspectives of nonmanagement, nonfamily directors bring fresh and independent thinking to important questions. Kurtz Bros., Inc., a landscape materials business in Cuyahoga Falls, Ohio, is a good example.

When the family members who run Kurtz Bros. decided to diversify into industrial materials two years ago, they forgot to consult the outside directors. When the three nonfamily board members learned of the plan, "they were pretty tough on us," recalls Lisa Kurtz, the company's president. "They told us we were fracturing our organization, and that we should stick to our knitting," which for Kurtz Bros. consists of selling top-soil, mulch, and other landscaping supplies. The family officers reconsidered and liquidated the new unit.

Source: Eugene Carlson, "Outside Directors Are an Asset Inside Small Companies," *The Wall Street Journal*, October 30, 1992, p. B2. Reprinted by permission of *The Wall Street Journal*, © 1992 Dow Jones & Company, Inc. All Rights Reserved Worldwide.

able candidates as board members. Suggestions may be obtained from the firm's accountant, attorney, banker, or other friends in the business community. Owners or managers of other, noncompeting small companies, as well as second- and third-level executives in large companies, are often willing to accept such positions. Before offering candidates positions on the board, a business owner would be wise to do some discreet checking.

Compensation of Directors

The amount of compensation paid to board members varies greatly, and some small firms pay no fees at all. However, a board member of a small firm would generally be paid between $200 and $300 monthly. The commitment usually involves one meeting per month. Board members also work at cultivating relationships within the community, an important activity. For the same services, a mid-sized company with about 500 employees might pay its board members $400 or so per month.

Relatively modest compensation for the services of well-qualified directors suggests that financial compensation is not the primary motivation for them. Some reasonable compensation appears appropriate, however, if directors are making important contributions.

An Alternative: An Advisory Council

In recent years, increased attention has been directed to the legal responsibilities of directors. Because outside directors may be held responsible for illegal company actions even though they are not directly involved in wrongdoing, some individuals are reluctant to accept directorships. Some small companies use an **advisory council** as an alternative to a board of directors. Qualified outsiders are asked to serve as advisers to the company. This group of outsiders then functions in much the same way as a board of directors does, except that its actions are advisory only.

The following account describes the potential value of an advisory council:

> *A seven-year-old diversified manufacturing company incurred its first deficit, which the owner-manager deemed an exception that further growth would rectify. Council members noted, however, that many distant operations were out of control and apparently unprofitable. They persuaded the owner to shrink his business by more than one-half. Almost immediately, the business began generating profits. From its reduced scale, growth resumed—this time soundly planned, financed, and controlled.[6]*

The legal liability of members of an advisory council is not completely clear.[7] However, a clear separation of the council from the board of directors is thought to lighten, if not eliminate, the personal liability of its members. Since it is advisory in nature, the council may pose less of a threat to the owner and possibly work more cooperatively than a conventional board.

advisory council
a group that functions like a board of directors but acts only in an advisory capacity

FEDERAL INCOME TAXES AND THE FORM OF ORGANIZATION

5 Explain how different forms of businesses are taxed by the federal government.

To help you understand the federal income tax system, we must first answer the twofold question "Who is responsible for paying taxes, and how is tax liability ascertained?" Businesses are taxed in the following ways:

- Self-employed individuals who operate a business as a sole proprietorship report income from the business on their individual federal income tax returns. They are then taxed at the rates set by law for individuals. The tax rates for a married couple reporting their income jointly are as follows:

Range of Taxable Income	Tax Rate (%)
$0–$35,800	15
$35,801–$86,500	28
$86,501–$140,000	31
$140,001–$250,000	36
Over $250,000	39

For example, assume that a sole proprietor, who is married and files a joint return with his or her spouse, has taxable income of $150,000 from a business. The taxes owed on this income would be $39,751, computed as follows:

	Income	×	Tax Rate	=	Taxes
First	$ 35,800		15%		$ 5,370
Next	50,700		28		14,196
Next	53,500		31		16,585
Remaining	10,000		36		3,600
Total	$150,000				$39,751

- A partnership reports the income it earns to the Internal Revenue Service, but it does not pay any taxes. The income is allocated to the partners according to their agreement. The partners each report their own share of the partnership income on their personal tax return and pay any taxes owed.

- The corporation, as a separate legal entity, reports its income and pays any taxes related to these profits. The owners (stockholders) of the corporation need only report on their personal tax returns any amounts paid to them by the corporation in the form of dividends. The current corporate tax rates are as follows:

Range of Taxable Income	Tax Rate (%)
$0–$50,000	15
$50,001–$75,000	25
$75,001–$10,000,000	34
Over $10,000,000	35

An additional 5 percent tax is imposed on taxable income between $100,000 and $335,000, as well as a 3 percent tax on income between $15,000,000 and $18,333,333.

For example, the tax liability for the K&C Corporation, which had $150,000 in taxable income, would be $41,750, calculated as follows:

	Income	×	Tax Rate	=	Taxes
First	$ 50,000		15%		$ 7,500
Next	25,000		25		6,250
Remaining	75,000		34		25,500
Total	$150,000				$39,250
Plus 5% surtax for income exceeding $100,000					2,500
[0.05 × ($150,000 − $100,000)]					
Total tax liability					$41,750

If the K&C Corporation paid a dividend to its owners in the amount of $40,000, the owners would need to report this dividend income when computing their personal income taxes. Thus, the $40,000 is taxed twice, first as part of the corporation's income and then as part of the owners' personal income. However, this double taxation could be avoided if the firm were a Subchapter S corporation.

The Subchapter S Corporation

The name **Subchapter S corporation** is derived from Subchapter S of the Internal Revenue Code, which permits a corporation to retain the limited-liability feature of a regular corporation, or **C corporation,** while being taxed as a partnership. To obtain S corporation status, a corporation must meet certain eligibility requirements:

- No more than 35 stockholders are allowed. Husband and wife count as one stockholder.
- All stockholders must be individuals or certain qualifying estates and trusts.
- Only one class of stock can be outstanding.
- The corporation must be a domestic one.
- No nonresident alien stockholders are permitted.
- The S corporation cannot own more than 79 percent of the stock of another corporation.

---

6 Describe the special features and restrictions of a Subchapter S corporation.

Subchapter S corporation
a type of corporation that is taxed by the federal government as a partnership

C corporation
a type of corporation that is taxed by the federal government as a separate legal entity

Once a corporation attains S status, it stops paying corporate income taxes and instead passes taxable income or loss on to the stockholders. This allows stockholders to receive dividends from the corporation without double taxation on the corporation's profit (once as corporate tax and again as personal tax).

A competent tax attorney should be consulted before making the S status election, as recent tax law changes have had considerable effect on the S corporation arrangement. A sample of the limitations of S corporation status under the reformed tax regulations are as follows:

- Except for certain exceptions, an S corporation must use the calendar year for tax reporting.
- Only stockholder employees owning less than 5 percent of the S corporation can borrow from the corporation's pension and profit-sharing plans.
- Medical-plan premiums paid by the S corporation and other fringe benefits received by stockholder employees are taxable income.
- An S corporation may be required to pay corporate tax if its passive income—income other than from operating the business—exceeds 25 percent of gross receipts.[8]

Despite these and other limitations, the S corporation has been particularly desirable to stockholders because of tax advantages. Specifically, tax rates in the 1980s and early 1990s were lower for individuals than for C corporations. However, the 1993 tax law changes raised tax rates for high-income individuals, including many owners of S corporations. They are now higher than C corporation tax rates—thus decreasing the attractiveness of the S corporation.

1 Describe the characteristics and value of a strong management team.

- A strong management team nurtures a business idea and helps provide the necessary resources to make it succeed.
- The skills of management team members should complement each other to form an optimal combination of education and experience.
- The management team should outline the organizational structure to be used.
- A small firm can improve its management by drawing on the expertise of outside professional groups.

2 Identify the common legal forms of organization used by small businesses and describe the characteristics of each.

- The most common legal forms of organization used by small businesses are the sole proprietorship, the partnership, and the corporation.
- In a sole proprietorship, the owner receives all profits and bears all losses. The principal disadvantage of this form is the owner's unlimited liability.
- A partnership should be established on the basis of a written partnership agreement. Partners can individually commit the partnership to binding contracts. In a limited partnership, general partners are personally liable for the debts of the business, while limited partners have limited personal liability as long as they do not take an active role in managing the business.
- Corporations are particularly attractive because of their limited-liability feature. The fact that ownership is easily transferable makes them well suited for combining the capital of numerous owners.

3 Identify factors to consider in making a choice among the different legal forms of organization.

- The key factors that affect the choice among different legal forms of organization are organizational costs, limited versus unlimited liability, continuity, transferability of ownership, management control, capability of raising new equity capital, and income taxes.

4 Describe the effective use of boards of directors and advisory councils.

- Boards of directors can contribute to small corporations by offering counsel and assistance to their chief executives.
- To be most effective, members of the board must be properly qualified, independent outsiders.
- One alternative to an active board of directors is an advisory council, whose members cannot be held personally liable for the company's actions.

5 Explain how different forms of businesses are taxed by the federal government.

- Self-employed individuals who operate a business as a sole proprietorship report income from the business on their individual tax returns.
- A partnership reports the income it earns to the Internal Revenue Service, but the partnership itself does not pay any taxes. The income is allocated to the owners according to their partnership agreement.
- The corporation reports its income and pays any taxes due on this income.

Continue on next page

6 Describe the special features and restrictions of a Subchapter S corporation.

- Subchapter S corporations are corporations that enjoy a special tax status that permits them to avoid corporate tax by passing taxable gains and losses on to individual stockholders.
- To qualify as a Subchapter S corporation, certain eligibility requirements must be met, most of which pose no problems for small companies.

New Terms and Concepts

management team *183*

sole proprietorship *186*

unlimited liability *186*

partnership *187*

articles of partnership *188*

agency power *189*

limited partnership *189*

general partner *190*

limited partner *190*

corporation *190*

legal entity *190*

corporate charter *190*

stock certificate *191*

pre-emptive right *191*

board of directors *195*

advisory council *199*

Subchapter S corporation *200*

C corporation *200*

ordinary income *202*

capital gains and losses *202*

Section 1244 stock *202*

Section 1244 Stock

For tax purposes, **ordinary income** is income earned in the everyday course of business. Salary is also considered ordinary income. **Capital gains and losses** are gains or losses incurred from the sale of property not used in the ordinary course of business, such as gains or losses from the sale of common stock.

Typically, capital losses may only be deducted from capital gains and may not be deducted from ordinary income. However, stock issued pursuant to Section 1244 of the Internal Revenue Code—**Section 1244 stock**—somewhat protects the stockholder in case of corporate failure. If such stock becomes worthless, the loss (up to $100,000 on a joint tax return) may be treated as an *ordinary* tax-deductible loss. Thus, when initially organizing a corporation, an owner would do well to consider issuing Section 1244 stock. Then, in the case of business failure, the owner could realize a tax savings that would not be allowed with regular stock.

ordinary income
income earned in the ordinary course of business, including any salary

capital gains and losses
gains and losses incurred from the sale of property not used in the ordinary course of business operations

Section 1244 stock
stock that offers some tax benefit to the stockholder in the case of corporate failure

DISCUSSION QUESTIONS

1. Why would investors tend to favor a new business that has a management team rather than a lone entrepreneur as its head? Is this preference justified?
2. Discuss the relative merits of the three major legal forms of organization.
3. Does the concept of limited liability apply to a sole proprietorship? Why or why not?
4. Suppose a partnership is set up and operated without formal articles of partnership. What problems might arise? Explain.
5. Explain why the agency power of partners is of great importance.
6. What is a Subchapter S corporation, and what is its advantage?
7. Evaluate the three major forms of organization in terms of management control by the owner and sharing of the firm's profits.
8. How might a board of directors be of value to management in a small corporation? What are the qualifications essential for a director? Is stock ownership in the firm a prerequisite for being a director?
9. What may account for the failure of most small corporations to use boards of directors as more than rubber stamps?
10. How do advisory councils differ from boards of directors? Which would you recommend to a small company owner? Why?

EXPERIENTIAL EXERCISES

1. Prepare a one-page résumé of your own qualifications to launch a term-paper typing business at your college or university. Add a critique that might be prepared by an investor evaluating your strengths and weaknesses as shown on the résumé.

2. Interview an attorney whose practice includes small businesses as clients. Inquire about the legal considerations involved in choosing the form of organization for a new business. Report your findings to the class.

3. Interview the partners of a local business. Inquire about their partnership agreement. Report your findings to the class.

4. Discuss with a corporate director, attorney, banker, or business owner the contributions of directors to small firms. Prepare a brief report of your findings. If you discover a particularly well-informed individual, suggest that person to your instructor as a possible speaker.

Exploring the

5. Do word searches on the Web for "sole proprietorship," "partnership," and "corporation." Look for materials that offer definitions of these terms and that give comparisons of these three forms of organization. Report your findings to the class.

You Make the Call

Situation 1 Ted Green and Mark Stroder became close friends as 16-year-olds when both worked part-time for Green's dad in his automotive parts store. After high school, Green went to college and Stroder joined the National Guard Reserve and devoted his weekends to his auto racing habit. Green continued his association with the automotive parts store by buying and managing two of his dad's stores.

In 1995, Green conceived the idea of starting a new business that would rebuild automobile starters, and he asked Stroder to be his partner in the venture. Stroder was somewhat concerned about working with Green because their personalities are so different. Green has been described as "outgoing and enthusiastic," while Stroder is "reserved and skeptical." However, Stroder was out of work at the time, and he agreed to the offer. He set up a small shop behind one of Green's automotive parts stores. Stroder does all the work; Green supplies the cash.

The "partners" realized the immediate need to decide on a legal form of organization. They agreed to name the business STARTOVER.

Question 1 How relevant are the individual personalities to the success of this entrepreneurial team? Do you think Green and Stroder have a chance to survive their "partnership"? Why or why not?

Question 2 Do you think it is an advantage or a disadvantage that the members of this team are the same age?

Question 3 Which legal form of organization would you propose for STARTOVER? Why?

Question 4 If Stroder and Green decide to incorporate, would they qualify as a Subchapter S corporation? If so, would you recommend this option? Why or why not?

Situation 2 Bob was the leading performer at a corporate-design firm; Clarence was the leader at its competitor. Deciding to work together, they both quit their jobs and started a firm.

Clarence argued that as the older of the two, with more experience, he was being exposed to greater risk than Bob. Therefore, Clarence negotiated to receive 51 percent of the firm and a compensation package based on each partner's own sales, net of expenses. As expected, Clarence earned more the first year. The next year, though, Bob unexpectedly sold more than Clarence and requested reconsideration of the terms. "I urged Clarence to regard me not as a risk anymore but as an asset." To which Clarence retorted, "Well, no asset's going to make more than *I* do." He hired a support team—for himself, not for Bob—and stopped sending Bob the figures on which their take-home pay was based. Bob accessed the information on the accounting department's computer and discovered that his partner had siphoned off more than $10,000. He confronted Clarence. "Okay, okay, I took it," his partner confessed. "But I deserved it; I had to manage the staff."

Source: Adapted from "Partner Wars," *Inc.*, Vol. 16, No. 6 (June 1994), p. 40.

Question 1 What mistake was made in the formation of this partnership?

Question 2 Is Clarence right in claiming that he should receive more than Bob?

Question 3 Do you see an ethical problem in this situation?

Question 4 If you were Bob, what would you do?

Continue on next page

Situation 3 For years, a small distributor of welding materials followed the practice of most small firms in treating the board of directors as merely a legal necessity. Composed of two co-owners and a retired steel company executive, the board was not a working board. The company was profitable and had been run with informal, traditional management methods.

The majority owner, after attending a seminar, decided that a board might be useful for more than legal or cosmetic purposes. Based on this thinking, he invited two outsiders—both division heads of larger corporations—to join the board. This brought the membership of the board to five. The majority owner believes the new members will be helpful in opening up the business to new ideas.

Question 1 Can two outside members in a board of five make any real difference in the way it operates?

Question 2 Evaluate the owner's choices for board members.

Question 3 What will determine the usefulness or effectiveness of this board? Do you predict that it will be useful? Why?

CASE 9
VMG Products (p. 618)

This case presents issues that relate to forming a limited partnership.

Alternative Cases for Chapter 9:
Case 12, "Walkers Machine Works," p. 624
Case 25, "The Martin Company," p. 660

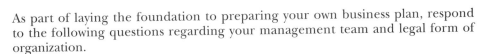
LAYING THE FOUNDATION
Asking the Right Questions

As part of laying the foundation to preparing your own business plan, respond to the following questions regarding your management team and legal form of organization.

Management Plan Questions

1. Who are the members of your management team?
2. What are the skills, education, and experience of each?
3. What other active investors or directors are involved, and what are their qualifications?
4. What vacant positions remain, and what are your plans to fill them?
5. What consultants will be used, and what are their qualifications?
6. What is the compensation package for each key person?
7. How is the ownership distributed?
8. How will employees be selected and rewarded?
9. What style of management will be used?
10. How will personnel be motivated?
11. How will creativity be encouraged?
12. How will commitment and loyalty be developed?
13. How will new employees be trained?
14. Who is responsible for job descriptions and employee evaluations?

Legal Plan Questions

1. Will the business function as a sole proprietorship, partnership, or corporation? If a corporation, will it be a C corporation or a Subchapter S corporation?
2. What are the liability implications of the legal form of organization chosen?
3. What are the tax advantages and disadvantages of this form of organization?
4. Where will the corporation be chartered?
5. If a corporation, when will it be incorporated?
6. What attorney or legal firm has been selected to represent the firm?
7. What type of relationship exists with the firm's attorney or law firm?
8. What legal issues are presently or potentially significant?
9. What licenses and/or permits may be required?
10. What insurance will be taken out on the business, the employees, and so on?

USING BizPlanBuilder

If you are using BizPlan*Builder,* refer to Part 3 for information that should be included in the business plan concerning building a management team and choosing a legal form of organization. Then turn to Part 2 for instructions on using the BizPlan software to write these sections of the plan.

Chapter 10

Choosing the Location and Physical Facilities

The Rosell Family

Spotlight on small business

The personal preferences of entrepreneurs often play an active role in their choice of a business location. In recent years, many entrepreneurs have fled big city offices to work in friendlier home environments. In 1988, Robert and Pat Rosell moved from Los Angeles, California to Bellevue, Washington, where they opened a business in their home. Their firm, Quality Media Resources, Inc. produces employee-training videos.

The Rosells' two children, both under five years old, are an integral part of this new life-style. A home-based business environment allows parents to read stories to their children, take them to school, and engage in other "normal" family activities not always possible in a two-wage-earner family. "It's wonderful to be a part of [our kids' lives]," says Pat, "to see all the important things happen on a daily basis."

What was the motivation for the move? "A work environment that supports our life-style" says Robert, "rather than a life-style that supports our work environment." Since the move, Quality Media Resources has added such prominent clients as Microsoft, Xerox, and Nintendo.

Source: Janean Huber, "Bright Lights, Small City," *Entrepreneur*, Vol. 22, No. 3 (March 1994), pp. 102–109. Reprinted with permission of *Entrepreneur* Magazine, March 1994.

A business concept takes on a visible form when an entrepreneur develops a business plan. It becomes even more tangible when the entrepreneur assembles the resources needed to implement the plan. Important resources at this stage are the business site and the necessary building and equipment. For some entrepreneurial ventures, the site may simply be a briefcase or desk space at home; for others, it may be a new freestanding building. Regardless, every entrepreneur should think seriously about the location decision. In this chapter, we address some of the major considerations in choosing a business location and physical facilities.

Looking Ahead

After studying this chapter, you should be able to:

1 Identify the general considerations affecting the choice of a business location.

2 Describe the process for making the location decision.

3 Identify the challenges of running a home-based business.

4 Explain how efficiency can be achieved in the layout of a physical facility.

5 Discuss the equipment and tool needs of small firms.

THE LOCATION DECISION

1 Identify the general considerations affecting the choice of a business location.

For many small businesses, choosing a location is a one-time decision—made only when the business is first established or purchased. Frequently, however, a business considers relocation to reduce operating costs, get closer to its customers, or gain other advantages. Also, as a business expands, it sometimes becomes desirable to begin additional operations at other locations. The owner of a custom drapery shop, for example, may decide to open a second unit in another section of the same city or even in another part of the state in order to increase the firm's customer base.

Some reference to a proposed location should be included in the business plan. The extent of this discussion will vary from venture to venture.

Importance of the Location Decision

The lasting effects of location decisions are what make them so important. Once a business is established, it is costly and often impractical, if not impossible, to pull up stakes and move. If the choice is particularly poor, the business may never be able to get off the ground, even with adequate financing and superior managerial ability (see Figure 10-1). This effect is so clearly recognized by national chains that they spend thousands of dollars investigating sites before establishing new stores. As we noted in Chapter 4, one of the reasons that franchising is such an attractive startup alternative is that franchisers will typically assist an entrepreneur in site selection.

The choice of a location is much more vital to some businesses than to others. For example, the site chosen for a dress shop can make or break the business because it must be convenient for customers. In contrast, the exact location of a painting contractor is of less importance, since customers do not need frequent access to the facility. Even painting contractors, however, may suffer from certain locational disadvantages. Some communities are more willing or able than others to invest resources to keep property in good condition, thereby providing better opportunities for painters.

Figure 10-1

*If a Business Plan Calls
for a Poor Location,
Prospects for a Successful
Venture Are Weak*

PEANUTS reprinted by permission of UFS, Inc.

Key Factors in Determining a Good Location

Only careful investigation of a potential site will reveal its good and bad features. However, four key factors guide the initial steps of the investigation process: personal preference, environmental conditions, resource availability, and customer accessibility. In a particular situation, one factor may be more important than the others, but each always has an influence. These factors are depicted in Figure 10-2.

Figure 10-2

Four Factors Deserve Careful Consideration in Determining a Good Business Location

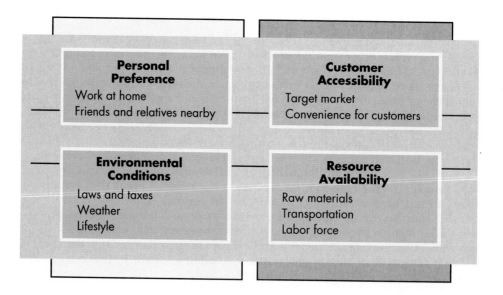

Action Report

TECHNOLOGICAL APPLICATIONS

Locating on the World Wide Web

A company located in a mall gives up a certain amount of independence: Its success depends as much on the popularity of the entire package of stores as it does on its own efforts. On the other hand, malls generate streams of prospective customers who otherwise might never have stopped by the store.

So it is with the "cybermall," a group of businesses that can be reached at a single World Wide Web address. Like their real-world counterparts, cybermalls can be developed around an anchor store, or they can simply be the home of many smaller businesses.

Bob and Arminda Alexander put a virtual version of their Hawaiian coffee-bean store in a cybermall earlier this year, when rent and other overhead sent expenses for their actual store, located on the island of Maui, skyrocketing.

For $1,000, a local Internet provider helped the Alexanders create a home page filled with color photographs and descriptions of their gourmet Kona beans. The home page could also process credit-card orders. But a big question remained: How would coffee shoppers know where to find Hawaii's Best Espresso Co.? Answer: Link the home page to a cybermall.

The Alexanders quickly realized that for just a few hundred dollars each month, they could link their home page to six cybermalls, including Downtown Anywhere and Planet-Hawaii. The company gets more than 1,000 visits by Web shoppers each day, producing $15,000 a month in orders. Business is so good that the couple recently closed the Maui shop.

"It's a gas to turn on a computer in the morning and have a couple hundred dollars of business be there waiting," crows Bob Alexander. "All we're doing on the Internet is the same as we did with the shop, except we're open 24 hours a day, and we don't have to be there."

Source: Rusty Weston, "Five Ways to Do Business on the Internet," *Inc. Technology*, Vol. 17, No. 13 (1995), p. 76.

PERSONAL PREFERENCE   As a practical matter, many entrepreneurs consider only their home community as a location. Frequently, the possibility of locating elsewhere never enters their minds. Just because an individual has always lived in a particular town, however, does not automatically make the town a satisfactory business location!

Even so, locating a business locally for personal reasons is not necessarily illogical. In fact, there are certain advantages. From a personal standpoint, the entrepreneur generally appreciates and feels comfortable with the atmosphere of the home community, whether it is a small town or a large city. From a practical business standpoint, the entrepreneur can more easily establish credit. The hometown banker can be dealt with more confidently, and other businesspersons may be of great service in helping evaluate a given opportunity. If potential customers live mainly in the locality, the prospective entrepreneur probably has a better idea of their tastes and preferences than an outsider would have. Relatives and friends may be the entrepreneur's first customers and may help to advertise his or her products and/or services. Personal preference, however, should not be allowed to take priority over obvious location weaknesses.

ENVIRONMENTAL CONDITIONS   A small business must operate within the environmental conditions of its location. These conditions can hinder or promote success. For example, weather is an environmental factor that traditionally affects the desirability of locations. Other environmental conditions, such as competition, laws, and leisure attractions, to name a few, are also part of the business environment. Consider hometown entrepreneur Steve Laing, founder of a career information magazine called *Beyond High School,* based in Eugene, Oregon. Laing likes running his business in scenic Oregon because he is hooked on the great outdoors. "What's nice about doing business in Eugene is the life-style factor," he says. "You have access to a lot of outdoor opportunities. I put in a lot of hours [at work]," he explains, "but I can take off at 2 P.M. and be on the river by 2:30."[1] Obviously, the best time to evaluate environmental conditions is prior to making a location commitment.

RESOURCE AVAILABILITY   Resources associated with operating a business should also be considered when selecting a location. Raw materials, land, water supply, labor supply, transportation, and communication facilities are some of the site-related factors that have a bearing on location. Raw materials and labor supply are particularly critical considerations in the location of a manufacturing business. In many cases, however, personal preference or environmental conditions may exert a strong influence on the final location decision and thus offset some resource advantages.

CUSTOMER ACCESSIBILITY   Frequently, the foremost consideration in selecting a location is customer accessibility. Retail outlets and service firms are typical examples of businesses that must be located so that access is convenient for target market customers.

Providing access for target market customers is especially important for retail stores and service firms. Choosing a location with abundant foot traffic or car traffic is essential for a business whose customers place a high priority on convenience.

Many products, such as snack foods and gasoline, are convenience goods, requiring a retail location close to target customers; otherwise, consumers substitute competitor brands. Many services, such as tire repair and banking services, are also classified as convenience items and require a location close to target customers. Once again, the precise location may be influenced strongly by other location factors.

As the entrepreneur conducts the site selection process, these four key factors should be uppermost in his or her mind. In the next section, we assume that these factors are equally important to an entrepreneur as he or she begins the actual site-selection process.

THE LOCATION SELECTION PROCESS

2 Describe the process for making the location decision.

For some businesses—a barbershop or drugstore, for example—there are many location options, as these businesses can operate successfully in most areas of the country. For other types of small businesses, however, entrepreneurs need to analyze prospective locations with extreme thoroughness. Location decisions cannot and should not be made haphazardly.

Choice of Region and State

The marketing of certain goods and services is more logically conducted in specific regions or even states. For example, a ski lodge is feasible only in an area with slopes and snow; a boat repair service is unlikely to locate in a state with insufficient water for boating. However, most new firms have the option of selecting among several regions.

THIRD-PARTY DATA   Various approaches can be used to evaluate regions of the country. In 1993, *The Wall Street Journal* ranked all U.S. states according to those that provided the most conducive environment for small business success. This ranking incorporated six evaluation factors developed by the Corporation for Enterprise Development, a nonprofit, small business research group in Washington, D.C.:

1. *State economic performance.* The better the economy, the better it can support new businesses. Includes, among other things, employment growth, unemployment rate, earnings growth, and income distribution.
2. *Business vitality.* The more vital and energetic the business community, the better the prospects for growth. Includes, among other things, the level of earnings from industries that compete with out-of-state companies, business closings, and number of new companies per worker.
3. *Development capacity.* This measures the resources needed by businesses to become and remain competitive. Includes, among other things, high school graduation rate, prevalence of scientists and engineers, financial resources, and quality and use of highways, mass transit, and medical care.
4. *Small business culture.* The greater the proportion of small businesses in a state, the more likely the business environment is conducive to new small businesses. Includes the percentage of businesses that have 20 or fewer employees, and the percentage that have 500 or fewer employees.
5. *State business assistance environment.* Measures the programs—including small business incubators, loan programs, and procurement programs—designed to assist in business formation.
6. *Balanced/fair tax and fiscal system.* The more rational and stable a tax system, the better for small business. Includes, among other things, the stability of revenue from taxes, existence of a "rainy day" fund, and the fairness of the tax burden.[2]

The top six states in *The Wall Street Journal* ranking were Colorado, Idaho, California, Utah, New Mexico, and Nebraska. Interestingly, Colorado, the overall winner, ranked 30th on state business assistance environment, while Nebraska, in sixth place overall, ranked first on this characteristic. The validity of ranking states with this system is, of course, subject to debate. Nevertheless, entrepreneurs should consult information of this nature as they evaluate regions and states. Other considerations in such an evaluation include nearness to the market, availability of raw materials and labor, and laws and tax policies.

NEARNESS TO THE MARKET Locating close to the center of the target market is desirable if other factors are approximately equal in importance. This is especially true for industries in which the cost of shipping a finished product is high relative to the product's value. For example, packaged ice and soft drinks require production facilities that are near consuming markets. And retailers always desire a location convenient to customers.

AVAILABILITY OF RAW MATERIALS If required raw materials are not abundantly available in all areas, a region in which these materials abound offers special locational advantages. The necessary use of bulky or heavy raw materials that lose much of their bulk or weight in the manufacturing process is a powerful force that affects location. A sawmill is an example of a business that must stay close to its raw materials in order to operate economically.

ADEQUACY OF LABOR SUPPLY A manufacturer's labor requirements depend on the nature of its production process. Available labor supply, wage rates, labor productivity, and a history of peaceful industrial relations are all particularly important considerations for labor-intensive firms. In some cases, the need for semiskilled or unskilled labor justifies locating in a surplus labor area. In other cases, firms find it desirable to seek a pool of highly skilled labor. For example, General Robert Mathis retired in 1982 after 34 years in the Air Force and moved with his wife to Bozeman, Montana, which he believed was an excellent place to start a business. His high-tech company, TMA Technologies, Inc., manufactures laser and computer "light scatter" equipment. Bozeman is home to Montana State University, from which John Stover, a professor and expert in optics technology, was recruited to work for TMA. Other skilled employees have also been lured to TMA from the university.[3]

LAWS AND TAX POLICIES Every entrepreneur seeks profits; therefore, all factors affecting the financial picture are of great concern. State and local governments can help or hinder a new business by their levying of unreasonably high taxes. State corporate income taxes are often a burden to business. Considerable variation in this tax exists across the United States, and only five states have no such tax. Table 10-1 lists sales tax rates and income tax rates for a sample of U.S. states. An example of one state with an advantageous tax policy is Wyoming. George Gault, director of economic and community development for the Wyoming Department of Commerce says, "We recruit small businesses because that's what we think fits in Wyoming communities," he says. He points out that the workers' compensation and property taxes in Wyoming are lower than in neighboring states. Wyoming also has no corporate income tax, personal income tax, or inventory tax.[4]

Choice of City

An entrepreneur wants to locate a new business in the right city in the best region. To make the correct decisions, the entrepreneur must analyze various cities in terms of the competitive situation, the availability of support services, and other such factors.

A few years ago, Bob Freese and three colleagues from 3M Corporation in St. Paul, Minnesota started a new high-tech firm, Alphatronix, to produce optical storage devices for computers. They were reluctant to locate in Minnesota because the cost of doing business there was high. Also, they believed it might be difficult for a startup to lure professional talent to such a cold climate. Therefore, they made a careful nationwide search of cities to find the best spot for their new company.

Alphatronix's Bob Freese and his partners looked carefully at Kansas City, as well as at other finalists such as Washington, D.C., and Salt Lake City. Various cities scored high on one or another criterion. Washington had a well-developed high-tech infrastructure; it

Tax Rates in Selected States | *Table 10-1* | - - - - - - - - - - - - - - - -

State	Rates		
	Sales Tax	**Personal Income Tax**	**Corporate Income Tax**
California	6%	1% of first $9,332 of taxable income to 11% of $424,761 and over for joint taxpayers and surviving spouses with dependents. An alternative tax of 8.5% (7% for tax years beginning after 1995) is also imposed.	9.3% of net income derived from business transactions in California except for banks and financial corporations
Connecticut	6%	4.5% of Connecticut taxable income	11.5% of net income, plus 3.1 mills per dollar of capital stock and surplus to the extent it exceeds the tax on net income. The rate is 11.25% in 1995 on value (minimum $250, maximum $1 million), 11% in 1996, 10.5% in 1997, and 10% in 1998.
Florida	6%*	None	5.5% of federal taxable income apportioned to Florida plus 3.3% alternative minimum tax. $5,000 of net income is exempt.
Illinois	6.25%*	3% of federal adjusted gross income with adjustments for individuals, estates, and trusts	4.8% of federal taxable income with adjustments
New Mexico	None	2.4% of taxable income not over $8,000 to 8.5% over $64,000 for married individuals filing jointly and surviving spouses	4.8% of first $500,000 of net income to 7.6% over $1 million. Qualified taxpayers may pay an alternative tax of 0.75% of gross receipts from New Mexico sales.
Rhode Island	7%	27.5% of first $15,000 of federal income tax liability to 25.05% of $75,528 or more of federal liability for married persons filing jointly	9% of net income
Tennessee	6%*	6%. Tax applies to interest and dividend income.	6% of net taxable income
Wyoming	4%*	None	None

*Plus an additional tax levied by county or municipal jurisdiction
Source: *Thorndike Encyclopedia of Banking and Financial Tables; 1995 Yearbook* (Boston: Warren, Gorham & Lamont, 1995). Prepared by Donald S. Benton.

also had high costs and a mixed quality of life. Salt Lake City had moderate costs and a high quality of life, but transportation was a problem: Reaching customers on the East Coast wouldn't be easy. The ultimate winner: Research Triangle Park, in the Raleigh-Durham area of North Carolina. "Other places in the country might look better in any given category," says Freese. "But when you begin looking at two or three criteria, this area just pops right up." [5]

At that time, Research Triangle Park housed about 60 high-tech companies and was expanding into 2,000 undeveloped acres.

Some cities are growing in both population and business activity, and the income level of their citizens is rising. In contrast, other cities are expanding slowly or even declining in population. Obviously, most businesses would prefer to locate in an area with a growing population.

Most small businesses are concerned about the nature and the amount of local competition. Manufacturers that serve a national market are an exception, but

Action Report

GLOBAL OPPORTUNITIES

Border Town: Good Location?

Laredo, Texas, a U.S.–Mexican border city of approximately 150,000, experiences more than one-third of all land traffic between the two countries. Many businesses in Laredo benefit from this location. Incomes are increasing in Mexico, and large numbers of Mexicans cross the border daily to take advantage of a wide selection of merchandise at cheaper prices. Laredo's Dillards, Sears, and Wal-Mart stores have the highest sales per square foot of any of their chains' stores in the country.

The fortunes of Laredo's small businesses have also grown with the increase in trade between the United States and Mexico. This economic boom has created a surge in transportation-related jobs, including short-haul truckers, custom brokers, freight forwarders, and warehouse workers. A decade ago, the homebuilding business of Robert Gutierrez was near insolvency. Now his firm, Armadillo Construction, is building cozy three-bedroom brick houses in Laredo as fast as it can. The 42-year-old Gutierrez proclaims that Laredo could be bigger than El Paso some day. "That giant sucking sound that Ross Perot talked about, that was jobs coming to Laredo," he says.

However, not all people in Laredo are this optimistic. James Giermanski, a trade expert at Laredo's Texas A&M International University, is concerned that free trade legislation may do more harm to small firms than good. "The economics of a border community are built on barriers to trade," he says. "When you take away those barriers, these cities may not be commercially viable."

Source: Christopher Palmeri, "Laredo's Giant Sucking Sound," *Forbes*, Vol. 153, No. 9 (April 25, 1994), pp. 78–81. Reprinted By Permission of *FORBES* Magazine © Forbes Inc., 1994.

overcrowding can occur in the majority of small business fields. The quality of competition also affects the desirability of a location. If existing businesses are not aggressive and do not offer the type of service reasonably expected by the customer, there is likely to be room for a newcomer. Published data can be used to shed light on this problem. The average population required to support a given type of business can be determined on a national or regional basis. By comparing the situation in a given city with these averages, an entrepreneur can get a better picture of the intensity of local competition.

Unfortunately, objective data of this type seldom produce unequivocal answers. There is no substitute for personal observation. The entrepreneur should also seek the opinions of those well acquainted with local business conditions. For example, wholesalers frequently have an excellent notion of the potential for additional retail establishments in a given line of business.

In choosing a city, the prospective entrepreneur should be assured of satisfactory police and fire protection, water and other utilities, public transportation, and communication technology. Unreasonably restrictive local ordinances constitute a major disadvantage. Some cities offer incentives, such as low-interest loans or a break in local property taxes, to new or expanding businesses. A city might also possess advantages related to civic, cultural, religious, and recreational affairs, which make it a better place in which to live and do business.

Communities that aggressively encourage small businesses are prime candidates for consideration. Arcata, California, located in Humboldt County on the state's northern coast, is such a city. In the late 1960s, logging and sawmills provided over 9,000 jobs in the county, but these industries declined over the next decade. In 1979, the city of Arcata established the Arcata Economic Development Corporation (AEDC) to foster economic development. By encouraging small business creation through loans and other incentives, the town of 16,000 has constructed a healthy and sustainable future. A few of the small businesses that have been attracted to Arcata are

- Cascade Forest Products, which manufactures and markets six different lines of packaged soil products. Begun in 1979 by entrepreneur Jim Sciaroni, the firm employs 35 workers and, after receiving a small loan from the Arcata Community Development Center, relocated to two new buildings encompassing 35,000 square feet.
- Yashi, a jewelry business formed by designer Holly Hosterman and industrial artist Paul Lubitz—both graduates of the local university, Humboldt State. The company employs over 50 artisans to produce its designs, which are sold around the world.
- Moonstone Mountaineering, Inc., started by Fred and Niki Williams, which specializes in handmade sleeping bags and clothing for backpacking. It employs almost 100 people and is based in Arcata's Aldergrove Industrial Park.[6]

Choosing a Specific Site

The entrepreneur's next step, after choosing a city, is to select a specific site in or near the city. Some critical factors to consider at this stage include costs, customer accessibility, neighborhood conditions, and the trend toward suburban development. In selecting a site, some firms—including most manufacturers, wholesalers, plumbing contractors, and painting contractors—stress operating costs and purchasing costs. It would be foolish for these firms to locate in high-rent districts.

Earlier, we stressed customer accessibility as an important consideration in selecting a location. This factor becomes critical when evaluating a specific site for many types of retail stores. For example, a shoe store or a drugstore may fail simply because it is on the wrong side of the street. Therefore, measurement of customer traffic—pedestrian or auto, depending on the nature of the business—is helpful in evaluating sites for some types of business. Terri Bowersock, owner of Terri's Consignment World, based in Mesa, Arizona, has commented on the perplexities of retail location:

> *"Find out where people shop, which roads they take," she says. "We discovered that in one area, people traveled from the east side of town to shop," but the people on the west side seldom shopped on the east side. . . . "We made a mistake with one store," says Bowersock. "We went for price and put [the store] in an area where annual incomes were about $20,000." After studying her customers at the other locations, she discovered that she needed an income level of at least $40,000 to be successful. So, for future stores, she selected the more-affluent areas.[7]*

Some site locations present special problems because of deteriorating conditions or the threat of natural disaster. For example, during the Midwestern floods in the summer of 1993, many small firms found themselves under several feet of water. While business opportunities exist in all geographical areas, the strengths and weaknesses of those areas must be evaluated.

Enterprise and Foreign Trade Zones

Many states offer businesses location incentives through a variety of strategies. One such strategy involves **enterprise zones,** which are established to bring jobs to eco-

enterprise zones
state-designated areas that are established to bring jobs to economically deprived areas through regulatory and tax incentives

Action Report

ENTREPRENEURIAL EXPERIENCES

Crime Rates Versus Rent Rates

The South Bronx in New York has a bad reputation. Its business climate rating is undesirable, to say the least. It has been described as "the landscape of the legendary police precinct known as Fort Apache, a place where churches surround themselves with fences topped with razor wire," but some entrepreneurs have chosen the South Bronx for their businesses because of low rents.

Nancy Lasher, industrial development director of the South Bronx Economic Development Corporation, says, "We've worked with 40 or 50 startups in the past three years." One of these was a computer equipment maker, Willow Peripherals, whose president is Jonathan Vall.

> *Willow moved from Manhattan in 1986 when the city government offered 8,100 square feet in a once-abandoned building in the South Bronx's Port Morris section for only $2 a square foot per year. "The space was wide open. There were tons of windows," Mr. Vall says. The rent has since climbed to about $3.50 a square foot.*
>
> *The location "has its ups and downs," Mr. Vall admits. Lack of other small technology companies in the neighborhood makes it hard to persuade vendor representatives to pay a visit. And hiring skilled help is a problem.*
>
> *"You put an ad in the New York Times. Somebody calls and says, 'Where are you?' You say the South Bronx. Next thing you hear is the dial tone," [he says].*
>
> *But, Mr. Vall says, "This is a place [where] you can keep your costs down." He notes that the city's wholesale flower market is moving a few blocks away. He downplays the crime factor—even while showing a visitor a hole in an interior wall caused by a toddler in a neighboring apartment house who fired a 9mm revolver out the window. The hole is surrounded by a small wooden frame and a label reading: "Genuine Bronx Bullet Hole."*

Once again, the entrepreneurial spirit finds an opportunity in the most unlikely place!

Source: Eugene Carlson, "South Bronx Address Can Give a Firm Reverse Cachet," *The Wall Street Journal*, August 12, 1993, p. B2. Reprinted by permission of *The Wall Street Journal*, © 1993 Dow Jones & Company, Inc. All Rights Reserved Worldwide.

nomically deprived areas. Their lure is regulatory and tax relief. Consider the benefits to the following three small businesses located in enterprise zones:

> *[Harold] Sarvetnick's company, Acrilex Inc., has been in the Jersey City Urban Enterprise Zone since 1989. Acrilex's 36 employees make and distribute about $8.2 million worth of acrylic sheets and related plastic products a year. Sarvetnick, president and owner, says the company's zone location has enabled it to take advantage of tax incentives, regulatory streamlining, and other breaks from the state. That $10,000 tax saving, for example, came about when Acrilex was exempted from New Jersey use taxes, which are similar to sales taxes, when it bought the $175,000 computerized router.*
>
> *[Roland] Christensen owns and runs Applied Composite, which forms high-tech materials into artificial limbs. A former aerospace engineer, Christensen converted some of the technology learned in that career to what he calls "another use" when he founded the company. The firm was located in what became the Sanpete County enterprise zone, in the center of Utah, where unemployment is about 9 percent. Applied Composite . . . has sales of nearly $2 million a year, and its work force . . . increased from 11 in 1985 to 25 [in*

1993]. Christensen has received a state tax credit of $700 to $1,000 per new hire toward the taxes owed by his corporation as a result of his location.

Connecticut, which oversees the South Norwalk enterprise zone, will pay [Tom] Gotthelf's company up to $1,500 for each of the new hires it plans [in 1993]—as many as three for the total incentive grant of $4,500. Says Gotthelf, 30, who took over the 5-year-old company after the death of his father in October [1992], "When you're a small business, every bit helps."[8]

It is best to view an enterprise zone as only a catalyst to help jump-start a small firm. It doesn't solve poor management problems or make up for an ill-conceived idea. Marilyn Rubin, a professor at the John Jay College of the City University of New York surveyed 1,000 companies in her state's enterprise zone program and found that 30 percent of the respondents said they wouldn't have expanded or located there without zone benefits.[9]

The U.S. government also provides a variety of programs to assist small firms. The foreign trade zone is one such effort. A **foreign trade zone** is a designated area within the United States where domestic and foreign goods may enter without being subject to customs duties or excise taxes. Although the first foreign trade zones in the United States were located at seaports, inland airport areas, such as a 9,600-acre tract at Alliance Airport in Fort Worth, Texas, have been established more recently.[10]

foreign trade zone
an area within the United States designated to allow foreign and domestic goods to enter without being subject to certain customs and excise taxes

HOME-BASED BUSINESSES

A **home-based business** is a small business that is based in the owner's home. Rather than renting or buying a separate building, the entrepreneur uses a basement, garage, or spare room for the business operation. According to one source, the number of home-based businesses in 1995 was estimated to be 12 to 15 million.[11]

Some businesses can operate in the home because of their modest space demands. Jill Shtulman, a 44-year-old copywriter, operates her one-person agency, JSA Creative Services, from her 18th-floor apartment, where she has two PCs, a laptop computer, a cordless telephone, a cellular phone, a fax machine, and an answering machine. In the beginning, Shtulman considered renting commercial office space. She found, however, that she would have to raise her fees to cover her rent and that she would lose her pricing edge.[12]

Some home-based businesses are Stage I firms, or beginning firms, that move out of the home when growth makes it necessary. Others continue to operate in the home indefinitely. For example, in 1982 Ed and Pat Endicott started the House of Thread & Woods in their home. At that time, the business used only two rooms. "Now our business occupies two bedrooms, our three-car garage, and a new room we built over the garage," says Pat. However, the Endicotts have no intentions of moving their home-based business.[13]

Many businesses operate in the home in order to allow the owners to focus more on family responsibilities. This was the case for Robert and Pat Rosell, featured in this chapter's opening. It was also true for Jane Edgington, who wanted to be at home to care for her newborn son Jeffrey during his early life. Her solution was to give up her position as a marketing research director for a publishing company in the Chicago area in 1992. Using a computer in a spare bedroom, she set up a home-based business as a freelance research analyst.

To function successfully, owners of home-based businesses need to establish both spatial and nonspatial boundaries between the business and the home. Without boundaries, the home and the business can easily interfere with each other. For example, an owner should set aside specific business space in the home and schedule definite hours for business matters. In fact, clients' calls may necessitate the ob-

3 Identify the challenges of running a home-based business.

home-based business
a business that maintains its primary facility in the residence of its owner

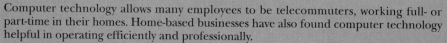

Action Report

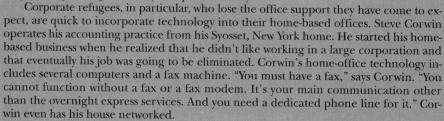

TECHNOLOGICAL APPLICATIONS

Technology Helps Home-Based Business

Computer technology allows many employees to be telecommuters, working full- or part-time in their homes. Home-based businesses have also found computer technology helpful in operating efficiently and professionally.

Corporate refugees, in particular, who lose the office support they have come to expect, are quick to incorporate technology into their home-based offices. Steve Corwin operates his accounting practice from his Syosset, New York home. He started his home-based business when he realized that he didn't like working in a large corporation and that eventually his job was going to be eliminated. Corwin's home-office technology includes several computers and a fax machine. "You must have a fax," says Corwin. "You cannot function without a fax or a fax modem. It's your main communication other than the overnight express services. And you need a dedicated phone line for it." Corwin even has his house networked.

Every room has an outlet he can plug a computer into, and they are all wired to his basement office. In other words, he can hook up a computer to a network connection in his bedroom and call up files on a computer in his home office. . . . All of Corwin's computers are portables, so he can carry work wherever he wants to be, and connecting a computer to the network is so simple that even his young children can do it.

Source: Ripley Hotch, "All the Comforts of a Home Office," *Nation's Business*, Vol. 81, No. 7 (July 1993), pp. 26–28. Reprinted by permission. Copyright 1993, U.S. Chamber of Commerce.

servance of regular business hours. While the owner needs to protect the business from undue family or home interference, he or she also needs to protect the home from unreasonable encroachment by the business. Since the owner never leaves the home to go to an office or place of business, he or she may find that either the business or the family absorbs every available waking moment.

The experience of Gail A. Smith shows that a home-based business doesn't work for everyone. In 1992, along with two partners, she started Inmedia in Dallas, Texas. The company designs interactive multimedia programs for marketing and training. Comfort and economy were the prime considerations of the partners in their decision to operate out of their homes. After only three months, however, the business moved to commercial office space. Smith offered the following five reasons for the change, and each is worthy of consideration by all entrepreneurs contemplating a home-based business:

1. *The need to "team."* Each partner had different strengths; we needed to work together on every project. Our success was based on a combination of our ideas. Separate home offices didn't provide easy access to one another.
2. *An ambitious business plan.* Capturing market share that was there for the taking— but only for a short time—meant pursuing new business at top speed. We had to hit our early sales targets to move forward. Working apart most of the time slowed us down.
3. *Client expectations.* Customers get frustrated when they can't get quick answers.

Working from home and not having access to a partner when needed made for longer response time.

4. *Focus.* It's easy to get distracted at home, to visit a neighbor, do laundry, or start dinner early. I had no time for that. Startups can't afford to take their eyes off the ball, even for a few minutes.

5. *Personal issues.* Home has always been my haven. I work long, intense days, but I escape to where I can pull back and approach work the next day with a fresh attitude. It's tough to get away when you know the business is down the hall.[14]

Zoning ordinances pose a potential problem for home-based businesses. Such local laws regulate the types of enterprises permitted to operate in various geographical areas. Some cities outlaw any type of home-based business within city limits.

David Hanania, founder and president of Home Business Institute, based in White Plains, New York, points out that many zoning laws, dating as far back as the 1930s, have never been updated. The intent of such laws is to protect a neighborhood's residential quality by preventing commercial signs and parking problems. Unfortunately, some entrepreneurs run up against these zoning laws. Just ask Georgia Patrick of Jefferson, Maryland; she faced criminal charges carrying possible fines of nearly $800,000 and prison time simply for operating The Communicators, Inc., her home-based marketing and communications consulting firm, which was considered by local authorities to be out of compliance with zoning regulations.[15]

zoning ordinances
local laws regulating land use

THE BUILDING AND ITS LAYOUT

4 Explain how efficiency can be achieved in the layout of a physical facility.

A business plan should describe the space in which a business will be housed. The plan may call for a new building or an existing structure. A new business ordinarily begins by occupying an existing building. Therefore, we exclude here the considerations involved in building a new structure. Because an existing structure may make a given site either suitable or unsuitable, the location decision must take building requirements into consideration.

Functional Requirements

When specifying building requirements, the entrepreneur must avoid committing to a space that is too large or too luxurious. At the same time, the space should not be too small or too austere for efficient operation. Buildings do not produce profits directly; they merely house the operations and personnel that produce the profits. Therefore, the ideal building is practical but, for most types of business, not pretentious.

The general suitability of a building for a given type of business operation relates to its functional character. For example, the floor space of a restaurant should normally be on one level. Other important factors are the age and condition of the building, fire hazards, heating and air conditioning, lighting and restroom facilities, and entrances and exits. Obviously, these factors are weighted differently for a factory operation than for a wholesale or retail operation. In any case, the comfort, convenience, and safety of the business's employees and customers must not be overlooked.

Federal legislation, discussed in Chapter 26, requires that all places of business be made accessible to individuals with physical disabilities. This may necessitate such modifications as widening doorways or building ramps.

Lease or Buy?

Assuming that a suitable building is available, the entrepreneur must decide whether to lease or buy such a facility. Although ownership confers greater freedom in the modification and use of a building, the advantages of leasing usually outweigh these considerations. Two reasons why most new firms should lease are the following:

1. A large cash outlay is avoided. This is important for a new small firm, which typically lacks adequate financial resources.
2. Risk is reduced by avoiding substantial investment and by postponing commitments for space until the success of the business is assured and the nature of building requirements is better known.

When entering into a leasing agreement, the entrepreneur should check the landlord's insurance policies to be sure there is proper coverage for various types of risks. If not, the renter should seek coverage under his or her own policy. It is also important to have the terms of the leasing agreement reviewed by an attorney. Sometimes, entrepreneurs are able to negotiate special clauses in a lease, such as an escape clause that allows the leasee to exit the agreement under certain conditions. An entrepreneur should not be unduly exposed to liability for damages that are caused by the gross negligence of others. In one case, a firm that wished to rent 300 square feet of storage space in a large complex of offices and shops found, on the sixth page of the landlord's standard lease, language that could have made the firm responsible for the entire 30,000-square-foot complex if it burned down, regardless of blame!

Space in a Business Incubator

business incubator
a facility that provides shared space, services, and management assistance to new businesses

In recent years, business incubators have sprung up in all areas of the country. A **business incubator** is an organization that rents space to new businesses or to people wishing to start businesses. Incubators are often located in recycled buildings, such as abandoned warehouses or schools. They serve fledgling businesses by making space available, offering management advice, and providing clerical assistance, all of which help lower operating costs. An incubator tenant can be fully operational the day after moving in, without buying phones, renting a copier, or hiring office employees.

The purpose of business incubators is to see new businesses hatch, grow, and leave the incubator. Most incubators, though not all, have some type of government or university sponsorship and are motivated by a desire to stimulate economic development.

Although the building space provided by incubators is significant, their greatest contribution is the business expertise and management assistance they provide. A more extensive discussion of incubators is included in Chapter 17.

Building Layout

A good layout involves an arrangement of physical facilities that contributes to efficient business operations. To provide a concise treatment of layout, we limit our discussion to layout problems specific to manufacturers (whose primary concern is production) and retailers (whose primary concern is customer traffic).

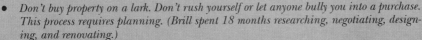

Action Report

QUALITY GOALS

Building Facilitates Quality Work

QUALITY

Owning a building gives an entrepreneur the ability to integrate many quality features into the business space, something that is not possible when leasing. Randi Brill, president of the Quarasan Group, an educational development firm with 28 employees, purchased and renovated a downtown building to house her business.

After leasing for several years, Brill decided she wanted to have creative control of her office space and to be better able to manage its costs. In leased space, she had a choice of two kinds of lights, neither of which she liked. In her own building, she chose the high-quality lighting needed by her designers, and she offset the higher cost by using less-expensive carpeting. She also had wiring installed for fiber optics that she plans to be using within five years. To those considering buying, she offers this advice:

- *Don't buy property on a lark. Don't rush yourself or let anyone bully you into a purchase. This process requires planning. (Brill spent 18 months researching, negotiating, designing, and renovating.)*
- *Get expert advice. (Brill had appraisals completed and paid structural engineers and designers to visit sites with her. She spent more than $10,000 to make sure that the building she bought could be made into the work space she wanted.)*
- *Have a realistic budget. If you feel strapped going in, buying is probably not for you.*

Brill also knows when the time to leave the business arrives, she can sell the firm and the building as a package or separately.

Source: "The Benefits of Buying a Building," *Nation's Business*, Vol. 81, No. 8 (August 1993), p. 10. Reprinted by permission. Copyright 1993, U.S. Chamber of Commerce.

FACTORY LAYOUT   The factory layout presents a three-dimensional space problem. Overhead space may be utilized for power conduits, pipelines for exhaust systems, and the like. A proper design of storage areas and handling systems should make use of space near the ceiling. Space must also be allowed for the unobstructed movement of products from one location to another.

The ideal manufacturing process would have a straight-line, forward movement of materials from receiving room to shipping room. If this ideal cannot be realized for a given process, backtracking, sidetracking, and long hauls of materials can at least be minimized, thereby reducing production delays.

Two contrasting types of layouts are used in industrial firms. A **process layout** groups similar machines together. Drill presses, for example, are separated from lathes in a machine shop using a process layout. The alternative, a **product layout**, arranges special-purpose equipment along a production line in the sequence in which each piece of equipment is used in processing. The product is moved progressively from one work station to the next. The machines are located at the work stations where they are needed for the various stages of production.

Smaller plants that operate on a job-lot basis cannot use a product layout, because such a layout demands too high a degree of standardization of both product and process. Thus, small machine shops are generally arranged on a process layout basis. Small firms with highly standardized products, such as dairies, bakeries, and car washes, however, can use a product layout.

process layout
a factory layout that groups similar machines together

product layout
a factory layout that arranges machines according to their roles in the production process

RETAIL STORE LAYOUT The objectives for a retail store layout include proper display of merchandise to maximize sales and customer convenience and service. Normally, the convenience and attractiveness of the surroundings contribute to a customer's continued patronage. Color, music, and even aroma are all important layout factors for a retail business. An efficient layout also contributes to lowering operating costs. Another objective involves the protection of a store's equipment and merchandise. In achieving all these objectives, the flow of customer traffic must be anticipated and planned.

A grid pattern and a free-flow pattern of store layout are the two most widely used layout designs.[16] A **grid pattern** is the plain, block-looking layout typical of supermarkets and hardware stores. It provides more merchandise exposure and simplifies security and cleaning. A **free-flow pattern** makes less efficient use of space but has greater visual appeal and allows customers to move in any direction at their own speed. Free-flow patterns result in curving aisles and greater flexibility in merchandise presentation.

Most retailers use a **self-service layout,** which permits customers direct access to the merchandise. Not only does self-service reduce the selling expense, but it also permits shoppers to examine the goods before buying. Today, practically all food merchandisers follow this principle.

Some types of merchandise—for example, magazines and candy—are often purchased on an impulse basis. Impulse goods should be placed at points where customers can see them easily, and some are typically displayed near the cash register. Products that customers need and for which they come to the store specifically may be placed in less conspicuous spots. Bread and milk, for example, are located at the back of a food store, with the idea that customers will buy other items as they walk down the store aisles.

Various areas of a retail store differ markedly in sales value. Customers typically turn to the right on entering a store, and so the right front space is the most valuable. The second most valuable areas are the center front and right middle spaces. Department stores often place high-margin giftwares, cosmetics, and jewelry in these areas. The third most valuable areas are the left front and center middle spaces; the left middle space is fourth in importance. Since the back areas are the least important as far as space value is concerned, most service facilities and the general office are typically found in the rear of a store. Certainly the best space should be given to departments or merchandise producing the greatest sales and profits. Finally, the first floor has greater space value than a higher floor in a multistory building.

Building Image

All new ventures, regardless of whether they are retailers, wholesalers, manufacturers, or service businesses, should be concerned with projecting the appropriate image to customers and the general public at large. The appearance of the workplace creates a favorable impression about the quality of a firm's product or service and, generally, about the way the business is operated.

Before making design changes, a business should think about the image it wants to convey, according to interior designer Sandy Lucas of the Bryan Design Associates, in Houston, Texas. Spring Engineers, Inc., a small, 50-employee business in Dallas, Texas, that makes springs for tools and other applications, hired Lucas to design a new facility. "We have a lot of vendors and suppliers coming to visit, and we often bring customers for tours of the machine shop," says president Kevin Grace. "It's very important that we make an impression that although we're a small business, we're a substantial one."[17]

---

grid pattern
a block-like type of retail store layout that provides for good merchandise exposure and simple security and cleaning

free-flow pattern
a type of retail store layout that is visually appealing and gives customers freedom of movement

self-service layout
a retail store layout that gives customers direct access to merchandise

EQUIPMENT AND TOOLS

5 Discuss the equipment and tool needs of small firms.

The final step in arranging for physical facilities involves the purchase or lease of equipment and tools. The types of equipment and tools required obviously depend on the nature of the business. We limit our discussion of equipment needs to the two diverse fields of manufacturing and retailing. Of course, even within these two areas, there is great variation in the need for tools and equipment.

Factory Equipment

Machines in the factory may be either general purpose or special purpose in character.

GENERAL-PURPOSE EQUIPMENT   **General-purpose equipment** requires a minimum investment and is well adapted to varied types of operations. Small machine shops and cabinet shops, for example, utilize this type of equipment. General-purpose equipment for metalworking includes lathes, drill presses, and milling machines. In a woodworking plant, general-purpose machines include ripsaws, planing mills, and lathes. In each case, jigs, fixtures, and other tooling items set up on the basic machine tools can be changed so that two or more shop operations can be accomplished. General-purpose equipment contributes the necessary flexibility in industries in which a product is so new that the technology has not yet been well developed or in which there are frequent design changes in a product.

general-purpose equipment
machines that serve many functions in the production process

SPECIAL-PURPOSE EQUIPMENT   **Special-purpose equipment** permits cost reduction for industries in which the technology is fully established and in which a capacity operation is more or less ensured by high sales volume. Bottling machines and automobile assembly-line equipment are examples of special-purpose equipment used in factories. A milking machine in a dairy is an example of special-purpose equipment used by small firms. A small firm cannot, however, ordinarily and economically use special-purpose equipment unless it makes a standardized product on a fairly large scale. Special-purpose machines using specialized tooling result in greater output per machine-hour of operation. The labor cost per unit of product is, therefore, lower. However, the initial cost of such equipment is much higher, and its resale value is little or nothing because of its highly specialized function.

special-purpose equipment
machines designed to serve specialized functions in the production process

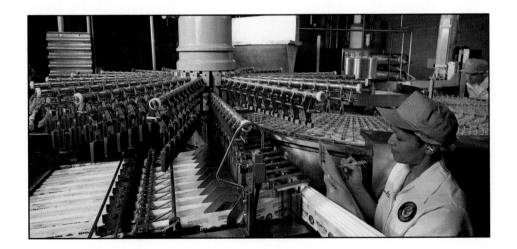

Some machinery, such as this assembly-line equipment for packaging ice cream, serves specific purposes. General-purpose equipment is usually more economical for a small firm, unless the firm makes a standardized product on a fairly large scale.

1 Identify the general considerations affecting the choice of a business location.

- The entrepreneur's personal preference is a practical consideration in selecting a location.
- Climate, competition, laws, and leisure attractions are types of environmental factors affecting the location decision.
- Resource requirements, such as availability of raw materials and transportation facilities, are important to location decisions.
- Customer accessibility is a key ingredient in the location decision of retail and service businesses.

2 Describe the process for making the location decision.

- Business publications such as *The Wall Street Journal* can be consulted for information about the attractiveness of various states as locations for small businesses.
- Three location considerations needing special attention when selecting a region or state are nearness to the market, availability of raw materials and labor, and laws and tax policies.
- In choosing a site, some firms must emphasize operating costs, while others must emphasize accessibility.

3 Identify the challenges of running a home-based business.

- Limitations of space in the home can restrict growth.
- Entrepreneurs need to introduce modern technology into the operation of their home-based businesses.
- Home-based businesses often require a balancing of business activities and family care.
- Zoning ordinances pose a potential problem for home-based businesses.

4 Explain how efficiency can be achieved in the layout of a physical facility.

- The general suitability of a building depends on the functional requirements of the business.
- Leasing avoids a large cash outlay, but buying increases freedom in modifying and using space.
- Business incubators provide a relatively inexpensive alternative to standard leasing arrangements.
- Good layout emphasizes productivity for manufacturers and customer accessibility for retailers.

5 Discuss the equipment and tool needs of small firms.

- Most small manufacturing firms must use general-purpose equipment, although some can use special-purpose equipment for standardized operations.
- Small retailers must have merchandise display racks and counters, mirrors, and other equipment.
- Display counters and other retailing equipment should create an atmosphere appropriate for customers in the retailer's target market.

Retail Store Equipment

Small retailers must have merchandise display racks or counters, storage racks, shelving, mirrors, seats for customers, customer pushcarts, cash registers, and other items necessary to facilitate selling. Such equipment may be costly, but it is usually less expensive than equipment for a factory operation.

If a store attempts to serve a high-income market, its fixtures should display the elegance and style expected by such customers. For example, polished mahogany showcases with bronze fittings lend a richness of atmosphere. Indirect lighting, thick rugs on the floor, and big easy chairs also contribute to the air of luxury. In contrast, for a store that caters to lower-income customers, luxurious fixtures create an atmosphere inconsistent with low prices. Such a store should concentrate on simplicity.

DISCUSSION QUESTIONS

1. What are the key attributes of a good business location? Which of these would probably be most important to a retail location? Why?
2. Is the hometown of the business owner likely to be a good location? Why? Is it logical for an owner to allow personal preferences to influence a decision about a business location? Why?
3. In the selection of a region, what types of businesses should place greatest emphasis on (a) markets, (b) raw materials, and (c) labor? In the choice of specific sites, what types of businesses must show the greatest concern with customer accessibility? Why?

4. Suppose that you are considering a location within an existing shopping mall. How would you go about evaluating the pedestrian traffic at that location? Be specific.
5. Under what conditions would it be most logical for a new firm to buy rather than rent a building for the business?
6. What types of factors should an entrepreneur evaluate when considering a home-based business? Be specific.
7. In a home-based business, there is typically some competition, if not conflict, between the interests of the home and those of the business. What factors would determine whether the danger is greater for the home or the business?
8. What is a business incubator and what advantages does it offer as a home for a new business?
9. When should the small manufacturer utilize (a) process layout, and (b) product layout? Explain.
10. Discuss the conditions under which a new small manufacturer should buy (a) general-purpose equipment, and (b) special-purpose equipment.

EXPERIENTIAL EXERCISES

1. Search for articles in business periodicals that provide site-evaluation rankings of states or cities. Report on your findings.
2. Identify and evaluate a local site that is now vacant after a business closure. Point out the strengths and weaknesses of that location for the former business, and comment on the part the location may have played in the closure.

New Terms and Concepts

enterprise zones *215*
foreign trade zone *217*
home-based business *217*
zoning ordinances *219*

business incubator *220*
process layout *221*
product layout *221*
grid pattern *222*
free-flow pattern *222*

self-service layout *222*
general-purpose equipment *223*
special-purpose equipment *223*

You Make the Call

Situation 1 A husband-and-wife team operates small department stores in two Midwestern towns with populations of about 2,000 each. Their clientele consists of the primarily blue-collar and rural populations of those two areas. After several years of successful operation, they have decided to open a third store in a town of 5,000 people. Most of the businesses in this larger town are located along a six-block-long strip—an area commonly referred to as "downtown." One attractive site for the store is in the middle of the business district, but the rental fee for that location is very high. Another available building was once occupied by Montgomery Ward but was vacated several years earlier. It is located on a block at one end of the business district. Other businesses on the same block include a TV and appliance store and some service businesses. Two clothing stores are located in the next block—closer to the center of town. The rent for the former Montgomery Ward store building is much more reasonable than the downtown site, a three-year lease is possible, and a local bank is willing to loan sufficient funds to accomplish necessary remodeling.

Question 1 Does the location in the middle of the business district seem to be substantially better than the other site?
Question 2 How might these owners evaluate the relative attractiveness of the two sites?
Question 3 To what extent would the department store benefit from having the service businesses and the TV and appliance business in the same block?
Question 4 What other market or demographic factors, if any, should the owners consider before opening a store in this town?

Situation 2 A business incubator rents space to a number of small firms that are just beginning operations or are fairly new. In addition to supplying space, the incubator provides a receptionist, computer, conference room, fax machine, and copy machine. In addition, it offers management counseling and assists new businesses in getting reduced advertising rates and reduced legal fees. Two clients of the incubator are (1) a jewelry repair, cleaning, and remounting service that does work on a contract basis for pawn shops and jewelry stores, and (2) a home health-care company that employs a staff of nurses to visit the homes of elderly people who need daily care but who cannot afford or are not yet ready to go to a nursing home.

Continue on next page

225

Question 1 Evaluate each of the services offered by the incubator in terms of its usefulness to these two businesses. Which of the two businesses seems to be a better fit for the incubator? Why?

Question 2 Do the benefits of the services offered seem to favor this location if rental costs are similar to rental costs for space outside the incubator? Why or why not?

Situation 3 Entrepreneur Mark King first began franchising his pest-control business, Wipe-Out, Inc., two years ago. Two of his franchisees currently operate the business from their homes. King has trained each entrepreneur to run a pest-control business and has explained to them how to network with potential customers.

The franchise fee and royalties are reasonably low—a $15,000 franchise fee and a 12 percent royalty rate. One of King's two franchisees, John Dortch, has already reached sales of $100,000 in just over a year.

King is concerned, however, about potential problems associated with running a home-based business of this type and wonders if it is ethical to continue selling franchises to be operated in a home-based environment.

Question 1 What do you think King sees as potential problems with home-based businesses?

Question 2 Would a pest-control business present more of a problem in any area than another type of home-based business?

Question 3 Is it ethical for King to continue selling franchises if any of these concerns are legitimate?

3. Interview a small business owner concerning the strengths and weaknesses of that business's location. Prepare a brief report summarizing your findings.

4. Visit three local retail stores and observe the differences in their layouts and flow of customer traffic. Prepare a report describing the various patterns and explaining the advantages of the best pattern.

CASE 10
Logan Beach (p. 619)

This case follows the owner of a new restaurant during the first few days after its opening and presents some lessons learned the hard way.

Alternative Cases for Chapter 10:
Case 7, "The Fantastic Catalogue Company," p. 610
Case 19, "Douglas Electrical Supply, Inc.," p. 642

LAYING THE FOUNDATION
Asking the Right Questions

As part of laying the foundation to preparing your own business plan, respond to the following questions regarding location and physical facilities.

Location Questions

1. How important are your personal reasons for choosing a location?
2. What environmental factors will influence your location decision?
3. What resources are most critical to your location decision?
4. How important is customer accessibility to your location decision?
5. How will the formal site evaluation be conducted?
6. What laws and tax policies of state and local governments have been considered?
7. Will a home-based business be a possibility?
8. What are the advantages and disadvantages of a home-based business?
9. Is an enterprise zone available in the area where you want to locate?

Physical Facility Questions

1. What are the major considerations regarding the choice of a new or existing building?
2. What is the possibility of leasing a building or equipment?
3. How feasible is it to locate in a business incubator?
4. What is the major objective of your building layout?
5. What types of equipment do you need for your business?

USING BizPlanBuilder

If you are using BizPlan*Builder*, refer to Part 2 for information about location and equipment that should be reflected in the business plan.

Accounting Statements and Financial Requirements

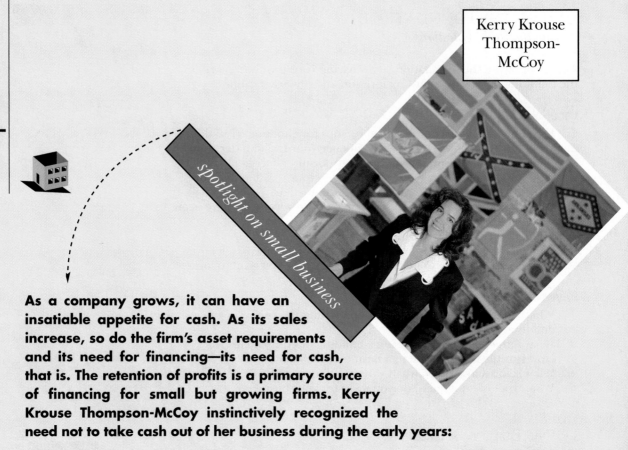

Chapter 11

Kerry Krouse
Thompson-
McCoy

spotlight on small business

As a company grows, it can have an insatiable appetite for cash. As its sales increase, so do the firm's asset requirements and its need for financing—its need for cash, that is. The retention of profits is a primary source of financing for small but growing firms. Kerry Krouse Thompson-McCoy instinctively recognized the need not to take cash out of her business during the early years:

Where a lot of entrepreneurs pull money out of their businesses, I never take much more than what I need to live. Of course, in the 19 years since I started Arkansas Flag & Banner, there hasn't always been much to take, but I am now at the point where I can see my strategy someday paying off in a big way.

With no money to work with and no credit to speak of, building an inventory was difficult. Every time I got an order, I spent the money providing one flag for the customer and one for stock.

As Arkansas Flag has grown into a full-service company, so, too, has the demand for money that has to be put back into the business. The company has 15 workers now with $1 million in sales. Things keep looking up and are almost at the point where I don't need more equipment to run with the big boys. Once I get to that point—and it has been a goal for the entire 19 years—I can invest a little bit more in my employees and maybe pay myself better, too.

Source: Kerry Krouse Thompson-McCoy, "A Time to Sew, a Time to Reap,"
Nation's Business, Vol. 82, No. 1 (January 1994), p. 6.

As we commented earlier, a good idea may or may not be a good investment opportunity. A good investment opportunity is represented by a product or service that creates a competitive advantage and meets a definite customer need. Whether such an investment opportunity in fact exists depends on (1) the level of profitability that can be achieved and (2) the size of the investment required to capture the opportunity. Therefore, projections of a venture's profits and its asset and financing requirements are essential factors in determining whether the venture is economically feasible. In order to make the necessary financial projections, an entrepreneur must first have a good understanding of financial statements.

ACCOUNTING STATEMENTS: TOOLS FOR DETERMINING FINANCING NEEDS

1 Describe the purpose and content of financial statements.

Financial statements, also called **accounting statements,** provide important information about a firm's performance and financial resources. The key statements are (1) an income statement, (2) a balance sheet, and (3) a cash flow statement. Understanding the purpose and content of financial statements is essential if the entrepreneur is to know the startup firm's financial requirements. By looking carefully at these statements, he or she will be better able to assess the financial implications of the plans for the startup.

financial statements (accounting statements) reports of a firm's financial performance and resources, including an income statement, a balance sheet, and a cash flow statement

The Income Statement

An **income statement,** or **profit and loss statement,** indicates the amount of profits generated by a firm over a given time period, often a year. In its most basic form, the income statement may be represented as follows:

$$\text{Sales} - \text{Expenses} = \text{Profits}$$

Thus, the income statement answers the question "How profitable is the business?" In providing this answer, the income statement reports financial information related to five broad areas of business activity:

1. Revenue derived from selling the company's product or service
2. Cost of producing or acquiring the goods or services to be sold
3. Operating expenses related to (a) marketing and distributing the product or service to the customer and (b) administering the business
4. Financing costs of doing business—namely, the interest paid to the firm's creditors
5. Payment of taxes

income statement (profit and loss statement) a financial report showing the profit or loss from a firm's operations over a given period of time

229

| Figure 11-1 | *The Income Statement: An Overview* |

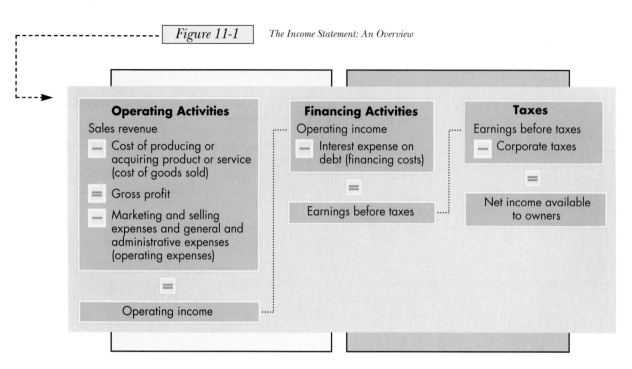

cost of goods sold
the cost of producing or acquiring goods or services to be sold by a firm

gross profit
sales less the cost of goods sold

operating expenses
costs related to general administrative expenses and marketing and distributing a firm's product or service

operating income (earnings before interest and taxes)
profits before interest and taxes are paid

financing costs
the amount of interest owed to lenders on borrowed money

net income available to owners (net income)
income that may be distributed to the owners or reinvested in the company

Figure 11-1 shows that the income statement begins with sales revenue, from which the **cost of goods sold,** or the cost of producing or acquiring the product or service, is subtracted to reflect the firm's **gross profit.** Next, **operating expenses,** consisting both of administrative expenses and selling and marketing expenses, are deducted to determine **operating income** (that is, **earnings before interest and taxes**). To this point, the firm's income has been affected solely by the first three activities listed above, which are considered the firm's operating activities. Note that no financing costs have been subtracted to this point.

From the company's operating income is deducted its **financing costs**—the company's interest expense on its debt. Next, the company's income taxes are calculated based on its earnings before taxes and the applicable tax rate for the amount of income reported.

The resulting figure, **net income available to owners** (frequently called **net income**), represents income that may be reinvested in the company or distributed to the company's owners—provided, of course, cash is available to do so. As we discuss later, a positive net income on an income statement does not necessarily mean that a firm has any cash—a surprising statement, but one you will come to understand.

It is important to note that some small firms sell their products or services on a cash basis only. In that case, there is a temptation *not* to report all income for tax purposes. Such an action is neither legal nor ethical.

Figure 11-2 provides an example of an income statement for the hypothetical FGD Manufacturing Company. The firm had sales of $830,000 for the 12-month period ending December 31, 1997. The cost of manufacturing its product was $540,000, resulting in a gross profit of $290,000. The firm had $190,000 in operating expenses, which included marketing expenses, general and administrative and depreciation. After the total operating expenses were subtracted, the firm's operating income (earnings before interest and taxes) amounted to $100,000. To this point, we have calculated the profits resulting only from operating activities, as opposed to financing decisions such as how much debt or equity is used to finance

Figure 11-2

*Income Statement for FGD
Manufacturing Company
for the Year Ending
December 31, 1997*

Sales revenue		$830,000
Cost of goods sold		540,000
Gross profit		$290,000
Operating expenses:		
Marketing expenses	$90,000	
General and administrative expenses	72,000	
Depreciation	28,000	
Total operating expenses		$190,000
Operating income (earnings before		
interest and taxes)		$100,000
Interest expense		20,000
Earnings before taxes		$ 80,000
Income tax (25%)		20,000
Net income		$ 60,000
Dividends paid		15,000
Change in retained earnings		$ 45,000

the company's operations. This figure represents the income generated by FGD assuming it to be an all-equity company—that is, a business without any debt.

Next, FGD's interest expense (the amount it paid for using debt financing) of $20,000 is deducted to arrive at the company's earnings (profits) before taxes of $80,000. Finally, income tax of $20,000 is subtracted, leaving a net income of $60,000. Note, below the income statement, that common dividends were paid by the firm to its owners in the amount of $15,000. The remaining $45,000 represents the profits that are retained within the business. (This amount appears as an increase in retained earnings on the balance sheet.)

The Balance Sheet

While an income statement reports the financial results of business operations over a period of time, a **balance sheet** provides a snapshot of a business's financial position at a specific point in time. Thus, a balance sheet captures the cumulative effects of earlier financial decisions. At the given point in time captured by the balance sheet, it will show the amount of all assets the firm owns, the liabilities (or debt) outstanding or owed, and the amount the owners have invested in the business (their equity). In its simplest form, a balance sheet follows this formula:

balance sheet
a financial report that shows a firm's assets, liabilities, and owners' equity at a specific point in time

$$\boxed{\text{Total assets}} = \boxed{\text{Outstanding debt} \ + \ \text{Owners' equity}}$$

Figure 11-3 provides a more complete picture of a balance sheet that is representative of a typical small firm. We now describe each of the three main components of the balance sheet: assets, outstanding debt, and owners' equity.

TYPES OF ASSETS   A company's assets, as shown on the left side of Figure 11-3, fall into three categories: (1) current assets, (2) fixed assets, and (3) other assets.

Current assets, or **working capital,** comprise those assets that are relatively liquid—that is, that can be converted into cash within a given operating cycle. Current assets primarily include cash, accounts receivable, inventories, and prepaid ex-

**current assets
(working capital)**
assets that will be converted into cash within a company's operating cycle

Figure 11-3

*The Balance Sheet:
An Overview*

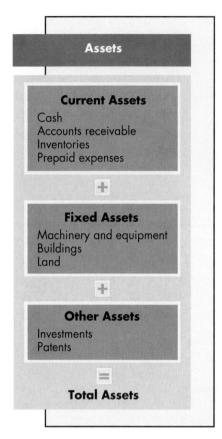

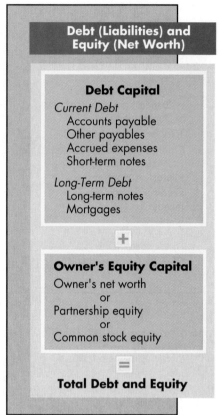

penses. Ineffective management of current assets is a prime cause of financial problems in companies. (We will discuss this issue more thoroughly in Chapter 23.)

Small retail stores generally adjust their inventory level on a seasonal basis. This San Francisco toy store, for example, stocks up on popular items for the pre-Christmas consumer rush-to-buy, using every inch of available shelf space.

accounts receivable
the amount of credit extended to customers that is currently outstanding

inventory
a firm's raw materials and products held in anticipation of eventual sale

- *Cash.* Every firm must have cash for current business operations. Also, a reservoir of cash is needed because of the unequal flow of funds into the business (cash receipts) and out of the business (cash expenditures). The size of this cash reservoir is determined not only by the volume of sales, but also by the predictability of cash receipts and cash payments.
- *Accounts receivable.* The firm's **accounts receivable** consists of payments due from its customers from previous credit sales. Accounts receivable can become a significant asset for firms that sell on a credit basis.
- *Inventories.* **Inventory** consists of the raw materials and products held by the firm for eventual sale. Although their relative importance differs from one type of business to another, inventories often constitute a major

part of a firm's working capital. Seasonality of sales and production levels affect the size of the minimum inventory. Retail stores, for example, may find it desirable to carry a larger-than-normal inventory during the pre-Christmas season.

- *Prepaid expenses.* A company often needs to prepay some of its expenses. For example, insurance premiums may be due before coverage begins, or rent may have to be paid in advance. For accounting purposes, **prepaid expenses** are recorded on the balance sheet as current assets and then shown on the income statement as operating expenses as they are used.

Fixed assets are the more permanent assets in a business. They might include machinery and equipment, buildings, and land. Some businesses are more capital-intensive than others—for example, a motel is more capital-intensive than a gift store—and, therefore, have more fixed assets.

The third category, **other assets,** includes such items as intangible assets. Patents, copyrights, and goodwill are intangibles. For a startup company, other assets may also include organizational costs—costs incurred in organizing and promoting the business.

TYPES OF FINANCING   We now turn to the right side of the balance sheet in Figure 11-3, headed "Liabilities (Debt) and Equity (Net Worth)," which indicates how the firm finances its assets. Financing comes from two main sources: debt (liabilities) and ownership equity. Debt is money that has been borrowed and must be repaid at some predetermined date. Ownership equity, on the other hand, represents the owners' investment in the company—money they have personally put into the firm without any specific date for repayment. Owners recover their investment by withdrawing money from the firm or by selling their interest in it.

Debt Capital   **Debt capital** is business financing provided by a creditor. As shown in Figure 11-3, it is divided into (1) current, or short-term, debt and (2) long-term debt. **Current debt,** or **short-term liabilities,** includes borrowed money that must be repaid within the next 12 months. Sources of current debt may be classified as follows:

- *Accounts payable.* **Accounts payable** represents credit extended by suppliers to a firm when it purchases inventories. The purchasing firm may have 30 or 60 days before paying for the inventory. This form of credit extension is also called **trade credit.**
- *Other payables.* **Other payables** include interest expenses and income taxes that are owed and will come due within the year.
- *Accrued expenses.* **Accrued expenses** are short-term liabilities that have been incurred, but not paid. For example, employees perform work that may not be paid for until the following week or month.
- *Short-term notes.* **Short-term notes** represent cash amounts borrowed from a bank or other lending source for a short period of time, such as 90 days. Short-term notes are a primary source of financing for most small businesses, as these businesses have access to fewer sources of capital than do their larger counterparts.

Long-term debt includes loans from banks or other sources that lend money for longer than 12 months. If a firm borrows money for 5 years to buy equipment, it signs an agreement—a long-term note—promising to repay the money in 5 years. If a firm borrows money for 30 years to purchase real estate, such as a warehouse or office building, the lender allows the real estate to stand as collateral for the loan. If the borrower is unable to repay the loan, the lender can take the real estate in settlement for the loan. This type of long-term loan is called a **mortgage.**

prepaid expenses
current assets that typically are used up during the year, such as prepaid rent or insurance

fixed assets
relatively permanent resources intended for use in the business

other assets
assets that are neither current nor fixed and may be intangible

debt capital
business financing provided by creditors

current debt (short-term liabilities)
borrowed money that must be repaid within 12 months

accounts payable (trade credit)
outstanding credit payable to suppliers

other payables
other short-term credit, such as interest payable or taxes payable

accrued expenses
short-term liabilities that have been incurred but not paid

short-term notes
cash amounts borrowed from a bank or other lending sources that must be repaid within a short period of time

long-term debt
loans from banks or other sources with repayment terms of more than 12 months

mortgage
a long-term loan from a creditor that pledges an asset, such as real estate, as collateral for the loan

owners' equity capital
owners' investments in a company, including the profits retained in the firm

Owners' Equity Capital   Owners' equity capital is simply money that owners invest in a business. They are *residual* owners; that is, creditors must be paid before the owners can retrieve any of their equity capital out of the income from the business. Also, if the company is liquidated, creditors are always paid first; then, the owners are paid.

The amount of ownership equity in a business is equal to (1) the amount of the owners' initial investment plus any later investments in the business and (2) the income retained within the business from its beginning, which equals the cumulative profits or earnings (net of any losses) over the life of the business, less any cash withdrawals by the owners. The second item (profits less withdrawals) is frequently called **retained earnings**—that is, earnings that have been reinvested in the business instead of being distributed to the owners. Thus, the owners' equity capital consists of the following:

retained earnings
profits less withdrawals (dividends)

$$\begin{array}{ccccccc} \text{Owners'} \\ \text{equity capital} \end{array} = \begin{array}{c} \text{Owners'} \\ \text{investment} \end{array} + \underbrace{\begin{array}{c} \text{Cumulative} \\ \text{profits} \end{array} - \begin{array}{c} \text{Owners'} \\ \text{cash withdrawals} \end{array}}$$

$$\text{or} \quad \begin{array}{c} \text{Owners'} \\ \text{equity capital} \end{array} = \begin{array}{c} \text{Owners'} \\ \text{investment} \end{array} + \begin{array}{c} \text{Earnings retained} \\ \text{within the firm} \end{array}$$

Figure 11-4

Balance Sheets for FGD Manufacturing Company for December 31, 1996 and December 31, 1997

	1996	1997	Change
Assets			
Current assets:			
Cash	$ 38,000	$ 43,000	$ 5,000
Accounts receivable	70,000	78,000	8,000
Inventories	175,000	210,000	35,000
Prepaid expenses	12,000	14,000	2,000
Total current assets	$295,000	$345,000	$ 50,000
Fixed assets:			
Gross plant and equipment	$760,000	$838,000	$ 78,000
Accumulated depreciation	355,000	383,000	28,000
Net plant and equipment	$405,000	$455,000	$ 50,000
Land	70,000	70,000	0
Total fixed assets	$475,000	$525,000	$ 50,000
Other assets:			
Goodwill and patents	30,000	50,000	20,000
TOTAL ASSETS	$800,000	$920,000	$120,000
Debt (Liabilities) and Equity			
Current debt:			
Accounts payable	$ 61,000	$ 76,000	$ 15,000
Income tax payable	12,000	15,000	3,000
Accrued wages and salaries	4,000	5,000	1,000
Interest payable	2,000	4,000	2,000
Total current debt	$ 79,000	$100,000	$ 21,000
Long-term debt:			
Long-term notes payable	146,000	200,000	54,000
Total debt	$225,000	$300,000	$ 75,000
Equity:			
Common stock	$300,000	$300,000	$ 0
Retained earnings	275,000	320,000	45,000
Total stockholders' equity	$575,000	$620,000	$ 45,000
TOTAL DEBT AND EQUITY	$800,000	$920,000	$120,000

Figure 11-5

*The Fit of the Income
Statement and the
Balance Sheet*

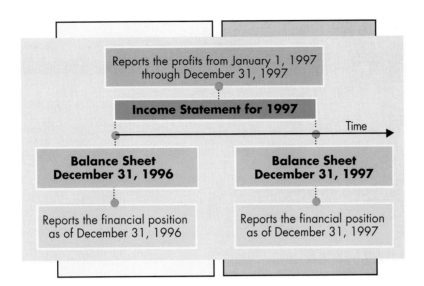

In summary, financing a new business entails raising debt capital and equity financing. The debt capital comes from borrowing money from financial institutions, suppliers, and other lenders. The equity financing comes from the owners' investment in the company, either from money invested in the firm or through profits retained in the business.

Figure 11-4 presents balance sheets for the FGD Manufacturing Company for both December 31, 1996 and December 31, 1997. By referring to the two balance sheets, you can see the financial position of the firm at the beginning *and* at the end of 1997.

The 1996 and 1997 balance sheets for FGD show that the firm began 1997 with $800,000 in total assets and ended the year with total assets of $920,000. These assets were financed 30 percent by debt and 70 percent by equity. About half of the equity came from investments made by the owners (common stock), and the other half came from reinvesting profits in the business (retained earnings). Also, note that the $45,000 increase in retained earnings equals the firm's net income for the year less the dividends paid to the owners, per the income statement in Figure 11-2 on page 231.

Let's now consider how the income statement and the balance sheet complement one another. Because the balance sheet is a snapshot of the firm's financial condition at a point in time and the income statement reports results over a given time period, both statements are required in order to have a complete picture of a firm's financial position. Figure 11-5 demonstrates how the balance sheet and the income statement fit together. If you want to know how a firm performed during 1997, you need to know the firm's financial position at the beginning of the year (balance sheet on December 31, 1996), its financial performance during 1997 (income statement for 1997) and its financial position at the end of 1997 (balance sheet on December 31, 1997).

The Cash Flow Statement[1]

It's important to note that while an income statement measures a company's profits, profits are not necessarily cash. Often, sales revenue is not received when earned and expenses are not paid when incurred, creating a difference between

cash flow statement
a financial report that shows changes in a firm's cash position over a given period of time

accrual-basis accounting
a method of accounting that matches revenues when they are earned against the expenses associated with those revenues

profits and cash flow. Although accounting profits have come to be used as the primary measure of a firm's performance, actual cash in the firm's bank account is important, too. Many entrepreneurs have been deceived by a good-looking income statement, only to discover that their companies are running out of cash. For this reason, the third key financial statement used by small businesses is the cash flow statement.

A **cash flow statement** presents the sources and uses of a firm's cash flows for a given period of time. It shows the change in cash amounts from period to period, thereby helping the owners and managers better understand how and when cash flows through the business. An income statement cannot provide this information, because it is calculated on an *accrual* basis rather than a *cash* basis. **Accrual-basis accounting** records income when it is earned, whether or not the income has been received in cash, and records expenses when they are incurred, even if money has not actually been paid out. For example, sales reported in the income statement include both cash sales and credit sales. Therefore, sales for a given year do not correspond exactly to the actual cash collected from sales. Similarly, a firm must purchase inventory, but some of the purchases are financed by credit rather than by immediate cash payment. Also, under the accrual system, the purchase of equipment that will last for more than a year is not shown as an expense in the income statement. Instead, the amount is recorded as an asset and then depreciated over its useful life. An annual **depreciation expense** (this is not a cash flow) is recorded as a way to match the use of the asset with sales generated from its use. **Cash-basis accounting,** on the other hand, reports income when cash is received and records expenses when they are paid.

The procedure for computing a firm's cash flow is depicted in Figure 11-6. Three steps are required:

1.   Convert the income statement from an accrual basis to a cash basis (operating activities).
2.   Compute investments made in fixed assets and other assets (investment activities).
3.   Determine cash received or paid to the firm's lenders and owners (financing activities).

The cash flow statement for FGD Manufacturing Company is presented in

depreciation expense
costs related to a fixed asset, such as a building or equipment, distributed over its useful life

cash-basis accounting
a method of accounting that reports transactions only when cash is received or a payment is made

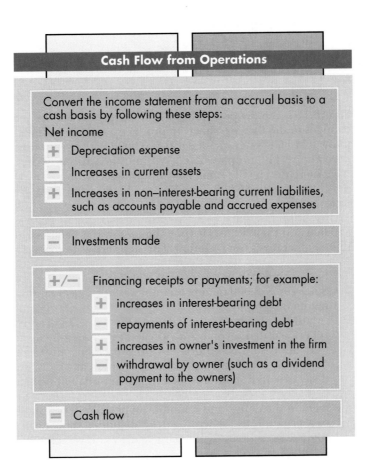

Figure 11-6

The Cash Flow Statement: An Overview

Cash Flow from Operations

Convert the income statement from an accrual basis to a cash basis by following these steps:

Net income

+   Depreciation expense

−   Increases in current assets

+   Increases in non–interest-bearing current liabilities, such as accounts payable and accrued expenses

−   Investments made

+/−   Financing receipts or payments; for example:

    +   increases in interest-bearing debt

    −   repayments of interest-bearing debt

    +   increases in owner's investment in the firm

    −   withdrawal by owner (such as a dividend payment to the owners)

=   Cash flow

Figure 11-7

Cash Flow Statement for FGD Manufacturing Company for the Year Ending December 31, 1997

Cash flow from operations

Net income (from the income statement)		$60,000
To reconcile net income to cash flow		
Add depreciation expense		28,000
Subtract the changes in current assets:		
Change in accounts receivable	($ 8,000)	
Change in inventories	(35,000)	
Change in prepaid expenses	(2,000)	(45,000)
Add the changes in non-interest-bearing current liabilities:		
Plus the change in accounts payable	$15,000	
Plus the change in income tax payable	3,000	
Plus the change in accrued wages	1,000	
Plus the change in interest payable	2,000	21,000
Cash flow from operations		$64,000

Cash flow from investment activities

Purchase of fixed assets	($78,000)	
Change in goodwill and patents	(20,000)	
Net cash used for investments		($98,000)

Cash flow from financing activities

Proceeds from long-term debt	$54,000	
Common stock dividends	(15,000)	
Net cash provided by financing activities		$39,000
Cash flow (change in cash)		$ 5,000

Figure 11-7. Simply put, it shows how the profits for the year combine with all the changes in the balance sheets to produce a change in the company's cash flow. We know that FGD's net income was $60,000 for the year ending December 31, 1997. (See Figure 11-2 on page 231.) Without the various accruals, the cash flow would have increased by the same amount. But according to FGD's balance sheets, cash only increased by $5,000. (See Figure 11-4 on page 234.) What's the reason for this difference?

As shown in Figure 11-7, the cash flow statement begins with the net income of $60,000 and then adjusts it (per changes in the balance sheets) to reflect the fact that net income is not cash flow. The steps are as follows:

1. Start with FGD's net income of $60,000.
2. Since the $28,000 in depreciation was not a cash outflow, add it to the $60,000 net income figure.
3. Adjust for changes in the balance sheets (see Figure 11-4 on page 234) that reflect accrued income and accrued expenses—income and expenses that were not cash transactions—by (a) subtracting any increases, or adding any decreases, in current assets and (b) adding any increases, or subtracting any decreases, in non-interest-bearing current liabilities. (Note the difference here between interest-bearing debt—such as short-term notes where interest is paid on the debt—and non-interest-bearing debt—such as accounts payable or accruals. Interest-bearing debt includes a short-term loan from the bank, which is considered a financing activity and is included later in the cash flow statement.)

For the FGD Manufacturing Company, these adjustments are as follows:

a. Accounts receivable increased by $8,000 ($78,000 – $70,000). This increase represents the amount of sales that were assumed to be received in cash but were not—a reduction in actual cash received. The company's inventory increased by $35,000 ($210,000 – $175,000), which represents products that were not sold, a reduction in cash. Prepaid expenses increased by $2,000 ($14,000 – $12,000). The company prepaid $2,000 in expenses that were not included in the income statement as expenses—again, a decrease in cash.

b. All of the current liabilities increased. Therefore, the cash figure must be adjusted upward because all expenses were not paid in cash. These increases in current liabilities are as follows:

| | December 31 | | |
	1996	1997	Change
Accounts payable	$61,000	$76,000	$15,000
Income tax payable	12,000	15,000	3,000
Accrued wages and salaries	4,000	5,000	1,000
Interest payable	2,000	4,000	2,000

With the foregoing adjustments, the **cash flow from operations,** equaling $64,000, has been calculated.

4. Compute the **cash flow from investment activities**—how much the company has invested in fixed assets and other assets. As shown in Figure 11-7, $98,000 was invested during 1997, including a $78,000 increase ($838,000 – $760,000) in fixed assets (note that this is the change in *gross,* not *net,* fixed assets) and a $20,000 increase ($50,000 – $30,000) for patents.

5. Calculate the **cash flow from financing activities,** which include borrowing, repaying debt, issuing new stock, and/or paying out dividends to the owners. FGD received a net positive cash flow from financing activities in the amount of $39,000. First, the company increased its long-term notes payable by $54,000 ($200,000 – $146,000). Second, the firm paid out $15,000 in common stock dividends to its owners. (The $15,000 dividend payment is shown below the firm's income statement in Figure 11-2 on page 231.)

At this point in developing the cash flow statement, every change in the balance sheet has been accounted for, except the $45,000 change in retained earnings:

$$\text{Change in retained earnings} = \text{Net income} - \text{Dividends paid}$$
$$= \$60,000 - \$15,000$$
$$= \$45,000$$

Since net income and dividend payments have already been included in the cash flow statement, the change in retained earnings can be ignored. To include it would be double counting.

The bottom line of the cash flow statement indicates that FGD generated $5,000 in cash flow during 1997, significantly below the reported net income of $60,000. The $55,000 difference between cash flow and net income results from all the changes in the balance sheet accounts that have no effect on net income.

The cash flow statement is the last type of financial statement you need to understand in order to develop projected financial statements, or what are known as **pro forma financial statements.** The purpose of pro forma statements is to answer two questions:

cash flow from operations
changes in a firm's cash position generated by day-to-day operations, including cash collections of sales and payments related to operations, interest, and taxes

cash flow from investment activities
changes in a firm's cash position generated by investments in fixed assets and other assets

cash flow from financing activities
changes in a firm's cash position generated by payments to a firm's creditors, excluding interest payments, and cash received from investors

pro forma financial statements
reports that provide projections of a firm's financial condition

1. What are the expected sales-expenses relationships for a proposed venture, and, given these relationships and the projected sales levels, how profitable is the firm likely to be?
2. What determines the amount and type of financing—debt versus equity—to be used in financing the new company?

Unless these questions are answered first, the search for specific sources of financing will probably meet with failure, not because the concept of the venture is flawed, but because the answers are essential to any new business's success. The remaining sections of this chapter provide the information necessary to address these two questions.

2 **Explain how to forecast a new venture's profitability.**

ASSESSING PROFITABILITY

A key question for anyone starting a new business is "How profitable is the venture likely to be?" In Chapters 22 and 23, we will look at this question in more detail. For now, however, our focus is on understanding how to forecast the firm's profits.

Profits reward an owner's investment in a company and constitute a primary source for financing future growth. The more profitable a company, the more funds it will have for growing. However, a profitable company does not necessarily have a high cash flow. For example, FGD Manufacturing Company had $60,000 in net income, but its cash flow was only $5,000. Even so, profits can help finance a firm's growth. Thus, an entrepreneur must understand the factors that drive profits, so that he or she can make the necessary profit projections. A company's net income, or profit, is dependent on four variables:

1. *Amount of sales.* The dollar amount of sales equals the price of the product or service times the number of units sold or the amount of service rendered. Most projections about a company's financial future are driven directly by assumptions regarding future sales.
2. *Cost of goods sold and operating expenses.* This variable includes (a) the cost of goods sold, (b) expenses related to marketing and distributing the product, and (c) general and administrative expenses. As far as possible, these expenses should be classified as those that do not vary with a change in sales volume (*fixed* operating expenses) and those that change proportionally with sales (*variable* operating expenses).

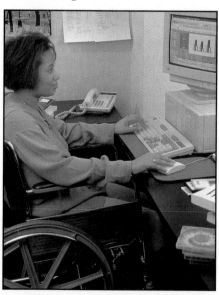

Computer-generated analyses, complete with bar graphs and pie charts, are useful in tracking profits and forecasting future profitability. Through "what-if" analysis, an entrepreneur can see the possible consequences of reducing prices or increasing inventory.

3. *Interest expense.* An entrepreneur who borrows money agrees to pay interest on the loan principal. For example, a loan of $25,000 for a full year at a 12-percent interest rate results in an interest expense of $3,000 for the year ($0.12 \times \$25,000$).
4. *Taxes.* A firm's income taxes are figured as a percentage of taxable income. As we discussed in Chapter 9, income tax rates increase as the amount of income increases. For projection purposes, the tax rates that are used are those applicable to the amount of income projected.

Let's consider an example that demonstrates how to estimate a new venture's profits. An entrepreneur is planning to start a new business, Oakcrest Products, Inc., that will make stair parts for luxury homes. A newly developed lathe will allow the firm to be more responsive to varying design specifications, in a very economical manner. Based on a study of potential market demand and expected costs-sales relationships, the following estimates for the first two years of operations have been made:

1. Oakcrest expects to sell its product for $125 per unit, with total sales for the first year projected at 2,000 units, or $250,000 ($125 × 2,000), and total sales for the second year projected at 3,200 units, or $400,000 ($125 × 3,200).
2. Fixed production costs (such as rent or building depreciation) are expected to be $100,000 per year, while fixed operating expenses (marketing expenses and administrative expenses) should be about $50,000. Thus, the total fixed cost of goods sold and fixed operating expenses will be $150,000.
3. The variable costs of producing the stair parts will be around 20 percent of dollar sales, and the variable operating expenses will be approximately 30 percent of dollar sales. In other words, at a selling price of $125 per unit, the combined variable costs per unit, both for producing the stair parts and for marketing them will be $62.50 [(0.20 + 0.30) × $125].
4. The bank has agreed to loan the firm $100,000 at an interest rate of 12 percent.
5. Assume that the income tax rate will be 25 percent; that is, taxes will be 25 percent of earnings before taxes (taxable income).

Given these estimates, Oakcrest's net income may be forecasted as shown in Figure 11-8.

Projecting the firm's income involved the following steps:

1. Calculations begin with the assumed sales projections (line 1).
2. The expected total cost of goods sold (line 4) and the total operating expenses (line 8) are computed for the projected level of sales. Subtracting these costs and expenses from sales provides the firm's operating profits, or earnings before interest and taxes (line 9).

	Year 1	Year 2	
Sales revenue	$250,000	$400,000	Line 1
Cost of goods sold:			
Fixed costs	$100,000	$100,000	Line 2
Variable costs (20% of sales)	50,000	80,000	Line 3
Total cost of goods sold	$150,000	$180,000	Line 4
Gross profits	$100,000	$220,000	Line 5
Operating expenses:			
Fixed expenses	$ 50,000	$ 50,000	Line 6
Variable expenses (30% of sales)	75,000	120,000	Line 7
Total operating expenses	$125,000	$170,000	Line 8
Operating profits	($ 25,000)	$ 50,000	Line 9
Interest expense (12% interest rate)	(12,000)	(12,000)	Line 10
Earnings before taxes	($ 37,000)	$ 38,000	Line 11
Taxes (25% of earnings before taxes)	0	(9,500)	Line 12
Net income	($ 37,000)	$ 28,500	Line 13

Figure 11-8

Projected Income Statements for Oakcrest Products, Inc.

Action Report

ENTREPRENEURIAL EXPERIENCES

A Company Failing from Too Much Success

Some firms fail because sales never become high enough to cover fixed costs, much less provide a good profit. Other firms fail because they are allowed to grow at a faster rate than can be sustained with available financing. That is, they fail to anticipate the cash flow requirements associated with high sales growth. The result can be disastrous, as the following situation illustrates:

> *When Harvey Harris started selling . . . personalized calendars in 1992, he anticipated strong demand. . . . But not so strong that it would ruin him.*
>
> *In January [1995], his Oklahoma City–based concern, Grandmother Calendar Co., went out of business. Mr. Harris blames the company's demise on an excess of success. "I'm a salesman, and a good one, [who] started this company up and it exploded and just went crazy," he told the* Daily Oklahoman.
>
> *In the period leading up to Christmas, things began to fall apart. Orders came in much faster than Mr. Harris could fill them, so he diverted money needed for day-to-day expenses to expand capacity, according to some employees. He leased more production and bought additional equipment. Output doubled to 300 calendars a day—but orders were coming in at a rate of 1,000 a day.*
>
> *Equipment began to fail from overuse. Output from the scanners overloaded the printers. And quality suffered, with Mr. Harris so desperate to speed up production that he allowed calendars with misspellings and poor color quality to be shipped anyway, says Johnna Pulis, a former scanner operator.*
>
> *In addition, the $20 for the basic item, which undercut most competitors by about $5, may have been too low, especially considering the complexity of the process.*
>
> *Looking back, Mr. Harris may have been insufficiently capitalized, having used his own savings and a loan from his father to get the business off the ground. Moreover, most customers paid for the additional options by credit card, and the credit-card companies didn't pay Grandmother until the finished product was shipped.*
>
> *When companies suddenly get a big influx of orders, working capital often runs out, management is strained, and computer systems get overloaded, says Gary Thompson, a principal with consulting firm Towers Perrin in Dallas. "It can all happen at once."*

Source: "A Company Failing from Too Much Success," *The Wall Street Journal*, March 17, 1995, p. B2.

3. The interest expense for each year (line 10) is calculated next. In this case, the annual interest expense is $12,000 (0.12 × $100,000).

4. The final computation is subtracting estimated income taxes. Here the tax rate is 25 percent of earnings before taxes. Note that taxes are zero for the first year because of the $37,000 loss. Typically, when a company has a loss from its operations, it owes no taxes for that year, and the tax laws allow it to apply the loss against income in following years. For simplicity, it is assumed here that the loss in the first year cannot be carried forward to the second year.

The computations in Figure 11-8 indicate that Oakcrest will lose $37,000 in its first year, followed by a positive net income of $28,500 in its second year. A startup company typically experiences losses for a period of time, frequently for as long as two or three years.[2] In a real situation, the entrepreneur would want to project the profits of a new company three to five years into the future, as opposed to the two-year projection for Oakcrest. However, this example does illustrate an approach for projecting profits, regardless of the length of the forecast.

A FIRM'S FINANCIAL REQUIREMENTS

3 Estimate the assets needed and the financing required for a new venture.

It is now time to shift attention from forecasting the startup's profits to estimating its financial requirements over the first few years. The specific needs of a proposed venture govern the nature of its initial financial requirements. If the firm is a food store, financial planning must provide for the building, cash registers, shopping carts, shelving, inventory, office equipment, and other items required for this type of operation. An analysis of capital requirements for this or any other type of business must consider how to finance (1) the necessary investments and expenses incurred to start the company and allow it to grow and (2) the owners' personal expenses if other income is not available for living purposes. Let's look at how an entrepreneur could estimate the financial requirements of a new venture.

Estimating a Firm's Financial Requirements

When estimating the magnitude of capital requirements for a startup, an entrepreneur might find a crystal ball useful. The uncertainties surrounding an entirely new venture make estimation difficult. Even for an established business, forecasting is never exact. Nevertheless, when seeking initial capital, the entrepreneur must be ready to answer the questions "How much financing is needed?" and "For what purpose?"

The amount of capital needed by new businesses varies considerably. High-technology businesses—such as computer manufacturers, designers of semiconductor chips, and gene-splicing companies—often require several million dollars in initial financing. Most service businesses, on the other hand, require very little initial capital.

An entrepreneur may use a double-barreled approach to estimating capital requirements by (1) using industry standard ratios to estimate dollar amounts and (2) cross-checking those dollar amounts by break-even analysis and empirical investigation. Robert Morris Associates, Dun & Bradstreet, banks, trade associations, and similar organizations compile industry standard ratios for numerous types of businesses. If standard ratios cannot be located, then common sense and educated guesswork must be used to estimate capital requirements.

ESTIMATING ASSET REQUIREMENTS   The key to effectively forecasting asset requirements is understanding the relationship between projected sales and needed assets. A firm's sales are the primary driving force of future asset needs. In other words, a sales increase causes an increase in a firm's asset requirements, which in turn creates a need for more financing. Figure 11-9 depicts these relationships.

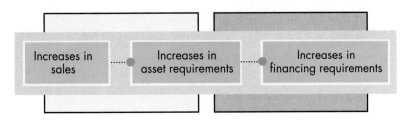

Figure 11-9

Sales-Assets Financing Relationships

Since asset needs tend to increase as sales increase, a firm's asset requirements may be estimated as a percentage of sales. Therefore, if future sales have been projected, a ratio of assets to sales can be used to estimate asset requirements. For example, if sales are expected to be $1 million and if assets in this particular industry tend to run about 50 percent of sales, a firm's asset requirements would be estimated to be $500,000 ($0.50 \times \$1,000,000$).

Although the assets-to-sales relationship varies over time and with individual firms, it tends to be relatively constant within an industry. For example, the assets-to-sales relationship for grocery stores is on average around 20 percent, compared to 65 percent for oil and gas companies.

This method, called the **percentage-of-sales technique,** is also used to project individual asset investments. For example, a typical relationship exists between the amount of accounts receivable and the amount of sales.

To illustrate use of the percentage-of-sales technique for forecasting purposes, consider the following example. Katie Dalton is planning to start a new business, Trailer Craft, Inc., to produce small trailers to be pulled behind motorcycles. After studying a similar company in a different state, she believes the business could generate sales of approximately $250,000 in the first year and have significant growth potential in following years. Based on her investigation of the opportunity, Dalton estimated the requirements for cash, accounts receivable, and inventories as a percentage of sales for the first year as follows:

Assets	*Percentage of Assets to Sales*
Cash	5
Accounts receivable	10
Inventories	25

Dalton searched for a manufacturing facility and found a suitable building for about $50,000. Given anticipated sales of $250,000 and the assets-to-sales relationships shown, the forecasted asset requirements for Trailer Craft are as follows:

Cash	$ 12,500	(5% of sales)
Accounts receivable	25,000	(10% of sales)
Inventories	62,500	(25% of sales)
Total current assets	$100,000	
Fixed assets (facility)	50,000	(Estimated cost)
Total assets required	$150,000	

Thus, Dalton might expect to need $150,000 in assets, some immediately and the rest as the firm continues its first year of operation. While the figures used to obtain this estimate are only rough approximations, the estimate should be relatively close if Dalton has identified the assets-to-sales relationships correctly and if sales materialize as expected. How to finance asset needs will be discussed later in this chapter, while specific options will be examined in Chapter 12.

It is important to note that the assets-sales relationship can also be expressed as a turnover ratio. The turnover ratio represents sales divided by assets, rather than assets divided by sales. For example, instead of saying that inventories will be about 25 percent of sales, we could say that the inventories will "turn over" four times per year. That is,

$$\frac{\text{Sales}}{\text{Inventories}} = 4$$

percentage-of-sales technique
a method to forecast asset investments and financing requirements

In our Trailer Craft example,

$$\frac{\$250,000}{\text{Inventories}} = 4$$

Therefore,

$$\text{Inventories} = \frac{\$250,000}{4} = \$62,500$$

Thus, Trailer Craft's inventories would equal $62,500, which is the same answer that was reached using the percentage-of-sales technique, just calculated a bit differently.

LIQUIDITY CONSIDERATIONS IN STRUCTURING ASSET NEEDS   The need for adequate working capital, as represented by a firm's **liquidity,** deserves special emphasis. A common weakness in small business financing is a disproportionately small investment in current assets relative to the investment in fixed assets. Too much money is thus tied up in assets that are difficult to convert to cash, and the business must depend on daily receipts to meet the obligations coming due from day to day. A slump in sales or unexpected expenses may force the firm into bankruptcy.

The lack of flexibility associated with investment in fixed assets suggests the desirability of minimizing this type of investment. For example, owners must frequently choose between renting or buying business property. For the majority of new small firms, renting is the better alternative. A rental arrangement not only reduces the initial cash outlay but also provides flexibility that is helpful if the business is more successful or less successful than anticipated.

liquidity
the ability of a firm to meet maturing debt obligations by having adequate working capital available

Identifying the Types of Financing

We have discussed the use of the relationship between assets and sales to estimate a firm's asset requirements. However, money must be found with which to purchase these assets. In other words, for every dollar of assets, there must be a corresponding dollar of financing. Certain guidelines, or principles, should be followed in financing a firm. Here are five such guidelines:

Leasing physical assets such as buildings and equipment frees up cash for daily business operations. It also allows the entrepreneur some flexibility should the business be less successful than anticipated.

Action Report

ENTREPRENEURIAL EXPERIENCES

Projecting Startup Financing Requirements

The development of a Pittsburgh, Pennsylvania company, AgRecycle, Inc., provides insight into the process of forecasting financial requirements. In the 1970s, Dan Eichenlaub (now president of AgRecycle) co-founded Eichenlaub, Inc., a landscape construction company. In 1988, the soils department of the company began producing limited quantities of compost made from yard debris and grass clippings from various job sites. Eichenlaub soon recognized that composting technology was beyond the scope of his landscaping business, both financially and in terms of staffing. That recognition led to the founding of AgRecycle in 1991.

To help with the startup, Eichenlaub enlisted Carla Castagnero, a friend and lawyer who was an environmental and safety consultant for USX Corporation. "We would work in the evenings and on weekends, investigating markets, composting technologies, and financial requirements," says Castagnero, vice-president of AgRecycle. "After about six months, we decided we either had to go for it full-time or abandon the idea."

Startup and operational costs needed from outside investment capital were estimated at close to $1 million. Eichenlaub and Castagnero raised the capital through individual investors, none of whom were involved in their industry. Bank financing was sought as well. To develop accurate pro forma statements, the partners talked with the managers of over 20 composting operations during actual site visits. Startup costs included $480,000 to prepare 10 acres of the 41-acre site leased by the company. AgRecycle also procured composting equipment costing close to $600,000. Ongoing expenses included the costs of fuel and repairs, lab testing of both raw materials and finished product, and disposal of rejects. The financial projections also had to recognize the seasonality of the composting business.

Eichenlaub and Castagnero were able to predict with reasonable accuracy the financial needs of AgRecycle, which could not have happened without some careful planning.

Source: Nora Goldstein, "When It Pays to Be Out Front," *In Business*, Vol. 16, No. 2 (March-April 1994), pp. 36–38.

1. The more assets needed by a firm, the greater its financial requirements. Thus, a firm that is growing rapidly in sales has greater asset requirements and, consequently, greater pressure to find the necessary financing.
2. A company should finance its growth in a way that maintains a proper degree of liquidity. A conventional measurement of liquidity is the current ratio, which compares a firm's current assets (mainly cash, accounts receivable, and inventories) to its current liabilities (short-term debt). The **current ratio** is calculated as follows:

current ratio a measure of a company's relative liquidity, determined by dividing current assets by current liabilities

$$\text{Current ratio} = \frac{\text{Current assets}}{\text{Current liabilities}}$$

For example, to ensure payment of short-term debts as they come due, an entrepreneur might maintain a current ratio of 2—that is, have current assets that are worth twice as much as current liabilities.

3. The amount of total debt that can be used in financing a business is limited by the amount of equity provided by the owners. A bank will not loan all the money needed to finance a company. Owners must put some of their own money into the venture. Thus, an initial business plan may specify that at least half of the firm's financing will come from equity and the remaining half will be financed with debt.

4. Some short-term debt arises spontaneously as the firm grows—thus the name **spontaneous financing.** These sources of financing increase as a natural consequence of an increase in the firm's sales. For example, an increase in sales requires more inventories, causing accounts payable to increase. Typically, spontaneous sources of financing average a certain percentage of sales.

5. There are two sources of equity capital: external and internal. The equity in a company comes initially from the investment the owners make in the firm. These funds represent **external equity.** After the company is in operation, additional equity may come from **profit retention,** as profits are retained within the company rather than distributed to the owners. This latter source is called **internal equity.** For the typical small firm, internal equity is the primary source of equity for financing growth. (Be careful not to think of retained profits as a big cash resource. As already noted, a company can have a large amount of earnings and no cash to reinvest. This problem will be discussed further in Chapters 22 and 23.)

In summary,

Total asset requirements	=	Total sources of financing	=	Profits retained within the business	+	Spontaneous sources of financing	+	External sources of financing

This equation captures the essence of forecasting financial requirements. The entrepreneur who thoroughly understands these relationships is better able to forecast his or her firm's financial requirements. Recall that for Trailer Craft, Inc., prospective owner Katie Dalton has projected asset requirements of $150,000 on the basis of $250,000 in sales (see page 244). In addition, Dalton has made the following observations:

- Earnings after taxes are estimated to be about 12 percent of sales; that is, $250,000 of sales should result in after-tax profits of $30,000 ($0.12 \times \$250,000$).
- Dalton has negotiated with a supplier to extend credit on inventory purchases; as a result, accounts payable will average about 8 percent of sales.
- Accruals (unpaid taxes or unpaid wages, for example) should run approximately 4 percent of annual sales.
- Dalton plans to incorporate the business and invest $40,000 of her personal savings in the venture in return for 10,000 shares of common stock.[3]
- The bank has agreed to provide a short-term line of credit of $20,000 to Trailer Craft, which means that the firm can borrow up to $20,000 as the need arises. However, when the firm has excess cash, it may choose to pay down the line of credit. For example, during the spring and summer, business is particularly brisk, and Trailer Craft may need to borrow the entire $20,000 to buy inventory and extend credit to customers. However, during the winter months, a slack time, less cash will be needed and the loan balance could possibly be reduced.
- The bank has also agreed to help finance the purchase of the building for manufacturing and warehousing the firm's product. Of the $50,000 needed, the bank will lend the firm $35,000, with the building serving as collateral for the loan. The loan will take the form of a 25-year mortgage.

spontaneous financing
short-term debts, such as accounts payable, that spontaneously increase in proportion to a firm's increasing sales

external equity
equity that comes initially from the owners' investment in a firm

profit retention
the reinvestment of profits in a firm

internal equity
equity that comes from retaining profits within a firm

- As conditions for loaning the money to Trailer Craft, the bank has imposed two restrictions: (1) the firm's current ratio should not fall below 1.75, and (2) no more than 60 percent of the firm's asset requirements should come from debt, either short-term or long-term (that is, total debt to total assets should be no more than 60 percent). Failure to comply with either of these conditions will result in the bank loans coming due immediately.

From the foregoing information, Dalton can estimate the financial sources for Trailer Craft as follows:

- Accounts payable: $0.08 \times \$250,000$ in sales = $20,000
- Accruals: $0.04 \times \$250,000$ in sales = $10,000
- Credit line: Per the agreement with the bank, Trailer Craft may borrow up to $20,000. Any additional financing must come from other sources.
- Long-term debt: The bank has agreed to loan Trailer Craft $35,000 for the purchase of real estate.
- Equity: By the end of the first year, the firm's equity should be around $70,000. This consists of the $40,000 originally invested in the company by the owner, plus the projected $30,000 in after-tax profits for the year. This $30,000 is to be retained within the company and not distributed to the owner.

Dalton can now formulate the projected debt and equity section of the firm's balance sheet. The balance sheet also reflects the financial requirements for the firm for the first year of business. These financial requirements are shown in the bottom portion of Figure 11-10, which shows Trailer Craft's projected balance sheet.

Two comments need to be made about the projected balance sheet in Figure 11-10. First, uses must always equal sources. Therefore, assets must equal debt plus equity. For Trailer Craft, asset requirements are estimated to be $150,000 by the end of the first year; thus, debt and equity must also total $150,000. For this to happen,

Figure 11-10

Projected Balance Sheet at the End of the First Year for Trailer Craft, Inc.

Assets:	
Cash	$ 12,500
Accounts receivable	25,000
Inventories	62,500
Total current assets	$100,000
Fixed assets (machinery)	50,000
Total assets	$150,000
Debt:	
Accounts payable	$ 20,000
Accruals	10,000
Credit line	15,000
Total current liabilities	$ 45,000
Long-term debt	35,000
Total debt	$ 80,000
Equity:	
Common stock	$ 40,000
Retained earnings	30,000
Total equity	$ 70,000
Total debt and equity	$150,000

only $15,000 of the $20,000 credit line is needed to bring the total debt and equity to $150,000. Second, if all goes as planned, Trailer Craft will be able to satisfy the banker's loan restrictions, in terms of both the current ratio and the debt-to-total-assets ratio. From the balance sheet, these ratios can be computed as follows:

$$\text{Current ratio} = \frac{\text{Current assets}}{\text{Current liabilities}}$$

$$= \frac{\$100,000}{\$45,000} = 2.22$$

and

$$\text{Debt-to-total-assets ratio} = \frac{\text{Total debt}}{\text{Total assets}}$$

$$= \frac{\$80,000}{\$150,000}$$

$$= 0.533, \text{ or } 53.3\%$$

The current ratio then is 2.22, above the bank's requirement of at least 1.75, and the debt ratio (debt as a percentage of total assets) is 53.3 percent, below the maximum limit imposed by the bank of 60 percent. Both outcomes fall within the bank's restrictions.

Finally, we should note that the forecasting process involves subjective judgment in terms of making predictions. The overall approach is straightforward—entrepreneurs make assumptions, and, based on these assumptions, they determine the financing requirements. But entrepreneurs may be tempted to overstate their expectations in order to acquire the necessary financing. There are two reasons not to fall prey to this temptation. First, not delivering on promises may place entrepreneurs in a situation where they are unable to honor future financial commitments. In such cases, it would be better not to have received the financing than to take the money and not repay it as promised. Second, intentionally overstating expectations to gain access to financing is unethical.

Provision for Personal Expenses

Provision must be made for the owner's personal living expenses during the initial period of operation of many startups. Whether or not these expenses are recognized as part of the business's capitalization, they must be considered in its financial plan. Inadequate provision for personal expenses will inevitably lead to a diversion of business assets and a departure from the financial plan. Therefore, failure to incorporate these expenses into the plan as a cash outflow raises a red flag to any prospective lender or investor.

Looking Back

1 Describe the purpose and content of financial statements.

- An income statement presents the financial results of a firm's operations over a given time period: the activities involved in selling the product, producing or acquiring the goods or services sold, operating the firm, and financing the firm.
- A balance sheet provides a snapshot of a firm's financial position at a specific point in time: the amount of assets the firm owns, the amount of outstanding debt, and the amount of owners' equity.
- The income statement does not measure a firm's cash flows, because it is calculated on an *accrual* basis rather than on a *cash* basis.
- A cash flow statement presents the sources and uses of a firm's cash flow for a given period of time; it involves calculating a firm's cash flow from operations, less cash invested in assets, plus or minus changes in cash from borrowing or repaying debt, plus cash from issuing new stock, less any payment of dividends.

2 Explain how to forecast a new venture's profitability.

- Estimation of a company's future profit begins with projecting anticipated level of sales.
- Fixed and variable operating expenses are based on the projected level of sales and then deducted from sales to obtain forecasted profit.

3 Estimate the assets needed and the financing required for a new venture.

- Funding for a new venture should cover its asset requirements and also the personal living expenses of the owner.
- A direct relationship exists between sales growth and asset needs; as sales increase, more assets and more financing are required.
- The two basic types of capital used in financing a company are debt financing and ownership equity.

New Terms and Concepts

financial statements (accounting statements) *229*

income statement (profit and loss statement) *229*

cost of goods sold *230*

gross profit *230*

operating expenses *230*

operating income (earnings before interest and taxes) *230*

financing costs *230*

net income available to owners (net income) *230*

balance sheet *231*

current assets (working capital) *231*

accounts receivable *232*

inventory *232*

prepaid expenses *233*

fixed assets *233*

other assets *233*

debt capital *233*

current debt (short-term liabilities) *233*

accounts payable (trade credit) *233*

other payables *233*

accrued expenses *233*

short-term notes *233*

long-term debt *233*

mortgage *233*

owners' equity capital *234*

retained earnings *234*

cash flow statement *236*

accrual-basis accounting *236*

depreciation expense *237*

cash-basis accounting *237*

cash flow from operations *239*

cash flow from investment activities *239*

cash flow from financing activities *239*

pro forma financial statements *239*

percentage-of-sales technique *244*

liquidity *245*

current ratio *246*

spontaneous financing *247*

external equity *247*

profit retention *247*

internal equity *247*

You Make the Call

Situation 1 In 1996, J. T. Rose purchased a small business, the Baugh Company. The firm has been profitable, but Rose has been disappointed by the lack of cash flow. He had hoped to have about $10,000 a year available for personal living expenses. However, there never seems to be much cash available for purposes other than business needs. In a recent visit, Rose asked you to examine the balance sheet shown below and explain why he is making a profit yet does not have any discretionary cash for personal needs. He observed, "I thought that I could take the profits and add depreciation to find out how much cash flow I was generating. However, that never seems to be the case. What's happening?"

Continue on next page

This chapter has presented a considerable amount of information regarding financial planning for a new company. The topics covered here will serve as a foundation for the entrepreneur's search for financing, which is examined in Chapter 12.

DISCUSSION QUESTIONS

1. What is the relationship between an income statement and a balance sheet?
2. Explain the purpose of the three main types of financial statements.
3. Distinguish among (a) gross profit, (b) operating profit (earnings before interest and taxes), and (c) net income (net profit).
4. Why are cash flow and profit not equal?
5. What determines a company's profitability?
6. Describe the process for estimating the amount of assets needed for a new venture.
7. Suppose that a retailer's estimated sales are $900,000 and the standard sales-to-inventory ratio is 6. What dollar amount of inventory should be planned on for the new business?
8. Distinguish between owners' equity capital and debt capital.
9. Distinguish between spontaneous and nonspontaneous financing and between internal and external equity.
10. How are a startup's financial requirements estimated?

EXPERIENTIAL EXERCISES

1. Interview an owner of a small firm about the financial statements used in his or her business. Ask the owner how important financial data are to decision making.
2. Acquire a small company's financial statements. Review the statements and describe the firm's financial position. Find out if the owner agrees with your conclusions.
3. Dun & Bradstreet and Robert Morris Associates compile financial information about many companies. They provide, among other information, income statements and balance sheets for an average firm in an industry. Go to the library and find one of these data sources. Then choose two industries and, for each industry, compute the following data:
    a. The percentage of firms' assets in each industry that are invested in (1) current assets and (2) fixed assets (plant and equipment)
    b. The percentage of the two industries' financing that comes from (1) spontaneous financing and (2) internal equity
    c. The cost of goods sold and the operating expenses as percentages of sales
    d. The total assets as a percentage of sales

    Given your findings, how would you summarize the differences between the two industries?

Balance Sheet for the Baugh Company for 1995 and 1996

	1995	1996
Cash	$ 8,000	$ 10,000
Accounts receivable	15,000	20,000
Inventory	22,000	25,000
Current assets	$45,000	$ 55,000
Gross fixed assets	50,000	55,000
Accum. depreciation	–15,000	–20,000
Net fixed assets	$35,000	$ 35,000
Other assets	12,000	10,000
Total assets	$92,000	$100,000
Accounts payable	$10,000	$ 12,000
Accruals	7,000	8,000
Short-term notes	5,000	5,000
Total short-term debt	$22,000	$ 25,000
Long-term debt	15,000	15,000
Total debt	$37,000	$ 40,000
Equity	55,000	60,000
Total debt and equity	$92,000	$100,000
Sales		$175,000
Cost of goods sold		–105,000
Gross profit		$ 70,000
Depreciation		–5,000
Administrative expenses		–20,000
Selling expenses		–26,000
Total operating expenses		$ 51,000
Operating income		$ 19,000
Interest expense		–3,000
Earnings before taxes		$ 16,000
Taxes		–8,000
Net income		$ 8,000

Question 1 From the information provided by the balance sheet, what would you tell Rose? (As part of your answer, develop a cash flow statement.)
Question 2 How would you describe the primary sources and uses of cash for the Baugh Company?

Continue on next page

Situation 2   Mary Watson, a mother and housewife, has always had a special interest in arts and crafts. For the last several years, she has created crafts at home and traveled occasionally to arts and crafts shows to sell her wares. Recently, Watson decided to open an arts and crafts shop to sell supplies and finished crafts. She lives in a small rural community and knows of other women who produce craft items that could supplement her own products. Watson believes her shop could be successful if several artists would display their work. She knows of a vacant building in town that would be an ideal location.

Question 1   What do you see as the nature of Watson's financial requirements?

Question 2   Is this venture too small to justify preparation of a financial plan? Why or why not?

Situation 3   The firm Trailer Craft, Inc., used as an example in this chapter, is an actual firm. Some of the facts were changed to maintain confidentiality. In reality, Stuart Hall has bought the company from its founding owners and is moving its operations to his hometown. Although we estimated the firm's asset needs and financing requirements, we have no certainty that these projections will be realized. The figures used represent the most likely case. However, Hall has also made some projections that he considers to be the worst-case and best-case sales and profit figures. If things do not go well, the firm might sell only $150,000 in its first year and earn only 10 percent on each sales dollar. However, if the potential of the business is realized, Hall believes that sales could be as high as $400,000, with a profit-to-sales ratio of 15 percent. If he needs any additional financing beyond the existing line of credit, he conceivably could borrow another $5,000 in short-term debt from the bank by pledging some personal investments. Any additional financing will need to come from Hall himself, by increasing his equity stake in the business.

Source: Personal visit with Stuart Hall. Permission granted to use as example, 1994. (Numbers are hypothetical.)

Question   Assuming that all the other relationships hold, as given in the discussion of Trailer Craft in this chapter, how will Hall's projections affect the balance sheet? Redo the balance sheet, and compare your results with the original projected balance sheet shown in Figure 11-10 (on page 248).

4. Obtain the business plan of a firm that is three to five years old. Compare the techniques used in the plan for forecasting the firm's profits and financing requirements with those presented in this chapter. If the information is available, compare the financial forecasts with the eventual outcome. What accounts for the differences?

Exploring the

5. Perform a word search on the Web for "small business financing." Report your findings to the class.

 CASE 11
WJP Partners (p. 622)

This case provides the necessary data to prepare pro forma financial statements for a small startup company.

Alternative Cases for Chapter 11:
Case 3, "Stitch Craft," p. 597
Case 6, "Robinson Associates, Inc.," p. 605
Case 22, "The Style Shop," p. 648
Case 23, "Barton Sales and Service," p. 653

LAYING THE FOUNDATION
Asking the Right Questions

As part of laying the foundation to preparing your own business plan, you will need to develop the following pro forma financial statements and accompanying information:

- Historical financial statements (if applicable) and five years of pro forma financial statements, including balance sheets, income statements, and cash flow statements
- Monthly cash budgets for one year in the future and quarterly for the second year. (See Chapter 22 for an explanation of cash budgets.)
- Profit and cash flow break-even analysis. (See Chapter 14 for an explanation of break-even analysis.)
- Financial resources required now and in the future, detailing the intended use of any funds being requested
- Underlying assumptions for all pro forma statements
- Current and planned investments by the owners and investors

USING BizPlanBuilder

If you are using BizPlan*Builder,* refer to Part 3 for information that should be included in the business plan as it relates to financial planning. Then turn to Part 2 for instructions on using the BizPlan software to prepare the pro forma financial statements.

Chapter 12

Finding Sources of Financing

Dr. Robin Potter

spotlight on small business

For nine months, Dr. Robin Potter searched for fellow visionaries to invest in his idea of a national health-care credit card. He schmoozed, and he networked. And he developed a marketing plan and a slide presentation and showed them to hundreds of investors in individual meetings.

By early 1989, Potter, a 42-year-old dentist from Overland Park, Kansas, had located about 20 individuals willing to invest a total of $700,000 to make his idea a going concern. By late 1993, nearly 10,000 physicians in 50 states were customers of PulseCard Inc. Each year, PulseCard transactions total more than $35 million.

Potter found what many entrepreneurs hunger for: bold individuals able and willing to provide enough capital to move a startup to the next phase. Known as "business angels," these investors are the only source of seed capital for many startups, beyond personal savings, friends, and relatives.

Potter, who gave up his dental practice to demonstrate to investors how serious he was about PulseCard, is certain his angels will be happy that they had confidence in him. "They believed I could do what I said I would do," he says.

Source: Dale D. Buss, "Heaven Help Us," *Nation's Business*, Vol. 81, No. 11 (November 1993), p. 29.

Looking Ahead

After studying this chapter, you should be able to:

1 Evaluate the choice between debt financing and equity financing.

2 Contrast the primary sources of financing used by startups and by existing firms.

3 Describe various sources of financing available to small firms.

4 Discuss the most important factors in the process of obtaining startup financing.

In Chapter 11, we answered two questions about financing a small company, especially a startup firm: *How much* financing will be needed? What *type* of financing might be available? In answering these two questions, we identified three basic types of financing: (1) spontaneous financing, which comes from sources that automatically increase with increases in sales; (2) profit retention, which requires owners to forego taking cash out of the business and let it remain within the firm to finance growth; and (3) external financing, which comes from outside investors. Once the necessary amount of financing is known, sources of funds must be identified. But before looking at specific sources, the entrepreneur must ask, "Should I use debt or equity financing?" Most capital sources specialize in providing either one or the other, but generally not both.

DEBT OR EQUITY FINANCING?

Assume that a firm needs $100,000 in outside financing. The firm can borrow the money (debt financing), issue common stock (equity), or use some combination of the two (debt and equity). The decision whether to use debt or equity financing depends to a large extent on the type of business, the firm's financial strength, and the current economic environment—that is, whether lenders and investors are optimistic or pessimistic about the future. It also depends on the owner's personal feelings about debt and equity. Given identical conditions, one entrepreneur will choose debt and another equity—and both can be right.

Choosing between debt and equity involves tradeoffs for owners with regard to potential profitability, financial risk, and voting control. Borrowing money (debt) rather than issuing common stock (owner's equity) increases the potential for higher rates of return to owners. Also, borrowing allows owners to retain voting control of the company. However, debt does expose them to greater financial risk. On the other hand, issuing stock rather than increasing debt limits the potential rate of return to the owners and requires them to give up some voting control in order to reduce risk.

The following discussion will consider each of these elements—potential profitability, financial risk, and voting control.

> **1** Evaluate the choice between debt financing and equity financing.

Potential Profitability

To illustrate how the choice between debt and equity affects potential profitability, let's consider some facts about the Somchai Company, a new firm that's still in the process of raising needed capital:

- The owners have already invested $100,000 of their own money in the new business. To complete the financing, they need another $100,000.

- If the owners raise the money needed by issuing common stock, new outside investors will receive 30 percent of the outstanding stock. (Even though these new investors will have contributed half the money required, they do not necessarily expect half the stock, because the original owners have contributed "sweat equity"—that is, time and effort to start the business.)
- If Somchai borrows the money, the interest rate on the debt will be 10 percent, or $10,000 in interest each year ($0.10 \times \$100,000$).
- Estimates suggest that the firm will earn $28,000 in operating profits (earnings before interest and taxes) each year, representing a 14 percent return on the firm's assets of $200,000 ($0.14 \times \$200,000 = \$28,000$).

If the firm issues stock, its balance sheet will read as follows:

Total assets	$200,000
Debt	$ 0
Equity	200,000
Total debt and equity	$200,000

But, if the firm borrows money, the balance sheet will appear as follows:

Total assets	$200,000
Debt (10% interest rate)	$100,000
Equity	100,000
Total debt and equity	$200,000

Given the above information and assuming no taxes (just to keep things simple), the firm's income statement under the two financing plans will be as follows:

	Equity	*Debt*
Operating income	$28,000	$28,000
Interest expense	0	10,000
Net income	$28,000	$18,000

As this income statement information reveals, net income is greater if the firm finances with equity rather than with debt. However, the rate of return on the owners' investment, which is more important than the absolute dollar income number, is greater when financing with debt. Using the following equation, we see that the owners' return on equity investment is 18 percent if debt is issued—and only 14 percent if equity is issued:

$$\text{Owners' return on equity investment} = \frac{\text{Net income}}{\text{Owners' investment}}$$

If equity is issued,

$$\text{Owners' return on equity investment} = \frac{\$28,000}{\$200,000} = 0.14, \text{ or } 14\%$$

If debt is issued,

$$\text{Owners' return on equity investment} = \frac{\$18,000}{\$100,000} = 0.18, \text{ or } 18\%$$

In other words, if equity financing is used, the owners will earn $14 for every $100 invested; if debt is used, however, the owners will earn $18 for every $100 invested. Thus, in terms of the rate of return on their investment, the owners are better off borrowing money at a 10 percent interest rate than issuing stock to new owners who will share in the profits.

As a general rule, as long as a firm's return on its assets (operating income ÷ total assets) is greater than the cost of the debt (interest rate), the owners' return on equity investment will be increased as the firm uses more debt. Somchai hopes to earn 14 percent on its assets but pay only 10 percent in interest for the debt financing. Using debt, therefore, increases the owners' opportunity to enhance the rate of return on their investment.

Financial Risk

If debt is so beneficial to the rate of return, why wouldn't Somchai's owners use even more debt and less equity? Then the rate of return on the owners' investment would be even higher. For example, if the Somchai Company financed with 90 percent debt and 10 percent equity—$180,000 in debt and $20,000 in equity—the firm's net income would be $10,000, computed as follows:

Operating income	$28,000
Interest expense (0.10 × $180,000)	18,000
Net income	$10,000

With $10,000 in net income and the owners' investment only $20,000, the return on the equity investment would be 50 percent ($10,000 ÷ $20,000).

However, in spite of this higher expected rate of return for the owners, there is a good reason to limit the amount of debt: *Debt is risky.* Debt is hard and demanding. One entrepreneur has likened it to ice—cold and hard. If the firm fails to earn profits, creditors still insist on their interest payments. Debt demands its pound of flesh from the owners regardless of their firm's performance. In an extreme case, creditors can force a firm into bankruptcy if it fails to honor its financial obligations.

Equity, on the other hand, is less demanding. If a firm does not reach its goal for profits, an equity investor must accept the disappointing results and hope for better results next year. Equity investors cannot demand more than what is earned.

Another way to view the negative side of debt is to contemplate what happens to the return on an equity investment if a company has a bad year. Let's consider what would happen if the Somchai Company experienced poor results. Instead of earning 14 percent on its assets as hoped, or $28,000 in operating profits, say the firm made a mere $2,000, or only 1 percent on its assets of $200,000. The owners' return would again depend on whether the firm used debt or equity to finance the second $100,000 investment in the company. The results would be as follows:

	Equity	*Debt*
Operating income	$2,000	$ 2,000
Interest expense	0	10,000
Net income	$2,000	($ 8,000)

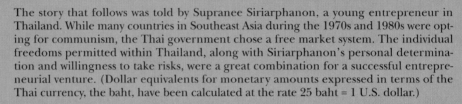

Action Report

ENTREPRENEURIAL EXPERIENCES

Building a Company with Debt: An Example from Thailand

The story that follows was told by Supranee Siriarphanon, a young entrepreneur in Thailand. While many countries in Southeast Asia during the 1970s and 1980s were opting for communism, the Thai government chose a free market system. The individual freedoms permitted within Thailand, along with Siriarphanon's personal determination and willingness to take risks, were a great combination for a successful entrepreneurial venture. (Dollar equivalents for monetary amounts expressed in terms of the Thai currency, the baht, have been calculated at the rate 25 baht = 1 U.S. dollar.)

I was born in Bangkok, Thailand—the youngest of 11 children of a Chinese family that immigrated into Thailand following World War II. . . . We were extremely poor, and as a small child, I worked as a laborer in my father's factory. However, I eventually attended King Mongkut's Institute of Technology, where I graduated with honors in architecture. Following graduation, I became the head designer for a furniture and interior decorating company. In 1989, my husband, Sompong Pholchareoncharit, and I started SPP Ceramics Co., Ltd., a ceramics manufacturer, located in Northern Thailand.

To begin, we invested 400,000 baht [$16,000] from personal savings and borrowed 500,000 baht [$20,000], with a house serving as collateral. We purchased land for the new business location worth 760,000 baht [$30,400]. Using the land as collateral, we acquired a 3 million baht [$120,000] loan from a local bank—2 million on a five-year payback and a 1 million baht line of credit. With the loan we built the facilities and a low-quality ceramic kiln from bricks, which left us with only 400,000 baht [a mere $16,000] for operating. The factory was opened in November 1989 with 25 employees.

We tried to compete in the domestic markets but found them to be very seasonal and price competitive. Sales occurred primarily at two times during the year—the new-year celebration and the "marrying season." . . . We could not compete effectively with the larger ceramics companies, where competition was based on price cutting and by giving better credit terms to customers. At one point, we were forced out of the market by a large competitor. Consequently, we were not being able to service our debt. . . .

To this point, I had kept my job in Bangkok, because with my salary I could pay the wages of 50 employees at the factory. But I came to realize that we either needed to close the company or I needed to quit my job and join my husband full-time at the company. So I resigned from my job.

When I came on full-time, I carefully studied our strengths and weaknesses. About then, I attended a ceramics show in Europe. At the show, I became convinced that by changing our strategies, we could compete in the European markets. . . .

Upon my return from Europe, we convinced our banker to loan us another 6 million baht [$200,000]. We then constructed the first fiber-glass kiln in Northern Thailand, receiving technical support from both the Thai and German governments.

The strategy worked. The changes allowed us to compete in the high end of the market in Europe, America, and Japan, which [was] much more profitable. . . . We were able to cash flow the operations, meet our loan payments, and even pull some money out of the business for personal financial security.

In 1995, we refinanced our loans to receive lower interest rates, this time borrowing 15 million baht [$600,000]—a 10 million baht term loan and a line of credit of 5 million baht. The loan came from the IFCT (Industrial Financial Corporation of Thailand, a financial institution that makes loans to small and mid-sized firms in Thailand). In making the loan, the IFCT valued the company at 24.5 million baht [almost $1 million], which means our net worth is something in the order of 9.5 million baht [$380,000], a significant amount in a developing country. And I sleep a lot better now, too.

Source: Based on personal interviews with Supranee Siriarphanon, August 1995.

If the added financing came in the form of equity, the rate of return would be 2 percent. But if debt was used, the rate of return would be a negative 8 percent. These rates of return on equity investment are calculated as follows:

If equity is issued,

$$\frac{\text{Net income}}{\text{Owners' investment}} = \frac{\$2,000}{\$200,000} = 0.01, \text{ or } 1\%$$

If debt is issued,

$$\frac{\text{Net income}}{\text{Owners' investment}} = \frac{-\$8,000}{\$100,000} = -0.08, \text{ or } -8\%$$

While Somchai's owners prefer debt if the firm does well, they would now choose equity. Thus, the use of debt financing not only increases potential returns when a company is performing well, it also increases the possibility of lower, even negative, returns if the company doesn't attain its goals in a given year. That is, debt is a two-edged sword—it cuts both ways. If debt financing is used and things go well, they will go *very* well—but if things go badly, they will go *very* badly. In short, debt financing makes doing business more risky.

Voting Control

The third element in choosing between debt and equity concerns the degree of control retained by owners. Most owners of small firms resist giving up control to outsiders.

For the Somchai Company, raising new capital through equity financing meant giving up 30 percent of the firm's ownership, with the original owners still controlling 70 percent of the stock. However, many small firm owners are reluctant to give away *any* of the company's stock. They do not want to be accountable in any way to minority owners, much less take a chance of eventually losing control of the business.

Given this aversion to losing control, many small business owners choose to finance with debt rather than with equity. They realize that debt increases risk, but it also permits them to retain all the stock and full ownership.

SOURCES OF FINANCING

The initial financing of a small business is often patterned after a typical personal financing plan. A prospective entrepreneur will first use personal savings and then try to access those of family and friends. Only if these sources are inadequate will the entrepreneur turn to more formal channels of financing, such as banks and outside investors.

Major sources of equity financing are personal savings, friends and relatives, private investors in the community, venture capitalists, and sale of stock in public equity markets (going public). Major sources of debt financing are individuals, business suppliers, asset-based lenders, commercial banks, and government-assisted programs.

Though the pool of capital available for startup companies may not be any larger in the 1990s than it was a decade earlier, the variety of options for financing is greater. As noted in *The Wall Street Journal*, "the greater variety of financing sources, with different missions and outlooks, makes it more likely that a venture will find money somewhere."[1]

> **2** Contrast the primary sources of financing used by startups and by existing firms.

Action Report

ENTREPRENEURIAL EXPERIENCES

Keeping Control of the Ownership of a Firm

One of the worst mistakes Bart Breighner believes he's made since founding Artistic Impressions, an art retail firm in Lombard, Illinois, nearly a decade ago, was undervaluing the stock he sold to raise early growth capital.

Breighner, the company's president, initially sold stock to five private investors. But as the company has grown (to $20 million in annual sales), that move has returned to haunt him. "I've offered several hundred thousand dollars to one investor who originally put in $45,000, but she just won't sell," he says. He has managed to buy out the other outside investors and restore his stake in the company to 87 percent.

Breighner concedes there's a bright side: "She doesn't hassle me, and she attends my shareholder meetings when I need her to." But he hopes to go public eventually, and he regrets having to shoulder all the business's financial risks only to have to share the ultimate rewards. Breighner says, "When I've had to borrow money, it's my name that's gone on the loan, not hers. I would have liked the opportunity to profit fully from the meteoric growth we've achieved."

Source: "Tomorrow's Loss," *Inc.*, Vol. 16, No. 14 (December 1994), p. 132.

In a study by the accounting firm Coopers & Lybrand, founders of 328 fast-growing businesses indicated that the average initial investment in a startup is $82,300. The primary sources for this money are shown in Figure 12-1. Clearly, the largest part of the money came from either personal savings or from family and friends.

A similar study by Ernst & Young, another accounting firm, surveyed entrepreneurs of existing firms with annual sales of less than $16 million. The owners of these firms were asked where they intended to acquire financial capital within the next 18 months. Figure 12-2 reports the responses from both firms with less than $6 million in sales and those with sales between $6 million and $16 million. It is encouraging to see that the owners of the smaller firms (sales less than $6 million) considered themselves to have options similar to those available to the larger firms (sales between $6 million and $16 million). Also, the differences between the responses of founding company owners (Figure 12-1) and existing company owners (Figure 12-2) are evident. First, for an existing company, the primary source of financing is cash flow from operations, which is not available for the startup business. Second, bank financing becomes more important with time. Third, the sale of equity—especially an issue of stock to the public—is an option generally not available to startups. Otherwise, many of the sources used by startups continue to be sources for established firms.

We now turn our attention to locating specific sources of financing and describing some of the conditions and terms that an entrepreneur must understand before obtaining the financing. Figure 12-3 gives an overview of the financial sources that are discussed in this chapter. Keep in mind, however, that the use of these and other sources of funds is not limited to initial financing. These sources are also frequently used to finance growing day-to-day operating requirements and business expansions.

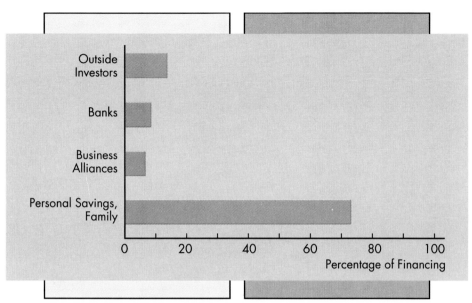

Figure 12-1

Sources of New Company Financing

Source: Adapted from Nick Galifianakis, "Dig Deep to Open Business," referencing Coopers & Lybrand study, *USA Today*, August 26, 1994, p. 1B.

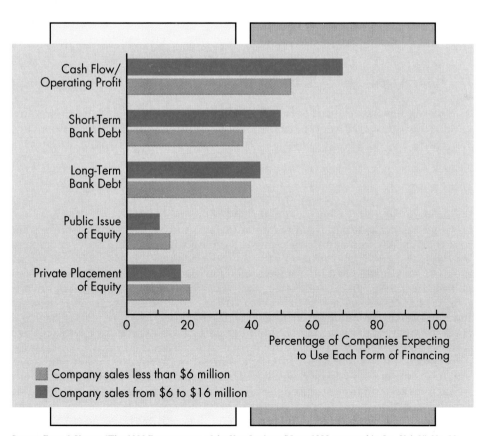

Figure 12-2

Sources of Financing for Existing Firms

Source: Ernst & Young, "The 1993 Entrepreneur of the Year Institute," June 1993, reported in *Inc.*, Vol. 15, No. 10, (October 1993), p. 40.

Figure 12-3

Sources of Funds

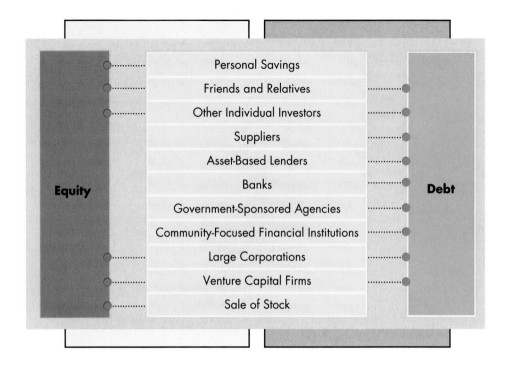

3   Describe various sources of financing available to small firms.

INDIVIDUALS AS SOURCES OF FUNDS

The search for financial support usually begins close to home. As we mentioned earlier, the aspiring entrepreneur frequently has three sources of early financing: (1) personal savings, (2) friends and relatives, and (3) other individual investors.

Personal Savings

It is imperative that the entrepreneur have some personal assets in the business, and these typically come from personal savings. Indeed, personal savings is the most frequently used source of equity financing when starting a new company. With few exceptions, the entrepreneur must provide an equity base. In a new business, equity is needed to allow for a margin of error. In its first few years, a company can ill afford large fixed outlays for debt repayment. Also, a banker—or anyone else for that matter—will not loan a company money if the entrepreneur does not have his or her own money at risk.

A problem for many people who want to start a business is lack of sufficient personal savings for this purpose. It can be very discouraging when the banker asks, "How much will you be investing in the business?" or "What do you have for collateral to secure the bank loan you want?" There is no easy solution to this problem, which is faced by many entrepreneurs. Nonetheless, many successful business owners who lacked personal savings for a startup found a way to accomplish their goal of owning their own company. But it does require creativity and some risk taking. It may also mean finding a partner who can provide the financing or friends and relatives who are willing to help.

Although personal savings is the preferred means of financing a startup, the entrepreneur frequently must look to other sources for early financing. One of the most widely used alternatives for financing is family and friends. When family and friends invest, however, they are likely to offer their opinion on management practices, sometimes to the chagrin of the entrepreneur.

Friends and Relatives

At times, loans from friends or relatives may be the only available source of new financing. Such loans can often be obtained quickly, as this type of financing is based more on personal relationships than on extensive financial analysis. However, friends and relatives who provide business loans sometimes feel that they have the right to offer suggestions concerning the management of the business. Also, hard business times may strain the bonds of friendship. Nevertheless, if relatives and friends are the only available source of financing, the entrepreneur has no other alternative. To minimize the chance of damaging important personal relationships, however, the entrepreneur should plan for repayment of such loans as soon as possible. In addition, any agreements made should be put in writing, as memories tend to become fuzzy over time. It's best to clarify expectations up front rather than be disappointed or angry later.

Other Individual Investors

A large number of private individuals invest in others' entrepreneurial ventures. These are mostly people who have moderate to significant business experience but may also be affluent professionals, such as lawyers and physicians. This source of financing has come to be known as **informal capital,** in that no established marketplace exists in which these individuals regularly invest. Somewhat appropriately, these investors have acquired the label of **business angels.** A few of the more well-recognized business angels are Ken Oshman, founder of the Rolm Corporation, Paul Allen, co-founder of Microsoft Corporation, and Warren Musser, founder of Safeguard Scientifics. These individuals alone have helped finance a large group of new companies. But even more important are the numerous private investors across the country who, without fanfare, invest in millions of new companies each year.

The total amount invested by business angels is not known with any certainty; however, it is very large. Two researchers who have studied small businesses, Gaston and Bell, have estimated that each year some 720,000 individuals make almost 500,000 investments in high-risk ventures, with the average investment being $67,000. Their findings suggest an annual flow of informal equity capital of $32.7 billion. Venture capitalists, formally operating as investment groups expressly inter-

informal capital funds provided by wealthy private individuals to high-risk ventures, such as startups

business angels private investors who finance new, risky, small ventures

Action Report

TECHNOLOGICAL APPLICATIONS

Searching for Investors on the World Wide Web

The World Wide Web would not yet be considered by most to be an effective way to identify prospective investors. But some companies—such as Prospector, an oil company located north of Houston, Texas with revenues of $8 million in 1995—are beginning to give it a try. David H. Mangum, a consultant for Prospector who helps match potential investors with exploration companies, was convinced that the chances of picking up the right kind of Web user were great enough to justify an investment in the Web.

> But after two months on the Web, Mangum had received no inquiries. "If you don't have flashing lights, people will just drive by you, and they won't know you're there," he says. He tried posting notes about the page elsewhere on the Internet—to no avail. Finally, Mangum guessed that his Internet provider wasn't doing enough to attract people to its Web sites. So he switched to a provider with more Web experience. During the first weekend, Mangum received 41 inquiries.
>
> Despite that encouraging sign, Prospector's president, Warren Evans, remains somewhat skeptical of the Web's likely payoff. "The users are just tire kickers. They're not there to invest." Still Evans says he is willing to sink $10,000 into the Web in the first year. After that, he will pull the plug if his advertising has not shown results.

Source: Steven Dickman, "Catching Customers on the Web," *Inc.*, Vol. 17, No. 4 (Summer 1995), p. 58.

ested in new growth companies, invest only $3 billion a year, with an average investment per business of about $1 million.[2]

The traditional path to informal investors is through contacts with business associates, accountants, and lawyers. Recently, more formal angel networks have taken shape. In forums across the country, entrepreneurs make presentations to groups of private investors gathered to hear about new ventures. For example, Venture Capital Network, Inc., based in Boston, receives proposals from potential investors and entrepreneurs and, for a fee, attempts to find a match. Such networks can greatly increase the odds of finding an investor. Other entrepreneurs are also a primary source of help in identifying prospective informal or private investors.

In addition to providing needed money, private investors frequently contribute know-how to a business. Many of these individuals invest in the type of business in which they have had experience. Although angel financing is easier to acquire than some of the more formal types of financing, informal investors can be very demanding. Thus, the entrepreneur must be careful in structuring the terms of the investor's involvement. A study by Freear, Sohl, and Wetzel investigated entrepreneurs' experiences with informal investors and summarized what the entrepreneurs would do differently:

- Try to raise more external equity earlier
- Work to present their case for funding more effectively
- Try to find more investors and to develop a broader mix of investors, with each one investing smaller amounts
- Be more careful in defining their relationships with individual investors before finalizing the terms of the agreement[3]

Action Report

ENTREPRENEURIAL EXPERIENCES

Looking for an Angel

Finding a wealthy individual to invest in a new venture is no easy task, as indicated by the following experience of an entrepreneur in search of a business angel in Milwaukee:

> So I began calling. Calls included investment bankers I knew; the head of a local foundation; the president of a small-business investment corporation; the head of a bank; the head of the venture-capital arm of the area's biggest utility; the chief of a publicly held concern known for buying and selling companies; an insurance-company CEO who is active in the community; the business schools of area universities; and the local Service Corps of Retired Executives, a Small Business Administration program.
>
> I ended up with a few leads. One was a huge local law firm where a handful of lawyers pool their capital and invest in clients' ventures. Another was an engineering professor who made a fortune consulting. There was a handful of members of old-money Milwaukee families who do some investing. I heard about a couple of investing groups. One was Wisconsin Venture Network, which invites entrepreneurs each month to make pitches to a group of about 20 lawyers, bankers, consultants, and investors who meet to discuss ventures and acquisitions.
>
> "It's difficult to track these people," says Doug Pavek, president of a local investment firm and head of the Adventurers. "They'll sneak up on an investment without telling you. They know what happens if they get identified: They get so many calls that that's all they would do all day long."

Source: Dale D. Buss, "Heaven Help Us," *Nation's Business*, Vol. 8, No. 11 (November 1993), p. 34.

BUSINESS SUPPLIERS AND ASSET-BASED LENDERS AS SOURCES OF FUNDS

Companies with which a new firm will have business dealings can be primary sources of funds for inventories and equipment. Both wholesalers and equipment manufacturers/suppliers can provide trade credit (accounts payable) or equipment loans and leases.

Trade Credit (Accounts Payable)

Credit extended by suppliers is very important to a startup. In fact, trade (or mercantile) credit is small firms' most widely used source of short-term funds. **Trade credit** is of short duration—30 days is the customary credit period. Most commonly, this type of credit involves an unsecured, open-book account. The supplier (seller) sends merchandise to the purchasing firm; the buyer then sets up an accounts payable for the amount of the purchase.

The amount of trade credit available to a new firm depends on the type of business and the supplier's confidence in the firm. For example, distributors of sunglasses provide business capital to retailers by granting extended payment terms on

trade credit
financing provided by a supplier of inventory to a given company, which sets up an account payable for the amount

sales made at the start of a season. The sunglass retailers, in turn, sell to their customers during the season and make the bulk of their payments to the distributors at or near the end of the season. If a retailer's rate of inventory turnover is greater than the scheduled payment for the goods, cash from sales may be obtained even before paying the supplier.

Equipment Loans and Leases

equipment loan
an installment loan from a seller of machinery used by a business

Some small businesses, such as restaurants, use equipment that may be purchased on an installment basis through an **equipment loan.** A down payment of 25 to 35 percent is usually required, and the contract period normally runs from three to five years. The equipment manufacturer or supplier typically extends credit on the basis of a conditional sales contract (or mortgage) on the equipment. During the loan period, the equipment cannot serve as collateral for another loan.

Instead of borrowing money from suppliers to purchase equipment, an increasing number of small businesses are beginning to lease equipment, especially computers, photocopiers, and fax machines.[4] Leases typically run for 36 to 60 months and cover 100 percent of the cost of the asset being leased, with a fixed rate of interest included in the lease payments. However, manufacturers of computers and industrial machinery, working hand-in-hand with banks or financing companies, are generally receptive to tailoring lease packages to the particular needs of customers.

It has been estimated that 80 percent of all companies lease some or all of their business equipment. Three reasons are commonly given for the increasing popularity of leasing: (1) the firm's cash remains free for other purposes; (2) lines of credit (a form of bank loan discussed later in this chapter) remain open; and (3) leasing provides a hedge against equipment obsolescence.

While leasing is certainly an option to be considered as a potential way to finance the acquisition of needed equipment, an entrepreneur should not simply assume that leasing is always the right decision. Only by carefully comparing the interest rates charged on a loan relative to the lease, the tax consequences of leasing versus borrowing, and the significance of the obsolescence factor can an owner make a good choice. Also, the owner must be careful about contracting for so much equipment that it becomes difficult to meet installment or lease payments.

Many small businesses, such as this manufacturer of toy parts, find that leasing equipment protects them against equipment obsolescence. However, the entrepreneur who leases too much equipment may find it difficult to meet monthly payments.

Asset-Based Lending

Asset-based lending is typically financing secured by working-capital assets. Usually, the assets used as loan collateral are accounts receivable or inventory. However, assets such as equipment (if not leased) and real estate can also be used. Asset-based lending is a viable option for young, growing businesses that may be caught in a cash-flow bind.

Of the several categories of asset-based loans, the most frequently used is factoring. **Factoring** is an option that makes cash available to a business before accounts receivable payments are received from customers. Under this option, a factor (many of these firms are owned by bank-holding companies) purchases the accounts receivable, advancing to the business from 70 percent to 90 percent of the amount of an invoice. The factor, however, does have the option of refusing to advance cash on any invoice considered questionable. The factor charges a servicing fee, usually 2 percent of the value of the receivables, and an interest charge on the money advanced prior to collection of the receivables. The interest charge may range from 2 percent to 3 percent above the prime rate. Jennifer Barclay, the founder of a profitable apparel business with sales of $5 million, was struggling to pay the firm's suppliers on time. The reason for the problem, according to Barclay: "Our customers weren't paying us fast enough." Her solution was to sell the firm's accounts receivables to a factor.[5]

Another form of asset-based lending is a loan that uses inventories for collateral. In this case, the loan amount is typically about 50 percent of the inventory value. Nonleased equipment may also be used as collateral for an asset-based loan, with the loan amount being between 50 and 100 percent of the equipment value, depending on the situation.

asset-based lending
financing secured by working-capital assets

factoring
obtaining cash by selling accounts receivable to another firm

COMMERCIAL BANKS AS SOURCES OF FUNDS

Commercial banks are the primary providers of debt capital to small companies. Although banks tend to limit their lending to providing for the working-capital needs of established firms, some initial capital does come from this source.

Types of Bank Loans

Three types of business loans that bankers tend to make are lines of credit, term loans, and mortgages.

LINES OF CREDIT   A **line of credit** is an informal agreement or understanding between the borrower and the bank as to the maximum amount of credit the bank will provide the borrower at any one time. However, under this type of agreement, the bank has no legal obligation to provide the stated capital. (A similar arrangement that does legally commit the bank is a **revolving credit agreement**.) The entrepreneur should arrange for a line of credit in advance of actual need because banks extend credit only in situations about which they are well informed. Attempting to obtain a loan on a spur-of-the-moment basis, therefore, is generally ineffective.

TERM LOANS   Given certain circumstances, banks will loan money on a five- to ten-year term. Such **term loans** are generally used to finance equipment with an economically useful life that corresponds with the loan's term. Since the economic benefits of investing in such equipment extend beyond a single year, a bank is will-

line of credit
an informal agreement between a borrower and a bank as to the maximum amount of funds the bank will provide at any one time

revolving credit agreement
a legal commitment by a bank to lend up to a maximum amount

term loan
money loaned for a five- to ten-year term, corresponding to the length of time the investment will bring in profits

ing to lend on terms that more closely match the cash flows to be received from the investment. It would be a mistake to borrow for a short term, such as six months, when the money is to be used to buy equipment that is expected to last for five years. *Failure to match the loan's payment terms with the expected cash inflows from the investment is a frequent cause of financial problems for many small firms.* We cannot overemphasize the importance of synchronizing cash inflows with cash outflows when structuring the terms of a loan.

MORTGAGES Mortgages, which represent a long-term source of debt capital, are of two types: chattel mortgages and real estate mortgages. A **chattel mortgage** is a loan for which certain items of inventory or other moveable property serve as collateral. The borrower retains title to the inventory but cannot sell it without the banker's consent. A **real estate mortgage** is a loan for which real property, such as land or a building, provides the collateral. Typically, these mortgages extend over 25 or 30 years.

> **chattel mortgage**
> a loan for which items of inventory or other moveable property serve as collateral

> **real estate mortgage**
> a long-term loan with real property held as collateral

Understanding a Banker's Perspective

To be effective in acquiring a loan, an entrepreneur needs to understand a banker's perspective about making loans. All bankers have two fundamental concerns when they make a loan: (1) how much income the loan will provide the bank, either in interest income and other forms of income, and (2) the possibility that the borrower will default on the loan. A banker is not interested in taking large amounts of risk and will, therefore, design loan agreements so as to reduce the risk to the bank.

In making a loan decision, a banker looks at the proverbial "five C's of credit": (1) the borrower's *character*, (2) the borrower's *capacity* to repay the loan, (3) the *capital* being invested in the venture by the borrower, (4) the *conditions* of the industry and economy, and (5) the *collateral* available to secure the loan.

It is imperative that the borrower's character be above reproach. A bad credit record or any indication of unethical behavior makes getting a loan extremely difficult. A borrower's capacity is measured by the banker's confidence in the firm's ability to generate the necessary cash flow to repay the loan. Mike Gilligan, a small business loan officer with Chase Manhattan Bank says, "We are cash flow lenders, so this is a key area of the loan request." On the matter of an owner's capital investment in the firm, Gilligan continues, "We look at the equity investment of the owners in the business. The more equity, the better."[6] The receptivity of a banker to a loan request also depends on the current economic conditions. In the late 1980s and early 1990s, many banks essentially quit making loans to small businesses, as a result of the savings and loan crisis. Federal regulators discouraged loans to the point that the top priority of many banks became to avoid making a bad loan. Numerous small companies with unblemished records had their loans cancelled, through no fault of their own. Finally, collateral is of key importance to bankers. Scott Day, a loan officer observes, "Collateral is a very important factor for all our small business loans. The amount of weight we place on the collateral depends on the whole package. In fact, it can be the determining factor in certain situations."[7]

Obtaining a bank loan requires cultivation of a banker and personal selling. A banker's analysis of a loan request certainly includes economic and financial considerations. However, this analysis is best complemented by a personal relationship between banker and entrepreneur. This is not to say that a banker would allow personal feelings to override the facts provided by a careful loan analysis. But, after all, a banker's decision whether to make a loan is in part driven by the banker's confidence in the entrepreneur as a person and a professional. Some intuition and sub-

Action Report

ENTREPRENEURIAL EXPERIENCES

Finding an Alternative to Bank Borrowing

What happens if a banker turns down your request for a business loan? If the business concept is sound, it may eventually survive, provided, of course, that the entrepreneur is an innovator with lots of determination. Sue Scott, a former sculptor and art gallery manager, is just such an entrepreneur. Bankers were skeptical about her business background and unwilling to back her when she wanted to start a business. She was determined to push ahead, however, and worked out a creative but highly unorthodox financing alternative.

Undaunted by the bankers' rejections, Scott got 25 credit cards and took a $1,000 cash advance on each. In August 1986, she started Primal Lite, an Emeryville, California maker of whimsical string lighting, that features anything from lobsters and lizards to cattle and laundry. (Scott's method of financing should *not* be viewed as a model. It involved extreme risk and would lead most new ventures to bankruptcy. In this case, however, her daring strategy somehow succeeded—she represents an exception to the rule.)

Primal Lite expected sales of $4 million in 1994, up from $2.5 million in 1993. People knowledgeable about the company say it could easily hit the $20 million mark by 1999. The company now offers 45 styles of string lights plus decorative night lights and Coca-Cola memorabilia. Its wares are sold in about 3,000 stores, including Macy's, Target, and Ace Hardware, and 20 percent of its revenues originate overseas—not a bad ending for an artist who couldn't get a banker to give her the time of day, much less grant her a loan.

Source: Steven B. Kaufman, "Business for Art's Sake," *Nation's Business*, Vol. 82, No. 9 (September 1994), pp. 13–14.

jective opinion based on past experience often play a role here. In view of this mixture of impersonal analysis and personal relationship, there are several things to remember when requesting a loan:

- Do not call on a banker for a business loan without an introduction by someone who already has a good relationship with the banker. Cold calling is not appropriate under these circumstances.
- Do not wait until there is a dire need for money. Such lack of planning is not perceived with favor by a prospective lender.
- A banker is not an entrepreneur or a venture capitalist. Do not expect a banker to show the same enthusiasm you may have for a venture.
- Develop alternative sources of debt capital; that is, visit with several banks. However, be sensitive to how a banker might feel about your courting more than one bank.

Also, a banker needs certain key questions answered before a loan will be made:

- What is the strength and quality of the management team?
- How has the firm performed financially?
- What is the venture going to do with the money?

- How much money is needed?
- When is the money needed?
- When and how will the money be paid back?
- Does the borrower have a good public accountant and attorney?
- Does the borrower already have a banking relationship?

Finally, a well-prepared written presentation—something like a shortened version of a business plan—is helpful, if not necessary. Capturing the firm's history and future in writing suggests that the entrepreneur has given thought to where the firm has been and is going. As part of this presentation, a banker expects a prospective borrower to provide detailed financial information in the following areas:

- Three years of the firm's historical financial statements, if available, including balance sheets, income statements, and cash flow statements
- The firm's pro forma financial statements (balance sheets, income statements, and cash flow statements), which include the timing and amounts of the debt repayment as part of the forecasts
- Personal financial statements, showing the borrower's personal net worth (net worth = assets − debt) and estimated annual income

Note that a banker will not make a loan without knowing the personal financial strength of the borrower. After all, in the world of small business, the owner *is* the business.

Selection of a Banker

The wide variety of services provided by banks make choosing a bank a critical decision. For a typical small firm, the provision of checking-account facilities and the extension of short-term (and possibly long-term) loans are the two most important services of a bank. Normally, loans are negotiated with the same bank in which the firm maintains its checking account. In addition, the firm may use the bank's safety deposit vault or its services in collecting notes or securing credit information. An experienced banker can also provide management advice, particularly in financial matters, to a new entrepreneur.

The location factor limits the range of possible choices of banks. For reasons of convenience when making deposits and conferring about loans and other matters, a bank should be located in the same general vicinity as the firm. All banks are interested in their home communities and, therefore, tend to be sympathetic to the needs of local business firms. Except in very small communities, two or more local banks are usually available, thus permitting some freedom of choice.

Banks' lending policies are not uniform. Some bankers are extremely conservative, while others are more willing to accept risks. If a small firm's loan application is neither obviously strong nor patently weak, its prospects for approval depend heavily on the bank's approach to small business accounts. Differences in willingness to lend have been clearly established by research studies, as well as by the practical experience of many business borrowers.

Negotiating the Loan

In negotiating a bank loan, four important issues must be resolved: (1) the interest rate, (2) the loan maturity date, (3) the schedule for repayment if payment is required over time, and (4) personal guarantees.

Action Report

ENTREPRENEURIAL EXPERIENCES

The Need for Understanding Loan Repayment Methods

When Mike Calvert purchased a Toyota dealership in Houston, Texas, he found it necessary to borrow most of the purchase price from a bank. He had thought that all the loan terms had been finalized until he went to the bank to sign the note. He was surprised to see that monthly payments on the note, according to the bank's computation, would be significantly more than he had expected. The reason: Calvert had calculated the loan payment by assuming equal monthly payments at about $51,000 per month. The bank, on the other hand, required repayment based on equal principal payments plus interest. As a consequence, monthly payments at the outset were to be $66,000, or $15,000 more than Calvert had expected. At the time, he was shocked and somewhat worried about having to meet such a large monthly fixed payment. Today, however, Calvert is thankful that he accepted the bank's repayment schedule, because he appreciates the current lower payments.

Source: Personal conversation with Mike Calvert, October 1995.

The interest rate charged by banks is usually stated in terms of the prime rate. The **prime rate** is the rate of interest charged by banks on loans to their most creditworthy customers. For instance, a banker may make a loan to a small business at a rate of "prime plus three," meaning that if the prime rate is 10 percent, the interest rate for the loan will be 13 percent. The interest rate can be a floating rate that varies over the loan's life—as the prime rate changes, the interest rate on the loan changes—or it can be fixed for the duration of the loan. Although a small firm should always seek a competitive interest rate, it should not overemphasize low interest at the expense of the other three considerations mentioned above.

As already noted, a loan's maturity should coincide with the use of the money—short-term needs require short-term financing, while long-term needs demand long-term financing. For example, since a line of credit is intended only to help a firm with its short-term needs, it is generally limited to a one-year maturity. However, some banks require that the firm "clean up" a line of credit one month each year. Because such a loan can be outstanding for only 11 months, the borrower can use the money to finance seasonal needs but not to provide permanent increases in working capital.

With a term loan, the schedule for repayment is generally arranged in one of two ways: (1) *equal* monthly or annual loan payments that cover both interest on the remaining note balance and the balance on the principal or (2) equal payments on the principal over the life of the loan plus the interest on the remaining balance. For example, assume that a firm is negotiating a $200,000 term loan to be repaid in annual payments over five years at an interest rate of 10 percent. If the lender specifies an *equal* amount to be paid each year to cover the interest due on the remaining balance of the loan plus a portion of the principal so that in five years the loan will be fully repaid, the annual payment will be $52,759.[8] If, on the other hand, the principal is to be repaid in equal amounts each year plus the amount of interest owed on the remaining principal, the payment in the first year will be $60,000, consisting of a $40,000 payment on principal ($200,000 ÷ 5 years)

prime rate
the interest rate charged by a commercial bank on loans to its most creditworthy customers

and an interest payment of $20,000 ($200,000 × 0.10). The amount of the annual payment will decline each year as the principal balance is paid down.

Which repayment plan is preferable? A banker will typically prefer that a company repay the loan in equal principal payments plus interest, causing the loan principal to be reduced more quickly in the early years. For an entrepreneur, the answer lies in the company's ability to service the repayment of the debt over time. Paying interest on the note balance plus a portion of the principal requires less cash outflow in the early years, which is usually the time when a new company cannot afford large fixed payments. On the other hand, if a firm can make the larger payments in the early years required by equal repayment of the principal plus interest, the payments will be less in later years, and the firm will have paid out less overall.

In addition to negotiating the timing and amount of loan repayments, an entrepreneur should be prepared to personally guarantee the loan. A banker wants the right to look at both the company's assets and the owner's personal assets before making a loan. If a company is formed as a corporation, the owner and the corporation are separate legal entities, allowing the owner to escape personal liability for the firm's debts—that is, the owner has **limited liability.** However, most banks are not willing to lend money to any small company without the owner's personal guarantee as well. As Glenda Frangenberg, a loan officer with Citizens Bank of Jonesboro, Arkansas, says, "It's a policy here that the principals of all closely held companies guarantee loans that we grant. If they aren't willing to back up the loan, then we probably aren't either."[9] Only after years of an ongoing relationship with a banker might an owner be exempt from a personal guarantee. In other words, while other elements are negotiable in structuring a loan, a banker typically will not negotiate the matter of a personal guarantee.

In conclusion, here are some of the primary reasons bankers give for denying an application for a business loan:

limited liability
the restriction of an owner's legal financial responsibilities to the amount invested in the business

- Bank's lack of familiarity with the business and its owners or with the industry in which the business operates
- Excessive business losses by the applicant
- Unwillingness on the part of the owners to guarantee the loan personally
- Insufficient collateral
- Inadequate preparation by the owners
- Past personal credit problems of the owners
- Government regulations that restrict certain types of lending
- Poor regional or national economic conditions[10]

GOVERNMENT-SPONSORED AGENCIES AS SOURCES OF FUNDS

Several government programs provide financing to small businesses. Federal and state governments have allocated increasing amounts of money to financing new businesses. Local governments have likewise increased their involvement in providing financial support to startups in their areas. Even though funds are available, however, they are not always easy to acquire. Time and patience on the part of the entrepreneur are required.

Federal Assistance to Small Businesses

The federal government has a long history of helping new businesses get started, primarily through the programs and agencies of the Small Business Administration.

SMALL BUSINESS ADMINISTRATION (SBA) LOANS   There are two basic types of Small Business Administration (SBA) loans: guaranty loans and direct loans. **Guaranty loans** are made by private lenders, usually commercial banks, and may be for as much as $750,000. The SBA guarantees 90 percent of such loans, for amounts not exceeding $155,000. For loans exceeding $155,000, the guaranty percentage is 85 percent. To obtain a guaranty loan, a small business must submit a loan application to a lender—such as a bank—who, after initial review, forwards the application to the SBA. Once the loan has been approved by the SBA, the lender disburses the funds.

The SBA also makes **direct loans.** This form of lending is available only if a small business has been unable to obtain a guaranty loan. This type of loan is usually limited to a maximum of $150,000.

SMALL BUSINESS INVESTMENT COMPANIES (SBICs)   In 1958, Congress passed the Small Business Investment Act. This act established privately owned capital banks, or **small business investment companies (SBICs)**, whose purpose is to provide long-term loans and/or equity capital to small businesses. SBICs are licensed and regulated by the SBA. They may obtain a substantial part of their capital from the SBA at attractive rates of interest.

Although SBICs may either lend funds or supply equity funds, the Small Business Investment Act places a strong emphasis on equity financing. An SBIC that provides equity financing may do so either by directly purchasing a small firm's stock or, more commonly, by purchasing the firm's convertible debentures (bonds), which may be converted into stock at the option of the SBIC.

SMALL BUSINESS INNOVATIVE RESEARCH (SBIR) PROGRAM   In 1993, Congress voted to increase the size of a program called **Small Business Innovative Research (SBIR)** to an estimated $1.4 billion. This program helps finance small firms that plan to transform laboratory research into marketable products. Qualifying for the program is based less on the potential profitability of a venture than on the likelihood that the firm will provide a product of interest to a particular federal agency.

State and Local Government Assistance

State and local governments are becoming increasingly involved in financing new businesses. The nature of the financing varies, but each program is geared to augment other sources of funding.

guaranty loan
money provided by a private lender, for which the Small Business Administration guarantees repayment

direct loan
money provided directly by the Small Business Administration

small business investment companies (SBICs)
privately owned banks, regulated by the Small Business Administration, that supply capital to small businesses

Small Business Innovative Research (SBIR) program
a government program that helps finance companies that plan to transform laboratory research into marketable products

Action Report

ENTREPRENEURIAL EXPERIENCES

Frustrations in Getting SBA-Guaranteed Money

To cut through the red tape of government-sponsored small business financing—particularly for exporters—you may need a chain saw. Zan Mengle, the chief financial officer for PlasmaQuest, a small firm that manufactures machines used to build semiconductors, has waded through the bureaucracy and successfully obtained financing for her company. One of Mengle's biggest frustrations was SBA's rigid requirements for a guarantee that would satisfy PlasmaQuest's need for financing.

After five months of negotiations, PlasmaQuest was able to obtain a five-year revolving credit line from Texas Commerce Bank, for which the SBA guaranteed $750,000 of the $1 million loan. "But to get a guarantee from the SBA, you have to fit the mold. The administration takes a 'cookie-cutter approach' and fails to recognize businesses' individual needs," Mengle says.

Throughout the negotiations, a lending officer had to act as a middleman because the SBA would not deal directly with PlasmaQuest. "They never wanted to talk to me, to understand why it couldn't be a cookie-cutter approach, to try to get them to understand our business," Mengle complains.

Source: Leigh Storpe, "Guaranteed Money," *Dallas Business Journal Strategies*, February 24, 1995, pp. B1–B2.

California was one of the first states to create a business and industrial development corporation to lend money to new businesses. Minnesota has provided $50 million to create Minnesota Technology, a source of financing for new technology companies located in the state. Massachusetts, Pennsylvania, and Maryland are among the states that have designated funding for local startups. Maryland, for example, in cooperation with three public-employee pension funds (mutual funds that invest the retirement savings of state employees) has committed over $19 million to a venture trust.[11]

Some large cities also provide funds for new business ventures. For example, Des Moines, Iowa has established a Golden Circle Loan Guarantee Fund to guarantee bank loans of up to $250,000 to small companies.

OTHER SOURCES OF FUNDS

The sources of financing that have been described thus far represent the primary avenues for obtaining money for many small firms. The remaining sources are generally of less importance but should not be ignored by an entrepreneur in search of financing.

Community-Based Financial Institutions

community-based financial institutions
lenders that provide financing to small businesses in lower-income communities for the purpose of encouraging economic development there

Community-based financial institutions are lenders that serve lower-income communities and receive funds from federal, state, and private sources. They are increasingly becoming a source of financing for smaller companies. During the first half of the 1990s, these organizations provided an estimated $250 million to startup firms.

The purpose of community-based financial institutions has been described as follows:

> Community-based lenders provide capital to enterprises that otherwise have little or no access to start-up funding—typically businesses with the potential to make modest profits, serve the community and create jobs, though lacking the promise of spectacular growth that venture funds demand.[12]

An example of a community-based financial institution is the Delaware Valley Reinvestment Fund, which provides financing for small companies in Philadelphia's inner-city area.

Large Corporations

In the past, large corporations have made a limited amount of funds available for investing in smaller companies when it is in their self-interest to maintain a close relationship with such a company. Larger firms are now becoming more involved in providing financing and technical assistance for smaller businesses. Harriet Michel, president of the National Minority Supplier Development Council, comments, "As corporations re-engineer themselves and down-size their operations, it's in their self-interest to ensure that their suppliers stay healthy."[13]

Examples of large corporations that have historically invested in smaller firms include such giants as J.C. Penney & Co., Ford Motor Company, General Motors Corporation, and American Telephone & Telegraph. More recently, large pharmaceutical and health-care corporations, such as SmithKline Beecham and Genentech, have started looking to smaller firms to develop technology more quickly than they have been able to do. For example, although Wendell Kelly and Dennis Garrett approached both banks and venture capitalists to seek financing for their new firm, Qualiticare Medical Services, Inc., it was only when they called on a prospective supplier, a pharmaceutical firm, that they received $4 million in financing.

Venture Capital Firms

Technically speaking, anyone investing in a new business venture is a venture capitalist. However, a **venture capitalist** is usually defined as a corporation or partnership that operates as an investment group. Most often, the investment takes the form of convertible debt or convertible preferred stock. In this way, the venture capitalists have senior claim over the owners and other equity investors, but they can also convert to stock and participate in the increased value of the company if it is successful. These investors generally try to limit the length of their investment to between five and seven years, though it is frequently closer to ten years before they are able to cash out.

In total, U.S. venture capital firms have about $50 billion invested in entrepreneurial ventures. However, the amount such firms invested each year during the late 1980s and early 1990s fluctuated from a low of $1 billion to as much as $5 billion. The amount of activity has largely reflected the ability of venture capitalists to earn attractive rates of return on their investments. In years when venture capitalists were making rates of return of some 40 percent or more, the money flowed into these investment companies. However, as rates of return declined in the late 1980s to as low as 7 percent—similar to the interest on a savings account—venture capitalists became discouraged and decreased their investments in new companies.

venture capitalist an investor or investment group that invests in new business ventures

Although venture capital as a source of financing receives significant coverage by the business media, few small companies ever receive this kind of funding. Fewer than 1 percent of the business plans received by any venture capitalist are eventually funded—not exactly an encouraging statistic. Failure to receive funding from a venture capitalist, however, does not suggest that the business plan is not a good one. Often, the venture is simply not a good fit for the investor. So before trying to compete for venture capital financing, the entrepreneur should try to assess whether the firm and the management team provide a good fit for that venture capitalist.

Stock Sales

Another way to obtain capital is by selling stock to outside individual investors through either private placement or public sale. In most cases, a business must have some history of profitability before its stock can be sold successfully.

Whether the owner is wise in using outside equity financing depends on the firm's long-range prospects. If there is opportunity for substantial expansion on a continuing basis and if other sources are inadequate, the owner may logically decide to bring in other owners. Owning part of a larger business may be more profitable than owning all of a smaller business.

private placement
the sale of a firm's capital stock to selected individuals

PRIVATE PLACEMENT   One way to sell common stock is through **private placement,** in which the firm's stock is sold to selected individuals, usually the firm's employees, the owner's acquaintances, members of the local community, customers, and suppliers. Finding outside stockholders can be difficult when a new firm is not known and has no ready market for its securities. However, when a stock sale is restricted to private placement, an entrepreneur can avoid many requirements of the securities laws.

initial public offering (IPO)
issuance of stock that is to be traded in public financial markets

PUBLIC SALE   Some small firms make their stock available to the general public —typically, *larger* small firms. This is commonly called going public, or an **initial public offering (IPO).** The reason often cited for a public sale is the need for additional working capital.

In undertaking a public sale of its stock, a small firm subjects itself to greater governmental regulation. Not only are there state regulations pertaining to the public sale of securities, but the federal Securities and Exchange Commission (SEC) also oversees such offerings.

Common stock may also be sold to underwriters, who guarantee the sale of securities. Compensation and fees paid to underwriters typically make the sale of securities in this manner expensive. Fees may range from 10 to 30 percent of the sale, with 18 to 25 percent being typical. In addition, options and other fees may cause the actual costs to run even higher. The reason for the high costs is, of course, the elements of uncertainty and risk associated with public offerings of the stock of small, relatively unknown firms.

4 Discuss the most important factors in the process of obtaining startup financing.

KEEPING THE RIGHT PERSPECTIVE

Amar Bhide, a professor at Harvard University who spent extensive time interviewing owners of some of the high-growth companies in the United States, learned that few of these companies had access to venture capital markets. Instead, they were most often required to boot-strap their financing—that is, to get it any way they could. Based on many interviews, Bhide warns of the real danger of becoming unduly focused on getting financing. While locating financial sources is certainly a critical issue, an entrepreneur should avoid losing sight of other matters important to business operations. Bhide offers the following recommendations to any aspiring entrepreneur who wants to start a business:

- Get operational. At some point, it is time to stop planning, and just make things happen.
- Go for quick break-even and high cash-flow–generating projects whenever possible.
- Fit growth goals to available personal resources.
- Have a preference for high-ticket, high-profit-margin products and services that can sustain direct personal selling.
- Start up with only a single product or service that satisfies a clear need.
- Forget about needing a crack management team with textbook credentials. The team can be developed as the venture develops.
- Focus on cash, rather than profits, market share, or anything else.
- Cultivate the banker.[14]

We believe Bhide's advice is worth consideration by anyone beginning the startup process.

DISCUSSION QUESTIONS

1. Explain the three factors that guide the choice between debt financing and equity financing.
2. Assume that you are starting a business for the first time. What do you feel are the greatest personal obstacles to obtaining funds for the new venture? Why?

Looking Back

1 Evaluate the choice between debt financing and equity financing.

- The basic types of financing are (1) spontaneous financing, (2) profit retention, and (3) external sources of financing.
- Choosing between debt and equity financing involves tradeoffs involving potential profitability, financial risk, and voting control.
- Borrowing money rather than issuing common stock (owners' equity) creates a potential for high rates of return to the owners and ensures voting control of the company but exposes the owners to greater financial risk.
- Issuing common stock rather than borrowing money results in lower potential rates of return to the owners and loss of some voting control but reduces their financial risk.

2 Contrast the primary sources of financing used by startups and by existing firms.

- A startup's sources of financing are usually close to home: personal savings, friends and relatives, and private investors in the community.
- Once a firm is operational and profitable, the primary source of financing is cash flow from operations.
- Bank financing is less important for a startup business than for an established company.
- Issuance of stock is generally not an option for startups.

3 Describe various sources of financing available to small firms.

- Business suppliers, a major source of financing for the small firm, can offer trade credit (accounts payable), equipment loans, and lease arrangements.
- Asset-based lending is financing secured by working-capital assets, such as accounts receivable or inventory.
- Commercial banks are the primary providers of debt financing to small companies, offering lines of credit, term loans, and mortgages.
- Government agencies at the federal, state, and local levels provide financing to small businesses.
- Community-based financial institutions, large corporations, venture capitalists, and stock sales represent other sources of financing for the small firm.

4 Discuss the most important factors in the process of obtaining startup financing.

- The entrepreneur should get operational as quickly as possible with a product or service that satisfies a clear need, even at the expense of raising capital.
- Quick break-even and high cash-flow–generating projects should be chosen whenever possible, with a preference for high-ticket, high-profit-margin products and services.
- Growth goals must be tailored to available personal financial resources.
- The entrepreneur must focus on cash—not profits, market share, or anything else.

New Terms and Concepts

informal capital *263*	real estate mortgage *268*	community-based financial institutions *274*
business angels *263*	prime rate *271*	venture capitalist *275*
trade credit *265*	limited liability *272*	
equipment loan *266*	guaranty loan *273*	private placement *276*
asset-based lending *267*	direct loan *273*	initial public offering (IPO) *276*
factoring *267*	small business investment companies (SBICs) *273*	
line of credit *267*		
revolving credit agreement *267*	Small Business Innovative Research (SBIR) program *273*	
term loan *267*		
chattel mortgage *268*		

You Make the Call

Situation 1 Too little working capital had been a constant problem at Plan-Graphics Inc., a consultant and designer of automated geographic information systems. But, in 1994, with 65 employees and seven offices worldwide, PlanGraphics faced a cash shortage that threatened to hit $1 million. Founder John Antenucci wasn't concerned. But his banker, Gordon Taylor, thought that amount was too much for a company barely doing $5 million in sales. Taylor, PlanGraphics's loan officer for the previous decade and a vice-president of Farmers Bank & Capital Trust, in Frankfort, Kentucky, wanted Antenucci to reduce his traveling expenses, shrink overhead, maximize profits, and give the bank good financial information. "You're not running a profitable operation," Taylor lectured, "and your balance sheet doesn't support your credit. My bank has gone as far as it will go." Indeed, the bank had gone even further. At the end of 1994, PlanGraphics had over-drawn its $800,000 line of credit by $300,000. If Taylor had returned those checks, he would have forced the company to close. But Antenucci wasn't alarmed: "Entrepreneurs come up against barriers. They're walls to some; to others, they're only hurdles."

Robert A. Mamis, "Me and My Banker," *Inc.*, Vol. 17, No. 3, (March 1995), p. 43.

Question 1 Antenucci and Taylor clearly have a different perspective about what needs to happen at PlanGraphics. Do you think this situation is common between an entrepreneur and a banker?

Question 2 Why do you think Antenucci and Taylor have such different views on the company's needs?

Question 3 What suggestions would you give Antenucci?

Continue on next page

3. If you were starting a new business, where would you start looking for capital? Would your answer depend on the nature of your new business?

4. Explain how trade credit and equipment loans provide initial capital funding.

5. Describe the different types of loans made by a commercial bank.

6. What does a banker need to know in order to decide whether to make a loan?

7. Distinguish between formal and informal venture capital.

8. Why might venture capital be an inappropriate type of financing for most small firms?

9. How does the federal government help with initial financing for small businesses?

10. Distinguish between a private placement and a public offering.

EXPERIENTIAL EXERCISES

1. Interview a local small business owner to determine how funds were obtained to start the business. Be sure you phrase questions so that they are not overly personal, and do not ask for specific dollar amounts. Report on your findings.

2. Interview a local banker to discuss the bank's lending policies for small business loans. Ask the banker to comment on the importance of a business plan to the bank's decision to loan money to a small business. Report on your findings.

3. Review recent issues of *Entrepreneur, Inc.,* or *Nation's Business,* and report on the financing arrangements of firms featured in these magazines.

4. Interview a stockbroker or investment analyst to learn his or her views regarding the sale of common stock by a small business. Report on your findings.

Exploring the

5. Find the home page on the Web for Wells Fargo Small Business Banking(http://www.wellsfargo.com/biz/bizfin/bizfin.html). Report to the class what financial services Wells Fargo is offering small firms.

 CASE 12
Walker Machine Works (p. 624)

This case evaluates financing arrangements for a new venture.

Alternative Cases for Chapter 12:
Case 9, "VMG Products," p. 618
Case 15, "Litter Ridder," p. 631

Situation 2   Jack Griggs is well on his way to starting a new venture—Max, Inc. He has projected a need for $350,000 in initial capital. He plans to invest $150,000 himself and either borrow the additional $200,000 or find a co-owner who will buy stock in the company. If Griggs borrows the money, the interest rate will be 12 percent. If, on the other hand, another equity investor is found, he expects to have to give up 60 percent of the company's stock. Griggs has also forecasted earnings of about 18 percent in operating income on the firm's total assets.

Question 1   Compare the results of the two financing options in terms of projected return on the owner's equity investment. Ignore any effect from income taxes.
Question 2   What if Griggs is wrong and the company only earns 5 percent in operating income on total assets?
Question 3   What must Griggs consider in choosing a source of financing?

Situation 3   James Ridings's firm, Craftmade International, Inc., sells ceiling fans. Originally, Ridings was a sales representative for a company that sold plumbing supplies. When the company added ceiling fans to its line, Ridings developed a number of customers who bought the fans. However, when the firm eliminated the ceiling fans from its line, Ridings had customers and nothing to sell them. Consequently, in 1985, he became partners with James Ivins, a sales representative for a firm that imported ceiling fans. They scraped together $30,000 and bought 800 fans from Taiwan, which were quickly sold. Encouraged, Ridings raised $45,000 to buy more fans. Again, they sold quickly. By the end of the first year, Ridings and Ivins had put together a sales force of 15 persons and were selling 3,000 fans per month. By 1989, the two men had started designing their own high-quality and high-profit-margin fans. Sales had grown to $10 million, and the firm was profitable. However, while the firm's sales were increasing at 50 percent per year, a problem developed: The firm ran into cash problems. At one critical point, Ridings had to persuade a supplier to accept stock in lieu of payment on a $224,000 order. Another time, Ridings and Ivins had to approach 16 bankers within a matter of a few days before finding someone who would loan them $100,000 to pay their bills.

Question 1   Craftmade International, Inc. is a successful firm when it comes to growing, but what are its owners overlooking?
Question 2   What steps would you suggest to Ridings and Ivins to solve their problems?

LAYING THE FOUNDATION
Asking the Right Questions

As part of laying the foundation for your own business plan, respond to the following questions regarding the financing of your venture:

- What is the total financing required to start up?
- How much money do you plan to invest in the venture? What is the source of this money?
- Will you need financing beyond what you personally plan to invest?
- If additional financing is needed for the startup, how will you raise it? How will the financing be structured—debt or equity? What will the terms be for the investors?
- Based on your pro forma financial statements, will there be a need for future financing within the first five years of the firm's life? If so, where will it come from?
- How and when will you arrange for investors to cash out of their investment?

USING BizPlanBuilder

If you are using BizPlan*Builder,* refer to Part 3 for information that should be included in the business plan as it relates to sources of financing. Then turn to Part 2 for instructions on using the BizPlan software with regard to sources of financing.

Part 4

13. **CONSUMER BEHAVIOR AND PRODUCT STRATEGY**

14. **PRICING AND CREDIT STRATEGIES**

15. **PROMOTION: PERSONAL SELLING, ADVERTISING, AND SALES PROMOTION**

16. **DISTRIBUTION CHANNELS AND GLOBAL MARKETS**

Chapter 13

Consumer Behavior and Product Strategy

spotlight on small business

Packaging is a valuable tool for a business that is trying to significantly increase demand for its product. The simple, but creative, marketing of Ronnybrook Farm in Ancramdale, New York reflects how a good packaging strategy works. In 1990, two brothers, Sid and Ronald Osofsky, were routinely selling cows' milk to a local cooperative. Because of depressed market conditions, however, the price of the milk was not covering their costs. "We knew we had to change in order to survive," says Sid.

Encouraged by Stephen James, a neighbor, Sid and Ron decided to target the nostalgia market by using different packaging. They hired a package design firm that recommended a "new" design featuring the type of milk bottle that had disappeared decades earlier.

Inside was, of course, just plain good milk, but it fetched twice what milk in ordinary cartons did. At $2.95 a quart (including a dollar deposit for the bottles), roughly twice the cost of regular milk, the brand actually developed a cult following in and around the New York metropolitan area.

The distinctive bottles gained tremendous publicity for Ronnybrook Farms when they appeared in the advertisements of a large telephone company and were displayed in the refrigerator of ABC's popular comedy *Home Improvement.*

Source: Lisa Gubernick, "Designer Dairy," *Forbes,* Vol. 154, No. 2 (July 18, 1994), pp. 294–295. Reprinted By Permission of *FORBES* Magazine © Forbes Inc., 1994.

In Chapter 8, we examined several marketing activities that have a direct impact on creating a successful venture—adopting the best marketing philosophy, collecting sound marketing information, and determining market potential. We also presented an outline of the components of a comprehensive marketing plan—product and/or service strategy, pricing strategy, promotional strategy, and distribution strategy. This part of the book, which comprises Chapters 13 through 16, develops each of these components more fully. The strategic ideas presented in this chapter are useful when planning marketing activities for both new and existing businesses.

Understanding the behavioral characteristics of target market customers helps build a foundation for sound product strategy. Therefore, we begin this chapter with an analysis of consumer behavior.

UNDERSTANDING THE CUSTOMER

1 Explain aspects of consumer behavior.

The most successful small business manager may well be the person who best understands her or his customers. The concepts of consumer behavior that we present here should help the marketing manager with this task. Figure 13-1 presents a model of consumer behavior structured around three major aspects: decision-making processes, psychological factors, and sociological factors.

Consumer Decision Making

One theory about consumer information processing holds that consumers are problem solvers. According to this theory, consumer decision making has four stages.

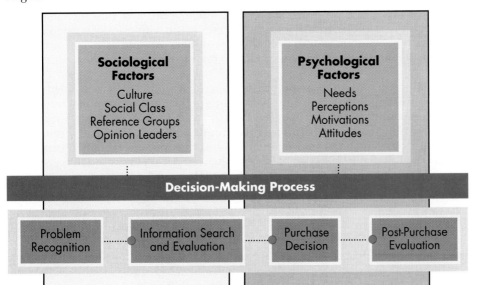

Figure 13-1

Simplified Model of Consumer Behavior

1. Problem recognition
2. Information search and evaluation
3. Purchase decision
4. Post-purchase evaluation

We use this widely accepted framework to examine consumer decision making among small business customers.

PROBLEM RECOGNITION   A generally accepted definition of problem recognition is that it is the mental state of a consumer in which a significant difference is recognized between the consumer's current state of affairs and some ideal state. Some problems are simply routine conditions of depletion, such as the desire for food when lunchtime arrives. Other problems occur much less frequently and may evolve slowly over time. The decision to replace the family dining table, for example, may take many years to develop.

A consumer must always recognize his or her problem before purchase behavior can begin. This stage cannot be avoided. However, many small firms develop marketing strategy as if consumers are functioning at later stages of the decision-making process. In reality, consumers may have not yet recognized a problem!

Many factors influence the recognition of a problem by consumers either by changing the actual state of affairs or by affecting the desired state. Here are a few examples:

- Changing financial status (a job promotion with a salary increase)
- Household characteristics (the birth of a baby)
- Normal depletion (using up the last tube of toothpaste)
- Product or service performance (breakdown of the VCR)
- Past decisions (poor repair service on car)
- Availability of products (introduction of a new product)

Once a market's situation with regard to problem recognition is understood, an entrepreneur can decide on the appropriate marketing strategy to use. In some situations, a small firm manager may need to *influence* problem recognition. For example, the Bron-Shoe Company is a family-owned firm that has been bronzing baby shoes for over 60 years. But today's "upscale parents now view such keepsakes as passé. Instead, they buy camcorders to preserve the memories of a video generation." Bron-Shoe attempted to influence consumers' desired state by contracting with independent sales representatives to go door-to-door to increase visibility of its product.[1]

In other situations, the small firm manager may simply *react* to problem recognition. For example, Safeguard Business Systems, Inc., moved from marketing only manual accounting systems materials—such as its One-Write check-writing systems—to selling computer forms and accounting software to its small business customers.[2] Research shows that many small business owners recognize that their actual accounting system falls short of their desired state. This problem recognition creates demand that Safeguard can pursue.

INFORMATION SEARCH AND EVALUATION   The second stage in consumer decision making involves consumers' collection and evaluation of appropriate information from both internal and external sources. The principal goal of search activity is to establish **evaluative criteria**—the features or characteristics of products or services that are used to compare brands. The small firm manager should understand which evaluative criteria customers use to formulate their evoked set.

evaluative criteria
the features of products that are used to compare brands

An **evoked set** is the group of brands that a consumer is both aware of and willing to consider as a solution to a purchase problem. Thus, the initial challenge for a new firm is to gain market *awareness* for its product or service. Only then will the brand have the opportunity to become part of consumers' evoked sets.

Developing market awareness was a huge challenge for entrepreneur Sheryl Leach, creator of Barney the Dinosaur. She attempted to break into a market stronghold of world-famous names such as Big Bird and Winnie-the-Pooh. In 1988, her small firm produced three children's videos featuring the Barney character, which were distributed to Toys "R" Us stores. Sitting on the shelf next to Disney and Sesame Street videos, "the [Barney] tapes mostly gathered dust. What we didn't realize is that exposure is so important," Leach said. When she later made a free distribution of videos to area preschools and day-care centers, sales started up immediately. The Barney character became a household companion of millions of youngsters.[3]

Creator Sheryl Leach had difficulty at first in developing awareness of her product in a market dominated by such giants as Disney, but eventually Barney the Dinosaur became a household name in millions of homes.

The decision to buy a new product will naturally take longer than a decision that involves a known product. For example, an industrial-equipment dealer with a new product may find it necessary to call on a prospective customer for a period of months before making the first sale.

PURCHASE DECISION Once consumers have evaluated brands in their evoked set and made their choice, they must still decide on how and where to make the purchase. A substantial volume of retail sales now come from nonstore settings such as mail-order catalogs and cable TV shopping channels. These outlets have created a complex and challenging environment in which to develop marketing strategy—particularly with regard to distribution decisions. Consumers attribute many different advantages and disadvantages to various shopping outlets, making it difficult for the small firm to devise a single correct strategy. Sometimes, however, simple recognition of these factors can be helpful.

Of course, not every purchase decision is planned prior to entering a store or looking at a mail-order catalog. Studies have shown that over 50 percent of most types of purchases from traditional retail outlets are not intended prior to entering the store. This fact places tremendous importance on store layout, sales personnel, point-of-purchase displays, and so forth.

POST-PURCHASE EVALUATION The consumer decision-making process does not terminate with a purchase. Small firms that desire repeat purchases from customers—and they all should—need to understand post-purchase behavior. Figure 13-2 illustrates several consumer activities that occur during post-purchase evaluation. We briefly comment on two of these activities—post-purchase dissonance and consumer complaints.

evoked set
brands that a person is both aware of and willing to consider as a solution to a purchase problem

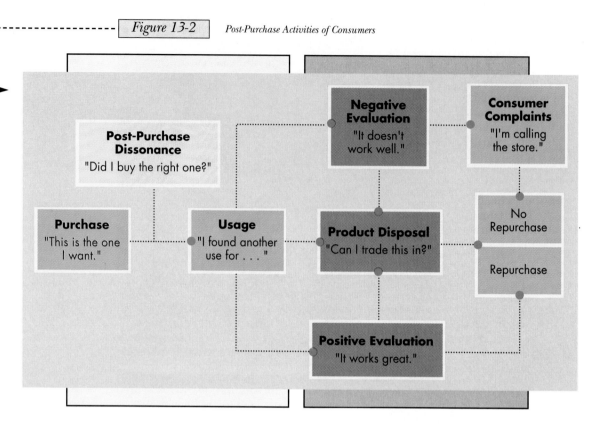

Figure 13-2   Post-Purchase Activities of Consumers

cognitive dissonance
the anxiety that occurs when a customer has second thoughts immediately following a purchase

Post-purchase dissonance is one type of **cognitive dissonance,** a tension that occurs immediately following a purchase decision when consumers have second thoughts as to the wisdom of their purchase. This anxiety is obviously uncomfortable to consumers and can negatively influence product evaluation and customer satisfaction. Small firms need to manage cognitive dissonance among their customers in whatever ways are most effective. For example, Clarke Otten, president of Professional Swedish Car Repair in Atlanta, Georgia allocates an hour or more each day to telephone recent customers to find out if they are happy with the car-repair services they received.[4]

In Chapter 7, we noted that U.S. consumers frequently experience dissatisfaction about their relationships with businesses. What do these consumers do when they are displeased? As Figure 13-3 shows, consumers have several options for dealing with their dissatisfaction. Six of the seven options threaten repeat sales. Only one—a private complaint to the offending business—is desirable to the business. These odds are not encouraging. Once again, they indicate the importance of quality customer service—both before and after a sale. Studies have shown that over 50 percent of dissatisfied customers will not deal again with the offending business and that almost all will tell other people about their bad experience.

To summarize the consumer decision-making process, Table 13-1 offers an example of a small firm's response to each stage.

Psychological Factors

The next major component of the consumer behavior model shown in Figure 13-1—psychological factors—may be labeled as intangible because they cannot be seen or touched. Such factors have been identified by the process of inference. The four

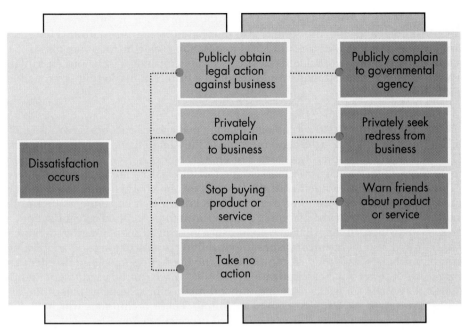

Source: Adapted from J. Singh, "Consumer Complaint Intentions and Behavior," *Journal of Marketing*, Vol. 52, No. 1 (January 1988), pp. 93–107.

Figure 13-3

Consumer Options for Dealing with Product or Service Dissatisfaction

psychological factors that have the greatest relevance to small businesses are needs, perceptions, motivations, and attitudes.

NEEDS   **Needs** are often defined as the basic seeds of (and the starting point for) all behavior. Without needs, there would be no behavior. Although there are innumerable consumer needs, we identify those needs as falling into four categories—physiological, social, psychological, and spiritual.

Needs are never completely satisfied, thereby ensuring the continued existence of business. A complicating characteristic of needs is the way in which they function together in generating behavior. In other words, various "seeds" (remember the definition) can blossom together, making it more difficult to understand which need is being satisfied by a specific product or service. Nevertheless, a careful assessment of the needs-behavior connection can be very helpful in developing marketing strategy. Different people buy the same product to satisfy different needs.

needs
the starting point for all behavior

Consumer Decision Stage	Business Owner's Action
Problem recognition (My old car is a junker.)	Mails to a list of tow-truck customers an advertising flyer entitled "Start a New Life with a New Vehicle"
Information search (I need to shop for a replacement car.)	Runs an ad in the newspaper showing business's "best buys"
Purchase decision (I know what I want if I can afford it.)	Promotes special financing in the automobile showroom
Post-purchase behavior (I hope I made a good decision to buy my new car.)	Sends a personal letter congratulating the customer on his or her wise decision

Table 13-1

A Car Dealer's Responses to the Consumer Decision-Making Process

For example, consumers purchase numerous food products in supermarkets to satisfy physiological needs. But food is also purchased in status restaurants to satisfy consumers' social and/or psychological needs. Some specific foods are also in demand by special market segments to satisfy certain consumers' religious (spiritual) needs. A needs-based strategy would result in a different marketing approach in each of these situations.

PERCEPTIONS   The second psychological factor, **perception,** encompasses those individual processes that ultimately give meaning to the stimuli that confront consumers. This meaning may be severely distorted or entirely blocked, however. Customer perception can cloud a small firm's marketing effort and make it ineffective.

Perception is a two-sided coin. It depends on the characteristics of both the stimulus and the perceiver. For example, it is known that consumers attempt to manage huge quantities of incoming stimuli through **perceptual categorization,** a process by which things that are similar are perceived as belonging together. Therefore, if a small business wishes to position its product alongside an existing brand and have it accepted as comparable, the marketing mix should reflect an awareness of perceptual categorization: A similar price can be used to communicate similar quality; a package design with a similar color scheme to that of the existing brand may be used to convey meaning. These techniques will help the customer fit the new product into the desired product category.

Small firms that use an existing brand name for a new product are relying on perceptual categorization to pre-sell the new product. On the other hand, if the new product is generically different or of a different quality, a unique brand name should be selected to avoid perceptual categorization.

If a consumer has strong brand loyalty to a product, it becomes difficult for other brands to penetrate that individual's perceptual barriers. Those competing brands are likely to have distorted images for that individual because of the pre-existing attitude. Perceptual mood thus presents a unique communication challenge.

MOTIVATIONS   Unsatisfied needs create tension within an individual. When this tension reaches a certain level, the individual becomes uncomfortable and is motivated to reduce the tension.

We are all familiar with hunger pains, which are manifestations of tension created by an unsatisfied physiological need. What directs a person to obtain food so that the hunger pains can be relieved? The answer is motivation. **Motivations** are goal-directed forces within humans that organize and give direction to tension caused by unsatisfied needs. Marketers cannot create needs, but they can create and offer unique motivations to consumers. If an acceptable reason for purchasing a product or service is provided, it will probably be internalized as a motivating force. The key for the marketer is to determine which motivation the consumer will perceive as acceptable in a given situation. The answer is found through an analysis of other consumer behavior variables.

Each of the other three classes of needs—social, psychological, and spiritual—is similarly connected to behavior via motivations. For example, when a person's social needs create tension due to incomplete satisfaction, a firm may show how its product can fulfill those needs by providing acceptable social motivations to that person. A campus clothing store might promote the styles that communicate that a college student has obtained group membership.

Understanding motivations is not easy. Several motives may be present in any situation, and motivations are often subconscious. However, they must be investigated if the marketing effort is to have an improved chance for success.

perception
the individual processes that give meaning to the stimuli that confront consumers

perceptual categorization
the perceptual process of grouping similar things to manage huge quantities of incoming stimuli

motivations
forces that give direction and organization to the tension of unsatisfied needs

ATTITUDES   Like the other psychological variables, attitudes cannot be observed, but everyone has them. Do attitudes imply knowledge? Do they imply feelings of good or bad, favorable or unfavorable? Does an attitude have a direct impact on behavior? If you answered yes to these questions, you were correct each time. An **attitude** is an enduring opinion that is based on a combination of knowledge, feeling, and behavioral tendency.

An attitude can be an obstacle or a catalyst in bringing a customer to a product. For example, consumers with the attitude that a local family-run grocery store has higher merchandise prices than a national chain may avoid the local store. Armed with an understanding of the structure of an attitude, a marketer can approach the consumer more intelligently.

Sociological Factors

The last component of the consumer behavior model is sociological factors. Among these social influences are culture, social class, reference groups, and opinion leaders, as Figure 13-1 on page 283 shows. Note that each of these sociological factors represents a different degree of group aggregation: Culture involves large masses of people; social classes and reference groups represent smaller groups; and, finally, an opinion leader is a single individual who exerts influence.

CULTURE   A group's social heritage is called its **culture.** This social heritage has a tremendous impact on the purchase and use of products. Marketing managers often overlook the cultural variable because its influences are so neatly embedded within the society. Culture is somewhat like air. You really do not think about its function until you are in water over your head! International marketers who have experienced more than one culture can readily attest to the reality of cultural influence.

The prescriptive nature of culture should most concern the marketing manager. Cultural norms create a range of product-related, acceptable behaviors that influence consumers in what they buy. Because culture does change, however, by adapting slowly to new situations, what works well as a marketing strategy today may not work a few years from now.

An investigation of culture within a narrower definitional boundary—by age, religious preference, ethnic orientation, or geographical location—is called *subcultural analysis.* Here, too, the unique patterns of behavior and social relationships concern the marketing manager. For example, the needs and motivations of the youth subculture are far different from those of the senior citizen subculture. Certain food preferences are unique to particular ethnic cultures. If small business managers familiarize themselves with cultures and subcultures, they can create better marketing mixes.

SOCIAL CLASS   Another sociological factor affecting consumer behavior is social class. **Social classes** are divisions in a society with different levels of social prestige. Important implications for marketing exist in a social class system. Different lifestyles correlate with different levels of social prestige, and certain products often become symbols of each type of life-style.

For some products, such as consumer packaged goods, social class analysis will probably not be very useful. For others, such as home furnishings, it may help explain variations in shopping and communication patterns.

Unlike a caste system, a social class system provides for upward mobility. For example, the status of parents does not permanently fix the social class of their child.

attitude
an enduring opinion based on knowledge, feeling, and behavioral tendency

culture
a group's social heritage, including behavior patterns and values

social classes
divisions in a society with different levels of social prestige

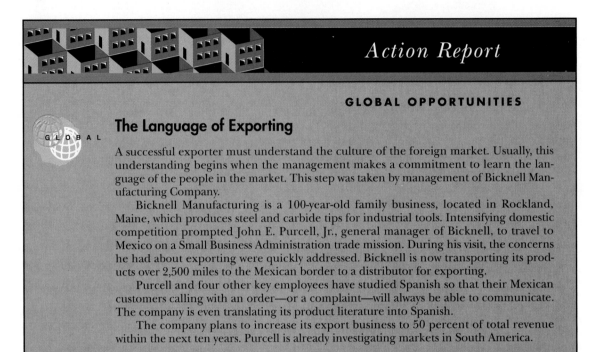

Occupation is probably the single most important determinant of social class. Other determinants that are used in social class research include possessions, source of income, and education.

REFERENCE GROUPS   Social class could, by definition, be considered a reference group. However, not every group is a reference group. Marketers are more generally concerned with small groups such as the family, the work group, a neighborhood group, or a recreational group. **Reference groups** are those groups that an individual allows to influence his or her behavior.

reference groups
groups that influence
individual behavior

The existence of group influence is well established. The challenge to the marketer is to understand why this influence occurs and how it can be used to promote the sale of a product. Individuals tend to accept group influence because of benefits they perceive as resulting from it. These perceived benefits allow the influencers various kinds of power. Five widely recognized forms of power are reward, coercive, referent, expert, and legitimate. Each of these power forms is available to the marketer.

Reward power and coercive power relate to a group's ability to give and to withhold rewards. Rewards can be material or psychological. Recognition and praise are typical psychological rewards. A Tupperware party is a good example of a marketing technique that takes advantage of reward power and coercive power. The ever-present possibility of pleasing or displeasing the hostess-friend tends to encourage the guest to buy.

Referent power and expert power involve neither rewards nor punishments. They exist because an individual attaches great importance to being like the group or perceives the group as being knowledgeable. Referent power causes consumers to conform to the group's behavior and to choose products selected by the group's members. Children will often be affected by referent power. Marketers can create a desire for products by using cleverly designed advertisements or packages. Consider the strategy of BertSherm Products, Inc., which markets Fun 'n Fresh deodorant sticks targeted to seven- to twelve-year-olds. Entrepreneur Philip B. Davis has been selling the deodorant with the campaign slogan "Be Cool in School." Children admit they purchase the deodorant not because of body odor but rather because using the deodorant makes them feel like an adult.[5]

Referent power exerts great sway over many teenagers. To create demand for a product, many marketers appeal to teenagers' susceptibility to group influence.

Legitimate power involves the sanctioning of what the individual ought to do. At the cultural level, legitimate power is evident in the prescriptive nature of culture. This type of power can also be used within smaller groups.

OPINION LEADERS   According to a certain communication theory, consumers receive a significant amount of information through individuals called **opinion leaders,** who are group members playing a key communications role.

Generally speaking, opinion leaders are knowledgeable, visible, and exposed to the mass media. A small business firm can enhance its own product and image by identifying with such leaders. For example, a farm-supply dealer may promote its products in an agricultural community by holding demonstrations of these products on the farms of outstanding local farmers, who are the community's opinion leaders. Also, department stores may use attractive students as models when showing campus fashions.

opinion leader
a group leader who plays a key communications role

PRODUCT MANAGEMENT

2   Describe the concepts of product life cycle and product development.

Product Versus Service Marketing

Traditionally, marketers have used the word *product* as a generic term to describe both goods and services. However, whether goods marketing and services marketing strategies are the same is questionable. As shown in Figure 13-4, certain characteristics—tangibility, production and consumption time separation, standardization, and perishability—define a number of differences between the two strategies. Based on these characteristics, for example, a pencil fits the pure goods end of the scale and a haircut fits the pure services end. The major implication of this distinction is that services present unique challenges to strategy development.[6]

Although we recognize the benefit of examining the marketing of services as a unique form of marketing, space limitations require that services be subsumed under the umbrella category of product marketing. Therefore, from this point on, a **product** is considered to include the total bundle of satisfaction that is offered to

product
a bundle of satisfaction—a service, a good, or both—offered to customers in an exchange transaction

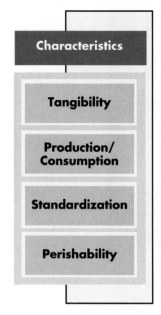

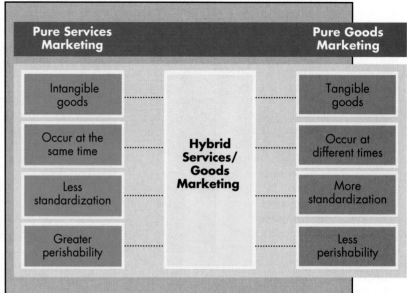

Figure 13-4 *Services Marketing Versus Goods Marketing*

customers in an exchange transaction—whether it be a service, a good, or a combination of the two. Also, a product includes not only the main element of the bundle, which is the physical product or core service, but also complementary components such as packaging or a warranty. Of course, the physical product or core service is usually the most important component. But, sometimes, that main element is perceived by customers to be similar for all products. Then, complementary components become the most important features of the product. For example, a particular cake-mix brand may be preferred by consumers, not because it is a better mix, but because of the unique toll-free telephone number on the package that can be called for baking hints. Or, a certain dry cleaner may be chosen over others because it treats customers with respect, not just because it cleans clothes exceptionally well.

Product strategy describes the manner in which the product component of the marketing mix is used to achieve the objectives of a firm. A **product item** is the lowest common denominator in a product mix. It is the individual item, such as one brand of bar soap. A **product line** is the sum of the individual product items that are related. The relationship is usually defined generically. Two brands of bar soap are two product items in one product line. A **product mix** is the collection of product lines within a firm's ownership and control. A firm's product mix might consist of a line of bar soaps and a line of shoe polishes. **Product mix consistency** refers to the closeness, or similarity, of the product lines. The more items in a product line, the more depth it has. The more product lines in a product mix, the greater the breadth of the product mix.

Once a marketing manager has gained a basic understanding of target market customers, he or she is better prepared to develop product strategy. Two concepts are extremely useful to the small business manager in developing and controlling the firm's product strategy—the product life cycle and product development. We briefly examine each of these prior to discussing small business product strategy.

product strategy
the way a product is marketed to achieve a firm's objectives

product item
the lowest common denominator in the product mix—the individual item

product line
all the individual product items that are related

product mix
a firm's total product lines

product mix consistency
the similarity of product lines in a product mix

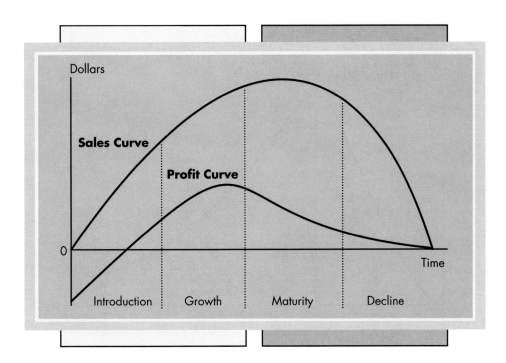

Figure 13-5

The Product Life Cycle

The Product Life Cycle

An important concept underlying sound product strategy is the product life cycle, which summarizes the sales and profits of a product from the time it is introduced until it is no longer on the market. The portrayal of the product life cycle in Figure 13-5 takes the shape of a roller-coaster ride, which is the way many entrepreneurs describe their experiences with the life cycles of their products. The initial stages are characterized by a slow and upward movement. The stay at the top is exciting but relatively brief. Then, suddenly, the decline begins, and the downward movement is rapid. Also, note the typical shape of the profit curve in the Figure 13-5. The introductory stage is characterized by losses, with profits peaking in the growth stage.

The product life-cycle concept is important to the small business manager for two reasons. First, it reminds a manager that promotion, pricing, and distribution policies should all be adjusted to reflect a product's position on the curve.[7] Second, it helps the manager see the importance of rejuvenating product lines whenever possible or switching to more promising offerings. This was the strategy of Gadi Rosenfeld and Dan Court when sales began to slip for their service—installing local-area computer networks in law offices. At one time, sales were high, but a flood of competition brought about a decline. By switching to a new product—CD-ROM storage systems—they cushioned the roller-coaster ride down the declining sales curve of the product life cycle.[8]

Product Development

As the product life-cycle concept suggests, a major responsibility of the entrepreneur is to introduce new products. This responsibility requires the entrepreneur to have a method for developing new products. In big business, committees or even

Figure 13-6

The Product Development
Curve

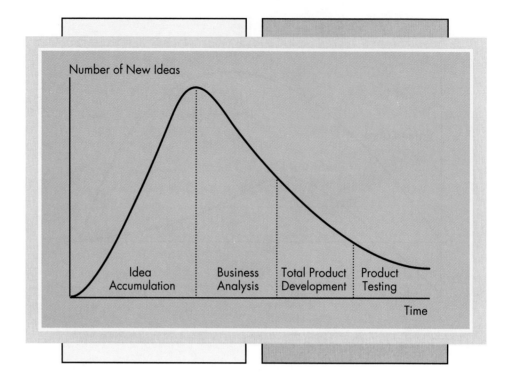

entire departments are created for that purpose. For both large and small firms, however, new product development needs to be a formalized process.

The entrepreneur usually views new-product development as a mountainous task. Therefore, Figure 13-6 shows the product development curve in the form of a mountain. The left slope of the mountain represents the gathering of a large number of ideas. Beginning at the mountain peak, these ideas are screened as the firm moves down the right slope toward the base of the mountain, which represents the retention of one product ready to be introduced into the marketplace.

IDEA ACCUMULATION   The first stage of the product development process—idea accumulation—involves increasing the pool of ideas under consideration. New products start with ideas, and these ideas have varied origins. Here are some of the many possible sources:

- Sales, engineering, or other personnel within the firm
- Government-owned patents, which are generally available on a royalty-free basis
- Privately owned patents listed in the *Official Gazette* of the U.S. Patent Office
- Other small companies that may be available for acquisition or merger
- Competitors' products and advertising
- Requests and suggestions from customers

BUSINESS ANALYSIS   Business analysis is the second stage in the product development process. Every new-product idea must be carefully studied in relation to several financial considerations. Cost and revenue are estimated and analyzed with techniques such as break-even analysis. Any idea failing to show that it can be profitable is discarded during the business analysis stage. Four key factors need to be considered when conducting a business analysis:

1. *Relationship to the existing product line.* Some firms intentionally add very different products to their product mix. However, in most cases, any product or product line added should be consistent with, or somehow related to, the existing product mix. For example, a new product may be designed to fill a gap in the company's product line or in the price range of the products it currently sells. If the product is completely new, it should have at least a family relationship to existing products. Otherwise, the new product may call for drastic and costly changes in manufacturing methods, distribution channels, type of promotion, or manner of personal selling.
2. *Cost of development and introduction.* One problem in adding new products is the cost of their development and introduction. Considerable capital outlays may be necessary, including expenditures for design and development, market research to establish sales potential and volume potential, advertising and sales promotion, patents, and the equipment and tooling that must be added. One to three years may pass before profits are realized on the sale of a contemplated new product.
3. *Personnel and facilities.* Obviously, having adequate skilled personnel and production equipment is better than having to add employees and buy equipment. Thus, introducing new products is typically more logical if the personnel and the required equipment are already available.
4. *Competition and market acceptance.* Still another factor to be considered when conducting a business analysis is the potential competition facing a proposed product in its target market. Competition must not be too severe. Some studies, for example, propose that new products can be introduced successfully only if 5 percent of the total market can be secured. The ideal solution, of course, is to offer a product that is sufficiently different or that is in a cost and price bracket that avoids direct competition.

TOTAL PRODUCT DEVELOPMENT   The next stage of product development—total product development—entails planning for branding, packaging, and other supporting efforts such as pricing and promotion. An actual prototype may be needed at this stage. After these components are considered, many new-product ideas may be discarded.

PRODUCT TESTING   The last step of the product development process is product testing. Through testing, the physical product should be proven acceptable. While the product can be evaluated in a laboratory setting, a limited test of market reaction to it should also be conducted. Consumer panels are sometimes used to evaluate a new product at this stage. However, the ultimate test of success will come in the marketplace.

PRODUCT STRATEGY ALTERNATIVES FOR SMALL BUSINESSES

3 Discuss alternative product strategies for small businesses.

Small business managers often lack a clear understanding of product strategy options. This creates ineffectiveness and conflict in the marketing effort. The major product strategy alternatives of a small business can be condensed into six categories, based on the nature of the firm's product offering and the number of target markets:

1. One product/one market
2. One product/multiple markets
3. Modified product/one market
4. Modified product/multiple markets
5. Multiple products/one market
6. Multiple products/multiple markets

Each alternative represents a distinct strategy, although two or more of these strategies can be pursued concurrently. Usually, however, a small firm will pursue the alternatives in basically the order listed here. Also, keep in mind that once any product strategy has been implemented, sales can be increased through certain additional growth tactics. For example, within any market, a small firm can try to increase sales of an existing product by doing any or all of the following:

- Convince *non-users* in the market to become customers
- Persuade current customers to *use more* of the product
- Alert current customers to *new uses* for the product

One Product/One Market

In the earliest stage of a new venture, the one product/one market product strategy is customary. Usually, an entrepreneur will try to carve out a strong market niche with a single basic product. This strategy was used by Bill Thomas, owner of W. Thomas Company, a pants distributor located in Reading, Pennsylvania. The company makes Bill's Khakis, which are sold to target market consumers entirely by mail order or wholesale. The first pair of pants was sold in January 1991. Concerning his one product/one market strategy, Thomas says:

> *I am also adding a few other colors and fabric weights, but I won't let those new products distract me. Bill's will concentrate on its bread and butter; that's how start-ups avoid being crushed by established giants. We'll live or die on khakis.*[9]

One Product/Multiple Markets

An extension of the first alternative is the one product/multiple markets strategy. With a small additional commitment in resources, the existing product can often be targeted to new markets. Extending a floor-cleaning compound from the commercial market into the home market is an example. Another example of this strategy is marketing a product abroad after first selling it domestically.

Modified Product/One Market

Customers seemingly anticipate the emergence of "new, improved" products. With the modified product/one market strategy, the original product is replaced, gradually phased out, or even left in the product mix while the new product is aimed at the original target market. If the existing product is to be retained, the impact of the modified product on its sales must be carefully assessed. It does little good to make an existing product obsolete unless the modified product has a higher profit margin. The product modification can involve a very minor change. For example, adding colored specks to a detergent can give the product new sales-attractive appeal. Some people criticize this type of product strategy, questioning the real value of such "improvements" and the ethics of claiming something is new when it is really not.

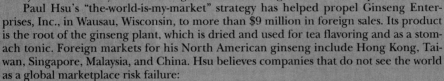

Action Report

GLOBAL OPPORTUNITIES

Growth Rooted in Global Markets

To grow and prosper, a firm must sometimes move beyond one product in a single market. It may need to identify additional target markets. A foreign market is one option.

Paul Hsu's "the-world-is-my-market" strategy has helped propel Ginseng Enterprises, Inc., in Wausau, Wisconsin, to more than $9 million in foreign sales. Its product is the root of the ginseng plant, which is dried and used for tea flavoring and as a stomach tonic. Foreign markets for his North American ginseng include Hong Kong, Taiwan, Singapore, Malaysia, and China. Hsu believes companies that do not see the world as a global marketplace risk failure:

I have purposely expanded my ginseng company to have a good mix of domestic and export sales. At this point, only a worldwide recession could crush the business. This kind of balance gives our company the ability to ride out a bad economy in one or more parts of the world.

Hsu moved from Taiwan to the United States in 1969. He began exporting North American ginseng to Asia in 1974. Hsu advises entrepreneurs to expand globally, adding that "a Made in the U.S.A. label still has a lot of prestige."

Source: Paul C. Hsu, "Profiting from a Global Mind-Set," *Nation's Business*, Vol. 82, No. 6 (June 1994), p. 6. Reprinted by permission. Copyright 1994, U.S. Chamber of Commerce.

Modified Product/Multiple Markets

A modified product can also be used to reach several markets. The modified product/multiple markets strategy, then, appeals to additional market segments. For example, a furniture manufacturer currently selling finished furniture to retail customers might market unfinished furniture directly to the do-it-yourself consumer.

Jim Zona, president of Pittsburgh Plastics Manufacturing, Inc., of Zelienople, Pennsylvania, is following a modified product/multiple markets strategy after considerable success with Gel Soles insoles for shoes, which sold 1.4 million pairs in 1993. These insoles are filled with glycerine and designed for everyday activities such as walking and working. But the company is now introducing an insole designed for a new market—sports consumers. Zona's company has also expanded into other gel-filled products, including a face mask and a neck wrap.[10]

Multiple Products/One Market

Current, satisfied customers make good markets for new additions to the product mix of a small business. Many products can be added that are more than product modifications but are generically similar to the existing products. For example, Zoom Telephonics originally produced a speed dialer, which was introduced in the early 1980s. Three years later, sales were over $5 million. When changes in the telephone industry depressed demand among consumers, Zoom successfully responded with a new related product—a modem.[11]

Action Report

TECHNOLOGICAL APPLICATIONS

Battling the Big Guys

A small company faces a big challenge when other firms are attracted to its market niche. What competitive tactics can the little guy use?

One small manufacturing firm's answer—add new products and improve manufacturing. In 1984, Tecnol Medical Products, Inc., a Fort Worth, Texas manufacturer of hospital supplies, found a niche—medical face masks. Tecnol transformed a single concept into a profitable line of masks that shield health-care workers from infection. "Big guys" such as Johnson & Johnson and 3M initially ignored the market but finally woke up and produced their own brands of specialty masks. However, Tecnol founders, Vance M. Hubbard and Kirk Brunson, were ready for the battle:

> *Tecnol's heavy spending on R&D and new-product development has allowed it to keep beating [larger firms] to the market with new products. Historically, face-mask manufacturing has been labor-intensive because it requires hand-sewing, but Tecnol engineered its own high-speed, automated equipment. The result: not only can Tecnol manufacture faster than rivals, but it also is the industry's lowest-cost supplier.*

To continue boosting sales, Tecnol next expanded in Europe.

Source: Stephanie Anderson, "Who's Afraid of J&J and 3M?" *Business Week* (December 5, 1994), pp. 66–68.

Multiple Products/Multiple Markets

Going after different markets with new but similar products is still another product strategy. This multiple products/multiple markets approach is particularly appropriate when there is concern that a new product may reduce sales of an existing product in a particular market niche. For example, a firm producing wood-burning stoves for home use might introduce a gas-burning furnace targeted for use in office buildings. Another example is the strategy of Lund International Holdings, a producer of sun visors and related equipment for trucks, based in Coon Rapids, Minnesota. For many years after its founding in 1972 in a chicken barn, sun visors were its only product. Lund later expanded to more than 20 other product lines, including bug shields, grills, and fender extensions. Its markets include automobile parts stores, body shops, and customizing shops.[12]

As another example, some cotton farmers are targeting the green products market with a new organic cotton—cotton grown without the use of chemical fertilizers, herbicides, or insecticides.[13] The fiber from this organically grown product is processed by special textile manufacturers and used in unbleached and undyed wearing apparel and mattresses.

Other Product Strategy Alternatives

The six options just discussed are the product strategies most commonly used by small firms. There are, of course, additional strategies. For example, a local dealer selling Italian sewing machines might add a line of microwave ovens—a generically unrelated product. A product strategy that includes a new product quite different from existing products can be very risky. However, this strategy is occasionally used by small businesses, especially when the new product fits existing distribution and sales systems or requires similar marketing knowledge.

Still another product strategy involves adding a new, unrelated product to the product mix to target a new market. This strategy has high risk, as a business is attempting to market an unfamiliar product in an unfamiliar market. For example, an electrical equipment service business added a private employment agency. If successful, this product strategy could build a hedge against volatile shifts in market demand. A business that sells both snowshoes and suntan lotion expects that demand will be high in one market or the other at all times.

One example of the multiple products/multiple markets strategy is targeting the green market with organically grown cotton, which is processed by special textile manufacturers and used in specialty household and clothing items.

BUILDING THE TOTAL PRODUCT OFFERING

4 Identify major marketing tactics that can transform a firm's basic product into a total product offering.

A major responsibility of marketing is to transform a basic product into a total product offering. For example, an idea for a unique new pen that has already been developed into a physical reality—the basic product—is still not ready for the marketplace. The total product offering must be more than the materials molded into the shape of the new pen. To be marketable, the basic product must be named, have a package, perhaps have a warranty, and be supported by other product components. We now examine a few of the components of a total product offering.

Branding

An essential element of a total product offering is a brand. A **brand** is a means of identifying the product—both verbally and symbolically. The name Xerox is a brand, as are the golden arches of McDonald's. Since a product's brand name is so important to the image of the business and its products, considerable attention should be given to the selection of a name.

brand
a verbal or symbolic means of identifying a product

In general, there are five rules to follow in naming a product:

1. *Select a name that is easy to pronounce and remember.* You want customers to remember your product. Help them with a name that can be spoken easily—for example, Curl Up and Dye (a hair salon) and Johnny on the Spot (a portable toilet service). An entrepreneur's own name should be carefully evaluated to ensure its acceptability before choosing it to identify a product. Dave Thomas, the founder of a major fast-food chain, successfully used his daughter's name for his company, Wendy's.
2. *Choose a descriptive name.* A name that is suggestive of the major benefit of the product can be extremely helpful. As a name for a tax preparation service, Brilliant Deductions correctly suggests a desirable attribute. Mug-A-Bug is also

Action Report

ENTREPRENEURIAL EXPERIENCES

What's in a Name?

Creative names build an image for a product that speaks to its target market. Sometimes, the name itself will help define the identity of the product.

This is exactly what happened when John Sundet, president of Snow Runner, Inc. in St. Paul, Minnesota, began thinking about a new identity for the company's recreational snow skates—ski boots with short runners. With the help of a consultant, Sundet began a month-long process working with focus groups, who showed a preference for the name Sled Dogs.

"This was an opportunity to create a new image for us," Sundet says. "The name tied in a north woods image and was comfortable because dogs are universally loved. And it allowed us to use dog vernacular to convey the freedom and excitement of the sport." Dogs, slang for feet, and sled, a fun way to get around in the snow, work together in a variety of ways.

Source: Roberta Maynard, "What's in a Name?" *Nation's Business*, Vol. 82, No. 9 (September 1994), p. 54. Reprinted by permission. Copyright 1994, U.S. Chamber of Commerce.

---

a creative name for a pest-control business. However, Rocky Road would be a poor name for a mattress!

3. *Use a name that can have legal protection.* Be careful to select a name that can be defended successfully. Do not risk litigation by copying someone else's brand name. A new soft drink named Professor Pepper would likely be contested by the Dr Pepper company. An attorney who specializes in trademarks should be hired to run a name search and then to register the tradename.

4. *Select names with promotional possibilities.* Exceedingly long names are not, for example, compatible with good copy design on billboards, where space is at such a premium. A competitor of the McDonald's hamburger chain is called Wuv's, a name that will easily fit on any billboard.

5. *Select a name that can be used on several product lines of a similar nature.* Customer goodwill is often lost when a name doesn't fit a new line. A company producing a furniture polish called Slick-Surface could not easily use the same name for its new sidewalk surfacing compound that purports to increase traction. The name Just Brakes for an auto service shop that repairs only brakes is excellent unless the shop later plans to expand into muffler repair.

A small business should also carefully select its trademark or service mark. **Trademark** and **service mark** are legal terms indicating the exclusive right to use a brand. These marks should be unique, easy to remember, and related to the product. For example, Liquid Paper, the trademark for a correction fluid, clearly relates to the product's function and is easy to remember.

Trademark registration for products in interstate commerce is handled through the U.S. Patent and Trademark Office under the authority of the Lanham Trademark Act, which also covers the registration of service marks. Chapter 26 provides further discussion of trademarks and their legal ramifications.

Once a trademark is selected by a business, it is important to protect its use. Two rules can help. First, be sure that the name is not carelessly used in place of

trademark
an identifying feature used to distinguish a manufacturer's product

service mark
a legal term indicating the exclusive right to use a brand to identify a service

Action Report

QUALITY GOALS

Quality Sells

QUALITY

A private branding strategy is used by large retailers when they buy products from manufacturers and then market the goods as their own brands. Favorable trends in private branding present opportunities for small manufacturers if they can meet the quality demands of their customers.

Drypers Corporation, in Houston, Texas, is a small firm that has profited from private branding. The seven-year-old manufacturer of disposable diapers produces private label products for several large supermarket chains. According to Dave Pitassi, a cofounder, success in private branding requires the right product, price, and marketing program. There are, however, additional considerations, according to Pitassi:

> *A product with the right sales potential is just the start, of course. Your line also must be comparable or superior* [in] *quality to the market leader. A retailer puts its own name on the line when it private labels your product, and it won't want that name to be sullied by inferior or inconsistent quality. If they're putting their name on your product, they want to make sure it lives up to their reputation.*

A retailer purchasing for a brand label wants assurance of product quality. Frequently, quality must be validated by an independent testing laboratory. Drypers, for example, assures quality with internal testing but also sends samples of its diapers to an outside laboratory for checks of absorbency quality.

Source: Jenny McCune, "Catch a Growing Wave," *Small Business Reports*, Vol. 19, No. 6 (June 1994), pp. 24–33.

the generic name. For example, Xerox tries to ensure that people say they are "copying" something rather than "xeroxing" it. Second, the business should inform the public that the brand is a brand by labeling it with the symbol ™ or, if the mark has been registered with the U.S. Trademark Office, the symbol ®. If the trademark is unusual or written in a special form, it is easier to protect.

Packaging

Packaging is another important part of the total product offering. In addition to protecting the basic product, packaging is a significant tool for increasing the value of the total product.

Mariani Packing Co., in San Jose, California, introduced new packaging for its dried fruit products, and eight months later found that sales had increased about 20 percent. "We have a pretty pure measurement of the package's success because we didn't change the price and we did no promotion of the product," says Mark Bagley, vice-president of marketing. "We invested our marketing funds in the packaging, and we are very, very pleased with the results."[14]

Consider for a moment some of the products you purchase. How many do you buy mainly because of a preference for package design and/or color? Innovative packaging is frequently the deciding factor for consumers. If a product is other-

1 Explain aspects of consumer behavior.

- It is helpful to view consumers as problem solvers who are going through several steps, from problem recognition to post-purchase behavior.
- Psychological factors affecting consumer behavior include needs, perceptions, motivations, and attitudes.
- Sociological factors affecting consumer behavior encompass culture, social class, reference groups, and opinion leaders.

2 Describe the concepts of product life cycle and product development.

- The product life cycle is a valuable tool for managing the product mix.
- The stages of the product life cycle are introduction, growth, maturity, and decline.
- The stages of new-product development are idea accumulation, business analysis, total product development, and product testing.

3 Discuss alternative product strategies for small businesses.

- Small business managers are often weak in their understanding of product strategy.
- The major product strategy alternatives can be condensed into six categories.
- Most entrepreneurs use a one product/one market strategy in the early stages of their ventures.
- Each product strategy is complemented by the growth options of convincing non-users to become customers, persuading current customers to use more, and alerting current customers to new uses for the product.

4 Identify major marketing tactics that can transform a firm's basic product into a total product offering.

- The five most important rules in naming a product are to select a name that is easy to pronounce and remember, is descriptive, can have legal protection, has promotional possibilities, and can be used on several products.
- Packaging is a significant tool for increasing total product value.
- A label is an important informative tool for product use, care, and disposal.
- A warranty can be valuable for achieving customer satisfaction.

wise very similar to competitive products, its package may create the distinctive impression that makes a sale. For example, having packaging materials that are biodegradable may distinguish a product from the competition. The original L'eggs packaging design is an example of creative packaging that sells well.

Labeling

Another part of the total product is its label. Labeling is particularly important to manufacturers, who apply most labels. A label serves several purposes. It often shows the brand, particularly when branding the basic product would be undesirable. For example, a furniture brand is typically shown on a label and not on the basic product. On some products, visibility of the brand is highly desirable; Calvin Klein jeans would probably not sell as well with the name labeled only inside the jeans.

A label is also an important informative tool for consumers. It can include information on product care and use. It can even include information on how to dispose of the product.

Laws on labeling requirements should be consulted carefully. Be innovative in your labeling information, and consider including information that goes beyond the specified minimum legal requirements.

Warranties

warranty
a promise that a product will do certain things or meet certain standards

A **warranty** is simply a promise that a product will do certain things or meet certain standards. It may be written or unwritten. All sellers make an implied warranty that the seller's title to the product is good. A merchant seller, who deals in goods of a particular kind, makes the additional implied warranty that those goods are fit for the ordinary purposes for which they are sold. A written warranty on a product is not always necessary. As a matter of fact, many firms operate without written warranties. They are concerned that a written warranty will only serve to confuse customers and make them suspicious.

The Magnuson-Moss Warranty Act of 1974 has had a strong impact on warranty practices. This law covers several warranty areas, including terminology. The most notable provisions affecting terminology relate to the use of the terms *full* and *limited* on an express warranty for a product that costs over $15.00. In order for a product to get a full warranty designation, the warranty must state certain minimum standards such as replacement or full refund after reasonable attempts at repair. Warranties not meeting all the minimum standards must carry the limited designation.

Warranties are important for products that are innovative, relatively expensive, purchased infrequently, relatively complex to repair, and positioned as high-quality goods. A business should use the following major considerations to rate the merits of a proposed warranty policy:

- Cost
- Service capability
- Competitive practices
- Customer perceptions
- Legal implications

In this chapter, we have analyzed consumer behavior and product strategy, and we have examined product management techniques with the ultimate goal of building the total product offering. Hopefully, these discussions will assist you in your personal entrepreneurial efforts.

DISCUSSION QUESTIONS

1. Briefly describe the four stages of the consumer decision-making process. Why is the first stage so vital to consumer behavior?
2. List the four psychological factors discussed in this chapter. What is their relevance to consumer behavior?
3. List the four sociological factors discussed in this chapter. What is their relevance to consumer behavior?
4. What factors are important to a small firm when conducting the business analysis stage of product development?
5. How does the modified product/one market strategy differ from the one product/multiple markets strategy? Give examples.

New Terms and Concepts

evaluative criteria *284*	attitude *289*	product item *292*
evoked set *285*	culture *289*	product line *292*
cognitive dissonance *286*	social classes *289*	product mix *292*
needs *287*	reference groups *290*	product mix consistency *292*
perception *288*	opinion leader *291*	brand *299*
perceptual categorization *288*	product *291*	trademark *300*
motivations *288*	product strategy *292*	service mark *300*
		warranty *302*

You Make the Call

Situation 1   After selling basic school supplies for 20 years as a manufacturer's representative, Bruce Shapiro created his own company to market more creative products for kids. Founded in 1989, Creative Works, located in Northbrook, Illinois, produces rulers, protractors, compasses, and more made from heavy-duty plastic. Shapiro has added fashion colors such as teal, purple, pink, and black to his line of 15 products. The durable plastic design and colors distinguish Creative Works products from those of competitors. Retailers such as Wal-Mart, Kmart, and Toys "R" Us stock the company's products.

Question 1   Is Creative Works pursuing more than one product strategy? If so, which ones?
Question 2   Would it be ethical to promote the fashion color items as "new and improved"? Why or why not?
Question 3   What aspects of consumer behavior are involved in the success of this marketing effort?

Situation 2   Paul McKinney is the owner and operator of a small restaurant located in the downtown area of Oklahoma City, Oklahoma. McKinney is a college graduate with a major in accounting. His ability to analyze and control costs has been a major factor in keeping his five-year-old venture out of the red. The restaurant is located in an old but newly remodeled downtown building. His business is based on high volume and low overhead. However, space limitations provide seating for only 25 to 30 people at one time. McKinney feels that customers stay too long after they've finished their meal, thereby tying up seating. He has considered using a small flashing light at each table to remind customers that it is time to move on. He is concerned that this method is too obvious and may create customer dissatisfaction.

Question 1   What is your opinion regarding McKinney's proposed flashing light system?
Question 2   What other suggestions to help increase turnover can you make? Why are your ideas better?
Question 3   What type of diversification strategy would be consistent with McKinney's restaurant business? Be specific.

Continue on next page

Situation 3 Judy Corwin has been test-marketing her new vending machine for almost a year. The machine, called Single-Smoke, dispenses individual cigarettes at 25 cents each. Corwin's target market is the occasional smoker and smokers short on cash. She plans to sell her product to restaurants and hotels, in part, because the machine has a unique design that takes up very little space. Corwin has invested over $200,000 of her own money in the project, including the cost of equipment to manufacture the vending machines. She plans to promote the product as helping "smokers kick the habit by forcing them to buy their cigarettes in single doses."

Question 1 Do you believe the name, Single-Smoke, is a good name? Why or why not?

Question 2 What factors should have been evaluated in selecting a name for this product?

Question 3 What consumer behavior concepts are relevant to this venture's success?

6. A manufacturer of power lawn mowers is considering the addition of a line of home barbecue equipment. What factors would be important in a decision of this type?

7. What are the three ways to achieve additional growth within each of the market strategies?

8. Select two product names, and then evaluate each with respect to the five rules for naming a product listed in this chapter.

9. Would a small business desire to have its name considered the generic name for the product area? Defend your position.

10. For what type of firm is the packaging of products most important? For what firms is it unimportant?

EXPERIENTIAL EXERCISES

1. Ask some owners of small firms in your area to describe their new product development processes. Report your findings.

2. For several days, make notes on your own shopping experiences. Summarize what you consider to be the best customer service you received.

3. Visit a local retail store and observe brand names, package designs, labels, and warranties. Report your thoughts to the class regarding good and bad examples.

4. Consider your most recent, meaningful purchase. Relate the decision-making process you used to the four stages of decision making presented in this chapter. Report your conclusions.

Exploring the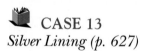

5. Visit three different companies' home pages on the Web. You might want to look under the Yahoo business directory (located at http://www.yahoo.com). Choose the home page that you like best and write a one-page summary describing the product(s) that the company offers.

CASE 13
Silver Lining (p. 627)

This case describes the product strategies of the entrepreneur who invented Rain-X, a wipe-on water repellent.

Alternative Cases for Chapter 13: Case 18, "Gibson Mortuary," p. 639
Case 24, "Fox Manufacturing," p. 657

Pricing and Credit Strategies

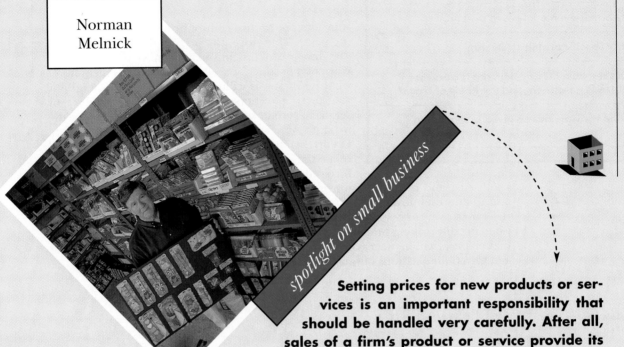

Norman
Melnick

spotlight on small business

Setting prices for new products or services is an important responsibility that should be handled very carefully. After all, sales of a firm's product or service provide its major source of revenue.

Norman Melnick, founder of Pentech International, based in Edison, New Jersey, treats the pricing task seriously. A manufacturer of innovative pens and pencils, he never "just slaps a price tag on his products." Melnick is convinced that sound pricing begins with knowing product costs.

Each year, Pentech introduces more than 24 new products, the majority of which achieve instant success. After a decade in business, Melnick has mastered the art of pricing. . . . [He] leaves no stone unturned, factoring in all the critical costs—raw materials, equipment and assembly line, shipping, staffing, even employee overtime.

After Melnick and his managers have a clear picture of product costs, they apply the desired profit margin, which gives them the selling price. If Melnick had not followed a careful pricing strategy, Pentech might have already been written off by competitors such as Bic and Papermate.

Source: Bob Weinstein, "Price Pointers," *Entrepreneur*, Vol. 23, No. 2 (February 1995), p. 48. Reprinted with permission from *Entrepreneur* Magazine, February 1995.

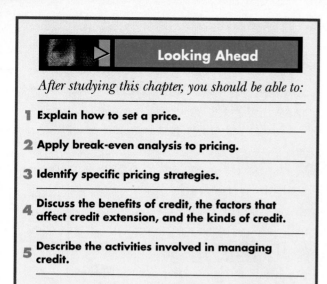

Looking Ahead

After studying this chapter, you should be able to:

1 Explain how to set a price.

2 Apply break-even analysis to pricing.

3 Identify specific pricing strategies.

4 Discuss the benefits of credit, the factors that affect credit extension, and the kinds of credit.

5 Describe the activities involved in managing credit.

start here

A product or service cannot be sold until it has a selling price. Therefore, the pricing decision is a necessary and critical task in small business marketing. The **price** of a product or service is the seller's measure of what he or she is willing to receive in exchange for transferring ownership or use of that product or service. A credit system is often required to place the product or service in a more competitive position. **Credit** involves an agreement between buyer and seller that payment for a product or service will be received at some later date.

Pricing and credit decisions are vital to the small firm because they directly affect both revenue and cash flow. Also, customers dislike price increases and often react negatively to restrictive credit policies. Therefore, care should be exercised when initially making pricing and credit decisions in order to reduce the likelihood that changes will be necessary. This chapter examines both the pricing decisions and the credit decisions of small firms.

---

1 Explain how to set a price.

SETTING A PRICE

price
a seller's measure of what he or she is willing to receive in exchange for transferring ownership or use of a product or service

credit
an agreement to delay payment for a product or service

Pricing is the systematic determination of the most appropriate price for a product. While setting just any price is easy, systematic pricing is complex and difficult. The total sales revenue of a small business is a direct reflection of two components: sales volume and price. Price is, therefore, half of the gross revenue equation. As a result, even a small change in price can drastically influence revenue. Consider the following situations (perfectly inelastic demand is assumed to emphasize the point):

Situation A
Quantity sold × Price per unit = Gross revenue
250,000   × $3.00   = $750,000

Situation B
Quantity sold × Price per unit = Gross revenue
250,000   × $2.80   = $700,000

The price per unit in Situation B is only $0.20 lower than that in Situation A. However, the total reduction in revenue is $50,000! Clearly, a small business can lose revenue unnecessarily if a price is set too low.

Pricing is also important because it indirectly affects sales quantity. In the situations just given, quantity sold was assumed to be independent of price—and it very well may be for a change in price from $3.00 to $2.80. However, a larger decrease or increase might substantially change the quantity sold. Pricing, therefore, has a dual influence on total sales revenue. It is important *directly* as one part of the gross revenue equation and *indirectly* through its impact on quantity demanded.

Before beginning a more detailed analysis of pricing considerations, we need to note that services are more difficult to price than products for at least two reasons:

Retailers must consider the three components of total cost in determining product pricing. Among its selling costs, a sporting goods store would have to factor in the cost of assembling a bicycle.

(1) It is difficult to estimate the cost of providing a service, and (2) since services are intangible, it is difficult to estimate demand. Our discussions will center on product pricing.

Cost Determination for Pricing

In a successful business, pricing must be sufficient to cover total cost plus some profit margin. (Remember the cost-oriented pricing of Pentech International in this chapter's opening.) Pricing, therefore, must be based on an understanding of the basic behavior of costs when production and sales change. **Total cost** includes three components, as illustrated in Figure 14-1. The first is the cost of goods (or services) offered for sale. An appliance retailer, for example, must include in the selling price the cost of the appliance and related freight charges. The second component is the selling cost, which includes the direct cost of the salesperson's time as well as the cost of advertising and sales promotion. The third component is the overhead cost that is applicable to the given product. Included in this cost are such items as warehouse storage, office supplies, utilities, taxes, and salaries. It is important not to overlook these cost classifications in the pricing process.

Costs behave differently as the quantity produced or sold increases or decreases. **Total variable costs** are those that increase as the quantity of product increases.

total cost
the sum of cost of goods sold, selling expenses, and general administrative expenses

total variable costs
costs that vary with the quantity produced or sold

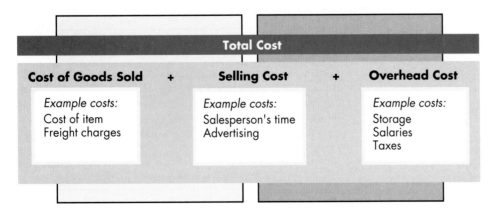

Total Cost		
Cost of Goods Sold +	**Selling Cost** +	**Overhead Cost**
Example costs: Cost of item Freight charges	*Example costs:* Salesperson's time Advertising	*Example costs:* Storage Salaries Taxes

Figure 14-1

The Three Components of Total Cost Are Used in Determining Pricing

total fixed costs
costs that remain constant as the quantity produced or sold varies

average pricing
an approach using average cost as the basis for setting a price

Material costs and sales commissions are typical variable costs that are incurred as a product is made and sold. **Total fixed costs** are those that remain constant at different levels of quantity sold. For example, an advertising campaign expenditure and factory equipment cost are fixed costs.

By understanding the behavior of different kinds of costs, a small business manager can reduce pricing mistakes. If all costs are incorrectly considered to behave in the same way, pricing can be inappropriate. Small businesses often disregard differences between fixed and variable costs and treat them identically for pricing. An approach called **average pricing** follows this dangerous practice. Average pricing divides the total cost over a previous period by the quantity sold in that period to arrive at an average cost, which is then used to set the current price. For example, consider the cost structure of a hypothetical firm selling 25,000 units of a product in 1997 at a sales price of $8.00 each (see Figure 14-2). The average unit cost at the 1997 sales volume of 25,000 units is $5.00 ($125,000 ÷ 25,000). The $3.00 markup provides a satisfactory profit margin at this sales volume.

However, consider the impact on profit if 1998 sales reach only 10,000 units and the selling price has been set at the same $3.00 markup, based on 1997's average cost (see Figure 14-3). At the lower sales volume (10,000 units), the average unit cost has increased to $9.50 ($95,000 ÷ 10,000). This increase is, of course, due to the constant fixed cost being spread over fewer units. Average pricing overlooks the reality of higher average costs at lower sales levels.

In certain circumstances, it may be logical to price at less than total cost as a special short-term strategy. For example, even if part of the production facilities of a business are idle, some fixed costs may be ongoing. In this situation, pricing should cover all marginal or incremental costs—that is, those costs specifically incurred to get additional business. In the long run, however, all costs must be covered.

Figure 14-2

Cost Structure of a Hypothetical Firm, 1997

Sales revenue (25,000 units @ $8)		$200,000
Total costs:		
Fixed costs	$75,000	
Variable costs ($2 per unit)	50,000	
		125,000
Gross margin		$ 75,000

$$\text{Average cost} = \frac{\$125,000}{25,000} = \$5$$

Figure 14-3

Cost Structure of a Hypothetical Firm, 1998

Sales revenue (10,000 units @ $8)		$80,000
Total costs:		
Fixed costs	$75,000	
Variable costs ($2 per unit)	20,000	
		95,000
Gross margin		$(15,000)

$$\text{Average cost} = \frac{\$95,000}{10,000} = \$9.50$$

Demand Factors in Pricing

Cost analysis provides a floor below which a price will not be set for normal purposes. However, it does not indicate by how much the "right" price should exceed that minimum figure. Demand factors must be considered before this can be determined.

THE NATURE OF INDUSTRY DEMAND   The price of a product will partially reflect the sensitivity of industry demand. *Elasticity* is the term used to describe this characteristic of a particular market. The effect that a change in price has on the quantity demanded is called **elasticity of demand.** A product is said to have **elastic demand** if an increase in its price *lowers* total revenue or a decrease in its price *raises* total revenue. A product is said to have **inelastic demand** if an increase in its price *raises* total revenue or a decrease in its price *lowers* total revenue.

In some industries, the demand for products is very elastic. When price is lower, the amount purchased increases considerably, thus providing higher revenue. For example, in the personal computer industry, a decrease in price will frequently produce a more than proportionate increase in quantity sold, resulting in increased revenue. For products such as salt, the demand is usually very inelastic. Regardless of its price, the quantity purchased will not change significantly because consumers use a fixed amount of salt.

The concept of elasticity of demand is important to a small firm because it suggests that inelastic demand within the industry provides an optimum situation for selling the firm's products. The small firm should seek to distinguish its product or service in such a way that small price increases will cause little resistance by customers and thereby result in increasing total revenue.

REFLECTING A FIRM'S COMPETITIVE ADVANTAGE   Several factors affect the demand for a product or service. One factor is the firm's competitive advantage. If consumers perceive the product or service as an important solution to their unsatisfied needs, they will demand more.

Only in rare cases are identical products and services offered by competing firms. In most cases, products are dissimilar in some way. Even if products are similar, the accompanying services typically differ. Speed of service, credit terms, delivery arrangements, personal attention from a salesperson, and willingness to stand behind the product are but a few of the factors that distinguish one product from another. The implications for pricing depend on whether a particular firm is inferior or superior to its competitors in these respects. Certainly, there is no absolute rule that a small business must conform slavishly with the prices of others. A unique combination of goods and services may well justify a higher price.

One pricing tactic that reflects competitive advantage is called prestige pricing. **Prestige pricing** is setting a high price to convey an image of high quality or uniqueness. Its influence varies from market to market and product to product. Higher-income markets are less sensitive to price variations than lower-income ones. Therefore, prestige pricing typically works better in these markets. Also, products sold to markets with low levels of product knowledge are candidates for prestige pricing. When customers know very little about product characteristics, they often use price as an indicator of quality. For example, a company selling windshield-washer fluid found that it could use prestige pricing for its product. The product cost pennies to manufacture and, therefore, could be profitable even if sold at a very low price that included a large markup. However, the firm recognized an opportunity and raised its price repeatedly, making the product extremely profitable.

elasticity of demand
the effect of a change in price on the quantity demanded

elastic demand
demand that changes significantly when there is a change in the price of a product

inelastic demand
demand that does not significantly change when there is a change in the price of a product

prestige pricing
setting a high price to convey the image of high quality or uniqueness

 *Action Report*

ENTREPRENEURIAL EXPERIENCES

Prestige Pricing

Sometimes entrepreneurs can successfully price a product well above cost because of its unique nature. Such is the case for Charles Bennett, of Branford, Connecticut, who sells Zymöl car wax.

Bennett and his wife, Donna, an analyst at a pharmaceutical company, adapted a homemade wax formula they discovered while vacationing in Germany. By experimenting with their electric coffeepot as a vat, they eventually decided on the Zymöl ingredients. An 8-ounce jar of the wax was originally priced at $19.95 but was later increased to $40!

> It takes a certain amount of brass to ask $40 for an 8-ounce jar of wax good for a dozen wax jobs. A 9.5-ounce can of Turtle Wax, by comparison, sells for about $7.50. Add to Bennett's basic 8-ounce jar some car cleaners and a towel and you've got a Zymöl starter kit, priced at $100. At the higher end, there's Zymöl Concours at $150 per 8-ounce jar, and Zymöl Destiny, priced at $450.

Does Bennett's wax create a winning shine? Ask the six winners at the 1990 Pebble Beach Car Show, whose cars were all shined with Zymöl.

Source: Jerry Flint, "Fruit Salad Car Wax," *Forbes*, Vol. 149, No. 9 (April 27, 1992), pp. 126–129. Reprinted By Permission of *FORBES* magazine © Forbes Inc., 1992.

Another dramatic example of pricing based on competitive advantage is found in the microwave popcorn market. In this market, niche customers are willing to pay a premium price for the convenience of microwave packaging—up to six times the price of conventional popcorn.[1]

---

2 Apply break-even analysis to pricing.

USING BREAK-EVEN ANALYSIS FOR PRICING

Break-even analysis entails a comparison of cost and demand estimates in order to determine the acceptability of alternative prices. Break-even analysis is typically explained by using formulas or graphs; we use a graphic presentation in this chapter. There are two steps in a comprehensive break-even analysis: (1) Examine revenue-costs relationships, and (2) incorporate sales forecasts into the analysis.

Examining Costs and Revenue

The objective of the first phase of break-even analysis is to determine the quantity at which the product, at an assumed price, will generate enough revenue to start earning a profit. Figure 14-4(a) presents a simple break-even chart reflecting this comparison. Total fixed costs are portrayed as a horizontal section, showing that they do not change with the volume of production. The variable-costs section slants upward, however, depicting the direct relationship of total variable costs to output.

Break-Even Charts for Pricing   Figure 14-4

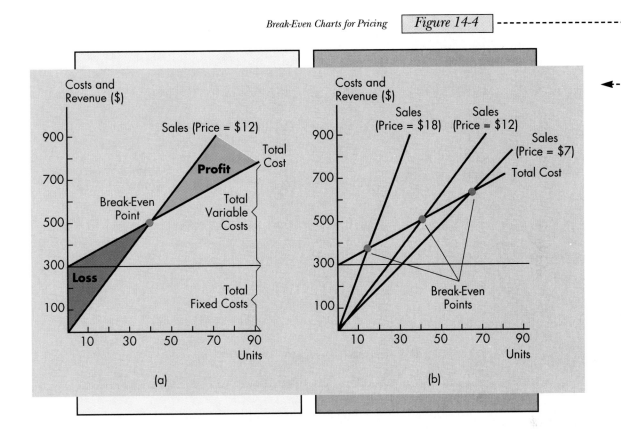

The area between the slanting total cost line and the horizontal base line thus represents the combination of fixed and variable costs. The shaded areas between the sales and total cost lines reveal the profit or loss position of the company at any level of sales. The point of intersection of these two lines is called the *break-even point*, because sales revenue equals total cost at this sales volume.

Additional sales lines at other prices can be charted to evaluate other break-even points. Such a flexible break-even chart is shown in Figure 14-4(b). The assumed higher price of $18 in Figure 14-4(b) yields a more steeply sloped sales line, resulting in an earlier break-even point. Similarly, the lower price of $7 produces a flatter revenue line, delaying the break-even point. Additional sales lines could be plotted to evaluate other proposed prices.

The break-even chart implies that quantity sold can increase continually (as shown by the larger and larger profit area to the right). This is misleading and should be clarified by adjusting the break-even analysis with demand data.

Adding Sales Forecasts

The indirect impact of price on quantity sold complicates pricing decisions. As noted earlier, demand for a product typically decreases as price increases. However, in exceptional cases, price may influence demand in the opposite direction, resulting in more demand for a product at higher prices. The estimated demand for a product at various prices needs to be incorporated into the break-even analysis. Marketing research can be used to estimate demand at various prices.

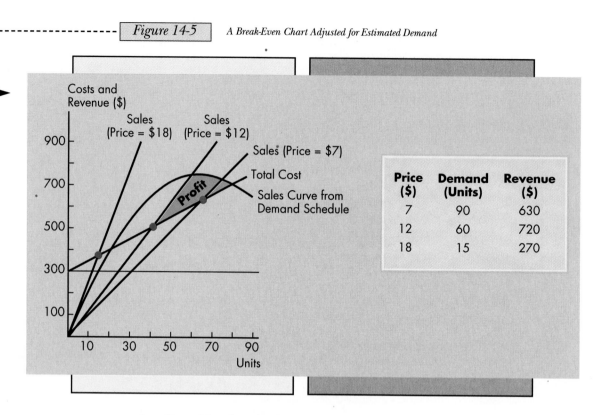

Figure 14-5   *A Break-Even Chart Adjusted for Estimated Demand*

Price ($)	Demand (Units)	Revenue ($)
7	90	630
12	60	720
18	15	270

An adjusted break-even chart that incorporates estimated demand is developed by using the initial break-even data and adding a demand curve. A demand schedule showing the estimated number of units demanded and total revenue at three prices is shown in Figure 14-5, along with a break-even chart on which the demand curve from these data is plotted. This graph allows a more realistic profit area to be identified. The break-even point in Figure 14-5 for a unit price of $18 corresponds to a quantity sold that appears impossible to reach at the assumed price, leaving $7 and $12 as feasible prices. Clearly, the optimum of these two prices is $12. The potential at this price is indicated by the profit area in the graph.

Markup Pricing

Up to this point, we have made no distinction between pricing by manufacturers and pricing by intermediaries—wholesalers and retailers. Since break-even concepts apply to all small businesses, regardless of their position in the distribution channel, such a distinction wasn't necessary. Now, however, we briefly present some of the pricing formulas used by the intermediaries. In the retailing industry, for example, where businesses often carry many products, markup pricing has emerged as a manageable pricing system. With this cost-plus approach to pricing, retailers are able to price hundreds of products much more quickly than they could with a system involving individual break-even analyses. In calculating the selling price for a particular item, a retailer adds a markup percentage to cover the following:

- Operating expenses
- Subsequent price reductions—for example, markdowns and employee discounts
- Profit

Markups may be expressed as a percentage of either the *selling price* or the *cost.* For example, if an item costs $6 and sells at $10, the markup of $4 represents 40 percent of the selling price [$4 (markup) ÷ $10 (selling price) × 100] or 66⅔ percent of the cost [$4 (markup) ÷ $6 (cost) × 100]. Here are the simple formulas used for markup calculations:

$$\text{Cost} + \text{Markup} = \text{Selling price}$$

$$\text{Cost} = \text{Selling price} - \text{Markup}$$

$$\text{Markup} = \text{Selling price} - \text{Cost}$$

$$\frac{\text{Markup}}{\text{Selling price}} \times 100 = \text{Markup expressed as a percentage of selling price}$$

$$\frac{\text{Markup}}{\text{Cost}} \times 100 = \text{Markup expressed as a percentage of cost}$$

If a seller wishes to convert markup as a percentage of selling price into a percentage of cost, or vice versa, the two formulas below are useful:

$$\frac{\text{Markup as a percentage of selling price}}{100\% - \text{Markup as a percentage of selling price}} \times 100 = \frac{\text{Markup as a}}{\text{percentage of cost}}$$

$$\frac{\text{Markup as a percentage of cost}}{100\% + \text{Markup as a percentage of cost}} \times 100 = \frac{\text{Markup as a percentage}}{\text{of selling price}}$$

SELECTING A PRICING STRATEGY

3 Identify specific pricing strategies.

Consideration of cost and demand data within a break-even analysis should create a better understanding of which prices are feasible for a specific product. The seemingly precise nature of break-even analysis, however, is potentially misleading for the small business manager. Such analysis is only one tool for pricing and does not by itself identify the most appropriate price. In other words, price determination must include consideration of market characteristics and the firm's current marketing strategy. We now describe several examples of pricing strategies that reflect these additional considerations.[2]

Penetration Pricing

A firm that uses a **penetration pricing strategy** prices a product or service lower than its normal, long-range market price in order to gain more rapid market acceptance or to increase existing market share. This strategy can sometimes discourage new competitors from entering a market niche if they mistakenly view the penetration price as a long-range price. Obviously, this strategy sacrifices some profit margin to achieve market penetration.

Skimming Pricing

A **skimming price strategy** sets prices for products or services at high levels for a limited period of time before reducing the price to a lower, more competitive level. This strategy assumes that certain customers will pay a higher price because they

penetration pricing strategy
a marketing approach that sets lower than normal prices to hasten market acceptance or to increase market share

skimming price strategy
a marketing approach that sets very high prices for a limited period before reducing them to more competitive levels

view a product or service as a prestige item. Use of a skimming price is most practical when there is little threat of short-term competition or when startup costs must be recovered rapidly.

Follow-the-Leader Pricing

A **follow-the-leader pricing strategy** sets a price for a product or service using a particular competitor as a model. The probable reaction of competitors is a critical factor in determining whether to cut prices below a prevailing level. A small business in competition with larger firms is seldom in a position to consider itself the price leader. If competitors view a small firm's pricing as relatively unimportant, they may permit a price differential to exist. On the other hand, some competitors may view a smaller price-cutter as a direct threat and counter with reductions of their own. In such a case, the small firm accomplishes very little.

Variable Pricing

Some businesses use a **variable pricing strategy** to offer price concessions to certain customers, even though they may advertise a uniform price. Concessions are made for various reasons, one of which is the customer's knowledge and bargaining strength. In some fields of business, therefore, pricing decisions involve two parts: setting a standard list price and offering a range of price concessions to particular buyers.

Flexible Pricing

Although many firms use total cost as the basis for their pricing decisions, a **flexible pricing strategy** takes into consideration special market conditions and the pricing practices of competitors. The following illustrates this point:

> The owner of a high-speed ferry service always charged $10 for a round-trip ticket between any two destinations. But the ferry was losing money due to low ridership during off-peak hours. The owner decided to differentiate her prices depending on the time of day, the type of rider and the competing modes of transportation in each of the ferry's destinations, such as cars, buses and commuter trains.
>
> She raised her round-trip price to an average of $12 during commuter and weekend hours—the ferry's busiest times. . . . For frequent users who couldn't afford the higher rate, she sold monthly passes that resulted in a round-trip price of less than $10. Off-peak riders, however, tended to view the ferry as homogeneous—a convenient way to get from one place to another. Thus, the owner lowered the price to an average of $8 during off-peak hours. As a result, ridership and revenues rose considerably and an annual loss became an annual profit.[3]

Price Lining

A **price lining strategy** determines several distinct prices at which similar items of retail merchandise are offered for sale. For example, men's suits (of differing quality) might be sold at $250, $300, and $600. The inventory level of the different lines depends on the income level and buying desires of a store's customers. A price lining strategy has the advantage of simplifying choice for the customer and reducing the necessary minimum inventory.

Action Report

ENTREPRENEURIAL EXPERIENCES

Pricing for the Season

Products that are subject to seasonal sales fluctuations present special production and pricing challenges. Alan Trusler, president of Aladdin Steel Products, in Colville, Washington, faced such a challenge—sales of his wood-burning stove predictably cooled off toward the end of winter's snowstorms. Trusler extended his selling season by offering his 350 dealers "discounts for the entire year if they stock stoves in the off-peak months—March through July, [and cash discounts] for buying early—8% off each invoice in March, 7% in April, 6% in May, on down." Aladdin grew over 400 percent from 1987 to 1991, and production began to run year-round.

Source: Susan Greco, "Rx for a Short Sales Season," *Inc.*, Vol. 14, No. 10 (October 1992), p. 29. Reprinted with permission, *Inc.* magazine, October 1992. Copyright 1992 by Goldhirsh Group, Inc., 38 Commercial Wharf, Boston, MA 02110.

What the Traffic Will Bear

The strategy of pricing on the basis of what the traffic will bear can be used only when the seller has little or no competition. Obviously, this strategy will work only for nonstandardized products or for situations in which competition is limited. For example, a food store might offer egg roll wrappers that its competitors do not carry. Busy consumers who want to fix egg rolls but have neither the time nor the knowledge to prepare the wrappers themselves will buy them at any reasonable price.

A Final Note on Pricing Strategies

In some situations, local, state, and federal laws must also be considered in setting prices. For example, the Sherman Antitrust Act generally prohibits price fixing. Most federal pricing legislation is intended to benefit small firms as well as consumers by keeping large businesses from conspiring to set prices that stifle competition.

If a small business markets a line of products—some of which may compete with each other—pricing decisions must consider the effects of a single product price on the rest of the line. For example, the introduction of a cheese-flavored chip will likely impact sales of an existing naturally flavored chip. Pricing can become extremely complex in these situations.

Constantly adjusting a price to meet changing marketing conditions can be both costly to the seller and confusing to buyers. An alternative approach is to make adjustments to the stated price and offer special price quotes. This can be achieved with a system of discounting designed to reflect a variety of needs. For example, a seller may offer a trade discount to a buyer (such as a wholesaler) because that buyer performs a certain marketing function for the seller (such as distribution). The stated, or list, price is unchanged, but the seller offers a lower actual price by means of a discount.

Pricing mistakes are not the exclusive domain of small businesses; large firms also make pricing errors. Remember that pricing is not an exact science. If the initial price appears to be off target, just make any necessary adjustment and keep going!

Discuss the benefits of credit, the factors that affect credit extension, and the kinds of credit.

4

OFFERING CREDIT

In a credit sale, the seller conveys goods or services to the buyer in return for the buyer's promise to pay. The major objective of granting credit is an expansion of sales—by attracting new customers and by increasing the volume and regularity of purchases by existing customers. Some retail firms—furniture stores, for example—invite the credit business of individuals who have established credit ratings. Credit records may be used for purposes of sales promotion through direct-mail appeals to credit customers. Adjustments and exchanges of goods are also facilitated through credit operations.

Benefits of Credit

If credit buying and selling did not benefit both parties to the transaction, their use would cease. Buyers obviously enjoy the availability of credit, and small firms, in particular, benefit from the extension of credit by their suppliers. Credit extended by suppliers provides small firms with working capital, often permitting the continuation of marginal businesses that might otherwise expire. There are additional benefits of credit to buyers:

- The ability to satisfy immediate needs and pay for them later
- Better records of purchases on credit billing statements
- Better service and greater convenience when exchanging purchased items
- Establishment of a credit history

Sellers extend credit to customers to obtain increased sales volume. Sellers expect the increased revenue to more than offset the costs of extending credit, so profits will increase. Other benefits of credit to sellers are as follows:

- Closer association with customers because of implied trust
- Easier selling through telephone and mail-order systems
- Smoother sales peaks and valleys, since purchasing power is always available
- Provision of a tool with which to stay competitive

Factors That Affect the Decision to Sell on Credit

An entrepreneur must decide whether to sell on credit or for cash only. In some cases, this decision is reduced to the question "Can the granting of credit to customers be avoided?" Credit selling is standard trade practice for many types of business; in other businesses, credit-selling competitors will always outsell a cash-selling firm.

Numerous factors bear on an entrepreneur's decision concerning credit extension. The seller always hopes to increase profits by allowing credit sales but must also consider the particular circumstances and environment of the firm.

TYPE OF BUSINESS Retailers of durable goods, for example, typically grant credit more freely than do small grocers who sell perishables. Indeed, most consumers find it necessary to buy big-ticket items on an installment basis, and such a product's life span makes installment selling possible.

CREDIT POLICY OF COMPETITORS Unless a firm offers some compensating advantage, it is expected to be as generous as its competitors in extending credit. Wholesale hardware companies and retail furniture stores are businesses that face stiff competition from credit sellers.

INCOME LEVEL OF CUSTOMERS   The income level of its customers is a significant factor in determining a retailer's credit policy. For example, a drugstore that is adjacent to a city high school would probably not extend credit to high school students, who are typically unsatisfactory credit customers because of their lack of maturity and income.

AVAILABILITY OF WORKING CAPITAL   There is no denying the fact that credit sales increase the amount of working capital needed by the business doing the selling. Open-credit and installment accounts tie up money that may be needed to pay business expenses.

Kinds of Credit

There are two broad classes of credit: consumer credit and trade credit. **Consumer credit** is granted by retailers to final consumers who purchase for personal or family use. However, a small business owner can sometimes use consumer credit to purchase certain supplies and equipment for use in the business. **Trade credit** is extended by nonfinancial firms, such as manufacturers and wholesalers, to customers that are other business firms. Consumer credit and trade credit differ with respect to types of credit instruments used, sources for financing receivables, and terms of sale. Another important distinction is that credit insurance is available for trade credit only.

CONSUMER CREDIT   The three major kinds of consumer credit accounts are open charge accounts, installment accounts, and revolving charge accounts. Many variations of these are also used.

Open Charge Accounts   When using an **open charge account,** a customer obtains possession of goods (or services) at the time of purchase, with payment due when billed. Stated terms typically call for payment at the end of the month, but customary practice allows a longer period for payment than that stated. There is no finance charge for this kind of credit if the balance of the account is paid in full at the end of the period. Customers are not generally required to make a down payment or a pledge of collateral. Small accounts at department stores are good examples of open charge accounts.

Installment Accounts   An **installment account** is a vehicle of long-term consumer credit. A down payment is normally required, and annual finance charges can be 20 percent or more of the purchase price. The most common payment periods are from 12 to 36 months, although automobile dealers often offer an extended payment period of 60 months. An installment account is useful for large purchases such as cars, washing machines, and TV sets.

Revolving Charge Accounts   A **revolving charge account** is a variation of the installment account. A seller grants a customer a line

consumer credit
credit granted by retailers to individuals who purchase for personal or family use

trade credit
financing provided by a supplier of inventory to a given company, which sets up an account payable for the amount

open charge account
a line of credit that allows the customer to obtain a product at the time of purchase, with payment due when billed

installment account
a line of credit that requires a down payment with the balance paid over a specified period of time

Selling on credit is standard practice for many types of businesses. Retail furniture stores that offer credit to their customers realize greater sales revenue than firms that make cash sales only.

Table 14-1

Commonly Used Trade Credit Terms

Credit Term	Explanation
3/10, net 60	Three percent discount if payment is made within the first 10 days; net (full amount) due by sixtieth day from invoice date
E.O.M.	Billing at end of month, covering all credit purchases during that month
C.O.D.	Amount due is to be collected upon delivery of the goods
2/10, net 30, R.O.G.	Two percent discount if payment is made within 10 days; net due by thirtieth day—however, both discount period and 30 days start from the date of receipt of the goods
2/10, net 30, E.O.M.	Two percent discount if payment is made within 10 days; net due by thirtieth day—however, both periods start from the end of the month in which the sale was made

revolving charge account
a line of credit on which the customer may charge purchases at any time, up to a pre-established limit

of credit and charged purchases may not exceed the credit limit. A specified percentage of the outstanding balance must be paid monthly, forcing the customer to budget and limiting the amount of debt that can be carried. Finance charges are computed on the unpaid balance at the end of the month. Credit cards offer this type of account. Because of their significance, credit cards are discussed in a separate section (see below).

TRADE CREDIT   Business firms may sell goods subject to specified terms of sale, such as 2/10, net 30. This means that a 2 percent discount is given by the seller if the buyer pays within 10 days of the invoice date. Failure to take this discount makes the full amount of the invoice due in 30 days. For example, with these terms, paying for a $100,000 purchase within 10 days of the invoice date would save 2 percent, or $2,000. Trade credit terms in common use are explained in Table 14-1.

Sales terms for trade credit depend on the kind of product sold and the buyer's and the seller's circumstances. The credit period often varies directly with the length of the buyer's turnover period, which obviously depends on the type of product sold. The larger the order and the higher the credit rating of the buyer, the better the sales terms will be, assuming that individual terms are fixed for each buyer. The greater the financial strength and the more adequate and liquid the working capital of the seller, the more generous the seller's sales terms can be. Of course, no business can afford to allow competitors to outdo it in reasonable generosity of sales terms. In many types of business, terms are so firmly set by tradition that a unique policy is difficult, if not impossible, for a small firm to implement.

CREDIT CARDS   Credit cards, sometimes referred to as *plastic money*, have become a major source of retail credit. As mentioned earlier, credit cards are usually based on a revolving charge account system. There are three basic types of credit cards, distinguished by their sponsor: bank credit cards, entertainment credit cards, and retailer credit cards.

Bank Credit Cards   The best-known bank credit cards are MasterCard and VISA. Figure 14-6 shows a credit card agreement issued by a credit union through a bank. Bank credit cards are widely accepted by retailers who want to offer credit but don't provide their own credit cards. Most small business retailers fit into this category. In return for a set fee (usually 2 to 5 percent of the purchase price) paid by the retailer, the bank takes the responsibility for making collections. Some banks charge annual membership fees to their cardholders. Also, cardholders are frequently able to receive cash up to the credit limit of their card.

Credit Card Agreement | Figure 14-6

LINE OF CREDIT (CREDIT CARD) AGREEMENT

_____ Credit Union

Address _____ , Texas
Street   City   Zip   County

BORROWER(S) _____ Account Number: _____

TERMS USED IN THIS AGREEMENT: "You" and "your" mean any person who signs this Agreement or uses the card. "The card" means any credit card issued to you or those designated by you under the terms of this Agreement. "Use of the card" means any procedure used by you, or someone authorized by you, to make a purchase or obtain a cash advance whether or not the purchase or advance is evidenced by a signed written document. "Unauthorized use of the card" means the use of the card by someone other than you who does not have actual, implied, or apparent authority for such use, and from which you receive no benefit.

EXTENSIONS OF CREDIT: If your application is approved, the Credit Union may, at its discretion, establish a MasterCard and/or VISA Card account in your name and cause one or more cards to be issued to you or those designated by you. In such an event, you authorize the Credit Union to pay for your account, all items reflecting credit purchases and cash advances obtained through use of the card.

CREDIT LIMITS: You promise that payments made for your account resulting from use of the card will, at no time, cause the outstanding balance in your account to exceed your credit limit as disclosed to you at the time you receive your card or as adjusted from time to time at the discretion of the credit union.

PROMISE TO PAY: You promise to repay the Credit Union all payments made for your account resulting from use of the card plus a **FINANCE CHARGE** on the unpaid balance. At the end of each monthly billing cycle, you will be furnished with a periodic statement showing (i) the "previous balance" (the outstanding balance in the account at the beginning of the billing cycle), (ii) the amount of all cash advances, purchases and **FINANCE CHARGES** posted to your account during the billing cycle, (iii) the amount of all payments and credits posted to your account during the billing cycle, and (iv) the "new balance" which is the sum of (i) and (ii) less (iii).

You agree to pay on or before the "payment due date" shown on the periodic statement either the entire "new balance" or a minimum payment equal to 5% of the "new balance," or $18.00, whichever is greater. If the "new balance" is $18.00 or less, you will pay in full.

COST OF CREDIT: You will pay a **FINANCE CHARGE** for all advances made against your account at the periodic rate of .049315% per day, which has a corresponding **ANNUAL PERCENTAGE RATE** of 18%. Cash advances incur a **FINANCE CHARGE** from the date they are posted to the account. New purchases will not incur a **FINANCE CHARGE** on the date they are posted to the account if you have paid the account in full by the due date shown on your previous monthly statement or if there was no previous balance. No additional **FINANCE CHARGE** will be incurred whenever you pay the account in full by the due date. The **FINANCE CHARGE** is figured by applying the periodic rate to the Balance Subject to **FINANCE CHARGE** which is the "average daily balance" of your account, including certain current transactions. The "average daily balance" is arrived at by taking the beginning balance of your account each day and adding any new cash advances, and, unless you pay your account in full by the due date shown on your previous monthly statement or there is no previous balance, adding in new purchases, and subtracting any payments or credits and unpaid **FINANCE CHARGES.** The daily balances for the billing cycle are then added together and divided by the number of days in the billing cycle. The result is the "average daily balance." Each **FINANCE CHARGE** is determined by multiplying the "average daily balance" by the number of days in the billing cycle and applying the periodic rates to the product. You may pay any amounts outstanding at any time without penalty for early payment.

CREDIT INSURANCE: If available, credit insurance is not required for any extension of credit under this Agreement. However, you may purchase any credit insurance available through the credit union and have the premium added to the outstanding balance in your account. If you elect to do so, you will be given the necessary disclosures and documents separately.

LIABILITY FOR UNAUTHORIZED USE: You may be liable for the unauthorized use of your card. You will not be liable for unauthorized use that occurs after you notify the Credit Union (or Credit Union's designee) orally or in writing, of the loss, theft, or possible unauthorized use. In any case, your liability will not exceed $50.00.

Action Report

TECHNOLOGICAL APPLICATIONS

TECHNOLOGY

Technology and Credit

Technology has an impact on many activities of small businesses, including the manner in which they manage financial transactions with customers. For example, banks are working with small businesses to develop point-of-sale systems for debiting customers, allowing small firms to better compete with larger ones.

> *Small businesses like White's of Florida have applied technology to the point of sale by making arrangements with banks that enable [its] stores to accept debit cards along with the traditional charge and revolving credit cards. . . . In a debit-card transaction the amount of the sale is deducted directly from the customer's checking account at the time of the purchase.*

Debbie White, who manages White's six-store chain, believes this system can provide the company with several benefits, "particularly the guarantee of payment."

Source: Joan C. Szabo, "The Changing World of Financial Services," *Nation's Business*, Vol. 82, No. 10 (October 1994), p. 24.

Entertainment Credit Cards   Well-known examples of entertainment credit cards are American Express and Diner's Club cards. These cards have traditionally charged an annual fee. Although originally used for services, these cards are now widely accepted for sales of merchandise. Just like bank credit cards, the collection of charges on an entertainment credit card is the responsibility of the sponsoring agency.

Retail Credit Cards   Many companies—for example, department stores, oil companies, and telephone companies—issue their own credit cards for specific use in their outlets or for purchasing their products or services from other outlets. Customers are usually not charged annual fees or finance charges if balances are paid each month.

---

5   Describe the activities involved in managing credit.

MANAGING THE CREDIT PROCESS

Unfortunately, many small firms pay little attention to their credit management systems until bad debts become a problem. Often this is too late. Credit management should precede the first credit sale (in the form of a thorough screening process) and then continue throughout the credit cycle. A comprehensive credit management program for a small business is discussed in the following sections.

Evaluating the Credit Status of Applicants

In most retail stores, the first step in credit investigation is having the customer complete an application form. The information obtained on this form is used as the basis for examining an applicant's creditworthiness. Perhaps the most important factor in determining a customer's credit limit is the customer's ability to pay the obligation when it becomes due. This requires an evaluation of the customer's financial resources, debt position, and income level. The amount of credit requested requires careful consideration. Drugstore customers need only small amounts of credit. On the other hand, business customers of wholesalers and manufacturers typically expect larger credit lines. In the special case of installment selling, the amount of credit should not exceed the repossession value of the goods sold. Automobile dealers follow this rule as a general practice.

THE FOUR CREDIT QUESTIONS   In evaluating the credit status of applicants, a seller must answer the following questions:

1. Can the buyer pay as promised?
2. Will the buyer pay?
3. If so, when will the buyer pay?
4. If not, can the buyer be forced to pay?

For credit to be approved, the answers to questions 1, 2, and 4 should be "yes" and the answer to question 3 should be "on schedule." The answers have to be based in part on the seller's estimate of the buyer's ability and willingness to pay. Such an estimate constitutes a judgment of the buyer's inherent creditworthiness.

Every applicant possesses creditworthiness in some degree, and extension of credit should not constitute a gift to the applicant. Instead, a decision to grant credit merely recognizes the buyer's credit standing. But the seller faces a possible inability or unwillingness to pay on the buyer's part. When evaluating an applicant's credit status, therefore, the seller must decide the degree of risk of nonpayment to assume.

THE FOUR C'S OF CREDIT   Willingness to pay is evaluated in terms of the four C's of credit: character, capital, capacity, and conditions.[4]

- *Character* refers to the fundamental integrity and honesty that should underlie all human and business relationships. For customers that are businesses, character is embodied in the business policies and ethical practices of the firm. Individual customers who are granted credit must be known to be morally responsible persons.
- *Capital* consists of the cash and other assets owned by the business or individual customer. A prospective business customer should have sufficient capital to underwrite planned operations, including an appropriate amount invested by the owner.
- *Capacity* refers to the customer's ability to conserve assets and faithfully and efficiently follow financial plans. A business customer should utilize its invested capital wisely and capitalize to the fullest extent on business opportunities.
- *Conditions* refer to such factors as business cycles and changes in price levels, which may be either favorable or unfavorable to the payment of debts. For example, the economic recession of the early 1990s placed a strong burden on both businesses' and consumers' abilities to pay their debts. Other adverse factors that might limit a customer's ability to pay include fires and other natural disasters, strong new competition, or labor problems.

Sources of Credit Information

One of the most important, and frequently neglected, sources of credit information is found in a customer's previous credit history. Properly analyzed, these records show whether the customer regularly takes cash discounts and, if not, whether the customer's account is typically slow. One small clothing manufacturer has every applicant reviewed by a Dun & Bradstreet–trained credit manager, who maintains a complete file of D&B credit reports on thousands of customers. Recent financial statements of customers are also on file. These reports, together with the retailer's own credit information, are the basis for decisions on credit sales, with heavy emphasis on the D&B credit reports. Nonretailing firms should similarly investigate credit applicants.

Manufacturers and wholesalers can frequently use a firm's financial statements as an additional source of information. Obtaining maximum value from financial statements requires a careful ratio analysis, which will reveal a firm's working-capital position, profit-making potential, and general financial health (as discussed in Chapter 22).

Pertinent data may also be obtained from outsiders. For example, arrangements may be made with other sellers to exchange credit data. Such credit information exchanges are quite useful to a seller for learning about the sales and payment experiences others have had with the seller's own customers or credit applicants.

Another source of credit information, particularly about commercial accounts, is the customer's banker. Some bankers are glad to supply credit information about their depositors, considering this to be a service that helps those firms or individuals obtain credit in amounts they can successfully handle. Other bankers feel that credit information is confidential and should not be disclosed in this way.

Organizations that may be consulted with reference to credit standings are trade-credit agencies and local credit bureaus. **Trade-credit agencies** are privately owned and operated organizations that collect credit information on businesses only, not individual consumers. After analyzing and evaluating the data, trade-credit agencies make credit ratings available to client companies for a fee. Dun & Bradstreet, Inc. is a nationwide, general trade-credit agency. Figure 14-7 shows a credit summary provided by its Small Business Services. Manufacturers and wholesalers are especially interested in Dun & Bradstreet's reference book and credit reports. Available to subscribers only, this reference book covers all U.S. businesses and provides a credit rating, an evaluation of financial strength, and other key credit information.

A **credit bureau** serves its members—retailers and other firms in a given community—by summarizing their credit experience with particular individuals. A local bureau can also broaden its service by affiliating with either the National Retail Credit Association or the Associated Credit Bureaus of America. These organizations make possible the exchange of credit information on persons who move from one city to another. Some bureaus do not require a business firm to be a member in order to get a credit report. The fee charged to nonmembers, however, is considerably higher than that charged to members. There are well over 1,000 automated credit bureaus, many of which are owned by either a private, independent party or a merchant association. Most credit bureaus operate on one of the three on-line data-processing networks: TRW, Inc. or Equifax, Inc. or Trans Union Credit Information Co. "The mission of the consumer reporting industry is to serve as an objective third-party provider of information to the companies and consumers involved in credit transactions," notes Walter R. Kurth, president of Associated Credit Bureaus.[5]

Aging of Accounts Receivable

Many small businesses can benefit from an **aging schedule,** which divides accounts receivable into age categories based on the length of time they have been outstanding. Typically, some accounts are current and others are past due. Regular use of an aging schedule allows troublesome trends to be spotted so that appropriate

---

trade-credit agencies
privately owned organizations that collect credit information on businesses

credit bureau
an organization that summarizes a number of firms' credit experiences with particular individuals

aging schedule
a categorization of accounts receivable based on the length of time they have been outstanding

Dun & Bradstreet's Credit Recommendation Summary | Figure 14-7 |

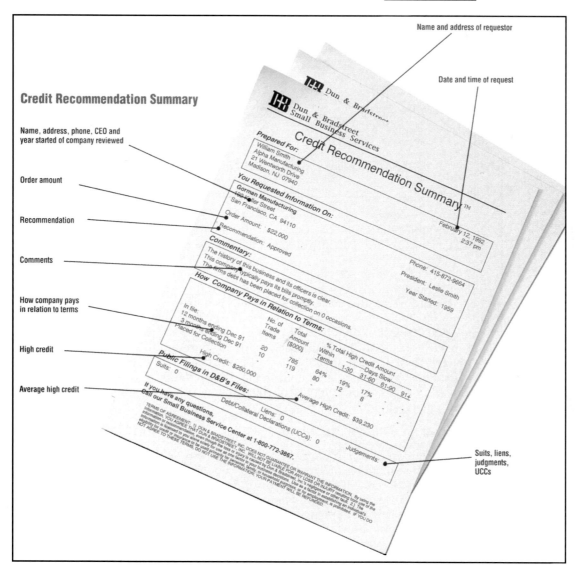

Source: Dun & Bradstreet, *Small Business Services Catalog*, p. 7. Copyright 1993 Dun & Bradstreet, Inc. All Rights Reserved. Reprinted with Permission.

actions can be taken. With experience, the probabilities of collecting accounts of various ages can be estimated and used to forecast cash conversion rates.

Figure 14-8 presents a hypothetical aging schedule for accounts receivable. According to the schedule, four customers have overdue credit, totaling $200,000. Only customer 005 is current. Customer 003 has the largest amount of overdue credit ($80,000). In fact, the schedule shows that customer 003 is overdue on all charges and has a past record of slow payment (indicated by the credit rating C). Immediate attention must be given to collecting from this customer. Customer 002 also should be contacted, because, among overdue accounts, this customer has the largest amount ($110,000) in the "Not Due" classification. Customer 002 could quickly have the largest amount overdue.

Figure 14-8

Hypothetical Aging Schedule for Accounts Receivable

	Customer Account Number					
Account status	001	002	003	004	005	Total
Days past due						
120 days	—	—	$50,000	—	—	$ 50,000
90 days	—	$ 10,000	—	—	—	10,000
60 days	—	—	—	$40,000	—	40,000
30 days	—	20,000	20,000	—	—	40,000
15 days	$50,000	—	10,000	—	—	60,000
Total overdue	$50,000	$ 30,000	$80,000	$40,000	$ 0	$200,000
Not due (beyond-discount period)	$30,000	$ 10,000	$ 0	$10,000	$130,000	$180,000
Not due (still in discount period)	$20,000	$100,000	$ 0	$90,000	$220,000	$430,000
Credit rating	A	B	C	A	A	—

Customers 001 and 004 require a special kind of analysis. Customer 001 has $10,000 more overdue than customer 004. However, customer 004's overdue credit of $40,000, which is 60 days past due, may well have a serious impact on the $100,000 not yet due ($10,000 in the beyond-discount period plus $90,000 still in the discount period). On the other hand, even though customer 001 has $50,000 of overdue credit, this customer's payment is only overdue by 15 days. Also, customer 001 has only $50,000 not yet due ($30,000 in the beyond-discount period plus $20,000 still in the discount period), compared to the $100,000 not yet due from customer 004. Both customers have an A credit rating. In conclusion, customer 001 is a better potential source of cash. Therefore, collection efforts should be focused on customer 004 rather than on customer 001, who may simply need a reminder of the overdue amount of $50,000.

Billing and Collection Procedures

Timely notification of customers regarding the status of their accounts is one of the most effective methods of keeping credit accounts current. Most credit customers pay their bills on time if the creditor provides them with the necessary information to verify their credit balance. Failure on the seller's part to send the correct invoices only delays timely payments. "The cornerstone of collecting accounts receivable on time is making sure you invoice your customers or send them their periodic billing statements promptly," says Robert M. Littman, a partner in the accounting firm of Saltz, Shamis & Goldfarb, Inc., in Akron, Ohio. "Keep a good pulse on the billing activity—the sooner you mail your invoice, the sooner the check will be in the mail."[6]

Overdue credit accounts are a problem because they tie up a seller's working capital, prevent further sales to the slow-paying customer, and lead to losses from bad debts. Even if a slow-paying customer is not lost, relations with this customer are strained for a time at least.

A firm extending credit must have adequate records and collection procedures if it expects prompt payments. Also, a personal acquaintance between seller and customer must not be allowed to tempt the seller to be less than businesslike in extending further credit and collecting overdue amounts. Given the seriousness of the problem, a small firm must know what steps to take and how far to go in collecting past-due accounts. It must decide whether to undertake the job directly or to turn it over to an attorney or a collection agency.

Perhaps the most effective weapon in collecting past-due accounts is the debtors' knowledge that their credit standing may be impaired. This impairment is

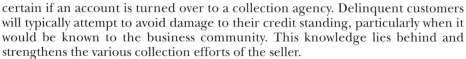

GLOBAL OPPORTUNITIES

Collecting from Overseas Customers

More and more small firms are selling to overseas markets. While getting cash up-front may be the ideal way to receive payment, it does not give many foreign customers the payment flexibility they want. Small firms that sell to foreign customers need some assurance that those customers will pay their bills if credit is extended. However, getting payments from overseas is somewhat complicated. The seller must therefore gather information on the various techniques for financing overseas sales.

Susan Corrales-Diaz, whose Orange, California company, Systems Integrated, began exporting six years ago, knew nothing about collecting overseas accounts until she was forced to learn. To educate herself, Corrales-Diaz began attending seminars and reading books. She learned about a "whole rainbow assortment of ways to get paid."

Source: Cynthia E. Griffin, "Foreign Exchange," *Entrepreneur*, Vol. 22, No. 10 (October 1994), pp. 58–60. Reprinted with permission from *Entrepreneur* Magazine, October 1994.

certain if an account is turned over to a collection agency. Delinquent customers will typically attempt to avoid damage to their credit standing, particularly when it would be known to the business community. This knowledge lies behind and strengthens the various collection efforts of the seller.

A small firm should deal compassionately with delinquent customers. A collection technique that is too threatening may not only fail to work but could also lose a customer or invite legal action. Consider the variety of collection philosophies and tactics shown in the following examples:

"I absolutely guarantee that I can outcollect the goons by being nice," declares Linda Russell, chief executive officer of CollectionCenter, Inc., of Rawlins, Wyoming. The 55-year-old grandmother of five says courtesy has always worked better. . . . The No. 1 rule: Never lose your cool. If a debtor launches into an X-rated rage . . . let him "vent" his frustrations and then say, "I understand how you feel. Let's talk about how we can solve the problem."[7]

Richard Ackerman, president of Credit Resolution Corp. of New York, deals mostly with commercial debtors. . . . Most are "honorable" . . . [but he] doesn't hesitate to turn the screws on those who aren't. . . . He pays 18 "operatives"—most of them beefy former security guards or policemen—to deliver notices.[8]

At Decoma Industries . . . the Vernon, California architectural firm . . . a red dot goes up next to the names of late-paying customers . . . says president Steve Notara. Notara mails or faxes the customer a copy of the invoice with a note saying work has stopped. Each day he personally calls the two most delinquent customers. Decoma . . . has never had a bad debt.[9]

Many business firms have found that the most effective collection procedure consists of a series of steps, each of which is somewhat more forceful than the preceding one. Although the procedure typically begins with a gentle written reminder, subsequent steps may include additional letters, telephone calls, regis-

1 Explain how to set a price.

- The revenue of a firm is a direct reflection of two components: sales volume and price.
- Price must be sufficient to cover total cost plus some margin of profit.
- A product's competitive advantage is a demand factor in setting price.
- A firm should examine elasticity of demand—the relationship of price and quantity demanded—when setting a price.

2 Apply break-even analysis to pricing.

- Analyzing costs and revenue under different price assumptions identifies the break-even point, the quantity sold at which total costs equal total revenue.
- The usefulness of break-even analysis is enhanced by incorporating demand forecasts.

3 Identify specific pricing strategies.

- Markup pricing is a generalized cost-plus system of pricing used by intermediaries with many products.
- Penetration pricing and skimming pricing are short-term strategies used when new products are first introduced into the market.
- Follow-the-leader, variable, and flexible pricing are special strategies that reflect the nature of the competition's pricing and concessions to customers.
- A price lining strategy simplifies choices for customers by offering a range of several distinct prices.
- State and federal laws must be considered when pricing, as well as any impact that price may have on other product line items.

4 Discuss the benefits of credit, the factors that affect credit extension, and the kinds of credit.

- Credit offers potential benefits to both buyers and sellers.
- Type of business, credit policies of competitors, income level of customers, and availability of adequate working capital affect the decision to extend credit.
- The two broad classes of credit are consumer credit and trade credit.

5 Describe the activities involved in managing credit.

- Evaluating the credit status of applicants begins with the completion of an application form.
- Pertinent credit data can be obtained from several outside sources, including formal trade-credit agencies such as Dun & Bradstreet and Equifax.
- An accounts receivable aging schedule can improve credit collection.
- A small firm should establish a formal policy for billing and collecting from charge customers.
- It is important that a small firm follow all relevant credit regulations.

tered letters, personal contacts, and referrals to collection agencies or attorneys.[10] The timing of these steps may be carefully standardized so that each one automatically follows the preceding one in a specified number of days.

Various ratios can be used to control expenses associated with credit sales. The best-known and most widely used expense ratio is the **bad-debt ratio,** which is computed by dividing the amount of bad debts by the total amount of credit sales. The bad-debt ratio reflects the efficiency of credit policies and procedures. A small firm may thus compare the effectiveness of its credit management with that of other firms. A relationship exists between the bad-debt ratio and the type of profitability, and the size of the firm. Small profitable retailers have a much higher bad-debt ratio than large profitable retailers do. Overall, the bad-debt losses of small business firms range from a fraction of 1 percent of net sales to percentages large enough to put them out of business!

Credit Regulation

The use of credit is regulated by a variety of federal and state laws. Prior to the passage of such legislation, consumers were often confused by credit agreements and were sometimes victims of credit abuse. Laws covering credit practices vary considerably from state to state. See Chapter 26 for a further discussion of these laws.

By far, the most significant piece of credit legislation is the federal Consumer Credit Protection Act. Part of this act is known as the 1968 Truth-in-Lending Act, and its two primary purposes are to inform consumers about terms of a credit agreement and to require creditors to specify how finance charges are

bad-debt ratio
a number obtained by dividing the amount of bad debts by the total amount of credit sales

computed. The act requires a finance charge to be stated as an annual percentage rate and requires creditors to specify the procedures for correcting billing mistakes.

Other federal legislation related to credit management includes the following:

- *The Fair Credit Billing Act* provides protection to credit customers in cases involving incorrect billing. A reasonable time period is allowed for billing errors to be corrected.

- *The Fair Credit Reporting Act* gives certain rights to credit applicants regarding reports prepared by credit bureaus.
- *The Equal Credit Opportunity Act* protects widowed and divorced women against credit denial because of lack of a credit history.
- *The Fair Debt Collection Practices Act* bans the use of intimidation and deception in collection.

Pricing and credit decisions are of prime importance to a small firm because of their direct impact on its financial health. Some entrepreneurs learn to make the best decisions through experience. Hopefully, the concepts presented in this chapter will help smooth the trip.

DISCUSSION QUESTIONS

1. How can average-cost pricing sometimes yield a "bad" price?
2. Explain the importance of fixed and variable costs to the pricing decision.
3. How does the concept of elasticity of demand relate to prestige pricing? Give an example.
4. If a firm has fixed costs of $100,000 and variable costs per unit of $1, what is the break-even point in units, assuming a selling price of $5 per unit?
5. What is the difference between a penetration pricing strategy and a skimming price strategy? Under what circumstances would each be used?
6. If a small business has conducted its break-even analysis properly and finds break-even volume at a price of $10 to be 10,000 units, should it price its product at $10? Why or why not?
7. What are the major benefits of credit to buyers? What are its major benefits to sellers?
8. How does an open charge account differ from a revolving charge account?
9. What is meant by the terms 2/10, net 30? Does it pay to take discounts when they are offered?

New Terms and Concepts

price 306	penetration pricing strategy 313	trade credit 317
credit 306	skimming price strategy 313	open charge account 317
total cost 307	follow-the-leader pricing strategy 314	installment account 317
total variable costs 307	variable pricing strategy 314	revolving charge account 318
total fixed costs 308	flexible pricing strategy 314	trade-credit agencies 322
average pricing 308	price lining strategy 314	credit bureau 322
elasticity of demand 309	consumer credit 317	aging schedule 322
elastic demand 309		bad-debt ratio 326
inelastic demand 309		
prestige pricing 309		

You Make the Call

Situation 1 Steve Jones is the 35-year-old owner of a highly competitive small business supplying temporary office help. Like most businesspeople, he is always looking for ways to increase profit. However, the nature of his competition makes it very difficult to raise prices for the temps' services, and reducing their wages makes recruiting difficult. Jones has, nevertheless, found an area where improvement should increase profits—bad debts. A friend and business consultant met with Jones to advise him on credit management policies. Jones was pleased to get this friend's advice, as bad debts were costing him about 2 percent of sales. Currently, Jones has no system of managing credit.

Question 1 What advice would you give Jones regarding the screening of new credit customers?
Question 2 What action should Jones take to encourage current credit customers to pay their debts? Be specific.
Question 3 Jones has considered eliminating credit sales. What are the possible consequences of this decision?

Situation 2 Mom's Monogram is a small firm that manufactures and imprints monogramming designs for jackets, caps, tee shirts, and other articles of clothing. The business has been in operation for two years. In the first year, sales reached $50,000. The next year, sales raced up to $300,000. Pricing of the firm's services has been based on a straight, cost-plus approach. Success has spawned plans to double plant and equipment. The owners have never spent money on advertising and believe that the expansion will double sales within the next three years. They plan to continue pricing their services using a cost-plus formula.

Continue on next page

327

Question 1 What problems may be encountered by this business if it continues to use cost-plus pricing?

Question 2 How can the firm's total costs be analyzed to ascertain its pricing strategy?

Question 3 What types of discounts might be offered to customers of Mom's Monogram? Be specific.

Situation 3 Paul Bowlin owns and operates a tree removal, pruning, and spraying business in a large metropolitan area with a population of approximately 200,000. The business started in 1975 and has grown to the point where Bowlin uses one and sometimes two crews with four or five employees on each crew. Pricing has always been an important tool in gaining business, but Bowlin realizes that there are ways to entice customers other than quoting the lowest price. For example, he provides careful cleanup of branches and leaves, takes out stumps below ground level, and waits until a customer is completely satisfied before taking payment. At the same time, he realizes his bids for tree removal jobs must cover his costs. In this industry, Bowlin faces intense price competition from operators with more sophisticated wood-processing equipment, such as chip grinders. Therefore, he is always open to suggestions about pricing strategy.

Question 1 What would the nature of this industry suggest about the elasticity of demand affecting Bowlin's pricing?

Question 2 What types of costs should Bowlin evaluate when he is determining his break-even point?

Question 3 What pricing strategies could Bowlin adopt to further his long-term success in this market?

Question 4 How can the high-quality of Bowlin's work be used to justify somewhat higher price quotations?

---

10. What is the major purpose of aging accounts receivable? At what point in credit management should this activity be performed? Why?

EXPERIENTIAL EXERCISES

1. Interview a small business owner regarding his or her pricing strategies. Try to ascertain whether the strategy being used reflects the fixed and variable costs of the business. Prepare a report of your findings.
2. Interview a small business owner regarding his or her policies for evaluating of credit applicants. Summarize your findings in a report.
3. Invite a credit manager from a retail store to speak to the class on the benefits and drawbacks of extending credit to customers.
4. Ask several small business owners in your community who extend credit to describe the credit management policies they use to collect bad debts. Report your findings to the class.

Exploring the

5. Write a one-page summary describing the credit information available on the Web at http://www.tiac.net/users/rooftop/crecol.html.

CASE 14
The Jordan Construction Account (p. 629)

This case examines a situation in which a credit customer is overdue on his account.

Alternative Cases for Chapter 14: Case 7, "The Fantastic Catalogue Company," p. 610
Case 15, "Litter Ridder," p. 631
Case 23, "Barton Sales and Service," p. 653

Promotion: Personal Selling, Advertising, and Sales Promotion

Chapter 15

Donna Cook

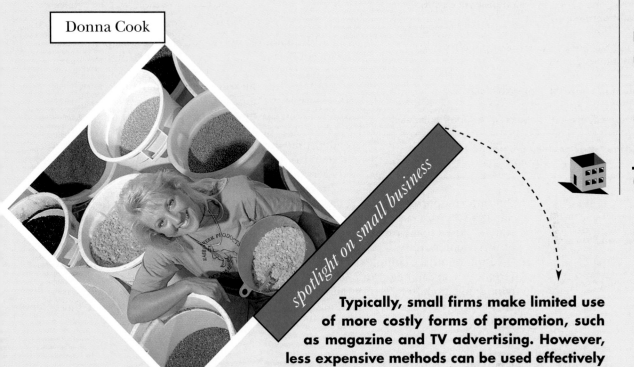

spotlight on small business

Typically, small firms make limited use of more costly forms of promotion, such as magazine and TV advertising. However, less expensive methods can be used effectively by creative entrepreneurs. Trade show exhibits, for example, are an economical promotional tool for reaching customers.

One entrepreneur who uses trade shows to promote her products is Donna Cook, owner of Rabbit Creek Products, in Louisburg, Kansas. Her wholesaler business markets gourmet food items to retailers. At trade shows, an attractive display lures customers to her booth.

Cook and her exhibit staffers all dress in matching T-shirts of shocking hot pink or aqua bearing the Rabbit Creek logo. . . . Another draw for Cook is her booth's buffet, which serves up samples of her 10-year-old company's 100-plus products, including muffin mixes and biscuit mixes.

The scent of Rabbit Creek's delectables attracts attendees to the booth, where staffers are ready to answer questions and take orders.

Source: Jayne Pearl, "Trick of the Trade Show," *Independent Business,* Vol. 5, No. 5 (September-October 1994), pp. 32–37. Reprinted with permission from *Independent Business* magazine, September-October 1994. Copyright 1994 by Group IV Communications, Inc., 125 Auburn Court, Suite 100, Thousand Oaks, CA 91362. All rights reserved.

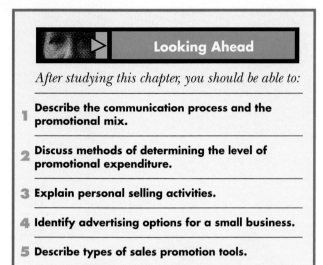

Looking Ahead

After studying this chapter, you should be able to:

1 Describe the communication process and the promotional mix.

2 Discuss methods of determining the level of promotional expenditure.

3 Explain personal selling activities.

4 Identify advertising options for a small business.

5 Describe types of sales promotion tools.

start here

The old adage "Build a better mousetrap and the world will beat a path to your door" highlights the importance of innovation in building a successful business but ignores the role of other marketing activities. For example, promotion is essential in informing customers about the new, improved "mousetrap" and how to get to the "door"! Customers may need to be persuaded that the new mousetrap is really better than their old one. Essentially, this process of informing and persuading is promotion.

promotion
persuasive communications between a business and its target market

Promotion consists of marketing communications that inform, persuade, and remind consumers of a firm's total product offering. Small businesses use promotion in varying degrees, with any given firm applying some or all of many promotional tools. The three promotional activities discussed in this chapter are personal selling, advertising, and sales promotion.

Promotion is a complex activity, to which most entrepreneurs are not attuned. However, you can begin to understand promotion by realizing that it is based on communication. In fact, promotion is worthless unless it communicates. Therefore, let's look at how promotional decisions need to be built on a correct understanding of the communication process.

1 Describe the communication process and the promotional mix.

PROMOTION AND THE COMMUNICATION PROCESS

Everyone communicates in some way each day. However, it is important to realize that communication is a process with identifiable components. As shown in Figure 15-1, every communication involves a source, a message, a channel, and a receiver. Part (a) in Figure 15-1 represents a personal communication—parents communicating with their daughter, who is away at college. Part (b) represents a small business communication—a company communicating with a customer. As you can see, there are many similarities between the two.

The receiver of the parents' message is their daughter. These parents have used three different channels for their messages: the mail, a personal conversation, and a special gift. The receiver for the small business message from the XYZ Company is the customer. The XYZ Company has used three message channels: a newspaper (advertising), a sales call (personal selling), and a business gift (sales promotion). The letter and advertising both represent nonpersonal communication. The parents' visit to their daughter and the sales call made by the company's representative are both forms of personal communications. Finally, the flowers and care package and the business gift are both special communication methods. The promotional efforts of a small firm, then, can be viewed simply as a special form of communication between the firm and its potential customers that relies on both personal and nonpersonal selling.

promotional mix
a blend of personal and nonpersonal promotional methods aimed at a target market

A **promotional mix** involves a blend of such personal and nonpersonal techniques. The mixture of the various promotional methods—advertising, personal selling, and sales promotion—is determined by three major factors. The first factor is the geographical nature of the market to be reached. A widely dispersed market tends to require mass coverage by advertising, in contrast to the more costly individual contacts of personal selling. On the other hand, if the market is local, with a relatively small number of customers, personal selling is more feasible.

Similarity of Personal and Small Business Communication Processes | *Figure 15-1* |

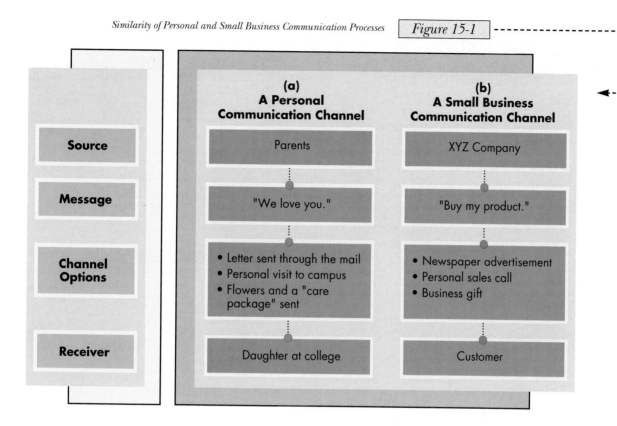

Second, a small business must identify its target customers. Shotgun promotion, which "hits" potential customers and nonpotential customers alike, is expensive and can be fine-tuned to some extent by analyzing audiences. The media can provide helpful profiles of their audiences. But, keep in mind that a small business cannot obtain a media *match* until it has carefully determined its target market.

The third factor that influences the promotional mix is the product's characteristics. If a product is of high unit value, such as a life insurance policy, personal selling will be a vital ingredient in the mix. Personal selling is also an effective method for promoting highly technical products, such as automobiles or street-sweeping machinery. On the other hand, sales promotion is more effective for a relatively inexpensive item, like razor blades.

There are, of course, other considerations that must be considered when developing a promotional mix. For example, the high total cost of the optimum mixture may necessitate substitution of a less expensive, and less than optimum, alternative. Nevertheless, promotional planning should determine the optimum mix. The entrepreneur can then make cost-saving adjustments, if necessary.

DETERMINING PROMOTIONAL EXPENDITURES

Unfortunately, no mathematical formula can answer the question "How much should a small business spend on promotion?" There are, however, some helpful approaches to solving the problem. Here are the most common methods of budgeting funds for small business promotion:

2 Discuss methods of determining the level of promotional expenditure.

Action Report

TECHNOLOGICAL APPLICATIONS

Are You Ready for the World Wide Web?

For many big companies, the Internet's World Wide Web is yet another way to serve customers and attract new business. And, in increasing numbers, smaller companies are exploring the numerous ways in which the Internet can help build and sustain business.

Before obtaining a web site, you must determine your business goals: What customers are you trying to attract? Is the Internet the right vehicle? What do you want to communicate? The answers to these questions will lead to consideration of various online strategies—each of which requires a different level of involvement and expense.

Online strategies range from the very simple—providing an E-mail address—to the very elaborate—using your web site as an entertainment magazine. Perhaps the most effective web presence for a small company is the brochure strategy. Like a printed brochure, the web site offers information about a company, its products, and its services. Potential customers who are given the company's Internet address can then read about it online. To attract new customers, an entrepreneur might look for related companies on the web that are not in direct competition with his or her company and ask them to link to the entrepreneur's site.

The newsletter strategy is another viable option for a small firm. In addition to telling customers about services and products, this forum can solicit feedback and suggestions and share information of interest. For example, "a veterinarian might want to put a newsletter on the site, keeping back issues for reference, adding detailed information about flea control during summer, giving links to dog-related sites and letting customers know where to find local pet sitters."

A word of caution: As with printed materials, the quality of an online strategy will reflect how much money is spent—the more elaborate the strategy, the greater the costs and the effort involved. The key to selecting the right Internet strategy is to know your goals.

Source: Rhonda M. Abrams, "Small Business Needs Realistic Goals Before Leaping into Cyberspace," *The Courier-Journal*, Louisville, KY, October 1, 1995, p. E3. Copyright 1995, Gannett Co., Inc. Reprinted with permission.

- Using a percentage of sales
- Deciding how much can be spared
- Spending as much as the competition does
- Determining what it will take to do the job

Using a Percentage of Sales

Earmarking promotional dollars based on a percentage of sales is a simple method for a small business to use. A company's own past experiences should be evaluated to establish a promotion/sales ratio. If 2 percent of sales, for example, has historically been spent on promotion, the company should budget 2 percent of forecasted sales for promotion. Secondary data can be checked to locate industry averages for comparison. One excellent source for finding out what firms are doing with their advertising dollars is the publication *Advertising Age*. Also, Leading National Advertisers, a research company, provides data on advertising expenditures by brand.

A major shortcoming of this method is an inherent tendency to spend more dollars on promotion when sales are increasing and less when they are declining. If promotion stimulates sales, then spending when sales are down seems desirable.

Deciding How Much Can Be Spared

A widely used piecemeal approach to promotional budgeting is to spend what's left over when all other activities have been funded. Sometimes, such a budget is nonexistent, and spending is determined only when a media representative sells an owner on a special deal. Such an approach to promotional spending should be avoided because it neglects analysis of promotional needs.

Spending as Much as the Competition Does

One technique builds a promotional budget that is based on that of the competition. If the small business can duplicate the promotional mix of close competitors, it will at least be reaching the same customers and spending as much as the competition. Obviously, if a competitor is a large business, this approach is not feasible. However, it can be used to react to short-run promotional tactics by small competitors. Unfortunately, this method results in the copying of mistakes as well as of successes, although it may enable a firm to remain competitive.

Determining What It Will Take to Do the Job

The preferred approach to estimating promotional expenditures is to decide what it will take to do the job. This method requires a comprehensive analysis of the market and the promotional alternatives. If reasonably accurate estimates are used, the amount that truly needs to be spent can be determined.

The best way for a small business to estimate promotional expenditures incorporates all four approaches, as represented by Figure 15-2. Start with an estimate of what it will take to do the job, and then look at the amount that represents a prede-

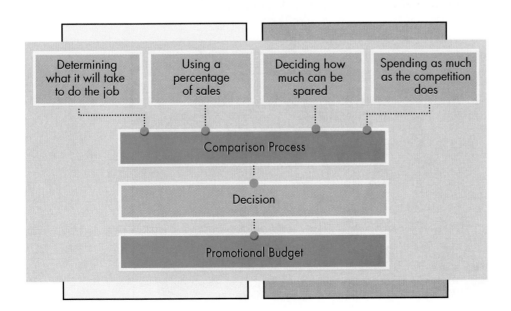

Figure 15-2

Four-Step Method for Determining a Promotional Budget

termined percentage of forecasted sales. Third, estimate what can be spared before examining what the competition is spending. Finally, make a decision regarding how much money your company will budget for promotional purposes.

PERSONAL SELLING TECHNIQUES FOR SMALL FIRMS

3   **Explain personal selling activities.**

personal selling
a sales presentation delivered in a personal, one-on-one manner

Many products require **personal selling,** which is promotion delivered in a one-on-one environment. It includes the activities of both the inside salespersons of retail, wholesale, and service establishments and the outside sales representatives who call on business establishments and final consumers.

Importance of Product Knowledge

Effective selling is built on a foundation of product knowledge. If a salesperson is well acquainted with a product's advantages, uses, and limitations, she or he can educate customers and successfully counter their objections. Most customers expect a salesperson to provide such information—whether the product is a camera, a coat, an automobile, paint, a machine tool, or an office machine. Customers are seldom experts on the products they buy; however, they can immediately sense a salesperson's knowledge or ignorance. Personal selling degenerates into mere order-taking when product knowledge is not possessed by the salesperson.

The Sales Presentation

prospecting
a systematic process of continually looking for new customers

The heart of personal selling is the sales presentation to the prospective customer. At this crucial point, an order is either secured or lost. A preliminary step leading to an effective sales presentation is **prospecting,** a systematic process of continually looking for new customers.[1]

TECHNIQUES OF PROSPECTING   One of the most efficient techniques for prospecting is to obtain *personal referrals*. Such referrals come from friends, customers, and other businesses. Initial contact with a potential customer is greatly facilitated by the ability to mention "You were referred to me by . . . ."

Salespersons who are knowledgeable about a product's characteristics are effective sellers, meeting customers' needs for information about the product's uses, advantages, and limitations.

Another technique for prospecting is to use *impersonal referrals,* such as media publications, public records, and directories. Newspapers and magazines, particularly trade magazines, can help identify prospects by reporting information on new companies entering the market, as well as on new products. Wedding announcements in a newspaper are impersonal referrals for a local bridal shop. Public records of property transactions and building permits can be impersonal referrals for, say, a garbage pick-up service, which might find prospective customers from those who are planning to build houses or apartment buildings.

Prospects can be identified without referrals through *marketer-initiated contacts.* Telephone calls or mail surveys, for example, isolate prospects. An author of this book used a mail questionnaire in a market survey conducted for a small business to identify prospects. The questionnaire, which asked technical questions about a service, concluded with the following statement: "If you would be interested in a service of this nature, please check the appropriate space below and your name will be added to the mailing list."

Finally, prospects can also be identified by recording *customer-initiated contacts.* Inquiries by a potential customer that do not lead to a sale result in that person being classified as a "hot prospect." Small furniture stores often require their salespeople to create a card for each person visiting the store. These prospects are then systematically contacted over the telephone. Records of these contacts are updated periodically.

PRACTICING THE SALES PRESENTATION   The old saying "Practice makes perfect" applies to a salesperson prior to making a sales presentation. A salesperson should make his or her presentation to a spouse, a mirror, or a tape recorder. He or she may want to use a camcorder to make a practice video. Practicing always improves a salesperson's success rate.

The salesperson should also be aware of possible objections to the product or service and be prepared to handle them. Although there is no substitute for actual selling experience, certain concepts can be helpful in dealing with customers' objections:

- *Comparing the products.* When the prospect is mentally comparing a product being used now or a competing product with the salesperson's product, the salesperson makes a complete comparison of the two by listing the advantages and disadvantages of each product.
- *Relating a case history.* The salesperson describes the experiences of another customer with the product or service.
- *Demonstrating the product.* A product demonstration gives a convincing answer to a product objection because the salesperson lets the product itself overcome the objection.
- *Giving a guarantee.* Often, a guarantee will remove the prospect's resistance. Guarantees assure prospects that they cannot lose by purchasing. The caution, of course, is that a guarantee must be meaningful and must provide for some recourse on the part of the prospect if the product does not perform as expected.
- *Asking questions.* "Why" questions are of value in separating excuses from genuine objections and in probing for hidden resistance. They are also useful in disposing of objections. Probing or exploratory questions are excellent in handling silent resistance. They can be worded and asked in a manner that appeals to a prospect's ego. By making a prospect do some thinking to convince the salesperson, questions of a probing nature get the prospect's full attention.
- *Showing what delaying a purchase might cost.* A common experience of salespeople is to obtain seemingly sincere agreements to the buying decisions concerning

need, product, source, and price, only to find that the prospect wants to wait some time before buying. In such cases, the salesperson can sometimes use pencil and paper to show conclusively that delay of the purchase will be expensive.

- *Admitting and counterbalancing.* Sometimes, a prospect's objection is completely valid because of some limitation in the salesperson's product. The only course of action in this case is for the salesperson to agree that the product does have the disadvantage to which the prospect is obviously objecting. Immediately after the acknowledgment, however, the salesperson should direct the prospect's attention to the advantages that overshadow the limitation.

- *Hearing the prospect out.* Some prospects object solely for the opportunity to describe how they were once victimized. The technique recommended for this type of resistance is that of empathetic listening.

- *Making the objection boomerang.* Once in a while, with expert handling, a salesperson can take a prospect's reason for not buying and convert it into a reason for buying. If the prospect says, "I'm too busy to see you," the salesperson might reply, "That's why you should see me—I can save you time."

- *Using the "Yes, but" technique.* The best technique for handling most resistance is the indirect answer known as the "Yes, but" method. Here are two examples of what a salesperson might say when using this technique: (1) "Yes, I can understand that attitude, but there is another angle for you to consider"; and (2) "Yes, you have a point there, but in your particular circumstances, other points are involved, too." The "Yes, but" method circumvents argument and friction. It respects the prospect's opinions, attitudes, and thinking and operates well when the prospect's point does not apply in a particular case.[2]

MAKING THE SALES PRESENTATION Salespersons must adapt their sales approach to customers' needs. A "canned" sales talk will not succeed with most buyers. For example, a person selling personal computers must demonstrate the capacity of the equipment to fill a customer's particular word-processing needs. Similarly, a boat salesperson must understand the special interests of particular customers and speak their language. Every sales objection must be answered explicitly and adequately.

Having raced the bikes he sells, this salesperson is well prepared to speak the customer's language. Possessing a personal interest in the product helps sellers understand the special needs of their customers.

Successful selling involves a number of psychological elements. A salesperson must realize that some degree of personal enthusiasm, friendliness, and persistence is required. Approximately 20 percent of all salespersons secure as much as 80 percent of all sales made because they persist and bring enthusiasm and friendliness to the task of selling.

Some salespersons have special sales techniques that they use with success. One automobile salesperson, for example, offered free driving lessons to people who had never taken a driver's training course or who needed a few more lessons before they felt confident enough to take the required driving tests. When such customers were ready to take the driving tests, this salesperson accompanied them to the driver examination grounds for moral support. Needless to say, these special efforts were greatly appreciated by new drivers who were in the market for cars.

Cost Control in Personal Selling

Both economical and wasteful methods exist for achieving the same volume of sales. For example, routing traveling salespersons economically and making appointments prior to arrival can conserve time and transportation expenses. The cost of an outside sales call on a customer may be considerable—perhaps hundreds of dollars—emphasizing the need for efficient, intelligent scheduling. Moreover, a salesperson for a manufacturing firm, say, can contribute to cost economy by stressing those products whose increased sales would give the factory a balanced production run. All products do not have the same margin of profit, however, and a salesperson can maximize profits by emphasizing high-margin product items.

Compensating Salespeople

Salespeople are compensated in two ways for their efforts: financially and nonfinancially. A good compensation program will allow its participants to work for both forms of reward. However, an effective compensation program recognizes that salespeople's goals may be different from entrepreneurs' goals. For example, an entrepreneur may seek nonfinancial goals that are of little importance to the salespeople.

NONFINANCIAL REWARDS   Personal recognition and the satisfaction of reaching a sales quota are examples of nonfinancial rewards recognized by salespeople. For example, many small retail businesses post the photograph of the top salesperson of the week or the month on a bulletin board for all to see. Plaques are also used for a more permanent record of sales achievements.

FINANCIAL REWARDS   Typically, financial compensation is the more critical factor for salespeople. Two basic plans for financial compensation are commissions and straight salary. Each plan has specific advantages and limitations.

Most small businesses would prefer to use commissions as compensation, because such an approach is simple and directly related to productivity. Usually, a certain percentage of sales generated by the salesperson represents his or her commission. A commission plan thereby incorporates a strong incentive into the selling activities—no sale, no commission! Also, with this type of plan, there is no drain on the firm's cash flow until a sale is made.

Salespeople have more security with the straight salary form of compensation, because their level of compensation is ensured, regardless of personal sales made. However, this method can potentially reduce a salesperson's motivation.

Combining the two forms of compensation can give a small business the most attractive plan. It is a common practice to structure combination plans so that salary represents the larger part of compensation for new salespeople. As a salesperson gains experience, the ratio is adjusted to provide more money from commissions and less from salary.

Action Report

ETHICAL ISSUES

Successful Professional Selling

All salespeople need to project the attitude that meeting the client's need is their number-one priority. Carroll Fadal, a highly successful life insurance salesman, who lives in Waco, Texas, discusses the need for such an attitude:

> *My sales career has been spent in life insurance. I need not tell you the typical image of the life insurance salesperson—a loud, pushy boor in bad clothes who will try to sell you a policy, any policy, whether you need it or not.*
>
> *Actually, there are some life insurance agents like that, but not nearly as many as some would have you believe. Upon entering the industry after a thirteen-year career in journalism, I was determined to be "set apart" from that caricature. My faith made that easier than I had imagined.*
>
> *Armed with very little knowledge, a lot of desire and a servant's attitude, I set about trying to sell life insurance professionally. My main goal in every client interview was to find out what he or she needed, then determine if I had a product that would fulfill that need. On more than one occasion, I had to tell the prospect that he didn't need any more life insurance. Imagine his surprise!*

Other factors such as education, diligence, honesty and perseverance are also important.

> *Temptation abounds. If one works on commission, the pressure to make a sale never goes away. At almost every juncture in the sales process, opportunities arise to shade the truth or to omit a seemingly insignificant detail. "Oh well, it's just a little thing, and if I bring it up, it might squirrel the deal," the thought goes.*
>
> *For every temptation to make the sale without full disclosure, for every desire to "massage the numbers" on a sales proposal, there is the small, still voice reminding us that we are to deal with people with integrity. It is my firm belief, borne out in experience, that in the long run, integrity wins.*
>
> *Clients want to know that they can count on what they've been told. It takes a lifetime to build a reputation for honesty and integrity; it takes only a moment's slip-up to ruin it.*

Source: Carroll Fadal, *Sales Leader*, Vol. 1, No. 2, The Center for Professional Selling, Baylor University, 1993.

Building Customer Goodwill

A salesperson must look beyond the immediate sale to build customer goodwill and to create satisfied customers who will patronize the company in the future. One way to accomplish this *relationship selling* is to display a good appearance, a pleasant personality, and good habits in all contacts with customers. A salesperson can also help build goodwill by understanding the customer's point of view. Courtesy, attention to details, and genuine friendliness will help gain the customer's acceptance.

Of course, high ethical standards are of primary importance in creating customer goodwill. Such standards rule out any misrepresentation and require confidential treatment of a customer's plans.

ADVERTISING CONSIDERATIONS FOR SMALL FIRMS

Advertising is the impersonal presentation of an idea that is identified with a business sponsor and is projected through mass media, including television, radio, magazines, newspapers, and billboards. Advertising is a vital part of small business marketing.

advertising
the impersonal presentation of a business idea through mass media

Table 15-1 reports the usage rates for various advertising media from a random survey of 130 small firms in Iowa.[3] As this study shows, small firms rely on a number of advertising media. Although television is shown to be used less frequently than other media, cable television, if available, may offer a channel for local advertising that is affordable and properly focused on a target market.

It is interesting to note that referrals (word-of-mouth advertising) are used by a large percentage of the sample. Referrals are possibly the most effective form of promotion because of their inherent credibility and low cost—they're free. Brooks O'Kane, president of Clear Vue Products in Lawrence, Massachusetts, evidently holds this view. He has decided to rely completely on word-of-mouth advertising to increase sales for his firm's window-cleaning product, Clear Vue. "I'm convinced that those customers who try it once will become repeat customers without the benefit of advertising. . . . Plus, for every one customer, I'm counting on bringing in three more of their friends," O'Kane says.[4]

Objectives of Advertising

As a primary goal, advertising seeks to sell by informing, persuading, and reminding customers of the existence or superiority of a firm's product or service. To be successful, it must rest on a foundation of product quality and efficient service—advertising can bring no more than temporary success to an inferior product. It must always be viewed as a complement to a good product and never as a replacement for a bad product.

The entrepreneur should not create false expectations with advertising. These expectations can effectively reduce customer satisfaction. Advertising may also accentuate a trend in the sale of an item or product line, but it seldom has the power

Table 15-1

Percentage of Small Firms Using Each Type of Advertising

Type of Advertising	Type of Firm					
	Retail (n = 52)		Service (n = 50)		Other (n = 30)	
	First Year of Operations (%)	1992 (%)	First Year of Operations (%)	1992 (%)	First Year of Operations (%)	1992 (%)
Referrals (word-of-mouth)	34.9	31.8	19.7	20.5	34.1	32.6
Newspaper	33.3	28.0	15.9	14.4	31.5	21.2
Telephone Directory	23.4	21.9	15.2	15.2	25.0	22.0
Radio	23.5	19.7	7.6	10.6	16.7	11.4
Flyers	15.2	11.4	8.3	10.6	12.9	11.4
Community Events	14.4	14.4	12.9	12.9	11.4	13.6
Television	3.8	6.8	1.5	3.0	1.5	2.3

Source: Howard E. Van Auken, B. Michael Doran, and Terri L. Rittenburg, "An Empirical Analysis of Small Business Advertising," *Journal of Small Business Management*, Vol. 30, No. 2 (April 1992), p. 90.

to reverse a trend. It must, consequently, be able to reflect changes in customer needs and preferences.

Advertising may appear, at times, to be a waste of money. It is expensive and adds little utility to the product. Nevertheless, the major alternative is personal selling, which is often more expensive and time-consuming.

Types of Advertising

product advertising
the presentation of a business idea designed to make potential customers aware of a product or service and their need for it

There are two basic types of advertising—product advertising and institutional advertising. **Product advertising** is designed to make potential customers aware of a particular product or service and their need for it. **Institutional advertising,** on the other hand, conveys information about the business itself. It is intended to keep the public conscious of the company and enhance its image.

institutional advertising
advertising designed to enhance a firm's image

The majority of small business advertising is of the product type. Retailers' advertisements, for example, stress products almost exclusively—weekend specials in a supermarket or sportswear sold exclusively in a women's shop. The same advertisement can convey both product and institutional themes, however. Furthermore, the same firm may stress its product in newspaper advertisements, while using institutional advertising in the telephone Yellow Pages. Decisions regarding the type of advertising to be used should be based on the nature of the business, industry practice, available media, and objectives of the firm.

Frequency of Advertising

Determining how often to advertise is an important and highly complex issue for a small business. Obviously, advertising should be done regularly, and attempts to stimulate interest in a company's products or services should be part of an ongoing promotional program. One-shot advertisements that are not part of a well-planned promotional effort lose much of their effectiveness in a short period and should be discouraged. However, deciding on the frequency of advertising involves a host of factors, both objective and subjective, and a wise entrepreneur will seek the advice of professionals.

Of course, some noncontinuous advertising, may be justified, such as advertising to prepare consumers for acceptance of a new product. Such advertising may also be used to suggest to customers new uses for established products or to promote special sales.

Where to Advertise

Most small firms restrict their advertising—either geographically or by class of customer. Advertising media should reach—but not overreach—a firm's present or desired target market. From among the many media available, a small business entrepreneur must choose those that will provide the greatest return for the advertising dollar.

The selection of the right combination of advertising media depends on the type of business and its current circumstances. A real estate sales firm, for example, may rely almost exclusively on classified advertisements in a local newspaper, supplemented by institutional advertising in the Yellow Pages of the telephone book. A transfer-and-storage firm may use a combination of radio, billboard, and Yellow Pages advertising to reach individuals planning to move household furniture. A small toy manufacturer may place greatest emphasis on television advertisements

Action Report

TECHNOLOGICAL APPLICATIONS

Scanner Technology Helps Small Firms

TECHNOLOGY

Small firms can benefit from technology just as much as large firms do—if they only give it a try. For example, scanners are being used by some entrepreneurs to assist selling and advertising efforts.

Scanners are like computer-friendly cameras. They take pictures of documents and artwork—pictures that your computer can use.

You can scan graphics (photographs, line drawings, slides, and overheads) or text (documents, magazines, books, etc.) and transfer them to your computer for use in a variety of printed materials.

"I scan a photograph of a prospective customer's property into my computer," says landscape designer and contractor P. J. Bale, owner of First State Inc. in Newcastle, Delaware. Then, using image-editing software, Bale adds trees, shrubs, flowers, pavers, and people—an image he prints onto glossy paper with a color printer so it looks like an actual photo. Customers find this visual so convincing, his success rate at closing sales has jumped from 70 to 90 percent.

Paul Thede, owner of Race Tech, a manufacturer of motorcycle suspensions in Pomona, California, uses his scanner for a different purpose—designing his own flyers and catalogs in-house. "I'm using outside agencies less, and I've lowered some of my costs 80 percent," says Thede.

Experts recommend a flatbed scanner for small business owners because of high-quality, efficiency, and reasonable prices.

Source: Alan S. Horowitz, "Scanners!" *Independent Business*, Vol. 6, No. 1 (January-February 1995), p. 50. Reprinted with permission from *Independent Business* magazine. January-February 1995. Copyright 1995 by Group IV Communications, Inc., 125 Auburn Court, Suite 100, Thousand Oaks, CA 91362. All rights reserved.

and participation in trade fairs. A local retail store may concentrate on display advertisements in a local newspaper. The selection should be made not only on the basis of tradition but also on an evaluation of the various ways to cover a firm's particular market.

A good way to build a media mix is to talk with representatives from each medium. A small business owner will usually find these representatives willing to recommend an assortment of media, not just the ones they represent. Before meeting with these representatives, the entrepreneur should study as much as possible about advertising in order to know both the weaknesses and the strengths of each medium. Table 15-2 summarizes important facts about several media. Study this information carefully, noting particularly the advantages and disadvantages of each medium.

Creating the Message

Most small businesses must rely on others' expertise to create their promotional messages. Fortunately, there are several sources for this specialized assistance: advertising agencies, suppliers, trade associations, and advertising media.

Table 15-2   *Media Summary*

Medium	Market Coverage	Type of Audience
Daily newspaper	Single community or entire metro area; zoned editions sometimes available	General; tends more toward men, older age group, slightly higher income and education
Weekly newspaper	Single community usually; sometimes a metro area	General; usually residents of a smaller community
Shoppers' guide	Most households in a single community; chain shoppers can cover a metro area	Consumer households
Telephone directory	Geographic area or occupational field served by the directory	Active shoppers for goods or services
Direct mail	Controlled by the advertiser	Controlled by the advertiser through use of demographic lists
Radio	Definable market area surrounding station's location	Selected audiences provided by stations with distinct programming formats
Television	Definable market area surrounding station's location	Varies with the time of day; tends toward younger age group, less print-oriented
Transit	Urban or metro community served by transit system; may be limited to a few transit routes	Transit riders, especially wage earners and shoppers; pedestrians
Outdoor (e.g., billboards)	Entire metro area or single neighborhood	General; especially auto drivers
Local magazine	Entire metro area or region; zoned editions sometimes available	General; tends toward better educated, more affluent

Source: Reprinted with permission from Bank of America, NT&SA, "Advertising Small Business," *Small Business Reporter*, Vol. 15, No. 2, Copyright 1981.

Advertising agencies can provide the following services:

- Furnishing design, artwork, and copy for specific advertisements and/or commercials
- Evaluating and recommending the advertising media with the greatest "pulling power"
- Evaluating the effectiveness of different advertising appeals
- Advising on sales promotions and merchandise displays
- Conducting market-sampling studies for evaluating product acceptance or determining the sales potential of a specific geographic area
- Furnishing mailing lists

Since advertising agencies may charge fees for their services, an entrepreneur must make sure that the return from those services will be greater than the fees paid. Quality advertising assistance can best be provided by a competent agency. Of course, with the high level of technology currently available to small business owners, creating print advertising in-house is becoming increasingly common for the small firm.

Other outside sources may also assist in formulating and carrying out promo-

Particular Suitability	Major Advantage	Major Disadvantage
All general retailers	Wide circulation	Nonselective audience
Retailers who service a strictly local market	Local identification	Limited readership
Neighborhood retailers and service businesses	Consumer orientation	A giveaway and not always read
Services, retailers of brand-name items, highly specialized retailers	Users are in the market for goods or services	Limited to active shoppers
New and expanding businesses; those using coupon returns or catalogs	Personalized approach to an audience of good prospects	High cost per thousand exposures
Businesses catering to identifiable groups: teens, commuters, housewives	Market selectivity, wide market coverage	Must be bought consistently to be of value
Sellers of products or services with wide appeal	Dramatic impact, wide market coverage	High cost of time and production
Businesses along transit routes, especially those appealing to wage earners	Repetition and length of exposure	Limited audience
Amusements, tourist businesses, brand-name retailers	Dominant size, frequency of exposure	Clutter of many signs reduces effectiveness of each one
Restaurants, entertainments, specialty shops, mail-order businesses	Delivery of a loyal, special-interest audience	Limited audience

tional programs. Suppliers often furnish display aids and even entire advertising programs to their dealers. Trade associations are also active in this area. In addition, the advertising media can provide some services offered by an ad agency.

SALES PROMOTION OPTIONS FOR SMALL FIRMS

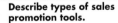

5 Describe types of sales promotion tools.

A **sales promotion** serves as an inducement to buy a certain product while typically offering value to prospective customers. Generally, a sales promotion includes any promotional technique other than personal selling, advertising, and public relations that stimulates the purchase of a particular good or service.

sales promotion
an inclusive term for any promotional techniques that are neither personal selling nor advertising

When to Use Sales Promotion

A small firm can use sales promotion to accomplish various objectives. For example, small manufacturers can use it to stimulate commitment among channel members—retailers and wholesalers—to market their product. Wholesalers can use sales promotion to induce retailers to buy inventories earlier than normally needed, and retailers, with similar promotional tools, may be able to persuade customers to make a purchase.

Sales Promotion Tools

Sales promotion should seldom comprise all the promotional efforts of a small business. Typically, it should be used in combination with personal selling and advertising. Here are some popular sales promotion tools:

- Specialties
- Publicity
- Trade show exhibits
- Sampling
- Coupons

- Premiums
- Contests
- Point-of-purchase displays
- Free merchandise

The scope of this book does not allow discussion of all of these tools. However, we will examine the first three sales promotion tools listed—specialties, publicity, and trade show exhibits.

SPECIALTIES   The most widely used specialty item is a calendar; other examples are pens, key chains, coffee mugs, and shirts. Actually, almost anything can be used as a specialty promotion, as long as each item is imprinted with the firm's name or other identifying slogan.

The most distinguishing characteristic of specialties is their enduring nature and tangible value. Specialties are referred to as the "lasting medium." As functional products, they are also worth something to recipients.

Specialties can be used to promote a product directly or to create goodwill for the company. Specialties are also excellent reminders of the company's existence.

Figure 15-3

Award-Winning Specialty Advertising Effort

Objective: To create awareness and initiate sales of a new product line.

Strategy & Execution: This exclusive banana importer was expanding into the distribution of a variety of fresh fruits and wanted to promote this to its existing accounts. Targeting 150 wholesaler customers, the advertiser's specialty advertising counselor developed a program involving the hand distribution of a magnetic spin-a-clip. The advertiser had new 800 numbers that spelled "bananas" and "fruit" and illustrated these on both sides of the magnetic roller with colorful fruit graphics. The sales force also hand-delivered a unique candy jar filled with fruit-shaped candies in fruit colors. A colorful brochure complemented the items.

Results: Reported reactions were excellent. The increased demand for the new fresh fruit product line and reorders for the spin-a-clip made the promotion a success.

Source: Promotional Products Association International.

Action Report

ETHICAL ISSUES

Community Involvement Gains Publicity

Sponsorship of events such as the Olympics or the Super Bowl costs giant corporations millions of dollars; however, it greatly enhances the visibility of their products. Sponsorship of smaller events such as the local high school yearbook or a community clean-up day costs much less and similarly benefits a small firm's image.

Local event sponsorship is an opportunity for a small business to say thank you to its customers. "At the very least, sponsoring an event allows you to show your company's best features to a highly qualified audience," says Linda Surbeck, president of a special event–planning firm in Lexington, Kentucky. "Along the way, you can achieve market awareness, favorable name recognition, and positive publicity," she says.

Consider the educational toy retailer, Thinker Toys, in Bellevue, Washington. Its owner, Brian Rekow, is helping underwrite a children's film festival at the local Children's Museum.

"The Thinker Toys logo will appear on programs, posters, and banners, and the store will be the only place to buy tickets on the east side of town. . . . I can't predict its success," says Rekow, "but I do have a sense that the relationship with the museum is right for our store and appropriate for our customer demographics. Sponsorships like these increase awareness about Thinker Toys and encourage people to come into the store and see what we're all about. And if they come in, they're likely to buy something."

Rekow's testimony suggests that sponsorship is a viable strategy that enables small companies to break through the clutter of traditional promotions and target their market niches.

Source: Alison Davis, "Big Events for Small Businesses," *Independent Business*, Vol. 3, No. 5 (May-June 1992), pp. 56–57. Reprinted with permission from *Independent Business* magazine, May-June 1992. Copyright 1992 by Group IV Communications, Inc., 125 Auburn Court, Suite 100, Thousand Oaks, CA 91362. All rights reserved.

For example, Carpenter Reserve Printing Co., in Cleveland, Ohio, uses a poster-calendar to create a lasting image among its customers:

The company's identity is tied to the image of an apple, obliquely suggesting that because of its distinctive qualities, the firm cannot be compared with any other, just as apples cannot be compared with oranges. Each limited-edition poster plays with that theme.

The posters are "eagerly anticipated" by customers each quarter, and many clients collect them, says Lynn Brewton, sales manager at Carpenter Reserve Printing. "It's been a great tool for us."[5]

Finally, specialties are personal: They are distributed directly to the consumer in a personal way; they can be used personally; and they have a personal message. Since a small business needs to retain its personal image, entrepreneurs can use specialties to achieve this objective. Figure 15-3 (on page 344) presents one award-winning specialty advertising campaign.

PUBLICITY Of particular importance to retailers because of its high visibility is **publicity.** Publicity can be used to promote both a product and a firm's image; it is a vital part of public relations for the small business. A good publicity program requires regular contacts with the news media.

publicity
information about a firm and its products or services that appears as a news item

1 Describe the communication process and the promotional mix.

- Every communication involves a source, a message, a channel, and a receiver.
- A promotional mix is a blend of personal and nonpersonal communication techniques.
- A promotional mix is influenced by three major factors—geographical nature of the market, identification of target customers, and the product's characteristics.

2 Discuss methods of determining the level of promotional expenditure.

- Earmarking promotional dollars based on a percentage of sales is a simple method for determining expenditures.
- Spending only what can be spared is a widely used approach to promotional budgeting.
- Spending as much as the competition does is a way to react to short-run promotional tactics of competitors.
- The preferred approach to determining promotional expenditures is to decide what it will take to do the job, while factoring in elements used in the other methods.

3 Explain personal selling activities.

- A sales presentation is a process involving prospecting, practicing the presentation, and then making the presentation.
- Salespeople are compensated in two ways—financially and nonfinancially.
- The two basic plans for financial compensation are commissions and straight salary.

4 Identify advertising options for a small business.

- Common media include television, radio, magazines, and newspapers.
- Product advertising is designed to promote a product or service, while institutional advertising conveys an idea regarding the business itself.
- A small firm must decide how often to advertise, where to advertise, and what the message will be.

5 Describe types of sales promotion tools.

- Sales promotion includes all promotional techniques other than personal selling and advertising.
- Typically, sales promotion tools should be used along with advertising and personal selling.
- Three widely used sales promotion tools are specialties, publicity, and trade show exhibits.

Although publicity is considered free advertising, this is not always an accurate profile of this type of promotion. Examples of publicity efforts that entail some expense include involvements with school yearbooks or youth athletic programs. While the benefits are difficult to measure, publicity is nevertheless important to a small business and should be used at every opportunity.

As an example, Pet Cards, Inc., in Baltimore, Maryland, creates cards designed for pet lovers to send to their favorite animals. These unique greeting cards are designed by the company's owners in their in-home office and feature special pet occasions, such as the birth of a new litter. These entrepreneurs found that advertising agencies were quoting a minimum of $200,000 to launch a campaign. They decided, therefore, to do the promotion themselves and began making phone calls to newspapers.

Our phone calls . . . produced several interviews, and we are hoping for more. The publicity seems to be working. One retailer put the cards away but then had to display them again because of customer requests generated by a newspaper article.[6]

TRADE SHOW EXHIBITS The use of trade show exhibits permits product demonstrations, or hands-on experience with a product. A customer's place of business is not always the best environment for product demonstrations during normal personal selling efforts. And advertising cannot always substitute for trial experiences with a product.

Trade show exhibits are of particular value to manufacturers. The greatest benefit of these exhibits is their potential cost savings over personal selling. Trade show groups claim that the cost of exhibits is less than one-fourth the cost of a sales call.[7] Small manufacturers also view exhibits as more cost-effective than advertising. Terk Technologies Corporation, located in New Rochelle, New York, manufactures FM radio antennas. Neil Terk, its president, was pleased with his strategy to exhibit at a large Chicago trade show. "It was absolutely the right decision," he says. "My sales now are spectacular."[8]

Hopefully, the discussions in this chapter have helped you understand the role that promotion plays in the marketing process. It is a complex activity, and entrepreneurs need to recognize their limitations in this area and seek professional advice when necessary.

DISCUSSION QUESTIONS

1. Discuss the parallel relationship that exists between a small business communication and a personal communication.
2. Discuss the advantages and disadvantages of each method of budgeting funds for promotion.
3. Outline a system of prospecting that could be used by a small camera store. Incorporate all the techniques presented in this chapter.
4. Why are a salesperson's techniques for handling objections so important to a successful sales presentation?
5. Assume you are going to "sell" your instructor in this course on the idea of eliminating examinations. Make a list of objections you expect to hear and how you would handle each objection.
6. What are some nonfinancial rewards that could be offered to salespeople?
7. What are the advantages and disadvantages of compensating salespeople by salary? By commissions? What is an acceptable compromise?
8. Refer to Table 15-2 (on pages 342–343) and list five advertising media that would give a small business the most precise selectivity. Be prepared to substantiate your list.
9. How do specialties differ from other sales promotion tools? Be specific.
10. Comment on this statement: "Publicity is free advertising."

New Terms and Concepts

promotion *330*	prospecting *334*	institutional advertising *340*
promotional mix *330*	advertising *339*	sales promotion *343*
personal selling *334*	product advertising *340*	publicity *345*

You Make the Call

Situation 1 The driving force behind Cannon Arp's new business was several bad experiences with his car. In fact, he had had six unpleasant experiences—two speeding tickets and four minor fender-benders. Consequently, his insurance rates more than doubled, which resulted in Arp's idea to design and sell a bumper sticker that read, "To Report Bad Driving, Call My Parents at. . . ." With a $200 investment, Arp printed 15,000 of the stickers, which contain space to write in the appropriate telephone number. Arp is now planning his promotion to support his strategy of distribution through auto parts stores.

Question 1 What role, if any, should personal selling have in Arp's total promotional plan?
Question 2 Arp is considering advertising in magazines. What do you think about this medium for his product?
Question 3 Of what value might publicity be for selling Arp's stickers? Be specific.

Situation 2 Cheree Moore owns and operates a small business that supplies delicatessens with bulk containers of ready-made salads. When served on salad bars, the salads appear to have been freshly prepared from scratch at the delicatessen. Moore wants additional promotional exposure for her products and is considering using her fleet of trucks as rolling billboards. If successful, she may even attempt to lease space on other trucks. Moore is concerned about the cost-effectiveness of the idea and whether the public will even notice the advertisements. She also wonders whether the image of her salad products might be hurt by this advertising medium.

Question 1 What suggestions can you provide that would help Moore make this decision?
Question 2 How could Moore go about determining the cost-effectiveness of this strategy?
Question 3 What additional factors should Moore evaluate before advertising on trucks?

Continue on next page

EXPERIENTIAL EXERCISES

1. Interview the owners of one or more small businesses, and determine how they develop a promotional budget. Classify the owners' methods into one or

Situation 3 Phil Damiani and Kenny Lee own and operate The Ooof Ball Company in Media, Pennsylvania. For four years, they have been establishing a market for their bouncy medicine ball, which is promoted as "building muscle while improving coordination." Their promotional task is continually handicapped by a minimal ad budget and an unproven product. Both Damiani and Lee believe their major challenge is to bring the product into the public eye and get people talking about it.

Question 1 What promotional techniques might be appropriate for this situation? Why?

Question 2 How important would a trade show exhibit be to this promotional effort?

Question 3 Do you believe word-of-mouth advertising would be especially important to this product? Why or why not?

more of the four categories described in this book. Report your findings to the class.

2. Plan a sales presentation with a classmate. One member of the team should role-play a potential buyer. Make the presentation in class, and ask the other students for a critique.

3. Select a small business advertisement from a local newspaper and evaluate its design and purpose.

4. Interview a media representative about advertising options for small businesses. Summarize your findings for the class.

Exploring the

5. Write a summary describing the information available on the Web in the area of small business advertising (use the word search option).

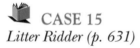 CASE 15
Litter Ridder (p. 631)

This case describes the initial promotional plan for a new product that is to be marketed directly to retailers.

Alternative Cases for Chapter 15: Case 8, "ScrubaDub Auto Wash," p. 614
Case 16, "NovaSoft Systems Inc.," p. 634

Distribution Channels and Global Markets

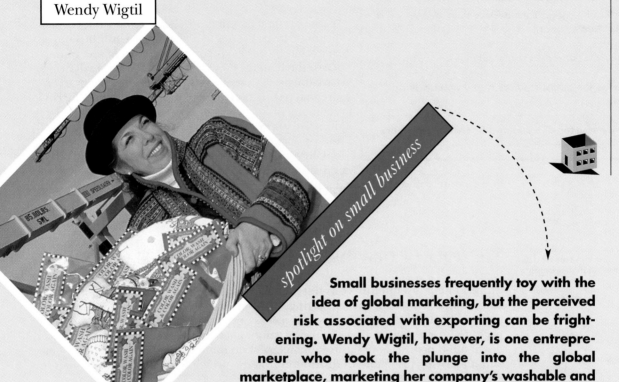

Wendy Wigtil

spotlight on small business

Small businesses frequently toy with the idea of global marketing, but the perceived risk associated with exporting can be frightening. Wendy Wigtil, however, is one entrepreneur who took the plunge into the global marketplace, marketing her company's washable and reusable cloth coloring books. "Exporting was critical for us, especially with the downturn here," says Wigtil, president of Barnyard Babies, Inc., located in Annapolis, Maryland.

Her toy company has six full-time employees and—depending on the workload—from 10 to 30 workers on contract who sew the cloth designs the company makes for children to color.

Wigtil's first orders were the result of an unsolicited inquiry from a foreign distributor at a trade show. That was in 1989, when her company was only three years old. Now, she sells her products in Japan, France, and Canada, and she'll soon expand to Brazil.

Wigtil is enthusiastic about future exporting opportunities for her company, which markets almost exclusively through distributors. "There are more intermediaries out there looking for American products," she says. The opening of new markets, such as the former Soviet bloc, is also creating huge global marketing opportunities.

Source: Roberta Maynard, "A Good Time to Export," *Nation's Business,* Vol. 82, No. 5 (May 1994), pp. 22–23. Excerpted by permission, *Nation's Business,* May 1994. Copyright 1994, U.S. Chamber of Commerce.

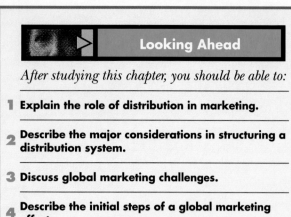

Looking Ahead

After studying this chapter, you should be able to:

1 Explain the role of distribution in marketing.

2 Describe the major considerations in structuring a distribution system.

3 Discuss global marketing challenges.

4 Describe the initial steps of a global marketing effort.

5 Identify sources of trade and financing assistance.

start here

As part of the marketing process, every product or service must be delivered to a customer. Until this physical exchange has been completed, purchasers cannot derive the benefits they seek. Therefore, a small firm's marketing system requires a distribution strategy to ensure that products arrive at the proper place at the correct moment for maximum customer satisfaction. Also, given today's global marketplace, small businesses may find opportunities in international marketing as they look beyond the domestic markets that have nurtured and sustained them. This chapter examines distribution channels as well as several aspects of global marketing.

THE ROLE OF DISTRIBUTION ACTIVITIES IN MARKETING

Entrepreneurs frequently consider distribution to be less glamorous than other marketing activities such as packaging, name selection, and promotion. Nevertheless, an effective distribution system is just as important to a small firm as a unique package, a clever name, or a creative promotional campaign. Prior to formalizing a distribution plan, a small business manager should understand and appreciate certain underlying principles of distribution. These principles apply to both domestic and international distribution.

Distribution Defined

distribution
physically moving products and establishing intermediary channels to support such movement

physical distribution (logistics)
the activities of distribution that result in the relocation of products

channel of distribution
a system of intermediaries that distribute a product

In marketing, **distribution** encompasses both the physical movement of products and the establishment of intermediary (middleman) relationships to guide and support such product movement. The activities involved in the physical movement form a special field called **physical distribution,** or **logistics.** The intermediary relationships are called **channels of distribution.**

Distribution is essential for both tangible and intangible goods. Since distribution activities are more visible for tangible goods (products), our discussion will focus on them. Most intangible goods (services) are delivered directly to the user. An income tax preparer and a barber, for example, serve clients directly. However, marketing a person's labor can involve channel intermediaries, as when, for example, an employment agency is used to provide temporary employees for an employer.

Functions of Intermediaries

Intermediaries exist to carry out necessary marketing functions and can often perform these functions better than the producer or the user of a product. Let's consider a producer of fruitcakes as an example illustrating the need for intermediaries. This producer can perform its own distribution functions—such as deliv-

Indirect distribution channels require intermediaries to perform marketing activities. This dairy products distribution center functions as an intermediary, delivering such items as milk and eggs to retail outlets.

ery—if the geographic market is extremely small, if customers' needs are highly specialized, and if risk levels are low. However, intermediaries may be a more efficient means of distribution if, for example, customers are widely dispersed or a need exists for special packaging and storage. Of course, many types of small firms, such as retail stores, also function as intermediaries. Four main functions of intermediaries are breaking bulk, assorting, providing information, and shifting risks.

BREAKING BULK　　Few individual customers demand quantities that are equal to the amounts manufacturers produce. Therefore, channel activities known as **breaking bulk** take the larger quantities produced and prepare them for individual customers. Wholesalers and retailers purchase large quantities from manufacturers, store these inventories, and then break bulk (sell them to customers in the quantities they desire).

ASSORTING　　Customers' needs are diverse, requiring many different products to satisfy. Intermediaries facilitate shopping for a wide variety of goods through the assorting process. **Assorting** consists of bringing together homogeneous lines of goods into a heterogeneous assortment. For example, a small business that produces a special golf club can benefit from an intermediary who carries many other golf-related products and sells to retail pro shops. It is much more convenient for a pro shop manager to buy from one supplier than from dozens of individual producers.

PROVIDING INFORMATION　　One of the major benefits of using an intermediary is information. Intermediaries can provide a producer with helpful data on market size and pricing considerations, as well as information about other channel members. They may even provide credit to final purchasers.

SHIFTING RISKS　　By using intermediaries called **merchant middlemen,** who take title to the goods they distribute, a small firm can often share or totally shift business risks. Other intermediaries, such as **agents and brokers,** do not take title to the goods.

breaking bulk
an intermediary process that makes large quantities of product available in smaller amounts

assorting
bringing together homogeneous lines of goods into a heterogeneous assortment

merchant middlemen
intermediaries that take title to the goods they distribute

agents and brokers
intermediaries that do not take title to the goods they distribute

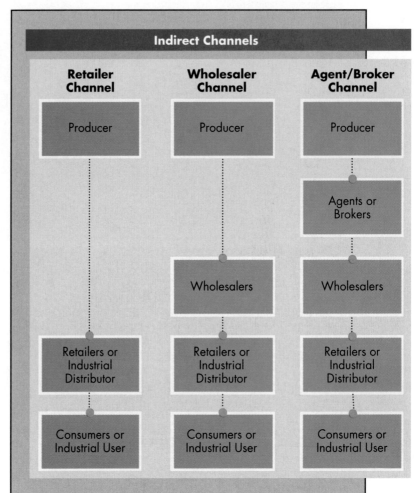

Figure 16-1   *Alternative Channels of Distribution*

Types of Channels of Distribution

A channel of distribution can be either direct or indirect. In a **direct channel** of distribution, there are no intermediaries; the product goes directly from producer to user. In an **indirect channel** of distribution, there may be one or more intermediaries between producer and user.

Figure 16-1 depicts the various options available for structuring a channel of distribution. Door-to-door retailing and mail-order marketing are familiar forms of the direct channel system for distributing consumer goods. The remaining channels shown in Figure 16-1 are indirect channels involving one, two, or three levels of intermediaries. As a final consumer, you are naturally familiar with retailers. Likewise, industrial purchasers are equally familiar with industrial distributors. Channels with two or three stages of intermediaries are probably the most typical channels used by small firms that have large geographic markets. Note that a small firm may use more than one channel of distribution—a practice called **dual distribution.**

direct channel
a distribution channel without intermediaries

indirect channel
a distribution channel with one or more intermediaries

dual distribution
a distribution system that involves more than one channel

Firms that successfully employ a single distribution channel may switch to dual distribution if an additional channel will improve overall profitability. For example, Avon, with its "Avon Calling" theme, symbolizes door-to-door product distribution. Recently, however, Avon announced a toll-free telephone number that customers may call to place orders. This additional distribution strategy reflects a cultural change—fewer women are at home to answer the "Avon Calling" message.[1]

STRUCTURING A DISTRIBUTION SYSTEM

One source of information about structuring a distribution system is competing businesses. The small business producer can observe their distribution systems for patterns in order to determine which system seems most practical. However, a small firm that is starting from scratch and wants to shape its own distribution system needs to give attention to several important considerations.

> **2** Describe the major considerations in structuring a distribution system.

Building a Channel of Distribution

Basically, there are three main considerations in building a channel of distribution: costs, coverage, and control.

COSTS   Entrepreneurs should not think that a direct channel is inherently less expensive than an indirect channel just because there are no intermediaries. A small firm may well be in a situation in which the least expensive channel is indirect. For example, a firm producing handmade dolls will probably not own trucks and warehouses for distributing its product directly to customers but will rely on established intermediaries because of the smaller total cost of distribution. Small firms should also look at distribution costs as an investment—spending money in order to make money. They should ask themselves whether the money they "invest" in intermediaries (by selling the product to them at a reduced price) would get the job done if they used direct distribution.

COVERAGE   Small firms often use indirect channels of distribution to increase market coverage. Let's consider a small manufacturer whose sales force can make 10 contacts a week. This direct channel provides 10 contacts a week with the final users of the product. Now consider an indirect channel involving 10 industrial distributors, each making 10 contacts a week with the final users of the product. With this indirect channel, and no increase in the sales force, the small manufacturer is able to expose its product to 100 final users a week.

CONTROL   A third consideration in choosing a distribution channel is control. A direct channel of distribution provides more control. With an indirect channel, a product may not be marketed as intended. A small firm must select intermediaries that provide the desired support.

Control is the main reason Robin Rose, of Robin Rose Ice Cream in Los Angeles, distributes her products directly to customers. The reputation of her ice cream depends on the freshness and quality of the product; therefore, she "has purposely remained small in order to control both the production and distribution of her ice cream."[2]

Action Report

GLOBAL OPPORTUNITIES

GLOBAL **Distribution Fails Venture**

The ultimate worth of a channel of distribution is determined by its ability to deliver a product to the right place at the right time. Sometimes, especially in the international marketplace, timely delivery can be a problem. Just ask Joe Reagan, owner of Reagan's Coffees, a coffee-supply company based in Springfield, Virginia, who decided to import bottled water from Ireland.

Reagan admits that he failed to properly investigate the distribution system that was to bring the bottled water to the U.S. market:

> *"What a mess. . . . The ship didn't come directly to the United States. They would fill it halfway up in Ireland with bottled water. Then it would go to one of the Scandinavian countries where they loaded up the rest of the boat with drugs." At every port of call, suspicious customs officers searched all of the ship's cargo for drugs. While rummaging through the crates containing . . . bottled water, officials often broke bottles or left them on the dock, where they froze and cracked before being reloaded.*

Initially, Reagan could not figure out why customs officials found his shipment so intriguing. For three years, he kept trying different ports before he found out that the boat wasn't coming directly from Ireland. Finally, Reagan understood the problem and abandoned the bottled-water venture.

Source: Timothy L. O'Brien, "Today's Lesson: Coffee and Water Don't Mix," *The Wall Street Journal*, October 16, 1992, p. R4. Reprinted by permission of *The Wall Street Journal*, © 1992 Dow Jones & Company, Inc. All Rights Reserved Worldwide.

The Scope of Physical Distribution

In addition to the intermediary relationships that make up a channel, there must also be a system of physical distribution. The main component of physical distribution is transportation. Additional components are storage, materials handling, delivery terms, and inventory management. The following sections briefly examine all these topics except inventory management, which is discussed in Chapter 20.

common carriers
transportation intermediaries available for hire to the general public

contract carriers
transportation intermediaries that contract with individual shippers

private carriers
shippers that own their means of transport

TRANSPORTATION   The major decision regarding transportation concerns what mode to use. Available modes of transportation are traditionally classified as airplanes, trucks, railroads, pipelines, and waterways. Each mode has unique advantages and disadvantages. The choice of a specific mode of transportation is based on several criteria: relative cost, transit time, reliability, capability, accessibility, and traceability.[3]

Transportation intermediaries are legally classified as common carriers, contract carriers, and private carriers. **Common carriers,** which are available for hire to the general public, and **contract carriers,** which engage in individual contracts with shippers, are subject to regulation by federal and/or state agencies. Shippers that own their means of transport are called **private carriers.**

STORAGE   Lack of space is a common problem for small businesses. When a channel system uses merchant middlemen or wholesalers, for example, title to the goods is transferred, as is responsibility for the storage function. On other occasions, the small business must plan for its own warehousing. If a firm is too small to own a private warehouse, it can rent space in public warehouses. If storage requirements are simple and do not involve much special handling equipment, a public warehouse can provide economical storage.

MATERIALS HANDLING   A product is worth little if it is in the right place at the right time but is damaged. Therefore, a physical distribution system must arrange for materials-handling methods and equipment. Forklifts as well as special containers and packaging are part of a materials-handling system.

DELIVERY TERMS   A small but important part of a physical distribution system is the terms of delivery. Delivery terms specify which party is responsible for several aspects of physical distribution:

- Paying the freight costs
- Selecting the carriers
- Bearing the risk of damage in transit
- Selecting the modes of transport

The simplest delivery term and the one most advantageous to a small business as seller is F.O.B. (free on board) origin, freight collect. These terms shift all the responsibility for freight costs to the buyer. Title to the goods and risk of loss also pass to the buyer at the time the goods are shipped.

GLOBAL MARKETING CHALLENGES

3 Discuss global marketing challenges.

Today, global marketing by small U.S. firms is becoming more commonplace. Certain opportunities abroad are simply more profitable than those at home. However, global marketing is not easy. If it were, the United States would not have such a large unfavorable balance of trade—importing more than it exports.

The challenges facing a small firm interested in global marketing can be better appreciated by considering the experiences and major obstacles encountered by entrepreneurs in international markets. The next two sections briefly examine these challenges.

Global Opportunity

A basic human characteristic is a tendency to shy away from the complex and shun the unfamiliar. Entrepreneurs have traditionally held this attitude regarding foreign markets. Why have small firms historically shunned international trade? One survey of more than 5,000 independent U.S. businesses found the factors given below to be major obstacles in exploring or expanding exports:

- Obtaining adequate, initial knowledge about exporting (72 percent)
- Identifying viable sales prospects abroad (61 percent)
- Understanding business protocols in other countries (57 percent)
- Selecting suitable target markets on the basis of the available information (57 percent)[4]

Nevertheless, many surveys indicate that U.S. entrepreneurs are pursuing international trade opportunities in increasing numbers. Consider the following statement from one recent survey as an example of this movement abroad:

> *A survey of almost 750 companies by Arthur Andersen & Co. and National Small Business United, a trade group, found that 20 percent of companies with fewer than 500 employees exported products and services [in 1994]. That's up from 16 percent in 1993 and 11 percent in 1992, the first year the survey was conducted.*[5]

Evidently, more and more small firms are accepting the international challenge. This is good news for all small firms, as well as government policy makers involved in solving U.S. trade problems. The following are two examples of small firms whose international involvement has been profitable:

> *Global American Television Inc. is not a big company, but it has big ambitions, especially overseas. . . . While maneuvering in the volatile and frustrating Russian market, however, this small TV production company faces stiff competition. . . . Yet Global American, with revenues of less than $500,000 a year, does plenty of high-profile business in Russia, often upstaging its bigger competitors, according to Edward Wierzbowski, co-owner with his wife, Pamela Roberts, of the Colrain, Massachusetts, company.*[6]

> *Three years ago, Rust Evader Corporation of Altoona, Pennsylvania, made a calculation that its rust-prevention devices for motor vehicles might have better potential abroad than here. Dan Emanuelson, president of the 37-employee firm, explained, "Overseas, automobiles are more expensive. People keep them longer. There are many backyard mechanics who like to tinker with their cars. They are more apt to keep their cars for 10 years. Overseas, there is less of the planned obsolescence that we have in this country." Rust Evader now sells most of its products overseas.*[7]

Clearly, small firms can be just as successful as large firms in international markets. The idea that global marketing is for big business only is extremely damaging to small firms' efforts to market abroad. Data regarding big business versus small business involvement in international markets is at best inconclusive.[8]

Understanding Other Cultures

As early as possible in global marketing efforts, an entrepreneur needs to study the cultural, political, and economic forces in foreign markets to determine which adjustments to domestic marketing strategies are required. It is important to remember that what may be acceptable in one culture may be considered unethical or morally wrong in another. When cultural lines are being crossed, even something as simple as a daily "Good Morning" greeting accompanied by a handshake may be misunderstood. The entrepreneur must evaluate the proper use of names and titles and be aware of different styles of do-

Global marketing efforts must take into account the cultural, political, and economic forces at work in host countries. The Japanese prefer to establish relationships based on mutual trust before conducting business.

Figure 16-2

Japanese Business Practices and Suggested Responses

Typical Japanese negotiating tactics:

- The Japanese usually respond to the other party's proposal rather than taking the initiative.
- They tend to single out specific elements and negotiate one element at a time rather than packaging a deal.
- The Japanese tend to maintain a relatively quiet response demeanor at meetings after stating their official position. They usually allow the other party enough maneuverability to keep giving bit by bit.
- Once a concession is made, it becomes the new baseline (without a counter-concession on their part), and they move on to the next item. Their strategy is usually to keep whittling away, one concession at a time.
- The Japanese use time and patience to wear down their opponent—consciously planning on long, drawn-out periods of successive meetings.
- Their negotiating team never has the authority to commit in a "give and take" type of approach. It is usually only authorized to receive offers and communicate prior authorized consensus positions.
- The Japanese tend to use the "bad guy" ploy extensively, that is, constantly referring to other organizations such as government agencies/authorities as demanding certain requirements or required concessions.

How to respond:

- Do not expect rapid progress.
- Learn to be quiet and accept long pauses in discussions. Outwait the Japanese until they respond constructively to your last proposal.
- Do not make successive individual concessions—insist on a package deal.
- Do not make a follow-on proposal with further concessions until the Japanese respond to the current proposal with concessions on their part. Set an agenda for the next meeting accordingly.
- Do not fall for the "cultural differences" ploy. Be polite but direct. You can expect the Japanese to understand Western business practices and culture. They should be prepared to compromise and accommodate on those issues you identify as absolutely essential. However, showing an appreciation of Japanese culture will help facilitate negotiations.
- Keep records on concessions by both parties.
- Have a speaker fluent in Japanese present at negotiations to preclude private discussions during meetings and to ensure the translations are accurate.
- Negotiate from a position of strength and confidence. The Japanese do not respond positively to real or perceived weakness, nor do they respond to idle threats and intimidation.

Source: Adapted from *Destination Japan*, U.S. Department of Commerce (Washington, DC: U.S. Government Printing Office, 1991).

ing business. For example, Figure 16-2 describes Japanese business negotiation practices and how to respond to them—valuable information for a small firm entering this international market.

When a foreign market is not studied carefully, costly mistakes may be made. For example, a U.S. mail-order concern offering products to the Japanese didn't realize that the American custom of asking customers for a credit-card number before taking their order would insult the Japanese. Later, a Japanese consultant told the company that people in Japan think that such an approach shows a lack of trust.[9] Additional examples highlighting the importance of understanding cultural differences include the following:

Forest Lumber Company of Meridian, Mississippi, which has only 15 employees, won business from the Japanese by being patient and building up confidence through personal relationships. Clyde Brooks, export sales manager for the foreign products broker and export management company, said that keeping your word "is particularly important in doing business with the Japanese, because they value personal relationships. I have done business with a Japanese trading company for 25 years, and I've never had a problem." In the beginning, Brooks doubted business with the Japanese would ever develop, because it took nearly a year to nail down a deal. However, perseverance paid off, and the company's "best response" is from Japan.[10]

An hour before an American company was to sign a contract with a Middle Eastern nation, the American executive met for tea with the responsible government official. The American propped his feet on a table with the soles facing his Arab host. The official became angry and left the room. Such an act is a grave insult in the Arab's culture. The contract was signed one year later.[11]

Trade Agreements

Differences in trading systems and import requirements of each country can make international trade difficult. To appreciate the problems that these differences create, let's consider the situation of Mentor O & O, Inc., a small manufacturer in Norwell, Massachusetts. Mentor produces diagnostic and surgical eye care equipment, which it markets internationally. It regularly modifies its products to meet rigid design specifications that vary from country to country. For example, an alarm bell on Mentor's testing device has an on/off switch that must be removed before it is acceptable in Germany.[12] This is typical of barriers to trade that exist throughout the world.

Free Trade Agreement (FTA) an accord that eases trade restrictions between the United States and Canada

The global market has recently entered a period of positive change with regard to trade barriers. In 1989, Canada and the United States signed the **Free Trade Agreement** (**FTA**), which calls for the elimination of most tariffs and other trade restrictions by January 1, 1998. The result should be an environment more conducive to trade between these two countries.[13]

North American Free Trade Agreement (NAFTA) an accord that removes Mexican tariffs from U.S.-made products

In 1993, the United States and Mexico signed the **North American Free Trade Agreement** (**NAFTA**).[14] Under NAFTA, all Mexican tariffs on products made in the United States will be phased out over a period of 15 years; almost half of these tariffs were removed on the agreement's effective date of January 1, 1994.

General Agreement on Tariffs and Trade (GATT) an international agreement that helps efforts to protect U.S.-patented products and reduces certain import tariffs

Also, November 1993 marked the official beginning of the 15-nation European Union (EU). For the last decade, businesses of all sizes have observed the preparations being made for a unified Europe. However, the fall of the Iron Curtain created a more complex world and has put certain pressures on the EU to admit Eastern European nations. The exact impact that this unification will have on small exporters is unknown.[15]

Effective on January 1, 1995, the **General Agreement on Tariffs and Trade (GATT)** was approved by Congress to add global muscle to efforts to stop the pirating of products having U.S. patents. GATT also reduces certain import tariffs.

4 Describe the initial steps of a global marketing effort.

INITIAL PREPARATIONS FOR GLOBAL MARKETING

Many activities prepare a small firm for a global marketing effort. Two, in particular, are vital for almost every international venture—researching the foreign market and setting up a sales and distribution plan.

Action Report

GLOBAL OPPORTUNITIES

What GATT Means to Small Business

Trade agreements, such as the General Agreement on Tariffs and Trade (GATT), benefit small firms in a number of ways. GATT is expected to reduce import tariffs and to create a better export environment. One area in which it is expected to have immediate impact is the protection of intellectual property.

> The intellectual-property protections included in the GATT agreement commit signatory countries to 7 years of protection for trademarks, 20 years for patents, and up to 50 years for copyrights, including those for films, music, and software.
>
> GATT is more than an acronym to Barbara Maxwell, marketing executive vice president and part owner of Synergy Software, in Reading, Pennsylvania. To her, the new accord under the General Agreement on Tariffs and Trade should help restore order to an international market where U.S. software creators alone lose about $2.5 billion a year when their works are pirated in other countries. "It's really crazy out there," she says.
>
> Synergy, an 11-year-old software publisher, suffered because of the lack of intellectual-property protections several years ago. A college professor in Italy at the time purchased and then duplicated one of the company's programs. What had been one copy became 1,200. Says Maxwell: "Everyone on the whole campus was using VersaTerm"—a program allowing easier access to the Internet, the global web of computer networks.
>
> Under Italian law at that time, Synergy had no way to recover any losses from the pirating of the software. "People told me to let it go. I didn't have a choice," says Maxwell. "Until [1993], there was no law that had the word 'software' in it. The best you could do in an Italian court was try to include software in some very old copyright laws that protected magazines."
>
> But now, under the new trade pact, Italy, as a GATT signatory, is required to provide legal protection for software and is, in fact, upgrading its protections under the agreement. Says Maxwell: "It will be much more reassuring for any smaller software developer to have things like GATT in place."

Source: John S. DeMott, "What GATT Means to Small Business," *Nation's Business*, Vol. 83, No. 3 (March 1995), pp. 53–54.

Researching a Foreign Market

Foreign-market research should begin by exhausting as many secondary sources of information as possible. The U.S. government offers an array of publications on how to locate and exploit global marketing opportunities. The Commerce Department's International Trade Administration (ITA) is the primary U.S. government agency responsible for assisting exporters. One of its more helpful publications, *U.S. Global Trade Outlook 1995–2000*, provides a global outlook. Figure 16-3 describes several ITA services.

One excellent publication about global marketing prepared by the federal government is *A Basic Guide to Exporting*, which is available from the Superintendent of Documents, U.S. Government Printing Office. Also available from the same source is the *Exporter's Guide to Federal Resources for Small Business*, which provides the reader with an overview of major federal export programs, as well as contact points for further information and help in finding expertise in utilizing these programs. The

| Figure 16-3 | *Export Services of the International Trade Administration* |

Export Counseling. Trade specialists are available at ITA district and branch offices for individualized export counseling.

Market Research. Analysts in foreign posts provide the United States & Foreign Commercial Service with timely, accurate, and in-depth marketing data on industrial sectors with high export potential in the most promising countries.

Agent/Distributor Service. A customized search for interested and qualified foreign representatives will identify up to six foreign prospects who have examined the U.S. firm's literature and expressed interest in representing it.

Commercial News USA. A monthly magazine promotes the products or services of U.S. firms to more than 110,000 overseas agents, distributors, government officials, and purchasers. Exporters may submit a black-and-white photo and a brief description of their product or service.

Comparison Shopping. A custom-tailored service provides firms with key marketing and foreign representation information about their specific products. Commerce Department staff conduct on-the-spot interviews to determine nine key marketing facts about the product, such as sales potential in the market, comparable products, distribution channels, going price, competitive factors, and qualified purchasers.

Foreign Buyer Program. Exporters can meet qualified foreign purchasers for their product or service at trade shows in the United States. The Commerce Department promotes the shows worldwide to attract foreign-buyer delegations, manages an international business center, counsels participating firms, and brings together buyer and seller.

Gold Key Service. A custom-tailored service is offered for U.S. firms planning to visit a foreign country. Offered by many overseas posts, it combines several services, such as market orientation briefings, market research, introductions to potential partners, an interpreter for meetings, and assistance in developing a sound market strategy and an effective follow-up plan.

Trade Opportunities Program. Companies are provided with current sales leads from overseas firms seeking to buy or represent their product or service. These leads are available electronically from the Commerce Department and are redistributed by the private sector in printed or electronic form.

World Traders Data Report. Custom reports evaluate potential trading partners. Such a report will include background information, standing in the local business community, creditworthiness, and overall reliability and suitability.

Overseas Catalog and Video-Catalog Shows. Companies can gain market exposure for their product or service without the cost of traveling overseas by participating in a catalog or video-catalog show sponsored by the Commerce Department. Provided with the firm's product literature or promotional video, an industry will display the material to select foreign audiences in several countries.

Overseas Trade Missions. Officials of U.S. firms can participate in a trade mission, which will give them an opportunity to confer with influential foreign business and government representatives. Commerce Department staff will identify and arrange a full schedule of appointments in each country.

Overseas Trade Fairs. U.S. exporters may participate in overseas trade fairs, which will enable them to meet customers face-to-face and also to assess the competition. The Commerce Department creates a U.S. presence at international trade fairs, making it easier for U.S. firms to exhibit and gain international recognition. The Department selects international trade fairs for special endorsement, called certification. This cooperation with the private show organizers enables U.S. exhibitors to receive special services designed to enhance their market promotion efforts. There is a service charge.

Matchmaker Events. Matchmaker Trade Delegations offer introductions to new markets through short, inexpensive overseas visits with a limited objective: to match the U.S. firm with a representative or prospective joint-venture/licensee partner who shares a common product or service interest. Firms learn key aspects of doing business in the new country and meet in one-on-one interviews the people who can help them be successful there.

Trade Information Center. A one-stop source for information on all federal government export assistance programs. Call 1-800-USA-TRADE.

Source: U.S. Department of Commerce, *Business America*, Vol. 113, No. 9 (Washington, DC: U.S. Government Printing Office, 1992).

Export Yellow Pages is a useful directory of export-trading companies and also lists over 12,000 U.S. firms involved in foreign trade.

Banks, universities, and other private organizations also provide information on exporting. A good example of such a service is The Export Hotline started in February 1992 by International Strategies of Boston. Essentially a fax-retrieval service, it offers export profiles on 68 countries and 50 industries. One company reported using the hotline information to make a $100,000 sale overseas. According to an International Strategies representative, over 15,000 companies have called the 800 USA-XPORT number.[16] In addition, Price Waterhouse, a public accounting firm, publishes a useful book entitled *The Expanding Into Exports Handbook*.

Talking with a citizen of a foreign country or even someone who has visited a potential foreign market can be a valuable way to learn something about it. International students studying at many universities can be contacted through faculty members who teach courses in the international disciplines.

One of the best ways to study a foreign market is to visit that market personally. Representatives of small firms can do this either individually or in organized groups. Entrepreneur Peter Johns is a good example of a small business owner who researched a foreign market on his own. His firm, Choices Unlimited, had obtained rights from over 20 U.S. companies to distribute their catalogs in Mexico City, but he could not find a good marketing study to determine the feasibility of the venture. Therefore, he went to Mexico City and toured affluent neighborhoods and shopping areas to evaluate market potential.

> *What he saw brightened his spirits: satellite dishes, imported sports cars, and women carrying Louis Vuitton handbags around. Drawing on those impressions, and other information he gathered on his own, he came to his own conclusion: His target market is about 300,000 families. . . . "That's called grass-roots marketing intelligence," says Mr. Johns.*[17]

Being a member of a trade mission sponsored by the Department of Commerce is another means of evaluating a foreign market. A trade mission is a planned visit to a potential foreign market to introduce U.S. firms to appropriate foreign buyers and to establish exporting relationships. These missions usually involve a group of from 5 to 10 business executives and are organized and planned to achieve maximum results in expanding exports. Members of the group typically pay their own expenses and share in the operating costs of the mission. Sometimes, foreign governments also sponsor trade missions for U.S. firms considering their markets. One small U.S. business owner went on such a trip sponsored by the Japanese government and found the experience worthwhile:

> *Richard Russell went a skeptic and came back a believer. His Tech Spray, Inc. of Amarillo, Texas, a maker of chemicals for the electronics industry, had tried to break into the Japanese market a decade earlier and "couldn't even get the products through customs." . . . Mr. Russell says he only accepted the invitation from the Japan External Organization to fly to Tokyo last August because the trip was free. To his surprise, he found the Japanese receptive. . . . The New York–born entrepreneur found a Japanese distributor, and it already has placed two test orders worth several thousand dollars.*[18]

Sales and Distribution Channels

Exporting is not the only way to be involved in international markets. In fact, licensing is the simplest strategy for conducting international trade. With only a small investment, a firm can penetrate a foreign market. **Licensing** is an arrangement that allows a foreign manufacturer to use the designs, patents, or trademarks

licensing
legally agreeing that a product may be produced in return for royalties

Figure 16-4

Additional Foreign Market Channels of Distribution

Sales Representatives or Agents. A sales representative is the equivalent of a manufacturer's representative here in the United States. Product literature and samples are used to present the product to the potential buyer. The representative usually works on a commission basis, assumes no risk or responsibility, and is under contract for a definite period of time (renewable by mutual agreement). This contract defines territory, terms of sale, method of compensation, and other details. The sales representative may operate on either an exclusive or a nonexclusive basis.

Foreign Distributor. A foreign distributor is a merchant who purchases merchandise from a U.S. manufacturer at the greatest possible discount and resells it for a profit. This would be the preferred arrangement if the product being sold requires periodic servicing. The prospective distributor should be willing to carry a sufficient supply of spare parts and maintain adequate facilities and personnel to perform all normal servicing operations. The U.S. manufacturer should establish a credit pattern so that more flexible or convenient payment terms can be offered. As with a sales representative, the length of association is established by contract, which is renewable if the arrangement proves satisfactory.

Foreign Retailer. Generally limited to the consumer product line, the foreign retailer relies mainly on direct contact by traveling sales representatives, although catalogs, brochures, and other literature can achieve the same purpose. However, even though direct mail would eliminate commissions and traveling expenses, a U.S. manufacturer's direct mail proposal may not receive proper consideration.

Selling Direct to the End User. Selling direct is quite limited and depends on the product. Opportunities often arise from advertisements in magazines receiving overseas distribution. This can often create difficulties because casual inquirers may not be fully cognizant of their country's foreign trade regulations. For several reasons, they may not be able to receive the merchandise upon arrival, thus causing it to be impounded and possibly sold at public auction, or returned on a freight-collect basis that could prove costly.

State-Controlled Trading Companies. State-controlled trading companies exist in countries that have state trading monopolies, where business is conducted by a few government-sanctioned and controlled trading entities. Because of worldwide changes in foreign policy and their effect on trade between countries, these companies can become important future markets. For the time being, however, most opportunities will be limited to such items as raw materials, agricultural machinery, manufacturing equipment, and technical instruments, rather than consumer or household goods. This is due to the shortage of foreign exchange and the emphasis on self-sufficiency.

Source: Adapted from U.S. Department of Commerce, *A Basic Guide to Exporting* (Washington, DC: U.S. Government Printing Office, 1992).

of the licenser. The practice of licensing helps overcome trade barriers surrounding exporting, because the product is produced in the foreign country. Michael Koss, CEO of Koss Corporation in Milwaukee, used licensing to diversify his stereo-headphone manufacturing company because "this seemed a good way to generate royalty income in the short run and cement a strategic partnership that could lead, over the long run, to joint ventures." His foreign licensee is the Dutch trading company Hagemeyer, which pays royalties to use Koss's brand name and logo. To ensure quality, Koss has "veto power over all product drawings, engineering specifications, first-product samples, and final products."[19]

A small firm can also participate in foreign-market sales via joint ventures and wholly owned subsidiaries in foreign markets. International joint ventures offer a greater presence abroad at less cost than that of establishing a firm's own operation or office in foreign markets. Some host countries may require that a certain

New Product Information Service (NPIS). This special service, offered by the Department of Commerce, can facilitate a direct selling effort to potential overseas customers. It enables U.S. companies interested in selling a new product overseas to submit appropriate data through Commerce Department district offices for placement in the Department's publication, *Commercial News USA*. This is distributed exclusively abroad through 240 U.S. Foreign Service posts. The new product data are extracted and reprinted in individual post newsletters that are tailored to local markets. Selected product information is also broadcast abroad by the International Communication Agency's Voice of America.

Commission Agents. Commission, or buying, agents are "finders" for foreign firms wanting to purchase U.S. products. These purchasing agents obtain the desired equipment at the lowest possible price and are paid a commission by their foreign clients.

Country-Controlled Buying Agents. Foreign government agencies or quasi-governmental firms, called country-controlled buying agents, are empowered to locate and purchase desired goods.

Export Management Companies. EMCs, as they are called, act as the export department for several manufacturers of noncompetitive products. They solicit and transact business in the name of the manufacturers they represent for a commission, salary, or retainer plus commission. Many EMCs carry the financing for export sales, ensuring immediate payment for the manufacturer's products. This can be an exceptionally good arrangement for small firms that do not have the time, personnel, or money to develop foreign markets but wish to establish a corporate and product identity internationally.

Export Merchants. Export merchants purchase products directly from the manufacturer and have them packed and marked to their specifications. They then sell overseas through their contacts, in their own names, and assume all risk for their accounts.

Export Agents. Export agents operate in the same manner as manufacturer's representatives, but the risk of loss remains with the manufacturer..

In transactions with export merchants and export agents, a seller is faced with the possible disadvantage of giving up control over the marketing and promotion of the product. This could have an adverse effect on future success.

percentage of manufacturing facilities be owned by nationals of that country, thereby forcing U.S. firms to operate through joint ventures. Other options for foreign distribution channels are identified in Figure 16-4.

Many firms find that foreign distributors, by first buying the product and then finding customers, offer a low-cost way to market products overseas. However, some foreign distributors are not strongly committed to selling an individual manufacturer's products. If a small firm mistakenly picks one of these distributors, sales may not grow as fast as they could. When B.D. Baggies, a New York–based men's shirt maker, first began marketing internationally, it contracted with the first foreign distributor that offered to sell its shirts in Europe. "Later, we found that the distributor wasn't right. They were selling our shirts to women's stores as a unisex product," explains Charles M. McConnell, president of B.D. Baggies. Subsequently, the firm carefully screened all distributors, and it is now doing good business in more than 40 countries.[20]

Action Report

TECHNOLOGY

TECHNOLOGICAL APPLICATIONS

The Global Link

As small businesses turn increasingly to global marketing opportunities, they perceive the advantage of integrating computers and other technology with their operations. One fairly new computer-based system—named IBEX for International Business Exchange and launched by the U.S. Chamber of Commerce and a group of businesses and trade associations—enables users to sell their products or buy supplies anywhere in the world. Here's how IBEX works:

- Once IBEX is installed in your computer, you enter your offer to buy or sell products or services on prepared electronic forms.
- IBEX then searches its system for potential matches and alerts you via fax to turn on your computer and examine potential offers.
- Then, through secure E-mail, you can make counteroffers, negotiate, or comment on the terms of the offer directly with the potential buyer or seller. At this stage, you can even deal with each other anonymously, without releasing company profiles. IBEX will indicate whether the parties are principal buyers and sellers or intermediaries.
- Once you and the other party agree on terms, you can check out each other's company profiles and use IBEX to tap into Dun & Bradstreet's vast database of company information, and even call references.
- After the deal is completed, IBEX can help you locate freight forwarders, bankers, accountants, or customs brokers.

One small business manager, Joan Gosciminski, of J. Moran Company, Inc. of Smithfield, Rhode Island, says she's "excited about the possibilities" of IBEX with regard to the freight-forwarding operations of her company. She is considering offering her company's services as a customs broker and international freight forwarder on the IBEX system.

Source: James Worsham, "A Global Reach for Small Firms," *Nation's Business*, Vol. 83, No. 10 (October 1995), p. 40. Excerpted by permission, *Nation's Business*, October 1995. Copyright 1995, U.S. Chamber of Commerce.

---

5 Identify sources of trade and financing assistance.

SOURCES OF TRADE AND FINANCING ASSISTANCE

Difficulty in getting trade information and arranging financing is often considered the biggest barrier to small business exporting. In reality, a number of direct and indirect sources of trade and financing information can help a small firm view foreign markets more favorably.

Private Banks

Commercial banks typically have a loan officer who is responsible for handling foreign transactions. Large banks may have a separate international department. Exporters use banks to issue commercial letters of credit and perform other financial activities associated with exporting.

A **letter of credit** is an agreement to honor a draft or other demand for payment when specified conditions are met. It helps assure a seller of prompt payment and may be revocable or irrevocable. An irrevocable letter of credit cannot be changed unless both the buyer and the seller agree to make the change. The pro-

letter of credit
an agreement to honor demands for payment under certain conditions

cedure typically followed when payment is made by an irrevocable letter of credit confirmed by a U.S. bank has these steps:

1. After exporter and buyer agree on the terms of sale, the buyer arranges for its bank to open a letter of credit. (Delays may be encountered if, for example, the buyer has insufficient funds.)
2. The buyer's bank prepares an irrevocable letter of credit, including all instructions to the seller concerning the shipment.
3. The buyer's bank sends the irrevocable letter of credit to a U.S. bank, requesting confirmation. The exporter may request that a particular U.S. bank be the confirming bank, or the buyer's bank will select one of its U.S. correspondent banks.
4. The U.S. bank prepares a letter of confirmation to forward to the exporter along with the irrevocable letter of credit.
5. The exporter carefully reviews all conditions in the letter of credit. The exporter's freight forwarder is generally contacted to make sure that the shipping date can be met. If the exporter cannot comply with one or more of the conditions, the buyer should be alerted at once.
6. The exporter arranges with the freight forwarder to deliver the goods to the appropriate port or airport.
7. When the goods are loaded, the freight forwarder completes the necessary documents.
8. The exporter (or the freight forwarder) presents to the U.S. bank documents indicating full compliance.
9. The bank reviews the documents. If they are in order, the documents are forwarded to the buyer's bank for review and transmitted to the buyer.
10. The buyer (or agent) gets the documents that may be needed to claim the goods.
11. A draft, which may accompany the letter of credit, is paid by the exporter's bank at the time specified or may be discounted if paid earlier.[21]

A letter of credit, as important as it is, is not an absolute guarantee of payment. Consider the experience of seafood exporter Michael Graham in the Russian Republic. Graham's firm, Ocean Traders of North America, obtained a letter of credit to back an export order for 16,000 tons of fish. The buyer's bank canceled the irrevocable letter of credit, admitting to a "technical error." In a letter of explanation, the Russian bank chairman says the deal was all a mistake.[22]

Factoring Houses

A factoring house, or factor, buys clients' accounts receivable and advances money to these clients. The factor assumes the risk of collection of the accounts. The Factors Chain International is an association representing factors from more than 25 countries.[23] Its efforts have helped make factoring services available on an international basis.

State Programs

More states each year are developing and implementing their own programs to help small companies under their jurisdiction finance exports.[24] For example, California guarantees repayment of 85 percent of loans used to finance receivables related to exports. C.M. Magnetics, of Santa Fe Springs, California, was a beneficiary of state assistance when the company needed capital to fill an order for its videotapes from China. "Without their help . . . we probably wouldn't be in business today," says President J. Carlos Maciel.[25]

Export Trading Companies

In 1982, President Reagan signed into law the Export Trading Company Act for the stated purpose of increasing U.S. exports of goods and services.[26] The act covers restrictions on trade financing and clarifies U.S. antitrust laws. Under the act, an Export Trading Company (ETC) can be organized to facilitate the exporting of goods and services produced in the United States. Affiliation with an ETC allows a small firm to employ the resources of an organization that has ongoing exporting expertise. At the end of 1995, only 125 ETCs had been certified. Their value to small firms is still in doubt. One study asking users of ETCs to evaluate their performance concluded that there is "a lack of congruence between [the] services small businesses desire from exporting intermediaries and the services ETCs perform well."[27]

The Export-Import Bank

To encourage U.S. businesses to sell overseas, the federal government created the Export-Import Bank (Eximbank) in 1934. Although historically of greatest use to large firms, in recent years Eximbank has overhauled its programs in order to benefit small firms. The following offerings are particularly helpful to small business exporters:

- *Export credit insurance.* An exporter may reduce its financing risks by purchasing export credit insurance. This insurance is available from Eximbank's agent, the Foreign Credit Insurance Association (FCIA). Policies include insurance for financing or operating leases, medium-term insurance, the new-to-export policy, insurance for the service industry, the umbrella policy, and multibuyer and single-buyer policies.
- *Working-capital guarantee.* The Working Capital Loan Guarantee Program assists small businesses in obtaining the necessary working capital to fund their export sales. The program guarantees working-capital loans extended by banks to eligible U.S. exporters with exportable inventory or export receivables as collateral.
- *Direct and intermediary loans.* Eximbank provides two types of loans: (1) direct loans to foreign buyers of U.S. exports and (2) intermediary loans to fund responsible parties that extend loans to foreign buyers of U.S. capital and quasi-capital goods and related services. Both programs cover up to 85 percent of the U.S. export value, with repayment terms of one year or more.
- *Guarantees.* Eximbank's guarantee provides repayment protection for private sector loans to creditworthy buyers of U.S. capital equipment and related services. The guarantee is available alone or with an intermediary loan. Most guarantees provide comprehensive coverage for both political and commercial risks, but coverage for political risks only is also available.

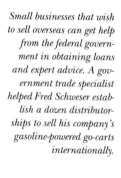

Small businesses that wish to sell overseas can get help from the federal government in obtaining loans and expert advice. A government trade specialist helped Fred Schweser establish a dozen distributorships to sell his company's gasoline-powered go-carts internationally.

Action Report

QUALITY GOALS

ISO 9000 Certification: Is It Worth It?

Among small businesses, there's an increasing emphasis on quality. In 1987, in Geneva, Switzerland, the International Organization for Standardization developed the ISO 9000 standards for voluntary application in both manufacturing and service organizations. Obtaining ISO 9000 certification is a signal that a firm is committed to producing quality products.

But is certification worth the cost? Consider one firm's efforts to attain ISO 9000 certification:

> *Dick Sunderland, the owner of D&S Manufacturing, in Westfield, Massachusetts, is seeking ISO 9000 certification "to get a leg up on the competition." Because of the cost of certification, though, Sunderland's ISO 9000 effort has stalled before really getting off the ground.*
>
> *Through contacts familiar with ISO 9000, Sunderland was able to gain some sense of where his company stood [with respect to] the ISO standards. An ISO 9000 consultant based in Europe ranked his company close to certification level.*
>
> *The task remaining for Sunderland before D&S was audited for certification was documenting what he was doing—that is, writing a quality-control manual that would meet ISO 9000 standards.*
>
> *The problem is that Sunderland says he can't do the work at his current staffing level of 25. He and a foreman can devote an average of five hours a week to the job, not enough to finish in what he considers a timely fashion. He can't afford to hire a full-time quality-control manager.*

Many small firms are in a similar situation regarding ISO 9000 certification. Nevertheless, as explained in Chapter 19, the benefits may well offset the initial trouble and costs.

Source: Michael Barrier and Amy Zuckerman, "Quality Standards the World Agrees On," *Nation's Business*, Vol. 82, No. 5 (May 1994), pp. 71–73.

- *Small business advisory service.* To encourage small businesses to sell overseas, Eximbank maintains a special office to provide information on the availability and use of export credit insurance, guarantees, and direct and intermediary loans to finance the sale of U.S. goods and services abroad.

Eximbank programs have been victims of recent budget cuts. One study found only 2 percent of all U.S. export transactions had Eximbank financing.[28]

Small Business Administration

The Small Business Administration (SBA) serves small U.S. firms primarily through its 107 regional, district, and branch offices. Small businesses that are either already exporting or interested in doing so can receive information through conferences and seminars, instructional publications, export counseling, and financial assistance. These are a few of the programs offered by the SBA to small firms:[29]

1 Explain the role of distribution in marketing.

- Distribution encompasses both the physical movement of products and the establishment of intermediary relationships to guide the movement of the products from producer to user.
- Four main functions of channel intermediaries are breaking bulk, assorting, providing information, and shifting risks.
- A distribution channel can be either direct or indirect. Some firms may successfully employ more than one channel of distribution.

2 Describe the major considerations in structuring a distribution system.

- Costs, coverage, and control are the three main considerations in building a channel of distribution.
- Transportation, storage, materials handling, delivery terms, and inventory management are the main components of a physical distribution system.

3 Discuss global marketing challenges.

- Recent surveys indicate that U.S. entrepreneurs are breaking new ground in foreign markets.
- Clearly, small firms can be just as successful as large firms in international markets.
- An entrepreneur needs to study cultural, political, and economic forces in a foreign market in order to understand why adjustments to domestic marketing strategies are needed.
- Differences among host countries in trading systems and import requirements make international trade difficult.

4 Describe the initial steps of a global marketing effort.

- Researching a foreign market should begin with a look at secondary data sources, such as *A Basic Guide to Exporting.*
- One of the best ways to study a foreign market is to visit it—either individually or as part of a trade mission.
- Licensing is the simplest and least costly strategy for conducting international business.
- A small firm can also participate in foreign-market sales via joint ventures or through foreign distributors.

5 Identify sources of trade and financing assistance.

- Private banks are a good source of assistance with financial matters associated with small business exporting.
- Increasingly, states are developing and implementing their own programs to help small firms in their efforts to export.
- The Export Trading Company Act was passed to facilitate the exporting of goods and services produced in the United States.
- The Export-Import Bank has several programs that are particularly helpful to small exporters.
- The Small Business Administration also provides exporting assistance.

- *Export counseling.* International trade officers in SBA regional and district offices provide advice and counseling on exporting. These professionals help small companies locate and utilize various government programs and guide them through the export process.
- *SCORE program.* One-on-one assistance is provided by members of the Service Corps of Retired Executives (SCORE), many of whom have years of practical experience in international trade. Specialists assist small firms in evaluating export potential and strengthening domestic operations by identifying financial, managerial, or technical problems.
- *SBDC and SBI programs.* Basic business counseling and assistance are offered through Small Business Development Centers (SBDCs), some of which are located at colleges and universities. Through Small Business Institutes (SBIs), business students from more than 450 colleges and universities provide in-depth, long-term counseling under faculty supervision to small firms.
- *Legal advice.* Through an arrangement with the Federal Bar Association (FBA), Export Legal Assistance Network (ELAN) provides free, initial consultations to small companies on the legal aspects of exporting. Advice is provided by qualified attorneys from the International Law Council of the FBA.
- *Financial assistance.* The SBA offers direct loans and loan guarantee programs to assist small U.S. exporters. To be eligible for an SBA loan, a businessperson must first attempt to secure a loan from a private bank, invest a reasonable amount of capital in the firm, and demonstrate that the loan can be paid back. The SBA provides guarantees of up to 85 percent of a private lending institution's loan to an eligible small firm as long as the total guaranteed by the SBA does not exceed its $750,000 statutory limit. However, the SBA can provide a maximum guarantee of 90 percent for loans less than $155,000.

- *Regular business loan program.* The SBA covers loans for acquisition or expansion of fixed assets and other working-capital purposes in amounts up to $750,000, with a maximum maturity of 25 years. Guarantees for general-purpose working-capital loans are usually limited to a maximum term of seven years.
- *Export Revolving Line of Credit program (ERLC).* The SBA has established the ERLC to encourage small U.S. businesses to export their products and services abroad. Any number of withdrawals and repayments can be made as long as the dollar limit of the credit is not exceeded and the disbursements are made within the stated maturity period. Proceeds can only finance labor and materials needed for manufacturing or wholesaling goods for export or for penetrating or developing foreign markets. The maximum maturity of an ERLC guarantee is 18 months, including all extensions.
- *Small Business Investment Company (SBIC) financing.* For an export company requiring more than $750,000, an SBIC-approved loan is a financing option.

DISCUSSION QUESTIONS

1. How does physical distribution differ from channels of distribution?
2. Why do small firms need to consider indirect channels of distribution for their products? Why involve intermediaries in distribution at all?
3. Discuss the major considerations in structuring a channel of distribution.
4. What are the major components of a physical distribution system?
5. Comment on the statement "Channel intermediaries are

New Terms and Concepts

distribution *350*	direct channel *352*	North American Free Trade Agreement (NAFTA) *358*
physical distribution (logistics) *350*	indirect channel *352*	
channel of distribution *350*	dual distribution *352*	General Agreement on Tariffs and Trade (GATT) *358*
breaking bulk *351*	common carriers *354*	licensing *361*
assorting *351*	contract carriers *354*	letter of credit *364*
merchant middlemen *351*	private carriers *354*	
agents and brokers *351*	Free Trade Agreement (FTA) *358*	

You Make the Call

Situation 1 Berney and Pat Anderson own and operate the Great Out-of-Doors Company, a manufacturing operation in Coleman, Colorado. Their principal product is a rifle sling. Berney conceived the product idea in 1995. One year later, he and his wife, Pat, took in two investors and began manufacturing. Currently, the plant has six employees producing the rifle sling and a few minor complementary products. Pat takes care of the accounting, and Berney supervises plant operations. Their rifle sling is patented and has been well received by those who have tried it. The nylon sling is produced with a 1-inch or 1½-inch strap and is available in 25 different colors. The firm has manufactured the sling for other brand-name sporting goods manufacturers and has also sold it under its own name—Sports Sling—in sporting goods stores.

Question 1 What do you see as the strong and weak points of the distribution channels the company is currently using?
Question 2 What additional channels would you recommend to the Andersons for consideration?
Question 3 Do you think exporting is a feasible alternative for the Andersons at this time? Why or why not?

Situation 2 John Adams is a veterinarian specializing in small-animal care in Jackson, Florida. For several years, he has supplemented his professional income by exporting products he has invented and patented. His best seller is a dog leash that he originally sold to other veterinarians in the United States. After placing a product release in a Department of Commerce publication, he received inquiries from foreign importers who wanted the product, and his exporting began. Based on his personal experiences with exporting, Adams is contemplating leaving his veterinary practice and becoming a full-time exporting distributor. He believes that a growing number of U.S. businesses do not want to get involved with the problems of the export business but would like the revenue from overseas markets. His services as a distributor should be attractive to these firms.

Question 1 Would you recommend that Adams leave his successful veterinary practice to pursue a career as an export distributor? Why or why not?
Question 2 What would you anticipate Adams's biggest problems will be if he makes the move he's considering?
Question 3 What private sources of assistance might he use?

Continue on next page

Situation 3 Researching a foreign market does not necessarily have to be an expensive effort. One economical source of good information is the pool of U.S. companies that sell related products abroad.

Fred Hansen, vice-president for marketing at Mardel Laboratories Inc. in Glendale Heights, Illinois, which makes water conditioners and other supplies for tropical-fish aquariums, hired a distributor in Hong Kong after contacting Penn Plax Plastics Inc., a Garden City [New York] company that sells plastic underwater plants. The company didn't compete with Mardel, but it knew both the distributor and the industry well.

Source: "It's a Small (Business) World," *Business Week* (April 17, 1995), pp. 96–101.

Question 1 Do you see any ethical conflict in providing distribution information to another firm under these circumstances?

Question 2 What other sources of global marketing information could Hansen consider?

6. How have trade agreements helped reduce trade barriers? Do you believe these efforts will continue?
7. Discuss the importance of a careful cultural analysis to a small firm that wishes to enter an international market.
8. What changes in a firm's marketing plan, if any, may be required when selling to foreign markets? Be specific.
9. What are some alternatives to exporting that provide involvement for small businesses in international markets? Which one(s) do you find most consistent with a small firm's situation? Why?
10. Explain the exporting assistance programs of Eximbank.

EXPERIENTIAL EXERCISES

1. Contact a local banker to discuss the bank's involvement with international marketing. Report your findings.
2. Interview two different types of local retail merchants to determine how the merchandise in their stores was distributed to them. Contrast the channels of distribution, and report your findings.
3. Review recent issues of *Entrepreneur, Inc.,* or *Nation's Business,* and report on articles that discuss international marketing.
4. Interview a local distributor concerning how it stores and handles the merchandise it distributes. Report your findings.

Exploring the

5. Search the Web for information regarding exporting. One site that can be accessed (http://www.dbisna.com./dbis/global/hglobal.html) is maintained by Dun & Bradstreet. Summarize the information that is available at this and any other site you may find.

CASE 16
NovaSoft Systems, Inc. (p. 634)

This case describes the global marketing of a small software firm that began its international strategy with a distributorship agreement.

Alternative Case for Chapter 16: Case 13, "Silver Lining," p. 627

Part 5

17. **PROFESSIONAL MANAGEMENT IN THE GROWING FIRM**

18. **MANAGING HUMAN RESOURCES**

19. **QUALITY MANAGEMENT AND THE OPERATIONS PROCESS**

20. **PURCHASING AND MANAGING INVENTORY**

21. **COMPUTER-BASED TECHNOLOGY FOR SMALL BUSINESSES**

Chapter 17

Professional Management in the Growing Firm

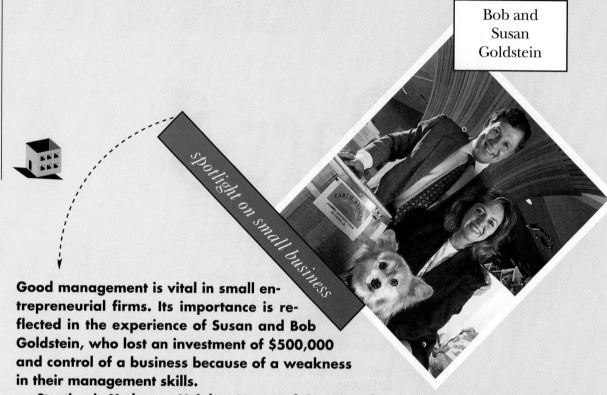

Bob and Susan Goldstein

spotlight on small business

Good management is vital in small entrepreneurial firms. Its importance is reflected in the experience of Susan and Bob Goldstein, who lost an investment of $500,000 and control of a business because of a weakness in their management skills.

Starting in Yorktown Heights, New York in 1979, the Goldsteins built a successful chain of six retail stores that sold health food for pets. Bob Goldstein, a veterinarian, had developed the pet food line to combat animal illnesses. Under pressure from financial backers to accelerate business growth, however, the Goldsteins expanded into areas that exceeded their management experience and skills. As losses mounted, other investors forced them out of the business they had started.

"The Goldsteins are typical of entrepreneurs who feel instinct is all you need," says Marge Lovero, director of the entrepreneurial center at Manhattanville College in Purchase, New York. Ms. Lovero, who has advised the Goldsteins, adds: *"Their first flush of business encouraged them to expand without planning. They charted too many courses without doing their homework."*

The Goldsteins learned from the costly experience of their first venture and have re-entered the retail market for pet health foods. In their new venture, Earth Animal, they are dedicated to professional management.

Source: Michael Selz, "Losing Control," *The Wall Street Journal*, October 16, 1992, pp. R6–7.

Organizations, even small ones, do not function on their own—they need to be managed. A small business will not run well, if at all, without proper direction and coordination of its activities. The management process enables production workers, salespeople, and others to collaborate effectively in serving customers. In this chapter, we examine the unique aspects of managing a small business and the transition to more professional management that becomes necessary in a growing firm.

Looking Ahead

After studying this chapter, you should be able to:

1 Discuss the distinctive features of small firm management.

2 Identify the various kinds of plans and approaches to planning.

3 Discuss the entrepreneur's leadership role.

4 Describe the nature and kinds of small business organization.

5 Discuss the ways in which control is exercised.

6 Describe the problem of time pressure and suggest solutions.

7 Explain the various types of outside management assistance.

DISTINCTIVE FEATURES OF SMALL FIRM MANAGEMENT

Even though managers in both large and small companies play similar managerial roles, their jobs differ in a number of ways. This is readily recognized by managers who move from large corporations to small firms and encounter an entirely different business atmosphere. Furthermore, a small firm experiences constant change in its organizational and managerial needs as it moves from point zero—its launching—to the point where it can employ a full staff of **professional managers.** Professional managers use more systematic and analytical methods, in contrast to the more haphazard techniques of those who lack their training and experience. In this section, we examine a number of distinctive features that challenge managers of small firms.

> **1** Discuss the distinctive features of small firm management.

professional manager
a manager who uses systematic, analytical methods of management

Prevalent Management Weaknesses in Small Firms

Although some large corporations experience poor management, small businesses seem particularly vulnerable to this weakness. Managerial inefficiency exists in tens (or even hundreds) of thousands of small firms. Many small firms are marginal or unprofitable businesses, struggling to survive from day to day. At best, they earn only a bare living for their owners. The reason for their condition is at once apparent to anyone who examines their operation. They operate, but it is an exaggeration to say that they are managed.

One successful entrepreneur who started several businesses candidly admitted his own inadequacies as a manager:

> *You name the mistake, and I made it during those years. I didn't pay enough attention to detail. I wasn't clear about responsibilities. I didn't hold people accountable. I was terrible at hiring. We had three chief financial officers in 10 years. We didn't start tracking cash flow until we were up to about $12 million in sales, and we went all the way to $25 million without developing an inventory system that worked. As a company, we lacked focus. Once, I brought in a consultant who asked our eight key people about the company's goals, and everyone gave a different answer.*[1]

Weaknesses of this nature are all too typical of small firms. The good news, however, is that poor management is neither universal nor inevitable.

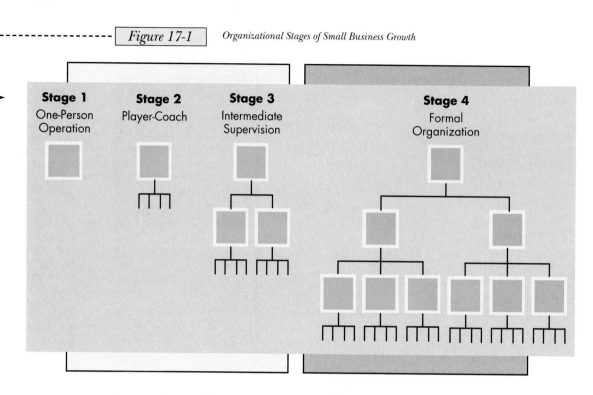

Figure 17-1 *Organizational Stages of Small Business Growth*

Stage 1 One-Person Operation

Stage 2 Player-Coach

Stage 3 Intermediate Supervision

Stage 4 Formal Organization

Constraints on Management in Small Firms

Managers of small firms, particularly new and growing companies, are constrained by conditions that do not trouble the average corporate executive: They must face the grim reality of small bank accounts and limited staff. A small firm often lacks the money for slick sales brochures. It cannot afford much in the way of market research. The shortage of cash even makes it difficult to employ an adequate number of secretaries and office assistants. Such limitations are painfully apparent to large firm managers who move into management positions in small firms.

Small firms typically lack an adequate specialized professional staff. Most small business managers are generalists, who lack the support of experienced professional specialists in market research, financial analysis, advertising, human resources management, and other areas. The manager in a small business must make decisions in these areas without the expertise that is available in a larger business. Later in this chapter, we note that this limitation may be partially overcome by using outside management assistance. Nevertheless, the shortage of internal professional talent is a part of the reality of managing entrepreneurial firms.

Stages of Growth and Implications for Management

As a newly formed business becomes established and grows, its organization and pattern of management change. To some extent, management must adapt to growth and change in any organization. However, the changes involved as a business moves through periods of "childhood" and "adolescence" are much more extensive than those that occur with the growth of a relatively mature business.

A number of experts have proposed models related to the growth stages of business firms.[2] These models typically describe four or five stages of growth and identify various management issues related to each of the stages. Figure 17-1 shows four stages in the organizational life of many small businesses. As firms progress from the minimum size of Stage 1 to the larger size of Stage 4, they add layers of management and increase the formality of operations. Even though some firms skip the first one or two stages by starting as larger businesses, thousands of small firms make their way through each of the stages pictured here.

In Stage 1, the firm is simply a one-person operation. Even though some firms begin with a larger organization, the one-person startup is by no means rare.

In Stage 2, the entrepreneur becomes a player-coach, which implies extensive participation in the operations of the business. In addition to performing the basic work—whether production, sales, writing checks, or record keeping—the entrepreneur must also coordinate the efforts of others.

In Stage 3, a major milestone is reached when an intermediate level of supervision is added. In many ways, this is a difficult and dangerous point for the small firm, because the entrepreneur must rise above direct, hands-on management and work through an intervening layer of management.

Stage 4, the stage of formal organization, involves more than increased size and multilayered organization. The formalization of management involves the adoption of written policies, preparation of plans and budgets, standardization of personnel practices, computerization of records, preparation of organization charts and job descriptions, scheduling of training conferences, institution of control procedures, and so on. While some formal management practices may be adopted prior to Stage 4 of a firm's growth, the stages outline a typical pattern of development for successful firms. Flexibility and informality may be helpful when a firm is first started, but its growth necessitates greater formality in planning and control. Tension often develops as the traditional easygoing patterns of management become dysfunctional. Great managerial skill is required to preserve a "family" atmosphere while introducing professional management.

As a firm moves from Stage 1 to Stage 4, the pattern of entrepreneurial activities changes. The entrepreneur becomes less of a doer and more of a manager, as shown in Figure 17-2.

Managers who are strong on "doing" skills are often weak on "managing" skills. As an example, a family wholesale business in New York ran into serious management problems as it expanded and became a designer jeans maker called Gitano Group Inc. The business was headed by a family member, Haim Dabah, who lacked the ability to control its growth.

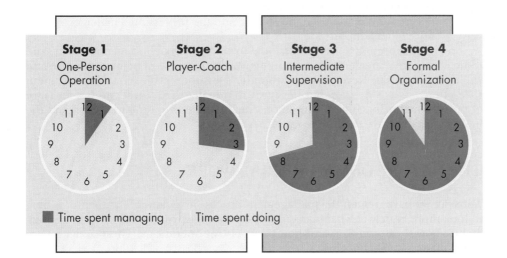

Figure 17-2

Use of Managerial Time at Various Stages of Business Growth

Table 17-1

*Typical Characteristics of
Founders and Professional
Managers*

Founders	Professional Managers
Innovative	Administrative
Intuitive	Analytical
Action-oriented	Planning-oriented
Focused on the long term	Focused on the short term
Bold	Cautious

> *There was no business plan, no budgeting, and no system to monitor the purchase and management of inventory. Admits Dabah: "The one thing I don't know how to do is make sure our systems, financial controls, and all that stuff work."*[3]

Firms that are too hesitant to move through these organizational stages and to acquire the necessary professional management limit their rate of growth. On the other hand, a small business may attempt to become a big business too quickly. The entrepreneur's primary strength may lie in product development or selling, for example, and a quick move into Stage 4 may saddle the entrepreneur with managerial duties and rob the organization of his or her valuable entrepreneurial talents.

The need for effective management becomes more acute as the business expands. Very small firms often survive in spite of weak management. To some extent, the quality of their products or services may offset deficiencies in their management. In the early days of business life, therefore, the firm may survive and grow even though its management is less than professional. Even in a very small business, however, defects in management place strains on the business and retard its development in some way.

Founders as Managers

Founders of new firms are not always good organization members. As we explained in Chapter 1, they are creative, innovative, risk-taking individuals who have the courage to strike out on their own. Indeed, they are often propelled into entrepreneurship by precipitating events, sometimes involving difficulty in fitting into conventional organizational roles. As a consequence, founders may fail to appreciate the value of good management practices. Their orientation frequently differs from that of professional managers. These differences, as outlined in Table 17-1, show the founder as more of a mover and shaker, and the professional manager, in contrast, as more of an administrator.

Some entrepreneurs are professional in their approach to management, and some corporate managers are entrepreneurial in the sense of being innovative and willing to take risks. Nevertheless, a founder's less than professional management style often acts as a drag on business growth. Ideally, the founder adds a measure of professional management without sacrificing the entrepreneurial spirit and the basic values that gave the business a successful start.

2 Identify the various kinds of plans and approaches to planning.

THE NATURE OF MANAGERIAL WORK

Thus far, we have treated the management process in a general way. Now it is time to look more closely at what managers do—how they plan, how they exercise leadership, how they organize, and how they control operations. These activities are called **management functions.**

Planning

The preparation of a formal business plan for a new business, as discussed in Chapter 6, is only the first phase of an ongoing process of planning that guides production, marketing, and other activities on a month-to-month and year-to-year basis. This section focuses on the ongoing planning process.

NEED FOR FORMAL PLANNING   Most small business managers plan to some degree. However, the amount of planning is typically less than ideal. Also, what little planning there is tends to be spotty and unsystematic—dealing with how much inventory to purchase, whether to buy a new piece of equipment, and other questions of this type. Specific circumstances affect the degree to which formal planning is needed, but most businesses would function more profitably by increasing their planning and making it more systematic.

The payoff from planning comes in several ways. First, the process of thinking through the issues confronting a firm and developing a plan can improve productivity. Second, planning provides a focus for a firm: Managerial decisions during a year can be guided by the annual plan, and employees can work consistently toward the same goal. Third, evidence of planning provides credibility with bankers, suppliers, and other outsiders.

KINDS OF PLANS   A firm's basic path to the future is spelled out in its **long-range plan,** also called a **strategic plan.** As we noted in Chapter 7, strategy decisions are concerned with such issues as market niche and/or features that differentiate the firm from its competitors. A long-range plan provides a foundation for the more specific plans explained below.

Short-range plans are action plans for one year or less that govern activities in production, marketing, and other areas. An important part of short-range operating plans is the **budget**—a document that expresses future plans in monetary terms. A budget is usually prepared one year in advance, with a breakdown by quarters or months. (Budgeting is explained more fully in Chapter 23.)

Other types of plans are less connected to the calendar and more concerned with the way things are done. **Business policies,** for example, are fundamental statements that serve as guides for managerial decision making. They include financial policies, personnel policies, and so on. A personnel policy may state, for example, that no employee may accept a gift from a supplier unless it is of nominal value.

Procedures are more specific and deal primarily with methodology—how something is to be done. In a furniture store, for example, a procedure might require the sale of furniture on credit to be approved by a credit manager prior to delivery to the customer. Once a work method is established, it may be standardized and referred to as a **standard operating procedure.**

MAKING TIME FOR PLANNING   Small business managers all too often succumb to the "tyranny of the urgent." Because they are busy putting out fires, they never get around to planning. Planning is easy to postpone and therefore easy for managers to ignore while concentrating on the more urgent issues of production and sales. And, like quarterbacks blindsided by blitzing linebackers, such managers may be bowled over by competitors.

Some discipline is necessary in order to reap the benefits of planning. Time and a degree of seclusion must be provided if significant progress is to be made. Planning is primarily a mental process. It is seldom done effectively in an atmosphere of ringing telephones, rush orders, and urgent demands for decision making.

---

management functions
the activities of planning, leading, organizing, and controlling

long-range plan (strategic plan)
a firm's overall plan for the future

short-range plans
plans that govern a firm's operations for one year or less

budget
a document that expresses future plans in monetary terms

business policies
basic statements that provide guidance for managerial decision making

procedures
specific methods followed in business activities

standard operating procedure
an established method of conducting a business activity

Action Report

ENTREPRENEURIAL EXPERIENCES

Setting Business Goals in a Small Foundry

Setting business goals is one part of managerial planning. Gregg Foster, owner of Elyria Foundry in Ohio, has introduced annual goal setting to provide a focus for the foundry's 290 employees. Each November, key managers gather and submit suggestions from their respective departments. At the December meeting of all employees, Foster announces next year's goals, stated in simple language. Here are one year's goals for customer service—one of five categories of goals:

- 100% on-time delivery
- Take every customer call
- 50 employees will visit customers
- All calls answered on second ring

Source: Leslie Brokaw, "One-Page Company Game Plan," *Inc.,* Vol. 15, No. 6 (June 1993), pp. 111–113.

EMPLOYEE PARTICIPATION IN PLANNING   Although a small business owner should personally spend time planning, this responsibility may be delegated to some extent, because some planning is required of all members of the enterprise. The larger the organization, the more important it is to delegate some planning; the owner can hardly specify in detail the program for each department.

The concept that the boss does the thinking and the employee does the work is misleading. Progressive managers have discovered that employees' ideas are often helpful in developing solutions to company problems. A salesperson, for example, is closer than his or her manager to the firm's customers and is usually better able to evaluate their needs and reactions.

3 Discuss the entrepreneur's leadership role.

Leading and Motivating

Like any endeavor involving people, a small firm needs an atmosphere of cooperation and teamwork among all participants. Fortunately, employees in small firms can collaborate effectively. In fact, the potential for good teamwork is enhanced in some ways by the smallness of the enterprise.

PERSONAL INVOLVEMENT AND INFLUENCE OF THE ENTREPRENEUR   In most small firms, employees get to know the owner-manager personally. This person is not a faceless unknown, but an individual whom employees see and relate to in the course of their normal work schedules. This situation is entirely different from that of large corporations, where most employees may never even see the chief executive. If the employer-employee relationship is good, employees in small firms develop strong feelings of personal loyalty to their employer.

In very small firms—those with 20 or fewer employees—extensive interaction is typical. As a firm grows, the amount of personal contact an employee may have with the owner naturally declines. Nevertheless, a significant personal relationship between the owner and employees is characteristic of most small businesses.

In a large corporation, the values of top-level executives must be filtered through many layers of management before they reach those who produce and sell the products. As a result, the influence of those at the top may be diluted by the process of going through channels. In contrast, personnel in a small firm receive the leader's messages directly. This face-to-face contact facilitates their understanding of the leader's stand on integrity, customer service, and other important issues.

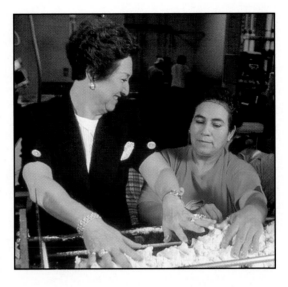

In small firms, significant personal relationships often exist between entrepreneur and employees. Employees in Ernestina Galindi's tortilla factory typically interact with the owner almost daily.

By creating an environment that encourages personal interaction, the leader of a small firm can get the best from his or her employees and also offer a strong inducement to prospective employees. For example, most professional managers prefer an organizational setting that minimizes office politics as a factor in getting ahead. By creating a friendly atmosphere that avoids the intrigue common in some organizations, an entrepreneur can build an environment that is very attractive to most employees.

LEADERSHIP THAT BUILDS ENTHUSIASM   Several decades ago, many managers were hard-nosed autocrats, giving orders and showing little concern for those who worked under them. Over the years, this style of leadership has given way to a gentler and more effective variety that emphasizes respect for all members of the organization and shows an appreciation for their potential. Progressive managers now seek some degree of employee participation in decisions affecting personnel and work processes.

In many cases, managers carry this leadership approach to a level called **empowerment.** The manager who uses empowerment goes beyond solicitation of employees' opinions and ideas by increasing their authority to act on their own and to decide things for themselves. Here is a description of worker empowerment at a small auto body shop called European Collision Center in Cambridge, Massachusetts:

empowerment
increasing employees' authority to make decisions or take action on their own

> *Bodymen take "ownership" of a car while it's in the shop, staying with it start to finish. No one looks over their shoulders: "There are a set of parameters, then they have to be responsible," says owner Wayne Stevenson. Workers are cross-trained to take on new tasks and sent back to school yearly to keep skills up to date. Customers love what they get, and Stevenson's traffic has doubled every year for five years.[4]*

Some companies carry employee participation a step further by creating self-managed **work teams.** In these groups, employees are assigned to a given task or operation, manage the task or operation without direct supervision, and assume responsibility for results. When work teams function properly, the number of supervisors needed decreases sharply.

work teams
groups of employees with freedom to function without close supervision

Work teams are often incorporated into management attempts to upgrade product quality. The Shelby Die Casting Company of Shelby, Mississippi used work teams to meet tough quality demands from its customers, big U.S. automakers, for

Action Report

ENTREPRENEURIAL EXPERIENCES

Upward Communication Gets Results

Upward communication is typically difficult, and in some companies it just doesn't happen. Robert Davies, founder and president of SBT Corporation in Sausalito, California, developed a special E-mail suggestion system that allows employees to pass along new ideas or make direct requests to the CEO. A number of suggestions commented on the company's formal dress code, and Davies actually listened:

> *Because I had always worked in places with a strict dress code, I didn't want to change it. But as suggestions for a more relaxed code kept making their way to me, I started to think that if it motivated my employees, why not?*
>
> *So last October, I reluctantly agreed to experiment with suspending the old dress code in favor of more casual attire. At the end of the year, we made it permanent.*
>
> *Interestingly, after trying the new system, I no longer feel comfortable in a suit and tie. Unless I'm giving a seminar or hosting an important guest, I usually wear a sweater and an open shirt.*
>
> *Best of all, the employees now find me more approachable because I feel more comfortable and don't look as intimidating. And that makes it easier, I think, for me to be receptive to their ideas, too. And when you have 80 people contributing, you have a veritable "idea factory." From the receptionist to the programmer, I never know who will give us the next great suggestion.*

In this case, a founder changed the rules because he heard and understood employees' concerns.

Source: Robert Davies, "Entrepreneur's Notebook: Managing by Listening," *Nation's Business*, Vol. 80, No. 9 (September 1992), p. 6.

QUALITY

alternator housings, engine covers, and the like.[5] When management first organized employees into teams to improve quality and make the plant profitable again, there was turmoil, because the method was entirely new to employees. As they gained experience, however, the teams functioned as intended, pinpointing problems and solving them in an orderly manner. After a year, the plant was profitable again, and the scrap rate had shrunk from 35 to 8 percent.

EFFECTIVE COMMUNICATION   Another key to a healthy organization is effective communication—that is, getting managers and employees to talk with each other and openly share problems and ideas. To some extent, the management hierarchy must be set aside so that personnel at all levels can speak freely with those higher up. The result is two-way communication—a far cry from the old-fashioned idea that managers give orders and employees simply carry them out.

To communicate effectively, managers must tell employees where they stand, how the business is doing, and what the company's plans for the future are. Negative feedback to employees may be necessary at times, but positive feedback is the primary tool for establishing good human relations. Perhaps the most fundamental concept managers need to keep in mind is that employees are people: They quickly detect insincerity but respond to honest efforts to treat them as mature, responsible individuals. In short, an atmosphere of trust and respect contributes greatly to good communication.

To go beyond having good intentions, a small firm manager can adopt any of the following practical techniques for stimulating two-way communication:

- Periodic performance review sessions to discuss employees' ideas, questions, complaints, and job expectations
- Bulletin boards to keep employees informed about developments affecting them and/or the company
- Suggestion boxes to solicit employees' ideas
- Staff meetings to discuss problems and matters of general concern

These methods and others can be used to supplement the most basic of all channels for communication—the day-to-day interaction between each employee and his or her supervisor.

Organizing

4 Describe the nature and kinds of small business organization.

While an entrepreneur may give direction through personal leadership, she or he must also define the relationships among the firm's activities and among the individuals on the firm's payroll. Without some kind of organizational structure, operations eventually become chaotic and morale suffers.

THE UNPLANNED STRUCTURE In small companies, the organizational structure tends to evolve with little conscious planning. Certain employees begin performing particular functions when the company is new and retain those functions as it matures. Other functions remain diffused over a number of positions, even though they have become crucial as a result of company growth.

This natural evolution is not all bad. Generally, a strong element of practicality characterizes organizational arrangements that evolve in this way. The structure is forged by the process of working and growing, rather than being derived from a textbook. Unplanned structures are seldom perfect, however, and growth typically creates a need for organizational change. Periodically, therefore, the entrepreneur should examine structural relationships and make adjustments as needed for effective teamwork.

ESTABLISHING A CHAIN OF COMMAND In a **line organization,** each person has one supervisor to whom he or she reports and looks for instructions. Thus, a single, specific chain of command exists, as illustrated in Figure 17-3. All employees are directly engaged in the business's work—producing, selling, or arranging financial resources. Most very small firms—for example, those with fewer than 10 employees—use this form of organization.

A **chain of command** implies superior-subordinate relationships with a downward flow of instructions, but it involves much more. It is also a channel for two-way communication. Although employees at the same level communicate among themselves, the chain of command is the official, vertical channel of communication.

An organizational problem occurs when managers or employees ignore formal lines of communication. In small firms, a climate of informality and flexibility makes it easy to short-circuit the chain of command. The president and founder of the business, for example, may absent-mindedly give instructions to salespersons or plant employees instead of going through the sales manager or the production manager. Similarly, an employee who has been with the entrepreneur from the beginning tends to maintain a direct person-to-person relationship rather than observing newly instituted channels of communication.

As a practical matter, adherence to the chain of command can never be perfect. An organization in which the chain of command is rigid would be bureaucratic and

line organization
a simple organizational structure in which each person reports to one supervisor

chain of command
the official, vertical channel of communication in an organization

Figure 17-3

Line Organization

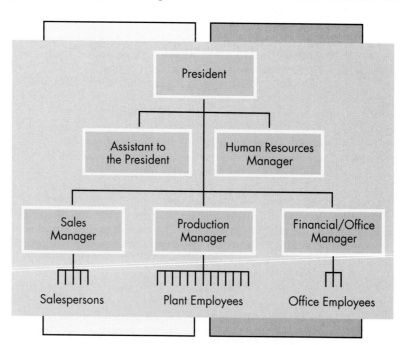

inefficient. Nevertheless, frequent and flagrant disregard of the chain of command quickly undermines the position of the bypassed manager.

A **line-and-staff organization** is similar to a line organization in that each person reports to a single supervisor. However, a line-and-staff structure also has staff specialists who perform specialized services or act as management advisers in specific areas (see Figure 17-4). Staff specialists may include a human resources manager, a production control technician, a quality control specialist, and an assistant to the president. Ordinarily, small firms grow quickly to a size requiring some staff specialists. Consequently, the line-and-staff organization is widely used in small business.

Line activities are those that contribute directly to the primary objectives of the small firm. Typically, these are production and sales activities. **Staff activities,** on the other hand, are supporting activities. Although both types of activities are important, priority must be given to line activities—those that earn the customer's

line-and-staff organization
an organizational structure that includes staff specialists who assist management

line activities
activities contributing directly to the primary objectives of a small firm

staff activities
activities that support line activities

Figure 17-4

Line-and-Staff Organization

dollar. The owner-manager must insist that staff specialists function primarily as helpers and facilitators. Otherwise, the firm will experience confusion as employees receive directions from a variety of supervisors and staff specialists. **Unity of command**—that is, the situation in which each employee is receiving direction from only one boss—will be destroyed.

INFORMAL ORGANIZATION   The types of structure that we have just discussed address the formal relationships among members of an organization. All organizations, however, also have informal groups composed of people with something in common, such as jobs, hobbies, carpools, or affiliations with civic associations.

Although informal groups are not a structural part of the formal organization, managers should observe them and evaluate their effect on the functioning of the total organization. An informal group, for example, may foster an attitude of working hard until the very end of the working day or doing the opposite—easing up and coasting the last half-hour. Ordinarily, no serious conflict arises between informal groups and the formal organization. An informal leader or leaders often emerge who will influence employee behavior. The wise manager understands the potentially positive contribution of informal groups and the inevitability of informal leadership.

Informal interaction among subordinates and managers can facilitate work performance and can also make life in the workplace more enjoyable for everyone. The value of compatible work groups to the individual became painfully clear to one college student who worked on a summer job:

> I was employed as a forklift driver for one long, frustrating summer. Soon after being introduced to my work group, I knew I was in trouble. A clique had formed and, for some reason, resented college students. During lunch breaks and work breaks, I spent the whole time by myself. Each morning, I dreaded going to work. The job paid well, but I was miserable.[6]

DELEGATING AUTHORITY   Through **delegation of authority,** a manager grants to subordinates the right to act or to make decisions. Delegating authority frees the superior to perform more important tasks after turning over less important functions to subordinates.

Although failure to delegate is found in all organizations, it is a special problem for the entrepreneur, whose background and personality often contribute to this problem. Frequently, the entrepreneur has organized the business and knows more about it than any other person working there. Furthermore, he or she must pay for mistakes made by subordinates. Thus, to protect the business, the owner is inclined to keep a firm hold on the reins of leadership.

Inability or unwillingness to delegate authority is manifested in numerous ways. For example, employees may find it necessary to clear even the most minor decision with the boss. A line of subordinates may be constantly trying to get the attention of the owner to resolve some issue that they lack authority to settle. This keeps the owner exceptionally busy, rushing from assisting a salesperson to helping iron out a production bottleneck to setting up a new filing system.

Delegation of authority is important for the satisfactory operation of a small firm and is absolutely a prerequisite for growth. An inability to delegate is the reason why many firms never grow beyond the small size that can be directly supervised in detail by the owner. One owner of a small restaurant operated it and achieved excellent profits. As a result of this success, the owner acquired a lease on another restaurant in the same area. During the first year of operating the second restaurant, the owner experienced constant headaches. Working long hours and trying to supervise both restaurants finally led the owner to give up the second one. This individual had never learned to delegate authority.

unity of command
a situation in which each employee's instructions come directly from only one immediate supervisor

delegation of authority
granting to subordinates the right to act or make decisions

Stephen R. Covey has distinguished between what he calls "gofer" delegation and "stewardship" delegation.[7] Gofer delegation refers to a work assignment in which the supervisor-delegator controls the details, saying "go for this" or "go do that." This is not true delegation. Stewardship delegation, on the other hand, focuses on results and allows the individual receiving an assignment some latitude in carrying it out. Only stewardship delegation provides the benefits of delegation for both parties.

span of control
the number of subordinates supervised by one manager

DECIDING HOW MANY TO SUPERVISE The **span of control** is the number of subordinates who are supervised by a manager. Although some authorities have stated that six to eight people are all that one individual can supervise effectively, the optimum span of control is actually a variable depending on a number of factors. Among these factors are the nature of the work and the manager's knowledge, energy, personality, and abilities. In addition, if the abilities of subordinates are better than average, the span of control may be enlarged accordingly.

As a very small firm grows and adds employees, the entrepreneur's span of control is extended. There is often a tendency to stretch the span too far—to supervise not only the first 5 or 6 employees but all employees added later. Eventually, a point is reached at which the attempted span exceeds the entrepreneur's reach—the time and effort he or she can devote to the business. It is at this point that the entrepreneur must establish intermediate levels of supervision and devote more time to management while moving beyond the role of player-coach.

5 Discuss the ways in which control is exercised.

Controlling

Organizations seldom function perfectly when executing plans. As a result, managers must monitor operations to discover deviations from plans and to make sure that the firm is functioning as intended. Managerial activities that check on performance and correct it when necessary are part of the managerial control function; they serve to keep the business on course.

The control process begins by establishing standards. This is evidence of the connection between planning and control, for it is through planning and goal setting that control standards are established. Goals are translated into norms by making them measurable. A goal to increase market share, for example, may be expressed as a projected dollar increase in sales volume for the coming year. An annual target like this may, in turn, be broken down into quarterly standards so that corrective action can be taken early if performance begins to fall below the projected amount.

While this example specifically illustrates growth and sales standards, performance criteria must be established in all areas of the business. In manufacturing, for example, product specifications provide predetermined standards that regulate the manufacturing process: A given dimension may be specified as fifteen inches with an error tolerance of plus or minus one-quarter inch.

Performance measurement occurs at various stages of the control process (see Figure 17-5). Performance may be measured at the input stage (perhaps to determine the quality of materials purchased), during the process stage (perhaps to determine if the product being manufactured meets quality standards), or at the output stage (perhaps to check the quality of a completed product).

Corrective action is required when performance deviates significantly from the standard in an unfavorable direction. To prevent the deviation from recurring, however, such action must be preceded by an analysis of the cause of the deviation. If the percentage of defective products increases, for example, a manager must determine whether the problem is caused by faulty raw materials, untrained workers,

Stages of the Control Process   Figure 17-5

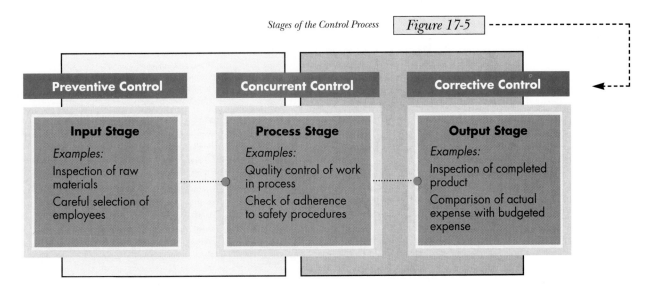

or some other factor. To be effective, corrective action must locate and deal with the real cause.

The cornerstone of financial control is the budget, in which cost and performance standards are incorporated. An expense budget for salespersons, for example, might include an item for travel expenses. At the end of a budget period, actual expenditures for travel can be compared with the budgeted amount. If there is a significant discrepancy, the matter is investigated and corrected. In this way, the budget serves as a device to control expenses.

Some very small businesses attempt to operate without a budget. However, even in these cases, the owner may have a rough idea of what cost and performance should be, may keep track of results, and may investigate when results seem out of line.

TIME MANAGEMENT

6 Describe the problem of time pressure and suggest solutions.

An owner-manager of a small firm spends much of the working day on the front line—meeting customers, solving problems, listening to employee complaints, talking with suppliers, and the like. She or he tackles such problems with the assistance of only a small staff. As a result, the owner-manager's energies and activities are diffused, and time is often her or his scarcest resource.

The Problem of Time Pressure

Many managers in small firms work from 60 to 80 hours per week. The hours worked by most new business owners are particularly long, as shown in Figure 17-6. A frequent and unfortunate result of such a schedule is inefficient work performance. Managers are too busy to see sales representatives who can supply market information on new products and processes. They are too busy to read technical or trade literature to discover what others are doing and what improvements might be adapted to their own use, too busy to listen carefully to employees' opinions and grievances, and too busy to give instructions properly and to teach employees how to do their jobs correctly.

Figure 17-6

Hours per Week Worked by New Business Owners

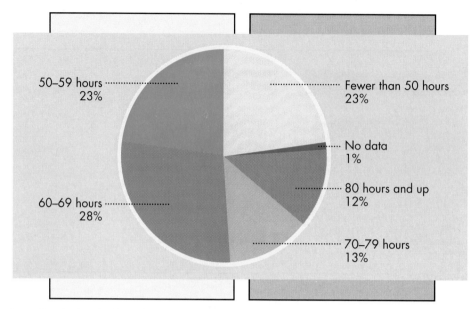

50–59 hours
23%

Fewer than 50 hours
23%

No data
1%

80 hours and up
12%

60–69 hours
28%

70–79 hours
13%

Source: Data developed and provided by the NFIB Foundation and sponsored by the American Express Travel Related Services Company, Inc.

Getting away for a vacation also seems impossible for some small business owners. In an extremely small firm, the owner may find it necessary to close the business during the period of his or her absence. Even in somewhat larger businesses, the owner may fear that the firm will not function properly if he or she is not there. Unfortunately, keeping his or her nose to the grindstone in this way may cost the entrepreneur dearly in terms of personal health, family relationships, and effectiveness in business leadership.

Time-Savers for Busy Managers

Part of the solution to the problem of time pressure is good organization. When possible, the manager should assign duties to subordinates who can work without close supervision. For such delegation to work, of course, a manager must first select and train qualified employees.

The greatest time-saver is effective use of time. Little will be accomplished if an individual flits from one task to another and back again. The first step in planning the use of time should be a survey of how much time is normally spent on various activities. Relying on general impressions is unscientific and likely to involve error. For a period of several days, or preferably several weeks, the manager should record the amounts of time spent on various types of activities during the day. An analysis of these figures will reveal the pattern of activities, the projects and tasks that use up the most time, and the factors responsible for wasted time. It will also reveal chronic time wasting due to excessive socializing, work on trivial matters, coffee breaks, and so on.

After eliminating practices that waste time, a manager can carefully plan his or her use of available time. A planned approach to a day's work or week's work is much more effective than a haphazard do-whatever-comes-up-first approach. This is true even for small firm managers whose schedules are interrupted in unanticipated ways.

One of a manager's biggest challenges is to use time effectively. Computer-based time management systems help managers establish priorities.

Many time management specialists recommend the use of a daily written plan of work activities. This plan may be a list of activities scribbled on a note pad or a formal schedule entered into a laptop computer, but it should reflect an establishing of priorities. By classifying duties as first, second, or third level of priority, the manager can identify and focus attention on the most crucial tasks.

Effective time management requires self-discipline. An individual may easily begin with good intentions and later lapse into habitual practices of devoting time to whatever he or she finds to do at the moment. Procrastination is a frequent thief of time. Many managers delay unpleasant and difficult tasks, retreating to trivial and less threatening activities and rationalizing that they are getting those items out of the way first in order to be able to concentrate better on the important tasks.

Some managers devote much time to meeting with subordinates. The meetings often just happen and drag on without any serious attempt by the manager to control them. The manager should prepare an agenda for these meetings, set starting and ending times, limit discussion to key issues, and assign any necessary follow-up to specific individuals. In this way, the effectiveness of business conferences may be maximized and the manager's own time conserved, along with that of other staff members.

OUTSIDE MANAGEMENT ASSISTANCE

7 Explain the various types of outside management assistance.

Given the managerial deficiencies we discussed earlier in this chapter, many entrepreneurs should consider the use of outside management assistance. Such outside assistance can supplement the manager's personal knowledge and the expertise of the few staff specialists on the company's payroll.

The Need for Outside Assistance

The typical entrepreneur is not only deficient in managerial skills but also lacks the opportunity to share ideas with peers. Although entrepreneurs can confide, to some extent, in subordinates, many experience loneliness. A survey of 210 owners revealed that 52 percent "frequently felt a sense of loneliness."[8] Moreover, this group reported a much higher incidence of stress symptoms than did those who said they did not feel lonely.

By using consultants, entrepreneurs can overcome some of their managerial deficiencies and reduce their sense of isolation. Furthermore, an insider directly involved in a business problem often cannot see the forest for the trees. In contrast, an outside consultant brings an objective point of view and new ideas, supported by a broad knowledge of proven, successful, cost-saving methods. The consultant can also help the manager improve decision making through better organization of fact gathering and the introduction of scientific techniques of analysis.

Sources of Management Assistance

Entrepreneurs who seek management assistance can turn to any of a number of sources, including business incubators, SBA programs, and management consultants. There are numerous other sources of knowledge and approaches to seeking needed management help. For example, owner-managers may increase their own skills by consulting public and university libraries, attending evening classes at local colleges, and considering the suggestions of friends and customers.

BUSINESS INCUBATORS   As we discussed in Chapter 10, a business incubator is an organization that offers both space and managerial and clerical services to new businesses. There are now several hundred incubators in the United States, and the number is growing rapidly. Most of them involve the participation of governmental agencies and/or universities, although some have been launched as purely private endeavors. The primary motivation in establishing incubators has been a desire to encourage entrepreneurship and thereby contribute to economic development.

Incubators offer new entrepreneurs on-site business expertise. Often, individuals who wish to start businesses are deficient in pertinent knowledge and lacking in appropriate experience. In many cases, they need practical guidance in marketing, record keeping, management, and preparation of business plans. Figure 17-7 shows the services that are available in a business incubator.

An incubator provides a supportive atmosphere for a business during the early months of its existence when it is most fragile and vulnerable to external dangers and internal errors. If the incubator works as it should, the fledgling business gains strength quickly and, within a year or so, leaves the incubator setting.

An incubator helped Derrick Johnson, who saw his sales nearly triple in 1991 when he moved his bulk-mail firm, Coastal Mail Service, from his home into the West Charlotte (North Carolina) Business Incubator.[9] The rent of $1.60 per square foot he paid there was far below the local market rate of $7 to $15, and the incubator's banking connections helped him secure an equipment loan for his business.

SMALL BUSINESS INSTITUTE (SBI)   In 1972, the Small Business Administration (SBA) implemented a program called the **Small Business Institute (SBI)** to make the consulting resources of universities available to small businesses. SBI teams of upper-division and graduate students, under the direction of a faculty member, work with owners of small firms in analyzing their business problems and devising solutions. The primary users of SBI consulting assistance are applicants for SBA loans, although the program is not restricted to such firms.

The program has mutual benefits: It provides students with a practical view of business management and supplies small firms with answers to their problems. The students who participate are typically combined in teams that provide a diversity of academic backgrounds. Individual teams, for example, may have different mem-

Small Business Institute (SBI)
an SBA-sponsored program making the consulting services of student teams available to small businesses

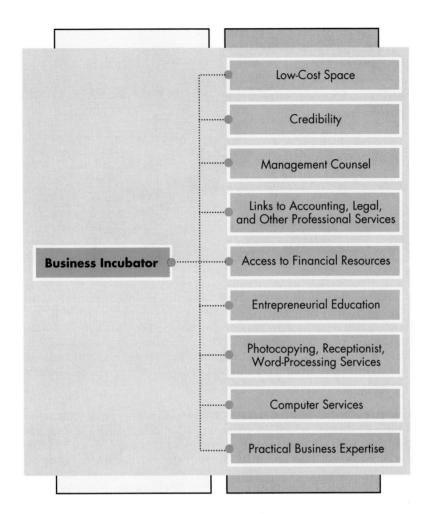

Figure 17-7

Services Provided by Business Incubators to New Firms

bers specializing in management, marketing, accounting, and finance. The enthusiasm of those participating in the program has been evident, and the SBI is considered one of the most successful consulting programs for small businesses.

Participating in an SBI assistance program, a team of students from Drake University helped Kane Manufacturing, a 24-employee family-owned business in Des Moines, Iowa, evaluate sales potential in Germany for its line of livestock products.[10] A 50-page report confirmed the hunch of the company's management that a market existed in Germany and also outlined the obstacles the business would face in marketing to European customers. The cost to the company for this evaluation was zero.

SERVICE CORPS OF RETIRED EXECUTIVES (SCORE)   Small business managers can obtain free management advice from a group called the **Service Corps of Retired Executives (SCORE)** by appealing to any SBA field office. SCORE is an organization of retired business executives who consult on current problems with small business managers. Functioning under the sponsorship of the SBA, SCORE provides an opportunity for retired executives to contribute to the business community and helps small business managers solve their problems. The relationship is thus mutually beneficial. Experience with SCORE may also encourage entrepreneurs to utilize paid consultants as their firms grow, by demonstrating the worth of consulting services.

Service Corps of Retired Executives (SCORE)
an SBA-sponsored group of retired executives who give free advice to small businesses

There are numerous stories of successful SCORE assistance to small firms. One entrepreneur, Peggy Harris, received counseling from a SCORE volunteer as she turned her crafts hobby into a business venture that involved teaching a no-sew technique for making drapes.[11] Taking the advice of the SCORE counselor, Harris started a line of credit with a local bank before she needed money. When cash was later required to produce a video of herself teaching the no-sew secrets, she had it available.

Small Business Development Centers (SBDCs)
university-affiliated centers offering consulting, education, and support to small businesses

SMALL BUSINESS DEVELOPMENT CENTERS (SBDCS)   **Small Business Development Centers (SBDCs),** which are patterned after the Agricultural Extension Service, are affiliated with colleges or universities as a part of the SBA's overall program of assistance to small business. SBDCs provide direct consultation, continuing education, research assistance, export services, and support to minority-owned firms. Their staff typically includes faculty members, SCORE counselors, professional staff, and graduate student assistants.

SBDC counselor John A. Boyd describes the type of assistance he provided to one entrepreneur:

> *Alice told me she had been a cook for 28 years in various restaurants (two totaled 21 years of service), and she wanted to start her own. As I worked through my list of standard questions, I began to find out that Alice had no particular target market in mind, had not yet developed a menu, only had a general idea about the price range, and had not considered the ambience or decor. She did, however, have a name, "Alice's Restaurant" (and you had to be an Arlo Guthrie fan to remember that).*
>
> *In a case such as this, I work very slowly with the client. Initially, I avoid discussing finances or pro forma financial statements because many people are afraid of numbers. In addition, one cannot do meaningful projections before the target market is determined. I also do not intimidate the client with all of the questions on the list, but attempt to assign three to five as homework for our next meeting. After Alice settled on the target market, location, menu and pricing, we started on more esoteric concepts such as ambience and decor. Eventually, we developed pro forma financial statements. It took over a year, but Alice's Restaurant eventually opened.[12]*

MANAGEMENT CONSULTANTS   Management consultants serve small businesses as well as large corporations. The entrepreneur should regard the services of a competent management consultant as an investment in improved decision making

Action Report

ENTREPRENEURIAL EXPERIENCES

Developing a Network

Pamela Barefoot admitted to being scared and not knowing much about business when she started Blue Crab Bay Co., a specialty foods and gift company in Onancock, Virginia. As a result, she began networking by reaching out for advice to business friends and others:

> From the start, I joined as many trade and business associations as I could and relied heavily on help from sources such as SBA's Service Corps of Retired Executives (SCORE) and the Virginia Department of Economic Development.
>
> Networking within the specialty-foods business in Virginia led to the formation of a trade group that gives me insights on working in this industry and gives my firm low-cost exposure through trade shows and group-sponsored advertising.
>
> Generally, I take new proposals to the members of my personal network. Armed with their experience and my knowledge of the direction I want for the company, I can make the kind of calculated, educated decisions that have fueled our growth; Blue Crab Bay Co. expects sales of about $680,000 this year.

Source: Pamela Barefoot, "Entrepreneur's Notebook: Developing a Network," *Nation's Business*, Vol. 80, No. 10 (October 1992), p. 6.

or cost reduction; many small firms could save as much as 10 to 20 percent of annual operating costs. The inherent advantage in the use of such consultants is suggested by the existence of thousands of consulting firms. They range from large, well-established firms to small one- or two-person operations. Two broad areas of services are rendered by management consultants:

1. Helping improve productivity and/or prevent trouble by anticipating and eliminating its causes
2. Helping a client get out of trouble

Business firms have traditionally used consultants to help solve problems they could not handle alone. A consultant may be used, for example, to aid in the design of a new computer-based management information system. An even greater service that management consultants provide is periodic observation and analysis, which keeps small problems from becoming large ones. This role of consultants greatly expands their potential usefulness. Outside professionals typically charge by the hour, so an owner should prepare as completely as possible before a consulting session or visit begins.

NETWORKS OF ENTREPRENEURS   Entrepreneurs also gain informal management assistance through **networking**—the process of developing and engaging in mutually beneficial relationships with peers. As business owners meet other business owners, they discover a commonality of interests that leads to an exchange of ideas and experiences. The settings for such meetings may be trade associations, civic clubs, fraternal organizations, or any situation that brings businesspeople into contact with one another. Of course, the personal network of an entrepreneur is not

networking
the process of developing and engaging in mutually beneficial relationships

1 Discuss the distinctive features of small firm management.

- Management weakness is prevalent in small firms.
- Small firm managers face special financial and personnel constraints.
- As a new firm grows, it adds layers of supervision and increases formality of management.
- As a firm grows, the entrepreneur must become more of a manager and less of a doer.
- Founders tend to be more action-oriented and less analytical than professional managers.

2 Identify the various kinds of plans and approaches to planning.

- Types of plans include strategic plans, short-range plans, budgets, policies, and procedures.
- Planning is easily neglected, and managers must exercise discipline to make time for it.
- A manager may improve planning by drawing on the ideas of employees.

3 Discuss the entrepreneur's leadership role.

- An entrepreneur exerts strong personal influence in a small firm.
- Progressive managers use participative management approaches such as empowerment and work teams.
- Effective communication is an important factor in building a healthy organization.

4 Describe the nature and kinds of small business organization.

- Organizational relationships that develop without formal planning require adjustment and greater planning as a firm grows.
- Firms with fewer than 10 employees typically use a line organization.
- As staff specialists are added to a growing firm, a line organization becomes a line-and-staff organization.
- Following the chain of command in organizations preserves unity of command.
- Managers who delegate authority successfully can devote their time to more important duties.
- The optimum span of control depends on such factors as the nature of the work and the abilities of subordinates.

Continue on next page

limited to other entrepreneurs, but those individuals may be the most significant part of that network.

A formally structured networking system called The Alternative Board (TAB) was started by businessman Allen Fishman. Fishman's company sets up advisory boards of about a dozen chief executives, who are usually owners of small, noncompeting companies.

They meet one morning a month, with a paid "facilitator," most often a semiretired entrepreneur, as guide. The cost is $2,000 a year for small companies and $3,000 for midsized ones. Tom Epstein, president of Continental Research, St. Louis, says that in his six months as a TAB member, "I've made my money back 10 times over."[13]

Networks of entrepreneurs are linked by several kinds of ties—instrumental, affective, and moral. An instrumental tie is one in which the parties find the relationship mutually rewarding—for example, exchanging useful ideas about certain business problems. An affective tie relates to emotional sentiments—for example, sharing a joint vision about the role of small business when faced with giant competitors or with the government. A moral tie involves some type of obligation—for example, a mutual commitment to the principle of private enterprise or to the importance of integrity in business transactions. In personal networks of entrepreneurs, affective and moral ties are believed to be stronger than instrumental ties.[14] This suggests that a sense of identity and self-respect may be a significant product of the entrepreneur's network.

OTHER BUSINESS AND PROFESSIONAL SERVICES A variety of business and professional groups provide management assistance. In many cases, such assistance is part of a business relationship. Sources of management advice include bankers, certified public accountants, attorneys, insurance agents, suppliers, trade associations, and chambers of commerce.

It takes initiative to draw on the management assistance available from such groups. For example, it is easy to confine a business relationship with a CPA to audits and financial statements, but the CPA can advise on a much broader range of subjects.

Besides offering advice on tax matters, a good accountant can help in a variety of situations. When you hire or fire, what benefits or severance package should you offer? When you're planning to open a new branch, will your cash flow support it? When you embark on a new sideline, will the margins be adequate? When you reduce insurance, what's the risk? When you factor receivables, how will it affect the balance sheet? When you take on a big account, what's the downside if you lose the account? Or when you cut expenses, how will the cuts affect the bottom line?[15]

As you can see from the examples given, potential management assistance often comes disguised as professionals and firms encountered in the normal course of business activity. By staying alert for and taking advantage of such opportunities, a small firm can strengthen its management and improve its operations with little, if any, additional cost.

5 Discuss the ways in which control is exercised.

- Managers exercise control by monitoring operations, in order to detect and correct deviation from plans.
- Business goals constitute the standards used in controlling.
- Performance may be measured at the input, process, or output stages of operation.
- Corrective action must be preceded by an analysis of the cause of the deviation from a standard.
- A budget is the cornerstone of financial control.

6 Describe the problem of time pressure and suggest solutions.

- Time pressure tends to create inefficiencies in the management of small firms.
- The greatest time-saver is effective use of time.
- A manager can reduce time pressure by such practices as eliminating wasteful activities and planning work carefully.

7 Explain the various types of outside management assistance.

- Outside management assistance can be used to remedy staff limitations.
- Business incubators provide guidance as well as space for beginning businesses.
- Three government-sponsored sources of assistance are the Small Business Institute, the Service Corps of Retired Executives, and Small Business Development Centers.
- Management assistance may also be obtained by engaging management consultants and by networking with other entrepreneurs.
- Business and professional groups such as bankers and CPAs also provide management assistance.

DISCUSSION QUESTIONS

1. Is it likely that the quality of management is relatively uniform in all types of small businesses? What might account for differences?
2. What are the four stages of small business growth outlined in this chapter? How do management requirements change as the firm moves through these stages?
3. Some professional football coaches have written game plans that they consult from time to time during games. If coaches need formal plans, does it follow that small business owners need them as they engage in their type of competition? Why?
4. Would most employees of small firms welcome or resist a leadership approach that sought their ideas and involved them in meetings to let them know what was going on? Why might some employees resist such an approach?
5. There is a saying that goes, "What you do speaks so loudly I can't hear what you say." What does this mean, and how does it apply to communication in small firms?

New Terms and Concepts

professional manager *373*

management functions *377*

long-range plan (strategic plan) *377*

short-range plans *377*

budget *377*

business policies *377*

procedures *377*

standard operating procedure *377*

empowerment *379*

work teams *379*

line organization *381*

chain of command *381*

line-and-staff organization *382*

line activities *382*

staff activities *382*

unity of command *383*

delegation of authority *383*

span of control *384*

Small Business Institute (SBI) *388*

Service Corps of Retired Executives (SCORE) *389*

Small Business Development Centers (SBDCs) *390*

networking *391*

You Make the Call

Situation 1   In one small firm, the owner-manager and his management team use various methods to delegate decision making to employees at the operating level. New employees are trained thoroughly when they begin, but no supervisor monitors their work closely once they have learned their duties. Of course, help is available as needed, but no one is there on an hour-to-hour basis to make sure employees are functioning as needed and that they are avoiding mistakes.

Occasionally, all managers and supervisors leave for a day-long meeting and allow the operating employees to run the business by themselves. Job assignments are defined rather loosely. Management expects employees to assume responsibility and to take necessary action whenever they see that something needs to be done. When employees ask for direction, they are sometimes simply told to solve the problem in whatever way they think best.

Question 1   Is such a loosely organized firm likely to be as effective as a firm that defines jobs more precisely and monitors performance more closely? What are the advantages and the limitations of the type of management style described above?

Question 2   How would such management methods affect morale?

Question 3   Would you like to work for this company? Why or why not?

Situation 2   A few years after successfully launching a new business, an entrepreneur found himself spending 16-hour days running from one appointment to another, negotiating with customers, drumming up new business, signing checks, and checking up as much as possible on his six employees. The founder realized that his own strength was in selling, but general managerial responsibilities were very time-consuming and interfered with his sales efforts. He even slept in the office two nights a week.

Continue on next page

6. What type of small firm might effectively use a line organization? When would its structure require change? To what type? Why?

7. Explain the relationship between planning and control in a small business. Give an example.

8. What practices can a small business manager use to conserve time?

9. What would be some advantages and drawbacks of a business incubator location for a startup retail firm?

10. Is the SBI program of greater benefit to the client firm or to the students involved?

EXPERIENTIAL EXERCISES

1. Interview a management consultant, SCORE member, SBI project director, or representative of a CPA firm to discuss small business management weaknesses and the willingness or reluctance of small firms to use consultants. Prepare a report on your findings.

2. Select a small business and diagram the organizational relationships in that firm. Report on any organizational problems that are apparent to you or that are recognized by the manager or others in the firm.

3. Most students have been employees (or volunteers) at some time. Prepare a report on your personal experiences regarding the leadership of and delegation of authority by a supervisor. Include references to the type of leadership exercised and to the adequacy of delegation, its clarity, and any problems involved.

4. Select an unstructured block of one to four hours in your schedule—that is, hours that are not regularly devoted to class attendance, sleeping, and so on. Carefully record your use of that time period for several days. Prepare a report summarizing your use of the time and outlining a plan to use it more effectively.

Exploring the

5. Consult the home page of the Small Business Administration on the Web at http://www.sbaonline.sba.gov. Prepare a one-page report summarizing the types of Small Business Development Center locations in your state and identifying the service location closest to your college or university.

CASE 17
Central Engineering (p. 636)

This case examines one entrepreneur's management style and the ways in which it hampered decision making.

Alternative Cases for Chapter 17:
Case 6, "Robinson Associates, Inc.," p. 605
Case 24, "Fox Manufacturing," p. 657

No matter how hard he worked, however, he knew that his people weren't organized and that many problems existed. He lacked the time to set personnel policies or to draw up job descriptions for his six employees. One employee even took advantage of the laxity and sometimes skipped work. Invoices were sent to customers late, and delivery schedules were sometimes missed. Fortunately, the business was profitable in spite of the numerous problems.

Question 1 Is this founder's problem one of time management or general management ability? Would it be logical to engage a management consultant to help solve the firm's problems?
Question 2 If this founder asked you to recommend some type of outside management assistance, would you recommend a SCORE counselor, an SBI team, a CPA firm, a management consultant, or some other type of assistance? Why?
Question 3 If you were asked to improve this firm's management system, what would be your first steps and your initial goal?

Situation 3 Time pressure faced by small business managers can affect relationships within a business and also spill over into family relationships. Faced with business pressures and deadlines, entrepreneurs may borrow time from the family to devote to the business. The following letter to *Family Business* advisor Marcy Syms expresses the pain felt by the wife of an overly busy small business owner:

> Dear Marcy:
>   The year I got married, my husband and his sister started a greeting-card business together. They have worked very hard for the past 15 years and now have a thriving company that has provided us with a lifestyle I only knew existed by reading magazines.
>   Over the years the company has hired good people to help manage its growth. So I keep telling my husband that there is now no excuse for not getting home in time to have dinner with me and the kids, and that we should plan a vacation together that's longer than a three-day weekend (and without a beeper!).
>   Every time I ask him to spend more time with the family, he seems to grow resentful. He tells me that I must be jealous of the business and his close relationship with his sister. I guess I am jealous to the extent that "our" family gets so little of his attention. I keep thinking that one day my husband may look around and notice that the kids are grown and I am gone.

Source: The letter is taken from "Ask Marcy Syms," *Family Business*, Vol. 4, No. 4 (Autumn 1993), p. 12.

Question 1 How are the entrepreneur's long hours beneficial to the family? How are they damaging?
Question 2 How can this entrepreneur solve his time management problem and spend more time with his family?
Question 3 What could the entrepreneur do to increase his wife's understanding and feeling of involvement in the business?

Managing Human Resources

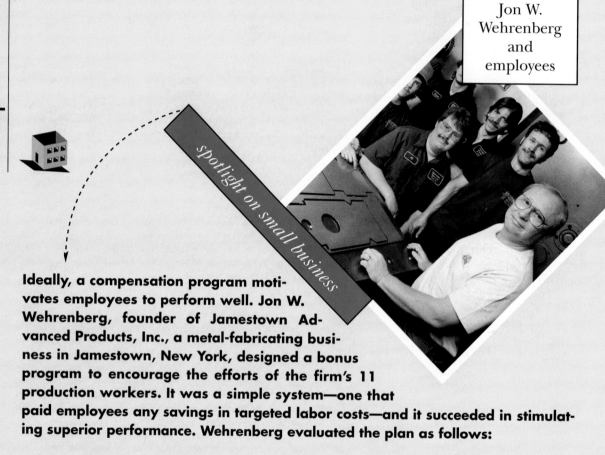

Chapter 18

Jon W. Wehrenberg and employees

spotlight on small business

Ideally, a compensation program motivates employees to perform well. Jon W. Wehrenberg, founder of Jamestown Advanced Products, Inc., a metal-fabricating business in Jamestown, New York, designed a bonus program to encourage the efforts of the firm's 11 production workers. It was a simple system—one that paid employees any savings in targeted labor costs—and it succeeded in stimulating superior performance. Wehrenberg evaluated the plan as follows:

> *As time went on, I could see the change in employees' attitudes. Before we were making bonus payments, workers didn't seem to care if we spent money on overtime because of a production snag. It was the company's nickel, not theirs. But once they crossed into bonus territory, they saw that production problems were costing them money, and they became very diligent about finding ways to improve.*

A compensation plan is just one component of human resources management. As the experience of Jamestown Advanced Products illustrates, a firm benefits when compensation arrangements, as well as other elements of the human resources program, are well managed.

Source: Jon W. Wehrenberg, "How My Company Learned to Run Itself," *Inc.*, Vol. 13, No. 1 (January 1991), pp. 54–60.

Capable, industrious, and congenial employees can create customer satisfaction and enhance business profits. To be effective, therefore, small firms must see employees as more than hired hands. Instead, they should regard them as valuable business resources.

Although small businesses cannot duplicate the personnel programs of such business giants as Wal-Mart and General Electric, they can develop approaches suitable for the 10, 50, or 100 employees on their payrolls. This chapter deals with the type of human resources management that works best for small firms.

RECRUITING PERSONNEL

When recruiting employees, a small firm competes with both large and small businesses. It cannot afford to let competitors take the cream of the crop. Aggressive recruitment requires the small firm to take the initiative in locating applicants and to search until enough applicants are available to permit wise choices.

Importance of People

Hiring the right people and eliciting their enthusiastic performance are essential factors in reaching the potential of any business. As Ellyn Spragins suggested, "With every person you hire, you determine how great your potential successes may be—or how awful your failures."[1]

Employees affect profitability in many ways. In most small firms, the attitudes of salespeople and their ability to serve customer needs directly affect sales revenue. Also, payroll is one of the largest expense categories for most businesses, having a direct impact on the bottom line. By recruiting outstanding personnel, therefore, a firm can improve its return on each payroll dollar.

Recruitment and selection of employees establish a foundation for a firm's ongoing human relationships. In a sense, the quality of employees determines the human potential of an organization. If talented, ambitious recruits can be attracted, the business, through good management, should be able to build a strong human organization.

Attracting Applicants to Small Firms

Competition in recruiting well-qualified business talent requires small firms to identify their distinctive advantages when making an appeal to outstanding prospects, especially to those seeking managerial and professional positions. Fortunately, small firm recruiters can advance some good arguments in favor of small business careers.

The opportunity for general management experience at a decision-making level is attractive to many prospects. Rather than toiling in obscure, low-level, specialized positions during their early years, capable newcomers can quickly move into positions of responsibility in well-managed small businesses. In such positions, they can see that their work makes a difference in the success of the company.

Small firms can structure the work environment to offer professional, managerial, and technical personnel greater freedom than they would normally have in big businesses. One example of a small company that created an atmosphere of this type is Stone Construction Equipment, Inc. of Honeoye, New York. This firm restructured the job of Stan Gerhart, who made metal engine covers for light machinery:

> *For 16 years, his job was to crank 'em out, put 'em on the shelf, punch out, and go home. Then Stone's new managers asked Gerhart to redesign his job from the ground up—and to run his one-man department as its own little business, dealing on his own with "vendors" and "customers" elsewhere in the shop. Today, Gerhart can point to a dozen time-saving or quality-assuring ideas he has come up with. "It makes my job a whole lot easier because I control my own destiny."*[2]

In this type of environment, individual contributions can be recognized rather than hidden under the numerous layers of a bureaucratic organization. In addition, compensation arrangements can be designed to create a powerful incentive. Flexibility in work scheduling and job-sharing arrangements are other possible lures. The value of any incentive as a recruiting advantage depends to some degree on the circumstances of the particular firm. From the standpoint of an applicant, ideally the firm should be growing and profitable. It should also have a degree of professionalism in its management that can be readily recognized by prospective employees.

Sources of Employees

To recruit effectively, the small business manager must know where and how to find qualified applicants. Sources are numerous, and it is impossible to generalize about the best source in view of variations in personnel requirements and quality of sources from one locality to another.

WALK-INS   A firm may receive unsolicited applications from individuals who walk into the place of business to seek employment. This is an inexpensive source for clerical and production jobs, but the quality of applicants may be mixed. If qualified applicants cannot be hired immediately, their applications should be kept on file for future reference. In the interest of good public relations, all applicants should be treated courteously, whether or not they are offered jobs.

SCHOOLS   Secondary schools, trade schools, colleges, and universities are desirable sources for certain classes of employees, particularly those who need no specific work experience. Some secondary schools and colleges have internship programs involving periods of work in business firms. These programs enable students to gain a measure of practical experience. Secondary and trade schools provide applicants with a limited but useful educational background. Colleges and universities can supply candidates for positions in management and in various technical and scientific fields. In addition, many colleges are excellent sources of part-time employees.

Action Report

ENTREPRENEURIAL EXPERIENCES

Using Flexible Schedules to Attract Applicants

Small firms can sometimes use flexible work schedules as a way to attract applicants. Although the nature of a firm's operations limits the degree to which it can use this incentive, one small food-processing company in Redmond, Washington has attracted employees in this way:

> *Ten years ago in their garage, partners Lynn Kirwan and Leigh Zwicker inaugurated Canterbury Cuisine, a . . . line of convenience foods and spices with homey names like Grandma Hannah's Sunday Beef Soup and Becka's Pumpkin Cake. The women offered other mothers in their neighborhood work schedules built around school schedules for their kids.*
>
> *Even though they now employ 20 people, have moved to larger facilities, and have sales of $1.5 million, the duo continues to offer work-time flexibility. Says Kirwan, "We use flexibility as a benefit. As women business owners with children ourselves, we know how difficult it is to find the time to go to the dentist and run errands."*

Source: Echo Montgomery Garrett, "Attack on Absenteeism," *Independent Business*, Vol. 5, No. 4 (July-August, 1994), pp. 21–22.

PUBLIC EMPLOYMENT OFFICES   State employment offices that are affiliated with the United States Employment Service offer at no cost to small businesses a supply of applicants who are actively seeking employment. These offices, located in all major cities, are for the most part a source of clerical workers, unskilled laborers, production workers, and technicians.

PRIVATE EMPLOYMENT AGENCIES   Numerous private agencies offer their services as employment offices. In some cases, employers receive their services without cost because the applicants pay a fee to the agency. However, most firms pay the agency fee if the applicant is highly qualified. Such agencies tend to specialize in people with specific skills, such as accountants, computer operators, or managers.

When filling key positions, small firms sometimes turn to executive search firms, called **headhunters,** to locate qualified candidates. Plasticolors, Inc., a small Ohio manufacturer of colorants for fiberglass plastics, successfully used an executive recruiter to fill the position of CEO, replacing the company's founder.[3] The recruiter spent about 45 hours interviewing directors and key employees before beginning the executive search, thereby developing a relationship with the company and an acquaintance with its managerial needs. Headhunters, who are paid by the company they represent, can make a wide-ranging search for individuals who possess the right combination of talents.

headhunter
a search firm that locates qualified candidates for executive positions

EMPLOYEE REFERRALS   If current employees are good employees, their recommendations of suitable candidates may provide excellent prospects. Ordinarily, employees will hesitate to recommend applicants unless they believe in their ability to do the job. Many small business owners say that this source provides more of their employees than any other. A few employers go so far as to offer financial rewards for employee referrals.

A small business manager may use various sources to find qualified applicants. One form of recruiting popular with small firms is help-wanted advertising, which usually takes the form of a sign in the store or an advertisement in the classifieds of local newspapers.

HELP-WANTED ADVERTISING   The "Help Wanted" sign in the window is one form of recruiting used by small firms. A similar but more aggressive form of recruiting consists of advertisements in the classified pages of local newspapers. Although the effectiveness of these forms has been questioned by some, many well-managed organizations recruit in this way.

TEMPORARY HELP AGENCIES   The temporary help industry, which is growing rapidly, supplies temporary employees (or temps) such as word processors, clerks, accountants, engineers, nurses, and sales clerks for short periods of time. By using agencies such as Kelly Services or Manpower, small firms can deal with seasonal fluctuations and absences caused by vacation or illness. As an example, a temporary replacement might be obtained to fill the position of an employee who is taking leave following the birth of a child—a type of family leave now mandated by law for some employees. In addition, use of temporary employees provides an introduction to individuals whose performance may justify an offer of permanent employment. Staffing with temporary employees is less practical when extensive training is required or continuity is important.

Describing Jobs to Be Filled

A small business manager should analyze the activities or work to be performed and determine the number and kinds of jobs to be filled. Knowing the job requirements permits a more intelligent selection of applicants for specific jobs, based on their individual capacities and characteristics.

Certainly the owner-manager should not select personnel simply to fit a rigid specification of education, experience, or personal background. Rather, she or he must concentrate on the ability of an individual to fill a particular position in the business. Making this determination requires an outline or summary of the work to be performed. A written summary of this type, as shown in Figure 18-1, is called a **job description.**

job description
a written summary of duties required by a specific job

Preparing job descriptions need not be a highly sophisticated process. The owner of White Glove Service Systems, in Phoenix, Arizona, simply asked employees to jot down what they did over a period of a few days.[4] The managers then looked for duplication of duties and for tasks that might have fallen through the cracks. In this relatively informal manner, they created job descriptions that spelled out duties recognized by the employees as well as the employer.

Duties listed in job descriptions should not be defined too narrowly. Job descriptions should minimize unnecessary overlap but avoid creating a "that's-not-my-job" mentality. Technical competence is as necessary in small firms as it is in a large business, but versatility and flexibility may be even more important. Engineers may occasionally need to make sales calls, and marketing people may need to pinch-hit in production.

Figure 18-1

*Job Description for Stock
Clerk in Retail Food Store*

Title: Stock Clerk
Primary Function: To stock shelves with food products and other items
Supervision Received: Works under direct supervision of store manager
Supervision Exercised: None
Duties:

1. Receive and store products in storage area.
2. Take products from storage, open outer wrapping, and place contents on store shelves.
3. Provide information and/or direction to customers seeking particular products or having other questions.
4. Monitor quantity of products on shelves and add products when supplies are low.
5. Perform housekeeping duties when special need arises—for example, when container is broken or products fall on the floor.
6. Assist cashiers in bagging products as needed during rush periods.
7. Assist in other areas or perform special assignments as directed by the store manager.

In the process of studying a job, an analyst should list the knowledge, skills, abilities, or other characteristics that an individual must have to perform the job. This statement of requirements is called a **job specification.** A job specification for the position of stock clerk might state that the incumbent must be able to lift 50 pounds and must have completed 10 to 12 years of school.

Job descriptions are mainly an aid in personnel recruitment, but they also have other uses. For example, they can give employees a focus in their work, provide direction in training, and supply a framework for performance review.

job specification
a list of skills and abilities needed by a job applicant to perform a specific job

EVALUATING PROSPECTS AND SELECTING EMPLOYEES

2 Identify the steps in evaluating job applicants.

An employer's recruitment activities merely locate prospects for employment. Subsequent steps are needed to evaluate these candidates and to select some as employees. An employer can minimize the danger of taking a blind, uninformed gamble on applicants of unknown quality by following the steps described in the next sections.

Step 1: Using Application Forms

The value of having prospective employees complete an application form lies in the form's systematic collection of background data that might otherwise be overlooked. The information recorded on an application form is useful in sizing up an applicant and serves as a guide in making a more detailed investigation of the applicant's experience and character.

An application form need not be elaborate or lengthy. However, care must be taken to avoid questions that may conflict with laws concerning unfair job discrimination. State and federal laws, which have been changing frequently, limit the use of many questions formerly found on application forms. Questions about race, color, national origin, religion, age, marital status, disabilities, or arrests are either prohibited or considered unwise unless the employer can prove their job-relatedness.

An employment interview is a crucial step in the selection process. It provides the employer with some idea of the potential employee's personality, intelligence, appearance, and job knowledge.

Step 2: Interviewing the Applicant

An interview permits the employer to get some idea of the applicant's appearance, job knowledge, intelligence, and personality. Any of these factors may be significant for the job to be filled. Although the interview is an important step in the selection process, it should not be the only step. Some managers have the mistaken idea that they are infallible judges of human nature and can choose good employees on the basis of interviews alone. Care must be taken in the interview process, as in designing application forms, to avoid questions that conflict with the law. If possible, applicants should be interviewed by two or more individuals in order to minimize errors in judgment.

Time spent in interviewing, as well as in other phases of the selection process, can save time and money later on. In today's litigious society, firing an employee has become quite difficult. A dismissed employee can bring suit even when an employer had justifiable reasons for dismissal.

The value of the interview depends on the interviewer's skill and methods. Any interviewer can improve his or her interviewing by following these generally accepted principles:

- Determine the job-related questions you want to ask the applicant before beginning the interview.
- Conduct the interview in a quiet atmosphere.
- Give your entire attention to the applicant.
- Put the applicant at ease.
- Never argue.
- Keep the conversation at a level suited to the applicant.
- Listen attentively.
- Observe closely the applicant's speech, mannerisms, and attire if these characteristics are important to the job.
- Try to avoid being unduly influenced by the applicant's trivial mannerisms or superficial resemblance to other people you know.

Employment interviews should be seen as a two-way process. The applicant is evaluating the employer while the employer is evaluating the applicant. In order

for the applicant to make an informed decision, he or she needs a clear idea of what the job entails and an opportunity to ask questions.

Step 3: Checking References and Other Background Information

Careful checking with former employers, school authorities, and other references can help avoid hiring mistakes, which can have serious consequences later. Suppose, for example, that you hired an appliance technician who later burglarized a customer's home. Checking the applicant's background for a criminal record might have prevented this unfortunate occurrence.

It is becoming increasingly difficult to obtain more than the basic facts concerning a person's background because of the potential for lawsuits brought against employers by disappointed applicants. However, reference checks on a prior employment record do not constitute infringements on privacy. A written letter of inquiry to these references is probably the weakest form of checking because most people will not put damaging statements in writing. Often, former employers or supervisors will speak more frankly when approached by telephone or in person.

For a fee, an applicant's history (financial, criminal, employment, and so on) may be supplied by private investigation agencies or credit bureaus. If an employer needs a credit report to establish an applicant's eligibility for employment, the Fair Credit Reporting Act requires that the applicant be notified in writing that such a report is being requested.

Step 4: Testing the Applicant

Many kinds of jobs lend themselves to performance testing. For example, an applicant may be given a data-entry test to verify speed and accuracy of keyboarding skills. With a little ingenuity, employers can improvise practical tests that are pertinent to many positions.

Psychological examinations may also be used by small businesses, but the results can be misleading because of difficulty in interpreting the tests or in adapting them to a particular business. In addition, the U.S. Supreme Court has upheld the Equal Employment Opportunity Commission's requirement that *any* test used in making employment decisions must be job-related.

Useful tests of any kind must meet the criteria of **validity** and **reliability.** If a test is valid, its results should correspond well with job performance; that is, the applicants with the best test scores should generally be the best employees. If a test is reliable, it should provide consistent results when used at different times or by various individuals.

validity
the extent to which a test assesses true job performance ability

reliability
the consistency of a test in measuring job performance ability

Step 5: Physical Examinations

A primary purpose of physical examinations is to evaluate the ability of applicants to meet the physical demands of specific jobs. Care must be taken, however, to avoid discriminating against those who are physically disabled. The Americans with Disabilities Act of 1990 (explained further in Chapter 26) requires employers to make "reasonable" adaptations to facilitate the employment of such individuals.

The law permits drug screening of applicants, and this can be included as part of the physical examination process. Since few small firms have staff physicians, most of them must make arrangements with a local doctor or clinic to perform physical examinations.

3 Describe the role of training for both managerial and nonmanagerial employees in the small firm.

TRAINING AND DEVELOPMENT

Once an employee has been recruited and added to the payroll, the process of training and development must begin. For this process, a new recruit is raw material, while the well-trained technician, salesperson, manager, or other employee represents a finished product.

Purposes of Training and Development

One obvious purpose of training is to prepare a new recruit to perform the duties for which he or she has been hired. There are very few positions for which no training is required. If an employer fails to provide training, the new employee must learn by trial and error, which frequently wastes time, materials, and money.

Training to improve skills and knowledge is not limited to newcomers. The performance of current employees can often be improved through additional training. In view of the constant change in products, technology, policies, and procedures in the world of business, continual training is necessary to update knowledge and skills—even in a small firm. Only with such training can employees meet the changing demands placed on them.

Both employers and employees have a stake in the advancement of qualified personnel to higher-level positions. Preparation for advancement usually involves developmental efforts—possibly of a different type than those needed to sharpen skills for current duties. Because personal development and advancement are prime concerns of able employees, a small business can profit from careful attention to this phase of the personnel program. The opportunity to grow and move up in an organization not only improves the morale of current employees but also offers an inducement for potential applicants.

Orientation for New Personnel

The developmental process begins with an employee's first two or three days on the job. It is at this point that a new person tends to feel lost and confused, confronted with a new physical layout, different job title, unknown fellow employees, different type of supervision, changed hours or work schedule, and/or a unique set of personnel policies and procedures. Any events that conflict with the newcomer's expectations are interpreted in light of his or her previous work experience, and these interpretations can foster a strong commitment to the new employer or lead to feelings of alienation.

Recognizing the new employee's sensitivity at this point, the employer can contribute to a positive outcome by proper orientation. Steps can be taken to help the newcomer adjust and to minimize feelings of uneasiness in the new setting.

In addition to explaining specific job duties, supervisors can outline the firm's policies and procedures in as much detail as possible. A clear explanation of performance criteria and the way in which an employee's work will be evaluated should be included in the discussion. The new employee should be encouraged to ask questions, and time should be taken to provide careful answers. The firm may facilitate the orientation process by providing the recruit with a written list of company practices and procedures in the form of an employee handbook. The handbook may include information about work hours, paydays, breaks, lunch hours, absences, holidays, names of supervisors, employee benefits, and so on. Since new employees are faced with information overload at first, it is good to schedule a follow-up orientation after a week or two.

Action Report

QUALITY GOALS

Better Quality Through Better Training

In 1994, Wainwright Industries, a family-owned manufacturer of metal parts in St. Peters, Missouri, won a Malcolm Baldrige National Quality Award—the most prestigious award given in the United States for quality performance in business. In 1990, the firm had been named as one of General Motors' top-quality suppliers.

What is the secret to Wainwright's success? The company's training program is a major contributor. Wainwright invests the equivalent of 7 percent of its payroll in training, roughly seven times the national average. In addition, the company listens to its customers, and it communicates quality goals and practices to its employees.

Source: Shelly Reese, "Wainwright Snags Awards by Listening," *USA Today*, October 19, 1994, p. 4B.

Training to Improve Quality

Employee training is an integral part of comprehensive quality management programs. Although quality management is concerned with machines, materials, and measurement, it also focuses attention on human performance. Thus, training programs can be designed to promote higher-quality workmanship.

To a considerable extent, training for quality performance is part of the ongoing supervisory role of all managers. In addition, special classes and seminars can be used to teach employees about the importance of quality and ways in which to produce high-quality work.

Robotron Corporation, a small manufacturer of heat-treatment machinery in Michigan, provides an example of the worth of quality training. Robotron's management discovered that 70 percent of its products had to be reworked.[5] Among other problems, some workers in a key operation were having difficulty reading blueprints. To deal with such problems, management established a broad quality management effort that included targeted programs to improve reading and math skills. In a short time, the company was able to substantially reduce the number of defects per unit reaching the final test department.

Training Nonmanagerial Employees

Job descriptions or job specifications, if they exist, may identify abilities or skills needed for particular jobs. To a large extent, such requirements regulate the type of training that is appropriate.

For all classes of employees, more training is accomplished on the job than through any other method. However, on-the-job training may not be very effective if it depends on haphazard learning rather than planned, controlled training programs. A system designed to make on-the-job training more effective is known as **Job Instruction Training.** The steps of this program are intended to help supervisors become more effective in training nonmanagerial employees.

1. *Prepare employees.* Put employees at ease. Place them in appropriate jobs. Find out what they already know about the job. Get them interested in learning it.

Job Instruction Training
a systematic step-by-step method for on-the-job training of nonmanagerial employees

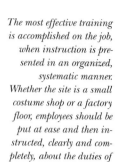

2. *Present the operations.* Tell, show, illustrate, and question carefully and patiently. Stress key points. Instruct clearly and completely, taking up one point at a time—but no more than the employees can master.
3. *Try out performance.* Test the employees by having them perform the jobs. Have the employees tell, show, and explain key points. Ask questions and correct errors. Continue until the employees know that they know how to do the job.
4. *Follow up.* Check on employees frequently. Designate the persons to whom the employees should go for help. Encourage questions. Get the employees to look for the key points as they progress. Taper off extra coaching and close follow-up.

Developing Managerial and Professional Employees

A small business has a particularly strong need to develop managerial and professional employees. Depending on its size, the firm may have few or many key positions. To function most effectively, the business must develop individuals who can hold these key positions. Incumbents should be developed to the point that they can adequately carry out the responsibilities assigned to them. Ideally, potential replacements should also be available for key individuals who may retire or leave for other reasons. The entrepreneur often postpones grooming a personal replacement, but this step is also important in ensuring a smooth transition in the firm's management.

Establishing a management training program requires serious consideration of the following factors:

• *Determine the need for training.* What vacancies are expected? Who needs to be trained? What type of training and how much training are needed to meet the demands of the job description?
• *Develop a plan for training.* How can the individuals be trained? Do they currently have enough responsibility to permit them to learn? Can they be assigned additional duties? Should they be given temporary assignments in other areas—for example, should they be shifted from production to sales? Would additional schooling be beneficial?

- *Establish a timetable.* When should training begin? How much can be accomplished in the next six months or one year?
- *Counsel employees.* Do the individuals understand their need for training? Are they aware of their prospects within the firm? Has an understanding been reached as to the nature of training? Have the employees been consulted regularly about progress in their work and the problems confronting them? Have they been given the benefit of the owner's experience and insights without having decisions made for them?

COMPENSATION AND INCENTIVES FOR SMALL BUSINESS EMPLOYEES

Compensation and financial incentives are important to all employees, and the small firm must acknowledge the central role of the paycheck and other monetary rewards in attracting and motivating personnel. In addition, small firms can offer several nonfinancial incentives that appeal to both managerial and nonmanagerial employees.

Wage or Salary Levels

In general, small firms find that they must be roughly competitive in wage or salary levels in order to attract well-qualified personnel. Wages or salaries paid to employees either are based on increments of time—such as an hour, a day, a month—or vary directly with their output. A compensation system based on increments of time is commonly referred to as **daywork.** Daywork is most appropriate for types of jobs in which performance is not easily measurable. It is the most common compensation system and is easy to understand and administer.

Financial Incentives

Incentive systems have been devised to motivate employees, particularly nonmanagerial employees, to increase their productivity. Incentive wages may constitute an employee's entire earnings or may supplement his or her regular wages or salary. The commission system often used to compensate salespeople is one type of incentive plan. In manufacturing, employees are sometimes paid according to the number of units they produce. While many incentive programs apply to employees as individuals, these programs may also involve the use of group incentives and team awards.

General bonus or profit-sharing plans are especially important for managerial or other key personnel, although such plans sometimes include lower-level personnel. These plans provide employees with a piece of the action, which may or may not involve assignment of shares of stock. A profit-sharing plan may simply entail a distribution of a specified share of the profits or a share of profits that exceed a target amount. Profit sharing provides a more direct work incentive in small companies than in large companies, because the connection between individual performance and company success can be more easily appreciated.

Performance-based compensation systems must be designed carefully if they are to work successfully. Such plans should be devised with the aid of a consultant and/or public accounting firm. Some distinctive features of good bonus plans are identified in the following list:

4 Explain the various kinds of compensation plans and the differences between daywork and incentives.

daywork
a compensation system based on increments of time

1. *Set attainable goals.* Incentive pay works best when workers feel they can meet the targets. Tying pay to broad measures such as companywide results leaves workers feeling frustrated and helpless.
2. *Set meaningful goals.* You can neither motivate nor reward by setting targets employees can't comprehend. Complex financial measures or jargon-heavy benchmarks mean nothing to most.
3. *Bring workers in.* Give them a say in developing performance measures and listen to their advice on ways to change work systems. Phase pay plans in gradually so employees have a chance to absorb them.
4. *Keep targets moving.* Performance-pay plans must be constantly adjusted to meet the changing needs of workers and customers. The life expectancy of a plan may be no more than three or four years.
5. *Aim carefully.* Know what message you want to send. Make sure that new scheme doesn't reward the wrong behavior. Linking bonuses to plant safety, for example, could encourage coverups.[6]

Fringe Benefits

fringe benefits
nonfinancial supplements to employees' compensation

Fringe benefits, which include payments for such items as Social Security, vacations, holidays, health insurance, and workers' compensation insurance, are expensive. According to a survey of 1993 compensation costs, the cost of fringe benefits amounted to 41.3 percent of payroll costs.[7] This means that for every dollar paid in wages, employers paid 41.3 cents for fringe benefits. (If the cost of fringe benefits were expressed as a percentage of total compensation costs—that is, payroll plus fringe benefits—the figure would be lower than 41.3 percent.) Small firms are somewhat less generous than large firms in providing fringe benefits for their employees. The same survey of compensation costs cited above reported that firms having fewer than 100 employees spent an amount equal to 35.7 percent of their payroll for such benefits. However it is calculated, the cost of fringe benefits is a substantial part of total labor costs for most small firms.

Even though fringes are expensive, a small firm cannot ignore them if it is to compete effectively for good employees. A small but growing number of small firms now use flexible benefits programs (or cafeteria plans) that allow employees to choose the type of fringe benefits they wish to receive.[8] All employees may receive a core level of coverage, such as basic health insurance, and then be allowed to choose how some amount specified by the employer is to be divided among additional options—for example, child care reimbursement, dental care, pension fund contributions, and additional health insurance.

Outside help in administering cafeteria plans is available to small firms that wish to avoid the detailed paperwork associated with them. Many small companies—including some with fewer than 25 employees—turn over the administration of their flexible benefits plans to outside consulting, payroll accounting, or insurance companies that provide such services for a monthly fee. In view of the increasing popularity of these plans and the wide availability of administrative services, it seems only a matter of time until many small firms will be offering flexible benefits.

Employee Stock Ownership Plans

employee stock ownership plans (ESOPs)
plans that give employees a share of ownership in the business

Some small firms have created **employee stock ownership plans (ESOPs),** by which they give employees a share of ownership in the business.[9] These plans may be structured in a variety of ways. For example, a share of annual profits may be designated for the benefit of employees and used to buy company stock, which is then placed in a trust for the employees.

ESOPs also provide a way for owners to cash out and withdraw from a business without selling the firm to outsiders. The owner might sell equity to the firm's employees, who can borrow funds at attractive rates for this purpose. In fact, tax advantages for both owners and employees make ESOPs an increasingly popular option.

SPECIAL ISSUES IN HUMAN RESOURCES MANAGEMENT

So far in this chapter, we have dealt with recruitment, selection, training, and compensation of employees. In addition to these primary activities, human resources management can involve a number of other general issues. These issues—leasing employees, dealing with labor unions, formalizing personnel management, and hiring a human resources manager—are the focus of this concluding section. (Legal constraints pertaining to human resources management are covered in Chapter 26.)

5 Discuss employee leasing, labor unions, and the formalizing of human resources management.

Leasing Employees

Leasing equipment or property has long been an accepted alternative to buying it. **Leasing employees,** as surprising as it may seem, has become a common alternative to employing them directly. An estimated 2,000 or more companies have emerged in recent years to lease personnel to small businesses.[10] For a fee of 1 to 5 percent of payroll, a personnel-leasing company writes paychecks, pays payroll taxes, and files necessary reports with government agencies. Although small firms using this service avoid certain paperwork, they do not usually escape the tasks of recruitment and selection. Typically, the employees of a small firm are simply shifted to the leasing company's payroll at some specified date. In most cases, the firm still determines who works, who gets promoted, and who gets time off.

Many employees like the leasing arrangement. Small employers are often able to provide better benefit packages in this way since leasing companies cover hundreds or thousands of employees and thus qualify for better rates. Of course, the small business must bear the cost of insurance and other benefits obtained through a leasing company, in addition to the company's basic service fee.

Some caution is necessary when selecting a leasing company. As leasing companies have proliferated in recent years, a number of them have run into financial trouble and left employers liable for unpaid claims. Some states have enacted legislation to protect employer-clients, and more regulation is likely.

Another note of caution pertains to the application of government regulations to small businesses. Very small employers are often excluded from specific regulations. For example, companies with fewer than 15 employees are exempt from the Americans with Disabilities Act. When these employees officially become part of a large leasing organization, however, the small firm using the leased employees becomes subject to the law.

leasing employees "renting" personnel from an organization that handles paperwork and benefits administration

Leasing personnel often allows small firms to obtain insurance benefits for their employees at a better rate. Thus they may be able to offer expanded benefit options to clerical workers and other non-managerial employees.

Action Report

ENTREPRENEURIAL EXPERIENCES

An Example of Employee Leasing

David Hinds's Van Tone Company in Dallas, Texas employs only 24 employees in the production of flavoring extracts. Faced with a drastic increase in workers' compensation and health insurance costs, Hinds turned to employee leasing.

> *Once he decided to pursue the leasing option, Hinds settled on Employers Resource Management Co., an employee-leasing company based in Boise, Idaho. The leasing company lowered his health premiums because it has access to cheaper, pooled rates not available to small employers. And it cut Hinds's workers' compensation costs because the leasing company's pool of workers had a better safety record—and therefore lower rates—than Hinds's own firm.*
>
> *Even as he cut costs, the leasing arrangement made it possible for Hinds to expand the benefits offered to his workers. The leasing company's health plan added dental and vision care as well as yearly physicals, and it offered a lower deductible and out-of-pocket annual maximum. In addition, Hinds's workers now have access to a credit union through the leasing firm.*

Source: Rosalind Resnick, "Leasing Workers," *Nation's Business*, Vol. 80, No. 11 (November 1992), pp. 20–28.

Dealing with Labor Unions

Most entrepreneurs prefer to operate independently and to avoid unionization. Indeed, most small businesses are not unionized. To some extent, this results from the predominance of small business in services, where unionization is less common than in manufacturing. Also, unions typically concentrate their primary attention on large companies.

However, labor unions are not unknown in small firms. Many types of small firms—building and electrical contractors, for example—negotiate labor contracts and employ unionized personnel. The need to work with a union formalizes and, to some extent, complicates the relationship between the small firm and its employees.

If employees wish to bargain collectively, the law requires the employer to participate in such bargaining. The demand for labor union representation may arise from employees' dissatisfaction with the work environment and employment relationships. By following enlightened human resources policies, the small firm can minimize the likelihood of labor organization or improve the relationship between management and union.

Formalizing Employer-Employee Relationships

As we explained earlier in this chapter, the management system of small firms is typically less formal than that of larger ones. A degree of informality can, in fact, constitute a virtue in small organizations. As personnel are added, however, the benefits of informality decline, and its costs increase. Large numbers of employees cannot be managed effectively without some system for regulating employer-employee relationships. This situation has been portrayed in terms of a family relationship: "House rules are hardly necessary where only two people are living. But add several children, and before long Mom starts sounding like a government regulatory agency."[11]

Growth, then, produces pressures to formalize personnel policies and procedures. The primary question is how much formality and how soon—a decision that involves judgment. Some matters should be formalized from the very beginning; on the other hand, excessive regulation can become paralyzing.

One way to formalize employer-employee relationships is to prepare a personnel policy manual, or employee handbook, which can meet a communication need by letting employees know the firm's basic ground rules. It can also provide a basis for fairness and consistency of management decisions affecting employees. The content of a policy manual may be as broad or narrow as desired. It may include an expression of company philosophy—an overall view of what the company considers important, such as standards of excellence or quality considerations. More specifically, personnel policies usually cover such topics as recruitment, selection, training, compensation, vacations, grievances, and discipline. Such policies should be written carefully, however, to avoid misunderstandings. In some states, an employee handbook is considered part of the employment contract.

Procedures relating to management of personnel may also be standardized. For example, a performance review system may be established and a timetable set up for reviews—perhaps an initial review after six months and subsequent reviews on an annual basis.

1 **Explain the importance of employee recruitment, and list some sources that can be useful for finding suitable applicants.**

- Recruitment of good employees contributes to customer service and to profitability.
- Small firms can attract applicants by stressing unique work features and opportunities.
- Recruitment sources include walk-ins, schools, public and private employment agencies, employee referrals, advertising, and temporary help agencies.
- Job descriptions outline the duties of the job; job specifications identify the skills needed by applicants.

2 **Identify the steps in evaluating job applicants.**

- Application forms help obtain background information from applicants.
- Additional evaluation steps are interviewing, checking references, and administering tests.
- The final evaluation step is often a physical examination.

3 **Describe the role of training for both managerial and nonmanagerial employees in the small firm.**

- Training enables employees to perform their jobs and also prepares them for advancement.
- An orientation program helps introduce new employees to the firm and work environment.
- Training is one component of a firm's quality management program.
- Training and development programs are applicable to both managerial and nonmanagerial employees.

4 **Explain the various kinds of compensation plans and the differences between daywork and incentives.**

- Small firms must be competitive in salary and wage levels.
- Daywork systems base compensation on increments of time.
- Incentive systems relate compensation to various measures of performance.
- Fringe benefit costs average 41.3 percent of payroll cost for all employers and 35.7 percent for employers having fewer than 100 employees.
- Employee stock ownership plans enable employees to own a share of the business.

5 **Discuss employee leasing, labor unions, and the formalizing of human resources management.**

- Small firms can reduce paperwork by transferring personnel to the payroll of a leasing company.
- Some small businesses must work with labor unions.
- As small firms grow, they must adopt more formal methods of human resources management.
- Employment of a human resources manager becomes necessary at some point as a firm continues to add employees.

411

New Terms and Concepts

headhunter *399*	reliability *403*	employee stock
job description *400*	Job Instruction	ownership plans
job	Training *405*	(ESOPs) *408*
specification *401*	daywork *407*	leasing
validity *403*	fringe benefits *408*	employees *409*

You Make the Call

Situation 1   The following is an account of one employee's introduction to a new job:

> It was my first job out of high school. After receiving a physical exam and a pamphlet on benefits, I was told by the manager about the dangers involved in the job. But it was the old-timers who explained what was really expected of me.
>
> The company management never told me about the work environment or the unspoken rules. The old-timers let me know where to sleep and which supervisors to avoid. They told me how much work I was supposed to do and which shop steward to see if I had a problem.

Question 1   To what extent should a small firm use "old-timers" to help introduce new employees to the workplace? Is it inevitable that newcomers will always look to old-timers to find out how things really work?

Question 2   How would you rate this firm's orientation efforts? What are its strengths and weaknesses?

Question 3   Assuming that this firm has fewer than 75 employees and no human resources manager, could it possibly provide any more extensive orientation than that described here? How? What low-cost improvements, if any, would you recommend?

Situation 2   Technical Products, Inc. distributes 15 percent of its profits quarterly to its eight employees. This money is invested for their benefit in a retirement plan and is fully vested after five years. An employee, therefore, has a claim to the retirement fund even if he or she leaves the company after five years of service.

The employees range in age from 25 to 59 and have worked for the company from 3 to 27 years. They seem to have recognized the value of the program. However, younger employees sometimes express a stronger preference for cash than for retirement benefits.

Continue on next page

Hiring a Human Resources Manager

A firm with only a few employees cannot afford a full-time specialist to deal with personnel problems. Some of the more involved human resources tools and techniques that are required in large businesses may be unnecessarily complicated for small businesses. As it grows in size, however, the small firm's personnel problems will increase in both number and complexity.

The point at which it becomes logical to hire a human resources manager cannot be specified precisely. In view of the increased overhead cost, the owner-manager of a growing business must decide whether the situation of the business would make it profitable to employ a personnel specialist. Hiring a part-time human resources manager—a retired personnel manager, for example—might be a logical first step in some instances.

Some conditions favor the appointment of a human resources manager in a small business:

- There are a substantial number of employees (100 or more is suggested as a guide).
- Employees are represented by a union.
- The labor turnover rate is high.
- The need for skilled or professional personnel creates problems in recruitment or selection.
- Supervisors or operative employees require considerable training.
- Employee morale is unsatisfactory.
- Competition for personnel is keen.

Until a human resources manager is hired, however, the owner-manager typically functions in that capacity. His or her decisions regarding selection, compensation, and other personnel issues will have a direct impact on the operating success of the firm.

DISCUSSION QUESTIONS

1. As a customer of small businesses, you can appreciate the importance of employees to their success. Describe an experience you've had in which an employee's contribution to his or her employer's success was positive and one in which it was negative.

2. What factor or factors would make you cautious about going to work for a small business? Could these reasons for hesitation be overcome by a really good small firm? How?

3. Under what conditions might walk-ins be a good source of employees?

4. Based on your own experience as an interviewee, what do you think is the most serious weakness in the interviewing process? How could this be remedied?

5. What steps and/or topics would you recommend for the orientation program of a printing firm with 65 employees?

6. Consider a small business with which you are well acquainted. Have adequate provisions been made to replace key management personnel when it becomes necessary? Is the firm using any form of executive development?

7. What problems are involved in using incentive pay systems in a small firm? How would the nature of the work affect management's decision concerning the use of such incentives?

8. Is the use of a profit-sharing system desirable in a small business? What major difficulties might lessen its effectiveness in providing greater employee motivation?

9. How does employee leasing differ from using a temporary help agency? What are the greatest benefits of employee leasing?

10. List the factors in small business operation that favor the appointment of a human resources manager. Should a human resources manager always be hired on a full-time basis? Why or why not?

Question 1 What are the most important reasons for structuring the profit-sharing plan as a retirement program?

Question 2 What is the probable motivational impact of this compensation system?

Question 3 How will an employee's age affect the appeal of this plan? What other factors are likely to strengthen or lessen its motivational value? Should it be changed in any way?

Situation 3 Ben Bronson, a small business owner, is concerned about proposals for health-care reform. The proposals seem to threaten his very livelihood—the modest profits from the business. Bronson provides no health coverage for his five employees, and the cost specified in recent legislative proposals was 3.5 percent of payroll. He wonders if he could survive such an increase in operating expenses.

On the other hand, Bronson worries about the employees without health coverage. Two of them have families, and serious illnesses would create major problems. "I think everyone should be protected," said Bronson, "but I don't know if I can afford it."

Question 1 What benefits, if any, would Bronson's firm receive from mandated health coverage?

Question 2 Should Bronson support or fight the proposed reforms?

Question 3 Should Bronson provide health coverage even if it is not mandated?

EXPERIENTIAL EXERCISES

1. Interview the director of the placement office for your college or university to determine the extent to which small firms use the office's services and to obtain the director's recommendations for improving college recruiting by small firms. Prepare a one-page summary of your findings.

2. Examine and evaluate the help-wanted section of a local newspaper. Summarize your conclusions and formulate some generalizations about small business advertising for personnel.
3. With another student, form an interviewer-interviewee team. Take turns interviewing each other as job applicants for a selected type of job vacancy. Critique each other's performance by using the interviewing principles outlined in this chapter.
4. With another student, take turns role-playing trainer and trainee using the Job Instruction Training method outlined in this chapter. Each student-trainer should select a simple task and teach it to the student-trainee. Jointly critique the teaching performance after each episode.

 CASE 18
Gibson Mortuary (p. 639)

This case explores the human resources problems encountered by one small family business.

Alternative Cases for Chapter 18: Case 4, "Operating a Kiosk Franchise," p. 600
Case 5, "The Brown Family Business," p. 603
Case 8, "ScrubaDub Auto Wash," p. 614
Case 14, "The Jordan Construction Account," p. 629
Case 19, "Douglas Electrical Supply, Inc.," p. 642
Case 24, "Fox Manufacturing," p. 657

Quality Management and the Operations Process

Larry Denny

spotlight on small business

Small firms can successfully implement quality management programs and reap benefits in the marketplace. Larry Denny demonstrated this fact by stressing quality in Den-Con, his Oklahoma City firm that makes oil-drilling equipment. Denny developed a quality management program in 1983, when Den-Con had only four employees.

Denny continued to focus on quality as the firm grew to 13 employees, and he used the firm's quality management program to get a toe-hold in the international market where Den-Con was competing against a well-established big firm.

When he entered the international marketplace, [Denny] recalls, he was trying to sell to multinational drilling contractors, in competition with a much larger company. Better delivery and lower prices alone wouldn't be enough; he had to find some way to make Den-Con credible despite its size. Den-Con's quality program "allowed us to go out to the industry and show people, when they questioned our credibility, that we knew what we were doing," he says.

The firm's attention to quality helped it survive and even prosper, despite the drop in world oil prices and the resulting decline in drilling.

Source: Michael Barrier, "Doing Well What Comes Naturally," *Nation's Business,* Vol. 80, No. 9 (September 1992), pp. 25–26.

After studying this chapter, you should be able to:

1 Explain the key elements of total quality management (TQM) programs.

2 Discuss the nature of the operations process for both products and services.

3 Describe the role of maintenance and the differences between preventive and corrective maintenance.

4 Explain how reengineering and other methods of work improvement can increase productivity and make a firm more competitive.

start here

Product quality and service quality are the keys to success and survival in today's competitive business environment. Customers expect quality, and a business can only offer its customers the quality created by its operations process—that is, by the activities that are involved in producing its goods or services. A small firm's long-term survival depends, therefore, on having an operations process that enables the firm to satisfy the quality demands of its customers in a cost-effective manner.

> 1 Explain the key elements of total quality management (TQM) programs.

TOTAL QUALITY MANAGEMENT

Terms such as *total quality management* and *zero defects* have become popular in recent years, reflecting an emphasis on quality by many modern managers. These managers understand that quality is more than a peripheral issue and that the quest for quality demands attention to all aspects of operations management.

Quality Goals of Today's Management

QUALITY

quality
the features of a product or service that enable it to satisfy customers' needs

The American Society for Quality Control defines **quality** as "the totality of features and characteristics of a product or service that bears on its ability to satisfy stated or implied needs." Quality has many different aspects. For example, a restaurant's customers base their perceptions of its quality on the taste of its food, the attractiveness of its decor, the friendliness and promptness of the servers, the cleanliness of the silverware, the type of background music, and numerous other factors. The operations process establishes a level of quality as a product is produced or a service is provided. Although cost and other considerations cannot be ignored, quality must constitute a primary focus of a firm's operations.

International competition has increasingly turned on quality differences. U.S. automobile manufacturers, for example, have begun to place greater emphasis on quality in their attempts to compete effectively with foreign producers. However, quality is not solely a concern of big business; the operations process of a small firm also deserves careful scrutiny. Many small firms have been slow to give adequate attention to the achievement of high quality. According to an editorial in *Business Week,* "many smaller companies have yet to achieve even a rudimentary understanding of how to achieve higher quality."[1] In examining the operations process, therefore, small business management must direct special attention to achieving superior product or service quality.

total quality management (TQM)
an all-encompassing management approach to providing high-quality products and services

An aggressive effort by a company to achieve superior quality is often termed **total quality management,** or **TQM.** Total quality management implies an all-encompassing, quality-focused management approach to providing products and services that satisfy customer requirements. Firms that implement TQM programs are making quality a major goal.

Many business firms merely give lip service to the achievement of high-quality standards. Others have introduced quality programs that have failed. The most

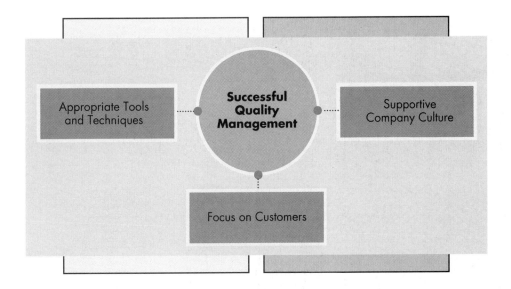

Figure 19-1

Essential Elements of Successful Quality Management

successful quality management efforts incorporate three elements—a focus on customers, a supportive company culture, and the use of appropriate tools and techniques, as shown in Figure 19-1.

Customer Focus of Quality Management

A firm's quality management efforts should focus on the customers who purchase its products or services. Such a focus adds realism and vigor to quality programs. Without such a focus, the quest for quality easily degenerates into an aimless search for some abstract, elusive ideal.

CUSTOMER EXPECTATIONS: THE DRIVING FORCE   Quality is ultimately determined by the extent to which a product or service satisfies customers' needs and expectations. Customers have quality expectations regarding both products (durability and attractiveness, for example) and services (speed and accuracy, for example). A customer is concerned with *product quality* when purchasing a camera or a loaf of bread, for example. In other cases, the customer's primary concern is *service quality*—the way in which an automobile is repaired, for example. Frequently, a customer expects some combination of *product and service quality*—when buying a lawnmower, a customer may be concerned with the performance of the lawnmower, the courtesy of the salesperson, the credit terms offered, and the terms of the warranty.

In thinking about customer quality requirements, therefore, managers must recognize that customers often have in mind specific standards that are relevant to the product or service being offered. Customer interviews yielded the following comments that illustrate the type of expectations customers have regarding three types of service businesses:

> **Automobile Repair Customers:** *Be Competent ("Fix it right the first time"); Explain Things ("Explain why I need the suggested repairs—provide an itemized list"); Be Respectful ("Don't treat me like I'm stupid").*
> **Hotel Customers:** *Provide a Clean Room ("Don't have a deep-pile carpet that can't be completely cleaned. . . . You can literally see germs down there"); Provide a Secure Room*

Action Report

QUALITY

QUALITY GOALS

Quality Management That Focuses on the Customer

A tenacious devotion to superior quality in a service business can lead to spectacular success. In 1940, three Mandel brothers (Mort, Joe, and Jack) founded Premier Industrial, a Cleveland-based business that distributes more than 200,000 parts ranging from electronic components and fasteners to industrial lubricants and chemicals. The company prospered and grew because of its singular dedication to pleasing its customers. The following is a description of the company's philosophy and practices:

> *Early on, the Mandel brothers decided to go after high-margin niches in the parts-distribution business and to make themselves indispensable to customers through superior service. Mort puts it a bit more forcefully: "Deeply built into this organization is the notion that it's really right to kill yourself for your customers, that that's the standard, not the exception."*
>
> *At Premier, this strategy means offering hard-to-find parts that other distributors won't keep in stock. It means superfast delivery, usually overnight but within just a few hours if the customer has an emergency. It means virtually never sending an order late—and phoning to apologize to the customer before he can call to complain if something does go wrong.*

Source: Lore Croghan, "Buckeye Billionaire," *Financial World*, Vol. 164, No. 8 (March 28, 1995), pp. 42–50.

("Good bolts and peephole on door"); *Treat Me like a Guest* ("It is almost like they're looking me over to decide whether they're going to let me have a room"); *Keep Your Promises* ("They said the room would be ready, but it wasn't at the promised time").
Equipment Repair Customers: *Share My Sense of Urgency* ("Speed of response is important. One time I had to buy a second piece of equipment because of the huge down time with the first piece"); *Be Competent* ("Sometimes I'm quoting stuff from their instruction manuals to their own people, and they don't even know what it means"); *Be Prepared* ("Have all the parts ready").[2]

A genuine concern for customer needs and customer satisfaction is a powerful force that energizes the total quality management effort of a business. If customer satisfaction is treated merely as a means of increasing profits, it tends to lose its impact. When the customer becomes the focal point in quality efforts, however, real quality improvement occurs, and profits tend to grow as a result.

LISTENING TO CUSTOMERS   Attentive listening can often provide information about customer satisfaction. Employees having direct contact with customers can serve as the eyes and ears of the business in evaluating quality levels and customer needs. Unfortunately, many managers are oblivious to the often subtle feedback from customers. Preoccupied with operating details, such managers do not listen to, let alone solicit, customers' opinions. Employees having direct contact with customers—servers in a restaurant, for example—are seldom trained or expected to obtain information about customers' quality expectations.

The marketing research methods of observation, interviews, and customer surveys, as described in Chapter 8, can be used to investigate customers' views re-

Focusing on customers is the most important element in quality management. Through her direct contact with customers, this server in a Brisbane, Australia restaurant can obtain information about customers' likes, dislikes, and expectations.

garding quality. Some businesses, for example, provide comment cards for their customers to use in evaluating service or product quality.

Organizational Culture and Total Quality Management

The values, beliefs, and traditional practices followed by members of a business firm may be described as the firm's **organizational culture.** Some firms are so concerned with quality levels that they will refund money if a service or product is unsatisfactory or will schedule overtime work to avoid disappointing a customer. Quality has become a primary value in such a business. Experts on quality management believe that such a culture is necessary for outstanding success.

A small business that adopts a total quality management philosophy commits itself to the pursuit of excellence in all aspects of its operations. Such dedication to quality is sometimes described as a cultural phenomenon—an organization-wide adoption of basic values related to quality. Time and training are required to build a TQM program that elicits the best efforts of everyone in the organization in producing a superior-quality product or service.

Total quality management goes beyond merely meeting existing standards. Its objective is **continuous quality improvement.** For example, if a production process has been improved to a level where there is only 1 defect in 100 products, the process must then be shifted to the next level and aim for a goal of no more than 1 defect in 200 or even 500 products. The ultimate goal is zero defects—a goal that has been popularized by many quality improvement programs. The leadership of a firm must become actively involved in its quest for quality if that type of effort is to be realized. Kenneth Ebel has emphasized the crucial role of company leadership:

> *Leadership is the key to excellence. The aim of management must be to help people to perform and improve their job. Leaders focus on improving the process, inform their management of potential problems, and act to correct problems. Leadership eliminates the need for production quotas which, by their very nature, focus attention away from quality. Leadership also means that fundamental changes in culture and actions occur first at the top of the organization.[3]*

organizational culture
patterns of behaviors and beliefs that characterize a particular firm

continuous quality improvement
a constant and dedicated effort to improve quality

benchmarking
studying the products, services, and practices of other firms, and using those examples to improve quality

A firm's efforts toward continuous quality improvement may include **benchmarking,** which is the process of identifying the best products, services, and practices of other businesses, carefully studying those examples, and using any insights gained to improve one's own operations. Simple types of benchmarking occur as owner-managers eat in competitive restaurants or shop in competitive stores. An example of more aggressive benchmarking is found in the reaction of a family business—Harry W. Schwartz Bookshops of Milwaukee, Wisconsin—to the vigorous competition of bookstore chains.[4] Managers visited book superstores, talked with other booksellers, watched customers shop, and even visited office-supplies superstores. By analyzing these other businesses, they were able to make substantial changes in their own operation, such as extending store hours, adopting a no-questions-asked return policy, bringing in authors to read from their books, providing comfortable chairs, and making freshly brewed coffee available to customers. The result was a more competitive and a more profitable business.

TQM Tools and Techniques

Various tools, techniques, and procedures are needed to support a total quality management program. Once the focus is on the customer and the entire organization is committed to providing top-quality products and services, operating methodology becomes important. Implementing a quality management program requires practical steps for training, counting, checking, and measuring progress toward quality goals. In this section, we discuss three important areas—employee participation, inspection processes, and use of statistical methods.

EMPLOYEE PARTICIPATION In most organizations, employee performance is a critical quality variable. Employees who work carefully obviously produce better-quality products than those who work carelessly. You may have heard the admonition "Never buy a car that was produced on Friday or Monday!" which conveys the idea that workers lack commitment to their work and are especially careless prior to and immediately after a weekend away from work. The vital role of personnel in producing a high-quality product or service has led managers to seek ways to actively involve employees in quality management efforts.

In Chapter 17, we referred to the concepts of work teams and empowerment of employees as approaches to building employee involvement in the workplace. Many businesses have adopted these ideas as part of their quality management programs. Japanese firms are particularly noted for their use of work teams. Many self-managed work teams, both in Japan and in the United States, monitor the quality level of their work and take any steps needed to continue operating at the proper quality level.

quality circle
a group of employees who meet regularly to discuss quality-related problems

Another device that utilizes the contributions of employees in improving the quality of products and services is the **quality circle.** Originated by the Japanese, it is widely used by small firms in the United States and other parts of the world. A quality circle consists of a group of employees, usually a dozen or fewer. They meet on company time, typically about once a week, to identify, analyze, and solve work-related problems, particularly those involving product or service quality. In some companies, employees can earn financial rewards or receive other recognition for quality improvements. For quality circles to function effectively, participating employees must be given appropriate training. Quality circles can help tap the potential of employees for enthusiastic and valuable contributions.

The contribution of quality circles to quality improvement has been demonstrated by the performance of Globe Metallurgical, Inc., a small business located in

Action Report

QUALITY GOALS

Quality Improvement Through Employee Participation

Marlow Industries, a Dallas, Texas producer of customized thermoelectric coolers, was a winner of the coveted Malcolm Baldrige National Quality Award in 1991. This award was created by an act of Congress in 1987 and is traditionally presented by the President of the United States at special ceremonies in Washington, D.C.

Raymond Marlow, the firm's president and CEO, emphasizes the importance of people in a small business quality program:

According to Marlow, a small business can achieve quality improvement through what he calls the three P's: persistence, patience, and pizza. He explain[s] that implementing quality is a long-term process and that any company needs the persistence to stick with it and lead the way. For the same reason, patience is critical. "It has to evolve," [says] Marlow. "It's a culture change and it takes time to do it." Pizza is the reward for employees. Marlow stresse[s] the importance of paying attention to employees, be it through pizza parties or other reward systems.

Marlow throws a lot of pizza parties for his employees, but that is only one of the 25 ways that the company rewards individuals and employee teams.

Source: "Small Wonders," *Quality Progress*, Vol. 25, No. 11 (November 1992), pp. 31–32.

Beverly, Ohio. This firm was one of three U.S. companies selected to receive the Malcolm Baldrige National Quality Award in 1988. Globe's use of employee participation is explained as follows:

Communication is a key. Every level of the company has a quality committee. Workers hash out issues in their own weekly "quality circles." Finally, in each of the company's two plants, still another committee, made up of the plant manager and department heads, assembles each morning to review the previous day's performance.[5]

INSPECTION: THE TRADITIONAL TECHNIQUE   Management's traditional method of maintaining product quality has been **inspection,** which consists of scrutinizing a part or a product to determine whether it is good or bad. An inspector typically uses gauges to evaluate important quality variables. For effective quality control, the inspector must be honest, objective, and capable of resisting pressure from shop personnel to pass borderline cases.

inspection
scrutinizing a product to determine whether it meets quality standards

Although the inspection processes described here are concerned with product quality, somewhat comparable steps can be used to evaluate service quality. Calls to customers of an auto repair shop, for example, could be used to measure the quality of the firm's repair services.

In manufacturing, **inspection standards** consist of design tolerances that are set for every important quality variable. These tolerances show the limits of variation allowable above and below the desired level of quality. Inspection standards must satisfy customer requirements for quality in finished products. Traditionally, inspection begins in the receiving room, when the condition and quantity of mate-

inspection standard
a specification of a desired quality level and allowable tolerances

rials received from suppliers is checked. Inspection is also customary at critical processing points—for example, *before* any operation that would conceal existing defects or *after* any operation that produces an excessive amount of defects. Of course, final inspection of finished products is of utmost importance.

Inspecting each item in every lot processed is called 100 percent inspection. It supposedly ensures the elimination of all bad materials in the process and all defective products prior to shipment to customers. Such inspection goals are seldom reached, however. This method of inspection is not only time-consuming, but also costly. Furthermore, inspectors often make honest errors in judgment, both by rejecting good items and by accepting bad items. Also, some types of inspection, such as opening a can of vegetables, destroy the product, making 100 percent inspection impractical.

In an inspection, quality characteristics may be measured as either attributes or variables. **Attribute inspection** determines quality acceptability based on attributes that can be evaluated and expressed as being in one of only two categories. A light bulb either lights or it doesn't. Similarly, a water hose can be inspected to see whether it leaks or doesn't leak.

Variable inspection, in contrast, determines quality acceptability by using variables expressed on a scale or continuum, such as weight. For example, a box of candy may be sold as containing a minimum of one pound of candy. An inspector may judge the product acceptable if its weight falls within the range of 16 ounces to 16.5 ounces.

attribute inspection
determining whether a product will or will not work

variable inspection
evaluating a product in terms of a variable such as weight or length

STATISTICAL METHODS   Controlling product and service quality can often be made easier, less expensive, and more effective by the use of statistical methods. As some knowledge of quantitative methods is necessary when developing a quality control method using statistical analysis, a properly qualified employee or outside consultant must be available. The savings made possible by using an efficient statistical method can often justify the consulting fees required to devise a sound plan.

Acceptance sampling involves taking random samples of products and measuring them against predetermined standards. Suppose, for example, that a small firm receives a shipment of 10,000 parts from a supplier. Rather than evaluating all 10,000 parts, the purchasing firm can check the acceptability of a small sample of parts and generalize about the acceptability of the entire order. The size of the sample affects the discriminating power of a sampling plan. The smaller the sample, the greater the danger of either accepting a defective lot or rejecting a good lot due to sampling error. A larger sample reduces this danger but increases the inspection cost. A well-designed plan strikes a balance, by simultaneously avoiding excessive inspection costs and minimizing the risk of accepting a bad lot or rejecting a good lot.

acceptance sampling
using a random sample to determine the acceptability of an entire lot

Statistical process control involves applying statistical techniques to control work processes. Items produced in a manufacturing process are not completely identical, although the variations are sometimes very small, and the items may seem to be exactly alike. Careful measurement, however, can pinpoint the differ-

statistical process control
using statistical methods to assess quality during the operations process

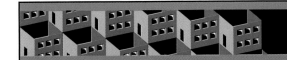

Action Report

QUALITY GOALS

Adopting Statistical Process Control

Small firms can sometimes improve their quality management by introducing statistical quality controls. When Robert Slass, president and owner of Rotor Clip Company in Somerset, New York, realized that his company needed to update its quality procedures for producing metal-stamped fasteners, he began researching the most recent quality control methods:

> *The area that needed the most updating was quality control. By this time, Japanese manufacturers' success with such techniques as statistical process control—or SPC—was well-documented. SPC is a statistical approach to monitoring a process with the use of graphs so that subtle changes can be detected and adjustments can be made before an unsatisfactory part is produced. This is in contrast to the former concept of quality control, which relied on inspection of parts after they were produced—when it was too late to make any meaningful adjustment to the process.*

Adopting statistical methods of quality control calls for an investment in time, training, and equipment. Slass elected to make that investment, and the benefits have been described as "enormous."

Source: Robert Slass, "The Hard Road Is the Best Road," *Nation's Business*, Vol. 78, No. 4 (April 1990), p. 6.

---

ences. Usually, these can be plotted in the form of a normal curve, which allows statistical control techniques to be applied.

The use of statistical analysis makes it possible to establish tolerance limits that allow for the inherent variation due to chance. When measurements fall outside these tolerance limits, however, the quality controller knows that there is a problem and must then search for the cause. The cause might be variations in the raw materials, machine wear, or changes in employees' work practices. Suppose, for example, that a candy maker is producing one-pound boxes of candy. Even though the weight varies slightly, each box must weigh at least 16 ounces. A study of the operations process has determined that the actual target weight must be 16.5 ounces to allow for the normal variation between 16 and 17 ounces. During the production process, a box is weighed every 15 or 20 minutes. If the weight of a box falls outside the tolerance limits—below 16 or above 17 ounces—the quality controller must immediately try to find the problem and correct it.

A **control chart** graphically shows the limits for a process that is being controlled. As current data are entered, it is possible to tell whether a process is under control or out of control. Control charts may be used for either variable or attribute inspections.

control chart
a graphic illustration of the limits used in statistical process control

International Certification

International recognition of a firm's quality management program can be obtained by meeting a series of standards, known as **ISO 9000,** developed by the International Organization for Standardization in Geneva, Switzerland. The certifi-

ISO 9000
the standards governing international certification of a firm's quality management procedures

cation process requires full documentation of a firm's quality management procedures as well as an audit to ensure that it is operating in accordance with those procedures. In other words, the firm must show that it does what it says it does. ISO 9000 certification can give a business credibility with purchasers in other countries and thereby ease entry into export markets. However, substantial costs are involved in obtaining it.

Certification of this type is particularly valuable for small firms, because they usually lack a global image as producers of high-quality products. Buyers in other countries, especially in Europe, look to this type of certification as an indicator of supplier reliability. Some large U.S. corporations, such as the Big Three automobile makers, require their domestic suppliers to conform to these standards. Small firms, therefore, may need ISO 9000 certification to sell more easily in international markets or to meet the demands of their domestic customers.

Quality Management in Service Businesses

The discussion of quality often focuses on a manufacturing process involving a tangible product. However, service businesses such as motels, dry cleaners, accounting firms, and automobile repair shops also need to maintain and improve quality. In fact, many firms offer a combination of tangible product and intangible services and, ideally, manage quality in both areas.

Service to customers may be effective or ineffective in a number of ways. Six factors positively influence customers' perception of service quality:

1. *Being on target.* Set and meet the customer's expectations. Do what was promised, when and where it was promised. Heighten the customer's awareness of the service provider's actions.
2. *Care and concern.* Be empathetic. Tune in to the customer's situation, frame of mind, and needs. Be attentive and willing to help.
3. *Spontaneity.* Empower service providers to think and respond quickly. Allow them to use their discretion and bend, rather than quote, procedures.
4. *Problem solving.* Train and encourage service providers to be problem solvers. Service providers have the customer's undivided attention when that person is experiencing a problem. A positive response to a problem will stick in the customer's mind. Capitalize on this opportunity to show the organization's capabilities.
5. *Follow-up.* Follow-up captures customers' attention and is often sincerely appreciated. It is associated with caring and professionalism, so follow up with flair and create a reputation for legendary service quality.
6. *Recovery.* Customers experiencing problems often have low expectations for their resolution; thus, they are exceedingly mindful and appreciative of speedy solutions. Making things right quickly is a powerful factor in creating an enduring image of high-quality service.[6]

Measurement problems exist in assessing the quality of a service. It is easier to measure the length of a piece of wood than the quality of motel accommodations. As noted earlier, however, methods can be devised for measuring the quality of services. A motel can maintain a record of the number of problems with travelers' reservations, complaints about cleanliness of rooms, and so on.

For many types of service firms, control of quality constitutes the most important managerial responsibility. All that such firms sell is service, and their future rests on customers' perceptions of the quality of that service.

THE OPERATIONS PROCESS

The **operations process,** or **production process,** consists of those activities necessary to get the job done—that is, to perform the work and create the quality expected by customers. To a great extent, both customer acceptance of a firm and its profitability will depend on the way the business manages its basic operations.

Nature of the Operations Process

An operations process is required whether a firm produces a tangible product, such as clothing or bread, or an intangible service, such as dry cleaning or entertainment. Examples are the production process in clothing manufacturing, the baking process in a bakery, the cleaning process in dry cleaning, and the performance process in entertainment. Operations processes differ for products and services, and they also differ from one type of product or service to another.

Despite their differences, these processes are similar in that they all change inputs into outputs. Inputs include money, raw materials, labor, equipment, information, and energy—all of which are combined in varying proportions depending on the nature of the finished product or service. Outputs are the products and/or services that a business provides to its customers. Thus, the operations process may be described as a conversion or transformation process. As Figure 19-2 shows, the operations process converts inputs of various kinds into products, such as baked goods, or services, such as window cleaning. A printing plant, for example, uses in-

Discuss the nature of the operations process for both products and services.

operations process (production process)
the activities that accomplish a firm's work

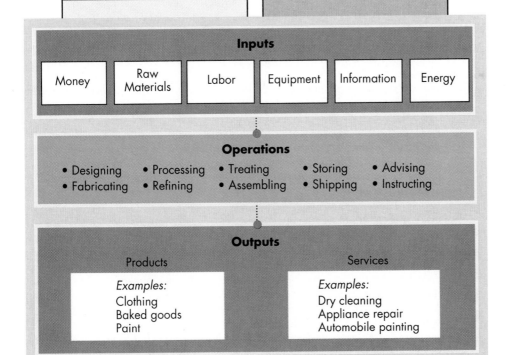

Figure 19-2

The Operations Process

puts such as paper, ink, the work of employees, printing presses, and electric power to produce printed material. Car-wash facilities and motor freight firms, which are service businesses, also use operating systems to transform inputs into car-cleaning and freight-transporting services.

operations management
the planning and control of the operations process

Operations management involves the planning and control of the conversion process. It includes acquiring inputs and then overseeing their transformation into the tangible products and intangible services desired by customers.

Manufacturing Versus Service Operations

Manufacturing operations result in tangible physical products, such as furniture or boats. In contrast, service operations produce intangible outputs, such as grass cutting by a lawn-care company or advice from a management consulting firm. The distinction between the two types of operations is somewhat fuzzy, as the two areas tend to overlap. A manufacturer of a tangible product, for example, may also extend credit and provide repair service; a restaurant, typically considered a service business, processes the food products that it serves.

Nevertheless, the operations of product-producing and service-producing firms differ in a number of ways. One of the most obvious differences is that greater customer contact typically occurs in a service firm. In a beauty shop, for example, the customer is a participant in the operations process as well as a user of the service. James B. Dilworth has identified and summarized four areas of difference as follows:

1. *Productivity generally is more easily measured in manufacturing operations than in service operations because the former provides tangible products, whereas the products of service operations are generally intangible. A factory that produces automobile tires can readily count the number of tires produced in a day. Repair service operations may repair or replace portions of a tangible product, but their major service is the application of knowledge and skilled labor. Advisory services may provide only spoken words, an entirely intangible product and one that is very difficult to measure.*

2. *Quality standards are more difficult to establish and product quality is more difficult to evaluate in service operations. This difference is directly related to the previous one. Intangible products are more difficult to evaluate because they cannot be held, weighed, or measured. We can evaluate a repair to a tangible product by comparing the product's performance after the repair with its performance before the repair. It is more difficult to know the worth of such a service [as] legal defense. No one knows for certain how the judge would have ruled had the attorney performed in some different manner.*

3. *Persons who provide services generally have contact with customers, whereas persons who perform manufacturing operations seldom see the consumer of the product. The marketing and customer relations aspects of a service often overlap the operations function. The doctor-patient relationship, for example, is often considered to be a very important component of the physician's services. In the service of hair care, the hairdresser-patron contact is necessary. The impact of discourteous salespersons or restaurant employees is of great concern in many establishments.*

4. *Manufacturing operations can accumulate or decrease inventory of finished products, particularly in standard product, repetitive production operations. A barber, in contrast, cannot store up haircuts during slack times so that he or she can provide service at an extremely high rate during peak demand time. Providers of services often try to overcome this limitation by leveling out the demand process. Telephone systems, for example, offer discount rates during certain hours to encourage a shift in the timing of calls that can be delayed.*[7]

Types of Manufacturing Operations

Manufacturing operations differ in the degree to which they are repetitive. Some factories produce the same product day after day and week after week. Other production facilities have great flexibility and often change the products they produce. Three types of manufacturing operations are job shops, repetitive manufacturing, and batch manufacturing.

Job shops are characterized by short production runs with only one or a few products being produced before shifting to a different production setup. Job shops use general-purpose machines. Each job may be unique, requiring a special set of production steps to complete the finished item. Machine shops exemplify this type of operation.

Firms that produce one, or relatively few, standardized products use **repetitive manufacturing,** which involves long production runs and is considered mass production. This process is associated with the assembly-line production of automobiles and other high-volume products. Highly specialized equipment can be employed, because it is used over and over again in manufacturing the same item. Few small business firms engage in repetitive manufacturing.

An intermediate type of production is called **batch manufacturing.** This involves more variety (and less volume) than repetitive manufacturing but less variety (and more volume) than job shops. A production run during batch manufacturing may produce a hundred standardized units and then be changed to accommodate another type of standardized product. The different products may all belong to the same family and use a similar production process. A bottling plant that fills bottles with several varieties of soft drinks is an example of batch manufacturing.

Planning and Scheduling Manufacturing Operations

In manufacturing, production control procedures are designed to achieve the orderly sequential flow of products through a plant at a rate commensurate with scheduled deliveries to customers. In order for this objective to be reached, it is essential that production bottlenecks be avoided and machines and personnel be utilized efficiently. Simple, informal control procedures are often used in small plants. If a procedure is simple and the output small, a manager can keep things moving smoothly with a minimum of paperwork. Eventually, however, any manufacturing organization experiencing growth will have to establish formal procedures to ensure production efficiency.

In planning the production process, the manager must first determine what raw materials and fabricated parts are needed. Consideration must then be given to such factors as the best sequence of processing operations, the number and kinds of machines and tooling items, and the output rate of each machine. Planning of this type can become quite complex for nonrepetitive manufacturing.

Once a given process has been thoroughly planned, the planner must schedule work by establishing timetables for each department and work center. In repetitive manufacturing, which involves large-scale production and is found in very few small factories, flow control is fairly simple and involves relatively little paperwork. However, in job shops and batch manufacturing, which involve small- to medium-volume production, more elaborate schedules are necessary. Keeping the work moving on schedule then becomes a major responsibility of shop supervisors.

Planning and Scheduling Service Operations

Since service firms are closely tied to their customers, they are limited in their ability to produce services and hold them in inventory for customers. An automobile

TECHNOLOGY

job shops
manufacturing operations in which short production runs are used to produce small quantities of unique items

repetitive manufacturing
the production of a large quantity of a standardized product by means of long production runs

batch manufacturing
a type of production that is intermediate in volume and variety of products between job shops and repetitive manufacturing

TECHNOLOGY

repair shop must wait until a car arrives, and a beauty shop cannot function until a customer is available. A retail store can perform some of its services, such as transportation and storage, but it, too, must wait until the customer arrives to perform other services.

Part of the scheduling task for service firms relates to the scheduling of employees' working hours. Restaurants, for example, schedule the work of servers to coincide with variations in customer traffic. In a similar way, stores and medical clinics increase their staff to meet times of peak demand. Other scheduling strategies of service firms focus on customers. Appointment systems are used by many automobile repair shops and beauty shops, for example. Service firms such as dry cleaners and plumbers take requests for service and delay delivery until the work can be scheduled. Still other firms, such as banks and movie theaters, maintain a fixed schedule of services and tolerate some idle capacity. Some businesses attempt to spread out customer demand by offering incentives for using services at off-peak hours—examples are an early-bird special at a restaurant or lower-price tickets for afternoon movies.

Plant Maintenance

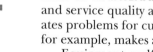

3 Describe the role of maintenance and the differences between preventive and corrective maintenance.

Murphy's Law states that if anything can go wrong, it will. In operating systems that use tools and equipment, there is indeed much that can go wrong. The maintenance function is intended to correct malfunctions of equipment and, as far as possible, to prevent such breakdowns from occurring.

T E C H N O L O G Y

ROLE OF MAINTENANCE Effective maintenance contributes directly to product and service quality and thus to customer satisfaction. Poor maintenance often creates problems for customers. A faulty shower or a reading lamp that doesn't work, for example, makes a motel stay less enjoyable for a traveler.

Equipment malfunctions and breakdowns not only cause problems for customers but also increase costs for the producing firm. Employees may be unproductive while repairs are being made, and expensive equipment may stand idle when it should be producing. Furthermore, improperly maintained equipment wears out more rapidly and requires early replacement, thus adding to the overall cost of operation.

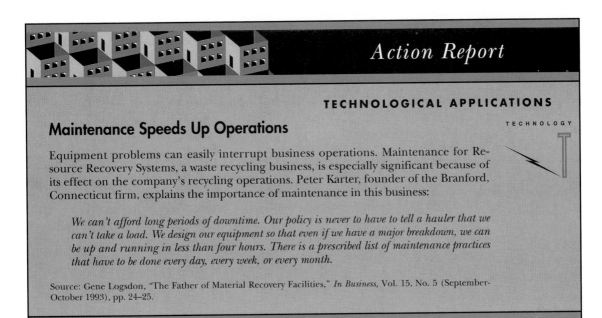

Source: Gene Logsdon, "The Father of Material Recovery Facilities," *In Business*, Vol. 15, No. 5 (September–October 1993), pp. 24–25.

The nature of maintenance work obviously depends on the type of operations process and the nature of the equipment being used. In an office, for example, machines that require maintenance include computers, fax machines, typewriters, copiers, and related office machines. Maintenance services are usually obtained on a contract basis—either by calling for repair personnel when a breakdown occurs or by scheduling periodic servicing. In manufacturing firms that use more complex and specialized equipment, the maintenance function is clearly much more difficult. In small plants, maintenance work is often performed by regular production employees. As a firm expands its facilities, it may add specialized maintenance personnel and eventually create a maintenance department.

TYPES OF MAINTENANCE   Plant maintenance activities fall into two categories: **Preventive maintenance** consists of the inspections and other activities intended to prevent machine breakdowns and damage to people and buildings, and **corrective maintenance** comprises both the major and the minor repairs necessary to restore equipment or a facility to good condition.

A small plant can ill afford to neglect preventive maintenance. If a machine is highly critical to the overall operation, it should be inspected and serviced regularly to preclude costly breakdowns. Frequent checking of equipment reduces industrial accidents, and installation of smoke alarms and/or automatic sprinkler systems minimizes the danger of fire damage. Preventive maintenance of equipment need not involve elaborate controls. Some cleaning and lubricating is usually done as a matter of routine. But for preventive maintenance to be truly effective, more systematic procedures are needed. A record card showing cost, acquisition date, periods of use and storage, and frequency of preventive maintenance inspections should be kept on each major piece of equipment.

Major repairs, which are a part of corrective maintenance, are unpredictable as to time of occurrence, repair time required, loss of output, and cost of downtime. Because of this unpredictability, some small manufacturers contract with other service firms for major repair work. In contrast, the regular occurrence of minor

preventive maintenance
the activities intended to prevent machine breakdowns and damage to people and facilities

corrective maintenance
the repairs necessary to restore equipment or a facility to good condition

breakdowns makes the volume of minor repair work reasonably predictable. Minor repairs can usually be completed easily, quickly, and economically by a firm's own employees.

GOOD HOUSEKEEPING AND PLANT SAFETY   Good housekeeping contributes to efficient operation, saves time in looking for tools, and keeps floor areas safe and free for production work. A firm's disregard for good housekeeping practices is reflected in its production record—good workmanship and superior quality are hard to achieve in an ill-kept plant.

The Occupational Safety and Health Act of 1970 (OSHA) requires employers to provide a place of employment free from hazards that are likely to cause death or serious physical harm. In other words, the building and equipment must be maintained in a way that minimizes safety and health hazards. Although very small firms have been relieved of some of OSHA's record-keeping requirements, they are still subject to the requirements of the law.

IMPROVING PRODUCTIVITY

Explain how reengineering and other methods of work improvement can increase productivity and make a firm more competitive.

4

A society's standard of living depends, to some extent, on its **productivity**—the efficiency with which inputs are transformed into outputs. Similarly, the competitive strength of a particular business depends on its productivity. In this section, we consider the approaches that can be used by small businesses to make them more competitive through improving their operations.

T E C H N O L O G Y

productivity
the efficiency with which inputs are transformed into outputs

The Importance of Improving Productivity

To remain competitive, a firm should constantly try to improve its productivity. Improvement efforts will vary greatly—some involve major reorganizations, and others are merely refinements of existing operations.

A business firm's productivity may be visualized as follows:

$$\text{Productivity} = \frac{\text{Outputs}}{\text{Inputs}} = \frac{\text{Goods and/or services}}{\text{Labor + energy + money + tools + materials}}$$

A firm improves its productivity by doing more with less. This can be accomplished in many different ways. For example, a small restaurant may improve the pastry making of its chef by sending the chef to cooking school, buying better ingredients, getting a better oven, or redesigning the kitchen.

At one time, productivity and quality were viewed as competitive, if not conflicting. However, production at a high-quality level reduces scrap and rework. Therefore, quality improvements, automation, and other improvements in operations methods are all routes to better productivity.

Improving productivity in the service sector is especially difficult, since it's a labor-intensive area, and managers have less opportunity for improvement by using automation. Nevertheless, small service firms can find ways to become more efficient. At one time, for example, customers in barber shops wasted time waiting for barbers who took them on a first-come, first-served basis. To improve the system, many shops started using an appointment schedule. A drop-in customer can still get service immediately if a barber isn't busy or else sign up for the first convenient appointment. Such a system smoothes out the barber's work schedule and reduces delays and frustration for customers.

Action Report

ENTREPRENEURIAL EXPERIENCES

Reengineering a Small Business

Small firms, such as Vortex Industries, have benefited from reengineering efforts. Vortex, a 130-employee, family-owned business in Costa Mesa, California that repairs and replaces warehouse doors, made the fundamental changes involved in reengineering even though its president, Frank Fulkerson, wasn't familiar with the terminology.

Fulkerson realized that the firm, which was experiencing stagnant sales and high overhead, had become very bureaucratic:

> *Each person was stuck in his or her little cut-out job. The receptionist only answered the phone. The material people only ordered and received. The billing clerk only billed. They each felt like what they did was such a small part of the equation that they didn't make a difference.*

Fulkerson reorganized the company by establishing semiautonomous branches and rearranging the duties of those who worked there. Individual managers were given areas of responsibility that previously had been divided among people in several rigid categories—sales, purchasing, and dispatching, for example. In this case, reengineering rescued the company from its financial problems and started a cycle of business growth.

Source: Michael Barrier, "Re-engineering Your Company," *Nation's Business*, Vol. 82, No. 2 (February 1994), pp. 16–22.

Reengineering for Improved Productivity

In the early 1990s, Michael Hammer and James Champy described a method for the restructuring of corporations so that they might serve their customers more effectively. In their best-selling book, *Reengineering the Corporation*, Hammer and Champy defined **reengineering** as "the fundamental rethinking and radical redesign of business processes to achieve dramatic improvements in critical, contemporary measures of performance, such as cost, quality, service, and speed."[8]

Reengineering is concerned with improving the way in which a business operates, whether that business is large or small. Hammer and Champy concentrated their early analysis on large corporations such as Wal-Mart, Taco Bell, and Bell Atlantic, which redesigned their rigid bureaucratic structures to become more efficient. Firms that engage in reengineering seek fundamental improvements as they ask questions about why they do the things they do in the way they do. They expect dramatic, radical change rather than minimal adjustments to traditional operating methods. Reengineering involves careful analysis of the basic processes followed by a firm in creating goods and services for customers.

Proponents of reengineering recommend evaluation of business operations at the most basic level. Reengineering alerts a firm's management to the danger of making small improvements in an inherently weak or outmoded operating system, by emphasizing thoroughness in the analysis of the firm's operations.

Reengineering's emphasis on basic processes is crucial and holds the potential for substantial improvements in operations. Like effective quality control efforts, it directs attention to activities that create value for the customer. Essentially, it asks how the operations process can be better managed, even if it means eliminating traditional departmental lines and specialized job descriptions.

reengineering
a fundamental restructuring to improve the operations process

Action Report

ENTREPRENEURIAL EXPERIENCES

Continuous Process Improvement in Doll Manufacturing

The continuing nature of productivity improvement is illustrated by the management efforts of the Alexander Doll Company of New York City. In 1995, the company's new owners started using the principles of continuous process improvement.

The first project, led by a team of 10 Alexander employees, examined the company's process for producing baby dolls. First, the team moved the work to one central location (operations had been spread over three floors), and then it created a simple production line. The results were astounding. The distance traveled by each doll during production was reduced from 630 feet to 40 feet, the time to complete a doll was shortened from 90 days to 90 minutes, and daily production per employee was increased from 8 to 25 dolls!

This project was the first of 65 planned improvement projects. Further refinements will occur as the company follows its policy of continuous process improvement.

Source: Roberta Maynard, "A Company Is Turned Around Through Japanese Principles," *Nation's Business*, Vol. 84, No. 2 (February 1996), p. 9.

Operations Analysis

Improving productivity for an overall operation involves an analysis of work flow, equipment, tooling, layout, working conditions, and individual jobs. For a specific manufacturing process, it means finding answers to questions such as these:

- Are the right machines being used?
- Can one employee operate two or more machines?
- Can automatic feeders or ejectors be used?
- Can power tools replace hand tools?
- Can the jigs and fixtures be improved?
- Is the workplace properly arranged?
- Is each operator's motion sequence effective?

laws of motion economy
guidelines for increasing the efficiency of human movement and tool design

Work methods can be analyzed for service or merchandising firms as well as for manufacturing. For example, a small plumbing company serving residential customers might examine its service vehicles to see whether they are equipped with the best possible assortment and arrangement of parts, tools, and supplies. In addition, the company might analyze the planning and routing of repair assignments to minimize unnecessary backtracking and waste of time.

motion study
an analysis of all the motions a worker makes to complete a given job

To be successful, work improvement and measurement require collaboration between employees and management. The assistance of employees is important to both the search for more efficient methods and the adoption of improved work procedures.

time study
the determination of a worker's average time to complete a given task

LAWS OF MOTION ECONOMY The **laws of motion economy** underlie any work improvement program—whether it is aimed at the overall operation of a plant or a single task. These laws concern work arrangement, the use of the human hands and body, and the design and use of tools. Examples of these laws follow:

- If both of a worker's hands start and stop their motion at the same time and are never idle during a work cycle, maximum performance is approached.
- If a worker makes motions simultaneously in opposite directions over similar paths, automaticity and rhythm develop naturally, and less fatigue is experienced.
- The method requiring the fewest motions generally is the best for performance of a given task.
- When a worker's motions are confined to the lowest practical classification, maximum performance and minimum fatigue are approached. Lowest classification means motions involving the fingers, hands, forearms, and torso.

A knowledge of the laws of motion economy will suggest various ways to improve work. For example, materials and tools should be placed so as to minimize movement of the torso and the extended arms.

METHODS OF WORK MEASUREMENT

There are several ways to measure work in order to establish a performance standard. **Motion study** consists of detailed observation of all the actual movements a worker makes to complete a job under a given set of physical conditions. From this study, a skilled observer should be able to detect any wasted movements, which can then be corrected or eliminated. **Time study,** which follows motion study, typically involves use of a stopwatch to determine an average time for performing a given task.

Another method of work measurement, which provides little operating detail but estimates the ratio of actual working time to downtime, is called **work sampling.** Originated in England by L.H.C. Tippett in 1934, work sampling involves random observations during which the observer simply determines whether a given worker is working or idle at that time. These observations are then tallied, and the tallies yield an estimate of the ratio of time spent working to time spent idle.

1 Explain the key elements of total quality management (TQM) programs.

- Quality of products or services is a primary goal of the operations process.
- Quality management efforts are focused on meeting customer needs.
- Effective quality management requires an organizational culture that places a high value on quality.
- Quality management tools and techniques include employee involvement, quality circles, inspections, and statistical methods.
- Service businesses can also benefit from use of quality management programs.

2 Discuss the nature of the operations process for both products and services.

- Operations, or production, processes vary from one industry to another, but they all change inputs into outputs.
- Service and manufacturing operations typically differ in the extent of contact with customers and the level of difficulty in establishing quality standards.
- Manufacturing operations include job shops, repetitive manufacturing, and batch manufacturing.
- Operations management involves planning and scheduling activities that transform inputs into products or services.

3 Describe the role of maintenance and the differences between preventive and corrective maintenance.

- Proper maintenance is necessary for efficient operation and achievement of quality performance.
- Preventive maintenance consists of activities needed to prevent breakdowns in machinery.
- Corrective maintenance involves repairs to restore equipment to good condition.
- Good housekeeping facilitates efficient operation and contributes to quality work.

4 Explain how reengineering and other methods of work improvement can increase productivity and make a firm more competitive.

- The competitive strength of a business depends on the level of its productivity.
- Reengineering involves restructuring firms by redesigning their basic work processes.
- Laws of motion economy can be applied to make work easier and more efficient.
- Work may be analyzed by motion study, time study, and work sampling.
- Productivity improvement requires continuous effort.

work sampling
a method of work measurement that estimates the ratio of working time to idle time

433

quality *416*

total quality management (TQM) *416*

organizational culture *419*

continuous quality improvement *419*

benchmarking *420*

quality circle *420*

inspection *421*

inspection standard *421*

attribute inspection *422*

variable inspection *422*

acceptance sampling *422*

statistical process control *422*

control chart *423*

ISO 9000 *423*

operations process (production process) *425*

operations management *426*

job shops *427*

repetitive manufacturing *427*

batch manufacturing *427*

preventive maintenance *429*

corrective maintenance *429*

productivity *430*

reengineering *431*

laws of motion economy *432*

motion study *432*

time study *432*

work sampling *433*

You Make the Call

Situation 1   A college professor opened a furniture shop in Maine and has watched it grow to $5 million in annual sales volume and 85 employees. The firm produces high-quality chairs, tables, and other items for the contract furniture market. Each piece is sanded and polished, sealed with linseed oil, and finished with paste wax. No stain, color, or varnish is added, and the furniture never needs refinishing.

As the firm has grown larger, it has begun to use the equivalent of mass production. Many of the original craftspeople have moved on and have been replaced by production workers. The founder is seeking to maintain quality through employee participation at all levels. He believes that quality can be maintained indefinitely if the company doesn't get too greedy. He has expressed his philosophy as follows:

> *We're still not driven by profit but by meaningful relationships* [among] *employees and between the producer and the user. It's a way of life. We throw out a lot of good stuff. If we had to produce something just to make a buck, I'd go back to teaching school.*

Source: Christopher Hyde, "The Evolution of Thomas Moser," *In Business*, Vol. 10, No. 4 (July–August 1988), pp. 34–37.

Continue on next page

Continuing Efforts Toward Improvement

Small business managers should recognize that productivity improvement requires more than a one-time effort. Studying operations methods and then taking specific steps to improve productivity should be seen as part of a continuing process. A given study can reach a conclusion that, ultimately, helps raise productivity, but the total system is never perfect and can always be improved.

The concept of continuous quality improvement—the idea that quality must constantly be improving—can be expanded to encompass the efficiency of operations. Those who run small businesses should always be trying to improve the quality of their products or services and also to produce them more efficiently.

DISCUSSION QUESTIONS

1. Defend the customer focus of quality management.

2. Explain what is meant by "total quality management."

3. A small manufacturer does not believe that statistical quality control charts and sampling plans are useful. Can traditional methods suffice? Can 100 percent inspection by final inspectors eliminate all defective products? Why or why not?

4. Describe the operations process for the following types of service firms: (a) management consultant, (b) barber shop, and (c) advertising agency.

5. How do operations processes differ for manufacturing firms and service firms?

6. Customer demand for services is generally not uniform during a day, week, or other period of time. What strategies can be used by service firms to better match the firm's capacity to perform services to customer demand for services?

7. Explain the difference between preventive and corrective maintenance. Evaluate the relative importance of each of these types of maintenance when (a) one or more major breakdowns have occurred in a small plant, and (b) shop

operations are running smoothly and maintenance does not face any major repair jobs.

8. How can improved housekeeping help raise productivity?
9. Explain the purpose and nature of reengineering.
10. Doing something rapidly and doing it well are often incompatible. How can quality improvement possibly contribute to productivity improvement?

EXPERIENTIAL EXERCISES

1. Visit a small manufacturing plant or service organization. Ask the manager to describe the operations process, the way operations are controlled, and the nature of maintenance operations. Prepare a brief report on your findings.
2. Outline the operations process involved in your present educational program. Be sure to identify inputs, operations, and outputs.
3. Assume that you are responsible for quality control in the publication of this textbook. Prepare a report outlining the quality standards you would use and the points of inspection you would recommend.
4. Outline, in as much detail as possible, your customary practices in studying for a specific course. Evaluate the methods you use, and specify changes that might improve your productivity.

 CASE 19

Douglas Electrical Supply, Inc.
(p. 642)

A wholesaler-distributor implements a total quality management program while simultaneously following management practices that alienate employees.

Alternative Cases for Chapter 19: Case 8, "ScrubaDub Auto Wash," p. 614
Case 10, "Logan Beach," p. 619

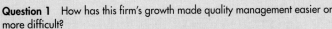

Question 1 How has this firm's growth made quality management easier or more difficult?
Question 2 The founder recognizes that people and relationships have a bearing on quality. What can he do to persuade or enable production employees to have the right attitude toward quality?
Question 3 The founder's comments suggest that profits and quality may be incompatible. When does making a buck lead to lower quality? Can or should this firm use financial incentives?

Situation 2 A retail dealer in plumbing equipment and fixtures for residential kitchens and bathrooms was unpacking a stainless steel double sink for a kitchen. On the bottom of the sink, she noticed a dent. It would never be seen, once the sink was installed. Furthermore, the dent would not interfere with the durability or the operating quality of the sink. It was possible that the customer would not even notice the dent, since the builder would make the installation.

The dealer was faced with a decision about selling a product with such a superficial defect. She pondered the profit implications and also the quality and ethical aspects of a dealer's responsibility.

Question 1 Should the dealer plan to sell the sink without informing the customer of the defect?
Question 2 What are the possible negative consequences of selling the dented sink?
Question 3 Suppose that the dealer decides to sell the sink as is and then the customer returns it. How should the dealer respond?

Situation 3 Broom making is a centuries-old craft. In the early 1980s, Thurman Scheumack started a small broom-making business in the foothills of the Ozark mountains. Although the workshop has only seven employees, including Scheumack and his wife, Rhonda, its output has grown to 20,000 brooms per year. Seventy-five percent of brooms produced is the standard kitchen model, and the rest have hand-carved faces in their handles. Some hand-carved brooms are sold through art galleries, and some are sold at tourist attractions such as Disneyland and Colonial Williamsburg at prices of up to $50 each.

The brooms are fashioned from broomcorn, a plant imported from Mexico. Most of the production equipment, initially built by Scheumack, is far from high-tech. Designed in the 1700s, the machinery runs on a system of hand- and foot-operated weights and levers. One concession to technology is a single electric motor that operates a pulley for a broom-winding machine.

Source: "Ozark Enterprise Handcrafts Brooms," *In Business,* Vol. 11, No. 1 (January-February 1989), p. 16.

Question 1 Should this firm attempt to modernize its equipment and update its manufacturing methods? Would motion study be relevant and useful?
Question 2 How would quality be defined for this type of product? How could quality be measured?

Purchasing and Managing Inventory

Chapter 20

Tom Asacker

Spotlight on small business

Small firms not only purchase raw materials, components, and products for resale, they also purchase business services—an arrangement known as outsourcing. This permits a firm to concentrate on what it can do best—its core competencies. Tom Asacker explains how his manufacturing company, Innovative Medical Systems Inc., in Manchester, New Hampshire, outsources many of its activities:

"We practice outsourcing both strategically and by necessity," says the 39-year-old Asacker, whose company sells devices for preventing sleep apnea (a common breathing disorder [that affects] sleep) as well as specialized mattresses designed to prevent bedsores. "I believe I improve my quality and responsiveness to the market by outsourcing to experts the things that I'm not expert at. And if I can get to the market fast with the highest-quality products using outsourcing, I've won for the long term, too."

Some of the activities performed by outside firms for Innovative Medical Sytems are product design, computer networking, payroll administration, direct mailing, and advertising placement.

Source: Dale D. Buss, "Growing More by Doing Less," *Nation's Business,* Vol. 83, No. 12 (December 1995), pp. 18–24.

Purchasing and inventory decisions in small firms are sometimes made rather haphazardly: When supplies drop to a noticeably low level, someone reorders. This is unfortunate, because the amount spent for raw materials or merchandise is often greater than that spent for other purposes, and the amount invested in inventory can tie up precious working capital. Moreover, the quality of items purchased for resale or as raw materials directly affects product quality and, possibly, its attractiveness to customers. Effective purchasing and inventory management are also closely related to the bottom line—that is, to the profitability of a small firm. For these reasons, purchasing and inventory decisions deserve careful attention from owner-managers of small firms.

PURCHASING PROCESSES AND POLICIES

The objective of **purchasing** is to obtain materials, merchandise, equipment, and services needed to meet production and/or marketing goals. Through effective purchasing, a firm secures all production factors except labor in the required quantity and quality, at the best price, and at the time needed.

purchasing
the process of obtaining materials, equipment, and services from outside suppliers

Importance of Purchasing

There is a direct correlation between the quality of finished products and the quality of raw materials used as inputs. For example, if tight tolerances are imposed on a product by design requirements, the manufacturer must acquire high-quality materials and component parts. Then, given a well-managed production process, excellent products will result. Similarly, the acquisition of high-quality merchandise makes a retailer's sales to customers easier and reduces the number of necessary markdowns and merchandise returns.

QUALITY

Purchasing can contribute to profitable operations when arrangements are made for delivery of goods at the time they are needed. In a small factory, failure to receive materials, parts, or equipment on schedule is likely to cause costly interruptions in production operations. Machines and personnel are kept idle until the items on order are finally received. And, in a retail business, failure to receive merchandise on schedule may mean loss of sales and, possibly, permanent loss of disappointed customers. Effective purchasing can also affect profits by securing the best price for a given piece of merchandise or raw material.

Shopping for the best price can be as worthwhile in business purchasing as it is in personal buying. Cost savings go directly to the bottom line. Therefore, purchasing practices that compare prices and seek out the best deal can have a major impact on the financial health of a business.

Note, however, that the importance of the purchasing function varies according to the type of business. In a small, labor-intensive service business—such as an accounting firm, for example—purchases of supplies are a very small part of the total operating costs. Such businesses are more concerned with labor costs than with the cost of supplies or other materials they may require.

The Purchasing Cycle

The purchasing cycle consists of the following steps: (1) receipt of a purchase requisition, (2) location of a source of supply, (3) issuance of a purchase order, (4) follow-up of a purchase order, and (5) verification of receipt of goods. By following these steps, a small business can minimize the added expenses incurred by haphazard procedures, such as overpayment due to overlooked discounts or payment of fraudulent invoices. Some firms, of course, can operate successfully on a relatively informal basis. If a firm is so small or if its business is of such a nature that it makes few purchases, it may function well without using the procedures described here. A growing firm, however, should avoid clinging too long to informal methods.

purchase requisition
a formal internal request that something be bought for a business

RECEIPT OF A PURCHASE REQUISITION   A **purchase requisition** is a formal, documented request from an employee or department that something be bought, such as raw materials for production, office supplies, or computers. In a small business, such requests are not always documented. However, financial control is improved if a firm purchases only on the basis of purchase requisitions.

LOCATION OF A SOURCE OF SUPPLY   A firm can locate suitable suppliers through information from sales representatives, advertisements, trade associations, word of mouth, and its own records of past supplier performance. The firm selects a specific supplier for a particular purchase by obtaining price quotations and, if the purchase is a major one, soliciting bids from a number of potential sources. The importance of maintaining good relationships with suppliers is discussed later in this chapter.

purchase order
a written form issued to a supplier to buy a specified quantity of some item or items

ISSUANCE OF A PURCHASE ORDER   The next step in the purchasing cycle is the issuance of a **purchase order.** A standard form, such as that shown in Figure 20-1, should be used for all buying operations. When the signed order is accepted by a supplier (vendor), it becomes a binding contract. In the event of a misunderstanding or a more serious problem, the written purchase order serves as the basis for adjustment.

Written purchase orders have saved money for Maitland Meeting Management, a meeting and convention planning firm in Kalispell, Montana:

> *"Once, before we started putting everything in writing, we got a shock from our printer,"* [Dottie Maitland] *says. "We dropped off some originals to have color copies made and I assumed that the printer's prices had stayed the same. But the bill was much more than I expected."*
>
> *So Maitland adopted a standard purchasing form. "We ask suppliers to write down their exact price and all related costs," she says. When a computer forms company added extra shipping costs to its delivery, Maitland won a reduction by sending a copy of the purchase order.*[1]

FOLLOW-UP OF A PURCHASE ORDER   It may be necessary to follow up on purchase orders to ensure that delivery occurs on schedule. This is particularly important when orders involve large dollar amounts, long lead times, and/or items that are critical in the production process. Some orders may require repeated checking to determine whether materials or merchandise will be available when needed.

VERIFICATION OF RECEIPT OF GOODS   A receiving clerk takes physical custody of incoming materials or merchandise, checks the general condition, and signs the carrier's release. Goods should be inspected to ensure an accurate count and the proper quality and kind of items. Inventory records that are computerized immedi-

Figure 20-1

A Purchase Order

DATE OF ORDER June 27, 1996	PURCHASE ORDER THE RED WING COMPANY, INC. Fredonia, NY 14063-4925	No. 05282 SHOW THIS NUMBER ON INVOICE

Byron Jackson & Company
4998 Michigan Avenue
Chicago, IL 60615-2218

SHIPPING INSTRUCTIONS
Mark purchase order number
on each piece in shipment

DELIVERY REQUIRED July 24	F.O.B. Chicago	ROUTING via NYC-Buffalo	TERMS 2/10, net 30

ITEM	QUANTITY & UNIT	DESCRIPTION	PRICE & UNIT
622	35 each	Spring assembly	$14.35 ea
230	200 each	Bearings	3.35 ea
272	70 each	Heavy duty relay 50V	7.50 ea
478	490 each	Screw set	.03 ea

ORIGINAL BILL OF LADING MUST ACCOMPANY ALL INVOICES FOR GOODS SHIPPED BY FREIGHT.
2% DISCOUNT FOR PAYMENT IN 10 DAYS WILL BE DEDUCTED FROM FACE OF INVOICE UNLESS
OTHERWISE SPECIFIED.

BY *Y. Yromboski*
Purchasing Agent

INVOICE IN DUPLICATE

ately reflect the increase in merchandise or materials. Sales or production personnel can then easily determine the volume on hand by checking the account in the computer.

Purchasing Policies and Practices

A small firm can systematize its purchasing by adopting appropriate purchasing policies and practices that can help control purchasing costs and contribute to good relationships with suppliers.

RECIPROCAL BUYING   Some firms sell to others from whom they also purchase. This policy of **reciprocal buying** is based on the premise that a company can secure additional orders by using its own purchasing requests as a bargaining weapon. Although the typical order of most small companies is not large enough to make reciprocal buying a potent weapon, purchasers do tend to give some weight to this factor. Of course, this policy would be damaging if it were allowed to obscure quality and price variations.

MAKING OR BUYING   Many firms face **make-or-buy decisions.** Such decisions are especially important for small manufacturing firms that have the option of making or buying component parts for the products they make. A less obvious make-or-buy

reciprocal buying
the policy of buying
from the businesses
to which a firm sells

**make-or-buy
decision**
a firm's choice between making or buying component parts
for its products

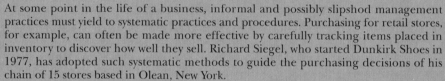

Action Report

TECHNOLOGY

TECHNOLOGICAL APPLICATIONS

Effective Purchasing Requires Proper Procedures

At some point in the life of a business, informal and possibly slipshod management practices must yield to systematic practices and procedures. Purchasing for retail stores, for example, can often be made more effective by carefully tracking items placed in inventory to discover how well they sell. Richard Siegel, who started Dunkirk Shoes in 1977, has adopted such systematic methods to guide the purchasing decisions of his chain of 15 stores based in Olean, New York.

> *Siegel believes in careful record keeping. He computerized his inventory-classification system more than 10 years ago by customer end use, style, size, color, store, and sales trends. "Any deviation in the numbers is the customer talking to us, saying she doesn't like the color, size selection, or style," he says. "Then we make adjustments in our merchandise."*

Sales records during preseason sales, for example, are scrutinized to provide guidance for further purchasing for the regular season. A systematic purchasing cycle and careful record keeping are obviously necessary as a basis for such purchasing.

Source: Meg Whittemore, "When Not to Go with Your Gut," *Nation's Business,* Vol. 81, No. 12 (December 1993), pp. 40–42.

choice exists with respect to certain services—for example, purchasing janitorial or car rental services instead of providing for those needs internally. Some reasons for making component parts, rather than buying them, follow:

- More complete utilization of capacity permits more economical production.
- The buyer has greater assurance of supply, with fewer delays caused by design changes or difficulties with suppliers.
- A secret design may be protected.
- Expenses are reduced by saving an amount equivalent to transportation costs and the supplier's selling expense and profit.
- Closer coordination and control of the total production process are allowed, thus facilitating operations scheduling and control.
- Higher-quality products than those available from suppliers can be produced.

Some reasons for buying component parts, rather than making them, are as follows:

- A supplier's part may be cheaper, because of the supplier's concentration on its production, which makes possible specialized facilities and greater efficiency.
- Additional space, equipment, personnel skills, and working capital are not needed.
- Less diversified managerial experience and skills are required.
- Greater flexibility is provided, especially in the manufacture of a seasonal item.
- In-plant operations can concentrate on the firm's specialty—finished products and services.
- The risk of equipment obsolescence is transferred to outsiders.

Action Report

TECHNOLOGICAL APPLICATIONS

Making Components Rather Than Buying Them

TECHNOLOGY

The decision as to whether a particular business should make or buy component parts depends on the specific circumstances. Lester Tabb, owner of a small, Florida-based company that produces an automatic gate opener known as the Mighty Mule, believes in making as many component parts as possible. Although his firm does not make the motor and battery used in the gate opener, it machines its own dies, does metal stamping, designs and builds electronic boards, and so on.

Tabb has described his reasons for preferring to make rather than buy many parts:

"When you are manufacturing something entirely new, as we are doing, you have to keep making changes as you go along. If you are relying on outside suppliers, change orders can mean lots of downtime, waiting for new parts. Doing everything we can in-house, we can do a turnaround in two weeks or less," [he says].

A second reason for working from scratch as much as possible, says Tabb, is that you maintain control [of] quality much better than when ordering in outside parts. Thirdly, looking to the future, Tabb believes that distribution, already worldwide, is going to expand....
"When you start getting into large quantities, you can save a lot of money through cost control if you are set up to do all the manufacturing yourself."

Source: Gene Logsdon, "Manufacturing Without a Pollution Trail," *In Business,* Vol. 15, No. 2 (March-April, 1993), pp. 32–33.

The decision to make or buy should be based on long-run cost and profit optimization, as it may be expensive to reverse. Underlying cost differences need to be analyzed carefully, since small savings from either buying or making may greatly affect profit margins.

OUTSOURCING   Closely related to the practice of buying, rather than making, component parts is the practice of purchasing outside services. **Outsourcing** involves the purchase of certain business services that are not part of a firm's competitive advantage. For example, a small company may contract with outside suppliers to provide accounting services, payroll services, janitorial services, equipment repair services, and so on. A firm can often reduce costs by taking advantage of the economies of scale and the expertise of outside service providers, rather than trying to provide all such services in-house. Also, because outside firms specialize in specific areas, they usually provide better service in those areas. Innovative Medical Systems, the small firm featured in this chapter's opener, makes extensive use of outsourcing in order to use the superior expertise of outside suppliers.

outsourcing
the purchase of business services, such as janitorial services, that are outside the firm's area of competitive advantage

PURCHASE DISCOUNTS   Cash discounts are granted by most sellers of industrial goods, although discount terms vary from one industry to another. The purpose of the seller's offering a purchase discount is to obtain prompt payment. The purchaser can also benefit financially by taking advantage of such discounts. The terms "2/10, net 30," for example, mean that the purchaser is entitled to a 2 percent dis-

Small firms often contract with outside suppliers for specialized services. Using an outside supplier to provide janitorial services, for example, is often more cost-effective than providing such services in-house.

count off the amount due if payment is made no later than the tenth day from the date of the invoice. After the 10-day discount period, the full amount is required, even if payment is delayed until the thirtieth day from the date of the invoice.

The effective annualized cost of not taking a discount can be significant. After all, with terms of 2/10, net 30, the purchaser is paying 2 percent to use the money for only 20 additional days. (The method for calculating the annual cost is explained in Chapter 23.) From an economic standpoint, therefore, prompt payment is desirable in order to avoid this additional cost. However, remember that payment of an invoice affects cash flow. If funds are extremely short, a firm may have no alternative but to wait and pay on the last possible day, in order to avoid an overdraft at the bank.

DIVERSIFYING SOURCES OF SUPPLY   There is a question of whether it is desirable to use more than one supplier when purchasing a given item. The somewhat frustrating answer is "It all depends." For example, one supplier is usually all that is necessary when buying a few rolls of tape. However, several suppliers might be involved when a firm is buying a component part to be used in hundreds of products.

A small firm might prefer to concentrate purchases with one supplier for any of several reasons:

- A particular supplier may be outstanding in its product quality.
- Concentrating purchases may lead to quantity discounts or other favorable terms of purchase.
- Orders may be so small that it is simply impractical to divide them.
- The purchasing firm may, as a good customer, qualify for prompt treatment of rush orders and receive management advice, market information, and financial leniency in times of emergency.
- A small firm may be linked to a specific supplier by the very nature of its business—if it is a franchisee, for example.

Other reasons favor diversifying rather than concentrating sources of supply:

- Shopping among suppliers enables the purchasing firm to locate the best source in terms of price, quality, and service.
- A supplier, knowing that competitors are getting some of its business, may try to provide better prices and service.
- Diversifying supply sources for key products provides insurance against interruptions caused by strikes, fires, or similar problems with sole suppliers.

Some firms compromise by following a policy by which they concentrate enough purchases to justify special treatment and, at the same time, diversify purchases sufficiently to maintain alternative sources of supply.

POOLING PURCHASES   Occasionally, a small business can save money by **pooling purchases** with other companies. Some small firms, for example, have developed cooperative plans for purchasing health insurance for their employees.[2] As another example, over 100 office-supply dealers, based in New York, have joined forces with a large independent wholesaler of office products to buy products directly from manufacturers.[3] This has enabled these smaller dealers to cope better with the expansion of office-supply superstores such as Staples.

pooling purchases
combining with other firms to buy materials or merchandise from a supplier

FORWARD BUYING   Forward buying involves purchasing in quantities greater than needed for normal usage or sales. It may be motivated by a number of considerations, such as protection from outages or delays caused by strikes or materials shortages and avoidance of anticipated price increases.

Purchasing excessive quantities to avoid anticipated higher prices creates a speculative risk. Price appreciation after such a purchase does produce inventory cost savings. However, decreases in the price will create excessive inventory costs. Unless it is very stable financially or a forthcoming price increase is virtually assured, a firm should avoid such speculative buying. Forward buying also adds to operating costs by increasing inventory size, thereby raising inventory carrying costs.

Forward buying runs counter to the concept of just-in-time inventory, which holds that inventory levels should, ideally, fall to zero. The just-in-time inventory system is discussed later in this chapter.

BUDGET BUYING   Budget buying simply means purchasing the quantities needed to meet estimated production or sales needs. Buying in such quantities ensures the maintenance of planned inventories and the meeting of schedule requirements without delays in production due to late deliveries. It represents the middle ground between just-in-time buying—with its planned minimal stocking of materials and occasional delays due to late deliveries—and forward buying—with its deliberate overstocking and resultant risk from seeking speculative profits. Budget buying is a conservative type of buying for small firms.

RELATIONSHIPS WITH SUPPLIERS

Before choosing a supplier, a purchaser must be thoroughly familiar with the characteristics of the materials or merchandise to be purchased, including details of construction, quality and grade, intended use, maintenance or care required, and the importance of style features. In manufacturing, the purchaser must also know how different grades and qualities of raw materials affect various manufacturing processes.

2 Explain the factors to consider in choosing suppliers and how to maintain good relationships with suppliers.

Selection of Suppliers

A number of considerations are relevant in deciding which suppliers to use on a continuing basis. Perhaps the most obvious of these are price and quality. Price differences are clearly significant, if not offset by quality or other factors.

Quality differences are sometimes difficult to detect. For some types of materials, statistical controls can be used to evaluate shipments from specific vendors. In this way, the purchaser obtains an overall quality rating for various suppliers. The purchaser can often work with a supplier to upgrade quality. If satisfactory quality cannot be achieved, the purchaser clearly has a reason for dropping the supplier.

Location becomes an especially important factor as a firm tries to reduce inventory levels and provide for rapid delivery of purchased items. A supplier's general

ENTREPRENEURIAL EXPERIENCES

A Mistake in Selecting a Supplier

Careful selection of suppliers is an important part of the purchasing process. An unwise choice of a supplier by Softub, a small builder of hot tubs in Chatsworth, California, illustrates the perils of making such a selection without adequate investigation.

Softub subcontracted the assembly of the motor, pump, and control unit that provide heat and jet action to its hot tubs. After meeting with the chosen supplier twice and receiving good reports from other customers, Softub CEO Tom Thornbury felt confident about the purchasing relationship. Before long, equipment failures surfaced during testing and, even worse, in customers' homes.

Soon after, the supplier went belly-up, and Softub was stuck servicing damaged tubs and trying to mollify the dealers that hadn't quit. Thornbury estimates the cost of the foul-up at about $500,000. "If we had done a better job of surveying our suppliers," he says, "this might not have happened."

The size of the assembly contract and its crucial role in Softub's overall performance justified more than a casual approach to supplier selection. To avoid other mistakes of this nature, Softub created an audit team to check out future supplier candidates thoroughly.

Source: Stephanie Gruner, "The Smart Vendor-Audit Checklist," *Inc.*, Vol. 17, No. 5 (April 1995), pp. 93–95.

---

reliability in supplying goods and services is also significant. The purchaser must be able to depend on the supplier to meet delivery schedules and to respond promptly to emergency situations.

Services offered by a supplier must also be considered. The extension of credit by suppliers provides a major portion of the working capital of many small firms. Some suppliers provide merchandising aids, plan sales promotions, and furnish management advice. During recessions, some small retailers have even received direct financial assistance from their major long-standing suppliers. Another useful service for some types of products is the provision of repair work by the supplier. A small industrial firm, for example, may select a supplier for a truck or diesel engine because the supplier has a reliable service department.

Building Good Relationships with Suppliers

Good relationships with suppliers are essential for firms of any size, but they are particularly important to small businesses. Perhaps the cornerstone of a good relationship is a small buyer's realization that the supplier is more important to it than the buyer (as a customer) is to the supplier. The buyer is only one among dozens, hundreds, or perhaps thousands buying from that supplier. Moreover, a small firm's volume of purchases over a year and the size of its individual orders are often so small that they could disappear without great loss to the supplier.

To implement the policy of fair play and to cultivate good relations, the small firm should try to observe the following purchasing practices:

- Pay bills promptly.
- Be on time for appointments with sales representatives and give them a full, courteous hearing.
- Do not abruptly cancel orders merely to gain a temporary advantage.
- Do not argue over prices, attempting to browbeat the supplier into special concessions and unusual discounts.
- Cooperate with the supplier by making suggestions for product improvement and/or cost reduction whenever possible.
- Give courteous, reasonable explanations when rejecting bids, and make fair adjustments in case of disputes.

If the volume of purchases is sufficiently large, small purchasers can build working partnerships with their suppliers. As an example, Peter Perry and Steve Pickett, who bought Denver-based Allwest Fire & Sound in 1990, have worked diligently to develop strong relationships with their suppliers. (Allwest assembles standard components—fire alarms, intercoms, closed-circuit television—into proprietary security systems for buildings of different sizes and functions.) Perry and Pickett have sought supplier training for Allwest employees:

"An awful lot of suppliers have bought into the idea that I constantly preach, that knowledge is power," Perry says, "and that one of the ways they can make us, and themselves, successful is to educate our people to an intense level of comfort with their product."[4]

Although price can never be completely ignored, emphasizing the development of cooperative relationships with qualified suppliers can pay substantial dividends to many small firms. Small business buyers should remember that although it takes a long time to build good relationships with suppliers, those relationships can be damaged by one ill-timed, tactless act.

OBJECTIVES OF INVENTORY MANAGEMENT

3 Identify the objectives of inventory management.

Inventory management is not glamorous, but it can make the difference between success and failure. The larger the inventory investment, the more vital proper inventory management is. The importance of inventory management, particularly in small retail or wholesale firms, is attested to by the fact that inventory typically represents a major financial investment by these firms. Both purchasing and inventory management have the same general objective: to have the right goods in the right quantities at the right time and place. Achieving this general objective requires pursuing more specific subgoals of inventory control, as shown in Figure 20-2.

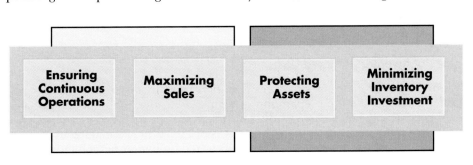

Figure 20-2

Objectives of Inventory Management

Ensuring Continuous Operations

Efficient manufacturing requires that work in process move on schedule. A delay caused by lack of materials or parts can cause the shutdown of a production line, a department, or even a whole plant. Such interruptions of scheduled operations are costly. Costs escalate when skilled workers and machines stand idle. Also, given a long production delay, fulfillment of delivery promises to customers may become impossible.

Maximizing Sales

Given adequate demand, sales are greater if goods are always available for display and/or delivery to customers. Most customers want to choose from an assortment of merchandise. Those customers forced to look elsewhere because of a narrow range of choices and/or stockouts—in which a customer looks for a product and finds an empty shelf—may be lost permanently. On the other hand, a small store might unwisely go to the other extreme and carry too large an inventory. Managers must walk the line between overstocking and understocking in order to retain customers and to maximize sales.

Protecting the Inventory

One of the essential functions of inventory control is to protect inventories against theft, shrinkage, or deterioration. The efficiency or wastefulness of storage, manufacturing, and handling processes affects the quantity and quality of usable inventory. For example, the more often an article is picked up and handled, the greater the risk that it will suffer physical damage. Also, inventory items that need special treatment can spoil or deteriorate if improperly stored.

Minimizing Inventory Investment

Effective inventory control allows firms to carry smaller inventories without causing disservice to customers or delays in processing. Therefore, inventory investment is lower, as are costs for storage space, taxes, and insurance. Inventory deterioration or obsolescence is less extensive as well.

---

4 Describe ways to control inventory costs and types of record-keeping systems used in inventory control.

CONTROLLING INVENTORY COSTS

It's easy to understand how effective control of inventory contributes to the bottom line—that is, to the profitability of a firm. It's more difficult to learn how to make effective inventory decisions that will minimize costs.

Types of Inventory-Related Costs

Minimizing inventory costs requires attention to many different types of costs. Order costs include the preparation of a purchase order, follow-up, and related bookkeeping expenses. Quantity discounts must also be included in such calculations. Inventory carrying costs are the costs associated with maintaining items in inventory and include interest that could be earned on money tied up in inventory and insurance premiums, storage rental, and losses due to obsolescence and pilferage. The costs of not having items in inventory include lost sales or production that is disrupted because of stockouts. Although stockout costs cannot be calculated as easily as other inventory costs, they are real.

ABC Inventory Analysis

Some inventory items are more valuable or more critical to a firm's operations than others. Therefore, they have a greater effect on costs and profits. Generally, managers should give their most careful attention to those inventory items entailing the largest investment.

One widely used approach, the **ABC method,** classifies inventory items into three categories based on value. A few high-value items in the A category account for the largest percentage of total dollars or are otherwise critical in the production process and, therefore, deserve close control. They might be monitored, for example, by an inventory system that keeps a running record of receipts, withdrawals, and balances of each such item. In this way, a firm avoids an unnecessarily heavy investment in costly inventory items. Category B items are less costly but deserve moderate managerial attention because they still make up a significant share of the firm's total inventory investment. Category C contains low-cost or non-critical items, such as paperclips in an office or nuts and bolts in a repair shop. Their carrying costs are not large enough to justify close control. These items might simply be checked periodically to be sure that a sufficient supply is available.

The purpose of the ABC method is to focus managerial attention on the most important items. The three categories could easily be expanded to four or more if that seemed more appropriate for a particular firm.

ABC method
a method of classifying items in inventory by relative value

Although use of a just-in-time inventory system can significantly reduce costs, an out-of-stock situation can seriously hamper operations. For this reason, factories must be careful to maintain some safety stock.

Action Report

ENTREPRENEURIAL EXPERIENCES

Limitations of the Just-in-Time Inventory System

Many small firms have reduced costs and increased profits by following a just-in-time philosophy for inventory management. Nevertheless, small firms sometimes encounter problems as they try to reap the benefits of such a system. The short production runs and large variety of products that are common in small businesses complicate the use of this method.

Allen-Edmonds Shoe Corporation of Port Washington, Wisconsin tried unsuccessfully to install a just-in-time system. It had difficulty getting suppliers to go along with its strategy of matching delivery to need. A bigger customer would have wielded more power, but the European tanneries supplying the calfskin hides that Allen-Edmonds used refused to handle the small batches needed to meet the firm's weekly production requirements. After losing money on this system and because of other related management changes, the firm gave up its goal of cutting inventory to the point suggested by the just-in-time model.

Source: Barbara Marsh, "Allen-Edmonds Shoe Tries 'Just-in-Time' Production," *The Wall Street Journal*, March 4, 1993, p. B2.

Reorder Point and Safety Stock

reorder point
the level at which additional quantities of items in inventory should be ordered

In maintaining inventory levels, a manager must decide on a point at which additional quantities will be ordered. Calculating the **reorder point** requires consideration of the time necessary to obtain a new supply, which, in turn, depends on supplier location, transportation schedules, and so on.

Because of difficulty in getting orders to arrive at the exact time desired and because of irregularities in withdrawals from inventory, firms typically maintain **safety stock.** Safety stock provides a measure of protection against stockouts caused by emergencies of one type or another.

safety stock
inventory maintained to protect against stockouts

two-bin method
a simple inventory control technique for indicating the reorder point

The **two-bin method** is a simple technique for implementing both of these concepts. Inventories are divided into two portions, or bins. When the first bin is exhausted, an order is placed to replenish the supply. The remaining bin includes safety stock and should cover normal needs until a new supply arrives.

Just-in-Time Inventory System

just-in-time inventory system
a system for reducing inventory levels to an absolute minimum

Reducing inventory levels remains a goal of all operations managers. The **just-in-time inventory system** attempts to cut inventory carrying costs by reducing inventory to an absolute minimum. Popularized as the *Kanban system* in Japan, the just-in-time system has led to cost reductions there and in other countries. Items are received, presumably, just as the last item of that type from existing inventory is placed into service. Many large U.S. firms have adopted some form of just-in-time system for inventory management, and small businesses can also benefit from its use.

Adoption of a just-in-time system necessitates close cooperation with suppliers. Supplier locations, production schedules, and transportation schedules must be carefully considered as all of these affect a firm's ability to obtain materials quickly and in a predictable manner—a necessary condition for using a just-in-time inventory system.

Some danger of possible failures exists in the just-in-time system. The result of out-of-stock situations when delays or mistakes occur may be interrupted production or unhappy customers. Most firms using the just-in-time inventory system maintain some safety stock to minimize difficulties of this type. Although safety stock represents a compromise of the just-in-time philosophy, it protects a firm against large or unexpected withdrawals from inventory and delays in delivery of replacement items.

Economic Order Quantity

If a firm could order merchandise or raw materials and carry inventory with no expenses other than the cost of these items, there would be no need to be concerned about what quantity to order at a given time. However, inventory costs are affected by both the cost of purchasing and the cost of carrying inventory—that is,

Total inventory costs = Total carrying costs + Total ordering costs

As we noted earlier, carrying costs include storage costs, insurance premiums, the cost of money tied up in inventory, losses due to spoilage or obsolescence, and other expenses of this type. Carrying costs increase as inventories increase in size. Ordering costs, on the other hand, include expenses associated with preparation and processing of purchase orders and expenses related to receiving and inspecting the purchased items. The cost of placing an order is a fixed cost, and total ordering costs increase, therefore, as a firm purchases smaller quantities more frequently. Also, quantity discounts, if available, favor the placement of larger orders.

The **economic order quantity** is that number of items that minimizes total inventory costs; it is the point labeled EOQ in Figure 20-3. Note that it is the lowest

economic order quantity
the quantity to be purchased that minimizes total inventory costs

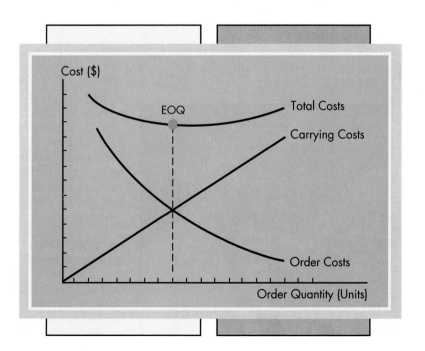

Determination of the Economic Order Quantity

Figure 20-4	Computer Printout for a Perpetual Inventory System

```
Item: Metal Eyelets            Maximum No. of Pairs            60,000
                               Reorder Point No. of Pairs      24,000
                               Minimum No. of Pairs            12,000
```

	Receipts			Issue			Balance on Hand		
Date	Pairs	Price per Pair	Cost	Pairs	Price per Pair	Cost	Pairs	Price per Pair	Cost
Jan. 1							14,000	$.00400	$ 56.00
2				2,500	$.00400	$10.00	11,500	.00400	46.00
3	48,000	$.00420	$201.60				59,500	.00416	247.60
3				2,000	.00416	8.32	57,500	.00416	239.28
4				2,100	.00416	8.74	55,400	.00416	230.54
7				2,000	.00416	8.32	53,400	.00416	222.22

Note: Minor discrepancies in the last column are due to 5-place rounding in the preceding column.

point on the total costs curve and that it coincides with the intersection of the carrying costs and order costs curves. In cases in which sufficient information on costs is available, this point can be calculated with some precision.[5] Even when the economic order quantity cannot be calculated with precision, a firm's goal is still to avoid both high ordering costs and high carrying costs.

Inventory Record-Keeping Systems

A small business needs a system for keeping tabs on its inventory—the larger the business is, the greater the need. Also, since manufacturers are concerned with three broad categories of inventory (raw materials and supplies, work in process, and finished goods), their inventory records are more complex than those of wholesalers and retailers. Although some record keeping is unavoidable, small firms should emphasize simplicity in their control methods. Too much control is as wasteful as it is unnecessary.

Many software programs are available to small businesses that wish to computerize their inventory. Using a bar-code scanner to take a physical inventory improves both the speed and the accuracy of the process.

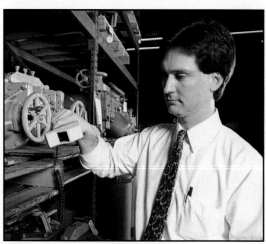

In most small businesses, inventory records are computerized. A large variety of software programs are available for this purpose; the manager, in consultation with the firm's accounting advisors, can select the software best suited for the particular business.

PHYSICAL INVENTORY CONTROL A **physical inventory system** involves an actual count of items on hand. The counting is done in physical units such as pieces, gallons, boxes, and so on. By using this method, a firm presum-

physical inventory system
a system for periodic counting of items in inventory

ably gains an accurate record of its inventory level at a given point in time. Some businesses have an annual shutdown to count everything—a complete physical inventory. Others use **cycle counting,** scheduling different segments of the inventory for counting at different times during the year. This simplifies the inventorying process and makes it less of an ordeal for the business as a whole. While most small businesses use their own employees to take a physical inventory, outside firms also provide this type of service. Some kinds of businesses—convenience stores, for example—often utilize these services.

In some businesses, the process of taking a physical inventory has been simplified by using computers and bar-code systems. Bar codes are the printed patterns of lines, spaces, and numerals that appear on certain products, which can be read with a hand-held wand that transmits data to a computer. Use of a bar-code system for inventory purposes benefited Tate Andale, a Baltimore-based metal-fabricating firm. Before bar coding was instituted at Tate Andale, taking inventory each year "required 24 people working two days," says Milt Thacker, the company's data-processing manager. "Then it would take 30 to 40 hours in the office to key in the data. With hand-held bar-code scanners, it takes four people eight hours in the warehouse, and manual data entry is eliminated. Not only do we save a tremendous amount of time, but the accuracy of our data is way up."[6]

1 Discuss purchasing policies and the basic steps in purchasing.

- Purchasing is important because it affects quality and profitability.
- Systematic purchasing involves a series of steps constituting the purchasing cycle: receiving a purchasing requisition, locating a supply source, issuing and following up on a purchase order, and verifying receipt of the goods.
- A key decision for manufacturers is whether to make or buy components.
- In outsourcing, a small firm contracts with outside suppliers for accounting, repair, or other services.
- Other purchasing policies relate to reciprocal buying, purchase discounts, and pooling purchases.

2 Explain the factors to consider in choosing suppliers and how to maintain good relationships with suppliers.

- Careful selection of suppliers identifies those offering the best price, quality, and services.
- Paying bills promptly and dealing professionally with suppliers contribute to good relationships.
- The product quality provided by a supplier affects the product quality of the purchasing firm.
- Building working relationships with suppliers can bring benefits, such as training provided by a supplier.

3 Identify the objectives of inventory management.

- Inventory management helps ensure continuous operations and maximize sales.
- Other inventory management objectives are protecting assets and minimizing inventory investment.

4 Describe ways to control inventory costs and types of record-keeping systems used in inventory control.

- Three categories of inventory costs are those related to purchasing, carrying inventory, and stockouts.
- ABC inventory analysis, the just-in-time inventory system, and the calculation of economic order quantities help minimize inventory costs.
- Inventory record-keeping systems include the physical inventory method and the perpetual inventory method.

PERPETUAL INVENTORY CONTROL   A **perpetual inventory system** provides an ongoing, current record of inventory items. It does not require a physical count. However, a physical count of inventory should be made periodically to ensure the accuracy of the system and to make adjustments for such factors as theft.

Records for a perpetual inventory system can be kept as computer files (see Figure 20-4) or on a card system. The records are used by routing and planning clerks to ensure an adequate supply of materials and parts to complete any given factory order. If a firm keeps accurate records of receipt and usage of materials, information on the number of units on hand will always be available. If each receipt and any withdrawal from inventory is costed, the dollar value of these units is also known.

Use of a perpetual inventory system is justifiable in both the small factory and the wholesale warehouse. Its use is particularly desirable for expensive and critical

cycle counting
counting different segments of the physical inventory at different times during the year

perpetual inventory system
a system for keeping a running record of inventory

New Terms and Concepts

purchasing *437*

purchase
requisition *438*

purchase order *438*

reciprocal
buying *439*

make-or-buy
decision *439*

outsourcing *441*

pooling
purchases *443*

ABC method *447*

reorder point *448*

safety stock *448*

two-bin method *448*

just-in-time inventory
system *448*

economic order
quantity *449*

physical inventory
system *450*

cycle counting *451*

perpetual inventory
system *451*

You Make the Call

Situation 1   Derek Dilworth, owner of a small manufacturing firm, is trying to rectify the firm's thin working capital situation by carefully managing payments to major suppliers. These suppliers extend credit for 30 days, and customers are expected to pay within that time period. However, the suppliers do not automatically refuse subsequent orders when a payment is a few days late. Johnson's strategy is to delay payment of most invoices for 10 to 15 days beyond the due date. Although he is not meeting the "letter of the law," he believes that the suppliers will go along with him rather than lose future sales. This practice enables Johnson's firm to operate with sufficient inventory, avoid costly interruptions in production, and reduce the likelihood of an overdraft at the bank.

Question 1   What are the ethical implications of Johnson's payment practices?

Question 2   What impact, if any, might these practices have on the firm's supplier relationships? How serious would this impact be?

Situation 2   In a sense, a temporary-help employment agency maintains an inventory of services in the form of personnel awaiting assignments. Excel, a temporary-help agency, has found that its inventory tends to disappear early each day. If assignments are not readily available, its temps accept work assignments from other agencies.

Excel wants to have personnel available the moment an employer requests help. Much of the time, calls from employers come in early on the same day that help is desired. The firm faces the problem of trying to match this unpredictable demand with its inventory of temps. If an employer's request comes in at 10:00 A.M., for example, Excel often finds that its best temps have already accepted assignments through other agencies. If Excel were to guarantee work for these temps, it would incur costs for their wages on days when enough demand failed to materialize.

Continue on next page

items—for example, those that could cause significant losses through theft or serious production delays.

Whatever inventory record-keeping system is used should function efficiently, thereby contributing to good overall management of the firm. Retention of customers and control of costs are both dependent on an accurate inventory record-keeping system.

DISCUSSION QUESTIONS

1. What conditions make purchasing a particularly vital function in a small business? Can the owner-manager of a small firm safely delegate purchasing authority to a subordinate? Explain.
2. Under what conditions should a small manufacturer either make component parts or buy them from others?
3. Compare the potential rewards and dangers of forward buying. Is forward buying more dangerous for a small firm or a large firm? Why?
4. What are the factors that govern a small manufacturer's selection of a supplier for a vital raw material?
5. In what ways is location a significant factor when choosing a supplier? Is the closest supplier usually the best choice?
6. Explain the following objectives of inventory management: (a) ensuring continuous operations, (b) maximizing sales; (c) protecting assets; and (d) minimizing inventory investment.
7. Suppose a small firm has excess warehouse space. What types of inventory carrying costs should be considered in deciding on how much inventory to hold? How would such costs differ for a firm that does not have excesssive storage space?
8. Explain and justify the use of the ABC method of inventory analysis. How would it work in an automobile repair shop?
9. What is the just-in-time inventory system? What are the advantages and disadvantages of using it in a small firm?

10. Explain the basic concept underlying the calculation of an economic order quantity.

EXPERIENTIAL EXERCISES

1. Interview an owner-manager regarding the purchasing procedures used in her or his business. Compare these procedures with the steps in the purchasing cycle outlined in this chapter.
2. Outline in detail the steps you took when making an important purchase recently—a purchase of more than $100, if possible. Compare these steps with the steps identified in this chapter as making up the purchasing cycle, and explain any differences.
3. Using the ABC inventory analysis method, classify some of your personal possessions into three categories. Include at least two items in each category.
4. Interview the manager of a bookstore about the type of inventory control system used in the store. Write a report that includes an explanation of the methods used to avoid buildup of excessive inventory and any use made of inventory turnover ratios (ratios that relate the dollar value of inventory with the volume of sales).

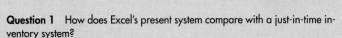

Question 1   How does Excel's present system compare with a just-in-time inventory system?

Question 2   Can the firm solve its problem by smoothing out demand in some way? How?

Question 3   Should the best temps be guaranteed work? How could this be arranged?

Question 4   If you were a consultant for this firm, what solution would you recommend for this problem?

Situation 3   The owner of a small food products company was confronted with an inventory control problem involving differences of opinion among his subordinates. His accountant, with the concurrence of his general manager, had decided to "put some teeth" into the inventory control system by deducting inventory shortages from the pay of route drivers who distributed the firm's products to stores in their respective territories. Each driver was considered responsible for the inventory on his or her truck.

When the first "short" paychecks arrived, drivers were angry. Sharing their concern, their immediate supervisor, the regional manager, first went to the general manager and, getting no satisfaction there, appealed to the owner. The regional manager argued that (1) there was no question about the honesty of the drivers; (2) he had personally created the inventory control system that is being used; (3) the system is admittedly complicated and susceptible to clerical mistakes by the driver and by the office; (4) the system had never been studied by the general manager or the accountant; and (5) it is ethically wrong to make deductions from the small salaries of honest drivers for simple record-keeping errors.

Question 1   What is wrong, if anything, with the general manager's approach to making sure that drivers do not steal or act carelessly? Is some method of enforcement necessary to ensure the careful adherence to the inventory control system?

Question 2   Is it wrong to deduct shortages from drivers' paychecks when the inventory records document the shortages?

Question 3   How should the owner resolve this dispute?

Exploring the

5. Consult Dun & Bradstreet's home page on the Web (http://www.dbisna.com). Prepare a one-page report summarizing and evaluating the type of information offered there concerning the management of supplier relationships.

 CASE 20
Mather's Heating and Air Conditioning (p. 644)

This case examines the difficulties experienced by a small heating and air-conditioning firm in dealing with a major supplier.

Alternative Cases for Chapter 20: Case 23, "Barton Sales and Service," p. 653
Case 26, "Diaper Dan," p. 662

Chapter 21

Computer-Based Technology for Small Businesses

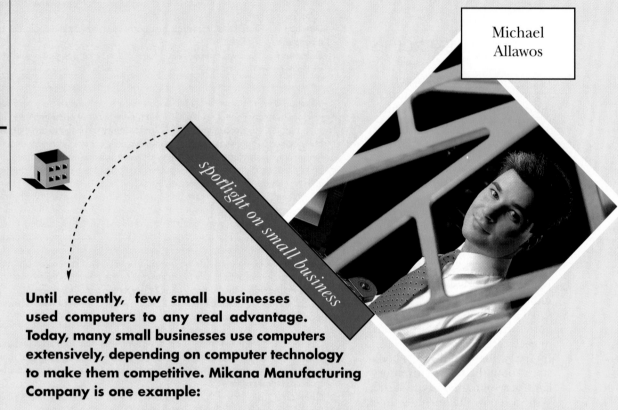

Michael Allawos

spotlight on small business

Until recently, few small businesses used computers to any real advantage. Today, many small businesses use computers extensively, depending on computer technology to make them competitive. Mikana Manufacturing Company is one example:

Michael Allawos's tool-and-die shop isn't very big. Housed in a tiny building in an industrial park in San Dimas, California, it makes metal parts for Northrop Grumman and Bristol-Myers Squibb Co. But it has big plans—and big-company technology on its side. On sales calls, Allawos whips out a laptop computer to confirm the status of a customer's order—and verify that all the materials for the job are on hand. Orders for new parts are dropped electronically into his job-tracking system, and a financial package traces to the penny the cost and profit for every order, every step of the way.

Allawos's Mikana Manufacturing Co. will close the year with not even $2 million in sales. But Mikana is just one small example of a quiet revolution in the way small companies view and use information technology. To Allawos, there was no choice: either automate or die. "If I hadn't been computerized in this last recession, I wouldn't have been competitive. My customers wouldn't have given me an opportunity to stay in business," he says.

Source: Gary McWilliams, "Special Report," *Business Week* (November 21, 1994), pp. 82–90.

Looking Ahead

After studying this chapter, you should be able to:

1 Identify basic applications of computer technology that are appropriate for small firms.

2 Describe the hardware and software components of an information-processing system.

3 Explain the role of computers in data communications.

4 Provide examples of computer-based office and production technology.

5 Outline the process for selecting the computer system best suited to a small firm's needs.

6 Discuss the ways in which computers may affect small businesses in the future.

In concept, a computer is a relatively simple device— a machine designed to follow instructions. In reality, a computer is a complex data-processing machine, vastly outperforming human beings in recording, classifying, calculating, storing, and communicating information. The widespread availability of inexpensive, powerful computer systems has made levels of automation that were once available only to large firms accessible to small firms as well.

OVERVIEW OF AVAILABLE TECHNOLOGY

Computer-based functions for small businesses are not limited to routine record-keeping activities. Diverse tasks such as desktop publishing, electronic communication with vendors and customers, and electronic banking are but a few of the new applications helping small businesses contain costs and improve services. The accuracy and speed of acquiring data have improved substantially with the use of computer systems. Today, more often than not, computers are playing a vital role in a small business, as Gary McWilliams of *Business Week* has described:

> *State-of-the-art digital technologies once available only to deep-pocketed big companies are making their way to mom-and-pop stores and garage shops. Once the last refuge of mechanical cash registers and shoe-boxed receipts, small businesses are latching onto sophisticated manufacturing, financial, and inventory management systems. Their operations are being transformed with easier-to-use software, cheap computer power, and global electronic networks. At the same time, small companies are getting a push from big businesses that have lost patience with old-fashioned ways. As a consequence, many of [the] 15 million small businesses [in the United States] are becoming as adept at exploiting technology as their bigger counterparts.*[1]

1 Identify basic applications of computer technology that are appropriate for small firms.

TECHNOLOGY

Financial and Marketing Applications

Many small businesses apply computer technology for tracking financial and marketing transactions with systems such as order entry, accounts receivable, accounts payable, payroll, and inventory management. The more sophisticated computerized financial systems are integrated so that duplication of data entry is minimized. Information is entered only once, with all subsystems providing data to an accounting system that produces financial statements such as income statements and balance sheets.

Many small businesses have access to an on-line, 24-hour-a-day information service capable of providing credit information about customers. Vendors' stock availability can also be ascertained on a timely basis through such telecommunications technology. In many cases, **electronic data interchange (EDI),** the exchange of data among businesses through computer links, is replacing the manual transmission of purchase orders and sales invoices.

electronic data interchange (EDI)
the exchange of data through computer links

Operations Applications

The manufacturing process has benefited greatly from computer technology. Powerful workstation units (personal computers with increased memory, faster processors, and high-resolution display monitors) are used in **computer-aided design (CAD)** and **computer-aided manufacturing (CAM).** Highly sophisticated CAD programs are used to prepare engineering drawings of new products, while CAM programs are used to control machines that cut, mold, and assemble products. Once requiring million-dollar investments, these types of equipment and programs are now within the reach of most small manufacturers. Both CAD and CAM are discussed in more detail later in this chapter.

Computer Networks

Office automation has grown dramatically with the popularity of local area networks. A **local area network (LAN)** is a connected series of computers, mainly personal computers, that are capable of communicating and sharing information within a limited geographic area, usually within one building or plant. Storage and output devices such as large magnetic disk drives and high-quality printers or plotters can be attached to the network. The capability of each personal computer on the network is enhanced by having access to the shared storage and output devices.

Applications such as electronic mail (discussed in more detail later in this chapter) have become more commonplace with the spread of LANs. Office personnel are less intimidated by personal computers, which are more user-friendly than larger computers. Also used in LANs, **work group software** facilitates the coordination of several employees working on a common project. Such software is more than a simple messaging system; it allows for efficient sharing of data and decisions among team members working toward a common goal.

The Internet

The Internet has something to offer all small business owners, not just those who are technologically advanced. Firms all over the world are using the Internet. In 1994, there were about 21,700 commercial "domains"—the Internet equivalent of storefront addresses—compared to 9,000 only three years earlier. Even more impressive is the fact that 3.2 million computers around the world were connected to the Internet in 1994, and that number is expected to increase to more than 100 million by 1999.[2] Firms using the Internet are developing entirely new ways of doing business—dealing directly with suppliers, industrial customers, and, potentially, millions of individual on-line shoppers.

Once considered too difficult for small business owners to use, the Internet is a powerful and cost-effective way to communicate with clients and associates, disseminate information on products, and learn the latest about what is happening in a given field. It is quickly becoming a significant tool for smaller companies seeking to be more competitive. The effective use of the Internet is independent of firm size, which means that a small company can look like a big company on the Internet.

Two primary uses of the Internet are electronic mail (E-mail) and the Web page. E-mail is a highly effective means of communicating with others anywhere in the world, and the message may be accompanied by a word-processing or spreadsheet file. The uses of E-mail and Web pages are illustrated by a hypothetical sce-

---

computer-aided design (CAD) the use of sophisticated computer systems to design new products

computer-aided manufacturing (CAM) the use of computer-controlled machines to manufacture products

local area network (LAN) an interconnected group of personal computers and related hardware located within a limited area

work group software computer programs that help coordinate the efforts of employees working together on a project

nario written by Michael Chorost, an owner of an Internet consulting firm. Chorost describes a typical day on the Internet as follows:

The World Wide Web can provide businesspeople with a wealth of information from around the globe. Home businesses benefit directly from establishing a Web page that attracts browsers—and potential customers—to a description of their products and/or services.

> *You sit down at your computer and log on to your Internet account. A soft beep informs you that you have E-mail (electronic mail) waiting. You select the message from your new business partner in Monterey. He wants your input on what to charge for local consulting fees. You created a price list last week, so you pull it up with your word processor and "cut-and-paste" the figures directly into your reply to him. For good measure, you send a copy of the message to your partner in Austin.*
>
> *Another message is from a client in San Antonio. He's quite pleased with the software your firm designed for him but needs documentation in both Spanish and English. For a project like this, you need to find a professional translator who specializes in technical documentation. So you post a message on the discussion group* soc.culture.mexican. american, *asking if anyone knows of a good technical translator. Dozens, perhaps even hundreds, of people will see your question each day, so the chances are good that someone will give you a lead.*
>
> *A third message is from a potential client in Houston, who wants more information on your products. You write a reply referring him to your company's "Web page," a document available to anyone with World Wide Web access. The World Wide Web is a vast worldwide collection of "pages" such as this.*
>
> *Your Web page has your company's logo on it, with text describing your services. It has buttons that can be clicked to bring up, among other things, your catalog with prices and photographs of your products, the answers to frequently asked questions, and sound clips of your own voice introducing yourself and inviting browsers to look around. At the bottom of this page is a form where browsers can type messages to you. Hundreds of people have browsed this Web page since you designed it, and you've gotten a number of good clients from it.*
>
> *You've been doing business in three cities today, and it's high-yield work: you have given important information to your colleague in Monterey, posted a call for information on translators, and directed a potential client to a rich source of information on your company, which he can access in a minute. You're still on your first cup of coffee.*
>
> *You decide next to spend a few minutes reading the new issue of the MAES National Magazine, which is published by the Society of Mexican-American Scientists and Engineers. This is also a Web page, which you reach by typing* http://loonytoons.tamu. edu/--keith/MAES/MAES_homepage.html *in your browsing program. You only need to type this the first time you want to reach the page; once you reach it, you can create a "bookmark" so you can reach the page again with just a mouse click.*
>
> *The magazine's brightly colored cover appears on screen, and below it are tidbits of text representing each of its articles. You click on the cover story. You learn that there are some new exhibitors in your fields and decide that you'd better check them out. You jot down their E-mail addresses in hopes of talking shop and maybe getting some new ideas. Then, just for fun, you read "The Science Behind the Camera," which discusses the making of Robert Rodriquez's film* El Mariachi.
>
> *Back to business. You're thinking of putting a new office in Houston but need to get a loan to do it. The Small Business Administration seems like a good place to start. Do they have a site on the Internet? A click of the mouse brings up a program that will search*

the entire Internet for anything you desire. You type Small Business Administration *and hit the Enter key. In a minute, the World Wide Web page for the SBA pops up, and you skim it for information about the types of loans available and the people to contact for further information. You fire off a quick E-mail message to one of them.*[3]

So goes the morning for a small business owner who relies on the Internet as a means of communicating quickly, effectively, and cheaply. However, Chorost's description of surfing the Internet does not mention one potential use of the Internet—selling.

In the past, selling a product or service electronically was a problem because of the difficulty in collecting payments. For security purposes, an electronic transaction must take place in a closed-loop system, so that a buyer's credit card information is protected from display on the Internet itself. Historically, the Internet has lacked the security features necessary to protect the credit card numbers needed for on-line shopping. However, several emerging Internet payment systems are overcoming this barrier.[4]

A small firm's failure to incorporate the Internet into its plans will soon be equivalent to not using a computer at all. The Internet is on its way to becoming an indispensable means by which small firms can reach large untapped markets and communicate with both suppliers and customers.

Desktop publishing provides a cost-effective way for small businesses to produce their own advertising brochures and newsletters. The design of the document appears on the computer monitor exactly as it will appear on the printed page—a quality known as WYSIWYG.

distributed processing
using two or more computers in combination to process data

COMPUTER SYSTEMS: HARDWARE AND SOFTWARE

Various types of computer systems exist for business applications, ranging from small, single-user personal computers to large multi-user systems. A computer system consists of the equipment (hardware) and the programs (software, or the instructions that control the steps the computer follows).

Types of Computers

Computers are classified into four broad categories. These categories are (1) personal computers (microcomputers), (2) minicomputers, (3) mainframe computers, and (4) supercomputers.

Many factors are involved in choosing the appropriate type of computer for a particular task. No one type is best suited for all applications; more than one type of computer can usually be used to accomplish the same result. Sometimes, the best solution is to use different types of computers linked together. For instance, a user might enter transaction data into a personal computer and then submit all of the data in a batch to a minicomputer or mainframe for processing. The use of two or more computers in combination to solve a problem is sometimes called **distributed processing.**

While larger companies use mainframes, and a few even have supercomputers, smaller firms generally use only personal computers and minicomputers. Thus, we will limit our discussion to these two types of hardware.

Action Report

TECHNOLOGICAL APPLICATIONS

Home-Based Entrepreneurs Increase Use of Computers

TECHNOLOGY

Home-based entrepreneurs are sharply expanding their use of computers and moving into increasingly sophisticated applications. Growing numbers of entrepreneurs in the United States are buying computers in order to start home-based businesses—John Stahle is one of them.

> *Four years ago, graphics designer John Stahle finally bought his first personal computer. It had a 9-inch black-and-white monitor, an internal speed of 7 megahertz and a minimum of supporting software. "It wasn't state-of-the-art, but I was able to work around it," said the New York home-based entrepreneur.*
>
> *Today, Mr. Stahle has moved up to a far more powerful personal computer, which runs at 68 megahertz and has a 16-inch color monitor. In addition, he works with three different sets of specialized software and has a fax, an external modem, a color printer, and an optional scanner. "The only [other] thing that I would love to do at home is do my own color proofs," said Mr. Stahle.*

For entrepreneurs such as Stahle, the expanded use of technology has meant better communications with customers, increased productivity, and time savings. Stahle noted, "What I can do in a half-hour once took me a day."

Source: Udayan Gupta, "Home-Based Entrepreneurs Expand Computer Use Sharply, Study Shows," *The Wall Street Journal*, October 13, 1995, p. B1.

PERSONAL COMPUTERS   **Personal computers (microcomputers)** are the least expensive and smallest computers. The term *personal computer* arose from the fact that the computer's operating instructions typically allow only one person at a time to use it. Personal computers can function in a stand-alone mode to enhance the productivity of one person or in a network with other personal computers.

Commercially, two large manufacturers of personal computers dominate the market—IBM and Apple. Additionally, several companies make IBM-compatible personal computers, or clones, which can use IBM-specific software. Historically, software created to be used on an IBM computer would not work on an Apple computer. However, many software producers provide versions of their programs for both types of computers. Also, Microsoft has developed user-friendly software known as Windows for IBMs and IBM compatibles that has minimized the differences between the IBM and Apple systems. Finally, IBM and Apple have jointly designed a personal computer, the Power PC, that can be used with either IBM or Apple software.

Typical software applications for a personal computer are word-processing programs for correspondence, spreadsheets for budgeting and graphs, and database programs for managing mailing lists. Tax preparation, financial statements, and project management are other tasks for which software applications exist.

Workstations are the most powerful personal computers. They have a special capability called **multitasking,** the ability to carry out more than one function at a time. For example, a secretary's workstation might need to simultaneously sort a

personal computer (microcomputer)
a small computer used by only one person at a time

workstations
powerful personal computers able to carry out multitasking

multitasking
the ability of a computer to carry out multiple functions at one time

large mailing list by zip code for bulk mailing purposes and receive an incoming facsimile (fax) transmission. More powerful operating system software gives workstations the multitasking feature.

minicomputer
a medium-sized computer that is capable of processing data input simultaneously from a number of sources

MINICOMPUTERS   A **minicomputer** affords multi-user accessibility to a common database. A small business with a high volume of credit sales requiring several clerks to enter data simultaneously in order to keep the billing and accounts receivable data current might need a minicomputer. The hardware of a minicomputer system is not very different from that of a personal computer, except that the minicomputer's memory and storage capacities are usually much larger. Each input device for a minicomputer may consist of only a keyboard and a monitor, which are connected to a common central processing unit. The operating system for a minicomputer is more complex than the same software for a personal computer. The operating system of a minicomputer must be capable of allocating processing time among simultaneous users.

throughput
the amount of work that can be done by a computer in a given amount of time

Local area networks have somewhat blurred the distinction between personal computers and minicomputers. Some of the multi-user functionality of a minicomputer can be replicated by a LAN. The **throughput,** or amount of work that can be done in a given amount of time, is usually higher for a correctly configured minicomputer than for a LAN. However, the overall price of the LAN may be lower. *There is always a trade-off between speed and cost when choosing a computer system.*

Both minicomputer and LAN environments usually require a high level of technical expertise on the part of the person managing the system. This requirement should be taken into consideration when evaluating the costs of alternative computer systems. Elaborate procedures may need to be implemented for such things as training and security. A minicomputer or LAN also requires formal daily backup of data (that is, a copy made and stored in another physical location) to guard against equipment malfunction or a natural disaster such as a fire. The data stored in a personal computer should be backed up as well, but the process is simpler because the volume of memory is much less for a stand-alone personal computer.

Computer Software

software
programs that provide operating instructions to a computer

The **software,** or operating instructions, of a computer system can be classified as either system software or application software.

system software
programs that control the internal functioning of a computer

SYSTEM SOFTWARE   System software provides instructions for the overall control of a computer's resources. The most common type of system software is the **operating system,** which controls the resources of a computer and the flow of information in and out of the computer. The operating system provides a link between the hardware and a specific application program, such as a customer billing system. For personal computers, the choices are limited with regard to operating systems. An IBM or IBM-compatible personal computer uses either the Disk Operating System (DOS) or OS/2. An IBM or IBM-compatible with multitasking capability must use OS/2. However, several choices of operating systems exist for minicomputers and especially mainframe. The preferred operating system is based on the type of work expected of the system.

operating system
the software that controls the flow of information in and out of a computer and links hardware to application programs

application software
programs that allow users to perform specific tasks on a computer

APPLICATION SOFTWARE   Application software refers to computer programs that perform specific types of functions for users. It can be classified as productivity packages or customized software.

Productivity Packages   Productivity packages include word-processing, spreadsheet, and database programs. With productivity packages, the user is not restricted to predefined functions but is free, within the bounds of the productivity package, to create original applications. For example, using a spreadsheet program, a small business owner might create a projected income statement in order to apply for a loan. The software might provide a template to facilitate the creation of the income statement. A **template** is essentially a blank form that a user simply fills with specific data in the assigned locations.

Word-processing programs allow the user to create, edit, and print documents that include text, graphics, and even scanned photos or artwork. Correspondence and office memorandums, for example, can be prepared by word processing. Spelling checkers and thesauruses have greatly extended the capabilities of word-processing programs. The mail-merge application, whereby a form letter is sent to a predefined list of customers on a regular basis, is a time-saving function of such a program. Some popular word-processing programs are *WordPerfect, Microsoft Word, Microsoft Word for Windows, ClarisWorks,* Ashton-Tate's *MultiMate Advantage,* and MicroPro's *WordStar.*

A **spreadsheet program** turns the computer screen into an electronic sheet of accounting paper divided into a grid of rows and columns. Applications involving calculations and graphs are best suited to a spreadsheet. By using the keyboard, the user can enter data into a **cell,** an intersection of a row and a column. These data entries can be titles, numbers, or formulas. Through these entries, applications such as budgets and loan schedules showing the amount of principal and interest in each payment can be prepared easily. Most spreadsheet programs have a list of powerful key words, known as *functions,* that allow for statistical and financial calculations, such as the return on an investment. "What if" scenarios can be played out in a spreadsheet to check the effect of changing assumptions in a financial analysis. Popular spreadsheet programs include *Lotus 1-2-3, Microsoft Excel,* Borland's *Quattro,* and Computer Associates' *SuperCalc.* Figure 21-1 provides an example of an electronic spreadsheet.

A **database program** is software that manages a file of related data, such as a customer list used for marketing purposes, containing a customer's name, address, date last contacted, and comments. New customers could be added, and data for existing customers could be modified easily. Mailing labels could be printed for mass mailings of advertisements. Popular database programs are Ashton-Tate's *dBase,* Symatec's *Q&A,* Borland's *Paradox,* and Microrim's *R:Base.*

Customized Software   Programs that allow a computer to process specific business functions such as billing, general ledger accounting, accounts receivable, and accounts payable are considered **customized software.** Customized software can be either purchased from another company or created in-house. Most small businesses do not need a full-time computer programmer but might engage one on a contract basis for special software customization needs. Some customized software packages have been tailored to the specific needs of particular kinds of small businesses. A general business system for an auto supply store, for example, is quite different from a system for a dentist. In some cases, a software vendor can offer modifications to adapt an existing software package to meet special needs. When purchasing customized packages, a business owner should find out whether modifications are possible and who would be responsible for making them.

Customized packages for small businesses are often a comprehensive system of programs that can be used individually or in combination. Typically, they are menu-driven systems on which the user simply selects a specific option from a series of choices. Mainly concerned with tracking data about customers, employ-

template
a pre-programmed form on which a user fills in blanks with specific data

word-processing program
application software that allows users to create, manipulate, and print text and graphics on a computer

spreadsheet program
application software that allows users to perform accounting and other numerical tasks on an electronic worksheet

cell
the intersection of a row and a column on a spreadsheet

database program
application software used to manage files of related data

customized software
application programs designed or adapted for use by a particular company or type of business

Figure 21-1 *Electronic Spreadsheet*

	A	B	C	D	E	F	G
1				Pro Forma Income Statement			
2							
3							
4							
5							
6	Year	1	2	3	4	5	
7							Total
8	Sales	$110,000	$121,000	$133,100	$146,410	$161,051	$671,561
9							
10	Cost of Goods Sold	82,500	90,750	99,825	109,808	120,788	503,671
11							
12	Gross Profit	27,500	30,250	33,275	36,603	40,263	167,890
13							
14	Operating Expenses						
15	Salaries	14,000	14,000	15,500	15,500	17,000	76,000
16	Commissions	2,750	3,205	3,328	3,660	4,026	16,789
17	Utilities	1,375	1,513	1,664	1,830	2,013	8,395
18	Telephone	2,200	2,420	2,662	2,928	3,221	13,431
19	Depreciation	1,500	1,500	1,500	1,500	1,500	7,500
20	Travel	3,025	3,328	3,660	4,026	4,429	18,468
21	Promotion	1,375	1,513	1,664	1,830	2,013	8,395
22	Payroll taxes	980	980	1,085	1,085	1,190	5,320
23							
24	Total Expenses	27,205	28,278	31,062	32,360	35,392	154,297
25							
26	Oper. Profit Before Taxes	295	1,973	2,213	4,243	4,870	13,593
27							
28	Taxes	89	592	664	1,273	1,461	4,078
29							
30	Profit After Taxes	207	1,381	1,549	2,970	3,409	9,515

ees, and assets such as inventories, these systems contain modules for payroll, order entry, billing, accounts receivable, accounts payable, general ledger accounting, and inventory management. Let's look more closely at each of these modules.

- The payroll function is often the first to be automated in a small business. A payroll program requires as input time sheets, wage rates, tax tables, and other information pertinent to calculating the salaries or wages of employees. The output of a payroll program includes paychecks or electronic transfers to employee bank accounts, updated year-to-date records detailing earnings and withholdings, and entries to the general ledger accounting system. At the end of each year, W-2 tax forms are printed for each employee.
- Order-entry programs are used for entering initial data concerning an order for merchandise or service. The ability to check against existing inventory levels to determine whether an order can be filled or a backorder is necessary is part of the program. An invoice detailing information about the order is its normal output. An order-entry program will often prepare a picking ticket specifying a list of merchandise to be selected from inventory.
- Billing programs are used to collect the data necessary to compile a periodic statement sent to customers. The statement lists a customer's previous balance

and any current charges or payments since the last statement was issued. A document to be returned with the payment also might be included.

- An accounts receivable program keeps track of the current amount owed to a business by its customers. The amount owed may also be aged into categories of less than 30 days, 30 to 60 days, 60 to 90 days, and over 90 days. This type of program can generate printed reports to identify customers who are not paying on a timely basis.

- An accounts payable program is used to track the amounts owed to vendors or suppliers and often to write checks to pay the bills. Some accounts payable programs are even sophisticated enough to question whether to make an early payment to qualify for a discount in view of projected cash needs.

- A general ledger accounting program performs the bookkeeping function for a business and prepares income statements, balance sheets, and cash flow statements as required. For just a few hundred dollars, a small business can computerize its accounting system with a general ledger program.

- An inventory management program maintains data about items in stock, including items available for sale by a distributor or component parts to be used in manufacturing. As items are received or sold (used), the quantity-on-hand amounts are adjusted. Sophisticated inventory management programs are integrated with order-entry and purchasing programs so that the quantities on hand can be adjusted automatically.[5]

COMMUNICATION AMONG COMPUTERS

3 Explain the role of computers in data communications.

The process of communicating data between two or more computers in different geographic locations is referred to as **telecommunications.** The resulting improvement in timeliness of information plays a crucial role in effective decision making.

telecommunications
the exchange of data among remote computers

communications control program
software that controls the flow of information between computers

terminal emulation
a communications mode that allows personal computers to exchange information with mainframes

network card
a circuit card required for computers on a local area network

file server
the computer that stores the programs and common data for a local area network

network control program
software that controls access to a local area network

Internal communications are simplified in a LAN office, where each user has access to the common database and programs shared by the personal computers within the network.

Speed and accuracy are increased when documents are transmitted electronically. Because of the increased need to exchange data rapidly, computers are becoming more standardized. In the future, few computers will exist in an unconnected, stand-alone mode.

Hardware and Software Requirements

A **communications control program** is necessary to connect a microcomputer through a telephone line to another microcomputer or to a larger host computer system, such as a minicomputer or mainframe. This type of program can provide access to public information service companies such as CompuServe and Prodigy, which offer such services as E-mail, stock prices, and airline schedules with reservation options. Some of the services are included in the monthly subscription fee, while others are obtained at additional cost. Most public information services also offer electronic bulletin boards where a user can give and receive information about a specific subject.

A communications control program also allows a personal computer to perform as though it were a terminal for a larger system. This mode of communication is often referred to as **terminal emulation,** and it provides small businesses with a means of communicating with vendors that have larger computer systems. *Crosstalk* and Hayes's *Smartcom II* are widely used communications control programs.

The linking of personal computers in a local area network (LAN) requires additional hardware and software. Each networked computer must have a special circuit card known as a **network card** in order to communicate on a LAN. At least one of the personal computers in the network must be dedicated as a **file server** to store the programs and common database that are shared by the different computers in the network. The file server is usually more powerful than the rest of the computers in the LAN in terms of processing speed, RAM memory, and disk storage capacity. Special software known as a **network control program** is also stored on the file server. The network control program provides security and controls access to the network. Two popular network control programs are Novell's *NetWare* and Microsoft's *LAN Manager.*

Telecommunications Applications

The **client/server model** has gained in popularity with the advent of local area networks, which are replacing minicomputer systems in many small businesses. In the conventional minicomputer environment, data and application programs are stored on a centralized system. Users log on to the centralized minicomputer and run application programs from it. When a number of users are logged on, the performance of the minicomputer can be seriously degraded. The terminal used in communicating with the minicomputer acts as a "dumb" communication device; no processing actually takes place there. In a client/server model, the user's personal computer (the client) runs or processes the application software locally, without waiting on a host computer. The client makes data requests to the server (a file server in the LAN), but the actual processing takes place at the client (personal computer) level. Response time and throughput can improve dramatically because the resources of a single CPU are not being divided among several users.

A major application of telecommunications technology is electronic data interchange (EDI), by which business documents such as purchase orders can be transmitted electronically rather than via such conventional means as mail or telephone. Orders are typically placed faster, and data-entry errors are reduced. Smaller inventories made possible by the speedier fulfillment of orders can also help improve profitability.[6]

Another use of telecommunications, **telecommuting,** allows employees to work at home by using a computer link. Some jobs, such as computer programming or technical writing, are well suited to telecommuting. Reduced employee fatigue (from long physical commutes) and decreased costs for office space are two of its benefits.

client/server model
a system whereby the user's personal computer (the client) obtains data from a central computer, but processing is done at the client level

telecommuting
working at home by using a computer link to the business location

OFFICE AND PRODUCTION TECHNOLOGY

Many computer-based products have helped office personnel become more productive. Local area networks allowing for information sharing and other "smart" devices have significantly changed how office work gets done.

4 Provide examples of computer-based office and production technology.

TECHNOLOGY

Computer-Based Office Technology

Local area networks have extended the technology of electronic mail to even the smallest businesses. **Electronic mail (E-mail)** allows users to send messages directly from one computer to another. Messages can be sent to a specific person or a predefined group of people. For example, a small business manager might want to send a message to only supervisory personnel. Also, computer-stored documents can be attached to the message. Most E-mail systems have an interface that works much like a simple word-processing program with a few special commands for receiving and transmitting messages.

Voice mail is another type of technology used in office communications. Voice mail is a computerized system that captures telephone messages and stores them on a magnetic disk. On returning to the office, the user can dial a number that will play back the calls. The voice mailbox can also be accessed from a remote telephone. For an office setting without a receptionist, voice mail is an attractive alternative.

Desktop publishing is the production of brochures, advertisements, manuals, and newsletters using a personal computer–based system. Pre-existing artwork, known as clip art, can be "pasted" electronically into documents, and photos or di-

electronic mail (E-mail)
text messages transmitted directly from one computer to another

voice mail
telephone messages stored by a computerized system

desktop publishing
the production of high-quality printed documents on a personal computer system

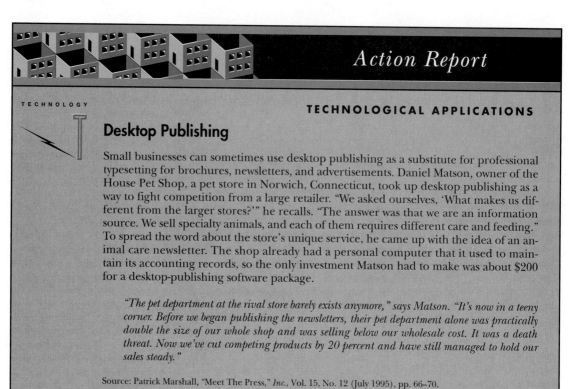

Action Report

TECHNOLOGY

TECHNOLOGICAL APPLICATIONS

Desktop Publishing

Small businesses can sometimes use desktop publishing as a substitute for professional typesetting for brochures, newsletters, and advertisements. Daniel Matson, owner of the House Pet Shop, a pet store in Norwich, Connecticut, took up desktop publishing as a way to fight competition from a large retailer. "We asked ourselves, 'What makes us different from the larger stores?'" he recalls. "The answer was that we are an information source. We sell specialty animals, and each of them requires different care and feeding." To spread the word about the store's unique service, he came up with the idea of an animal care newsletter. The shop already had a personal computer that it used to maintain its accounting records, so the only investment Matson had to make was about $200 for a desktop-publishing software package.

"The pet department at the rival store barely exists anymore," says Matson. "It's now in a teeny corner. Before we began publishing the newsletters, their pet department alone was practically double the size of our whole shop and was selling below our wholesale cost. It was a death threat. Now we've cut competing products by 20 percent and have still managed to hold our sales steady."

Source: Patrick Marshall, "Meet The Press," *Inc.*, Vol. 15, No. 12 (July 1995), pp. 66–70.

WYSIWYG
acronym for "What You See Is What You Get"

facsimile (fax) machine
a device that transmits and receives copies of documents via telephone lines

fax modem
a circuit board that allows a document to be sent from a computer disk to another computer or a fax machine

multimedia
a combination of text, graphics, audio, and video in a single presentation

agrams can be scanned and then incorporated. Desktop publishing systems can greatly reduce the need for the services of graphic artists and professional printers. Desktop publishing requires a more powerful personal computer than does routine word processing. The computer monitor should be large enough to accommodate full-page composition and should possess the quality known as WYSIWYG. **WYSIWYG** stands for "What You See Is What You Get" and means that what appears on the monitor is what the document will look like when it is printed. A fast microprocessor is needed in order to rapidly update the display on the monitor when changes are made. A larger-than-normal hard disk is required in desktop publishing because documents that include photos or artwork take up large amounts of disk storage space. A laser printer is necessary to produce a high-quality final copy. Laser printers offer many different font styles and sizes, allowing for near-typeset quality.

Few businesses operate today without the services of a **facsimile (fax) machine.** A fax machine transmits or receives copies of physical documents across standard telephone lines. Most fax machines print about one to four pages per minute. A recent innovation for personal computers is a device known as a fax modem. A **fax modem** is a circuit board installed in a personal computer that allows the sender to transfer documents on a computer disk directly to a fax machine or to another personal computer having a fax modem. This eliminates printing the document and then feeding it into a fax machine. Incoming faxes can be stored on disk and printed later. A fax modem cannot completely replace a regular fax machine, because users may still need to transfer documents that are not stored on disk.

Multimedia technology and presentation software merge text, graphics, audio, and video into a single presentation. The presentation can be viewed on a regular computer monitor or through a large-screen projection system. Multimedia presentations are popular at trade shows for promoting products or services. Such a presentation can be made interactive, with the viewer selecting different paths through the presentation. Multimedia technology is also useful in developing computer-assisted training materials. An employee can watch a video clip on a new process and then take a test to measure his or her comprehension. Remedial training can then be provided for the questions missed. All of this can be done with a single multimedia presentation.

Computer-Based Production Technology

As we noted at the beginning of the chapter, many small manufacturers use computer-aided design (CAD) and computer-aided manufacturing (CAM). Used to automate the design process for new products, a CAD system consists of a powerful workstation coupled with a drawing pad or a touch-sensitive monitor activated with a light pen. A designer or engineer can draw an on-screen model of the product, which can then be rotated to provide different views. The CAD system can even be used to test the product by simulating real-world stresses and strains on the model.

In computer-aided manufacturing (CAM), computers are used in the actual manufacturing process. For example, computers may monitor temperatures and pressures with sensors and automatically make adjustments based on certain guidelines, or they may control machines that cut and mold materials based on a model design. As an example of the use of CAM, robots are used in such processes as painting and welding. As another example, Gerber Garments Technology has developed computer software to be used in designing and cutting patterns for clothing manufacturers.

The manufacturing process also uses computer-based technology for **material requirement planning (MRP).** MRP systems produce a bill-of-materials document based on a firm's production schedule. The bill-of-materials document specifies the quantity of each component needed and when it is needed. This information is merged with inventory and purchasing data to provide the necessary materials on a timely basis. MRP systems can place orders for inventory items and minimize time wasted while waiting for critical parts to arrive.

material requirement planning (MRP) controlling the timely ordering of production materials by using computer software

Computer-based technology can save time as well as research and development dollars by permitting researchers to simulate conditions that might affect the product in the real world. Engineers find that using a computer-aided design (CAD) system, such as the one shown, allows them to develop concepts more quickly.

PURCHASING AND MANAGING TECHNOLOGY

A small business owner-manager who is considering the use of a computer system should analyze the potential benefits, estimate the costs, and work out an appropriate plan. There are no quick and easy procedures to follow in this decision process. Each business will have a unique set of requirements.

Assessing Feasibility

When considering a computer system, a small business owner-manager should first conduct a feasibility study to determine whether the firm has a sufficient workload or efficiency problem to justify the expense of a computer. The cost/benefit analysis may be difficult, but it is the most important step in the decision-making process. The analysis can be performed by the owner-manager or by an outside computer consultant. Feasibility should be assessed on both a technical basis and a cost basis. The technical feasibility will determine whether current technology exists to satisfy the firm's particular needs. The cost feasibility will ascertain whether the cost of the computer system is justified, based on the benefits received.

The feasibility study may indicate that the firm should not adopt an integrated computer system. However, with the decreased cost of computers, it is hard to imagine a small business that would not benefit from some level of automation.

Considering the Options

If the feasibility study justifies the use of a computer system, a choice must be made among several options: using a service bureau, using a time-sharing relationship, leasing a computer, or buying a computer.

service bureaus
firms that use their computer systems to process data for business customers

SERVICE BUREAUS　　**Service bureaus** are firms that receive data from business customers, use their computer systems to perform the data processing required, and then return the processed information to the customers. Service bureaus charge a fixed fee for the use of their computers. For a small firm with a need to perform a single application and a lack of experience with computers, the service bureau represents a logical first choice.

Using a service bureau has several advantages. The user avoids an investment in equipment that will soon become obsolete and having to hire specially trained personnel. Some service bureaus provide guidance to make it easier for novice users to start and expand computer usage. The disadvantages of using a service bureau include slow turnarounds on processed information, divulgence of confidential information to outside parties, and difficulties in working with outsiders unfamiliar with the user's procedures.

time sharing
accessing the capabilities of a powerful computer system by paying a variable fee for the privilege of using it

TIME SHARING　　**Time sharing** allows a business to use the capabilities of an appropriate computer system without buying or leasing. A business pays a variable fee for the privilege of using the computer system and must have at least one terminal in order to input and receive data. The terminal is connected to the time-sharing computer over the telephone line via a modem.

Early time-sharing systems provided computer time for professionals who knew how to program a computer. Today, time sharing is more frequently used to run existing programs to process data for a company. The time-sharing option is a good first or second step for small firms that decide to computerize.

The advantages of time sharing include maintenance of control over company records, use of more sophisticated application programs, and lower installation cost. Possible disadvantages include increasing variable costs, work delays when other customers are using the system, and the need for the user to have some computer ability.

LEASING A COMPUTER   Leasing a computer generally means possessing and using it without buying it. The most common leasing arrangement is the full payback lease. Usually, lease periods are fairly long (around eight years). A shorter lease period may be more expensive, but it reduces the possibility of having to stick with outdated equipment. With the rapid advances that are occurring in computer technology, some users claim that computer equipment becomes obsolete every two years!

Two advantages of leasing are access to an appropriate computer system without a large initial investment and the availability of consulting help from the leasing company's specialists. The disadvantages of leasing relate to the length of the lease period and the possibility of having to use outdated equipment. In addition, leasing a computer requires the lessee to have some personnel who are skilled in computer use.[7]

BUYING A COMPUTER   The advantages of buying a computer system are that the small firm has total control of and unlimited access to the computer and that depreciation expense reduces the owner's taxable income. Although a new computer system will not save a troubled business, it can help a successful business become more successful. The disadvantages are the significant cost of buying a computer system, the need for trained personnel to run the programs, the cost of maintaining the hardware, and the possible obsolescence of the equipment.

For small firms that purchase a computer system, the key to success is a carefully planned approach. The following steps outline a systematic approach:

Step 1: Learn About Computers   Be aware that computerization will require much time and thought. Visit other firms that are already using computers for similar applications. Ask for a vendor demonstration, and perhaps hire a consultant or a data-processing manager with experience; at the least, put someone in charge of overseeing the process.

Step 2: Analyze the Manual System   Examine all transactions that involve routine actions to find more efficient procedures, if possible. Involve as many employees as possible in analyzing the manual system because early participation by those who will use the new system will improve the chances of success. Detailed study of the areas of the business that might be computerized will help clarify computer needs. This information allows computer vendors to propose ways to computerize a company efficiently.

Step 3: Clearly Define the Expectations for the Computer System   After reviewing the manual system, decide what the computer system is expected to do, immediately and for five years into the future. Be specific about the functions the computer will perform—for example, processing mailing lists, payroll preparation, inventory control, or sales analyses. Possible sources of help in determining exact needs are other small businesses, computer consultants, or an employee with computer experience.

Step 4: Compare Costs and Benefits   It is easy to estimate the costs of current manual systems, but it is difficult to estimate the costs of computerization. Obtain estimates from several vendors. And remember to consider hidden costs, such as employee stress during the conversion.

Step 5: Establish a Timetable for Installing the Computer System   Plan to install the computer system on a five-year schedule. It is best to automate the simplest manual operations first. Be sure to allow enough time for each computerized operation to be implemented and tested completely. Be aware that the transition will be slow and be willing to adjust the timetable from time to time as unexpected problems occur.

Step 6: Write a Tight Contract   Both the purchaser and the vendor should be willing to sign a formal agreement that specifies the functions the computer system is expected to perform. The specifications should contain details rather than general summaries of expected performance. Requirements for equipment servicing should also be clearly specified, as well as what is required of the vendor before each step in the payment schedule. It is usually unwise to agree to field-test innovative equipment. It's best to purchase equipment and programs that have been working in other small businesses.

Step 7: Obtain Programs First, Then the Hardware   It is important for the first-time computer buyer to look first at the programs needed, not the hardware. There are several options for obtaining the necessary programs:

- Obtain programs that are already working at similar small businesses.
- Hire a programmer to write customized programs.
- Hire a consultant who has created programs that can be adapted to serve most of the necessary functions.

Figure 21-2

Resistance to Computerization Is Usually Short-Lived

"I don't want to talk to a middleman . . . put me straight through to the computer!"

From *The Wall Street Journal*—Permission, Cartoon Features Syndicate.

An owner-manager must make the decision about which alternative is best for his or her business. Once the necessary programs are identified, the most economical hardware to run those programs can be obtained.

Step 8: Prepare Your Employees for Conversion   Any employees affected by the decision to buy a computer system should be involved in the decision from the very beginning. It is common for employees to resist computerization because they feel that the computer is a threat to their jobs. Assure employees that the change will be beneficial to the business and, consequently, beneficial to them. People who are unwilling to become involved can be moved to other departments, if possible. All employees, from top management to clerical workers, must support the computerization for a successful transition to take place (see Figure 21-2).

Step 9: Make the Conversion   First, carefully assign the responsibilities for the conversion process. The conversion period will require overtime because daily work must continue. Second, remember to convert the manual operations one at a time. If possible, run the manual system parallel with the computer system until rough spots are ironed out. Third, be patient and remember that problems will occur. Do not plan on using the system until it is functioning effectively.

Step 10: Reap the Benefits   The goal of the transition to computerized operations is to obtain the following benefits:

- More timely, accurate, economical, and extensive information
- Better organization of information
- Current information on costs and sales
- Current information on inventory levels
- Better cash control

Evaluating and Maintaining the System

After a computer system has been installed and is in use, the process of evaluation and maintenance begins. Only when the system is in actual use will most problems surface. Some problems may be corrected with updates of the software, and sometimes temporary fixes may be necessary. The software vendor or contract programmers can make the necessary program modifications. New legislation or business reorganization can also require such modifications.

TRENDS IN COMPUTER-BASED TECHNOLOGY

Small companies are entering the information age just as corporate America did a decade ago; the trend is irreversible. According to the National Federation of Independent Businesses, in 1980, only 25 percent of small firms used computers. By 1990, this number had increased to 68 percent. In 1994, computer purchases increased by 14 percent.[8]

Computer manufacturers view small business as the next great untapped market. Thomas Martin, an executive with Dell Computers, notes:

> *The smaller guys are adopting new technologies faster than our larger accounts. . . . The payoff that larger companies have already seen from effective technology use—higher productivity, quality improvements, and faster turnaround—should start kicking in for small businesses in the second half of the 1990s.*[9]

Discuss the ways in which computers may affect small businesses in the future.

6

TECHNOLOGY

1 Identify basic applications of computer technology that are appropriate for small firms.

- Computer technology is used extensively in small businesses for tracking financial and marketing transactions.
- Computer-aided design (CAD) and computer-aided manufacturing (CAM) systems are widely used by small manufacturers.
- Office automation has grown dramatically with the popularity of local area networks.
- Smaller companies are exploring the different ways in which the Internet can help build and sustain business.

2 Describe the hardware and software components of an information-processing system.

- Computers are categorized as personal computers (microcomputers), minicomputers, mainframes, and supercomputers. Small firms primarily use personal computers and minicomputers.
- Customized software is used for such tasks as payroll processing, order entry, billing, accounts receivable, accounts payable, general ledger accounting, and inventory management.
- Productivity software consists of programs for word processing, spreadsheet analysis, and database management.

3 Explain the role of computers in data communications.

- Electronic data interchange (EDI) allows small businesses to place orders with vendors and to access information services.
- Telecommuting allows employees to work at home by using a computer link.

4 Provide examples of computer-based office and production technology.

- Office technology has improved through the use of E-mail, voice mail, desktop publishing, facsimile machines and modems, and multimedia capabilities.
- Small manufacturers have benefited from computer-aided design (CAD), computer-aided manufacturing (CAM), and material requirement planning (MRP) software.
- Multimedia technology and presentation software merge text, graphics, audio, and video into a single presentation.

Continue on next page

The trend suggests that the number of businesses with LANs is certain to rise in the near future as such networks become cheaper and easier to use. The increased use of telecommunications will no doubt dominate new computer applications for small businesses.

Higher levels of software integration will allow computers and software systems to "speak" to one another more easily than they can currently. For example, a single data update such as changing a customer's address will change the information in all the necessary data files. The ability to "cut and paste" information from one application to another will make computer systems more productive.

Computer networks will be used to conduct electronic meetings. In conventional meetings, some participants may feel intimidated and fail to participate. A computer network will allow anonymous participation, if so desired. Research is now being conducted to determine whether any loss in meeting effectiveness occurs when participants are unable to react to the visual cues and body language that a face-to-face meeting provides.

Business presentations and employee training will benefit from the increased merging of computer and television technology in the form of multimedia software. Multimedia capabilities will allow for more varied applications in the future.

Geographic information systems (GIS) will become widely used to create "smart" maps. A small business will be able to connect a physical map with a customer database and carry out "what if" analyses with the output in map form. Decisions about optimal shipping routes and new store locations will be improved through GIS.

geographic information systems (GIS) programs that connect a physical map with a customer database

A recent Gallup survey, commissioned by SyQuest Technology Inc., a Fremont, California maker of computer peripherals, surveyed 1,002 owners of home-based businesses. Here are some of the findings of the study:

- Nearly one-third of the businesses surveyed own more than one computer, with about 13 percent of those having three or more computers.
- In addition to computers, a majority of the home-based businesses own printers, modems, or fax modems. Forty percent of these home businesses own removable data storage, and 19 percent own scanners.

- Entrepreneurs are commonly using their computers for such functions as desktop publishing, data storage and analysis, and sales and marketing. More than 80 percent use their computers for billing and accounting.
- A majority of home-based businesses had upgraded their equipment since they first began using computers. However, only a small number of these businesses expect to make additional purchases in the next 12 months.
- Thirty percent of home-based businesses have access to the Internet, and 15 percent are networked with other users.
- Nearly 40 percent of the entrepreneurs expect to use their computers to order materials on-line. Twenty-six percent expect to be networked to other offices and about one in five expects to use the Internet to advertise or sell products.[10]

Given the accelerated pace of computer use, small business owners and managers must be computer-literate and able to determine which computer technology will best help their businesses in a cost-effective way—or forfeit a competitive edge in the future.

DISCUSSION QUESTIONS

1. What is meant by the term *distributed processing*?
2. What are the advantages of multitasking?
3. What are the four categories of computer hardware?
4. What are the two types of software?
5. Give an example of the usefulness of a spreadsheet program.
6. What role does a modem play in a computer system?
7. What are the advantages of connecting personal computers in a local area network (LAN)?
8. What is EDI? How do small businesses use EDI?

5 **Outline the process for selecting the computer system best suited to a small firm's needs.**

- The process for selecting a computer system includes assessing feasibility, considering the available options, and evaluating and maintaining the system.
- The small business has several options for computerization: using a service bureau, time sharing, leasing a computer, or buying a computer.

6 **Discuss the ways in which computers may affect small businesses in the future.**

- To maintain a competitive advantage, today's small business manager needs to be computer and telecommunications literate.
- Computers will soon affect every aspect of a small company's operations, including electronic meetings, business presentations, and employee training.
- Geographic information systems will improve business decisions regarding shipping routes and potential locations for a new store or plant.

New Terms and Concepts

electronic data interchange (EDI) 455

computer-aided design (CAD) 456

computer-aided manufacturing (CAM) 456

local area network (LAN) 456

work group software 456

distributed processing 458

personal computer (microcomputer) 459

workstations 459

multitasking 459

minicomputer 460

throughput 460

software 460

system software 460

operating system 460

application software 460

template 461

word-processing program 461

spreadsheet program 461

cell 461

database program 461

customized software 461

telecommunications 464

communications control program 464

terminal emulation 464

network card 464

file server 464

network control program 464

client/server model 465

telecommuting 465

electronic mail (E-mail) 465

voice mail 465

desktop publishing 465

WYSIWYG 466

facsimile (fax) machine 466

fax modem 466

multimedia 466

material requirement planning (MRP) 467

service bureaus 468

time sharing 468

geographic information systems (GIS) 472

Situation 1 Rick's Hardware carries over 15,000 line items from over 200 vendors. A time-sharing arrangement for billing and accounts receivable is currently the only computerized operation. The only way to tell whether a particular line item is in stock is to have a clerk physically search for the item. The owner-manager, Rick Johnson, believes too much inventory is not selling. Store clerks need access to current stock levels and pricing information simultaneously for handling over-the-counter sales and sales called in by outside salespersons. Johnson is considering installing an in-house computer system for the company. Several departments of the company will need access to the computer information system throughout the workday.

Question 1 What is the first step that Johnson should take in exploring further computerization?

Question 2 Discuss two types of computer systems that might be used by Rick's Hardware.

Question 3 Which type of application software, customized or productivity, would be appropriate for Rick's Hardware?

Situation 2 Rather than having separate offices, a group of eight independent insurance agents have decided to share overhead by occupying a single office complex. They plan on sharing a reception area and office equipment such as a photocopier and fax machine. Each agent has his or her own personal computer. The agents have expressed an interest in having access to a laser printer and some common insurance-related databases. They would also like access to E-mail, since they will work together with some clients.

Question 1 Explain what can be done to connect the agents' individual personal computers. What additional hardware and software will be required?

Question 2 What can the agents use as an alternative to a standard fax machine for transmitting computer-generated documents to clients?

Situation 3 Alan Wills is a co-owner of Do Rags, Inc. The firm designs and sells headwear, clothing, and accessories for active life-styles. Its product mix consists of ski headwear, summer headwear, and screen-printed tee-shirts, which it sells to retailers. Wills believes the firm could increase its sales significantly by advertising on the Internet. However, he doesn't know how to use the Internet. In fact, his ideas have come largely from talking to a friend who spends a lot of time "surfing the Internet."

Question 1 Would using the Internet be a good idea for Do Rags?

Question 2 How might Wills investigate the feasibility of using the Internet for his business?

---

9. Discuss the advantages and disadvantages of (a) service bureaus, (b) time-sharing systems, (c) leasing computers, and (d) buying computers.

10. List and discuss the steps a small business owner-manager should take when buying a computer system for the first time.

EXPERIENTIAL EXERCISES

1. Conduct a personal interview with a local small business manager who uses a computer system in his or her firm. Determine what types of hardware the business owns and why. Report your findings to the class.

2. Try to find a local small firm that does not yet use a computer. Interview the owner to determine whether she or he has ever considered computerizing the firm. Determine what reservations the owner has about purchasing a computer. Report your findings to the class.

3. Contact a local computer store owner or a salesperson representing a computer manufacturer, and ask him or her to demonstrate the hardware and software that small businesses might use. Bring copies of the sales literature to class.

4. Interview the manager of a local small firm to determine whether its computer applications are productivity packages, customized software, or both. Summarize your findings.

 CASE 21
Franklin Motors (p. 646)

This case looks at the decision-making process for a small firm that is considering a change from using a service bureau to purchasing an in-house computer system.

Part 6

22. **EVALUATING FINANCIAL PERFORMANCE**

23. **WORKING-CAPITAL MANAGEMENT AND CAPITAL BUDGETING**

24. **RISK AND INSURANCE MANAGEMENT**

Evaluating Financial Performance

Chapter 22

Max Klein

spotlight on small business

The importance of an effective accounting system cannot be overstated. When Max Klein bought Mike's Meat Market in Nashua, New Hampshire in 1987, he inherited a paper-and-pencil accounting system and outside payroll preparation for his 11 employees by a firm that charged extra for weekend work—which was necessary for the Monday paydays Klein insisted on. To eliminate the outside firm's weekend preparation charges, he brought the payroll work in-house, costing him free time on Sundays.

Klein eliminated working on Sundays by adopting a computerized accounting system, *One-Write Plus.* Almost immediately, weekly payroll chores "went from taking more than two hours Sunday after work to about 15 to 30 minutes," Klein says.

The understanding he has gained of his market's cash flow and the confidence he has in the accuracy of the tax forms generated are indirect benefits of computers, Klein says. The accounting software "lets us know where we are, and we don't incur any type of penalties to the government. . . . I just can't say enough about it."

"Small business owners . . . have become tremendously more sophisticated about knowing how their business functions," says Ted Needleman, editor of *Accounting Technology.* "A lot of that is [a result of] their maintaining good financial records." Moreover, he says, entrepreneurs are demanding—and getting—management information from their accounting systems.

Source: Ripley Hotch, "Accounting Programs That You Can More Than Count On," *Nation's Business,* Vol. 33, No. 6 (June 1995), pp. 45, 46.

After studying this chapter, you should be able to:

1 Identify the basic requirements for an accounting system.

2 Explain two alternative accounting options.

3 Describe the purpose of and procedures related to internal control.

4 Evaluate a firm's liquidity.

5 Assess a firm's operating profitability.

6 Measure a firm's use of debt or equity financing.

7 Evaluate the rate of return earned on the owners' investment.

Managers must have accurate, meaningful, and timely information if they are to make good decisions. This is particularly true concerning financial information about a firm's operations. Experience suggests that inadequacy of the accounting system is a primary factor in small business failures. Owner-managers of small firms sometimes feel that they have less need for financial information because of their personal involvement in day-to-day operations. Such a belief is not only incorrect but also dangerously deceptive.

In this chapter, we first examine the basic ingredients of an effective accounting system. Then, we suggest how to use accounting data to draw conclusions about a firm's financial performance.

ACCOUNTING ACTIVITIES IN SMALL FIRMS

1 Identify the basic requirements for an accounting system.

Most small business owner-managers are not expert accountants—nor should they expect to be. But every one of them should know enough about the accounting process, including financial statements, to recognize which accounting methods are best for their company.

Basic Requirements for Accounting Systems

An accounting system structures the flow of financial information to develop a complete picture of a firm's financial activities. Conceivably, a few very small firms may not require formal financial statements. Most small firms, however, need at least monthly financial statements, which should be computer-generated. The benefits of using a computer in developing financial information are so great and the cost so low that it makes little sense to do otherwise.

FULFILLMENT OF ACCOUNTING OBJECTIVES   Regardless of its level of sophistication, any accounting system for a small business should accomplish the following objectives:

- Provide an accurate, thorough picture of operating results
- Permit a quick comparison of current data with prior years' operating results and budgetary goals
- Offer financial statements for use by management, bankers, and prospective creditors
- Facilitate prompt filing of reports and tax returns to regulatory and tax-collecting government agencies
- Reveal employee fraud, theft, waste, and record-keeping errors

GENERALLY ACCEPTED ACCOUNTING PRINCIPLES   In seeking to develop and interpret financial statements, an owner-manager must remember that certain generally accepted accounting principles, or GAAPs, govern the preparation of such statements. For example, the principle of *conservatism* guides accountants; thus, an accountant will typically choose the most conservative method available. For example, inventories are reported at the lower of either cost or current market value. Another principle governing the preparation of statements is *consistency,* meaning that a given item on a statement will be handled in the same way every month and every year so that comparability of the data will be assured. Also, the principle of *full disclosure* compels an accountant to insist that all liabilities be shown and all material facts be presented. This principle is intended to prevent misleading any investor who might read the firm's financial statements.

AVAILABILITY AND QUALITY OF ACCOUNTING RECORDS   An accounting system provides the framework for managerial control of a firm. The effectiveness of the system basically rests on a well-designed and well-managed record-keeping system. In addition to the financial statements intended for external use with bankers and investors (the balance sheet, the income statement, and the cash flow statement), internal accounting records should be kept. The major types of internal accounting records and the financial decisions to which they are related are as follows:

- *Accounts receivable records.* Records of receivables are vital not only for decisions on credit extension but also for accurate billing and for maintaining good customer relations. An analysis of these records will reveal the effectiveness of a firm's credit and collection policies.
- *Accounts payable records.* Records of liabilities show what the firm owes to suppliers, facilitate the taking of cash discounts, and allow payments to be made when due.
- *Inventory records.* Adequate records are essential for the control and security of inventory items. In addition, they supply information for use in purchasing, maintenance of adequate stock levels, and computation of turnover ratios.
- *Payroll records.* Payroll records show the total salaries paid to employees and provide a base for computing and paying payroll taxes.
- *Cash records.* Carefully maintained records showing all receipts and disbursements are necessary to safeguard cash. They provide essential information about cash flows and cash balances.
- *Fixed asset records.* Fixed asset records show the original cost of each asset and the depreciation taken to date, along with other information such as the condition of the asset.
- *Other accounting records.* Among the other accounting records that are vital to the efficient operation of a small business are the insurance register (showing all policies in force), records of leaseholds, and records of the firm's investments outside of its business.

USE OF COMPUTER SOFTWARE PACKAGES   Computer software packages can be used to provide the accounting records discussed earlier. Most of the software packages include the following features:

- A checkbook that automatically calculates a firm's cash balance, prints checks, and reconciles the account with the bank statement at month's end
- Automatic preparation of income statements, balance sheets, and cash flow statements
- A cash budget that compares actual expenditures with budgeted expenditures
- Preparation of subsidiary journal accounts—accounts receivable, accounts payable, and other high-activity accounts

In addition, numerous software packages fulfill specialized accounting needs such as graphing, cash flow analysis, and tax preparation. The small business owner can choose from a wide variety of useful software.

Action Report

ENTREPRENEURIAL EXPERIENCES

He Asks to Be Audited—Often

For many small firms, the use of an outside accountant cannot be justified based on the benefits received relative to the cost. But even when it may make sense, some firms will not hire an outside accountant until they feel pressure from their bankers.

Anthony Miranda, president of Protocol Telecommunications, made the decision to hire an outside accountant to perform regular audits on his company—even before he was required to do so by his banker. Miranda pays the accountant a monthly retainer of $1,000 to audit the company's annual financial statements and to supervise the preparation of the company's quarterly financial statements. "I wanted there to be no question then—or at any time—that our financial information was misstated or less than fully disclosed," he says.

"Our bankers were impressed by our decision to upgrade our financial reports without any requirements from them," Miranda recalls. "That has helped us expand our credit line as necessary."

Source: Jill Anfresky Fraser, Ed., "He Asks to Be Audited—Often," *Inc.*, Vol. 16, No. 14 (December 1994), p. 132.

There are an almost unlimited number of options in terms of accounting software that is appropriate for a small firm. However, a small group of programs are most widely used. In the September 1995 issue of *PC World*, Theresa W. Carey featured the six leaders in the entry-level category of accounting software programs. In beginning the comparisons, Carey states:

Now is the time for all you small business owners to dump that pastiche of Post-it notes, pencils, paper—and faith—you've been using to keep track of your company's finances. Today's Windows accounting programs, aimed at small businesses, without an accountant on staff, can help you do the job faster and smarter, with less jargon, more guidance, and features that make it easier to enter and use your financial data.[1]

The six programs, which range in cost between $100 and $300, are *DacEasy, Great Plains' Profit, M.Y.O.B., QuickBooks, Peachtree Accounting*, and *Simply Accounting*. While these programs have been well tested and widely used, considerable care should be taken in buying either software or hardware. The chance of acquiring computer equipment or programs that do not fit a firm's needs is still significant.

OUTSIDE ACCOUNTING SERVICES   As an alternative to record keeping by an employee or a member of the owner's family, a firm may have its financial records kept by a certified public accountant or by a bookkeeping firm or service bureau that caters to small businesses. Very small firms often find it convenient to have the same person or agency keep their books and prepare their financial statements and tax returns.

Numerous small public accounting firms offer complete accounting services to small businesses. The services of such accounting firms are usually offered at a lower cost than are those of larger accounting firms. However, larger accounting firms have begun paying closer attention to the accounting needs of small businesses. Although their fees are higher than those of the accountant down the street, discounts are usually available. While fees are an important consideration in selecting an accountant, other major factors, such as whether the accountant has experience in the particular industry in which the entrepreneur is operating, play a large part in this decision.[2]

Mobile bookkeepers also serve small firms in some areas, bringing a mobile office that includes computer equipment to a firm's premises, where they obtain the necessary data and prepare the financial statements. Use of mobile bookkeeping can be a fast, inexpensive, and convenient approach to filling certain accounting needs.

Alternative Accounting Options

2 Explain two alternative accounting options.

Accounting records can be kept in just about any form as long as they provide users with needed data and meet legal requirements. Very small firms have some options in selecting accounting systems and accounting methods. We examine two such accounting options—cash versus accrual accounting, and single-entry versus double-entry systems—in the following sections. These two alternatives represent only the most basic issues in developing an accounting system.

CASH VERSUS ACCRUAL ACCOUNTING   The major distinction between cash and accrual accounting is the point at which a firm reports revenue and expenses. The **cash method of accounting** is easier to use and reports revenue and expenses only when cash is received or payment is made. In contrast, with the **accrual method of accounting,** revenue and expenses are reported when they are incurred, regardless of when the cash is received or payment is made.

cash method of accounting (cash-basis accounting) a method of accounting that reports transactions only when cash is received or a payment is made

accrual method of accounting (accrual-basis accounting) a method of accounting that matches revenues when they are earned against the expenses associated with those revenues

The cash method of accounting is sometimes selected by very small firms, as well as those firms whose receivables move slowly and who want to help their cash flow by avoiding the payment of taxes on income not yet received. However, the cash method does not ultimately provide an accurate matching of revenue and expenses. Also, the accounting principle of consistency would consider alternating between a cash method and an accrual method of accounting to be unacceptable. On the other hand, the accrual method of accounting matches revenue when earned against expenses associated with it. The accrual method, while involving more record keeping, is preferable because it provides a more realistic measure of profitability within an accounting period.

SINGLE-ENTRY VERSUS DOUBLE-ENTRY SYSTEMS   A single-entry record-keeping system is occasionally still found in the very small business. It is not, however, a system recommended for firms that are striving to grow and achieve effective financial planning. A single-entry system neither incorporates a balance sheet nor directly generates an income statement. A **single-entry system** is basically a checkbook system of receipts and disbursements.

single-entry system a checkbook system of accounting reflecting only receipts and disbursements

double-entry system a self-balancing accounting system that uses journals and ledgers

Introductory accounting textbooks usually provide information on setting up a **double-entry system.**[3] This type of accounting system provides a self-balancing mechanism that consists of two counterbalancing entries for each transaction recorded. It also uses record-keeping journals and ledgers, which can be found in most office supply retail stores. However, relatively simple computerized systems that are appropriate for most small firms are currently available.

Internal Control

As already noted, an effective accounting system is vital to a firm's success. Without the information provided by an accounting system, management cannot make informed decisions. However, the quality of a firm's accounting system is dependent on the effectiveness of internal controls that exist within the firm. **Internal control** is a system of checks and balances that plays a key role in safeguarding a firm's assets and in enhancing the accuracy and reliability of its financial statements. The importance of internal control has long been recognized in large corporations. However, some owners of smaller companies are concerned about the cost of a system of internal control or feel that such a system is not applicable for a small company. Nothing could be further from the truth.

Building internal controls within a small company is difficult, but no less important than for a large company. The absence of internal controls significantly increases the chances not only of fraud and theft but also of bad decisions based on inaccurate and untimely accounting information. Effective internal controls are also necessary for an audit by independent accountants. Certified public accountants are unwilling to express an opinion about a firm's financial statements if adequate internal controls are lacking.

Although a complete description of an internal control system is beyond the scope of this book, it is important to understand the concept. For example, one internal control is separation of employees' duties, so that the individual maintaining control over an asset is not the same person recording transactions in the accounting ledgers. That is, an employee who collects cash from customers should not be allowed to reconcile the bank statement. Here are some other examples of internal control:

- Identifying the various types of transactions that require the owners' authorization
- Establishing a procedure to ensure that checks presented for signature are accompanied by complete supporting documentation
- Limiting access to accounting records
- Sending bank statements directly to the owner
- Safeguarding blank checks
- Requiring all employees to take regular vacations so that any irregularity is likely to be revealed
- Controlling access to the computer facilities[4]

The importance of developing an effective system of internal control cannot be overemphasized. Extra effort may be needed to implement internal controls in a small company in which business procedures are informal and the segregation of duties is difficult because of the limited number of employees. Even so, it is best to try to develop such controls. An accountant may be of assistance in minimizing the problems that can result from the absence of internal controls.

3 Describe the purpose of and procedures related to internal control.

internal control
a system of checks and balances that safeguards assets and enhances the accuracy and reliability of financial statements

A working system of checks and balances is important to every business, large or small. Such a system decreases the chance of employee theft. For example, a business that uses internal controls would be sure that someone other than the cashier takes the cash deposits to the bank.

Action Report

ENTREPRENEURIAL EXPERIENCES

How Internal Controls Helped Solve Cash Flow Problems

Effective internal controls can do more than prevent fraud—they can make a firm more efficient in its operations. Bob Martin owns and manages Martin Distribution, a rapidly growing sports novelty company in its third year of operation, with 25 employees and total assets of over $3 million. Recently, although sales forecasts for the future indicate continued growth, the company experienced cash flow problems.

Martin hired a local CPA to study the situation. The accountant discovered the following problems:

- In the last three years, the average collection time on the firm's accounts receivable had increased from 30 days to 48 days, and the percentage of accounts receivable that were actually collected had decreased.
- Accounts receivable write-offs also increased during the same period by 67 percent.
- From the company's bank statements and deposit slips, the accountant determined that numerous deposits had been made by the company's office manager with a "less cash" notation. In addition, deposits were not being made on a regular basis.

A significant factor in the problem was a lack of internal controls. Credit policies were relaxed, cash handling was sloppy, and daily deposits were not made. To cover daily expenditures, cash was extracted from bank deposits.

The solution to the problem was relatively simple. The accountant suggested implementing several controls:

- A thorough investigation of the creditworthiness of prospective customers before extending credit
- Controls to help ensure that sales orders would not be filled without prior credit approval
- Periodic reviews of credit limits for existing customers
- Cash deposited intact on a daily basis

After approximately three months, the percentage of accounts receivable collected increased significantly. Bad debts and returns decreased, and profit margins increased. In addition, strict accountability was established for cash collections and miscellaneous daily cash expenditures.

Source: Jack D. Baker and John A. Marts, "Internal Control for Protection and Profits," *Small Business Forum*, Vol. 8, No. 2 (Fall 1990), p. 32. Adapted with permission.

ASSESSING A FIRM'S FINANCIAL PERFORMANCE

If an effective accounting system is in place, a firm's owner must determine how to use the data it generates most productively. If an owner has a good accounting system but does not use it, the owner is a little like Mark Twain's description of a person who does not read: "He who does not read is no better off than he who cannot read." We now offer a framework for interpreting financial statements that, hopefully, will clarify such statements for those persons who never took an accounting course or who had difficulty in such a course in college.

Since management decisions may affect a firm positively or negatively, an owner needs to understand the financial effect that those decisions may have. Ultimately, the results of operating decisions appear in a company's financial statements.

The exact methods used to interpret financial statements can vary, with the perspective of the interpreter determining what areas are emphasized. For example, a banker might assign more importance to some facts in making a loan decision than an entrepreneur would when analyzing the financial statements. But whatever perspective is taken, the issues are fundamentally the same and may be captured in the following four questions:

1. Does the company have the capacity to meet its short-term financial commitments ("short-term" meaning one year or less)?
2. Is the company producing adequate operating profits on its assets?
3. How is the company financing its assets?
4. Are the owners (stockholders) receiving an acceptable return on their equity investment?

The answers to these questions require restating the income statement data and the balance sheet data into relative terms, or **financial ratios.** Only in this way can comparisons be made with other firms or industry averages and across time. Typically, we use industry averages or norms published by companies such as Dun & Bradstreet, Robert Morris Associates, or Standard & Poor for comparison purposes.[5] Table 22-1 shows the industry norms for the computer and software retailing industry, as reported by Robert Morris Associates. Robert Morris Associates compiles financial ratios for banks to use in their analysis of companies seeking loans. As shown in the table, the ratios are reported by firm size.

financial ratios
restatements of selected income statement and balance sheet data in relative terms

---

Table 22-1

Financial Ratios for Retail Computer and Software Stores (Industry Code No. 5734)

	Firm Size by Total Assets		
	Less than $500,000	**$500,000 to $2 Million**	**$2 Million to $10 Million**
Current ratio	1.6	1.5	1.3
Quick ratio	1.0	.9	.9
Accounts receivable turnover	11.4	9.5	8.0
Inventory turnover*	12.3	10.7	14.8
Operating income return on investment[†]	12.0%	9.9%	14.3%
Gross profit margin	36.0%	31.8%	31.3%
Operating profit margin	2.8	2.6	3.9
Fixed asset turnover	47.0	38.2	53.0
Total asset turnover	4.3	3.8	3.7
Debt/equity	3.1	2.8	2.7
Return on equity (before tax)	30.9%	22.1%	26.7%

*Based on cost of goods sold.

†Not reported in the RMA data, but computed by multiplying the operating profit margin times the total asset turnover.

Source: Adapted from RMA 1995 *Annual Statement Studies* published by Robert Morris Associates, Philadelphia, Pa. Copyright Robert Morris Associates 1995. Note: RMA cautions that the Studies be regarded only as a general guideline and not as an absolute industry norm. This is due to limited samples within categories, the categorization of companies by their primary Standard Industrial Classification (SIC) number only, and different methods of operations by companies within the same industry. For these reasons, RMA recommends that the figures by used only as general guidelines in addition to other methods of financial analysis.

4 Evaluate a firm's liquidity.

liquidity
the ability of a firm to meet maturing debt obligations by having adequate working capital available

Can the Firm Meet Its Financial Commitments?

The **liquidity** of a business is defined as the firm's ability to meet maturing debt obligations. That is, does a firm now have or will it have in the future the resources to pay creditors when debts come due?

This question can be answered in two ways: (1) by comparing the firm's assets that are relatively liquid in nature with the debt coming due in the near term, or (2) by examining the timeliness with which liquid assets are being converted into cash.

MEASURING LIQUIDITY: APPROACH 1 The first approach to measuring liquidity compares cash and the assets that should be converted into cash within the year against the debt (liabilities) that is coming due and will be payable within the year. The assets here are the current assets, and the debt consists of the current liabilities in the balance sheet. Thus, the following measure, called the **current ratio,** estimates a company's relative liquidity:

current ratio
a measure of a company's relative liquidity, determined by dividing current assets by current liabilities

$$\text{Current ratio} = \frac{\text{Current assets}}{\text{Current liabilities}}$$

Furthermore—remembering that the three primary current assets include cash, accounts receivable, and inventories—we can make this measure of liquidity more restrictive by excluding inventories, the least liquid of the current assets, in the numerator. This revised ratio is called the **acid-test ratio,** or **quick ratio**:

acid-test ratio (quick ratio)
a measure of a company's liquidity that excludes inventories

$$\text{Acid-test ratio} = \frac{\text{Current assets} - \text{Inventories}}{\text{Current liabilities}}$$

We can demonstrate computation of the current ratio and the acid-test ratio by returning to the financial statements for the FGD Manufacturing Company that were presented in Chapter 11. For ease of reference, the income statement and the balance sheets for the company are reproduced in Figures 22-1 and 22-2.

Figure 22-1

Income Statement for FGD Manufacturing Company for the Year Ending December 31, 1997

Sales revenue		$830,000
Cost of goods sold		540,000
Gross profit		$290,000
Operating expenses:		
Marketing expenses	$90,000	
General and administrative expenses	72,000	
Depreciation	28,000	
Total operating expenses		$190,000
Operating income		$100,000
Interest expense		20,000
Earnings before taxes		$ 80,000
Income tax (25%)		20,000
Net income		$ 60,000

	1996	1997
Assets		
Current assets:		
Cash	$ 38,000	$ 43,000
Accounts receivable	70,000	78,000
Inventories	175,000	210,000
Prepaid expenses	12,000	14,000
Total current assets	$295,000	$345,000
Fixed assets:		
Gross plant and equipment	$760,000	$838,000
Accumulated depreciation	355,000	383,000
Net plant and equipment	$405,000	$455,000
Land	70,000	70,000
Total fixed assets	$475,000	$525,000
Other assets:		
Goodwill and patents	30,000	50,000
TOTAL ASSETS	$800,000	$920,000
Debt (Liabilities) and Equity		
Current debt:		
Accounts payable	$ 61,000	$ 76,000
Income tax payable	12,000	15,000
Accrued wages and salaries	4,000	5,000
Interest payable	2,000	4,000
Total current debt	$ 79,000	$100,000
Long-term debt:		
Long-term notes payable	146,000	200,000
Total debt	$225,000	$300,000
Common stock	$300,000	$300,000
Retained earnings	275,000	320,000
Total stockholders' equity	$575,000	$620,000
TOTAL DEBT AND EQUITY	$800,000	$920,000

Figure 22-2

Balance Sheets for FGD Manufacturing Company December 31, 1996 and December 31, 1997

Calculations of the current ratio and the acid-test ratio for 1997, as well as the corresponding industry norms or averages as would be reported by Robert Morris Associates, follow:

$$\text{Current ratio} = \frac{\text{Current assets}}{\text{Current liabilities}}$$

$$= \frac{\$345,000}{\$100,000} = 3.45$$

Industry norm = 2.70

$$\text{Acid-test ratio} = \frac{\text{Current assets} - \text{Inventories}}{\text{Current liabilities}}$$

$$= \frac{\$345,000 - \$210,000}{\$100,000} = 1.35$$

Industry norm = 1.25

In terms of the current ratio and the acid-test ratio, FGD Manufacturing is more liquid than the average firm in its industry. FGD has $3.45 in current assets relative to every $1 in current liabilities (debt), compared to $2.70 for a "typical" firm in the industry. The company has $1.35 in current assets less inventories per $1 of current debt, compared to the industry norm of $1.25. While both ratios indicate that the company is more liquid than the industry norm, the current ratio appears to suggest more liquidity than the acid-test ratio. Why might this be the case? Simply put, FGD has more inventories relative to current debt than do most other firms. Which ratio should be given greater weight depends on the actual liquidity of the inventories. We shall return to this question shortly.

MEASURING LIQUIDITY: APPROACH 2 The second view of liquidity examines a firm's ability to convert accounts receivable and inventory into cash on a timely basis. The conversion of accounts receivable into cash may be measured by computing how long it takes on average to collect the firm's receivables. That is, how many days of sales are outstanding in the form of accounts receivable? We answer this question by computing the **average collection period:**

average collection period
the average time it takes a firm to collect its accounts receivable

$$\text{Average collection period} = \frac{\text{Accounts receivable}}{\text{Daily credit sales}}$$

If we assume that all sales are credit sales, as opposed to some cash sales, the average collection period in 1997 for FGD Manufacturing is 34.3 days, compared to an industry norm of 35 days:

$$\text{Average collection period} = \frac{\text{Accounts receivable}}{\text{Daily credit sales}}$$

$$= \frac{\$78,000}{\$830,000 \div 365} = 34.30$$

Industry norm = 35

Thus, the company collects its receivables in about the same number of days as the average firm in the industry. It appears that accounts receivable are of reasonable liquidity when viewed from the perspective of the length of time required to convert receivables into cash.

accounts receivable turnover
the number of times accounts receivable "roll over" during a year

We can reach the same conclusion by determining the **accounts receivable turnover,** that is, by measuring the number of times that accounts receivable are "rolled over" during a year. For example, FGD Manufacturing turns its receivables over 10.64 times a year:

$$\text{Accounts receivable turnover} = \frac{\text{Credit sales}}{\text{Accounts receivable}}$$

$$= \frac{\$830,000}{\$78,000} = 10.64$$

Industry norm = 10.43

We can also measure the accounts receivable turnover by dividing 365 days by the average collection period: $365 \div 34.30 = 10.64$.

Whether the average collection period or the accounts receivable turnover is used, the conclusion is the same: FGD Manufacturing is comparable to the average firm in the industry in terms of the collection of receivables.

Financial ratios, such as inventory turnover, are used to measure a firm's liquidity. The frequency with which this nursery owner is able to turn over his inventory and the price he puts on his product will affect the firm's bottom line.

We now need to determine how many times FGD Manufacturing is turning over its inventories during the year. The answer provides some insight into the liquidity of FGD's inventories. The **inventory turnover** is calculated as follows:

$$\text{Inventory turnover} = \frac{\text{Cost of goods sold}}{\text{Inventory}}$$

inventory turnover the number of times inventories "roll over" during a year

Note that sales in this ratio are shown at the company's cost, as opposed to the full market value when sold. Since the inventory (the denominator) is at cost, it is desirable to measure sales (the numerator) on a cost basis also to avoid a biased answer. (As a practical matter, however, sales are often used instead of cost of goods sold by most suppliers of industry norm data. Thus, for consistency in comparisons, it is often necessary to use the sales figure.)

The inventory turnover for FGD Manufacturing, along with the industry norm, follows:

$$\text{Inventory turnover} = \frac{\text{Cost of goods sold}}{\text{Inventory}}$$

$$= \frac{\$540,000}{\$210,000} = 2.57$$

Industry norm = 4.00

This analysis reveals a significant problem for FGD Manufacturing. The company is carrying excessive inventory, possibly even some obsolete inventory. That is, it generates only $2.57 in sales (at cost) for every $1 of inventory, compared to $4 in sales at cost for the average firm. It is now more obvious why the current ratio made the company look better than the acid-test ratio: FGD Manufacturing's inventory is a larger component of its current ratio than is the inventory of other firms. So, the current ratio for FGD Manufacturing is not totally comparable with the industry norm.

Is the Firm Producing Adequate Operating Profits on Its Assets?

The second question to be considered is vitally important to a firm's investors: Are operating profits—profits that will be available for distribution to all the firm's investors—sufficient relative to the total amount of assets invested? Figure 22-3 provides an overview of the computation of the rate of return on all capital invested in a firm, whether it comes from creditors or common stockholders. The total capital from various investors becomes the firm's total assets. These assets are invested for the express purpose of producing operating profits—profits that are then distributed to creditors and stockholders. A comparison of operating profits and total invested assets reveals the rate of return that is being earned on all the capital.

The profits—and, more importantly, cash flows—are then shared by each investor or investment group based on the terms of its investment agreement. Based on the amount of profits flowing to each investor, the rate of return on its respective investments can be computed.

operating income return on investment (OIROI)
a measure of operating profits relative to total assets

operating income (earnings before interest and taxes)
profits before interest and taxes are paid

MEASURING A FIRM'S RETURN ON INVESTMENT   The first step in analyzing a firm's return on investment is finding the rate of return on the total invested capital (capital from all investors)—a rate of return that is independent of how the company is financed (debt versus equity). The answer is arrived at by calculating the **operating income return on investment (OIROI),** which is measured by comparing a firm's **operating income (earnings before interest and taxes)** to its total invested capital or total assets. We compute the operating income return on investment as follows:

Figure 22-3

Return on Invested Capital: An Overview

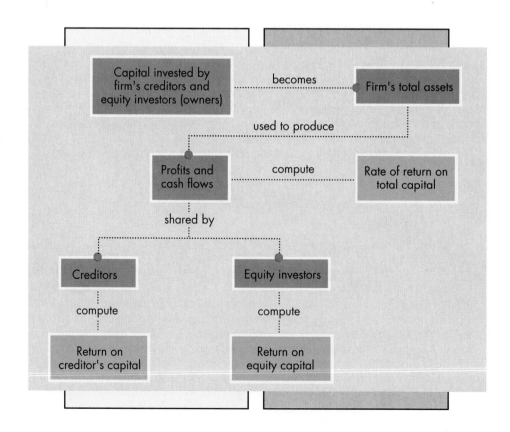

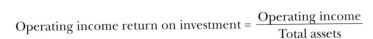
$$\text{Operating income return on investment} = \frac{\text{Operating income}}{\text{Total assets}}$$

The operating income return on investment for FGD Manufacturing for 1997 and the corresponding industry norm are as follows:

$$\text{Operating income return on investment} = \frac{\text{Operating income}}{\text{Total assets}}$$

$$= \frac{\$100,000}{\$920,000} = 0.1087, \text{ or } 10.87\%$$

$$\text{Industry norm} = 13.2\%$$

It is evident that FGD Manufacturing's return on total invested capital is less than the average rate of return for the industry. For some reason, FGD's managers are generating less operating income on each dollar of assets than are their competitors.

UNDERSTANDING THE RETURN-ON-INVESTMENT RESULTS   The owners of FGD Manufacturing should not be satisfied with merely knowing that they are not earning a competitive return on the firm's assets. They should also want to know *why* the return is below average. To gain more understanding, the owners could separate the operating income return on investment into two important components: the operating profit margin and the total asset turnover.

The **operating profit margin** is calculated as follows:

operating profit margin
a ratio of operating profits to sales

$$\text{Operating profit margin} = \frac{\text{Operating profits}}{\text{Sales}}$$

The operating profit margin shows how well a firm manages its income statement—that is, how well a firm manages the activities that affect its income. There are five factors, or driving forces, that affect the operating profit margin and, in turn, the operating income return on investment:

1. The number of units of product or service sold (volume)
2. The average selling price for each product or service unit (sales price)
3. The cost of manufacturing or acquiring the firm's product (cost of goods sold)
4. The ability to control general and administrative expenses (operating expenses)
5. The ability to control expenses in marketing and distributing the firm's product (operating expenses)

These influences should be apparent from analysis of the income statement and consideration of what is involved in determining a firm's operating profits or income.

The second component of a firm's operating income return on investment is the **total asset turnover,** which is calculated as follows:

total asset turnover
a measure of the efficiency with which a firm's assets are used to generate sales

$$\text{Total asset turnover} = \frac{\text{Sales}}{\text{Total assets}}$$

This financial ratio indicates how efficiently management is using the firm's assets to generate sales—that is, how well the firm is managing its balance sheet. If Company A can generate \$3 in sales with \$1 in assets compared to Company B's \$2 in sales per asset dollar, then Company A is using its assets more efficiently in generating sales. This is a major determinant in the firm's return on investment.

By taking the product of the two foregoing financial ratios, the operating income return on investment can be restated:

$$\text{Operating income return on investment} = \frac{\text{Operating profits}}{\text{Sales}} \times \frac{\text{Sales}}{\text{Total assets}}$$

or

$$\text{OIROI} = \text{Operating profit margin} \times \text{Total asset turnover}$$

Separating the operating income return on investment into its two factors—the operating profit margin and total asset turnover—better isolates a firm's strengths and weaknesses when it is attempting to identify ways to earn a competitive rate of return on its total invested capital.

FGD Manufacturing's operating profit margin and total asset turnover can be computed as follows:

$$\text{Operating profit margin} = \frac{\text{Operating profits}}{\text{Sales}}$$

$$= \frac{\$100,000}{\$830,000} = 0.1205, \text{ or } 12.05\%$$

$$\text{Industry norm} = 11\%$$

$$\text{Total asset turnover} = \frac{\text{Sales}}{\text{Total assets}}$$

$$= \frac{\$830,000}{\$920,000} = 0.90$$

$$\text{Industry norm} = 1.20$$

Then, for FGD Manufacturing,[6]

$$\text{Operating income return on investment} = \text{Operating profit margin} \times \text{Total asset turnover}$$

or

$$\text{OIROI}_{\text{FGD}} = 0.1205 \times 0.90 = 0.1085, \text{ or } 10.85\%$$

And, for the industry,

$$\text{OIROI}_{\text{Ind}} = 0.11 \times 1.20 = 0.132, \text{ or } 13.2\%$$

Clearly, FGD Manufacturing is competitive when it comes to managing its income statement—keeping costs and expenses in line relative to sales—as reflected by the operating profit margin. In other words, its managers are performing satisfactorily in managing the five driving forces of the operating profit margin. However, the firm's total asset turnover shows why its managers are less than competitive in terms of operating income return on investment. The firm is not using its assets efficiently; its managers are not managing the balance sheet well. FGD Manufacturing's problem is that it generates slightly less than $0.90 in sales per dollar of assets, while the competition produces $1.20 in sales from every dollar in assets.

The analysis should not stop here, however. It is clear that FGD's assets are not being used efficiently, but the next question should be "Which assets are the problem?" Is this firm overinvested in all assets, or mainly in accounts receivable or inventory or fixed assets? To answer this question, we must examine the turnover ratios for each asset. The first two ratios— accounts receivable turnover and inventory turnover—were calculated earlier. The third ratio, **fixed asset turnover,** is found by dividing sales by fixed assets. Thus, these three financial ratios are as follows:

fixed asset turnover
a financial ratio that measures the relationship of sales to fixed assets

Turnover Ratio		FGD Manufacturing	Industry Norm
$\dfrac{\text{Accounts receivable}}{\text{turnover}}$ =	$\dfrac{\text{Credit sales}}{\text{Accounts receivable}}$	$\dfrac{\$830,000}{\$78,000} = 10.64$	10.43
Inventory turnover =	$\dfrac{\text{Cost of goods sold}}{\text{Inventory}}$	$\dfrac{\$540,000}{\$210,000} = 2.57$	4.00
Fixed asset turnover =	$\dfrac{\text{Sales}}{\text{Fixed assets}}$	$\dfrac{\$830,000}{\$525,000} = 1.58$	2.50

FGD Manufacturing's problems are now clearer. The company has excessive inventories, which was evident earlier. Also, it is too heavily invested in fixed assets for the sales being produced. It appears that these two asset categories are not being managed well. Consequently, FGD Manufacturing is experiencing a lower than necessary operating income return on investment.

We have shown how to analyze a firm's ability to earn a satisfactory rate of return on its total investment capital. To this point, we have ignored the firm's financing decisions as to whether it should use debt or equity and the consequence of such decisions on the owners' return on the equity investment. The analysis must now move to how the firm finances its investments.

How Is the Firm Financing Its Assets?

6 Measure a firm's use of debt or equity financing.

We shall return to the issue of profitability shortly. Now, however, we turn our attention to the matter of how the firm is financed. That is, are the firm's assets financed to a greater extent by debt or by equity? To answer this question, we will use two ratios (although many others could be used). First, we must determine what percentage of the firm's assets are financed by debt—including both short-term and long-term debt. (The remaining percentage must be financed by equity.) As discussed in an earlier chapter, the use of debt, or **financial leverage,** can increase a firm's return on equity, but with some risk involved. The **debt ratio** is calculated as follows:

financial leverage
the use of debt in financing a firm's assets

debt ratio
the ratio of total debt to total assets

$$\text{Debt ratio} = \frac{\text{Total debt}}{\text{Total assets}}$$

(The same relationship can be stated as the **debt-equity ratio,** which is total debt divided by total equity, rather than total debt divided by total assets. Either ratio leads to the same conclusion.)

debt-equity ratio
the ratio of total debt to total equity

For FGD Manufacturing in 1997, debt as a percentage of total assets is 33 percent, compared to an industry norm of 40 percent. The computation is as follows:

$$\text{Debt ratio} = \frac{\text{Total debt}}{\text{Total assets}}$$

$$= \frac{\$300,000}{\$920,000} = 0.33, \text{ or } 33\%$$

Industry norm = 40%

Thus, FGD Manufacturing uses somewhat less debt than the average firm in the industry, which means that it has less financial risk.

A second perspective on a firm's financing decisions can be gained by looking at the income statement. When a firm borrows money, it is required, at a minimum, to pay the interest on the debt. Thus, determining the amount of operating income available to pay the interest provides a firm with valuable information. Stated as a ratio, the computation shows the number of times the firm earns its interest. Thus, **times interest earned** ratio is commonly used when examining debt position. This ratio is calculated as follows:

times interest earned
the ratio of operating income to interest charges

$$\text{Times interest earned} = \frac{\text{Operating income}}{\text{Interest expense}}$$

For FGD Manufacturing, the times interest earned ratio is

$$\text{Times interest earned} = \frac{\text{Operating income}}{\text{Interest expense}}$$

$$= \frac{\$100,000}{\$20,000} = 5.00$$

Industry norm = 4.00

FGD Manufacturing is better able to service its interest expense than most comparable firms. Remember, however, that interest is not paid with income but with cash. Also, the firm may be required to repay some of the debt principal as well as the interest. Thus, times interest earned is only a crude measure of a firm's capacity to service its debt. Nevertheless, it gives a general indication of the firm's debt capacity.

7 Evaluate the rate of return earned on the owners' investment.

Are the Owners Receiving Adequate Return on Their Investment?

return on equity
the rate of return that owners earn on their investment

The last question looks at the accounting return on the owners' investment, or **return on equity.** We must determine whether the earnings available to the firm's owners (or stockholders) are attractive when compared to the returns of owners of similar companies in the same industry. The return on the owners' equity can be measured as follows:

$$\text{Return on equity} = \frac{\text{Net income}}{\text{Common equity}}$$

The return on equity for FGD Manufacturing in 1997 and the return for the industry are as follows:

$$\text{Return on equity} = \frac{\text{Net income}}{\text{Common equity}}$$

$$= \frac{\$60,000}{\$620,000}$$

$$= 0.097, \text{ or } 9.7\%$$

Industry norm = 12.5%

It appears that the owners of FGD Manufacturing are not receiving a return on their investment equivalent to that of owners of competing businesses. Why not? In this case, the answer is twofold. First, FGD Manufacturing is not as profitable in its operation as its competitors. (Recall that the operating income return on investment was 10.87 percent for FGD Manufacturing, compared to 13.2 percent for the industry.) Second, the average firm in the industry uses more debt, causing the return on equity to be higher, provided, of course, that the firm is earning a return on its investments that exceeds the cost of debt (the interest rate). However, the use of debt does increase a firm's risk.[7]

Summary of Financial Ratio Analysis

To review the use of financial ratios in evaluating a company's financial position, all ratios for the FGD Manufacturing Company for 1997 are presented in Figure 22-4. The ratios are grouped by the issue being addressed: liquidity, operating profitability, financing, and owners' return on equity. Recall that two ratios are used for more than one purpose—the turnover ratios for accounts receivable and inventories. These ratios have implications for both the firm's liquidity and its profitability; thus, they are listed in both areas. Note, also, that the table shows both average collection period and accounts receivable turnover. Typically, only one of these ratios is used in analysis, since they represent different ways to measure the same thing. Presenting the ratios together, however, provides an overview of our discussion.

Looking Back

1 Identify the basic requirements for an accounting system.

- An accounting system structures the flow of financial information to develop a complete picture of financial activities.
- The system should be objective, follow generally accepted accounting principles, and supply information on a timely basis.
- In addition to the balance sheet, income statement, and cash flow statement, an accounting system should provide records that account for cash, accounts receivable, inventories, accounts payable, payroll, and fixed assets.

2 Explain two alternative accounting options.

- Accounting systems may use either cash or accrual methods and be structured as either single-entry or double-entry systems.
- With a cash method of accounting, transactions are recorded only when cash is received or a payment is made; the accrual method of accounting matches revenue earned against the expenses associated with it.
- A single-entry system is basically a checkbook system of receipts and disbursements, supported by sales tickets and disbursement receipts; a double-entry system of accounting incorporates journals and ledgers and requires that each transaction be recorded twice.

3 Describe the purpose of and procedures related to internal control.

- Internal control refers to a system of checks and balances designed to safeguard a firm's assets and enhance the accuracy of financial statements.
- Some examples of internal control procedures are separation of employees' duties, limiting access to accounting records and computer facilities, and safeguarding blank checks.
- Building internal controls within a small business is difficult but important.

4 Evaluate a firm's liquidity.

- Liquidity is a firm's capacity to meet its short-term obligations.
- One measure of a firm's liquidity is a comparison of its liquid assets (cash, accounts receivable, and inventories) and its short-term debt, by using the current ratio or the acid-test ratio.
- A second measure of liquidity is determining the time it takes to convert accounts receivables and inventories into cash, by using the accounts receivable turnover and the inventory turnover.

Continue on page 495

Figure 22-4

*Financial Ratio Analysis
for FGD Manufacturing
Company*

Financial Ratios/FGD Manufacturing	**Industry Norm**

Firm liquidity

Current ratio = $\dfrac{\text{Current assets}}{\text{Current liabilities}} = \dfrac{\$345{,}000}{\$100{,}000} = 3.45$ — 2.70

Acid-test ratio = $\dfrac{\text{Current assets} - \text{Inventories}}{\text{Current liabilities}} = \dfrac{\$345{,}000 - \$210{,}000}{\$100{,}000} = 1.35$ — 1.25

Average collection period = $\dfrac{\text{Accounts receivable}}{\text{Daily credit sales}} = \dfrac{\$78{,}000}{\$830{,}000 \div 365} = 34.30$ — 35.00

Accounts receivable turnover = $\dfrac{\text{Credit sales}}{\text{Accounts receivable}} = \dfrac{\$830{,}000}{\$78{,}000} = 10.64$ — 10.43

Inventory turnover = $\dfrac{\text{Cost of goods sold}}{\text{Inventory}} = \dfrac{\$540{,}000}{\$210{,}000} = 2.57$ — 4.00

Operating profitability

Operating income return on investment = $\dfrac{\text{Operating income}}{\text{Total assets}} = \dfrac{\$100{,}000}{\$920{,}000} = 10.87\%$ — 13.20%

Operating profit margin = $\dfrac{\text{Operating profits}}{\text{Sales}} = \dfrac{\$100{,}000}{\$830{,}000} = 12.05\%$ — 11.00%

Total asset turnover = $\dfrac{\text{Sales}}{\text{Total assets}} = \dfrac{\$830{,}000}{\$920{,}000} = 0.90$ — 1.20

Accounts receivable turnover = $\dfrac{\text{Credit sales}}{\text{Accounts receivable}} = \dfrac{\$830{,}000}{\$78{,}000} = 10.64$ — 10.43

Inventory turnover = $\dfrac{\text{Cost of goods sold}}{\text{Inventory}} = \dfrac{\$540{,}000}{\$210{,}000} = 2.57$ — 4.00

Fixed asset turnover = $\dfrac{\text{Sales}}{\text{Fixed assets}} = \dfrac{\$830{,}000}{\$525{,}000} = 1.58$ — 2.50

Financing

Debt ratio = $\dfrac{\text{Total debt}}{\text{Total assets}} = \dfrac{\$300{,}000}{\$920{,}000} = 33.00\%$ — 40.00%

Times interest earned = $\dfrac{\text{Operating income}}{\text{Interest}} = \dfrac{\$100{,}000}{\$20{,}000} = 5.00$ — 4.00

Return on equity

Return on equity = $\dfrac{\text{Net income}}{\text{Common equity}} = \dfrac{\$60{,}000}{\$620{,}000} = 9.70\%$ — 12.50%

DISCUSSION QUESTIONS

1. Explain the accounting concept that income is realized when earned, whether or not it has been received in cash.
2. Should entrepreneurs have an outside specialist set up an accounting system for their start-ups or do it themselves? Why?
3. What are the major types of records required in a sound accounting system?
4. What are the major advantages of a double-entry accounting system over a single-entry system?
5. What is liquidity? Differentiate between the two approaches given in this chapter to measure liquidity.
6. Explain the following ratios:
   a. Operating profit margin
   b. Total asset turnover
   c. Times interest earned
7. What is the relationship among these ratios: operating income return on investment, operating profit margin, and total asset turnover?
8. What would be the difference between using operating profit and using net income when calculating a firm's return on investment?
9. What is financial leverage? When should it be used and when should it be avoided? Why?
10. What determines a firm's return on equity?

5 **Assess a firm's operating profitability.**

- Operating profitability is evaluated by determining if the firm is earning a good return on its total assets, as computed by the operating income return on investment.
- The operating income return on investment can be separated into two components—the operating profit margin and the total asset turnover—to gain more insight into the firm's operating profitability.

6 **Measure a firm's use of debt or equity financing.**

- Either the debt ratio or the debt-equity ratio can be used to measure how much debt a firm uses in its financing mix.
- A firm's ability to cover interest charges on its debt can be measured by the times interest earned ratio.

7 **Evaluate the rate of return earned on the owners' investment.**

- Owners' return on investment is measured by dividing net income by the common equity invested in the business.
- The return on equity is a function of (1) the firm's operating income return on investment less the interest paid and (2) the amount of debt used relative to the amount of equity financing.

New Terms and Concepts

cash method of accounting *480*

accrual method of accounting *480*

single-entry system *480*

double-entry system *480*

internal control *481*

financial ratios *483*

liquidity *484*

current ratio *484*

acid-test ratio (quick ratio) *484*

average collection period *486*

accounts receivable turnover *486*

inventory turnover *487*

operating income return on investment (OIROI) *488*

operating income (earnings before interest and taxes) *488*

operating profit margin *489*

total asset turnover *489*

fixed asset turnover *491*

financial leverage *491*

debt ratio *491*

debt-equity ratio *491*

times interest earned *492*

return on equity *492*

Situation 1 Having worked for several different businesses over the last 30 years, Mary and Matt Townsel are now in their early retirement years. To supplement their Social Security income, they operate a newspaper delivery service that has more than 600 customers in the retirement/vacation village in which they live. Mary's major contribution to the business partnership, in addition to rolling papers early each morning, is bookkeeping. Mary has recently purchased a computer to assist with the accounting records. She is therefore looking for someone to write a software program for the business.

Question 1 What types of accounting records do you believe Mary should maintain? Why?

Question 2 Will a computer benefit Mary's record-keeping task? How?

Situation 2 The following letter was written by a parent about her son:

My son was caught with his hand in the cookie jar. He has been working with me in our car dealership for the past two years, and I have been very proud of some of the ideas he has come up with to save us money and increase efficiency. Most of the other men we work with seem to respect him, not only because he's my son but because he is a talented salesman with true leadership qualities. It's because he's such a good salesman that I have allowed him to pad his expense reports. Well, I didn't exactly allow it; I simply let it go, since it didn't amount to much at first, and [I] hoped that he would eventually stop doing it. Now his expenses have gotten so inflated, our bookkeeper asked me what to do about the charges. I'm not sure how to handle this. I don't want to embarrass my son, but now that others know about it, I can't let it continue.

Source: "Confronting a Son Who Pads His Expenses," *Family Business*, Vol. 5, No. 3 (Summer 1994), p. 9.

Question 1 Given that the parent owns the business and knew what the son was doing, should the son's actions still be considered wrong?

Question 2 Do you agree with the parent's handling of this situation up to this point?

Question 3 What should the parent do now?

Question 4 What internal controls should be established to prevent padding either by the son or by others in the firm from recurring?

Situation 3 In 1994, Joe Dalton purchased the Baugh Company. Although the firm has consistently earned profits, little cash has been available for other than business needs. Before purchasing Baugh, Dalton thought that cash flows were generally equal to profits plus depreciation. However, this does not seem to be the case. The financial statements (in thousands) for the Baugh Company, 1995–1996, are presented on the next page.

The industry norms are given below for financial ratios.

Financial Ratios	Industry Norms	Financial Ratios	Industry Norms
Current ratio	2.50	Operating profit margin	8.0%
Acid-test ratio	1.50	Total asset turnover	2.00
Average collection		Fixed asset turnover	7.00
period	30.00	Debt-equity ratio	1.00
Inventory turnover	6.00	Times interest earned	5.00
Operating income		Return on equity	14.0%
return on investment	16.0%		

Continue on next page

EXPERIENTIAL EXERCISES

1. Interview a local CPA who consults with small firms about his or her experiences with small business accounting systems. Report to the class on the levels of accounting knowledge the CPA's clients appear to possess.

2. Contact several very small businesses and explain your interest in their accounting systems. Report to the class on their level of sophistication—such as whether they use a single-entry system, a computer, or an outside professional.

3. Find out whether your public or university library subscribes to a financial service that provides industry financial ratios. Ask for Robert Morris Associates or Dun & Bradstreet. If the library does not subscribe to either of these two services, ask whether it subscribes to another financial service that provides industry norms. When you find a source, select an industry and bring a copy of the ratios to class for discussion of the information.

4. Locate a small company in your community that will allow you to use its financial statements to perform a financial ratio analysis. You will need to decide on the industry that best represents the firm's business for comparative data and then find the norms in the library. Also, you may need to promise confidentiality to the company's owners by changing all names on statements.

CASE 22
The Style Shop (p. 648)

This case describes how the owner of a women's clothing store uses comparative financial statements in her decision making.

Alternative Case for Chapter 22:
Case 11, "WJP Partners," p. 622

Balance Sheet
(in thousands)

Assets	1995	1996
Current assets:		
Cash	$ 8	$ 10
Accounts receivable	15	20
Inventory	22	25
Total current assets	$45	$ 55
Fixed assets:		
Gross plant and equipment	$50	$ 55
Accumulated depreciation	15	20
Total fixed assets	$35	$ 35
Other assets	12	10
TOTAL ASSETS	$92	$100
Debt (Liabilities) and Equity		
Current debt:		
Accounts payable	$10	$ 12
Accruals	7	8
Short-term notes	5	5
Total current debt	$22	$ 25
Long-term debt	15	15
Total debt	$37	$ 40
Equity	55	60
TOTAL DEBT AND EQUITY	$92	$100

Income Statement, 1996
(in thousands)

Sales revenue		$175
Cost of goods sold		105
Gross profit		$ 70
Operating expenses:		
Marketing expenses	$26	
General and administrative expenses	20	
Depreciation	5	
Total operating expenses		$ 51
Operating income		$ 19
Interest expense		3
Earnings before taxes		$ 16
Income tax		8
Net income		$ 8

Question 1 Why doesn't Dalton have cash for personal needs? (As part of your analysis, develop a cash flow statement as discussed in Chapter 11.)
Question 2 Evaluate the Baugh Company's financial performance, given the financial ratios for the industry.

Working-Capital Management and Capital Budgeting

Greg Garvis

spotlight on small business

One important task of working-capital management is monitoring the flow of cash into and out of the firm. Mistakes in cash management can be as damaging as declining sales volume and can sometimes force a business to close its doors.

BankTemps, a small firm that supplies temporary employees to banks in Nashville, Tennessee, has experienced major cash-flow problems. "My biggest miscalculation," says owner Greg Garvis, "occurred in underestimating the costs associated with added staff due to growth. Also, I had assumed that year-end numbers reflected actual cash needs throughout the year."

Garvis discovered instead that receivables in the temporary-employment industry fluctuate markedly. In the third month of 1991, they surged to $65,000, from a monthly norm of $23,000 in 1990. Taken by surprise, Garvis had to raise money from friends and relatives to cover the salaries and taxes of his employees.

A similar pattern of catch-up unfolds every year. It remains a cash-flow challenge, which is magnified by BankTemps's 75 percent annual sales growth. In several months during 1993, receivables soared more than $100,000 over annualized monthly projections. However, Garvis's friends and relatives no longer have to foot the bill. Having proved his creditworthiness, he is currently cushioned by a $250,000 revolving line of bank credit.

Source: Robert A. Mamis, "Seed Capital: The 12-Step Program," *Inc.*, Vol. 16, No. 2 (February 1994), pp. 34–36.

Looking Ahead

After studying this chapter, you should be able to:

1 Describe the working-capital cycle of a small business.

2 Identify the important issues in managing a firm's cash flows.

3 Explain the key issues in managing accounts receivable, inventory, and accounts payable.

4 Discuss the techniques commonly used in making capital budgeting decisions.

5 Determine the appropriate cost of capital to be used in discounted cash flow techniques.

6 Describe the capital budgeting practices of small firms.

start here

In Chapter 22, we suggested that an owner needs to manage the firm's income statement carefully, which requires managing expenses relative to the firm's level of sales. Owners and managers must also effectively administer the firm's balance sheet, by managing both investments in working capital and long-term investments. In this chapter, we will consider the investment decisions of a firm. We will first discuss the management of working capital—that is, the management of short-term assets and liabilities—and then present the process for making decisions on long-term investments, such as those for equipment and buildings.

THE WORKING-CAPITAL CYCLE

Ask the owner of a small company about financial management and you will hear about the joys and tribulations of managing cash, accounts receivable, inventories, and accounts payable. **Working-capital management**—managing short-term assets (current assets) and short-term sources of financing (current liabilities)—is extremely important to most small firms. A perfectly good business opportunity can be destroyed by ineffective management of a firm's short-term assets and liabilities.

> *It's the lifeblood of business, the high-octane fluid that courses through the enterprise, kindling dreams, fueling growth and providing the energy needed to maintain a company's forward momentum. It is hard to come by, difficult to track, and has the maddening habit of leaking away just when it's needed most.*
>
> *The substance in question is, of course, cash, also known as working capital. It is an obsession with every businessperson, from the fledgling entrepreneur who desperately needs it to jump start an idea, to the proprietor of a multi-million-dollar company who wants to expand production.[1]*

Thus, the key issue in working-capital management is to avoid running out of cash. And understanding how to manage cash requires knowledge of the working-capital cycle.

Net working capital consists primarily of three assets—cash, accounts receivable, and inventories—and two sources of short-term debt—accounts payable and accruals.[2] A firm's **working-capital cycle** is the flow of resources through these accounts as part of the firm's day-to-day operations. The steps in a firm's working-capital cycle are as follows:

1. Purchase or produce inventory for sale, which increases accounts payable—assuming the purchase is a credit purchase—and increases inventories on hand.
2. a. Sell the inventory for cash, which increases cash, or
   b. Sell the inventory on credit, which increases accounts receivable.
3. a. Pay the accounts payable, which decreases accounts payable and decreases cash.
   b. Pay operating expenses and taxes, which decreases cash.

---

1 Describe the working-capital cycle of a small business.

working-capital management
the management of current assets and current liabilities

net working capital
the sum of a firm's current assets (cash, accounts receivable, and inventories) less current liabilities (accounts payable and accruals)

working-capital cycle
the daily flow of resources through a firm's working-capital accounts

499

Figure 23-1 Working-Capital Cycle

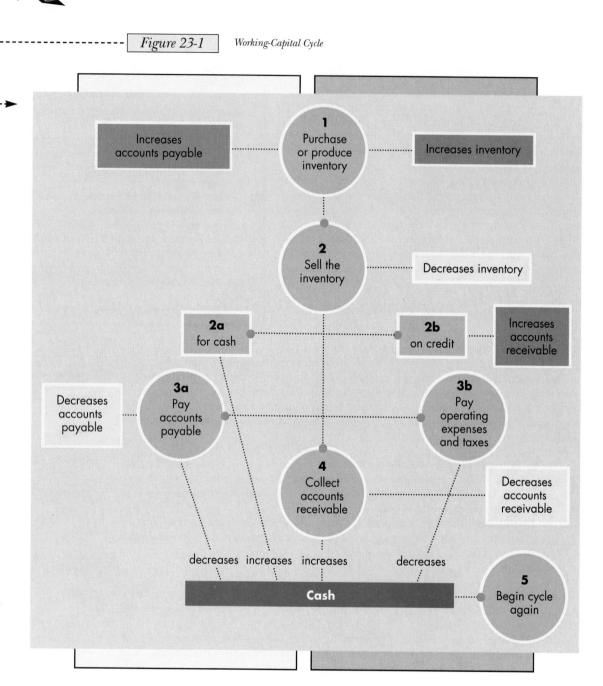

4. Collect the accounts receivable when due, which decreases accounts receivable and increases cash.
5. Begin the cycle again.

Figure 23-1 shows this cycle graphically.

Depending on the industry, the working-capital cycle may be long or short. For example, it is short and repeated quickly in the grocery business and is longer and repeated more slowly in an automobile dealership.

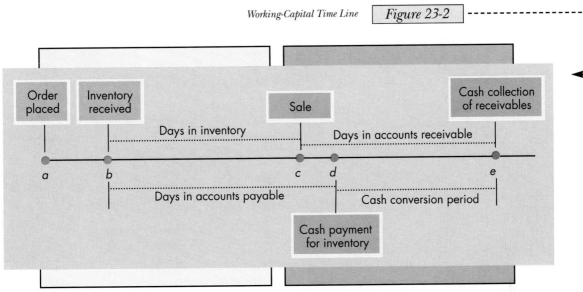

Working-Capital Time Line — Figure 23-2

Source: Terry S. Maness and John T. Zietlow, *Short-Term Financial Management* (New York: West Publishing, 1993), p. 14.

Timing and Size of Working-Capital Investments

It is imperative that owners of small companies understand the working-capital cycle, in terms of both the timing of investments and the size of the investment required, such as the amount invested in inventories and accounts receivable. An owner's failure to understand these relationships underlies many of the financial problems of small companies.

Figure 23-2 shows the chronological sequence of a hypothetical working-capital cycle. The time line reflects the order in which events unfold, beginning with investments in inventories and ending with collection of accounts receivable. The key dates in the figure are represented as follows:

Day *a:* Inventory is ordered in anticipation of future sales.
Day *b:* Inventory is received.
Day *c:* Inventory is sold on credit.
Day *d:* Accounts payable come due and are paid.
Day *e:* Accounts receivable are collected.

The investing and financing implications of the working-capital cycle reflected in Figure 23-2 are as follows:

- Money is invested in inventory from day *b* to day *c.*
- The supplier provides financing for the inventories from day *b* to day *d.*
- Money is invested in accounts receivable from day *c* to day *e.*
- Financing of the firm's investment in accounts receivable must be provided from day *d* to day *e.* This time span, called the **cash conversion period**, represents the number of days required to complete the working-capital cycle, ending with the conversion of accounts receivable into cash. During this period, the firm no longer has the benefit of financing (accounts payable) provided by the supplier. The longer this period lasts, the greater the potential cash-flow problems for the firm.

cash conversion period
the time required to convert paid-for inventories and accounts receivable into cash

Action Report

ENTREPRENEURIAL EXPERIENCES

The Cash-Flow Quagmire

Managing working capital, especially cash flow, is a critically important task in most small firms. Mary Baechler, cofounder and president of Racing Strollers, a $5 million company, learned to manage cash flow the hard way. When the firm started in 1984, its management systems were simple. Rapid growth initially masked the working-capital problems that were developing. Baechler explains her response when she was confronted by cash-flow trouble:

> *I took a statement home and spent a Saturday reading it, every line, the way I used to. I wanted to throw up. We'd had a record year. We'd hit all our profit goals. All our employees had worked their hearts out, and they had done everything we had asked them to do. And we had fallen off the cliff.*
>
> *We needed to raise money and quickly. And while I was looking outside, the money was on the inside. [I] hired an outside consultant, [and] he asked me, "Why are you trying to raise money?" My reply, "I have to." "No, you don't," he said. "Why don't you collect what's owed you?"*
>
> *None of us thought to look where we should have gone first: accounts receivable. A couple hundred thousand dollars were late, and no one had had the time to collect them. So we brought back a former employee whose specialty was collection, and she went to work. We had money coming in quicker than I could have put a deal together.*

Source: Mary Baechler, "The Cash-Flow Quagmire," *Inc.*, Vol. 16, No. 10 (October 1994), pp. 25, 26.

Examples of Working-Capital Management

Figure 23-3 offers two examples of working-capital management by companies with contrasting working-capital cycles: Pokey, Inc. and Quick Turn Company. On August 15, both companies buy inventory that they receive on August 31, but the similarity ends there. Pokey, Inc. must pay its supplier for the inventory on September 30, before eventually reselling it on October 15. It collects from its customers on November 30. As you can see, the company must pay for the inventory two months prior to collecting from its customers. The company's cash conversion period—the time required to convert the paid-for inventories and accounts receivable into cash—is 60 days. The company's managers must find a way to finance this investment in inventories and accounts receivable, or they will have to deal with cash-flow problems. Furthermore, although increased sales should produce higher profits, they will compound the cash-flow problem.

Now consider Quick Turn Company's working-capital cycle in the bottom portion of Figure 23-3. Compared to Pokey, Inc., Quick Turn Company has an enviable working-capital position. By the time Quick Turn must pay for its inventory purchases (October 31), it has sold its product (September 30) and collected from its customers (October 31). Thus, there is no cash conversion period, because the supplier is essentially financing Quick Turn's working-capital needs.

To gain an even better understanding of the working-capital cycle, let's look again at Pokey, Inc. In addition to the working-capital time line shown for Pokey in Figure 23-3, consider the following information about the firm:

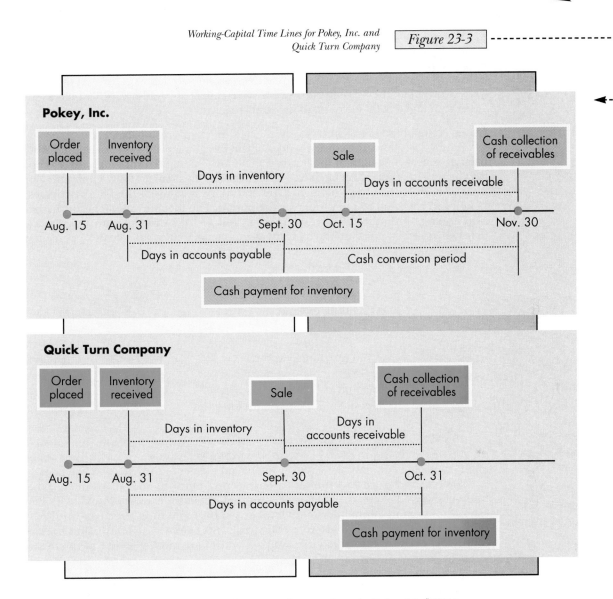

Working-Capital Time Lines for Pokey, Inc. and Quick Turn Company | Figure 23-3

Pokey, Inc.

Order placed | Inventory received | Sale | Cash collection of receivables

Days in inventory | Days in accounts receivable

Aug. 15 | Aug. 31 | Sept. 30 | Oct. 15 | Nov. 30

Days in accounts payable | Cash conversion period

Cash payment for inventory

Quick Turn Company

Order placed | Inventory received | Sale | Cash collection of receivables

Days in inventory | Days in accounts receivable

Aug. 15 | Aug. 31 | Sept. 30 | Oct. 31

Days in accounts payable

Cash payment for inventory

- Pokey, Inc. is a new company, having started operations in July with $300 in long-term debt and $700 in common stock.
- On August 15, the firm's managers ordered $500 in inventory, which was received on August 31 (per Figure 23-3). The supplier allowed Pokey 30 days from the time the inventory was received to pay for the purchase; thus, inventories and accounts payable both increased by $500 when the inventory was received.
- On September 30, the firm paid for the inventory; both cash and accounts payable decreased by $500.
- On October 15, the merchandise was sold on credit for $900; sales (in the income statement) and accounts receivable increased by that amount.
- During the month of October, the firm incurred operating expenses (selling and administrative expenses) in the amount of $250, to be paid in early November; thus, operating expenses (in the income statement) and accrued expenses increased by $250. (An additional $25 in accrued expenses resulted from accruing the taxes owed on the firm's earnings.)

- Also in October, the firm's accountants recorded $50 in depreciation expense, meaning that accumulated depreciation on the balance sheet increased to $50.
- In early November, the accrued expenses were paid, which resulted in a $250 decrease in cash along with an equal decrease in accrued expenses. At the end of November, the accounts receivable were collected, yielding a $900 increase in cash and a $900 decrease in accounts receivable.

(Note: None of the events in October affected the firm's cash balance.)

Figure 23-4 shows the consequences of the foregoing events on Pokey's monthly balance sheets—changes in the balance sheet are highlighted for emphasis. Except for changes in retained earnings and taxes payable, the changes for each month can be traced directly to the events that transpired. As a result of the firm's activities, Pokey, Inc. reported $75 in profits for the period. The income statement for the period ending November 30 would appear as follows (disregarding any interest expense incurred on outstanding debt and assuming an income tax rate of 25 percent):

Sales revenue		$900
Cost of goods sold		500
Gross profit		$400
Operating expenses:		
Cash	$250	
Depreciation	50	
Total operating expenses		$300
Operating income		$100
Income tax (25%)		25
Net income		$ 75

The $75 in profits is therefore reflected as retained earnings in the balance sheet to make the figures balance. Also, the $25 in taxes shown in the income statement results in taxes payable of $25 in the balance sheet in October and November.

The data in Figure 23-4 point to a serious problem—the negative effect of the transactions on Pokey's cash balances. Although the business was profitable, Pokey ran out of cash in September and October (−$100) and didn't recover until November, when the receivables were collected. This 60-day cash conversion period represents a critical time when the company must find another source of financing if it is to survive.

Figure 23-4

End-of-Month Balance Sheets for Pokey, Inc.

	July	August	September	October	November
Cash	$ 400	$ 400	−$ 100	−$ 100	$ 550
Accounts receivable	0	0	0	900	0
Inventory	0	500	500	0	0
Fixed assets	600	600	600	600	600
Accumulated depreciation	0	0	0	−50	−50
TOTAL ASSETS	$1,000	$1,500	$1,000	$1,350	$1,100
Accounts payable	$ 0	$ 500	$ 0	$ 0	$ 0
Accrued wages and salaries	0	0	0	250	0
Taxes payable	0	0	0	25	25
Long-term debt	300	300	300	300	300
Common stock	700	700	700	700	700
Retained earnings	0	0	0	75	75
TOTAL DEBT AND EQUITY	$1,000	$1,500	$1,000	$1,350	$1,100

The somewhat contrived examples of Pokey and Quick Turn make an important point. The owner of a small company must understand the working-capital cycle of his or her firm. The fundamental lesson of these examples has been expressed succinctly by one practitioner: "Get your customers to pay you as soon as possible (preferably in advance). Get your vendors to let you take your sweet time paying them (preferably within several months)."[3]

An understanding of the working-capital cycle provides a basis for examining the primary components of working-capital management: cash, accounts receivable, inventory, and accounts payable.

MANAGING CASH FLOW

2 Identify the important issues in managing a firm's cash flows.

It should be clear to you by now that the core of working-capital management consists of monitoring cash flow. Cash is constantly moving through a healthy business. It flows in as customers pay for products or services, and it flows out as payments are made to suppliers. The typically uneven nature of cash inflows and outflows makes it imperative that they be properly understood and regulated.

The Nature of Cash Flows

A firm's net cash flow may be determined quite simply by examining its bank account. Monthly cash deposits less checks written during the same period equal a firm's net cash flow. If deposits for a month add up to $100,000 and checks total $80,000, the firm has a net positive cash flow of $20,000. The cash balance at the end of the month is $20,000 higher than it was at the beginning of the month. Figure 23-5 graphically represents the flow of cash through a business; it includes not only the cash flows that arise as part of the firm's working-capital cycle (shown in Figure 23-1), but other cash flows as well, such as those from purchasing fixed assets and issuing stock. More specifically, the red dots in Figure 23-5 reflect the inflows and outflows of cash that relate to the working-capital cycle, while the black dots represent other, longer-term cash flows.

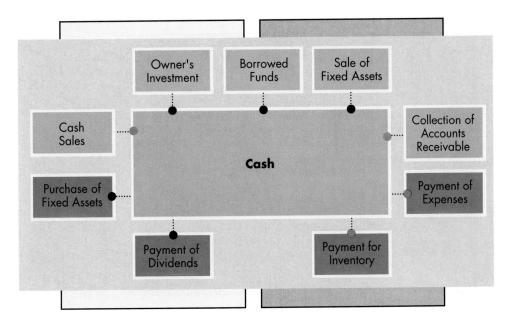

Figure 23-5

Flow of Cash Through a Business

It is necessary in calculating net cash flows to distinguish between sales revenue and cash receipts. They are seldom the same. Revenue is recorded at the time a sale is made but does not affect cash at that time unless the sale is a cash sale. Cash receipts, on the other hand, are recorded when money actually flows into the firm, often a month or two after the sale. Similarly, it is necessary to distinguish between expenses and disbursements. Expenses occur when materials, labor, or other items are used. Payments (disbursements) for these expense items may be made later, when checks are issued.

Net Cash Flow and Net Profit

In view of the characteristics just noted, it should come as no surprise that net cash flow and net profit are different. Net cash flow is the difference between cash inflows and outflows. Net profit, in contrast, is the difference between revenue and expenses. Failure to understand this distinction can play havoc with a small firm's financial well-being.

One reason for the difference is the uneven timing of cash disbursements and the expensing of those disbursements. For example, the merchandise purchased by a retail store may be paid for (a cash disbursement) before it is sold (when it becomes recognized as a cost of goods sold). On the other hand, labor may be used (an expense) before a paycheck is written (a cash disbursement). In the case of a major cash outlay for building or equipment, the disbursement shows up immediately as a cash outflow. However, it is recognized as an expense only as the building or equipment is depreciated over a period of years.

Similarly, the uneven timing of sales revenue and cash receipts occurs because of the extension of credit. When a sale is made, the transaction is recorded as revenue; the cash receipt is recorded when payment for the account receivable is received 30 or 60 days later. We observed this fact earlier as part of the working-capital cycle.

Furthermore, some cash receipts are not revenue and never become revenue. When a firm borrows money from a bank, for example, it receives cash without receiving revenue. When the principal is repaid to the bank some months later, cash is disbursed. However, no expense is recorded, because the firm is merely return-

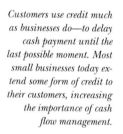

Customers use credit much as businesses do—to delay cash payment until the last possible moment. Most small businesses today extend some form of credit to their customers, increasing the importance of cash flow management.

Action Report

ENTREPRENEURIAL EXPERIENCES

Profits but No Cash

A manager needs to monitor both profits and cash flow. Otherwise, the company's checking account may run dry at the same time its income statement is showing a profit.

The president of a small midwestern manufacturing company made the mistake of concentrating exclusively on the firm's monthly profit-and-loss statements—statements that showed profits of $5,000 on sales of $100,000. He assumed that cash balances would not be a problem. However, after the president received a call from an irate creditor who had not been paid, he discovered that his company had, indeed, held up payment on a number of bills because of a cash shortage. Concentration on the income statement alone had led to neglect of cash-flow analysis and to the embarrassing surprise that the company's sales dollars had not made it to the bank in time to pay the bills.

Source: Ron D. Richardson, "Managing Your Company's Cash," *Nation's Business*, Vol. 74, No. 11 (November 1986), pp. 52–54.

ing money that was borrowed. Any interest on the loan that was paid to the bank would, of course, constitute both an expense and a cash disbursement.

It is imperative that small firms manage cash flows as carefully as they manage revenue, expenses, and profits. Otherwise, they may find themselves insolvent, while showing handsome paper profits. More businesses fail because of lack of cash than lack of profits.

The Growth Trap

Some firms experience rapid growth in sales volume; a firm's income statement may simultaneously reflect growing profits. However, rapid growth in sales and profits may be hazardous to the firm's cash. A **growth trap** can occur, because growth tends to soak up additional cash more rapidly than such cash can be generated in the form of additional profits.

growth trap
a cash shortage resulting from rapid growth

Inventory, for example, must be expanded as sales volume increases; additional dollars must be expended for merchandise or raw materials to accommodate the higher level of sales. Similarly, accounts receivable must be expanded proportionally to meet the increased sales volume. Obviously, a growing, profitable business can quickly find itself in a financial bind—growing profitably, while going broke at the bank.

The growth problem is particularly acute for small firms. Quite simply, it is easier to increase a small firm's sales by 50 percent than those of a Fortune 500 firm. This fact, combined with the difficulty a small firm may have in obtaining funds externally, highlights the detrimental effect that the growth trap can have on small businesses, unless cash is managed carefully.

In short, the need for additional financing in a high-growth company may exceed the company's available resources, even though it is profitable. Without additional resources, the company's cash balances may decline sharply, leaving it in a precarious financial position.

Cash Budgeting

Cash budgets are tools for managing cash flow. They differ in a number of ways from income statements. Income statements take items into consideration before they affect cash—for example, expenses that have been incurred but not yet paid and income earned but not yet received. In contrast, cash budgets are concerned specifically with dollars as they are received and paid out.

By using a cash budget, an entrepreneur can predict and plan the cash flow of a business. No single planning document is more important in the life of a small company, either for avoiding cash-flow problems when cash runs short or for anticipating short-term investment opportunities if excess cash becomes available.

To better understand the process of preparing a cash budget, let's consider the example of the Carriles Corporation, a manufacturer of cartons. Its owner, Catalina Carriles, wishes to develop a monthly cash budget for the next quarter (July–September) and has made the following forecasts.

- Historical and predicted sales are as follows:

Historical Sales		Predicted Sales	
April	$ 80,000	July	$130,000
May	100,000	August	130,000
June	120,000	September	120,000
		October	100,000

- Of the firm's sales dollars, 40 percent is collected the month of sale, 30 percent one month after sale, and the remaining 30 percent two months after sale.
- Inventory is purchased one month before the sales month and is paid for in the month it is sold. Purchases equal 80 percent of projected sales for the next month.
- Cash expenses have been estimated for wages and salaries, rent, utilities, and tax payments, all of which are reflected in the cash budget.
- The firm's beginning cash balance for the budget period is $5,000. This amount should be maintained as a minimum cash balance.
- The firm has an $80,000 line of credit with its bank at an interest rate of 12 percent annually (a 1 percent monthly rate). The interest owed is to be paid monthly.
- Interest on a $40,000 bank note (with the principal due in December) is payable at an 8 percent annual rate for the three-month period ending in September.

Based on the information above, Carriles has used a computer spreadsheet to prepare a monthly cash budget for the three-month period ending September 30. Figure 23-6 shows the results of her computations, which involved the following steps:

1. Determine the amount of collections each month, based on the projected collection patterns.
2. Estimate the amount and timing of the following cash disbursements:
   a. Inventory purchases and payments. The amount of the purchases is shown in the boxed area of the table, with payments being made one month later.
   b. Rent, wages, taxes, utilities, and interest on the long-term note
   c. The interest to be paid on any outstanding short-term borrowing. For example, the table shows that for the month of July Carriles would need to borrow $10,600 to prevent the firm's cash balance from falling below the $5,000 acceptable minimum. Assume that the money will be borrowed at

Carriles Corporation Three-Month Cash Budget
for July–September

Figure 23-6

	May	June	July	August	September
Monthly sales	$100,000	$120,000	$130,000	$130,000	$120,000
Cash receipts			40%		
Cash sales for month			$ 52,000	$52,000	$48,000
1 month after sale		30%	36,000	39,000	39,000
2 months after sale	30%		30,000	36,000	39,000
Step 1 Total collections			$118,000	$127,000	$126,000
Purchases (80% of sales)		$104,000	$104,000	$96,000	$80,000
Cash disbursements					
Step 2a Payments on purchases			$104,000	$104,000	$96,000
Rent			3,000	3,000	3,000
Wages and salaries			18,000	18,000	16,000
Step 2b Tax prepayment			1,000		
Utilities (2% of sales)			2,600	2,600	2,400
Interest on long-term note					800
Step 2c Short-term interest (1% of short-term debt)				106	113
Total cash disbursements			$128,600	$127,706	$118,313
Step 3 Net change in cash			–$ 10,600	–$ 706	$ 7,687
Step 4 Beginning cash balance			5,000	5,000	5,000
Step 5 Cash balance before borrowing			–$ 5,600	$ 4,294	$ 12,687
Step 6 Short-term borrowing (payments)			10,600	706	–$ 7,687
Ending cash balance			$ 5,000	$ 5,000	$ 5,000
Step 7 Cumulative short-term borrowing			$ 10,600	$ 11,306	$ 3,619

the end of July and that the interest will be payable at the end of August. The amount of the interest in August is $106, or 1 percent of the $10,600 cumulative short-term debt outstanding at the end of July.

3. Calculate the net change in cash (cash receipts less cash disbursements).
4. Determine the beginning cash balance (ending cash balance from the prior month).
5. Compute the cash balance before short-term borrowing (net change in cash for the month plus the cash balance at the beginning of the month).
6. Calculate the short-term borrowing or repayment—the amount borrowed if there is a cash shortfall for the month or the amount repaid on any short-term debt outstanding.
7. Compute the cumulative amount of short-term debt outstanding, which also determines the amount of interest to be paid in the following month.

As you can see, the company does not achieve a positive cash flow until September. Short-term borrowing must be arranged, therefore, in both July and August. By preparing a cash budget, Carriles can anticipate these needs and avoid any nasty surprises that might otherwise occur.

When a small business has idle funds, the cash should be invested. The cash budget anticipates such occasions. If unexpected excess funds are generated, they should also be used to take advantage of the many short-term investment opportunities that are available. Certificates of deposit and money market certificates are just two of the numerous means of putting excess cash to work for a firm.

3 Explain the key issues in managing accounts receivable, inventory, and accounts payable.

MANAGING ACCOUNTS RECEIVABLE

Chapter 14 discussed the extension of credit by small firms and the managing and collecting of accounts receivable. This section considers the impact of credit decisions on working capital and particularly on cash flow. The most important factor in managing cash well within a small firm is the ability to collect accounts receivable quickly.

How Accounts Receivable Affect Cash

Granting credit to customers, although primarily a marketing decision, directly affects a firm's cash account. By selling on credit and thus allowing customers to delay payment, the selling firm delays the inflow of cash.

The total amount of customers' credit balances is carried on the balance sheet as accounts receivable—one of the firm's current assets. Of all noncash assets, accounts receivable are closest to becoming cash. Sometimes called "near cash," accounts receivable are typically collected and become cash within 30 to 60 days.

The Life Cycle of Receivables

The receivables cycle begins with a credit sale. In most businesses, an invoice is then prepared and mailed to the purchaser. When the invoice is received, the purchaser processes it, prepares a check, and mails the check in payment to the seller.

Under ideal circumstances, each of these steps is taken in a timely manner. Obviously, delays can occur at any stage of this process. Some delays result from inefficiencies within the selling firm. One small business owner found that the shipping clerk was batching invoices before sending them to the office for processing, delaying the preparation and mailing of invoices to customers. Of course, this practice also postponed the day on which the customers' money was received and deposited in the bank so that it could be used to pay bills. John Convoy, a cash-flow consultant and former treasurer of several small firms, explains it this way: "Most overdue receivables are unpaid because of problems in a company's organization. Your cash-flow system is vulnerable at points where information gets transferred—between salespeople, operations departments, accounting clerks—because errors disrupt your ability to get paid promptly."[4]

Credit management policies, practices, and procedures affect the life cycle of receivables and the flow of cash from them. It is important for small business owners, when establishing credit policies, to consider cash-flow requirements as well as the need to stimulate sales. A key goal of every company should be to minimize the average time it takes customers to pay their bills. By streamlining administrative procedures, a company can speed up the task of sending out bills, thereby generating cash faster. Here are some examples of credit-management practices that can have a positive effect on a company's cash flow:

- Minimize the time between shipping, invoicing, and sending notices on billings.
- Review previous credit experiences to determine impediments to cash flow, such as continued extension of credit to slow-paying or delinquent customers.
- Provide incentives for prompt payment by granting cash discounts or charging interest on delinquent accounts.
- Age accounts receivable on a monthly or even a weekly basis to identify quickly any delinquent accounts.

- Use the most effective methods for collecting overdue accounts. For example, prompt phone calls to overdue accounts can improve collections considerably.
- Use a **lock box**—a post-office box for receiving remittances. The firm's bank maintains a post-office box to which customers send their payments. The bank empties the lock box frequently and immediately deposits any checks into the firm's account.

lock box
a post-office box for receiving remittances from customers

Accounts-Receivable Financing

Some small businesses can speed up the cash flow from accounts receivable by borrowing against them. By financing receivables, they can often secure the use of their money 30 to 60 days earlier than would be possible otherwise. Although this practice was once concentrated largely in the garment business, it has expanded to many other types of small businesses, such as manufacturers, food processors, distributors, home building suppliers, and temporary employment agencies. Such financing is provided by commercial finance companies and by some banks.

Two types of accounts-receivable financing are possible. The first type uses a firm's **pledged accounts receivable** as collateral for a loan. Payments received from customers are forwarded to the lending institution to pay off the loan. In the second type of financing, a business sells its accounts receivable to a finance company, a practice known as **factoring**. The finance company thereby assumes the bad-debt risk associated with receivables it buys.

The obvious advantage of accounts-receivable financing is the immediate cash flow it provides for firms that have limited working capital. As a secondary benefit, the volume of borrowing can quickly be expanded proportionally to match a firm's growth in sales and accounts receivable.

A drawback to this type of financing is its high finance cost. Interest rates typically run several points above the prime interest rate, and factors charge a fee to compensate them for their credit-investigation activities and for the risk that customers may default in payment. Another weakness is that pledging accounts receivable may limit a firm's ability to borrow from a bank by removing a prime asset from its available collateral.

pledged accounts receivable
accounts receivable used as collateral for a loan

factoring
obtaining cash by selling accounts receivable to another firm

MANAGING INVENTORY

Inventory is a "necessary evil" in the financial management system. It is "necessary" because supply and demand cannot be managed to coincide precisely with day-to-day operations. Inventory is an "evil" because it ties up funds that are not actively productive.

Freeing Cash by Reducing Inventory

Inventory is a bigger problem for some small businesses than for others. The inventory of many service firms, for example, consists of only a few supplies. A manufacturer, on the other hand, has several inventories—raw materials, work in process, and finished goods. Also, retailers and wholesalers, especially those with high inventory turnover rates such as those in grocery distribution, are continually involved in solving inventory-management problems.

For years, David Schwartz and Alvin Domitz, owners of Harry W. Schwartz Bookshops in Milwaukee, simply ordered the books they expected to sell, no matter how long the volumes remained on the shelves. Eventually, spurred by their

Inventory management can be a complex and disheartening task for small business owners. Computerizing the inventory system of small bookstores, such as this one in Westport, Connecticut, frees up capital that can then be used for catalogs and other sales initiatives.

banker and a shortage of available working capital, Schwartz and Domitz developed a new computerized inventory system and came to recognize inventory as a double-edged sword. By ordering in small batches and tracking sales closely, they were able to increase inventory turnover by nearly 50 percent, which released capital for more productive uses.[5]

Chapter 20 discussed several ideas related to purchasing and inventory management that are designed to minimize inventory carrying costs and processing costs. The emphasis in this section is on practices that will minimize average inventory levels, thereby releasing funds for other applications. The correct minimum level of inventory is the level needed to maintain desired production schedules or a required level of customer service. A concerted effort to manage inventory can trim inventory excess and pay handsome dividends. For example, the Boston-based Superior Pet Products Company tightened its inventory policies and freed up about $400,000 in capital. This released capital also meant a savings of $80,000 in interest expense, which was being paid to finance the inventory.[6]

Monitoring Inventory

One of the first steps in managing inventory is to discover what's in inventory and how long it's been there. Too often, items are purchased, warehoused, and essentially forgotten. A yearly inventory for accounting purposes is inadequate for good inventory control. Items that are slow movers may sit in a retailer's inventory beyond the time when markdowns should have been applied.

Computers can provide assistance in inventory identification and control. The use of physical inventories may still be required, but only to supplement the computerized system.

Controlling Stockpiling

Some small business managers tend to overbuy inventory for several reasons. First, an entrepreneur's enthusiasm may forecast greater demand than is realistic. Second, the personalization of the business-customer relationship may motivate a manager to stock everything customers want. Third, a price-conscious manager may overly subscribe to a vendor's appeal: "Buy now; prices are going up."

Stockpiling is not bad per se. Improperly managed and uncontrolled stockpiling may, however, greatly increase inventory carrying costs and place a heavy drain on the funds of a small business. Managers must exercise restraint.

MANAGING ACCOUNTS PAYABLE

Cash-flow management and accounts-payable management are intertwined. As long as a payable is outstanding, the buying firm can keep cash equal to that amount in its own checking account. When payment is made, however, that firm's cash account is reduced accordingly.

Although payables are legal obligations, they can be paid at various times or even renegotiated in some cases. Therefore, financial management of accounts payable hinges on negotiation and timing.

Negotiation

Any business is subject to emergency situations and may find it necessary to request of its creditors postponement of its payable obligations. Usually, creditors will cooperate in working out a solution because they want the firm to succeed.

Timing

The saying "Buy now, pay later" is the motto of many entrepreneurs. By buying on credit, a small business is using creditors' funds to supply short-term cash needs. The longer creditors' funds can be borrowed, the better. Payment, therefore, should be delayed as long as acceptable under the agreement.

Typically, accounts payable (trade credit) involves payment terms that include a cash discount. With trade-discount terms, paying later may be inappropriate. For example, terms of 3/10, net 30 offer a 3 percent potential discount. Table 23-1 shows the possible settlement costs over the credit period of 30 days. Note that for a $20,000 purchase, a settlement of only $19,400 is required if payment is made within the first 10 days ($20,000 less the 3 percent discount of $600). Between day 11 and day 30, the full settlement of $20,000 is required. After 30 days, the settlement cost may exceed the original amount, as late-payment fees are added.

The timing question then becomes "Should the account be paid on day 10 or day 30?" There is little reason to pay $19,400 on days 1 through 9, when the same amount will settle the account on day 10. Likewise, if payment is to be made after day 10, it makes sense to wait until day 30 to pay $20,000.

Table 23-1

An Accounts-Payable Timetable

Timetable (days after invoice date)	Settlement Costs for a $20,000 Purchase (terms: 3/10, net 30)
Day 1 through 10	$19,400
Day 11 through 30	$20,000
Day 31 and thereafter	$20,000 + possible late penalty and deterioration in credit standing

By paying on the last day of the discount period, the buyer saves the amount of the discount offered. The other alternative of paying on day 30 allows the buyer to use the seller's money for an additional 20 days by forgoing the discount. As Table 23-1 (on page 513) shows, the buyer can use the seller's $19,400 for 20 days at a cost of $600. The annualized interest rate can be calculated as follows:

$$\text{Annualized rate} = \frac{\text{Days in year}}{\text{Net period} - \text{Cash discount period}} \times \frac{\text{Cash discount \%}}{100 - \text{Cash discount \%}}$$

$$= \frac{365}{30 - 10} \times \frac{3}{100 - 3}$$

$$= 18.25 \times 0.030928$$

$$= 0.564, \text{ or } 56.4\%$$

By failing to take a discount, a business typically pays a high rate for use of a supplier's money—56.4 percent per annum in this case. Payment on day 10 appears to be the most logical choice. Recall, however, that the payment also affects cash flow. If funds are extremely short, a small firm may have to pay on the last possible day in order to avoid an overdraft at the bank.

We now shift the discussion from management of a firm's working capital to management of its long-term assets—equipment and plant—or what is called capital budgeting.

CAPITAL BUDGETING

Discuss the techniques commonly used in making capital budgeting decisions.

capital budgeting analysis
an analytical method that helps managers make decisions about long-term investments

Capital budgeting analysis helps managers make decisions about long-term investments. In developing a new product line, for example, a firm needs to expand its manufacturing capabilities and to buy the inventory required to make the product. That is, it makes investments today with an expectation of receiving profits or cash flows in the future, possibly over 10 or 20 years.

Some capital budgeting decisions that might be made by a small company include the following:

- Develop and introduce a new product that shows promise but requires additional study and improvement.
- Replace a company's delivery trucks with newer models.
- Expand sales activity into a new territory.

Capital budgeting decisions must be carefully weighed by the small business owner to determine the value of future benefits to the firm. The owner of Klosterman Bakery decided to invest in updating the firm's delivery trucks with newer models.

- Construct a new building.
- Hire several additional salespersons to intensify selling in the existing market.

Although the owner of a small business does not make long-term investment decisions frequently, capital budgeting is still important. Correct investment decisions will add value to the firm. A wrong capital budgeting decision, on the other hand, may prove fatal to a small firm.

Capital Budgeting Techniques

Three techniques for making capital budgeting decisions are considered here. They all attempt to answer one general question: Do the future benefits from an investment exceed the cost of making the investment? However, each of the techniques answers this question by focusing on a different specific question. The techniques and the specific question each addresses can be stated as follows:

1. *Accounting return on investment.* How many dollars in average profits are generated per dollar of average investment?
2. *Payback period.* How long will it take to recover the original investment outlay?
3. *Discounted cash flow.* How does the present value of future benefits from the investment compare to the investment outlay?

Three simple rules are used in judging the merits of an investment. Although these may seem trite, the rules state in simple terms the best thinking about the attractiveness of an investment.

1. The investor prefers more cash rather than less cash.
2. The investor prefers cash sooner rather than later.
3. The investor prefers less risk rather than more risk.

ACCOUNTING RETURN ON INVESTMENT   A small firm invests to earn profits. The **accounting return on investment technique** compares the average annual after-tax profits a firm expects to receive with the average book value of the investment.

$$\text{Accounting return on investment} = \frac{\text{Average annual after-tax profits per year}}{\text{Average book value of the investment}}$$

accounting return on investment technique
a technique that evaluates a capital expenditure based on the average annual profits relative to the average book value of an investment

The average annual profits can be estimated by adding the after-tax profits expected over the life of the project and dividing by the number of years the project is expected to last. The average book value of an investment equals the average of the initial outlay and the estimated final project salvage value. To make an accept-reject decision, the owner compares the calculated return to a minimum acceptable return, which is usually based on past experience.

As an illustration of the use of the accounting return on investment, assume that you are contemplating buying a piece of equipment for $10,000 and depreciating it over four years to a book value of zero (it will have no salvage value). Further assume that you expect the investment to generate after-tax profits each year as follows:

Year	After-Tax Profits
1	$1,000
2	2,000
3	2,500
4	3,000

The accounting return on the proposed investment is calculated as follows:

$$\text{Accounting return on investment} = \frac{\dfrac{(\$1,000 + \$2,000 + \$2,500 + \$3,000)}{4}}{\dfrac{(\$10,000 + \$0)}{2}}$$

$$= \frac{\$2,125}{\$5,000} = 0.425, \text{ or } 42.5\%$$

For most people, a 42.5 percent profit rate would seem outstanding. Assuming the calculated accounting return on investment of 42.5 percent exceeds your minimum acceptable return, you will accept the project. If not, you will reject the investment, provided, of course, that you have confidence in the technique.

Although the accounting return on investment is easy to calculate, it has two major shortcomings. First, it is based on *accounting profits* rather than *actual cash flows* received. An investor should be more interested in the future cash produced by the investment than in the reported profits. Second, the accounting return technique ignores the time value of money. Thus, although it is a popular technique, the accounting return on investment fails to satisfy any of the three rules already mentioned concerning the investor's preference for receiving more cash sooner with less risk.

payback period technique
a capital budgeting technique that measures the amount of time it takes to recover the cash outlay of an investment

PAYBACK PERIOD   The **payback period technique**, as the name suggests, measures how long it will take to recover the initial cash outlay of an investment. It deals with cash flows as opposed to accounting profits. The merits of any project are judged on whether the initial investment outlay can be recovered in less time than some maximum acceptable payback period. For example, an owner may not want to invest in any project that requires more than five years to recoup the investment. Assume that the owner is studying an investment in equipment with an expected life of 10 years. The investment outlay will be $15,000, with depreciation of the cost of the equipment on a straight-line basis, or $1,500 per year. If the owner makes the investment, the annual after-tax profits can be estimated as follows:

Years	After-Tax Profits
1–2	$1,000
3–6	2,000
7–10	2,500

To determine the after-tax cash flows from the investment, the owner would merely add back the depreciation of $1,500 each year to the profit. The reason for adding the depreciation to the profit is that it was deducted when the profits were calculated (as an accounting entry), even though it was not a cash outflow. The results, then, would be as follows:

Years	After-Tax Cash Flows
1–2	$2,500
3–6	3,500
7–10	4,000

By the end of the second year, the owner will have recovered $5,000 of the investment outlay ($2,500 per year). By the end of the fourth year, another $7,000, or $12,000 in total, will have been recouped. The additional $3,000 can be recovered in the fifth year, when $3,500 is expected. Thus, it will take 4.86 years [4 years + ($3,000 ÷ $3,500)] to recover the investment. If the maximum acceptable payback is more than 4.86 years, the owner will accept the investment.

Many managers and owners of companies use the payback technique in evaluating investment decisions. Although it uses cash flows, rather than accounting profits, the payback period technique has two significant weaknesses. First, it does not consider the time value of money (cash is preferred sooner rather than later). Second, it fails to consider the cash flows received after the payback period (more cash is preferred, rather than less).

DISCOUNTED CASH FLOW   Managers can avoid the deficiencies of the accounting return on investment and payback period techniques by using discounted cash flow analysis. Discounted cash flow techniques take into consideration the fact that cash today is more valuable than cash received one year from now (time value of money). For example, interest can be earned on cash that can be invested immediately; this is not true for cash to be received later.

The **discounted cash flow (DCF) techniques** compare the present value of future cash flows with the investment outlay. Such an analysis may take the form of either of two methods: net present value or internal rate of return.

The **net present value (NPV)** method estimates the current value of the cash that will flow into the firm from the project in the future and deducts the amount of the investment being made today. To find the present value of the expected future cash flows to be received, we discount them back to the present at the firm's cost of capital, where the cost of capital is equal to the investors' required rate of return. If the net present value of the investment is positive (that is, if the present value of future cash flows discounted at the return rate required to satisfy the firm's investors exceeds the initial outlay), the project is acceptable.

The **internal rate of return (IRR)** method estimates the rate of return that can be expected from a contemplated investment. For the investment outlay to be attractive, the internal rate of return must exceed the firm's cost of capital—the return rate required to satisfy the firm's investors.

The use of DCF techniques is explained and illustrated in Appendix 23B at the end of this chapter. (Appendix 23A will familiarize you with the concept and application of time value of money.)

We have presented several approaches for evaluating investment opportunities. Discounted cash flow techniques can generally be trusted to provide a more reliable basis for decisions than does the accounting return on investment or the payback period. However, use of DCF techniques requires determination of the appropriate discount rate. The discount rate—often called the cost of capital or, more precisely, the weighted cost of capital—is an issue that deserves careful attention.

Determining a Firm's Cost of Capital

The **cost of capital** is the rate of return a firm must earn on its investments in order to satisfy its debt holders and its owners. An investment with an internal rate of return below the cost of capital—a rate of return that is less than what creditors and owners require—will decrease the value of the firm and the owner's equity value. An investment with an expected rate of return above the cost of capital, on the other hand, will increase the owner's equity value. Although determining a firm's cost of capital is extremely important for effective financial management, few small business owners are aware of the concept, much less able to estimate their firm's cost of capital.

MEASURING COST OF CAPITAL   Calculation of a firm's cost of capital is based on the opportunity cost concept. An **opportunity cost** is the rate of return an owner could earn on another investment with similar risk. For example, a small business owner contemplating an expansion would want to know the rate of return that

---

discounted cash flow (DCF) technique
a capital budgeting technique that compares the present value of future cash flows with the cost of the initial investment

net present value (NPV)
the present value of future cash flows less the initial investment outlay

internal rate of return (IRR)
the rate of return a firm expects to earn on a project

5 Determine the appropriate cost of capital to be used in discounted cash flow techniques.

cost of capital
the rate of return required to satisfy a firm's investors

opportunity cost
the rate of return that could be earned on another investment of similar risk

Action Report

GLOBAL OPPORTUNITIES

Deciding on a Capital Investment

In Southeast Asia, a woman who marries into a Chinese family becomes an integral part of that family and usually lives with other family members. If the family owns a business, she is expected to work in the firm. Such was the case for Sirikarn Saksripanith, a Thai woman who married Sittichai Saksripanith, a member of a Chinese family that owned a ceramics manufacturing firm.

After working for the firm for a time, Sirikarn began making suggestions for improvements, but her ideas were seldom implemented. She eventually decided that she was prepared to operate her own plant. So, she and her husband approached his parents to indicate their desire to break away from the family business. Even though this meant that they would be in direct competition with Sittichai's family, the parents not only gave their blessing but provided the land for the new facility. With the land as collateral, Sirikarn borrowed money to build the plant. The new firm was successful almost at the outset. She then considered building a second plant. Her financial projections for the new plant are shown below in baht (25 baht equals 1 U.S. dollar).

Monthly Pro Forma Income Statement		*Projected Initial Investment*	
Sales revenue	2,451,000	Land	6,000,000
Cost of goods sold	1,710,000	Plant	11,468,000
Gross profit	741,000	Ceramic oven	4,000,000
Operation expenses:	114,000	Other ceramic equipment	8,170,000
Depreciation	213,166	Office equipment	500,000
Operating income	413,834	Other office equipment	1,150,000
Interest expense	200,000	Equipment installation	1,000,000
Earnings before taxes	213,834	Other startup expenses	3,000,000
Income taxes	64,150	Total investment outlay	35,288,000
Monthly net income	149,684		

Sirikarn used the accounting rate of return—income relative to the size of the investment—to decide whether to invest. Based on her projections, the decision was made to build the plant. Her bank helped with the financing, and she began construction in 1995. By year's end, the plant was in full operation.

At the time of her evaluation, Sirikarn did not know about the net present value method of analysis—a technique that she later wished she had used.

Source: Personal interview with Sirikarn Saksripanith in Lampang, Thailand, August 1995.

---

could be earned elsewhere with the same amount of risk. If the owner could earn a 15 percent return on the money by investing it elsewhere, then the expansion investment should not be made unless it is expected to earn at least 15 percent. The 15 percent rate of return is the opportunity cost of the money and, therefore, should be the cost of capital for the firm's equity investors.

The cost of capital should recognize all permanent sources of finance, including debt and ownership equity. That is, a **weighted cost of capital** is needed. For example, assume that a firm expects to finance future investments with 40 percent

weighted cost of capital
the cost of capital adjusted to reflect the relative costs of debt and equity financing

debt and 60 percent equity. Further assume that the opportunity cost of funds supplied by debt holders (that is, the current interest rate) is 10 percent. However, since the interest paid by the firm is tax deductible and the firm's tax rate is 25 percent, the after-tax cost of the money is only 7.5 percent [$0.10 \times (1 - 0.25)$]. If the opportunity cost of capital for the owners is thought to be 18 percent, the firm's weighted cost of capital is 13.8 percent:

	Weight	Cost	Weighted Cost
Debt	40%	7.5%	3.0%
Equity	60	18.0	10.8
Total	100%		13.8%

The 13.8 percent rate becomes the discount rate used in present value analysis, assuming that future investments will be financed on average by 40 percent debt and 60 percent equity and that the riskiness of the future investments will be similar to the riskiness of the firm's existing assets.

The greatest difficulty in measuring a company's weighted cost of capital is estimating the cost of owners' equity. Debt holders receive their rate of return mostly through the interest paid to them by the company, and the cost estimation is relatively straightforward. The required return for the owners is another matter, however. Although some of their expected returns are in the form of dividends received, most are derived from the increase in the firm's value, or what is generally called capital gains.

In measuring the cost of equity for a large, publicly traded company, an analyst uses market data to estimate the owners' required rate of return. However, since a small firm is owned either by a family or by a specific small group of investors, the owners' required rates of return can be determined by direct inquiry. As long as the owners are informed about competitive rates in the marketplace, they can set the required rate of return.

USING THE COST OF DEBT AS AN INVESTMENT CRITERION   The weighted cost of capital may be fine in theory, but what if a company could borrow the entire amount needed for an investment in a new product line? Is it really necessary to use the weighted cost of capital, or can the decision simply be based on the cost of the debt providing the funding?

Consider the Poling Corporation. The firm's owners believe they could earn a 14 percent rate of return by purchasing $50,000 in new equipment to expand the business. Although the firm tries to maintain a capital structure with equal amounts of debt and equity, it can borrow the entire $50,000 from the bank at an interest rate of 12 percent. Any time the return on the investment is greater than the cost of the debt financing, using debt will increase a firm's net income. In this case, the expected return on investment is 14 percent and the cost of debt financing is 12 percent. The increase in net income comes from the use of **favorable financial leverage**, investing at a rate of return that exceeds the interest rate on borrowed money.

The owners of the firm have also estimated the required rate of return for their funds to be 18 percent. However, since Poling can finance the purchase totally by debt, the owners have decided to make the investment and finance it by borrowing the money from the bank at 12 percent.

The following year, Poling's owners find another investment opportunity costing $50,000, but with an expected internal rate of return of 17 percent—better than the previous year's 14 percent. However, when they approach the bank for financing, they find it unwilling to lend the company any more money. In the words of the banker, "Poling has used up all of its debt capacity." Before the bank

favorable financial leverage
benefit gained by investing at a rate of return that is greater than the interest rate on a loan

will agree to fund any more loans, the owners must either contribute more of their own money in the form of common equity or find some new investors to invest in the business. However, since the investment does not meet the owners' required rate of return of 18 percent, they believe there is no other option than to reject the investment.

What is the moral of the story for Poling? Intuitively, we know that Poling's owners made a mistake. Making the investment in the first year denied the firm the opportunity to make a better decision in the second year.

A more general conclusion is that a firm should never use a single cost of financing as the criterion for making capital budgeting decisions. When a firm uses debt, it implicitly uses up some of its debt capacity for future investments; only when it complements the use of debt with equity will it be able to continue to use more debt in the future. Thus, business owners should always use a weighted cost of capital that recognizes the need to blend equity with debt over time.

Capital Budgeting Practices of Small Firms

> **6** Describe the capital budgeting practices of small firms.

A 1963 study of capital budgeting practices in small firms in Iowa asked owners how they went about analyzing capital budgeting projects. The findings were not encouraging. Fifty percent of the respondents said they used the payback technique. Even worse, 40 percent of the firms used no formal analysis at all.[7] However, 30 years ago, even large firms were not using discounted cash flow techniques to any great extent.

When 200 small companies with net worths between $500,000 and $1 million were surveyed in a 1983 study, an examination of their approaches for evaluating the merits of proposed capital investments revealed that only 14 percent used any form of a discounted cash flow technique, 70 percent used no DCF approach at all, and 9 percent used no formal analysis of any kind.[8] Although it is encouraging to note that the practice of not relying on any formal analysis has declined significantly, small businesses are still not using net present value (DCF) analysis.

Why are so few small businesses using DCF? Since the 1983 study dealt with firms having net worths under $1 million, a significant number of the owners probably had not been exposed to these financial concepts. However, the cause for such limited use of DCF tools probably rests more with the nature of the small firm it-

Although many small business owners do not give high priority to long-term planning, such planning is essential in avoiding liquidity problems. At regular budget meetings, such as this one in Raleigh, North Carolina, executives can develop strategies and forecasts to prevent undercapitalization.

self. We suggest that several more important reasons exist, including the following:

- For many owners of small firms, the business is an extension of their lives: Business events affect them personally. The same is true in reverse: What happens to the owners personally affects decisions about the firm. The firm and its owners are inseparable. We cannot fully understand decisions made about a firm without being aware of the personal events in the owners' lives. Consequently, nonfinancial variables may play a significant part in owners' decisions. For instance, the desire to be viewed as a respected part of the community may be more important to an owner than the present value of a business decision.
- The undercapitalization and liquidity problems of a small firm can directly affect the decision-making process, and survival often becomes the top priority. Long-term planning is, therefore, not viewed by the owners as a high priority in the total scheme of things.
- The greater uncertainty of cash flows within a small firm makes long-term forecasts and planning seem unappealing and even a waste of time. The owners simply have no confidence in their ability to predict cash flows beyond two or three years. Thus, calculating the cash flows for the entire life of a project is viewed as a futile effort.
- The value of a closely held firm is less easily observed than that of a

publicly held firm whose securities are actively traded in the marketplace. Therefore, the owner of a small firm may consider the market-value rule of maximizing net present values irrelevant. Estimating the cost of capital is also much more difficult for a small firm than for a large firm.

- The smaller size of a small firm's projects may make net present value computations less feasible in a practical sense. The time and expense required to analyze a capital investment are generally the same, whether the project is large or small. Therefore, it is relatively more costly for a small firm to conduct such a study.
- Management talent within a small firm is a scarce resource. Also, the owner-managers frequently have a technical background, as opposed to a business or

1 **Describe the working-capital cycle of a small business.**

- The working-capital cycle begins with the purchase of inventory and ends with the collection of accounts receivable.
- The cash conversion period is critical because it is the time period during which cash-flow problems can arise.

2 **Identify the important issues in managing a firm's cash flows.**

- A firm's cash flows consist of cash flowing into a business (through sales revenue, borrowing, and so on) and cash flowing out of the business (through purchases, operating expenses, and so on).
- Profitable small companies sometimes encounter cash-flow problems by failing to understand the working-capital cycle or failing to anticipate the negative consequences of growth.
- Cash inflows and outflows are reconciled in the cash budget, which involves forecasts of cash receipts and expenditures.

3 **Explain the key issues in managing accounts receivable, inventory, and accounts payable.**

- Granting credit to customers, primarily a marketing decision, directly affects a firm's cash account.
- A firm can improve its cash flow by speeding up collections from customers, minimizing inventories, and delaying payments to suppliers.
- Some small businesses can speed up the cash flow from accounts receivable by borrowing against them.
- A concerted effort to manage inventory can trim inventory fat and free cash for other uses.
- Accounts payable, a primary source of financing for small firms, directly affect a firm's cash-flow situation.

4 **Discuss the techniques commonly used in making capital budgeting decisions.**

- Capital budgeting is the process of planning long-term expenditures.
- The most popular capital budgeting techniques among small businesses are the payback period and the accounting return on investment methods.
- The discounted cash flow techniques—net present value and internal rate of return—provide the best accept-reject decision criteria in capital budgeting analysis.

Continue on next page

5 Determine the appropriate cost of capital to be used in discounted cash flow techniques.

- The cost of capital is the discount rate used in determining a project's net present value.
- The cost of capital equals the investors' opportunity cost of funds.
- Few small firms make use of the concept of cost of capital.
- A firm should not use cost of debt as a substitute for the cost-of-capital criterion in making investment decisions.

6 Describe the capital budgeting practices of small firms.

- A 1983 study revealed that only 14 percent of small firms used any type of a discounted cash flow technique and 9 percent used no formal analysis at all.
- The very nature of small firms may explain, to some degree, why they seldom use the conceptually richer and more effective techniques for evaluating long-term investments.

New Terms and Concepts

working-capital management *499*

net working capital *499*

working-capital cycle *499*

cash conversion period *501*

growth trap *507*

cash budget *508*

lock box *511*

pledged accounts receivable *511*

factoring *511*

capital budgeting analysis *514*

accounting return on investment technique *515*

payback period technique *516*

discounted cash flow (DCF) technique *517*

net present value (NPV) *517*

internal rate of return (IRR) *517*

cost of capital *517*

opportunity cost *517*

weighted cost of capital *518*

favorable financial leverage *519*

compound value of a dollar *524*

---

finance orientation. The perspective of owners is influenced greatly by their backgrounds.

The foregoing characteristics of a small firm and its owners have a significant effect on the decision-making process within the firm. The result is often a short-term mindset, caused partly by necessity and partly by choice. However, the owner of a small firm should make every effort to use discounted cash flow techniques and to be certain that contemplated investments will, in fact, provide returns that exceed the firm's cost of capital.

DISCUSSION QUESTIONS

1. a. List the events in the working-capital cycle that directly affect cash and those that do not.
   b. What determines the length of a firm's cash conversion period?
2. a. What are some examples of cash receipts that are not sales revenue?
   b. Explain how expenses and cash disbursements during a month may be different.
3. How may a seller speed up the collection of accounts receivable? Give examples that may apply to various stages in the life cycle of receivables.
4. Suppose that a small firm could successfully shift to a just-in-time inventory system—an arrangement in which inventory is received just as it is needed. How would this affect the firm's working-capital management?
5. How do working-capital management and capital budgeting differ?
6. Contrast the different techniques that can be used in capital budgeting analysis.
7. Could a firm conceivably make an investment that would increase its earnings but reduce the firm's value?
8. Define internal rate of return.
9. a. Find the accounting return on investment for a project that costs $10,000, will have no salvage value, and has expected annual after-tax profits of $1,000.
   b. Determine the payback period for a capital investment that costs $40,000 and has the following after-tax profits. (The project outlay of $40,000 would be depreciated on a straight-line basis to a zero salvage value.)

Year	After-Tax Profits
1	$4,000
2	5,000
3	6,000
4	6,500
5	6,500
6	6,000
7	5,000

10. *a.* Define cost of capital. Why is it important?
    b. Why do we compute a *weighted* cost of capital?

EXPERIENTIAL EXERCISES

1. Interview the owner of a small firm to determine the nature of the firm's working-capital time line. Try to estimate the cash conversion period.
2. Interview a small business owner or credit manager regarding the extension of credit and/or the collection of receivables in that firm. Summarize your findings in a report.
3. Identify a small company in your community that has recently expanded. Interview the owner of the firm about the methods used in evaluating the expansion.
4. Either alone or with a classmate, approach an owner of a small company about getting data on a current problem or one the company encountered at some time in the past, to see whether you would reach the same decision as the owners did.

 CASE 23
Barton Sales and Service (p. 653)

This case looks at the financial performance of a small air-conditioning and heating services company, with emphasis on its working-capital policies.

Alternative Case for Chapter 23: Case 14, "The Jordan Construction Account," p. 629

You Make the Call

Situation 1 A small firm specializing in the sale and installation of swimming pools was profitable but devoted very little attention to managing its working capital. It had, for example, never prepared or used a cash budget. To be sure that money was available for payments as needed, the firm kept a minimum of $25,000 in a checking account. At times, this account grew larger, once totaling $43,000. The owner felt that this practice of cash management worked well for a small company because it eliminated all the paperwork associated with cash budgeting. Moreover, it had enabled the firm to pay its bills in a timely manner.

Question 1 What are the advantages and weaknesses of the minimum cash balance practice?
Question 2 There is a saying, "If it's not broke, don't fix it." In view of the firm's present success in paying bills promptly, should it be encouraged to use a cash budget? Defend your answer.

Situation 2 Ruston Manufacturing Company is a small firm selling entirely on a credit basis. It has experienced successful operation and earned modest profits. Sales are made on the basis of net payment in 30 days. Collections from customers run approximately 70 percent in 30 days, 20 percent in 60 days, 7 percent in 90 days, and 3 percent bad debts. The owner has considered the possibility of offering a cash discount for early payment. However, the practice seems costly and possibly unnecessary. As the owner has put it, "Why should I bribe customers to pay what they legally owe?"

Question 1 Is a cash discount the equivalent of a bribe?
Question 2 How would a cash discount policy relate to bad debts?
Question 3 What cash discount policy, if any, would you recommend?
Question 4 What other approaches might be used to improve cash flow from accounts receivable?

Situation 3 Return to the Action Report featuring Sirikarn Saksripanith, the young Thai woman who decided to build a new ceramics plant. Her analysis was based on the projected net income relative to the size of the investment. Review the data as they are presented in the Action Report.

Question 1 Do you see any weakness or inadequacy in the data as presented?
Question 2 Compute the accounting return on investment—to do so, you must convert the monthly income to annual income.
Question 3 From the financial data, do you think Saksripanith should have made the investment?

APPENDIX 23A
TIME VALUE OF MONEY: FINDING THE PRESENT VALUE OF A DOLLAR

This appendix briefly explains the concept of time value of money—that is, a dollar today is worth more than a dollar received a year from now. To logically compare projects and financial strategies, we must move all cash flows back to the present.

The Departure Point

The starting point for finding the present value of future cash flows is represented in the following equation:

$$FV_n = PV(1 + i)^n$$

where

FV_n = future value of the investment at the end of n years

PV = present value or original amount invested at the beginning of the first year

i = annual interest (or discount) rate

n = number of years during which the compounding occurs

The above equation can be used to answer the following question: If you invested $500 today (PV = $500) at an annual interest rate of 8 percent ($i = 0.08$), how much money would you have (future value, or FV_n) in five years ($n = 5$)? If interest is compounded annually (interest is earned on the interest each new year), the answer is

$$FV_n = \$500(1 + 0.08)^5$$
$$= \$500(1.4693)$$
$$= \$734.65$$

Thus, if you invested $500 today at 8 percent, compounded annually, you would have $734.65 at the end of five years. This procedure is called calculating the **compound value of a dollar.**

compound value of a dollar
the increasing value of a dollar over time resulting from interest earned both on the original dollar and on the interest received in prior periods

The Present Value of a Dollar

Determining the present value—that is, the value in today's dollars of a sum of money to be received in the future—involves inversing the compounding process just described. Restructuring the equation shown above to solve for the present value of a dollar, yields

$$PV = \frac{FV_n}{(1 + i)^n}$$
$$= FV_n \left[\frac{1}{(1 + i)^n} \right]$$

where PV is now the present value of a future sum of money, FV_n is the future value of the money to be received in year n, and i is the interest rate.

Thus, the present value of $1,200 to be received in 7 years, assuming an interest rate of 10 percent, is

$$PV = FV_n \left[\frac{1}{(1+i)^n} \right]$$

$$= \$1,200 \left[\frac{1}{(1+0.10)^7} \right]$$

$$= \$1,200(0.5132)$$

$$= \$615.84$$

Rather than solving for the present value by using this equation, we may instead use Appendix B at the end of the book, in which the computations within the brackets have already been performed to yield the present value interest factors for year n and interest rate i, or $PVIF_{i,n}$.

$$PVIF_{i,n} = \left[\frac{1}{(1+i)^n} \right]$$

Suppose that we want to calculate the present value of $2,000 to be received in 12 years, with an interest rate of 14 percent:

$$PV = \$2,000(PVIF_{14\%,12\,yr})$$

Appendix B, in the row for 12 years and the column for the interest rate of 14 percent, shows the present value interest factor to be 0.208. So,

$$PV = \$2,000(0.208)$$

$$= \$416$$

Therefore, the present value of $2,000 to be received in 12 years is $416, assuming an interest rate of 14 percent. In other words, we would be indifferent to receiving $416 today or $2,000 in 12 years.

The Present Value of an Annuity

An annuity is a series of equal dollar payments for a specified number of years. That is, a 10-year annuity of $200 yields $200 each year for 10 years. Alternatively, we could say that an annuity involves depositing or investing an equal sum of money at the end of each year for a certain number of years and allowing it to grow at the stated interest rate.

To find the present value, PV, of a three-year annuity of $600 (received each year) at an interest rate of 13 percent, we could perform the following operation:

$$PV = \frac{\$600}{(1+0.13)^1} + \frac{\$600}{(1+0.13)^2} + \frac{\$600}{(1+0.13)^3}$$

Using the present value interest factors from Appendix B, we may find the present value as follows:

$$PV = \$600(\text{PVIF}_{13\%,1\text{ yr}}) + \$600(\text{PVIF}_{13\%,2\text{ yr}}) + \$600(\text{PVIF}_{13\%,3\text{ yr}})$$
$$= \$600(0.885) + \$600(0.783) + \$600(0.693)$$
$$= \$531 + \$469.80 + \$415.80$$
$$= \$1,416.60$$

We could also find the present value of $1,416.60 in the following way:

$$PV = \$600(0.885 + 0.783 + 0.693)$$
$$= \$600(2.361)$$
$$= \$1,416.60$$

Also, rather than looking up the three present value interest factors individually, we can find the interest factor for an entire annuity in an interest factor table. A table of present value interest factors for an annuity is provided in Appendix C. If $\text{PVIFA}_{i,n}$ represents the present value interest factor for an annuity of n years at an interest rate of i and if the annual amount each year is defined as PMT, the equation for finding the present value of an annuity is as follows:

$$PV = PMT(\text{PVIFA}_{i,n})$$

Thus, if we want to find the present value of a 15-year annuity in the amount of $3,000 each year, at an interest rate of 18 percent, the solution is as follows:

$$PV = PMT(\text{PVIFA}_{i,n})$$
$$= \$3,000(\text{PVIFA}_{18\%,15\text{ yr}})$$

Locating 15 years and an 18 percent interest rate in Appendix C, we determine the interest factor for the annuity to be 5.092. Thus, the present value of the annuity is $15,276, computed as follows:

$$PV = \$3,000(5.092) = \$15,276$$

Using the foregoing explanation and the table values shown in Appendix B and Appendix C, you will be able to find the present value of future dollars to solve finance problems important to the owner of a small company. However, an even better approach is to use a good financial calculator or a computer spreadsheet.

APPENDIX 23B
DISCOUNTED CASH FLOW TECHNIQUES: COMPUTING A PROJECT'S NET PRESENT VALUE AND INTERNAL RATE OF RETURN

Chapter 23 described the concept of discounted cash flow analysis for capital budgeting decisions and introduced the two techniques commonly used—net present value and internal rate of return. This appendix builds on that description and provides a more in-depth explanation of these two techniques.

Net Present Value

To measure a project's *net present value (NPV)*, we estimate today's value of the dollars that will flow in from the project in the future and deduct the amount of the investment being made. That is, we discount the future after-tax cash flows back to their present value and then subtract the initial investment outlay. The computation may be represented as follows:

$$\text{Net present value} = \left(\begin{array}{c}\text{Present value of future}\\ \text{after-tax cash flows}\end{array}\right) - \left(\begin{array}{c}\text{Initial}\\ \text{investment outlay}\end{array}\right)$$

If the net present value of the investment is positive (that is, if the present value of future cash flows exceeds the initial outlay), we accept the project. Otherwise, we reject the investment.

The actual computation for finding the net present value follows:

$$NPV = \left[\frac{ACF_1}{(1+k)^1} + \frac{ACF_2}{(1+k)^2} + \frac{ACF_3}{(1+k)^3} + \cdots + \frac{ACF_n}{(1+k)^n}\right] - IO$$

where

$$NPV = \text{net present value of the project}$$
$$ACF_t = \text{after-tax cash flow in year } t$$
$$n = \text{life of the project in years}$$
$$k = \text{discount rate (required rate of return)}$$
$$IO = \text{initial investment outlay}$$

To see how to compute the net present value, assume that we are evaluating an investment in equipment that will cost $12,000. The equipment is expected to have a salvage value of $2,000 at the end of its projected life of five years. The investment is also expected to provide the following after-tax cash flows as a result of increased product sales:

Years	After-Tax Cash Flows
1	$1,500
2	2,500
3	4,000
4	4,000
5	3,000

These cash flows, plus the $2,000 in expected salvage value, can be represented graphically on a time line as follows. (Note that the after-tax cash flow in the fifth year includes both the $3,000 cash flow from operating the project and the $2,000 expected salvage value.)

(Cash inflows)	$1,500	$2,500	$4,000	$4,000	$5,000
	↓	↓	↓	↓	↓
	Year 1	Year 2	Year 3	Year 4	Year 5

(Outlays) $12,000

Further assume that the firm's required rate of return—or cost of capital, as it is often called—is 14 percent. As explained in Chapter 23, a firm's *cost of capital,* which is used as the discount rate, is the rate the firm must earn to satisfy its investors. Given this information, we can compute the investment's net present value as follows:

$$NPV = \left[\frac{\$1,500}{(1+0.14)^1} + \frac{\$2,500}{(1+0.14)^2} + \frac{\$4,000}{(1+0.14)^3} + \frac{\$4,000}{(1+0.14)^4} + \frac{\$5,000}{(1+0.14)^5} \right] - \$12,000$$

Using the present value interest factors ($PVIF_{k,n}$) for discount rate k and year n in Appendix B, we find the net present value of the investment to be −$1,099, calculated as follows:

$$NPV = \$1,500(PVIF_{14\%,1\ yr}) + \$2,500(PVIF_{14\%,2\ yr}) + \$4,000(PVIF_{14\%,3\ yr})$$
$$+ \$4,000(PVIF_{14\%,4\ yr}) + \$5,000(PVIF_{14\%,5\ yr}) - \$12,000$$
$$= \$1,500(0.877) + \$2,500(0.769) + \$4,000(0.675) + \$4,000(0.592)$$
$$+ \$5,000(0.519) - \$12,000$$
$$= \$10,901 - \$12,000 = -\$1,099$$

A financial calculator could also be used to solve for the present value of the project. (Such computations are shown in Figure A23-1 for a Hewlett Packard calculator Model 17B II and for the Texas Instruments BAII Plus.)

Since the net present value of the proposed investment is negative (that is, the present value of future cash flows is less than the cost of the investment), the investment should not be made. The negative net present value shows that the investment would not satisfy the firm's required rate of return of 14 percent. Only if the present value of future cash flows were greater than the $12,000 investment outlay would the firm's required rate of return be exceeded.

Internal Rate of Return

In the preceding example, we calculated the net present value and found it to be negative. Given the negative net present value, we concluded, and rightfully so, that the project would not earn the 14 percent required rate of return. But we did not take the next logical step and ask what rate would be earned, assuming our projections are on target. The *internal rate of return (IRR)* provides that answer by measuring the rate of return we expect to earn on the project.

PROBLEM:

Years	After-Tax Cash Flows
0	−$12,000
1	1,500
2	2,500
3	4,000
4	4,000
5	5,000

SOLUTION:

Hewlett Packard 17B II

1. Select the FIN menu and then the CFLO menu; clear memory if FLOW(0) = ? does not appear.
2. Enter the investment outlay, CF_0, as follows: 12,000 $\boxed{+/-}$ $\boxed{\text{INPUT}}$
3. Enter the first year after-tax cash flow, CF_1, as follows: 1,500 $\boxed{\text{INPUT}}$
4. Now the calculator will inquire if the $1,500 is for period 1 only. Press $\boxed{\text{INPUT}}$ to indicate that the cash flow is for one year only. If the $1,500 were expected for three years consecutively, you would press "3" and $\boxed{\text{INPUT}}$ to indicate three years of cash flows.
5. Enter the remaining CFs, with $\boxed{\text{INPUT}}$ followed each time by another $\boxed{\text{INPUT}}$ to indicate that each cash flow is for one year only.
6. Press $\boxed{\text{EXIT}}$ and then $\boxed{\text{CALC}}$.
7. Enter 14 $\boxed{\text{I\%}}$ to indicate the discount rate.
8. Press $\boxed{\text{NPV}}$ to find the project net present value of −$1,095.49.

Texas Instruments BAII Plus

1. Press $\boxed{\text{CF}}$ to select cash flow worksheet.
2. Press $\boxed{\text{2nd}}$ $\boxed{\text{CLR}}$ to clear memory.
3. Enter the investment outlay, CFo, as follows: 12,000 $\boxed{+/-}$ $\boxed{\text{ENTER}}$
4. Enter the first year after-tax cash flow, C01, as follows: $\boxed{\downarrow}$ 1,500 $\boxed{\text{ENTER}}$ $\boxed{\downarrow}$
5. Enter the frequency number, F01. Key in "1" and press $\boxed{\text{ENTER}}$ to indicate that the cash flow is for one year only. (If the $1,500 were expected for three years consecutively, you could have pressed "3" and $\boxed{\text{ENTER}}$ to indicate three years of cash flows.)
6. Repeat steps 4 and 5 to enter the other after-tax cash flows.
7. Press $\boxed{\text{NPV}}$ 14 $\boxed{\text{ENTER}}$ to indicate the discount rate of 14%.
8. Press $\boxed{\downarrow}$ $\boxed{\text{CPT}}$ to compute the NPV of −$1,095.49.

To calculate the internal rate of return, we must find the discount rate that gives us a zero net present value. At that rate, the present value of future cash flows just equals the investment outlay. Using the previous example, we need to determine the discount rate that causes the present value of future cash flows to equal $12,000, the cost of the investment. In other words, we need to find the internal rate of return that satisfies the following condition:

$$\left(\begin{matrix}\text{Present value of future} \\ \text{after-tax cash flows}\end{matrix}\right) - \left(\begin{matrix}\text{Initial} \\ \text{investment outlay}\end{matrix}\right) = \$0$$

or

$$\begin{pmatrix} \text{Present value of future} \\ \text{after-tax cash flows} \end{pmatrix} = \begin{pmatrix} \text{Initial} \\ \text{investment outlay} \end{pmatrix}$$

If ACF_t is the after-tax cash flow received in year t, IO is the amount of the investment outlay, and n is the life of the project in years, the internal rate of return, IRR, is the discount rate, where

$$\left[\frac{ACF_1}{(1 + IRR)^1} + \frac{ACF_2}{(1 + IRR)^2} + \frac{ACF_3}{(1 + IRR)^3} + \cdots + \frac{ACF_n}{(1 + IRR)^n} \right] - IO = \$0$$

For the previous example, the IRR can be found as follows:

$$\left[\frac{\$1,500}{(1 + IRR)^1} + \frac{\$2,500}{(1 + IRR)^2} + \frac{\$4,000}{(1 + IRR)^3} + \frac{\$4,000}{(1 + IRR)^4} + \frac{\$5,000}{(1 + IRR)^5} \right] - \$12,000 = \$0$$

We cannot solve for the internal rate of return directly. We must either try different rates until we discover the rate that gives us a zero net present value or use a financial calculator and let it compute the answer for us. Let's look at the first approach, which uses the present value table in Appendix B.

As already noted, finding the internal rate of return using the present value table involves a trial-and-error process. We must try new rates until we find the discount rate that causes the present value of future cash flows to just equal the initial investment outlay. If the internal rate of return is somewhere between rates in the table, we must then use interpolation to estimate the rate.

From the example, we know that a 14 percent discount rate causes the present value of future cash flows to be less than the initial outlay, and we would not earn 14 percent if we made the investment. We will, therefore, want to try a lower rate. Let's arbitrarily select 12 percent and see what happens:

$$NPV = \left[\frac{\$1,500}{(1 + 0.12)^1} + \frac{\$2,500}{(1 + 0.12)^2} + \frac{\$4,000}{(1 + 0.12)^3} + \frac{\$4,000}{(1 + 0.12)^4} + \frac{\$5,000}{(1 + 0.12)^5} \right]$$
$$- \$12,000$$

Using the table of present value interest factors in Appendix B, we find the net present value at a discount rate of 12 percent to be –$449.

$$NPV = \$1,500(0.893) + \$2,500(0.797) + \$4,000(0.712) + \$4,000(0.636)$$
$$+ \$5,000(0.567) - \$12,000$$
$$= \$11,559 - \$12,000 = -\$449$$

Since the net present value is still negative, we know that the rate is even lower than 12 percent. So let's try 10 percent.

$$NPV = \left[\frac{\$1,500}{(1 + 0.10)^1} + \frac{\$2,500}{(1 + 0.10)^2} + \frac{\$4,000}{(1 + 0.10)^3} + \frac{\$4,000}{(1 + 0.10)^4} + \frac{\$5,000}{(1 + 0.10)^5} \right]$$
$$- \$12,000$$

$$= \$1,500(0.909) + \$2,500(0.826) + \$4,000(0.751) + \$4,000(0.683)$$
$$+ \$5,000(0.621) - \$12,000$$
$$= \$12,270 - \$12,000 = \$270$$

Given a positive net present value ($270), we know that the internal rate of return is between 10 percent and 12 percent. Since the internal rate of return is less than the firm's required rate of return of 14 percent, we reject the investment. (Note: Any time the net present value is positive, the internal rate of return will be greater than the company's required rate of return. Conversely, any time the net present value is negative, the internal rate of return will be less than the company's required rate of return.)

To find the internal rate of return using either the Hewlett Packard 17B II or the Texas Instruments BAII Plus, repeat the steps taken in Figure A23-1. Then, on either calculator, press $\boxed{\text{IRR}}$. The answer will be 10.74 percent. Rather than entering the data again to compute the IRR, we could have solved for the NPV and the IRR while the data were still in the calculator. An even better approach is to use a computer spreadsheet, such as Excel or Lotus, to solve the problem.

Capital Budgeting: A Comprehensive Example

Let's consider one more example, using the various capital budgeting techniques on a single project. Suppose that it is the end of 1996 and you are considering a capital expenditure of $25,000 to invest in a new product line. The cost of the investment includes $15,000 for equipment and $10,000 in working capital (additional accounts receivable and inventories). The investment would have a five-year life (1997–2001), after which the equipment would have a zero salvage value. The cost of the equipment would be depreciated over the five years on a straight-line basis. The working capital would need to be maintained for the five years but could then be liquidated, with the firm recovering the full $10,000 in 2001. That is, all accounts receivable would be collected and the inventories liquidated. The projected income statements and after-tax cash flows for the next five years are given in Figure A23-2.

Relying on the data in Figure A23-2, we can use each of the evaluation techniques as follows:

1. *Accounting return on investment*

$$\text{Accounting return on investment} = \frac{\text{Average annual after-tax profits per year}}{\text{Average book value of the investment}}$$

$$= \frac{\displaystyle\sum_{t=1}^{n} \left(\frac{\text{Expected after-tax profit in year } t}{n} \right)}{\dfrac{(\text{Initial outlay} + \text{Expected salvage value})}{2}}$$

$$= \frac{\dfrac{(\$3,000 + \$4,500 + \$6,000 + \$6,000 + \$6,000)}{5}}{\dfrac{(\$25,000 + \$10,000)}{2}}$$

$$= \frac{\$5,100}{\$17,500} = 0.2914, \text{ or } 29.14\%$$

| Figure A23-2 | Projected Income Statements and Cash Flows—Comprehensive Example |

	1996	**1997**	**1998**	**1999**	**2000**	**2001**
Sales revenue		$30,000	$35,000	$40,000	$40,000	$40,000
Cost of goods sold		18,000	21,000	24,000	24,000	24,000
Gross profits		$12,000	$14,000	$16,000	$16,000	$16,000
Operating expenses:						
Marketing expenses		5,000	5,000	5,000	5,000	5,000
Depreciation expense		3,000	3,000	3,000	3,000	3,000
Operating profits		$ 4,000	$ 6,000	$ 8,000	$ 8,000	$ 8,000
Taxes		1,000	1,500	2,000	2,000	2,000
Earnings after taxes		$ 3,000	$ 4,500	$ 6,000	$ 6,000	$ 6,000
Plus depreciation		3,000	3,000	3,000	3,000	3,000
Plus working capital						10,000
After-tax cash flows	−$25,000	$ 6,000	$ 7,500	$ 9,000	$ 9,000	$19,000
Book value of the investment:						
Working capital	$10,000	$10,000	$10,000	$10,000	$10,000	$ 0
Equipment	15,000	12,000	9,000	6,000	3,000	0
Total book value	$25,000	$22,000	$19,000	$16,000	$13,000	$ 0

2. *Payback period*

Year	After-Tax Cash Flow	Cumulative Cash Flows to Be Recovered
1	$ 6,000	$ 6,000
2	7,500	13,500
3	9,000	22,500
4	9,000	31,500 ($6,500 over investment)

$$\text{Payback period} = 3 + \left(\frac{\$2,500}{\$9,000} \right) = 3.28 \text{ yr}$$

3. *Net present value*

$$\text{NPV} = \left[\frac{\text{ACF}_1}{(1+k)^1} + \frac{\text{ACF}_2}{(1+k)^2} + \frac{\text{ACF}_3}{(1+k)^3} + \cdots + \frac{\text{ACF}_n}{(1+k)^n} \right] - \text{IO}$$

$$= \left[\frac{\$6,000}{(1+0.15)^1} + \frac{\$7,500}{(1+0.15)^2} + \frac{\$9,000}{(1+0.15)^3} + \frac{\$9,000}{(1+0.15)^4} + \frac{\$19,000}{(1+0.15)^5} \right]$$
$$- \$25,000$$

Using a financial calculator, we find the net present value to be $6,398.
(The same answer could be found, subject to rounding differences, by using
Appendix B.)

4. *Internal rate of return*

$$\left[\frac{ACF_1}{(1+IRR)^1} + \frac{ACF_2}{(1+IRR)^2} + \frac{ACF_3}{(1+IRR)^3} + \cdots + \frac{ACF_n}{(1+IRR)^n}\right] - IO = \$0$$

$$\left[\frac{\$6{,}000}{(1+IRR)^1} + \frac{\$7{,}500}{(1+IRR)^2} + \frac{\$9{,}000}{(1+IRR)^3} + \frac{\$9{,}000}{(1+IRR)^4} + \frac{\$19{,}000}{(1+IRR)^5}\right]$$

$$- \$25{,}000 = \$0$$

Using a financial calculator, we find the internal rate of return to be 23.6 percent.

Risk and Insurance Management

spotlight on small business

Donna and
Joseph Dubé

All small business retailers face some degree of risk. Without insurance, damage to physical assets or their loss can prove particularly detrimental to a small business, and the loss can be more than financial. Donna and Joseph Dubé can attest to some of the problems associated with business risks.

After surviving a deep recession in New England and a statewide banking crisis, the Wickford, Rhode Island couple faced yet another disaster: The building that housed their gourmet food business suffered an electrical fire, which left it just a shell.

"We lost everything," Donna says. Until then, she had regarded the Dubés' retail business as a means of survival. But the fire taught her something: "I felt a great loss—not just financially," she says. "That's when I realized that I *loved* the business and that I wanted to stay in the business."

Fortunately, the Dubés were insured and were able to get the business running again in three months.

Source: Sharon Nelton, "Gourmet Food for Thought," *Nation's Business* (May 1994), p. 20.

start here

It is said that "Nothing is certain except death and taxes." Entrepreneurs might extend this adage: "Nothing is certain except death, taxes, and small business risks." In Chapter 1, we noted the moderate risk-taking propensities of entrepreneurs and their desire to exert some control over the risky situations in which they find themselves. As a consequence, they seek to minimize business risks as much as possible. The first step in managing business risks is understanding the different types of risks and alternatives for reducing them.

DEFINING AND CLASSIFYING RISK

Simply stated, **risk** is "a condition in which there is a possibility of an adverse deviation from a desired outcome that is expected or hoped for."[1] Applied to a small business situation, risk translates into losses associated with company assets and the earning potential of the company. Here, the term *asset* includes not only inventory and equipment but also such factors as the firm's employees and its reputation.

Small business risks can be classified in several ways. One simple approach groups them by cause of loss. For example, fire, personal injury, theft, and fraud would be key categories. Another approach identifies business risks by grouping them into two categories: generally insurable (for example, fire loss) and largely uninsurable (for example, product obsolescence).

A third classification approach, the one used in this chapter, emphasizes the asset-oriented focus of business risks by categorizing them into four areas: market-oriented risks, property-oriented risks, personnel-oriented risks, and customer-oriented risks. Although a substantial loss in any one of these four areas could devastate a small business, the first category—market-oriented risk—is primarily the result of market pressures and competition, which were discussed in previous chapters. Thus, we will look only at the last three categories of risk in this chapter. Figure 24-1 (see page 536) illustrates these risk categories and their components, with bankruptcy shown as the ultimate small business risk. This section examines the three forms of risk and identifies possible alternatives for dealing with them.

risk
the chance that a situation may end with loss or misfortune

Risks Associated with Property

Property-oriented risks involve tangible and highly visible assets. When these physical assets are lost or destroyed, they are quickly missed. Fortunately, many property-oriented risks are insurable; they include fire, natural disasters, burglary and business swindles, and shoplifting.

FIRE Buildings, equipment, and inventory items can be totally or partially destroyed by fire. Of course, the degree of risk and potential for loss are different for each type of business. For example, industrial processes that are hazardous or that involve explosives, combustibles, or other flammable materials increase this particular risk.

Figure 24-1

The Wheel of Misfortune

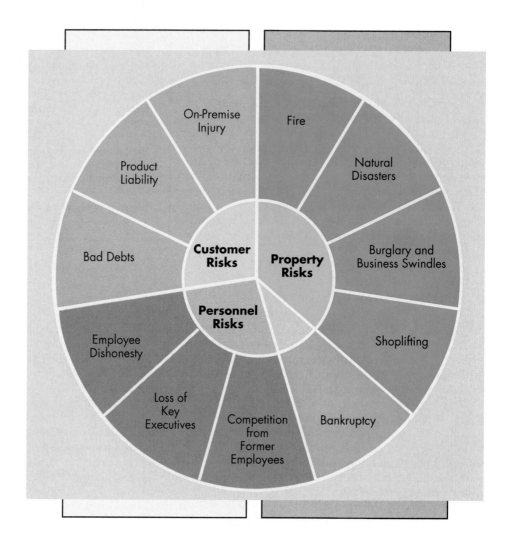

Fire not only causes direct property loss but also interrupts business operations. Although a firm's operations may be halted, such fixed expenses as rent, supervisory salaries, and insurance fees continue. To minimize losses arising from business interruptions, a firm might, for example, have alternative sources of electric power, such as its own generators, for use in times of emergency.

NATURAL DISASTERS Floods, hurricanes, tornadoes, and hail are often described as "acts of God" because of human limitations in foreseeing and controlling them. Like fire, natural disasters may interrupt business operations. Although a firm can take certain preventive measures—for example, locating in an area not subject to flood damage—little can be done to avoid natural disasters.

Small businesses rely heavily on insurance in coping with natural disaster losses. Insurance for flood damage to buildings may be purchased, but only through a federal flood insurance program—and only in areas that have agreed to practice land-use management. Flood damage to movable property is also insurable; for example, automobile policies usually provide insurance to cover flood damage to a vehicle. Similar insurance coverage can be acquired for losses incurred because of severe wind conditions. In 1992, Hurricane Andrew hit the southeastern United

Action Report

ENTREPRENEURIAL EXPERIENCES

Coping with a Natural Disaster

The Hawkeye Lumber Company in Muscatine, Iowa, on the banks of the Mississippi River, was prepared for the worst—or so its manager, Wayne Lindley, thought. Although Lindley took precautions to try to minimize disaster, he found that he had underestimated Mother Nature.

It started seeping into the yard on a Sunday. By Tuesday, it was in the office, and when the Mighty Mississippi finally crested 11 days later, the water inside the Muscatine, Iowa branch of the Hawkeye Lumber Co. was more than four feet deep.

At first, Lindley thought the office records were high enough off the floor to be safe. But as the predictions rose of how high the crest would reach, he and some other employees donned waders and went in to rescue files and furnishings, loading them on a boat and taking them to higher ground.

"We operated off of my kitchen table for about a week and a half," he says. Then they moved to a temporary office up the hill from the store.

"We're losing in the neighborhood of $6,000 to $7,000 a day in sales, and that's been going on for three weeks now," Lindley said. By early August, the water was gone, and the damage was still being assessed. "It's going to be sizable is all I can tell you," said Lindley.

Hawkeye Lumber was just one of thousands of small to medium-size businesses victimized by the Mississippi floodwaters in 1993. The cost of the disaster was not limited to property damage but also included lost business, which can mean an inability to meet payroll and other fixed expenses. The end result can even be having to close the business.

Source: Sharon Nelton, "Prepare for the Worst," *Nation's Business* (September 1993), pp. 20–28.

States, resulting in insurance claims that exceeded $30 billion. Also in 1992, the Los Angeles earthquake proved almost as devastating as Hurricane Andrew, damaging at least 100,000 businesses. Of those businesses damaged, 90,000 sought financial assistance from the Small Business Administration.

BURGLARY AND BUSINESS SWINDLES   The unauthorized entering of premises with the intent to commit a crime such as the removal of cash or merchandise is called burglary. Although insurance should be carried against losses from burglary, a small business may find it helpful to install a burglar alarm system or arrange for private security services.

Business swindles cost firms thousands of dollars each year. Small firms are particularly susceptible to swindles, such as bogus office-machine repairers, phony charity appeals, billing for listings in nonexistent directories, sale of advertising space in publications whose nature is misrepresented, and advance-fee deals. Risks of this kind are avoidable only through the alertness of the business manager.

SHOPLIFTING   It is estimated that as many as 60 percent of consumers may shoplift at some point during their lives. In the United States, there are more than 200 million shoplifting incidents a year. Few shoplifters are professional thieves; most are consumers who shoplift only sporadically.[2] *Even so, the loss to retailers is enormous, not simply through the direct loss of goods, but also because of the cost of security.*

Shoplifting occurs primarily on sales floors or at checkout counters of retail stores. On the sales floor, nonprofessional shoplifters steal goods that can be quickly and easily hidden inside clothing, a backpack, or a handbag. Professional shoplifters—those for whom crime is a primary source of income—are much more skillful. Cleverly designed devices, such as clothing with large hidden pockets and shielded shopping bags for transporting merchandise with antitheft tags past detection gates, help the professional shoplifter conceal items both small and large.

Various precautionary measures may be taken by small businesses to minimize shoplifting. One business publication offered a list of the top ten antishoplifting tactics:

1. Training employees is crucial. "Shoplifting is a constant problem for us," says Ed Sherman, owner of Sherman's Inc., a Tulsa, Oklahoma variety store. "It costs us a lot of money." Sherman's solution is to train employees in customer service. "An attentive sales force is the best deterrent to shoplifting," says Sherman, "because the shoplifter's first requirement is privacy."

2. Post signs around the store warning potential thieves that you will prosecute and then follow up on that threat. Katy Culmo, owner of By George, a women's clothing store in Austin, Texas, maintains that the best shoplifting defense is a strong offense. She cultivates a reputation for being hard on thieves. "An ambivalent approach makes you a target," Culmo says. Her clothes bear tags that sound an alarm if not removed at the cash register, and she trains her staff to catch and detain shoplifters.

3. Hang convex mirrors to eliminate blind aisles, and install alarms on emergency exits.

4. Display expensive items in security cases. Place "targeted" merchandise—those items most at risk—near checkout stands. Howard Laves, owner of Benolds, a jewelry store in Austin, Texas, uses cameras and alarms to deter shoplifters. "We show expensive pieces one at a time," he says. When a thief is caught, Laves prosecutes.

5. Reduce clutter; arrange merchandise so that unexplained gaps on shelves can be easily detected.

6. Channel the flow of your customers past the cashier, and block off unused checkout stands.

7. Attend to the needs of your customers. Be visible, be available, and be attentive.

8. Monitor fitting rooms and employee-only areas.

9. Consider using uniformed or plain-clothed store detectives, two-way mirrors, electronic sales tags, and TV cameras.

10. Ask the police to do a "walk-through" of your store to pinpoint vulnerable areas.[3]

Understanding the type of person who shoplifts can help a manager better understand the problem. The following profile of a shoplifter was developed by the Council of Better Business Bureaus:

Most shoplifters are amateurs rather than professionals. Juvenile offenders, who, according to the Small Business Administration, account for about 50 percent of all shoplifting, may steal on a dare or simply for kicks. Impulse shoplifters include many "respectable" people who have not premeditated their thefts but instead succumb to the temptation of a sudden chance, such as an unattended dressing room or a blind aisle in a supermarket. Alcoholics, vagrants, and drug addicts are often clumsy and erratic in their behavior but

may be violent as well—their apprehension is best left to the police.
*Kleptomaniacs, motivated by a com-
pulsion to steal, usually have little
or no actual use for the items they
steal and in many cases could well
afford to pay for them. All of these
types of amateur shoplifters can be
relatively easy to spot. The professional shoplifter, on the other hand,
is usually highly skilled at the business of theft. Professionals generally
steal items that can be resold quickly
to an established fence, and they
tend to concentrate on high-demand
consumer goods such as televisions,
stereos, and other small appliances.
Even the professional, however, can
be deterred from theft by a combination of alert personnel and effective
store layout.*[4]

*Shoplifters come from all
walks of life. To help identify potential shoplifters,
small business managers
should familiarize them-
selves with the profile of
each type of shoplifter.*

Shoplifters, then, are as varied as
customers in general. The problem
of shoplifting can, in part, be reduced by learning how to recognize
the profile of each type of shoplifter, which is not an easy task.

Risks Associated with Personnel

Personnel-oriented losses occur through the actions of employees. Employee theft
is an illegal and intentional act against the business and constitutes a major concern for many small businesses. A physically sick or injured employee can also
cause a business loss. The three primary types of personnel-oriented risks are dishonesty of current employees, former-employee competition, and loss of key executives. Most employee-oriented risks are insurable.

EMPLOYEE DISHONESTY   One form of employee dishonesty is theft. Estimates of
the magnitude of employee theft are difficult to make and tend to vary considerably. Small businesses are particularly vulnerable to theft because they tend to be
lax in establishing antitheft controls.

Thefts by employees may include not only cash but also inventory items, tools,
scrap materials, postage stamps, and the like. Possibilities exist for forgery, raising
the amounts on checks, and other fraudulent practices. For example, a trusted
bookkeeper may collude with an outsider to have presented for payment bogus invoices or invoices that are double or triple the correct amount. The bookkeeper
may approve such invoices for payment, write a check, and secure the manager's
signature. Consider the following incident. A company hired a bookkeeper who

had excellent academic credentials. The company didn't suspect any problems until the employee left town two years later. Although the bookkeeper had recorded accounts as paid, creditors were claiming that the company owed thousands of dollars in past-due accounts. The company discovered that the employee had been drawing extra payroll checks by forging signatures. She had also altered amounts on her expense reimbursement checks. The company determined that the bookkeeper had been keeping money intended for creditors, while sending the creditors small amounts to buy time.[5]

Bonding employees—that is purchasing from a bonding company insurance that will protect the purchasing firm against a loss from employee fraud or embezzlement—is one way to counter the cost of employee dishonesty. However, a firm's most effective protection against employee fraud is to develop a comprehensive system of internal control.[6]

COMPETITION FROM FORMER EMPLOYEES   Good employees are hard to get; they are even harder to keep. When a business experiences employee turnover—and it always will—there may be risks associated with former employees. Salespeople, beauticians, and other employees often take business with them when they leave. The risk is particularly acute with turnover of key executives, as they are likely candidates to start a competing business or to leave with trade secrets.

Most companies are very sensitive to the activities of former employees. Consider the following situation. Assume that you work for a company that makes equipment and supplies used in oil fields. Through your job, you meet Hank Sorens, who owns a company that sells parts to your employer. You begin ordering parts from a second company owned by Sorens. In time, you and Sorens form your own corporation. You quit your job and begin competing with your former employer, which may elect to sue you and Sorens for misappropriating its manufacturing procedures and other alleged trade secrets. Courts have frequently awarded significant sums in such cases.

One common practice to help avoid this kind of employee-oriented risk is to require employees to sign employment contracts that clearly set forth the employee's promise not to disclose certain information or use it to compete against the employer.

LOSS OF KEY EXECUTIVES   Every successful small business has one or more key executives. These employees could be lost through death or through attraction to other employment. If key personnel cannot be successfully replaced, a small firm may suffer appreciably as the result of the loss of their services.

In addition to valuable experience and skill, key executives may have specialized knowledge that is vital to the successful operation of a firm. Consider the case of one manufacturer, who was killed in an auto accident at the age of 53. His processing operations involved the use of a secret chemical formula that he had personally devised and divulged to no one because of his fear of losing the formula to competitors. He had not reduced it to writing anywhere, even in a safety-deposit box. Not even his family knew the formula. As a result of his sudden death, the firm went out of business within six months. Expensive special-purpose equipment had to be sold as junk. All that his widow salvaged was about $60,000 worth of bonds and the Florida residence that had been the couple's winter home.

At least two solutions are available to a small firm that may be faced with this situation. The first solution is buying life insurance, which is discussed later in this chapter. The second is developing replacement personnel. A potential replacement should be groomed for every key position, including the position of the owner-manager.

Risks Associated with Customers

Customers are the source of profit for small businesses, but they are also the center of an ever-increasing amount of business risk. Much of this risk is attributable to on-premise injuries and product liability.

ON-PREMISE INJURIES   Customers may initiate legal claims as a result of on-premise injuries. Because of high in-store traffic, this risk is particularly acute for small retailers. Personal injury liability of this type may occur, for example, when a customer breaks an arm by slipping on icy steps while entering or leaving the store. An employer is, of course, at risk when employees suffer similar fates; but customers, by their sheer numbers, make this risk more significant.

Another form of on-premise risk arises from inadequate security, which may result in robbery, assault, or other violent crimes. The number of on-premises liability cases involving violent crimes has "doubled during the past five years to about 1,000 annually," according to estimates by Liability Consultants, Inc., a security consulting firm in Framingham, Massachusetts.[7] Victims, often customers, look to the business to recover their losses. Consider the freelance photographer who was assaulted during her stay at a motel. Fortunately, the woman survived, but she sued the motel; its insurers paid $10 million to settle the suit.[8]

Good management of this kind of customer-oriented risk requires a regular check of the premises for hazards. The concept of preventive maintenance applies to management of this risk factor.

PRODUCT LIABILITY   Recent product liability court decisions have broadened the scope of this form of risk. No reputable small business would intentionally produce a product that would harm a customer, but good intentions are weak defenses in liability suits.

A product liability suit may be filed when a customer becomes ill or sustains physical or property damage from using a product made or sold by a company. Class-action suits, together with individual suits, are now widely used by consumers in product liability cases. Some types of businesses operate in higher-risk markets than others. For example, the insulation business has been targeted with numerous claims based on the physical effects of asbestos on those exposed to it.

"Right now, a small business can be wiped out by one punitive-damage award," says Victor Schwartz, counsel to the Product Liability Alliance, in Washington, D.C. "The rules on punitive damage in most states are open-ended, the standards are vague, and there are no limits on the amounts of money for which a company can be sued."[9]

RISK MANAGEMENT

Risk management consists of all efforts designed to preserve the assets and earning power of a business. Since risk management has grown out of insurance management, the two terms are often used interchangeably. Actually, risk management has a much broader meaning, covering both insurable and uninsurable risks and including noninsurance approaches to reducing all types of risks.

Risk management in a small firm differs from risk management in a large firm in several ways. For one thing, insurance companies aren't always eager to insure small firms and may even turn them down in some cases. Also, in a large firm, the responsibilities of risk management are frequently assigned to a specialized staff manager. In contrast, the manager of a small business is usually its risk manager.

2 Explain how risk management can be used in coping with business risks.

risk management ways of coping with risk that are designed to preserve assets and the earning power of a firm

Action Report

ENTREPRENEURIAL EXPERIENCES

Avoiding Insurer Roadblocks

Today, an entrepreneur may be required to do more than simply take out insurance for theft. He or she also needs to know what is required in case of a loss.

Mark Moerdler, executive vice-president of MDY Advanced Technologies, learned that $90,000 worth of computers and equipment had been stolen from his company. Consequently, Moerdler filed a claim with the insurers. However, the insurance company delayed payment for nearly a year and, according to Moerdler, never repaid anything resembling the extent of the firm's loss. Based on his experience, Moerdler offers this advice:

- When you negotiate your coverage, get a full description in writing of whatever documentation your insurers will expect you to file should you have any claims.
- Don't act alone. Moerdler says, "Bring in a lawyer at the first sign of delay. I wasted months by not involving our lawyer until the insurer offered us a $.50-on-the-dollar settlement."
- Take serious measures if your insurer is uncooperative. According to Moerdler, "What finally scared the insurer into acting was our threat to report the incident to the state insurance commissioner. That's the kind of action that produces results."
- Comparison shop for an insurer. And don't sign up based on price alone. "When it's time for us to renew, I plan to question many insurers about their claims-filing procedures," Moerdler says.

Source: Jill Andresky Fraser, Ed., "Avoid Insurer Roadblocks," *Inc.*, Vol. 17, No. 5 (April 1995), p. 115.

Generally, small businesses have been slow to focus on managing risk. Ric Yocke, a consultant in risk management with the accounting firm of Ernst & Young, says, "I think it's easier for a small company not to address risk management because people wear so many hats. It's not something that requires immediate attention—until something happens."[10] In practicing risk management, a small business manager needs to identify the different types of risks faced by her or his business and find ways to cope with them.

Once a manager is fully aware of the sources of risk, programs of risk management can be developed. Three basic programs for coping with risks can be pursued individually or in combination: (1) preventive risk reduction, (2) self-insurance, and (3) risk sharing. Many small businesses rely solely on sharing business risks by purchasing insurance when they should be using the options in combination.

Preventive Risk Reduction

Small business risks of all kinds can be reduced with sound, commonsense management. Preventive maintenance applied to risk management calls for the elimination of circumstances and situations that create risk. For example, a small firm needs to take every possible precaution to prevent fires, including the following:

- *Use of safe construction.* The building should be made of fire-resistant materials, and the electrical wiring should be adequate to carry the maximum load of electrical energy that will be imposed. Fire doors and insulation should be used where necessary.
- *Installation of a completely automatic sprinkler system.* If an automatic sprinkler system is available, fire insurance rates will be lower—and the fire hazard itself definitely will be reduced.
- *Provision of an adequate water supply.* Ordinarily, securing an adequate water supply requires a location in a city with water sources and water mains, as well as a pumping system that will ensure the delivery of any amount of water needed to fight fires. Of course, a company may provide its own water storage tanks or private wells.
- *Institution and operation of a fire-prevention program involving all employees.* A fire-prevention program must have top-management support, and its emphasis must always be on keeping employees conscious of fire-safety measures. Regular fire drills for all employees, including both building evacuation and practice of actual firefighting procedures, may be undertaken.

Self-Insurance

Intelligent personal financial planning usually involves the practice of "saving for a rainy day." This concept should also be incorporated into small business risk management. This form of risk management is frequently called self-insurance. Although it is a difficult practice to follow in a business, it will pay dividends.

Self-insurance can take a general or specific form. In its general form, a part of the firm's earnings is earmarked for a contingency fund against possible future losses, regardless of the source. In its specific form, a self-insurance program designates funds to individual loss categories such as property, medical, or workers' compensation. Some firms have begun to rely heavily on self-insurance. However, self-insurance plans need to be approved and monitored to protect the interests of those covered.

self-insurance
designating part of a firm's earnings as a cushion against possible future losses

An area in which small firms are moving toward self-insurance is medical coverage for employees. A 1991 survey by a benefits consulting firm found that 22 percent of firms with between 100 and 500 employees were self-insured, compared with only 8 percent in a 1988 study.[11]

Obviously, self-insurance is not affordable for every small firm. One insurance specialist, Lori Raffel, director of the stop-loss division of Mutual Group, offers a general rule of thumb: A company should have a net worth of at least $250,000 and at least 25 employees to be self-funded.[12] Moreover, very few

Discussions with various insurance representatives will help a small business owner determine sources of risk and develop a risk management program specifically designed for his or her company.

Figure 24-2

Risk-Taking Begins Early

Source: From *The Wall Street Journal*—Permission, Cartoon Features Syndicate.

firms can practice unlimited self-insurance, especially when it comes to liability claims. Unless a small company has insurance to cover losses above a certain level, any large loss could put it out of business (see Figure 24-2).

Risk Sharing

A rapid increase in insurance premiums in the 1980s—particularly for general liability coverage—resulted in the inability of many small businesses to obtain affordable insurance.[13] Nevertheless, insurance still provides one of the most important means of sharing business risks. A sound insurance program—the topic of the next section—is imperative for the proper protection of a business.

Regardless of the nature of a business, risk management is a serious issue. Too often in the past, small businesses paid insufficient attention to insurance matters and failed to acquire skill in analyzing risk problems. Today, such a situation is unthinkable. The small business manager must take an active role in structuring an insurance package for his or her firm.

INSURANCE FOR THE SMALL BUSINESS

Many small firms carry insufficient insurance protection. The entrepreneur often comes to such a realization only after a major loss. Good risk management requires careful study of insurance policies in advance of a loss rather than after a loss has occurred.

Action Report

Thinking Risk Management

Business owners are learning that, in order to keep insurance costs down, they must take an active role and become their own risk managers. They can no longer afford to sit back and wait for suggestions from insurance agents. Instead, they need to formulate and offer their own ideas.

Acting on his own instincts, Larry Joiner, owner of West Coast Roofing and Waterproofing Co. in Naples, Florida, rearranged his insurance coverage by raising damage deductibles on his building and cutting back on vehicle-damage insurance. Because his roofing company could be swept away by a hurricane coming off the Gulf of Mexico, Joiner modified his coverage to use premium dollars more effectively. "You've got to be alert," says Joiner, "and you've got to care about these insurance details yourself."

Laura Reid, owner of the Fish Mart Inc. in West Haven, Connecticut, is another business owner acting as her own risk manager. Wholesaling about $5 million worth of animals and tropical fish a year, Reid raised the deductibles on her fleet of a dozen delivery trucks in order to reduce her auto premium. By starting safety classes for her drivers, she also cut the weekly $1,200 workers' compensation insurance premium to a reasonable $500. "I learned long ago," Reid says, "that you've really got to think carefully about what your doctor does, what your lawyer does, even what your insurance agent does."

Both Joiner and Reid have saved substantially by becoming risk managers.

Source: John S. DeMott, "Think Like a Risk Manager," *Nation's Business* (June 1995), pp. 30–31.

Basic Principles of a Sound Insurance Program

What kinds of risks can be covered by insurance? What kinds of coverage should be purchased? How much coverage is adequate? Unfortunately, there are no clear-cut answers to these questions. A reputable insurance agent can provide valuable assistance to small firms in evaluating risks and designing proper protection plans, but an entrepreneur should become as knowledgeable about available insurance as possible. Basic principles in evaluating an insurance program include identifying business risks to be insured, limiting coverage to major potential losses, and relating premium costs to probability of loss.

> **3** Explain basic principles in evaluating an insurance program and the fundamental requirements for obtaining insurance.

IDENTIFYING BUSINESS RISKS TO BE INSURED   Although the most common insurable risks were pointed out earlier, other less obvious risks may be revealed only by careful investigation. A small firm must first obtain risk coverages required by law or contract, such as workers' compensation insurance and automobile liability insurance. As part of the risk-identification process, plant and equipment should be reevaluated periodically by competent appraisers in order to ensure that adequate insurance coverage is maintained.

LIMITING COVERAGE TO MAJOR POTENTIAL LOSSES   A small firm must determine the magnitude of loss that it could bear without serious financial difficulty. If the firm is sufficiently strong, it may decide to avoid unnecessary coverage by covering only those losses exceeding a specified minimum amount. It is important, of course, to guard against underestimating the severity of potential losses.

RELATING PREMIUM COSTS TO PROBABILITY OF LOSS   Because insurance companies must collect enough premiums to pay the actual losses of insured parties, the cost of insurance must be proportional to the probability of occurrence of the insured event. As the loss becomes more certain, premium costs become so high that a firm may find that insurance is simply not worth the cost. Thus, insurance is most applicable and practical for *improbable* losses—that is, situations where the probability that the loss will occur is low, but the overall cost of the loss would be high.

Requirements for Obtaining Insurance

Before an insurance company is willing to underwrite possible losses, the particular risk and the insured firm must meet certain requirements.

THE RISK MUST BE CALCULABLE   The total overall loss arising from many insured risks can be calculated by means of actuarial tables. For example, the number of buildings that will suffer fire damage each year can be predicted with some accuracy. An insurance company can determine appropriate insurance rates only if the risks can be calculated.

THE RISK MUST EXIST IN LARGE NUMBERS   A particular risk must occur in sufficiently large numbers and be spread over a wide enough geographical area to permit the law of averages to work. A fire insurance company, for example, cannot afford to insure only one building or even all the buildings in one town. It would have to insure buildings in many towns and cities before it would be assured of an adequate, safe distribution of risk.

THE INSURED PROPERTY MUST HAVE COMMERCIAL VALUE   An item that possesses only sentimental value cannot be insured. For example, an old family photo that is of no value to the public may not be included among insured items whose value can be measured in monetary terms.

THE POLICYHOLDER MUST HAVE AN INSURABLE INTEREST IN THE PROPERTY OR PERSON INSURED   The purpose of insurance is reimbursement of actual loss, not creation of profit for the insured. For example, a firm could insure a building worth $70,000 for $500,000, but it could collect only $70,000, the actual worth of the building, in case of loss. So, insuring for an amount higher than actual value is simply a waste of money, with no benefit to the insured. Similarly, a firm cannot obtain life insurance on its customers or suppliers.

Types of Insurance

4 Identify types of insurance coverage.

Several classifications of insurance and a variety of coverages are available from different insurance companies.[14] Each purchaser of insurance should seek a balance among coverage, deductions, and premiums. Since the trend is toward higher and higher premiums for small businesses, the balancing act is becoming even more critical.

COMMERCIAL PROPERTY COVERAGE   Commercial property insurance provides protection from losses associated with damage to or loss of property. Causes of property loss that can be covered include fire, explosion, vandalism, broken glass, business interruption, and employee dishonesty.

    Most entrepreneurs recognize the need for protection against fire and maybe a few other, more traditional losses. However, few small business owners realize the value of business interruption insurance. **Business interruption insurance** protects

business interruption insurance
coverage of lost income and certain expenses while the business is being rebuilt

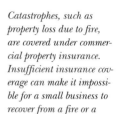

Catastrophes, such as property loss due to fire, are covered under commercial property insurance. Insufficient insurance coverage can make it impossible for a small business to recover from a fire or a flood.

companies during the period necessary to restore property damaged by an insured risk. Coverage pays for lost income and certain other expenses of rebuilding the business. John Donahue, vice president of the commercial insurance division of The Hartford Insurance Company, says that the biggest mistake small companies make "is in not having sufficient . . . coverage that protects them against some catastrophe, such as a flood or fire, which would close down their business; while standard property insurance will pay to replace a building and its contents, it will not cover the payroll and other expenses that must be paid during the three or four months the factory is being rebuilt."[15] Trying to reconstruct what never was makes proving the extent of lost profits difficult.

Dishonesty insurance covers such traditional areas as fidelity bonds and crime insurance. Employees occupying positions of trust in handling company funds are customarily bonded as protection against their potential dishonesty. The informality and highly personal basis of employment in small firms make it difficult to realize the value of such insurance. That is, the potential for loss of money or other property through the dishonesty of persons other than employees, which can be covered by crime insurance, is easier to accept psychologically.

Many commercial property policies contain a **coinsurance clause**. Under this clause, the insured agrees to maintain insurance equal to some specified percentage of the property value at the time of actual loss—80 percent is quite typical. In return, the insured is given a reduced rate. If the insured fails to maintain the 80 percent coverage, only part of the loss will be reimbursed. To see how a coinsurance clause determines the amount paid by the insurer, let's assume that the physical property of a business is valued at $50,000. If the business insures the property for $40,000 (or 80 percent of the property value) and incurs a fire loss of $20,000, the insurance company will pay the full amount of $20,000. However, if the business insures the property for only $30,000 (which is 75 percent of the specified minimum), the insurance company will pay only 75 percent of the loss, or $15,000.

SURETY BONDS   **Surety bonds** insure against the failure of another firm or individual to fulfill a contractual obligation. They are frequently used in connection with construction contracts.

dishonesty insurance
coverage to protect against employees' crimes

coinsurance clause
part of an insurance policy that requires the insured to maintain a specific level of coverage or to assume a portion of any loss

surety bonds
coverage to protect against another's failure to fulfill a contractual obligation with the insured

credit insurance
coverage to protect against abnormal bad-debt losses

CREDIT INSURANCE **Credit insurance** protects businesses from abnormal bad-debt losses—for example, losses that result from a customer's insolvency due to tornado or flood losses, depressed industry conditions, business recession, or other factors. Credit insurance does not cover normal bad-debt losses that are predictable on the basis of business experience. Insurance companies compute the normal rate on the basis of industry experience and the loss record of the particular firm being insured.

Credit insurance is available only to manufacturers and wholesalers, not to retailers. Thus, only trade credit may be insured. There are two reasons for this. The more important reason is the relative ease of analyzing business risks compared with analyzing consumer risks. The other reason is that retailers have a larger number of accounts receivable, which are smaller in dollar amount and provide greater risk diversification, so credit insurance is less acutely needed.

The collection service of an insurance company makes available legal talent and experience that may otherwise be unavailable to a small firm. Furthermore, collection efforts of insurance companies are generally considered superior to those of regular collection agencies.

The credit standing of a small firm may be enhanced when it uses credit insurance. The small firm can show a banker that steps have been taken to avoid unnecessary risks; thus, it might obtain more favorable consideration in securing bank credit.

Credit insurance policies typically provide for a collection service on bad accounts. Although collection provisions vary, a common provision requires the insured to notify the insurance company within 90 days of the past-due status of an account and to turn it in for collection after 90 days.

Although the vast majority of policies provide general coverage, policies may be secured to cover individual accounts. A 10 percent, or higher, coinsurance requirement is included to limit the coverage to approximately the replacement value of the merchandise. Higher percentages of coinsurance are required for inferior accounts in order to discourage reckless credit extension by insured firms. Accounts are classified according to ratings by Dun & Bradstreet or other recognized agencies, and premiums vary with these ratings.

general liability insurance
coverage against suits brought by customers

employer's liability insurance
coverage against suits brought by employees

workers' compensation insurance
coverage that obligates the insurer to pay employees for injury or illness related to employment

COMMERCIAL LIABILITY INSURANCE Commercial liability insurance has two general classes: general liability and employers' liability/workers' compensation. **General liability insurance** covers businesses' liability to customers injured on the premises or injured off the premises by the product sold to them. General liability insurance does not cover injury to a firm's own employees. However, employees using products such as machinery purchased from another manufacturer can bring suit under product liability laws against the equipment manufacturer.

Employer's liability insurance is required by most states to insure employees. All states have workers' compensation laws. As the titles imply, **employer's liability insurance** provides protection for the insured business against suits brought by employees who suffer injury, and **workers' compensation insurance** obligates the insurer to pay eligible employees for injury or illness related to employment.

key-person insurance
coverage that protects against the death of a firm's key personnel

risk-retention group
an insurance company started by a homogeneous group of entrepreneurs or professionals to provide liability insurance for its members

KEY-PERSON INSURANCE By carrying **key-person insurance**, a small business can protect itself against the death of key personnel. Such insurance may be written on an individual or group basis. It is purchased by a firm, with the firm being the sole beneficiary.

Most small business advisers suggest term insurance for key-person insurance policies, primarily because of lower premiums. How much key-person insurance to buy is more difficult to decide. Face values of such policies usually begin around $50,000 and may go as high as several million dollars. Bayshore Metals of San Francisco, for example, has two $500,000 policies on its partners, while Reebok International has a $50 million policy to cover its key executives.[16]

INSURANCE COOPERATIVES Another means by which a small business can share its risk is to join with other, similar firms in an insurance cooperative. This option was made possible with the passage in 1981 of the federal Product Liability Risk Retention Act, which allows organizations to form special risk-retention groups or join together as a purchasing group.[17]

A **risk-retention group** is an insurance company started by a homogeneous group of entrepreneurs or professionals. The group provides liability insurance for its members. A **purchasing group** is any unincorporated group of firms that has as its purpose purchasing liability insurance for the firms in the group. A purchasing group is subject to less regulation than a risk-retention group. Prior to passage of the 1981 act, it was almost impossible for these cooperatives to function in a nonlicensing state.

The Risk Retention Amendments of 1986 broadened the scope of risk-retention and purchasing groups by allowing a group to provide any commercial liability coverage to its members who face a common risk. A cooperative effort to share risks with other small businesses is not necessarily a viable option for all small firms. It does, however, offer another alternative for coping with business risk.

DISCUSSION QUESTIONS

1. Which of the different classifications of business risks is the most difficult for the small firm to control? Why? Which is the least difficult to control? Why?
2. If you were shopping in a small retail store and somehow sustained an injury such as a broken arm, under what circumstances would you sue the store? Explain.
3. Do you think some firms are hesitant to enter formal bankruptcy proceedings even though they might be able to save the business? Why?

Looking Back

1 Explain what risk is and classify business risks according to the assets they affect.

- Risk is a condition in which there is a possibility of an adverse deviation from a desired outcome.
- From an asset-oriented perspective, insurable business risks can be categorized into property-oriented risks, personnel-oriented risks, and customer-oriented risks.

2 Explain how risk management can be used in coping with business risks.

- Risk management is concerned with protection of the assets and the earning power of a business against accidental loss.
- The three ways to manage business risks are (1) reduce the risk, or avoid it altogether if the loss would be devastating to the firm; (2) increase savings to cover possible future losses; and (3) transfer the risk to someone else by carrying insurance.

3 Explain basic principles in evaluating an insurance program and the fundamental requirements for obtaining insurance.

- Basic principles of insurance include (1) identifying the business risks to be insured, (2) limiting coverage to major potential losses, and (3) relating the cost of premiums to the probability of loss.
- Fundamental requirements for obtaining insurance include the following: (1) the risk must be calculable, (2) the risk must exist in large numbers, (3) the insured property must have commercial value, and (4) the policyholder must have an insurable interest in the property or person insured.

4 Identify types of insurance coverage.

- Commercial property coverage provides protection from losses associated with damage to or loss of property.
- Surety bonds insure against the failure of another firm or individual to fulfill a contractual obligation.
- Credit insurance protects businesses from abnormal bad-debt losses.
- Commercial liability insurance includes general liability insurance, which covers business liability to customers injured on the premises or injured off the premises by the product sold to them; employer's liability insurance, which provides protection against suits brought by employees who suffer injury; and workers' compensation insurance, which obligates the insurer to pay eligible employees for injury or illness related to employment.
- Key-person insurance provides protection against the death of key personnel in the firm.
- An insurance cooperative can be a risk-retention group, which is an insurance company started by a homogeneous group of entrepreneurs or professionals to provide liability insurance for its members, or a purchasing group, which is any unincorporated group of firms that has the purpose of purchasing liability insurance for group members.

purchasing group
an unincorporated group of firms that purchases liability insurance for its members

risk *535*

risk
management *541*

self-insurance *543*

business interruption
insurance *546*

dishonesty
insurance *547*

coinsurance
clause *547*

surety bonds *547*

credit insurance *548*

general liability
insurance *548*

employer's liability
insurance *548*

workers'
compensation
insurance *548*

key-person
insurance *548*

risk-retention
group *548*

purchasing
group *549*

You Make the Call

Situation 1 The Amigo Company manufactures motorized wheelchairs in its Bridgeport, Michigan plant under the supervision of Alden Thieme. Alden is the brother of the firm's founder, Allen Thieme. The company has 100 employees and does $10 million in sales a year. Like many other firms, Amigo is faced with increased liability insurance costs. Although it is contemplating dropping all coverage, it realizes that the users of its product are individuals who have already suffered physical and emotional pain. Therefore, if an accident occurred and resulted in a liability suit, a jury might be strongly tempted to favor the plaintiff. In fact, the company has already experienced litigation. A woman in an Amigo wheelchair was killed by a car on the street. Because the driver of the car had no insurance, Amigo was sued.

Question 1 Do you agree that the type of customer to whom the Amigo Company sells should influence its decision regarding insurance?

Question 2 In what way, if any, should the outcome of the firm's current litigation impact Amigo's decision about renewing its insurance coverage?

Question 3 What options does Amigo have if it drops all insurance coverage? What is your recommendation?

Situation 2 Pansy Ellen Essman is a 42-year-old grandmother who is chairman of a company, based in Atlanta, Georgia, that does $5 million in sales each year. Her company, Pansy Ellen Products, Inc., grew out of a product idea that Essman had as she bathed her squealing, squirming granddaughter in the bathroom tub. Her idea was to produce a sponge pillow that would cradle a child in the tub, thus freeing the caretaker's hands to clean the baby. Since production of this initial product, the company has expanded its product line to include nursery lamps, baby food organizers, strollers, and hook-on baby seats. Essman has seemingly managed her product mix risk well. However, she is concerned that other sources of business risk may have been ignored or slighted.

Question 1 What types of business risk do you think Essman might have overlooked? Be specific.

Question 2 Would a risk-retention group be a good possibility for this company? Why or why not?

Question 3 What kinds of insurance coverage should this type of company carry?

Continue on next page

4. What are the basic ways to cope with risk in a small business?

5. Can a small firm safely assume that business risks will never turn into losses sufficient to bankrupt it? Why or why not?

6. When is it logical for a small business to utilize self-insurance?

7. List several approaches for combatting the danger of theft or fraud by employees and also by outsiders.

8. Under what conditions would life insurance on a business executive constitute little protection for a business? When is such life insurance helpful?

9. Are any kinds of business risks basically human risks? If so, who are the people involved?

10. Is the increase in liability claims and court awards of special concern to small manufacturers? Why?

EXPERIENTIAL EXERCISES

1. Locate a recent issue of a business magazine in which you can read about new small business startups. Select one new firm that is marketing a product and another that is selling a service. Compare their situations relative to business risks. Report on your analysis to the class.

2. Contact a local small business owner and obtain his or her permission to conduct a risk analysis of the business. Report to the class on the business's situation in regard to risk and what preventive or protective actions you suggest.

3. Contact a local insurance company and arrange to conduct an interview with the owner or one of the agents. Determine in the interview the various types of coverage the company offers for small businesses. Write a report on your findings.

4. Assume that upon graduation you enter your family's business or obtain employment with an independent business in your hometown. Further assume that after five years of employment you leave the business to start your own competing business. Make a list of the considerations you would face regarding leaving the business with trade secrets after just five years of experience.

 CASE 24
Fox Manufacturing (p. 657)

This case reviews the events and the owner's actions following the loss of a firm's manufacturing plant from a fire.

Situation 3 H. Abbe International, owned by Herb Abbe, is a travel agency and freight forwarder located on the 28th floor of New York's World Trade Center. When the World Trade Center was bombed, the firm was forced to relocate its 2 computers and 11 employees. Moving into the offices of a client, Abbe worked from this temporary location for a month before returning to his regular offices. The disruption cost him about $70,000 in lost business and moving expenses. In addition, he had to lay off four employees.

Question 1 What are the major types of risk faced by a firm such as H. Abbe International? What kind of insurance will cover these risks?
Question 2 What kind of insurance would have helped Abbe cope with the loss resulting from the bombing? In making the decision to purchase this kind of insurance, what questions must be answered regarding the amount and terms of insurance to be purchased?
Question 3 Would you have recommended that Abbe purchase insurance that would have covered his losses in this case?

Part 7

25. **SOCIAL AND ETHICAL ISSUES**

26. **WORKING WITHIN THE LAW**

Chapter 25

Robert L. Wahlstedt, Lee Johnson, Dale Merrick

spotlight on small business

Corporate codes of ethical conduct are often viewed with skepticism. To some, they appear to be ideals that are compromised as soon as profits are threatened. Here is one observer's testimony about a small company in Minnesota that not only maintains a written code of ethics but also practices what it preaches:

I'm delighted to report that I've stumbled across a Twin Cities company that not only has committed itself in writing to ethical treatment of employees, customers, and suppliers, but has spent 20 years demonstrating in rather dramatic fashion that it actually means what it says.

Allow me to introduce you to Reell Precision Manufacturing Corporation (RPM), a privately held Vadnais Heights company that, among other odd notions, places the well-being of its 100 employees and their families above unfettered profit growth.

This firm's code of ethics specifies that its commitments to its workers come before short-term profits and that conflicts between the job and the family are to be resolved in favor of the family. Because jobs come before profits, there has never been an economic layoff. As a further example of the firm's commitment to the family, RPM does not ask employees to travel on weekends to take advantage of lower airline fares.

Source: Dick Youngblood, "A Firm That Means What It Says About Ethical Conduct," *Minneapolis–St. Paul Star Tribune*, December 28, 1992, p. 2D. Reprinted with permission of the *Minneapolis–St. Paul Star Tribune*.

Looking Ahead

After studying this chapter, you should be able to:

1 Explain the impact of social responsibilities on small businesses.

2 Describe the special challenges of environmentalism and consumerism.

3 Identify contextual factors that affect ethical decision making in small businesses.

4 Describe practical approaches for applying ethical precepts in small business management.

Small business firms must earn profits while simultaneously acting as good citizens. Indeed, they must earn profits if they are to survive and to continue to provide their products and/or services. However, the free enterprise system does not grant firms the freedom to disregard the welfare of the broader society. Some social expectations are written into law, and others are recognized voluntarily by firms. Small business owners, therefore, must understand their firms' social obligations and the ethical rules by which they must function.

SOCIAL RESPONSIBILITIES AND SMALL BUSINESS

In today's business world, public attention is focused on the social responsibilities of business organizations. The public's concern is rooted in a new awareness of the role of business in modern society. In a sense, the public regards a firm's managers as its trustees and expects them to act accordingly in protecting the interests of suppliers, employees, customers, and the general public, while making a profit. Obligations of this nature are called **social responsibilities**.

How Small Firms View Their Social Responsibilities

Conservation, fair hiring practices, consumerism, environmental protection, and public safety are popular themes in the news media today. The extent to which small businesses are sensitive to these issues varies greatly. One study asked small business owners and managers, "How do you see your responsibilities to society?"[1] In response, 88 percent mentioned at least one type of social obligation, whereas only 12 percent felt that they had no specific responsibilities or did not know how to respond to the question. The majority who recognized social responsibilities cited obligations to customers, employees, and the community, as well as a general responsibility to act ethically. On the basis of these responses, it is evident that most small business owners are aware that their firms function within the context of the broader society.

A few entrepreneurs have displayed an unusually strong commitment to the betterment of society. Judy Wicks, who operates Philadelphia's thriving White Dog Cafe, attaches high priority to various social causes. Her company, for example, contributes about 10 percent of after-tax profits to projects and causes.

> *Her pet projects include a mentoring program in which staff members work on-site with disadvantaged high school kids interested in the hospitality industry; a "sister" restaurant project to promote minority-owned restaurants in Philadelphia; and an international "sister" restaurant program—with related tours—in Nicaragua, Vietnam, and Cuba.*[2]

Entrepreneurs and businesses that express such a high degree of social concern are more often the exception than the rule. Even so, many—perhaps most—small firms are recognized as good citizens in their communities.

1 Explain the impact of social responsibilities on small businesses.

social responsibilities ethical obligations to customers, employees, and the general community

Action Report

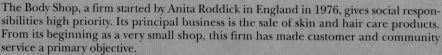

ETHICAL ISSUES

Social Objectives in an Entrepreneurial Firm

The Body Shop, a firm started by Anita Roddick in England in 1976, gives social responsibilities high priority. Its principal business is the sale of skin and hair care products. From its beginning as a very small shop, this firm has made customer and community service a primary objective.

One example of this commitment is The Body Shop's efforts to protect the environment by using products that are biodegradable, recycling waste, using recycled paper, offering discounts to customers who return plastic bottles, and providing biodegradable carrier bags. To better serve its customers, The Body Shop places a greater emphasis on health and well-being than on beauty, avoids high-pressure selling, seeks to provide adequate product information, keeps packaging at a minimum so that customers pay only for the product, and uses a range of container sizes so that customers can buy only what they need.

Source: *What Is The Body Shop?*, a brochure distributed in The Body Shop stores.

Given that small business owners have some awareness of their social obligations, how do they compare with big business CEOs in their views of social responsibility? The evidence is limited, but entrepreneurs who head small, growth-oriented companies seem to be more narrowly focused on profits and, therefore, seem less socially sensitive than are CEOs of large corporations. A study that compared small business entrepreneurs with large business CEOs concluded the following:

> The entrepreneurial CEOs were found to be more economically driven and less socially oriented than their large-firm counterparts. Apparently, CSR [corporate social responsibility] is a luxury many small growth firms believe they cannot afford. Survival may be the first priority.[3]

Nevertheless, these entrepreneurs were not totally self-centered. According to the study, they were just somewhat less sensitive to social issues than were the CEOs of large corporations.

In defense of small firm owners, we should note that they are spending their own money rather than corporate funds. It is easier to be generous when spending someone else's money. Furthermore, small business philanthropy often takes the form of personal contributions by business owners.

It is apparent, then, that entrepreneurs differ in the importance they attach to social obligations. Most accept some degree of social responsibility, but, perhaps due to financial pressures, many also show concern about a possible trade-off between social responsibility and profits.

Social Responsibilities and Profit Making

Small firms, as well as large corporations, must reconcile their social obligations with their need to earn profits. Meeting the expectations of society can be expensive. Protective legislation, varying from state to state and frequently changing, often increases the cost of doing business. For example, small firms must sometimes purchase new equipment or make costly changes in operations in order to protect the environment. Here are some examples of environmental costs facing small businesses in the 1990s:[4]

- Gas stations may need to install hydrocarbon-blocking devices on gas pumps.
- Auto repair shops may incur additional costs to dispose of hazardous waste.
- Restaurants may need containment units to collect hydrocarbon emissions from charcoal grills.
- Bakeries may require equipment to control the ethanol that is produced by yeast while dough is fermenting and released during baking.
- Motels may need to install water-efficient equipment to reduce water usage.
- Small food-processing plants may need to modify packaging to make it biodegradable or to make recycling possible.

From these examples, it is evident that acting in the public interest often requires the expenditure of money, with a consequent reduction in profits. There are limits, therefore, to what particular businesses can afford.

Fortunately, many types of socially responsible action can be consistent with a firm's long-term profit objective. Indeed, some socially desirable practices—honesty in advertising, for example—entail no additional costs. Some firms actually thrive by making a special point of their dedication to certain social objectives. Walnut Acres, for example, is a Pennsylvania farming business that specializes in the production and distribution of organically grown foods. Organic farming avoids the use of pesticides and chemical fertilizers, thereby protecting the environment and the health of consumers. This firm has expanded to the point that it employs about 100 people; it had sales of about $8 million in 1995.[5] The success of Walnut Acres shows that environmental protection and profits are not always in conflict. In this case, the firm prospered as customers were attracted by its socially responsible farming methods.

Some degree of goodwill is earned by socially responsible behavior. A firm that consistently fulfills its social obligations makes itself a desirable member of the community and may attract customers because of that image. Conversely, a firm that scorns its social responsibilities may find itself the object of restrictive legislation and discover that its employees lack loyalty to the business. To some extent, therefore, socially responsible practices can have a positive impact on profits.

Recognition of a social obligation does not change a profit-seeking business into a charitable organization. Earning a profit is absolutely essential. Without profits, a firm is not in any position to recognize its social responsibilities. However, although profits are essential, they are not the only factor of importance.

Environmental costs associated with meeting a firm's social responsibilities often reduce profits. The profits of this bakery suffered when it had to install equipment to control the release of ethanol during baking.

Action Report

ETHICAL ISSUES

Affordable Social Contributions

A small firm's contributions to the welfare of a community are restricted by the firm's economic resources. Some firms have avoided severe financial strain in their efforts to do good by contributing their expertise or services instead of money. One such example is Longfellow Clubs, a health and recreation company in Wayland, Massachusetts.

Laury Hammel, general manager and principal owner of the company, donates the use of health-club facilities to children with special needs. In one program, about 25 handicapped children learn to play tennis weekly. Similar programs are conducted in swimming and basketball, all without cost to the children or the agency that oversees the program.

Source: Ellyn E. Spragins, "Making Good," *Inc.*, Vol. 15, No. 5 (May 1993), p. 116.

> **2** Describe the special challenges of environmentalism and consumerism.

THE SPECIAL CHALLENGES OF ENVIRONMENTALISM AND CONSUMERISM

Social issues impacting businesses are numerous and diverse. Business firms are expected—at various times and by various groups—to help solve social problems, even in peripheral areas such as education, crime, ecology, and poverty. In this section, we discuss environmentalism and consumerism, two topics of immediate concern to small businesses.

Environmental Issues

In recent decades, the deterioration of the environment has become a matter of widespread concern. One source of pollution has been firms that discharge waste into streams, contaminants into the air, and noise into the areas surrounding their operations. **Environmentalism**—the effort to preserve and redeem the environment—thus directly affects all business organizations.

> **environmentalism**
> the effort to protect and preserve the environment

The interests of small business owners and environmentalists are not necessarily, or uniformly, in conflict. Some business leaders, including those in small business, have consistently worked and acted for the cause of conservation. For example, many small firms have taken steps to landscape and otherwise improve the appearance of plant facilities. Others have modernized their equipment and changed their procedures to reduce air and water pollution. Some small businesses have actually been in a position to benefit from the general emphasis on ecology. For example, those companies whose products are harmless to the environment are preferred by customers over competitors whose products pollute. Also, some small firms are involved in servicing pollution-control equipment. Auto repair shops, for example, may service pollution-control devices on automobile engines.

Other small firms, however, are adversely affected by efforts to protect the environment. Livestock feeding lots, cement plants, pet-food processors, and iron foundries are representative of industries that are especially vulnerable to extensive environmental regulation. The cost impact of such regulation on businesses of

this type is often severe. Indeed, the required improvements can force the closure of some firms. Many small foundries, for example, were forced to close because of costly environmental controls.

A firm's ability to pass higher costs on to its customers depends on the market situation, and it is ordinarily quite difficult for a small business to do so. Resulting economic hardships must, therefore, be recognized as a cost of pollution control and evaluated accordingly. Effective pollution control is especially hard on a small, marginal firm with obsolete equipment. Environmental regulation may simply hasten the inevitable closing of such a firm.

The level at which governmental regulation originates poses another potential problem for small businesses. State or local legislation may prove discriminatory by forcing higher costs on a local firm than on its competitors, which are located outside the regulated territory. The immediate self-interest of a small firm, therefore, is best served by legislation that applies at the highest or most general level. A federal regulation applies to all U.S. firms and thereby avoids giving competitive advantages to low-cost polluters in other states.

Consumer Issues

At one time, the accepted philosophy of business was expressed as "Let the buyer beware." In contrast, today's philosophy forces the seller to put more emphasis on meeting customers' expectations. Today's buyers expect to purchase products that are safe, reliable, durable, and honestly advertised. These expectations are the core of a current movement known as **consumerism** and have influenced various types of consumer legislation. The Magnuson-Moss Warranty Act, for example, imposes special restrictions on sellers, such as requiring that any written warranties be available for inspection rather than being hidden inside a package.

consumerism
a movement that stresses the needs of consumers and the importance of serving them honestly and well

To some extent, small firms stand to gain from the consumerism movement. Attention to customer needs and flexibility in meeting those needs have traditionally been strong assets of small firms. Their managers have close relationships with customers and thus are able to know and respond easily to their needs. To the extent that these positive features have been realized in practice, the position of small businesses has been strengthened. And to the extent that small firms can continue to capitalize on customers' desire for excellent service, they can reap rewards from the consumerism movement.

Building a completely safe product and avoiding all errors in service are almost impossible goals to reach. Moreover, the growing complexity of products makes their servicing more difficult. A mechanic or repairperson must know a great deal more to render satisfactory service today than he or she needed two or three decades ago. Rising consumer expectations, therefore, provide a measure of risk as well as opportunity for small firms. The quality of their management determines the extent to which small firms realize opportunities and avoid threats to their success.

THE SMALL BUSINESS CONTEXT FOR ETHICAL DECISIONS

3 Identify contextual factors that affect ethical decision making in small businesses.

Stories in the news media concerning insider trading, fraud, and bribery usually involve large corporations. However, ethical problems are clearly not confined to big business. In the less publicized, day-to-day life of small businesses, decision makers face ethical dilemmas and temptations to compromise principles for the sake of business or personal advantage. In this section, we discuss some of the ethical issues facing small firms.

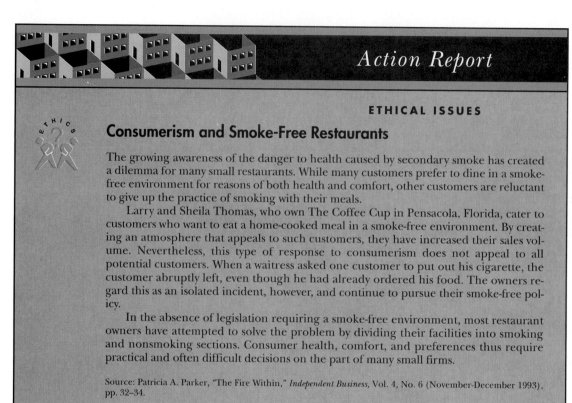

Action Report

ETHICAL ISSUES

Consumerism and Smoke-Free Restaurants

The growing awareness of the danger to health caused by secondary smoke has created a dilemma for many small restaurants. While many customers prefer to dine in a smoke-free environment for reasons of both health and comfort, other customers are reluctant to give up the practice of smoking with their meals.

Larry and Sheila Thomas, who own The Coffee Cup in Pensacola, Florida, cater to customers who want to eat a home-cooked meal in a smoke-free environment. By creating an atmosphere that appeals to such customers, they have increased their sales volume. Nevertheless, this type of response to consumerism does not appeal to all potential customers. When a waitress asked one customer to put out his cigarette, the customer abruptly left, even though he had already ordered his food. The owners regard this as an isolated incident, however, and continue to pursue their smoke-free policy.

In the absence of legislation requiring a smoke-free environment, most restaurant owners have attempted to solve the problem by dividing their facilities into smoking and nonsmoking sections. Consumer health, comfort, and preferences thus require practical and often difficult decisions on the part of many small firms.

Source: Patricia A. Parker, "The Fire Within," *Independent Business*, Vol. 4, No. 6 (November-December 1993), pp. 32–34.

Kinds of Ethical Issues in Small Firms

ethical issues
practices and policies involving questions of right and wrong

Ethical issues are those practices and policies that involve questions of right and wrong. Such questions go far beyond what is legal or illegal. Many small business relationships call for decisions regarding honesty, fairness, and respect.

Only a naive person would argue that small business is pure in terms of ethical conduct. In fact, there is widespread recognition of unethical and even illegal small business activity. While the extent of unethical conduct cannot be measured, an obvious need for improvement in small, as well as large, businesses exists.

One glaring example of poor ethics practiced by some small businesses is fraudulent reporting of income and expenses for income tax purposes. This unethical conduct includes skimming—that is, concealing some income—as well as improperly claiming certain business expenses. We do not mean to imply that all or even most small firms engage in such practices. However, tax evasion does occur within small firms, and the practice is sufficiently widespread to be recognized as a general problem.

The Internal Revenue Service regularly uncovers cases of income tax fraud. For example, the John E. Long family, the largest promoter of country folk art shows in the nation, was forced to pay millions in back taxes, and four members of the family were given prison terms for tax law violations.[6] The Longs did not record the cash they collected for admission. Instead, they deposited into corporate accounts only checks received from such sources as renting booths and publishing a magazine. Unfortunately for the Longs, the IRS discovered 2,000 unreported deposits that members of the family had made into 37 different accounts. The Longs had reported that their business was losing money, when, in fact, it was doing very well.

Cheating on taxes represents only one type of unethical business practice. Questions of right and wrong permeate all areas of business decision making. Understanding the scope of the problem requires comprehension of the way in which ethical issues affect decisions in marketing, management, and finance.

When making marketing decisions, an owner is confronted with a variety of ethical questions. For example, advertising content must sell the product or service but also tell "the truth, the whole truth, and nothing but the truth." Salespeople must walk a fine line between persuasion and deception. In some types of small business, a salesperson might obtain contracts more easily by offering improper inducements to buyers or by joining with competitors in rigging bids.

Through management decisions, an owner affects the personal and family lives of employees. Issues of fairness, honesty, and impartiality surface in decisions and practices regarding hiring, promotions, salary increases, dismissals, layoffs, and work assignments. In communicating with employees, an owner may be truthful, vague, misleading, or totally dishonest. Of course, employees also have ethical obligations to their employers—for example, to do "an honest day's work."

In making financial and accounting decisions, an owner must decide the extent to which he or she will be honest and candid in reporting financial information. The owner should recognize that outsiders such as bankers and suppliers depend on a firm's financial reports to be accurate.

Comparatively little is known about the types of ethical issues that are most troublesome for small business owners. As an initial step in exploring this largely unknown area, we asked respondents to a nationwide survey of small firms the following question: "What is the most difficult ethical issue that you have faced in your work?" As might be expected, the question precipitated a wide variety of responses, which have been grouped into the categories shown in Table 25-1. The number of difficult issues given by the respondents total 166; the number for each grouping is indicated.

These responses provide a rough idea of the great diversity of ethical issues faced by members of small businesses. As you can see, a major category of concerns relates to customers, clients, and competitors. This category is followed by one concerned with management processes and relationships. Management relationship issues are especially disturbing because they reflect the moral fiber or culture of the firm, including deficiencies in management actions and commitments.

Vulnerability of Small Firms

Walking the straight and narrow may be more difficult and costly on Main Street than it is on Wall Street.[7] That is, small firms may face greater temptations and pressures to act unethically as a direct result of their smallness. For example, a lack of resources may make it difficult for owners of a small firm to resist extortion by public officials.

> *Professor William Baxter of the Stanford Law School notes that for such owners, delayed building permits or failed sanitation inspections can be "life-threatening events" that make them cave in to bribe demands. By contrast, he adds, "the local manager of Burger King is in a much better position" to tell these people to get lost.[8]*

The small firm may also be at a disadvantage in competing with larger competitors that have superior resources. As a result, the firm's owner may be tempted to rationalize bribery as a way of offsetting what seems to be a competitive disadvantage and securing an even playing field.

Table 25-1

*Difficult Ethical Issues
Facing Small Firms*

Issue	Number of Respondents	Responses
Relationships with customers, clients, and competitors (relationships with outside parties in the marketplace)	56	"Avoiding conflicts of interest when representing clients in the same field" "Putting old parts in a new device and selling it as new" "Lying to customers about test results"
Management processes and relationships (superior-subordinate relationships)	30	"Reporting to an unethical person" "Having to back up the owner/CEO's lies about business capability in order to win over an account and then lie more to complete the job" "Being asked by my superiors to do something that I know is not good for the company or its employees"
Employee obligations to employer (employee responsibilities and actions that in some way conflict with the best interests of the employer)	26	"Receiving kickbacks by awarding overpriced contracts or taking gratuities to give a subcontractor the contract" "Theft of corporate assets" "Getting people to do a full day's work"
Relationships with suppliers (practices and deceptions that tend to defraud suppliers)	18	"Vendors want a second chance to bid if their bid is out of line." "Software copyright issues" "The ordering of supplies when cash flows are low and bankruptcy may be coming"
Governmental obligations and relationships (compliance with governmental requirements and reporting to government agencies)	17	"Having to deal with so-called anti-discrimination laws which in fact force me to discriminate" "Bending state regulations" "Employing people who may not be legal [citizens] to work"
Human resource decisions (decisions relating to employment and promotion)	14	"Whether to lay off workers who [are] surplus to our needs and would have a problem finding work or to deeply cut executive pay and perks" "Sexual harrassment" "Attempting to rate employees based on performance and not personality"
Environmental and social responsibilities (business obligations to the environment and society)	5	"Whether to pay to have chemicals disposed of or just throw them in a dumpster" "Environmental safety versus cost to prevent accidents" "Environmental aspects of manufacturing"

Source: Justin Longenecker, Joseph A. McKinney, and Carlos W. Moore, "Ethical Attitudes, Issues, and Pressures in Small Business." Paper presented at the International Council for Small Business Conference, Sydney, Australia, June 1995.

The temptation for entrepreneurs to compromise ethical standards as they strive to earn profits is evident in the results of a study of entrepreneurial ethics.[9] In this study, entrepreneurs were compared with other business managers and professionals on their views about various ethical issues. Respondents were presented with sixteen vignettes, each describing a business decision having ethical overtones, and were asked to indicate the degree to which they found each action compatible with their own ethical views by checking a seven-point scale ranging from 1 (never acceptable) to 7 (always acceptable). Here is one vignette: "An owner of a small firm obtained a free copy of a copyrighted computer software program from a business friend rather than spending $500 to obtain his own program from the software dealer."

For the most part, all respondents in this study, including entrepreneurs, expressed a strong moral stance. They condemned decisions that were ethically questionable as well as those that were clearly illegal. For all vignettes, the mean response ratings for both entrepreneurs and other respondents were less than 4 (sometimes acceptable), thus indicating some degree of disapproval. For nine of the sixteen vignettes, there were no significant differences between the responses of entrepreneurs and those of others. For the remaining seven vignettes, however, the responses of the entrepreneurs were significantly different. In five cases, the entrepreneurs appeared significantly less moral (more approving of questionable conduct) than the other respondents.[10] Each of these situations involved an opportunity to gain financially by taking a profit from someone else's pocket. For example, entrepreneurs were more willing to condone collusive bidding and the duplicating of copyrighted computer software without payment to the manufacturer for its use.

Obviously, a special temptation exists for entrepreneurs who are strongly driven to earn profits. However, this issue must be kept in perspective. Even though the entrepreneurs appeared less moral than the other business respondents in their reactions to five ethical issues, the majority of the entrepreneurs were significantly *more* moral in their responses to two other issues in which there was no immediate profit impact.[11] One of these issues involved an engineer's decision to keep quiet about a safety hazard that his employer had declined to correct.

Evidence shows, then, that most entrepreneurs display a general ethical sensitivity, but that some show vulnerability in issues that directly affect profits. While business pressures do not justify unethical behavior, they help explain the context for decisions involving ethical issues. Ethical decision making often calls for difficult choices by the entrepreneur.

PUTTING ETHICAL PRECEPTS INTO PRACTICE

4 Describe practical approaches for applying ethical precepts in small business management.

Having discussed the kinds of ethical issues confronting small firms and their special vulnerability, we turn now to the practical matter of achieving ethical performance. In discussing this process, we must consider the underlying values of a firm's business culture, the nature of its leadership, and the guidance provided to employees.

Underlying Values and Business Ethics

underlying values
unarticulated ethical beliefs that provide a foundation for ethical behavior

Business practices viewed as right or wrong by a firm's leaders or employees reflect that firm's **underlying values.** An employee's beliefs affect what that employee does on the job and how she or he acts toward customers and others. Certainly, people sometimes speak more ethically than they act. Despite any verbal posturing, however, actual behavior can provide clues to a person's underlying system of basic values. Behaviors may reflect a commitment or lack thereof to honesty, respect, and truthfulness—to integrity in all of its dimensions.

Values that serve as a foundation for ethical behavior in business are based on personal views of the universe and the role of humankind in that universe. Such values, therefore, are part of basic philosophical and/or religious convictions. In the United States, Judeo-Christian values have traditionally served as the general body of beliefs underlying business behavior, although there are examples of ethical behavior based on principles derived from other religions. Since religious and/or philosophical values, or the lack thereof, are reflected in the business practices of firms of all sizes, a leader's personal commitment to certain basic values is important in determining the ethical climate in a small firm.

As one example of the way a leader's basic values affect business practices, consider the company featured in this chapter's opening—Reell Precision Manufacturing Corporation.[12] The founders of this firm share a religious belief that shapes their approach to conducting business. They have involved company personnel in discussing ethical issues by forming a committee called "The Forum," a group of four management and nine rank-and-file representatives who meet weekly to discuss corporate policy. As a part of their deliberations, the members of this group examine basic religious teachings as they relate to practical business ethics. Within one period of a few weeks, for example, they invited a rabbi, a priest, and a Lutheran minister to address the group on the subject of applying religious values in the business arena.

One observer of the firm and its operations described its leaders' approach to applying religious values as follows:

> *Their original corporate directions statement talked unabashedly about "a personal commitment to God, revealed in Jesus Christ," and about following "the will of God" in business dealings. But that seemed a bit much to some employees who did not share their strong convictions, so the matter was tossed to The Forum.*
>
> *The result: Most of the religious language was excised—although the founders insisted on keeping the thought that the business is based on "practical application of Judeo-Christian values." The reasoning was simple, Wahlstedt [the president and one of the partners] said: "I don't see how you can approach the subject of ethics without relating it to some base of values."*[13]

The way in which these values influence this firm's business practices—reducing profits, for example, rather than laying off employees—was noted earlier.

It seems apparent that a deep commitment to certain basic values leads to behavior that is widely appreciated and admired. Without such a commitment on the part of small business leadership, ethical standards can easily be compromised.

Ethical Leadership

Entrepreneurs who care about ethical performance in their firms can use their influence as leaders and owners to encourage and even insist that everyone in their firms display honesty and integrity in all operations. Ethical values are established by leaders in all organizations, and those at lower levels take their cues regarding proper behavior from the pronouncements and conduct of the top level.

In a small organization, the ethical influence of a leader is more pronounced than it is in a large corporation, where leadership can become diffused. In a large corporation, the chief executive must exercise great care to make sure that his or

Action Report

ETHICAL ISSUES

Herman Miller's Reputation for Integrity

A company's reputation for integrity reflects a leadership with strong underlying values and a deep commitment to doing what is right. A classic example is found in one of the nation's best-known family businesses—Herman Miller, Inc., a manufacturer of fine office furniture, based in Zeeland, Michigan. Although the founding family is no longer active in management, the business still reflects its values. Established in 1923 by D. J. DePree, the firm was later headed for many years by his son, Max DePree. Its reputation as a well-managed company rests not only on its superb products—acclaimed by some as the highest-quality office furniture made anywhere—but also on its integrity in relationships with employees, customers, and others. Here is an outsider's assessment of the company and the ethical leadership of Max DePree:

> *Herman Miller is a place with integrity. Max defines integrity as "a fine sense of one's obligations." That integrity exhibits itself in the company's dedication to superior design, to quality, to making a contribution to society—and in its manifest respect for its customers, investors, suppliers, and employees.*

One of the ways in which this firm's integrity is demonstrated is by its treatment of employees. For many years, Herman Miller has used a system known as the Scanlon Plan to share with employees the financial gains resulting from productivity improvements. As the use of this plan illustrates, the values of the DePree family have been built into the operating practices of this firm.

Source: The assessment of Herman Miller, Inc. was made by James O'Toole, University of Southern California, and appears in the foreword to Max DePree, *Leadership Is an Art* (East Lansing: Michigan State University Press, 1987), pp. xvii–xviii.

her precepts are shared by those in the various divisions and subsidiaries. Some corporate CEOs have professed great shock on discovering behavior at lower levels that conflicted sharply with their own espoused principles. Leaders of large corporations are also responsible to stockholders, most of whom focus more attention on corporate profits than corporate ethics. The position of an entrepreneur is much simpler. Recall the Reell Precision Manufacturing Corporation, in which owner-managers were able to base difficult decisions on their underlying ethical values.

The potential for high ethical standards in small firms is obvious. An entrepreneur who believes strongly in honesty and truthfulness can insist that those principles be followed throughout the organization. In effect, the founder or head of a small business can say "My personal integrity is on the line, and I want you to do it this way!" Such statements are easily understood. And such a leader becomes even more effective when he or she backs up such statements with appropriate behavior. In fact, a leader's behavior—rather than his or her stated philosophy—has the greater influence on employees. In Herman Miller, Inc., for example, the ethical values of the founder and his son obviously permeated and continue to characterize this firm's operation.

In summary, the personal integrity of a founder or owner is the key to a firm's ethical performance. The dominant role of this one person or leadership team affords that person or team a powerful voice in the ethical performance of the small firm.

Pressure to Act Unethically

Employees of small firms sometimes face pressure to act in ways that conflict with their own sense of what is right and wrong. The pressure may come from various sources. For example, a salesperson may face pressure to compromise personal ethical standards in order to make a sale. Or, in some cases, an employee may feel pressured by his or her boss to act unethically—a condition guaranteed to produce an organizational culture that is soft on ethics.

Fortunately, most employees of small firms do not face such pressures. However, pressure to violate personal standards is not unknown. In a survey of individuals holding managerial and professional positions in small firms, respondents reported feeling the following degrees of pressure to act unethically:[14]

No pressure	67.2%
Slight pressure	29.0%
Extreme pressure	3.8%

While it is encouraging to note that two-thirds of the respondents reported an absence of pressure to compromise personal standards, the fact that one-third of the respondents experienced either slight or extreme pressure is disturbing. The stringency of a person's ethical standards is, of course, related to that person's perception of pressure to act unethically. That is, a person with low ethical standards would probably encounter few situations that would violate such standards. Conversely, a person with high ethical standards would find more situations that might violate his or her personal norms. The ideal is to develop a business environment in which the best ethical practices are consistently and uniformly encouraged.

Developing a Code of Ethics

As a small firm grows, the personal influence of the entrepreneur inevitably declines. Personal interactions between owner and employees occur less and less. Consequently, as the business grows larger, the entrepreneur's basic ethical values simply cannot be expressed or reinforced as frequently or consistently as they once were.

code of ethics
official standards of employee behavior formulated by a firm

At some point, therefore, the owner-manager of a firm should formulate a **code of ethics,** similar to that of most large corporations. This code should express the principles to be followed by employees of the firm and give examples of these principles in action. A code of ethics might, for example, prohibit acceptance of gifts or favors from suppliers but point out the standard business courtesies, such as free lunch, that might be accepted without violating the policy.[15]

If a code of ethics is to be effective, employees must be aware of its nature and convinced of its importance. At the very least, they should read and sign it. However, as a firm grows larger and new employees are less familiar with the firm's ethics, training becomes necessary to ensure that the code is well understood and taken seriously. It is also imperative, of course, that management operate in a manner consistent with its own principles and deal decisively with any infractions.

Better Business Bureaus

In any sizable community, all types of ethical and unethical business practices can be found. Some firms use highly questionable practices—for example, **bait advertising,** which is a deceptive offer to sell a product at an attractive price in order to lure in customers and then convince them to purchase more expensive products. Other firms are blatantly dishonest in the products or services they provide—for example, replacing auto parts that are perfectly good.

Because unethical operations reflect adversely on honest members of the business community, privately owned business firms in many cities have banded together to form Better Business Bureaus. The purpose of such organizations is to promote ethical conduct on the part of all business firms in the community.

Specifically, a Better Business Bureau's function is twofold: (1) It provides free buying guidelines and information about a company that a consumer should know *prior to* completing a business transaction, and (2) it attempts to solve questions or disputes concerning purchases. As a result, unethical business practices often de-

bait advertising an insincere offer to sell a product or service at a very low price in order to entice customers, only to switch them later to the purchase of a more expensive product or service

---

Bait Advertising and Selling

A "bait" offer is an alluring but insincere offer to sell a product or service [that] the advertiser does not intend to sell. Its purpose is to switch consumers from buying the advertised merchandise or service in order to sell something else, usually at a higher price or on a basis more advantageous to the advertiser.

a. No advertisement should be published unless it is a bona fide offer to sell the advertised merchandise or service.

b. The advertising should not create a false impression about the product or service being offered in order to lay the foundation for a later "switch" to other, more expensive products or services, or products of a lesser quality at the same price.

c. Subsequent full disclosure by the advertiser of all other facts about the advertised article does not preclude the existence of a bait scheme.

d. An advertiser should not use or permit the use of the following scheme practices:
- refusing to show or demonstrate the advertised merchandise or service;
- disparaging the advertised merchandise or service, its warranty, availability, services and parts, credit terms, etc.;
- selling the advertised merchandise or service and thereafter "unselling" the customer to make a switch to other merchandise or service;
- refusing to take orders for the advertised merchandise or service or to deliver it within a reasonable time;
- demonstrating or showing a defective sample of the advertised merchandise; or
- having a sales compensation plan designed to penalize salespersons who sell the advertised merchandise or service.

e. An advertiser should have on hand a sufficient quantity of advertised merchandise to meet reasonably anticipated demands, unless the advertisement discloses the number of items available. If items are available only at certain branches, their specific locations should be disclosed. The use of "rainchecks" is no justification for inadequate estimates of reasonably anticipated demand.

f. Actual sales of the advertised merchandise or service may not preclude the existence of a bait scheme since this may be merely an attempt to create an aura of legitimacy. A key factor in determining the existence of "bait" is the number of times the merchandise or service was advertised compared to the number of actual sales of the merchandise or service.

Figure 25-1

Better Business Bureau Code of Advertising

Source: Reprinted with permission of the Council of Better Business Bureaus, from "Code of Advertising," copyright 1985. Council of Better Business Bureaus, Inc., 4200 Wilson Blvd., Arlington, VA 22203.

1 Explain the impact of social responsibilities on small businesses.

- Most small businesses recognize some social responsibilities, especially to customers, employees, and communities.
- Socially acceptable actions create goodwill in the community and can attract customers.
- Some socially responsible practices are expensive, while others are cost-free.
- The need of small firms to remain profitable limits their ability to adopt costly social programs.

2 Describe the special challenges of environmentalism and consumerism.

- Many small businesses protect the environment, and some contribute positively by providing environmental services.
- Some small firms, such as pet-food processers, are adversely affected by environmentalism.
- By requiring the seller to meet consumer expectations, the consumerism movement creates problems for some small businesses but provides opportunities for those businesses that serve their customers well.

3 Identify contextual factors that affect ethical decision making in small businesses.

- Ethical issues go beyond what is legal or illegal and include more general questions of right and wrong.
- The limited resources of small firms make them especially vulnerable to allowing or engaging in unethical practices.
- Income tax cheating by some small firms is an especially visible form of bad ethics.
- The most troublesome ethical issues for small businesses involve relationships with customers, clients, and competitors; management processes and relationships; and employees' obligations to their employers.

4 Describe practical approaches for applying ethical precepts in small business management.

- The underlying values of business leaders and the examples those leaders set by their actions are powerful forces that affect ethical performance.
- Managers of small firms should seek to create an ethical climate that reduces or eliminates pressures on individual employees to compromise their ethical standards.
- Some small firms develop codes of ethics to provide guidance for their employees.
- Many small businesses join Better Business Bureaus to promote ethical conduct throughout the business community.

cline in a community served by a Better Business Bureau. Figure 25-1 presents a section of the code of advertising ethics developed by the Better Business Bureaus.

The creation of Better Business Bureaus reflects an initiative on the part of independent firms to encourage ethical conduct within the business community. Actions of this type and voluntary commitment to ethical performance within individual firms tend to receive less press coverage than the ethical failures of some business leaders. However, ethical performance achieved in these ways greatly contributes to the effective functioning of the private enterprise system.

DISCUSSION QUESTIONS

1. This chapter's opening referred to RPM's intention to cut short-term profits rather than lay off employees. How can this be justified in a competitive enterprise system in which the goal of the business is profits?
2. To what extent do small business owners recognize their social responsibilities? Could you defend the position of those who say they have no social responsibility? If so, how?
3. Why might small business CEOs focus more attention on profit and less on social goals than large business CEOs?
4. Give some examples of expenditures required on the part of small business firms to protect the environment.
5. Should all firms use biodegradable packaging? Is your answer the same if you know that its use adds 25 percent to the price of a product?
6. What is skimming? How do you think owners of small firms might attempt to rationalize such a practice?

7. Give an example of an unethical business practice that you have personally encountered.

8. Based on your experience as an employee, customer, or other observer of some particular small business, how would you rate its ethical performance? On what evidence or clues do you base your opinion?

9. Explain the connection between underlying values and ethical business behavior.

10. Give some examples of the practical application of a firm's basic commitment to supporting the family life of its employees.

EXPERIENTIAL EXERCISES

1. Visit or telephone the nearest Better Business Bureau office to research the types of unethical business practices it has uncovered in the community and the ways in which it is attempting to support ethical practices. Report briefly on your findings.

2. Employees sometimes take sick leave when they are merely tired, and students sometimes miss class for the same reason. Separate into groups of four or five, and prepare a brief statement showing the nature of the ethical issue (if any) in each of these practices.

3. Examine a recent issue of *The Wall Street Journal* or another business periodical and report briefly on some ethical problem in the news. Could this type of ethical problem occur in a small business? Explain.

4. Interview a small business manager to discover how (or whether) environmental issues affect the manager's firm. Does the firm face any special governmental restrictions? Are there costs involved?

New Terms and Concepts

social responsibilities *555*

environmentalism *558*

consumerism *559*

ethical issues *560*

underlying values *563*

code of ethics *566*

bait advertising *567*

You Make the Call

Situation 1   At one time, Ben Cohen, founding partner of Ben & Jerry's Homemade, Inc. (purveyor of all natural ice cream), considered selling his share of the business. He decided instead to keep his ownership share and run the business in a socially responsible way. Operating differently from a traditional business apparently gives him a greater sense of purpose as an entrepreneur. Cohen took the following actions at the time: Because he felt strongly that "the community should prosper right along with the company," he engineered a $5.1 million equity offering pitched first to Vermonters and, a year later, to fellow ice cream fanatics nationwide; $500,000 from the offering helped start a nonprofit foundation that, bolstered by 15 percent of Ben & Jerry's pretax profits, supports local causes. Internally, Cohen also instituted a five-to-one salary-ratio cap, whereby the lowliest line employee cannot make any less than 20 percent of what top management makes.[16]

Source: "Double Fudge—Ben & Jerry's: A Double Scoop of Business Style," *Inc.*, Vol. 8, No. 5 (May 1986), p. 52.

Question 1   Is selling equity in a Vermont-based business to Vermonters more socially responsible than selling equity to people in other states?
Question 2   In what way is the salary cap a socially responsible policy?
Question 3   Is a business that sells double fudge ice cream to overweight customers acting in a socially responsible way?

Situation 2   A software firm sells its product to retailers and dealers for resale to end users. It has been a slow year, and profits are running behind those of a year ago. One way to increase sales is to persuade dealers to stock more inventory. This is achievable by exaggerating total product demand to dealers by presenting them with an extremely optimistic picture of the size and effectiveness of the company's promotional program. This action should encourage dealers to build larger inventories sooner than they would normally. The software itself is regarded as a good product, and the producer simply wishes to build sales by putting its best foot forward in this way.

Question 1   Is the software firm acting ethically if it attempts to increase sales in this way?
Question 2   If this approach is sound ethically, is it also good business?
Question 3   What course of action do you recommend? Why?

Continue on next page

Situation 3 A self-employed commercial artist reports taxable income of $7,000. Actually, her income is considerably higher, but much of it takes the form of cash for small projects and is easy to conceal. She considers herself part of the "underground economy" and defends her behavior as a tactic that allows her small business to survive. If the business were to close, she argues, the government would receive even less tax revenue.

Question 1 Is the need to survive a reasonable defense for the practice described here?

Question 2 If the practice of concealing income is widespread, as implied by the phrase "underground economy," is it really wrong?

 CASE 25
The Martin Company (p. 660)

This case describes a conflict between two brothers who were managers in a family-owned firm—a conflict that involves issues of fairness, right, and wrong.

Working Within the Law

Bill Slater

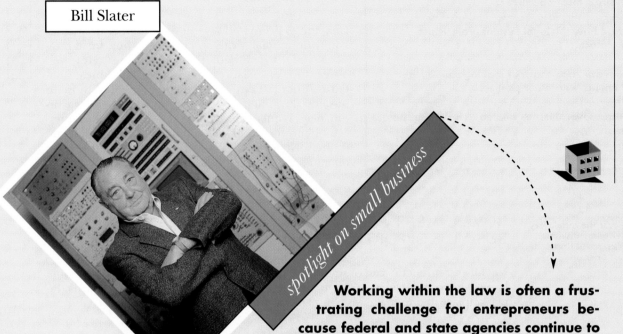

spotlight on small business

Working within the law is often a frustrating challenge for entrepreneurs because federal and state agencies continue to churn out regulations, often with forms for reporting and inspectors to ensure compliance. Bill Slater, owner of Apex Electronics in Sun Valley, California, is fed up with the situation. He escapes some federal regulations by intentionally staying small.

Slater is making sure his business doesn't grow beyond its current 10 employees. "I wouldn't go any higher because then we'd come under the federal and California OSHA [Occupational Safety and Health Administration]," he declares.

However, Slater has not been as successful in escaping state regulators. For 40 years, Apex recycled aluminum cans. Then a California law was passed.

[It requires] all recyclers to have state licenses and to collect glass, paper and plastic as well as aluminum. Slater didn't want to devote space to those materials, given the rock-bottom prices his buyers would pay for them. "It would cost 10 times as much to take it in as I'd get back," he says. But when state inspectors brought in a box of plastic bottles and he said he didn't buy bottles, he lost his recycling license.

Now, Apex can't even recycle aluminum.

Source: Jan Easter Bahls, "Seeing Red," *Entrepreneur*, Vol. 22, No. 6 (June 1994), p. 104. Reprinted with permission from *Entrepreneur* Magazine, June 1994.

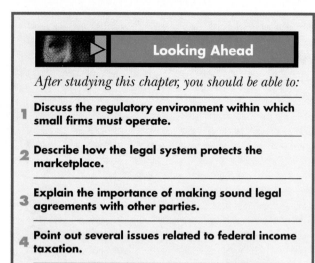

start here

Looking Ahead

After studying this chapter, you should be able to:

1 Discuss the regulatory environment within which small firms must operate.

2 Describe how the legal system protects the marketplace.

3 Explain the importance of making sound legal agreements with other parties.

4 Point out several issues related to federal income taxation.

Chapter 25 presented several social and ethical issues confronting small firms and discussed how small businesses might deal with these challenges. However, observance of social responsibilities and ethical standards is not left entirely to the discretion of those in business. Federal laws, as well as state laws and local ordinances, regulate business activity in the public interest. Therefore, this chapter examines the legal framework of regulation within which business firms operate.

---

1 Discuss the regulatory environment within which small firms must operate.

GOVERNMENT REGULATION AND SMALL BUSINESS OPPORTUNITY

Not all entrepreneurs can or want to be lawyers. Nevertheless, they must have some knowledge of the law in order to appreciate how the legal system safeguards the marketplace and to make wise business decisions.

The Burden of Regulation

Government regulation has grown to the point at which it imposes a real hardship on small firms, both domestically and abroad. To some extent, problems arise from the seemingly inevitable red tape and bureaucratic procedures of governments. However, the sheer magnitude of regulation is a major problem.

An interesting perspective on the situation is offered by a recent president of the National Federation of Independent Business in the introduction to a book entitled *Small Business Under Siege:*

> *In America, the growing belief in a government fix for every problem is leading quickly to a system in which individuals who have never started or run a business are issuing regulation after regulation telling small business owners whom they can hire and what they must be paid. These same elected officials and bureaucrats—most of whom have never met a payroll—are piling on mandatory employee benefits, employment guidelines, workplace regulations and compliance paperwork overload.*
>
> *This belief in a government fix for every problem has created a web of regulations and accompanying regulatory bureaucracy which often frightens the owners of even the fairest, safest and healthiest workplaces. It has created a system that can destroy jobs and family businesses in order to save drainage ditches and obscure fish.*
>
> *This belief in a government fix for every problem has led us to a society in which the majority of American people, when asked, say without considering the broader implications that, yes, the government should require employers to provide this or that new benefit. (The misinformed assumption, of course, is that employers can provide these benefits with no impact on jobs or the salaries of current employees.)*
>
> *In the end, this belief in a government fix for every problem is leading our nation to the ultimate choice between government dictates and the free market.*[1]

The results of two recent studies point out the strong feelings of small business owners regarding government regulations:

[The] *1993 Survey of Mid-Sized Businesses by National Small Business United (NSBU) and the Arthur Andersen Enterprise Group shows business owners rank regulatory burdens and federal taxes third and fourth out of the 10 biggest challenges to future growth.*[2]

In a 1993 survey of 250 midsized manufacturers, Chicago-based Grant Thornton Accountants and Management Consultants found that 81 percent listed "reduced regulation" as the change that would be most beneficial to their companies.[3]

Another study published in *Small Business Reports* found that from 1989 to 1992 the government tax and regulatory burden per worker increased 34 percent while the business profit per worker declined 22 percent. The authors of this study name four specific regulations as the major contributors to the increased burden: the 1989 minimum-wage increase, the 1990 Americans with Disabilities Act, the 1990 amendments to the Clean Air Act, and the 1991 Civil Rights Act. The study concluded, "Federal government policies since 1989 amount to nothing less than economic crib death, suffocating jobs in the cradle of small business."[4] Other spokespersons for small business agree with this assessment. "The current level of regulation is so high, and so complicated, and so intrusive that it's strangling business and suppressing productivity," according to Brink Lindsey, director of regulatory studies for the Cato Institute in Washington, D.C.[5]

Thomas D. Hopkins, of the Rochester Institute of Technology in Rochester, New York, estimates that in 1991 federal regulations cost taxpayers over $400 billion—more than $4,200 per household.[6] Since regulation also occurs at state and local levels, the total cost of regulation is even greater than this figure suggests. Regulatory costs at the state and local levels are virtually impossible to estimate. Nevertheless, it is important to recognize that states are extremely active in establishing regulatory policies.

Another burden imposed on small businesses by the government is taxes. Taxes have a direct impact on small business cash flow and, therefore, represent a costly drain on the financial health of small firms. The federal income tax is the most publicized, but certainly not the only tax facing small firms. States raise funds from citizens and businesses through the use of state income taxes, sales taxes, and other forms of revenue production.

A small firm must work within state laws if it is to avoid legal problems. Major differences among state regulations compound the difficulty of this task. Consider the following state sales tax rules:

Tennessee imposes a sales tax on mandatory tips added to a customer's bill. Minnesota taxes the preparation of a floral arrangement by a florist or nursery. Maryland now applies its sales tax to cellular telephones, telephone answering machines, pay-per-view television, newspapers, and prescribed cat and dog food; Missouri considers trophy fees charged to guests at a wild game ranch taxable, and North Carolina deems water-treatment equipment subject to sales tax.[7]

It is difficult for an entrepreneur to stay abreast of state laws. Fortunately, state chambers of commerce are able to provide small firms with regulatory information. The U.S. Chamber of Commerce offers a publication entitled *Staff Directory—State Chambers of Commerce and Associations of Commerce and Industry,* which provides the addresses of all state chambers of commerce. Also, the newly formed National

Action Report

ENTREPRENEURIAL EXPERIENCES

Regulations Apply Brakes to New Product

Entrepreneurs face rules and regulations that are designed to protect the public interest but that sometimes serve to frustrate their efforts to operate a business. Entrepreneur Phillip Ramos, Jr., founder of Philatron International, Inc. in Santa Fe Springs, California, is a good example. Federal regulations recently halted efforts to market his new product.

Ramos invented a new coiled air-brake hose for attaching the braking system of a trailer to the back of a heavy-duty truck. Ramos maintains that his design is more durable than existing designs and provides superior performance. After introducing the product in 1991, Philatron sold more than 45,000 units within the first few months.

Customers obviously liked the new hose, but the product had a major problem: It did not meet federal safety requirements, which specified that such a hose be able to "withstand prolonged immersion in very hot oil." Philatron argued that this rule was an outdated requirement passed decades ago when tractor-trailer designs were different. Philatron's biggest critics, its competitors, disagreed with this argument.

With the assistance of several members of Congress and the U.S. Small Business Administration, Philatron persuaded the National Highway Traffic Safety Administration to rule in June 1992 that the critics' complaints "aren't relevant to the real-world safety performance" of the hose. This ruling saved Philatron from an expensive product recall, but it did not allow the company to resume sales.

Source: John R. Emshwiller, "Maker of Air-Brake Hoses Is Seeking Regulatory Relief," *The Wall Street Journal*, February 10, 1993, p. B1. Reprinted by permission of *The Wall Street Journal*, © 1993 Dow Jones & Company, Inc. All Rights Reserved Worldwide.

Resource Center for State Laws and Regulations has a 50-state network to help firms respond to proposed new taxes, laws, and regulations.

One strategy to escape the burden of regulation is to stay small, since very small firms are frequently exempt from regulations. However, the fact that our system of laws and regulations restricts business growth seems anti-American to many observers.

Not all laws are detrimental to small business. We will now briefly examine some of the beneficial aspects of regulation.

Benefits from Regulations

Regulation of small business activity is not all bad. A business world without some degree of regulation would surely be chaotic, and some degree of regulation is of general social value. Therefore, small firms should recognize the value of regulatory policies and show some willingness to shoulder the burden. Eugene Kimmelman, legislative director of the Consumer Federation of America, says, "It's hypocritical for small business to seek tax relief and loans from the government to boost their position in the marketplace and then to decry any costs imposed on them to protect the health, safety, and other needs of their employees and customers."[8]

Some entrepreneurs acknowledge that government regulation can occasionally create profit-making opportunities. New regulations sometimes spawn a market niche for a new product. For example, when the Environmental Protection Agency announced standards for automobile replacement-market catalytic converters, Perfection Automotive Products, in Livonia, Michigan, saw an opportunity to expand its product mix. Perfection's management says, "The new legislation created a market for replacement models that could be made more cheaply because they wouldn't have to last as long in aging vehicles. . . . [The company's sales have] significantly increased because of the catalytic-converter market."[9]

Finally, consider the new service of Clean Duds franchisees, which are actively pursuing new clients after the Occupational Safety and Health Administration issued a new rule requiring medical professionals to clean their uniforms more thoroughly. Under the rule, dental and medical offices, blood banks, ambulance services, mortuaries, and other similar businesses must clean apparel that could transmit blood-borne diseases. Philip Akin, CEO of Clean Duds, says the new business has been extremely profitable.[10]

Very small firms may find that they are exempt from some regulations—a situation that creates a favorable competitive situation for them. (Recall the strategy of the firm featured in this chapter's opening.) However, size requirements to qualify for exempt status vary from law to law.

Government Reaction to Regulatory Criticism

Recognition of the burdensome nature of small business regulation at the federal level has led to a number of legislative attempts to alleviate the problem. The **Regulatory Flexibility Act** of 1980, for example, requires federal agencies to assess the impact of proposed regulations on small businesses. These agencies are required to reduce paperwork requirements and to exempt small firms or simplify rules whenever possible. Somewhat similar legislation was enacted with the **Paperwork Reduction Act** of 1980. This act created the Office of Information and Regulatory Affairs (OIRA), which is overseen by the Office of Management and Budget. Unfortunately, in 1990, a U.S. Supreme Court decision drastically reduced the power of the act.

Another law recognizing the regulatory plight of small firms is the **Equal Access to Justice Act** of 1980. Strengthened in 1985, this law mandates the federal government to reimburse court costs to small firms that win cases against regulatory agencies. Incorporated and unincorporated businesses, partnerships, and organizations having a net worth of less than $7 million are eligible for recovery of attorneys' fees.

The immediate concern for small businesses is knowing what laws they must obey and how they can operate within these laws. Therefore, the remaining sections of this chapter cover laws that influence small business operations. Although only a sampling of laws and legal issues is possible in a single chapter, we have attempted to include both old and new legislation that impact small businesses.

Regulatory Flexibility Act
legislation that protects small firms from excessive federal regulation by simplifying rules and reducing paperwork

Paperwork Reduction Act
legislation that simplifies regulatory rules for small businesses

Equal Access to Justice Act
legislation requiring that small businesses be reimbursed for legal expenses in cases won against regulatory agencies

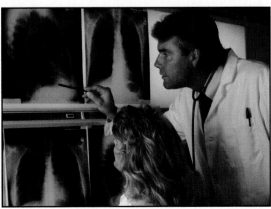

While government regulations can create a financial burden for some small businesses, they provide opportunity for others. A new OSHA ruling requiring more thorough cleaning of medical uniforms created new business for the Clean Duds franchise.

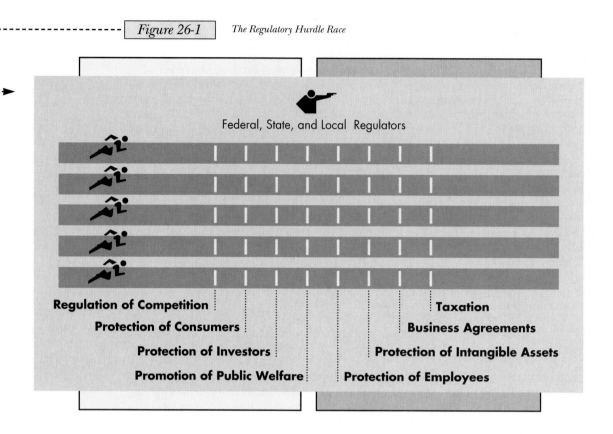

Figure 26-1 The Regulatory Hurdle Race

Federal, State, and Local Regulators

Regulation of Competition
Protection of Consumers
Protection of Investors
Promotion of Public Welfare

Taxation
Business Agreements
Protection of Intangible Assets
Protection of Employees

Figure 26-1 summarizes the legal issues selected for inclusion here. The regulatory areas are represented symbolically as hurdles facing the five entrepreneurs as they run the business race. Also, note that the starter—representing federal, state, and local regulatory agencies—is on the sidelines watching the race to be sure it is run legally. Although regulatory agencies are not discussed specifically in this chapter, they are important to a small firm's efforts to function within the law.

2 Describe how the legal system protects the marketplace.

GOVERNMENT REGULATION AND PROTECTION OF THE MARKETPLACE

The types of regulation are endless, affecting the ways in which small firms pay their employees, advertise, bid on contracts, dispose of waste, promote safety, and care for the public welfare. Of necessity, the discussion here will be limited to a few key areas of regulation.

This section emphasizes broad areas of government regulation of the marketplace—regulation of competition, protection of consumers, protection of investors, and promotion of public welfare—and includes discussions concerning regulation of employee rights and protection of a firm's intangible assets. The last two sections of the chapter look at business agreements and the issue of taxation. Because government regulation can be overwhelming, all small firms should seek guidance through the regulatory maze from professional legal counsel.

Regulation of Competition

A fully competitive economic system presumably benefits consumers, who can buy products and services from those firms that best satisfy their needs. Of the various laws intended to maintain a competitive economy, perhaps the best known are the federal antitrust laws, especially the Sherman Antitrust Act of 1890 and the Clayton Act of 1914. Both acts were designed to promote competition by eliminating artificial restraints on trade.

Although the purpose of federal and state antitrust laws is noble, the results leave much to be desired. One would be naive to think that small business need no longer fear the power of oligopolists that would control markets. Antitrust laws prevent some mergers and eliminate some unfair practices, but giant business firms continue to dominate many industries.

To some extent, at least, antitrust laws offer protection to small firms. The Robinson-Patman Act of 1936, an amendment to the Clayton Act, prohibits price discrimination by manufacturers and wholesalers in dealing with other business firms. In particular, the law is designed to protect independent retailers and wholesalers in competition with large chains. Quantity discounts may still be offered to large buyers, but the amount of the discounts must be justified financially by the seller on the basis of actual costs. Vendors are also forbidden to grant disproportionate advertising allowances to large retailers. The objective of this act is to prevent large purchasers from obtaining unreasonable discounts and other concessions merely because of their superior size and bargaining power.

The effectiveness of the Robinson-Patman Act and its benefits to small businesses have been debated. Some experts have argued that it discourages both large and small firms from cutting prices. Others say that this act makes it harder to expand into new markets and to pass on to customers the cost savings on large orders.

Since women-owned business firms have become a growing part of the economy, the federal government has recognized the possibility of discriminatory barriers. Therefore, Congress has created legislation such as the **Women's Business Ownership Act** of 1988 to encourage fair opportunities for women owners in the free enterprise system. Programs initiated under the authority of this act are intended to promote the interests of women-owned small businesses, in part by removing discriminatory barriers to obtaining capital.

The **Foreign Corrupt Practices Act** and later amendments to the act impact competitive practices internationally by restricting payments to foreign officials that may be interpreted as bribes. Some argue that this act places U.S. entrepreneurs at a disadvantage.

Women's Business Ownership Act
legislation intended to further the interests of women-owned firms and remove discriminatory barriers

Foreign Corrupt Practices Act
legislation making it illegal to pay bribes to foreign officials

Protection of Consumers

Consumers benefit indirectly from the freedom of competition provided by the laws just discussed. In addition, consumers are given various forms of more direct protection by federal, state, and local legislation.

The Wheeler-Lea Act of 1938 gave the Federal Trade Commission (FTC) a broad mandate to attack unfair or deceptive practices in commerce. The FTC's original focus on antitrust practices has been expanded through the years to cover a wide range of business activities: labeling, safety, packaging, and advertising of products; truth-in-lending; fair credit reporting; equal credit opportunity; and many others. States have also enacted laws and created consumer protection agencies to deal with unfair or deceptive practices. A few examples of the types of trade practices scrutinized by the Federal Trade Commission are the labeling of goods as

Safety standards are set by the Consumer Product Safety Commission to protect consumers against unreasonable risk of injury. Such standards ensure the safety of toys for infants and children.

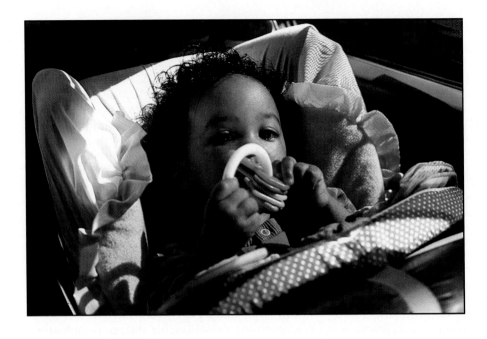

"free" or "handmade," misleading advertising that offers "bargains" by pretending to reduce unused regular prices, and bait and switch advertising.

The passage of the **Telephone Consumer Protection Act** in 1991 was another effort to protect consumers. The problem addressed by this legislation is unrestricted telemarketing, which many individuals feel is an invasion of privacy. The act places restrictions on the use of automated telephone equipment in telemarketing.

The **Nutrition Labeling and Education Act** of 1990 is an example of federal labeling regulation. Every food product covered by the law must have a standard nutrition label, listing the amounts of calories, fat, salt, and nutrients. The law also addresses the veracity of advertising claims such as "low salt" or "fiber prevents cancer." Some experts estimate the labeling costs at thousands of dollars per product.

As still another measure to protect the public against unreasonable risk of injury, the federal government enacted the Consumer Product Safety Act of 1972. This act created the Consumer Product Safety Commission to set safety standards for toys and other consumer products and to ban those goods that are exceptionally hazardous.

Telephone Consumer Protection Act legislation that offers consumers protection from intrusive telemarketing

Nutrition Labeling and Education Act legislation that requires producers to carry labels disclosing nutritional information on food packaging

Protection of Investors

To protect the investing public against fraudulent activities in the sale of stocks and bonds, both federal and state laws regulate the issuance and public sale of securities. To this end, the federal government enacted the Securities Act of 1933 and the Securities Exchange Act of 1934. The Securities Exchange Act established the powerful Securities and Exchange Commission to enforce the regulations implemented by both acts.

Most small businesses are excluded from extensive regulation under federal law because of the private nature of much of their financing and the small amounts involved. However, they are subject to state **blue-sky laws**, which cover registration of new securities; licensing of dealers, brokers, and salespersons; and prosecution of individuals charged with fraud in connection with the sale of stocks and bonds.

blue-sky laws state laws that protect investors from securities fraud

Promotion of Public Welfare

Other laws are designed to benefit the welfare of the public. Local ordinances, for example, establish minimum standards of sanitation for restaurants to protect the health of patrons. Zoning ordinances protect communities from unplanned development.

Environmental protection legislation—at federal, state, and local levels—deals with air pollution, water pollution, solid waste disposal, and handling of toxic substances. As discussed earlier, environmental laws adversely affect some small firms, although they occasionally provide opportunities for others.

The decade of the 1990s is shaping up as a period of strong emphasis on environmental protection. The 1990 amendments to the federal **Clean Air Act** of 1970, for example, put pressure on states to develop better systems for vehicle emissions testing. This, in turn, has required small service stations to make additional investments in testing equipment. The Clean Air Act requires that Freon—a contributor to the destruction of the earth's ozone layer—be recycled from automobile and business air-conditioning systems.

The **Americans with Disabilities Act** (ADA) was passed by Congress in 1990 to bar discrimination against people with disabilities. The act is enforced by the Equal Employment Opportunity Commission. Its provisions bar discrimination against qualified job applicants with disabilities. Businesses with as few as 15 employees must comply with the act's hiring, firing, and promotion policies. The act also requires reasonable accommodation for a disabled person to perform the job; "public accommodation" is also required of all businesses regardless of size.

State governments restrict entry into numerous professions and types of businesses by establishing licensing procedures. For example, physicians, barbers, pharmacists, accountants, lawyers, and real estate salespersons must be licensed. Insurance companies, banks, and public utilities must seek entry permits from state officials. Although licensing protects the public interest, it also tends to restrict the number of professionals and firms in such a way as to reduce competition and increase prices paid by consumers.

Note that there is a difference between licensing that involves a routine application and licensing that prescribes rigid entry standards and screening procedures. The fact that the impetus for much licensing comes from within the affected industry suggests a need for careful scrutiny of licensing proposals to avoid merely protecting a private interest and restricting entry into a field of business. In fact, a case can be made for the regulation of almost any business. However, failure to limit such regulation to the most essential issues undermines freedom of opportunity to enter a business and thereby provide an economic sevice to the community.

Clean Air Act
federal legislation regulating air pollutants

Americans with Disabilities Act
legislation that guarantees disabled people equal access to employment, as well as access to public places

The Americans with Disabilities Act prohibits discrimination against the disabled in both public areas and the workplace. Those with disabilities are assured of access to all public buildings.

Action Report

ETHICAL ISSUES

ADA Requirements Taste Bad to a Small Business

The saying "There is no free lunch" took on a unique meaning to entrepreneur Patricia Wangsness and her husband after they remodeled their Vienna, Virginia store in order to open a Manhattan Bagel shop. The location they chose had previously been occupied by another type of business and, therefore, had to be extensively revamped, at a total cost of $70,000.

The Wangsnesses estimate that they wound up spending around $20,000, or about 30 percent of the total, on ADA-related construction requirements. That figure embraces custom-made cabinets that are low enough, and recessed enough, and two restrooms large enough, to accommodate wheelchairs.

The Wangsnesses would have spent money on cabinets and restrooms in any event, but meeting the ADA's requirements raised the cost significantly. For example, they had to spend an additional $2,000 to alter previously approved plans and make the restroom doors open in instead of out. That change created a problem: When the doors opened in, there was not room enough for a wheelchair in front of the sink. Thus, the restrooms had to be enlarged, by moving a wall 18 inches farther into the store.

When that wall was moved, the Wangsnesses had to give up revenue-generating space: With smaller restrooms, there would have been room for another row of tables—and thus room for would-be customers who cannot find a seat on busy weekend mornings. There is no way to calculate how much business has been lost, the proprietors say.

Pat Wangsness wants all her customers to have convenient access, but "it's very hard for a small business to dig out from under that kind of expense," she says. In the first three months after the remodeled store opened, 15,000 customers were served—only 1 was in a wheelchair.

Source: Michael Barrier, "Unfunded and Unloved," *Nation's Business*, Vol. 83, No. 4 (April 1995), p. 40. Excerpted by permission, *Nation's Business*, April 1995. Copyright 1995, U.S. Chamber of Commerce.

Protection of Employee Rights

Occupational Safety and Health Act
legislation that regulates the safety of workplaces and work practices

Civil Rights Act
legislation prohibiting discrimination based on race, color, sex, religion, or national origin

Business employees are U.S. citizens first and employees second. Therefore, employees are afforded protection from robbery, assault, and other crime at work just as they are at home. In addition, some laws—for example, the Occupational Safety and Health Act of 1970, the Civil Rights Act of 1991, and the Family and Medical Leave Act of 1993—have been designed primarily for employees and potential employees.

The **Occupational Safety and Health Act** of 1970 created the Occupational Safety and Health Administration (OSHA) to ensure safe workplaces and work practices. OSHA continues, through a structured procedure, to establish additional health and safety standards as it deems necessary.

The **Civil Rights Act** of 1964, amended by the Civil Rights Act of 1991, prohibits employment discrimination based on race, color, sex, religion, or national origin. The 1991 Civil Rights Act allows employers to be tried by juries in employment discrimination cases. Workers may now recover punitive damages in sexual harassment cases involving intentional discrimination. Those workers who win a civil rights suit can receive punitive awards ranging from $50,000 (from employers with 100 or fewer employees) to $300,000 (from employers with over 500 employees).[11] The act does exempt firms with fewer than 15 employees. Some entrepreneurs may limit their firms' growth to maintain exempt status.

The **Family and Medical Leave Act** of 1993 was passed and signed into law by President Clinton in February 1993. The law applies to firms with 50 or more employees and requires such firms to allow workers as much as 12 weeks of unpaid leave for adoption of a child, childbirth, or other specified family needs. The worker must have been employed by the firm for 12 months and have worked at least 1,250 hours. Furthermore, the employer must continue health-care coverage during the leave and guarantee that the employee can return to the same or a comparable job. During the first year of this law's application, Labor Department officials reported that approximately 90 percent of employee complaints of noncompliance were resolved with a simple phone call to employers.[12]

Family and Medical Leave Act
legislation that assures employees of unpaid leave for childbirth or other family needs

Protection of a Firm's Intangible Assets

In addition to managing and protecting its physical assets, a business must protect its intangible assets, which include trademarks, patents, copyrights, and trade dress. These four assets are portrayed in Figure 26-2.

TRADEMARKS A **trademark** is a word, name, symbol, device, slogan, or any combination thereof that is used to distinguish a product sold by one manufacturer or merchant. In some cases, a color or scent also can be part of a trademark.[13] Small manufacturers, in particular, often find it desirable to feature an identifying trademark in advertising.

trademark
an identifying feature used to distinguish a manufacturer's product

Since names that refer to products are trademarks, potential names should be investigated carefully to ensure that they are not already in use. Given the complexity of this task, many entrepreneurs seek the advice of specialized attorneys who are experienced in trademark registration.

Some entrepreneurs may conduct the trademark search personally by using the Trademark Search Library of the U.S. Patent and Trademark Office (PTO) in Arlington, Virginia. The PTO provides its depository libraries with CD-ROMs containing the database of registered and pending marks. It also publishes a booklet entitled *Basic Facts About Registering a Trademark,* which is available at no cost by calling 703-308-HELP. Such publications can also be accessed through the Internet.

Common law recognizes a property right in the ownership of trademarks. However, reliance on common-law rights is not always adequate. For example, Microsoft Corporation, the major supplier of personal computer software, claimed it had common-law rights to the trademark *Windows* because of the enormous industry recognition given the product. Nevertheless, when Microsoft filed a trademark application in 1990 seeking to gain exclusive rights to the name *Windows,* the U.S. Patent and Trademark Office rejected the bid, claiming that the word was a generic term and therefore in the public domain.[14]

Registration of trademarks is permitted under the federal Lanham Trademark Act, making protection easier if infringement is attempted. The act was revised in November 1989 and now allows trademark rights to begin with merely an "intent to use," along with the filing of an application and the payment of fees. Prior to this revision, a firm had to have already used the mark on goods shipped or sold. A trademark registration remains effective for 10 years and may be renewed for

Figure 26-2

A Firm's Intangible Assets

additional 10-year periods. Application for such registration can be made to the U.S. Patent and Trademark Office.

A small business must use a trademark properly in order to protect it. Two rules can help. One rule is to make every effort to see that the trade name is not carelessly used in place of the generic name. For example, the Xerox company never wants people to say that they are "xeroxing" something when they are using one of its competitors' copiers. Second, the business should inform the public that the trademark *is* a trademark by labeling it with the symbol ™. If the trademark is registered, the symbol ® or the phrase "Registered in U.S. Patent and Trademark Office" should be used.

PATENTS   A **patent** is the registered, exclusive right of an inventor to make, use, or sell an invention. The two primary types of patents are utility patents and design patents. A **utility patent** covers a new process or protects the function of a product. A **design patent** covers the appearance of a product and everything that is an inseparable part of the product. Utility patents are granted for a period of 17 years, while

patent
the registered, exclusive right of an inventor to make, use, or sell an invention

utility patent
registered protection for a new process or a product's function

design patent
registered protection for the appearance of a product and its inseparable parts

Action Report

GLOBAL OPPORTUNITIES

The Laws Abroad

In recent years, franchising laws have taken effect in many foreign countries. This has created an unresolved legal question as to whether franchisors continue to be bound by Federal Trade Commission and individual state rules when operating in foreign countries. Andrew P. Loewinger, an international franchising attorney in Washington, D.C., recommends that franchisors seeking to operate abroad devote attention to several legal issues:

- *Trademarks.* Because piracy is a problem in some countries, trademark registration should be the first item of international business. It's not uncommon for a company wishing to expand abroad to discover that someone else has already applied to register its trademark.
- *The structure of the deal.* A critical decision is how to structure the international expansion—directly, through a joint venture, or by using a master franchisee. Each option has financial, tax, and legal implications. An important consideration is the taxation of franchise fees in the host country.
- *Local laws.* Some foreign jurisdictions require the franchisor to pay termination fees to a franchisee when the franchise arrangement is being ended. Others restrict certain foreigners from operating certain types of businesses (a prohibition that could apply to a prospective franchisee), or they may restrict the outflow of hard foreign currency.
- *Dispute-resolution provisions.* Because foreign courts have no obligation to enforce a judgment from a U.S. court against a foreign party, contracts should contain a clause outlining the means of dispute resolution, which usually is arbitration.

Source: Andrew P. Loewinger, "The Laws Abroad," *Nation's Business*, Vol. 83, No. 10 (October 1995), p. 72. Excerpted by permission, *Nation's Business*, October 1995. Copyright 1995, U.S. Chamber of Commerce.

---

design patents are effective for 14 years. Patent law also provides for **plant patents**, which cover any distinct and new variety of plants.

Items that may be patented include machines and products, improvements on machines and products, and original designs. Some small manufacturers have patented items that constitute the major part of their product line. Indeed, some businesses such as Polaroid and IBM can trace their origins to a patented invention. Small business owners preparing a patent application often retain a patent attorney to act for them.

Figure 26-3 is a patent description appearing in the government publication *The Official Gazette of the U.S. Patent & Trademark Office.* As you can see, the advertising cap nameplate received its patent on April 2, 1991. This is a very simple idea and not necessarily one that will be profitable for the inventor—but it might be.

Lawsuits concerning patent infringements are costly and should be avoided, if possible. Finding the money and legal talent with which to enforce this legal right is one of the major problems of patent protection in small business. Monetary damages and injunctions are available, however, if an infringement can be proved.

For many years, patent infringement decisions were appealed to 12 circuit courts. Each court had its own interpretation of patent law, resulting in much

plant patent
registered protection for for any distinct and new variety of plant

Figure 26-3 *Patent Description*

United States Patent [19]
Pizzacar

[54] **ADVERTISING CAP NAMEPLATE**

[76] Inventor: **Anthony Pizzacar,** 160 Greenway West, New Hyde Park, N.Y. 11040

[21] Appl. No.: **417,204**

[22] Filed: **Oct. 4, 1989**

[51] Int. Cl.⁵ **A42B 1/24**

[52] U.S. Cl. ....**2/199;** 2/197; 2/185 R; 2/DIG. 6

[58] **Field of Search** ....2/174.4–174.8, 2/181, 181.2, 181.4, 182.1–182.7, 183, 184.5, 197, 209.3, 209.4, 199, 185 R, DIG. 6; 40/329

[56] **References Cited**

U.S. PATENT DOCUMENTS

525,287	8/1894	Ruth	2/185 R
676,293	6/1901	Wright	2/185 R
1,294,595	2/1919	Allen	40/329
1,559,917	11/1925	Schnebel	2/183
1,808,966	6/1931	Morgan	2/181
2,181,446	11/1939	Ames	2/171.4

[11] **Patent Number:** **5,003,640**

[45] **Date of Patent:** **Apr. 2, 1991**

4,776,043	10/1988	Coleman	2/185 R
4,872,218	10/1989	Holt	2/197
4,905,406	3/1990	Warner	2/199

FOREIGN PATENT DOCUMENTS

444667	6/1936	United Kingdom	2/185 R

Primary Examiner—William A. Cuchlinski, Jr.
Assistant Examiner—Alvin Wirthlin
Attorney, Agent, or Firm—Michael I. Kroll

[57] **ABSTRACT**

An advertising cap for a user has a back, a headband, a pair of straps disposed at the back of the conventional cap for adjustment of the size of the headband of the conventional cap, an advertising cap nameplate for concealing the pair of straps after the headband of the conventional cap is adjusted, and structure for removably mounting the advertising cap nameplate so that the advertising cap nameplate may be changed depending upon the preference of the user.

8 Claims, 2 Drawing Sheets

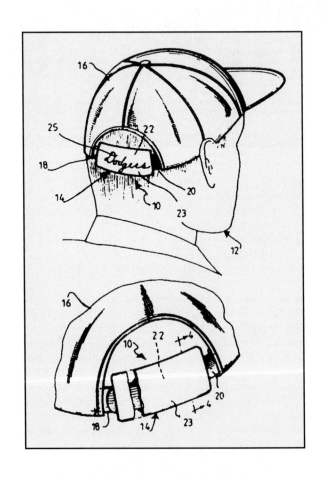

Action Report

ENTREPRENEURIAL EXPERIENCES

Seeking Patent Protection

Legal aspects of the patent process are often perplexing to applicants. However, the potential benefits of a patent encourage entrepreneurs to work within the law to receive the protection they deserve. Entrepreneur Barbara Stenger's story provides an inspirational example of the rewards of persistent effort:

> *Barbara Stenger, a home-based business owner in Brimfield, Illinois, was turned down when she first sought patent protection for a three-ring binder index for recipes. . . . "[The patent office] sent back copies of five old patents, saying, 'Yours isn't something new,'" she says.*
>
> *Rather than accept that determination, she appealed the denial and succeeded in showing that her index was in fact the first of its kind. "I never give up easily," Stenger says.*
>
> *Her experience demonstrates that an initial rejection to a patent application is not necessarily final. The U.S. Patent Office has a built-in mechanism for applicants wanting a second opinion—the Board of Patent Appeals.*
>
> *The appeals process begins with the applicant's filing of a notice to appeal, which is followed by the filing of a brief setting forth the applicant's reasons for the appeal. In addition, a request for a formal hearing might be filed. For what the Patent Office terms "small entities"— individuals and unincorporated businesses—the fee for filing the notice of appeal is $135, and it's the same for filing the brief. The request for a formal hearing carries a fee of $115.*

Source: "A First Refusal Isn't Necessarily Final," *Nation's Business*, Vol. 81, No. 2 (February 1993), p. 10. Excerpted by permission, *Nation's Business*, February 1993. Copyright 1993, U.S. Chamber of Commerce.

confusion about what was and was not legal. However, in 1982, the U.S. Court of Appeals for the Federal Circuit was formed, and all patent appeals are now directed to this court, which has "often demonstrated a heavy bent in favor of the rights of patent owners and has put teeth into patent laws in reinterpreting them."[15]

COPYRIGHTS A **copyright** is the exclusive right of a creator (author, composer, designer, or artist) to reproduce, publish, perform, display, or sell work that is the product of that person's intelligence and skill. According to the Copyright Act of 1976, the creator of an original work receives copyright protection for the duration of the creator's life plus 50 years. A "work made for hire" is protected for 100 years from its creation or 75 years from publication, whichever is shorter. Copyrights are registered in the Copyright Office of the Library of Congress.

Under the Copyright Act of 1976, copyrightable works are automatically protected from the moment of their creation. However, any work distributed to the public should contain a copyright notice. The notice consists of three elements (which can also be found on the copyright page of this book):

1. The symbol ©
2. The year the work was published
3. The copyright owner's name

copyright
the exclusive right of a creator to reproduce, publish, or sell his or her own works

The law provides that copyrighted work cannot be reproduced by another person or persons without authorization. Even photocopying of such work is prohibited, although an individual may copy a limited amount of material for such purposes as research, criticism, comment, and scholarship. A copyright holder can sue a violator of her or his copyright for damages.

TRADE DRESS   A small business may also possess a valuable intangible asset called trade dress. **Trade dress** describes those elements of a firm's distinctive operating image not specifically protected under a trademark, patent, or copyright. Trade dress is the "look" that a firm creates to establish its marketing advantage. For example, if the employees of a pizza retailer dress as prison guards and prisoners, a "jailhouse" image could become uniquely associated with this business and, over time, become its trade dress. One court has defined trade dress as "the total image of a product, including features such as size, shape, color or color combinations, texture, graphics, or even particular sales techniques."[16] Although there are currently no statutes covering trade dress, the courts are beginning to recognize the value of this asset.

> **trade dress**
> elements of a firm's distinctive image not covered by a trademark or patent

BUSINESS AGREEMENTS AND THE LAW

> **3** Explain the importance of making sound legal agreements with other parties.

An entrepreneur should be careful in structuring agreements with individuals and businesses. Because today's society seems to encourage lawsuits and legal action toward others, entrepreneurs must understand such basic elements of law as contracts, agency relationships, and negotiable instruments, just to name a few (see Figure 26-4).

Contracts

Managers of small firms frequently make agreements with employees, customers, suppliers, and others. If the agreements are legally enforceable, they are called **contracts.** For a valid contract to exist, the following five requirements must be met:

> **contracts**
> agreements that are legally enforceable

1. *Voluntary agreement.* A genuine offer must be accepted unconditionally by the buyer.
2. *Competent contracting parties.* Contracts with parties who are under legal age, insane, seriously intoxicated, or otherwise unable to understand the nature of the transaction are typically voidable.
3. *Legal act.* The subject of the agreement must not be in conflict with public policy, as it would be in a contract to sell an illegal product.
4. *Consideration.* The parties must exchange something of value, known in legal terms as *consideration.*
5. *Form of contract consistent with content.* Contracts may be written or oral, but under the **statute of frauds** contracts for the following must be in written form: sales transactions of $500 or more, sales of real estate, and actions that cannot be performed within one year after the contract is made. The existence of an oral contract must be demonstrable in some way; otherwise, it may prove difficult to establish.

> **statute of frauds**
> a law under which specific agreements must be made in writing

If one party to a contract fails to perform in accordance with the contract, the injured party may have recourse to certain remedies. Occasionally, a court will require specific performance of a contract when money damages are not adequate. However, courts are generally reluctant to rule in this manner. In other cases, the

Basic Elements of Law   Figure 26-4

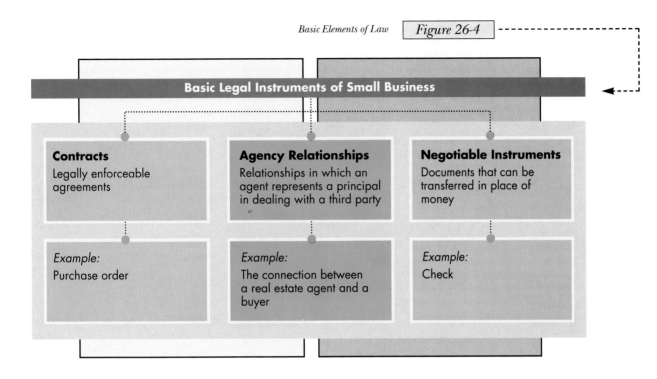

Basic Legal Instruments of Small Business

Contracts
Legally enforceable agreements

Example:
Purchase order

Agency Relationships
Relationships in which an agent represents a principal in dealing with a third party

Example:
The connection between a real estate agent and a buyer

Negotiable Instruments
Documents that can be transferred in place of money

Example:
Check

injured party has the right to rescind, or cancel, the contract. The most frequently used remedy takes the form of money damages, which are intended to put the injured party in the same condition that he or she would have been in had the contract been performed.

Agency Relationships

An **agency relationship** is an arrangement whereby one party—the agent—represents another party—the principal—in contracting with a third person. Examples of agents are the manager of a branch office who acts as an agent of the firm, a partner who acts as an agent for the partnership, and a real estate agent who represents a buyer or seller.

Agents differ in the scope of their authority. The manager of a branch office is a general agent with broad authority. A real estate agent, however, is a special agent with authority to act only in a particular transaction.

The principal is liable to a third party for the performance of contracts made by the agent acting within the scope of his or her authority. The principal is also liable for fraudulent, negligent, and other wrongful acts of an agent that are executed within the scope of the agency relationship.

An agent has certain obligations to the principal. In general, the agent must accept the orders and instructions of the principal, act in good faith, and use prudence and care in the discharge of agency duties. Moreover, the agent is liable if he or she exceeds stipulated authority and causes damage to the third party as a result. An exception occurs when the principal ratifies, or approves, the act, whereupon the principal becomes liable.

It is apparent that the powers of agents can make the agency relationship a potentially dangerous one. For this reason, small firms should exercise care in selecting agents and clearly stipulate their authority and responsibility.

agency relationship
an arrangement in which one party represents another party in dealing with a third party

Negotiable Instruments

Credit documents that can be transferred from one party to another in place of money are known as **negotiable instruments.** Examples of negotiable instruments are promissory notes, drafts, trade acceptances, and ordinary checks. When a negotiable instrument is in the possession of an individual known as a holder in due course, it is not subject to many of the challenges possible in the case of ordinary contracts. For this reason, a small firm should secure instruments that are prepared in such a way as to make them negotiable. In general, the requirements for a negotiable instrument are as follows:

- There must be a written, signed, unconditional promise or order to pay.
- The amount to be paid in money must be specified.
- The instrument must provide for payment on demand, at a definite time, or at a determinable time.
- The instrument must be payable to the bearer or to the order of someone.

THE CHALLENGE OF TAXATION

Tax evasion accounts for a big part of underpaid federal income taxes, but some underpayment is unintentional and due to the complexity of tax laws. Even an honest mistake can bring the IRS to your business. "Nothing strikes the fear of God in people like receiving a letter from the IRS," says Thomas Sherman, a tax partner in the Coopers & Lybrand firm.[17] Most audits are triggered by IRS computers using a special "score" that is based on relationships of various items on the tax return. Also, certain deductions may be scrutinized in some years because of related court decisions. For example, a 1993 Supreme Court decision restricted the types of business activity that can qualify for home-office deductions. This will likely call attention to these expenses in future audit analyses. Because small firms are often accused of being major tax offenders, they need professional tax advice to ensure that all taxes are paid properly.[18]

Many issues have arisen since the passage of the Tax Reform Act of 1986 and, more recently, the Budget Reconciliation Act of 1993. A complete presentation of tax issues involving small firms would fill several books. The federal government provides Publication 334 each year as a tax guide for small businesses—a document that exceeds 200 pages in length!

Figure 26-5 summarizes the various federal taxes for which a small firm may be liable. It also indicates what type of business organization is liable for each tax, the numbers of the necessary forms, and the filing dates. It's easy to see how all these filing requirements can tend to depress and confuse a small business manager! In March 1994, the Commissioner of the Internal Revenue Service established the IRS Office of Small Business Affairs to serve as the national IRS contact with small businesses, to recommend changes to regulations and administrative practices that cause undue burden or inequity, and to address issues that are important to both small businesses and the IRS.

Table 26-1 summarizes selected federal tax regulations relating to small business issues. The issues chosen for inclusion here are those that have been significantly impacted by the Tax Reform Act of 1986 and subsequent rulings.

Several personal computer tax-preparation software packages, such as *TurboTax,* are available to assist entrepreneurs who choose to prepare their own tax returns. These programs can be tremendously helpful to small business owners as they make their way through the complicated IRS forms.[19] They virtually eliminate the math errors commonly associated with tax preparation. Most of these programs also allow taxpayers to file returns electronically.

*Federal Taxes and Tax Filing Requirements Facing
Small Businesses*   **Figure 26-5**

Some of the federal taxes for which a sole proprietor, a corporation, or a partnership may be liable are listed below. If a due date falls on a Saturday, Sunday, or legal holiday, it is postponed until the next day that is not a Saturday, Sunday, or legal holiday. A statewide legal holiday delays a due date only if the IRS office where you are required to file is located in that state. For more information, see Publication 509, *Tax Calendars for 1996.*

You may be liable for:	If you are:	Use Form:	Due on or before:
Income tax	Sole proprietor	Schedule C or C-EZ (Form 1040)	Same day as Form 1040
	Individual who is a partner or S corporation shareholder	1040	15th day of 4th month after end of tax year
	Corporation	1120 or 1120-A	15th day of 3rd month after end of tax year
	S corporation	1120S	
Self-employment tax	Sole proprietor, or individual who is a partner	Schedule SE (Form 1040)	File with Form 1040
Estimated tax	Sole proprietor, or individual who is a partner or S corporation shareholder	1040-ES	15th day of 4th, 6th, 9th months of tax year, and 15th day of 1st month after the end of tax year
	Corporation	1120-W (worksheet) 8109 (to make deposits)	15th day of 4th, 6th, 9th and 12th months of tax year
Annual return of income	Partnership	1065	15th day of 4th month after end of tax year
Social security and Medicare (FICA taxes) and the withholding of income tax	Sole proprietor, corporation, S corporation, or partnership	941 8109 (to make deposits)	4-30, 7-31, 10-31, and 1-31 See Chapter 33
Providing information on social security and Medicare taxes (FICA taxes) and the withholding of income tax	Sole proprietor, corporation, S corporation, or partnership	W-2 (to employee) W-2 and W-3 (to the Social Security Administration)	1-31 Last day of February
Federal unemployment (FUTA) tax	Sole proprietor, corporation, S corporation, or partnership	940-EZ or 940 8109 (to make deposits)	1-31 4-30, 7-31, 10-31, and 1-31, but only if the liability for unpaid tax is more than $100
Information returns for payments to non-employees and transactions with other persons	Sole proprietor, corporation, S corporation, or partnership	See Chapter 36	Forms 1099—to the recipient by 1-31 and to the Internal Revenue Service by 2-28 Other forms— see Chapter 36
Excise taxes	Sole proprietor, corporation, S corporation, or partnership	See Chapter 35	See the instructions to the forms

Source: 1995 *Tax Guide for Small Business,* Publication 334, Internal Revenue Service, Washington, DC, 1995.

Table 26-1

*Highlights of Federal
Income Tax Regulations
for Small Businesses*

Topics	Regulations
Accounting Period	A partnership is now required to conform its tax year to the tax year of either its majority partners, its principal partners, or a calendar year, in that order, unless it can establish a business purpose for using a different year.
	An S corporation must now use as its tax year a year that ends on December 31 (the calendar year), unless the corporation establishes a business purpose for using a different tax year or makes a section 444 election.
	A new corporation establishes its tax year when it files its first income tax return. It can use either a calendar year or a fiscal year as its tax year.
Accounting Methods	The cash method may not be used by corporations (other than S corporations), partnerships having a corporation (other than an S corporation) as a partner, or by tax shelters. An exception allows farming businesses with gross receipts of $25 million or less, qualified personal service corporations, and entities with average annual gross receipts of $5 million or less to continue using the cash method. This exception does not include tax shelters.
	IRS consent is required to change accounting methods.
Going into Business Costs	Costs such as conducting market surveys, travel to look over various business possibilities, and fees to have a lawyer organize a business or an accountant set up your record-keeping system cannot be deducted as business expenses but rather must be amortized.
	If a business wishes to amortize startup expenditures, it must make an election to do so. Generally, these costs are deducted in equal amounts over a period of 60 months or more.
Depreciation	The maximum section 179 deduction for a trade or business property is $17,500.
	A new depreciation method applies to tangible property placed in service after 1986. This system, which is referred to as the modified accelerated cost recovery system (MACRS), has eight classes of property with depreciation periods ranging from 3 to 20 years.
Business Expenses	A small business may deduct advertising expenses if they are reasonable and related to the business activities. A business cannot deduct the cost of advertising if its purpose is to influence legislation. Expenses for public service advertising, such as encouraging people to contribute to the Red Cross, are deductible.
	If a business is located in the taxpayer's home, expenses associated with the part of the home used exclusively and regularly as the principal place of business can be deducted. Also, you may be allowed to deduct expenses for use of part of your home as a daycare facility or as a place to store inventory you sell in your business.
	Generally, you can deduct only 50 percent of your business meals and entertainment expenses. You can deduct no more than $25.00 for business gifts you give directly or indirectly to any one person during your tax year.

Source: Excerpted from *Tax Guide for Small Business,* Publication 334, Internal Revenue Service, Washington, DC, 1995, and David R. Evanson, "A New Balancing Act," *Entrepreneur,* Vol. 21, No. 10 (October 1993), p. 29.

We have discussed only the tax burden on a small firm that results from federal taxation. Of course, state, county, and local governments also have taxing authority. In many situations, these taxes are more troublesome than the federal income tax. Even when a small firm has no taxable income, it will usually have taxes to pay. For example, each of the following taxes or fees is levied by a nonfederal agency:

- Sales taxes
- School property taxes
- Motor fuel taxes
- Incorporation fees
- Business license fees
- State income taxes

Despite its laws and tax regulations, there is still no place like the United States for the entrepreneurial spirit. We expect you to be a part of that spirit. Best of luck.

DISCUSSION QUESTIONS

1. In what ways do the regulatory requirements of government conflict with the interests of small business?
2. Why is government regulation burdensome to small firms?
3. Is it inherently unfair to accord special attention to small firms in formulating government regulations?
4. How does the Americans with Disabilities Act impact small firms? Be specific.
5. What is meant by agency relationships?
6. Discuss the legal protection afforded by trademarks. Does registration guarantee ownership?
7. Name the types of patents. What kinds of fees should a small firm expect to pay for a patent?
8. What is a copyright? How can copyrighted materials be protected?
9. What is trade dress? What is the legal status of trade dress?
10. For what kinds of taxes, in addition to the income tax, may a small firm be liable?

Looking Back

1 Discuss the regulatory environment within which small firms must operate.

- The growth of government regulation imposes a hardship on small firms.
- Taxes have a direct impact on small business cash flow.
- Certain government regulations create profit-making opportunities.
- The federal government has passed legislation to help alleviate the burdensome nature of small business regulation.

2 Describe how the legal system protects the marketplace.

- Antitrust laws offer protection to small firms.
- Consumer protection laws include provisions covering nutrition labeling of food products and safety standards for toys.
- Laws also exist for protection of investors and promotion of the public welfare.
- Numerous laws for the protection of employees impact small firms.
- The legal system provides protection for trademarks, patents, copyrights, and trade dress.

3 Explain the importance of making sound legal agreements with other parties.

- Agreements that are legally enforceable are called contracts.
- In an agency relationship, the principal is liable for the commitments and also the misdeeds of the agent.
- Credit instruments that can be transferred are known as negotiable instruments and should be secured.
- The current trend toward litigation highlights the need for entrepreneurs to carefully craft each agreement they make.

4 Point out several issues related to federal income taxation.

- Tax evasion accounts for a big part of tax shortfalls in the United States.
- Small firms are liable for a variety of federal taxes.
- Many personal computer tax-preparation software packages are available to provide tax assistance to entrepreneurs.

New Terms and Concepts

Regulatory Flexibility Act *575*

Paperwork Reduction Act *575*

Equal Access to Justice Act *575*

Women's Business Ownership Act *577*

Foreign Corrupt Practices Act *577*

Telephone Consumer Protection Act *578*

Nutrition Labeling and Education Act *578*

blue-sky laws *578*

Clean Air Act *579*

Americans with Disabilities Act *579*

Occupational Safety and Health Act *580*

Civil Rights Act *580*

Family and Medical Leave Act *581*

trademark *581*

patent *582*

utility patent *582*

design patent *583*

plant patent *583*

copyright *585*

trade dress *586*

contracts *586*

statute of frauds *586*

agency relationship *587*

negotiable instruments *588*

You Make the Call

Situation 1 A manufacturer refused to buy back a dealer's unsold inventory, citing a written contract with the dealer. One clause of the contract did indeed make repurchase by the manufacturer optional. The dealer, however, argued that he had a prior oral agreement with the manufacturer that it would repurchase unsold inventory. Adding a further complication was the fact that the manufacturer had neither signed nor dated the contract when the dealer signed it. Also, the dealer's minimum inventory requirements were left blank, and the contract failed to mention other details.

Question 1 Does the dealer appear to have a strong legal case to force the manufacturer to repurchase the inventory?

Question 2 How would an attorney be useful in this case?

Situation 2 Alice Landers is president of her own company, Nationwide Drinks, Inc., which she founded in 1980 to produce and market a natural soda that she formulated in her kitchen. The company grew and prospered over its first 10 years of operation, but a major problem emerged when Landers saw a television commercial promoting a new natural soda that an industry giant was introducing at $0.20 below her soda's price. Landers was concerned about the new competition, but she was most distressed that the bottle design was almost identical to Nationwide Drink's. She sued the competitor, charging infringement of her design—even though she had no formal ownership of a copyright or trademark. A federal judge granted Nationwide Drinks a preliminary injunction.

Question 1 What arguments should Landers present to the court?

Question 2 Do you predict that the large competitor will eventually win by forcing Nationwide Drinks to face huge legal costs? Why or why not?

Question 3 In your opinion, what course of action should Landers have taken to avoid this situation? Can a small firm such as Nationwide Drinks afford to pursue your recommendation?

Situation 3 Joseph Tallon, Jr. created a new process to kill termites. Along with his brothers, he runs Tallon Termite in southern California, where 50 percent of the houses are believed to have some termite infestation. Their unique treatment process involves applying liquid nitrogen to the inside of walls, which lowers the temperature of the wood to –20° F and freezes the termites. Although the treatment is expensive, its selling point is its safety, since the nitrogen dissipates quickly. Many Californians have opted for Tallon's less disruptive treatment, which does not require the "tenting" of a home as do some other pesticide treatments.

Source: Damon Darlin, "A Chilling Tale," *Forbes*, Vol. 154, No. 1 (July 4, 1994), pp. 116–117. Reprinted By Permission of *FORBES* Magazine © Forbes Inc., 1994.

Question 1 What sorts of regulatory red tape might Tallon Termite encounter?

Question 2 What laws could actually help the demand for this new process?

Question 3 Would you suggest a patent or trademark for this business? Why or why not?

EXPERIENTIAL EXERCISES

1. Interview a local attorney regarding her or his patent or trademark work for small business clients. Report on the problems the lawyer has faced in this work.
2. Interview a local business owner—a manufacturer, if possible—about his or her strategy to protect the intangible assets of the business.
3. Interview a local lawyer, and determine what areas of law she or he considers most vital to small firm managers. Report your findings to the class.
4. Interview a tax accountant, and determine the major tax issues for her or his small business clients. Report your findings to the class.

Exploring the

5. Using the word search feature, enter "small business taxes." Write a one-page summary describing the information you find.

 CASE 26
Diaper Dan (p. 662)

This case describes the experiences of an entrepreneur as he develops a diaper service business.

King's Beauty Supply

Personal Qualities in Entrepreneurship

Twelve years ago, Tae Wan Cho said goodbye to his native South Korea and set off, he says, "for more opportunity and freedom in the United States." He left behind a wife and two daughters so he could fully focus on launching a business. What business, he had no idea. He also had no capital and no credit rating. He spoke little English.

Cho, who had worked in an import-export business, stayed in Harrisonville, Missouri, with an American friend who had served in South Korea. He read in a trade magazine about strong growth in sales of hair-care products for African Americans and decided to open a store in St. Louis. One factor in locating there was the metropolitan area's affordability.

He applied for a $10,000 loan from a local bank but was turned down. He then borrowed $3,000 from the friend in Harrisonville and $2,000 from his landlord in St. Louis.

Cho signed a lease for 500 square feet of space on the first floor of a vacant downtown building, where the second floor was condemned. "It was all I could afford," he says. He called the store King's Beauty Supply "because King is a common and respected name in the African-American community," and he painted the name on the window.

The first day, Cho sold $40 worth of merchandise; the first month, he rang up $3,000 in sales. But he couldn't afford to heat his shop

that first winter, and much of his merchandise froze. Cash flow was such a severe problem that he could stock only two items of many of his products. He decided everything he made would be reinvested into the business.

"I spent no money on myself," he says. "I paid my bills before I ate. I had no radio, no television, no chair, no sofa, no bed. I did not turn on the heat or the air conditioning in my apartment because I knew I couldn't pay the bills. All I had was a blanket and a 10-year-old Ford Pinto."

Cho spent his weekends in the Pinto, driving to Kansas City, Missouri, to buy the products he would sell during the week because he couldn't afford the freight charge for truck delivery. He bought as much as the Pinto would hold, about $1,000 worth of shampoos, conditioners, relaxants, and gels.

For three years, he lived this way, working seven days a week, 10 hours a day. Whether he was selling or sweeping in the store, hauling merchandise, or shivering in his apartment, he recalls, he was thinking about the business.

Finally confident that he could make a living, he sent for his family. Shortly after they arrived, he opened a second store, which his wife, Young Suk, managed.

Today, Cho, 52, operates nine retail stores in St. Louis and sells his products wholesale all over the United States. His company, King's Beauty Supply Distributor, Inc. generated $7 million in sales in 1993, and Cho expects sales of $8 million to $10 million this year.

Source: Cheryl Jarvis, "When Sacrifice Equals Success," *Nation's Business*, Vol. 82, No. 7, pp. 14–16. Reprinted by permission, *Nation's Business*, July 1994. Copyright 1994, U.S. Chamber of Commerce.

From the old, unheated shop, the company has grown to occupy a 30,000-square-foot warehouse. Huge trucks arrive daily, with as much as $100,000 in merchandise.

Cho now has a $1 million line of credit at the same bank that turned him down for a loan years before.

He attributes his success not only to hard work but also to a good reputation and advertising. "In the beginning," he says, "manufacturers wouldn't see me because I was so small and I knew nothing about the product I was selling. So I started studying the labels, questioning the manufacturers on the phone, and talking a lot to my customers. I made it a high priority to become knowledgeable about what I was selling."

The strategy worked. Manufacturers started coming, and they brought with them advertising allowances for their products. A standard practice among retail owners was to take the allowance—about 3 to 5 percent of the wholesale price—and distribute inexpensive fliers that cost less than the allowance, then pocket the rest. But Cho used every penny for television, radio, and newspaper advertising.

At one radio station's suggestion, he started in-store promotions. While the station advertised and organized these events, Cho got the manufacturers to pay for the prizes, which have ranged from tickets to rock concerts to a trip to the Bahamas. Hundreds of consumers flock to these once-a-month Saturday events and consistently generate the company's biggest sales.

Today, Cho and his family are nestled in a 4,300-square-foot home in an affluent St. Louis suburb. In the garage are a Mercedes-Benz for him and a Jaguar for his wife, Young Suk, who, as vice president of the company, manages the stores and staff. The couple's plans include distributing in China and countries in Africa; profit sharing for their 51 employees; and, in five years, taking the cross-cultural company public.

"When I started out," says Cho, "I had no idea that I could do this well. But I still have a long way to go and a lot more to learn."

Questions

1. What entrepreneurial characteristics do you see in Tae Wan Cho? Which characteristic seems to be most important to his success?
2. What rewards seem to have attracted him to an entrepreneurial career? What evidence do you find for your opinion?
3. What kind of refugee is Tae Wan Cho, and what bearing did this have on his success?
4. Evaluate Tae Wan Cho's preparation for entrepreneurship. How did it affect the process of starting a new business?

Construction Equipment Dealership

Weighing a Career with IBM Against Running the Family Business

As Professor Alan Stone talked on the telephone, he watched his graduate assistant, Jerry Westin, shifting nervously in his chair. When Stone had completed his call, the following conversation with Jerry took place.

Professor Stone: Sorry we were interrupted, Jerry! You said you have a problem. How can I help you?

Jerry: Dr. Stone, I'll be finishing my M.B.A. next month, and I still haven't been able to decide which job offer to accept. Two of the companies want answers next week, so I simply have to make some decisions.

Professor Stone: Well, Jerry, you will have to make the final determination yourself, but we can certainly discuss the various alternatives. As a matter of curiosity, did any of the consulting work we did for IBM ever result in a job offer?

Jerry: Yes, sir! IBM has offered me a really intriguing project-planning job in their National Marketing Division in Atlanta at $47,800. I would have a lot of responsibility from the start, and I would be coordinating the efforts of personnel from several functional departments. If all went well, they have indicated I'd probably have a good chance to be the head of product development for the entire division. Of course, they would pay all moving expenses, and they really have a package of fringe benefits.

Professor Stone: That sounds awfully good! What else do you have?

Jerry: Samsonite, Shell Development, and Boise Cascade. If my wife has her way, we'll go to San Francisco with Boise Cascade. My only question is, can two people live in San Francisco on $44,000 a year?

Professor Stone: Say, what about the family business? Have you given up the idea of being the biggest construction equipment dealer in Billings, Montana?

Jerry: No, sir, not really! As a matter of fact, that's one of the complicating factors. I've been getting some pressure to go back to Billings.

Professor Stone: How do you mean, Jerry?

Jerry: Well, I never really noticed how subtle Dad has been until I started thinking about it. As far as I can recall, he has never specifically said that he thought I should come into the business. But he always said that the opportunity was there if I wanted to take it. His classic statement is how good the business and Billings have been to the family, and I think it is fair to say he influenced me to go to Iowa State, his alma mater, and even to major in accounting. My uncle, who is the accountant in our company, is retiring this year, and I see now that I was probably being prepared all along for that position.

Professor Stone: Does your mother voice an opinion?

Jerry: Yes, sir! She voices more than an opinion! To give you an idea, the last time I talked to her about some of the job offers, she burst into tears and said that it would break my father's heart if

Source: This case was prepared by John E. Schoen of Texas A&M University. Reprinted with permission.

I didn't join the business. She said they built the business for me and that they hadn't worked all those years to turn it over to some stranger. Since my uncle has to retire because of his health, she accused me of turning my back on Dad just when he needs me the most. By the time she finished, she had me feeling confused, miserable, and mad!

Professor Stone: Mad?

Jerry: Yeah! Mom made some statements about Carol, my wife. Mom thinks Carol is trying to persuade me not to go back to Billings because it's too small and I'd be too close to the family. I suppose I wouldn't have been so angry if it hadn't been partially the truth!

Professor Stone: You mean your wife doesn't want to go to Billings?

Jerry: Oh, I'm sure she'll go if that's what I decide to do, but I think she'd greatly prefer San Francisco. She is from Seattle and likes all the bright lights and activity in big cities. In addition, she has a degree in interior design and the opportunities for employment and learning would be greater in San Francisco than any of the other places, particularly Billings. She has worked to help put me through school for the last two years, so I may owe this to her. She also believes it would be better for me to stand on my own two feet and asks why I went for an M.B.A. if all I was going to do was join the family business. She made me mad, too, last week when she said the worst thing she can imagine is eating at my folks' house three times a week.

Professor Stone: What about the Shell and the Samsonite offers?

Jerry: Oh, they're really just offers I've had. It is basically San Francisco, IBM, or home!

Professor Stone: Well, Jerry, you do seem to have a problem. Can you compare the nature of the work in each job?

Jerry: Yes, sir! The IBM job looks very interesting, and the possibilities for advancement are good. Boise Cascade, on the other hand, has a typical cost accounting position. I suppose it would be all right for a couple of years while Carol does her thing and we see if we like San Francisco, but something else would have to come along eventually!

Professor Stone: What about your work in the family business?

Jerry: That's the funny part of it! Everything about the IBM offer—the salary, fringes, authority, prestige, promotion possibilities, and so forth—appeals to me, but I like the family business, too. I mean I've grown up in the business;

I know and like the employees, customers, and suppliers; and I really like Billings. Of course, I'd be working as an accountant for awhile; but I would eventually succeed my father, and I've always thought I'd like to run the business someday.

Professor Stone: What about salary in the family business?

Jerry: That's a part I've forgotten to tell you! Last week, my uncle was in town, and even he was dropping broad hints about the family looking forward to our return to Billings and how he will give me a short orientation and then "get the heck outa Dodge." His parting comment was that he was certain Dad would match anything the big companies could do on starting salary.

Professor Stone: Even $47,800?

Jerry: Apparently! Well, there it is, Dr. Stone! What do you think? I've got to let IBM know by the end of the month.

Professor Stone: I don't know, Jerry. Could you go with IBM or Boise Cascade for a couple of years and then go back to the family business?

Jerry: I thought of that possibility, but I think that if I'm going to go with the family business, this is the right time. Uncle Phil is retiring, so there is a position; and I know Dad was a little hesitant about the M.B.A. versus getting experience in the family business. Dad is approaching 60, and the business is hitting all-time highs, so I believe he will try to sell it if I go somewhere else. No, I think it's now or never!

Professor Stone: Well, you were right about one thing, Jerry. You do have a dilemma! This reminds me of the cases in management textbooks—no easy solution! Good luck, and let me know your decision.

Jerry: Thanks, Prof!

Questions

1. What are the major advantages offered by a big business career with IBM?
2. How competitive is the family business career opportunity with the IBM offer?
3. Does Jerry Westin have an obligation to provide leadership for the family business?
4. What obligation does Jerry have to his wife in view of her background, education, and career interests?
5. Should Jerry simply do what he wants to do? Does he know what he wants to do?
6. In view of the conflict between Jerry's own interests and those of his wife, what should his career choice be?

Stitch Craft

Buying a Small Business

Helen and Martha, recent graduates of the School of Fabric Design at Webster University, are interested in going into business in a field that will utilize their education. They both have been steady customers of Stitch Craft, a nationally franchised business, since it opened a year ago, and they both know Peggy and Susan, the owners. Helen and Martha have learned from Peggy that the store is doing quite well for having been in business only a year. Just the other day, while Martha was shopping in Stitch Craft, she was approached by Susan, who told her that she and Peggy were considering selling the business. Susan said the reason they wished to sell was that they had overextended themselves in terms of time availability and were having difficulties maintaining their homes, children, outside interests, and the business simultaneously. Since Helen and Martha had expressed an interest in the business and had experience in fabric design, Peggy and Susan thought they should be given the first chance to buy the business.

Helen and Martha are quite excited about this prospect and make an appointment to meet with Peggy and Susan. At this meeting, they are shown the entire business, from inventory procedures to ringing out the cash register at night. They are quite impressed and are eager to proceed with the takeover. When they discuss finances, Helen and Martha are told that, since the business is only one year old, Peggy and Susan are only asking them to assume the existing balance of the SBA loan and pay the invoice price of the inventory, plus $20,000 for the fixtures, leasehold improvements, and franchise fee. Helen and Martha don't know anything about finances, so they have come to you with a copy of Stitch Craft's income statement from last year and this month's income and balance sheets. (See Figures C3-1, C3-2, and C3-3.)

Other points that have come up in your discussion with Helen and Martha are that they have contacted the Stitch Craft Corporation, which granted Peggy and Susan the franchise, and were informed that they could indeed take over the remaining nine years of the franchise agreement. Martha also explained that the Stitch Craft brand is nationally known for quality and style, which accounts for its rapid acceptance in the Webster City market. Helen and Martha have given a great deal of thought to the store's current location, which is in a strip mall on the south end of town. The store's customers are mainly from the higher-income northwest section of town. Helen and Martha feel the store should be moved to a location that is closer to the market. If they buy the business, they plan to move the store at the end of the current lease, which expires in two years. However, they have options to extend the lease for six years after the current lease expires should they decide not to move. The landlord has agreed to turn over Peggy and Susan's lease to Helen and Martha without alteration.

Source: This case was prepared by Professor Carl Schweser of the University of Iowa.

Questions

1. Your job is to review the current financial statements and all the data presented to you and make a recommendation on whether Helen and Martha should buy Stitch Craft.

2. What counteroffer would you recommend they make if you feel the current asking price is not attractive?

Figure C3-1

Stitch Craft Income Statement for 1995

	Stitch Craft	Industry Data (% of Sales)
Sales		
Fabric	$144,376	82.0
Patterns/books	16,871	10.0
Sewing classes	6,932	7.0
Other	1,621	1.0
Total sales	$169,800	100.0
Cost of goods sold	79,300	51.0
Gross profit	$ 90,500	49.0
Expenses		
Wages	$ 30,600	14.0
Supplies	2,575	1.0
Rent	15,000	7.5
Utilities	2,880	1.5
Advertising	9,572	5.5
Displays	2,220	1.0
Travel	375	1.0
Phone	1,550	0.5
Services	1,875	0.5
Royalty fee (4.5% of sales)	7,436	4.5
Depreciation and amortization	4,128	2.0
Interest	7,185	1.0
Other	5,654	5.0
Total expenses	$ 91,050	45.0%
Income before taxes & owners' draw	($ 550)	4.0%

Figure C3-2

Stitch Craft Income Statement for January

Sales	$6,750
Cost of goods	3,649
Gross margin	$3,101
Operating expenses	6,001
Net income (loss)	($2,900)

Note: January/February sales are lowest in year. October/November sales are highest.

Current assets		
Cash on hand		$ 400
Cash in the bank		(1,245)
Accounts receivable		0
Inventory		
Fabrics	$20,372	
Notions	3,900	
Patterns/books	2,190	
Sewing machines	1,345	$27,807
Prepaid rent		1,250
Total current assets		$28,212
Fixed assets		
Fixtures	$12,000	
Less accumulated depreciation	(1,300)	
		$10,700
Leasehold improvements	$11,760	
Less accumulated depreciation	(1,820)	
		$ 9,940
Franchise	$12,500	
Less amortization	(1,352)	
		$11,148
Total fixed assets		31,788
TOTAL ASSETS		$60,000
Current liabilities		
Accounts payable—trade	$21,873	
Withholdings payable	550	
Sales tax payable	202	
Total current liabilities		$22,625
Long-term liabilities		
SBA loan—balance due		
($50,000 over 7 years @ 15%)		$46,025
Equity		
Capital—Peggy Ralson	($ 275)	
Add current income/loss	(1,550)	
Training expense draw	(2,500)	
Plus other withdrawals	(0)	
New balance		($ 4,325)
Capital—Susan Keightly	($ 275)	
Add current income/loss	(1,550)	
Training expense draw	(2,500)	
Plus other withdrawals	(0)	
New balance		($ 4,325)
Total equity		($ 8,650)
TOTAL LIABILITIES AND EQUITY		($60,000)

Operating a Kiosk Franchise

An Entrepreneur Tries Franchising

"Run Our Store," read the ad in the paper. The advertising business had been a little slow, so my career as a broadcast writer and producer was in a bit of a slump. With the holiday season approaching, I was looking for opportunities to make some extra money. Besides, I had always wanted to try retail—so I called.

The opportunity was a short-term (six- to eight-week) franchise selling various products—from car seat covers to slippers—through kiosks. For $15, the company overnighted me a sales package with a videotape. I watched it, read the material, checked out the company at the library and visited the mall. The company had predetermined a mall in my area through an agreement with a national mall ownership company, and also negotiated and paid for the kiosk space.

The company offered two franchise levels, priced at $3,000 and $15,000. The initial investment was more of a "security deposit," and would be returned to me as long as my books balanced and my business was well-managed, among other things. The higher the investment, the greater the percentage of sales I could keep. Since I was just testing my retail wings, I chose the lower level.

Since my wife has her own career, and I needed at least one other full-time staffer, I contacted my sister-in-law to see if she would be interested in being my employee. She was.

Decision time. With an attitude of "nothing ventured, nothing gained," we took the plunge.

After all, the company buys back any unsold merchandise and returns the deposit, so what did we have to lose?

THE ADVENTURE BEGINS

Next week on Wednesday, the phone rang and the company said they would be happy to do business with us. The operations manual would be arriving soon. We were to read it all, then contact the mall to introduce ourselves and find out when we could construct the kiosk.

Thursday, the mall called to say that our inventory and kiosk had arrived and had to be moved soon, since they had no storage available. "How much is there?" I asked. "There are 39 boxes," the voice replied. Wow!

The instruction manual said to check all the merchandise . . . but I hadn't gotten to that part of the manual yet. It just seemed like common sense to inventory the boxes. As I soon found out, that's one of the secrets in any business—just use common sense. I had to make sure the box contents and the bill of lading (the list of what was supposed to be there) agreed, or I would be short the difference. After a long afternoon, I was sure it was all there. And I wondered, "Will I ever be able to sell all this?"

Source: John Coriell, "My Life as a Franchise," *Entrepreneur,* Vol. 22, No. 1 (January 1994), pp. 90–95. Reprinted with permission from *Entrepreneur* Magazine, January 1994.

I had been under the impression that the franchisor would help me construct the 10- by 10-foot kiosk. I sure didn't know how it went together. I soon found out, however, that I was responsible for providing the able bodies for its construction.

Thursday night, four of us arrived at the mall to start building and preparing to open the kiosk Friday morning. After opening numerous boxes, we realized the assembly instructions were missing from our manual. The company faxed the instructions to us the next afternoon.

From 9 o'clock Saturday night till 3:30 Sunday morning, the same four able bodies were busy. We constructed the kiosk, installed the lighting, and attached the canvas siding and signs. Then we completely stocked the unit, working out the product display design ourselves. (The instructions for that were also missing.) After it was all finished, we collapsed.

Sunday, November 22, 1992, at noon, our kiosk opened—along with the rest of the mall. We found out that when you operate in a mall, you are open whenever the mall is. At first, we were unsure of all the procedures, not to mention what all the merchandise was for (or was called). It went like this: "Ah, the price for what? Let me check . . . too much? Well, thanks for stopping by." People were constantly moving items around, and we were constantly picking up after them.

Then came the sales, and more questions arose: Have I filled out the sales slip correctly? How do I check out the credit card or verify a check? Most of this kind of information should be provided by the franchisor, and a lot of it was covered in the manual; however, some decisions inevitably fell into our laps. I rented a portable cellular phone to call in credit card verification. It was handy, but I don't think I used it enough to justify the cost.

Week one began with my sister-in-law opening, me closing, and my wife helping out when she could. I quickly found out I needed a schedule and more employees.

Seeking prospective employees, I checked with other businesses and the mall office. And, to my surprise, four or five people simply showed up asking for work. I had them fill out a copy of an application form I borrowed from another kiosk business.

I had plenty of questions about personnel. Should I verify the application information? How much and when do I pay them? The fran-

chisor suggested a small hourly wage combined with a percentage commission. I hired two of the applicants.

They worked hard, but it wasn't long before I was in the throes of the full "employer experience." "I'm sick . . . my full-time job made me work overtime . . . I have a dead battery." Good employee relationships and management are especially important in a short-term franchise, since you don't have the time to make mistakes when breaking people in.

Another consideration was how to handle employees' taxes. Due to the small size of their income over the six weeks, we didn't have to withhold any federal tax, but Social Security withholding was a must. I filed the form and deposited the cash from daily sales at the bank for both Social Security and our company's cash flow. I didn't forget to obtain 1099 tax forms (sort of like a W-2) to be sent to employees at the end of the year. Other paperwork: obtaining a federal employer ID number and opening a separate deposit-only bank account, as the franchisor required.

I needed office supplies and an old car seat to display a seat cover. I also had to solve the storage problem. Without any mall storage, where do you put new merchandise and the empty boxes for reshipping the kiosk and leftover merchandise? My sister-in-law's nearby garage did the trick.

After only four (long) days we said, "Oh, thank goodness, it's Thanksgiving—a day off." And it was just beginning.

Week two consisted of getting our sales legs. We studied the customers and tried to judge the right time to approach them and what to say. Too soon and they flee; too late and they lose interest. Although the franchisor offered some helpful sales tips, selling is an art, and to a great extent, relying on your instincts is a good bet.

Daily and weekly sales and inventory reports had to be sent to the franchisor. We took inventory every evening; it was time-consuming, but helped us know where we stood. It was also a good crosscheck on the weekly sales reports— and during those early slow periods, it kept us busy.

By week three we were making friends with other mall merchants. Being in the center of the aisle, we were in the midst of the action. It was like moving into a new neighborhood. Soon, we were on a first-name basis with the assistant mall manager and mall security guards—a good idea.

Sales continued to be slow despite our best efforts. I thought the product might be a bit pricey for the area—a steel town with a slow economy. But we had known this going in, and still decided to go for it.

The franchisor required some pictures of our setup and displays, and told us we had one of the best-looking kiosks they'd ever seen. Our sales had doubled each week; but we were still behind where we should have been. The franchisor said, "Be patient; it's just the seasonal pattern. It will happen."

In week four, the franchisor decreed a mandatory "50 percent off" sale. They had never done that kind of sale before, so some of the procedural information we received was confusing. Sales picked up, but 50 percent off the price also means 50 percent off the profit. New merchandise shipments came in, though sometimes the inventory we got wasn't what we were expecting—or even wanted.

Week five, 'twas the week before Christmas, and the people, the activity and the noise level all increased to a frenzy. Shoppers knew what they wanted and went for it—fast. We became experts at filling out sales slips.

Those mall hours were turning into extremely long days because the mall was open later than usual. The increased sales volume made the usually manageable closing paperwork a nightmare. We were busy day and night. Scheduling employees was even more important at this point to maximize personnel and still control payroll costs. I still had only two employees plus my sister-in-law.

Week six brought the day after Christmas—the biggest return and shopping day of all. After the flurry, however, sales quickly diminished—a good thing, because our inventory had diminished, too.

Finally, it was time to wrap up the enterprise. I contacted mall management to find out when we could pack up. Once again we gathered a few willing bodies to help. I notified the trucking company to pick up the boxes, returned the display car seat to its junkyard home, and discontinued the overnight delivery service that had picked up the paperwork each Monday and shipped it to the franchisor. Last, but not least, a copy of the bill of lading, signed by the trucker who picked up the boxes, had to be faxed to the franchisor that day.

Questions

1. What type of franchise evaluation process should this entrepreneur have undertaken prior to making his decision?
2. Do you agree with his "nothing ventured, nothing gained" attitude?
3. Evaluate the training and other services of this franchisor.
4. What type(s) of franchise training could have benefited this entrepreneur?

The Brown Family Business

Defining Work Opportunities for Family Members in a Family Firm

For 56 years, the Brown family has operated an agricultural products business in central Texas. As the business has grown, family leaders have attempted to preserve family relationships while operating the business in a profitable manner. At present, five members of the second generation, three members of the third generation, and one member of the fourth generation are active in the business. Other members of the family, of course, have ownership interests and a concern about the firm even though they are pursuing other careers.

In the interest of building the business and also preserving family harmony, the family has developed policies for entry and career opportunities for family members. The human resource policies governing family members are shown below.

FAMILY PHILOSOPHY CONCERNING THE FAMILY AND WORK OPPORTUNITIES

1. A family working together as one unit will always be stronger than individuals or divided units.
2. Family is an "umbrella" that includes all direct descendants of P. and L. Brown and their spouses.

3. The Brown family believes that a career with Brown Bros. is only for those who
    - Believe in working for their success;
    - Believe that rewards they receive should come from the work they have done;
    - Believe in working for the company versus working for a paycheck; and
    - Believe that everyone must work to provide an equal and fair contribution for the good of the whole business.
4. While work opportunities and career opportunities with the family business will be communicated to all family members, there will be no guarantee of a job in the family business for any member of the family at any time.
5. A family member working in the family business, whether in a temporary or a long-term career position, will be offered work and career counseling by a supervisor or officer/family member (depending on the job level). However, the family member/employee is not guaranteed a job or a career position. His or her job performance and qualifications must be the primary factor determining whether the family member will be allowed continued employment.
6. While the family business is principally agriculture-related, there are many jobs that both men and women can perform equally and safely.
7. Compensation will be based on comparable positions held by other employees.

Source: This case was prepared by Nancy B. Upton, founder of the Institute for Family Business, Baylor University.

COMMITTEE ON FAMILY EMPLOYEE DEVELOPMENT

1. Review, on an annual basis, policies for entry and recommend changes.
2. Receive notices of positions available and communicate to all family members.
3. Review, on an annual basis, evaluations of family members' performance, training provided, outside training programs attended, and goals and development plans. Offer counseling to upper management when appropriate.
4. Committee composed of three persons— one of four Brown brothers in the business; one of seven non-operating Browns; one of spouses of eleven Browns.

The general criteria for having a career at Brown Bros. are given in Table C5-1.

Questions

1. What are the key ideas embodied in the statement of philosophy concerning the family and work opportunities?
2. Evaluate each of the criteria specified for a management career in the firm. Which, if any, would you change or modify?
3. Evaluate the structure and functions of the committee on family employee development.

Table C5-1

Criteria for a Career at Brown Bros.

	Mid- Management Positions	Upper-Management Positions
Personal:		
No criminal record	Required	Required
No substance abuse	Required	Required
Education:		
High school	Required	Required
College degree (2.5 on a 4-point system)	Recommended	Required
Work experience with others:		
While completing college	Recommended	Recommended
After completing college (one to three years)	Recommended	Required

Robinson Associates, Inc.

Business Plan for a New Venture

This case presents a business plan for a proposed management consulting firm. This plan was prepared by a graduate student in business who set up the firm to support himself both during and after his period of graduate study. A few details, such as name and location, have been changed, but the situation is real.

Business Plan for
David R. Robinson
Minneapolis, Minnesota

SCOPE OF THE BUSINESS

Personal

I plan to start a business consulting service in conjunction with USA Consultants (a nationwide business consulting firm).

History of USA Consultants

USA is over 30 years old. It originated in Boston and Atlanta. It started out as P. Miller Management Consultants. The name changed to USA in

1972. Paul Miller III is the current president of USA, which has over 160 consultants in more than 50 cities.

SPECIFIC AREAS OF FOCUS

Company (Brochure Available on Request)

1. Analysis Phase
2. Implementation Phase (selected examples)
   a. Marketing programs
   b. Organization planning
   c. Personnel training programs
   d. Cost reduction programs
   e. Loan package preparation
   f. Inventory control systems
   g. Financial control and reporting
   h. Mergers and acquisitions
   i. Strategic business planning
   j. Business evaluation

Personal

With my accounting background (CPA–inactive) and current experience consulting with small businesses, I would concentrate on:

1. Analysis phase
2. Implementation phase—especially on:
   a. Organization planning

Source: This case was prepared by Philip R. Carpenter.

b. Loan package preparation
c. Strategic business planning
d. Financial control and reporting systems
3. USA continuing education programs in various areas in which I could update my skills.

GOALS

Personal

1. I plan to begin the business July 1 and operate it part-time for three months. I will limit my hours to 32 per week. I will still be eligible for full-time benefits including health insurance and tuition remission. I will go into the business full-time starting October 1.
2. I plan to continue pursuing a Ph.D. in business administration. This is entirely compatible with the consulting business. (See attached projected cash flow statements [Table C6-1].)

Financial

I plan to reach the following cumulative gross billing goals [Table C6-2]:

Six months	$ 22,500
Twelve months	$ 86,500
Eighteen months	$137,000
Twenty-four months	$191,000

MANAGEMENT CAPABILITY

See attached résumé [Figure C6-1].

Strong Points

1. Four years of consulting experience with Small Business Development Centers.
2. Admitted to Ph.D. program at the university in business administration. Major: Management; minor: International Business, with current G.P.A. of 4.0, out of possible 4.0.
3. Accepted by USA. USA advertised in *The Wall Street Journal, Inc.,* and *USA Today.* To date, they have received over 3,000 applications but approved only 158.

4. Education will be continued through schooling and USA's continuing education program.

MARKETING

Competition

External:

1. Review of the Minneapolis–St. Paul *Webb's Directory* on management consultants shows no direct competition.
2. Typically, consultants specialize in one to three areas. No firm can offer the wide range of services that USA can.

Internal: There are two other USA consultants in the Minneapolis–St. Paul area. One started his business in December of last year, and the second is just starting. Both are on the Minneapolis side of the river. There appears to be plenty of room in the market for a third USA consultant.

Customer Analysis

USA billing rates are $125/hour to $300/hour. These rates will preclude very small businesses from using my services in most cases. The firms that appear to be best suited for using a USA consultant would be firms with 30 to 400 employees. These firms can be identified through the use of *Webb's Directory* and various other publications.

Reaching the Customer

There are three primary methods to reach customers:

1. *Salesperson.* USA will assist the consultant in hiring and training.
2. *MAS services to small accounting firms.* USA works with accounting firms that do not have an MAS department to provide them with consulting services.
3. *Personal contacts.* Extensive contacts have been developed on both sides of the river and will be used to assist in identifying potential customers.

Table C6-1

Cash Flow Projections for David R. Robinson Family

Item	July	Aug.	Sept.	Oct.	Nov.	Dec.
Husband	$1,396	$1,396	$1,396	$ 0	$ 0	$ 0
Wife	$ 783	$ 783	$ 783	$ 783	$ 783	$ 783
USA	$ 0	$ 625	$ 935	$1,560	$2,500	$3,125
Subtotal	$2,179	$2,804	$3,114	$2,343	$3,283	$3,908
Expenses	$3,300	$3,300	$3,400	$3,500	$3,600	$3,700
Overage (Shortage)	($1,121)	($ 496)	($ 286)	($1,157)	($ 317)	$ 208

Item	Jan.	Feb.	Mar.	Apr.	May	June
Husband	$ 0	$ 0	$ 0	$ 0	$ 0	$ 0
Wife	$ 783	$ 783	$ 783	$ 0	$ 0	$ 0
USA	$2,500	$4,125	$4,125	$ 5,250	$6,375	$6,375
Other	$ 0	$ 0	$ 0	$ 7,500	$ 0	$ 0
Subtotal	$3,283	$4,908	$4,908	$12,750	$6,375	$6,375
Expenses	$5,500	$3,800	$3,900	$ 4,000	$3,800	$3,900
Subtotal	($2,217)	$1,108	$1,008	$ 8,750	$2,575	$2,475

Summary of Overages (Shortages)	
July	($1,121)
August	($ 496)
September	($ 286)
October	($1,157)
November	($ 317)
December	$ 208
January	($2,217)
Additional cash needed	($5,386)

Table C6-2

Projected Billable Hours for First Year

Month	Hours	Billings	Compensation (@ 50%)
July	10	$ 1,250	$ 625
August	15	$ 1,875	$ 938
September	25	$ 3,125	$ 1,563
October	40	$ 5,000	$ 2,500
November	50	$ 6,250	$ 3,125
December	40	$ 5,000	$ 2,500
January*	55	$ 8,250	$ 4,125
February	55	$ 8,250	$ 4,125
March	70	$10,500	$ 5,250
April	85	$12,750	$ 6,375
May	85	$12,750	$ 6,375
June	75	$11,250	$ 5,625
Totals		$86,250	$43,125

*Pay review is conducted every six months—expect increase to $150/hour. After $50,000 in cumulative gross billings, consultant receives $7,500 deposit back. This should occur about the end of March.

CAREER OBJECTIVE

To make optimal use of my organizational analysis and human relations abilities to become a skilled consultant to businesses.

This will result in:

- More coordinated organizations
- Increased job satisfaction/productivity

QUALIFIED BY

Training and over 10 years of experience, encompassing:

- Organizational skills
- Human relations
- Leadership skills
- Financial analysis
- Reporting

ACHIEVEMENTS

Organizational Skills

- Effectively worked with the Small Business Development Center (SBDC) director to present a highly rated conference on SBDCs for state and federal government personnel.
- Supervised and coordinated other staff accountants in the preparation of audited financial statements.
- Coordinated with volunteer personnel to achieve a very successful fund drive.
- Developed and presented in coordination with other area procurement specialists two highly rated seminars.

Human Relations

- Quickly developed an atmosphere of trust with established clients through careful consideration of their accounting and tax needs.
- Successfully assisted two business partners in planning, starting, and operating their own small business.
- Provided clear direction to several small businesses, which enabled them to successfully bid on government contracts.

Leadership Skills

- Effectively taught a government procurement seminar in a concise and clear manner to small business owners.
- Successfully started and developed a Procurement Assistance Center that helped local businesses obtain over $1,000,000 in government contracts in just over two years.

Financial Analysis

- Developed and successfully implemented annual budgets for the SBDC and Procurement Assistance Center for over two years.
- Thoroughly completed audits and prepared financial statements for corporations with assets up to $2,000,000.
- Developed an accounting system for the Chaplain Fund that provided more complete documentation and permitted audits to be completed in half the expected time.

Reporting

- Coordinated development of successful funding proposals for the local SBDC and Procurement Assistance Center.
- Thoroughly prepared two nominations for awards, one national and one state, which resulted in the nominees' receiving the rewards.
- Gathered information regarding a specific question by the Chaplain Fund council, then translated this information into a short, understandable format that permitted an immediate, well-informed decision.

Continued

Figure C6-1

Continued

EXPERIENCE
State University, Minnesota (June 1989–Present)
Procurement specialist/small business counselor/graduate assistant
Bellhaven Hospital (November 1987–May 1989)
Advanced staff auditor
Moore, Synder CPA, Inc. (December 1986–June 1987)
Staff accountant
Harry C. Reynolds & Co. (January 1985–November 1986)
Staff accountant
U.S. Army (1980–1984)
Fund custodian, Chaplain Fund, Illinois
Chapel activities specialist, Korea
Funds clerk, Chaplain Fund, Texas

EDUCATION
B.S. in Accounting, State University, Ohio
M.A. in industrial/organizational psychology, State University, Minnesota
(thesis title: Comparative Psychological Characteristics of Entrepreneurs vs.
Small Business Owners)

OTHER
Licensed as a CPA (inactive) in Minnesota.

Market Trends

Many businesses today are downsizing. Typically, the person that businesses are outplacing is in middle management. Businesses will still have the same problems as before. Businesses will then turn to a consultant to assist in solving these problems.

FINANCIAL

Amount Needed:

$ 7,500	Initial deposit*
$ 1,000	Supplies**
$ 4,000	Working capital***
$12,500	Bank financing
$ 9,500	Personal collateral (certificate of deposit)
$22,000	Total

*To be refunded when $50,000 in gross billings have been achieved.
**Supplies include *Webb's Directory*, file cabinet, office supplies, shelving, business subscriptions, and business phone.
***See attached cash flow statement for details.

Questions

1. Which part of this business plan would impress a potential investor most favorably?
2. What are the most serious concerns or questions a potential investor might have after reading this plan?
3. What additional information should be added to strengthen the plan?
4. What changes could be made in the format or wording of the plan to enhance its communication effectiveness?
5. As a banker, would you make a working-capital loan to this business? Why or why not?

The Fantastic Catalogue Co.

Gaining a Competitive Advantage in the Mail Order Market

It would be quite a wedding; the nuptials would take place in the stone chapel at the school from which the bride and groom had graduated. A reception for 400 guests would follow at the seaside home of the bride's parents. And from start to finish, the festivities would be imbued with Gatsby-esque elegance and style. Kathleen Mahoney, the bride herself, would see to that.

"I researched every aspect of it to the *n*th degree," she says, recalling the year of preparation. "I went haywire. I looked at 20 guest books, 20 bridesmaids' gifts, 20 different goblets, and so on. I wanted everything to be perfect."

Only the finest items would do, and finding them was frustrating. "There's a decentralized flow of information and goods in the wedding industry," Mahoney says. "There was no source for the upscale bride to find all the high-quality, tasteful wedding accessories she'd need." Her search took her to some 50 stores from Boston to San Francisco—gift shops, bridal boutiques, stationery stores.

All of which got her thinking. And by the time Mahoney and Ozzie Ayscue were married in June 1990, she had a new business on her hands. One-stop shopping for brides—the idea seemed irresistible. "It made intuitive sense to me, from my own experience," says Mahoney, 31. "I did some research with friends, and it made sense to everyone."

With 2.5 million weddings a year in the United States, a huge and lucrative market beckoned. The most promising targets, Mahoney reasoned, were career women, brides age 26 and up. They'd have the discretionary income to purchase topflight wedding goods but not the time to hunt for them.

How best to capitalize on the opportunity? She had dismissed a retail store as too limiting—hers was a national concept. A catalog, though, could put the products right at brides' fingertips. Mahoney was a catalog nut—she loved them. She didn't know the first thing about publishing one, she admits, but she figured she could learn.

The timing was fortunate. Mahoney was at American Express in Manhattan, in the direct-mail travel business. Ayscue was working for a travel-industry startup in San Francisco, where the couple had decided to settle. In late 1989 Mahoney left American Express and moved west, itching to take a crack at the catalog game.

It's no cakewalk to start a consumer catalog from scratch. Typically, retailers branch into mail order to augment established store-based operations. Other merchants tiptoe into the field by first advertising a few items in magazines. That's a cost-effective way of learning what sells while building a buyer file. Gradually, their product lines expand to fill full-blown catalogs. That's how Lands' End got started, for example.

One impediment to launching cold is capital. Catalogs inhale money. One might open a retail store for, say, $50,000, but that won't even get you off the ground in the catalog trade. It can easily cost $150,000 or more to get that first

Source: Jay Finegan, "Made to Order," *Inc.*, Vol. 14, No. 5 (May 1993), pp. 74–84. Reprinted with permission, *Inc.* magazine (May 1993). Copyright 1993 by Goldhirsh Group, Inc., 38 Commercial Wharf, Boston, MA 02110.

book in the mail, and follow-on editions are needed to build a buyer file. First come production costs for photography, copy writing, layout, and design—the "creative" end of the business. Then come costs for list rental, photographic color separation, printing, fulfillment, data processing, and postage. And even before that first order comes in, a startup needs to stock most of the featured items.

Mind you, all that happens before you know if the phone will ever ring. What if all the recipients throw your catalog in the trash? By definition, a startup has zero name recognition. And with an estimated 9,000 consumer catalogs in the country, mailing hundreds of millions of copies, it's easy to get lost in the clutter. Given that saturation, catalogs are creeping into ever smaller niches, staking out tiny franchises in hopes of survival.

Even so, most of them don't last long. Industry lore is replete with tales of first-timers who sank $1 million or more into a black hole before calling it quits. The market is ruthless in weeding out the glut. According to Leslie Mackenzie, publisher of *The Directory of Mail Order Catalogs*, between 1,000 and 1,500 of them fail or cease operations every year.

It is a business, analysts stress, in which you must get everything right. For instance, you might have terrific merchandise, a superb shipping operation, and a good mailing list. But you drop the ball on the creative—the product photos and the copy don't quite click. In that case, says consultant Bill Nicolai, "you are toast. It's a very tricky business, but it's one where sharp entrepreneurs can find their way in."

As Mahoney mapped her plans, she felt confident. A private investor had promised her $1 million, for 30 percent of the company, plus a $500,000 loan. That would sustain business for two years or more. The wedding niche, moreover, seemed solid. "I knew in my heart it was a good idea, so I didn't do much formal market research other than some demographics," she says.

She presented her concept to Jeff Haggin, chairman of the MoreNow Corp., a catalog-production firm in Sausalito, California. Over the years, MoreNow had handled the creative work for many prominent catalogers—Smith & Hawken, Sierra Club, and dozens more. Haggin knew the industry cold, and he thought Mahoney's idea had real merit.

That's all she needed to hear. And thus was born, in February 1990, The Wedding Fantastic, Inc.

With that start date, the earliest Mahoney could mail her first catalog would be July. That wasn't optimal. The big wedding season is spring and summer, and she would miss most of it. But impatient to get something into the market, she plunged in, headquartered in her San Francisco apartment.

Ayscue pitched in and joined the company in July as copresident. Two years as an analyst with Morgan Stanley had given him strong number-crunching skills. He'd handle strategic planning, statistical analysis, and financial management, while Mahoney concentrated on merchandising and marketing. Working with list brokers, she identified between 3.5 million and 10 million rentable names that met her demographic profile. Industry wisdom has it that you must mail at least 100,000 books to get a reasonable response. To reach her target market, she rented 100,000 names from Bloomingdale's, Williams Sonoma, Victoria's Secret, Neiman-Marcus, and 16 other upscale catalogers. She also rented from bridal-magazine subscriber lists. "I wanted to reach not just brides but brides' mothers, aunts, and shower throwers," she says.

From each list she rented a "cell" of 5,000 names. As a rule, names rent for about a dime each for onetime use, with rates rising to 15¢ depending on the number of "selects." That is, a renter can request names based on such factors as the timing, frequency, and monetary value of the customers' catalog purchases. Mahoney shot for people who had ordered through the mail in the previous six months, a common select.

The use of competing cells is key. It allows a cataloger to see which lists work best, so that when more names are needed, one can mine deeper into good ones. Essentially, a cataloger cold calls people in their mailboxes, and on average only 1.66 percent of the prospects respond. In other words, for every 100 catalogs mailed to rented names, better than 98 yield no sales. And those who do respond place smaller orders than established buyers.

To succeed, a mail-order operator must build a buyer file so that repeat customers represent a substantial percentage of total circulation. That can take several years. In Mahoney's model, the critical mass would be reached in 1994, when, she calculated, 12 percent of the 7 million people receiving her catalog would be buyers. That's the point at which her business would turn profitable. Her plan projected net sales that year of $12.5 million, with purchases averaging $95. That translates to more than 131,500 orders, enough that the company could amortize its costs over a far larger business base. General operating expenses, for example, would shrink from 41 percent of net sales in 1991 to 8 percent in 1994. Publicity expenses—creative work, color separation, printing, list rental—would drop from 89.5 percent of sales to 30 percent. And net income would rise from a 1991 loss of $837,000 to a positive $484,000.

Economies of scale work their magic all over the place once catalogs grow large, but reaching the magic number of 236,000 was, and remains, an ambitious goal. By comparison, Gump's, an old-line San Francisco gift cataloger, has a buyer file of about 100,000 names.

Pressing on, Mahoney contracted with MoreNow for production and arranged to have the book printed by Alden Press, a catalog specialty house in Elk Grove Village, Illinois. Fulfillment—everything from inventory storage to order taking to product packing—was farmed out to a small San Francisco company. United Parcel Service would handle deliveries.

Time was short. To get the catalog out in July, all the merchandise had to be selected and turned over to MoreNow by April 1, to start photography. It was a crash project, but Mahoney made it. Just three weeks after she and Ayscue exchanged vows, 100,000 copies of the inaugural edition of The Wedding Fantastic hit the mail.

It was very classy, a glossy, beautifully designed 32-pager featuring pretty much everything an upscale bride would need except a gown and a groom. Most items were the fruits of Mahoney's research for her own nuptials. There was a personalized Limoges porcelain ring box ($125), an heirloom-quality moiré hatbox ($298), a lace picture frame ($85), and even a sterling-silver service for the wedding cake (knife and server, $95 each).

The other half of the equation called for putting wedding gifts right in the catalog, to make it a complete wedding resource. They included some of Mahoney's personal favorites, among them a sterling ice-cream scoop ($95), a Zen rock garden ($48), and a birdhouse shaped like a Victorian manor ($145)—"mainstream products," she says, "but with a twist." In all, the catalog had 120 handpicked items.

Established catalogers know from experience how much inventory to carry. Startups don't know which items will be best-sellers and which will be dogs, and guessing wrong either way can be costly. "That's one of the hardest things we do," says Ayscue. "If you overstock, you are stuck with products. If you understock, you have to back-order and you might not make the sale." Going conservative, Mahoney went with a bare-bones inventory.

Competing not on price but on quality and uniqueness, she marked the products up 60 percent on average. On shipping and handling charges she aimed for break-even. The order form listed an 800 number and a fax number and allowed payment by check, money order, or credit card. On page three, a chatty "Dear brides" letter from Mahoney touted her commitment to top-quality goods and superb customer service, plus a full refund-exchange policy.

Getting that first book out was pricey. MoreNow's bill for the creative was $74,000—over $2,300 per page. Color separation added another $30,000. Alden charged $0.22 each for the 112,000 copies printed (there were some extras), and postage totaled $24,640. The combined in-the-mail cost came to $153,000, excluding list rental.

So handsome was the book that it won second prize that year in a new-catalog competition. "Even the most cynical of readers cannot help but be charmed by the catalog's sentimental approach to weddings," gushed trade journal *Catalog Age.*

The problem, however, was meager response, well below the 1.66 percent industry average for prospects. Response fell further when Mahoney "dropped" the second batch, 88,000, in September 1990, and further still when 127,000 went out in November. On the up side, however, the average order was $90, against an industry average of $61.

The new, updated spring edition hit the mail in three volleys, in February, March, and May of 1991. With 40 pages, it featured new items as well as top sellers from the first book. A total of 501,000 copies went out, half of them in May. With timing on the edition's side, the response rates climbed across the board. The new mailings generated sales of $917 per 1,000 catalogs, versus $547 for the first edition. Still, the response rate remained discouragingly below the industry standard, and the average order dipped to $81. "The wedding books were very narrowly targeted," Mahoney says now, "but we were taking a shotgun approach."

Needing something with broader appeal, she and Ayscue brought forth in September 1991 a brand-new catalog—The Christmas Fantastic. Weddings were seasonal, so why not launch a sister publication for the hottest shopping time of the year?

Working again with MoreNow, they developed a 32-page version known in the trade as a "slim jim." By virtue of its dimensions, 6 inches by 11 inches, it was cheaper to print and mail. To give the new catalog a better product mix, Mahoney and her employee sidekick, Georgina Sanger, scoured gift shows all over the country and developed several exclusives with California artists.

As with the wedding catalog, the products in The Christmas Fantastic were eclectic and fairly expensive. The new book featured about 150 items, everything from personalized tree ornaments and stockings to a hand-painted "kitty privy" and a $795 "Grand Mr. President" desk set. There were books and CDs, festive party invitations, even a beer-brewing kit. Some old favorites encored—the silver ice-cream scoop, the Victorian birdhouse, and the Zen rock garden.

The company sent out a test quantity of 112,000 catalogs in three mailings (early returns provide a "product read" that removes some inventory guesswork), and this time it hit pay dirt. The response rate topped the national norm, orders averaged $97, and sales per 1,000 catalogs mailed hit $1,584, beating the industry standard by $566.

So compelling were the overall economics that Mahoney and Ayscue retooled, shifting entirely away from the bridal market and into the gift business. There will be no new The Wedding Fantastic this spring, although some of its products are featured in full-page ads in bridal magazines, and a leftover 10,000 copies are available for $3 each. Instead, they launched another new catalog—The Celebration Fantastic—and changed their name to The Fantastic Catalogue Company.

The newest book, a 32-page slim jim, is billed as a way to "celebrate life's special occasions with romance, whimsy and imagination!" While some core items remain—the birdhouse, for one—the new catalog is heavy on unusual gifts for Easter, Mother's Day, Father's Day, graduations, anniversaries, and new babies. Its 120 items include everything from a complete gourmet picnic hamper for six ($525) to donkey and elephant earrings for election years ($34). Like Mahoney's other books, it strikes an upscale and upbeat tone.

"We think now we are sending the right message to the right people," she says. "Our targeting is getting more refined."

If The Celebration Fantastic yields results comparable with the Christmas edition's, as Mahoney expects, she will have a strengthening, nonseasonal business and a more secure foothold in the $2-billion mail-order consumer gift market.

But as they say, that's a big if. Having virtually abandoned the wedding niche, she is stepping into a gift sector already sated with some 630 catalog companies, many of them large and resource rich. The Fantastic Catalogue Co. has to establish itself fast. "We need to become the household name, the completely trusted brand name for this whole celebration segment," Mahoney says.

To do that she feels she has to expand quickly. She'd like to circulate a million copies of The Christmas Fantastic this fall to aggressively build her buyer file from its current 15,000 names. But with the initial financing of $1.5 million fast depleting, that hinges on raising $1.25 million or so by summer. And another $1 million will be needed in 1993 to move The Celebration Fantastic beyond the test phase.

As the company expands and Mahoney increasingly understands exactly who her customer is, she has begun to focus on servicing that customer better. Toward that end she brought the company's fulfillment operations in-house early this year, a move that will require more employees and might produce as-yet-unseen complications.

Questions

1. Do you think Mahoney has correctly assessed the basic nature of the competition she faces? Why or why not?
2. What is the competitive advantage Mahoney is trying to create? Do you agree with this appeal? Why?
3. What market segmentation strategy is The Fantastic Catalogue Co. following?
4. How can this firm use customer service to gain a competitive advantage?
5. Do you think Mahoney leaped before looking? What should she have done differently?

Case 8

ScrubaDub Auto Wash

Waxing Philosophical

Imagine charging more than competitors for a number of your services, yet maintaining a higher market share and profit margin. ScrubaDub Auto Wash, based in Natick, Massachusetts, does just that. With eight locations and sales of more than $5 million, ScrubaDub is the largest auto-wash chain in the Boston area. And the company has continued its growth—posting annual sales increases of 10 percent in recent years—despite a long-lasting and punishing recession in its home state.

"Nineteen ninety-two was an absolutely disastrous year for the economy in Massachusetts, but it was one of the best years we ever had," recounts Marshall Paisner, who owns and operates the chain with his wife, Elaine, and their sons, Dan and Bob.

Their secret? ScrubaDub combines an expertise in the science of cleaning cars with a flair for the art of marketing. The company has turned an otherwise mundane chore—getting the car washed—into a pleasant service interlude. Employees sweat the details that define the experience for customers, and the company tracks [customers'] buying habits to improve customer service and boost sales. ScrubaDub then backs up its work with guarantees, ensuring that customers are satisfied with the results.

In short, ScrubaDub's managers and employees think from the customer's point of view, says Paul M. Cole, vice president of marketing services at the Lexington, Massachusetts, office of Mercer Management Consulting Inc. The ScrubaDub staff looks beyond the moment to anticipate how customers will feel about the company's services and its long-term role in the community . . . from the performance guarantees to Halloween charity events. "They're looking for every opportunity to demonstrate concern for customers," Cole says.

DETAILS AND DATA

Better yet, ScrubaDub didn't need the resources of an industry giant to create its marketing and service programs. Instead, the 100-plus-employee company has focused on cutting overhead—by automating functions such as cash management—to free up funds to invest in labor, computer operations and customer service.

Here are seven lessons from the car-wash chain that might apply to your business as well:

Pay attention to the details. Just as the hospitality industry wants travelers to feel pampered, the Paisners want customers to view the car-wash service as a pleasant experience. The first clues to this service philosophy: flower beds decorate the entrance to the wash, neatly groomed employees greet customers courteously, and car owners receive little treats such as peanuts as they enter the cleaning tunnel.

Inside, the cars are cleaned by an equipment system the Paisners configured for the most effective treatment possible (as opposed to the

Source: Jo-Ann Johnston, "Waxing Philosophical," *Small Business Reports,* Vol. 19, No. 6 (June 1994), pp. 14–19. Reprinted with permission.

standard systems used by some competitors) and scrubbed with a soap that's exclusive to the chain. Meanwhile, any kids on board may be delighted to see cartoon characters like Garfield or Bart Simpson mounted on poles inside the tunnel. These familiar characters help calm children who are frightened when the washing machine descends on their family car—and thus allow their parents to relax. (Of course, kids like to be scared around Halloween, so then the chain decorates its tunnels like haunted houses.)

Once drivers emerge from the wash, they can go to a waiting room and get free coffee if they want the insides of their cars cleaned. Some customers—depending on the make of their car and the level of service they've chosen—have their wheels cleaned with a toothbrush. Others can go to the "satisfaction center," a final service checkpoint, for any extra attention they feel the car needs. The goal is to make sure customers feel well taken care of when they drive out of the lot.

Know the customer. ScrubaDub's marketing and service programs rely heavily on the tracking of customers' buying habits. For example, the company develops vehicle histories of its "club members," who spend $5.95 for a membership pass that entitles them to certain specials, such as a free wash after 10 paid cleanings. ScrubaDub uses a computer database to track the frequency of these customers' visits and the services purchased. Each time a member visits, an employee scans a bar-code sticker that's placed on the vehicle's window and logs information into the database.

Behind the scenes, the company analyzes the vehicle histories, along with other sales and profit data, to track buying habits and identify sales opportunities. To punch up its relatively slow business in the evening hours, for example, ScrubaDub introduced a "night wash" special with a $1 savings and doubled its volume. And if a review of the data shows that certain club members haven't been to the store for a while, the company sends out a "We miss you letter" to invite them back.

More recently, ScrubaDub has moved its vehicle histories out of the back office and onto the car-wash lot to improve its customer service. Now, when club members enter the car wash, sales advisors can call up their histories on a computer terminal. That way, they can address customers by name and remind them of services they've purchased before, such as an undercarriage wash, a special wax treatment, or a wheel cleaning.

What's more, employees can now use the histories to suggest service upgrades. If a customer usually gets a regular wash, for example, a sales advisor might recommend an undercarriage wash if the car has been coated by heavily salted roads. ScrubaDub counts on these special options to generate income above the base price of $5.95 (the average purchase above that level is $1.60), but it also wants employees to suggest only those services appropriate to the vehicle and the customer. The point-of-sale histories help guide the sales advisor to the customer's buying preferences.

Mine new prospects. ScrubaDub is always on the lookout for new prospects, using both mass-market means (such as radio jingles) and more targeted approaches to draw them in. New car buyers are obvious prospects, so the company works with local car dealers to distribute 30-day passes for free washes to their customers. To reach new home buyers, another target group, ScrubaDub uses an outside service to generate names from property-transfer records, then sends [those buyers] coupons for its services.

Last year, the company also launched a direct-mail campaign to reach people with $75,000 or more in income and homes close to one of its locations. The $30,000 mailing invited [those people] to become club members, who tend to be steady customers and purchase more add-on services. The mailing yielded more than 1,000 new members and generated a $45,000 return in its first year.

Fix the problems. If a customer believes the car wash has damaged his or her car in any way, the manager can spend up to $150 in labor or merchandise to fix the problem, no questions asked. Even if ScrubaDub is not at fault, the Paisners don't want customers driving away with a sour memory. When one customer's tire began to leak, for example, an employee spotted it, helped the customer change the tire and got the leaky one repaired. After a problem is fixed, says Elaine Paisner, ScrubaDub sends the customer "a little warm fuzzy" of flowers, cookies, or candy.

It also backs up its work with guarantees. Customers who purchase the basic wash can get a rewash if they're not satisfied, while club members are entitled to some added protection. In exchange for these customers' loyalty and investment, ScrubaDub offers them a free replacement wash if it rains or snows within 24 hours after they've left the lot. With some of the more expensive treatments, customers are guaranteed a clean car for three days. If the driver goes through a puddle or parks under a flock of pigeons, the company will wash the car again for free.

The benefit of such guarantees? They help a company stay competitive by acknowledging that a bad service experience eats away at a customer's good will, says Christopher W. L. Hart, president of TQM Group, a Boston consulting firm. Of course, this forces a company to determine what services it can afford to guarantee and to improve operations so that mistakes are the exception. But the cost of fulfilling guarantees should be viewed as a marketing investment and a second chance to make a good impression, not as a loss. "View it as something to celebrate," says Hart.

Monitor customer satisfaction. The Paisners use a variety of feedback mechanisms to evaluate the quality of their service at the eight locations. These include comment cards available to all customers and special reports which the managers personally ask some drivers to fill out each month. In addition, ScrubaDub recently added a new service questionnaire for customers getting the insides of their cars cleaned. This feedback mechanism, which a ScrubaDub manager adopted from a noncompeting operator, allows the company to make sure its inside-cleaning service is as detailed as customers expect.

Together, these forms give ScrubaDub enough feedback to rate overall customer satisfaction and calculate it on an index ranging to 100. To supplement its own research, the company also employs an outside firm to send people through the car wash and generate professional "shoppers' reports" on their experiences.

Use training and incentives to ensure good service. If you want high-quality service, says Paisner, then get the message across with your hiring, training, and pay practices. His company tries to set itself apart from competitors by hiring well-groomed employees, for example, and Paisner believes you get what you ask for in the recruiting process. "If you expect clean-cut kids who are willing to wear shirts and ties, you're going to get them," he says.

Once hired, employees go through various training modules in a classroom setting—an unusual practice in the car-wash business—to make sure service will be consistent from location to location. New employees also must meet the approval of their coworkers, since the staff at each location is viewed as a team with its own sales and expense goals to meet.

Indeed, up to half of employees' pay is tied to such goals; the incentive-pay proportion for each individual varies according to the sales and management content of his or her job. (Managers' incentive pay is more heavily weighted toward incentives than that of employees who vacuum the cars.) The teams also compete for contest awards, based on specific sales goals and their satisfaction ratings from customer feedback mechanisms.

Finally, several employees from each location join an improvement team that meets regularly to discuss new ways to enhance customer service. Employees recently designed a new "QuickShine" program, aimed at 4 percent of customers, comprised of a wax treatment that's applied in 25 minutes and provides 90 days of protection.

Demonstrate respect for the community. One of the subtler ways ScrubaDub impresses customers is by being a good neighbor. In these days of environmental awareness, ScrubaDub reclaims some of the water used and treats the dirt that's eliminated for recycling as fill. And the company links its decorated Halloween tunnels—always a neighborhood attraction—to the problem of child poverty and homelessness. ScrubaDub donates a portion of its sales over a three-day period to nearby homeless shelters that use the cash to buy winter clothes for their young clients.

CONTINUOUS IMPROVEMENTS

There's a final lesson to be drawn from ScrubaDub's operations, says Cole of Mercer Management. As inventive as the company has been, the managers didn't always start from scratch in devising ways to improve their marketing and customer service. Instead, they adapted ideas from other industries for their own use. Doctors and dentists, for instance, use cartoon characters to make kids happier. And many industries, including airlines and long-distance telephone companies, use sophisticated databases to track customers' buying habits and create new marketing programs.

The important point is to foster curiosity and a constant desire to improve among employees—an objective that's well within reach of small companies. "Small business can be at the cutting edge. It doesn't require monolithic companies with huge resources and lines of MBAs," says Cole.

Paisner, for his part, believes that the companies best poised for long-term growth are those committed to keeping new ideas in the pipeline. "There's no such thing as staying the same anymore. You have to be prepared to improve all the time," he says.

Questions

1. Which type of marketing philosophy has ScrubaDub adopted? Do you think this is the best choice? Why or why not?
2. What methods of marketing research were used by ScrubaDub? What additional research could it do to better understand its customers?
3. Do you think the promotional activities of ScrubaDub could be improved and/or extended? Explain.
4. What kind of forecasting method do you believe would be most appropriate to estimate ScrubaDub's market potential?

Case 9

VMG Products

Formation of a Limited Partnership

As a salesman of industrial adhesives, Timothy Wagner discovered a business opportunity in the disposable diaper market. Although two companies (Procter and Gamble and Kimberly-Clark) dominated the market, Wagner believed that a low-cost producer located in the Pacific Northwest should be able to compete effectively in that area. He and two associates prepared a 60-page business plan and took it to William N. Prater, Jr., head of Weatherly Private Capital, an investment firm in Seattle. Prater helped them establish a limited partnership.

> *The three founders would be one of two general partners in the venture. Weatherly would be the other—acting in an administrative role, just to assuage investors who might be nervous about the founders' youth and lack of experience, Prater had explained. Neither one would put any significant cash into the deal; that would come from the limited partners. In return, the limiteds would be first in line for a payback, getting nearly all the net income from the diaper line until they had recovered their original investment. Then their share would decline, stepwise, until they had earned seven times their capital. At that point the founders would get 60 percent of the partnership's income, the limiteds 30 percent, and Weatherly 10 percent.*
>
> *Right there, Prater had said, was the beauty of the partnership structure. If he had set up a corporation right away, the founders would have had to give up most of the equity just to attract capital. This way, they could work themselves up from 1 percent to what amounted to 60 percent ownership.*

The partnership agreement provided that the two general partners were supposed to agree before they took significant action. The limited partners had no day-to-day authority, but they had the power, if it came to that, to kick out either or both general partners.

Questions

1. What makes such an ownership arrangement attractive to limited partners?
2. What are the advantages for Wagner and his two associates?
3. What are the disadvantages for Wagner and his two associates?

Source: Reprinted with permission, *Inc.* magazine, April 1987. Copyright 1987 by Goldhirsh Group, Inc., 38 Commercial Wharf, Boston, MA 02110.

Logan Beach

Sleepless in Chicago

It's the day before Virginia Lewey opens her first business, a cafe . . . called Logan Beach. And as she runs through her chores, the former lawyer is full of confidence.

"I have a little nagging feeling," she says, "that this isn't brain surgery."

But that evening, panic strikes. While preparing chicken salad at about 10 P.M., she notices that the chicken isn't sufficiently cooked. "My first day, and I kill people!" she says fretfully. She discards the salad and drops it from her opening menu. Not long afterward, the cafe's coffee maker, which she bought used, breaks down. And sometime around 3 A.M., the printer attached to her personal computer jams while printing the menus.

The next morning, Ms. Lewey arrives at the cafe at 6 o'clock to meet her milk supplier. He never appears.

Such are the trials of launching a new venture—an experience that can shatter anyone's illusions about the joys of owning a business.

Like many new owners, the 40-year-old Ms. Lewey chose entrepreneurship in the hope of finding a freer lifestyle. She gave up a six-figure income as a law partner and invested $28,000 to open Logan Beach this past summer. She dreamed of wearing jeans to work, blasting rock music, taking afternoon naps and luring a hip, bustling clientele by word-of-mouth.

Source: Barbara Marsh, "Sleepless in Chicago," *The Wall Street Journal.* October 15, 1993. p. R18. Reprinted by permission of *The Wall Street Journal,* ©1993 Dow Jones & Company, Inc. All Rights Reserved Worldwide.

However, Ms. Lewey quickly discovered how surprisingly tough it is to run a small business. Her sales during the first seven days never rose above a trickle. On Friday night at the end of the first week, she counted five tables empty out of eight and confessed, "I thought there would be more people by now."

Ms. Lewey got off to a rocky start by opening before she had worked out all the kinks. Clark Wolf, a New York restaurant consultant, recommends that new owners first practice on their friends, inviting them in before the opening to try everything on the menu at a discounted price. This gives the owner a chance to train the staff, alert suppliers, develop efficient routines—and make the inevitable missteps without turning off the public.

Another problem is that Ms. Lewey ignored some marketing basics. Consultants find it incredible that Logan Beach lacks a visible sign. The cafe's name, painted on the front window, rises from ground level to waist height—ensuring that passing drivers can't see it. Moreover, the storefront itself is barely noticeable, being situated on a street that gets little foot traffic and is just off a square where vagrants tend to congregate.

Nevertheless, some say the cafe's best asset is Ms. Lewey herself. Customers remark on her warm, friendly manner. She chats as easily with the weekend yuppie crowd and their kids as she does with the Hispanic professionals grabbing a business lunch and the young hipsters who linger over evening coffee. If she can learn from her early errors, consultants say, she will improve her cafe's chance of success.

As it is for many new business owners, Ms. Lewey's opening date was a moving target. She originally aimed for May, but she misjudged the time required to remodel her 674-square-foot storefront. Inexperience slowed her down, as she herself pried out floor staples, combed secondhand shops for furnishings and experimented with the color scheme—first painting a navy stripe on the wall and then covering it with pale gold.

The final result? A striking, cozy spot with a high ceiling, wood floor, two couches, and local artists' works on the walls. There are 20 chairs and eight tables, each sporting a lamp and flowered tablecloth.

But the two months of remodeling delays cost Ms. Lewey $1,500 in rent for June and July, without any sales to offset the expense. She hoped that her opening week would change all that. Here's how the first couple of days went:

Friday, July 30. A city inspector visits Logan Beach—two weeks later than expected—and says she'll recommend Ms. Lewey for a business license. Thrilled, the new proprietor decides to open the next day, rather than wait however long it might take for written approval. Although restaurants often open with only such verbal approvals, consultants note that Ms. Lewey risked being closed down for operating without a license. (She has since received her license.)

Saturday, July 31. After her struggles with the chicken, the computer printer, and the coffee maker, and her fruitless wait for the milkman, Ms. Lewey opens her cafe at 10 A.M. Her menu lists a variety of specialty coffees and other beverages, muffins, bagels, fruit, sandwiches, and pastries, with prices ranging from $0.75 for milk to $4.25 for a sandwich of sliced turkey breast with cheese.

Within minutes, the cafe fills with professionals and their young children. Ms. Lewey is inundated with orders for chocolate milk and espresso drinks. She has no help: The friends she called yesterday, looking for volunteers, aren't here yet.

As the wait for service stretches uncomfortably, a friend in the crowd pitches in at the espresso machine. He doesn't know how to adjust the milk temperature, though, and serves the "hot cappuccino" lukewarm.

The milk supply dwindling, Ms. Lewey sends her friend's wife out for emergency provisions. But soon the counter is overflowing with duplicate items, for by the time the woman returns with her order, the volunteers are finally arriving with theirs. As everyone scrambles, both the groceries and the customers go unattended. This is hardly the way Ms. Lewey imagined her first half hour in business, and she later admits to feeling embarrassed about having been caught so off guard.

That evening, she notices that her coffee grinder isn't working properly. A volunteer figures he will remove its bean container to adjust the machine. But he doesn't know that he should first close the container's trap, where beans flow into the grinding mechanism. As he lifts the container, the cafe floor is showered with beans.

Sunday, August 1. Afternoon business is so slow that Ms. Lewey has little to do but sit listening to marketing tips from a local customer, retired from a retailing career.

But Ms. Lewey is skeptical. She dismisses as "hokey" such standard techniques as a highly publicized grand opening. Her advertising effort consists of a token $25 ad placed in a local community group's yearbook. Meanwhile, she is relying on an artist friend to donate his time designing fliers. She plans to sponsor a local theater's reading of "Waiting for Godot" in mid-August, though she doesn't expect to make such occasions regular events.

Monday, August 2. Ms. Lewey's early-morning commuter rush amounts to one woman. In a way, though, that's a blessing, because the machines aren't cooperating.

Ms. Lewey's first employee, Mary Lou Raiz, tests the faulty coffee maker. Scalding water sprays out of the top. In the meantime, the ice machine below the counter has stopped working. Ms. Lewey calls for servicing; two repairmen arrive promptly, tinker, and depart.

Later, during lunch, a customer points out that there are dark particles in his ice. Ms. Lewey theorizes that coffee grounds have fallen into the ice machine. At night, she looks more carefully and finds other grit in the machine that she can't identify. The coffee maker still isn't working, either.

Giving up on both, she decides to rely instead on a small coffee maker brought from home and her backup ice machine in the cafe's kitchen.

Tuesday, August 3. Operationally, the cafe starts to click. Ms. Raiz, a former truck-stop owner, has lunch fixings prepared by 7:30 A.M.—four hours earlier than on Monday. A caterer arrives for the first time. Now Ms. Lewey can add pasta salad, cold potato soup, gazpacho, and lemon and mocha dessert bars to the short menu.

Customers compliment her. Mario Ortiz, a coffee lover, can't say enough about the house blend. Mr. Ortiz's nephew David tries a cucumber-and-cream-cheese sandwich, then orders two more. Margaret McCombs, a real-estate agent who is reading as she eats, says she hates the rock music playing but will be back anyway because Ms. Lewey seems nice.

For the day, Ms. Lewey's cash-register total hits a new high of $279—and her spirits rise. She aims to average $1,000 a day within six weeks.

Questions

1. Which key location factors did Ms. Lewey ignore? Explain.
2. Was Ms. Lewey's decision to remodel wise? Why or why not?
3. What recommendations, regarding the cafe's facility and equipment, might have helped overcome some of the problems she experienced?

WJP Partners

Projecting Financial Requirements

Mary Jo Wright is a sophomore English major attending Southern University, a small liberal arts college in southern Florida. She is president of the journalism club, which is where she first met her dorm roommate and good friend Sarah Jane Poe. Poe is a junior computer science major. Wright and Poe have been discussing the possibility of a new business venture. After months of brainstorming, they have agreed to start a venture that would offer students and local businesses help in preparing term papers and reports. Both young entrepreneurs recently attended a local seminar entitled "How to Start a New Business." From this experience, they realized the need for preparing pro forma financial statements to obtain necessary financing and also to help them better visualize the merits of the venture.

RESEARCH FINDINGS

Research indicates an unfulfilled demand for quality report-preparation services on campus. Market projections estimate a potential volume of 19,200 reports a year from Southern University students. Additionally, there are over 100 small businesses within two miles of the university that have indicated an interest in the service.

The majority of the students at Southern University are enrolled in classes that require two or three reports each semester, ranging from 5 to 50 pages in length. The venture's secondary target market consists of businesses in the nearby city of Emmett, Florida, which has an SMA (Standard Metropolitan Area) population of approximately 150,000. There are two office building complexes within two miles of the university, each containing over 50 small businesses.

STATEMENT OF FINANCIAL ASSUMPTIONS

Drawing on their findings, Wright and Poe have made the following observations:

1. Sales projections related to the preparation of student reports and term papers are based on the following assumptions:
   a. Eighty percent of the 12,000 students at the university, or 9,600 students, prepare at least two reports each 12-month period. This gives a projection of 19,200 reports (9,600 × 2 = 19,200).
   b. The firm will get 3 percent of student market in the first year, which will increase to 5 percent and 7 percent in the following two years, respectively.

c. Student reports will average 16 pages in length, for which the firm will receive $20 per report.

2. Revenue forecasts associated with the businesses needing the firm's services are based on the following assumptions:

a. Sixty percent of the 100 local businesses will need at least 10 reports each 12-month period.

b. The firm will obtain 6 percent of the business market in the first year, which will increase to 10 percent and 12 percent in the following two years, respectively.

c. Business reports will average 30 pages in length, for which the firm will receive $40 per report.

3. On average, students will want one copy of their report in addition to the original; businesses will want five copies. The firm will charge $0.06 a page for copies.

4. Practically all copies of reports will be bound, for a charge of $1 per copy.

5. The effective income tax rate will be 20 percent.

6. The firm will extend credit to its business customers. Accounts receivable should be about 15 percent of annual business sales, and inventories should run about 12 percent of annual total sales. However, suppliers are expected to provide credit to the firm, which is estimated at 6 percent of annual sales.

7. The average cost of producing each report is estimated to be $12 in labor and $0.50 in materials.

Wright and Poe have an option for a rent-free office in the university's student activities building. This arrangement was negotiated based on an understanding that they will provide the university with a special pricing schedule after 12 months of operation.

The initial operation will include two personal computers with word-processing, spreadsheet, and database software. One laser printer and two photocopying machines will also be needed. The total equipment costs will be as follows:

Computers	$12,000
Printers and copiers	$ 5,000
Total equipment costs	$17,000

The equipment will be depreciated on a straight-line basis over a five-year life expectancy.

Financing is expected to come from the following sources:

- As the founders, Wright and Poe will each invest $2,000 in the business.
- Additional equity will be raised in the amount of $4,000 from an outside investor: $3,000 will be invested at startup and the remaining $1,000 at the conclusion of the first year of operations.
- The National Bank of Emmett has agreed to loan the firm $3,000, to be repaid within one year, but with the option to renew each year, provided the business is doing well. The interest rate is expected to be 9 percent.
- The $17,000 in equipment will be purchased with a down payment of $7,000; the remaining balance will be paid off at $2,000 in principal per year, plus interest due on the remaining balance at an interest rate of 10 percent.

Question

Given the above information, help Wright and Poe prepare pro forma income statements, balance sheets, and cash flow statements for the first three years of their operation.

Walker Machine Works

Financing Arrangements for a New Venture

Jim Walker was a management consultant on an indefinite assignment with a medium-size plastics company. He was also studying for an M.B.A. degree at a nearby university. He had thought that the consultant position would be challenging and would add a dimension of practical experience to his academic background. But, after several months, Walker had become very disenchanted with his job. Although he seemed to have a lot of freedom in his duties, he began to realize that his reports and suggestions would not be translated into meaningful results and solutions, as the company's management was interested only in maintaining the status quo. His efforts to help the company were largely ignored and overlooked. It seemed as though his job was quickly becoming nothing more than an exercise in futility.

Walker discussed the situation with a few friends, most of whom urged him to seek a more fulfilling position with another company. But he had another idea—why not start a small company of his own? He had toyed with this idea for the past couple of years, and there was no better time than the present to give it a try. At the very least, it would be a real test of his managerial abilities.

After a few days and considerable thought, Walker came up with several potential ventures. The most promising idea involved the establishment of a machine shop. Before entering college, he had worked as a general machinist for two years and had acquired diversified experience operating a variety of lathes, milling machines, presses, drills, grinders, and more. And he really enjoyed this type of work; it satisfied some sort of creative urge he felt.

Very comprehensive and systematic research of the local market revealed a definite need for a high-quality machine shop operation. Walker was confident that he had adequate knowledge of machining processes (and enough ambition to find out what he didn't know), and that his general business education was a valuable asset. The problem was money. The necessary machinery for a small shop would cost about $12,000, and Walker had only about $3,000 in savings. Surely he could borrow the money or find someone willing to invest in his venture.

A visit to one of the local banks was less than productive. The vice-president in charge of business investments was quite clear: "You don't have a proven track record. It would be a big risk for us to lend so much money to someone with so little actual experience." Walker was very disappointed but unwilling to give up yet. After all, there were six other banks in town, and one of them might be willing to lend him the money.

Source: This case was prepared by Richard L. Garman.

FINANCING PROPOSAL 1

The banker had suggested that Walker contact Russ Williams, the president of a local hydraulics company, who, the banker felt, might be interested in investing some money in the venture. It was certainly worth a try, so Walker called Williams and made an appointment to see him.

Williams had been involved in manufacturing for over 40 years. As a young man, he had begun his career as Walker had—in the machine shop. After several years of experience as a journeyman machinist, Williams had been promoted to shop supervisor. After rising steadily through the ranks, he had been promoted to president of the hydraulics company only two years ago.

Walker knew little about Williams or his background. Nevertheless, he soon found him to be pleasant in nature and very easy to talk to. Walker spent about an hour presenting his business plan to Williams, who seemed impressed with the idea. Although Williams's time and energies were currently committed to an expansion project for the hydraulics company, he indicated that he might be interested in contributing both money and management to Walker's venture. As Walker rose to leave, Williams proposed a 50-50 deal and asked Walker to think it over for a few days.

FINANCING PROPOSAL 2

A few days later, Stan Thomas came by to see Walker. They had been good friends for about a year and had even roomed together as undergraduates. Thomas had talked with his father about Walker's idea and perhaps had glorified the venture's possibilities a little. His father was intrigued with the plan and had offered to meet with Walker to discuss a potential partnership.

Phil Thomas, Stan's father, was a real estate investor who owned his own agency. Although he had been in business only a few years, he was very successful and was constantly looking for new investment prospects. After looking over the business plan and some pro forma financial statements that Walker had prepared, he agreed that it might be a worthwhile venture. "I'll contribute all of the capital you need and give you a fair amount of freedom in running the business. I know that most investors would start out by giving you only 10 or 15 percent of the equity and then gradually increase your share, but I'll make you a better deal. I'll give you 40 percent right off the bat, and we'll let this be a sort of permanent arrangement," he said. Walker said he'd think it over for a few days and then let Mr. Thomas know.

Walker didn't know quite what to do. He had several options to choose from, and he wasn't sure which one would be best. The sensible thing to do would be to talk to someone who could offer good advice. So, he went to the business school to talk to a professor he knew fairly well.

FINANCING PROPOSAL 3

Walker found Professor Wesley Davis in his office and described the situation to him. The professor was an associate dean and a marketing specialist. Although he had no actual manufacturing experience, he had edited some publications for the Society of Manufacturing Engineers. Thus, he had at least a general knowledge of the machining processes involved in Walker's proposed business.

The professor had been aware of Walker's interest in starting a business and frequently inquired about the progress he was making. At the end of their discussion, Walker was surprised to hear the professor offer to help by investing some of his own money. "It sounds like you have an excellent idea, and I'd like to see you give it a try. Besides, a little 'real-world' experience might be good for an old academic type like me," said the professor. "And I would suggest bringing in Joe Winsett from the accounting department. I know that neither of us relishes keeping books. Besides, Joe is a CPA and could provide some valuable assistance. I'll talk to him if you like." The professor suggested that the equity be split into equal thirds, giving Walker the first option to increase his share of the equity. That is, he would be the first source of financing for any additional capital needed, thereby increasing his proportionate share of the stock and his ownership percentage.

Questions

1. Evaluate the backgrounds of the possible partners in terms of the business and management needs of the proposed firm.

2. Evaluate the three financing proposals from the standpoint of Walker's managerial control of the firm and the support or interference he might experience.
3. Compare Walker's equity position under each of the three proposals.
4. What are some important characteristics to look for in a prospective business partner?
5. Which option should Walker choose? What reasons can you give to defend your answer?

Silver Lining

Developing a New Product Strategy

It was a dark and stormy night. Actually, it was a few hundred dark and stormy nights that finally pushed Howard Ohlhausen toward a new discovery, a new business . . . and clear windshields forever. The president of Unelko Corp. created Rain-X, a wipe-on water repellent that makes raindrops bead up and blow away, and has windshield-wiper makers anxiously mopping their brows. So far, more than 100 million bottles have been sold in 46 countries around the world, and Unelko is now known as a pioneer in developing commercial products that repel water, protect surfaces, and prevent fogging.

[Ohlhausen], a U.S. Air Force electronic countermeasures officer during the Korean War, remembers dreaming of a product that would repel water from airplane windshields. The aircraft flew at low altitudes to escape radar detection; the trade-off was flying underneath swollen rain clouds. "Windshield wipers just didn't do the job," he recalls, "so takeoffs and landings were always treacherous."

Still, the demands of civilian life, including marriage and a baby, deterred [Ohlhausen] from his dream. After leaving the Air Force, he joined his father's business in Chicago, processing and exporting scrap textile, and frequently traveled on business through Europe, Africa, and Asia.

During one particular takeoff, the rain was

so severe that the pilot couldn't get the wheels off the ground. As [Ohlhausen] sat on that soggy runway in East Africa, the old dream of an easy-to-apply water repellent came rushing back. "It became an obsession," he admits.

While his contemporaries spent their free time golfing and socializing, [Ohlhausen] holed up in the library, studying glass properties and repellent techniques. He got up early to drive to his small lab, mixing all kinds of chemicals, sometimes with method . . . but often with madness.

"I didn't know what wouldn't work," says [Ohlhausen], who claims that at any time he could have "turned left instead of right" and never found the right formula. A helping hand came from the Illinois Institute of Technology, which offered to conduct commercial tests for [Ohlhausen] during his advanced research and development phase.

Finally, after six years of mixing and fixing [Ohlhausen] came up with several repellent formulas that gave satisfactory results. In early 1979, as he drove in a heavy rain, the Rain-X on his windshield working beautifully, he said to himself, "It's now or never." Patents in hand, he was ready to strike out on his own.

MAKING A SPLASH

Ever methodical, [Ohlhausen] made sure his family's textile business was in good shape before he left. Then, in June 1979, he rented a tiny

Source: Erika Kotite, "Silver Lining," *Entrepreneur* (July 1994), pp. 201–202. Reprinted with permission from *Entrepreneur* Magazine, July 1994.

office and warehouse and sat facing his son David, who was in the business with him. "We looked at each other and said, 'Okay, now what?'" recalls [Ohlhausen], 62.

They first went after the government market, which at the time used a complicated four-step process to coat airplane and helicopter windshields. Called Repcon, their product caught on and eventually reached nearly every Air Force installation in the country. The public, however, was a tougher sell.

"You have to really educate people," explains David, 39, who is vice president of Unelko and general manager of the automotive division. To that end, [Ohlhausen] would approach service stations, toting a mirror, a spray bottle, and a case of Rain-X. If no rain was forecast, he'd douse his car with a hose. Bottle by bottle, case by case, father and son heightened awareness of their product, hoping satisfied customers would start asking their favorite automotive stores to stock Rain-X.

Reaction to the product was astounding, as evidenced by thousands of letters from satisfied, even reverential, customers. David boasts that some of the letters are from people who had never written a thank-you note about a product before. "The letters are what really makes this business gratifying," he says. "We're truly helping people solve a problem."

STORMY WEATHER

Yet while consumers saw clearly how amazing Rain-X was, retailers were slower to come in out of the rain. The Ohlhausens were unknowns in an industry accustomed to dealing with big, established companies. "It's an irony in our society," says [Ohlhausen]. "America celebrates newness, yet when you have a truly revolutionary product, no one is willing to take a chance on it."

When [Ohlhausen] tried to market a product that would make concrete and masonry more water repellent, he managed to get an appointment with a managing partner of a major architectural firm, who told him to come back in five years after treating a building with it . . . if the building was still standing. "We kept hearing objections such as, 'We've never heard of it or gotten calls for it,'" says Howard. "Well, how could they have? It was brand new!"

Nevertheless, father and sons (by this time, David's brothers Steven and Michael had also joined the business) doggedly pursued their dream of selling Rain-X all over the world, even if they had to do it bottle by bottle. Slowly, one by one, retailers started to sign on.

Rain-X's eventual success paved the way for wider acceptance of the Ohlhausens' other products, including an anti-fog and nonstick coating called Invisible Shield that protects porcelain, glass and ceramic from dirt buildup. By the time Invisible Shield was ready for distribution three years ago, Unelko had enough market presence to persuade retailers like Kmart, Builder's Square, and Home Depot to stock the new product. The company once disparagingly dubbed "Howard's Folly" had arrived.

Now located in Scottsdale, Arizona, Unelko has more than 100 employees who manufacture and market its products full time. And the Ohlhausen family has shifted into high gear: David works on national accounts, Howard handles international sales, Steven manages the household division, and Michael directs the commercial and industrial division.

All of them are proud of how far Unelko has come since its shoestring beginnings 15 years ago. "Three things can limit you: a bad product, no money, and bad management," says David. "We didn't have a problem with any of these." David, for one, says he can't imagine a life working for someone else. "If I weren't doing this," he says, "I'd be one of the other leading entrepreneurs you write about. . . . That's what America is all about!"

Questions

1. Evaluate the name Rain-X using the characteristics of a good name discussed on pages 299–300.

2. Which product strategy did Ohlhausen follow with the initial introduction of Rain-X?

3. What product strategies were used to expand the Unelko's product mix?

4. What aspects of consumer behavior might explain the reluctance of retailers to stock Rain-X?

The Jordan Construction Account

Extending Credit and Collecting Account Receivables

Bob McFarland was the president and principal stockholder of Iowa Tractor Supply Company, a farm and construction equipment distributor located in Marshalltown, Iowa. The firm employed 27 persons, and in 1991 sales and net profit after taxes reached all-time highs of $3.4 million and $81,500, respectively. The firm's ending net worth for 1991 was slightly in excess of $478,000.

McFarland was highly gratified by these figures, as 1991 was the first full year with Barry Stockton serving as general manager. Although the company had been in operation since 1957, it had prospered only from the time McFarland had purchased it in 1969. Having been a territorial sales manager for the John Deere Company, he was able to obtain that account for Iowa Tractor, and it typically contributed two-thirds or more of the annual sales volume. After struggling successfully for 10 years to build Iowa Tractor into a profitable firm, McFarland decided that it was time to take things a little easier. Accordingly, he promoted Stockton and delegated many of his day-to-day duties to him. Fortunately, Stockton seemed to do an outstanding job, and, during the summer of 1992, McFarland felt secure enough about leaving the business to spend six weeks in Europe with his wife.

One day, shortly after McFarland returned to work, his accountant, Marvin Richter, approached with several ledger cards in his hand.

Source: This case was prepared by John E. Schoen of Texas A&M University.

Richter entered the office, carefully closed the door, and began to speak earnestly:

Mr. McFarland, I think you should look at these accounts receivable, particularly Jordan Construction. I've been telling Barry to watch out for Jordan for two months, but he just says they're good for it eventually. I got the latest Dun & Bradstreet monthly report today, which didn't look very good, so I've called Standifer Equipment in Ames and the Caterpillar branch at Cedar Rapids. Jordan seems to have run up some pretty good bills with both of them, and Carter at Standifer said some of the contractors in Des Moines think that the two jobs Jordan got on Interstate 80 are just too big for it to handle. If Jordan can't finish those jobs, we are going to be in trouble! Carter says Standifer's probably going to put Jordan on C.O.D. and call in the rental equipment.

McFarland examined the data for a few minutes, asked Richter several questions before dismissing him, and then summoned Stockton to his office. The following dialogue took place:

McFarland: Barry, I've just been looking over the sheets on Jordan, and the amount really scares me. Apparently, they are over 90 days on nearly $21,000, between 30 and 90 days on another $17,000, and the total due is more than $45,000. Payments on their account have been dropping off since April, and last month they barely covered the interest on the amount outstanding.

Stockton: I know, Bob, I've been over to talk to old man Jordan twice in the last three weeks. He admits they are having some trouble with those jobs on the interstate, but he claims it is only temporary. I hate to push him too hard because he's bought a lot of equipment from us over the years.

McFarland: That's right, Barry, but we're talking about $45,000! At this rate, we'll soon have more money in Jordan's business than he does! I'm not so sure we shouldn't put Jordan on C.O.D. until he makes some substantial payments on their account.

Stockton: I don't think so, Bob! Old man Jordan has a real mean streak, and the first time I went over there he really cussed me out for even questioning his account. He reminded me that he had been a good customer for more than 10 years, and he threatened to cut us off if we put any pressure on him.

McFarland: Yes, but you've heard that before, Barry. Here we are, contributing capital to his business involuntarily; we never get a share of his profits if he succeeds, but we sure get a share of the losses if he goes belly-up. Barry, I don't want any $45,000 losses!

Stockton: Well, I won't say that Jordan doesn't have some problems, but our sales manager thinks it'll be all right. It's just that if we put Jordan on C.O.D. or pick up the rental equipment and they make it, I'm sure they'll never spend another dollar here.

McFarland: Harry thinks they'll be okay?

Stockton: Yes, sir.

McFarland: Get Harry in here!

In a few minutes, Stockton returned with Harry Reiser, the sales manager for Iowa Tractor. The following dialogue took place between McFarland and Reiser:

Reiser: Barry says you wanted to talk to me?

McFarland: That's right, Harry. We've just been discussing Jordan Construction, and I'd like to get any information you have.

Reiser: Well, Jordan is a pretty good customer, of course. I rented him two tractor-backhoes last month. There are some rumors about the interstate jobs, but I don't think there's much to it because Jordan was talking about buying a couple of crawler tractors last Friday. I think we have a good chance to get those crawlers if that joker over at Ames doesn't sell his below cost.

McFarland: Just a minute. You rented Jordan some backhoes last month?

Reiser: Yes, sir, two model 310-A's.

McFarland: How much are we getting for those units?

Reiser: $1,400 a month each, and I think we have a good chance to convert them to a sale if Jordan gets six months' rent into them.

McFarland: Did you check with anybody before you put those units out with Jordan?

Reiser: Well, I think I asked Barry. No, I think he was busy that day. I'm really not certain, but Jordan Construction is one of our best accounts, isn't it?

McFarland: That's what we are trying to determine, Harry. Did you know that Jordan's accounts receivable is over $45,000?

Reiser: No! That's great! I knew we'd really been selling there. I'm sure those rumors . . .

McFarland: And did you know that $38,000 of the $45,000 is past due and $21,000 is over 90 days?

Reiser: Oh!

McFarland then turned to Stockton and said, "Barry, I think we've established what Harry knows about Jordan. Why don't we get Marvin in here and see what information he has. Then I think the four of us need to decide the best approach to getting as much of our money back as soon as possible."

Questions

1. Evaluate the quality of the information provided to McFarland by each of his subordinates.
2. Evaluate the alternatives for resolving the Jordan situation.
3. What action should McFarland take regarding the Jordan account?
4. How could McFarland improve the credit and collections procedures of Iowa Tractor to minimize problems of this nature?
5. Evaluate the performances of Richter, Stockton, and Reiser in handling the Jordan account. Do the circumstances warrant any type of disciplinary action?

Litter Ridder

Finding the Best Promotional Mix for a New Product

It is often said that necessity is the mother of invention. Don and Marsha Hostetler found necessity to be an unpleasant household chore. Don and Marsha liked cats, but they hated cleaning the cat litter box.

Don decided there must be a better way. In 1993, he developed "Litter Ridder," a disposable cat litter box. The cat owner need never see or smell cat litter again. He or she can merely replace the old box each week with a new one. The box is made of two cardboard pieces. The bottom piece holds the cat litter, and the top piece pops up to form a covering over the litter. The cat can easily go in and out of the enclosed litter box.

Don's architectural drafting background helped him not only to design the product but also to design and build a small assembly line to produce Litter Ridder. Marsha proved to be a hard-nosed negotiator with suppliers, and this helped minimize costs of materials.

Don and Marsha needed assistance in two primary areas: finance and marketing. They found three local investors to provide the initial financial support. One was an attorney, and the other two (father and son) were owners of a professional services firm. Don said the investors were chosen because they made the first offers to finance the business. None of the investors

Source: This case was prepared by Philip R. Carpenter. He gratefully acknowledges the support of the St. Louis University Small Business Development Center and Don Kirchgessner of the St. Louis County Enterprise Center.

had marketing expertise, but their financial support gave Don and Marsha the resources they needed to set up production facilities, begin production, and develop a marketing strategy.

The four major grocery chains operating in the St. Louis area were Schnucks, Dierbergs, Shop 'N Save, and National. Schnucks and Dierbergs were upscale stores patronized by affluent customers. Shop 'N Save was a discount grocer drawing lower-income customers. National was positioned in the middle in terms of customer appeal.

Litter Ridder was sold in the upscale Schnucks and Dierbergs stores throughout the greater St. Louis area. In order to get Litter Ridder into the stores, Don approached the respective buyers and showed them a sample of Litter Ridder. Both buyers readily agreed to put the product on their shelves. There were no wholesalers or food brokers involved in the process. For Schnucks, Don delivered Litter Ridder to a central warehouse; for Dierbergs, he delivered to each store.

Marketing was not a high priority. A total of eight ads were placed in local newspapers. One was placed with the *St. Louis Post-Dispatch* (a daily paper), four with *The Riverfront Times* (a free weekly paper distributed throughout the metropolitan St. Louis area), and three were placed with the *Ladue News* (Ladue is the wealthiest suburb in the St. Louis area). The company was also featured in 13 public relations articles appearing in the *Post-Dispatch* and several suburban newspapers.

Don, Marsha, and the other investors intended to advertise on television, but funds ran low before such ads could be developed. Radio advertising was not considered viable. The investors believed that Litter Ridder was a product best advertised by using visual media.

The retail price of Litter Ridder was $3.85 per box. Competition included national and generic brands of cat litter such as the following:

Brand	Bag Size	Price
Tidy Cat 3	25 pounds	$3.50
Fresh Step	16 pounds	$4.59
Generic	25 pounds	$1.79–2.29

A 25-pound bag would typically last three or four weeks (changing the litter once a week), while Litter Ridder would last one week. Customers who bought Litter Ridder were concerned not with minimizing costs, but with convenience and avoiding the unpleasant sights and odors related to ordinary litter.

In early 1995, in-store demonstrations were held by store personnel; Don and Marsha had no say in which employees would demonstrate the product. However, they did send an instruction sheet on how to present Litter Ridder. The results from demonstrations were discouraging. Several customers made negative remarks regarding the product. Discount coupons were offered, but the response was low. As if these problems weren't enough, one of the product demonstrators was quite negative toward Litter Ridder during the demonstration.

Sales were increasing slowly (see Table C15-1). No sales were recorded in May because the stores had made large purchases in April in anticipation of increased sales after the in-store demonstrations. Sales volume was still well below the break-even point. Don thought the price might be too high. He spent time redesigning the box and was able to reduce the cost of production significantly.

After current inventory was used up, Don planned to begin production of the new box. He planned to pass on the cost savings to the supermarkets. There was a positive response from the supermarket buyers. They said they would in turn pass on the savings by reducing Litter Ridder's price. Don started the lower pricing in June.

Don thought that by expanding the market, the firm could increase sales. Visiting a large regional grocer in Indianapolis, he found himself unprepared for the detailed questions concerning pricing, delivery, food brokers, discounting, and couponing asked by the grocer's buyers.

By June 1996, the investors were becoming restless. While the father and son were willing to be patient and stick it out, the lawyer was not. He wanted out, and he persuaded the other two to join him. The investors had been supporting the business on a modified pay-as-you-go plan. They had each made an equal initial investment. When this sum was gone, they had paid the monthly expenses of the business. They stopped paying the monthly expenses at the end of June. Their total investment in the corporation was $52,000, which was split evenly among them. Don and Marsha had invested no cash in the business. The agreement was that their share would be 25 percent in the event the business was sold.

Don and Marsha believed there was potential for a new investor. Don had been reviewing patent applications for products similar to Litter Ridder. One day, he came across an application from the local St. Louis area. When Don called the person who had applied for the patent, he found someone interested in possibly providing financial and marketing assistance for Litter Ridder. The discussion had remained at a preliminary stage.

Table C15-1 *Litter Ridder Sales History*

Sales	December 95 Dollars	Units	January 96 Dollars	Units	February 96 Dollars	Units	March 96 Dollars	Units	April 96 Dollars	Units	May 96 Dollars	Units	June 96 Dollars	Units
Schnucks	$423	144	$846	288	$1058	360	$1058	360	$2328	792	$0	0	$1332	720
Dierbergs	$133	43	$151	49	$ 231	75	$ 408	131	$ 478	73	$0	0	$ 204	105
Total	$556	187	$997	337	$1289	435	$1466	491	$2806	865	$0	0	$1536	825

Don and Marsha stopped production in June and planned to sell their three-month backlog of product. During this time, they planned to make some difficult decisions regarding Litter Ridder's future.

Questions

1. How important is personal selling to marketing a cat litter box?

2. What types of objections from retailers should the Hostetlers anticipate?

3. What features of this product should be advertised?

4. Evaluate the Hostetlers' sales and promotional efforts. Suggest types of advertising and advertising media that might be most appropriate.

Case 16

NovaSoft Systems Inc.

Not So Innocent Abroad

With the homes they'd pledged for seed capital on the line and the seed money running thin, Sureyya "Ray" Ciliv and Robin Hillyard, engineer-founders of a software startup outside Boston, planned to test a business basic: Sales generate cash. However, another business basic—a stock-market crash—intervened. NovaSoft Systems Inc. was down to its last $250 when the panic of 1987 hit, reducing its chances of attracting risk capital to nil.

CEO Ciliv and chief technical officer Hillyard didn't dare begin marketing in the United States without resources. So they decided to begin marketing overseas without resources. As novice owners of a nearly broke company, they nonetheless had an asset no one abroad did—the latest technology in computer-based engineering document management systems. They would prove their product could sell and then ride that momentum back to the United States.

"When you market in the United States," Ciliv notes, "you have to advertise and do PR and attend large trade shows—all of which costs money. Then you have to build a sales organization, but salespeople don't become 100 percent productive for maybe nine months, and that's also a cost. The usual routine is to make an investment, then wait for a return. But if you don't have the cash to make that investment, obviously, you don't have a choice." Accordingly, he invested what remained in NovaSoft's treasury in a ticket to Europe.

The strategy called for establishing distributorship agreements with, Ciliv says, "solid, well-staffed companies that already had sales forces and support organizations in place and were dealing with the kind of companies that would be our target customers." Ciliv began in Rome. "Italians would be open-minded and spontaneous," the Turkish-born Ciliv had theorized.

His instincts were right. In July 1988, hardly two months after NovaSoft had begun operations, he closed a deal with Italcad, a large Italian distributor of computer-aided design and computer-aided manufacturing equipment. It wasn't a hard sell, Ciliv says. The company even gave him a quick $100,000 up front. "It was supplying other products and could anticipate the appeal of ours within its customer base. Any kind of agreement—even a royalty advance—represented little risk to it; essentially, it had already done the market research." Within weeks, Italcad had placed NovaSoft's systems with Fiat.

Buoyed by that debut, Ciliv convinced Hewlett Packard that running his software would show off the manufacturer's hardware to good advantage. While Ciliv was presenting a NovaSoft program at a Hewlett-Packard booth at a large trade exhibition in Germany, some executives from the international conglomerate Siemens, based in Munich, happened by. The company arranged to send a representative to NovaSoft's U.S. facilities to evaluate the technology. "That," Ciliv recalls, "was unnerving. We

Source: Robert A. Mamis, "Not So Innocent Abroad," *Inc.*, Vol. 15, No. 9 (September 1993), pp. 110–111. Reprinted with permission, *Inc.* magazine (September 1993). Copyright 1993 by Goldhirsh Group, Inc., 38 Commercial Wharf, Boston, MA 02110.

were just a handful of people working out of a dinky office in the back of a warehouse. I was afraid the guy would turn back, but he came in and announced, 'I don't care about your size—extraordinary technology comes out of ordinary offices.'"

The cost of signing with Siemens was rock-bottom: the price of a hotel room during the convention week. And, revels Ciliv, who devoted the following four weeks to carving out the deal's fundamentals, "we didn't have to surrender a thing. Siemens wasn't our only option. We told them we could go to Philips or some other big company just as easily." In fact, NovaSoft still can. Although Siemens is obliged to purchase a minimum dollar amount of software for resale each year, the German license isn't exclusive, and NovaSoft is entitled to offer its products to anyone else in the country. But it's not likely to, inasmuch as the contract also calls for NovaSoft to supply products for Siemens to sell under Siemens's own label. In another low-budget appearance, NovaSoft's document-management and work flow–management software so impressed a Venezuelan oil corporation that it bought a $145,000 system for its sprawling refinery on the spot. When Ciliv later sought a Venezuelan distributor, his leverage was bolstered by being able to deliver a ready-made customer.

Within two years, NovaSoft had established distributor relations in Italy, Belgium, and Germany. Each deal provided for an advance against sales. "Initial agreements in strategic relationships are extremely important," Ciliv contends. "You have to be careful not to give away your future for the sake of the present." Advance royalties are indicated because such royalties prove that your proposed partner is taking you seriously. If a company doesn't commit cash, it risks nothing and could simultaneously agree to distribute products from 100 sellers without the other 99 knowing. "By the time you discover they haven't bothered with yours," Ciliv cautions, "it's a year later, and you've lost."

Next, Ciliv looked for a market in Japan. Having no idea whom to seek for a strategic partner in Japan, he phoned the Japanese consulate in Boston, asked for a list of companies serving the engineering market, and wrote to the president of the one that seemed most promising. "If you have a good product and can communicate its potential," he reckoned, "a sound businessperson anywhere in the world has to answer." Sure enough, one did. The cold-callee, Mutoh-Kogyo, a Tokyo-based company, said it would be pleased to send a strategy-planning unit directly to Boston.

The business protocol that followed, however, wasn't so direct. "Whereas other countries respond to a product's technical features, in Japan that's not the principal issue for the end-user," Ciliv discovered. "The relationship with the vendor is more important. Japanese customers are very conservative. They like to purchase from people they've been doing business with for a long time." His recommendation: "Don't even think of opening your own sales office there."

Questions

1. Will the international experiences of NovaSoft be beneficial to its domestic marketing? Why or why not?
2. What type of cultural understanding may have aided NovaSoft's marketing effort?
3. What alternative distribution systems could potentially have been developed by NovaSoft?

Central Engineering

How an Entrepreneur's Management Practices Hampered Decision Making

Henry and Jami Wolfram, a husband-and-wife team, owned and operated Central Engineering, a heating and air conditioning firm located in Huntsville, Alabama. The business prospered during the six years they owned it, and it served both residential and commercial accounts.

ORGANIZATION STRUCTURE

Figure C17-1 shows the simple organization structure of the firm. Henry served as general operations manager. As the business grew, more and more responsibility fell on his shoulders. Although Jami assumed some of the burden by acting as treasurer and supervising the office work, Henry was personally involved in most of the key decisions. Henry's son, Jeff Wolfram, had started at Central Engineering as a worker on an installation crew. Later, he moved into the position of estimator-salesperson and acted as manager whenever his father was out of town.

THE BOTTLENECK

An unfortunate consequence of Henry's growing workload was the creation of a bottleneck at the very top of the business. Since he was a key person, his judgment seemed indispensable to many actions. As a result, decisions were some-times delayed, waiting for his attention. Others in the organization sometimes found themselves waiting in line to get a chance to talk with him. And Henry found himself rushed, with insufficient time to think carefully about some aspects of the business. In addition, he would have liked to devote a little more time to family, church, and personal interests.

REVIEW OF CUSTOMER BILLING

One task that required Henry's attention was his personal review of invoices before they were sent to customers. When a management consultant asked why this was necessary, the following dialogue took place:

Henry: I really need to take a last look before bills are sent out. For example, on construction jobs, there may be additions or extras that were included after we made the original bid.
Consultant: On regular service calls, is there a similar chance of an error?
Henry: That's right. For instance, maybe the worker left something off the work order. The worker may say he has done this and this and this, but, over here on the materials list, he has some items that don't match up or that are missing from what he said he's done.

Source: Personal communication.

Organization Structure of Central Engineering | Figure C17-1

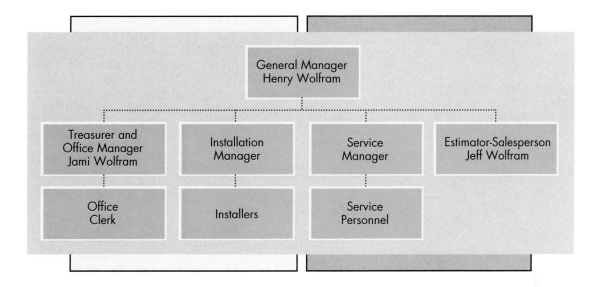

Consultant: Can you tell me how many hours in a day or week are required for this?

Henry: Well, it cuts into a lot of time. This is part of another problem. The office is too open, with Jeff and his customers in the same office with me. I just don't have any place where I can concentrate on this type of work. I think that, when we get that physical arrangement changed, it will help some.

Consultant: So, how many hours a week does this take?

Henry: Sometimes, we stay here at night or come in Saturday to do this. But I suppose it might run 8 or 10 hours a week.

Consultant: Is there anybody else who could do this?

Henry: Well, on service calls, Jami can usually spot such discrepancies. She is getting enough experience that she can recognize them.

Consultant: What is Jeff's role? Could he do this?

Henry: He's an estimator and does sales work. He doesn't quite have the experience yet. Well, he might be close to being capable. But he's pretty busy. Also, I have a service manager who could catch a lot of these things when the orders are turned in. But he doesn't manage that carefully. I have a more aggressive manager in installation who is better at catching things like this.

The general theme in Henry's discussion with the management consultant was the diffi-culty of resolving the time-management problem. Henry recognized the burden this placed on him personally and on the business, but there seemed to be no obvious answer at this stage in the life of the firm.

REVIEW OF ACCOUNTS PAYABLE

Henry also tried to look over all payments being made by accounts payable. His discussion with the management consultant regarding this function follows:

Henry: These payments need to be checked over because we may be charged too much on some bills.

Consultant: How does that happen?

Henry: On particular jobs, we may get special pricing. Say I'm working on a bid. I may pick up a phone and say to the supplier, "We need some special pricing. Here's what we're up against, and we need the special pricing to get this job." And if they give us the special pricing, we should pay accordingly.

Consultant: And you can't depend on them to bill you at that special price?

Henry: I don't think it's anything intentional. But they give it to their clerks to bill, and they may overlook the special pricing that was promised. So, if we don't catch it, we lose it.

HENRY'S DILEMMA

The responsibilities relative to accounts receivable and accounts payable were typical of the overall situation. In many aspects of the business, Henry felt compelled to give his personal attention to the issues and the decisions that needed to be made. In a sense, he felt trapped by the very success and work that accompanied the operation of the business. He enjoyed the work, every minute of it, but occasionally he wondered why there was no obvious solution to his dilemma.

Questions

1. Is Henry Wolfram's personal involvement in the various specific aspects of the business necessary? Or is it a matter of habit or of simply enjoying doing business that way?
2. What changes would be necessary to extricate Henry from the checking of customer invoices before they are mailed?
3. If you were the consultant, what changes would you recommend?

Gibson Mortuary

Human Resources Problems in a Small Family Business

Gibson Mortuary was founded in 1929 and has become one of the best-known funeral homes in Tacoma, Washington. One of its most persistent problems over the years has been the recruitment and retention of qualified personnel.

BACKGROUND OF THE BUSINESS

Gibson Mortuary is a family business headed by Ethel Gibson, who owns 51 percent of the stock. As an active executive in the business, Ethel is recognized as a community leader. She has served in various civic endeavors, been elected to the city council, and served one term as mayor.

The mortuary has built a reputation as one of the finest funeral homes in the state. The quality of its service over the years has been such that it continues to serve families over several generations. While large corporations have bought up many mortuaries in recent years, Gibson Mortuary continues to remain competitive as an independent family firm—a "family serving families." Funeral homes in general have recently become the target of public criticism, and books such as *The American Way of Death* reflect adversely on this type of business. Nevertheless, Gibson Mortuary has withstood this threat by its determined, consistent effort to provide the best

Source: Personal communication; names have been disguised.

possible customer service. In its most recent year, it conducted 375 funerals, which places it in the top 9 percent of all funeral homes in the nation when measured in terms of volume of business.

Ethel's son, Max Gibson, entered the business after completing military service and became general manager of the firm. He is a licensed funeral director and embalmer. Both mother and son are active in the day-to-day management of the firm.

RECRUITMENT AND RETENTION PROBLEM

Perhaps the most difficult problem facing Gibson Mortuary is the recruitment and retention of qualified personnel. The image of the industry has made it difficult to attract the right caliber of young people as employees. Many individuals are repelled by the idea of working for an organization in which they must face the fact of death daily. In addition, the challenges raised by social critics reflect poorly on the industry and conveyed to many people the impression that funeral homes are profiting from the misery of those who are bereaved.

One source of employees is walk-in applicants. Also, Gibson Mortuary works through local sales representatives who often know of people who might be considering a change in their careers.

As a small business, Gibson Mortuary presents fewer total opportunities than a larger company or even a funeral home chain. The fact that it is a family business also suggests to prospective employees that top management will remain in the family. It is apparent to all that the two top management spots are family positions. However, Ethel and Max (who is 49 years old) are the only family members employed, so there is some hope for the future for nonfamily employees.

TRAINING PROBLEM

Gibson Mortuary uses two licensed embalmers—Max and another individual. The pressure of other managerial work has made it difficult for Max to devote sufficient time to this type of work.

Any individual interested in becoming a licensed embalmer has to attend mortuary college (mortuary science programs are part of some community-college programs) and serve a two-year apprenticeship. The apprenticeship can be served either prior to or after the college training. Gibson Mortuary advises most individuals to take the apprenticeship prior to the college training so that they can evaluate their own aptitude for this type of career.

Gibson Mortuary prefers its personnel to be competent in all phases of the business. The work involves not only embalming, but also making funeral arrangements with families and conducting funerals and burials. However, some part-time employees only assist in conducting funerals and do not perform preparatory work.

PERSONAL QUALIFICATIONS FOR EMPLOYMENT

All employees who meet the public and have any part in the funeral service need to be able to interact with others in a friendly and relaxed but dignified manner. The personalities of some individuals are much better suited to this than those of others. Ethel describes one of the problem personalities she had to deal with as follows:

> In the first place, he didn't really look the part for our community here. He was short and stocky, too heavy for his height. His vest was too short, and he wore a big cowboy buckle! Can't you see that going over big in a mortuary! He wanted to stand at the door and greet people as they came. We do furnish suits, so we tried to polish off some of the rough edges.
>
> But he was still too aggressive. He became upset with me because I wouldn't get him any business cards immediately. One day I had to send him to the printers, and he came back and said, "While I was there, I just told them to make some cards for me. I'll pay for them myself." I said to him, "Willis, you go right back there and cancel that order! When you are eligible for cards, I'll have them printed for you." We couldn't have him at that point scattering his cards with our name all over town.

Another young applicant made an impressive appearance but lacked polish. His grammar was so poor that he lacked the minimal skills necessary for any significant contact with the public.

Two characteristics of employment that discourage some applicants are the irregular hours and the constant interruptions that are part of the life of a funeral director. A funeral director might start to do one thing and then find it necessary to switch over to another, more urgent matter. Also, some night and weekend duty in the work schedule is required.

SOLVING THE HUMAN RESOURCES PROBLEMS

Although Gibson Mortuary has not completely solved its need for qualified personnel, the business is working at it. While waiting for the right person to come along, Gibson Mortuary started another apprentice prior to any college training. In addition, it is following up on a former apprentice who worked during summer vacations while attending mortuary college. The business also employs a part-time minister as an extra driver. In these ways, Gibson Mortuary is getting along, but it still hopes to do a better job in personnel staffing.

Questions

1. Evaluate the human resources problems facing this firm. Which appears most serious?

2. How can Gibson Mortuary be more aggressive in recruitment? How can it make itself more attractive to prospective employees?

3. Does the fact that Gibson Mortuary is a family firm create a significant problem in recruitment? How can the firm overcome any problems that may exist in this area?

4. Assuming that you are the proper age to consider employment with Gibson Mortuary, what is the biggest question or problem you would have as a prospective employee? What, if anything, might the Gibsons do to deal with that type of question or problem?

Douglas Electrical Supply, Inc.

Conflicting Messages in TQM

Jim Essinger is a management consultant and training specialist from St. Louis who specializes in continuous process improvement and total quality management. Each month, he goes to Springfield, Illinois and provides three days of training to employees of a privately owned electrical wholesaler-distributor, Douglas Electrical Supply, Inc.

Most of the employees attending this fourth session are from the Springfield branch and have either gone back to the office or to their favorite restaurants during the lunch break. Jim has noticed that one of the class members from out of town is alone in the coffee shop of the hotel where the training sessions are conducted, and he has invited the young man to join him for lunch. The nervousness of his young companion is apparent to Jim, and he decides to ask a few questions.

Jim: Tony, you seem a little distracted; is there something wrong with your lunch?

Tony: Oh, it's not that, Jim. I . . . I'm having a problem at work, and it kind of relates to the training you are doing with us.

Jim: Really? Tell me about it.

Tony: Well, as you might know, I drive a van for the company, delivering electrical products and materials to our customers.

Jim: You work at the Quincy branch, right?

Tony: Yes. I drive about 250 miles a day, all over western Illinois, making my deliveries.

Jim: I see.

Tony: About seven weeks ago, I was making a big delivery at Western Illinois University in Ma-

comb. A lady pulled out in front of me, and I had to brake hard and swerve to miss her!

Jim: You didn't hit her?

Tony: No! She just drove off . . . . I don't think she ever saw me. Anyway, I had a full load of boxes, pipe, conduit, and a big reel of wire. The load shifted and came crashing forward. Some of it hit me hard in the back and on the back of my head.

Jim: Were you injured?

Tony: I'm not sure if I was ever unconscious, but I was stunned. Some people stopped and helped me get out of the van. I was really dizzy and couldn't get my bearings. Eventually, they called an ambulance. The paramedics took me to the hospital, and the doctors kept me for two days while they ran some tests.

Jim: Did you have a concussion?

Tony: Yes, I had some cuts and a slight concussion. My wife was really upset, and she made me stay home for the rest of the week. We have two little kids under four, and she wants me to quit and get a safer job.

Jim: She wants you to quit?

Tony: Yes! Sooner or later, all of the drivers get hit or have close calls. When you have a full load, those loads can shift and do a lot of damage. When I get in the van lately, especially when I have pipe or big reels of wire, I'm frightened. My wife is scared for me. I don't want to be killed or paralyzed, or something!

Source: This case was prepared by John E. Schoen of Texas A&M University.

Jim: I can understand your concern, Tony. What can the company do to protect you? Can you put in some headache racks or heavy-gauge metal partitions in the van that would keep the load from hitting you if it shifts?

Tony: That's exactly what I was thinking! I've been talking with some of the other drivers during our TQM sessions. We've learned that we can get heavy-gauge partitions that would keep us safe built for about $350 per vehicle.

Jim: Good! Have you talked to management about making the modifications?

Tony: Yes, I had all the information and talked to my boss in Quincy, Al Riess. However, he hardly seemed to listen to me. When I pressed the issue, he said the company had nearly 30 vans, counting the ones in Chicago and northern Illinois, and that the company could not afford to spend $10,000 for headache racks, partitions, or anything else! Al finally said that I was just being paranoid, that I should drive more carefully, and that I should definitely stop talking to the other drivers if I valued my job.

Jim: You mean he threatened you?

Tony: You could say that. He said to keep my mouth shut and just drive . . . or else!

Jim: Tony, is there someone else you could talk to about this problem? It would seem to me that one injury lawsuit would certainly cost the company more than the modifications you're proposing.

Tony: Well, there's the problem! You know how expensive the TQM training is . . . and all of us "little people" were actually excited about TQM and continuous process improvement when the owners and you first talked to us. We believed management was changing and was really interested in our ideas and suggestions. We thought maybe they cared about us after all.

Jim: Well, I believe the owners do want to change the culture and improve the operations.

Tony: Maybe it's different in Chicago and northern Illinois, Jim, but the guys in Peoria and Springfield are like military types and are really into control. I think they're authoritarians—is that the right term?

Jim: Yes, authoritarians, autocrats . . . .

Tony: Al Riess, my boss, is the son-in-law of Bob Spaulding, who heads our division. As you probably know, Bob has a real bad temper and nobody crosses him twice, if you know what I mean. Bob is particularly sensitive about Al—because everyone knows Al doesn't have much ability and we're losing money at the Quincy branch.

Jim: Okay, I see your problem with going to Bob. Is there a safety officer or anyone at headquarters who could logically be brought into this situation?

Tony: I don't know! The owners seem to have a lot of confidence in Bob and give him a free hand in the management of our division. No, I don't see much hope of change. It makes the TQM training pretty hollow and kind of a crock! No offense, Jim!

Jim: No, I see what you mean, Tony.

Tony: See, I have eight years invested in this company! I used to like my job and driving the van. But, now, I'm afraid, my wife is afraid . . . .

Jim: Sure, I can understand where you're coming from! Let me ask you a question. How many van drivers are there in the entire company?

Tony: I'm not absolutely sure. There are 17 drivers in our division, and I believe 13 to 15 drivers in the north. About 30 vans and drivers would be close to the correct numbers.

Jim: Are any of the drivers in a union?

Tony: None of us in this area, but all of the truck and van drivers in the north are Teamsters.

Jim: Aha! Have any of you ever talked to those drivers about this safety issue?

Tony: Oh, I see where you're coming from. . . .

Jim: Hang on! That might be your fallback position, but you won't necessarily be protected if you're regarded as a troublemaker. Let me think about ways I might be able to intercede in a functional way.

Tony: Gee, that would be great if you could. I mean we like our jobs, but we've got to be safe and we've got to be heard when it is a matter of life and death!

Questions

1. How is driver safety related to total quality management (TQM)?
2. On the basis of this conversation, what is your impression of the organizational culture at Douglas Electrical? How would you expect this to affect the TQM program? What could management do to strengthen the culture?
3. What are the positive features of the firm's TQM program?
4. What is the proper role of a TQM consultant? Should Jim Essinger attempt to intervene in the management process by discussing safety issues?

Case 20

Mather's Heating and Air Conditioning

Selecting and Dealing with Suppliers

Fred Mather operates a small firm that sells and services heating and air-conditioning systems. Over the years, the firm has changed from relying primarily on one supplier—Western Engineering—to a more balanced arrangement involving three suppliers. In the following discussion with a consultant, Mather describes some points of friction in his dealings with Western Engineering.

Mather: Western Engineering is so big that it can't be customer-oriented. Why, with my firm, they've probably lost $600,000 or $700,000 worth of business just because of their inflexibility!

Consultant: They can't bend to take care of your needs?

Mather: Right. They're not flexible. And part of it, of course, is due to the sales reps they have. They just blew our account. We sold Western equipment mostly until we just got disgusted with them.

Consultant: Did the situation just deteriorate over time?

Mather: Yes, it did. Finally, after a good period of time, I started getting on them. I'm kind of temperamental. I finally just made up my mind—although I didn't tell them—that in the future our policy would be to sell other equipment, too. In essence, what we've done since then is sell more Marshall Corporation and Solex equipment than we have Western.

Consultant: What bothered you about Western Engineering?

Mather: It's really a combination of things. For example, the sales rep, instead of creating a feeling that he was going to try to take care of you and work with you and be for you, was always on the opposite side of the fence. It was really strange. Western had certain items that were special quotes to help us be competitive. Well, he was always wanting to take different items off the special quote list every time there was a price change. But we needed every item we could get. This is a very competitive area.

Consultant: What other kinds of problems did he create?

Mather: He wouldn't get the paperwork done. And another example is the sign in front of the business. We bought that sign when we bought the business, and we paid Western for it. About a year later, the rep came back and said, "Western has a new policy. The sign can no longer belong to the owner, so we will return the money you paid for the sign." I said, "Now that you have operated on my money for a year, the sign doesn't belong to me?" I went along with it, but it was the idea of the thing. They tell you one thing and then do something else.

Consultant: Were there other special incidents that occurred?

Source: Personal communication.

Mather: One time, we got a job involving $30,000 or $40,000 worth of equipment. I told the rep it *appeared* that we had the job. We had a verbal contract, but the deal wasn't final. The next thing I knew, the equipment was sitting in Central Truck Lines out here. I hadn't ordered the equipment or anything. Fortunately, we did get the contract. But we weren't ready for the equipment for two more months and had no place to put it. And I ended up paying interest. It irritated me to no end.

Consultant: Was that what made you lean toward the other suppliers?

Mather: The final straw was the Park Lake project—a four-story renovation. I had designed the heating and air-conditioning system myself. I called the rep, intending to use Western equipment, and requested a price. So he called back and gave me a lump sum. There were lots of different items, and they were broken down into groups. I asked him to price the items by groups to provide various options to the purchaser. He replied, "We can't break it out." I said, "What do you mean, you can't break it out?" He said something about company policy. I really came unglued, but he never knew.

Consultant: What did you do about it?

Mather: As soon as I quit talking with him, I picked up the phone and called the Marshall Corporation rep. In just a few hours, we had prices that were broken down as I wanted them. The total price turned out to be $2,500 more, but I bought it! That was the end of Western Engineering as our sole supplier.

Questions

1. What services did Fred Mather expect from his supplier? Were these unreasonable expectations?

2. Evaluate Mather's reaction when the Western Engineering rep declined to give him a breakdown of the price. Was Mather's decision to pay $2,500 more for the other equipment a rational decision?

3. Was Western Engineering at fault in shipping the $30,000 or $40,000 worth of equipment on the basis of an oral commitment and in the absence of a purchase order? What should Mather have done about it?

4. Are the deficiencies that bother Mather actual weaknesses of Western Engineering or are they caused by the sales rep?

5. Should Mather continue to use three separate suppliers or concentrate purchases with one of them?

Franklin Motors

Selecting a Computer System

Franklin Motors, a new and used car dealer, currently uses a service bureau for limited data processing, including payroll and general ledger accounting applications. The service bureau provides either payroll checks or electronic direct deposits for Franklin's employees. At the end of the year, W-2 tax statements are provided for the employees. The software of the service bureau is programmed to produce a profit/loss statement and a balance sheet only once each quarter. All other data-processing tasks are currently done manually.

Until now, the management of Franklin Motors did not think the firm could afford the hardware, software, and personnel necessary to run an in-house computer system. Several factors have caused management to reconsider buying a computer system. First, Franklin's primary supplier has requested that the company obtain the necessary technology for placing orders and checking stock availability electronically. This will require at least one personal computer with a modem for communicating data to the manufacturer through a standard telephone line. Second, the accounting reports from the service bureau are often so late that they are useless in planning and budgeting decisions. Management feels that the timeliness and accuracy of important reports would be improved if the work were done in-house. In addition, the cost of a multi-user system has dropped so substantially that even small businesses can afford them, and the newer computer systems re-

quire fewer technically skilled employees than the older systems did.

The management of Franklin Motors asked the controller, Bob Mathis, to head a team to conduct a feasibility study and to evaluate the alternative solutions. The results of the feasibility study showed that the company had a desperate need for a new information system for management and clerical employees. Mathis's team narrowed the computer vendor choices to two firms. Each of the competing firms offered a turnkey system that included installation, training, and an 800 number for troubleshooting problems. (A turnkey computer system is supposed to be like a new car in that the user merely has to turn the key in order to use it.) One of the systems is based on a centralized minicomputer with multiple terminals. The terminals are simply input devices that rely on the central processing unit (CPU) of the minicomputer. The other vendor has configured a local area network (LAN) of personal computers. The personal computers in the network can be used either as input devices for the management information system or as stand-alone computers with their own processors. The LAN solution would allow the use of popular applications software, such as word processors and spreadsheets, and desktop publishing.

The vendor proposing the minicomputer solution can provide excellent recommendations from several companies with installations of the same system. The vendor proposing the LAN solution has had only one installation, since this alternative involves newer technology. The LAN-based system did not receive as high a recommendation as the minicomputer vendor's system. The LAN vendor explained that the system was being tested and corrected in a live environment for the first time. Many of the problems with the LAN system have been corrected and shouldn't pose a problem with the second installation. The costs of the two systems are practically the same.

Questions

1. Which alternative should Mathis recommend to management and why?
2. What problems will occur as a result of acquiring an in-house computer system, and how can these problems be avoided or managed?

Case 22

The Style Shop

A "Tough Guy" Uses Financial and Accounting Information for Decisions

A friend of mine recently said that 1996 is going to be the year of the tough guys, and that's right. It's for guys and gals who care enough to put everything they've got into what they're doing, and do their best. It's not the year for sitting around and letting everyone else do it for them. It's a good year for challenge and productivity because there is still money there, and there are still people who are ready to spend it. It's up to the tough guys, to the ones who merit being the ones with whom that money is spent!

Dorothy Barton, sitting at her desk in the small office just off the Style Shop sales floor, pondered this quotation, which had caught her eye as she leafed through the latest edition of the *Dallas Fashion Retailer*.

Women's ready-to-wear is a rough business. It had been particularly rough, however, for the Style Shop owner. Barton had seen sales fall 12.5 percent from 1994 to 1995; but, more significantly, her net profit plunged 62.5 percent over the same period. She spent untold hours on the sales floor catering to her customers, in the office appealing to manufacturers to ship the next season's orders even though current orders had not yet been paid, and at the Dallas Apparel Mart buying the fashions she hoped would fit the needs and desires of her customers. At the same time, she was spending many hours each week trying to help her husband get his infant construction business off the ground.

She remembered hearing one "expert" say, "This is not a time for pessimism, nor a time for

optimism. This is a time for realism." And, an economic forecaster had indicated that he saw a good future in the industry. Customers, he had noted, are buying a little more cautiously right now. They are still buying—just looking at things a little more carefully.

"But what is 'realism' for me?" Barton asked herself. "Am I one of the tough guys who can stick it out and be one of those 'with whom the money is spent'?"

LOCATION AND BACKGROUND

The Style Shop opened its doors on February 12, 1969, in Lufkin, Texas. In 1984, it moved to the Angelina Mall. The mall contains a major discount chain store, two full-line department stores, and a number of specialty shops. Located nearby are a twin cinema, a motel, and a junior college. The mall serves as the hub of a trade area that extends over a radius of more than 100 miles. The only shopping centers comparable to the Angelina Mall at the time were in Houston, which is 120 miles to the southwest, and Dallas, which is 166 miles to the northwest.

Barton began with the Style Shop as a part-time accountant in March 1977. She became a 50-50 partner when the new shop opened in

Source: This case was prepared by Janelle C. Ashley, Dean, School of Business, Stephen F. Austin State University.

1984 and purchased the 50 percent belonging to her partner in January 1994. She now operates the business as a sole proprietorship.

HISTORY PRIOR TO 1994

Personnel

The Style Shop employed four full-time clerks, one tailor, and a housekeeper. A former employee and Barton's teenage daughter were frequently called in for part-time work during peak seasons.

Flo Gates had been with the shop for 10 years. She worked as a clerk and floor manager and accompanied Barton to the Dallas Apparel Mart. The other three clerks had been with the Style Shop from one to three years each. Personnel turnover and apathy had been problems in the past, but Barton was quite pleased with her present work force.

Policies

The Style Shop operated with no formal, written policies. Personnel were paid wages and benefits comparable to other workers in similar capacities in Lufkin. They enjoyed a great deal of freedom in their work, flexibility in hours of work, and a 20 percent discount on all merchandise purchased in the shop.

Competition

For its size, Lufkin had an average number of retail outlets carrying ladies' ready-to-wear. Several department stores and other specialty shops carried some of the same lines the Style Shop did, but they were all comparable in price. The Style Shop did handle several exclusive lines in Lufkin, however, and enjoyed the reputation of being the most prestigious women's shop in town. Its major competition was a similar, but

Comparative Statement of Income   **Figure C22-1**

	1991	1992	1993	1994	1995
Sales revenue	$200,845.43	$213,368.15	$216,927.31	$217,969.59	$190,821.85
Cost of goods sold	132,838.30	133,527.91	131,900.84	138,427.14	121,689.74
Gross profit	$ 68,007.13	$ 79,840.24	$ 85,026.47	$ 79,542.45	$ 69,132.11
Operating expenses	60,727.46	70,051.29	67,151.58	69,969.93	65,438.20
Net income	$ 7,279.67	$ 9,788.95	$ 17,874.89	$ 9,845.52	$ 3,693.91

Comparative Balance Sheets   **Figure C22-2**

Item	1991	1992	1993	1994	1995
Current assets*	$38,524.93	$ 70,015.11	$ 66,749.78	$ 58,530.44	$ 68,458.34
Inventory	23,039.00	37,971.00	33,803.00	36,923.00	35,228.00
Fixed assets	7,314.58	86,504.94	83,924.45	80,534.06	63,943.67
TOTAL ASSETS	$45,839.51	$156,520.05	$150,674.23	$139,064.50	$132,402.01
Current debt	$35,892.81	$ 19,586.45	$ 20,161.93	$ 31,587.57	$ 55,552.70
Long-term debt	0	39,042.90	33,680.07	26,841.76	20,003.45
Total debt	$35,892.81	$ 58,629.35	$ 53,842.00	$ 58,429.33	$ 75,556.15
Equity	9,946.70	97,890.70	96,832.23	80,635.17	56,845.86
TOTAL DEBT AND EQUITY	$45,839.51	$156,520.05	$150,674.23	$139,064.50	$132,402.01

*Current-asset figures include the amounts shown for inventory.

larger, specialty shop with a fashion shoe department in neighboring Nacogdoches, 19 miles away.

Inventory Control

The Style Shop used the services of Santoro Management Consultants, Inc., of Dallas, for inventory control. Inventory management reports generated by computer were received each month, broken down into 23 departmental groupings. These reports showed beginning inventory, sales and purchases for the month and year to date, markdowns, ending inventory, and various other information. The cost of the services was $110 per month.

Financial Position

It is often quite difficult and sometimes next to impossible to evaluate the true financial position of a single proprietorship or a partnership, because of the peculiarities that are either allowed or tolerated in accounting practices for these forms of ownership. This becomes evident in looking at the Style Shop's five-year comparative income statement (Figure C22-1) and the comparative balance sheets (Figure C22-2), plus a more detailed income statement for 1995 (Figure C22-3) and the 1995 balance sheet (Figure C22-4). Key business ratios (median) for women's ready-to-wear stores are also given for comparative purposes in Table C22-1.

Two explanatory comments about these statements are necessary. First, the jump in fixed assets between 1991 and 1992 (see Figure C22-2) and the subsequent changes were due in large part to the inclusion of personal real estate on the partnership books. Second, the long-term liability initiated in 1992 was an SBA loan. Caught in a period of declining sales (due in part to the controversy over styles) and rapidly rising expenses in the new mall location, the Style Shop owners found themselves in a financial bind in late 1990 and 1991. They needed additional funds both for working capital and fixed invest-

---

Figure C22-3

*1995 Income Statement
for Year Ended
December 31, 1995*

Sales revenue		$190,821.85
Cost of goods sold:		
Beginning inventory	$ 36,923.00	
Purchases	119,994.74	
	$156,917.74	
Ending inventory	35,228.00	121,689.74
Gross profit		$ 69,132.11
Operating expenses:		
Advertising	$ 3,034.63	
Auto expense	1,509.63	
Bad debts	(439.83)	
Depreciation	1,580.49	
Freight, express, delivery	2,545.90	
Heat, light, power, and water	1,847.96	
Insurance	1,431.80	
Interest expense	4,064.25	
Legal and accounting	2,034.74	
Rent	11,220.40	
Repairs	528.98	
Salary	26,227.69	
Suppliers	5,138.11	
Tax (Payroll)	1,656.18	
Income tax	604.62	
Telephone	784.67	
Dues and subscriptions	601.89	
Travel	1,066.09	65,438.20
Net income		$ 3,693.91

Assets
Current assets:
Cash	$ 4,923.92
Accounts receivable	21,306.42
Inventory	35,228.00
Cash value of life insurance	7,000.00
Total current assets	$ 68,458.34

Fixed assets:
Furniture and fixtures	$37,749.94	
Auto and truck	9,500.00	
Real estate	20,000.00	
Boat and motor	2,000.00	
Office equipment	2,500.00	
Jewelry	2,000.00	
Gross fixed assets	$73,749.94	
Less: Allowance for depreciation	9,806.27	
Net fixed assets		$ 63,943.67
TOTAL ASSETS		$132,402.01

Debt (Liabilities) and Equity
Current debt:
Accounts payable	$ 30,413.12
Accrued payroll tax	825.64
Accrued sales tax	1,193.94
Note payable—due in one year	9,420.00
Note payable—real estate	10,700.00
Note payable—auto	3,000.00
Total current debt	$ 55,552.70
Note payable—due after one year	20,003.45
Total debt	$ 75,556.15
Equity	56,845.86
TOTAL DEBT AND EQUITY	$132,402.01

Figure C22-4

1995 Balance Sheet for December 31, 1995

Key Business Ratios for Women's Ready-to-Wear Stores

Table C22-1

Ratio	1991	1992	1993	1994	1995
Current assets ÷ Current liabilities	2.50	2.38	2.51	2.81	2.65
Net profit ÷ Net sales	2.18%	1.86%	1.81%	2.30%	2.05%
Net profit ÷ Net worth	8.73%	7.14%	6.86%	8.53%	8.92%
Net sales ÷ Total assets	3.78	3.76	3.95	3.96	3.82
Net sales ÷ Net working capital	4.49	4.90	4.73	4.92	4.61
Net sales ÷ Inventory	6.10	6.70	6.60	6.70	6.70
Net sales ÷ Fixed assets	11.50	12.00	12.50	11.00	12.00
Current liabilities ÷ Net worth	56.5%	54.5%	51.0%	49.2%	49.4%
Total liabilities ÷ Net worth	125.80	124.10	104.00	100.10	98.50
Inventory ÷ Net working capital	78.3%	71.1%	76.7%	72.3%	73.0%

Note: Average collection period was not computed. Necessary information as to the division between cash sales and credit sales was available in too few cases to obtain an average collection period that would be usable as a broad guide.

ments. Since a big jump in sales was anticipated in the new location, additional working capital was necessary to purchase the required inventory. The new tenants also desired cash to purchase fixed assets in the form of display fixtures for the new store. They obtained this money through a local bank in the form of an SBA-insured loan.

THE STYLE SHOP, 1996

"Certainly, there is no longer an arbiter of the length of a skirt or the acceptance of different styles," Barton mused. "The economic picture is looking brighter. The experts tell us there will be more disposable personal income and a lower rate of inflation. Yet this is a time for realism. Am I tough enough?"

Questions

1. Using the Style Shop's comparative financial statements for 1991–1995, evaluate the following:
   a. The firm's liquidity
   b. The firm's profitability
   c. The firm's use of debt financing
   d. The return on equity
2. Why can't you use the four-question approach to assessing a firm's financial performance exactly as suggested in this chapter? What modifications are required?
3. Should Barton keep the business or sell it? What are the primary factors to be considered in reaching such a decision?

Barton Sales and Service

Managing a Firm's Working Capital

The owners of Barton Sales and Service, based in Little Rock, Arkansas, were John and Joyce Barton. John served as general manager, and Joyce as office manager. The firm sold General Electric, Carrier, and York air-conditioning and heating systems to both commercial and residential customers and serviced these and other types of systems. Although the business had operated successfully since the Bartons purchased it in 1988, it continued to experience working-capital problems.

BARTON'S FINANCIAL STRUCTURE

The firm had been profitable since the Bartons purchased it. Profits for 1993 were the highest for any year to date. Figure C23-1 shows the income statement for Barton Sales and Service for that year.

The balance sheet as of December 31, 1993, for Barton Sales and Service is shown in Figure C23-2. Note that the firm's equity was somewhat less than its total debt. However, $10,737 of the firm's liabilities was a long-term note payable to a stockholder. This note was issued at the time the Bartons purchased the business, with payments going to the former owner.

BARTON'S CASH BALANCE

A minimum cash balance is necessary in any business because of the uneven nature of cash inflows and outflows. John explained that they need a substantial amount in order to "feel comfortable." He believed that it might be possible to reduce the present balance by $5,000 to $10,000, but he stated that it gave them some "breathing room."

BARTON'S ACCOUNTS RECEIVABLE

The trade accounts receivable at the end of 1993 were $56,753, but at some times during the year the accounts receivable were twice this amount. These accounts were not aged, so the firm had no specific knowledge of the number of overdue accounts. However, the firm had never experienced any significant loss from bad debts. The accounts receivable were thought, therefore, to be good accounts of a relatively recent nature.

Customers were given 30 days from the date of the invoice to pay the net amount. No cash discounts were offered. If payment was not received during the first 30 days, a second statement was mailed to the customer and monthly carrying charges of one-tenth of 1 percent were added. The state usury law prohibited higher carrying charges.

Figure C23-1

Barton Sales and Service
Income Statement for
the Year Ending
December 31, 1993

Sales revenue	$727,679
Cost of goods sold	466,562
Gross profit	$261,177
Selling, general & administrative expenses (including officers' salaries)	189,031
Earnings before taxes	$ 72,086
Income tax	17,546
Net income	$ 54,540

Figure C23-2

Balance Sheet for Barton
Sales and Service for
December 31, 1993

Assets	
Current assets:	
Cash	$ 28,789
Trade accounts receivable	56,753
Inventory	89,562
Prepaid expenses	4,415
Total current assets	$179,519
Loans to stockholders	41,832
Autos, trucks, and equipment, at cost, less accumulated depreciation of $36,841	24,985
Other assets:	
Goodwill	16,500
TOTAL ASSETS	$262,836
Debt (Liabilities) and Equity	
Current debt:	
Current maturities of long-term notes payable*	$ 26,403
Trade accounts payable	38,585
Accrued payroll taxes	2,173
Income tax payable	13,818
Other accrued expenses	4,001
Total current debt	$ 84,980
Long-term notes payable*	51,231
Total stockholders' equity	126,625
TOTAL DEBT AND EQUITY	$262,836

*Current and long-term portions of notes payable:

	Current	Long-Term	Total
• 10% note payable, secured by pickup, due in monthly installments of $200, including interest	$ 1,827	$ 1,367	$ 3,194
• 10% note payable, secured by equipment, due in monthly installments of $180, including interest	584	0	584
• 6% note payable, secured by inventory and equipment, due in monthly installments of $678, including interest	6,392	39,127	45,519
• 9% notes payable to stockholder	0	10,737	10,737
• 12% note payable to bank in 30 days	17,600	0	17,600
	$26,403	$51,231	$77,634

On small residential jobs, the firm tried to collect from customers when work was completed. When a service representative finished repairing an air-conditioning system, for example, he or she presented a bill to the customer and attempted to obtain payment at that time. However, this was not always possible. On major items such as unit changeouts—which often ran as high as $2,500—billing was almost always necessary.

On new construction projects, the firm sometimes received partial payments prior to completion, which helped to minimize the amount tied up in receivables.

BARTON'S INVENTORY

Inventory accounted for a substantial portion of the firm's working capital. It consisted of the various heating and air-conditioning units, parts, and supplies used in the business.

The Bartons had no guidelines or industry standards to use in evaluating their overall inventory levels. They believed that there *might* be some excessive inventory, but, in the absence of a standard, this was basically an opinion. When pressed to estimate the amount that might be eliminated by careful control, John pegged it at 15 percent.

The firm used an annual physical inventory that coincided with the end of its fiscal year. Since the inventory level was known for only one time in the year, the income statement could be prepared only on an annual basis. There was no way of knowing how much of the inventory had been used at other points and, thus, no way to calculate profits. As a result, the Bartons lacked quarterly or monthly income statements to assist them in managing the business.

Barton Sales and Service was considering changing from a physical inventory to a perpetual inventory system, which would enable John to know the inventory levels of all items at all times. An inventory total could easily be computed for use in preparing statements. Shifting to a perpetual inventory system would require the purchase of proper file equipment, but the Bartons believed that that cost was not large enough to constitute a major barrier. A greater

expense would be involved in the maintenance of the system—entering all incoming materials and all withdrawals. The Bartons estimated that this task would necessitate the work of one person on a half-time or three-fourths-time basis.

BARTON'S NOTE PAYABLE TO THE BANK

Bank borrowing was the most costly form of credit. Barton Sales and Service paid the going rate, slightly above prime, and owed $17,600 on a 90-day renewable note. Usually, some of the principal was paid when the note was renewed. The total borrowing could probably be increased if necessary. There was no obvious pressure from the bank to reduce borrowing to zero. The amount borrowed during the year typically ranged from $10,000 to $25,000.

The Bartons had never explored the limits the bank might impose on borrowing, and there was no clearly specified line of credit. When additional funds were required, Joyce simply dropped by the bank, spoke with a bank officer, and signed a note for the appropriate amount.

BARTON'S TRADE ACCOUNTS PAYABLE

A significant amount of Barton's working capital came from its trade accounts payable. Although accounts payable at the end of 1993 were $38,585, the total payable varied over time and might be double this amount at another point in the year. Barton obtained from various dealers such supplies as expansion valves, copper tubing, sheet metal, electrical wire, and electrical conduit. Some suppliers offered a discount for cash (2/10, net 30), but Joyce felt that establishing credit was more important than saving a few dollars by taking a cash discount. By giving up the cash discount, the firm obtained the use of the money for 30 days. Although the Bartons could stretch the payment dates to 45 or even 60 days before being "put on C.O.D.," they found it unpleasant to delay payment more than 45 days because suppliers would begin calling and applying pressure for payment.

Their major suppliers (Carrier, General Electric, and York) used different terms of payment. Some large products could be obtained from Carrier on an arrangement known as "floor planning," meaning that the manufacturer would ship the products without requiring immediate payment. The Bartons made payment only when the product was sold. If still unsold after 90 days, the product had to be returned or paid for. (It was shipped back on a company truck, so no expense was incurred in returning unsold items.) On items that were not floor-planned but were purchased from Carrier, Barton paid the net amount by the 10th of the month or was charged 18 percent interest on late payments.

Shipments from General Electric required payment at the bank soon after receipt of the products. If cash was not available at the time, further borrowing from the bank became necessary.

Purchases from York required net payment without discount within 30 days. However, if payment was not made within 30 days, interest at 18 percent per annum was added.

CAN GOOD PROFITS BECOME BETTER?

Although Barton Sales and Service had earned a *good* profit in 1993, the Bartons wondered whether they were realizing the *greatest possible* profit. Slowness in the construction industry was affecting their business somewhat. They wanted to be sure they were meeting the challenging times as prudently as possible.

Questions

1. Evaluate the overall performance and financial structure of Barton Sales and Service.
2. What are the strengths and weaknesses in this firm's management of accounts receivable and inventory?
3. Should the firm reduce or expand its bank borrowing?
4. Evaluate Barton's management of trade accounts payable.
5. Calculate Barton's cash conversion period. Interpret your computation.
6. How can Barton Sales and Service improve its working-capital situation?

Fox Manufacturing

Responding to Disaster

The end of the workday on May 12, 1990, was like any other—or so Dale Fox thought when he closed up shop for the night. But 12 hours later, an electrical fire had destroyed Fox Manufacturing Inc.'s only plant, in Albuquerque, New Mexico. The damage exceeded $1.5 million.

"It was the largest fire New Mexico had seen in years. About 37 fire trucks were at the scene trying to put out the fire. We made local and national news," recalls Fox, president of the family-owned manufacturer and retailer of southwestern-style and contemporary furniture. The fire was especially devastating since all orders from the company's three showrooms were sent to the plant. Normally, the furniture was built and delivered 10 to 12 weeks later.

Such a disaster could force many companies out of business. But just eight weeks after the fire, the first piece of furniture rolled off the Fox assembly line in a brand new plant in a new building. The company even managed to increase sales that year. And now, just three years later, the company has emerged stronger than ever. Annual sales average between $3.5 million and $5 million.

How did Fox Manufacturing manage literally to rise from the ashes? It forged an aggressive recovery plan that focused not only on rebuilding the business, but also on using the untapped skills of employees and an intensive

Source: Don Nichols, "Back in Business," *Small Business Report*, Vol. 18, No. 3 (March 1993), pp. 55–60. Adapted by permission of publisher, from *Small Business Report*, March/1993 © 1993. American Management Association, New York. All rights reserved.

customer relations campaign. Indeed, with more than $1 million in unfilled orders at the time of the fire, Fox offered extra services to retain its customer base. Dale Fox also took advantage of his close relationships with his financial and legal experts to help manage the thicket of legal and insurance problems that arose after the fire.

RISING FROM THE ASHES

Recovering from this disaster, and getting the company up and running again, was a particularly grueling experience for Fox and his employees. Having to complete the monumental task in just eight weeks added to the pressure. "We had no choice," says Fox. "Because we had more than $1 million in orders, we had to get back in production quickly so we wouldn't lose that business."

Fox found himself working up to 20 hours a day, seven days a week. One of his first tasks was finding a new building to house his manufacturing facility. Remodeling the old site—and the requisite tasks of clearing debris, rebuilding, and settling claims with the insurance company—would take too long and hold up the production of new furniture. At the same time, however, he had to quickly replace all the manufacturing equipment lost in the fire. He decided to hit the road, attending auctions and other sales across the country in search of manufacturing equipment, including sanders, glue machines, molding machines, and table saws. Unfortunately, all the company's hand-drawn furniture designs and cushion patterns also perished in the fire and had to be redrawn because no backup copies existed.

TAPPING EMPLOYEE TALENT

Although Fox initially laid off most of his hourly workers, he put the company's 15 supervisors to work building new work tables that would be needed once manufacturing resumed. They did the work at an empty facility loaned to Fox by a friend. At the same time, the company's drafts-men—working in a rented garage—started re-drawing the furniture designs, this time using a computer. (It took nearly a year to redraw all the designs lost in the fire.) To check frame configu-rations and measurements, they had to tear apart showroom furniture. A handful of hourly employees also started tearing apart cushions to redraw the patterns.

When Fox found the new building—the for-mer home of a beer distributor—two weeks after the fire, he started rehiring the 65-plus hourly employees to help with the remodeling. Fox knew what construction skill—carpentry, plumb-ing, metalworking, or painting—each had to of-fer because the day he laid them off he had them fill out a form listing such skills. "If I had gone through the process of having contractors bid on the work, we never would have reopened as fast as we did. Plus, our employees needed the work to feed their families," says Fox.

Within five weeks of the fire, Fox had re-hired most employees. The employees, who were paid the same hourly rate they earned be-fore the fire, proved to be competent and coop-erative. Like Fox, they often worked up to 20 hours a day because they were aware of their boss's ambitious timetable for reopening.

STAYING IN CLOSE CONTACT WITH CUSTOMERS

Fox's salespeople started calling customers the day of the fire to explain what had happened and assure them that the company planned to bounce back quickly. Just days later, Fox's two sons called the same customers to reinforce that message and let them know that the Fox fam-ily appreciated their patience. In subsequent weeks, customers received three or four more calls or letters that updated them on the com-pany's progress. Fox even rented billboard space in Albuquerque to advertise that the company planned to be manufacturing furniture again soon.

"If we hadn't kept in such close contact with our customers, we probably would have lost 50 percent of the orders," Fox says. But Fox's strat-egy paid off handsomely; the company lost less than 3 percent of its pre-fire orders. That's an amazingly low percentage, especially since some customers had to wait up to 36 weeks for deliv-ery, instead of the usual 10 to 12 weeks.

Customers had good reason to be patient: When they placed their orders, they were re-quired to pay a 25 percent to 33 percent deposit. After the fire, as a goodwill gesture, the com-pany agreed to pay them 1 percent per month on the deposited money until their orders were filled. To calculate his customers' interest, Fox started from the order date, not the fire date. And rather than simply deduct the interest from the final amount due, Fox wrote each customer a check, so they could see exactly how much money they had earned.

Because Fox also kept his suppliers in-formed, most of them continued filling the com-pany's orders after the fire and told Fox not to worry about paying until his operation was in full swing again. "Factors were the only people we had any problem with," says Fox. "Once they found out about the fire, they wanted money that wasn't even due yet."

RELYING HEAVILY ON PROFESSIONAL EXPERTISE

During a normal year, Fox pays his CPA and lawyer to handle such tasks as tax planning and consulting on leases, insurance, and operations. Together, their bills run about $25,000 to $30,000. The year of the fire, however, Fox Man-ufacturing's accounting bill topped $50,000; the legal bill was over $75,000. As far as Fox is con-cerned, it was money well spent: "Without their help, I couldn't have gotten back in business as quickly as I did."

Fox called his CPA and his lawyer as soon as he got news of the Saturday-morning fire. While the firemen battled the blaze, the three met with key management employees to develop a come-back plan. During subsequent weeks, his accountant and lawyer assumed so much responsibility for valuing lost assets and haggling with the insurance company that Fox felt comfortable leaving the city to travel around the country buying manufacturing equipment.

One early decision was to apply for a $1 million loan to buy the new building. The CPA put together all the paperwork necessary for the bank to approve it—such as a financial analysis, a cash flow statement, and profit projections. He also played a key role in helping Fox's in-house accountant determine the value of the inventory, machinery, and work in progress destroyed in the fire, which totaled about $800,000.

His involvement lent credibility to the numbers that were generated and quelled any concerns or doubts that the insurance companies had. "It was very important to have an outside CPA firm verify the numbers. If we had tried to just throw some numbers together ourselves, we could have been in over our heads in arguments with insurance companies," Fox says.

Even so, settling insurance claims was difficult, and that's where Fox's lawyer earned his money. For example, what the insurance company thought it would cost to replace the old plant was less than half of what Fox claimed. One figure over which they disagreed was the cost of replacing the electrical wiring. The insurance company estimated that it would cost $30,000; Fox and his lawyer insisted it would cost $120,000. The lawyer had a local electrician familiar with the Fox plant verify that Fox's estimate was accurate. The insurance company finally settled the claim at Fox's value.

"Dealing with the insurance company was a constant battle. There are a lot of things they won't tell you unless you bring it up," Fox warns. Indeed, it was his lawyer, not the insurance company, who pointed out that Fox was entitled to $25,000 for the cost of cleaning away debris and $2,000 to replace shrubbery that was destroyed.

And, even after they settled the claim on Fox's business-interruption insurance, it took much longer than expected to get the final $750,000 payment. Fox finally had to call his insurance company with an ultimatum: "If I didn't get the check, I told them my lawyer and I were going to Santa Fe the next day to a file a formal complaint with the insurance commissioner. I got the check."

Painfully aware that another disaster could strike at any time, Fox now takes risk management to a justified extreme. He doesn't leave anything to chance and takes numerous safety precautions that will make it easier for the company to rebound should it be dealt a similar setback again. What happened to Fox Manufacturing can happen to any company—other companies would do well to follow Dale Fox's lead.

Question

What are some basic disaster precautions that Fox could have taken to minimize the chances of the loss incurred and the consequences of the disaster?

The Martin Company

Ethical Issues in Family Business Relationships

In 1951, John and Sally Martin founded AFCO, a wholesaling firm in the construction industry. The firm grew beyond expectations, and, by 1969, sales exceeded $25 million. As a result, the Martin family prospered financially.

Beginning in 1961, the Martins's children started working for AFCO. The two oldest sons, David and Jess, along with their sister's husband, Jackson Faulkner, eventually assumed key managerial roles within the firm. The other children worked for the firm in operations and/or were beneficiaries of the firm's success through dividends on their stock. John Martin came to visualize the firm as a family effort that would benefit the family for generations to come.

In 1969, John Martin and Jackson Faulkner were killed in an airplane crash while flying in the company plane on business. The issue of firm leadership had to be resolved quickly for the sake of the firm's future. David and Jess, both in their late forties, were the obvious candidates. AFCO's board of directors, which included both family members and outsiders, eventually chose David, the older of the two sons, to be the firm's president.

Over time, conflicts and disagreements between David and Jess became increasingly frequent. Jess, who was the firm's vice-president for sales, considered David to be uninformed about the firm's customers. And, whenever he approached David about a problem within the company, Jess felt that he was treated as the bearer of bad news. David, on the other hand, perceived Jess to be undermining his authority

as president. At one point, David confronted Jess regarding actions that David considered to be no less than insubordination. He advised Jess that repeating such actions would result in his dismissal, even though they were brothers. When a similar event occurred sometime later, David met with the board and indicated that he planned to fire Jess. The board concurred, and Jess was subsequently terminated from the firm.

Jess was angered and hurt by David's decision, and he immediately appealed to other family members, especially their mother, to help settle the differences. Even though their mother agreed with Jess, efforts at reconciliation were unsuccessful.

In 1984, after about a year of bickering, David approached Jess and offered to buy his shares in the company for $1 per share. Jess rejected the offer but said he would sell at $1.75 per share—approximately $800,000 in total. David borrowed the money and bought Jess's shares.

At this time, David was expanding the company's operations through acquisitions of other firms. In 1988, at the peak of "merger mania," when financial groups were using heavy debt financing to buy companies, David was offered $20 per share for the firm. By this time, a large portion of the shares were held by employees in the form of an employee stock ownership plan.

Source: Personal communication.

In a stockholders' meeting, a decision was made to sell the company because the price offered was too attractive to refuse.

When Jess learned about the sale, he was furious. Not only had David fired him, but he had now sold the shares that Jess had originally inherited for more than ten times what Jess had received. Jess felt he had been robbed of his heritage by his own brother, who first took away his rightful place within the firm and now was making huge profits off "his" shares.

The conflict still has not been resolved. David does not think he has done anything wrong, either legally or ethically. Jess, however, continues to believe that he has been treated unfairly by a brother who placed his own personal welfare above that of the family. Meetings with independent mediators and counselors have yielded nothing in the way of reconciliation. Jess intends to continue pursuing the issue in every way possible, but David has decided that nothing can be gained from further discussion.

Questions

1. Did David act professionally and ethically in firing Jess?
2. Was the purchase of shares from Jess at $1.75 each a fair deal?
3. Is Jess's complaint that he was robbed valid?
4. Evaluate the founders' record in building and managing the firm in the light of later developments.
5. Can you suggest a solution to the animosity and conflict that has developed in this family?

Diaper Dan

Environmental Regulations Create Demand

As career switches go, few have been as bold as Daniel Gold's. Two years ago, as a Manhattan lawyer, Gold was operating in the high-octane arena of corporate takeovers. His days were filled with proxy contests, greenmail strategies, and junk-bond machinations. But like a refugee from *The Bonfire of the Vanities,* he abandoned his Fifth Avenue law office for an earthier field of play. Now Gold is better known as Diaper Dan.

It happened that Gold was looking to get out of law and start a business of his own. If he needed a push, the collapse of the junk-bond market provided one. In seven-and-a-half years of legal work, he had reviewed thousands of prospectuses, and he had a few ideas about what businesses he might want to try. He had a couple of false starts. In April 1989, Gold started his first business, Vision Capital Associates, Inc., a venture capital consulting firm that still exists but has no active clients. That summer he opened a West Hampton, New York, restaurant called Crabby Dan's, but after one week of operation he closed it because he was unable to secure a permit.

Restless and anxious for a big hit, Gold continued to cast about for business opportunities. The idea that most fascinated him was hatched as he roamed malls and department stores. "There were baby carriages everywhere," he says. "I figured there was a birth boom under way, and I thought there might be something in the baby market."

In his orderly, lawyerly way, Gold went to a library and did some research. The country was,

indeed, in the midst of a baby boom. Births had risen steadily from 3.7 million in 1986 to 3.9 million in 1988. By 1989, when Gold began his research, they were topping 4 million and fast approaching the magnitude of the postwar explosion's peak years.

What particularly intrigued Gold, however, was that most of the media coverage also mentioned diapers. Some 17.1 billion paper and plastic diapers are sold each year in the United States, Gold learned, and they end up in the trash. More than 1 billion tons of wood pulp and 70 tons of plastic are used annually to make a product that lasts a few hours. With the average disposable-diapered tyke going through some 8,000 diapers before being toilet trained, each contributes nearly 2 tons of refuse to the country's overburdened landfills. The disposable diapers make up only about 2 percent of municipal solid waste, but they have come to symbolize a throwaway society run amok. Cotton diapers, on the other hand, are the original curbside recyclables. And, given the solid-waste space shortage, the debate has reached such a pitch that a number of state legislatures are on the verge of taxing disposable diapers or banning them outright. If there was a market begging to be served, Gold's research showed, this was it.

Since their introduction in the mid-1960s, disposable diapers had captured 85 to 90 per-

Source: Jay Finegan, "Diaper Dan," *Inc.,* Vol. 13, No. 3 (March 1991), pp. 80–89. Reprinted with permission, *Inc.* magazine (March 1991). Copyright 1991 by Goldhirsh Group, Inc., 38 Commercial Wharf, Boston, MA 02110.

cent of the market. They had become a $3.5 billion industry for Procter & Gamble (Pampers and Luvs), Kimberly-Clark (Huggies), and Weyerhaeuser (private labels), and they had driven countless diaper-delivery services out of business. Only about 200 delivery services remained at the time of Gold's research, mostly mom-and-pop outfits with a handful of trucks.

But, as environmentally concerned new parents began turning to cloth diapers, the surviving services were swamped with demand. The landfill brouhaha had a big hand in the revival, and so did new technology. Cloth diapering was easier than ever—Velcro tabs on the covers had replaced safety pins—and new deodorants minimized diaper-pail odor. Moreover, Gold notes, there was a return to basics among upscale mothers over 30 having their first child—they had a sense that it was stylish and more healthful for the baby to wear natural fibers. Diaper services had always been cheaper than disposables, about $10 to $14 a week for the service versus $15 to $20 for disposables. But now it was a matter of choice, not economics.

Right from the start, Gold knew he wouldn't be content with just running a few diaper vans around the capital area. His background suggested something more ambitious. He had completed college in just two years. At California Western School of Law in San Diego, he had served as editor of the *California Western International Law Journal* and won awards in national moot-court competition. He had gone on to pick up an M.B.A. and was already at work on a master's degree in taxation. "A headhunter told me to quit going to school," Gold says with a laugh. "He said my parents were already proud of me."

Gold had spoken to several venture capitalists about investing in the company, but no one took him seriously. "You're a lawyer, Dan," one said, shrugging. "What do you know about the diaper business?" Convinced that startups spend too much time and money trying to raise financing, Gold simply obtained a $50,000 bank loan on his personal guarantee and added $25,000 of his own cash.

With a total capitalization of $75,000, Gold was hardly able to invest the kind of money required for high-volume laundry equipment. He decided to do something unusual in the industry—farm out the dirty diapers to an outside party. After exploring his options, he settled on

Virginia Linen Service, part of a company that has 13 operations in six eastern states and the District of Columbia. Virginia Linen Service, rigged with a state-of-the-art, continuous-batch tunnel washing-and-drying system, was a 10-minute drive from Diaper Dan's own location, in suburban Maryland. In addition, the service had some experience laundering diapers, having done it for years before the advent of disposables.

In March 1990, Gold locked up a three-year contract with Virginia Linen to handle his and only his diapers within a 50-mile radius of the Washington Monument. There was only one catch: "It's an exclusive provided he builds the volume that makes it worth our while," said Virginia Linen's owner and chief executive, Donald Struminger. "If he doesn't build that volume, then he will not have an exclusive contract. He has not yet reached the point where we'd be satisfied to continue, but he is moving along on the projection curve that we set when we made the agreement."

Finally, Gold planned to introduce a name-brand Diaper Dan's diaper for retail sale. Most cloth diapers sold in the United States are manufactured domestically by Dundee Mills and Gerber Childrenswear. Cotton diapers are also produced in India, Pakistan, Peru, and Venezuela. But Gold was convinced that the best, the most absorbent, and the cheapest diapers came from China. Chinese cotton products exported to the United States are restricted by U.S. textile quotas, but Gold already had contacted a U.S. agent about securing for him a reliable supply of Chinese diapers.

With his plan complete, Gold got down to work, analyzing other diaper services in the Washington area and listing customers' complaints. Foremost was a health matter: People seemed concerned about getting back strangers' diapers. Gold resolved that concern by hanging a net in each client's diaper pail. His delivery person simply yanks out the net, fastens it with a giant safety pin (engraved with the customer's account number), and tosses it in the van. The diapers are washed right in the net and returned clean and folded to the same family. Another complaint was that women were mistrustful of male delivery people; Gold solved that one by planning to employ as many female drivers as possible.

Gold and partner Dana Goldman set up operations in a 3,000-square-foot warehouse in an industrial park just off the Capital Beltway—for a mere $250-a-month rent—and they were soon ready to roll. They had thousands of Chinese diapers, a driver, and a 12-foot van that had been carefully customized to segregate dirty diapers from clean ones and from the ancillary products. The truck is decorated with a Dapper Dan–style logo—a baby sporting a top hat and a cane, like an infant Fred Astaire.

Gold set conservative projections. He forecast 400 customers by the end of his first year, with an average of 600 in the second and 1,000 in the third year. If those numbers held true and if the add-on products sold as well as he expected, revenue would rise from $442,500 the first year to $1.7 million in the third, with before-tax income climbing from $35,125 to $362,037.

Questions

1. Which laws described in Chapter 26 of this book may be applicable to this business venture?

2. Is Gold's exclusive agreement with the laundry service wise? Why or why not?

3. What trademarks, patents, or copyrights may be involved in this business?

4. What types of taxes do you expect Gold's business will have to pay? Be specific.

Sample Business Plan

Ph. 409-383-0000

**SiBôn
Beverage Corporation**
P.O. Box 1927
202 Simmons Way
Jasper, Texas 75951-1927
1-800-755-0000

Fax: 409-383-0000

EXECUTIVE SUMMARY

The "New Age" beverage market is the result of a spectacular boom in demand for drinks that have nutritional value, are made from environmentally safe ingredients, and use water that comes from deep, clear, clean springs free of chemicals and pollutants. SiBôn Beverage Corporation ("SiBôn") will produce and market a full line of sparkling fruit drinks, flavored waters, and sports drinks of the highest quality and purity. These drinks have taste appeal similar to that of soft drinks, while using the most healthful fruit juices, natural sugars, and the purest spring water—the hallmark of the New Age drink market.

New Age beverages are relatively new in the $28 billion soft drink market, growing in sales from $117 million (wholesale) in 1985 to over $1 billion in 1993. The industry has grown tenfold in sales in less than two years, and demand has simply outpaced supply. The product is distinguished by rich natural fruit concentrates, spring waters, and all natural ingredients. A New Age drink is defined as a beverage that is perceived by consumers as (1) healthy, allowing consumers to feel good about themselves, and (2) a natural product, free of artificial ingredients, preservatives, and flavors.

SiBôn projects gross sales and earnings as follows:

	1994	*1995*	*1996*
Gross sales	$1,446,731	$5,082,302	$8,095,825
Pre-tax income	($ 169,719)	$ 307,146	$1,261,782

SiBôn proposes to finance its building and land, located in the Jasper Industrial Park, with an acceptable Jasper Bank, using a financial guarantee from the Jasper Economic Development Corporation (JEDC). The following business plan details SiBôn's projected operations to support JEDC's guarantee.

BUSINESS PLAN

History

In 1985, David Rault, president of U.S. Aquarius, Inc., purchased 110 acres of land in Stewartstown, New Hampshire with the intent of building a plant to produce bottled pure spring water and sparkling fruit juice drinks.

For several years, Mr. Rault and his wife, Mary Jo, consulted geologists and hydrologists to determine the best way to secure a long-term supply of the purest spring water. In addition, the Raults spent time and money developing formulas for plain and sparkling water fruit drinks and an isotonic sports drink. They subsequently applied for and were issued a trademark for each of their products.

In 1989, Mr. Rault placed a purchase option on a defunct Coca-Cola bottling plant in Bunkie, Louisiana. The purchase of the 30,000-square-foot plant and equipment gave rise to considerable obstacles. First, the equipment proved not to be satisfactory and was sold off to pay part of the debt incurred acquiring the property. In 1990, Mr. Rault and an investor attempted to finance the plant with a $2,000,000 loan. After 18 months of negotiation and over $125,000 in fees spent in an unsuccessful attempt to obtain the loan, the development was put on hold until proper financing could be arranged.

In 1993, Mr. Rault met with Kenneth R. Barnett of the Cypress Investment Group to determine if funding for the Company could be completed. After months of research and visits and discussions with people in the industry, the Cypress Investment Group made a commitment to raise the necessary funds to capitalize the Company and begin operations.

In February 1994, Mr. Barnett introduced a proposal to Robert J. Caskey of Jasper, Texas to relocate the Company to Jasper, and, in April 1994, SiBôn Beverage Corporation was authorized by the state of Texas to begin operations.

Product Description

The product line will consist of

1. Aquaria, which is pure spring water from Buck Springs in Jasper, Texas.
2. SiBon, which is a carbonated natural fruit drink in four flavors, using pure fruit concentrates (not flavoring) and pure spring water. Since the carbonation is lighter than that of most sweetened competitors, SiBon uses less sweetener and has approximately 50 percent of the calories of a typical soft drink (68 calories per 12-ounce bottle). The Nutrasweet drink has only 2 calories per bottle.
3. Zingo, which is a lightly carbonated, fruit-flavored drink that tempts the palate by presenting a new taste in four flavors. Zingo will be as clear and pure as spring water.
4. Peppy-K, which is an isotonic sports drink bottled in four flavors with a new energy formula composed of a finely tuned balance of fruit juice flavors, vitamins and minerals, and electrolytes and carbohydrates. SiBôn is in negotiations with the inventor of the formula to license the Company with the exclusive worldwide right to market the formula in the beverage industry.

Aquaria and Peppy-K, packaged in plastic bottles to prevent breakage, will be targeted toward active people. SiBon and Zingo will be sold in glass bottles to prolong carbonation and retain flavor. Beverages in plastic bottles lose carbonation more quickly and tend to absorb the taste of the plastic. If market changes require a change in the containers, making the adaptation will simply be a matter of printing new labels—no changes will be required in the production equipment. If there is demand for flavors other than the present projected flavors, again making the adaptation will simply be a matter of changing the fruit concentrates and printing new labels.

The spring water used in production will come from Buck Springs in Jasper, Texas. These natural flowing springs have the purest water quality and were the prime reason for locating the plant in Jasper.

Quality control is of paramount concern to the Company in all aspects of its business, but particularly in regard to the springs. The water will be tested daily at the springs, tested a second time when it is received at the bottling facility, and tested a final time as a finished product after bottling.

The Company has two reliable sources for fruit concentrate. Both firms have a long history of dependably providing quality fruit concentrates to the beverage industry. One of the firms has provided assistance to the Company in developing formulas and samples for testing for over three years.

Formulas and Trademarks

David Rault originated the formulas for Aquaria, SiBon, and Peppy-K, with the exception of the special energy-boosting formula for Peppy-K. He and his wife, Mary Jo, officially registered the labels as trademarks and have transferred all formulas and trademarks to SıBôn Beverage Corporation.

Market Analysis

John C. Maxwell, Jr., *Beverage Industry* analyst, defines New Age beverages as nonalcoholic drinks containing natural ingredients without preservatives that are perceived by consumers as healthy alternatives to traditional soft drinks. Included are natural sodas, sparkling juices, and still or sparkling beverage waters that are either unflavored or flavored with juices or essences. According to Maxwell, "the New Age category is expected to grow in excess of 10 percent in volume in 1995 and should capture about 2 percent of the soft drink market." The premium-priced New Age market is expected to produce $1 billion in wholesale dollar sales in 1995, up from $117 million in 1985.

The Bottled Water Market report, a consumer survey of bottled water–purchasing behavior from Business Trend Analysts, Inc., indicates that health concerns and taste are the most important reasons for purchasing still and sparkling bottled water. Today's consumer is better educated and receives more information about his or her health than consumers at any other time in U.S. history. Consumers are demanding better products, packaging, and delivery systems to enhance their modern life-style.

Business Trend Analysts projects that bottled water production in the United States will increase annually by 9.6 percent between 1991 and 2001. SıBôn is prepared to participate in this unprecedented expected growth of the New Age beverage market for the balance of this decade.

Market Definition

The Texas and Louisiana regional market for New Age beverages offers an unusual opportunity to produce and distribute a high-quality, fresh-tasting, sparkling fruit juice drink. Studies and reports by Beverage Marketing, the industry standard marketing research firm, and by *Beverage Industry* and *Beverage World,* the leading industry magazines, show high anticipated growth in the southeastern and southwestern United States for the balance of this decade for New Age beverages.

New Age beverages are sold in most retail outlets where soft drinks are sold—supermarkets, vending machines, convenience stores/gas marts/mom-and-pop operations, warehouse clubs, and restaurants.

Consumption of soft drinks, beer, wine, and liquor has consistently declined for the past eight years, according to all industry authorities. At the same time, the New Age category has been the fastest growing of any beverage category, including bottled water, averaging over 40 percent annual growth since 1985. Most of the major players in beverages, particularly liquor producers, have tried to make inroads into this market, without much success. The reason is simply that consumers perceive liquor as they do colas—high in sodium, high in calories, and not as thirst quenching as New Age products.

Distribution

New Age products are distributed through food brokers, beverage distributors, or directly by the manufacturer. Getting a new product on supermarket shelves requires a manufacturer or its representative to pay slotting fees to reserve shelf space. In addition, expensive media campaigns are required, especially if a product is to be distributed on a national basis. However, grocery and supermarket sales represent only 20 percent of the market.

SiBôn will distribute the majority of its products through beverage and food distributors, which will have an exclusive marketing area in which to represent the Company. For the past two years, Mr. Rault and Lloyd L. Simmons have been meeting with many distributors' representatives who are willing to sign an exclusive distribution agreement with the Company when it is ready to deliver the final product.

The Company has hired four regional district managers, located in Texas, Oklahoma, Louisiana, and Mississippi, who will begin taking distributor applications on September 1, 1996. SiBôn has already received a letter of intent from two distributors that would require 17,500 cases per month of initial distribution. The projected break-even point is 18,600 cases per month. The following bottlers and distributors have expressed interest in distributing the Company's products as soon as possible:

Buck Springs	10,000 to 20,000 cases/month
Shreveport Beverage Distributors	7,500 cases/month

All American Bottling Corporation has 16 Royal Crown Cola bottling plants. This major bottler is seeking a fruit drink that will increase its profits. A list of its distribution centers follows.

States	Number of Sales Centers	Percentage of Area Covered
Alabama	2	12%
Georgia	1	4
Illinois	3	10
Indiana	2	20
Kentucky	3	50
Minnesota	3	65
Mississippi	5	70
North Dakota	2	70

States	Number of Sales Centers	Percentage of Area Covered
Ohio	2	10
Oklahoma	1	18
South Dakota	2	65
Tennessee	5	65
Virginia	2	20
Washington, D.C.	2	100
West Virginia	3	30
Wisconsin	4	65

Areas in which All American has less than 50 percent coverage require additional distributors to deliver to areas and stores not served.

Additional direct-deliver distributors that have expressed interest in distributing Company products are

Tulsa 7-Up, northeast Oklahoma
Little Dixie Distributing, southeast Oklahoma
Lawton 7-Up, southwest Oklahoma
Pope Distributing, northwest Oklahoma
Clark Bottling/Distributing, central Mississippi, Louisiana, and western Kentucky

Food brokers that are interested in distributing Company products are

W. J. Jones, Oklahoma and the Texas panhandle
Acosta Sales, Alabama
Tennessee Valley Marketing, eastern Tennessee
J. A. Richardson, North Carolina and South Carolina

Competition

As with any consumer-oriented product, competition for sales requires dedicated focus and resources. The New Age beverage market is a highly competitive arena with premium-priced products. The competition is taken very seriously by all New Age beverage producers. The following competitive issues have been given careful consideration by the management of SIBÔN:

- *Capital resources.* A well-capitalized company can weather market aberrations, miscalculations, and new competitive products in the marketplace. Major companies such as Coca-Cola, Pepsi, and Perrier are well positioned to participate in this market.
- *Technological advances.* New high-speed computerized bottling equipment has allowed bottlers to cut costs. New processing equipment has introduced innovative products to the market.
- *Distribution methods.* The largest producer of New Age beverages, Clearly Canadian, does not have any production facilities in the United States; all product sold in the United States is contract bottled. In management's opinion, problems and delays in filling orders result when the contract bottler is busy bottling its own product. When a company experiences extended delays in getting the product on the shelf for sale, market share is quickly eroded.
- *Marketing strategy.* Major competitors spend 8 to 9 percent of sales on advertising and marketing, trying to capture a larger share of this $1 billion market.

The Company's initial strategy is to offer distributors what they want most—more profit per case sold (see SiBôn's marketing strategy).

- *Consumer acceptability.* A majority of consumers will purchase a new product because of the appeal of the label or a special advertising offer or coupon. It is extremely important to establish and maintain consumer confidence in the product. This is accomplished through eye-catching labels, bottles, and point-of-sale advertising (see SiBôn's marketing strategy).

Marketing Strategy

SiBôn's marketing strategy is to produce a superior spring water, sparkling fruit juice, and isotonic sports drink made with the purest spring water and the highest-quality fruit concentrates available. By providing distributors, wholesalers, and retailers with more profit per case sold and more service and support than they might expect, the Company will establish a strong regional distributor network by laying a foundation for national distribution.

Comprehensive Plan

The overall marketing plan for SiBôn's products is based on the following objectives:

1. Establish a financially strong, regional New Age beverage company by providing initial capital funding for the Company through private investor contributions
2. Work with the city and county of Jasper and the state of Texas to establish more jobs, an enhanced economic development, and a better community in which to work and play
3. Produce unique-tasting pure spring water and fruit concentrate products to meet today's health-conscious consumers' demands for a better alternative to colas
4. Create an exclusive distributor network that will participate in a greater share of the profits from retail sales and will therefore help the Company grow faster
5. Capture 1 percent of the regional market share in less than three years (estimated to be $7,600,000 in the third year)

Product Strategy

The product strategy for the Company is to establish a wholesale distribution channel for SiBôn's products through beverage brokers and independent distributors servicing regional chain stores, convenience stores, grocers, health food stores, restaurants, institutional food service contractors, and other retailers operating in the southwestern and southeastern United States.

The Company will issue exclusive distributor agreements to qualified distributors to represent SiBôn's products in a specific area. These distributors will be required to promote the products through local advertising, shelf locations in grocery stores and supermarkets, and point-of-sale advertisements in the form of display racks at the ends of aisles and cracker barrels filled with Company products.

Initially, there are no plans to advertise the products on billboards or through any other media such as television, radio, or newspaper. All advertising will be dedicated to assisting the exclusive distributor network in establishing product identification through point-of-sale displays, coupons, and in-store marketing samplers. Special promotions will be mainly by coupons and product sampling.

The formulas for Aquaria, SiBon, and Zingo are complete. Labels for the products are in the final design stage and have been approved by the Louisiana FDA. The way a product initially looks and feels is very important in appealing to consumers. Professional designers will assure the right product identity on an ongoing basis.

Public Relations

No public relations promotions are anticipated initially. All efforts of management will be dedicated to providing support to distributors and the retailers selling the Company's products.

Strategy Review

A review of the corporate marketing strategy will be undertaken on a monthly basis and a report presented to the Board of Directors.

Pricing and Profitability

The prices for the Company's products will be determined first and foremost by competitive pricing of similar products in our marketing area. The Company will depend on its management and the distributor network to determine fair pricing.

It is projected that the net profit per case will be minimal for the first two years while the Company pays back the line of credit (see Financial Projections).

Margin Structure

The margin of profit per case is different for each of SiBôn's products.

	Aquaria	*SiBon*	*Peppy-K*	*Zingo*
Retail price	$16.56	$15.72	$15.36	$14.10
Wholesale price	12.42	11.79	11.52	10.58
Distributor price	10.42	9.79	9.52	8.58
Manufacturing cost	5.30	4.91	7.28	6.28
Gross margin	5.12	4.88	2.24	2.30

The retail margin will average 23 percent, or $3.25 per case; the distributor margin will average 18 percent, or $2.00 per case.

Costs

The estimated cost of manufacturing all Company products will be consistent. The cost of each product includes spring water, fruit flavor or concentrate, carbonation, Nutrasweet or high-fructose corn syrup, preservative, bottles, caps, and labels. Other expenses include labor, plant and equipment, general and administrative costs, bank-debt payback, and corporate overhead.

Some factors that may affect costs include the following (also see Financial Projections):

- Changes in product formulation
- A change in containers
- Freight rates for hauling spring water or delivering the product

Location

The plant site is located on five acres in the Jasper Industrial Park, at the intersection of Highway 190 and Highway 63 in the city of Jasper, Texas. It is approximately 140 miles northeast of Houston and 230 miles southeast of Dallas. Jasper's population is approaching 8,000 residents, the majority of whom are employed in the timber industry. The city and the county have a substantial semi-skilled labor force available for employment.

Facilities

SiBôn's plant will consist of three buildings:

1. *Warehouse and production.* A metal building that will contain 6,000 square feet of production area and 24,000 square feet of warehouse space
2. *Office.* A building containing 4,000 square feet of space that will house the corporate headquarters of SiBôn
3. *Bunkhouse.* A 750-square-foot, two-room hotel in which truck drivers can stay overnight or catch a nap while their trucks are being loaded

Logistics

The plant site will be serviced mainly by trucks. Receipt of raw materials and delivery of Company products will be by truck on the main highways connecting Jasper with other major cities. Rail siding is not available or required.

Production and Manufacturing

The processing of Aquaria, SiBon, Zingo, and Peppy-K simply requires the right bottling, labeling, and packaging equipment. Raw materials necessary for production are pure spring water, natural fruit flavors and concentrates, high-fructose corn syrup or Nutrasweet, carbonation, and preservatives. Additionally, bottles, caps, and labels are required.

An agreement has been reached with Buck Springs in Jasper, Texas to supply pure spring water at an agreed contract price in 6,000-gallon tanker loads. An additional water supply is readily available in the surrounding Jasper area.

The fruit concentrates and flavorings will be supplied by Flavoring, A.B. of Sweden. Through its U.S. representative, David Packard, Flavoring, A.B. assisted Mr. Rault by providing samples for comparative testing of potential formulas for Company products. The Company will have a second supplier available to provide the concentrates and flavorings should they not be available from Flavoring, A.B.

EQUIPMENT Production equipment will include a completely automated bottling line capable of filling 400 bottles per minute, or approximately 250,000 cases per month, with an eight-hour shift. On the bottling line, pallets of bottles will be unpacked; bottles will then be washed, filled, labeled, capped, and packed in cartons and cases for shipping.

TECHNICAL SPECIFICATIONS   All piping must be stainless steel, and all electrical wiring must be three phase. There are no hazardous materials in the manufacturing process. The plant meets all federal requirements with respect to clean air, water, toxic emissions, and noise abatement.

INVENTORY REQUIREMENTS   Inventory will be ordered in sufficient quantities to produce 60,000 cases of product per week. Lead times will vary from one week to eight weeks for delivery of the various raw materials. More inventory will have to be ordered during the high-volume months of April through September.

PRODUCTION STANDARDS   Quality is controlled by assigning a batch number to each product manufactured. Test samples are made prior to mixing and during and after production runs. As product is delivered, numbers are matched by computer to keep accurate records and maintain quality control.

    The Company's safety programs are based on National Soft Drink Association standards and OSHA regulations.

INTEGRATION (MAKE VERSUS BUY)   The Company will produce all products for sale at the plant site, with the exception of 1- and 2.5-gallon bottles of spring water. An agreement has been reached with Buck Springs to produce these large-size bottles and attach the Aquaria label.

EMPLOYEES   Line employees include a forklift operator, uncaser, filler operator, syrup blender, caser, and packer. Staff employees include a production manager, computer operator/bookkeeper, and quality control person. Six to eight employees will work in the plant on each shift. They will all be trained by working on the job.

    All hiring and screening will be done by David Rault and Lloyd Simmons. Each new employee will be given a physical, drug test, hepatitis shots, and reading and manual dexterity tests. All employees will be required to wear hard hats, ear plugs, back supports, and rubber boots to prevent injury.

    Production procedures will use the team method, with all employees crosstrained for all skills. All employees will sign a nondisclosure agreement with regard to the formulas for all Company products.

PACKAGING   The final steps in the manufacturing process are important in establishing the desired image for each product. SɪBôN's labels have eye-catching appeal, as do all point-of-sale materials and literature for distributors.

Management

Robert J. Caskey, Chairman of the Board, provides experience and direction to the Company and its officers.

Kenneth R. Barnett, President and CEO, is responsible for the overall financial and fiscal growth of the Company; he reports directly to the Chairman of the Board and the Board of Directors.

David Rault, Executive Vice President and COO, coordinates all production schedules, hires employees, orders all raw materials, and oversees shipping and receivables. He plans, develops, and establishes policies and objectives of the business organization in accordance with board directives and the corporation charter.

Lloyd L. Simmons, Vice President of Sales, manages all sales activities of the Company and directs staffing, training, and performance evaluations to develop and control the sales program. He coordinates sales territories, quotas, and goals and advises dealers, distributors, and clients concerning sales and advertising. He has over 32 years of experience in the beverage industry with major bottling companies in all phases of production and market analysis.

Shareholders and Directors

Following is a list of the Company's shareholders.

Shareholders	Number of Shares	
Robert J. Caskey, Director	38,000	(38%)
Kenneth R. Barnett, Director	20,000	(20%)
David Rault, Director	15,000	(15%)
Mary Jo Rault	15,000	(15%)
Frank Z. Johnston	10,000	(10%)
Shannon Caskey, Director	1,000	(1%)
Edward Soderstrom, Director	1,000	(1%)
Total Shares	100,000	(100%)

FINANCIAL PROJECTIONS

**SiBôn Beverage Corporation
Balance Sheet for July 31, 1996**

Assets
Current assets:

Cash	$ 176,760.27
Accounts receivable	250.00
Inventory	50,000.00
	$ 227,010.27

Fixed assets:

Land*	$ 46,940.00
Building construction in progress*	563,666.68
Production equipment*	278,450.16
Furniture, fixtures, computer hardware and software	111,432.60
Automotive equipment	21,594.23
	$1,022,083.67

Other assets:

Organization expense	$ 95,607.72
Financing costs	200,000.00
Formulas	25,000.00
Label design, trade names, and trademarks	21,057.70
	$ 341,665.42
TOTAL ASSETS	$1,590,759.36

Debt (Liabilities) and Equity

Current debt:

Accrued interest	$	3,402.52
Current portion of long-term debt		4,089.15
	$	7,491.67

Long-term debt:[†]

Note payable to First Bank & Trust East Texas under a
$1,500,000 line of credit guaranteed by Robert J. Caskey;
such guarantee secured by all real, personal, and
intangible property other than a 1995 Plymouth Voyager $1,330,000.00

Note payable to First Bank and Trust East Texas, payable
in 36 equal monthly installments of $411.70, including
interest thereon and commencing June 24, 1996, less
the current portion of $4,089.15 secured by a 1995
Plymouth Voyager   8,398.56

      1,338,398.56

Total debt		$1,345,890.23

Equity:

Capital stock, common $0.01 par value; 1,000,000 shares authorized; 100,000 shares issued and outstanding	$	1,000.00
Paid in capital in excess of par value		249,000.00
Retained earnings	(	5,130.87)
Total stockholders' equity	$	244,869.13
TOTAL DEBT AND EQUITY		$1,590,759.36

---

* SiBôn Beverage Corporation was incorporated in the state of Texas on April 22, 1996 for the purpose of constructing a bottling plant in Jasper, Texas and then producing and marketing a full line of sparkling fruit drinks, flavored waters, and sports drinks under the trade names of SiBon, Aquaria, Zingo, and Peppy-K. It is expected that the plant will be fully completed and equipped and ready to run in September 1996, at a total cost of approximately $1,040,000, including land. Until such time as the plant becomes operational, virtually all costs are being capitalized.

† The note payable to First Bank and Trust East Texas bears interest at ½% over prime rate, payable quarterly on April 15, July 15, October 15, and January 15 of each year prior to maturity. The entire unpaid principal balance and accrued but unpaid interest owed, if not paid sooner, is due and payable on or before April 15, 1999.

    The installment note payable to First Bank and Trust East Texas bears interest at 8%, for a total finance charge of $1,683.10, which together with the principal of $13,138.10 is included in the original amount of the note. The first two payments on the installment note were timely made on July 31, 1996.

SiBôn Beverage Corporation
Net Income by Quarter

		May–June 1996	Jul–Sept 1996	Oct–Dec 1996	Total
Cases Produced					
Aquaria	(16 oz.)	0	5,625	14,063	19,688
	(1.5 ltr.)	0	5,625	14,063	19,688
SiBon	(11 oz.)	0	13,125	39,375	52,500
	(23 oz.)	0	13,125	39,375	52,500
Peppy-K	(20 oz.)	0	0	2,813	2,813
	(36 oz.)	0	0	2,813	2,813
Zingo	(11 oz.)	0	0	0	0
	(23 oz.)	0	0	0	0
TOTAL CASES PRODUCED		0	37,500	112,502	150,000
Gross Sales					
Aquaria	(16 oz.)	0	$ 58,613	$ 146,531	$ 205,144
	(1.5 ltr.)	0	50,513	126,281	176,794
SiBon	(11 oz.)	0	124,950	374,850	499,800
	(23 oz.)	0	128,494	385,481	513,975
Peppy-K	(20 oz.)	0	0	26,775	26,775
	(36 oz.)	0	0	24,244	24,244
Zingo	(11 oz.)	0	0	0	0
	(23 oz.)	0	0	0	0
TOTAL GROSS SALES		0	$362,570	$1,084,163	$1,446,731
Less promotional allowances		0	(18,750)	(56,250)	(75,000)
Net Sales		0	$343,820	$1,027,913	$1,371,731
Cost of Sales (Schedule A)		0	$216,804	$ 660,902	$ 877,706
Gross Profit from Sales		0	$127,016	$ 367,010	$ 494,025
Selling, General and Administrative Expenses					
Salaries and wages		$ 28,500	$ 54,950	$ 79,350	$ 162,800
Payroll taxes		4,560	12,696	12,696	29,952
Commissions		0	3,000	9,000	12,000
Royalties		0	0	0	0
Office supplies		500	2,000	1,500	4,000
Insurance		1,500	9,900	9,900	21,300
Legal, accounting, and professional fees		102,000	15,000	15,000	132,000
Advertising		10,000	25,000	15,000	50,000
Postage, dues, and subscriptions		0	200	300	500
Freight out		0	18,750	56,250	75,000
Amortization		14,298	21,447	21,447	57,192
Travel and entertainment		7,000	21,000	37,500	65,500
Equipment rental		1,500	3,000	3,000	7,500
Research and development		0	5,000	0	5,000
Other taxes		0	0	0	0
Interest		3,688	21,344	10,469	35,500
Miscellaneous		0	2,500	3,000	5,500
TOTAL SELLING, G & A EXPENSE		$173,546	$215,787	$ 274,412	$ 663,744
Net Income Before Income Taxes		($173,546)	($ 88,772)	$ 92,598	($ 169,719)
Net Profit per Case		$ 0.00	$ 0.84	$ 1.12	$ 0.49
Income Tax		$ 0.00	$ 0.00	$ 0.00	$ 0.00
NET INCOME		($173,546)	($ 88,772)	$ 92,598	($ 169,719)

SiBôn Beverage Corporation
Net Income by Quarter

		Jan–Mar 1997	Apr–June 1997	Jul–Sept 1997	Oct–Dec 1997	Total
Cases Produced						
Aquaria	(16 oz.)	11,156	17,719	22,313	14,438	65,625
	(1.5 ltr.)	11,156	17,719	22,313	14,438	65,625
SiBon	(11 oz.)	27,563	39,375	44,625	28,875	140,438
	(23 oz.)	27,563	39,375	44,625	28,875	140,438
Peppy-K	(20 oz.)	2,231	3,544	4,463	2,888	13,125
	(36 oz.)	2,231	3,544	4,463	2,888	13,125
Zingo	(11 oz.)	3,675	14,175	17,850	11,550	47,250
	(23 oz.)	3,675	14,175	17,850	11,550	47,250
TOTAL CASES PRODUCED		89,250	141,750	178,500	115,500	525,000
Gross Sales						
Aquaria	(16 oz.)	$116,248	$ 184,629	$ 232,496	$ 150,439	$ 683,813
	(1.5 ltr.)	100,183	159,114	200,366	129,649	589,313
SiBon	(11 oz.)	262,395	374,850	424,830	274,890	1,336,965
	(23 oz.)	269,837	385,481	436,879	282,686	1,374,883
Peppy-K	(20 oz.)	21,242	33,737	42,483	27,489	124,950
	(36 oz.)	19,233	30,547	38,467	24,890	113,138
Zingo	(11 oz.)	31,513	121,551	153,064	99,041	405,169
	(23 oz.)	35,317	136,222	171,539	110,996	454,073
TOTAL GROSS SALES		$855,968	$1,426,131	$1,700,123	$1,100,080	$5,082,302
Less promotional allowances		(44,625)	(70,875)	(89,250)	(57,750)	(262,500)
Net Sales		$811,343	$1,355,256	$1,610,873	$1,042,330	$4,819,802
Cost of Sales (Schedule A)		$520,261	$ 824,763	$ 975,793	$ 659,205	$2,980,022
Gross Profit from Sales		$291,082	$ 530,493	$ 635,080	$ 383,125	$1,839,780
Selling, General and Administrative Expenses						
Salaries and wages		$ 99,188	$ 99,188	$ 99,188	$ 99,188	$ 396,750
Payroll taxes		14,600	14,600	14,600	14,600	58,402
Commissions		8,211	13,041	16,422	10,626	48,300
Royalties		0	0	0	0	0
Office supplies		1,500	1,500	2,000	1,500	6,500
Insurance		9,900	8,100	9,900	9,900	37,800
Legal, accounting, and professional fees		15,000	15,000	15,000	15,000	60,000
Advertising		30,000	30,000	30,000	30,000	120,000
Postage, dues, and subscriptions		1,500	1,500	1,500	1,500	6,000
Freight out		44,625	70,875	89,250	57,750	262,500
Amortization		21,447	21,447	21,447	21,447	85,788
Travel and entertainment		45,000	45,000	45,000	45,000	180,000
Equipment rental		3,000	3,500	3,000	3,000	12,500
Research and development		7,500	7,500	7,500	7,500	30,000
Other taxes		1,000	0	0	0	1,000
Interest		16,500	10,875	0	0	27,375
Miscellaneous		7,500	7,500	7,500	7,500	30,000
TOTAL SELLING, G & A EXPENSE		$326,471	$ 349,626	$ 362,307	$ 324,511	$1,362,915
Net Income Before Income Taxes		($ 35,389)	$ 180,867	$ 272,773	$ 58,614	$ 307,146
Net Profit (Loss) per Case		($ 0.48)	$ 1.28	$ 1.52	$ 0.39	$ 0.68
Income Tax		$ 1,908	$ 36,173	$ 54,555	$ 14,374	$ 107,010
NET INCOME		($ 37,296)	$ 144,694	$ 218,218	$ 44,240	$ 200,136

SiBôn Beverage Corporation
Net Income by Quarter

		Jan–Mar 1998	Apr–June 1998	Jul–Sept 1998	Oct–Dec 1998	Total
Cases Produced						
Aquaria	(16 oz.)	18,063	28,688	36,125	23,375	106,250
	(1.5 ltr.)	18,063	28,688	36,125	23,375	106,250
SiBon	(11 oz.)	36,125	57,375	72,250	46,750	212,500
	(23 oz.)	36,125	57,375	72,250	46,750	212,500
Peppy-K	(20 oz.)	3,613	5,738	7,225	4,675	21,250
	(36 oz.)	3,613	5,738	7,225	4,675	21,250
Zingo	(11 oz.)	14,450	22,950	28,900	18,700	85,000
	(23 oz.)	14,450	22,950	28,900	18,700	85,000
TOTAL CASES PRODUCED		144,500	229,500	289,000	187,000	850,000
Gross Sales						
Aquaria	(16 oz.)	$ 188,211	$ 298,924	$ 376,423	$ 243,568	$1,107,125
	(1.5 ltr.)	162,201	257,614	324,403	209,908	954,125
SiBon	(11 oz.)	343,910	546,210	687,820	445,060	2,023,000
	(23 oz.)	353,664	561,701	707,328	457,683	2,080,375
Peppy-K	(20 oz.)	34,391	54,621	68,782	44,506	202,300
	(36 oz.)	31,140	49,457	62,280	40,299	183,175
Zingo	(11 oz.)	123,909	196,796	247,818	160,353	728,875
	(23 oz.)	138,865	220,550	277,729	179,707	816,850
TOTAL GROSS SALES		$1,376,290	$2,185,873	$2,752,581	$1,781,082	$8,095,825
Less promotional allowances		(72,250)	(114,750)	(144,500)	(93,500)	(425,000)
Net Sales		$1,304,040	$2,071,123	$2,608,081	$1,687,582	$7,670,825
Cost of Sales (Schedule A)		$ 804,936	$1,238,205	$1,537,205	$1,024,633	$4,604,979
Gross Profit from Sales		$ 499,104	$ 832,918	$1,070,876	$ 662,948	$3,065,846
Selling, General and Administrative Expenses						
Salaries and wages		$ 119,025	$ 119,025	$ 119,025	$ 119,025	$ 476,100
Payroll taxes		19,044	19,044	19,044	19,044	76,176
Commissions		15,028	23,868	30,056	19,448	88,400
Royalties		0	0	0	0	0
Office supplies		1,500	1,500	2,000	1,500	6,500
Insurance		9,900	9,900	9,900	9,900	39,600
Legal, accounting, and professional fees		7,500	7,500	10,000	7,500	32,500
Advertising		45,000	45,000	45,000	45,000	180,000
Postage, dues, and subscriptions		1,500	1,500	1,500	1,500	6,000
Freight out		72,250	114,750	144,500	93,500	425,000
Amortization		32,697	32,697	32,697	32,697	130,788
Travel and entertainment		60,000	60,000	60,000	60,000	240,000
Equipment rental		3,000	3,000	3,000	3,000	12,000
Research and development		7,500	7,500	7,500	7,500	30,000
Other taxes		1,000	0	0	0	1,000
Interest		0	0	0	0	0
Miscellaneous		15,000	15,000	15,000	15,000	60,000
TOTAL SELLING, G & A EXPENSE		$ 409,944	$ 460,284	$ 499,222	$ 434,614	$1,804,064
Net Income Before Income Taxes		$ 89,160	$ 372,634	$ 571,654	$ 228,334	$1,261,782
Net Profit per Case		$ 0.55	$ 1.59	$ 1.98	$ 1.13	$ 1.31
Income Tax		$ 22,290	$ 93,158	$ 142,913	$ 57,084	$ 315,445
NET INCOME		$ 66,870	$ 279,475	$ 428,740	$ 171,251	$ 946,336

Robert J. Caskey
Employment History

Robert J. Caskey has lived in Jasper, Texas for 38 years and has been an active participant and leader in the business, civic, cultural, and local communities. He has demonstrated expertise in management, planning, and implementation at Visador Company and on the Board of Directors of a number of corporations, hospitals, and institutions of higher learning.

A brief history of Mr. Caskey's business experience follows:

1953–1956   **El Paso Molding Company, Inc.**
Vice President and General Manager

Mr. Caskey managed 35 employees who made pre-hung door parts and finger-jointed moldings.

1956–1959   **Visador Mouldings, Inc.**
Vice President

As supervisor of 60 employees, Mr. Caskey began a lumber yard and kiln-drying system on behalf of the company.

1959–1964   **Visador Company** (a partnership)
Partner

Mr. Caskey was in charge of production, purchasing, and personnel; he later took on the added responsibility of credit manager for the company. During this period, Mr. Caskey was the designer of all plant expansion, and the company grew to over 200 employees.

1964–1988   **Visador Company** (a corporation)
President and Chief Executive Officer

Under Mr. Caskey's leadership, Visador's sales grew from $3 million to $48 million, while the company expanded to four manufacturing locations and four distribution centers with almost 700 employees.

Kenneth R. Barnett
Employment History

Mr. Barnett has been in the investment and financial planning industry in Houston, Texas for over 23 years. His experience includes representing key executives of Fortune 500 companies, professional athletes, professionals, and small business owners in virtually all areas of financial and investment management. He has a Bachelor of Science degree in Biology/Chemistry and is a Certified Financial Planner.

Some of Mr. Barnett's accomplishments follow:

- Held the position of Account Manager and Tax Shelter Manager with Paine, Webber, Jackson & Curtis
- Founded and built the largest financial planning and consulting firm in Houston, Texas; provided total financial, investment, and estate planning for corporation executives, professional athletes, and entrepreneurs; negotiated and structured complex investment transactions in oil and gas, real estate, and private enterprise on behalf of clients

- Founded the fourth-largest single-family residential investment management company in Houston, Texas; structured and completed the registration of a $50 million public limited partnership to provide mortgage funds on residential investment properties. The company had over 30 employees located in three states, with annual sales in excess of $15 million.
- Has evaluated over 150 investment, financial, and business proposals annually on behalf of clients, accountants, and attorneys

David Rault
Employment History

Academic Degrees   B.S., M.B.A.

1958–1960   **Loeb Rhodes**

Corporate Analyst

Evaluated existing companies controlled by Loeb Rhodes and new companies for acquisitions and mergers

1960–1970   **International Business Machine Corp.**

Branch Manager

Progressed from Systems Analyst to Salesman to Branch Manager, Federal Systems Division while at IBM; handled all specifications and bidding for main-frame computers; became the direct liaison for the company with the federal government, overseeing its purchases and installations

1970–1981   **Harbinger Homes**

President and Founder

Oversaw the building of over 5,000 homes and office distribution warehouses in the Greater Houston area

1982–1991   **Business Automation**

President and Founder

Supervised the selling and installation of multi-user computer systems. The company had an exclusive contract with Western Union to install and service all equipment in the state of Texas.

1991–Present   **U.S. Aquarius, Inc.**

President

Created formulas, trademarks, and business plan to start a New Age beverage company

Mr. Rault's expertise is in evaluating, building, and managing companies through mergers, acquisitions, and liquidations and in assisting insolvent companies in getting back in the black. He has in-depth knowledge of the aerospace, wholesale, liquor, food brokerage, food distribution, and insurance industries.

Lloyd L. Simmons
Employment History

Mr. Simmons has been in the beverage industry for 32 years. His employment has successfully progressed through the years in the following manner:

Pepsi Cola, Oklahoma

> Started in production and was promoted to increasing responsibilities in the warehouse, vending service, and repair areas. Held the positions of Key Account Manager, Merchandising Manager, Sales Manager, and General Sales Manager over five branches.

Oklahoma Beverage Distributors and Bottlers

> *Northeast Division Manager*
>
> Supervised six sales centers and the fountain supply company

Pepsi Cola, Arkansas

> *Division Manager*

Bryant Beverage (Division of Mid-South Bottling)

Vice President

> Managed all bottling and sales operations and two branch operations. His branch won the Highest Profit/Case and Highest Increased Market Share awards from Mid-South Bottling. Won the Cappy Award for the highest percentage increase in market share in the southeast region from Pepsi. Won the Kalab T. Branum (inventor of Pepsi) Award for quality assurance in production.

Arkansas Beverage (Division of Mid-South Bottling)

> *Vice President of Sales and Division Manager*

Denver Coca-Cola

> *Division Manager*
>
> Managed the number one division in every area—product turnover, sales increase, fewest days of work missed, no job injuries, and sales record for a single month

Murray Distributing

> *Consultant to Paul Murray in acquiring Royal Crown plants*

InterBevCo.

> *Operations Manager*
>
> Set up new plant. Promoted to Division Manager in Alabama.

Willow Springs Bottled Water Company

> *Division Manager*
>
> Supervised sales of bottled water in four states and the wholesale division dealing with food and beverage brokers

Royal Crown Cola, Oklahoma

Franchisee/Owner with two partners

Sold the company to All American Bottling

U.S. Aquarius, Inc.

Vice President of Sales

Moved to Louisiana to start operations of new bottling plant

Cenla Water Company

Sales Manager

Supervised distribution of Kempwood bottled water in five Louisiana parishes

Present Value of $1

n	1%	2%	3%	4%	5%	6%	7%	8%	9%	10%
1	.990	.980	.971	.962	.952	.943	.935	.926	.917	.909
2	.980	.961	.943	.925	.907	.890	.873	.857	.842	.826
3	.971	.942	.915	.889	.864	.840	.816	.794	.772	.751
4	.961	.924	.888	.855	.823	.792	.763	.735	.708	.683
5	.951	.906	.863	.822	.784	.747	.713	.681	.650	.621
6	.942	.888	.837	.790	.746	.705	.666	.630	.596	.564
7	.933	.871	.813	.760	.711	.665	.623	.583	.547	.513
8	.923	.853	.789	.731	.677	.627	.582	.540	.502	.467
9	.914	.837	.766	.703	.645	.592	.544	.500	.460	.424
10	.905	.820	.744	.676	.614	.558	.508	.463	.422	.386
11	.896	.804	.722	.650	.585	.527	.475	.429	.388	.350
12	.887	.789	.701	.625	.557	.497	.444	.397	.356	.319
13	.879	.773	.681	.601	.530	.469	.415	.368	.326	.290
14	.870	.758	.661	.577	.505	.442	.388	.340	.299	.263
15	.861	.743	.642	.555	.481	.417	.362	.315	.275	.239
16	.853	.728	.623	.534	.458	.394	.339	.292	.252	.218
17	.844	.714	.605	.513	.436	.371	.317	.270	.231	.198
18	.836	.700	.587	.494	.416	.350	.296	.250	.212	.180
19	.828	.686	.570	.475	.396	.331	.277	.232	.194	.164
20	.820	.673	.554	.456	.377	.312	.258	.215	.178	.149
21	.811	.660	.538	.439	.359	.294	.242	.199	.164	.135
22	.803	.647	.522	.422	.342	.278	.226	.184	.150	.123
23	.795	.634	.507	.406	.326	.262	.211	.170	.138	.112
24	.788	.622	.492	.390	.310	.247	.197	.158	.126	.102
25	.780	.610	.478	.375	.295	.233	.184	.146	.116	.092
30	.742	.552	.412	.308	.231	.174	.131	.099	.075	.057
40	.672	.453	.307	.208	.142	.097	.067	.046	.032	.022
50	.608	.372	.228	.141	.087	.054	.034	.021	.013	.009

n	11%	12%	13%	14%	15%	16%	17%	18%	19%	20%
1	.901	.893	.885	.877	.870	.862	.855	.847	.840	.833
2	.812	.797	.783	.769	.756	.743	.731	.718	.706	.694
3	.731	.712	.693	.675	.658	.641	.624	.609	.593	.579
4	.659	.636	.613	.592	.572	.552	.534	.516	.499	.482
5	.593	.567	.543	.519	.497	.476	.456	.437	.419	.402
6	.535	.507	.480	.456	.432	.410	.390	.370	.352	.335
7	.482	.452	.425	.400	.376	.354	.333	.314	.296	.279
8	.434	.404	.376	.351	.327	.305	.285	.266	.249	.233
9	.391	.361	.333	.308	.284	.263	.243	.225	.209	.194
10	.352	.322	.295	.270	.247	.227	.208	.191	.176	.162
11	.317	.287	.261	.237	.215	.195	.178	.162	.148	.135
12	.286	.257	.231	.208	.187	.168	.152	.137	.124	.112
13	.258	.229	.204	.182	.163	.145	.130	.116	.104	.093
14	.232	.205	.181	.160	.141	.125	.111	.099	.088	.078
15	.209	.183	.160	.140	.123	.108	.095	.084	.074	.065
16	.188	.163	.141	.123	.107	.093	.081	.071	.062	.054
17	.170	.146	.125	.108	.093	.080	.069	.060	.052	.045
18	.153	.130	.111	.095	.081	.069	.059	.051	.044	.038
19	.138	.116	.098	.083	.070	.060	.051	.043	.037	.031
20	.124	.104	.087	.073	.061	.051	.043	.037	.031	.026
21	.112	.093	.077	.064	.053	.044	.037	.031	.026	.022
22	.101	.083	.068	.056	.046	.038	.032	.026	.022	.018
23	.091	.074	.060	.049	.040	.033	.027	.022	.018	.015
24	.082	.066	.053	.043	.035	.028	.023	.019	.015	.013
25	.074	.059	.047	.038	.030	.024	.020	.016	.013	.010
30	.044	.033	.026	.020	.015	.012	.009	.007	.005	.004
40	.015	.011	.008	.005	.004	.003	.002	.001	.001	.001
50	.005	.003	.002	.001	.001	.001	.000	.000	.000	.000

n	21%	22%	23%	24%	25%	26%	27%	28%	29%	30%
1	.826	.820	.813	.806	.800	.794	.787	.781	.775	.769
2	.683	.672	.661	.650	.640	.630	.620	.610	.601	.592
3	.564	.551	.537	.524	.512	.500.	.488	.477	.466	.455
4	.467	.451	.437	.423	.410	.397	.384	.373	.361	.350
5	.386	.370	.355	.341	.328	.315	.303	.291	.280	.269
6	.319	.303	.289	.275	.262	.250	.238	.227	.217	.207
7	.263	.249	.235	.222	.210	.198	.188	.178	.168	.159
8	.218	.204	.191	.179	.168	.157	.148	.139	.130	.123
9	.180	.167	.155	.144	.134	.125	.116	.108	.101	.094
10	.149	.137	.126	.116	.107	.099	.092	.085	.078	.073
11	.123	.112	.103	.094	.086	.079	.072	.066	.061	.056
12	.102	.092	.083	.076	.069	.062	.057	.052	.047	.043
13	.084	.075	.068	.061	.055	.050	.045	.040	.037	.033
14	.069	.062	.055	.049	.044	.039	.035	.032	.028	.025
15	.057	.051	.045	.040	.035	.031	.028	.025	.022	.020
16	.047	.042	.036	.032	.028	.025	.022	.019	.017	.015
17	.039	.034	.030	.026	.023	.020	.017	.015	.013	.012
18	.032	.028	.024	.021	.018	.016	.014	.012	.010	.009
19	.027	.023	.020	.017	.014	.012	.011	.009	.008	.007
20	.022	.019	.016	.014	.012	.010	.008	.007	.006	.005
21	.018	.015	.013	.011	.009	.008	.007	.006	.005	.004
22	.015	.013	.011	.009	.007	.006	.005	.004	.004	.003
23	.012	.010	.009	.007	.006	.005	.004	.003	.003	.002
24	.010	.008	.007	.006	.005	.004	.003	.003	.002	.002
25	.009	.007	.006	.005	.004	.003	.003	.002	.002	.001
30	.003	.003	.002	.002	.001	.001	.001	.001	.000	.000
40	.000	.000	.000	.000	.000	.000	.000	.000	.000	.000
50	.000	.000	.000	.000	.000	.000	.000	.000	.000	.000

n	31%	32%	33%	34%	35%	36%	37%	38%	39%	40%
1	.763	.758	.752	.746	.741	.735	.730	.725	.719	.714
2	.583	.574	.565	.557	.549	.541	.533	.525	.518	.510
3	.445	.435	.425	.416	.406	.398	.389	.381	.372	.364
4	.340	.329	.320	.310	.301	.292	.284	.276	.268	.260
5	.259	.250	.240	.231	.223	.215	.207	.200	.193	.186
6	.198	.189	.181	.173	.165	.158	.151	.145	.139	.133
7	.151	.143	.136	.129	.122	.116	.110	.105	.100	.095
8	.115	.108	.102	.096	.091	.085	.081	.076	.072	.068
9	.088	.082	.077	.072	.067	.063	.059	.055	.052	.048
10	.067	.062	.058	.054	.050	.046	.043	.040	.037	.035
11	.051	.047	.043	.040	.037	.034	.031	.029	.027	.025
12	.039	.036	.033	.030	.027	.025	.023	.021	.019	.018
13	.030	.027	.025	.022	.020	.018	.017	.015	.014	.013
14	.023	.021	.018	.017	.015	.014	.012	.011	.010	.009
15	.017	.016	.014	.012	.011	.010	.009	.008	.007	.006
16	.013	.012	.010	.009	.008	.007	.006	.006	.005	.005
17	.010	.009	.008	.007	.006	.005	.005	.004	.004	.003
18	.008	.007	.006	.005	.005	.004	.003	.003	.003	.002
19	.006	.005	.004	.004	.003	.003	.003	.002	.002	.002
20	.005	.004	.003	.003	.002	.002	.002	.002	.001	.001
21	.003	.003	.003	.002	.002	.002	.001	.001	.001	.001
22	.003	.002	.002	.002	.001	.001	.001	.001	.001	.001
23	.002	.002	.001	.001	.001	.001	.001	.001	.001	.000
24	.002	.001	.001	.001	.001	.001	.001	.000	.000	.000
25	.001	.001	.001	.001	.001	.000	.000	.000	.000	.000
30	.000	.000	.000	.000	.000	.000	.000	.000	.000	.000
40	.000	.000	.000	.000	.000	.000	.000	.000	.000	.000

Present Value of an Annuity of $1 for *n* Periods

n	1%	2%	3%	4%	5%	6%	7%	8%	9%	10%
1	.990	.980	.971	.962	.952	.943	.935	.926	.917	.909
2	1.970	1.942	1.913	1.886	1.859	1.833	1.808	1.783	1.759	1.736
3	2.941	2.884	2.829	2.775	2.723	2.673	2.624	2.577	2.531	2.487
4	3.902	3.808	3.717	3.630	3.546	3.465	3.387	3.312	3.240	3.170
5	4.853	4.713	4.580	4.452	4.329	4.212	4.100	3.993	3.890	3.791
6	5.795	5.601	5.417	5.242	5.076	4.917	4.767	4.623	4.486	4.355
7	6.728	6.472	6.230	6.002	5.786	5.582	5.389	5.206	5.033	4.868
8	7.652	7.326	7.020	6.733	6.463	6.210	5.971	5.747	5.535	5.335
9	8.566	8.162	7.786	7.435	7.108	6.802	6.515	6.247	5.995	5.759
10	9.471	8.983	8.530	8.111	7.722	7.360	7.024	6.710	6.418	6.145
11	10.368	9.787	9.253	8.760	8.306	7.887	7.499	7.139	6.805	6.495
12	11.255	10.575	9.954	9.385	8.863	8.384	7.943	7.536	7.161	6.814
13	12.134	11.348	10.635	9.986	9.394	8.853	8.358	7.904	7.487	7.103
14	13.004	12.106	11.296	10.563	9.899	9.295	8.746	8.244	7.786	7.367
15	13.865	12.849	11.938	11.118	10.380	9.712	9.108	8.560	8.061	7.606
16	14.718	13.578	12.561	11.652	10.838	10.106	9.447	8.851	8.313	7.824
17	15.562	14.292	13.166	12.166	11.274	10.477	9.763	9.122	8.544	8.022
18	16.398	14.992	13.754	12.659	11.690	10.828	10.059	9.372	8.756	8.201
19	17.226	15.679	14.324	13.134	12.085	11.158	10.336	9.604	8.950	8.365
20	18.046	16.352	14.878	13.590	12.462	11.470	10.594	9.818	9.129	8.514
21	18.857	17.011	15.415	14.029	12.821	11.764	10.836	10.017	9.292	8.649
22	19.661	17.658	15.937	14.451	13.163	12.042	11.061	10.201	9.442	8.772
23	20.456	18.292	16.444	14.857	13.489	12.303	11.272	10.371	9.580	8.883
24	21.244	18.914	16.936	15.247	13.799	12.550	11.469	10.529	9.707	8.985
25	22.023	19.524	17.413	15.622	14.094	12.783	11.654	10.675	9.823	9.077
30	25.808	22.397	19.601	17.292	15.373	13.765	12.409	11.258	10.274	9.427
40	32.835	27.356	23.115	19.793	17.159	15.046	13.332	11.925	10.757	9.779
50	39.197	31.424	25.730	21.482	18.256	15.762	13.801	12.234	10.962	9.915

n	11%	12%	13%	14%	15%	16%	17%	18%	19%	20%
1	.901	.893	.885	.877	.870	.862	.855	.847	.840	.833
2	1.713	1.690	1.668	1.647	1.626	1.605	1.585	1.566	1.547	1.528
3	2.444	2.402	2.361	2.322	2.283	2.246	2.210	2.174	2.140	2.106
4	3.102	3.037	2.974	2.914	2.855	2.798	2.743	2.690	2.639	2.589
5	3.696	3.605	3.517	3.433	3.352	3.274	3.199	3.127	3.058	2.991
6	4.231	4.111	3.998	3.889	3.784	3.685	3.589	3.498	3.410	3.326
7	4.712	4.564	4.423	4.288	4.160	4.039	3.922	3.812	3.706	3.605
8	5.146	4.968	4.799	4.639	4.487	4.344	4.207	4.078	3.954	3.837
9	5.537	5.328	5.132	4.946	4.772	4.607	4.451	4.303	4.163	4.031
10	5.889	5.650	5.426	5.216	5.019	4.833	4.659	4.494	4.339	4.192
11	6.207	5.938	5.687	5.453	5.234	5.029	4.836	4.656	4.487	4.327
12	6.492	6.194	5.918	5.660	5.421	5.197	4.988	4.793	4.611	4.439
13	6.750	6.424	6.122	5.842	5.583	5.342	5.118	4.910	4.715	4.533
14	6.982	6.628	6.303	6.002	5.724	5.468	5.229	5.008	4.802	4.611
15	7.191	6.811	6.462	6.142	5.847	5.575	5.324	5.092	4.876	4.675
16	7.379	6.974	6.604	6.265	5.954	5.669	5.405	5.162	4.938	4.730
17	7.549	7.120	6.729	6.373	6.047	5.749	5.475	5.222	4.990	4.775
18	7.702	7.250	6.840	6.467	6.128	5.818	5.534	5.273	5.033	4.812
19	7.839	7.366	6.938	6.550	6.198	5.877	5.585	5.316	5.070	4.843
20	7.963	7.469	7.025	6.623	6.259	5.929	5.628	5.353	5.101	4.870
21	8.075	7.562	7.102	6.687	6.312	5.973	5.665	5.384	5.127	4.891
22	8.176	7.645	7.170	6.743	6.359	6.011	5.696	5.410	5.149	4.909
23	8.266	7.718	7.230	6.792	6.399	6.044	5.723	5.432	5.167	4.925
24	8.348	7.784	7.283	6.835	6.434	6.073	5.747	5.451	5.182	4.937
25	8.442	7.843	7.330	6.873	6.464	6.097	5.766	5.467	5.195	4.948
30	8.694	8.055	7.496	7.003	6.566	6.177	5.829	5.517	5.235	4.979
40	8.951	8.244	7.634	7.105	6.642	6.233	5.871	5.548	5.258	4.997
50	9.042	8.305	7.675	7.133	6.661	6.246	5.880	5.554	5.262	4.999

Present Value of an Annuity of $1 for *n* Periods

n	21%	22%	23%	24%	25%	26%	27%	28%	29%	30%
1	.826	.820	.813	.806	.800	.794	.787	.781	.775	.769
2	1.509	1.492	1.474	1.457	1.440	1.424	1.407	1.392	1.376	1.361
3	2.074	2.042	2.011	1.981	1.952	1.923	1.896	1.868	1.842	1.816
4	2.540	2.494	2.448	2.404	2.362	2.320	2.280	2.241	2.203	2.166
5	2.926	2.864	2.803	2.745	2.689	2.635	2.583	2.532	2.483	2.436
6	3.245	3.167	3.092	3.020	2.951	2.885	2.821	2.759	2.700	2.643
7	3.508	3.416	3.327	3.242	3.161	3.083	3.009	2.937	2.868	2.802
8	3.726	3.619	3.518	3.421	3.329	3.241	3.156	3.076	2.999	2.925
9	3.905	3.786	3.673	3.566	3.463	3.366	3.273	3.184	3.100	3.019
10	4.054	3.923	3.799	3.682	3.570	3.465	3.364	3.269	3.178	3.092
11	4.177	4.035	3.902	3.776	3.656	3.544	3.437	3.335	3.239	3.147
12	4.278	4.127	3.985	3.851	3.725	3.606	3.493	3.387	3.286	3.190
13	4.362	4.203	4.053	3.912	3.780	3.656	3.538	3.427	3.322	3.223
14	4.432	4.265	4.108	4.962	3.824	3.695	3.573	3.459	3.351	3.249
15	4.489	4.315	4.153	4.001	3.859	3.726	3.601	3.483	3.373	3.268
16	4.536	4.357	4.189	4.033	3.887	3.751	3.623	3.503	3.390	3.283
17	4.576	4.391	4.219	4.059	3.910	3.771	3.640	3.518	3.403	3.295
18	4.608	4.419	4.243	4.080	3.928	3.786	3.654	3.529	3.413	3.304
19	4.635	4.442	4.263	4.097	3.942	3.799	3.664	3.539	3.421	3.311
20	4.657	4.460	4.279	4.110	3.954	3.808	3.673	3.546	3.427	3.316
21	4.675	4.476	4.292	4.121	3.963	3.816	3.679	3.551	3.432	3.320
22	4.690	4.488	4.302	4.130	3.970	3.822	3.684	3.556	3.436	3.323
23	4.703	4.499	4.311	4.137	3.976	3.827	3.689	3.559	3.438	3.325
24	4.713	4.507	4.318	4.143	3.981	3.831	3.692	3.562	3.441	3.327
25	4.721	4.514	4.323	4.147	3.985	3.834	3.694	3.564	3.442	3.329
30	4.746	4.534	4.339	4.160	3.995	3.842	3.701	3.569	3.447	3.332
40	4.760	4.544	4.347	4.166	3.999	3.846	3.703	3.571	3.448	3.333
50	4.762	4.545	4.348	4.167	4.000	3.846	3.704	3.571	3.448	3.333

n	31%	32%	33%	34%	35%	36%	37%	38%	39%	40%
1	.763	.758	.752	.746	.741	.735	.730	.725	.719	.714
2	1.346	1.331	1.317	1.303	1.289	1.276	1.263	1.250	1.237	1.224
3	1.791	1.766	1.742	1.719	1.696	1.673	1.652	1.630	1.609	1.589
4	2.130	2.096	2.062	2.029	1.997	1.966	1.935	1.906	1.877	1.849
5	2.390	2.345	2.302	2.260	2.220	2.181	2.143	2.106	2.070	2.035
6	2.588	2.534	2.483	2.433	2.385	2.339	2.294	2.251	2.209	2.168
7	2.739	2.677	2.619	2.562	2.508	2.455	2.404	2.355	2.308	2.263
8	2.854	2.786	2.721	2.658	2.598	2.540	2.485	2.432	2.380	2.331
9	2.942	2.868	2.798	2.730	2.665	2.603	2.544	2.487	2.432	2.379
10	3.009	2.930	2.855	2.784	2.715	2.649	2.587	2.527	2.469	2.414
11	3.060	2.978	2.899	2.824	2.752	2.683	2.618	2.555	2.496	2.438
12	3.100	3.013	2.931	2.853	2.779	2.708	2.641	2.576	2.515	2.456
13	3.129	3.040	2.956	2.876	2.799	2.727	2.658	2.592	2.529	2.469
14	3.152	3.061	2.974	2.892	2.814	2.740	2.670	2.603	2.539	2.477
15	3.170	3.076	2.988	2.905	2.825	2.750	2.679	2.611	2.546	2.484
16	3.183	3.088	2.999	2.914	2.834	2.757	2.685	2.616	2.551	2.489
17	3.193	3.097	3.007	2.921	2.840	2.763	2.690	2.621	2.555	2.492
18	3.201	3.104	3.012	2.926	2.844	2.767	2.693	2.624	2.557	2.494
19	3.207	3.109	3.017	2.930	2.848	2.770	2.696	2.626	2.559	2.496
20	3.211	3.113	3.020	2.933	2.850	2.772	2.698	2.627	2.561	2.497
21	3.215	3.116	3.023	2.935	2.852	2.773	2.699	2.629	2.562	2.498
22	3.217	3.118	3.025	2.936	2.853	2.775	2.700	2.629	2.562	2.498
23	3.219	3.120	3.026	2.938	2.854	2.775	2.701	2.630	2.563	2.499
24	3.221	3.121	3.027	2.939	2.855	2.776	2.701	2.630	2.563	2.499
25	3.222	3.122	3.028	2.939	2.856	2.776	2.702	2.631	2.563	2.499
30	3.225	3.124	3.030	2.941	2.857	2.777	2.702	2.631	2.564	2.500
40	3.226	3.125	3.030	2.941	2.857	2.778	2.703	2.632	2.564	2.500
50	3.226	3.125	3.030	2.941	2.857	2.778	2.703	2.632	2.564	2.500

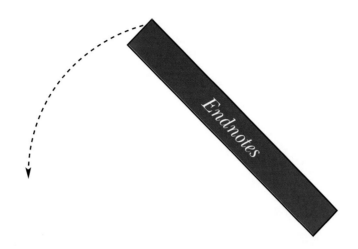

Endnotes

Chapter 1

1. Michael Barrier, "Adversity Brings Opportunity," *Nation's Business*, Vol. 81, No. 4 (April 1993), pp. 31–34.

2. Toddi Gutner, "Nostalgia Sells," *Forbes*, Vol. 149, No. 9 (April 27, 1992), pp. 102–103. Adapted from *FORBES* magazine by permission. © Forbes Inc., 1992. (Sales and profit data have been updated.)

3. Matthew Schifrin, "Know Thy Customer," *Forbes*, Vol. 151, No. 10 (May 10, 1993), pp. 122–123.

4. Ibid., p. 122.

5. Ibid., p. 123.

6. The account of Proctor and Gardner Advertising is taken from a telephone conversation with a company official in 1994; and Jill Bettner and Christine Donahue, "Now They're Not Laughing," *Forbes*, Vol. 132, No. 12 (November 21, 1983), p. 124.

7. Edward O. Wells, "What CEOS Make," *Inc.*, Vol. 17, No. 12 (September 1995), p. 46.

8. "Poll: Most Like Being Own Boss," *USA Today*, May 6, 1991. For a scholarly study confirming the importance of a quest for independence as a motivational factor, see Marco Virarelli, "The Birth of New Enterprises," *Small Business Economics*, Vol. 3, No. 3 (September 1991), pp. 215–223.

9. Dorothy J. Gaiter, "You'll Have to Leave. I'm Cold," *The Wall Street Journal*, November 22, 1991, p. R4.

10. Larry Mahar, "A Second Career for the Fun of It," *Nation's Business*, Vol. 79, No. 1 (January 1991), p. 10. Reprinted by permission, *Nation's Business*, January 1991. Copyright 1991, U.S. Chamber of Commerce.

11. "PC Greetings," *Independent Business*, Vol. 5, No. 2 (March–April 1994), p. 16.

12. Frances Huffman, "Burnout Blues," *Entrepreneur*, Vol. 18, No. 2 (February 1990), p. 78.

13. For a review of this topic, see Arnold C. Cooper and F. Javier Gimeno Gascon, "Entrepreneurs, Processes of Founding, and New-Firm Performance," in Donald L. Sexton and John D. Kasarda (eds.), *The State of Entrepreneurship* (Boston: PWS-Kent, 1992), pp. 308–309.

14. David C. McClelland, *The Achieving Society* (New York: Free Press, 1961). Also see David C. McClelland and David G. Winter, *Motivating Economic Achievement* (New York: Free Press, 1969); and Bradley R. Johnson, "Toward a Multidimensional Model of Entrepreneurship: The Case of Achievement Motivation and the Entrepreneur," *Entrepreneurship Theory and Practice*, Vol. 14, No. 3 (Spring 1990), pp. 39–54.

15. Robert H. Brockhaus, Sr., and Pamela S. Horwitz, "The Psychology of the Entrepreneur," in Donald L. Sexton and Raymond W. Smilor (eds.), *The Art and Science of Entrepreneurship* (Cambridge: Ballinger, 1986), p. 27.

16. McClelland, op. cit., Chapter 6.

17. See Brockhaus and Horwitz, op. cit., p. 27; and Rita Gunther McGrath, Ian C. MacMillan, and Sari Scheinberg, "Elitists, Risk-Takers, and Rugged Individualists? An Exploratory Analysis of Cultural Differences between Entrepreneurs and Non-Entrepreneurs," *Journal of Business Venturing*, Vol. 7, No. 2 (March 1992), pp. 115–135.

18. J. B. Rotter, "Generalized Expectancies for Internal Versus External Control of Reinforcement," *Psychological Monographs*, 1966a. A more recent review is given in Brockhaus and Horwitz, op. cit., pp. 25–48.

19. Russell M. Knight, "Entrepreneurship in Canada." Paper presented at the annual conference of the International Council for Small Business, Asilomar, California, June 22–25, 1980.

20. Bruce G. Posner, "The Education of a Big-Company Man," *Inc.*, Vol. 16, No. 7 (July 1994), pp. 64–69.

21. Suzanne Oliver, "The Shiksa Chef," *Forbes*, Vol. 151, No. 11 (May 24, 1993), pp. 66–68.

22. "Your Toes Know," *In Business*, Vol. 10, No. 3 (May–June 1988), p. 6.

23. *The State of Small Business: A Report of the President 1993* (Washington, DC: U.S. Government Printing Office, 1993), p. 63.

24. "Women Entrepreneurs: 'A Pretty Big Game,'" *Nation's Business*, Vol. 80, No. 8 (August 1992), p. 53.

25. *The State of Small Business*, op. cit., p. 253.

26. Steven B. Kaufman, "Building Blocks of Success," *Nation's Business,* Vol. 82, No. 5 (May 1994), p. 18.

27. Norman R. Smith, *The Entrepreneur and His Firm: The Relationship Between Type of Man and Type of Company* (East Lansing: Bureau of Business and Economic Research, Michigan State University, 1967). Also see Norman R. Smith and John B. Miner, "Type of Entrepreneur, Type of Firm, and Managerial Motivation: Implications for Organizational Life Cycle Theory," *Strategic Management Journal,* Vol. 4, No. 4 (October–December 1983), pp. 325–340; and Carolyn Y. Woo, Arnold C. Cooper, and William C. Dunkelberg, "The Development and Interpretation of Entrepreneurial Typologies," *Journal of Business Venturing,* Vol. 6, No. 2 (March 1991), pp. 93–114.

28. Martha E. Mangelsdorf, "Behind the Scenes," *Inc.,* Vol. 14, No. 10 (October 1992), p. 72.

Chapter 2

1. *The State of Small Business: A Report of the President 1993* (Washington, DC: U.S. Government Printing Office, 1993), p. 36.

2. "Importing Can Help a Firm Expand and Diversify," *Nation's Business,* Vol. 83, No. 1 (January 1995), p. 11.

3. "The Rise and Rise of America's Small Firms," *The Economist* (January 21, 1989), p. 67.

4. Bennett Harrison, *Lean and Mean: The Changing Landscape of Corporate Power in the Age of Flexibility* (New York: Basic Books, 1994), p. 13.

5. The first four factors noted here are included in Zoltan J. Acs and David B. Audretsch, *Innovation and Small Firms* (Cambridge, MA: MIT Press, 1990), pp. 3–5.

6. Tatiana Pouschine and Manjeet Kripalani, "I Got Tired of Forcing Myself to Go to the Office," *Forbes,* Vol. 149, No. 11 (May 25, 1992), p. 104.

7. *The State of Small Business: A Report of the President 1988* (Washington, DC: U.S. Government Printing Office, 1988), p. 38.

8. David L. Birch, *Job Creation in America* (New York: Free Press, 1987).

9. Acs and Audretsch, op. cit., p. 151.

10. For a criticism of Birch's work, see Harrison, op. cit., Chapter 2; also see Bruce A. Kirchoff, *Entrepreneurship and Dynamic Capitalism: The Economics of Business Firm Formation and Growth* (Westport, CT: Praeger Publishers, 1994), Chapter 6, for an analysis that supports Birch's work.

11. "The 'Job Generation Process' Revisited: An Interview with Author David L. Birch," *ICSB Bulletin,* Vol. 25, No. 4 (February 1993), p. 6.

12. Jeffrey A. Timmons, *New Venture Creation,* 4th ed. (Burr Ridge, IL: Irwin, 1994), p. 5.

13. Zoltan J. Acs, "Where New Things Come From," *Inc.,* Vol. 16, No. 5 (May 1994), p. 29. Also see a National Science Foundation study in U.S. Congress, Joint Hearings before the Select Committee on Small Business and other committees, *Small Business and Innovation,* August 9–10, 1978, p. 7. For a more recent analysis, see John A. Hansen, "Innovation, Firm Size, and Firm Age," *Small Business Economics,* Vol. 4, No. 1 (March 1992), pp. 37–44. Also, see Harrison, op. cit., Chapter 3, questioning the innovative superiority of small firms.

14. "Sorrell Ridge Makes Smucker Pucker," *Forbes,* Vol. 143, No. 12 (June 12, 1989), pp. 166–168.

15. *The State of Small Business: A Report of the President 1987* (Washington, DC: U.S. Government Printing Office, 1987), p. 105.

16. Dun & Bradstreet issues an annual publication entitled *Business Failure Record.*

17. Kirchoff, op. cit., pp. 167–168.

18. Albert Shapero, "Numbers That Lie," *Inc.,* Vol. 3, No. 5 (May 1981), p. 16.

19. Graham Hall, "Reasons for Insolvency Amongst Small Firms—A Review and Fresh Evidence," *Small Business Economics,* Vol. 4, No. 3 (September 1992), pp. 237–249.

Chapter 3

1. Leslie Brokaw, "How to Start an *Inc. 500* Company," *Inc. 500* (Special Issue), 1994, p. 52.

2. Ibid., pp. 57–59.

3. Kevin Helliker, "Smile: That Cranky Shopper May Be a Store Spy," *The Wall Street Journal,* November 30, 1994, p. B1.

4. Amar Bhide, "Bootstrap Finance: The Art of Start-ups," *Harvard Business Review,* November–December 1992, pp. 109–117.

5. Brent Bowers, "Well, It Sounded Like a Great Idea," *The Wall Street Journal,* October 16, 1992, p. R4.

6. Stanford L. Jacobs, "Asian Immigrants Build Fortune in U.S. by Buying Cash Firms," *The Wall Street Journal,* October 1, 1984, p. 29.

7. If you are not familiar with the concept and process of discounting cash flows to their present value, read Appendix 23B.

8. The ideas presented in this section are taken from Leslie Brokaw, "The Truth About Start-ups," *Inc.,* Vol. 15, No. 3 (March 1993), pp. 56–64.

Chapter 4

1. *Franchise Fact Sheet,* International Franchise Association, July 25, 1994, p. 4.

2. Ibid.

3. Meg Whittemore, "Succeeding with Multiple Locations," *Nation's Business,* Vol. 82, No. 10 (October 1994), p. 66.

4. *The State of Small Business: A Report of the President 1993* (Washington, DC: U.S. Government Printing Office, 1993), p. 117.

5. For an empirical study of franchising advantages, see Alden Peterson and Rajiv P. Dant, "Perceived Advantages of the Franchise Option from the Franchisee Perspective: Empirical Insights from a Service Franchise," *Journal of Small Business Management,* Vol. 28, No. 3 (July 1990), pp. 46–61.

6. *The State of Small Business,* op. cit., p. 127.

7. As reported in Jeffrey A. Tannenbaum, "Chain Reactions," *The Wall Street Journal,* October 15, 1993, p. R6.

8. Erika Kotite, "Is Franchising for You?" *Franchise & Business Opportunities 1995, Entrepreneur* (Special Issue), p. 17.

9. As reported in McDonald's First Quarter Report, 1991.

10. Tannenbaum, op. cit., p. R6.

11. Cynthia E. Griffin, "Global Warning," *Entrepreneur,* Vol. 23, No. 1 (January 1995), p. 118.

12. James H. Amos, Jr., "Trends and Developments in International Franchising," *The Franchising Handbook,* American Management Association, 1993, p. 463.

13. See Jeffrey A. Tannenbaum, "More Franchisers Include Profit Claims in Pitches," *The Wall Street Journal,* August 20, 1991, p. B1.

14. Janean Huber, "Faking a Claim," *Entrepreneur,* Vol. 22, No. 10 (October 1994), p. 174.

15. Meg Whittemore, "A Consultant Who Has Gone the Distance," *Nation's Business,* Vol. 78, No. 5 (May 1990), p. 70.

16. "Warning Signs," *Franchise & Business Opportunities 1995, Entrepreneur* (Special Issue), pp. 24–25.

17. John R. Wilke, "Fraudulent Franchisers Are Growing," *The Wall Street Journal,* September 21, 1990, p. B1.

Chapter 5

1. Pat B. Alcorn, *Success and Survival in the Family-Owned Business* (New York: McGraw-Hill, 1982), p. 107.

2. Peter Davis, "Realizing the Potential of the Family Business," *Organizational Dynamics,* Vol. 12 (Summer 1983), pp. 53–54.

3. John Robben, "Have Toys, Will Travel: My Father's Journey," *Family Business,* Vol. 4, No. 1 (Winter 1993), p. 63.

4. W. Gibb Dyer, Jr., *Cultural Change in Family Firms* (San Francisco: Jossey-Bass, 1986), Chapter 2.

5. Marie-Jeanne Juilland, "The Good, the Bad, and the Ugly," *Venture,* Vol. 10, No. 1 (January 1988), p. 42.

6. "Brawl in the Family at Johnson Products," *Business Week* (March 23, 1992), p. 34.

7. Katy Danco, *From the Other Side of the Bed: A Woman Looks at Life in the Family Business* (Cleveland, OH: Center for Family Business, 1981), p. 21.

8. Nancy Upton, *Transferring Management in a Family-Owned Business* (Washington, DC: U.S. Small Business Administration, 1991), p. 6.

9. For an earlier extended treatment of this topic, see Justin G. Longenecker and John E. Schoen, "Management Succession in the Family Business," *Journal of Small Business Management,* Vol. 16 (July 1978), pp. 1–6.

10. Colette Dumas, "Integrating the Daughter into Family Business Management," *Entrepreneurship Theory and Practice,* Vol. 16, No. 4 (Summer 1992), p. 47.

11. Leon A. Danco, *Inside the Family Business* (Cleveland, OH: Center for Family Business, 1980), pp. 198–199.

Chapter 6

1. Mark Stevens, "Seven Stops to a Well-Prepared Business Plan," *Executive Female,* Vol. 18, No. 2 (March 1995), p. 30.

2. Kenneth Blanchard and Spencer Johnson, *The One-Minute Manager* (New York: William Morrow, 1982).

3. Stanley R. Rich and David Gumpert, *Business Plans That Win $$$: Lessons from the MIT Forums* (New York: Harper & Row, 1985), p. 22.

4. Ibid., p. 23.

5. Adapted from Phillip Thurston, "Should Smaller Companies Make Formal Plans?" *Harvard Business Review* (September–October 1983), p. 163.

6. *An Entrepreneur's Guide to Developing a Business Plan* (Chicago: Arthur Andersen and Company, 1990).

Chapter 7

1. Karl H. Vesper, *New Venture Strategies,* rev. ed. (Englewood Cliffs, NJ: Prentice-Hall, 1990), p. 192.

2. "IB Owners," *Independent Business* (July–August 1994), p. 19.

3. Ibid., p. 18.

4. Allen Conway, Sr., "When the Customer Needs It Yesterday," *Nation's Business,* Vol. 82, No. 4 (April 1994), p. 6.

5. Michael E. Porter, *Competitive Advantage* (New York: Free Press, 1985), p. 5.

6. Michael E. Porter, "Know Your Place," *Inc.,* Vol. 13, No. 9 (September 1992), pp. 90–93.

7. John Case, "How to Launch an *Inc. 500* Company," *Inc.,* Vol. 14, No. 10 (October 1992), p. 91.

8. Michael Selz, "Start-Up Tries to Break the Club's Lock on Car Security," *The Wall Street Journal,* October 24, 1994, p. B1.

9. John Pierson, "There's Mulch Ado About Composting in the Round," *The Wall Street Journal,* December 2, 1992, p. B1.

10. Cynthia E. Griffin, "Wee the People," *Entrepreneur,* Vol. 22, No. 8 (July 1994), p. 213.

11. Michael Barrier, "A Global Reach for Small Firms," *Nation's Business,* Vol. 82, No. 4 (April 1994), p. 66.

12. Jeffrey A. Tannenbaum, "New Magazine Targeting Poor Instead of Wealthy," *The Wall Street Journal,* November 7, 1994, p. B1.

13. Sharon Nelton, "Beating Back the Competition," *Nation's Business,* Vol. 82, No. 9 (September 1994), p. 24.

14. Roberta Maynard, "Rich Niches," *Nation's Business,* Vol. 81, No. 11 (November 1993), p. 39.

15. Amar Bhide, "How Entrepreneurs Craft Strategies That Work," *Harvard Business Review,* Vol. 72, No. 2 (March–April 1994), p. 154.

16. Michael E. Porter, *Competitive Advantage* (New York: Free Press, 1985), p. 5.

17. Erika Kotite, "Watch Your Back," *Entrepreneur,* Vol. 22, No. 8 (August 1994), pp. 112–117.

18. Gayle Sato Stodder, "Sole Survivor," *Entrepreneur,* Vol. 22, No. 10 (October 1994), pp. 112–117.

19. "(Can't Get No) Satisfaction," *Entrepreneur,* Vol. 21, No. 11 (November 1993), p. 12.

20. Carl Sewell and Paul B. Brown, "Customers for Life," *Family Business,* Vol. 1, No. 10 (November 1990), pp. 39–40.

21. John Case, "Total Customer Service," *Inc.,* Vol. 16, No. 1 (January 1994), pp. 52–61.

22. Paul B. Brown, "You Get What You Pay For," *Inc.,* Vol. 12, No. 10 (October 1990), p. 155.

23. For an overview of the principles of TQM, see Richard J. Schonberger, "Is Strategy Strategic? Impact of Total Quality Management on Strategy," *Academy of Management Executive,* Vol. 6, No. 3 (August 1992), pp. 80–87.

24. Patricia A. Galagan, "How to Get Your TQM Training on Track," *Nation's Business,* Vol. 80, No. 10 (October 1992), p. 26.

25. Joan Koob Cannre, with Donald Caplin, *Keeping Customers for Life* (New York: AMACOM, 1991), p. 237.

26. Jay Finegan, "The Rigorous Customer-Complaint Form," *Inc.,* Vol. 16, No. 3 (March 1994), p. 101.

Chapter 8

1. For an excellent article describing the role of marketing in entrepreneurship, see Gerald E. Hills and Raymond W. LaForge, "Research at the Marketing Interface to Advance Entrepreneurship Theory," *Entrepreneurship Theory and Practice,* Vol. 16, No. 3 (Spring 1992), pp. 33–59.

2. For more discussion of this point, see Oren Harari, "The Myths of Market Research," *Small Business Reports,* Vol. 19, No. 7 (July 1994), pp. 48–52.

3. Udayan Gupta, "Costly Market Research Pays Off for Biotech Start-up," *The Wall Street Journal,* August 2, 1993, p. B2.

4. "Marketing Research and the Small Business," *Small Business Success,* Vol. III, 1990, p. 38. Reprinted with permission from *Small Business Success,* published by Pacific Bell Directory in partnership with the U.S. Small Business Administration.

5. William Bak, "Read All about It," *Entrepreneur,* Vol. 22, No. 1 (January 1994), pp. 50–53.

6. Erskine Bowles, "Help Is Online," *Entrepreneur,* Vol. 22, No. 10 (October 1994), p. 168.

7. William Bak, "Read All about It," *Entrepreneur,* Vol. 22, No. 1 (January 1994), pp. 50–53. Reprinted with permission from *Entrepreneur* Magazine, January 1994.

8. Joshua Hyatt, "Steal This Strategy," *Inc.,* Vol. 13, No. 2 (February 1991), pp. 49–57.

9. Gayle Sato Strodder, "Right Off Target," *Entrepreneur,* Vol. 22, No. 10 (October 1994), p. 56.

10. Fleming Meeks, "And Then the Designer Left," *Forbes,* Vol. 150, No. 13 (December 7, 1992), pp. 162–164.

11. William Bak, "Hot Spots," *Entrepreneur,* Vol. 21, No. 6 (June 1993), pp. 56–57.

12. Richard Phalon, "Thin in the Wrong Places," *Forbes,* Vol. 149, No. 12 (June 8, 1992), pp. 62–63.

Chapter 9

1. Michael Barrier, "Creator of Habits," *Nation's Business,* Vol. 81, No. 11 (November 1993), p. 64.

2. U.S. Internal Revenue Service, *Statistics of Income, Corporation Income Tax Returns, and Statistics of Income Bulletin* (Washington, DC: U.S. Internal Revenue Service, 1993).

3. "The *Inc.* FaxPoll: Are Partners Bad for Business?" *Inc.,* Vol. 14, No. 2 (February 1992), p. 24.

4. Joshua Hyatt, "Reconcilable Differences," *Inc.,* Vol. 13, No. 4, p. 87. Reprinted with permission, *Inc.* magazine (April 1991). Copyright 1991 by Goldhirsh Group, Inc., 38 Commercial Wharf, Boston, MA 02110.

5. Gardner W. Heidrick, "Selecting Outside Directors," *Family Business Review,* Vol. 1, No. 3 (Fall 1988), p. 271. Copyright 1988 by Jossey-Bass Inc., Publishers.

6. Harold W. Fox, "Growing Concerns: Quasi-Boards—Useful Small Business Confidants," *Harvard Business Review,* Vol. 60, No. 1 (January–February 1982), p. 164.

7. Fred A. Tillman, "Commentary on Legal Liability: Organizing the Advisory Council," *Family Business Review,* Vol. 1, No. 3 (Fall 1988), pp. 287–288.

8. Based on discussion in Ted S. Frost, "Opting for 'S' Status, *D & B Reports* (November–December 1987), p. 6.

Chapter 10

1. Debra Phillips, "25 Best Cities for Small Business," *Entrepreneur,* Vol. 22, No. 10 (October 1994), p. 107.

2. Eugene Carlson, "Most Likely to Succeed," *The Wall Street Journal,* October 15, 1993, p. R10.

3. Toddi Gutner, "High Tech in Montana," *Forbes,* Vol. 150, No. 14 (December 21, 1992), p. 130.

4. Leah Ingram, "The State of Entrepreneurship: Wyoming," *Entrepreneur,* Vol. 22, No. 3 (March 1994), p. 143.

5. John Case, "The Best Places in America to Own a Business," *Inc.,* Vol. 14, No. 8 (August 1992), p. 38.

6. David Riggle, "The Best Place in the U.S. to Make It on Your Own," *In Business,* Vol. 16, No. 2 (March–April 1994), pp. 20–27.

7. Roberta Maynard, "Branching Out," *Nation's Business,* Vol. 82, No. 11 (November 1994), p. 53.

8. John S. DeMott, "Recasting Enterprise Zones," *Nation's Business,* Vol. 81, No. 2 (February 1993), p. 16.

9. Ibid., p. 21.

10. Heather C. Million, "Foreign Trade: Deep in the Heart of Texas," *Today's CPA,* Vol. 18, No. 3 (November–December 1992), pp. 25–28.

11. Personal telephone conversation with the National Association of Home-Based Businesses, November 9, 1995.

12. Barbara Marsh, "The Way It Works," *The Wall Street Journal,* October 14, 1994, p. R8.

13. Barbara Brabec, "Home Office Hints," *Independent Business,* Vol. 5, No. 3 (May–June 1994), p. 70.

14. Gail A. Smith, "When Not to Work Out of the Home," *Nation's Business,* Vol. 82, No. 7 (July 1994), p. 10.

15. Janean Huber, "Combat Zone," *Entrepreneur,* Vol. 22, No. 9 (September 1994), p. 100.

16. A discussion of these two layout patterns can be found in J. Barry Mason, Morris L. Mayer, and J. B. Wilkinson, *Modern Retail Theory and Practice,* 6th ed. (Homeword, IL: Richard D. Irwin, 1993), Chapter 16.

17. Roberta Maynard, "Could Your Shop Use a Face-Lift?" *Nation's Business,* Vol. 82, No. 8 (August 1994), p. 47.

Chapter 11

1. The cash flow statement is important for a firm of any size, small or large. But for many small firms, a monthly cash budget may be of even greater importance. The preparation of a cash budget is explained in Chapter 22 and should be used in conjunction with a cash flow statement.

2. As part of the financial projections, investors want to know the sales level required for a firm to break even in terms of profits. Measuring a firm's break-even point, while important from a financial perspective, is also needed in pricing its product or services. The pricing issue is addressed in Chapter 14. We will defer our discussion about break-even analysis until that time.

3. There is no economic rationale for 10,000 shares; it could just as easily have been 20,000 shares. In either case, the total value of the equity ownership would be the same; only the value per share would be different.

Chapter 12

1. Udayan Gupta, "Beyond the Banks," *The Wall Street Journal,* October 15, 1993, p. R7.

2. R. J. Gaston and S. E. Bell, *The Informal Supply of Capital* (Washington, DC: Office of Economic Research, U.S. Small Business Administration, 1988).

3. John Freear, Jeff A. Sohl, and William E. Wetzel, "Raising Venture Capital: An Entrepreneur's View of the Process." Paper presented at the Babson College Entrepreneurship Research Conference, 1993.

4. The information in this section regarding leasing comes from Janet L. Willen, "Should You Lease Office Equipment?" *Nation's Business,* Vol. 83, No. 5 (May 1995), p. 59.

5. Bruce G. Posner, "How to Pick a Factor," *Inc.,* Vol. 6, No. 2 (February 1992), p. 89.

6. J. Tol Broome, Jr., "A Loan at Last?" *Nation's Business,* Vol. 82, No. 8 (August 1994), p. 42.

7. Ibid.

8. Computing the annual payment of $52,759 requires using the present value function of a financial calculator or referring to Appendix C at the end of this book. To use the appendix, look up the interest factor for an interest rate of 10 percent for 5 years, which is 3.791. Then solve for payment by using the following equation:

Amount of loan = (Payment) (Interest factor)

$200,000 = (Payment) (3.791)

Payment = $52,757

The $2 difference from the amount shown in the example ($52,759 versus $52,757) is due to rounding differences between using a financial calculator and using the table values. The calculator answer is more accurate.

9. Broome, op.cit., p. 43.

10. Ibid.

11. Gupta, op. cit., p. R7.

12. Ibid.

13. Ibid.

14. Amar Bhide, "Bootstrap Finance: The Art of Startups," *Harvard Business Review*, Vol. 70, No. 6 (November–December 1992), pp. 117–118.

Chapter 13

1. James S. Hirsch, "Bron-Shoe Tries to Polish Image of an Old-Line Business," *The Wall Street Journal*, May 9, 1991, p. B2.

2. David J. Jefferson, "Manual-Ledger Maker's Strategy: Sell to the Small," *The Wall Street Journal*, September 26, 1991, p. B2.

3. Karen Blumenthal, "How Barney the Dinosaur Beat Extinction, Is Now Rich," *The Wall Street Journal*, February 28, 1992, p. B2; and Mimi Swartz, "Invasion of the Giant Purple Dinosaur," *Texas Monthly* (April 1993), p. 176.

4. "Presidential Hot Line," *Inc.*, Vol. 13, No. 2 (February 1991), p. 76.

5. Timothy L. O'Brien, "BertSherm Aims Its Deodorant at Pre-Adolescent Set," *The Wall Street Journal*, July 16, 1992, p. B2.

6. See Charles W. Lamb, Joseph F. Hair, Jr., and Carl McDaniel, *Principles of Marketing* (Cincinnati, OH: South-Western, 1994). An excellent discussion of the uniqueness of services is provided in Chapter 11.

7. Lamb, Hair, and McDaniel, op. cit. A detailed presentation of these policies can be found in Chapter 9.

8. Martha E. Mangelsdorf, "Growing with the Flow," *Inc. 500* (Special Issue), 1994, p. 90.

9. Bill Thomas, "Developing Passion for a Product," *Nation's Business*, Vol. 81, No. 12 (December 1993), p. 9.

10. Alyssa Gabbay, "The Sole of a True Inventor," *Waco Tribune-Herald*, December 2, 1994, p. 4C.

11. John R. Wilkie, "In Niches, Necessity Can Be the Mother of Reinvention," *The Wall Street Journal*, April 30, 1991, p. B2.

12. Justin Martin, "Lund International Holdings," *Fortune*, Vol. 130, No. 7 (October 3, 1994), p. 148.

13. See Calvin Pigg, "Organic Cotton: A Mix of Old and New," *Southwest Farm Press*, September 17, 1992, p. 14.

14. Roberta Maynard, "What a Difference a Package Makes," *Nation's Business*, Vol. 82, No. 2 (February 1994), p. 8.

Chapter 14

1. Bob Weinstein, "Price Pointers," *Entrepreneur*, Vol. 23, No. 2 (February 1995), p. 50.

2. For an excellent discussion of price setting, see Charles W. Lamb, Jr., Joseph F. Hair, Jr., and Carl McDaniel, *Principles of Marketing* (Cincinnati, OH: South-Western, 1994), Chapter 19.

3. Robert J. Calvin, "The Price Is Right," *Small Business Reports*, Vol. 19, No. 6 (June 1994), p. 13.

4. Based on Tracy L. Penwell, *The Credit Process: A Guide for Small Business Owners* (New York: Federal Reserve Bank of New York, 1994), p. 9.

5. Daniel B. Klein and Jason Richner, "What You Should Know about Credit Ratings," *Consumers' Research*, Vol. 75, No. 9 (September 1992), p. 11.

6. Richard J. Maturi, "Collection Dues and Don'ts," *Entrepreneur*, Vol. 20, No. 1 (January 1992), p. 326.

7. Brent Bowers, "Bill Collectors Thrive Using Kinder, Gentler Approach," *The Wall Street Journal*, March 2, 1992, p. B2.

8. Ibid.

9. "Red Alert," *Inc.*, Vol. 12, No. 12 (December 1990), p. 148.

10. For an example of a well-written collection letter, see "The Ideal Collection Letter," *Inc.*, Vol. 13, No. 2 (February 1991), pp. 60–61.

Chapter 15

1. For a more detailed discussion of prospecting, see Lawrence B. Chonko and Ben M. Enis, *Professional Selling* (Boston: Allyn and Bacon, 1993), Chapter 9.

2. Joseph Hair, Francis Notturno, and Frederick A. Russ, *Effective Selling*, 8th ed. (Cincinnati, OH: South-Western, 1991), pp. 254–355.

3. Howard E. Van Auken, B. Michael Doran, and Terri L. Rittenburg, "An Empirical Analysis of Small Business Advertising," *Journal of Small Business Management*, Vol. 30, No. 2 (April 1992), p. 90.

4. Suzanne Alexander, "For Cleaner Maker, Madison Avenue Is Just a Street," *The Wall Street Journal*, October 5, 1990, p. B2.

5. "How to Keep Your Name on the Minds of Clients," *Nation's Business*, Vol. 80, No. 9 (September 1992), p. 10.

6. Mary Jane Brand and Bitten Norman, "Greetings with a Playful Purpose," *Nation's Business*, Vol. 78, No. 7 (July 1990), p. 6.

7. Leslie Bloom, "Trade Show Selling Tactics," *In Business*, Vol. 10, No. 4 (July–August 1988), p. 43.

8. Jeffrey A. Tannenbaum, "Trade Shows Can Pay Off for New Firms," *The Wall Street Journal*, January 11, 1989, pp. B1–B2.

Chapter 16

1. Jeffrey A. Trachtenberg, "Avon's New TV Campaign Says, 'Call Us,'" *The Wall Street Journal*, December 28, 1992, p. B1.

2. *Something Ventured: An Entrepreneurial Approach to Small Business Management*, Episode 115 of a telecourse produced by INTELECOM (818-796-7300).

3. A good discussion of modes of transportation is found in Charles W. Lamb, Jr., Joseph F. Hair, Jr., and Carl McDaniel, *Principles of Marketing* (Cincinnati, OH: South-Western, 1994), Chapter 14.

4. Roger E. Axtell, "International Trade: A Small Business Primer," *Small Business Forum*, Vol. 10, No. 1 (Spring 1992), p. 47.

5. "It's a Small (Business) World," *Business Week* (April 17, 1995), p. 97.

6. Stephen J. Simurda, "Trade Secrets," *Entrepreneur*, Vol. 22, No. 5 (May 1994), p. 99.

7. U.S. Department of Commerce, "The ABCs of Exporting," *Business America*, Vol. 113, No. 9 (Washington, DC: U.S. Government Printing Office, 1992), p. 4.

8. An interesting analysis of firm size and exporting behavior is found in Abbas Ali and Paul M. Swiercz, "Firm Size and Export Behavior: Lessons from the Midwest," *Journal of Small Business Management*, Vol. 29, No. 2 (April 1991), pp. 71–78.

9. Julie Amparano Lopez, "Going Global," *The Wall Street Journal*, October 16, 1992, p. R20.

10. U.S. Department of Commerce, op. cit., p. 7.

11. Charles F. Valentine, "Blunders Abroad," *Nation's Business*, Vol. 44, No. 3 (March 1989), p. 54.

12. Roger Thompson, "EC92," *Nation's Business*, Vol. 77, No. 6 (June 1989), p. 18.

13. A more detailed analysis of the FTA is found in "The Canada–United States Free Trade Agreement and Its Implication for Small Business," *Journal of Small Business Management*, Vol. 28, No. 2 (April 1990), pp. 64–69.

14. A comprehensive analysis of NAFTA is presented in the U.S. Chamber of Commerce publication *A Guide to the North American Free Trade Agreement: Implications for U.S. Business.*

15. One interesting analysis is Saeed Samiee, "Strategic Considerations of the EC 1992 Plan for Small Exporters," *Business Horizons*, Vol. 33, No. 2 (April 1990), pp. 48–52.

16. Bill Holstein, "An Export Service of Great Import," *Business Week* (September 28, 1992), p. 138.

17. Dianna Solis, "Grass-Roots Marketing Yields Clients in Mexico City," *The Wall Street Journal*, October 24, 1991, p. B2.

18. Brent Bowers, "To Sell to the Japanese, Meet with Them Face to Face," *The Wall Street Journal*, March 12, 1992, p. B2.

19. Jill Andresky Fraser, "Structuring a Global Licensing Deal," *Inc.*, Vol. 14, No. 11 (November 1992), p. 45.

20. Lopez, op. cit., p. R20.

21. U.S. Department of Commerce, *A Basic Guide to Exporting* (Washington, DC: U.S. Government Printing Office, 1992), p. 13-2.

22. Eugene Carlson, "Entrepreneurs Risk Stumbling as They Rush into Russia," *The Wall Street Journal*, May 15, 1992, p. B2.

23. For further discussion of factoring, see R. Michael Rice, "Four Ways to Finance Your Exports," *The Journal of Business Strategy* (July–August 1988), pp. 30–31.

24. For addresses and telephone numbers of state offices providing export assistance, see U.S. Department of Commerce, "The ABCs of Exporting," *Business America*, Vol. 113, No. 9 (Washington, DC: U.S. Government Printing Office, 1992), pp. 28–29.

25. Ibid.

26. For a complete description of the Export Trading Company Act, see U.S. Department of Commerce, *The Export Trading Company Guidebook* (Washington, DC: U.S. Government Printing Office, 1987).

27. Alex F. DeNoble, Richard M. Castaldi, and Donald M. Moliver, "Export Intermediaries: Small Business Perceptions of Services and Performance," *Journal of Small Business Management*, Vol. 27, No. 2 (April 1989), pp. 33–41.

28. Martha E. Mangelsdorf, "Unfair Trade," *Inc.*, Vol. 13, No. 4 (April 1991), p. 33.

29. U.S. Department of Commerce, "A Directory of Export Services," *Business America*, Vol. 113, No. 9 (Washington, DC: U.S. Government Printing Office, 1992), pp. 10–11.

Chapter 17

1. Jim Schell, "In Defense of the Entrepreneur," *Inc.*, Vol. 13, No. 5 (May 1991), p. 30.

2. The best-known model is found in Neil C. Churchill and Virginia L. Lewis, "The Five Stages of Small Business Growth," *Harvard Business Review* (May–June 1983), pp. 3–12. A more recent study was conducted by Kathleen M. Watson and Gerhard R. Plaschka, "Entrepreneurial Firms: An Examination of Organizational Structure and Management Roles Across Life Cycle Stages," *Proceedings*, United States Association for Small Business and Entrepreneurship, Baltimore, Maryland, October 13–16, 1993.

3. "Is This Any Way to Run the Family Business?" *Business Week* (August 24, 1992), pp. 48–49.

4. "Special Report: Rethinking Work," *Business Week* (October 17, 1994), p. 77.

5. Michael Barrier, "Adversity Brings Opportunity," *Nation's Business*, Vol. 81, No. 4 (April 1993), pp. 31–34.

6. Personal communication from a student of one of the authors.

7. Stephen R. Covey, *The 7 Habits of Highly Effective People* (New York: Simon & Schuster, 1990), pp. 173–179.

8. David E. Gumpert and David P. Boyd, "The Loneliness of the Small Business Owner," *Harvard Business Review*, Vol. 62, No. 6 (November–December 1984), p. 19.

9. Bradford McKee, "A Boost for Start-ups," *Nation's Business*, Vol. 80, No. 8 (August 1992), pp. 40–42.

10. "First-Class Export Help," *Inc.*, Vol. 15, No. 10 (October 1993), p. 30.

11. Mike Copeland, "Score One for Free Enterprise," *Waco Tribune-Herald*, February 28, 1993.

12. John A. Boyd, "A Business Advisor's Guide to Counseling Theories," *Small Business Forum*, Vol. 11, No. 1 (Spring 1993), pp. 52–54.

13. "Small Firms Get Help from Advisory Boards," *The Wall Street Journal*, September 23, 1991, p. B1.

14. Bengt Johannisson and Rein Peterson, *The Personal Networks of Entrepreneurs.* Paper presented at the Third Canadian Conference, International Council for Small Business, Toronto, Canada, May 23–25, 1984.

15. Howard Scott, "Getting Help from Your Accountant," *IB Magazine*, Vol. 3, No. 3 (May–June 1992), p. 38.

Chapter 18

1. Ellyn E. Spragins, "Hiring Without the Guesswork," *Inc.*, Vol. 14, No. 2 (February 1992), p. 81.

2. John Case, "The Best Small Companies to Work for in America," *Inc.*, Vol. 14, No. 11 (November 1992), p. 93.

3. Barbara Rudolph, "Make Me a Match," *Inc.*, Vol. 13, No. 4 (April 1991), pp. 116–117.

4. Diane P. Burley, "Making Job Descriptions Pay," *Independent Business*, Vol. 5, No. 2 (March–April 1994), pp. 54–56.

5. Joan C. Szabo, "Training Workers for Tomorrow," *Nation's Business*, Vol. 81, No. 3 (March 1993), p. 22.

6. "Bonus Pay: Buzzword or Bonanza?" *Business Week* (November 14, 1994), pp. 62–63.

7. Roger Thompson, "Benefit Costs Hit Record High," *Nation's Business*, Vol. 83, No. 2 (February 1995), p. 36.

8. Roger Thompson, "Switching to Flexible Benefits," *Nation's Business*, Vol. 79, No. 7 (July 1991), pp. 16–23.

9. Joan C. Szabo, "Using ESOPs to Sell Your Firm," *Nation's Business*, Vol. 79, No. 1 (January 1991), pp. 59–60.

10. Timothy L. O'Brien, "Rise in Employee Leasing Spurs Scams," *The Wall Street Journal*, March 22, 1994, p. B1.

11. "Do You Need an Employee Policy Manual?" *In Business*, Vol. 10, No. 4 (July–August 1988), p. 48.

Chapter 19

1. "How to Spread the Gospel of Quality," *Business Week* (November 30, 1992), p. 122.

2. Adapted from Leonard L. Berry, A. Parasuraman, and Valarie A. Zeithaml, "Improving Service Quality in America: Lessons Learned," *Academy of Management Executive*, Vol. 8, No. 2 (May 1994), p. 36.

3. Kenneth E. Ebel, *Achieving Excellence in Business* (Milwaukee, WI: American Society for Quality Control, 1991), pp. 12–13.

4. Tom Ehrenfeld, "The New and Improved American Small Business," *Inc.*, Vol. 17, No. 1 (January 1995), pp. 34–48.

5. Donald C. Bacon, "How the Baldrige Winners Did It," *Nation's Business*, Vol. 77, No. 1 (January 1989), p. 32.

6. Ken Myers and Jim Buckman, "Beyond the Smile: Improving Service Quality at the Roots," *Quality Progress*, Vol. 25, No. 12 (December 1992), p. 57.

7. James B. Dilworth, *Operations Management: Design, Planning, and Control for Manufacturing and Services* (New York: McGraw-Hill, 1992), pp. 13–14.

8. Michael Hammer and James Champy, *Reengineering the Corporation* (New York: HarperCollins, 1994), p. 32.

Chapter 20

1. John Hawks, "Buying Right," *Independent Business*, Vol. 5, No. 6 (November–December 1994), p. 61.

2. Roberta Maynard, "The Power of Pooling," *Nation's Business*, Vol. 83, No. 3 (March 1995), pp. 15–22.

3. Laurel Touby, "The Big Squeeze on Small Businesses," *Business Week* (July 19, 1993), pp. 66–67.

4. Michael Barrier, "Call It 'Supplier Satisfaction,'" *Nation's Business*, Vol. 82, No. 5 (May 1994), pp. 56–57.

5. For formulas and calculations related to the economic order quantity, see an operations management textbook, such as James B. Dilworth, *Operations Management* (New York: McGraw-Hill, 1992), pp. 375–379.

6. Leila Davis, "Wider Uses for Bar Codes," *Nation's Business*, Vol. 77, No. 3 (March 1989), p. 34.

Chapter 21

1. Gary McWilliams, "Special Report," *Business Week* (November 21, 1994), p. 82.

2. John Verity, "The Internet: How It Will Change the Way You Do Business," *Business Week* (November 14, 1994), p. 80.

3. Michael Chorost, "What Can the Internet Do for My Business?" *Hispanic*, Vol. 8, No. 2 (March 1995), pp. 68–69.

4. See Roberta Maynard, "Small Business Meets the Internet," *Nation's Business* (May 1995), p. 11.

5. Ripley Hotch, "The Most Desired, Troubling Categories of Programs," *Nation's Business*, Vol. 78, No. 9 (September 1990), pp. 50–53.

6. James A. O'Brien, *Management Information Systems—A Managerial End User Perspective* (Homewood, IL: Richard D. Irwin, 1993), pp. 306–308.

7. Nancy Nichols, "Lease or Buy," *Inc.*, Vol. 13, No. 10 (October 1991), pp. OG60–OG62.

8. McWilliams, op. cit., pp. 82–90.

9. Ibid.

10. Udayan Gupta, "Home-Based Entrepreneurs Expand Computer Use Sharply, Study Shows," *The Wall Street Journal*, October 13, 1995, p. B1.

Chapter 22

1. Theresa W. Carey, "Bean Counting Made Easy," *PC World*, Vol. 13, No. 9 (September 1995), pp. 164–176.

2. See Jill Andresky Fraser, "Accounting Search," *Inc.*, Vol. 14, No. 10 (October 1992), p. 11.

3. See, for example, Charles Horngreen and Tom Harrison, *Principles of Accounting*, 2nd ed. (Englewood Cliffs, NJ: Prentice Hall, 1995).

4. Jack D. Baker and John A. Marts, "Internal Control for Protection and Profits," *Small Business Forum*, Vol. 8, No. 2 (Fall 1990), p. 29.

5. Dun & Bradstreet annually publishes a set of 14 key financial ratios for each of 125 types of businesses. Robert Morris Associates, the association of bank loan and credit officers, publishes a set of 16 key financial ratios for over 350 types of businesses. In both cases, the ratios are classified by industry and by firm size to provide a basis for more meaningful comparisons.

6. When we computed FGD's operating income return on investment earlier, we found it to be 10.87 percent. Now it is 10.85 percent. The difference is the result of rounding.

7. The relationship of a firm's return on equity to its operating profitability and the use of debt was explained in detail in Chapter 11. You may want to return to that discussion.

Chapter 23

1. "Working Capital," *Inc.*, Vol. 17, No. 6 (May 1995), p. 35.

2. Accruals are not considered in terms of managing working capital. Accrued expenses, although shown as a short-term liability, primarily result from the accountant's efforts to match revenues and expenses. There is little that could be done to "manage accruals."

3. Robert A. Mamis, "Money In, Money Out," *Inc.*, Vol. 15, No. 3 (March 1993), p. 100.

4. "Cash Flow: Who's in Charge," *Inc.*, Vol. 15, No. 11 (November 1993), p. 140.

5. "Working Capital," *Inc.*, Vol. 17, No. 6 (May 1995), p. 38.

6. "How to Unlock Your Company's Hidden Cash," *Inc.*, Vol. 2, No. 7 (July 1980), p. 64.

7. Robert M. Soldofsky, "Capital Budgeting Practices in Small Manufacturing Companies," in Dudley G. Luckett (ed.), *Studies in the Factor Markets for Small Business Firms* (Washington, DC: Small Business Administration, 1964).

8. L. R. Runyon, "Capital Expenditure Decision Making in Small Firms," *Journal of Business Research*, Vol. 11, No. 3 (September 1983), pp. 389–397.

9. To find the internal rate of return using either the Hewlett Packard 17B II or the TI BAII Plus, repeat the steps taken in Figure A23-1. Then for either calculator, press IRR. The answer will be 10.74 percent. Rather than having to enter the data again to compute the IRR, we could have solved for the NPV and the IRR while the data were still in the calculator. An even better approach is to use a computer spreadsheet, such as Excel or Lotus, to solve the problem.

Chapter 24

1. Emmett J. Vaughan, *Fundamentals of Risk and Insurance*, 6th ed. (New York: John Wiley & Sons, 1992), p. 5.

2. David Strutton, Scott J. Vitell, and Lou E. Pelton, "Making an Impact on the Shoplifter," *International Journal of Retail & Distribution Management*, Vol. 23, No. 2 (March 22, 1995), p. 12.

3. Joe Dacy II, "They Come to Steal," *Independent Business*, Vol. 3, No. 5 (September–October 1992), pp. 24–29.

4. Reprinted with permission of the Council of Better Business Bureaus, from *How to Protect Your Business*, copyright 1992. Council of Better Business Bureaus, Inc., 4200 Wilson Blvd., Arlington, VA 22203.

5. Dorothy Simonelli, "A Small Owner's Guide to Preventing Embezzlement," *Independent Business* (September–October 1992), pp. 30–31.

6. For a thorough discussion of these controls, see Neil H. Snyder and Karen E. Blair, "Dealing with Employee Theft," *Business Horizons*, Vol. 32, No. 3 (May–June 1989), pp. 27–34.

7. Barbara Marsh, "Small Businesses Face Problem from Crime Lawsuits," *The Wall Street Journal,* February 1, 1993, p. B2.

8. Terri Thompson, David Hage, and Robert F. Black, "Crime and the Bottom Line," *U.S. News & World Report* (April 13, 1992), p. 56.

9. Joan C. Szabo, "The Maze of Product Liability," *Nation's Business,* Vol. 78, No. 6 (June 1990), p. 62.

10. Jane Easter Bahls, "The Rewards of Risk Management," *Nation's Business,* Vol. 78, No. 9 (September 1990), p. 61.

11. Edward Felsenthal, "Self-Insurance of Health Plans Benefits Firms," *The Wall Street Journal,* November 11, 1992, p. B1.

12. Dale Buss, "Can You Afford to Self-Insure?" *Independent Business,* Vol. 4, No. 1 (January–February 1993), p. 40.

13. See, for example, the discussion in Archer W. Huneycutt and Elizabeth A. Wibker, "Liability Crisis: Small Businesses at Risk," *Journal of Small Business Management,* Vol. 26, No. 1 (January 1988), pp. 25–30.

14. Much of the terminology used here to describe the different types of insurance is consistent with that used in the Portfolio Program, suggested by the Insurance Services Office, a national rating bureau that publishes rates for property and liability insurance. This program introduced simplified policy terminology, effective January 1, 1986.

15. Nancy McConnell, "Business Insurance Good News and Bad News," *Venture,* Vol. 10, No. 9 (September 1988), p. 64.

16. John S. DeMott, "Key People, Key Protection," *Nation's Business,* Vol. 81, No. 3 (March 1993), p. 43.

17. For an excellent discussion of the Product Liability Risk Retention Act, see John Harkavy, "The Risk Retention Act of 1986: The Options Increase," *Risk Management,* Vol. 34, No. 3 (March 1987), pp. 22–34.

Chapter 25

1. Erika Wilson, "Social Responsibility of Business: What Are the Small Business Perspectives?" *Journal of Small Business Management,* Vol. 18, No. 3 (July 1980), pp. 17–24.

2. Janet Falon, "Juggling Act," *Business Ethics,* Vol. 8, No. 2 (March–April 1994), p. 13.

3. Kenneth E. Aupperle, F. Bruce Simmons III, and William Acar, "An Empirical Investigation into How Entrepreneurs View Their Social Responsibilities." Paper presented at the Academy of Management Meetings, San Francisco, California, August, 1990.

4. Some of these examples are cited in Bradford McKee, "Small Firms Pay for Clear Air," *Nation's Business,* Vol. 79, No. 3 (March 1991), p. 54.

5. Personal communication with Walnut Acres's management, January 1996.

6. Janet Novack, "You Know Who You Are, and So Do We," *Forbes,* Vol. 153, No. 8 (April 11, 1994), pp. 88–92.

7. This possibility is advanced by Michael Allen in "Small-Business Jungle," *The Wall Street Journal,* June 10, 1988, p. 19R.

8. Ibid.

9. Justin G. Longenecker, Joseph A. McKinney, and Carlos W. Moore, "Egoism and Independence: Entrepreneurial Ethics," *Organizational Dynamics,* Vol. 16, No. 3 (Winter 1988), pp. 64–72.

10. These differences were significant at the .05 level.

11. These differences were also significant at the .05 level.

12. Dick Youngblood, "A Firm That Means What It Says About Ethical Conduct," *Minneapolis–St. Paul Star Tribune,* December 28, 1992, p. 2D.

13. Ibid. Reprinted with permission of the *Minneapolis–St. Paul Star Tribune.*

14. Nationwide survey of business professionals conducted by Justin G. Longenecker, Joseph A. McKinney, and Carlos W. Moore in 1993.

15. Sample codes can be obtained from Ethics Resource Center, Inc., 1025 Connecticut Avenue, N.W., Washington, DC 20036.

16. Ben & Jerry's has since acquired a new president, and the 20 percent salary ratio no longer applies.

Chapter 26

1. Jack Faris, ed., *Small Business Under Siege* (Nashville, TN: Hammock Publishing, 1994), pp. 4–5.

2. Erika Kotite, "Call to Action," *Entrepreneur,* Vol. 22, No. 7 (July 1994), p. 95.

3. Jane Easter Bahls, "Seeing Red," *Entrepreneur,* Vol. 22, No. 6 (June 1994), p. 106.

4. Reported in "Crippling Regulations," *Small Business Reports,* Vol. 18, No. 4 (April 1993), p. 5.

5. David Warner, "Regulations' Staggering Costs," *Nation's Business,* Vol. 80, No. 6 (June 1992), p. 50.

6. David Warner, "How Do Federal Rules Affect You?" *Nation's Business,* Vol. 80, No. 5 (May 1992), p. 56.

7. Timothy D. Schellhardt, "Tax Changes by States Vex Small Concerns," *The Wall Street Journal,* June 17, 1992, p. B2.

8. Jeanne Saddler, "Small Businesses Complain That Jungle of Regulations Threatens Their Futures," *The Wall Street Journal,* June 11, 1992, p. B1.

9. Jeffrey A. Tannenbaum, "Government Red Tape Puts Entrepreneurs in the Black," *The Wall Street Journal,* June 12, 1992, p. B2.

10. Michael Selz, "Medical-Apparel Rule Is Boon for Laundries," *The Wall Street Journal,* August 14, 1992, p. B1.

11. "Here Comes the Fallout," *Independent Business,* Vol. 3, No. 7 (January–February 1992), p. 44.

12. Laura M. Litvan, "Family Leave Rules Issued," *Nation's Business,* Vol. 83, No. 2 (February 1995), p. 40.

13. See Junda Woo, "Trademark Law Protects Colors, Court Rules," *The Wall Street Journal,* February 25, 1993, p. B1; Junda Woo, "Product's Color Alone Can't Get Trademark Protection," *The Wall Street Journal,* January 5, 1994, p. B2; and Paul M. Barrett, "Color in the Court: Can Tints Be Trademarked?" *The Wall Street Journal,* January 5, 1995, p. B1.

14. G. Pascal Zachary, "Microsoft Loses Bid for a Trademark on the Word *Windows* for PC Software," *The Wall Street Journal,* February 25, 1993, p. B9.

15. Steven D. Glazer, "Patents: A Stake in the Future," *Nation's Business,* Vol. 82, No. 3 (March 1994), p. 36.

16. Maxine Lans Retsky, "The ABCs of Protecting Your Package," *Marketing News* (October 9, 1995), p. 12.

17. Rick Wartzman, "Don't Wave a Red Flag at the IRS," *The Wall Street Journal,* February 24, 1993, p. C1.

18. Cary Henrie, "Notes from the Underground Economy," *Business Week* (February 15, 1993), p. 99.

19. A good discussion of two of these software programs is found in Walter S. Mossberg, "These Two Programs Offer Some Relief in Taxing Situations," *The Wall Street Journal,* March 11, 1993, p. B1.

PHOTO CREDITS

479   © Amy Etra
481   © Jeff Greenberg
487   © PhotoDisc
498   © Stephen Ramsey
506   Photography by Alan Brown/Photonics Graphics
512   © Susan Lapides/Woodfin Camp and Associates
518   Courtesy of Sirikarn Saksripanith
520   © Charles Grupton/The Stock Market
534   © 1994 Rick Friedman/Black Star
537   © David Sutton/ZUMA
539   © Richard Hutchings/PhotoEdit
543   © Billy Barnes/PhotoEdit

554   Courtesy Reell Precision Manufacturing Corporation
556   Ted Thai/*Time Magazine*
557   © Tom Tracy/The Stock Market
558   © David Zadig
565   © 1989 Michael Melford
571   © Janise Witt
579   © Chuck Savage/The Stock Market
580   © T. Michael Keza/*Nation's Business*
582   Upper right: Courtesy *Adweek*; lower right: Photography by Photonics Graphics
585   Roark Johnson/Gamma Liaison

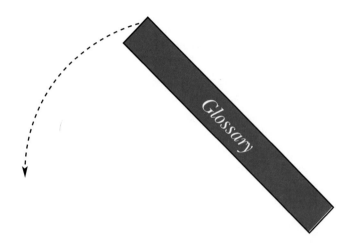

Glossary

A

ABC method a method of classifying items in inventory by relative value

acceptance sampling using a random sample to determine the acceptability of an entire lot

accounting return on investment technique a technique that evaluates a capital expenditure based on the average annual profits relative to the average book value of an investment

accounts payable (trade credit) outstanding credit payable to suppliers

accounts receivable the amount of credit extended to customers that is currently outstanding

accounts receivable turnover the number of times accounts receivable "roll over" during a year

accrual method of accounting (accrual-basis accounting) a method of accounting that matches revenues when they are earned against the expenses associated with those revenues

accrual-basis accounting *see* accrual method of accounting

accrued expenses short-term liabilities that have been incurred but not paid

acid-test ratio (quick ratio) a measure of a company's liquidity that excludes inventories

advertising the impersonal presentation of a business idea through mass media

advisory council a group that functions like a board of directors but acts only in an advisory capacity

agency power the ability of any partner to legally bind in good faith the other partners

agency relationship an arrangement in which one party represents another party in dealing with a third party

agents and brokers intermediaries that do not take title to the goods they distribute

aging schedule a categorization of accounts receivable based on the length of time they have been outstanding

Americans with Disabilities Act legislation that guarantees disabled people equal access to employment, as well as access to public places

application software programs that allow users to perform specific tasks on a computer

area developers individuals or firms that obtain the legal right to open several franchised outlets in a given area

articles of partnership a document that states explicitly the rights and duties of partners

artisan entrepreneur a person who starts a business with primarily technical skills and little business knowledge

asset-based lending financing secured by working-capital assets

asset-based valuation approach determination of the value of a business by estimating the value of its assets

assorting bringing together homogeneous lines of goods into a heterogeneous assortment

attitude an enduring opinion based on knowledge, feeling, and behavioral tendency

attractive small firm any small firm that provides substantial profits to its owner(s)

attribute inspection determining whether a product will or will not work

average collection period the average time it takes a firm to collect its accounts receivable

average pricing an approach using average cost as the basis for setting a price

B

bad-debt ratio a number obtained by dividing the amount of bad debts by the total amount of credit sales

bait advertising an insincere offer to sell a product or service at a very low price in order to entice customers, only to switch them later to the purchase of a more expensive product or service

balance sheet a financial report that shows a firm's assets, liabilities, and owners' equity at a specific point in time

batch manufacturing a type of production that is intermediate in volume and variety of products between job shops and repetitive manufacturing

benchmarking studying the products, services, and practices of other firms and using those examples to improve quality

benefit variables variables that distinguish market segments according to the benefits sought by customers

blue-sky laws state laws that protect investors from securities fraud

board of directors the governing body of a corporation, elected by the stockholders

brand a verbal or symbolic means of identifying a product

breakdown process a forecasting method that begins with a macro-level variable and works down to the sales forecast

breaking bulk an intermediary process that makes large quantities of product available in smaller amounts

budget a document that expresses future plans in monetary terms

buildup process a forecasting method that identifies all potential buyers in submarkets and adds up the estimated demand

business angels private investors who finance new, risky, small ventures

business format franchising an agreement whereby the franchisee obtains an entire marketing system and ongoing guidance from the franchisor

business incubator a facility that provides shared space, services, and management assistance to new businesses

business interruption insurance coverage of lost income and certain expenses while the business is being rebuilt

business plan a document containing the basic idea underlying a business and related considerations for starting up

business policies basic statements that provide guidance for managerial decision making

buyout purchasing an existing business

C

C corporation a type of corporation that is taxed by the federal government as a separate legal entity

capital budgeting analysis an analytical method that helps managers make decisions about long-term investments

capital gains and losses gains and losses incurred from the sale of property not used in the ordinary course of business operations

capitalization rate a figure, determined by the riskiness of current earnings and the expected growth rate of future earnings, that is used to assess the earnings-based value of a business

cash budget a planning document strictly concerned with the receipt and payment of dollars

cash conversion period the time required to convert paid-for inventories and accounts receivable into cash

cash flow from financing activities changes in a firm's cash position generated by payments to a firm's creditors, excluding interest payments, and cash received from investors

cash flow from investment activities changes in a firm's cash position generated by investments in fixed assets and other assets

cash flow from operations changes in a firm's cash position generated by day-to-day operations, including cash collections of sales and payments related to operations, interest, and taxes

cash flow statement a financial report that shows changes in a firm's cash position over a given period of time

cash flow–based valuation approach determination of the value of a business by a comparison of the expected and required rates of return on the investment

cash method of accounting (cash-basis accounting) a method of accounting that reports transactions only when cash is received or a payment is made

cash-basis accounting *see* cash method of accounting

cell the intersection of a row and a column on a spreadsheet

chain of command the official, vertical channel of communication in an organization

channel of distribution a system of intermediaries that distribute a product

chattel mortgage a loan for which items of inventory or other moveable property serve as collateral

Civil Rights Act legislation prohibiting discrimination based on race, color, sex, religion, or national origin

Clean Air Act federal legislation regulating air pollutants

client/server model a system whereby the user's personal computer (the client) obtains data from a central computer, but processing is done at the client level

code of ethics official standards of employee behavior formulated by a firm

cognitive dissonance the anxiety that occurs when a customer has second thoughts immediately following a purchase

coinsurance clause part of an insurance policy that requires the insured to maintain a specific level of coverage or to assume a portion of any loss

common carriers transportation intermediaries available for hire to the general public

communications control program software that controls the flow of information between computers

community-based financial institutions lenders that provide financing to small businesses in lower-income communities for the purpose of encouraging economic development there

competitive advantage a benefit that exists when a firm has a product or service that is seen by its target market as better than that of a competitor

compound value of a dollar the increasing value of a dollar over time resulting from interest earned both on the original dollar and on the interest received in prior periods

computer-aided design (CAD) the use of sophisticated computer systems to design new products

computer-aided manufacturing (CAM) the use of computer-controlled machines to manufacture products

consumer credit credit granted by retailers to individuals who purchase for personal or family use

consumerism a movement that stresses the needs of consumers and the importance of serving them honestly and well

continuous quality improvement a constant and dedicated effort to improve quality

contract carriers transportation intermediaries that contract with individual shippers

contracts agreements that are legally enforceable

control chart a graphic illustration of the limits used in statistical process control

copyright the exclusive right of a creator to reproduce, publish, or sell his or her own works

corporate charter the document that establishes a corporation's existence

corporate refugee a person who leaves big business to go into business for himself or herself

corporation a business organization that exists as a legal entity

corrective maintenance the repairs necessary to restore equipment or a facility to good condition

cost of capital the rate of return required to satisfy a firm's investors

cost of goods sold the cost of producing or acquiring goods or services to be sold by a firm

credit an agreement to delay payment for a product or service

credit bureau an organization that summarizes a number of firms' credit experiences with particular individuals

credit insurance coverage to protect against abnormal bad-debt losses

cultural configuration the total culture of a family firm, made up of the firm's business, family, and governance patterns

culture a group's social heritage, including behavior patterns and values

current assets (working capital) assets that will be converted into cash within a company's operating cycle

current debt (short-term liabilities) borrowed money that must be repaid within 12 months

current ratio a measure of a company's relative liquidity, determined by dividing current assets by current liabilities

customer profile a description of potential customers

customer satisfaction strategy a marketing plan that emphasizes customer service

customized software application programs designed or adapted for use by a particular company or type of business

cycle counting counting different segments of the physical inventory at different times during the year

D

database program application software used to manage files of related data

daywork a compensation system based on increments of time

debt capital business financing provided by creditors

debt ratio the ratio of total debt to total assets

debt-equity ratio the ratio of total debt to total equity

delegation of authority granting to subordinates the right to act or make decisions

demographic variables specific characteristics that describe customers and their purchasing power

depreciation expense costs related to a fixed asset, such as a building or equipment, distributed over its useful life

design patent registered protection for the appearance of a product and its inseparable parts

desktop publishing the production of high-quality printed documents on a personal computer system

direct channel a distribution channel without intermediaries

direct forecasting a forecasting method that uses sales as the predicting variable

direct loan money provided directly by the Small Business Administration

discounted cash flow (DCF) technique a capital budgeting technique that compares the present value of future cash flows with the cost of the initial investment

dishonesty insurance coverage to protect against employees' crimes

distributed processing using two or more computers in combination to process data

distribution physically moving products and establishing intermediary channels to support such movement

distribution function a small business activity that links producers and customers

double-entry system a self-balancing accounting system that uses journals and ledgers

dual distribution a distribution system that involves more than one channel

Dun & Bradstreet a company that researches and publishes business credit information

E

earnings-based valuation approach determination of the value of a business based on its potential future earnings

economic competition a situation in which businesses vie for sales

economic order quantity the quantity to be purchased that minimizes total inventory costs

elastic demand demand that changes significantly when there is a change in the price of a product

elasticity of demand the effect of a change in price on the quantity demanded

electronic data interchange (EDI) the exchange of data through computer links

electronic mail (E-mail) text messages transmitted directly from one computer to another

employee stock ownership plans (ESOPs) plans that give employees a share of ownership in the business

employer's liability insurance coverage against suits brought by employees

empowerment increasing employees' authority to make decisions or take action on their own

enterprise zones state-designated areas that are established to bring jobs to economically deprived areas through regulatory and tax incentives

entrepreneur a person who starts and/or operates a business

entrepreneurial team two or more people who work together as entrepreneurs

environmentalism the effort to protect and preserve the environment

Equal Access to Justice Act legislation requiring that small businesses be reimbursed for legal expenses in cases won against regulatory agencies

equipment loan an installment loan from a seller of machinery used by a business

ethical issues practices and policies involving questions of right and wrong

evaluative criteria the features of products that are used to compare brands

evoked set brands that a person is both aware of and willing to consider as a solution to a purchase problem

executive summary a section of the business plan, written to convey a clear and concise picture of the proposed venture

external equity equity that comes initially from the owners' investment in a firm

external locus of control believing that one's life is controlled more by luck or fate than by one's own efforts

F

facsimile (fax) machine a device that transmits and receives copies of documents via telephone lines

factoring obtaining cash by selling accounts receivable to another firm

failure rate the proportion of businesses that close with a loss to creditors

family business a company in which family members are directly involved in the ownership and/or functioning

family council an organized group of family members who gather periodically to discuss family-related business issues

Family and Medical Leave Act legislation that assures employees of unpaid leave for childbirth or other family needs

family retreat a gathering of family members, usually at a remote location, to discuss family business matters

favorable financial leverage benefit gained by investing at a rate of return that is greater than the interest rate on a loan

fax modem a circuit board that allows a document to be sent from a computer disk to another computer or a fax machine

file server the computer that stores the programs and common data for a local area network

financial leverage the use of debt in financing a firm's assets

financial plan a section of the business plan providing an account of the new firm's financial needs and sources of financing and a projection of its revenues, costs, and profits

financial ratios restatements of selected income statement and balance sheet data in relative terms

financial statements (accounting statements) reports of a firm's financial performance and resources, including an income statement, a balance sheet, and a cash flow statement

financing costs the amount of interest owed to lenders on borrowed money

fixed asset turnover a financial ratio that measures the relationship of sales to fixed assets

fixed assets relatively permanent resources intended for use in the business

flexible pricing strategy a marketing approach that offers different prices to reflect demand differences

follow-the-leader pricing strategy a marketing approach that sets prices using a particular competitor as a model

Foreign Corrupt Practices Act legislation making it illegal to pay bribes to foreign officials

foreign refugee a person who leaves his or her native country and becomes an entrepreneur in a new country

foreign trade zone an area within the United States designated to allow foreign and domestic goods to enter without being subject to certain customs and excise taxes

founder an entrepreneur who brings a new firm into existence

franchise the privileges in a franchise contract

franchise contract the legal agreement between franchisor and franchisee

franchisee an entrepreneur whose power is limited by a contractual relationship with a franchising organization

franchising a marketing system revolving around a two-party legal agreement, whereby the franchisee conducts business according to terms specified by the franchisor

franchisor the party in a franchise contract who specifies the methods to be followed and the terms to be met by the other party

Free Trade Agreement (FTA) an accord that eases trade restrictions between the United States and Canada

free-flow pattern a type of retail store layout that is visually appealing and gives customers freedom of movement

fringe benefits nonfinancial supplements to employees' compensation

G

General Agreement on Tariffs and Trade (GATT) an international agreement that helps efforts to protect U.S.-patented products and reduces certain import tariffs

general liability insurance coverage against suits brought by customers

general manager an entrepreneur who functions as an administrator of a business

general partner the partner with unlimited personal liability in a limited partnership

general-purpose equipment machines that serve many functions in the production process

geographic information systems (GIS) programs that connect a physical map with a customer database

grid pattern a block-like type of retail store layout that provides for good merchandise exposure and simple security and cleaning

gross profit sales less the cost of goods sold

growth trap a cash shortage resulting from rapid growth

guaranty loan money provided by a private lender, for which the Small Business Administration guarantees repayment

H

headhunter a search firm that locates qualified candidates for executive positions

high-potential venture (gazelle) a small firm that has great prospects for growth

home-based business a business that maintains its primary facility in the residence of its owner

I

income statement (profit and loss statement) a financial report showing the profit or loss from a firm's operations over a given period of time

indirect channel a distribution channel with one or more intermediaries

indirect forecasting a forecasting method that uses variables related to sales to project the sales forecast

inelastic demand demand that does not significantly change when there is a change in the price of a product

informal capital funds provided by wealthy private individuals to high-risk ventures, such as startups

initial public offering (IPO) issuance of stock that is to be traded in public financial markets

inspection scrutinizing a product to determine whether it meets quality standards

inspection standard a specification of a desired quality level and allowable tolerances

installment account a line of credit that requires a down payment with the balance paid over a specified period of time

institutional advertising advertising designed to enhance a firm's image

internal control a system of checks and balances that safeguards assets and enhances the accuracy and reliability of financial statements

internal equity equity that comes from retaining profits within a firm

internal locus of control believing that one's success depends upon one's own efforts

internal rate of return (IRR) the rate of return a firm expects to earn on a project

inventory a firm's raw materials and products held in anticipation of eventual sale

inventory turnover the number of times inventories "roll over" during a year

ISO 9000 the standards governing international certification of a firm's quality management procedures

J

job description a written summary of duties required by a specific job

Job Instruction Training a systematic step-by-step method for on-the-job training of nonmanagerial employees

job shops manufacturing operations in which short production runs are used to produce small quantities of unique items

job specification a list of skills and abilities needed by a job applicant to perform a specific job

just-in-time inventory system a system for reducing inventory levels to an absolute minimum

K

key-person insurance coverage that protects against the death of a firm's key personnel

L

laws of motion economy guidelines for increasing the efficiency of human movement and tool design

leasing employees "renting" personnel from an organization that handles paperwork and benefits administration

legal entity a business organization that is recognized by the law as having a separate legal existence

letter of credit an agreement to honor demands for payment under certain conditions

licensing legally agreeing that a product may be produced in return for royalties

limited liability the restriction of an owner's legal financial responsibilities to the amount invested in the business

limited partner a partner who is not active in the management of a limited partnership and who has limited personal liability

limited partnership a partnership with at least one general partner and one or more limited partners

line activities activities contributing directly to the primary objectives of a small firm

line of credit an informal agreement between a borrower and a bank as to the maximum amount of funds the bank will provide at any one time

line organization a simple organizational structure in which each person reports to one supervisor

line-and-staff organization an organizational structure that includes staff specialists who assist management

liquidation value approach determination of the value of a business based on the money available if the firm were to liquidate its assets

liquidity the ability of a firm to meet maturing debt obligations by having adequate working capital available

local area network (LAN) an interconnected group of personal computers and related hardware located within a limited area

lock box a post-office box for receiving remittances from customers

long-range plan (strategic plan) a firm's overall plan for the future

long-term debt loans from banks or other sources with repayment terms of more than 12 months

M

major industries the eight largest groups of businesses as specified by the U.S. Department of Commerce

make-or-buy decision a firm's choice between making and buying component parts for the products it makes

management functions the activities of planning, leading, organizing, and controlling

management plan a section of the business plan describing the key players in a new firm and their experience and qualifications

management team managers and other key persons who give a company its general direction

marginal firm any small firm that provides minimal profits to its owner(s)

market a group of customers or potential customers who have purchasing power and unsatisfied needs

market analysis evaluation process that encompasses market segmentation, marketing research, and sales forecasting

market segmentation division of a market into several smaller groups with similar needs

market-based valuation approach determination of the value of a business based on the sale prices of comparable firms

marketing mix product, pricing, promotion, and distribution activities

marketing plan a section of the business plan describing the user benefits of the product or service and the type of market that exists

marketing research gathering, processing, reporting, and interpreting market information

master licensee firm or individual acting as a sales agent with the responsibility for finding new franchisees within a specified territory

matchmakers specialized brokers who bring together buyers and sellers of businesses

material requirement planning (MRP) controlling the timely ordering of production materials by using computer software

merchant middlemen intermediaries that take title to the goods they distribute

minicomputer a medium-sized computer that is capable of processing data input simultaneously from a number of sources

modified book value approach determination of the value of a business by adjusting book value to reflect differences between the historical cost and the current value of the assets

mortgage a long-term loan from a creditor that pledges an asset, such as real estate, as collateral for the loan

motion study an analysis of all the motions a worker makes to complete a given job

motivations forces that give direction and organization to the tension of unsatisfied needs

multimedia a combination of text, graphics, audio, and video in a single presentation

multiple-unit ownership a situation in which a franchisee owns more than one franchise from the same company

multisegmentation strategy recognizing different preferences of individual market segments and developing a unique marketing mix for each

multitasking the ability of a computer to carry out multiple functions at one time

N

need for achievement a desire to succeed, where success is measured against a personal standard of excellence

needs the starting point for all behavior

negotiable instruments credit documents that are transferable from one party to another in place of money

net income available to owners (net income) income that may be distributed to the owners or reinvested in the company

net present value (NPV) the present value of future cash flows less the initial investment outlay

net working capital the sum of a firm's current assets (cash, accounts receivable, and inventories) less current liabilities (accounts payable and accruals)

network card a circuit card required for computers on a local area network

network control program software that controls access to a local area network

networking the process of developing and engaging in mutually beneficial relationships

niche marketing choosing market segments not adequately served by competitors

normalized earnings earnings that have been adjusted for unusual items, such as fire damage

North American Free Trade Agreement (NAFTA) an accord that removes Mexican tariffs from U.S.-made products

Nutrition Labeling and Education Act legislation that requires producers to carry labels disclosing nutritional information on food packaging

O

Occupational Safety and Health Act legislation that regulates the safety of workplaces and work practices

open charge account a line of credit that allows the customer to obtain a product at the time of purchase, with payment due when billed

operating expenses costs related to general administrative expenses and marketing and distributing a firm's product or service

operating income (earnings before interest and taxes) profits before interest and taxes are paid

operating income return on investment (OIROI) a measure of operating profits relative to total assets

operating plan a section of the business plan describing the new firm's facilities, labor, raw materials, and processing requirements

operating profit margin a ratio of operating profits to sales

operating system the software that controls the flow of information in and out of a computer and links hardware to application programs

operations management the planning and control of the operations process

operations process (production process) the activities that accomplish a firm's work

opinion leader a group leader who plays a key communications role

opportunistic entrepreneur a person who starts a business with both sophisticated managerial skills and technical knowledge

opportunity cost the rate of return that could be earned on another investment of similar risk

ordinary income income earned in the ordinary course of business, including any salary

organizational culture patterns of behaviors and beliefs that characterize a particular firm

other assets assets that are neither current nor fixed and may be intangible

other payables other short-term credit, such as interest payable or taxes payable

outsourcing the purchase of business services, such as janitorial services, that are outside the firm's area of competitive advantage

owners' equity capital owners' investments in a company, including the profits retained in the firm

P

Paperwork Reduction Act legislation that simplifies regulatory rules for small businesses

partnership a voluntary association of two or more persons to carry on, as co-owners, a business for profit

patent the registered, exclusive right of an inventor to make, use, or sell an invention

payback period technique a capital budgeting technique that measures the amount of time it takes to recover the cash outlay of an investment

penetration pricing strategy a marketing approach that sets lower than normal prices to hasten market acceptance or to increase market share

percentage-of-sales technique a method to forecast asset investments and financing requirements

perception the individual processes that give meaning to the stimuli that confront consumers

perceptual categorization the perceptual process of grouping similar things to manage huge quantities of incoming stimuli

perpetual inventory system a system for keeping a running record of inventory

personal computer (microcomputer) a small computer used by only one person at a time

personal selling a sales presentation delivered in a personal, one-on-one manner

physical distribution (logistics) the activities of distribution that result in the relocation of products

physical inventory system a system for periodic counting of items in inventory

piggyback franchising the operation of a retail franchise within the physical facilities of a host store

plant patent registered protection for any distinct and new variety of plant

pledged accounts receivable accounts receivable used as collateral for a loan

pooling purchases combining with other firms to buy materials or merchandise from a supplier

precipitating event an event, such as losing a job, that moves an individual to become an entrepreneur

pre-emptive right the right of stockholders to buy new shares of stock before they are offered to the public

prepaid expenses current assets that typically are used up during the year, such as prepaid rent or insurance

prestige pricing setting a high price to convey the image of high quality or uniqueness

preventive maintenance the activities intended to prevent machine breakdowns and damage to people and facilities

price a seller's measure of what he or she is willing to receive in exchange for transferring ownership or use of a product or service

price lining strategy a marketing approach that sets a range of several distinct merchandise price levels

primary data market information that is gathered by the entrepreneur through various methods

prime rate the interest rate charged by a commercial bank on loans to its most creditworthy customers

private carriers shippers that own their means of transport

private placement the sale of a firm's capital stock to selected individuals

pro forma financial statements reports that provide projections of a firm's financial condition

procedures specific methods followed in business activities

process layout a factory layout that groups similar machines together

product a bundle of satisfaction—a service, a good, or both—offered to customers in an exchange transaction

product advertising the presentation of a business idea designed to make potential customers aware of a product or service and their need for it

product item the lowest common denominator in the product mix—the individual item

product layout a factory layout that arranges machines according to their roles in the production process

product line all the individual product items that are related

product mix a firm's total product lines

product mix consistency the similarity of product lines in a product mix

product strategy the way a product is marketed to achieve a firm's objectives

product and trade name franchising a franchise relationship granting the right to use a widely recognized product or name

productivity the efficiency with which inputs are transformed into outputs

products and/or services plan a section of the business plan describing the product and/or service to be provided and explaining its merits

professional manager a manager who uses systematic, analytical methods of management

profit retention the reinvestment of profits in a firm

promotion persuasive communications between a business and its target market

promotional mix a blend of personal and nonpersonal promotional methods aimed at a target market

prospecting a systematic process of continually looking for new customers

publicity information about a firm and its products or services that appears as a news item

purchase order a written form issued to a supplier to buy a specified quantity of some item or items

purchase requisition a formal internal request that something be bought for a business

purchasing the process of obtaining materials, equipment, and services from outside suppliers

purchasing group an unincorporated group of firms that purchases liability insurance for its members

Q

quality the features of a product or service that enable it to satisfy customers' needs

quality circle a group of employees who meet regularly to discuss quality-related problems

R

real estate mortgage a long-term loan with real property held as collateral

reciprocal buying the policy of buying from the businesses to which a firm sells

reengineering a fundamental restructuring to improve the operations process

reference groups groups that influence individual behavior

refugee a person who becomes an entrepreneur to escape an undesirable situation

Regulatory Flexibility Act legislation that protects small firms from excessive federal regulation by simplifying rules and reducing paperwork

reliability the consistency of a test in measuring job performance ability

reorder point the level at which additional quantities of items in inventory should be ordered

repetitive manufacturing the production of a large quantity of a standardized product by means of long production runs

replacement value approach determination of the value of a business based on the cost necessary to replace the firm's assets

retained earnings profits less withdrawals (dividends)

return on equity the rate of return that owners earn on their investment

revolving charge account a line of credit on which the customer may charge purchases at any time, up to a pre-established limit

revolving credit agreement a legal commitment by a bank to lend up to a maximum amount

risk the chance that a situation may end with loss or misfortune

risk management ways of coping with risk that are designed to preserve assets and the earning power of a firm

risk premium the difference between the required rate of return on a given investment and the risk-free rate of return

risk-retention group an insurance company started by a homogeneous group of entrepreneurs or professionals to provide liability insurance for its members

S

safety stock inventory maintained to protect against stockouts

sales forecast a prediction of how much will be purchased within a market during a defined time period

sales promotion an inclusive term for any promotional techniques that are neither personal selling nor advertising

SBA standards the standards set by the Small Business Administration (SBA) that specify the size limits for small firms

secondary data market information that has been previously compiled by others

Section 1244 stock stock that offers some tax benefit to the stockholder in the case of corporate failure

segmentation variables the parameters used to distinguish one form of market demand from another

self-insurance designating part of a firm's earnings as a cushion against possible future losses

self-service layout a retail store layout that gives customers direct access to merchandise

serendipity the faculty for making desirable discoveries by accident

service bureaus firms that use their computer systems to process data for business customers

Service Corps of Retired Executives (SCORE) an SBA-sponsored group of retired executives who give free advice to small businesses

service function an activity in which small businesses provide repair and other services that aid larger firms

service mark a legal term indicating the exclusive right to use a brand to identify a service

short-range plans plans that govern a firm's operations for one year or less

short-term notes cash amounts borrowed from a bank or other lending sources that must be repaid within a short period of time

single-entry system a checkbook system of accounting reflecting only receipts and disbursements

single-segmentation strategy recognizing the existence of several distinct market segments, but pursuing only the most profitable segment

size criteria criteria by which the size of a business is measured

skimming price strategy a marketing approach that sets very high prices for a limited period before reducing them to more competitive levels

Small Business Development Centers (SBDCs) university-affiliated centers offering consulting, education, and support to small businesses

Small Business Innovative Research (SBIR) program a government program that helps finance companies that plan to transform laboratory research into marketable products

Small Business Institute (SBI) an SBA-sponsored program making the consulting services of student teams available to small businesses

small business investment companies (SBICs) privately owned banks, regulated by the Small Business Administration, that supply capital to small businesses

small business marketing identifying target markets, assessing their potential, and delivering satisfaction

social classes divisions in a society with different levels of social prestige

social responsibilities ethical obligations to customers, employees, and the general community

software programs that provide operating instructions to a computer

sole proprietorship a business owned and operated by one person

span of control the number of subordinates supervised by one manager

special-purpose equipment machines designed to serve specialized functions in the production process

spontaneous financing short-term debts, such as accounts payable, that spontaneously increase in proportion to a firm's increasing sales

spreadsheet program application software that allows users to perform accounting and other numerical tasks on an electronic worksheet

staff activities activities that support line activities

stages in succession phases in the process of transferring leadership from parent to child in a family business

standard operating procedure an established method of conducting a business activity

startup creating a new business from scratch

statistical process control using statistical methods to assess quality during the operations process

statute of frauds a law under which specific agreements must be made in writing

stock certificate a document specifying the number of shares owned by a stockholder

strategic decision a decision regarding the direction a firm will take in relating to its customers and competitors

Subchapter S corporation a type of corporation that is taxed by the federal government as a partnership

supply function an activity in which small businesses function as suppliers and subcontractors for larger firms

surety bonds coverage to protect against another's failure to fulfill a contractual obligation with the insured

System A franchising a franchising system in which a producer grants a franchise to a wholesaler

System B franchising a franchising system in which a wholesaler is the franchisor

System C franchising the most widely used franchising system in which a producer is the franchisor and a retailer is the franchisee

system software programs that control the internal functioning of a computer

T

telecommunications the exchange of data among remote computers

telecommuting working at home by using a computer link to the business location

Telephone Consumer Protection Act legislation that offers consumers protection from intrusive telemarketing

template a pre-programmed form on which a user fills in blanks with specific data

term loan money loaned for a five- to ten-year term, corresponding to the length of time the investment will bring in profits

terminal emulation a communications mode that allows personal computers to exchange information with mainframes

throughput the amount of work that can be done by a computer in a given amount of time

time study the determination of a worker's average time to complete a given task

time sharing accessing the capabilities of a powerful computer system by paying a variable fee for the privilege of using it

times interest earned the ratio of operating income to interest charges

total asset turnover a measure of the efficiency with which a firm's assets are used to generate sales

total cost the sum of cost of goods sold, selling expenses, and general administrative expenses

total fixed costs costs that remain constant as the quantity produced or sold varies

total quality management (TQM) an all-encompassing management approach to providing high-quality products and services

total variable costs costs that vary with the quantity produced or sold

trade credit financing provided by a supplier of inventory to a given company, which sets up an account payable for the amount

trade dress elements of a firm's distinctive image not covered by a trademark or patent

trade-credit agencies privately owned organizations that collect credit information on businesses

trademark an identifying feature used to distinguish a manufacturer's product

transfer of ownership the final step in conveyance of power from parent to child, that of distributing ownership of the family business

two-bin method a simple inventory control technique for indicating the reorder point

Type A ideas startup ideas to provide customers with an existing product not available in their market

Type B ideas startup ideas to provide customers with a new product

Type C ideas startup ideas to provide customers with an improved product

U

underlying values unarticulated ethical beliefs that provide a foundation for ethical behavior

Uniform Franchise Offering Circular (UFOC) a document accepted by the Federal Trade Commission as satisfying its franchise disclosure requirements

unity of command a situation in which each employee's instructions come directly from only one immediate supervisor

unlimited liability owner's liability that extends beyond the assets of the business

unsegmented strategy defining the total market as a target market

utility patent registered protection for a new process or a product's function

V

validity the extent to which a test assesses true job performance ability

variable inspection evaluating a product in terms of a variable such as weight or length

variable pricing strategy a marketing approach that sets more than one price for a good or service in order to offer price concessions to various customers

venture capitalist an investor or investment group that invests in new business ventures

voice mail telephone messages stored by a computerized system

W

warranty a promise that a product will do certain things or meet certain standards

weighted cost of capital the cost of capital adjusted to reflect the relative costs of debt and equity financing

Women's Business Ownership Act legislation intended to further the interests of women-owned firms and remove discriminatory barriers

word-processing program application software that allows users to create, manipulate, and print text and graphics on a computer

work group software computer programs that help coordinate the efforts of employees working together on a project

work sampling a method of work measurement that estimates the ratio of working time to idle time

work teams groups of employees with freedom to function without close supervision

workers' compensation insurance coverage that obligates the insurer to pay employees for injury or illness related to employment

working-capital cycle the daily flow of resources through a firm's working-capital accounts

working-capital management the management of current assets and current liabilities

workstations powerful personal computers able to carry out multitasking

WYSIWYG acronym for "What You See Is What You Get"

Z

zoning ordinances local laws regulating land use

Index

A

ABC method, 447
Acceptance sampling, 422
Accola, Harlan, 121
Accounting. *See also* Accounting systems
    accrual-basis, 236
    cash-basis, 237
Accounting return on investment technique, 515–516
Accounting services, 479–480
Accounting software, 478–479
Accounting statements. *See* Financial statements
Accounting systems, 236–237, 477–480
    alternative, 480
    basic requirements of, 477–480
    cash versus accrual, 480
    double-entry, 480
    internal control of, 481–482
    and managerial control, 478
    single-entry, 480
Accounts payable, 233, 265–266, 655
    management of, 513–514
Accounts receivable, 232, 653
    aging of, 322–324
    collecting, case study of, 629–630
    management of, 510–511
Accounts-receivable financing, 511
Accounts-receivable turnover, 486, 494
Accrual method of accounting, 480
Accrual-basis accounting, 236
Accrued expenses, 233
Achievement, need for, 9
Acid-test ratio, 484, 494
Ackerman, Richard, 325

Acrilex Inc., 216
Acs, Zoltan J., 29
Advertising, 339–343
    assistance in, 341–343
    bait, 567
    frequency of, 340
    help-wanted, 400
    institutional, 340
    media, 340–341, 342–343
    objectives of, 339–340
    product, 340
Advertising Age, 332
Advisory council, 198–199
Agency power, 189
Agency relationship, 587
Agents, 351
Aging schedule, 322
AgRecycle, Inc., 246
A.J. & Co. Big and Tall, 150
Akin, Philip, 575
Aladdin Steel Products, 315
Alden Press, 612
Alexander, Arminda, 209
Alexander, Bob, 209
Alexander Doll Company, 432
Allawos, Michael, 454
Allen, Paul, 263
Allen-Edmonds Shoe Corporation, 448
Allwest Fire & Sound, 445
Alphatronix, 212
American Legal Distributors, 87–88
American Society for Quality Control, 416
Americans with Disabilities Act, 403, 409, 573, 579

Andreesson, Marc, 142
Annuity, 525
Antitrust laws, 577
Apex Electronics, 571
Apple, 459
Application software, 460
Applied Composite, 216
Area developers, 68
Arkansas Flag & Banner, 228
Armadillo Construction, 214
Arthur Andersen and Company, 71, 122, 356
Arthur Andersen Enterprise Group, 573
Articles of partnership, 188–189
Artis, Henry, 141
Artisan entrepreneur, 18
Artistic Impressions, 260
Asacker, Tom, 436
Asset(s)
    current, 231
    fixed, 233
    intangible, protection of, 581–586
    other, 233
    requirements for, estimating, 243–245
    types of, 231–233
Asset-based lending, 267
Asset-based valuation approach, 54
Associated Credit Bureaus of America, 322
Assorting, 351
Atlantic Publication Group, Inc., 148
AT&T Small Business Study, 129
Attitude, 289
Attractive small firms, 18
Attribute inspection, 422

Aubin, Leslie, 176
Auburn Farms, Inc., 26
Audretsch, David B., 29
Average collection period, 486, 494
Average pricing, 308
Ayscue, Ozzie, 610–613

B

Babbage's, 51
Bad-debt ratio, 326
Baechler, Mary, 99, 502
Baechler, Phil, 99
Bagley, Mark, 301
Bait advertising, 567
Balance sheet, 231–235, 485
Bank(s)
    exporting assistance from, 364–365
    as source of financing, 260, 267–272
Bank credit cards, 318–319
Bank loans, types of, 267–268
Banker(s)
    perspective of, in loan decision,
        268–270
    selection of, 270
    as source of credit information, 322
BankTemps, 498
Bar-code system, 451
Barefoot, Pamela, 391
Barney the Dinosaur, 285
Barnyard Babies, Inc., 349
*Basic Facts About Registering a Trade-
    mark*, 581
Basic Guide to Exporting, A, 359,
    362–363
Baskin-Robbins, 73
Batch manufacturing, 427
Baxter, William, 561
Bayshore Metals, 548–549
B. D. Baggies, 363
Bell, S. E., 263
Benchmarking, 420
Benefit variables, 147
Bennett, Charles, 310
Benolds, 538
BertSherm Products, Inc., 291
Better Business Bureaus, 567–568
Beyond High School, 210
Bhide, Amar, 48, 276
Bicknell Manufacturing Company, 290
Bihn, Adele, 98–99
Billing procedures, 324
Biosite Diagnostics, Inc., 163–164
Birch, David L., 16, 29
Biver, John, 184
BizPlan*Builder*, 130, 133, 134, 135,
    136, 158, 181, 205, 227, 253, 280
Blanchard, Kenneth, 118
Blickenstaff, Kim, 164
Blue Chip Enterprises, 3

Blue Crab Bay Co., 391
Blue-sky laws, 578
Blum, Rodney, 184
Board of directors, 195–199
    compensation of, 198
    contribution of, 196–197
    selection of, 197–198
Body Shop, The, 556
Bonding employees, 540
Bonds, surety, 547
Bowersock, Terri, 215
Boyd, John A., 390
Branches Medical Inc., 94
Brand, 73, 299–300
Breakdown process, 172
Break-even analysis, application to
        pricing, 310–313
Break-even point, 311
Breaking bulk, 351
Breighner, Bart, 260
Brent, Emma Lou, 152
Brero Construction, 16
Brewton, Lynn, 345
Brill, Randi, 221
Brokers, 351
Brokow, Leslie, 61–62
Bron-Shoe Company, 284
Brooks, Clyde, 358
Brown, Louis, Jr., 137
Brunson, Kirk, 298
Bryan Design Associates, 222
Budget, 377, 385
    cash, 508–509
Budget buying, 443
Budget Reconciliation Act, 588
Buffett, Warren, 15
Building(s), 219–222
    business incubator and, 220
    functional requirements of, 219
    image of, 222
    layout of, 220–222
    lease or buy decision and, 220
Buildup process, 173
Burger Street, 47
Burglary, 537
Burkhard, Alan, 174
Business
    purchase of. *See* Buyout
    valuation of. *See* Valuation
Business angels, 263
Business culture, underlying values of,
        563–564
Business failure. *See* Failure, business
Business format franchising, 68
Business incubator, 220, 388–389
Business interruption insurance,
        546–547, 659
Business plan, 114–131
    content of, 123–128
    definition of, 115

extent of planning in, 120–122
    internal use of, 117
    investor's perspective and, 118–120
    need for, 116–120
    for new business, case study of,
        605–609
    and outsiders, 117–118
    preparation of, 122–131
    sample, 665–682
Business Plan Writing, 129
Business policies, 377
Business swindles, 537
Buying
    budget, 443
    forward, 443
    versus leasing, 220, 469
    versus making, 439–441
    reciprocal, 439
Buyout, 43, 50–61
    case study of, 597–599
    evaluating existing business for,
        52–54
    negotiating and closing, 60–61
    reasons for, 51–52
By George, 538

C

C corporation, 200
    income taxes and, 194, 200
CAD. *See* Computer-aided design
Cafe Nicholson, 7
Calvert, Mike, 271
CAM. *See* Computer-aided manufac-
    turing
Campau, Mary Beth, 165
Canterbury Cuisine, 399
Capital
    cost of, 517–519
    debt, 233
    equity, 247
    informal, 263
    working, 231
Capital budgeting, 514–522
    accounting return on investment,
        515–516
    comprehensive example of, 531–533
    discounted cash flow and, 517
    payback period and, 516–517
    in small firms, 520–522
    techniques in, 515–517
Capital budgeting analysis, 514
Capital gains and losses, 202
Capital Southwest Corporation, 119
Capitalization rate, 57
Carey, Theresa W., 479
Carpenter Reserve Printing Co., 345
Cascade Forest Products, 215
Cash budget, 508–509
Cash conversion period, 501

Cash flow, 502
  from financing activities, 239
  from investment activities, 239
  managing, 505–509
  nature of, 505–506
  net, 506
  from operations, 239, 260
Cash flow–based valuation approach, 58
Cash flow statement, 235–240
Cash method of accounting, 480
Cash-basis accounting, 237
Castagnero, Carla, 246
Cato Institute, 573
C&B Industrial Safety, Inc., 2
Cell, 461, 611
Certified public accountant, 481, 482
Chain of command, 381
Chain-ratio method, 172
Champy, James, 431
Channel of distribution, 350
Chattel mortgage, 268
Cho, Tae Wan, 593–594
Choices Unlimited, 361
Christensen, Roland, 216
Ciliv, Sureyya, 634–635
City, choice of, 212–215
City Family, 148
Civil Rights Act
  of 1964, 580
  of 1991, 573, 580
Clayton Act, 577
Clean Air Act, 573, 579
Clean Duds, 575
Clear Vue Products, 339
Client/server model, 465
C.M. Magnetics, 365
Coastal Mail Service, 388
Code of ethics, 566
Coffee Cup, The, 560
Cognitive dissonance, 286
Coinsurance clause, 547
Coldwater Creek, 5
Cole, Paul M., 614, 616–617
Collection procedures, 324–326
CollectionCenter, Inc., 325
Commercial News USA, 363
Commercial property insurance,
  546–547
Commissions, 337, 407
Common carriers, 354
Communication
  chain of command and, 381
  among computers, 463–465
  between managers and employees,
    380–381
  and promotion, 330–331
Communications control program, 464
Communism, fall of, and economic com-
  petition, 31
Community respect, 616

Community-based financial institutions,
  274–275
Compensation, 407–409. See also Incentives
  of salespeople, 337
Competition
  basic nature of, 138–140
  economic, 31
  from former employees, 540
  global, 32
  government regulation of, 577
  as profiled in marketing plan, 176–177
  stimulation of, 31–32
Competitive advantage, 137–155
  case study of, 610–613
  definition of, 138
  demand and, 309
  strategies for, 140–142
Competitive Advantage, 139, 149
Compound value of a dollar, 524
Computer(s). See also Computer software, Internet
  buying, 469–471
  communication among, 463–465
  evaluating and maintaining, 471
  hardware and software requirements
    for, 464
  leasing, 469
  personal, 459–460
  selection of, case study of, 646–647
  telecommunications applications for,
    465
  types of, 458–460
  use of, by home-based entrepreneurs,
    459, 473
  use of, in inventory monitoring,
    450–451, 512
  use of, in marketing, 615
Computer networks, 456, 472
Computer software, 459, 460–463
  accounting, 478–479
  application, 460
  customized, 461
  global marketing of, case study of,
    634–635
  system, 460
  tax preparation, 588
  work group, 456
Computer-aided design (CAD), 456, 467
Computer-aided manufacturing (CAM),
  456, 467
Computer-based technology
  financial and marketing applications
    of, 455
  operations applications of, 456
  purchasing and managing of,
    468–471
  trends in, 471–473
  use of, in office, 465–467
  use of, in production, 467

Computerware, Inc., 95
Connecticut Mutual Life Insurance, 4
Conner, Carla, 2
Consumer, protection of, 577–578
Consumer behavior, 283–291
  and decision-making process,
    283–286
  psychological factors in, 286–289
  sociological factors in, 289–291
Consumer credit, 317
Consumer Credit Protection Act, 326
Consumer Federation of America, 574
Consumer Product Safety Act, 578
Consumer Product Safety Commission,
  578
Consumerism, 559
Continental Research, 392
Continuous improvement, 616–617
Continuous process improvement, 432
Continuous quality improvement,
  419–420, 434
Contract(s), 586–587
  franchise, 68, 76, 83–85
Contract carriers, 354
Control chart, 423
Convoy, John, 510
Conway, Allen, Sr., 139
Cook, Donna, 329
Cookie Bouquet, 74
Cookies By Design, 74, 76, 77
Coopers & Lybrand, 260, 588
Copyright, 585–586
Copyright Act, 585
Coriell, John, 600–602
Corporate charter, 190
Corporate refugee, 11
Corporation(s), 190–193
  board of directors of, 195–199
  C, 200
  as source of financing, 275
  Subchapter S, 194, 200
Corporation for Enterprise Development,
  211
Corrales-Diaz, Susan, 325
Corrective maintenance, 429
Corwin, Steve, 218
Cost(s)
  in building channel of distribution,
    353
  of debt, as investment criterion,
    519–520
  distribution, 353
  environmental, 557
  financing, 230
  franchise, 76, 77
  of government regulations, 573
  inventory, 446–447, 449
  opportunity, 59, 517, 519
  and pricing, 307–308
  total, 307

Cost(s) (cont.)
  total fixed, 308
  total variable, 307
Cost analysis, 307–309
Cost of capital, 517, 528
  measuring, 517–519
  weighted, 518
Cost of goods sold, 230
Cost-advantage strategy, 140–141
CottageCare, 42
Council of Better Business Bureaus, 538
CPA. *See* Certified public accountant
Crabby Dan's, 662
Cracker Barrel Old Country Store, 4–5
Credit, 316–320
  benefits of, 316
  case study of, 629–630
  commonly used terms in, 318
  consumer, 317
  definition of, 306
  four C's of, 321
  kinds of, 317–320
  selling on, 316–317
  and technology, 320
  trade, 233, 317, 318
Credit bureau, 322
Credit cards, 318–320
Credit insurance, 548
Credit management, 320–326
  evaluating status of applicants and, 320–321
  sources of credit information and, 321–322
Credit regulation, 326–327
Credit Resolution Corp., 325
Cruise Holidays International, 66, 75, 78, 80, 81, 82
Culmo, Katy, 538
Cultural configuration, 96–97
Cultural differences, global marketing and, 356–358
Culture, 289
  organizational, 96, 419
Current assets, 231
Current debt, 233
Current ratio, 246, 484, 494
Cushing, Randy, 159
Customer(s)
  buying habits of, 615
  delinquent, 325
  expectations of quality by, 417–418
  risks associated with, 541
Customer profile, 175
Customer satisfaction strategy, 151
  case study of, 615–616
Customer service
  evaluating, 155
  management of, 150–155
Customer-initiated contacts, 335

Customized software, 461
Cycle counting, 451

D

Dabah, Haim, 375
Data Marketing, Inc., 99
Database program, 461
Davies, Robert, 380
Davis, Peter, 95
Davis, Philip B., 291
Daywork, 407
Debt, 257, 258
  current, 233
  long-term, 233
Debt capital, 233
Debt ratio, 491, 494
Debt-equity ratio, 491
Decision making
  as hampered by management style, case study of, 636–638
  use of financial and accounting information in, case study of, 648–652
Decoma Industries, 325
Delegation of authority, 383–384
Dell, Michael, 14
Dell Computer Corporation, 14, 471
DeLuca, Frank, 8
Demand
  as created by environmental regulations, case study of, 662–664
  elastic, 309
  elasticity of, 309
  inelastic, 309
Demographic variables, 147
Den-Con, 415
Denny, Larry, 415
Denny's Restaurant, 73
Depreciation expense, 237
DePree, D. J., 565
DePree, Max, 565
Design, computer-aided, 456, 467
Design patent, 582
Desktop publishing, 465–466
D. H. Blair & Co., 114
Diaper Dan, 662–664
DiBella, Jack, 236
Dilworth, James B., 426
Direct channel, 352
Direct forecasting, 174
Direct loan, 273
Direct-mail campaign, 615
Directory of Mail Order Catalogs, The, 611
Discount Labels, 139
Discounted cash flow (DCF) techniques, 517, 520, 527–533
Dishonesty, employee, 539–540
Dishonesty insurance, 547

Distributed processing, 458, 459
Distribution, 350–355
  definition of, 350
  dual, 352
  functions of intermediaries in, 350–352
  physical, scope of, 354–355
  structuring of a system for, 353–355
Distribution channels
  in foreign market, 361–363
  types of, 352–353
Distribution costs, 353
Distribution function, 32–33
Distributorship agreement, case study of, 634–635
Domitz, Alvin, 511–512
Donahue, John, 547
Double-entry system, 480
Drypers Corporation, 301
D&S Manufacturing, 367
Dual distribution, 352
Dubé, Donna, 534
Dubé, Joseph, 534
Dun & Bradstreet, 35, 36, 37, 167, 243, 322, 323, 364, 483
Dun & Bradstreet Information Services, 165
Duncan, Max, 140–141
Dunkirk Shoes, 440
Dunning, Dale, 139
DuPont, Pierre, 94
Dyer, W. Gibb, Jr., 96

E

Earnings
  normalized, 57
  retained, 234
Earnings before interest and taxes, 230
Earnings-based valuation approach, 57
Ebel, Kenneth, 419
Economic competition, 31
Economic order quantity, 449–450
Edgington, Jane, 217
Edmark, Tomima, 30
Edwards, Keith L., 30
Efficiency, of small business, 33–34
Eichenlaub, Dan, 246
Eidson, DeWayne, 44, 46
Elastic demand, 309
Elasticity of demand, 309
Electronic Controls Co., 155
Electronic data interchange (EDI), 455, 465
Electronic mail, 167, 456–458, 465
Elkins, Linda T., 129
Elliott, Fred, 79
E-mail. *See* Electronic mail
Emanuelson, Dan, 356

Employee(s)
 alienation of, case study of, 642–643
 bonding of, 540
 compensation of, 407–409
 in competition with former employer,
  540
 computers and, 471
 dishonesty of, 539–540
 incentives for, 616
 leasing of, 409–410
 nonfamily, in a family firm, 103–104
 nonmanagerial, training of, 405–406
 orientation of, 404
 percentage of, in small firms, 27
 pressure on, to act unethically, 566
 protection of, 580–581
 recruitment of, 397–401
 recruitment and retention of, case
  study of, 639–641
 scheduling of, 428
 selection of, 401–403
 sources of, 398–400
 training and development of,
  404–407, 616
Employee handbook, 411
Employee improvement team, 616
Employee participation
 in management, 379, 420–421
 in planning, 378
Employee stock ownership plans
 (ESOPs), 408–409
Employer's liability insurance, 548
Employers Resource Management Co.,
 410
Employment agencies
 private, 399
 public, 399
Employment interview, 402–403
Empowerment, 379
Endicott, Ed, 217
Endicott, Pat, 217
Engineering Data Systems, 184
Enterprise zones, 215–217
Entrepreneur(s), 2–20
 artisan, 18
 characteristics of, 9–12
 college-age, 14
 definition of, 3
 government regulations and, 574
 home-based, computer use by, 459,
  473
 leadership role of, 378–379
 management style of, case study of,
  636–638
 need for outside assistance of,
  387–388
 networks of, 391–392
 opportunistic, 18–19

 successful examples of, 4–6
 women as, 15–17
Entrepreneurial ethics, 563
Entrepreneurial opportunities, 3–6
 age and, 12–13, 14
 hobbies as, 46
Entrepreneurial team, 18–20
Entrepreneur's Guide to Developing a
 Business Plan, An, 122
Entrepreneurship
 drawbacks of, 8–9
 kinds of, 15–20
 personal qualities in, case study of,
  593–594
 preparation for, 14–15
 readiness for, 12–15
 rewards of, 5, 6–8
Environmental costs, 557, 558–559
Environmental Protection Agency, 575
Environmental regulation, 558–559, 579
 creation of demand by, case study of,
  662–664
Environmentalism, 558–559, 616
Epstein, Tom, 392
Equal Access to Justice Act, 575
Equal Credit Opportunity Act, 327
Equal Employment Opportunity Commis-
 sion, 403, 579
Equifax, Inc., 322
Equipment, 223–224
 general-purpose, 223
 retail store, 224
 special-purpose, 223
Equipment loan, 266
Equity, 257
 external, 247
 internal, 247
 return on, 492–494
Ernst & Young, 123, 260, 542
Ethical issues, 560–563
 in family business, case study of,
  660–661
 kinds of, 560–561
Ethical leadership, 564–566
Ethics, code of, 566
EthoGraphics, 149
European Collision Center, 379
European Union (EU), 358
Evaluative criteria, 284
Evans, Warren, 264
Event, precipitating, 13
Evins, Dan, 4–5
Evoked set, 285
Executive summary, 123
Executives, key, loss of, 540
Eximbank. See Export-Import Bank
Expanding into Exports Handbook, The,
 361

Expenses
 accrued, 233
 depreciation, 237
 operating, 230
 personal, provision for, 249
 prepaid, 233
Export Hotline, The, 361
Export Legal Assistance Network, 368
Export management companies, 363
Export Revolving Line of Credit (ERLC)
 program, 369
Export Trading Company (ETC), 366
Export Trading Company Act, 366
Export Yellow Pages, 361
Exporter's Guide to Federal Resources
 for Small Business, 359
Export-Import Bank, 366
Exporting. See Exporting assistance,
 Global marketing
Exporting assistance, 364–369
 from factoring houses, 365
 federal programs for, 366–369
 from private banks, 364–365
 state programs for, 365
External equity, 247
External locus of control, 10

F

Facsimile machine, 466
Factor, 365
Factoring, 267, 511
Factors Chain International, 365
Factory equipment, 223
Factory layout, 220–221
Fadal, Carroll, 338
Fadal Engineering Company, 34
Failure, business, 9
 causes of, 36–37
 costs of, 35–36
 rate of, 34–35, 70–71
Fair Credit Billing Act, 326
Fair Credit Reporting Act, 327, 403
Fair Debt Collection Practices Act, 327
Family and Medical Leave Act, 580, 581
Family business(es), 91–110
 advantages of, 94–95
 conflicts in, case study of, 660–661
 versus corporate career, case study of,
  595–596
 culture of, 96–97
 definition of, 92
 ethical issues in, case study of,
  660–661
 human resources problems in, case
  study of, 639–641
 leadership succession in, 97
 need for good management in,
  102–103

Family business(es) (cont.)
  nonfamily employees in, 103–104
  and overlap with family, 92–94
  roles and relationships in, 98–102
  transfer of ownership of, 108–110
  and work opportunities for family
    members, case study of, 603–604
Family council, 104
Family retreat, 104
Fantastic Catalogue Co., The, 610–613
Faucet Outlet, 142
Favorable financial leverage, 519
Fax machine, 466
Fax modem, 466
Federal Bar Association (FBA), exporting
  advice from, 368
Federal income tax. *See* Taxes
Federal Prison Industries, Inc., 176
Federal Trade Commission (FTC), 85,
  577, 583
Feedback Plus, 46
Fiddler, Jerry, 182
File server, 464
Financial leverage, favorable, 491
Financial performance, assessment of,
  482–494
Financial plan, 126
Financial ratios, 483, 487–494
Financial requirements, initial, for
  startups, 243–249
Financial risk, 257–259
Financial statements, 229–240,
  482–483
  use of, in decision making, case study
    of, 648–652
Financing
  accounts-receivable, 511
  of assets, 491–492
  debt versus equity, 255–259
  identifying types of, 245–249
  sources of, 259–276
  spontaneous, 247
  for a startup, case study of, 624–626
  types of, 233–235
Financing costs, 230
Finch, Harold, 42
Fish, Christopher, 164
Fish Mart Inc., 545
Fishman, Allen, 392
Fixed asset turnover, 491, 494
Fixed assets, 233
Flexible pricing strategy, 314
Flexible schedules, as recruitment tool,
  399
Follow-the-leader pricing strategy, 314
Forecasting, sales, 170–171, 175
  direct, 174
  indirect, 174
  limitations of, 171–172

process methods of, 172–174
use of percentage-of-sales technique
  in, 244
Foreign Corrupt Practices Act, 577
Foreign Credit Insurance Association
  (FCIA), 366
Foreign market. *See* Global marketing
Foreign refugee, 11
Foreign trade zone, 217
Forest Lumber Company, 358
Forward buying, 443
Founder, 17
  as manager, 376
  personal integrity of, 564–566
"Frameables," 8
Franchise(s), 68. *See also* Franchising
  cost of, 76, 77
  investigation of, 79–83
  locating, 78
  operating benefits of, 73
  purchasing of, case study of,
    597–599
  selling of, 83
Franchise Annual, The, 82
Franchise consultants, 82–83
Franchise Consulting Group, The, 71
Franchise contract, 68, 83–85
  restrictions on growth in, 76
Franchise Opportunities Guide, 81–82
Franchise Opportunities Handbook, 73,
  81
Franchisee(s), 17, 67–68
  as source of information, 81
Franchising, 66–88
  advantages of, 70–76
  business format, 68
  case study of, 600–602
  definition of, 67
  evaluating opportunities in, 78–83
  frauds in, 85–88
  laws on, in foreign countries, 583
  limitations of, 76–78
  piggyback, 68
  product and trade name, 68
  systems of, 68–69
  terminology of, 68
Franchisor(s), 67–68
  financial assistance provided by, 73
  information profiles of selected, 74–75
  as source of information, 79–81
  training provided by, 71–73
Frangenberg, Glenda, 272
Frauds
  franchising, 85–88
  income tax, 560–561
Free Trade Agreement (FTA), 358
Freear, John, 264
Free-flow pattern, 222
Freese, Bob, 212

Friends, as source of financing, 263
Fringe benefits, 408
Frye, Tom, 148

G

Galindi, Ernestina, 379
Garrett, Dennis, 275
Garvis, Greg, 498
Gaston, R. J., 263
Gault, George, 212
Gazelle, 18
Geis, Donald W., 32
General Agreement on Tariffs and Trade
  (GATT), 358, 359
General liability insurance, 548
General manager, 17
General partner, 189–190
General-purpose equipment, 223
Geographic information systems (GIS),
  472
Gerhart, Stan, 398
Ginseng Enterprises, Inc., 297
Gitano Group Inc., 375
Global Alliance of Travel Entrepreneurs,
  236
Global American Television Inc., 356
Global marketing, 355–358
  case study of, 634–635
  initial preparations for, 358–363
  sales and distribution channels in,
    361–363
  trade agreements and, 358
  understanding other cultures and,
    290, 356–358
Globe Metallurgical, Inc., 420
Goals, 384
Gold, Daniel, 662–664
Goldman, Dana, 663
Goldstein, Bob, 372
Goldstein, Susan, 372
Gordon, Theodore J., 30
Gosciminski, Joan, 364
Gotthelf, Tom, 217
Government regulation(s)
  benefits from, 574–575
  burden of, 572–574, 575–576
  of competition, 577
  costs of, 573
  as profit-making opportunity, case
    study of, 662–664
  protection of consumers by, 577–578
  protection of employees by, 580–581
  protection of intangible assets by,
    581–586
  protection of investors by, 578
  protection of marketplace and,
    576–586
Government-sponsored agencies, as
  sources of financing, 273–274

Graham, Michael, 365
Grand Rapids Spring & Wire Products, 153
Grandmother Calendar Co., 242
Grant Thornton Accountants and Management Consultants, 573
Gregg, Rose, 87–88
Grid pattern, 222
Gross profit, 230
Growth
  and implications for management, 375–376
  restrictions on, in franchise contract, 76
  stages of, 374–375
Growth trap, 507
Guarantees, 615–616
Guaranty loan, 273
Gumpert, David E., 119
Gutierrez, Robert, 214

H

Hagemeyer, 362
Haggin, Jeff, 611
Hall, Robert J., 44
Hammel, Laury, 558
Hammer, Michael, 431
Hanania, David, 219
Harris, Harvey, 242
Harris, Peggy, 390
Harris, Richard, 192
Harrison, Bennett, 28
Harry W. Schwartz Bookshops, 420, 511–512
Hart, Christopher W. L., 616
Hartford Insurance Company, The, 547
Hawkeye Lumber Company, 537
Headhunter, 399
Healthy Planet Products, 8
Heinrich, Murray P., 98–99
Heller, Stephen, 176
Hendricks, Elias, 146
Hendricks, Gaynell, 146
Henry, Vickie, 46
Herman Miller, Inc., 565
High-potential venture, 18
Hillyard, Robin, 634–635
Hiltronics, 176
Hindman, Jim, 62
Hinds, David, 410
Hobbies, as entrepreneurial opportunity, 46
Holiday Inn, 71, 73
Home Business Institute, 219
Home-based business(es), 217–219
  computer use in, 459, 473
  technology and, 218
  zoning ordinances and, 219

Hopkins, Thomas D., 573
Hosterman, Holly, 215
House of Thread & Woods, 217
House Pet Shop, 466
Hsu, Paul, 297
Hubbard, Vance M., 298
Hull, Edwin, Jr., 141
Hull Industries, Inc., 141
Human resources management, 396–412. *See also* Employee(s)
  formalizing employer-employee relationships and, 410–411
  labor unions and, 410
  leasing employees and, 409–410
  problems in a family business and, case study of, 639–641
Human resources manager, 412

I

IBM, 459
IFA. *See* International Franchise Association
Impersonal referrals, 335
Improvement team, 616
Imtech, 114
Inc., 19–20, 46, 61
Inc. 500 firms, 45, 61–62
Incentives
  employee stock ownership plans (ESOPs) as, 408–409
  financial, 407–408, 616
  fringe benefits as, 408
Income
  net, 230
  operating, 230
  ordinary, 202
Income statement, 229–231, 484
Income taxes. *See* Taxes
Independence, 7
  loss of, in franchise, 77–78
Indirect channel, 352
Indirect forecasting, 174
Inelastic demand, 309
Informal capital, 263
Initial public offering (IPO), 276
Injury, on-premise, 541
Inmedia, 218
Innovative Medical Systems Inc., 436, 441
Inspection, 421–422
  attribute, 422
  variable, 422
Inspection standards, 421–422
Installment account, 317
Institute for Family Business, 104
Institutional advertising, 340
Insurance, 534–551
  business interruption, 546–547, 659

case study of, 657–659
commercial property, 546–547
credit, 548
dishonesty, 547
employer's liability, 548
general liability, 548
key-person, 548–549
requirements for obtaining, 546
small business, 544–549
workers' compensation, 548
Insurance cooperatives, 549
Integrity, 4
Integrity Industries, 140–141
Internal control, 481
Internal equity, 247
Internal locus of control, 10
Internal rate of return (IRR), 517, 528–531
Internal Revenue Service, 25, 588. *See also* Taxes
  income tax fraud and, 560–561
International Business Exchange, 364
International Franchise Association, 81, 86
International Organization for Standardization, 367, 423
International Strategies, 361
International trade, 26. *See also* Global marketing
International Trade Administration, 359, 360
Internet, 14, 142, 165, 209, 264, 332, 456–458, 473
Interviewing, of job applicants, 402–403
Inventory. *See also* Inventory management
  amount of, case studies of, 612, 655
  definition of, 232–233
Inventory costs, 446–447, 449
Inventory management, 511–513
  and ABC analysis, 447
  and just-in-time system, 448–449
  objectives of, 445–446
  record-keeping systems for, 450–452
  and two-bin method, 448
Inventory turnover, 487, 494
Investor(s). *See also* Venture capitalist
  individual, as source of financing, 263–264
  perspective of, 118–120
  protection of, 578
Investment
  identifying and evaluating opportunities for, 48–49
  return on, 492–493
IRS Office of Small Business Affairs, 588
ISO 9000, 367, 423–424
Italcad, 634

J

J. B. Dollar Stretcher, 7
J. Moran Company, 364
Jackson, Mary Anne, 13
James, Stephen, 282
Jamestown Advanced Products, Inc., 396
Jenkins, Marvin, 148
Jiffy Lube, 62
Job applicants, evaluating, 401–403
Job application form, 401
Job description, 400–401
Job Instruction Training, 405–406
Job opportunities, 29
Job shops, 427
Job specification, 401
Johns, Peter, 361
Johnson, Derrick, 388
Johnson, Lee, 554
Johnson, Spencer, 118
Johnson family, 101
Johnson Products Company, 101
Joiner, Larry, 545
Joint ventures, international, 362–363
JoLene Company, 32
JSA Creative Services, 217
Junior's, 47
Just-in-time inventory system, 448–449

K

Kahl, Jack, 168
Kanban system, 448
Kane Manufacturing, 389
Karter, Peter, 429
Kelly, Wendell, 275
Kelly Services, 400
Key-person insurance, 548–549
Kilmer, Jim, 11–12
Kimmelman, Eugene, 574
King's Beauty Supply, 593–594
Kirchoff, Bruce A., 35
Kirwan, Lynn, 399
Klein, Max, 476
Klosterman Bakery, 514
Knight, Russell M., 11–12
Koss, Michael, 362
Koss Corporation, 362
Kovalcik, John, Jr., 95
Kurth, Walter R., 322
Kurtz, Lisa, 198
Kurtz Bros., Inc., 198
Kushell, Edward, 71
Kusin, Gary, 51
Kwik-Kopy Printing, 72, 75

L

Labeling, 302
Labor supply, and location selection, 212

Labor unions, 410
Laing, Steve, 210
Lanham Trademark Act, 300, 581
Lasher, Nancy, 216
Laves, Howard, 538
Laws of motion economy, 432–433
Layout, building, 220–222
  factory, 220–221
  retail store, 222
Layton, Marcia, 129
Layton & Co., 129
Leach, Sheryl, 285
Leadership
  ethical, 564–566
  role of, in quality management, 419
Leading National Advertisers, 332
Leases, 266
Leasing
  of buildings, 219–220
  of computers, 469
  of employees, 409
Legal entity, 190
Letter of credit, 364–365
Lewey, Virginia, 619–621
Liability
  limited, 272
  product, 541
  unlimited, 186
Liability Consultants, Inc., 541
Licensing, 361–362, 579
Life cycle, product, 293
Life-style satisfaction, 7–8
Limited liability, 272
Limited partner, 190
Limited partnership, 189–190
  case study of, 618
Lindberg, Bob, 150
Lindley, Wayne, 537
Lindsey, Brink, 573
Line activities, 382
Line of credit, 267, 271
Line organization, 381
Line-and-staff organization, 382
Link, Lawrence, 22
Link, Linda, 22
Link-a-Rink, 159
Lipscomb, Bill, 169
Liquidation value approach, 55
Liquidity, 245, 484
  measuring, 484–487, 494
Littman, Robert M., 324
Loan(s)
  bank, 267–268
  banker's perspective about, 268–270
  direct, 273
  equipment, 266
  guaranty, 273
  line of credit, 267
  negotiation of, 270–272

Small Business Administration, 273
  term, 267
Loan repayment methods, 271–272
Local area network (LAN), 456, 460, 464, 646–647
Location(s), 207–210
  and choice of specific site, 215
  customer accessibility and, 210
  enterprise and foreign trade zone and, 215–217
  environmental conditions and, 210
  importance of, 207
  key factors in determining, 208–210
  personal preference in, 209–210
  resource availability and, 210
Lock box, 511
Locus of control
  external, 10
  internal, 10
Loewinger, Andrew P., 583
Logan Beach, 619–621
Logistics, 350
London, Mike, 66
Long, John E., 560–561
Longfellow Clubs, 558
Long-range plan, 377
Long-term debt, 233
Lowrey, Pierce, Jr., 114
Lubin, Daniel, 114
Lubitz, Paul, 215
Lucas, Sandy, 222
Lund International Holdings, 298

M

Maciel, J. Carlos, 365
Mackenzie, Leslie, 611
Mad Butcher's Salsa, 139
Madway, Bill, 170
Madway Business Research, Inc., 170
Magnifete, 84
Magnuson-Moss Warranty Act, 302, 559
Mahar, Hazel, 8
Mahar, Larry, 8
Mahoney, Kathleen, 610–613
Mail surveys, for marketing research, 168
Mail-order marketing, 352
  case study of, 610–613
Maintenance, 428–430
  computer, 471
  corrective, 429
  preventive, 429
Maitland, Dottie, 438
Maitland Meeting Management, 438
Major industries, 25
Make-or-buy decision, 439–441
Malcolm Baldrige National Quality Award, 405, 421

Management
  accounts-payable, 513–514
  accounts-receivable, 510–511
  cash flow, 505–509
  conflicting messages in, case study of, 642–643
  credit, 320–326
  customer service, 150–155
  family business, 102–105
  human resources, 396–412
  inventory, 445–452
  operations, 426
  outside assistance and, 387–393
  product, 291–295
  risk, 541–544, 545
  small firm, 373–376, 636–638
  time, 385–387
  working-capital, 499, 502–505, 653–656
Management consultants, 390–391
Management functions, 376–385
  controlling, 384–385
  leading and motivating, 378–381
  organizing, 381–384
  planning, 377–378
Management plan, 125
Management style, case study of, 636–638
Management team, 183–185
  building of, 183–185
  outside assistance for, 185
  value of, 183
Manager(s)
  development of, 406–407
  founders as, 376
  human resources, hiring of, 412
  leadership approaches of, 379–381
  professional, 373
  time pressure and, 385–386
  timesavers for, 386–387
Manco, Inc.,168
Mandel family, 418
Mangum, David H., 264
Manhattan Bagel, 580
Manpower, 400
Manufacturing
  batch, 427
  computer-aided, 456, 467
  planning and scheduling, 427
  repetitive, 427
  types of, 427
Marcus, Stanley, 151
Mardirossian, Aris, 78
Marginal firm, 17–18
Mariani Packing Co., 301
Market(s)
  definition of, 147, 170
  estimating potential of, 170–174
  global, 297

ingredients of, 170
  mail-order, case study of, 610–613
  product strategies in, 295–299
Market analysis, 159, 161, 175
Market niche. See Niche, market
Market segmentation, 142–147
  definition of, 142
  need for, 142–143
  segmentation variables and, 147
  strategies for, 143–146
  targeted, 615
Market-based valuation approach, 56
Marketer-initiated contacts, 335
Marketing
  consumer orientation in, 161–162
  global, 355–358, 634–635
  niche, 147–150
  product versus service, 291–292
  role of distribution in, 350–353
  small business, 160–162
Marketing advantage strategy, 141–142
Marketing mix, 161
Marketing plan, 125
  components of, 175–178
  importance of, case study of, 614–617
Marketing research, 162–178
  steps in, 165–170
Marketing strategy, in marketing plan, 177–178
Markup pricing, 312–313
Marlow, Raymond, 421
Marlow Industries, 421
Martin, Bob, 482
Martin, David, 83
Martin, Thomas, 471
Martin Distributorship, 482
Mass marketing, 143
Master licensee, 68
Matchmakers, 52
Material requirement planning, 467
Mathis, Robert, 212
Matson, Daniel, 466
Maxwell, Barbara, 359
McCain Foods Limited, 93
McClelland, David C., 9
McCombs, Margaret, 621
McConnell, Charles M., 363
McCurry, James, 51
McDonald's, as franchise, 72, 73, 74, 76, 83
MDY Advanced Technologies, 542
Melnick, Norman, 305
Mengle, Zan, 274
Mentor O & O, Inc., 358
Mercer Management Consulting Inc., 614, 616
Merchant middlemen, 351
Mergerstat Review, 56
Merrick, Dale, 554

Michel, Harriet, 275
Microcomputer, 459
Micros Systems, Inc., 137
Microsoft Corporation, 263, 581
Mighty Mule, 441
Mikana Manufacturing Company, 454
Mike's Meat Market, 476
Minchak, Bob, 7
Minicomputer, 460, 646–647
Minnetonka, 150
Miranda, Anthony, 479
Mister Donut, as franchise, 72
MIT Enterprise Forum, 50, 119
Modified book value approach, 54
Moerdler, Mark, 542
Money, time value of, 524–526
Moonstone Mountaineering, Inc., 215
MoreNow Corp., 611, 612, 613
Mortgage, 233
  chattel, 268
  real estate, 268
Motion economy, laws of, 432–433
Motion study, 432–433
Motivations, 288
MRP. See Material requirement planning
Multimedia, 466–467
Multiple-unit ownership, 68
Multisegmentation strategy, 144–145
Multitasking, 459
Musser, Warren, 263
Mutual Group, 543

N

Naisbitt, John, 147
National Federation of Independent Business, 45, 176, 471, 572
National Highway Traffic Safety Administration, 574
National Minority Supplier Development Council, 274
National Retail Credit Association, 322
National Small Business United, 356, 573
Nation's Business, 4
Needs, 287
  for achievement, 9
Negotiable instruments, 588
Neiman-Marcus, 151
Net cash flow, 506
Net income available to owners, 230
Net present value (NPV), 517, 527–528
Net profit, 506–507
Net working capital, 499
Netscape Communications Corp., 142
Network card, 464
Network control program, 464
Networking, 391
New Product Information Service, 363

New York Stock Exchange, 59
Niche, market
  maintaining potential of, 149–150
  selection of, 147–149
Niche marketing, 147–150
Nicholson, John, 7
Nicolai, Bill, 611
Normalized earnings, 57
North American Free Trade Agreement
  (NAFTA), 79, 358
North American Securities Administra-
  tors Association, 85
Northwest Industrial Coatings, 164
Notara, Steve, 325
NovaSoft Systems Inc., 634–635
Nutrition Labeling and Education Act,
  578

O

Occupational Safety and Health Act,
  430, 580
Occupational Safety and Health Admin-
  istration (OSHA), 571, 575
Ocean Traders of North America, 365
OCS Consulting Services, 46
Odell, Pat, 45
Odwalla, Inc., 143
Office of Information and Regulatory Af-
  fairs (OIRA), 575
Office of Management and Budget, 575
Office technology, computer-based,
  465–467
*Official Gazette of the U.S. Patent &
  Trademark Office, The,* 583
Ohlhausen, Howard, 627–628
O'Kane, Brooks, 339
Once Upon A Child, 73
Open charge account, 317
Operating expenses, 230
Operating income, 230, 488
Operating income return on investment
  (OIROI), 488–491, 494
Operating plan, 125
Operating profit margin, 489, 494
Operating profitability, assessing,
  488–491, 494
Operating system, 460
Operations, manufacturing versus service,
  426
Operations analysis, 432–434
Operations management, 426
Operations process, 425–430
Opinion leader, 291
Opportunistic entrepreneur, 18–19
Opportunity cost, 59, 517, 519
Ordinary income, 202
Organization, 381–384
  informal, 383

line, 381
  line-and-staff, 382
Organizational culture, 96, 419
Orientation, of new employees, 404
Ortiz, Mario, 621
Oshman, Ken, 263
Osofsky, Ronald, 282
Osofsky, Sid, 282
Other assets, 233
Other payables, 233
Otten, Clarke, 286
Outsourcing, 441
Owners' equity capital, 234
Ownership
  selecting form of, 193–195
  types of, 185–193

P

Packaging, 301–302
Paisner family, 614
Paperwork Reduction Act, 575
Partner(s)
  general, 189–190
  limited, 190
  qualifications of, 187–188
  rights and duties of, 188–189
Partnership, 187–190
  articles of, 188–189
  income taxes and, 194, 199–200
  limited, 189–190
  termination of, 189
Patent, 582–585
  design, 582
  plant, 583
  utility, 582
Payback period technique, 516–517
Pence, Ann, 5
Pence, Dennis, 5
Penetration pricing strategy, 313
Pentech International, 305
Percentage-of-sales technique, 244
Perception, 288
Perceptual categorization, 288
Perfection Automotive Products, 575
Performance criteria, 384
Performance measurement, 384–385
Performance testing, 403
Perpetual inventory system, 450,
  451–452
Perry, Peter, 445
Personal computer, 459
Personal referrals, 334
Personal savings, as source of financing,
  260–261, 262
Personal selling, 334–338
  building customer goodwill through,
  338
  cost control in, 337

definition of, 334
  product knowledge and, 334
  sales presentation and, 334–337
Pet Cards, Inc., 346
Phelps Country Bank, 152
Philatron International, Inc., 574
Physical distribution, 350
Physical examinations, of job applicants,
  403
Physical inventory system, 450–451
Pickett, Steve, 445
Piggyback franchising, 68
Pittsburgh Plastics Manufacturing, Inc.,
  297
Pivot Corporation, 173
Placers, The, 174
Planning, 377–378
Plant maintenance, 428–430
Plant patent, 583
Plant safety, 430
PlasmaQuest, 274
Plasticolors, Inc., 399
Pledged accounts receivable, 511
Poe, Sheri, 150
Policies, business, 377
Pooling purchases, 443
Porter, Michael, 139, 140, 149
Potter, Dr. Robin, 254
Power, referent, 290–291
Prater, William N., Jr., 618
Precipitating event, 13
Pre-emptive right, 191
Premier Industrial, 418
Prepaid expenses, 233
Present value of an annuity, 525–526
  of $1 for *n* periods, table for,
  687–690
Present value of a dollar, 524–525
  table for, 683–686
Prestige pricing, 309, 310
Preventive maintenance, 429
Price, definition of, 306
Price lining strategy, 314
Price Waterhouse, 361
Price-to-earnings ratio, 56
Pricing, 306–310
  average, 308
  break-even analysis and, 310–313
  cost determination for, 307–308
  demand factors in, 309–310
  flexible, 314
  follow-the-leader, 314
  markup, 312–313
  penetration, 313
  prestige, 309, 310
  sales forecasts and, 311–312
  seasonal, 315
  selecting a strategy for, 313–315
  skimming, 313–314

variable, 314
and what traffic will bear, 315
Primal Lite, 269
Primary data, 168
Prime rate, 271
Private carriers, 354
Private placement, 276
Pro forma statements, 126, 239
preparation of, case study of, 622–623
Procedures, 377
Process layout, 221
Procter & Gamble, 150
Proctor, Barbara Gardner, 5–6
Proctor and Gardner Advertising, 5–6
Product, definition of, 291–292
Product advertising, 340
Product and trade name franchising, 68
Product development, 293–295
Product innovation, by small firms, 29–31
Product item, 292
Product layout, 221
Product liability, 541
Product Liability Alliance, 541
Product Liability Risk Retention Act, 549
Product life cycle, 293
Product line, 292
Product management, 291–295
Product mix, 292
Product mix consistency, 292
Product quality, 301
Product strategy, 292, 295–299
case study of, 627–628
Production process, 425
Production technology, computer-based, 467
Productivity, 430–434
definition of, 430
importance of improving, 430
reengineering for, 431
Productivity packages, 461
Products and/or services plan, 125
Professional manager, 373
Professional Swedish Car Repair, 286
Profit(s)
gross, 230
as incentive for entrepreneurship, 6–7
net, 506–507
operating, 488–491
Profit and loss statement. See Income statement
Profit making
as a result of government regulations, 575
social responsibilities and, 556–557
Profit retention, 247
Profitability
assessing, 240–243

potential, 255–257
Profit-sharing plan, 407
Promotion. See also Advertising, Personal selling, Sales promotion
communication process and, 330–331
definition of, 330
determining level of expenditure for, 331–334
Promotional mix, 330
for new product, case study of, 631–633
Prospecting, 334
Prospector, 264
Protocol Telecommunications, 479
Public welfare, 579
Publicity, 345–346
PulseCard Inc., 254
Purcell, John E., Jr., 290
Purchase discounts, 441–442
Purchase order, 438, 439
Purchase requisition, 438
Purchasing, 437
policies and practices in, 439–443
Purchasing cycle, 438–439
Purchasing group, 549

Q

Qualiticare Medical Services, Inc., 275
Quality
as competitive advantage, 612
definition of, 416
differences in and international competition, 416
employee training and, 405
entrepreneurial opportunities and, 3–4
ISO 9000 certification and, 367
price as indicator of, 309
product, 301
Quality circle, 420
Quality management
customer focus of, 417–419
in service businesses, 424
Quality Media Resources, Inc., 206
Quarasan Group, 221
Quick ratio, 484

R

Rabbit Creek Products, 329
Race Tech, 341
Racing Strollers, 502
Raffel, Lori, 543
Raftery, Thomas W., 176
Ragan, Wayne, 192
Rain-X, 627–628
Raiz, Mary Lou, 620, 621
Ramos, Phillip, Jr., 574

Reach Strategic Venture Partner program, 165
Reagan, Joe, 354
Reagan's Coffees, 354
Real estate mortgage, 268
Receivables, life cycle of, 510–511
Reciprocal buying, 439
Reed family, 94
Reell Precision Manufacturing Corporation, 554, 563, 565
Reengineering, 431
Reengineering the Corporation, 431
Reference groups, 290
References, checking of, 403
Referrals, 339
Refugee, 10–12
corporate, 11–12
foreign, 11
Regulation. See Government regulation(s)
Regulatory Flexibility Act, 575
Reid, Laura, 545
Rekow, Brian, 345
Relatives, as source of financing, 263
Reliability, 403
Reorder point, 448
Repcon, 628
Repetitive manufacturing, 427
Replacement value approach, 55
Required rate of return. See Cost of capital
Resource Development Group, 8
Resource Recovery Systems, 429
Retained earnings, 234
Return on equity, 492–494
Return on investment, operating income, 488–491
Revolving charge account, 317
Revolving credit agreement, 267
Rich, Stanley R., 119
Richards, Mary, 91
Risk(s)
customer-associated, 541
definition of, 535
for entrepreneurs, 9–10
financial, 257–259
personnel-oriented, 539–540
preventive reduction of, 542–543
property-oriented, 535–539
sharing of, 544
Risk management, 541–544, 545
case study of, 657–659
Risk premium, 59
Risk Retention Amendments, 549
Risk-retention group, 548–549
Robben, John, 96
Robert Morris Associates, 243, 483, 485
Roberts, Pamela, 356
Robin Rose Ice Cream, 353

Robinson-Patman Act, 577
RobToy, Inc., 96
Roddick, Anita, 556
Rolm Corporation, 263
Ronnybrook Farm, 282
Rose, Robin, 353
Rosell, Pat, 206, 217
Rosell, Robert, 206, 217
Rosenfield, George, 108
Rosenfield, Sheryl, 108
Rotor Clip Company, 423
Rotter, J. B., 10
Russell, Linda, 325
Russell, Richard, 361
Rust Evader Corporation, 356
Rykä, 150

S

Safeguard Business Systems, Inc., 284
Safeguard Scientifics, 263
Safety, plant, 430
Safety stock, 448
Saksripanith, Sirikarn, 518
Salary levels, 407
Sale of equity, 260
Sales forecast, 170–171
    and pricing, 311–312
Sales presentation, 335–337
Sales promotion, 343–346
    tools of, 344–346
Sales tax, 573
Salespeople, compensation of, 337
Salmore, Stanley, 54
Saltz, Shamis, & Goldfarb, Inc., 324
Sam Ash Music Corporation, 102
San Luis Sourdough Co., 152
Sanculi, Ron, 139
Sanger, Georgina, 613
Sarvetnick, Harold, 216
Saul, Marvin, 47
SBA. See Small Business Administration
SBT Corporation, 380
Schiff, Arthur, 148
Schwartz, David, 511–512
Schwartz, Victor, 541
Sciaroni, Jim, 215
Scott, Sue, 269
ScrubaDub Auto Wash, 614–617
Secondary data, 165
Secter, Richard, 176
Section 1244 stock, 202
Securities Act, 578
Securities and Exchange Commission
    (SEC), 276, 578
Securities Exchange Act, 578
Segmentation variables, 147
Seiff, Kenneth, 173
Selden, Andrew C., 81

Self-confidence, 10
Self-insurance, 543–544
Self-service layout, 222
Serendipity, 46
Service bureau, 468, 646
Service business, quality management
    in, 424
Service Corps of Retired Executives
    (SCORE), 167, 368, 389–390
Service function, 33
Service mark, 300
Service operations, planning and sched-
    uling, 427–428
Sewell, Carl, 152
Sewell Village Cadillac, 152
Shapero, Albert, 36
Shelby Die Casting Company, 379–380
Sherman, Ed, 538
Sherman, Thomas, 588
Sherman Antitrust Act, 315, 577
Sherman's Inc., 538
Shoplifting, 537–539
Short-range plans, 377
Short-term liabilities, 233
Short-term notes, 233
Shtulman, Jill, 217
SiBön Beverage Corporation, 44,
    665–682
Siegel, Richard, 440
Siemens, 634–635
Single-entry system, 480
Single-segmentation strategy, 146
Siriarphanon, Supranee, 258
Site, selection of, 211–217
6-Twelve Convenient Mart, Inc., 78
Size criteria, 23
Skimming price strategy, 313–314
Skypix, 121
Slass, Robert, 423
Slater, Bill, 571
Small business(es), 22–37
    accounting activities in, 477–482
    advertising considerations for,
        339–343
    advisory council and, 198–199
    attracting applicants to, 397–398
    buying, case study of, 597–599
    capital budgeting practices of,
        520–522
    choice of location of, 207–210
    computer-based technology for,
        455–473
    consumer issues and, 559
    and contribution to big business, 32–33
    definition of, 23–24
    efficiency of, 33–34
    environmental issues and, 558–559
    ethical issues in, 560–563
    federal assistance to, 273

    federal taxes on, 589–590
    government regulation of, 572–576
    home-based, 217–219
    insurance for, 544–549
    in international trade, 26
    and legal forms of organization,
        185–195
    legal instruments of, 586–588
    management weaknesses in, 373
    nonfederal taxes on, 591
    number of, 25–26
    pressures to act unethically in,
        561–563
    as producer of goods and services,
        24–28
    product strategies for, 295–299
    relative economic importance of,
        26–27
    sales promotions and, 343–346
    site selection and, 211–217
    social responsibilities and, 555–557
    special contributions of, 29–34
    state and local assistance in financing
        for, 273–274
    trends in activity of, 28
    use of outside directors in, 196–197
Small Business Administration (SBA), 5,
    165, 185, 367–369, 537, 538,
    574
    loans by, 273
    size standards of, 23–24
Small Business Development Centers
    (SBDCs), 368, 390
Small Business Innovative Research
    (SBIR) program, 273
Small Business Institute (SBI), 368,
    388–389
Small business investment company
    (SBIC), 273, 369
Small business marketing, 160–161
Smith, Gail A., 218
Smith, Norman R., 18–19
Smith, Tim, 119
Snelson, Barbara, 91
Snelson, Julie, 91
Snow Runner, Inc., 300
Social classes, 289
Social responsibilities, 555
    definition of, 555
    and profit making, 556–557
    small firms' view of, 555–556
Softub, 444
Software. See Computer software
Sohl, Jeff A., 264
Sole proprietorship, 186–187
    case study of, 649
    income taxes and, 194, 199
Sorrell Ridge, 32
Span of control, 384

Special-purpose equipment, 223
Spiegel, Susan, 91
Spontaneous financing, 247
Spouses, in family business, 101–102
SPP Ceramics Co., Ltd., 258
Spragins, Ellyn, 397
Spreadsheet program, 461
Spring Engineers, Inc., 222
Staff activities, 382
Staff Directory—State Chambers of Commerce and Associations of Commerce and Industry, 573
Stages in succession, 105–107
Stahle, John, 459
Standard Industrial Classification (SIC) code, 173
Standard operating procedure, 377
Standard & Poor, 483
Startup(s), 43–50
    case study of, 610–613
    evaluation criteria for, 48–49
    financing for, case study of, 624–626
    preparing pro forma statement for, case study of, 622–623
    successful, characteristics of, 61–63
Startup ideas
    hobbies as, 46
    kinds of, 44–45
    refinement of, 50
    sources of, 45–47
Statistical methods, use in controlling quality, 422–423
Statistical process control, 422–423
Statute of frauds, 586
Steak-Out, 83
Steins, 22
Steltenpohl, Greg, 143
Stenger, Barbara, 585
Stevens, Mark, 118
Stevenson, Wayne, 379
Stidman, Linda, 91
Stiles, Natalie, 45–46
Stock certificate, 191
Stock ownership plans, for employees, 408–409
Stock sales, as source of financing, 260, 276
Stockholders
    death or withdrawal of, 191–193
    limited liability of, 191
    rights and status of, 191
Stockpiling, controlling of, 512–513
Stone Construction Equipment, Inc., 398
Strategic decision, 148
Strategic niche, entrepreneurs and, 6
Strategic plan, 377
Strategic planning, and family council, 104–105
Struminger, Donald, 663

Stuecher, David, 463
Subchapter S corporation, 200–201
    income taxes and, 194
Subcultural analysis, 289
Succession, in family business, 105–110
    available family talent and, 105
    cultural patterns and, 97
    stages in, 105–107
    transfer of ownership and, 108–110
Sullivan, Dan, 142
Sunderland, Dick, 367
Sundet, John, 300
Superior Pet Products Company, 512
Suppliers
    building good relationships with, 444–445
    just-in-time system and, 448–449
    selecting and dealing with, case study of, 644–645
    selection of, 443–444
    as source of financing, 265–266
Supply, sources of
    diversification of, 442
    location of, 438
Supply function, 33
Surety bonds, 547
Surveys, 165–166, 168–169
Synergy Software, 359
SyQuest Technology Inc., 422
System A franchising, 68
System B franchising, 69
System C franchising, 69
System software, 460
Systems Integrated, 325

T

Tabb, Lester, 441
Taco Bueno, 47
Tarhill, Mike, 192
Tasco Corporation, 108
Tate Andale, 451
Taylor, Scott, 184
Tax Reform Act, 588
Taxes, 573, 588–591
    and business site selection, 212–213
    computer software packages for preparation of, 588
    evasion of, 560–561
    federal, 573, 589–590
    and form of organization, 194, 199–202
    nonfederal, 591
    sales, 573
Tech Spray, Inc., 361
Technology
    computer-based, feasibility study of, 468
    and credit, 320

Tecnol Medical Products, Inc., 298
Telecommunications, 463–464
Telecommuting, 465
Telephone Consumer Protection Act, 578
Template, 461
Temporary help agencies, 400
Terk, Neil, 346
Terk Technologies Corporation, 346
Term loan, 267, 271
Terminal emulation, 464
Terri's Consignment World, 215
Thacker, Milt, 451
The Alternative Board (TAB), 392
Thede, Paul, 341
Thinker Toys, 345
Thomas, Bill, 296
Thomas, Larry, 560
Thomas, Sheila, 560
Thompson, Bill, Jr., 92
Thompson, Chris, 91
Thompson-McCoy, Kerry Krouse, 228
Thompson's Plumbing Supply, 92
Thornbury, Tom, 444
Throughput, 460
Time management, 385–387
Time sharing, 468–469
Time study, 432–433
Time value of money, 524–526
Times interest earned, 492, 494
Timmons, Jeffrey A., 30
Tippett, L. H. C., 433
TMA Technologies, Inc., 212
Tolerance limits, 423
TopsyTail, 30
Total asset turnover, 489, 494
Total cost, 307
Total fixed costs, 308
Total product offering, 299–303
Total quality management (TQM), 416–424
    conflicting messages in, case study of, 642–643
    customer service and, 153–155
    definition of, 153
    international certification of, 423–424
    organizational culture and, 419–420
    tools and techniques for, 420–423
Total variable costs, 307
TQM. *See* Total quality management
TQM Group, 616
Trade agreements, 358
Trade credit, 233, 265–266, 317, 318
Trade dress, 586
Trade mission, 361
Trade show exhibits, 346
Trade-credit agencies, 322
Trademark, 73, 300, 581–582
Trademark Search Library, 581

Training
   employee, 404–407
   provided by franchisor, 71–73
Trans Union Credit Information Co., 322
Transfer of ownership, 108–110
Transportation, as component of physical
   distribution, 354
Trusler, Alan, 315
Truth-in-Lending Act, 326
TRW, Inc., 322
TumbleBug, 141
TurboTax, 588
Two-bin method, 448
Type A startup ideas, 44
Type B startup ideas, 44
Type C startup ideas, 44

U

Underlying values, 563–564
Unelko Corp., 627–628
Unicor, 176
Uniform Franchise Offering Circular
   (UFOC), 85
United States Employment Service, 399
Unity of command, 383
Unlimited liability, 186
Unsegmented strategy, 143–144
Upton, Nancy, 104
U.S. Chamber of Commerce, 4, 573
U.S. Department of Commerce, 24–25,
   30, 173
   export services of, 361, 362–363
   franchise guidelines of, 73, 79
U.S. Global Trade Outlook 1995–2000,
   359
U.S. Patent and Trademark Office, 300,
   581, 582
U.S. Patent Office, 585
Utility patent, 582

V

Validity, 403
Vall, Jonathan, 216
Valuation
   asset-based, 54–55
   cash flow–based, 58
   determination of, in buyout, 54–60
   earnings-based, 57–58
   market-based, 56–57
   nonquantitative factors and, 60

Van Tone Company, 410
Variable inspection, 422
Variable pricing strategy, 314
Variables, benefit, 147
Venture capital firms, as source of financ-
   ing, 275–276
Venture Capital Network, Inc., 264
Venture capitalist, 275
Vesper, Karl H., 138
Virginia Linen Service, 663
Vision Capital Associates, Inc., 662
VMG Products, 618
Voice mail, 465
Voting control, 259

W

W. Thomas Company, 296
Wage levels, 407
Wagner, Timothy, 618
Wahlstedt, Robert L., 554, 563
Wainwright Industries, 405
Wall Street Custom Clothiers, 139
Walnut Acres, 557
Wangsness, Patricia, 580
Warranty, 302–303
Watson, Shelagh, 84
Waugh, Bill, 47
Weatherly Private Capital, 618
Web page. *See* Internet
Weber, Claudette, 16
Wedding Fantastic, Inc., The, 611
Wee Care Academy, Inc., 146
Wegman, Danny, 151
Wegmans Food Markets, 151
Wehrenberg, Jon W., 396
Weighted cost of capital, 518, 519
Weinstock, Carol, 149
West, David, 152
West, Linda, 152
West Coast Roofing and Waterproofing
   Co., 545
Wetzel, William E., 264
Wharton Applied Research Center, 95
"What You See Is What You Get," 466
Wheeler-Lea Act, 577
White, Debbie, 320
White Dog Cafe, 555
White Glove Service Systems, 400
White's of Florida, 320
Wicks, Judy, 555

Wierzbowski, Edward, 356
Wigtil, Wendy, 349
Williams, Fred, 215
Williams, Nancy, 91
Williams, Niki, 215
Willow Peripherals, 216
Wilmer, David, 182
Wilson, Bruce, 8
Wind River Systems, 182
Windows (Microsoft), 581
Winner International Corporation, 141
Wolf, Clark, 619
Women entrepreneurs, 15–17
Women's Business Ownership Act, 577
Word-processing programs, 461
Work group software, 456
Work measurement, 433
Work sampling, 433
Work teams, 379, 420
Workers' compensation insurance, 548
Working capital, 231
Working Capital Loan Guarantee Pro-
   gram, 366
Working-capital cycle, 499–505
   timing and size of investments and,
   501
Working-capital management, 499
   case study of, 653–656
   examples of, 502–505
Workstations, 459
World Wide Web. *See* Internet
Worthington Foods, Inc., 176
WYSIWYG, 466

Y

Yashi, 215
Yocke, Ric, 542

Z

Zawacki, Jim, 153
Zimmer, Ed, 155
Zona, Jim, 297
Zoning ordinances, 219
Zoom Telephonics, 297
Zuncker, Leigh, 399
Zymöl, 310